D1116927

CONSTITUTIONAL AND POLITICAL HISTORY OF PAKISTAN

Hamid Khan

OXFORD
UNIVERSITY PRESS

Great Clarendon Street, Oxford OX2 6DP

Oxford University Press is a department of the University of Oxford. It furthers the University's objective of excellence in research, scholarship, and education by publishing worldwide in

Oxford New York

Athens Auckland Bangkok Bogotá Buenos Aires Calcutta Cape Town Chennai Dar es Salaam Delhi Florence Hong Kong Istanbul Karachi Kuala Lumpur Madrid Melbourne Mexico City Mumbai Nairobi Paris São Paulo Shanghai Singapore Taipei Tokyo Toronto Warsaw

with associated companies in Berlin Ibadan

Oxford is a registered trade mark of Oxford University Press in the UK and in certain other countries

First published 2001

ISBN 0 19 579341 2

Printed in Pakistan at
Mas Printers, Karachi.
Published by
Ameena Saiyid, Oxford University Press
5-Bangalore Town, Sharae Faisal
PO Box 13033, Karachi-75350, Pakistan.

This work is dedicated to the

People of Pakistan

whose rights would not have been trampled upon had the ruling elite faithfully followed the constitutional and democratic path set for the nation by its founder Quaid-e-Azam Muhammad Ali Jinnah

CONTENTS

Part II
CONSTITUTIONAL AND POLITICAL DEVELOPMENTS FROM AUGUST 1947 TO OCTOBER 1958

Part V
THE BHUTTO REGIME: DECEMBER 1971 TO JULY 1977

TABLE OF CASES

Abdul Baqi Baluch v Government of Pakistan, PLD 1968 S.C. 313
Abdul Ghani Khan v Government of West Pakistan, PLD 1968 Lahore 1244
Abdul Hamid Khan v The District Magistrate, Larkana PLD 1973 Karachi 344
Abdus Saboor Khan v Karachi University, PLD 1966 S.C. 536
Abington School District v Schempp, 374 U.S. 203 (1963)
Abrar Hassan v Government of Pakistan, PLD 1976 S.C. 315
Abul Ala Maudoodi v Government of West Pakistan, PLD 1964 S.C. 673
Aftab Ahmad Khan Sherpao v The Governor of NWFP, PLD 1990 Peshawar 192
Ahmad Tariq Rahim v Federation of Pakistan, PLD 1990 Lahore 505
Ahmad Tariq Rahim v Federation of Pakistan, PLD 1991 Lahore 78
Ahmad Tariq Rahim v Federation of Pakistan, PLD 1992 S.C. 646
Akhunzada Behrawar Saeed v Justice Sajjad Ali Shah, 1998 SCMR 173
Akhunzada Behrawar Saeed v Justice Sajjad Ali Shah, 1998 SCMR 115
Al-Jehad Trust v Federation of Pakistan, PLD 1996 S.C. 324
Al-Jehad Trust v Federation of Pakistan, PLD 1997 S.C. 84
Al-Jehad Trust v Federation of Pakistan, PLJ 1997 S.C. 209
Asad Ali v Federation of Pakistan, PLD 1998 S.C. 161
Asad Ali v Federation of Pakistan, 1998 SCMR 122
Asad Ali v Federation of Pakistan, 1998 SCMR 119
Asad Ali v Federation of Pakistan, 1998 SCMR 15
Asma Jilani v Government of the Punjab, PLD 1972 S.C. 139

Begum Nazir Abdul Hamid v Pakistan, PLD 1974 Lahore 7
Benazir Bhutto v Farooq Ahmad Khan Leghari, PLJ 1998 S.C. 27 = PLD 1998 S.C. 388
Benazir Bhutto v Federation of Pakistan, PLD 1988 S.C. 416
Benazir Bhutto v Federation of Pakistan, PLD 1989 S.C. 66
Board of Foreign Mission v Government of the Punjab, PLJ 1987 S.C. 464

Christian Educational Endowment Trust v Deputy Commissioner, PLJ 1987 S.C. 473

Darvesh M. Arbey v Federation of Pakistan, PLD 1977 Lahore 846

Everson v Board of Education, 330 U.S.1 (1947)

F.B. Ali v The State, PLD 1975 S.C. 506
Fakhre Alam v The State, PLD 1973 S.C. 525
Farooq Ahmad Khan Leghari v Federation of Pakistan, PLD 1999 S.C. 57

Fazlul Quadir Chowdhry v Syed Shah Nawaz, PLD 1966 S.C. 105
Fazlul Quadir Chowdhry v Muhammad Abdul Haque, PLD 1963 S.C. 486
Federal Government of Pakistan v M.D. Tahir, 1990 SCMR 189
Federation of Pakistan v Hazoor Bukhsh, PLD 1983 FSC 255
Federation of Pakistan v Maulvi Tamizuddin Khan, PLD 1955 F.C. 240
Federation of Pakistan v Ali Ahmad Hussain Shah, PLD 1955 F.C. 522
Federation of Pakistan v Saeed Ahmad Khan, PLD 1974 S.C. 151
Federation of Pakistan v Ch. Manzoor Elahi, PLD 1976 S.C. 430
Federation of Pakistan v Shaukat Ali Mian, PLD 1999 S.C. 1026
Federation of Pakistan v Haji Muhammad Saifullah Khan, PLD 1989 S.C. 166
Federation of Pakistan v Aftab Ahmad Khan Sherpao, PLD 1992 S.C. 723
Federation of Pakistan v Ghulam Mustafa Khar, PLD 1989 S.C. 26
Fida Muhammad v Province of NWFP, PLD 1973 Peshawar 156

Ghulam Mustafa Khar v Pakistan, PLD 1988 Lahore 49
Government of East Pakistan v Rowshan Bijaya Shaukat Ali Khan, PLD 1966 S.C. 286
Government of NWFP v Said Kamal Shah, PLD 1986 S.C. 360
Government of Sindh v Sharaf Faridi, PLD 1994 S.C. 105
Government of West Pakistan v Begum Agha Abdul Karim Shorish, Kashmiri PLD 1969 S.C. 14

Habiba Jilani v Federation of Pakistan, PLD 1974 Lahore 153
Habib-ul-Wahab-al Khairi v Sh. Shaukat Ali, PLD 1976 Lahore 373
Hakam Qureshi v Judges of the Lahore High Court, PLD 1976 S.C. 713
Hakim Khan v Government of Pakistan, PLD 1992 S.C. 595
Hamid Sarfaraz v Federation of Pakistan, PLD 1979 S.C. 991
Hazoor Bakhsh v Federation of Pakistan, PLD 1981 FSC 145

In re: Complaint of malpractices in Constituency No. NA-57, Sargodha-V, PLD 1977 Journal 164
In re: Complaint of malpractices in Constituency No. NA-76 Lyallpur-IX, PLD 1977 Journal 190
In re: Complaint of malpractices in Constituency No. NA-80 Lyallpur-XIII, PLD 1977 Journal 187
In re: Complaint of malpractices in Constituency No. NA-89 Kasur-I, PLD 1977 Journal 198
In re: Suo Moto Constitutional Petition, 1994 SCMR 1028
In re: The Constitutional Petition No. 248-Q of 1997, 1998 SCMR 127
Indo-Pakistan Corporation Ltd. Lahore v Government of Pakistan, PLD 1975 Lahore 1058
Islamic Republic of Pakistan v Abdul Wali Khan, M.N.A. PLD 1976 S.C. 57

Jamal Shah v Member Election Commission, Government of Pakistan, Lahore, PLD 1966, S.C. 1

Kanayalal v The State, PLD 1977 Karachi 675
Khalid Malik v Federation of Pakistan, PLD 1991 Karachi 1
Khan Iftikhar Hussain Khan of Mamdot v Province of Punjab, PLD 1950 F.C. 15
Khan Muhammad Yusuf Khan Khattak v S.M. Ayub, PLD 1973 S.C. 160

Liaquat Hussain v Federation of Pakistan, PLD 1999 S.C. 504
Liaquat Ali v Government of Sindh, PLD 1973 Karachi 78

M. Yamin Qureshi v Islamic Republic of Pakistan, PLD 1980 S.C.22
M.A. Khuhro v Federation of Pakistan, PLD 1950 Sindh 49
M.D. Tahir v Federal Government, 1989 Civil Law Cases 1369
M.H. Khondkar v The State, PLD 1966 S.C. 140
M.H. Shamim v Secretary Establishment Division, Government of Pakistan, 1981 PLC (C.S.) 337
Mahmood Khan Achakzai v Federation of Pakistan, PLD 1997 S.C. 426
Malik Ghulam Jilani v Government of West Pakistan, PLD 1967 S.C. 373
Manzoor Ahmad Wattoo v Federation of Pakistan, PLD 1997 Lahore 38
Martial Law Administrator v Muhammad Niaz, PLD 1979 S.C. 921
Maulana Abdus Sattar Khan Niazi v The State, PLD 1974 Lahore 324
Maulana Musahib Ali v The State, PLD 1975 Karachi 909
Maulvi Tamizuddin Khan v Federation of Pakistan, PLD 1955 Sindh 96
Mehram Ali v Federation of Pakistan, PLJ 1998 S.C. 1415
Mian Abdul Majeed v Province of Punjab, 1994 CLC 1244
Mir Hassan v The State, PLD 1969 Lahore 786
Mirza Khurshid Ahmad v Government of Punjab, PLD 1992 Lahore 1
Muhammad Abdul Haque v Fazlul Quadir Chowdhry, PLD 1963 Dacca 669
Muhammad Akram Shaikh v Federation of Pakistan, PLD 1989 S.C. 229
Muhammad Anwar Durrani v Province of Baluchistan, PLD 1989 Quetta 25
Muhammad Aslam v Punjab Government, NLR 1995 Civil 630
Muhammad Ikram Choudhry v Mian Muhammad Nawaz Sharif, 1998 SCMR 176
Muhammad Nawaz Sharif v President of Pakistan, PLD 1993 S.C. 473
Muhammad Niaz v Martial Law Administrator, PLD 1979 Quetta 179
Muhammad Safdar v The State, PLD 1974 Lahore 200
Muhammad Sharif v Federation of Pakistan PLD 1988 Lahore 725
Mujibur Rehman v Federal Government of Pakistan, PLD 1985 Federal Shariat Court 8
Mumtaz Ali Bhutto v Deputy Martial Law Administrator, PLD 1979 Karachi 307
Murlidhar v University of Karachi, PLD 1966 S.C. 841
Muzaffar Qadir v The District Magistrate, Lahore, PLD 1975 Lahore 1198

Nasir Ahmed v The State, PLJ 1993 S.C.1
Nasir Ahmed v The State, PLJ 1992 Criminal Cases (Lahore) 427
Nasirullah Khan Babar v Chief of the Army Staff, PLD 1979 Peshawar 23
National Bank of Pakistan v Wafaqi Mohtasib, PLD 1992 Karachi 339
Nawab Begum v Home Secretary, Government of the Punjab, PLD 1974 Lahore 344
Nawabzada Mohsin Ali Khan v Government of NWFP, PLD 1993 Peshawar 207
Nusrat Bhutto v Chief of Army Staff, PLD 1977 S.C. 657

Parvez Elahi v Province of Punjab, PLD 1993 Lahore 518
Parvez Elahi v Province of Punjab, PLD 1993 Lahore 595
President v Justice Shaukat Ali, PLD 1971 S.C. 585
Province of East Pakistan v Muhammad Mehdi Ali Khan, PLD 1959 S.C. 387

Qazi Muhammad Anwar Barlas v Secretary Establishment Division, Government of Pakistan, 1981 PLC (C.S.) 330

Reference by His Excellency the Governor-General, PLD 1955 F.C. 435

Sabir Shah v Federation of Pakistan, PLD 1994 S.C. 738
Sakina Bibi v Federation of Pakistan, PLD 1992 Lahore 99
Sarfraz Ali Khan v The Crown, PLD 1951 F.C. 41
Sharaf Faridi v Federation of Islamic Republic of Pakistan, PLD 1989 Karachi 404
Shaukat Ali Mian v Federation of Pakistan, 1999 CLC 607
Sir Edward Snelson v The Judges of the High Court of West Pakistan, PLD 1961 S.C. 237
State v Dosso, PLD 1958 S.C. 533
State v Shaukat Ali Advocate, PLD 1976 Lahore 355
State v Shaukat Ali Advocate, PLD 1976 Lahore 714
State v Tariq Aziz MNA, 2000 SCMR 751
State v Yusaf Lodhi, PLD 1973 Peshawar 25
State v Ziaur Rahman, PLD 1973 S.C. 49
State v Zulfiqar Ali Bhutto, PLJ 1978 Criminal Cases (Lahore) 1
State v Zulfiqar Ali Bhutto and others, PLD 1978 Lahore 523
Supreme Court Advocates-on-Record Association v Union of India, AIR 1994 S.C. 268
Syed Iqbal Haider v Federation of Pakistan, 1998 SCMR 179
Syed Iqbal Haider v Federation of Pakistan, 1998 SCMR 181
Syed Masroor Ahsan v Ardeshir Cowasjee, PLD 1998 S.C. 823

Tahir Beg v Syed Kausar Ali Shah, PLD 1976 S.C. 504
Tajjamal Hussain Malik v Federal Government of Pakistan, PLD 1981 Lahore 462
Tamizuddin Ahmed v Government of East Pakistan, PLD 1964 Dacca 795

PREFACE

As Pakistan entered the last decade of the twentieth century, I thought that there was a need for a narrative of the constitutional history of Pakistan, spanning fifty years of its existence. The only book of substance on the subject was written by G.W. Chaudhry titled *Constitutional Development in Pakistan*. Its first edition had appeared in 1959 and the second in 1969. No serious effort has been made to write on such an important subject for so many decades.

Pakistan has had a most unusual and turbulent constitutional experience in the era following the departure of the British from India. In over half a century of its existence, Pakistan has experienced democratic and military regimes, pseudo democracy and quasi dictatorship, and even a civilian Martial Law. For outsiders, the constitutional history of Pakistan may make an interesting story, but for those who have lived through the experience, it is extremely painful. It amounts to living perpetually in a laboratory wherein all kinds of constitutional experiments are being conducted by whosoever is in control of the State for the time being. It is a story of ambitious and adventurous generals; manipulative and crafty bureaucrats; self-serving and crooked politicians; and pliable and self-centered judges. It is a horrifying spectre of a new nation with formidable prospects being ruined by its own leaders.

It is obvious that constitutional history cannot be read and understood in a void. Constitutional developments can only be understood in the context of the political events shaping them. Therefore, constitutional and political developments have to be dealt with concurrently so that they can be comprehended in their true perspective. Hence a narrative of constitutional history has to include the political developments. I have in this study focused on such political developments in Pakistan which have had some direct or indirect bearing on constitutional developments.

I initiated this project in the early 1990s with the plan of publishing it by 1997, when Pakistan would complete fifty years of its independence. I wrote the first draft of its earlier chapters in 1992, but research and writing was moving rather slowly due to my professional engagements. The project took off in 1994, primarily due to the interest taken in it by Dr D. Conrad of the South Asia Institute, University of Heidelberg, who was instrumental in the grant of a fellowship to me by the Friedrich Ebert Foundation to work on the project at the South Asia Institute, Heidelberg. My stay at the Institute during the summer of 1994 gave me ample opportunity to collect material for the project because the library is rich in literature on South Asian history, law, and political science. I spent the summer of the following year working on the project in the Law library of Madison Building in the Library of Congress, Washington DC. By this time, I had written the first draft of the book but it required a good deal of revision. I was given this opportunity by the British Council, Lahore which extended a research grant for the project at the Oxford and London Universities.

I spent my summer vacations in 1996 working in the libraries of Oxford University and the School of Oriental and African Studies (SOAS) at the University of London. I also used the India Office Library in London during this period. These libraries afforded me an opportunity to review the entire manuscript and add to it from other research made during this period.

I sent a manuscript of the book to the Oxford University Press (OUP), Karachi in early 1997 for evaluation by its experts. Since the manuscript was voluminous, it took a few months to hear from the OUP. However, I was overjoyed to learn in October 1997 that the OUP had agreed to undertake the publication of the book. By this time, I had already requested I.A. Rehman of the Human Rights Commission of Pakistan (HRCP) to take a look at my work. It was very kind of him to have gone through the voluminous manuscript painstakingly. He also made certain valuable suggestions for improving the quality of the work. In this period, I added new chapters updating the manuscript to 30 June 1998. The complete manuscript was finally sent to the OUP in July 1998.

The book is divided into eight parts, the first part covers the pre-Independence period; the second part covers the period from August 1947 to October 1958 when martial law was imposed throughout the country for the first time; the third part covers the Ayub era (October 1958 to March 1969) and ends with the fall of Ayub; the fourth part pertains to a brief yet very critical period of the Yahya regime from March 1969 to December 1971 ending with the break up of Pakistan; the fifth part covers the Bhutto period (December 1971 to July 1977) ending with the imposition of martial law by Zia; the sixth part covers the Zia regime ending with the death of Zia in August 1988; the seventh part relates to the post-Zia period; and the eighth and final part relates to a discussion of constitutional and political issues in Pakistan over the fifty years of its existence.

The editorial process undertaken by the OUP editorial staff has indeed been a very educative experience for me. The editorial therapy of the book had taken quite a long time and it was indeed tedious and laborious work. The quality of the book owes a lot to this elaborate and intensive effort by the editorial team of the OUP.

I owe so much to so many people for this work. I owe the most to Dr Dietrich Conrad of the South Asia Institute, Heidelberg, who initially encouraged me to undertake this project, helped me obtain the Ebert fellowship in 1994, and provided me with all the facilities at the South Asia Institute in the summer of 1994, which included stay at the Institute, unlimited use of the library, and complete access to his own office at the Institute. His advice was instrumental in shaping the research project. I owe special thanks to my friend, Javed A. Khokhar, Attorney-at-Law, with whom I stayed in Washington DC in the summers of 1993 and 1995 while doing research for the book at the Library of Congress. I am thankful to the British Council, Lahore, for the research grant to work on the book at the libraries of the Oxford and London Universities. I am deeply indebted to Professor Bernard Rudden of the Oxford University for facilitating my stay as his guest at the Brasenose College and for providing me with access to the Oxford University library. I am also indebted to Dr

David Taylor of SOAS for arranging my stay in London and for facilitating the use of the SOAS library at the University of London.

I owe deep gratitude to I.A. Rehman of HRCP who gave a lot of his valuable time to read and edit the manuscript and made very valuable suggestions. I am thankful to Mrs Rukhsana Ahmad who endeavoured to have the book published in England. It was the volume of the book that discouraged British publishers from undertaking such an expensive project. I am indebted to my friend and partner, Afzal Hayat Mufti, for introducing me to the British Council, Lahore and for making my stay at Oxford and London comfortable during the summer of 1996. I am thankful to Dr Klaus Klennert and Dr Hans-Joachim Esderts, Resident Representatives of the Friedrich Ebert Foundation in Islamabad, for facilitating the award of an Ebert fellowship to me for the summer of 1994.

I am grateful to Muhammad Zakaullah, former Registrar, Supreme Court of Pakistan and former Secretary, Pakistan Law Commission, for providing me access to the Supreme Court library and for allowing me to obtain photocopies of the extracts of relevant debates of the Constituent Assembly. I owe a debt of gratitude to Abdul Wahid Siddiqui who worked very hard in transferring the manuscript to a computer hard disc and then preparing floppies with back-up arrangements. The manuscript went through several revisions and modifications over a period of three years and Siddiqui carried out all revisions and modifications faithfully and with precision.

I am thankful to Ms Samina Choonara, Editor, OUP Lahore, for undertaking and supervising the painstaking work of editing the manuscript. The publication of the book owes a lot to her coordinating efforts. I also owe thanks to Ms Uzma Gilani and Ms Daleara Hirjikaka, members of the editorial staff of OUP Karachi for looking after the editorial process of the book in Karachi. I am deeply indebted to Mrs Ameena Saiyid, Managing Director of OUP, for accepting the book for publication.

Hamid Khan

PART I

PRE-PARTITION CONSTITUTIONAL AND POLITICAL HISTORY

1

THE STATE OF UNDIVIDED INDIA

The earliest Muslims to travel to India may have sailed from Arabia in the lifetime of Prophet Muhammad (PBUH). For centuries, Arab traders and sailors had been familiar with the ports of western India. Some of them settled there, and it seems that certain rajas of Madras, whose prosperity depended on the maritime trade, encouraged their youthful subjects to become Muslims and learn navigation.[1] The descendants of these Arabs and the converts are still to be found on the Malabar coast. However, the Muslims' arrival in the Indian subcontinent in great numbers started with their invasion of Sindh in AD 712 under the leadership of Muhammad bin Qasim. The Muslims followed in waves of conquest until Delhi fell to Muslim forces under Shahabuddin Muhammad Ghori in 1192.

The Delhi Sultanate was founded by Qutubuddin Aibak in 1206 and Muslim power continued to expand until it reigned supreme over the entire subcontinent. Five Turkish/Afghan dynasties ruled Delhi till 1526. The Muslim sultans belonging to these dynasties ruled by decrees (*farmans*). The sultan was the chief executive, sole legislator, and the chief judge of the land. The powers of executive, legislature, and judiciary were concentrated in him. He administered justice to both Muslim and non-Muslim subjects. The Hindus acquired the status of *dhimmies*; persons who, while retaining their own religion, were exempted from military service on payment of a poll tax.[2] The Delhi sultans, however, preferred adherance to the principles of Islamic law while administering justice to their subjects. Nevertheless, the unrestrained power of the sultan and his whims and wishes were the law of the land. Each sultan divided his territory into provinces (*subas*), run by provincial governors (*subedars*). Magnificent and luxurious courts, rewards for obedience, suppression of dissent, pious dispositions, and instilling fear and awe in the hearts of the ruled, rather than seeking the consent of the people, were the chief traits of such rule.[3]

The Mughals: Founders of Modern Administration

The Turko-Afghan Muslim dynasties were succeeded by the Mughals. Babur, the first Mughal to rule the Indian subcontinent, came from a small kingdom in Turkistan. He defeated the last of the Turko-Afghan dynasties, the Lodhis, and laid the foundation of the Mughal empire. The period of its first six emperors (1526–1707) is known for the glory and power of the Mughals. These emperors are known for laying the foundation of the modern administration of India and for introducing a system of agricultural revenue administration which still prevails in India and Pakistan.

Akbar (1556–1605), subdued the entire subcontinent except the extreme south, and ruled over Afghanistan as well. He tried to unite Muslims and Hindus by adopting a policy of appeasement towards his Hindu subjects. He accepted in marriage, for himself as well as for his son, women of Hindu Rajput chieftains. He prohibited the levy of taxes on Hindu pilgrims and the collection of *Jizya*, the differential tax (or protection tax), claimed from non-Muslims. Cow slaughter was made illegal. He even founded a new religion, *Din-e-Illahi,* synthesizing Muslim and Hindu faiths. This religion, however, did not survive him.

For transacting the affairs of the state, Mughal emperors appointed heads of various departments: the Imperial Household under the Khan-e-Saman; the Imperial Exchequer under the Diwan; the Military Pay Department under the Mir Bakhshi; the Judiciary under the Chief Qazi; Religious Endowment and Charities under the Sadurs Sudar; and the Mohtasib, who censored public morals. Qazi Courts usually followed the interpretations of divine law by eminent Muslim jurists. The Mughal empire was initially divided into twelve provinces and finally into fifteen during the reign of Aurangzeb. The provinces were further divided into districts and sub-divisions. The Mughal government freely borrowed and adopted Persio-Arabic rules of governance and mixed them with elements and institutions of Hindu empires of yore. The Mughals were prone to centralization. Despite their despotic disposition, most emperors never allowed their imperial rule to degenerate into unbearable tyranny for the masses.[4]

Aurangzeb (1658–1707), was the last of the great Mughals. He tried to rule strictly in accordance with the tenets of Islam. He re-introduced *Jizya* for non-Muslim subjects but it was made clear that the objective was to allow non-Muslims to buy exemption from military service. He did not dismiss non-Muslims from his service because he believed that religion had no concern with the secular business of administration. One of his achievements, for which he is particularly remembered, is a detailed compilation of Muslim laws known as *Fatawa-Alamgiri*.

After the death of Aurangzeb, the Mughal empire quickly fell into decay. Although it survived in name until 1857, it slowly disintegrated and became ineffective. In 1739, Delhi was sacked by invaders from Persia led by Nadir Shah. The Marathas became a power to be reckoned with until they were crushed by Ahmed Shah Abdali in the third battle of Panipat in 1761.

The British, French, Portuguese, and the Dutch fought amongst themselves for domination of the subcontinent until finally the British got the better of the other colonialists. In the weakened Mughal empire, successor states were created in Bengal, Oudh, Rohilkand, Hyderabad, and Mysore, led by Muslim rulers. Sikhs dominated the Punjab for some time. The British East India Company, after disposing of their European rivals, dealt with the Muslim, Hindu, and Sikh rulers of the states one by one. However, the rulers of Mysore, Hyder Ali and Tipu Sultan, did put up a stiff resistance and kept the British at bay for some time. By the middle of the nineteenth century, the British East India Company completely dominated the Indian subcontinent. The last attempt at throwing off the British yoke failed in 1857 when the Company's forces fought back and suppressed the mutiny of Indian soldiers (known as the War of Independence). The last of the Mughal emperors, Bahadur Shah Zafar, was formally deposed. Simultaneously, the East India Company's rule was brought to an end and India was made a colony of the British Crown.

The Mughals had ruled by decree with the emperor concentrating all executive, legislative, and judicial powers in himself. The status of the subjects and the justice administered to them depended largely on the disposition of the sovereign and the calibre and integrity of men appointed by him as administrators and judges.

No written constitutions are known to have existed during the Muslim rule of India from 1206 to 1857. Governments were run more or less on the principles of monarchy. The eldest son was expected to succeed his father as sultan or emperor. However, there were no fixed rules of imperial succession. On the death or decline of almost every emperor, there was a fratricidal war until the strongest claimant eradicated all possible threats and proclaimed himself emperor.

Although the emperor or sultan was the repository of all powers of State, day to day administration was carried out by his appointed governors and justice was administered by his appointed judges (Qazis). Judgments were given at different levels in different matters by either the head of the family, village, caste, the court of the guild, the governor of the province, the minister of the king, or even the king himself.[5] Litigation was brief and the execution of the judgment was swift.

British Expansionism in India

The desire of the British to trade with India and South East Asia grew out of their need to import spices. On 31 December 1600, Queen Elizabeth I granted a charter, for fifteen years initially, to the Governor and company of Merchants of London trading into the East Indies. The Charter authorized the London Company to trade freely into and from the East Indies.[6]

This Charter provides, *inter alia,*

> that it shall and may be lawful to and for them, or the more Part of them, being so assembled, and that shall then and there be present, in any such Place or Places, whereof the Governor or his Deputy for the time being, to be one, to make, ordain and constitute such, and so many reasonable laws, Constitutions, Orders and Ordinances, as to them, or the greater Part of them, being then and there present, shall seem necessary and convenient, for the good Government of the Company, and of all Factors, Masters, Mariners and other Officers, employed or to be employed in any of their Voyage and for the better Advancement and Continuance of the said Trade and Traffic.[7]

It appears from this that since the Company was formed mainly for the purpose of sea-trade, and not for any territorial acquisition or sovereignty over a foreign country, power to make maritime emergency regulations was granted. This is somewhat similar to the power of modern subordinate legislation.[8]

Besides the legislative function of the Governor and Company, it had immediate judicial function. It was empowered to 'lawfully impose, ordain, limit and provide such Pains, Punishments and Penalties, by Imprisonment of Body, or by Fines and Amercements, or by all or any of them, upon and against all Offenders, contrary to such Laws, Constitutions, Orders and Ordinances, or any of them.'[9]

Emperor Jahangir allowed the Company to trade with India and to manage the Company's factory in Gujarat without any interference from the central government but subject to the approval of the local Viceroy, Prince Khurram, who did not raise any question regarding this grant. He was in the habit of upholding the Company's interest in the local area. Gradually, the Company managed to establish factories in different parts of India, particularly in the coastal areas of the country. Throughout the seventeenth century, it was one of the basic aims of the Company to acquire territorial control by establishing factories in important trade and political centres of India.[10]

This Charter was renewed by King James I in 1609 for perpetuity. However, it could be cancelled at any time by a royal decree, after giving three years' notice to the Company. Charles II issued a new Charter in 1661 increasing the authority of the Company and making it more effective. In 1683, the Company was empowered to declare war on and to conclude peace with any ruler. Consequent to this, the Company was also granted the right to raise, arm, train, and muster a strong army. In 1686, the Company established its own royal mint. Around 1698, the British government wanted to raise a loan, and therefore auctioned the monopoly of trade in the East Indies. As the Company could not raise the requisite amount, it was wound up and a new Company was formed similar to the old one.[11]

The establishment of the New East India Company coincided with the disintegration of the Mughal empire after the death of Aurangzeb in 1707. As mentioned earlier, after struggling with rival colonialists from France and Holland, the Company succeeded in driving them out and establishing its own supremacy over a large part of India. To begin with, the Company established its administrative control over Bombay. After the battle of Plassey and Buxor, it extended its control and administration to Bengal, Bihar, and Orissa. On the fall of Seringapatam in the fourth Mysore war in 1799, the last real resistance to the expansionism of the Company offered by the Sultans of Mysore also collapsed and the Company continued to extend its hegemony over the subcontinent without much resistance.

The story of British expansionism in India is quite intriguing. The island and port of Bombay was ceded to the British Crown in 1661 by the Portuguese sovereignty as part of the dower of Catherine of Braganza. It was granted to the East India Company by a Charter of 1669 for the yearly rent of ten pounds. Patna, ancient Pataliputra, the Palibothra of Megasthenes, was the seat of one of the Company's factories in Bengal as early as 1620. Dhaka, so called from the Dakh or Buten frondosa trees of the neighbourhood, was occupied by Dutch, English, and French factories in the seventeenth century. The right to establish a factory at Balasore (Bal Eshwar, 'Strength of God') was granted to the Company in 1642, 1645, and in 1646, in return, as the story goes, for medical services rendered to Shah Jehan (1627–58), and to his Viceroy, the Nawab of Bengal, Sultan Shuja (1639–60), by Surgeon Gabriel Broughton of the Company's ship, Hopewell. Additional privileges were awarded to the Company due to the presence of their factories at Hugli and Balasore. It was to Balasore that the Pippli factory was transferred in 1642.[12]

English settlement in Calcutta began in August 1690. A local rebellion prepared the ground for fortifying the Company's factory at Sutanati in 1698. Earlier, in 1696, the Company had purchased the right to own land over the three villages of Sutanati, Calcutta, and Gavindpur for an annual payment of 1200 rupees. The fortified factory at Sutanati was named after the then King of England as Fort William.[13]

In 1717, Sir John Surman obtained three decrees from the Mughal emperor, Farrukhsiyar, which were addressed to the viceroys of Gujarat, Hyderabad, and Bengal. The Company acquired several valuable rights through these *farmans*. 'A compensation of 10,000 rupees was accepted for customs and dues at Surat; the rupees coined in Bombay by the Company were to be valid in the imperial dominions. The position in Madras was regularized . . . and the right to trade free of dues in Bengal subject to the annual payment of 3000 rupees was established'.[14]

In 1757, the victory of Plassey by Clive paved the way for British rule in India. Their supremacy was further established when Mir Qasim lost the battle of Buxor in 1764. The year 1765 marked a turning point in Anglo-Indian history when the Company was empowered to collect revenue on behalf of the Mughal emperor, Shah Alam, and to administer fiscal law for the purpose in Bengal, Bihar, and Orissa.[15] So, in the legal sense, the Company did not acquire 'territorial sovereignty' over these provinces in 1765. Admittedly, in the name of fiscal administration, the Company had acquired territorial sovereignty and the Mughal emperor was nothing but its shadow. However, if the term 'territorial sovereignty' is used in a loose sense, then the Company acquired this authority not in 1765 under the grant of Diwani but immediately after the victory of Plassey in 1757. Because of this development, the Company played the role of kingmaker in the eastern provinces of India. It exerted so much political influence over the succession to the throne of Murshidabad that all the Nawabs of Bengal, Bihar, and Orissa did not dare protest against the rule of the Company over these territories. The fact was that they were puppets in the hands of the Company. Besides, the power of the Mughal emperor was on the decline and Shah Alam had no other alternative but to please the Company by granting Diwani in 1765.

This was the beginning of the ascendancy and sovereignty of the East India Company over India which ultimately culminated in direct British rule.

Legislative Control by the British Parliament

The expansion of the Company's rule in India made it imperative for the British government to find ways and means to supervise such control. This resulted in legislation being passed by the British Parliament. The Act of 1773 granted the British government powers to regulate the affairs of the Company in India.[16] Apart from making extensive provisions for internal management of the Company, it endorsed the appointment of Warren Hastings as the first Governor-General of India along with his four counsellors.[17] Provisions were made for the establishment of a Supreme Court of Judicature at Fort Williams and for its effective jurisdiction.[18] This Act left much to be desired because it was inherently vague and unclear. It did not make clear the division of powers between the British government and the Company and became a useless piece of legislation in the face of swiftly changing circumstances in India. The Amending Act of 1781 was passed to remove the defects in the parent Act but all the difficulties were not removed.[19]

These Acts were followed by what is known as Pitt's India Act of 1784, whereby the supreme authority was placed in the hands of the British government of the day which acted through a Board of Control. It introduced a dual control system under two bodies, the Board of Control and the Court of Directors.[20] The Governor-General of India was accountable to both of these bodies which made his position difficult and the administration under him cumbersome. The Act of 1786 made Cornwallis Governor-General of India as well as the Commander-in-Chief of the Indian military forces with the power to override his Council.[21] In 1788, the Declaratory Act was passed vesting full powers and supremacy in the Board of Control, thus transferring power to the Crown.[22] The Charter Act of 1793 empowered the Governor-General of India and the Governors of the Indian Provinces to override their respective Councils.[23] The Governor-General was given direct control over the Presidencies of Calcutta, Madras, and Bombay.[24]

Further provisions were made to regulate the government of British territories in India and for better administration of India under the Government of India Act, 1800.[25] This Act provided for the establishment of a Supreme Court of Judicature at Madras.[26] Provisions were also made for jurisdiction of Courts in Bengal, Madras, and Bombay.[27] The Charter Act of 1813 expressly proclaimed the sovereignty of Britain over India and the Company was reduced to an administrative organization.[28] The Government of India Act 1833, fully declared the authority of the Crown, restricting the trade monopoly of the Company till 30 April 1854, and led to the codification of laws for India.[29] The Government of India Act of 1853 further reduced the authority of the Company by reducing the number of directors from twenty-four to eighteen and by introducing six nominees of the British government on the Board of Directors.[30] During this period, the Company kept expanding its control over the Indian subcontinent. Around 1856, the Company controlled the entire subcontinent except the Princely states which also accepted the overlordship of the Company. The Princely states that tried to tow an independent line were forcibly brought under control. The last symbol of Mughal power, Bahadur Shah Zafar, was removed from office in 1857.

The dual control system introduced by Pitt's India Act of 1784 continued up to 1858 when it was abolished and replaced by the Secretary of State for India. The uprising of Indian soldiers in 1857 provided a pretext for the British government to assume direct control over India. The Act of 2 August 1858 ended the regime of the East India Company and with it the dual control system. The Board of Directors of the Company held its last meeting after the said Act and formally handed over to its British sovereign the vast empire it had built in India with skill, cunning, and enterprise. The Company created history by proving that a skilful trading company could take over a vast country, rather a subcontinent, fraught with internal strife, power rivalries, religious animosities, and lack of central authority.

Although colonization of India had been completed by the East India Company by 1858, the British government formally assumed control over the administration of India after a Proclamation issued by Queen Victoria on first November, 1858.[31] Under this Proclamation, civil and military officials in the service of the Company were retained and all treaties and engagements made with the native princes of India by the Company were protected. The Proclamation promised the Indians some fundamental rights. These included: freedom of religion, safeguard against discrimination on the basis of race or creed, or in services; equal and impartial protection of the law; and protection of property rights inherited from ancestors. The Proclamation also extended recognition to the ancient rights, usages, and customs of India.

The Government of India Act, 1858

In order to administer India in accordance with the Proclamation, the British Parliament passed the Government of India Act in 1858.[32] It was, in effect, a constitutional document for colonial India. Under this Act, the territories under the control and administration of the Company were transferred to and vested in the Crown. The Secretary of State, who was to sit in Parliament, was empowered to exercise powers that were previously exercised by the Company or the Board of Control (which was abolished).[33] A Council, consisting of fifteen members, was established by the Act. The council was to conduct all business relating to the Government of India in the United Kingdom under the direction of the Secretary of State.[34] The Secretary of State could override the opinion of the majority of the Council but had to record reasons for doing so.[35] The expenditure of the revenues of India was made subject to the control of the Secretary of State and the Council.[36] The accounts for each financial year were to be laid before the British Parliament.[37] The Secretary of State could sue or be sued in India as well as in England in the name of the Secretary of State in Council as a body corporate.[38] All acts and provisions in force at the time were saved and continued in force and made applicable.[39] The Secretary of State and members of the Council were indemnified against any personal liability regarding the performance of their official duties and all liabilities, costs, and damages in respect thereof were to be paid out of the revenues of India.[40]

The Government of India Act, 1858 was amended in 1859 and the Governor-General of India, Governors and certain officers (authorized by the Secretary of State and the Council) were empowered to sell and dispose of all real and personal estate in India which was vested in the Crown and to execute any contracts in this behalf.[41]

The Indian Councils Act, 1861

The Government of India Act, 1858 was concerned with the business of the Government of India to be transacted in the United Kingdom. It made no provision for the administrative set-up in India. It was therefore necessary to provide for an internal framework for the administration of India and to incorporate the native population in the administration. Decentralization of authority was also deemed necessary.

With these objectives in view, the Indian Councils Act was passed in 1861 to make provisions for the Council of the Governor-General and for the Local Government of the Presidencies and Provinces of India.[42] The Council of the Governor-General was composed of five members, three to be appointed by the Secretary of State with the concurrence of a majority of the members of his Council. The other two were appointed by the Crown, one being a barrister and the other the Commander-in-Chief of the Armed Forces in India.[43] In addition to these five ordinary members of the Council, the Governor-General was empowered to nominate six to twelve additional members to his Council for making laws and regulations.[44] The Council of the Governor-General was empowered to make, repeal, amend, or alter any laws and regulations for India subject to the assent of the Governor-General or the Crown.[45] The Governor-General was also empowered to make Ordinances having the force of law in cases of urgent necessity.[46]

Provision was also made for the composition of Councils for the Governors of the Presidencies of Madras and Bombay. These Councils could frame laws and regulations for their respective Presidencies subject to the assent of the Governor concerned.[47] The Governor-General could constitute new provinces, alter provincial boundaries,[48] and appoint Lieutenant-Governors and their Councils for such provinces.[49]

Constitutional Developments between 1861 and 1909

While the Indian Councils Act, 1861 did provide a framework for legislation and administration within India, it was not an exhaustive piece of constitutional legislation. The gaps in the Act were filled by various laws of constitutional importance. The East India (High Courts of Judicature) Act, 1861, provided for the establishment of High Courts in Calcutta, Bombay, and Madras.[50] Judges of the High Courts held their offices at the Crown's pleasure.[51] Upon establishment of the High Courts of Calcutta, Madras, and Bombay, the Supreme Courts of Sudder Dewany Adawlut and Foujdary Adawlut at these places were abolished and their jurisdiction stood vested in these High Courts.[52] These High Courts exercised all such civil, criminal, admiralty, vice-admiralty, testamentary, intestate and matrimonial jurisdiction, original and appellate, and powers which were granted to them by the Crown under the Letters Patents.[53] These High Courts had powers to superintend and to frame the Rules of Practice for courts subordinate to them.[54] Provision was also made for the establishment of a High Court in the North-western Provinces.[55]

The Indian Councils Act, 1861 was amended to enlarge the powers of the Governor-General of India-in-Council at meetings for making laws and regulations and to amend the law respecting the territorial limits of the several presidencies and lieutenant-governorships in India.[56] The Governor-General was given the power to make laws and regulations for all British subjects, whether in the service of the Government of India or not, including those within the princely states of India.[57] The Governors of the presidencies and Lieutenant-Governors of the provinces were conferred powers to draft laws and regulations for the governments of the territories under them for the assent of the Governor-General.[58] The Governors and Lieutenant-Governors were made ex-officio members of the Governor-General's Council for the purpose of such laws and regulations.[59] The Governor-General was empowered to override the opinion of the majority of his Council but any two or more members of such a dissentient majority could record their dissent and notify it to the Secretary of State.[60] The Governor-General, with the sanction of the Secretary of State, was empowered to make appointments to certain offices without certificate from the Civil Service Commission.[61]

The Indian Councils Act, 1892 was enacted in order to amend the Indian Councils Act, 1861.[62] The number of additional members of the Governor-General's Council was raised from six to twelve, to ten to twenty. This Act opened the way for the appointment of Indian residents as additional members of the Councils of the Governor-General, governors of the presidencies, or lieutenant-governors of the provinces.[63] The local legislature of any province was empowered to repeal or amend any law or regulation as to that province.[64]

The Muslims of India bore the main brunt of defeat in the 1857 war of independence. Three sons of the last Mughal Emperor, Bahadur Shah Zafar, were shot dead and their heads presented to the Emperor. The Emperor was exiled for life to Rangoon. A number of *ulema* who had given *fatwas* of *jehad* against the British were either killed or deported for life. Muslims in Delhi were particularly victimized and the city fell into a quagmire of illiteracy and backwardness.[65] Muslims were not allowed to enter Delhi. As Mirza Ghalib[66] bemoaned in one of his famous letters, 'while birds and animals can come to Delhi, Muslims cannot'.

The British exaggerated the Muslims' responsibility for, and their role in, the Indian uprising of 1857. Muslims, therefore, not only lost their empire, but also had to face the agony of persecution by the British conquerors. The state of the Muslims in India immediately after 1857 has been aptly described by Chaudhri Muhammad Ali in the following words:

> Too proud to cooperate with the victor, too sullen to adjust themselves to the new circumstances, too embittered to think objectively, too involved emotionally with the past to plan for the future, Muslim society in the decades following the events of 1857 presented a picture of desolation and decay.[67]

Hindus, on the other hand, were forging ahead in all fields of life. Of the 240 Indian pleaders admitted to the Calcutta Bar between 1852 and 1868, only one was a

Muslim. There were no covenanted officers or High Court judges from amongst the Muslims. In all of the government gazetted appointments in the province of Bengal, only 92 out of the 1338 posts were held by Muslims.[68] In 1878, there were 3155 Hindus as opposed to 57 Muslims holding graduate and post-graduate degrees.[69]

In these difficult times, when Muslims in India were sliding into ignorance and retrogression, a towering figure, Syed Ahmad Khan, possessing great foresight and courage, appeared on the scene. He advised his fellow Muslims to seek adjustment with western ideas and took steps to restore mutual trust between the British and the Muslims by defending Muslims against British charges of disloyalty. Syed Ahmed was convinced that the only hope for the advancement of the Muslim community lay in their acquisition of western learning, especially the sciences. To achieve this he established the Mohammadan Anglo-Oriental College (subsequently the Aligarh University) in 1875. To meet the demand of the Muslim community for Islamic education, Syed Ahmad ensured that although the teaching at the college was in English and the main curriculum western, both Arabic and religious instruction were made compulsory subjects. The College was successful not only in Syed's immediate objective, but also produced candidates for the higher ranks of government service, as well as Muslim political leaders such as Maulana Muhammad Ali, Khawaja Nazimuddin, and Liaquat Ali.

Syed Ahmad's contribution to the political cause of Indian Muslims was formidable. As a member of the Governor-General's Legislative Council from 1878, he successfully campaigned for separate nomination of Muslims to the local self-government institutions which were created by Lord Rippon. He was one of the original exponents of the two nation theory and believed that Hindus and Muslims could not have an equal share in power. Syed Ahmad opposed the demands of the Indian National Congress for the enlargement of the representative government in India and the recruitment of Indians for government service by open competitive examination. In his view, representative government was inexpedient for a country inhabited by two different nations, Hindus and Muslims. Regarding competitive examinations, he believed that Muslims had not yet acquired sufficient knowledge of the English language and other modern sciences to adequately compete with others.[70]

An important political development during this period was the formation of the Indian National Congress in 1885, on the initiative of Allan Octavian Hume, a retired British official, and under the presidency of the Viceroy, Lord Dufferin. The Party originally intended to throw up a cadre of native politicians beholden to the British rulers to help the latter improve administration, but, with the passage of time, the Congress grew into the most powerful political organization in India. Although a number of Muslims joined the Congress, many influential Muslim leaders, including Syed Ahmad, advised them against it. Muslim leaders were afraid that in a Congress dominated by Hindus, Muslims would be at a disadvantage.

The partition of Bengal in 1905 embittered relations between Hindus and Muslims. The reason for partition was mainly administrative. In those days Bengal included the present Bihar and Orissa, and it was difficult to administer such a large area and population with one Governor. The agrarian economy of Bengal was dominated by the capitalists of Calcutta, and this was hindering local initiative for progress and industrialization. The partition of Bengal was meant to lead to greater administrative efficiency and to encourage local initiative. The Muslims of Bengal welcomed partition, but the Hindus bitterly opposed it. The latter thought that it would weaken their economic and political position. Violent agitation by Hindu members of the Congress convinced the Muslims that they had to create their own political force and leadership. The British government, under pressure from Hindus, later annulled the partition of Bengal in 1911.[71]

The fears of Hindu domination within the Congress and the situation arising from the agitation against the partition of Bengal were addressed by some influential Muslim leaders by forming the All-India Muslim League in Dhaka in 1906 with the aim of protecting political and other rights of Indian Muslims. The All-India Muslim League was later recognized as the political body representing Indian Muslims which later spearheaded the Pakistan movement.

Another development during this period was the Muslims'demand for separate electorates at all levels of government, district boards, municipalities, and legislative councils. They drew the attention of the Viceroy to the fact that in the United Provinces, while Muslims constituted 14 per cent of the population, they had not secured a single seat under joint franchise.[72] These views were communicated to the Viceroy by a Muslim delegation led by the Agha Khan in 1906. The delegation requested that Muslims be granted separate electorates in future reforms. The Viceroy, Lord Minto, assured them that he was entirely in accord with their case and agreed to extend favourable consideration to their demand for a separate electorate.

The Minto-Morely Reforms, 1909–1919

By 1909, there was widespread political awakening amongst the Indians. Active political participation of Indians was reflected in the formation and influence of political parties such as the Indian National Congress and the All-India Muslim League. So much so, that the local self-government reforms introduced by Lord Rippon did not meet the political aspirations of the Indian people who wanted greater participation in government, provincial as well as central, at the highest levels.

One factor which contributed to movements for greater reform was the triumph of Japan in the Russo-Japanese War of 1904–5. Japan's victory raised the hope in the hearts of the Indians that India, too, could become a great power. There was also a change in public opinion in Britain with the Liberals' accession to power in 1906. They did not subscribe to the archaic notions of an endless wardship of a permanently adolescent India.[73] Another factor was the growing strength of Indian public opinion. The demand for greater participation in government became more and more pronounced after the Viceroyalty of Lord Curzon (1899–1905), who had an autocratic style of governance and disregarded Indian opinion.

The British government considered it advisable not to ignore the rapidly changing political atmosphere in India. In 1907, Lord Minto, the Viceroy, disclosed in the

Legislative Council that the people of India would be given greater opportunity to express their views on administrative methods. In December 1904, Lord Morley, the Secretary of State, introduced his famous Bill in the British Parliament which was passed in 1909 as the Indian Councils Act. This Act is popularly known as the Minto-Morley reforms.

The Indian Councils Act, 1909

The Indian Councils Act, 1909 enlarged the size of Legislative Councils of the Governor-General and the Governors of various Provinces,[74] which included the nominated as well as elected members. Indians became entitled to nomination or election as members of these Legislative Councils, subject to conditions laid down in the regulations made by the Governor-General with the approval of the Secretary of State.[75]

The functions of the Legislative Councils were increased and individual members in the Imperial Legislative Council could move resolutions relating to alteration in taxation. Matters of general public interest could also be discussed in the Legislative Councils and members could ask questions and supplementary questions.

In the rules framed under this Act, official majority was given up in the Provincial Legislative Councils, though working majorities were maintained. Official majority was, however, maintained in the Central Legislature. In the provinces, university senators, landlords, district boards, municipalities and Chambers of Commerce were to elect members of the Legislative Councils. Muslims were given separate representation and Muslim members of the legislature were to be elected by Muslims alone. The demand for a separate electorate was thus accepted.

These reforms did not satisfy the Indians. Although elections to Legislative Councils were introduced, the number of voters was limited due to strict qualifications of property and education imposed on franchise. Further, the system of election was indirect. The people were to elect members of local bodies who were to elect members of electoral colleges who, in turn, were to elect members of the provincial legislatures. The members of the Provincial Legislature were to elect members of the Imperial Legislature. These reforms also made no change in the composition of the executive though the legislatures could criticize its actions. The Act gave great weight to vested interests by giving special representation to landlords, chambers of commerce and other influentials. There was official majority in the Imperial Council. Non-official majorities in the provincial councils were nullified by the fact that they included nominated members. While parliamentary reforms were introduced, no responsibility was given to the councils. In short, the reforms led to a lot of confusion. The result was widespread criticism of the government[76] though some of it was thoughtless and irresponsible.

The inadequacy of the reforms of 1909 and the resultant discontent and disappointment of the people gave rise to revolutionary and terrorist activities. The reversal in 1911 of the 1905 partition of Bengal annoyed the Muslims. They saw it as a concession to the Hindus who had challenged the government. The undoing of the province of East Bengal meant that Muslims would lose their majority and once again be dominated by the more advanced Hindu community.[77] It was a clear breach of assurances and commitments made by the British regarding the inviolability of the partition. The years following the cancellation of the partition of Bengal marked a turning point in the history of Indian Muslims. It could be argued that the seeds of Pakistan were sown by this one event.

During the World War that broke out in August 1914, British India and the princely states contributed 1,302,000 combatants and non-combatants (such as labour corps) to the imperial forces.[78] The political fallout in India was a strengthening of the demand for free institutions. Turkey's entry in the War on the side of the central European powers made a deep and disturbing impression on the Muslim community in India, which considered itself to be a part of a universal religious brotherhood.

By 1916, hopes of a speedy and conclusive British victory in the War had disappeared and disillusionment had set in. This realization brought the Muslim League close to the Congress. In the Lucknow Pact of 1916, the Muslim League and the Congress agreed to urge Britain to announce self-governance to the people of India and substantial reforms after the War as a step towards that goal. The Lucknow Pact settled the proportionate election of representatives of Muslims and Hindus in the provincial and all-India legislatures.

Before his death in 1915, Gokhale had prepared a scheme of reforms to be given to India after the War,[79] the main feature of which was the grant of provincial autonomy. It was recommended that four-fifths of the members of Provincial Legislative Councils should be elected and half the members of the Executive Council or Cabinet of the Governor should be Indians.

The Secretary of State for India, Edwin Montague, and the Viceroy, Lord Chelmsford, jointly prepared a report on Indian constitutional reforms known as the Montagu-Chelmsford Report. Published in July 1918, the Report identified four objectives:[80]

1. Complete popular control, as far as possible, in local bodies.
2. Immediate steps towards responsible government to be taken in the provinces.
3. The Indian Legislative Council to be made more representative while the Government of India remained wholly responsible to the British Parliament.
4. The control of Parliament and the Secretary of State over the Government of India and the provincial governments to be relaxed.

The Report recommended 'responsible government' at the provincial level and authority was no longer to be concentrated at the centre. An important outcome of the report was the setting up of the Chamber of Princes on 8 February 1921. The Chamber included 108 leading princes and twelve additional members elected by group voting from amongst the rulers of 127 other states. The Viceroy presided, and the Princes annually elected their own Chancellor and Pro-Chancellor. A standing committee of seven members was formed to advise the Viceroy on matters referred to the committee by him.[81] The Chamber was given no executive powers but it was an important step forward in co-operation between ruling princes and the paramount British power.

The Montagu-Chelmsford Report met with a mixed response. Extremists denounced it as entirely unacceptable, while the moderates, whose policy was to secure self-government for India within the empire by constitutional agitation, welcomed it and decided to co-operate with the government. The Muslims were disappointed. They believed that they had done better in the Congress-League Scheme known as the Lucknow Pact than what was being offered in the Montford Report.

It was on the basis of the Montford report that the Government of India Bill was introduced in the House of Commons by Montague in June, 1919. The object of the Bill, said Montague, was the conciliation of the Indians. He emphasized the Bill's importance as the promise held out to the Indians for reforms after the end of the First World War.[82] It was passed by the British Parliament on 18 December 1919 and received the Royal Assent five days later.

The Government of India Act, 1919

The preamble of the Government of India Act, 1919 stated that it was the declared policy of the British Parliament to provide for increasing association of Indians in every branch of administration and for the gradual development of self-governing institutions, with a view to the progressive realization of responsible government in British India. However, it said, progress in giving effect to this policy could only be achieved in successive stages.[83]

Some of the main provisions of the Government of India Act, 1919 were as under:

1. The Act provided that the Secretary of State for India was to be paid out of British revenues.[84] The Secretary of State continued to possess and exercise the powers of superintendence, direction, and control over the affairs of India. The Governor-General of India was obliged to carry out the orders of the Secretary of State.
2. The Act set up a bicameral legislature at the centre in place of the Imperial Council consisting of one House.[85] The two Houses were called the Central Legislative Assembly and the Council of State.
3. Direct elections were provided for both Houses of the Central Legislature though the franchise was very restricted.[86]
4. The duration of the term for the Central Legislative Assembly was three years, and for the Council of State five years, which could be extended by the Governor-General.[87] The Governor-General had the power to summon, prorogue, and dissolve the Houses of the Central Legislature. He could also address both Houses.[88]
5. The Central Legislature had the power to make laws for all of British India, for Indian subjects wherever they might be, and for all persons employed in the defence forces. It could also repeal or amend laws for the time being in force. However, prior sanction of the Secretary of State-in-Council was required to pass a law abolishing any High Court.[89] Prior sanction of the Governor-General was required to introduce Bills on the following subjects:[90]

(a) The public debt or public revenues of India.
(b) Religion or religious rites and usages of British subjects in India.
(c) Discipline or maintenance of the land, naval, or air forces.
(d) Relations of the Government of India with foreign states or Indian states.
(e) Any measure repealing or amending any Act of legislature or any Ordinance passed by the Governor-General.

The Governor-General could also prevent consideration of a Bill or a part of it if, in his opinion, it 'affects the safety or tranquility of British India, or any part thereof'.[91]

6. The Governor-General could issue an Ordinance for a period of six months which had the same force and effect as an Act of the Central Legislature. He had the power of veto over the Bills passed by the Central Legislature. He could withhold his assent and return a Bill for reconsideration.[92] He could also reserve the Bill for the signification of His Majesty's pleasure. The Crown could disallow any Bill passed by the Indian legislature or Ordinance issued by the Governor-General.
7. The Central Budget was presented before the Central Legislature in the form of demands for grants. There were certain non-votable items which were not open to discussion unless the Governor-General so allowed. All other items were submitted to vote. In an emergency, the Governor-General was empowered to authorize such expenditure as, in his opinion, was necessary for the safety or tranquility of British India or any part thereof.[93]

Diarchy in the Provinces

A partially responsible government was introduced in the provinces in the form of a diarchy, that is, dual government. The executive of the provinces was divided into two parts, one responsible to the legislature and the other responsible to the British Parliament through the Governor and the Governor-General.[94] Departments such as education, local self-government, public health, public works, industries and so on, known as transferred subjects, were allocated to ministers who were elected members of the Provincial Legislature. Departments such as police, administration, finance, land revenue administration, irrigation and canals described as reserved subjects, were headed by nominated officials, generally ICS officers (taken from the executive council of the Governor), who were responsible only to the Governor.[95] The transferred departments were also indirectly controlled by reserved departments, because they depended for revenue on the finance department, a reserved subject. The Governor headed both reserved as well as transferred departments and could easily override the decision of his minister or a member of his executive Council. No principle of Cabinet or collective responsibility was introduced in the working of the provinces.[96]

This system of diarchy, which operated from 1921 to 1937 in the provinces, had many drawbacks. The division of administration into two parts within the same province was contrary to the principles of efficient administration. The division of subjects into reserved and transferred was confusing and haphazard. Many initiatives and reforms were lost in red-tapism. The ministers, who were representatives of the people, and members of the executive council, who were mostly bureaucrats, did not generally pull together. The position of a minister was weak and vulnerable. He was accountable to two masters, the Governor and the Legislative Council and could be dismissed by the Governor or turned out by a vote of no-confidence passed by the legislature. Secretaries of the transferred departments who were bureaucrats had direct access to the Governor and cared very little for the ministers. The Secretary of Finance was very powerful and the ministers were dependent on him for allocation of funds to their departments. As a member of the Indian Civil Service and usually British, he had no sympathy for the aspirations of the Indians as represented by the ministers and cared more for the needs of reserved departments.[97] The economy in India also changed for the worse in the 1920s, which did not give the diarchy an adequate chance. The system was not taken seriously by the Indians whose expectations were higher. They were not content with their restricted involvement in public administration.

Inspite of these drawbacks, diarchy worked in some provinces. There were joint deliberations between the two parts of government in some departments. It proved to be a transitional stage between bureaucracy and responsible government. Considering the general restlessness and discontent in post-war India, the Act was an experimental adventure in Indian constitutional history.[98]

Central and Provincial Legislatures and their Powers

Two separate lists were drawn up under the Act, one containing central and the other provincial subjects.[99] The central list included defence, foreign and political relations, public debts, tariffs and customs, posts and telegraphs, patents and copyright, currency and coinage, communications including railways, aircraft, waterways, commerce and shipping, civil and criminal law and procedure, major courts, quarantine, and so on. The provincial list included local self-government, public health, sanitation and medical administration, education, public works, water supplies and irrigation, land revenue administration, famine relief, agriculture, forests, co-operative societies, law and order including justice, police and jails. There was no concurrent list but all the residuary subjects were to fall within the domain of the centre. In case of doubt, the Governor-General and not the courts, decided whether a particular subject did or did not belong to a province.

The sources of revenue for the centre were customs, income tax, non-alcoholic excise including salt, opium, railways, posts and telegraphs, currency and coinage, and tributes from the Indian states. The sources of revenue for the provinces were land revenue, irrigation, excise on alcoholic liquors, stamps, registration fees, forests, and minerals. The provinces could also impose taxes on succession, betting, gambling, advertisements, and amusements. The raising of loans by the provinces inside India needed special sanction of the Governor-General, while for a loan sought outside

India the prior permission of the Secretary of State was needed. The provinces were given a certain amount of money out of the proceeds of the income tax collected by the central government while the provincial governments made contributions to the centre to meet its deficit.[100]

Under the Act of 1919, the Central Legislature had two chambers: the Council of State and the Legislative Assembly. The Council of State was the upper house and was composed of 60 members, 34 elected and the remaining nominated. Of the 26 nominated members, not more than 20 could be officials. Of the 34 elected members, 19 were elected by general constituencies and the rest by communal and special constituencies; eleven Muslims, one Sikh and three Europeans. Elections were direct but the franchise was extremely restricted. For instance, United Provinces (UP) elected seven members but only those paying 5000 rupees as land revenue or 1000 rupees as income tax could cast their votes. The total number of electors in all of British India for the Council of State in 1925 did not exceed 17,000.[101]

The Legislative Assembly was the lower house and had 145 members; 26 were officials, 14 nominated non-officials, and the remaining 105 elected. Out of the elected members, 53 were elected from the general seats, thirty Muslims, two Sikhs, nine Europeans, seven landlords, and four from Indian commerce. Qualifications of voters differed from province to province. For instance, in UP a person owning a house with annual rental value of rupees 160 could vote in urban constituencies and a person paying land revenue of rupees 150 annually could vote in rural constituencies. The total franchise for electing members of the Legislative Assembly in the year 1926 was only 1,128,331 throughout British India.[102]

The Central Legislature had the power to make laws for all subjects and servants of the Crown in British India. It could not make any law affecting the powers of the Secretary of State for India or the Governor-General. It could not make laws affecting the public debt of India, religious rights or usages, armed forces and foreign relations.[103] The budget was simultaneously laid before both Houses and discussed thoroughly but the right to vote was given only to members of the Lower House. There were votable and non-votable items in the budget. The main non-votable items were the salary of the Governor-General and the funds allocated to the defence, foreign affairs, and political department. Votable items accounted for only 20 per cent of the total budget and even in those the Governor-General had overriding powers. The executive was not responsible to the legislature. The Central Legislature could exercise some influence on the administration at the time of discussion on the annual budget or by passing resolutions from time to time.

The provincial legislatures were all unicameral and were called Legislative Councils.

Political Developments, 1919–1935

The period from 1919 to 1935 was very important and turbulent from the standpoint of political and constitutional developments in India. The Indian National Congress, in its annual session in 1919, condemned the Montford Reforms as 'inadequate, unsatisfactory and disappointing'.[104] It called on the British government to take immediate steps to establish a fully responsible government in India.

Satyagraha

Political trouble started with the passing of the Anarchical and Revolutionary Crimes Act, 1919, based on the Report of the Rowlatt Committee headed by Justice Sidney Rowlatt. This Act provided for speedy trial of offences by a special court consisting of three High Court judges. This court could meet in camera and could take into consideration evidence not otherwise admissible under the Evidence Act. No appeal was provided against the decision of the court. Provincial governments were also given wide powers in matters of arrest, searches and seizures, confinement of suspects, censorship, and so on.[105] The Act was bulldozed through the Central Legislature by the official majority despite strong opposition and warnings by every single non-official Indian member, elected or nominated. Muhammad Ali Jinnah resigned from the Central Legislature in protest.

M.K. Gandhi launched a movement of *Satyagraha* against the Act and called for country-wide strikes. Although he intended to start a peaceful and non-violent movement against this Draconian law, the movement led to violent protests and disorders and a number of people in Delhi and Ahmadabad were killed by police firing. The worst incident occured in Amritsar where, on 13 April 1919, under the orders of Army Commander, Brigadier-General Dyer, troops opened indiscriminate fire on a peaceful but large public meeting in the Jallianwala Bagh. Four hundred people died in this incident and another 1200 were wounded. In order to control further outbreaks of violence, Martial Law was declared in some districts of the Punjab from 15 April to 11 June 1919. Gandhi decided to call off *Satyagraha* because of the violence and killings it had unleashed.

Khilafat Movement

During the First World War, Lloyd George, the Prime Minister of Britain, made a solemn promise to Indian Muslims that Turkey would not be deprived of the lands of Asia Minor and Thrace, populated predominantly by people of Turkish stock. This promise was not kept and Turkey was deprived of her homelands in the terms settled for the armistice. Thrace was given to Greece and the Asian portions of the Turkish empire were divided amongst Britain and France as mandated territories. A High Commission was appointed with a view to deprive the Sultan of all his powers.

Muslims in India were enraged by these events and the Ali brothers, Maulana Muhammad Ali and Shaukat Ali, launched what they called the Khilafat Movement and approached Gandhi for help. Gandhi seized this opportunity to lead the Muslims in India. He threatened to launch a movement of non-cooperation if the terms of peace with Turkey did not meet the sentiments of Indian Muslims. The Khilafat

Movement came to an end in 1923 when Mustafa Kamal Ataturk seized power in Turkey and expelled the British, French, and Greek forces from Asia Minor and Thrace.

Non-cooperation Movement

In a special session held in Calcutta in September 1920, the Congress passed a resolution in favour of a movement for non-cooperation with the government as well as a boycott of the councils (as reformed by the 1919 Act). Gandhi was to lead this movement. In the Nagpur session of Congress, the programme of non-cooperation was discussed and decided according to Gandhi's wishes, despite strong opposition from Bengal and Maharashtra. Jinnah opposed the resolution and was jeered by a throng of Gandhi supporters at the meeting. He decided to leave the Congress after the Nagpur session.

The Prince of Wales, who visited India in November and December 1921, was met with mass protests and boycotts in Bombay and Calcutta. Several Indian leaders were jailed. The Viceroy, Lord Reading, offered to negotiate with the Indian leaders. He was willing to discuss provincial autonomy and diarchy in the centre in return for an end to the non-coperation movement. This offer was not accepted by Gandhi and, in the Ahmadabad session of the Congress held in December 1921, he promised home rule within a year. Gandhi was arrested in March 1922 for propagating sedition and was sentenced to six years in prison.

The Hunter Committee Report on the Jallianwala incident also created unrest. The report justified imposition of Martial Law in the Punjab, and General Dyer's responsibility for hundreds of deaths was treated as a mere error of judgment.

The Simon Commission

In September 1925, a resolution was carried in the Central Assembly advising the British government to make fundamental changes in the Constitution of India, making the government fully responsible. It also called for a round table conference, representing all interests, to prepare a detailed scheme to be placed before the Legislative Assembly for approval and submission to the British Parliament. In November 1927, the British government appointed a commission, composed entirely of Englishmen and headed by Sir John Simon, to inquire into the working of the system of government, the growth of education, and the development of representative institutions in British India. The Commission was also asked to report on the desirability of establishing the principles of responsible government and extension, modification, or restriction of the degree of responsible government then existing under the Act of 1919.

The Simon Commission was boycotted by political parties and other representative organizations in India. Resolutions were passed condemning the exclusion of Indians from the Commission. The day the Commission landed in India, a country-wide *hartal* was observed. The Commission was greeted with black flags and no one, including the Central Assembly, co-operated with the Commission. Thus a step taken ostensibly to appease and pacify Indians produced contrary results.

The Report of the Simon Commission was published in May 1930. It considered the ultimate constitutional framework for the whole of India as a federation, and the place of the provinces in that set-up. The Report declared that the framework could not be unitary and must be federal, not merely in response to the growth of provincial loyalties, but because it was only in a federation that the Indian states could be expected in due course of time to unite with British India. The Report made the following recommendations:

1. Diarchy should be abolished in the provinces and provincial administration should be entrusted to ministers responsible to their legislatures. Franchise should be expanded and the legislature enlarged.
2. Each province should be given a Legislative Council of its own and its representation in the Central Legislature should be strengthened.
3. At the centre, the Central Legislature should be refashioned on the federal principle. The members of the Federal Assembly or the Lower House should be representatives of the provinces and elected by the Provincial Councils. The elections and nominations to the Councils of States should also be on a provincial basis.
4. As far as the Central Executive was concerned, no substantial change was recommended. The entire government could continue to be composed of official nominees and it was not responsible to the legislature. There was to be no diarchy at the centre.
5. The Report said that an All-India Federation would be set up in the distant future.[106]

The Report was, generally condemned by Indians.

The Nehru Report

After the boycotting of the Simon Commission, an all-parties conference was formed to propose a constitution for India. It held its meeting in Bombay in May 1928 and appointed a committee headed by Pandit Motilal Nehru to consider and determine the principles of a Constitution for India. The Report of the all-parties conference, commonly known as the Nehru Report, was published in August 1928.

The Nehru Report proposed a fully responsible government both at the centre and in the provinces. It proposed that the provinces be assigned enumerated functions, whereas residuary powers were to be assigned to the government of India. The Central Legislature should be bicameral, composed of a Senate and a House of Representatives. The Senate should consist of two hundred members elected by the Provincial Legislative Councils, through proportional representation with a single transferable vote. The House of Representatives would have a membership of five hundred. The members were to be elected by means of joint non-communal constituencies on the basis of adult franchise. The distribution of seats amongst the provinces, both in the case of the Senate and the House of Representatives, was to be proportionate to population. In ordinary legislation, both the chambers were to possess equal powers, but with regard to Money Bills, the House of Representatives was to be given the supreme power. No measure affecting the discipline or maintenance of any part of the military forces was to be introduced except on the recommendation of the Defence Committee consisting of ministers and military experts.

The Governor-General was to be appointed by the British government. He was to be paid out of Indian revenues and his salary was not to be altered during the tenure of office. The Governor-General was to act on the advice of his executive council. The Prime Minister was to be appointed by the Governor-General and other ministers were to be appointed by him on the advice of the Prime Minister. The Executive Council was to be collectively responsible to Parliament. The Governor-General-in-Council was to appoint High Commissioners and other representatives similar to those appointed in Canada and other dominions.

Military services were to be guaranteed their existing rights and privileges but in the civil services, the legislatures were to have full powers to make laws and regulations. The central government was to exercise the same rights and discharge the same obligations towards the Indian states, arising out of treaties or otherwise, as the government of India had hitherto exercised or discharged.

The government of a province was to be vested in the Governor to be appointed by the King. He was to be paid out of provincial revenues. The Governor was to act on the advice of the Provincial Executive Council whose number was not to exceed five. The Chief Minister was to be appointed by the Governor and other members of the Executive Council were to be appointed by him on the advice of the Chief Minister. Legislative Councils in the provinces were to be reconstituted on the basis of joint electorate and adult franchise. The North-West Frontier Province, Sindh, and Balochistan were to have the same status and form of government as other major provinces.

Provisions were to be made for a Supreme Court consisting of the Lord President and other justices of the Supreme Court who were to be appointed by the Governor-General-in-Council, but were not to be removed from office except on an address from both Houses of Parliament praying for such removal on the ground of misbehaviour or incapacity. The Supreme Court was to have both original and appellate jurisdiction. Provision was also made for preferring appeals to the King-in-Council under certain circumstances.

The Governor-General-in-Council was to appoint a Committee of Defence, consisting of the Minister of Defence, the Minister of Foreign Affairs, the Commander-in-Chief, the Commander of Air Forces, the Commander of Naval Forces, the Chief of General Staff, and two other experts. The functions of the Defence Committee would be to advise the government and the various departments concerned on questions of defence and general policy.

The Report provided for the fundamental rights, nineteen in number, which were to be embodied in the Constitution. Fundamental rights were to guarantee freedom of life, liberty, property, speech, assembly, and freedom of conscience and religion. They also guaranteed all citizens the right to free elementary education and equality before the law as well as equal civil rights. There were to be no penal laws of a discriminatory nature. No person would by reason of his religion, caste, or creed suffer in any way in public employment, office of power or honour, and in the exercise of any trade or calling. All citizens were to have an equal right of access to and use of public roads, public wells, and all other places of public resort. Parliament was to make suitable laws for the maintenance of health of all citizens and for securing a living wage for every worker, as well as laws for the protection of motherhood, the welfare of children, and the economic consequences of old age, infirmity, and unemployment. Finally, men and women were to have equal rights as citizens.

The Report proposed joint electorates with reserved seats for minorities on population basis with the right to contest for additional seats. There were to be no reserved seats for any community in the provinces of Punjab and Bengal, and it was suggested that full protection should be given to the religious and cultural interests of the Muslim community. New provinces were to be created on the basis of language.[107]

The Nehru Report was considered and accepted by the all-parties conference held in Lucknow on 28 August 1928. A large section of Muslims, however, rejected the proposal of communal representation on the basis of joint electorates. The Indian National Congress, in its session on 31 December 1928, accepted the Nehru Report.

Jinnah's Fourteen Points

In March 1929, the Muslim League held its meeting in Delhi. It was at this forum that Jinnah presented his Fourteen Points as the minimum Muslim demand for any political settlement. The Muslim League, rejecting the Nehru Report, passed a resolution adopting the Fourteen Points, which are given below:

1. The form of the future Constitution should be federal in structure with residuary powers vested in the provinces.
2. A uniform measure of autonomy should be granted to all the provinces.
3. All legislatures, central and provincial, and other elected bodies in the country should be constituted on the definite principle of adequate and effective representation of minorities in every province without reducing the majority in any province to a minority or even equality.
4. In the central legislature, Muslim representation should not be less than one-third.
5. Representation of communal groups should continue to be based on separate electorates, but the option to abandon separate electorate in favour of a joint electorate at any time, should be given to every community.

6. Any territorial redistribution that might at any time be necessary should not in any way affect the Muslim majority in the Punjab, Bengal, and North-West Frontier Provinces.
7. Full religious liberty, that is, liberty of belief, worship, and observance, propaganda, association and education should be guaranteed to all communities.
8. No Bill or resolution or any part thereof should be passed in any legislative or any elected body if three-fourths of the members of a community in that particular body opposed such a Bill, resolution or part thereof on the ground that it would be injurious to the interests of that community, or alternatively such other methods should be devised which might practically deal with such cases.
9. Sindh should be separated from the Bombay Presidency.
10. Reforms should be introduced in the North-West Frontier Province and Balochistan on the same footing as in other provinces.
11. Provision should be made in the Constitution giving Muslims an adequate share along with the other Indians in all the services of the state and in local self-governing bodies having due regard to the requirements of efficiency.
12. The Constitution should embody adequate safeguards for the protection of Muslim culture and for the promotion of Muslim education, language, religion, personal laws, and Muslim charitable institutions and for their due share in the grants-in-aid given by the state and by self-government bodies.
13. No Cabinet, either central or provincial, should be formed without there being at least one-third Muslim ministers.
14. No change should be made in the Constitution by the central legislature except with the concurrence of the states constituting the Indian federation.[108]

Civil Disobedience Movement and Round Table Conference

The Viceroy, Lord Irwin, was convinced that it was not possible to maintain unrepresentative central government for all times to come. He conferred with the newly formed Labour government in England and made a statement in October 1929 that the ultimate goal of India's constitutional progress was the attainment of dominion status.

The views of Indians and the British government differed on the subject. Indians demanded a Constituent Assembly to draft a Constitution for India. Gandhi and Lord Irwin met to iron out the differences but did not succeed and the civil disobedience movement was launched in March 1930. Thousands of people all over the country deliberately violated laws and courted arrest. Repression was in full force. Ordinances were issued in quick succession by the government to meet the situation. Editors and proprietors of newspapers and printing presses were arrested and fined. There seemed to be a complete breach between the government and the nationalist movement in the country.[109]

After the publication of the Simon Commission Report and its condemnation by the people of India, the British government called the first round table conference in London. The conference met in November 1930. As the Congress leaders were in jail, the government appointed those men belonging to other parties, communities, and interests to represent India whom it considered predisposed towards it. It was not considered advisable to proceed with the work of the final form of the future Constitution of India in the absence of the representatives of the Indian National Congress; therefore, it was decided to call a second round table conference and, in the meanwhile, efforts were made towards a reconciliation between Congress and government. Consequently, Gandhi withdrew the civil disobedience movement and the famous Gandhi-Irwin Pact was signed in March 1931.

At the second round table conference, many problems were considered but no solution could be conclusively reached. Consequently, the work was referred to various committees which were required to submit detailed reports. As regards the question of communal representation, the British government said it had been obliged to give its own award.

The third round table conference, in November 1932, was called by the British Government rather reluctantly as it was of the opinion that the remaining work on the draft of the Indian Constitution could be done in India. The session of the third round table conference lasted from 17 November to 24 December. The Labour Party did not co-operate in the deliberations and the Indian National Congress was unrepresented in this session. Delegates to the Conference merely discussed the reports of the various committees appointed by the second round table conference and decided a few more points.[110]

Communal Award and the Poona Pact

As the Indians could not arrive at any settlement, Ramsay MacDonald issued his famous award known as the Communal Award on 26 August 1932. The scope of this award was purposely confined to the arrangements to be made for the representation of British Indian communities in provincial legislatures. Consideration of representation to the central legislature was deferred for the time being since it involved a question of the representation of Indian states which needed further discussion.

According to the Award, elections to the seats allocated to the Muslim, European, and Sikh constituencies were to be held separately by voting on separate communal electorates covering the whole area of a province. Special provisions were made for excluded areas. Provision was to be made in the new Constitution of India to allow the revision of electoral arrangements after a lapse of ten years with the assent of the communities affected, for the ascertainment of which suitable means were to be devised. All qualified voters who were not voters in the Muslim, Sikh, Indian, Christian, Anglo-Indian, or European constituencies, were entitled to vote in a general constituency. Seven seats were reserved for the Marathas in certain selected plural-member general constituencies in Bombay. Members of the depressed classes who were qualified to vote were given a general constituency. However, special seats were to be reserved for them to be filled by election from special constituencies in which only members of the depressed classes electorally qualified were entitled to vote. Any person voting in such a special constituency was also entitled to vote in a general constituency.

The election of Indian Christians was to be held by voting in separate communal constituencies. Anglo-Indians were to vote on communal lines. Women were also given special representation. Electors of a particular community were to elect their quota. Special seats were allotted to commerce and industry as well as mining and planting which were to be filled up by election through the Chamber of Commerce and other associations. Their details were to be worked out later. Seats allotted to land holders were to be filled by their constituencies.

The government reserved the right of making slight variations in the number of seats given to various communities with a view to facilitating the work of delimitation of constituencies. However, the proportion was not to be materially changed.

Gandhi, in a letter written in March 1932 to Sir Samuel Hoare, Secretary of State for India, had warned that he would resist with his life the grant of separate electorates to the depressed classes. When the British government refused to move in the matter and the condition of Gandhi became serious on account of his fast unto death, Indian leaders made up their mind to modify the Award by mutual agreement. Negotiations took place and ultimately the Poona Pact was signed in September 1932, and was accepted by the government.

The Poona Pact reserved seats for depressed classes out of the general electoral seats in the provincial legislature as follows. Madras 30, Bombay with Sindh 15, Punjab 8, Bihar and Orissa 18, CP 20, Assam 7, Bengal 30, and UP 20. The total number of reserved seats for the depressed classes was thus 148.

The depressed classes were to have representation in the central legislature on the principle of joint electorate and seats were to be reserved for them in the same way as in the case of the provinces. 18 per cent of the general seats for British India were to be reserved for them. They were also to be given fair representation in the local bodies and in the public services, subject to educational qualifications.[111]

NOTES

1. Symonds, Richard, *Making of Pakistan*, published in Pakistan by arrangement with Faber & Faber Ltd. London, Allied Book Corporation, Karachi, Hyderabad, 1966, p. 190.
2. Ibid., p. 20.
3. Maluka, Zulfikar Khalid, *The Myth of Constitution in Pakistan*, Oxford University Press, 1995, p. 83.
4. Ibid., pp. 84-5.
5. Durant, Will, 'Our Oriental Heritage', *The Story of Civilization: Part 1*, Simon and Schuster, New York, 1954, p. 483.
6. Queen Elizabeth's Charter 1600, printed in *Constitutional Documents (Pakistan)*, Volume 1, 1964, pp. 1-20.

7. Ibid.
8. Saharay, H.K., *A Legal Study of Constitutional Development in India*, 1970, Nababharat Publishers, 72 Mahatma Gandhi Road, Calcutta, 1970, p. 36.
9. *Supra*, note 6.
10. *Supra*, note 8, p. 37.
11. Bokhari, Abrar Husain, *Constitutional History of Indo-Pakistan*, M. Mohammad Suleman Qureshi & Sons, Lahore, 1964. p. 2.
12. Birdwood, Sir George, *Report of the Old Records of India Office*, pp. 85-6, cited by Saharay, H.K. *Supra*, note 8, p. 38.
13. *Supra*, note 8, p. 38.
14. Keith, A.B., *A Constitutional History of India, 1600-1935*, Central Book Depot, Allahabad, 1937, p. 26.
15. *Supra*, note 6, p. 44.
16. *The East India Company Act 1773*, printed in *Constitutional Documents* (*Pakistan*), Volume 1, 1964, pp. 1-20.
17. Ibid., para X.
18. Ibid., paras XIII, XIV, XV, and XVI.
19. *Supra*, note 8, p. 3.
20. *The East India Company Act 1784*, printed in *Constitutional Documents* (*Pakistan*), Volume 1, 1964, pp. 52-100.
21. *Supra*, note 8, p. 4.
22. Ibid.
23. *The Charter Act 1793*, printed in *Constitutional Documents* (*Pakistan*), Volume 1, 1964, pp. 218-34.
24. Ibid., paras XXXIX and XL.
25. *The Government of India Act 1800*, printed in *Constitutional Documents* (*Pakistan*), Volume 1, 1964, pp. 218-24.
26. Ibid., para II.
27. Ibid., para XXIII.
28. *Supra*, note 8, p. 4.
29. *The Government of India Act 1833*, printed in the *Constitutional Documents* (*Pakistan*), Volume 1, 1964, pp. 249-303.
30. *The Government of India Act 1853*, printed in the *Constitutional Documents* (*Pakistan*), Volume 1, 1964, pp. 303-25.
31. Queen Victoria's Proclamation of 1 November 1858, printed in *Constitutional Documents* (*Pakistan*), Vol. 1, 1964, pp. 328-31.
32. *The Government of India Act 1858*, printed in *Constitutional Documents* (*Pakistan*), Vol. 1, 1964, pp. 332-62.
33. Ibid., Article III.
34. Ibid., Article XIX.
35. Ibid., Article XXV.
36. Ibid., Article XLI.
37. Ibid., Article LIII.
38. Ibid., Article LXV.
39. Ibid., Article LXIV.
40. Ibid., Article LXVIII.
41. Article 1 of the *Government of India (Amendment) Act 1859*, printed in *Constitutional Documents* (*Pakistan*), Volume 1, pp. 362-5.
42. *The Indian Council's Act 1861*, printed in *Constitutional Documents* (*Pakistan*), Volume 1, pp. 366-90.
43. Ibid., Section 3.
44. Ibid., Section 10.
45. Ibid., Sections 19, 20 and 22.
46. Ibid., Section 23.

47. Ibid., Section 38 & 39.
48. Ibid., Section 47.
49. Ibid., Section 45 & 46.
50. *East India (High Courts of Judicature) Act 1861*, printed in *Constitutional Documents (Pakistan)*, Volume 1, 1964, pp. 390-98, Section 2.
51. Ibid., Section 4.
52. Ibid., Section 8 & 10.
53. Ibid., Section 9.
54. Ibid., Section 15.
55. Ibid., Section 15.
56. *The Government of India Act 1865*, printed in *Constitutional Documents (Pakistan)*, Volume 1, 1964, pp. 399-400.
57. Ibid., Section 1.
58. *The Government of India Act 1870*, printed in *Constitutional Documents (Pakistan)*, Volume 1, 1964, pp. 403-406, Section 1.
59. Ibid., Section 3.
60. Ibid., Section 5.
61. Ibid., Section 6.
62. *The Indian Councils Act 1892*, printed in *Constitutional Documents (Pakistan)*, Volume I, Edition 1964, pp. 408-13.
63. Ibid., Section 1.
64. Ibid., Section 5.
65. Khurshid, Sorraya, 'The Great Mutiny', *The Nation*, Lahore, 2 November 1990, citing contemporary English writers. She also quotes a correspondent of the *Calcutta Review*, an English magazine, who wrote in 1859, 'five years back when I went to Delhi, I was rather amazed to see a great number of magazines and journals, which are no more published now.'
66. A famous poet and man of letters.
67. Ali, Chaudhri Mohammad, *The Emergence of Pakistan*, published by Services Book Club, 1988 and printed in Pakistan by Wajidalis (Pvt) Ltd., 65-Kot Lakhpat Industrial Estate, Lahore, Pakistan p. 7.
68. These figures are taken from the book of Symonds, *supra*, note 1, p. 26.
69. *Supra*, note 67, pp. 7-8, citing Ram Gopal, *Indian Muslims: A Political History* (Asia Publishing House, Bombay), 1959, p. 34.
70. Ahmad, Sir Syed, *The Present State of Indian Politics*, extracts of which have been reproduced by Symonds, *supra*, note 1, p. 31.
71. Shahab, Rafiullah, *History of Pakistan*, Sang-e-Meel Publications, Lahore, 1992.
72. Sayeed, Khalid Bin, Pakistan - the Formative Phase, published by Oxford University Press, Karachi, 1968, pp. 29-30.
73. Smith, Vincent A., *The Oxford History of India*, 1981, Oxford University Press, Karachi, p. 764.
74. *The Indian Councils Act 1909*, printed in the *Constitutional Documents (Pakistan)*, Vol. I, 1964, pp. 413-19. *See* Section 1 and First Schedule.
75. Ibid., Section 6, p. 417.
76. Mahajan, V.D., *History of Indo-Pakistan*, 1985, pp. 279-81.
77. Sayeed, Khalid Bin, *Pakistan - The Formative Phase 1857-1948*. *Supra*, note 72, p. 31.
78. Dunbar, Sir George, *A History of India*, first published in 1936, reprinted in 1990, published by Low Price Publications, Delhi, p. 598.
79. This scheme was published in August 1917 and is known as 'Gokhale's Political Testament'.
80. Dunbar, Sir George, *supra*, note 78, pp. 600-601.
81. Ibid., pp. 601-604.
82. Bokhari, Abrar Husain, *Constitutional History of Indo-Pakistan*, *supra*, note 11, p. 44.
83. *The Government of India Act 1919*, printed in the *Constitutional Documents (Pakistan)*, Vol. I, 1964, pp. 513-74. *See* Preamble.

84. *The Government of India Act 1919*, Section 30.
85. Ibid., Section 17.
86. Ibid., Sections 18 and 19.
87. Ibid., Section 21.
88. Ibid.
89. Ibid., Sections 24, 25, 26, and 27.
90. Ibid., Section 25.
91. Ibid., Section 25 (8).
92. Ibid., Section 24.
93. Ibid., Section 25.
94. Ibid., Section 1.
95. Ibid.
96. Kapur, Anup Chand, *Constitutional History of India (1765-1970)*, Niraj Prakashan, New Delhi 1970, pp. 346-8.
97. Ibid., pp. 343 to 346.
98. Saharay, H.K., *A Legal Study of Constitutional Development of India*, Nababharat Publishers, Calcutta, 1970, p. 133.
99. *Supra*, note 83, Section 1.
100. *Supra*, note 11, p. 63 to 65.
101. Ibid., pp. 70-71.
102. Ibid., pp. 71-2.
103. Ibid., p. 72.
104. Ibid., p. 81.
105. *Supra*, note 96, p. 323.
106. *Supra*, note 11, p. 90.
107. *Supra*, note 96, pp. 357-9.
108. Ibid., pp. 359-60.
109. *Supra*, note 11, p. 89.
110. Ibid., pp. 91, 92 & 96.
111. Ibid., pp. 92, 94.

2

A COLONIAL CONSTITUTION

When the scheme regarding the future Constitution of India was worked out, the British government issued a document known as the 'White Paper' in March 1933. It stated that the basic idea of the new Indian Constitution would be diarchy at the centre and responsible government in the provinces. In April 1933, a Joint Select Committee of the British Parliament was appointed with Lord Linlithgow as its chairman, to examine and report on government proposals contained in the White Paper. The Committee submitted its report in December 1934. The fundamentals given in the White Paper were not changed but many changes in the structure of the federal and provincial legislatures and other matters were recommended. A bill was drafted on the basis of the recommendations in the report which was passed by both Houses of the British Parliament by July 1935 and received the Royal assent in August 1935.[1] It was called the Government of India Act, 1935.

The broad principles on which the Act was based were the autonomy of the provinces and the powers of their legislatures to make the legislatures almost wholly elective, to introduce the principles of a Cabinet system at the provincial level, and to enlarge participation of Indians in the government at the centre. Thus the foundation was laid on which a new Constitution could be built.

The Government of India Act, 1935

The Act was a comprehensive statute running into 321 sections and two schedules. It was a comprehensive written Constitution given to India by its colonial masters. The special features of the Act were:

i. The polity of India was reconstituted on a federal basis, although the Constitution of India was unitary and the provincial governments derived their powers by devolution from the central government and discharged their functions under the superintendence, direction, and control of the Governor-General and ultimately the Secretary of State for India. The Act thus created a federation.
ii. Partial responsibility in the form of a diarchy at the centre was introduced.
iii. The provinces were granted autonomy and responsible government.
iv. The Governor-General of India and the Governors of the provinces were granted extensive powers by way of safeguards, reservations, special responsibilities, overriding powers, and so on.

v. New institutions like the Federal Court, Federal Railway Authority, the Reserve Bank of India (the Central Bank), and the Public Service Commissions for the federation and the provinces were created under the Act.

vi. Burma was separated from India.

vii. The Act prescribed the method whereby a state could join the federation and also provided for the legal consequences which followed from such an accession. The ruler of a state desiring to federate could execute an instrument of accession on behalf of himself, his heirs, and his successors, defining therein matters in which the state agreed to federate and thereby accepting the jurisdiction of the federation in all such matters. The Crown could refuse to accept an Instrument of Accession if it was inconsistent with the scheme of the federation. But once a state had acceded to the federation and was approved by the Crown, it could not secede from the federation.

viii. The area of federal jurisdiction extended to the whole of British India including the states that had acceded. In relation to the provinces, there was a three-fold division of functions and the subjects were divided into the federal, provincial, and concurrent lists. The federal legislature alone had the power to make laws with respect to the matters enumerated in the federal list. The subjects enumerated in the provincial list were within the exclusive domain of the provincial legislatures. Both the federal and provincial legislatures were competent to make laws on subjects enumerated in the concurrent list. In case of conflict and inconsistency, the federal law prevailed and the law of the province or state was void to the extent of such repugnancy.[2]

The Federal Executive

The executive power and authority of the federation was vested in the Governor-General as he was the representative of the Crown. The Crown in turn issued an Instrument of Restrictions to the Governor-General which contained directions as to the way in which he could exercise the authority conferred upon him. The extent of the executive authority of the federation included:[3]

(a) matters with respect to which the federal legislature had power to make laws;
(b) raising in British India on behalf of the Crown naval, military, and air forces and the governance of the King's forces borne on the Indian establishment, and
(c) exercise of such rights, authority, and jurisdiction as were exercisable by the Crown by treaty, grant, usage, sufferance, or otherwise in and in relation to the tribal areas.

However, the jurisdiction of the federal government was subject to two limitations. Firstly, the federal executive authority did not extend in any province to matters except those expressly provided in the Act with respect to which the provincial legislature had the power to make laws. Secondly, it extended to a federated state subject to such limitations as might be specified in its Instrument of Accession. The executive authority of the ruler of a federated state was, however, to continue to be exercisable in that state regarding matters with respect to which the federal legislature had the power to make laws, except in so far as it was excluded by virtue of a federal law.

The Governor-General, as head of the federal executive, had supreme command of the military, naval, and air forces in India. This command, however, was subject to the power of His Majesty to appoint a Commander-in-Chief, to exercise in relation to those forces such functions as might be assigned to him.

The federal government was not concerned with the powers connected with the exercise of the functions of the Crown in its relations with the Indian states. These were exercisable by His Majesty's representative appointed for the purpose, but His Majesty could appoint one person to fill both the offices of the Governor-General and Representative of the Crown in relation to Indian states.

The Government of India Act, 1935 established diarchy at the centre. Administrative functions with respect to defence, ecclesiastic affairs, foreign relations except relations between the federation and any part of His Majesty's dominions, and the tribal areas, were to be exercised by the Governor-General at his discretion. To assist him in the exercise of these functions, the Governor-General was empowered to appoint councillors not exceeding three in number. The salaries and conditions of service of the councilors were to be prescribed by His Majesty-in-Council. They were responsible to the Governor-General alone and were in no way responsible to the federal legislature for any act done by them in the exercise of their duties.

All other executive powers were to be exercised by the Governor-General with the help and advice of the Council of Ministers, subject to the exercise by the Governor-General of special powers and responsibilities. The number of ministers was not to exceed ten. Ministers were to be chosen by the Governor-General to hold office during his tenure. It was stipulated in the Act that ministers should be chosen from amongst the members of the federal legislature and that a minister who for a period of six consecutive months was not a member of either chamber of the federal legislature, should at the expiry of that period cease to be a minister. The ministers were to get such salaries as might be determined by an act of the legislature and in the absence of it as fixed by the Governor-General, provided that the salary of a minister was not to vary during his term of office. The Governor-General, at his discretion, might preside at meetings of the Council of Ministers. The control of ministers over the administration of transferred departments was subject to the following limitations:

1. Ministers had no right to tender advice on matters in respect of which the Governor-General was required to act at his discretion;
2. In cases where the Governor-General was empowered to exercise his individual judgment; and
3. When the Governor-General acted in the exercise of powers entrusted to him in the discharge of his special responsibilities.

In all matters which involved his special responsibilities, the Governor-General was required to exercise his individual judgment as to the action to be taken. He could, however, seek ministerial advice, but he need not act thereupon.

The matters in which the Governor-General had a special responsibility were:[4]

(a) the prevention of any grave menace to the peace or tranquility of India or any part thereof;
(b) the safeguarding of the financial stability of the federal government;
(c) the safeguarding of the legitimate interests of minorities;
(d) the securing to, and to the dependants of, persons who were or had been members of the public services, any rights provided or preserved for them by or under the Act and the safeguarding of their legitimate interests;
(e) the securing in the sphere of executive action of the purposes which the provision of Chapter III of Part V of the Act of 1935 (which dealt with commercial discrimination) were designed to secure in relation to legislation;
(f) the prevention of action which would subject goods of United Kingdom or Burmese origin imported into India to discriminatory or penal treatment;
(g) the protection of the rights of any Indian state and the rights and dignity of the Ruler thereof; and
(h) the securing of the due discharge of his functions with respect to matters in relation to which he was by or under the Act of 1935 required to act at his discretion, or to exercise his individual judgment, was not prejudicial or impeded by any course of action taken with respect to any other matter.

In order to assist him in the discharge of his special responsibility for safeguarding the financial stability and credit of the federal government, the Governor-General was empowered to appoint a Financial Adviser. This official could also give advice to the federal government, whenever consulted, upon any matter relating to finance. The Financial Adviser held office at the pleasure of the Governor-General, who also determined his salary and conditions of service. The Governor-General also appointed the Advocate-General and fixed his remuneration in the exercise of his individual judgment.

If a question arose regarding whether any matter was or was not one in which the Governor-General was required to act in his individual judgment, the decision of the Governor-General was final. The Governor-General was answerable only to the Secretary of State of India in all matters in which he acted upon his discretion or exercised his individual judgment.

All executive action of the federal government was expressed to be taken in the name of the Governor-General, who also made rules for the more convenient transaction of the business of the government and for the allocation of business among the ministers.

The Federal Legislature

The Federal Legislature was to be bicameral and it consisted of the King, represented by the Governor-General, and the two Chambers, the Council of State, and the House of Assembly.[5] The Council of State was to consist of 156 representatives of British

India, and not more than 104 representatives of the Indian states.[6] Out of 156 seats to be filled by the representatives of British India, 150 seats were to be allocated to governors' provinces and chief commissioners' provinces. There were 75 general seats, 6 for scheduled castes, 4 in the Punjab for Sikhs, 49 Muslims, 6 women, 7 European, 2 Indian Christians and one Anglo-Indian. Six seats were to be filled by persons chosen by the Governor-General at his discretion. The Council of State was to be a permanent body, not subject to dissolution, but one-third of its members were to retire every third year.

The House of Assembly was to consist of 250 representatives of British India and not more than 125 representatives of the Indian states. The life of the House of Assembly was five years, unless sooner dissolved. The Governor-General could, at his discretion, from time to time summon, prorogue, and address the chambers or send messages or dissolve the House of Assembly provided that the chambers be summoned to meet at least once every year. The principle of direct election was adopted. Indirect election was retained for the representatives of the Anglo-Indian, European, and Indian Christian communities. The representatives of the Indian states were to be appointed by the rulers of the states concerned. The allocation of seats among the statesmen was to be determined according to the principle of relative rank and importance of the state as indicated by the dynastic salute and other factors.

The Joint Select Committee rejected the proposal of direct election of representatives to the House of Assembly and this recommendation was accepted by Parliament. Hence under the Act, the House of Assembly was to be elected by the provincial assemblies. Allocation of seats among the Indian states was to proceed on the principle that the number of seats allotted to each state or group of states should be proportionate to their population. Every minister or councillor had the right to speak in, and otherwise participate in, the proceedings of either chamber, any joint sitting of the chambers, and any committee of the legislature of which he might be named a member.

The Council of State and the House of Assembly were to choose from among their members respectively a President and a Speaker to preside over these chambers. A member holding office as President or as a Speaker was to vacate his office if he ceased to be a member of the chamber over which he presided. He could at any time resign his office and he might be removed from his office by a resolution of the Council or Assembly, as the case might be, passed by a majority of all its then members.

Bills other than financial bills could originate in either chamber. In general, a bill was not to be deemed to have been passed by the chambers of the legislature unless it had been agreed to by both chambers.[7] If a Bill passed by one chamber was rejected by the other, or it did not agree to the amendments made in the Bill, or more than six months had elapsed from the date of the reception of the Bill by the other chamber and it had not been passed by that chamber, the Governor-General could summon a joint sitting of both the chambers for the purpose of deliberating and voting on the Bill. But in case of a Finance Bill or a Bill which affected the discharge of his functions in so far as he was required to act at his discretion or to exercise his individual judgment, he could summon a joint sitting, even though the above conditions had not been fulfilled.

After the Bill had been passed by both the chambers, it was presented to the Governor-General, who: might give his assent in the name of His Majesty; withhold his assent; reserve the Bill for the signification of the King's pleasure; return it to the chambers with a message to reconsider the Bill or any specified provision, or to move any such amendment to the Bill as indicated therein.

A Bill reserved for the signification of the King's pleasure could not become an Act unless and until, within twelve months from the day on which it was presented to the Governor-General, the Governor-General had known by notification that the King had assented thereto. Power was reserved by the Crown to disallow any Act assented to by the Governor-General.

At the start of every financial year, the Governor-General was to put before both chambers an 'annual financial statement' giving the estimated receipts and expenditure of the federation for that year.[8] The estimates of expenditure embodied in the annual financial statement to show separately (a) the sums required to meet expenditure charged upon the revenues of the federation, and (b) the sums required to meet other expenditure proposed to be made from the revenues of the federation. The following items were charged on the revenues of the federation:

1. the salary and allowances of the Governor-General and other expenditure relating to his office for which provision was required to be made by order in Council;
2. debt charges for which the federation was liable including interest, sinking fund charges and redemption charges, and other expenditure relating to the raising of loans and the service of redemption of debt;
3. the salaries and allowances of Ministers, Councillors, the Financial Adviser, the Advocate-General, Chief Commissioners, and the staff of the Financial Adviser;
4. the salaries, allowances, and pensions payable to the Judges of the Federal Court, and the pensions payable to the Judges of High Courts;
5. expenditure for the purpose of the discharge by the Governor-General of his functions with respect to reserved subjects;
6. expenditure on the discharge of the functions of the Crown in its relations with Indian states;
7. any grants connected with the administration of any areas in a province which were for the time being excluded areas;
8. any sums required to satisfy any judgment, decree, or award of any court or arbitral tribunal; and
9. any expenditure declared by an Act of Parliament or any Act of the Federal Legislature to be so charged.

Any question on whether any proposed expenditure fell within a class of charges on the revenue of the federation was to be decided at the Governor-General's discretion.

The items of expenditure so charged upon the revenues of the federation were not to be submitted to the vote of the legislature. Some of them, however, could be discussed in either chamber, but these items did not include the salary and allowances of the Governor-General and the sums payable to His Majesty in respect of expenses incurred in the discharge of the functions of the Crown in its relations with the Indian states. All other estimates which were not charged on the revenues of the federation were to be submitted in the form of demands for grants in the Federal Assembly and thereafter to the Council of State. Either chamber had the power to assent or refuse to assent to any demand, or assent to any demand subject to a reduction of the specified amount; but where the Assembly had refused to assent to any demand, that demand was not to be submitted to the Council of State unless the Governor-General so directed. Also, where the Assembly had assented to a demand subject to a reduction in the amount specified therein, a demand for the reduced amount only was to be submitted to the Council of State, unless the Governor-General directed otherwise. If the two chambers differed with respect to any demand, the Governor-General could summon the two chambers to meet in a joint sitting for the purpose of deliberating and voting upon the demand to which they had disagreed. The decision of the majority of the members of both chambers present and voting at the joint sitting was deemed to be the decision of the two chambers.

If the demand was assented to by both the chambers it then required the Governor-General to authenticate it. If the chambers however, had not assented to a demand for a grant or had assented subject to a reduction of the amount specified therein, the Governor-General could change the decision if, in his opinion, he felt that the refusal or reduction would affect the due discharge of any of his special responsibilities, and could include or restore the amount as he might deem necessary in order to enable him to discharge that responsibility. The schedule so authenticated was to be laid before both chambers, but it was neither open to discussion nor to vote.

The Act placed a number of restrictions on the legislative powers of the Federal Legislature. These restrictions were set out in section 108 which provided: unless the Governor-General in his discretion thinks fit to give his previous sanction, there shall not be introduced into, or moved in, either chamber of the Federal Legislature any Bill or amendment which:

(a) repeals, amends, or is repugnant to any provisions of any Act of Parliament extending to British India; or
(b) repeals, amends, or is repugnant to any Governor-General's or Governor's Act or any ordinance promulgated at his discretion by the Governor-General or a Governor; or
(c) affects matters in respect of which the Governor-General is by or under the Act, required to act at his discretion; or
(d) repeals, amends, or affects any Act relating to any police force; or
(e) affects the procedure for criminal proceedings in which European and British subjects are concerned; or
(f) subjects persons not resident in British India to greater taxation than persons resident in British India, or subjects companies not wholly controlled or

managed in British India to greater taxation than companies wholly controlled or managed therein; or

(g) affects the grant of relief from any federal tax or income in respect of income taxed or taxable in the United Kingdom.

The Federal Legislature had no power (a) to make any law affecting the sovereign or the Royal family, or the succession to the Crown, or the sovereignty, dominion, or suzerainty of the Crown in any part of India, or the law of British nationality, or the Army Act, the Air Force Act, or the Naval Discipline Act, or the Law of Prize or Prize courts; or (b) except in so far as was expressly permitted by any subsequent provisions of the Act of 1935, to make any law amending any provision of this Act, or any Order in Council made thereunder, or any rules made under this Act by the Secretary of State, or by the Governor-General or a Governor in his discretion, or in the exercise of his individual judgment; or (c) except in so far as was expressly permitted by the Government of India Act to make any law derogating from any prerogative right of the King to grant special leave to appeal from any court.[9]

No federal law was valid which contravened the provision made in the Government of India Act against discriminatory legislation. Restrictions were also imposed on the authority of both the Federal and Provincial Legislatures to pass discriminatory legislation in certain matters against British subjects domiciled, British trading companies incorporated, and ships registered, in the United Kingdom. If the Governor-General using his discretion certified that the discussion of a Bill, clause, or amendment would affect the discharge of his special responsibility for the prevention of any grave menace to the peace or tranquility of India, he might at his discretion direct that no further proceedings should be taken in relation to it.

The Governor-General was invested with extraordinary powers of legislation and could issue ordinances having the same force and effect as an Act of the Federal Legislature assented to by the Governor-General. The Act made a distinction between functions in the discharge of which the Governor-General was required by the law to act at his discretion or to exercise his individual judgment, and other functions. In respect to the former, the Governor-General could at any time, at his discretion, promulgate such ordinance as in his opinion the circumstances of the case would required subject to the following conditions:

1. The maximum period for which an ordinance could remain in force was six months. But it could be extended, by a subsequent ordinance, for a further period not exceeding six months.
2. When the operation of an ordinance was extended for a further period, it was to be communicated forthwith to the Secretary of State for India and it was to be laid by him before each House of Parliament.
3. The ordinance, like the Act of the Federal Legislature, was subject to disallowance by the King.
4. In respect of their subject matter, ordinances were governed by the same limitations as applied to Acts of the Federal Legislature. If and so far as an

ordinance made a provision which the Federal Legislature would not be competent to enact, it was void.

The Governor-General was also empowered to promulgate ordinances during the recess of the legislature. It was provided that if at any time when the Federal Legislature was not in session and the Governor-General was satisfied that circumstances existed which rendered it necessary for him to take immediate action, he could promulgate such ordinances as the circumstances appeared to him to require. An ordinance promulgated under such circumstances was to be laid before the Federal Legislature and it ceased to operate at the expiry of six weeks from the re-assembly of the legislature, or, if before the expiry of that period resolutions disapproving of it were passed by both chambers, upon the passing of the second of those resolutions.[10] It was also subject to the power of His Majesty to disallow Acts as if it was an Act of the Federal Legislature assented to by the Governor-General. An ordinance could be withdrawn at any time by the Governor-General, and if it was an ordinance extending a previous ordinance for a further period, it was to be communicated forthwith to the Secretary of State, who would put it before each House of Parliament.

The Governor-General was also empowered to make laws in the form of Governor-General's Acts at his discretion in matters relating to functions in which he was required to act at his discretion or to exercise his individual judgment. The exercise of this power was subject to the following limitations:

(a) The Governor-General was required to explain by message to both the chambers the circumstances which in his opinion rendered legislation essential. He could either enact forthwith, as a Governor-General's Act, a Bill containing such provisions as he considered necessary, or attach to his message a draft of the Bill which he considered necessary. When he attached a draft to his message, he might at any time after the expiry of one month enact, as the Governor-General's Act, the Bill proposed by him to the chambers either in the form of the draft communicated to them or with such amendments as he deemed necessary. But before so doing, he was to consider any address which might have been presented to him by either chamber with reference to the Bill or to any suggested amendment.

(b) The Act was to be communicated forthwith to the Secretary of State and it was to be laid by him before each House of Parliament.

(c) It was subject to disallowance by the Crown.

The Act contained special provisions enabling the Governor-General to act promptly in the event of a breakdown in the constitutional machinery. If at any time the Governor-General felt that a situation had arisen in which the government of the federation could not be carried on in accordance with the provisions of the Act, he could using his discretionary powers, issue a Proclamation declaring that his functions now be extended to all or any of the powers vested in or exercisable by any federal body or authority, other than the Federal Court. Such a proclamation was to be communicated to the Secretary of State for India and laid by him before each House of Parliament. The proclamation was to cease to operate at the expiry of six months unless before the expiry of that period it had been approved by a resolution of both Houses of Parliament in which case it continued in force for a further period of twelve months from the date on which it would otherwise have ceased to operate. If, at any time, the government of the federation had for a period of three years been carried on under such a proclamation, then, at the expiry of such a period, the proclamation would cease to have effect and the government of the federation was to be carried on in accordance with the provisions of the Act of 1935. If the Governor-General by a proclamation assumed to himself any power of the federal legislature to make laws, any law made by him in the exercise of that power would continue to have effect until two years had elapsed from the date on which the proclamation ceased to have effect, unless sooner repealed or re-enacted by the Act of the appropriate legislature.[11]

The Federal Court

Under the Government of India Act, 1935, a Federal Court was to be established.[12] It was to be the interpreter and guardian of the Constitution and a tribunal for determination of disputes between the constituent units of the federation.

The Federal Court was to consist of a Chief Justice and not more than six puisne judges who were to be appointed by the King to remain in office till the age of sixty-five. The King could increase the number of judges on presentation of an address by the Federal Legislature to the Governor-General for submission to the King. For appointment as a judge, one had to be either a judge of a High Court in British India or in a federated state for at least five years, a Barrister of England or Northern Ireland of at least ten years' standing, a member of the Faculty of Advocates in Scotland of at least ten years' standing, or had to be for at least ten years a pleader of a High Court in British India, or in a federated state or of two or more such courts in succession. For appointment as Chief Justice of India, it was necessary that one should be a Barrister or Pleader of at least fifteen years' standing. A judge could be removed from his office by His Majesty on the ground of misbehaviour or infirmity of mind or body, if the Judicial Committee of the Privy Council, on a reference made to them by His Majesty, recommended his removal.

The court's jurisdiction was three-fold: original jurisdiction, appellate jurisdiction in appeals from High Courts in British India, and advisory jurisdiction. The court exercised original jurisdiction in any dispute between any two or more of the following parties; the federation, any of the provinces, or any of the federated states, if and in so far as the dispute involved any question (whether of law or fact) on which the existence or extent of a legal right depended, provided that the said jurisdiction did not extend to a dispute to which the state was a party, unless the dispute:

i. concerned the interpretation of the Act of 1935, or of an Order in Council made thereunder, or the extent of the legislative or executive authority vested in the federation by virtue of the Instrument of Accession of that state; or

ii. it arose under an agreement made, under an administrative relation between the federation and states in Part VI of the Act, in relation to administration in that state of a law of the federal legislature, or otherwise concerned some matters with respect to which the federal legislature had power to make laws; or
iii. it arose under any agreement made after the establishment of the federation, with the approval of His Majesty's Representative for the exercise of the functions of the Crown in its relations with Indian states; being an agreement which expressly provided that the jurisdiction of the Federal Court would extend to such a dispute.[13]

The appellate jurisdiction of the Federal Court extended to appeals from any judgment or decree or final order of a High Court in British India, if the High Court certified that the case involved a substantial question of law as to the interpretation of the Act of 1935, or any Order in Council made thereunder.[14] An appeal also rested in the Federal Court from a High Court in a federated state on the ground that a question of law had been wrongly decided, being a question which concerned the interpretation of the Act of 1935, or of an Order in Council made thereunder or the extent of the legislative or executive authority vested in the federation by virtue of the Instrument of Accession of that state, or arose under an agreement made under Part VI (the administrative relations between federation and states) in relation to the administration in that state of a law of the federal legislature.[15]

The appellate jurisdiction of the Federal Court was extended to some civil cases also by an Act of the Federal Legislature provided that no appeal lay unless the amount of the claim or subject matter in dispute was not less than 50,000 rupees or such other sum not less than 15,000 rupees as was specified in the Act, or special leave of the Federal Court had been obtained.[16]

The Federal Court was also invested with advisory jurisdiction. The Governor-General could, at his discretion, refer to the Federal Court any question of law of special public importance for consideration and report.

An appeal could be brought to the Privy Council (His Majesty-in-Council) from a decision of the Federal Court:[17]

(a) given in the exercise of its original jurisdiction any dispute which concerned the interpretation of the Act of 1935, or of an Order in Council made thereunder, or the extent of the legislative or executive authority vested in the federation by virtue of the Instrument of Accession of any state, or arose under an agreement made under Part VI (Administrative relations between federation, provinces, and states) of the Act of 1935, in relation to the administration in any state of a law of the Federal Legislature, without leave, and
(b) in any case, by leave of the Federal Court or of His Majesty-in-Council.

Provincial Governments

With the separation of Orissa from Bihar and Sindh from Bombay, and the severance of Burma from British India, there were eleven Governor's provinces, namely:

Madras, Bombay, Bengal, the United Provinces, the Punjab, Bihar, the Central Provinces and Berar, Assam, the North-West Frontier Province, Orissa, and Sindh. Section 290 provided that the Crown by Order in Council might create a new province, increase the area of any province, diminish the area of any province, and alter the boundaries of any province. It was, however, provided that before the draft of any such Order was laid before Parliament, the Secretary of State would take steps for ascertaining the views of the Federal Legislature as also of the government and the legislature of the province which was to be affected by such an order. These preliminary consultations were to be directed towards both the proposal to make the Order and the provisions to be inserted therein.

In form, the executive authority of a province was similar to that at the centre and it was to be exercised on behalf of the Crown by a Governor. The Governor received his appointment from the King by a commission under the Royal Sign Manual and was constitutionally responsible to the Governor-General. An Instrument of Instructions was issued to each Governor on the assumption of office.

Subject to the provisions of the Act of 1935, the executive authority of each province extended to matters with respect to which the legislature of the province had power to make laws. The administration of the province might, for purposes of convenience, be grouped under three heads:

(a) functions in the discharge of which the Governor was required to act on the advice of the Council of Ministers;
(b) functions in the discharge of which he was required to exercise his individual judgment; or
(c) functions in respect of which he was required to act at his discretion.

Where a question arose regarding whether a given matter fell in one category or another, the decision of the Governor was final and the validity of anything done by the Governor could not be called into question on the ground that he ought or ought not to have acted at his discretion.

It was provided that even though the Governor could act at his discretion, he should exercise his functions with the help and on the advice of a Council of Ministers.[18] The ministers were chosen and summoned by the Governor and they held office at his pleasure. The Act provided that if a person appointed minister was for a period of six months not a member of the Provincial Legislature, he ceased to be a minister at the expiry of that period. The salaries of the ministers were determined by an Act of the provincial legislature and until then fixed by the Governor, provided that the salary of a minister was not to vary during his term of office. The Governor could, if he so wished, preside at the meetings of the Council of Ministers.

In the exercise of the functions left to his discretion or to his individual judgment, the Governor was required to act in accordance with the directions given to him by the Governor-General. But the validity of anything done by him could not be called into question on the ground that it was contrary to the directions so issued. Before giving his directions, the Governor-General was required to satisfy himself that nothing in the directions required the Governor to act in any manner inconsistent with the Instrument of Instructions issued to him by His Majesty with the approval of both the Houses of Parliament.

The Governor was entrusted with the following special responsibilities, in the exercise of which he acted in his individual judgment:

i. the prevention of any grave menace to the peace or tranquility of the province or any part thereof;
ii. the safeguarding of the legitimate interests of minorities;
iii. the securing to, and to the dependants of, persons who were or had been members of the public services, any rights provided or preserved for them by or under the Act, and the safeguarding of their legitimate interests;
iv. the securing in the sphere of executive action of the purposes which the provisions of Chapter III of Part V of the Act (which dealt with discrimination) were designed to secure in relation to legislation;
v. the securing of the peace and good government of areas which by or under the provisions of the Act were declared to be partially excluded areas;
vi. the protection of the rights of any Indian state and the rights and dignity of the Ruler thereof; and
vii. the securing of the execution of orders or directions lawfully issued to him under Part VI of the Act (which dealt with administrative relations) by the Governor-General at his discretion.[19]

The Governor of the Central Provinces and Berar was also to have the special responsibility of securing that a reasonable share of the revenues of the province was expended in or for the benefit of Berar. The Governor of any province which included an excluded area, was to have the special responsibility of securing that the due discharge of his function in respect of excluded areas was not prejudiced or impeded by any course of action taken in respect of any other matter. A Governor who was discharging any function as an agent for the Governor-General also had the special responsibility of securing that the due discharge of his function was not prejudiced or impeded by any course of action taken with respect to any other matter. The Governor of Sindh was to have the special responsibility of securing the proper administration of the Lloyd Barrage and Canals Scheme.

The Governor, exercising his individual judgment, would appoint a person, being a person qualified to be appointed a High Court Judge, to be the Advocate-General for the province. He held office during the pleasure of the Governor, received such remuneration as he might determine, and performed such duties of a legal character as might from time to time be referred or assigned to him by the Governor. When a proposal was made to the Governor to make, amend, or approve any rules or orders relating to the police and affecting in his opinion the organization or discipline of that force, he was to exercise his individual judgment with respect to that proposal.

The following were the more important functions in the exercise of which the Governor was required to act at his discretion: appointment and dismissal of ministers, determination of their salaries (unless fixed by an Act of the legislature), allocation of business among ministers, presiding at meetings of the Council of Ministers, and the making of rules for the transaction of the business of the provincial government.

If it appeared to the Governor of a province that the peace or tranquility of the province was endangered by the activities of persons committing, or conspiring to commit, crimes of violence intended to overthrow the government, the Governor could, if he thought that the circumstances of the case required him so to do, take action and pass directives at his discretion for the purpose of combating those operations. While any such directive was in force, the Governor could appoint an official as a temporary member of the provincial legislature, but without the right to vote, to act as his mouthpiece and take part accordingly in the proceedings of the chamber or chambers, at any joint sitting of the chambers and any of the committee of the legislature of which he might be named a member by the Governor.

Provincial Legislatures

In every province, there was to be a legislature which was to consist of the King, represented by the Governor and one or two chambers. The provinces of Madras, Bombay, Bengal, the United Provinces, Bihar, and Assam had bicameral legislatures, whereas the remaining five provinces had unicameral legislatures. Where there were two chambers of the provincial legislature, one was known as the Legislative Council and the other as the Legislative Assembly, and where there was only one chamber, it was known as the Legislative Assembly. The composition of the chamber or chambers of the legislature of a province was such as was specified in relation to that province.[20]

Representation in the Legislative Assembly of each province was based mainly on the allocation of seats to various communities and to specified interests. There were separate electorates for Muslims, Sikhs, Indian Christians, Anglo-Indians, and Europeans. The details of the distribution of seats were based upon the Communal Award, with such modifications as had been rendered necessary, first by the later proposal to create a new province of Orissa, and, secondly, by the Poona Pact.

The Communal Award did not contain proposals for the composition of Legislative Councils. The composition of Legislative Councils was, however, based upon the same principles as the Communal Award. As these were to be much smaller bodies than the Legislative Assemblies it was, therefore, not possible to provide in them for the exact equivalence of all the interests represented in the Legislative Assemblies. But the Act provided for the inclusion of a certain number of seats to be filled by nomination by the Governor at his discretion with a view to redressing any possible inequality or for securing some representation for women.

The Legislative Council was a permanent body, one-third of its members retiring once in every three years. It was not subject to dissolution. The Legislative Assembly, unless sooner dissolved, continued for five years. Membership of both the federal legislature and the provincial legislature at the same time was prohibited. If a person was chosen a member of both legislatures then, at the expiration of such period as might have been specified in rules made by the Governor of the Province, that person's seat in the provincial legislature was to become vacant, unless he or she had previously resigned his or her seat in the federal legislature.

With respect to other matters such as the appointment of a Speaker of Legislative Assembly and, in provinces with bicameral legislature, of a President of Legislative Council, voting, disqualification for membership, privileges and financial procedure, the provisions of the Act relating to the provinces were practically identical with those which applied to the same matters in the federal legislature.

A Bill passed by the Legislative Assembly, in provinces with unicameral legislatures and by both the chambers in provinces with bicameral legislatures, was presented to the Governor who was empowered to use his discretion either to give his assent to it in the name of the King, or to withhold assent, or to reserve it for the consideration of the Governor-General. A Bill reserved for the consideration of the Governor-General might be assented to by him in the name of the King or he might withhold his assent or reserve it for the signification of the King's pleasure.

Even when a Bill had received the assent of the Governor or the Governor-General, it could be disallowed by the King within twelve months from the date of such assent. A measure thus disallowed was to be duly notified by the Governor concerned.

No discussion could take place in the provincial legislature with respect to the conduct of any Judge of the Federal Court or of a High Court in British India or in a federal state in the discharge of his duties. If the Governor certified that discussion of a Bill introduced or proposed to be introduced, or any specified clause or a Bill, or of any amendment moved or proposed to be moved to a Bill, would affect the discharge of his special responsibility for the prevention of a grave menace to the peace and tranquility of the province, or any part thereof, he could at his discretion direct that no proceedings or no further proceedings should be taken in relation to the Bill, clause, or amendment and effect would be given to that direction.

Limitation on the Legislative Power of the Provincial Legislatures

Provincial legislature had the power to make laws for the province or for any part thereof in respect of any of the matters enumerated in List II (Provincial) or List III (Concurrent). It had no power to make any law affecting the sovereignty or dominion of the Crown over any part of India, or amending any provision of the Government of India Act, 1935, or derogating from the prerogative right of the King to grant special leave to appeal to any court. It had, moreover, no power to pass any law of a discriminatory nature against any British subject or company carrying on business in the province. The prior sanction of the Governor-General, using his discretion, was required for the introduction into the legislature of any Bill or amendment which:

(a) Repealed, amended, or was repugnant to any provisions of any Act of Parliament extending to British India; or
(b) repealed, amended, or was repugnant to any Governor-General's Act, or any ordinance promulgated at his discretion by the Governor-General, or

(c) affected matters in respect of which the Governor-General was by or under the Government of India Act, required to act at his discretion; or
(d) affected the procedure for criminal proceedings in which European British subjects were concerned.

Without the previous sanction of the Governor, no Bill or amendment could be introduced or moved which:
1. Repealed or amended or was repugnant to any Governor's Act, or any ordinance promulgated at his discretion; or
2. repealed or amended or affected any Act relating to any police force.

Special Provisions Relating to Financial Bills

No Financial Bill could be moved or introduced except on the recommendation of the Governor nor could it be introduced in the Legislative Council. A Financial Bill, as defined in the Act, was a Bill:
(a) for imposing or increasing any tax; or
(b) for regulating the borrowing of money or the giving of any guarantee by the province or for amending the law with respect to any financial obligations undertaken or to be undertaken by the province; or
(c) for declaring any expenditure to be expenditure charged on the revenues of the province or for increasing the amount of such expenditure.

The annual financial statement or Budget was laid before the chamber or chambers for discussion. Voting was done only in the Assembly and for that purpose distinction was made between the items relating to expenditure charged on the revenues of the province and other expenditure. The following items of expenditure were declared by the Act[21] to be expenditure on the revenues of India and expenditure so charged was not submitted to the vote of the Assembly, though it could be discussed, except in case of expenditure under the following clauses:
(a) The salary and allowances of the Governor and other expenditure relating to his office for which provision was required to be made by order in Council;
(b) debt charges, including interest, sinking fund charges, and redemption charges;
(c) the salaries and allowances of Ministers, the Advocate-General, and the Judges of the High Court;
(d) expenditure for excluded areas;
(e) sums required to satisfy any judgment, decree, or award of any court on arbitral tribunal;
(f) any other expenditure so charged by this Act or any Act of the provincial legislature.

Where any question arose whether a proposed expenditure did or did not fall within any of the above clauses, it was to be decided by the Governor, whose decision was final.

The expenditure not charged on the revenues of the province was submitted in the form of demands for grant to the Legislative Assembly. It was expressly laid down in the Act that no demand for grant could be made except on the recommendation of the Governor. The Assembly had the power to assent to, or refuse, or reduce the amount specified in any demand but the Governor was empowered to restore and treat as sanctioned any such proposed expenditure in whole or in part if in the opinion of the Governor the same was necessary for the due discharge of his special responsibilities.

The Governor, like the Governor-General, possessed the power to promulgate ordinances during the recess of the legislature. He could promulgate ordinances at any time in any matter using his discretion or individual judgment to make laws in the form of Governor's Act. An ordinance issued by the Governor or a Governor's Act, had the same force and effect as an Act of the provincial legislature. The Governor was also given special powers to make regulations for territories declared by the King as 'excluded areas' or 'partially excluded area'. The administration of excluded areas was carried on by the Governor at his discretion. No Act made by the federal legislature or a provincial legislature applied to an excluded area unless the Governor had so decided, with such exceptions and modifications as he considered necessary. The Governor could also make regulations for the peace and good government of such an area which might repeal or amend any federal or provincial act or any existing Indian law applicable to it. Such regulations were required to be submitted forthwith to the Governor-General and had no effect until assented to by him. These were subject to disallowance by the King like an Act of the provincial legislature.[22]

The Governor was also given special powers in case of the failure of the constitutional machinery in the province. If, at any time, the Governor believed that a situation had arisen in which the government of the province could not be carried on in accordance with the provisions of the Government of India Act, 1935 he could, using his discretion by Proclamation, declare that he had assumed upon himself all or any of the powers vested in or exercisable by any provincial body or authority other than a High Court, subject to the following conditions:[23]

1. No Proclamation declaring the failure of the constitutional machinery could be issued without the concurrence of the Governor-General.
2. The Proclamation was to be forthwith communicated to the Secretary of State and it was to be laid by him before both Houses of Parliament.
3. The Proclamation ceased to operate on the expiry of six months unless its continuance had been approved by resolution of both Houses of Parliament, but no such Proclamation could in any case remain in force for more than three years.
4. Any law made by the Governor when the Proclamation was in force continued to have effect for a period of two years after the expiry of the Proclamation, unless sooner repealed or enacted by an Act of the appropriate legislature.

Formation of Ministries in the Provinces

The federal part of the Constitution was not largely put into operation but the provincial part came into force on 1 April 1937. In the provincial elections, the Congress Party had won the majority of the seats in eight provinces. Initially, the Congress refused to form the governments. However, later on, when an assurance was given that the Governors would not use their special powers, the Congress formed ministries in the provinces where the Party was returned in majority. The Muslim League did not do well in these elections and secured only 51 out of a total of 482 seats reserved for Muslims. The Muslim League offered to join the Congress ministries, but on honourable terms. This was not acceptable to the Congress who demanded that the Muslim League should cease to function as a separate group in the legislature and should come under the control of the Congress high command. The Muslim League refused such humiliating terms offered by a power drunk party.

The Congress ministries functioned from July 1937 to October 1939. In September 1939, the Second World War broke out and Britain declared war on Germany. The Governor-General declared India a belligerent country on the side of Britain and the Allies. Neither the central legislature nor the provincial governments were consulted over this. The Congress was in a dilemma and as a protest asked its ministers in the provincial governments to resign in protest. Provincial autonomy thus came to an end all of a sudden. No other group could form the ministries consequently, the Governors suspended the Constitution in the eight provinces where Congress had been in office. Section 93 of the Act came into operation and the Governors carried on the entire work of administration with the help of their advisers. Parliamentary government came to an end and the rule of the Governors began which lasted till until the end of the war. This was done by amending the Act because the Governor's Proclamations of Emergency could not last longer than six months under the Act of 1935. The Defence of India Rules was in force throughout India during the Second World War. It restricted the powers of the ministers in other provinces where. Governors began to force their will upon the ministers in the day-to-day administration. Mr Allah Bux, the Chief Minister of Sindh, was dismissed from the office of premiership although he enjoyed the confidence of the legislature. This was an act of great constitutional impropriety. The resignation of Mr Fazlul Haq, prime minister of Bengal, was also obtained under similar circumstances.

Role of the Governors

Initially, the Governors did not interfere in the day-to-day affairs of the provincial administration. As time passed, differences between the Governors and the ministers began to surface. In the case of Bihar and UP, differences arose between the Governors and the Congress ministries on the question of the release of political prisoners. The Governors refused to release political prisoners on the grounds that peace and tranquility of India was likely to be disturbed thereby. When the Governor-

General consulted the other provinces, they also opposed the release of political prisoners in Bihar and in the UP. The result was that the Congress ministries in those two provinces resigned and a deadlock was created. As the Government of India was not prepared to take the matter to the extreme, a via-media was found to suit the parties. It was decided to allow the release of political prisoners but in stages. It was declared that the cases of the individual prisoners were to be examined on merit and then action was to be taken. The result was that the British government was able to save its face and the Congress ministries were able to release political prisoners. The Congress ministries in Bihar and UP resumed office and this event had a very healthy effect on other Governors in Congress majority provinces.

In the Punjab, the Governor played an important part in the administration of the province. When the Governor was consulted by the Governor-General in 1938 on the question of the release of political prisoners in Bihar and in the UP, the Governor of the Punjab wrote back that the peace and tranquility of the Punjab was likely to be disturbed if the prisoners were released. This he did without consulting the Chief Minister or the members of his Cabinet. Sikandar Hayat Khan, Chief Minister of the Punjab, had to admit in the Assembly that he had not been consulted at all. Despite the provincial government, the police and secret service of the Raj operated in the Punjab and in Bengal. In Bengal, thousands of people were put behind bars without any trial. Allah Bux, the Chief Minister of Sindh, was dismissed by the Governor on the frivolous ground that he had given up his title of Khan Bahadur. This was done in-spite of the fact that he had the backing of the majority of the members of the legislature at the time of his dismissal.

The provinces were thus not really free from interference by the central government in administrative, legislative, or financial matters. The federal legislature could frame laws for the provinces, the Governor-General could interfere in matters of administration. The Governors of the provinces were also subject to the control of the Governor-General and, had to exercise their authority in such a way that there could be no encroachments on the federation or the Governor-General. The legislatures were also not free. At every step, safeguards came in and provincial autonomy became merely a farce. Provincial autonomy in the strict sense of the term was not granted by the Constitution. The safeguards became vital encroachments on it and they were construed and applied according to the convenience of the centre. The special powers of the Governors proved to be a hindrance to the growth of responsible government in the provinces.

The Muslims had a bitter experience in the provinces having Congress ministries. The Congress Party was totally exposed in these two years by its ministries in the eight provinces where Muslims suffered discrimination and rough treatment at their hands. It is no surprise that the Muslims in India rejoiced and celebrated a day of deliverance when these ministries resigned in 1939. It is said that the experience with those ministries was one of the major causes behind the Lahore Resolution of 23 March 1940 (later called 'The Pakistan Resolution'), seeking an independent state for Muslims in India.

It cannot be denied that the Government of India Act, 1935 was not a perfect piece of legislation. It fell far short of the aspirations and demands of the people of India. Some of its shortcomings and defects were:

1. Indians were not given control over the government of their country. They could not change or amend their Constitution. This was a serious drawback and a large number of states did not join the federation.
2. Indian states were given a privileged position under the Constitution. The representation given to them both in the Council of State and the Federal Assembly was more than what was due to them on the basis of their territory, population, and the contributions made by them to the revenues of the federal government. While the members from British India were to be elected by the people, the Indian princes were allowed to nominate their quota. Critics pointed out that as the Indian princes were under the control of the political department of the Government of India and did what they were directed to do, their representatives were obviously under the control of the British government. They could not dare to vote against their masters. The nominees from the Indian states could be used by the British government in India to serve their own interest and stop the progress of the country.
3. It was against the canons of democracy to have indirect elections to the federal assembly.
4. Indians resented the control which exercised by the Secretary of State for India over the Indian Civil Service, the Indian Police Service, and other All-India Services.
5. Even though the Indian Army got the lion's share of the Indian budget, Indians were given absolutely no control over it, as defence was a reserved subject.
6. The discretionary powers of the Governors reduced provincial autonomy to a farce. Those powers and responsibilities frustrated the powers and functions of the provincial legislature and the executive. The Governor was made the sole judge to decide whether any particular matter fell within his discretionary scheme or affected any of his special responsibilities. The Governor could become a virtual dictator of the province within the letter of the law.
7. The powers of the provincial legislatures were very restricted. The upper chambers were deliberately made reactionary bodies.

NOTES

1. Bokhari, Abrar Husain, *Constitutional History of Indo-Pakistan*, 1964, M. Mohammad Suleman Qureshi & Sons, Lahore, pp. 96-7.
2. *The Government of India Act 1935*, Seventh Schedule and Sections 99, 100, 101, 102, 103 and 107.
3. *Government of India Act 1935*, Section 8.
4. Ibid., Section 12.
5. Ibid., Section 18.
6. Ibid., Schedule I.
7. Ibid., Section 30, 31.

8. Ibid., Section 33 to 37.
9. Ibid., Section 110.
10. Ibid., Section 42.
11. Ibid., Section 45.
12. Ibid., Section 200.
13. Ibid., Section 204.
14. Ibid., Section 205.
15. Ibid., Section 207.
16. Ibid., Section 206.
17. Ibid., Section 208.
18. Ibid., Section 50.
19. Ibid., Section 52.
20. Ibid., Fifth Schedule.
21. Ibid., Section 78.
22. Ibid., Section 88.
23. Ibid., Section 45.

3

COUNTDOWN TO PARTITION

Although both the Congress and the Muslim League were critical of the Government of India Act, 1935, they decided to participate in the elections during the first weeks of 1937. Their electoral programmes were similar and it was expected that they would be able to co-operate in the provinces as they were already doing in the central assembly. The results of the elections shattered all such hopes. The Congress obtained outright majorities in five out of eleven provincial assemblies and was the largest party in two others. Congress ministries were formed in Bombay, Madras, Central Provinces, United Provinces, Bihar, Orissa, and the North-West Frontier Province. In Bengal and the Punjab, coalition governments were formed under the leadership of Muslims who were members neither of the Congress nor of the League. In the North-Western Frontier Province, Dr Khan Sahib, a Muslim nationalist, allied himself with the Congress but in the Hindu majority provinces where the League captured a substantial number of Muslim seats, it confidently expected to be asked to form coalition ministries with the Congress. Jinnah, as Chairman of the League's Election Board, made it clear that co-operation with the Congress was desired provided that it was a general coalition between independent parties. This expectation of the League was well founded, particularly in the United Provinces where the League's candidates had run on a common platform with the Congress and had won more Muslim seats than any other party and had received, what it considered to be, definite assurance of a coalition before the elections. When the election results were declared and Congress found itself in an overall majority, it offered the League terms which no independent political party could have accepted. Leaguers would be taken into the Cabinet only if the party dissolved its parliamentary organization and if all its representatives became members of the Congress. Thereafter, all policy decisions would be made by a majority vote of the Congress Party. Obviously, such humiliating terms were not acceptable to the League.

The main reason why the Muslim League did not do well in the elections was because, for a number of years, it had been divided into factions. By 1931, Jinnah was so disgusted with the state of Indian politics that he decided to settle in England. He was only persuaded to return to India to take charge of the Muslim League a little more than a year before the elections. When he toured India in 1936, he found that Muslim leaders who were entrenched in the provinces were extremely reluctant to follow an all-India Muslim policy.[1] In the Punjab, Fazl-i-Hussain had organized the Unionist Party which comprised Muslims and some Hindus and Sikhs. The Unionist Party secured a majority in the elections under Fazl-i-Hussain, succeeded by Sikandar

Hayat Khan. In Bengal, Fazlul Haq had formed the Krishak Proja Party and was able to head a coalition government which included the Muslim League and the independent scheduled castes group. Sindh was absorbed in factional politics and the 35 Muslim members of the Provincial Assembly were divided into four groups. In the North-West Frontier Province, the Red Shirts, led by Abdul Ghaffar Khan, had aligned themselves with the Congress and had won 19 of the 50 seats in the Provincial Assembly. After the death of the first chief minister of the provincial government, Sir Abdul Qayyum Khan, a Congress coalition ministry came into existence under Dr Khan Sahib, the brother of Abdul Ghaffar Khan. Only in the provinces where the Muslims were in a minority was the Muslim League in a better position. In Assam, it won a fair number of seats and a coalition ministry, under Mohammad Saadullah, was formed. Its greatest success was, however, in the United Provinces where it captured 29 seats, about 80 per cent of the seats it contested. No Muslim was elected from the United Provinces on the Congress ticket.[2]

The leaders of Congress, now drunk with victories, insisted that the Congress was the sole national organization and denied the existence of any other party. This was in effect an attempt to claim the right to be recognized as the sole inheritor of power from the British. Jawaharlal Nehru declared in March 1937 'there are only two forces in India today, British Imperialism and the Indian Nationalism as represented by the Congress'. Jinnah reminded him immediately that there was a third party to be reckoned with, the Muslims. On coming into power, Congress ministries immediately ordered the hoisting of the Congress flag on government buildings. Singing *Bande Matram* was made compulsory in the legislative assemblies and educational institutions.[3] Hindi was introduced in schools and colleges. Vidya Mandir Educational Scheme, which was introduced to confuse the Muslims about Islamic ideology, was put into practice. The Congress imposed its will on the Muslim minorities. The slaughter of cows was prohibited, the *Azaan* was forbidden, and attacks on worshippers and mosques became frequent. The use of beef was prohibited in areas where it had the sanction of tradition and custom. If a Muslim slaughtered a cow for sacrifice, he was killed, his house burnt, and his women and children assaulted. The Hindus refused to act on the various clauses of the Lucknow Pact which envisaged the participation of Muslims. This attitude disturbed Jinnah who still had hopes of Hindu-Muslim unity. He then decided to devote his life for a separate homeland for the Muslims.

The Pakistan (Lahore) Resolution, 1940

What occurred between 1937 and 1940 was an eye-opener for Muslims in India. The way Congress ministries in various provinces treated Muslims convinced them that they had to struggle for a separate homeland. One of the founders of Hindu Mahasabha, Lala Lajpat Rai, suggested the partition of India between Hindus and Muslims as early as 1924. Savarkar, the President of Mahasabha, frequently referred to Hindus and Muslims as 'two nations'. Iqbal had placed the idea of a Muslim state before the League in 1930. Rehmat Ali had coined the name of 'Pakistan' in 1933 and campaigned indefatigably for its creation ever since.

Even though the Hindus and Muslims had lived together for centuries, they were distinctly apart. Even within the same village, they lived in different parts. A Muslim did not eat with a Hindu or marry into his family. His food, his dress, his name, and often his profession, was distinctly Muslim and when he died he was buried, whereas the Hindu was burnt. Therefore, in 1937, when Congress ministers, in home-spun dress, sat in the Secretariat and controlled British revenue officials, magistrates, and police officers, whilst the Congress flag with its spinning wheel, flew on government buildings, they could not bring together the two communities. However hard the Congress leaders tried to make it otherwise, Congress was an overwhelmingly Hindu organization. Hence, when a Muslim was told by League organizers of the wrong which his brethren were suffering under Congress raj, they were ready to unite and fight for their rights. The suggestion of Hindu domination was intolerable. Once Muslims believed that Islam was in danger, no talk of communal weightage and safeguards could move them. The admirable economic and social reforms instituted by the Congress seemed totally irrelevant to the Muslims. They understood that if the British were leaving, there must either be a Hindu or a Muslim rule, and were thus ready to follow a leader who claimed to save them from Hindu rule.

In this background, the All India Muslim League held its session in Lahore on 23 March 1940, in which the famous Lahore Resolution (now called the 'Pakistan Resolution') was adopted. The Resolution runs as under:

> RESOLVED that it is the considered view of this session of the All India Muslim League that no Constitutional Plan would be workable in this country or acceptable to Muslims, unless it is designed on the following basic principle, namely, the geographically contiguous units are demarcated into regions which should be so constituted, with such territorial readjustments as may be necessary, that the areas in which the Muslims are numerically in a majority as in the North Western and Eastern Zones of India, should be grouped to constitute 'independent states', in which the constituent units shall be autonomous and sovereign.
>
> That adequate, effective, and mandatory safeguards should be specifically provided in the constitution for minorities in these units and in these regions for the protection of their religious, cultural, economic, political, administrative, and other rights and interests in consultation with them. And in other parts of India, where the Musalmaans are in a minority, adequate, effective, and mandatory safeguards shall be specially provided in the constitution for them and other minorities for the protection of their religious, cultural, economic, political, administrative, and other rights and interests in consultation with them.
>
> This session further authorizes the Working Committee to frame a scheme of constitution in accordance with these basic principles providing for the assumption finally by the respective regions of all powers such as defence, external affairs, communications, customs, and such other matters as may be necessary.

Jinnah, in his famous address on the occasion, gave clear expression to the basic concept underlying the resolution. Some of the extracts from his address are reproduced below:

> It has always been taken for granted mistakenly that the Musalmaans are a minority. The Musalmaans are not a minority. The Musalmaans are a nation by any definition. What the military Government of India for 150 years has failed to achieve cannot be realized by the imposition of Central Federal Government except by means of armed force. The problem in India is not of an inter-communal character but manifestly of an international one and it must be treated as such. The Hindus and Muslims belong to two different civilizations which are based mainly on conflicting ideas and conceptions. To yoke together two such nations under a single state, one as a numerical minority and the other as a majority, must lead to growing discontent and final destruction of any fabric that may be so built up for the government of such a state.

This was the famous two-nation theory which aroused so much controversy but formed the basis of the Pakistan Resolution.

No one can argue that the Lahore Resolution was a complete or coherent statement of Muslim demands. It appears on the face of it an incomplete and contradictory statement. Its flaws were eventually exploited by Mountbatten and the Congress to justify the partition of Bengal and the Punjab. It was also used as the basis of the Six-Point Programme spelled out by Mujibur Rehman in 1966 which ultimately led to the break up of Pakistan in 1971. It can, however, be said in defence of the Resolution that perhaps it was the only statement on which Jinnah could get consensus of the Muslim community all over India. There were, after all, contradictions between Muslim interests in majority and minority provinces, and between an apparently separatist demand for autonomous Muslim states and the need for a centre capable of ensuring the interests of Muslims in the rest of India.[4]

Second World War and the Termination of Congress Ministries

The Second World War broke out on 1 September 1939, when Nazi Germany attacked Poland, and Britain and France declared war on Germany. The attitudes of the Congress and the League towards the British government during the Second World War were very different. Congress provincial ministries in Madras, Central Provinces, Bihar, United Provinces, Bombay, Orissa, and North-West Frontier Province resigned in October 1939 after passing identical resolutions in the assemblies of these provinces, deploring the 'Declaration of War without the consent of the Indian people' and calling for the immediate treatment of India as 'an independent nation entitled to frame her own Constitution'. As the war continued, the Congress demand for immediate independence became more strident. In October 1940, Gandhi launched an individual civil disobedience campaign in which Congressmen were nominated by him to make speeches opposing India's participation in the war and to court imprisonment. In the course of this, national leaders such as Patel and Nehru, together with most of the former Congress provincial ministers, were arrested. There was a general jail delivery in 1941, but after the failure of Stafford Cripps' Mission in 1942, Congress declared open rebellion sanctioning a mass struggle on non-violent lines on the widest possible scale against 'an imperialist and authoritarian government'. As a result, the Congress Working Committee remained in jail from August 1942 until June 1945, and Gandhi was detained between August 1942 and May 1944.

The League's attitude towards the government throughout the war was one of limited co-operation. A working committee resolution in September 1939 expressed deep sympathy for Poland, England, and France, but it urged that the Indian Muslim troops should on no account be used to fight against Muslims. It also demanded fair treatment for the Arabs in Palestine, called for justice for Muslims in the Congress ruled provinces, and for the abandonment of the federal part of the Government of India Act, 1935. On all these points, they received a measure of satisfaction, and although the League refused to support the war effort unless the government firmly committed itself in favour of Pakistan, its provincial ministries gave quiet assistance.

The League gained by the absence of Congress from the political scene. At one point or another, there were League ministries in Bengal, the Punjab, Sindh, the North-West Frontier, and Assam. In the remaining provinces, the assemblies were prorogued and the administration was carried on by British Governors with official advisers. Jinnah, regularly re-elected as President of the League, strongly asserted party discipline. When the Viceroy appointed the Muslim provincial premiers as members of the National Defence Council in 1941, Jinnah obtained their immediate resignations because the invitations had not come through party channels. By doing so, he lost the allegiance of Fazlul Haq, Premier of Bengal, but the League was strengthened for Fazlul Haq was replaced by the loyal Leaguer, Nazimuddin. Similarly, although in the Punjab Khizar Hayat Khan defied Jinnah and remained premier of a coalition government even on his expulsion from the League, he lost the support of a great part of the Muslim electorate. In this way, Jinnah was able to assert party authority over Muslim politics throughout India.

The Cripps' Mission, 1942

In March 1942, it appeared to many people in India that the Japanese could over-run India with the same ease with which they had conquered South-East Asia. Subhas Chandra Bose, who had escaped from India in 1940, began organizing the Indian National Army with Indian prisoners-of-war captured by the Japanese.

It was in these circumstances that the British government sent a prominent member of the War Cabinet, Sir Stafford Cripps, to India with a draft declaration for discussion with Indian leaders. He arrived in Delhi on 23 March 1942, had discussions with Indian leaders, and departed a fortnight later without achieving anything. The draft declaration which Cripps brought with him promised a Constituent Assembly consisting of elected representatives from the provinces and nominated representatives from the Indian states immediately upon the cessation of hostility. It also gave an understanding on behalf of the British government to accept and implement the Constitution framed by the Constituent Assembly, provided that any province or state would be free either to adhere or not to adhere to the new provisions. Meanwhile, the British government would retain control of the defence of India as part of the world war effort, but invited the immediate and effective participation of leaders of the principal section of the Indian people in the task of organizing the military, moral, and material resources of India.[5]

The Congress rejected the offer on the advice of Gandhi, who regarded it as a post-dated cheque of a failing bank. The Muslim League also rejected it because it did not concede Pakistan unequivocally. Of the Congress leaders, only Rajgopalachari favoured acceptance of Cripps' offer and the formation of a national front for prosecuting the war. He clearly saw that the main obstacle in the way of India's freedom and national security was lack of agreement between the Congress and the Muslim League. Under his leadership, Congress members in the Madras legislature passed a resolution in April 1942, recommending acceptance of Pakistan in principle. The leaders in control of Congress rejected the proposal and Rajgopalachari was driven into exile.[6]

Regardless of the fate of Cripps' offer, it cannot be denied that it was the best one made uptil then. It conceded to the proposed Indian union the liberty to secede from the British Commonwealth. The framing of the new Constitution was to rest solely in Indian hands. But its acceptance was subject to the fulfilment of British obligations. If Indians could not become free as a single state, they were allowed to become free as two or more units. Leaders of the principal sections of the Indian people were invited to participate in the Councils of India, the Commonwealth, and the United Nations. The depressed classes rejected the proposal on the ground that the necessary safeguards were not provided for their interests. The scheme failed because it was to be accepted or rejected as a whole and there was no room given for negotiations or adjustments. There was no indication that the British government was prepared to part with power. The failure of the Cripps' Mission brought a lot of discontent throughout India.

The 'Quit India' Movement

On the failure of the Cripps' Mission, Gandhi began to press for an immediate withdrawal of the British from India and the transfer of power to the Congress without a prior settlement with any other party. According to him, the presence of the British in India was an invitation to Japan to invade it. Their withdrawal would remove such bait. Even if it did not, he thought that India would be in a better position to cope with the invasion. These ideas were formally adopted by the All India Congress committee meeting held in Bombay on 8 August 1942, in the famous 'Quit India' Resolution which demanded the withdrawal of British power from India and authorized the starting of a mass struggle, on non-violent lines, on the widest possible scale. Gandhi called the resolution open rebellion. This time, the government did not take time to act. Gandhi and other Congress leaders were arrested and Congress committees were declared to be unlawful associations. Widespread disorder soon broke out. Railways, post offices, telegraph and telephone systems, and police stations were attacked. By the end of November 1942, 940 lives had been lost and property worth one million pounds sterling had been destroyed. Other political parties and the bulk of the population kept away from this movement.

The Muslim League saw in these actions an attempt to coerce the British into handing over power to a Hindu oligarchy led by the Congress Party. The Muslims were not any less insistent on the attainment of independence but they felt that the purpose of the Congress agitation was to bring about the establishment of Hindu raj and to deal a death blow to the Muslim goal of Pakistan. To Gandhi's slogan of 'Quit India', Jinnah replied, 'Divide and Quit'.

In February 1943, Gandhi went on a twenty-one day fast. For some time, it appeared as if his life was in danger and great pressure was put on the Viceroy to release him unconditionally. Three members of the Viceroy's Executive Council resigned on this issue, but the government stood firm and Gandhi gave up.

When Lord Wavell succeeded Lord Linlithgow as Viceroy in the fall of 1943, the war was turning clearly in favour of the Allies. India was the base for the South East Asia Command and the strain of supplying the large military forces, particularly American, British, and Indian, with provisions and equipment was telling on the Indian economy. The shortage of shipping, fall in imports, dislocation of the transport system by the heavy movement of men and material for the Burma front, restricted supplies available for civilian consumption and, above all, the financing of the war effort in India by printing currency led to a rapid rise in price and serious inflationary pressures. The worst sufferer was Bengal which was ravaged by a severe famine in 1943. Peasants who had been induced by high prices to sell rice died of starvation in millions. The congestion of transport channels delayed supplies, rationing was introduced tardily, and the central government did not intervene till a later stage when the Viceroy, Lord Wavell, gave personal attention to the problem.[7]

In May 1944, Gandhi was released on medical grounds. Soon afterwards, he wrote to the Viceroy offering renunciation of the civil disobedience programme and full co-operation in the war effort by the Congress if a declaration of immediate Indian independence was made and a national government responsible to the central assembly was formed. During the earlier years of the war when the British were sustaining reverse after reverse, Gandhi had objected to Indian participation, giving a fundamental religious principle of *Ahinsa* (non-violence) as the reason. Now, with Allied victory assured, *Ahinsa* was conveniently laid aside so that Congress could gain its political goal.

The belief that the end of the war was in sight stimulated political activity in response to the general public desire for a settlement of Hindu-Muslim differences, and talks took place between Gandhi and Jinnah in September 1944. Gandhi wanted to persuade Jinnah that the idea of Pakistan was absurd. Jinnah was in dead earnest and explained painstakingly that the demand of Pakistan was based on the two-nation theory. Gandhi maintained that India was one nation and saw in the Pakistan Resolution nothing but ruin for all of India. In his opinion, if Pakistan had to be conceded, the areas in which the Muslims were in an absolute majority should be demarcated by a commission approved by both the Congress and the League, and the wishes of all the adult inhabitants of these areas should be ascertained through a referendum. This proposal meant, in effect, that power over India had to be first transferred to the Congress which, thereafter, would allow Muslim majority areas that voted for separation to be constituted not as an independent sovereign state but as part of an Indian federation. In the process, the Punjab and Bengal provinces with a Muslim majority would be partitioned. Gandhi contended that his offer conceded the substance of the Lahore Resolution. Jinnah did not agree and the talks broke down.

The Simla Conference—Wavell's Plan (1945)

Soon after the end of the war in Europe in May 1945, Viceroy Lord Wavell decided to hold a political conference to which he invited Congress and Muslim League representatives, provincial premiers, and some other leaders. He proposed an interim central government in which all portfolios, except that of war, should be held by Indians. There was to be a parity of representation between Muslims and caste Hindus.

The conference began in Simla on 25 June and lasted till 14 July, but it failed to achieve anything. There was a deadlock over the Muslim League's demand that all five Muslim members of the executive council should be taken from the League. The Viceroy said he was prepared to include four members of the Muslim League, but the fifth should be a Punjabi Muslim who did not belong to the League. Behind this apparently minor divergence of views lay serious political dispute. When the Premier of the Punjab, Sikandar Hayat, died in 1942, he was succeeded by Khizar Hayat Tiwana, who lacked the suppleness of his predecessor and soon fell out with Jinnah over the status of the Muslim League in the Punjab. In his stand against the Muslim League, Tiwana was supported by feudal Muslim elements, the Hindus, and Sikhs of the Unionist Party and the British Governor, Sir Bertrand Glancy. All of them ignored the rising influence of the Muslim League amongst the Muslim intelligentsia and masses of the Punjab. Landed interests, with a strong tradition of loyalty to the powers that be, were blind to the signs of the times. The Viceroy's insistence on a non-Leaguer from Punjab was in accordance with the advice given him by the British and Hindu officials to support Khizar Hayat Tiwana in his stand against the League. He was also supported by the Congress which denied the League's claim to be the sole representative of Muslims. When Jinnah stood firm, the conference broke down.

Elections to Provincial and Central Legislatures, 1945–46

The Second World War came to an end with the surrender of Japan on 15 August 1945. British general elections at the end of July resulted in a large Labour majority. Congress leaders who had cultivated close relations with the leaders of the Labour Party over the years felt elated at this unexpected turn of events and immediately started exploiting their position of vantage. British policy had consistently favoured the maintenance of India as a single administrative and political entity. Conservatives like Lord Linlithgow had emphasized it as much as had the soldier statesman, Lord Wavell. Congress leaders expected even stronger support from the Labour Party on this issue which was dividing the Congress and the Muslim League.

The issue was put to test at the general elections for the provincial and central legislatures in the winter of 1945–46. Both Congress and the Muslim League exerted themselves to the utmost because the constitutional future of India depended on the outcome of these elections. The results showed a decisive victory for the idea of Pakistan. The League won all Muslim seats in the Central Assembly and 446 out of a total 495 Muslim seats in provincial assemblies. The Congress won a similar victory in the Hindu constituencies and came to power in all the provinces that had a Hindu majority. In Bengal, the Muslim League won 113 out of a total 119 Muslim seats, and was able to form a ministry with Huseyn Shaheed Suhrawardy as Chief Minister. In the Punjab, the Muslim League captured 79 out of 86 Muslim seats. In Sindh, a Muslim League ministry was formed. Only in the North-West Frontier Province did the League fall short of a majority by winning only 17 out of a total of 36 Muslim seats and the Congress formed a ministry under Dr Khan Sahib.[8]

The 1946 elections proved conclusively that the Muslim League alone represented the Muslims of India, but this only increased the hostility of the Congress towards it. Instead of recognizing the representative character of the Muslim League and coming to terms with it, the Congress persisted in its policy of dividing the Muslims and denying political power to the trusted representatives of the Muslim community even in the provinces where Muslims were in a majority. In this way, Congress deepened Muslim suspicions, intensified communal discord, and made an amicable settlement impossible.

The Cabinet Mission Plan, 1946

On 9 February 1946, the British government announced its decision to send a special mission to India consisting of three Cabinet Ministers to seek, in association with Viceroy Lord Wavell and in consultation with Indian leaders, an agreement on constitutional issues. The Cabinet Mission consisting of Lord Pethwick-Lawrence, the Secretary of State for India, Sir Stafford Cripps, the President of the Board of Trade, and A.V. Alexander, the first Lord of Admiralty, arrived in New Delhi on 24 March 1946. At that time, there were serious differences on constitutional issues between the Congress and Muslim League. The Congress wanted a single Constituent

Assembly to draw up a Constitution for an all-India federal government and legislatures dealing with foreign affairs, defence, communications, fundamental rights, currencies, customs, and planning as well as such other subjects as, on scrutiny, might be found to be intimately allied to them. The Muslim League had passed a resolution demanding that the six provinces of Bengal and Assam in the north-east, and the Punjab, North-West Frontier Province, Sindh and Balochistan in the north-west, be constituted into a sovereign independent state of Pakistan and that two separate constitution-making bodies be set up by the peoples of Pakistan and Hindustan for the purpose of framing their respective Constitutions.

The Cabinet Mission conducted individual negotiations with the top leaders of the two parties and, in early May 1946, arranged a joint meeting in Simla in which both Congress and the Muslim League were duly represented. However, neither party accepted the proposals of the other. The fundamental issue was whether there should be one sovereign state for the whole subcontinent, or two independent states. Either solution involved the presence of minorities and both the Congress and the Muslim League agreed that minorities should receive adequate constitutional protection. Indeed, this was the only common ground. The mediation of the Cabinet Mission could not bridge the gulf between them.

On 16 May 1946, the Cabinet Mission and the Viceroy published a statement containing their own solution to the constitutional problem. The focal point of the plan was the preservation of the single state. On administrative, economic, and military grounds, they rejected the proposal for two independent sovereign states. The Mission could see no justification for including within a sovereign Pakistan those districts of the Punjab, Bengal, and Assam in which the population was predominantly non-Muslim. The Mission, however, saw force in the apprehension of Muslims that their cultural, political, and social life may submerge in a purely unitary India dominated by Hindus.

The Cabinet Mission, therefore, made the recommendation that the new Constitution of India should be made on the following lines:

1. There should be a Union of India, embracing both British India and the Princely states which should deal with the following subjects: foreign affairs, defence, and communications, and should have the powers necessary to raise the finances required for these subjects.
2. India was to be divided into three Zones—A, B, and C. Zone B was to consist of the Punjab, Sindh, and North-West Frontier Province. Zone C was to consist of Bengal and Assam. Zone A was to consist of the rest of the provinces of India. These zones were to settle the provincial constitution for the provinces included in each section. They were also to decide whether group constitution should be set up for these provinces and, if so, with what subjects it should deal. The representatives of these zones of India and the Princely States were then to re-assemble and settle the Union Constitution.
3. Regarding the constitution-making machinery, it was provided that the Legislative Assemblies of the provinces would elect the members of that body on the basis of one representative for one million of the population. Muslim

and Sikh legislators were to elect the quota of their communities determined on the basis of population. Others were to elect the representatives for the rest of the population.

4. The Union should have an executive and a legislature constituted of representatives from British India and the Princely States. Any question raising a major communal issue in the legislature should require for its decision a majority of the representatives present and voting of each of the two minor communities as well as a majority of all the members present and voting.
5. All subjects other than the Union subjects and all residuary powers would vest in the provinces.
6. The states would retain all subjects and powers other than those ceded to the Union.
7. Provinces would be free to form groups with executives and legislatures, and each group could determine the provincial subjects to be taken in common.
8. The Constitution of the Union and of the group would contain a provision whereby any province could, by a majority vote of its Legislative Assembly, call for a reconsideration of the terms of the Constitution after an initial period of ten years and at ten yearly intervals thereafter.[9]

An interim government representing the major parties had to be formed by the Viceroy to carry on the administration. The paramountcy of the British government over the Princely States would lapse when the Indian Union came into being and it would be for each state to negotiate its future relationship with the Union.

On 6 June 1946, the Muslim League, satisfied that Muslim interests would be safeguarded because of the grouping proposal, accepted the plan and agreed to join the interim government 'in the hope that it would ultimately result in the establishment of a complete Pakistan'; and after obtaining an assurance from the Viceroy that 'we shall go ahead with the plan, so far as circumstances permit, if either party accepts'.[10] On 26 June, the Congress accepted the constitution-making part of the plan but refused to join the interim government. As a result, the plan was shelved and the Cabinet Mission then adjourned further discussions of the interim government until elections for the Constituent Assembly had taken place. Meanwhile, the Viceroy formed a caretaker government of civil servants.

Maulana Abul Kalam Azad, who was the President of the Congress at that time, favoured the Cabinet Mission Plan and paid tribute to the way in which the Mission conducted the negotiations.[11] According to him, the acceptance of the Cabinet Mission plan by both Congress and Muslim League was a glorious event in the history of the freedom movement in India. It is unfortunate that Maulana Azad decided to retire as the President of Congress in 1946 despite the general feeling in the party that since he had conducted the negotiations till then, he should be charged with the task of bringing them to a successful close and implementing them.[12] Azad chose Nehru as his successor, a step he regretted later because it was Nehru who sabotaged the plan. He stated that the Congress had agreed only to participate in the Constituent Assembly and regarded itself free to change or modify the Cabinet Mission plan as it thought best. Nehru was wrong and the matters settled in the plan could not be the changed unilaterally by Congress without the consent of the other parties to the agreement.[13] Jinnah immediately issued a statement that this declaration of Nehru demands a review of the whole situation. The Muslim League, according to him, had accepted the plan as it was assured that the Congress had also accepted the scheme and that the plan would be the basis of the future Constitution of India. Since the Congress President had declared that the Congress could change the scheme through its majority in the Constituent Assembly, this would mean that the minorities were placed at the mercy of the majority.[14]

The Congress under the presidency of Nehru destroyed the scheme painstakingly worked out through negotiations with the Cabinet Mission. Viceroy Wavell lamented, 'We have in fact been outmanoeuvred by the Congress, and this ability of Congress to twist words and phrases and to take advantage of any slip in wording is what Jinnah has all along feared, and has been the reason for his difficult attitude'.[15] On 28 June, the Cabinet Mission trio flew back to England, its mission unaccomplished.

Direct Action Plan and the Interim Government

The Muslim League regarded the failure of the Cabinet Mission plan as a direct breach of the promise held out by the Viceroy. Jinnah's view that since Congress had rejected the Mission plan, the Viceroy should call upon the League to form the government, was correct. The League also accused the Viceroy of having promised that the interim government would consist of five Congress, five League, and two other members, but subsequently, this proposal was modified to include six Congress, five League, and three other members. The League also strongly challenged the good faith of the Congress in accepting the long-term proposals citing the statement of Nehru on 10 July that 'the big probability is that there will be no grouping'.[16]

The League thus withdrew its acceptance of the proposal, called on all Muslims to renounce their titles, and decided on a campaign of 'Direct Action' to achieve Pakistan and to get rid of the slavery under the British. There was no other course open to the Muslim League because otherwise there would be Hindu domination at the centre in times to come. The resolution of 'Direct Action' authorized the working committees of the League to prepare a programme immediately. 16 August was fixed as 'Direct Action Day' when Hindu-Muslim communal riots broke out in Calcutta on an unprecedented scale. In Calcutta alone, four thousand people were killed, another five thousand were killed in Bihar, and there were fifty thousand homeless refugees in East Bengal.[17]

The Congress withdrew its objection to entering the interim government, and on 24 August, the Viceroy's Council was re-formed with all its members nominated by Congress, with Nehru as its vice president. The Congress government at the centre did not act to prevent communal riots and Muslim interests suffered due to their lack of representation at the centre. The Muslim League then decided to join the interim government and in October 1946, five League nominees led by Liaquat Ali Khan, including scheduled caste Hindus, entered the interim government.

Constituent Assembly and Attlee's Statement, February 1947

Elections to the Constituent Assembly had taken place in July 1946 and the Constituent Assembly met for the first time in New Delhi in December 1946. Out of 296 members, Congress and its allies secured 212 seats, and the League 73 seats. The Muslim League refused to participate in its deliberations. Jinnah and Nehru were invited to London, where an attempt was made to reconcile conflicting interpretations of the Mission's plan, and to induce the League to take part in the proceedings of the Assembly. Meanwhile, Congress was proceeding with constitution-making in the absence of the League and on 22 January1947, the 'Objective Resolution' was passed.

On 31 January 1947, the Muslim League passed a resolution protesting that the Congress, instead of postponing the sittings of the Assembly until fundamental points of principle had been settled, had not only acted on its own interpretation of the Cabinet Mission plan but had forced decisions in the Assembly which were clearly outside the scope of the plan. The 'Objective Resolution', passed by the Constituent Assembly on 22 January, had proclaimed an independent federal republic. Rules of procedure had been made in violation of the directions in the plan which envisaged that the central Constitution was not to be considered until the provincial and regional (group) constitutions had been settled. The League, therefore, called upon the British government to declare that the plan had failed.

On 20 February 1947, Attlee, the British Prime Minister, made an important declaration. He announced that the British government would grant full self-government to British India by June 1948 at the latest. In the meantime, according to the statement, preparatory measures would be put in hand in advance and legislation would be introduced in due course to give effect to the final transfer of power. The British government would negotiate an agreement regarding matters arising out of the transfer of power with representatives of those to whom they propose to transfer power. The future of the Princely States had to wait until the date of final transfer of power. It was also announced that Lord Mountbatten was to succeed Lord Wavell as the Viceroy of India, who would be entrusted with the task of transferring power into Indian hands.

The Mountbatten Plan, June 1947

Lord Mountbatten reached New Delhi on 24 March 1947 and declared that he would complete the work of transfer of power into Indian hands within the next few months in consultation with Indian leaders. On his arrival, he was faced with a desperate situation. The central Cabinet was so divided as to be almost impotent; in the Punjab, the Unionist government was tottering under the attack of the Muslim League; and in the North-West Frontier, there was a Muslim League civil disobedience campaign. All over the country, fierce communal clashes were taking place and private armies were being formed for the final struggle for power. The civil services were bitterly divided on communal lines and headed by dispirited Englishmen, anxious to retire.

British troops were already being repatriated, and the morale of the Indian Army was uncertain.[18] It was evident that the unity of India could not be maintained. Mountbatten started a new series of conferences and talks with the Congress, Muslim League, and Sikh leaders. He tried to persuade Jinnah to join the Constituent Assembly, but without success. After all, Jinnah understood the consequences because it would have meant submission and capitulation to brute majority as the League was outnumbered by the Congress by 73 to 199. Mountbatten later claimed that he had worked 'hand in glove' with Indian leaders at every step of development of the new plan, but this claim is not substantiated from the writings of a number of British authors who had access to the inner story of the transfer of power. It is now quite clear that his final draft for the transfer of power was prepared in consultation with Mountbatten's Hindu constitutional adviser, V.P. Menon, and that this draft had been shown only to Nehru. The Muslim League and its leaders were not taken into confidence at the time of making the final draft.[19]

On 3 June 1947, the British government accepted the principle of the partition of India and undertook to hand over dominion status, to the successor governments on 15 August with the implicit right to secede from the Commonwealth.

The Mountbatten Plan of 3 June 1947, did not elaborate any constitutional proposals. It outlined the procedure to ascertain the wishes of the people of those areas in which the majority of representatives boycotted the Constituent Assembly and whether their Constitution should be framed by the existing Constituent Assembly or by a new and separate Constituent Assembly, in other words to determine whether they wished to join Pakistan or not. In Bengal, the Punjab, and Sindh, the choice was left to the members of the provincial legislative assemblies. But the assemblies of Bengal and the Punjab would each meet in two parts, one representing the Muslim majority districts and the other the Hindu majority districts. Each part would vote separately on the questions, whether or not the province should be partitioned and if so which Constituent Assembly the areas it represented should join. But there was also a provision that if any member of the Legislative Assembly so demanded, a vote of the whole should be taken if the two parts decided to remain united. If in either part of the Legislative Assembly the verdict went in favour of partition, the province would be provisionally divided on the basis of Muslim majority and non-Muslim districts. Thereafter, a boundary commission would demarcate the boundaries of the two parts of the province on the basis of contiguous majority areas of Muslim and non-Muslim.

The North-West Frontier Province presented a problem. Though it was a Muslim majority province it still had a Congress ministry in power. The responsibility of making the crucial decision of joining India or Pakistan could not fairly be entrusted to the Provincial Assembly, in which Hindu and Sikh minorities, though counting only eight per cent of the population, had been given no less than twelve seats out of a total of fifty. It was, therefore, necessary to give the province an opportunity of deciding whether it wished to form a part of Pakistan. Hence the plan provided that the Viceroy, in consultation with the provincial government, should arrange for a referendum of the electors to the Assembly.

If the decision in Bengal should go in favour of partition, a similar referendum would be held in Muslim majority districts of Sylhet in Assam province. Special administrative arrangements were made to determine the wishes of the people of Balochistan.

The new plan concluded with an announcement which promised to make the transfer of power much simpler and even earlier than June 1948. The decision was to introduce legislation during the current session of the British Parliament for the transfer of power in 1947 on a dominion status basis to either one or two successor authorities according to the decision taken under the plan. This would be without prejudice to the right of the Constituent Assemblies to decide in due course whether India or Pakistan should remain within the British Commonwealth. It soon became known that 15 August 1947 was the date on which the British would hand over power.

Both the Congress and the Muslim League accepted the plan. The Muslim majority parts of India decided in favour of Pakistan. By the end of June, the procedure for deciding on the unity or partition of Bengal and the Punjab had been worked out, in each case it had resulted in a verdict in favour of partition. That Sindh and Balochistan would vote to join Pakistan was never in doubt. The Sindh Assembly registered this decision on 26 June, 1947 and in Balochistan there was a unanimous vote in favour of Pakistan. The referendum in the North-West Frontier Province and in the district of Sylhet similarly resulted in favour of Pakistan. In Punjab, Khizar Hayat Tiwana, who headed the Unionist ministry, resigned making way for the Nawab of Mamdot, leader of the Muslim League in Punjab, to form the government.

It may be pointed out here that the partitioning of Bengal and the Punjab was a painful act. The percentage of Muslim population in Bengal was 55 and in the Punjab 57.[20] Both the provinces ought to have joined Pakistan as a whole. Perhaps the vagueness of the Lahore Resolution led to the partitioning of these provinces. Reportedly, Mountbatten pointed out to League leaders that the area of Pakistan, as envisaged in the Lahore Resolution, did not include the entire provinces of Punjab, Bengal, and Assam because the Lahore Resolution carefully used the phrase 'areas in which the Muslims are numerically in a majority as in the north-western and eastern zones of India'. If the framers of the Lahore Resolution had been clear and confident about Muslim majority in the entire provinces of Punjab, Bengal, and Assam, they would have been more specific. Accordingly, Mountbatten argued, the Muslim League could not oppose the partition of these provinces as this was clearly hinted at by the Lahore Resolution which used the term 'areas' without clearly defining what provinces the term 'areas' constituted.[21]

The increasing tempo which marked the new plan, as compared to the Cabinet Mission plan, was further accelerated by the Indian Independence Bill. Within one month, the Bill was drafted, referred to the Viceroy, and discussed by him with the Congress and League leaders, so that on 4 July, it was introduced in the British parliament. On 18 July, only fourteen days after its introduction, the Bill received the Royal assent. On the day after the Indian Independence Act was passed, the legal birth of the new dominions was marked by the splitting of the interim government in New Delhi into two groups, representing the two successor governments—India and Pakistan.[22]

Lord Mountbatten went to Karachi to formally inaugurate the new state of Pakistan on 14 August 1947.

The Independence Act, 1947

The Independence Act, 1947 was enacted to give effect to the Mountbatten Plan of 3 June 1947. He formalized and legalized what had been held out by the British government as a promise to the people of India. The Act provided for the partition of India and the establishment of two independent dominions to be known as India and Pakistan, with effect from the 15 August 1947.[23] The British government was to cease to have control over the affairs of the dominions, provinces, or any part of the dominions after 15 August 1947. With the end of the sovereignty of the British government over the Indian states, treaties and agreements between the British and any of the authorities in the tribal areas also lapsed.[24]

The salient features and the provisions of the Act are enumerated below:

1. A Governor-General was provided for each of the new dominions who was to be appointed by the Crown, subject to the law of the legislature of either of the new dominions; the same person could be Governor-General of both the new dominions.[25]
2. The legislatures of the two dominions were made fully sovereign and were given powers to make laws having extra-territorial jurisdiction. The Governor-General of each dominion had full power to assent. No Act of Parliament of the United Kingdom on or after 15 August could extend to any of the new dominions.[26]
3. The Constituent Assembly of each of the dominions was given the power to frame a Constitution; pending which each of the dominions and all provinces and other parts thereof were to be governed as nearly as could be in accordance with the Government of India Act, 1935. The Governor-General of each dominion was empowered till 31 March 1948[27] to make necessary omissions, additions, adaptations, and modifications in the provisions of the Government of India Act, 1935 and of the Orders in Council, rules and other instruments made thereunder.[28] After 31 March 1948 (later extended to 31 March 1949), the Constituent Assembly of a dominion had the power to make such modification or adaptation. Until a new Constitution was framed for each dominion, the existing Constituent Assemblies were temporarily made the dominion legislatures.
4. The office of the Secretary of State for India was abolished[29] and the provisions of the Government of India Act, 1935 relating to appointments to the Civil Service or civil posts under the Crown by the Secretary of State ceased to operate. However, all those who had been appointed by the Secretary of State before 15 August 1947 to the Civil Service of the Crown or those who had been appointed as Judges of the Federal Court or a High Court before such date were to continue as such in either of the dominions.[30]

5. The Indian armed forces were divided between the two dominions and the Governors-General were to make provision for such division for the command and governance of those forces.[31] British forces in India, including His Majesty's Air Force and Naval Force, were not to form part of the Indian forces on or after 15 August 1947.[32]
6. The existing Instruments of Instructions to the Governor-General and the Governors of the provinces would lapse and they would act without such Instruments.[33]
7. The laws of British India and of the several parts thereof existing immediately before 15 August 1947 would, as far as applicable and with necessary adaptations, continue as the laws of each of the new dominions and the several parts thereof until other provisions were made by laws of the legislature of the dominion in question or by any other legislature or other authority having power in that behalf.[34]
8. The province of Bengal, as constituted under the Government of India Act, 1935, ceased to exist and in its place were constituted two provinces known as East Bengal and West Bengal. The District of Sylhet was to form part of the new province of East Bengal and the boundaries of these two provinces were to be determined by the award of a boundary commission appointed by the Governor-General of British India.[35]
9. The province of the Punjab, as constituted under the Government of India Act, 1935 ceased to exist and in its place two new provinces were constituted to be known as West Punjab[36] and East Punjab. The boundaries of the two new provinces were to be determined by a boundary commission appointed by the Governor-General of British India and, until such determination, the districts specified in the Second Schedule of the Act were to be treated as territories comprising the new province of West Punjab. The remaining territories in the province of the Punjab at the time of the passing of the Act were to comprise the territories of the new province of East Punjab.[37]

The Princely States of India

As discussed above, the Indian Independence Act, 1947 terminated all treaties and agreements between the British government and the rulers of Indian states as of 15 August 1947. Lord Mountbatten, at a press conference held on 4 June 1947, said that the Indian states had been independent in treaty relations with the British and with the lapse of paramountcy, they would assume an independent status and were absolutely free to choose to join one Constituent Assembly or the other, or make some other arrangement.[38]

There were 562 states throughout British India. Pakistan was contiguous with only fourteen, which included the State of Jammu and Kashmir. The rest were geographically linked with the Indian Union. On the question of whether the states could become independent, there was a difference of opinion between the Congress and the Muslim League. The Congress maintained that since the states did not have the means to establish international relations or to declare war, they could not become sovereign independent states and should enter the political structure of one or the other dominion government. The League felt that the states were under no compulsion to join either dominion and should be left free to decide for themselves. However, Jinnah said it was in the mutual interest of the states and the dominion governments to make necessary adjustments.[39] Moreover, there was real conflict of interest over the two largest states, Kashmir and Hyderabad. Kashmir, contiguous to Pakistan, had a Muslim majority and a Hindu ruler. Hyderabad, contiguous to India, had a Hindu majority and a Muslim ruler. India wanted to hold on to both Kashmir and Hyderabad. Kashmir was an integral part of the Muslim concept of Pakistan. Hyderabad, which had been ruled by a Muslim dynasty from the days of the Mughal Empire, occupied a special place in the sentiments of Muslim India. Muslim League leaders were in deep sympathy with Hyderabad's desire to be independent.

With the persuasion of Mountbatten and the skill of V.P. Menon, secretary to the concerned department, and the cunning of Sardar Patel, the minister in charge, the accession of the states to India continued and the fear of possible balkanization of India was put to rest. V.P. Menon drew up an instrument of accession for defence, external affairs, and communications and a standstill agreement to cover existing arrangements for customs, currency, and similar matters. Sardar Patel assured the Princes that their states would be autonomous but for the three above subjects. The scheme was simple and statesmanlike. Instead of entering into long and difficult negotiations with each individual state, every state was confronted with two standard documents from which no variation was allowed. It was in the obvious interest of most states to enter into a standstill agreement but they were told that this was not possible without an instrument of accession. Sardar Patel and V.P. Menon handled the Princes firmly and skilfully but the real credit for manoeuvering them into signing the instrument of accession goes to Mountbatten's diplomacy.[40] He addressed the Chamber of Princes on 25 July 1947 in his capacity as Crown Representative and gave a reception on 28 July. On both occasions, he advised, canvassed, and persuaded the Princes to sign the instrument of accession in favour of the dominion of India.

By contrast, he did nothing for Pakistan although as Crown Representative he owed an equal duty to both dominions. On the contrary, in every disputed case of accession, he threw his weight in favour of India. He also played a major role in the occupation of Jammu and Kashmir by the Indian forces. When Mountbatten learnt that the states of Jodhpur and Jaisalmer wanted to accede to Pakistan, he intervened and told the Maharaja of Jodhpur that although from a purely legal standpoint he could accede to Pakistan, his action would conflict with the principles underlying the partition of India. He was scared into believing that serious communal trouble might break out in his state. Consequently, both Jodhpur and Jaisalmir acceded to India. He paid little heed to the principle underlying the partition of India 'when he accepted the accession to Indian dominion of Kapurthala which had Sikh rulers but 64 per cent of the population was Muslim'.[41]

In marked contrast to the spate of accession to the Indian dominion, no state acceded to Pakistan before 15 August. The states that were contiguous to West

Pakistan and had a Muslim majority and Muslim rulers were quite a few, Bahawalpur, Khairpur, Kalat, Las Bela, Kharan, Makran, Dir, Swat, Amb and Chitral. Bahawalpur acceded to Pakistan on 3 October 1947, followed by Khairpur, Chitral, Swat, Dir, and Amb during the next few months. The States of Las Bela, Makran, Kharan, and Kalat, after protracted negotiations, acceded to Pakistan by the end of March 1948.[42]

Junagarh, a state with a Muslim ruler but a majority of Hindu subjects, acceded to Pakistan. It was a coastal state situated on the coast of Gujarat and Kathiawar and could easily maintain its link with Pakistan through sea of no more than three hundred miles. The Prime Minister of India protested to the Prime Minister of Pakistan stating, in a telegram, that the population of Junagarh was 80 per cent Hindu and was opposed to such accession. He was, however, willing to accept the verdict of the people of the state on this question, provided plebiscite was held under the joint supervision of the Indian and Junagarh governments. Since Pakistan did not accept this suggestion, Indian troops marched into Junagarh and seized it by force.[43] This logic was conveniently reversed in the case of the State of Jammu and Kashmir.

The Princes, who were lured into signing the instruments of accession in favour of India, met a sad end. They lost control of their states, even their own assets, in a few years and their states were absorbed into the contiguous state provinces of the Indian Union.

The haste in the implementation of the partition plan accomplished within two-and-a-half months led to hectic negotiations. It has been widely felt that the decision to advance the date of the transfer of power from June 1948 to August 1947 was a disastrous error of judgment. In two-and-a-half months, a new federal government had to be set up in Karachi and the services and assets of the Indian government and of three provincial governments had to be divided. On 15 August, authority was handed over to provincial governments whose boundaries had not been defined, half of whose police and administrative services were in the process of transfer, and East Punjab did not even have a temporary capital. This chaotic situation led to mass murders, abductions, and arson in every district of the Punjab which the authorities had neither the will nor the capacity to check.

The matter of accession of states remained unsettled, leading to permanent conflict between India and Pakistan over the state of Jammu and Kashmir, resulting in repeated hostilities between the two neighbouring countries. Pakistan was suddenly saddled with the colossal problem of settling 10 million refugees due to the disturbances that led to an exchange of population between West Punjab and East Punjab, coupled with a million deaths and abductions. It seems that every effort was made to create problems for Pakistan at its very inception with the expectation on the part of Indian Congress that it would soon collapse under the burden of its problems.

Another misfortune that befell Pakistan at the crucial stage of transfer of power was that the incumbent Governor-General of India was biased and unfair towards Pakistan, and partial towards India. It is an acknowledged fact of history that Mountbatten was very friendly to Nehru and hostile to Jinnah. He expressed his dislike for Jinnah in a number of statements and even in his memoirs.[44] He did everything to inconvenience the Muslim League leadership and to help the Indian Congress. Mountbatten ensured that the birth of Pakistan was made as painful as possible.

NOTES

1. Ali, Chaudhri Mohammad, *The Emergence of Pakistan*, Services Book Club, 1988.
2. Ibid., p. 28.
3. Ibid., pp. 29-30.
4. Jalal, Ayesha, *The Sole Spokesman: Jinnah, the Muslim League and the Demand for Pakistan*, 1985, p. 59, Cambridge University Press, Cambridge.
5. *Supra*, note 1, pp. 42-3.
6. Ibid., p. 44.
7. Ibid., p. 45-6.
8. Ibid., p. 48.
9. Bokhari, Abrar Husain, *Constitutional History of Indo-Pakistan*, 1964, M. Mohammad Suleman Qureshi & Sons, pp. 175-6.
10. Viceroy's letter to Mr Jinnah, 4 June 1946, reproduced in Bannerjee, *Making of the Indian Constitution*, Volume I (Documents).
11. Azad, Maulana Abul Kalam, *India Wins Freedom*, 1959, Orient Longmans, Calcutta, p. 151.
12. Ibid., p. 152.
13. Ibid., p. 155.
14. Ibid., pp. 155-6.
15. Note by Wavell for the Cabinet Delegation, reproduced by Ayesha Jalal in her book *The Sole Spokesman*, *supra*, note 4, p. 206.
16. Statement at Press Conference in Bombay. Text in Bannerjee, *Making of the Indian Constitution*, Vol. I (Documents), p. 241.
17. Symond, Richard, *Making of Pakistan*, Faber & Faber Ltd., London, 1966, p. 69. Statistics given by Sir Stafford Cripps in the House of Commons, 12 December 1946.
18. Ibid., p. 70.
19. Choudhry, G.W., *Constitutional Development in Pakistan*, 1969, printed by Lowe & Brydone (Printers) Ltd., London, p. 17.
20. These figures are taken from the book of Chaudhri Mohammad Ali, *The Emergence of Pakistan*, p. 26.
21. Sayeed, Khalid Bin, *Pakistan: The Formative Phase*, 1960, Pakistan Publishing House, Karachi, p. 125.
22. Ibid., pp. 17 to 19.
23. *Indian Independence Act, 1947*, Sec.1. See *Constitutional Documents* (*Pakistan*) Volume III, published by Government of Pakistan, Karachi, 1964, p. 3.
24. Ibid., Section 7.
25. Ibid., Section 5.
26. Ibid., Section 6.
27. The date was extended to 31 March 1949 by the Indian Independence (Amendment) Act, 1948, Section 2.
28. Ibid., Sections 8 and 9.
29. However, the Secretary of State would continue to perform functions as under Section 14 as respects the management of and the making of payments in respect of government debt.
30. *Supra*, note 23, Section 10.
31. Ibid., Section 11.
32. Ibid., Sections 12 & 13.
33. Ibid., Section 18(4).
34. Ibid., Section 18(3).
35. Ibid., Section 3.
36. For the words 'West Punjab', the words 'the Punjab' were substituted by the Indian Independence (Amendment) Act, 1950, Section 2.

37. *Supra*, note 23, Section 4. It is interesting to note that the District of Gurdaspur is included in West Punjab in the Second Schedule.
38. Ali, Ch. Mohammad, *The Emergence of Pakistan*, Services Book Club 1988, p. 228.
39. Ibid., p. 229.
40. Ibid., p. 231.
41. Ibid., p.234.
42. Ibid., pp. 235-6.
43. Bokhari, Abrar Husain, *Constitutional History of Indo-Pakistan*, 1964, p. 189.
44. Larry Collins and Dominique Lapierre, *Freedom at Midnight*, 1975, Harper Collins Publishers, Great Britain. See pp. 125-6, 129-32, 150, and 232.

PART II

CONSTITUTIONAL AND POLITICAL DEVELOPMENTS FROM AUGUST 1947 TO OCTOBER 1958

4

THE BIRTH OF A NATION AND THE DEATH OF JINNAH

Among the original members of the Constituent Assembly, Muhammad Ali Jinnah[1] was the most eminent. He was not only the Governor-General and President of the Constituent Assembly, but the architect and founder of Pakistan. Under his dynamic leadership, Muslims of the subcontinent were united. His had been the amazing achievement of raising the Muslim League in just ten years (1937–47) from a poorly organized party, representing a minority of a minority, to a political force which could successfully challenge the British and Hindus combined. When Jinnah took up the leadership of the Muslim League in 1937, he found the Muslims of India a demoralized and weak lot without leadership or organization, and surrounded by an intolerant and arrogant Hindu majority which possessed vast resources in numbers, wealth, and propaganda. Within a short period, he became the accredited leader of the Muslims who affectionately bestowed on him the title of Quaid-e-Azam, the great leader.

After being elected the first president of the Constitutent Assembly on 11 August 1947, Jinnah delivered his memorable presidential address. It is indeed one of his most important speeches in which he clearly outlined the ideal and concept of Pakistan, its constitutional structure, and the hopes and aspirations of its people. Also clearly spelt out were the two main functions of the Constituent Assembly; framing the future Constitution of Pakistan and its functioning as a sovereign body being the federal legislature of Pakistan.

The first duty of the government, he declared, was maintenance of law and order and protection of life, property, and religious beliefs of the citizens. He identified bribery and corruption (which he called 'a poison'), black-marketing, nepotism, and jobbery as the greatest evils afflicting society which had to be stamped out. He called upon the majority and minority communities in Pakistan, Muslims and Hindus respectively, to bury the hatchet, forget the past, and co-operate with each other. He exhorted them to concentrate on the well being of the people, especially of the poor. He declared that all citizens of Pakistan, regardless of their colour, caste or creed, would enjoy equal rights, privileges, and obligations.

> I cannot emphasize it too much. We should begin to work in that spirit and in course of time all these angularities of the majority and minority communities, the Hindu community and the Muslim community—because even as regards Muslims you have Pathans, Punjabis,

> shias, sunnis and so on and among the Hindus you have Brahmans, Vashnavas, Khatris, also Bengalees, Madrasis, and so on—will vanish. Indeed if you ask me this has been the biggest hindrance in the way of India to attain the freedom and independence and but for this, we would have been free peoples long ago. No power can hold another nation, and specially a nation of 400 million souls in subjection; nobody could have conquered you, and even if it had happened, nobody could have continued its hold on you for any length of time but for this. Therefore, we must learn a lesson from this.[2]

He then proceeded to affirm the right to religious freedom in the following words:

> You are free; you are free to go to your temples, you are free to go to your mosques or to any other places of worship in this state of Pakistan. You may belong to any religion or caste or creed—that has nothing to do with the business of the state.
>
> Now, I think we should keep that in front of us as our ideal and you will find that in course of time, Hindus would cease to be Hindus and Muslims would cease to be Muslims, not in the religious sense, because that is the personal faith of each individual, but in the political sense as citizens of the state.

It is evident from this speech that Jinnah's prescription for the Constitution of Pakistan included guarantees that: one, all citizens of Pakistan would be equal regardless of their belief, caste, or creed; two, that all citizens would be guaranteed freedom to practise whatever religion they believed in; three, that all religious, sectarian, ethnic, linguistic, and other similar distinctions would cease to mattter in political sense, and the Constitution would ensure that the nation should progress regardless of such distinctions; and, four, that Pakistan would not be a theocratic state and religion would be a citizen's private and personal matter.

In short, Jinnah visualized Pakistan as a modern, progressive, and democratic state whose energies would be harnessed towards the uplift of the people, especially the masses and the poor, and evils such as corruption, bribery, black-marketing, nepotism, and jobbery would be stamped out. This was a re-affirmation of what Jinnah had told Doon Campbell, Reuter's correspondent in New Delhi in 1946:

> The new state would be a modern democratic state with sovereignty resting in the people and the members of the new nation having equal rights of citizenship regardless of their religion, caste, or creed.[3]

The Interim Constitution: Adaptation of the Government of India Act, 1935

Under the provisions of the Indian Independence Act, 1947, the Government of India Act, 1935 became, with certain adaptations, the working Constitution of Pakistan.[4] The Pakistan (Provisional Constitution) Order, 1947 established the federation of

Pakistan which included (1) the four provinces of East Bengal, West Punjab, Sindh, and the North-West Frontier Province; (2) Balochistan; (3) any other areas that might with the consent of the federation be included therein; (4) the capital of the federation, Karachi; and (5) such Indian states that might accede to the federation.

Under the original Act of 1935, the position of the Governor-General was unique. As the representative of the British Crown in India, he was invested with the final political authority in the country and given the widest discretionary powers and special responsibilities. As the representative of the British Crown, he could also exercise such prerogatives as the Crown might delegate to him. The supreme command of the land, naval, and air forces was vested in him. In the exercise of his functions, the Governor-General was to be aided and advised by a council except in relation to powers relating to (1) defence, external affairs, and ecclesiastical affairs; (2) the administration of British Balochistan; and (3) such other matters as were left by the Act to his discretion and in which the ministers had no constitutional right to advise. The Act also imposed upon the Governor-General certain wide and important special responsibilities in the sphere of the ministries which he was to discharge in his 'individual judgment'. In such matters, the ministry concerned had the right to tender advice but the Governor-General could reject it. Regarding the exercise of all other powers vesting in the Governor-General, the ministers were given the final word. The reason for vesting such wide and discretionary powers in the Governor-General was described by the joint parliamentary committee as 'the vital importance in India of a strong executive'. These discretionary powers and the special responsibilities were restricted through an amendment in the Indian Independence Act, 1947. Under Section 8(c) of the Act of 1947, the powers of the Governor-General or any Governor to act at his discretion or to exercise his individual judgment lapsed from 15 August 1947. The Governor-General was presumed to act on the advice of his ministers. But, under the Government of India Act of 1935, as adapted in Pakistan, the Governor-General continued to enjoy wide and substantial powers. He was the executive head of the federation and all executive actions of the federal government had to be taken in his name. Some of the key appointments were to be made by the Governor-General. Thus he had the right to appoint the prime minister and other federal ministers. The council of ministers would hold office during his pleasure.[5] The Governor-General also had the power to appoint the principal military officers, Governors of the provinces, the Advocate-General of the federation, the Chief Justice and other judges of the Federal Court, and many other important officials.

The Governor-General had the power to summon and prorogue the federal legislature. He could also assent to bills passed by the federal legislature or send them back for reconsideration. His sanction was required for bills or amendments relating to a number of specific matters. Bills affecting the coinage or currency of the federation or the Constitution or functions of the State Bank of Pakistan could be introduced into the federal legislature only with the sanction of the Governor-General.[6] The Governor-General also had the positive power of legislation by Ordinance which had the same force of law as an Act of the federal legislature. Such ordinances, however, had to be first laid before the federal legislature for approval. If the federal legislature should take no action, they would continue to have the force of law. The Governor-General also had enormous powers of control over the provincial governments. Part of this authority was derived from his supervisory power over the Governors' actions. In the exercise of his functions with respect to choosing, summoning, and dismissing the provincial ministers, a Governor was under the general control of the Governor-General.[7]

While the list of the powers of the Governor-General under the Act of 1935 were comprehensive, no discretionary power was left with the Governor-General under the Act as adapted in Pakistan. With effect from 14 August 1947, all governmental activity was brought under the control of the Cabinet which was responsible to the Constituent Assembly. The Governor-General's powers enumerated above were presumed to be exercised on the advice of the Cabinet.

The original plan of one Constituent Assembly for all of India had to be discarded because of differences between the Hindus and the Muslims, and two Constituent Assemblies were created, one for India and the other for the new dominion of Pakistan. The inaugural session of the Constituent Assembly of Pakistan was held in Karachi from 10 to 14 August 1947. J.N. Mandal, a member of the minority community from East Pakistan, was unanimously elected as temporary chairman on the first day of the session. Jinnah was subsequently elected unopposed as president of the Constituent Assembly on 11 August.

Under the Indian Independence Act, the Constituent Assembly was given two separate functions: to prepare a Constitution and to act as the Federal Legislative Assembly of Pakistan until such time that a Constitution came into effect. The powers and functions of the central legislature under the Government of India Act, 1935, were conferred on the Constituent Assembly. The Constituent Assembly could, however, amend the Indian Independence Act or the Government of India Act, 1935, and no Act of the British Parliament could be extended to Pakistan without legislation by the Constituent Assembly. The Constituent Assembly originally consisted of sixty-nine members; subsequently, its strength was raised to seventy-four. The states of Bahawalpur, Khairpur, and Balochistan and the tribal areas were given additional seats on their accession to Pakistan.[8]

There were only two parties in the Constituent Assembly—the Muslim League to which all the Muslim members, with the exception of two, belonged; and the Congress largely representing twelve million Hindus. Muslim League, the largest party in the Constituent Assembly, had fifty-nine seats. Its members from East Pakistan were mostly drawn from the middle class while those from West Pakistan included several big landlords. Among its members were the principal associates of Jinnah in the movement for Pakistan such as the first prime minister, Liaquat Ali Khan, and Khawaja Nazimuddin who succeeded Jinnah as Governor-General and later on became prime minister after the death of Liaquat in 1951. Some of the members were academics, such as I.H. Qureshi, Mohammad Husain, and Omar Hayat Malik. Though there was no organized Muslim political opposition party in the Constituent Assembly, there was some divergence of views within the Muslim League. On the left was

Iftikharuddin, a former Congressman and a Communist by repute. He was Oxford educated and an eloquent speaker. On the right were the religious critics, of whom the most influential though moderate one was Maulana Shabbir Ahmed Osmani, who died at the end of 1949. The only Muslims in the Constituent Assembly who were not Muslim Leaguers were Abdul Ghaffar Khan of the North-West Frontier Province, the leader of the Khudai Khidmatgars (servants of God), who had in alliance with the Congress opposed the creation of Pakistan, and A.K. Fazlul Haq, a former chief minister of Bengal with nearly half a century of political experience.[9]

Basic Principles and Other Important Committees

The Constituent Assembly set up several committees and sub-committees to carry out its task of framing a Constitution. Amongst these was the Basic Principles Committee, the most important one. It was appointed on 12 March 1949, when the Objectives Resolution was passed by the Constituent Assembly. Its task was to report in accordance with the Objectives Resolution on the main principles of the future Constitution. It consisted of twenty-four members and it could co-opt not more than ten, not necessarily from amongst members of the Constituent Assembly. The Basic Principles Committee set up three sub-committees:

1. Sub-committee on federal and provincial constitutions and distribution of powers.
2. Sub-committee on franchise.
3. Sub-committee on the judiciary.

The Basic Principles Committee empowered the sub-committees to co-opt technical experts, up to two or three, as advisers who would not, however, have the right to vote. The sub-committees were further allowed to tour various parts of Pakistan to collect information and take evidence if and when necessary. The Basic Principles Committee submitted its interim report on 7 September 1950, and its final report in December 1952.

Another important committee of the Constituent Assembly was on 'Fundamental Rights of the Citizens of Pakistan' and on 'Matters Relating to Minorities'. Set up in the inaugural session of the Constituent Assembly on 12 August 1947, it was authorized to add certain members, who were not necessarily from amongst the Constituent Assembly. This was done with a view to giving representation to the communities, such as Christians, who were not adequately represented in the Constituent Assembly. The committee, as mentioned above was divided into two sections, one dealing with 'Fundamental Rights' and the other with 'Matters Relating to Minorities'. The interim report of the former was adopted by the Constituent Assembly in 1950, and the final report in 1954. The discussion of 'Matters Relating to Minorities' took a long time because of the complexity of its task and the time taken in obtaining the opinions of minority communities. Many memoranda and suggestions were received by the committee. The question of joint or separate electorates entailed lengthy discussions.[10]

Two other committees of the Constituent Assembly were, the 'State Negotiating Committee,' to deal with the representation of the Princely States which had acceded to Pakistan, and the 'Tribal Areas Negotiating Committee' which dealt with matters relating to the tribal areas.[11]

Despite the paramount position of the Governor-General, the Interim Constitution envisaged a parliamentary form of government headed by a prime minister. A council of ministers was provided for with joint responsibility to the federal legislature.[12] The daily business of the federal government was run by the prime minister with the assistance of the council of ministers.

Under Section 8(i) of the Act of 1947, the powers and functions of the federal legislature were to be exercised by the Constituent Assembly which was to hold regular sessions.[13] It was a unicameral legislature presided over by a Speaker, or in his absence, the Deputy Speaker.[14]

Each province was headed by a Governor who was to be appointed by the Governor-General and served at his pleasure.[15] Parliamentary form of government was also provided for the provinces. There was to be a council of ministers headed by the chief minister. The provincial legislatures, also unicameral, had a life of five years unless dissolved earlier.[16] A long list of disqualifications for membership of the provincial legislature included the holding of any office of profit, insolvency, lunacy, dismissal from government service, conviction for moral turpitude, and so on.[17]

The Governor-General was vested with the power to promulgate ordinances in cases of an emergency. An ordinance could authorize expenditure from the revenues of the federation. Ordinances promulgated before 31 December 1949 were not required to be laid before the federal legislature but after such date, they were required to be so laid and would expire on a resolution or disapproval or at the expiry of six weeks from the reassembly of the legislature.[18]

The Governors were also empowered to promulgate ordinances when provincial legislatures were not in session and circumstances appeared to them to require immediate action. The ordinances were required to be laid before the provincial legislatures and expired on resolution of disapproval or at the expiry of six weeks from the reassembly of such legislatures.[19]

The Interim Constitution provided for a Federal Court consisting of the Chief Justice of Pakistan and not more than six puisne judges, all to be appointed by the Governor-General. A judge could not be removed except on the ground of misbehaviour or of infirmity of mind or body on the report of the Judicial Committee of the Privy Council. For appointment as judge to the Federal Court, a person had to be either a judge of a High Court for at least five years or a Barrister or pleader of a High Court of at least ten years standing. The Chief Justice had to have fifteen years standing and could only be taken from amongst Barristers or pleaders or judges of High Courts who had been such Barristers or pleaders at the time of their own appointment.[20] The Federal Court had original jurisdiction in the matter of disputes between the federation and any of the provinces, provided such dispute related to a question of legal right.[21] The Federal Court had appellate jurisdiction over the High Courts.[22] The law declared by the Federal Court or Privy Council was binding on all courts in Pakistan.[23] The Governor-General had the power to refer any question of law of public importance for the opinion of the Federal Court, and the court was to report on such reference in terms of the opinion of majority of judges present at the hearing of the case.[24]

Two High Courts were constituted under the Interim Constitution, the Dhaka High Court (for East Bengal) and the Lahore High Court (for the Punjab). Each High Court had to consist of a Chief Justice and a number of judges, fixed and appointed by the Governor-General. To qualify for appointment as a judge of a High Court, a person had to be a Barrister or pleader of any High Court of ten years standing, a member of the civil service for at least ten years, out of which he ought to have been a district judge for at least three years or ought to have held a judicial office for at least ten years. A judge could only be removed on the grounds of misbehaviour, or infirmity of mind or body, by the Governor-General if the Federal Court so reported on a reference being made to it.[25] The High Courts retained their powers and jurisdiction that they exercised prior to the establishment of the federation.[26] Later on, the High Courts were vested with the jurisdiction to issue writs in the nature of *habeas corpus, mandamus*, prohibition, *quo warranto*, and *certiorari*.[27] In addition to the High Courts in Lahore and Dhaka, the Chief Court of Sindh continued to function in Karachi for the province of Sindh. There was also a Court of Judicial Commissioner in Peshawar which had the functions of a chief court for the North-West Frontier Province (NWFP).

Partition of Punjab: The Carnage and Refugee Problem

At the beginning of August 1947, widespread rioting broke out in the Punjab which intensified as the date of the partition of India drew near. There is considerable evidence to show that the riots were started by the Sikhs and the Rashtriya Swayam Sevak Sangha.[28] On the announcement of the partition plan in March 1947, and the resignation of Khizar Hayat ministry, Master Tara Singh, the Sikh leader, openly called for violent resistance. He stood at the steps of the Legislative Assembly Chamber in Lahore, rattled his *kirpan* (sword or dagger), and raved, 'This will decide'.[29] Unfortunately, that was the opening of a horrible chapter of carnage in Punjab. There was immediate retaliation by the Muslims. Ian Morrison, correspondent of *The London Times*, reported from Jullundur on 24 August:

> More horrible than anything we saw during the war, is the universal comment of experienced officers, British and Indian, on the present slaughter in East Punjab. The Sikhs are clearing East Punjab of Muslims, butchering hundreds daily, forcing thousands to flee westward, burning Muslim villages and homesteads, even in their frenzy burning their own. This violence has been organized from the highest level of Sikh leadership, and it is being done systematically, sector by sector.[30]

According to another report:

> On 15 August the day of liberation was strangely celebrated in the Punjab. During the afternoon, a Sikh mob paraded a number of Muslim women naked through the streets of Amritsar, raped them, and then hacked some of them to pieces with Kirpans and burned the others alive.[31]

There is substantial evidence that rioting in West Punjab was a repercussion of the massacre in East Punjab. Auchinleck, in his farewell letter to Major-General Rees, commander of Punjab Boundary Forces, referred to the massacre in East Punjab and stated 'the whole movement was undoubtedly planned long beforehand and soon gave rise to inevitable repercussions in the West Punjab'.[32] In September 1947, widespread violence and disturbance broke out against Muslims in Delhi, forcing a large number of them to flee to Pakistan, particularly to Karachi which was swarming with refugees from Delhi.

The situation in the Punjab was grim. Whole sections of Lahore, Amritsar, Sheikhupura, Jullundur, and indeed most of the principal cities of the Punjab were in flames. In the villages, armed bandits plundered, burned, massacred, and raped women. Thousands of women—Muslim, Hindu, and Sikh—were abducted, never to be seen again by their relatives. The Punjab Boundary Force, containing both Muslim and non-Muslim troops and commanded by British senior officers, was utterly incapable of maintaining peace. Its troops refused to fire on members of their own communities. It had to be disbanded, leaving the armies of Pakistan and India responsible for their respective area. The Muslims living in Sikh states in East Punjab met the worst fate. They did not even have protection of the Indian Army.[33] Abul Kalam Azad stated from personal knowledge that some members of the former undivided Indian Army killed Hindus and Sikhs in Pakistan and Muslims in India.[34] In Kapurthala state, with a Sikh ruler, Muslims were in a majority. All of them were either killed or driven out. Those who survived were harassed by guerilla groups, went without food and sleep, and encountered unprecedented floods along the escape routes. More were drowned than slaughtered and very few could reach Pakistan.[35]

The Governments of India and Pakistan, having failed to stop the slaughter, decided at the end of August to assist the complete evacuation of Muslims from East Punjab and of non-Muslims from West Punjab. A Joint Military Evacuation Organization was set up in Lahore. Mixed guards were provided for the refugee camps as well as armed escorts for foot, railway, and motor convoys.[36] Within a matter of weeks, over twelve million people had left their homes and gone forth on foot, by bullock-cart, by railway, by car, and by plane to seek shelter and safety in the other dominion. They had no earthly possessions save the clothes they wore and, more often than not, these were in tatters. They had seen babies killed, corpses mutilated, and women dishonoured. Death had stalked them on the way. Tens of thousands had died on the road of starvation and disease, or had been killed by Sikh murder gangs.[37] The Pakistan government estimated that in the exchange of population, excluding those from Kashmir, approximately 6,500,000 refugees came into Pakistan. Of these,

5,200,000 came from East Punjab and East Punjab states, 360,000 from Delhi and the remainder from other parts of northern India.[38] It is believed that about 1,000,000 Muslims lost their lives or were abducted. The number of refugees West Punjab had to accommodate exceeded by some 1,700,000 the number of refugees who had left.[39] The main burden of rehabilitating refugees was borne by West Punjab which lay in the path of incoming refugees. Other provinces did not fully co-operate in settling refugees in their provinces though there were evacuee properties available in those provinces as well.

Under the circumstances, the central government was compelled to assume powers for settling refugees and a proclamation under Section 102 of the adapted Government of India Act, 1935 was issued on 27 August 1948 as under:

> Whereas the economic life of Pakistan is threatened by circumstances arising out of the mass movement of population from and into Pakistan, a state of emergency is hereby declared.[40]

The next day, it was decided that out of the large number of refugees in West Punjab's camps, Sindh must absorb 200,000, the NWFP 100,000, Bahawalpur, Khairpur, and the Balochistan 100,000, and West Punjab was to settle an additional 100,000. These plans were only partially successful. According to the 1951 census, the number of refugees settled in Sindh was 540,000 as against 900,000 evacuees; and in NWFP 51,000 had been settled against 269,000 evacuees.[41] The economic dislocation caused further problems. West Punjab obtained a considerable surplus of agriculturists, weavers, potters, shoe-makers, and other artisans. It lost 10 per cent of its traders and 90 per cent of its sweepers. In the villages, the agricultural credit system disappeared with the Hindu money lenders.[42]

In the first year of its existence, Pakistan faced the colossal problem of settling the refugees that constituted nearly one-fourth of West Pakistan's total population. The task of framing a Constitution receded into the background, and Pakistan lost the opportunity of gaining from the guidance of Jinnah. Besides tackling the pressing problem of refugees, he had to launch the central and provincial governments virtually from scratch, and his health was fast deteriorating.

A good part of the blame for the carnage in Punjab lies with Mountbatten. He deliberately avoided disclosing the details of the Boundary Commission Award to political leaders until 18 August, three days after the grant of dominion status.[43] His tactic of postponing the Award did nothing to prevent a violent eruption in the Punjab. It was a complete failure of responsible political leadership which brought anarchy to the Punjab. While Punjab writhed and turned in blood, Mountbatten coldly claimed credit for having accomplished, in less than two-and-a-half months, one of the 'greatest administrative operations in history'.[44]

The Kashmir Issue

As if the refugee problem was not enough to divert the attention of the government of Pakistan from constitution-making, the state of Jammu and Kashmir posed a threat to the stability of the new nation with seemingly endless hostility between India and Pakistan. The state had about 80 per cent Muslims, but its ruler was Hindu. The Indian government secured, under questionable circumstances, an instrument of accession from the Hindu Maharaja on 27 October 1947, thus opening the way to India's military intervention in Kashmir. Under Mountbatten's direct guidance, airborne units of the Indian Army landed in Srinagar, thus halting the advance of liberation forces outside Srinagar. This was most shocking to the people of Pakistan because from the time the Lahore Resolution of 1940 was passed, Kashmir had been regarded as an essential part of Pakistan, both politically and economically. The government of Pakistan resisted the popular clamour, particularly in the West Punjab, for open armed intervention, and proposed to India in the meeting held on 1 November 1947 between the Governors-General of the two dominions, that fighting should be stopped and a plebiscite should be held under the joint control of India and Pakistan. India did not respond positively to this proposal and claimed Kashmir as its territory.

The matter was taken up before the Security Council of the United Nations where charges and counter-charges were made by the two countries. A five-power commission was sent out by the United Nations to offer its good offices to bring about a settlement. Pakistan was compelled to send its regular troops to counter a massive Indian offensive against the liberation forces and Azad Kashmir in the spring of 1948. Despite pressure from extremists, both India and Pakistan desisted from an all-out war and fighting remained localized. In 1949, in pursuance of a resolution of the United Nations Security Council calling upon India and Pakistan to withdraw their forces from Kashmir so that the United Nations could hold a free, fair, and impartial plebiscite to determine the will of the people of Jammu and Kashmir, a cease-fire was secured by the UN commission. Contrary to its commitment, India declined to abide by the UN resolutions.

Jinnah's Death, September 1948

Jinnah had been suffering from consumption of the lungs and in the last three years of his life the disease became serious. It was a well-kept medical secret, for had it been known that Jinnah was terminally ill, the Congress and the British might have dragged on the process of independence and transfer of power and thus would have ensured that Pakistan never came into existence. During the last two years of his life, Jinnah was sustained largely by his will and determination to see Pakistan become a reality. He worked day and night first to see Pakistan become an independent state and then to attend to the grave challenges that confronted Pakistan in its infancy. As a result of poor health, normal work became impossible for him. The last public function that he attended, against medical advice, was the opening ceremony of the State Bank of Pakistan on 1 July 1948.

Jinnah spent his last days in Ziarat, a remote Balochistan hill station about fifty miles from Quetta. His condition rapidly worsened and by the beginning of September he had pneumonia as well as tuberculosis and cancer of the lungs.[45] On 9 September, his doctors gave up hope but such was his devotion to duty and love for Pakistan that even in a state of unconsciousness he was heard muttering aloud:

> The Kashmir Commission have an appointment with me today; why haven't they turned up? Where are they?[46]

Jinnah was flown to Karachi on 11 September 1948. He was carried in an army ambulance from the Air Force base at Mauripur, Karachi, where his plane had landed at 4:15 p.m. The ambulance broke down after covering about five miles with Jinnah's pulse going down rapidly. 'Nearby stood hundreds of huts belonging to the refugees who went about their business, not knowing that their Quaid, who had given them a homeland, was in their midst, lying helpless'.[47] He died shortly afterwards. Wrapped in a simple shroud, he was buried the next day in Karachi. Millions of Pakistanis wept for him. They truly felt orphaned.

Considerable evidence is available to show that in his last days, Jinnah was let down by his colleagues. Although he had chosen Liaquat Ali Khan as the first prime minister of Pakistan, he had started regretting his decision. Liaquat proved to be a less forceful personality than what the times demanded, and Jinnah had to assume some of his functions.[48] His relations with his closest colleagues also deteriorated rapidly in the final months of his life. As he grew weaker and daily more conscious of the imminence of death, he was less patient with inefficiency and ineptitude, more easily angered by the usual excuses for not getting things done. Before dying, Jinnah naturally wanted to see significant progress in the struggling infant land. Relations between the Governor-General and his Prime Minister could not have been less strained in that era of unrelieved national calamity and stress, financial stringency, and virtual war. Liaquat reportedly wrote to Jinnah in January 1948 and offered to 'resign' as Prime Minister after learning from his wife that Jinnah had angrily and openly expressed dissatisfaction with his work. Jinnah expressed equal frustration and disgust at the way the Nawab of Mamdot, then Chief Minister of the Punjab, 'was uninterested in the fate of refugees'. He called Mamdot and Governor Mudie to Karachi in May and told Mamdot, who had been his right arm in winning the Punjab for the League, that 'he was useless as a Chief Minister', to which Mudie reported, 'was only too true. He [Jinnah], therefore, nominated Mian Mumtaz Daultana' to take control of the Punjab ministry, but Daultana 'refused, protesting that he had complete confidence in Mamdot... I [Mudie] knew and he [Daultana] knew that if he did become Chief Minister, Mamdot would just about cut his throat. Jinnah was very angry and the meeting was adjourned... Jinnah... rounded on me... "Your policy is weak. You've lost your nerve." I asked what his orders for me were. He said "None". I then asked what his advice to me would be as a friend. He replied "Wash your hands of them, as I am going to do." It was clear... that Jinnah was far from well. Indeed, he had to lie down immediately after our meeting.'[49]

When, in his last days, Liaquat visited Jinnah in Ziarat, he told his sister, Fatima Jinnah in a trembling voice, 'Do you know why he has come? He wants to know how serious my illness is, how long I will last.'[50]

Jinnah is recognized as the sole spokesman of Indian Muslims in united India. From the late 1930s, his main concern was the arrangement by which power at the centre was to be shared once the British quit India.[51] But if Jinnah and the League were to play their part at the centre, they needed a mandate from the Muslims in the provinces. This mandate was finally won in the elections of 1946. It would be unfair to Jinnah to regard him as a communal leader. He was far above that. It is alleged by his detractors that he used the communal card as a political tactic, not an ideological commitment.[52] In fact, he used the communal factor for none of the purposes. His outlook was much wider and his political thinking far too liberal. His primary concern was thwarting the domination of a brute Hindu majority in united India and to let the Muslim majority provinces and areas form a modern state where they could prosper unhindered by fear and prejudice.

Jinnah as Governor-General: A Review

There was serious debate in the early years of Pakistan about Jinnah's decision to become the new state's first Governor-General. Some people argued that Mountbatten should have been accepted as the Governor-General of both the dominions because this made him bitterly hostile to Pakistan. The distribution of assets and liabilities, which was the number one priority of the Governor-General, should have been entrusted to an impartial arbitrator. This would have gone in Pakistan's interest. Mountbatten's position was unenviable because he had assured the British government that Jinnah would opt for a common Governor-General. Jinnah's decision, therefore, seemed a personal insult to him.[53] There were tangible factors, such as the accession of the states, the Kashmir question, and the award of the Boundary Commission in which the balance was tilted against Pakistan by Mountbatten, with momentous consequences.

It has been alleged by Sardar Shaukat Hayat Khan in his *Memoirs* that there was a conspiracy to dissuade Jinnah from accepting Mountbatten as common Governor-General of the two dominions of India and Pakistan. His version is:

> When it became known that Mountbatten desired to be the common Governor-General of India and Pakistan for six months, to win a laurel for himself, and also as a gesture of respect for the Crown, it alarmed Liaquat and those close to him. They feared that Mountbatten might persuade Mr Jinnah to be the Prime Minister for the interim period. They planned a telegraphic blitz against Mountbatten.
>
> I was present in Gul-e-Raana when this operation was being finalized. I was present attending the Capital Selection Committee and Mumtaz was present for the Committee

deliberating about the selection of Pakistan's flag. Nawabzada asked both of us and Chaudhri Mohammad Ali, his Secretary, to stay for luncheon. The whole matter was thrashed out in my presence. It was planned to despatch telegrams to Quaid-i-Azam, maligning Mountbatten and saying that Mountbatten could not be relied upon, as he had close relations with Nehru and his family.

I vehemently disagreed, knowing Mountbatten's vanity. I told them that if the Muslim League turned him down he would jump at becoming the Governor-General solely of India. He could create many problems and handicaps for Pakistan. I, therefore, asked for an interview with the Quaid which unfortunately was granted a few days later.

At our meeting the Quaid turned round to me and said, 'Shaukat, look at the thousands of telegrams I have received on the subject. You, Nawab Ismail, Nawab of Bhopal, and Sardar Abdur Rab Nishtar are the only exceptions, opposing it. How could I ignore the general trend?'

I said, 'Sir, I have a feeling that this campaign has been engineered'. I told him that knowing Mountbatten as a Commander I felt that this decision would be catastrophic for Pakistan because he could do a tremendous amount of damage by accepting the sole Governor-Generalship of India.

I argued that we still had to divide our defence supplies and other assets. Moreover, the Sikhs were up in arms and the eighteen regiments of British troops under his command would never be utilized by Mountbatten just as the Governor-General of India. It could open the floodgates of a holocaust against the Muslims.

I think we lost Kashmir mainly on this account, because Mountbatten changed the Radcliffe Award. This has been confirmed recently by Mr Beaumont, of the Indian Civil Service, Secretary to Radcliffe, who admitted the change was made on account of political expediency! This was also confirmed by the map Radcliffe left with the Governor of the Punjab showing the majority Muslim district of Gurdaspur which was arbitrarily attached to India against all Principles that were laid down as the basis for division, thus creating a connection between India and Kashmir. Similarly, Ajnala tehsil of Amritsar and two tehsils of Ferozpur were wrongfully attached to India. Ferozpur just to appease the Maharaja of Bikaner, because the headworks of Bikaner canal was situated on the Pakistan side of the border at Mianwala, again ignoring the very basis of partition. Similarly, we lost the major arsenal at Ferozpur.

All this was on account of the ghastly decision of not permitting Mountbatten to be a common Governor-General, because the Quaid was impressed by the dishonest telegraphic offensive which proved disastrous for Pakistan. The Quaid, unfortunately, ignored the fact that his writ would have always prevailed in Pakistan as Gandhi's would be in India, even without their holding the office of the Governor-General.

India, on the contrary, gladly accepted Lord Mountbatten. It won for them the advantage of Mountbatten's friendship and British Commerce as well as their goodwill. Where Pakistan was concerned we suffered on account of this short-sighted decision without fully considering the consequent disadvantage to the nation. This proves that Jinnah was human; he could make mistakes. He suffered from frailties like any other human. He was not infallible or free of all faults, which according to wise men is an attribute only of Prophets.'[54]

It is said on good authority that Mountbatten wanted to be the first Governor-General of Pakistan. When told that Jinnah would be Pakistan's first Governor-General, he protested that he (Jinnah) had picked the wrong job:

> Under the British constitutional process which would prevail in the two dominions, it was the Prime Minister who had all the power. The Governor-General's role was a symbolic one akin to the sovereign's with no real power attached to it.

His argument did not move Jinnah. 'In Pakistan,' he coldly replied, 'I will be Governor-General and the Prime Minister will do what I tell him to do'.[55]

Although the argument in favour of accepting Mountbatten as the common Governor-General for India and Pakistan is attractive, time has confirmed Jinnah's wisdom in keeping Pakistan out of Mountbatten's hands. Mountbatten had never made any secret of his belief that the division of the subcontinent into two separate states had been a tragic ending to British rule. In Britain, the government and the opposition were advocating reunion of Pakistan with India with one voice.[56] Indeed, Hodson reveals in *The Great Divide* that Mountbatten had in fact worked out a plan by which he hoped to recapture lost ground. He referred to the proposed new nation as 'this mad Pakistan' at the time of conceding the League demand which shows his intense disapproval of the division of India.[57] Accepting him as the common Governor-General might have spelled the end of Pakistan as a sovereign state and would have ensured its absorption back into India. Thus, Jinnah's decision helped preserve Pakistan against the machinations of those who were plotting its extinction.[58] It was obvious that Mountbatten would spend less time in Karachi than in Delhi, the bigger capital, and that while in the latter city, he would have been so near his friend Nehru as to be influenced by him who detested the idea of Pakistan.[59] Mountbatten was extremely close to Nehru and he helped the Indian administration at the request of Nehru and Patel by becoming the head of the Emergency Committee.[60] He could thus hardly be an even-handed Governor-General of both the dominions.

A question keeps coming back: Why Jinnah did not give a Constitution to put to an end to all the controversy that followed? With the benefit of hindsight it can said be that it would have been highly desirable if he had done that. He was a democrat in every sense of the word and did not wish to pre-empt the Constituent Assembly. Some of his remarks on the subject are worth noting:

> The Constituent Assembly may take some time to accomplish its task of framing the final constitution of our state. It is a stupendous task and it may take 18 months or, two years before it can come into full operation.[61]

> Pakistan is now a sovereign state absolute and unfettered and the Government of Pakistan is in the hands of the people. Until we finally frame our constitution which, of course, can only be done by the Constituent Assembly, our present provisional constitution based on the fundamental principles of democracy not bureaucracy or autocracy, or dictatorship, must be worked.[62]

Qadeeruddin Ahmad, former Chief Justice of West Pakistan High Court, says:

> I personally do not believe that he thought in terms of permanently binding the coming generation to any specific constitutional pattern. This was against his democratic temperament and inconsistent with his legal acumen.[63]

Another reason that prevented Jinnah's intervention in constitution-making was the heavy burden of dealing with the refugee problem and the Kashmir dispute. Had these stupendous problems not befallen the nation in its infancy, Jinnah might have goaded the Constituent Assembly into concluding its task expeditiously.

Nevertheless, Jinnah did indicate the broad guidelines for Pakistan's Constitution in various statements and speeches. Had these guidelines been followed in the right spirit, Pakistan might not have landed itself in the constitutional morass it finds itself in today. Jinnah desired to see Pakistan a true democracy based on equality and freedom for all citizens regardless of their religion, colour, or creed; devoted to development and progress; free from religious, sectarian, ethnic, provincial, linguistic, and racial prejudices, and with the guarantee of freedom of religion to the minorities.

NOTES

1. Jinnah was by now aclaimed as 'Quaid-e-Azam', the Great Leader, by Indian Muslims.
2. *Quaid-e-Azam Mohammad Ali Jinnah, Speeches and Statements as Governor-General of Pakistan, 1947-48.* Published by Government of Pakistan, Ministry of Information and Broadcasting, Directorate of Films & Publications, Islamabad, 1989, pp. 42 to 47.
3. Quoted by Mohammad Munir, *From Jinnah to Zia*, published by Vanguard Books Ltd., Davis Road, Lahore, 1980, p. 29.
4. Section 8 of the *Indian Independence Act, 1947.*
5. *Government of India Act, 1935* as adapted as Interim Constitution, Section 10.
6. Ibid., Section 153.
7. Ibid., Section 51.
8. Choudhry, G.W., *Constitutional Development in Pakistan*, 1969, Longman Group Ltd., London, p. 19.
9. Ibid., p. 20.
10. Ibid., p. 21.
11. Ibid., p. 22.
12. Ibid., Section 9.
13. Ibid., Sections 18 and 19.
14. Ibid., Section 22.
15. Ibid., Section 48.
16. Ibid., Section 61.
17. Ibid., Section 69.
18. Ibid., Section 42.
19. Ibid., Section 88.
20. Ibid., Section 200.
21. Ibid., Section 204.
22. Ibid., Section 205.
23. Ibid., Section 212.
24. Ibid., Section 213.
25. Ibid., Section 220.
26. Ibid., Section 223.
27. Ibid., Section 223 A.
28. See appendices to '*The Sikh Plan*' and '*The Sikhs in Action*', published by the West Punjab Government, Lahore, 1948.

29. Khan, Muhammad Zafarullah, *The Forgotten Years: Memoirs of Sir Muhammad Zafrullah Khan.* Edited by A.H.Batalvi, 1991, Vanguard Books, Lahore, p. 139.
30. Stephens, Ian, *Pakistan: Old Country, New Nation*, 1963, p. 183, Ernest Benn Limited, London.
31. Ali, Chaudhri Mohammad. *The Emergence of Pakistan*, Services Book Club, 1958 p. 256, quoting John Cornell Auchinleck (London, Cassell, 1959) p. 906.
32. Ibid., p. 258.
33. There are witnesses who say that at places, Indian Army units provided protection and even cover of artillery fire to the Sikh bands attacking Muslim villages in East Punjab.
34. Azad, Maulana Abul Kalam, *India Wins Freedom*, 1959, Orient Longmans, Calcutta, p. 202.
35. Symonds, Richard, *Making of Pakistan*, 1966, Allied Book Corporation, Karachi, p. 83.
36. Ibid.
37. Ali, Chaudhri Mohammad, *The Emergence of Pakistan, supra*, note 31, p. 261.
38. Symonds, Richard, *supra*, note 35, p. 83.
39. Ali, Ch. Mohammad, *supra*, note 31, p. 264.
40. Ibid., p. 267.
41. Ibid., pp. 267-8.
42. Symond, Richard, *supra*, note 35, p. 84.
43. Jalal, Ayesha, *The Sole Spokesman: Jinnah, the Muslim League and the Demand for Pakistan* 1985, Cambridge University Press, Cambridge, p. 293.
44. Ibid, referring to Mountbatten's address to the Indian Constituent Assembly at New Delhi, 15th August 1947.
45. Wolpert, Stanley, *Jinnah of Pakistan*, 1984, Oxford University Press, p. 368.
46. Ibid., quoting Dr Ilahi Bakhsh, *Last Days*, p. 40.
47. Ibid., quoting Fatima Jinnah, *My Brother*, p. 369.
48. Salim, Ahmad. *Pakistan of Jinnah: The Hidden Face*. 1993, Brothers Publishers, Lahore, p. 23.
49. Wolpert, Stanley, Jinnah of Pakistan, *supra*, note 45, pp. 360-361 quoting Sir Francis ('Frank') Mudie's 'Report' was dictated shortly before his death and is preserved in India Office Library in London, MSS EUR, 33.
50. Ibid., p. 365, quoting Pirzada, *Last Days of the Quaid*, p. 6.
51. Jalal, Ayesha, *The Sole Spokesman, supra*, note 43, pp. 4-5.
52. Ibid., p. 5.
53. Khan, Wali, *Facts are Facts: The Untold Story of India's Partition*, 1987, Vikas Publishing House, New Delhi, p. 135.
54. Khan, Sirdar Shaukat Hayat, *The Nation that Lost its Soul*. 1995. Jang Publishers, Lahore, pp. 169-71.
55. Collins, Larry and Lapierre, Dominique, *Freedom at Midnight*. 1975, Harper Collins Publishers Great Britain. p. 232.
56. Burke, S. M., 'Quaid-e-Azam's decision to become Pakistan's first Governor-General: Its pros and its cons', page 306. It is an article published in *World Scholars* on Quaid-e-Azam Mohammad Ali Jinnah, edited by Dr Ahmad Hasan Dani, Quaid-e-Azam University, Islamabad, 1979.
57. Hodson, H.U., *The Great Divide*, London, 1969, p. 523.
58. Ibid.
59. Stephens, Ian, *Pakistan-Old Country New Nation, supra*, note 31, pp. 176-7.
60. Khan, Salahuddin, *Had there been no Jinnah*. 1989, Pan Graphics, Islamabad, pp. 160-62.
61. Speech at Sibi Durbar; 14 February 'New Era of Progress for Baluchistan', *supra*, note 6, p. 139.
62. Address to a gathering of the Civil Officers of Baluchistan at Sibi; February 14, 1948, *supra*, note 2, p. 143.
63. Ahmad, Qadeeruddin, *Pakistan - Facts and Fallacies*, 1979, Royal Book Company, Karachi, p. 170.

5

THE OBJECTIVES RESOLUTION, 1949

The first significant step towards the framing of a Constitution was taken by the Constituent Assembly in March 1949 when it passed a resolution on the 'Aims and Objects of the Constitution', popularly known as the Objectives Resolution. It laid the foundation of the Constitution and indicated the broad outlines of its structure. It was described as the most important occasion in the life of Pakistan, next in importance only to the achievement of independence. The Resolution and the debate on it are of great interest because they bring out the political philosophy of the then government of Pakistan and of its principal critics. The Resolution was moved by Liaquat Ali Khan and the leading members of the Cabinet and the opposition participated in the debate.

The text of the Resolution as passed by the Constituent Assembly was:

'In the name of Allah, the Beneficent, the Merciful:

Whereas sovereignty over the entire universe belongs to God Almighty alone and the authority which He has delegated to the state of Pakistan through its people for being exercised within the limits prescribed by Him is a sacred trust;

This Constituent Assembly representing the people of Pakistan resolves to frame a constitution for the sovereign independent State of Pakistan;

Wherein the state shall exercise its powers and authority through the chosen representatives of the people;

Wherein the principles of democracy, freedom, equality, tolerance, and social justice as enunciated by Islam shall be fully observed;

Wherein the Muslims shall be enabled to order their lives in the individual and collective spheres in accordance with the teachings and requirements of Islam as set out in the Holy Quran and the *Sunnah*;

Wherein adequate provision shall be made for the minorities freely to profess and practise their religions and develop their cultures; Wherein the territories now included in or in accession with Pakistan and such other territories as may hereafter be included in or accede to Pakistan shall form a federation wherein the units will be autonomous with such boundaries and limitations on their powers and authority as may be prescribed;

Wherein shall be guaranteed fundamental rights including equality of status, of opportunity and before law, social, economic and political justice, and freedom of thought, expression, belief, faith, worship, and association, subject to law and public morality;

Wherein adequate provision shall be made to safeguard the legitimate interests of minorities and backward and depressed classes;

Wherein the independence of the Judiciary shall be fully secured;

Wherein the integrity of the territories of the federation, its independence and all its rights including its sovereign rights on land, sea, and air shall be safeguarded;

So that the people of Pakistan may prosper and attain their rightful and honoured place amongst the nations of the world and make their full contribution towards international peace and progress and happiness of humanity.'

Liaquat explained the concept and the spirit behind the Resolution in his speech before the Constituent Assembly while introducing the Resolution on 7 March 1949. Some important extracts from his speech are:[1]

> We, the people of Pakistan, have the courage to believe firmly that all authority should be exercised in accordance with the standards laid down in Islam so that it may not be misused. All authority is a sacred trust, entrusted to us by God for the purpose of being exercised in the service of man, so that it does not become an agency for tyranny or selfishness. I would, however, point out that this is not a resuscitation of the dead theory of divine right of kings or rulers, because, in accordance with the spirit of Islam, the preamble fully recognizes the truth that authority has been delegated to the people, and to none else, and that it is for the people to decide who will exercise that authority.
>
> For this reason it has been made clear in the Resolution that the state shall exercise all its powers and authority through the chosen representatives of the people. This is the very essence of democracy, because the people have been recognized as the recipients of all authority and it is in them that the power to wield it has been vested. This naturally eliminates any danger of the establishment of a theocracy.
>
> You should notice, Sir, that the Objectives Resolution lays emphasis on the principles of democracy, freedom, equality, tolerance, and social justice, and further defines them by saying that these principles should be observed in the constitution as they have been enunciated by Islam. It has been necessary to qualify these terms because they are generally used in a loose sense. It has, therefore, been found necessary to define these terms further in order to give them a well-understood meaning. Whenever we use the word democracy in the Islamic sense, it pervades all aspects of our life, it relates to our system of government and to our society with equal validity, because one of the greatest contributions of Islam has been the idea of the equality of all men. Islam recognises no distinctions based upon race, colour, or birth. Similarly, we have a great record in tolerance, for under no system of government, even in the Middle Ages, have the minorities received the same consideration and freedom as they did in Muslim countries. When Christian dissentients and Muslims were being tortured and driven out of their homes, when they were being hunted as animals and burnt as criminals—even criminals have never been burnt in Islamic society—Islam provided a haven for all who were persecuted and who fled from tyranny. It is a well-known fact of history that when anti-semitism turned the Jews out of many a European country, it was the Ottoman Empire which gave them shelter. The greatest proof of the tolerance of Muslim peoples lies in the fact that there is no Muslim country where strong

minorities do not exist, and where they have not been able to preserve their religion and culture. It is the tolerance which is envisaged by Islam, wherein a minority does not live on sufferance, but is respected and given every opportunity to develop its own thought and culture, so that it may contribute to the greater glory of the entire nation. In the matter of social justice as well, Sir, I would point out that Islam has a distinct contribution to make. Islam envisages a society in which social justice means neither charity nor regimentation. Islamic social justice is based upon fundamental laws and concepts which guarantee to men a life free from want and rich in freedom. It is for this reason that the principles of democracy, freedom, equality, tolerance, and social justice have been further defined by giving to them a meaning which, in our view, is deeper and wider than the usual connotation of these words.

Muslims shall be enabled to order their lives in the individual and collective spheres in accordance with the teachings and requirements of Islam as set out in the Holy Quran and the *Sunnah*. It is quite obvious that no non-Muslim should have any objection if the Muslims are enabled to order their lives in accordance with the dictates of their religion. You would also notice, Sir, that the sate is not to play the part of a neutral observer, wherein the Muslims may be merely free to profess and practise their religion, because such an attitude on the part of the state would be the very negation of the ideals which prompted the demand of Pakistan, and it is these ideals which should be the corner-stone of the state which we want to build. The state will create such conditions as are conducive to the building up of a truly Islamic society, which means that the state will have to play a positive part in this effort.

In our desire to build up an Islamic society, we have not ignored the right of the non-Muslims. Indeed, it would have been un-Islamic to do so, and we would have been guilty of transgressing the dictates of our religion if we had tried to impinge upon the freedom of the minorities. In no way will they be hindered from professing or protecting their religion or developing their cultures. The history of the development of Islamic culture itself shows that the cultures of the minorities, who lived under the protection of Muslim states and empires contributed to the richness of the heritage which the Muslims built up for themselves. I assure the minorities that we are fully conscious of the fact that if the minorities are able to make a contribution to the sum total of human knowledge and thought, it will redound to the credit of Pakistan and will enrich the life of the nation. Therefore, the minorities may look forward, not only to a period of the fullest freedom but also to an understanding and appreciation on the part of the majority which has always been such a marked characteristic of Muslims throughout the history.

Mr President, it has become fashionable to guarantee certain fundamental rights, but I assure you that it is not our intention to give these rights with one hand and take them away with the other. I have said enough to show that we want to build up a truly liberal government where the greatest amount of freedom will be given to all its members. Everyone will be equal before the law, but this does not mean that his personal law will not be protected. We believe in the equality of status and justice. It is our firm belief and, we have said this from many a platform, that Pakistan does not stand for vested interests or the wealthy classes. It is our intention to build up an economy on the basic principles of Islam which seeks a better distribution of wealth and the removal of want. Poverty and backwardness—all that stands in the way of the achievement of his fullest stature by man—must be eradicated from Pakistan.

We believe that no shackles can be put on thought and, therefore, we do not intend to hinder any person from the expression of his views. Nor do we intend to deprive anyone of his right of forming associations for all lawful and moral purposes. In short, we want to base our polity upon freedom, progress, and social justice. We want to do away with social distinctions, but we want to achieve this without causing suffering or putting fetters upon the human mind and lawful inclinations.

Sir, there are a large number of interests for which the minorities legitimately desire protection. This protection this Resolution seeks to provide. The backward and depressed classes are our special charge. We are fully conscious of the fact that they do not find themselves in their present plight for any fault of their own. It is also true that we are not responsible by any means for their present position. But now that they are our citizens, it will be our special effort to bring them upto the level of other citizens, so that they may bear the responsibilities imposed by their being citizens of a free and progressive state, and share them with others who have been more fortunate than themselves. We know that so long as any section, amongst our people are backward, they will be a drag upon society and, therefore, for the purpose of building up our state, we must necessarily look to the interests of these sections.

As soon as the Resolution was moved, a non-Muslim member, Prem Hari Barma, proposed 'that the Motion be circulated for eliciting public opinion thereon by the 30 April, 1949.'[2]

This motion was vehemently supported by another non-Muslim member, Sris Chandra Chattopadhyaya, in the following words:[3]

Mr President, I rise to support the amendment for circulation of the Resolution for eliciting public opinion. I want to make a few observations about the amendment. First, in the course of the last 18 months, that have passed after the partition, no 'Objectives Resolution' was brought forward. In fact after 14 August 1947, when Pakistan became a sovereign state, we thought no such Resolution was necessary at all. The thing that matters is the constitution itself and not a theoretical resolution on the aims and objects of the constitution. In fact, not even a committee of this House was formed to consider this Resolution. In India they had an Objectives Resolution because the Britishers were still there, and it was necessary to tell the people and the world what her constitution would be like after the British left. Even that was before August 1947, when the sovereignty was made over to the people of Pakistan and India. In some countries there have been Objectives Resolutions after a bloody revolution because everything was in a chaos. But the case is different here in Pakistan. Some 18 months ago, Britishers had left and we are now free to do as we like. And we have been going on without any Objectives Resolution for so long. As a matter of fact, I understand, the Sub-Committee on Fundamental Rights have already finalized their Report. There was no difficulty to recommend Fundamental Rights even without this Objectives Resolution. The fact is that it is the actual constitution that will matter and a theoretical resolution like the one before us may not be necessary at all. So long as we had an idea that the constitution would be based on the eternal principles of equality, democracy, and social justice. We thought that religion and politics would not be mixed up. That was the declaration of Quaid-e-Azam Muhammad Ali Jinnah in this House. But the Resolution before us has a religious basis. We got notice of it some four days back. We have not been able to understand fully the implications of some of the paragraphs of the Resolution. They require study, consultation, deliberation with our friends, both Muslims and non-Muslims, and the citizens of our country who are our masters. We are their servants. But the time given to us for the purpose has been too short. Frankly speaking, for example, what the Resolution means and implies in the Preamble, *viz*, that:- 'Sovereignty over the entire universe belongs to God Almighty alone and the authority which He has delegated to the state of Pakistan through its people for being exercised within the limits prescribed by Him is a sacred trust;' is a thing for which we require time to study it and understand before accepting or modifying it in any way. Then come to paragraph four: 'Wherein the principles of democracy, freedom, equality, tolerance, and social justice, as enunciated by Islam, shall be fully observed.' has been mentioned. This again is not clear to us—the non-Muslims. We need time to study it, in consultation with our friends in East Bengal and for the sake of clarification. In fact when we left East Bengal this time we had no idea that such a Resolution was to be brought forward. There was no indication of it in the Agenda papers circulated.

Liaquat opposed the motion which was put to vote that very day, 7 March 1949, and defeated.

Proposed Amendments

The days following the moving of the Objectives Resolution generated a lively discussion in which some non-Muslim members of the Constituent Assembly, namely Bhupendra Kumar Datta, Professor Raj Kumar Chakravarty, Prem Hari Barma, Kamini Kumar Datta, and Birat Chandra Mandal, participated vigorously and raised a large number of objections to the Resolution. These members also moved a large number of amendments which are reproduced below:[4]

1. 'That the paragraph beginning with the words "Whereas sovereignty over the entire universe..." and ending with the words "...is a sacred trust" be omitted.'
2. 'That in the paragraph beginning with the words "Whereas sovereignty over the entire universe..." for the words "State of Pakistan through its people" the words "people of Pakistan" be substituted.'
3. 'That in the paragraph beginning with the words "Whereas sovereignty over the entire universe..." the word "within the limits prescribed by Him" be omitted.'
4. 'That in the paragraph beginning with the words "This Constituent Assembly..." after the word "independent" the word "democratic" be inserted.'
5. 'That after the paragraph beginning with the words "This Constituent Assembly...", the following new paragraphs be inserted:-

   "Wherein the national sovereignty belongs to the people of Pakistan;

   Wherein the principle of the state is government of the people, for the people, and by the people".'
6. 'That for the paragraph beginning with the words "Wherein the state shall exercise...", the following paragraph be substituted:-

"Wherein the elected representatives of the people—in whom shall be centered and in whom shall belong legislative as well as executive authority—shall exercise their powers through such persons as are by law authorized to do so. The elected representatives shall control acts of Government and may at any time divest it of all authority".'

7. 'That in the paragraph beginning with the words "Wherein the principles of democracy...", the words "as enunciated by Islam" be omitted.'
8. 'That in the paragraph beginning with the words "Wherein the principles of democracy..." after the words "as enunciated by Islam", the words "and as based upon eternal principles", be inserted.'
9. 'That in the paragraph beginning with the words "Wherein the principles of democracy..." after the words "as enunciated by Islam", the words "and other religions", be inserted.'
10. 'That in the paragraph beginning with the words "Wherein the principles of democracy..." after the words "as enunciated by Islam", the words "but not inconsistent with the Charter of the Fundamental Human Rights of the United Nations Organization", be inserted.'
11. 'That in the paragraph beginning with the words "Wherein the Muslims shall be..." for the words "Muslims shall", the words "Muslims and non-Muslims shall equally" be substituted.'
12. 'That in the paragraph beginning with the words "Wherein the Muslims shall be...", for the words "Islam as set out in the Holy Quran and the *Sunnah*", the words "their respective religions" be substituted.'
13. 'That in the paragraph beginning with the words "Wherein the Muslims shall be...", after the words "Holy Quran and the *Sunnah*", the following be added:-

    'in perfect accord with non-Muslims residing in the State and in complete toleration of their culture and social and religious customs".'
14. 'That for the paragraph beginning with the words "Wherein adequate provision shall be made for the minorities", the following paragraph be substituted:-

    'Wherein shall be secured to the minorities the freedom to profess and practise their religions and develop their cultures and adequate provision shall be made for it".'
15. 'That in the paragraph beginning with the words "Wherein shall be guaranteed...", after the word "guaranteed", the words "and secured to all the people of Pakistan" be inserted.'
16. 'That in the paragraph beginning with the words "Wherein adequate provision shall be made to safeguard...", for the words "and depressed classes", the words "classes and Scheduled Castes" be substituted.'
17. 'That in the paragraph beginning with the words "Wherein adequate provision shall be made to safeguard..." between the words "backward" and "depressed classes", the words "and labouring" be inserted.'

The Debate on Religious Minorities

Out of the long speeches made by the non-Muslim members of the Constituent Assembly, the speech of Birat Chandra Mandal,[5] made on 9 March 1949, was an eloquent and representative one for the minorities and is reproduced below:

> Sir, since the beginning of the session, I have not had the opportunity of opening my lips, but today I thought that I should say something on the subject which, in my opinion, appears to be very very important and from the international point of view, I think it is really very important. I want to say that the Great Prophet Muhammad was born in Arabia and Islam also first appeared in Arabia. I think even in that country, there is a constitution in which we do not see that the principles of administration or constitution have been based on Islam. Then, Sir, I want to impress upon the House that Turkey is the most powerful Muslim country in the world. There also we do not find that the constitution has been based on Islamic principles. Then, Sir, I hear that *ulemas* are insisting on this principle of Islam. Are there not *pandits* in India who could not insist on political thinkers of India to adopt such a constitution. Are there not Bishops in England nor in America — or in any other country which is dominated by Christians on the face of the globe, where these *ulemas*, I mean the Bishops, have voice. The constitution has all along been and everywhere on the face of the globe established on democracy and specially on the economic thinking of the political people of individual countries. But, Sir, I find a great deviation in our beloved Pakistan. It is a newly built up dominion. The founder of this dominion most unequivocally said that Pakistan will be a secular state. That great leader of ours never said that the principles of constitution will be based on Islam. So, I want to tell, the Honourable Prime Minister of our state through you, Sir,that we are going to commit a serious blunder, a very serious blunder, and we are going to do something which is unprecedented in the history of the world. Sir, I want to impress upon him this point that he has forgotten to think about the past. In the world, constitutions have been framed since long ago. We have got our independence recently and so that Prime Minister might say, 'Oh, these are the things of the past? Nowhere on the face of the globe we find a constitution which has been based on the principles of a particular religion.' Hindus also have not done so on the basis of religion. It was the great Quaid-e-Azam who had given the dominion to Hindus. During the last 800 years, there has been no Hindu dominion on the face of the globe. There was a Christian dominion, there was a Muslim dominion, but there was no Hindu dominion on the face of the globe at least during the last 800 years. But it was our Quaid-e-Azam who created a Hindu dominion along with a Muslim dominion. But to my mind, I think, the Honourable the Prime Minister is leading us to commit a serious blunder. We have forgotten the past. He has forgotten to think of the past records of the world. He is only considering the present and he is not at the same time considering that what posterity will think of us. The whole world is gradually progressing and all the civilized countries of the world are progressing. Why is it that our Pakistan should not keep pace with the advancement of other countries of the world. I live in Pakistan. I have been known to the Honourable President for the last 30 years and I have had opportunities of working with almost all the big Muslim leaders of Bengal. I never had any opposition with regard to religion because I have all along been friendly with the Muslim community. I am not for Christians, not for Hindus, and not for Persians. But I am for the state, I say that my state will be guilty of framing a constitution which posterity will condemn. I believe from the core of my heart

that most progressive people will be born after our death. Mr Liaquat Ali Khan will die and I will die, but there will be a posterity which will outlive us. Do you not see that even the ladies are working on progressive lines?The world is progressing. Today we are fighting that he is a Muslim, he is a Hindu, he is a Christian, he is a Buddhist in Pakistan. But the time will come when people will not believe in their individual religions. Nobody will believe in these things. Now nobody is willing to have a constitution based on Islam or Hinduism or Christianity and nobody is willing to do anything in the name of religion.

So, I say, please look forward and make the constitution in such a way that you may not have to repent afterwards. Remember 'uneasy lies the head that wears the Crown'. So the responsibility lies on the head that moves the Resolution. I request the Honourable Prime Minister through the Chair to consider again and again before finally coming to any conclusion whether we should adopt this Resolution at all. I would like to give you this advice in the interests of the state and not in the interests of the Hindus or Christians or Buddhists or Musalmans or Parsees. The state has got no religion. Individuals might have religion, but the state has got no religion. So, in the interests of the state, of which I am an humble member, I bring it to your notice through the President that you will be held responsible because you are the sponsor of this Resolution not only to the countries in the world which have made their constitutions in the past but also to the posterity who will think of making their constitutions in the future. So, I tell you again and again to ponder over this Resolution before you finally adopt it.

Bhupendra Kumar Datta also made an eloquent speech while opposing the Objectives Resolution. Some extracts from his speech are reproduced below:[6]

'Sir, we are here by the will of the people of our newly-won independent state of Pakistan to draw up a constitution for its future governance. Although all powers of an independent state emanate from the sovereign powers of its people, certain laws, rules and regulations must guide and control the relations between the people and the state. Such laws, rules, and regulations have in the modern world come within the domain of matters, political. The relations between a state and its citizens may be, and have been throughout the ages, of diverse forms, but whatever the forms, they are subject properly of politics. On the other hand, the relation between man and God comes within the sphere of religion.'

'The two—reason and faith—may blend together perfectly. But we allow each to work separately in order that each may grow to its fullest maturity so that a higher synthesis of the two may be attained—a mellower blending. Even in the evolution towards that ultimate end, the two may be working hand in hand but unobtrusively.'

'Politics, as I have said, Sir, belongs to the domain of reason. But as you intermingle it within religion, as this Preamble to the nobly conceived Resolution does, you pass into the other sphere of faith. The same is done in the paragraph on 'Sovereignty' on page 13 of the 1 volume of Select Constitutions of the World, circulated by the Constituent Assembly Office. Thereby, on the one hand, you run the risk of subjecting religion to criticism, which will rightly be resented as sacreligious; on the other hand, so far as the state and state policies are concerned, you cripple reason, curb criticism. Political institutions—particularly modern democratic institutions—as we all know, Sir, grow and progress by criticism, from broader to still broader basis. As long as you remain strictly within the region of politics, criticism may be free and frank, even severe and bitter.'

'But as you bring in religion, or things as matters of faith, you open the door ajar for resentment of criticism. You then leave it to absolutism to fling it wide open. Sir, I feel—I have every reason to believe—that were this Resolution to come before this House within the life-time of the great creator of Pakistan, the Quaid-i-Azam, it would not have come in its present shape. Even with you, Sir, the Honourable mover of this Resolution at the helm of affairs in the state, I have no fear that criticism will be stilled or absolutism will find a chance to assert itself.'

'But, Sir, we are framing a constitution, which will outlive us, may be, even many of our succeeding generations. So, as far as human reason can guard against it, let us not do anything here today that may consign our future generations to the furies of a blind destiny. May be, may God forbid it, but some day, perhaps even within our lifetime—extremely troublous times as we live in—a political adventurer, a Yanshikai, or a Bacheha-i-Sakao may find a chance to impose his will and authority on this state. He may find a justification for it in this Preamble. To the people of our state, he may justify his claim on the clause in it that refers to the delegation of the Almighty's authority to the state through its people. He has only to forge a further link and get it delegated through the state to himself and declare that he is the ruler of Pakistan, anointed by his Maker.'

Mian Mohammad Iftikharuddin also opposed the Resolution, but for other reasons. Extracts from his speeches are as under:[7]

What I am trying to stress is that the words used in this Resolution do not mean anything. This Resolution is not the product of the League Party in this House. This Resolution is supposed to be the voice of the seventy million people of our country. This Resolution is supposed to be their voice, and I have every right to criticize it because I feel that we are taking upon ourselves a tremendous responsibility which we are not discharging properly.

Had we given the world a proper Islamic constitution, a fine ideology, a new way of achieving real democracy, I think, we would have performed a great task. On this occasion, I have a right to say—and I am not doing this to blame any member or any section of this House,—I am saying as is, perhaps, as progressive, as revolutionary, as democratic, and as dynamic as that of any other state or ideology. I do hope that even at this stage this House, realizing its great responsibility, will incorporate in its Objectives Resolution those principles which will make real democracy possible. And if it fails to do that, at this stage, I do hope it will do so in the actual constitution and then the world will know what we really mean by the Islamic conception of democracy and social justice.

Dr Ishtiaq Husain Qureshi, Maulana Shabbir Ahmed Osmani, Sardar Abdur Rab Khan Nishtar, Nazir Ahmad, Dr Omar Hayat Malik, Nur Ahmad, Dr Mohammad Husain, Begam Shaista, and Chaudhry Mohammad Zafarullah Khan spoke in support of the Resolution and opposed the amendments moved in it. Dr Ishtiaq Husain Qureshi tried to reassure non-Muslims in the following words:[8]

In the end, Sir, I would suggest that instead of dwelling upon fear, instead of saying that we, by underhand means, are trying to keep the minorities in a subservient position, it would be much better to trust the majority, because the ultimate guarantee of the well-being of a minority is not the inclusion in the constitution or in the Objectives Resolution of certain principles. They must be enunciated, it is quite true, but the real guarantee is the behaviour of the people, and so far as the people in Pakistan are concerned the majority of them are Muslims. They have a great faith in Islam and are likely to be motivated in their actions by their faith. It is for their benefit that we are saying, 'you are a rising nation today; being a rising nation you should not get drunk with this power that you have achieved anew; remember the fact that all power is a sacred trust'. There are too many examples, Sir—and I need not quote them here—of peoples who have come into their own and have achieved power and then have misused it, and, therefore, at a time when new power is obtained by peoples it is fit and proper that they should be reminded of the moral and ethical principles which should always guide them in the use of authority. Therefore, Sir, I should have thought that the Preamble and the various other clauses of the Resolution which my friends want to get amended and modified, should have really assured them, should have given them the guarantee, the promises of a free and prosperous life that they seek and that in no way can amendments to this Resolution prove a better guarantee.

Maulana Shabbir Ahmed Osmani expressed his views to support the Objectives Resolution as under:[9]

Islam has never accepted the view that religion is a private affair between man and his creator and as such has no bearing upon the social or political relations of human beings. Some other religious systems may expound this theory and may, incidentally, be too idealistic to possess a comprehensive and all-embracing code of life. But Islam has no use for such false notions and its teachings are in direct contradiction to them. The late Quaid-e-Azam made the following observations in the letter he wrote to Gandhiji in August, 1944:

'The Quran is a complete code of life. It provides for all matters, religious or social, civil or criminal, military or penal, economic or commercial. It regulates every act, speech and movement from the ceremonies of religion to those of daily life, from the salvation of the soul to the health of the body; from the rights of all to those of such individual, from the punishment here to that in the life to come. Therefore, when I say that the Muslims are a nation, I have in my mind all physical and metaphysical standards and values.'

In 1945, Jinnah observed in an Eid Day message to the Muslims—

'Every Mussalman knows that the Quran is not confined to religious and moral duties. The Quran is the dearest possession of the Muslims and their general code of life—a religious, social, civil, commercial, military, judicial, criminal and penal Code. Our Prophet has enjoined on us that every Mussalman should possess a copy of the Quran and study it carefully so that it may promote our material as well as individual welfare.'

The Quaid-e-Azam gave frequent expression to such ideas. In the face of such unequivocal and repeated declarations, is it not fit to say that religion has got nothing to do with politics or that if the Quaid-e-Azam had been alive, the Resolution would not have come up before this House.

I think Gandhiji was fully conscious of this fact when he advised the Congress Ministers in 1937 to follow in the footsteps of Hazrat Abu Bakar and Hazrat Umar. The Quaid-e-Azam too was referring to the basic principle of our constitution when he observed in the course of his presidential address delivered at a conference of the All-India Students Federation at Jullundur in 1943:-

'In my opinion our system of government was determined by the Quran some 1350 years ago.'

In his letter to the Pir Sahib of Manki Sharif in November 1945, he clearly stated:

'It is needless to emphazise that the Constituent Assembly which would be predominantly Muslim in its composition, would be able to enact laws for Muslims, not inconsistent with the shariat laws and the Muslims will no longer be obliged to abide by the un-Islamic laws.'

Sardar Abdur Rab Khan Nishtar, who was one of the closest associates of Jinnah, stoutly defended the Resolution and made the following remarks in his speech on 10 March 1949.[10]

The first and the main opposition was voiced against the Preamble of the Resolution and the basic idea that was put forward in support of the adverse criticism was that politics is different from religion; politics should be divorced from religion and politics should have nothing to do with the religion. Both have different spheres and thereafter, they should not be mingled together in the affairs of the state. Well, Sir, so far as this point is concerned, the world knows, and particularly those who belong to the Indo-Pak continent know it very well, that on this point there is a fundamental difference between the Muslims and the non-Muslims. I can well understand the reason for that difference. Maybe the non-Muslims who advocate divorce between religion and politics look at this point from the point of view of their own religion. May be their religion lays down that religion is only a matter which concerns the relations of a man with his creator and thus far and no further. But we, the Muslims and our Leader, the former Leader of the Muslims, the Quaid-e-Azam, have declared it from thousands of platforms that our outlook on life and of life is quite different from the outlook of our friends. We believe that our religion governs not only our relations with God, but also our activities in other spheres of life. We have always described it, and rightly described it, as a complete code of life. Therefore, if in spite of this knowledge and in spite of the controversy that has been going on for years in the Indo-Pak subcontinent, it is expected of us today to accept that philosophy which has been advanced by my friends who have opposed the Preamble, I would submit it is too much. That is not our belief. Our view about this point is quite different. So, let there be no misunderstanding on that point. But this in no way affects them.

As I understand it, Sir, it will be a constitution which will be a purely democratic constitution in that meaning of the term which the Muslims know. It means that even the humblest will have the right to criticize the highest. May I tell my learned friends over there that they must have heard the word *Jihad* which has been a subject of criticism the other day in India. It was wrongly translated as mere holy war or crusade. In Islam for a humble person to utter truth in the face of an oppressor king or ruler is the greatest *Jihad.* With this principle of Islam, with such a principle of freedom and with the principle of equality and with all the explanations and illustrations that have been given in the Resolution, I personally, Sir, have no doubt whatsoever that it will be constitution where the voice of the people will be supreme and that no person will be entitled to arrogate to himself the authority of the people. As a matter of fact, one phrase 'within the limits prescribed by Him' which has been objected to by the other side, obviates the possibility of any individual arrogating to himself power or authority in Pakistan because one of the main limitations which has been laid down in Islam with regard to constitution is this that the ruling authority in a Muslim country cannot be a king, it cannot be a dictator. This is one of the limitations prescribed by God.

Mr Barma suggested that it should be stated in the clause that 'the Muslims and non-Muslims equally shall be enabled', he has not understood the implications of his amendment, otherwise he would have never made this suggestion. Muslims will be in a majority in this country. There is no harm if it is stated that the state should create conditions, whereby the Muslims are enabled to live the life of a good Muslim; but if you allow the government, which of necessity, will mostly be composed of people belonging to Muslim community to interfere with your religion or regulate, your religious affairs, you would be sorry for it. The Mussalmans may not abuse it—I am sure they would not abuse it—but to provide so is not in your interest. Who has to enforce this provision who has to regulate it and who has to create those conditions? It is the government and what would be the complexion of the government, at any rate, the overwhelming complexion of the government? It is not in your interest. If I had been a non-Muslim and such a proposal had been suggested to me I would have protested against it. What has been provided for the minorities is the freedom to profess and the freedom to practise their own religions and the freedom to develop their own cultures. Therefore, I would submit that so far as that amendment is concerned, it is not in the interest of minorities. After all, I am also a fellow citizen of non-Muslims of Pakistan and I have to see that their interests do not suffer.

Another remark which was made by one of the members was that soon after the Quaid-e-Azam's death you have confronted us with this Resolution as if we have done something against the wishes of the Quaid-e-Azam. It is correct that the Quaid-e-Azam had given pledges to the minorities but Quaid-e-Azam had also given pledges to the majority. Pakistan was demanded with a particular ideology, for a particular purpose and this Resolution, that has been moved, is just in accordance with those solemn pledges which Quaid-e-Azam and the leaders of the Muslim League gave to the majority as well as to the minorities. We have done nothing and none of us dare do anything which goes against the declarations of the Quaid-e-Azam.

Chaudhry Mohammad Zafarullah Khan, Foreign Minister of Pakistan, in his speech of 12 March 1949 before the Constituent Assembly supporting the motion, tried to allay the fears and apprehensions of the minorities in the following words:

We are told that man has been created in the image of God. Inasmuch as God neither has nor assumes physical or material shape or form, obviously the image of God must have only a metaphorical significance, namely, that man has been endowed with a reflection of divine attributes, and that the purpose of his terrestrial existence is to develop those attributes. It is for that purpose that man has been granted dominion, again in a limited sense, over the physical universe. In other words, the physical universe has been created to subserve the purpose of man's spiritual, moral, and physical evolution. It follows, therefore, that whatever authority man has been invested with in respect of the universe, is delegated authority to be used only for the purpose and to the end stated.

To the opening statement in the Preamble that sovereignty over the entire universe belongs to God Almighty alone, I do not conceive that any person believing in God could take exception. The rest of the Preamble, though based on the assumption that all authority, political or otherwise, which man has been invested with, has been delegated by the Supreme Ruler and must be exercised within the limits said by Him, is designed to emphazise that political authority vested in a people and by them entrusted to the State is a sacred trust and must be exercised and administered in that spirit. Some controversy has been raised as to whether that authority rests primarily in the people or in the state. From the Islamic point of view, there can be no doubt that such authority or sovereignty as Islam concedes to mankind, vests in the people and in the Quran it is the people who are commanded to entrust that authority into the hands of those who are in every respect fit to exercise it. The state is the servant of the people and is like any other instrument in any other sphere brought into being for the purpose of serving the people.

Resolution Adopted

Winding up the debate on the Motion of Objectives Resolution on 12 March 1949, Liaquat made the following remarks re-assuring the non-Muslims.[11]

Sir, my Honourable friends, the Leader of the Congress Party had a visit from some *ulemas*. He did not tell us whether it was that they had come in search of knowledge to him or whether he had gone in search of knowledge to them. But I presume that this visit was paid by certain *ulemas* according to him from Lahore on their own initiative and they left certain literature with him, which seems to have upset my Honourable friend, who is very seldom upset. I can quite understand why this visit and why these handing over of this literature was done. There are some people here who are out to disrupt and destroy Pakistan and these so-called *ulemas* who have come to you they have come with that particular mission of creating doubts in your mind regarding the bonafides of the Mussalmans of Pakistan. Do not, for God's sake, lend your ear to such mischievous propaganda.

I want to say and give a warning to this element which is out to disrupt Pakistan, that we shall not brook it any longer. They have misrepresented the whole ideology of Islam to you. They are in fact enemies of Islam while posing as friends and supporters of Islam.

Sir, my friend said that these people told him that in an Islamic state — that means a state which is established in accordance with this Resolution — no non-Muslim can be the head of the administration. This is absolutely wrong. A non-Muslim can be the head of the administration under a constitutional government with limited authority that is given under the constitution to a person or an institution in that particular state. So here again these people have indeed misled him. He has by his remarks told the non-Muslims here that if this Resolution is passed, there is no place for them in Pakistan. This, Sir, as I said is not the type of statement that one would expect from one who professes to be a true and real Pakistani. Sir, let me tell my Honourable friend that the greatest guarantee that the non-Muslims can have, they will get only through this Resolution and through no other manner and, therefore, I would request him not to be misled by interested persons and do not think for a moment that this Resolution is really intended or will really result, in driving out the non-Muslims from Pakistan or reducing them to the position of—as he described hewers of wood and drawers of water. In a real Islamic society, let me tell you, Mr President, there are no classes of hewers of wood and drawers of water. The humblest can rise to the highest position. As a matter of fact, let me tell you, Mr President, what we have provided here for minorities I only wish that the sister dominion of India had provided similar concessions and similar safeguards for the minorities in India. Here, we are guaranteeing you your religious freedom, advancement of your culture, sanctity of your personal laws, and equal opportunities, as well as equality in the eye of the law. What have they done on the other side? No question of culture. As a matter of fact, the personal law of Muslims is not to be recognized in India. That is the position.

Sir, my Honourable friend, Mr B. C. Mandal, told me that posterity will curse me for bringing forward this Resolution. Let me tell my friend, if we succeed in building Pakistan on the basis of this Resolution, we shall be able to create conditions that posterity instead of cursing me, will bless me.

Sir, I would just once again tell my friends, on the other side, that whether you believe us or whether you do not believe us; whether you desire it or whether you do not desire it, as long as you are citizens of Pakistan, we are determined to do the right thing by you for the simple reason that our religion tells us to do so; for the simple reason that we are trying to build up this state on morality and on higher values of life than what materialism can provide.

At the conclusion of the speech all the amendments proposed by the non-Muslim members were put to the vote of the Constituent Assembly. These amendments were rejected by the House by ten against twenty-one.[12] The members who voted for the amendments were:

1. Mr Prem Hari Barma
2. Prof. Raj Kumar Chakravarty
3. Mr Sris Chandra Chattopadhyaya
4. Mr Akshay Kumar Dass
5. Mr Bhupendra Kumar Datta
6. Mr Jnanendra Chandra Majumdar
7. Mr Birat Chandra Mandal
8. Mr Bhabesh Chandra Nandy
9. Mr Dhananjoy Roy
10. Mr Harrendra Kumar Sur

The names of those members who voted against the amendments are:

1. Mr A. M. A. Hamid
2. Maulana Mohd Abdullah-el Baqui
3. Mr Abul Kasem Khan
4. Maulana Mohd Akram Khan
5. Mr Fazlur Rahman
6. Prof. Ishtiaq Husain Qureshi
7. Mr Liaquat Ali Khan

8. Dr Mohammad Husain
9. Mr Nur Ahmad
10. Mr Serajul Islam
11. Maulana Shabbir Ahmed Osmani
12. Khwaja Shahabuddin
13. Begum Shaista Suhrawardy Ikramullah
14. Mr Nazir Ahmad Khan
15. Sheikh Karamat Ali
16. Dr Omar Hayat Malik
17. Begum Jahan Ara Shah Nawaz
18. Sir Mohd Zafarullah Khan
19. Sardar Abdur Rab Khan Nishtar
20. Khan Sardar Bahadur Khan
21. Pirzada Abdus Sattar Abdur Rahman

After voting on the amendments, the main Resolution was placed before the Constituent Assembly and was adopted.[13]

It is unfortunate that there was a division on the Resolution along communal lines. Muslim members voted against the amendments and non-Muslim members voted for the amendments. One cannot escape the conclusion that the Resolution might have sown the seeds of suspicion, alienation, and distrust among the minorities against the majority. It might have been more prudent to accept some of the amendments proposed by the members representing the minorities in order to reach an understanding with them so that the Resolution could have been passed by consensus. It cannot be denied that some of the proposed amendments were quite reasonable and moderate and their point of view ought to have been accommodated in the larger national interest.

NOTES

1. *The Constituent Assembly of Pakistan Debates*, Volume V-1949, pp. 2-7.
2. Ibid., p. 8.
3. Ibid., p. 9.
4. Ibid., pp. 98, 99 & 100.
5. Ibid., pp. 48-9.
6. Ibid., pp. 13-17.
7. Ibid., pp. 54 & 55.
8. Ibid., pp. 42 & 43.
9. Ibid., pp. 44, 45 & 46.
10. Ibid., pp. 55, 56, 59, 60, 61 & 62.
11. Ibid., pp. 94-8.
12. Ibid., pp. 98, 99 & 100.
13. Ibid., pp. 100 & 101.

6

CONTROVERSIES WITHIN THE CONSTITUENT ASSEMBLY

After Jinnah's death, the crucial issue to be decided was whether the Governor-General should be the constitutional head of state with the Prime Minister and his Cabinet exercising real executive power or otherwise. At that time, Liaquat Ali Khan wielded real power. He chose to remain prime minister which meant that the Cabinet form of government was to become effective. Khawaja Nazimuddin, who became the second Governor-General, appeared to be willing to assume the customary privileges of the office without Jinnah's real power. He was 'delightful, honest, respected, and not very dynamic'. The position of the Governor-General during this period was similar to that in other dominions—he became the constitutional figurehead while real power was exercised by the Prime Minister and his cabinet. This harmony continued until the death of Liaquat Ali Khan on 16 October 1951.[1]

During the period immediately following Jinnah's death, there developed a fierce competition for influence, wealth, power, and prestige between the various political interests and personalities. The arena in which this competition first manifested itself was the organization for framing the Constitution which was to give formal expression to Pakistan's polity. It was here that Jinnah's guiding hand was especially missed because he would have been able, to enforce upon all the interested parties a due sense of proportion to moderate selfish aspirations and, above all, to convince the elite that the drawing up of a constitution presented a task which the nation must quickly undertake. What counted far more with the politicians and members of the Constituent Assembly was how power was to be divided between the centre and the provinces and between East and West Pakistan; how far the shape of a modern state could be squared with the principles of Islam; and how the different competing interests—landlords, religious leaders, businessmen, industrialists—could receive recognition of their claim to power and influence.[2]

When Jinnah died, he could, in the nature of things, have no real successor, but Liaquat Ali Khan who continued as Prime Minister, inherited a share of his leader's prestige and remained in office until his assassination in 1951. The nation-wide authority which Jinnah had exercised disappeared just at the moment when it was needed to sublimate regional and personal jealousies into a sustained effort for the common good. Before he died, Jinnah had delivered a series of stern warnings against the dangers which 'provincialism' held for the future of the nation.[3] It was this spirit of partisanship which haunted and frustrated Liaquat Ali Khan throughout his term of office. His authority was not unchallenged and some of his colleagues were too ambitious to accept his advice. Some of his ministers began to form their own groups of supporters in the Assembly and even to communicate their own views to the press when they differed from the majority opinion in the Cabinet. All this considerably hampered the Prime Minister in his task of consolidating the work which Jinnah had begun and weakened the prestige of the central government throughout the country.[4]

Basic Principles Committee and its Interim Report

After the passing of the Objectives Resolution in 1949, the Constituent Assembly set up a number of committees and sub-committees to work out the details of the Constitution on the principles as laid down in the Objectives Resolution. The Basic Principles Committee was the most important one. It had twenty-four members who were not required to be members of the Constituent Assembly. It set up three sub-committees:

1. Sub-Committee on federal and provincial constitutions and distribution of powers;
2. Sub-Committee on franchise; and
3. Sub-Committee for judiciary.

The Basic Principles Committee also set up a special committee for 'Talimaat-i-Islamia', which consisted of reputed Islamic scholars to advise on matters arising out of the Objectives Resolution. Another special committee was assigned the task of recommending appropriate nomenclatures.[5]

Without finalizing its recommendations regarding several other matters such as financial allocations, nomenclatures, qualifications of the head of the state, and so on, the Basic Principles Committee presented to the Assembly an interim report.[6]

The first draft Constitution, as prepared by the Basic Principles Committee, was presented to the country by Liaquat Ali Khan in 1950. Its salient features were:

1. The Objectives Resolution was to be incorporated in the Constitution as a directive principle of state policy and was not to prejudice the incorporation of fundamental rights in the Constitution.[7]
2. There was to be a head of state, to be elected for five years by a joint session of both the Houses of central legislature. He was not to be a member of either House and, if so, he had to cease to be a member after his election. A person could not be elected head of state for more than two full terms.[8] He was to appoint the commanders-in-chief and officers of the armed forces. His discretionary powers were confined to granting clemency and appointment of election tribunals.[9]
3. The Head of the state was to appoint as Prime Minister a member of the central legislature who commanded the confidence of both houses of the central legislature jointly. Ministers were to be appointed on the advice of the Prime Minister.[10]

4. The central legislature was to consist of two houses:
   (a) the house of units representing the legislatures of the units;
   (b) the house of the people elected by the people.[11]

   The report did not give a full picture of the composition and size of the house of the people as the sub-committee on franchise had not completed its work by 1950. But it was made clear that the existing provinces, including Balochistan, should have equal representation in the house of units. It was further laid down that the two houses of the federal legislature should have equal powers and in the case of a dispute on any question, a joint session of both houses should be summoned for taking the final decision thereon.[12] The power to convene a joint session was to be vested in the head of the state and to be exercised in the following cases:[13]
   (a) Conflict between the houses of the legislature;
   (b) Election and removal of the Head of the State;
   (c) Consideration of the budget and other money Bills; and
   (d) Consideration of a motion of no-confidence in the Cabinet.

   It was recommended that the Cabinet would be responsible to both the houses of the legislature. Thus the first draft provided for a bicameral system with equal representation of the various units in the upper house and equality of powers between the two houses. Of course, if the popular house should have greater numbers, it would be in a stronger position, but this was not made clear, the strength of the two houses being undefined. The dissolution of the central legislature was to take place on the advice of the Prime Minister.[14]

5. There was to be a head of the province for each province to be appointed by the head of the state and was to hold office during the latter's pleasure.[15]
6. The head of the province was to appoint as Chief Minister a member who commanded a majority in the provincial legislature. Other ministers were to be appointed on the advice of the Chief Minister.[16]
7. There was to be one house of legislature in each province elected by the people for a period of five years. It could be dissolved on the advice of the Chief Minister.[17]
8. The head of the state and the heads of the provinces were given powers to promulgate ordinances during the period when the legislature concerned was not in session.[18]
9. Urdu was to be the national language of the state.[19]

The reaction to the first draft Constitution was most unfavourable in East Pakistan. The main point of criticism related to the quantum of representation in the proposed central legislature. All the units were given an equal number of seats in the upper house. East Pakistan, where a majority of the country's population lived, had equal representation with each of the four provinces in West Pakistan thus reducing the representation of the majority of the population in Pakistan to one-fifth. This fact assumed great importance because the upper house was vested with powers equal to that of the lower house. It was thus apprehended that the majority of the people might be converted into a minority. East Pakistanis also did not favour the idea of Urdu being the only state language.[20]

A provincial convention was held in Dhaka on 4 and 5 November 1950, offering an alternative Constitution. It recommended a republican form of government, having two autonomous regional governments for the eastern and western units and one central parliament on the basis of population with powers to deal with foreign affairs, currency, and defence. Meanwhile, the East Bengal members of the Constituent Assembly, including A. K. Fazlul Haq, described the apprehensions of the people of East Bengal as 'groundless' in a joint statement issued from Karachi on 13 October 1950.[21] They did not share the anxiety that East Bengal's majority in the central legislature would be converted into a minority and that the powers of the provincial government would be seriously curtailed. However, it cannot be denied that there was widespread agitation in East Pakistan. The East Pakistan Muslim League Working Committee in a meeting held on 29 October 1950, took note of widespread feelings among people of the province on certain recommendations of the Basic Principles Committee and suggested a 'drastic amendment of the report'. It particularly stressed that in setting up the federal structure of Pakistan, the geographical position of East Bengal should be seriously considered. At the East Pakistan Muslim League Council meeting which was attended by Liaquat Ali Khan, some members described the report as 'terribly anti-Bengali'. The agitation in East Bengal obliged the Constituent Assembly to postpone its deliberations. Liaquat announced in the Constituent Assembly on 21 November 1950 that postponement was desired for the purpose of enabling the Basic Principles Committee to examine and consider any concrete and definite suggestions that might be made by the people regarding the basic principles of the Constitution.[22]

Report of the Committee on Fundamental Rights and Matters Relating to Minorities

The committee on the fundamental rights of citizens submitted its report before the Constituent Assembly which was accepted in 1950.

The proposed Constitution guaranteed the right to all citizens including the 11 million members of the minority communities in a population of 76 million to apply to the Supreme Court for enforcement of their fundamental rights. Following the model of some of the new constitutions of the world, the constitution-makers guaranteed certain fundamental rights to the citizens, both Muslims and non-Muslims in Pakistan. The fundamental rights included the following important provisions: equality of all citizens before the law; equal protection of law to all citizens; no discrimination on grounds of religion, race, caste, sex, or place of birth with regard to access to places of public entertainment, recreation, welfare, or utility. Every qualified citizen would be eligible for induction in the services of the state irrespective of religion, race, caste, sex, descent, or place of birth. Every citizen was guaranteed freedom of speech, conscience, expression, association, profession, occupation, trade, or business. No community would be prevented from providing religious instruction to the pupils of its own community and the personal law of every community was guaranteed. No person would be compelled to pay any special taxes the proceeds of which would be specifically appropriated for the propagation of any religion other than his. (The non-Muslim members of the Constituent Assembly often expressed the apprehension that in an 'Islamic state', Islam would be propagated and maintained with public money and that the non-Muslims would be forced to pay taxes for this purpose.) Further, it was provided that there would be no discrimination against any community in the matter of exemption from or concession in taxes granted with respect to religious institutions. No discrimination in admission to educational institutions would be permitted. The report of the fundamental rights of citizens received favourable comments both inside and outside the Constituent Assembly. It was quite a comprehensive list of rights and Liaquat could claim, with some justification, that 'all the essential rights have been provided'.[23]

In addition to these fundamental rights which were applicable to Muslims and non-Muslims alike, special safeguards for minorities were provided in the Constitution. The Committees on Fundamental Rights set up a sub-committee on matters relating to minorities at its first meeting held in 1948. The Minorities Committee included representation from all groups of the minority population. The sub-committee issued the following questionnaire to important individuals and organizations in the country with a view to ascertaining the views of the public on this complicated question:

1. What should be the political safeguards of a minority in the centre and in the provinces?
2. What should be the economic safeguards of a minority in the centre and in the province?
3. What safeguards should be provided for a minority with regard to matters religious, educational, social, and cultural?
4. What methods are suggested to make the safeguards effective?
5. Should any of the safeguards be eliminated later and if so, how, when, and under what circumstances?
6. Any other remarks or suggestions with regard to safeguards for a minority.

The suggestions received from the public were numerous and often divergent. They were circulated in a consolidated form to the members of the sub-committee which made its decision in the light of suggestions and proposals received from the public.[24]

Some of the Hindu leaders had maintained that they did not want any safeguards, but regardless of what they said, it was clear from the beginning that safeguards were needed for the religious minorities, particularly when the Constituent Assembly decided to have an Islamic Constitution. In one of the memoranda submitted to the

Constituent Assembly by the minority communities, it was demanded that the Hindus should get representation in the legislature not only according to their numbers but also some 'weightage' should be given to them. For instance, in East Bengal, where the Hindus constituted about 23 per cent of the entire population, it was demanded that they should get 41 per cent of the seats in the East Bengal legislature.[25]

Other safeguards considered essential for the minorities were as follows:[26]

1. They should be protected from the threat of physical persecution. In the months following partition, there were riots in India and Pakistan resulting in the death of members of the minorities but by 1950 Pakistan could justly point out that not a single communal riot had taken place in that year. Meanwhile, in India, not a single year had passed since partition without riots and physical persecution of the minority community of Muslims. There was at that time no threat of physical persecution of the minorities in Pakistan. This was freely admitted by the minorities themselves.
2. Religious minorities must possess freedom of conscience in its widest sense. That has already been provided in the fundamental rights of citizens by 1950.
3. Minorities which differ from the majority in language and culture should have the right to run their own schools provided, of course, that they conformed to the general regulations of the government regarding education and that such schools were not used to inculcate a spirit of hostility to the majority of the state. This was also clearly provided in the fundamental rights.

In its final report on the minorities' rights, the Constituent Assembly added the following safeguards in addition to those already provided for in the fundamental rights:

1. 'Any minority residing in the territory of Pakistan or any part thereof having a distinct language, script, or culture of its own should not be prevented from conserving the same.
2. 'The state shall not discriminate in granting aid to educational institutions, discriminate against any educational institution merely on the ground that it is mainly maintained by a religious minority.
3. 'There shall be a Minister for Minority Affairs both at the centre and in the provinces to look after the interests of the minorities and to see that the safeguards provided in the constitution for the minorities are duly observed'.[27]

The Assassination of Liaquat Ali Khan, October 1951

After the death of Jinnah, the mantle of leadership fell upon the shoulders of Liaquat Ali Khan. Although Liaquat could not maintain harmony among divergent interest groups which confronted him, he kept the reputation of being an honest man. However, his moderation and refusal to rush into rash courses offended the extremist. His acceptance of a peaceful solution of the Kashmir dispute, his negotiations with Nehru over the protection of religious minorities and the resettlement of the refugees, and his eagerness to rationalize Indo-Pakistan relations in the interest of both countries, offended extremists and religious fanatics. His opponents, backed by the Press, attacked his wife for not observing *purdah*. These attacks were most unfortunate because she was a remarkable lady, earnestly working for the amelioration of the conditions of women so that they could enjoy equal status with men and play their legitimate role in society. The attacks on her were essentially intended to embarrass Liaquat.[28]

Liaquat earned personal enmity based on religious fanaticism which might have been the reason behind his assassination in Rawalpindi on 16 October 1951 while he was addressing a public meeting. His assassin was killed on the spot by the security forces thus destroying all evidence. There were rumours at the time that political rivals might have plotted to remove him but the most searching inquiries by an expert loaned by Scotland Yard failed to connect the individual assassin with any interest group in political circles.[29]

Liaquat's death was a blow to Pakistan because he was the last real link with Jinnah. His political stock and long experience were beyond doubt. Although he lost Jinnah's confidence to some extent in the latter's last days[30] and was accused of complicity in the alleged rigging of the Punjab provincial elections in 1951, he stood head and shoulders above Jinnah's other companions. Liaquat Ali Khan was responsible for persuading Jinnah to return to India to lead the Muslim League.[31] His services during the freedom movement as Jinnah's chief deputy cannot be over-emphasized. Chaudhry Mohammad Zafarullah Khan, Pakistan's first foreign minister and a colleague of Liaquat in the cabinet, recalled him in these words:

> Liaquat Ali Khan was a good chief to work with. He was pro-nothing and anti-nothing, but looked on everything from the point of view of Pakistan. I could never detect any kind of bias in his temperament, either for or against persons or causes or any other thing. He was a devoted public servant in the real sense of the term. During the four years we worked together, I never had the slightest cause to doubt any Cabinet member's loyalty to him.[32]

He was succeeded as prime minister by Khawaja Nazimuddin, the Governor-General at that time. Ghulam Muhammad, who had been Finance Minister from the earliest days of Pakistan, was selected as Governor-General.

Report of the Basic Principles Committee, 1952

As discussed earlier, the first report of the Basic Principles Committee was severely criticized, particularly in East Pakistan. By postponing its consideration in accordance with the wishes of the people, Liaquat acted in a democratic way. The report was referred back to the Constituent Assembly on which they invited proposals and suggestions from the public by January 1951 and a sub-committee was appointed to examine them. The sub-committee made its report to the Basic Principles Committee in July 1952, and it was presented as the second draft to the Constituent Assembly by the then Prime Minister[33] Nazimuddin on 22 December 1952.

Salient Features of the Report:

1. The Objectives Resolution was adopted as a Preamble to the proposed Constitution.
2. The head of the state was required to be a Muslim and to be elected for a term of five years at a joint sitting of both the houses of the federal legislature.[34] The head of state could not hold office consecutively for more than two full terms.[35]
3. The Prime Minister was to be appointed by the head of the state who also appointed the other ministers on the advice of the Prime Minister.[36] The Council of Ministers was to be collectively responsible to the House of the People only.[37]
4. The proposed federal legislature under the second draft comprised two houses of parliament as in the first draft. The House of Units was to consist of 120 members. The legislature of East Bengal was to elect sixty of their members according to the principle of proportional representation by means of a single transferable vote. West Pakistan seats were to be allocated as follows, also to be elected according to the principle of proportional representation by means of a single transferable vote by their respective legislatures:[38]

Punjab	27
Sindh	8
North-West Frontier	6
Tribal areas	5
Bahawalpur	4
Balochistan	2
Baloch states	2
Khairpur	2
Capital of Federation	4
	60

The house of the people was to consist of 400 members, of whom 200 were to be directly elected from East Bengal, and 200 from West Pakistan. The seats allowed to West Pakistan were divided as follows:

Punjab	90
Sindh	30
North-West Frontier	25
Tribal areas	17
Bahawalpur	13
Balochistan	5
Baloch States	5
Khairpur	4
Capital of Federation	11
	200

Under the second draft, the House of the People was to enjoy the real authority; the House of Units could only recommend revision of hasty legislation. All Money Bills had to originate in the House of the People. In case of any conflict between the houses, joint sittings of both were provided for in which a simple majority would decide the issue.

The second draft brought the principle of parity between East and West Pakistan as most important contribution towards solving the problem of representation and it claimed to 'bring about a constitutional balance of power as well as of responsibilities' between the two wings of Pakistan.

5. Seats were to be allocated to communities in the House of the People.[39] The single-member territorial constituencies were to be drawn in such a manner as to ensure that within a unit or the capital of the federation, all the constituencies of a particular community could have, as far as possible, equal number of votes.[40] Out of 200 seats allocated to East Bengal, 153 were reserved for Muslims, 24 for scheduled castes, 20 for other Hindus, 1 for Christians, and 2 for Buddhists. Out of 90 seats allocated to Punjab, 88 were reserved for Muslims and 2 for Christians. There was no seat reserved for the minorities in the NWFP, Tribal Areas, Bahawalpur state, Balochistan, Balochistan states, and Khairpur State. Out of 30 seats allocated to Sindh (minus Karachi Federal Area), 27 were reserved for Muslims, 2 for Scheduled Castes, and 1 for other Hindus. For the Karachi Federal Area, 11 seats were allocated, 10 for Muslims and 1 seat for Parsis.[41] The allocation of reserved seats for the minorities necessarily required preparation of separate electorates. The members of the Basic Principles Committee representing the minorities, namely S. C. Chattopadhyaya, B.K. Datta and Prem Hari Barma, recorded their dissent against this provision of allocation of seats to the communities.
6. For each of the provinces, states, capital of federation, and tribal area, the word 'unit' was used. There was to be a head of the unit for each unit appointed by the head of state serving at his pleasure for the maximum period of five years at a time.[42]
7. The Chief Minister of each unit was to be appointed by the head of the unit and other Ministers were to be appointed on the advice of the Chief Minister.[43]
8. For each unit, there was to be a unicameral legislature composed of members chosen by direct election. The number of members of the legislature of a unit was to vary between 75 and 350 as determined by a law of the federal legislature which was also to provide for the actual number of seats to be reserved for various communities on the basis of population as far as practicable.[44] The ministers in the units were to be collectively responsible to the legislatures of the units.[45]
9. The head of the state was to have the power to promulgate ordinances during the period when the federal legislature was not sitting. However, an ordinance was to be laid before the federal legislature and would expire six weeks from its reassembly.[46] Similar provision was made in respect of the heads of the units regarding promulgation of ordinances.[47]

10. The authority to dissolve the House of the People was vested in the head of the state, normally to be exercised on the advice of the council of ministers. Where no ministry could command confidence of the House of the People, the head of the state was to be authorized to dissolve the house of the people in exercise of his discretion and hold fresh elections.[48] Similar provision was made for the heads of the units in regard to the dissolution of their respective legislatures.[49]
11. The judiciary was to be headed by the Supreme Court of Pakistan consisting of a Chief Justice and two to six other judges. The Chief Justice was to be appointed by the head of the state and other Judges were to be appointed by the head of the state after taking into consideration the recommendations made by the Chief Justice.[50] The qualifications for appointment as Judge of the Supreme Court was to be five years as a Judge of a High Court or being Barrister or Advocate of twelve years standing.[51] Provisions were also made for acting Chief Justice and ad hoc Judges.[52] The original jurisdiction of the Supreme Court existed in case of dispute between the Federal Government and one or more units or between two or more units.[53] Appellate jurisdiction was to be conferred in criminal, civil, and other matters against the judgments, decrees or final orders of a High Court.[54] The decisions of the Supreme Court were to be final and binding on all authorities, executive and judicial, which were required to act in its aid.[55] There were provisions for special leave to appeal against any judgment, decree, or order of a High Court; review of its own Judgments and orders; and advisory jurisdiction on reference by the head of the state.[56] Judges of the Supreme Court could not be removed, except on the ground of misbehaviour or infirmity of mind or body on reference from the head of state. The alleged ground was to be enquired into by a Bench of three judges of that court.[57]
12. There was to be a High Court for each of the units of East Bengal, the Punjab, Sindh and the NWFP.[58] Every judge of a High Court was to be appointed by the head of the state on the recommendations of the Chief Justice of the Supreme Court, who in the case of appointment of a judge, other than Chief Justice of the High Court, was required to consult the Chief Justice of the High Court concerned before making his recommendations.[59] The qualifications for appointment as a judge of a High Court were to be a Barrister or Advocate of any High Court of ten years standing; a member of former Indian Civil Service of at least ten years standing having been a District Judge for at least three years; having been a judicial officer for at least ten years; or, in the opinion of the head of the state, a distinguished jurist.[60] A Judge could only be removed on the ground of misbehaviour or infirmity of body or mind if the Supreme Court, on reference made by the head of the state, recommends his removal.[61] There were also provisions for appointment of acting Chief Justice and Additional Judges.[62] The High Courts were to have all such jurisdictions, including appellate and revisional, which they had before commencement of the Constitution, but such jurisdiction was subject to variation by the

appropriate legislature.[63] In addition, the High Courts were to be conferred with powers to issue writs in the nature of habeas corpus, mandamus, prohibition, quo warranto and *certiorari*.[64]

13. There were guarantees to be provided to the civil servants of the federation and the units against dismissal, removal, or reduction in rank without opportunity to show cause.[65]
14. Directive Principles of State Policy were to be made part of the Constitution.[66]

Like the first draft of the Constitution presented in September 1950, the second draft, though more exhaustive as compared to the first one, evoked the same response. This time, the reaction in the Punjab was extremely unfavourable. Critics saw no logic in treating a single unit, East Bengal, of equal importance with all other units put together and regarded it as a violation of the federal principle under which all the units, large or small, should get equal representation in the Upper House, as is the case in the United States and some other federations. The Press in the Punjab, with few exceptions, joined in a chorus of protest against the second draft. *Nawa-i-Waqt*, a leading Lahore daily, in its editorial of 28 December 1952, opposed the parity formula on the ground that it was likely to result in the permanent domination of one province (East Bengal) over all other provinces of Pakistan. A symposium was held in Lahore on 11 January 1953, under the auspices of the Local Government Institute. The speaker of the Punjab Legislative Assembly, the provincial ministers, and other leaders took part in it. The constitutional draft was subjected to adverse criticism, particularly the parity formula. It was pointed out that parity was an injustice in that East Pakistan was one province while West Pakistan had nine different units.[67]

The critics seemed to overlook the fact that East Pakistan had a larger population than the total of nine units of West Pakistan put together. The composition and lesser powers of the Upper House were also attacked. The Punjab leaders demanded representation in the Lower House to be on the basis of population and in the Upper House to be on the basis of equality of the units, and for the two Houses to have equal powers. It may be recalled here that these provisions of the first draft had been attacked in East Bengal, and the Constitution-framers had to modify those proposals to meet their demands. Although the new proposals were opposed in the Punjab, reaction to the second report was not unfavourable in the smaller units of West Pakistan. For instance, at a meeting held in Peshawar on 30 December 1952, the Chief Minister of the NWFP and other leaders expressed a favourable opinion on the second draft.[68] The opposition to the second report in the Punjab forced the Constituent Assembly to postpone its deliberations for an indefinite period. The country seemed to face a constitutional deadlock of great magnitude. National unity was threatened. For some time it appeared that no compromise was possible which would be acceptable to the two wings of Pakistan.

An analysis of the second draft and the main objections to it reveal that while some of the objections, as in the case of the first draft, were inspired by a deliberate intention to create a constitutional deadlock, there were obvious defects in the new proposals. They may be summarized as follows:

1. The draft did not acknowledge in a democratic way the fact that East Bengal had a majority of the total population of the country.
2. It did not pay due respect to the fact that West Pakistan had the major part of the country's territory.
3. By giving to the Upper House a composition identical to that of the Lower House, it made the former a weak replica of the House of the People and reduced its utility.
4. The lack of a constitutional provision in case the two Houses were unable to resolve a conflict in joint session.[69]

Anti-Ahmediya Movement, Martial Law, and Dismissal of Nazimuddin's Government

In the provincial elections held in Punjab in 1951, the Muslim League led by Mian Mumtaz Daultana emerged victorious. With support from Jamiat-i-Ulema-i-Islam, the Ahrars and, above all, with the help of the government machinery, it won 153 seats which later increased to 166. Only 52 per cent of the total votes were cast.[70] To everyone's amazement, and as an indication that the opposition's charges of election fraud were not baseless, the League somehow managed to win fifteen of the twenty-three urban seats.[71] Daultana was elected unopposed as Chief Minister and the leader of the League's parliamentary party. The Punjab soon faced serious food shortages, partly created by landlords who had turned hostile due to the modest reforms made by the Daultana government in favour of agricultural tenants. By mid-1952, speculation and hoarding had played havoc with the provincial distribution machinery. The provincial government decided to requisition wheat but to no avail since the biggest hoarders were almost without fail the political bigwigs of the Muslim League.

Shortage of food was not the only crisis looming on the horizon. Fringe groups, religious or lay, had been waiting for an opportune moment to swing into action. Soaring grain prices and, in some areas, the complete absence of wheat, together with longer standing grievances, presented a perfect scenario. It was the Ahrars who took the lead because they were the most adept of the religious opportunists at creating mischief and because their electoral deal with the Daultana ministry provided a cover to their activities, however dangerous and reprehensible. Whatever else they may have been, the Ahrars were not innovators. Short of ideas on how to go about acquiring political prominence, they stuck to themes which had a proven appeal to the religious conservatism of the people. In a campaign that was to lay the foundations of religious intolerance in Pakistan, the Ahrars reverted to their favourite target—reviling the Ahmediya community and demanding that they be declared a minority.[72]

The Ahmedis (whom their opponents also refer to as Mirzais or Qadianis) were a close-knit community who believed that Mirza Ghulam Ahmad (1835–1908) was a prophet or *nabi*, though subservient to Prophet Muhammad (PBUH). This belief was regarded as blasphemous by the Muslims for having infringed upon the cardinal principle of Islam regarding the finality of the prophethood of Hazrat Muhammad

(PBUH). A group of Mirza Ghulam Ahmad's followers based in Lahore called the Lahori Party did not subscribe to the claim of his prophethood. Nevertheless, they were targets of anti-Ahmediya sentiments. These sentiments, where they existed, had material and political rather than purely religious moorings. The Ahmedis, by and large, were better off than the vast majority of the faithful; they held prominent positions in government service and also in the professions. The Foreign Minister, Zafarullah Khan, was the most influential member of the sect and, naturally, the main target of the Ahrar onslaught.

Anyone with the ability to think could see that the Ahrars were merely seeking to restore a public image marred by their outspoken opposition to the Pakistan demand. They attracted simple minded people by alleging, in the Punjab, that Kashmir had been denied to Pakistan because Chaudhry Zafarullah Khan, like many other Ahmedies, was in league with the British. This allegation was advanced by some other interested quarters who wanted the removal of Chaudhry Zafarullah Khan as Foreign Minister of Pakistan. For many others, the anti-Ahmediya movement provided an opportunity to have other Ahmedis holding key positions removed from the positions held by them at the centre as well as in the provinces.

With a mixture of ambivalence and active connivance with the educated section of society, the field was left wide open for an agitation that was to result in the downfall of not one but two governments. By the summer of 1952, when the food shortage was beginning to be felt, illiterate or at best half-educated audiences throughout the province were held spellbound by the fiery and flawless oratory of Ahrar leaders like Ata Ullah Shah Bokhari, Qazi Ehsan Ahmed Shujabadi, Mohammad Ali Jullunduri, and Sahibzada Faiz-ul-Hasan. The gist of the speeches was more or less the same. Their fulmination left the Ahmedis in a virtual state of siege, their properties were burned and looted, excited crowds murdered members of the sect, and mock funerals of Zafarullah topped the list of local entertainments. No decisive steps were taken to quash the Ahrar menace, despite a clear realization on the part of top officials in the Punjab police that the agitation with its criminal overtones was a potential forerunner to anarchy. The blame rests squarely with the Punjab ministry, in the first instance, and on the central government in the final analysis.[73]

In his most enigmatic political phase ever, Daultana not only protected but encouraged a movement that cut through the very fabric of his progressive views. The reasons for this intriguing volte-face are complex and unedifying. The Ahrar agitation was seen by Daultana as an opportunity to browbeat the central government into submitting to the Punjab's economic and, by late 1952, constitutional demands. If successful, Daultana could hope to replace Nazimuddin or Zafarullah at the centre, thus fortifying his position within the province. These Machiavellian calculations were implicit in the dramatic policy turns taken by the Punjab Chief Minister against the advice of his principal henchmen in the provincial administration. In July 1952, Daultana finally gave in to pressure from Qurban Ali Khan, the Inspector-General of the Punjab police, to impose section 144 in certain districts in the province. While this prevented the Ahrars from holding meetings, it also encouraged them to close ranks with other religious and like-minded groups. On 13 July, an All-Parties Muslim

Convention in Lahore endorsed Ahrar demands. Far from being unsettled by these developments, Daultana saw them as evidence of support for his pro-Ahrar policy. So on 21 July, upon receiving limp assurances from Ahrar leaders disavowing violence, Daultana lifted section 144, prefacing it with a public statement that since the finality of prophethood was an article of faith for all Muslims the issue of declaring Ahmedis a minority should be taken up by the Constituent Assembly. Within less than a week the council of the Punjab Muslim League had adopted a resolution by a vote of 264 against eight in support of the anti-Ahmediya agitation. In what is proof of Daultana's hand in the phrasing of the resolution, the final decision was left to the 'mature judgement of the leadership of the Pakistan Muslim League and the Constituent Assembly'.[74]

Thus Ahrars, who had opposed the creation of Pakistan, became the vanguard of the anti-Ahmediya movement that was joined by Jamaat-i-Islami, the Jamiatul Ulema-i-Pakistan, and Jamiat-i-Ulema-i-Islam. Somehow, the situation favoured various politicians for reasons of their own. For the religious groups, this was an opportunity to force the central government to bend to their demands for an 'Islamic Constitution'; for Daultana and his associates, a thinly disguised ploy to detract attention from a worsening food situation, not to mention an excuse to extract a more acceptable constitutional deal for the Punjab; and for Nazimuddin and his inner coterie, a highly dangerous tactic to muffle all opposition by appearing to come down on the side of religion.[75]

The anti-Ahmediya agitation and Nazimuddin's vacillating role created a clear gulf between him and other politicians on one hand, and senior civil and military officials, on the other. Nazimuddin tried to fall back on the religious appeal in an effort to confront colossal problems facing his government. He was mistaken in this because the politicians using Islam for their political ends did not have wide support amongst the masses. But he had thrown in his lot with them. He prevailed upon the Basic Principles Committee to welcome in its midst a team of *ulema*, the Talimaat Islam board, to advise and guide on religious matters. He even toyed with the idea of giving in to the demands of the anti-Ahmediya movement, a line of thinking which invited a strong rebuke from the Governor-General who was indignant about the Prime Minister's reluctance to openly support Zafarullah and issue a public condemnation of the attacks on his person and community.[76]

The bureaucratic-military combine was averse to the introduction of a retrograde section of society into the power structure. The introduction of the *ulemas* into the Basic Principles Committee as advisers pleased no one. While there were charges of surrender to *mullahism* and the religious bodies were unhappy at being restricted to the position of advisers, insisting on a bigger slice of the pie. This situation provided an ideal opportunity for Washington to make inroads into the civil and military bureaucracy of Pakistan in order to lure Pakistan to join the Middle Eastern Defence Pact. This move was met with immediate favour by the military and civil bureaucracy. Having contributed in no uncertain terms to the central government's lack of credibility in American eyes, the bureaucratic-military axis had now to consider ways of restoring their confidence in the Pakistan government. In early March 1953, the eruption of anti-Ahmediya riots in the Punjab provided an opening. On 6 March, after failing to get sanction from Karachi, General Azam, the Area Commander, had 'taken over [apparently] on his own', imposing martial law in Lahore and ensuring the dismissal of Daultana's ministry. General Ayub, Commander-in-Chief of the Pakistan the Army, proved that the army would not let politicians or religious idealogues lead the country to anarchy. The message to Washington was more than implicit; the army was Pakistan's main, perhaps the only, hope. It had to be strengthened. Left to unruly politicians, Pakistan could crumble.[77]

The central government's budget created further complications. Because of stringent financial conditions austerity measures were adopted, including the slashing down of the defence budget by one-third. Military leaders did not like that and, in fact, demanded supplementary appropriation for defence following the imposition of martial law in Lahore. The unpopularity of the budget gave the bureaucratic-military axis the opening they had been searching for. An emergency food conference was called in Karachi to discuss the worsening situation in the country. In the presence of an uncharacteristically taciturn Governor-General, senior civil servants joined the Commander-in-Chief in levelling abuses at the Prime Minister.

Sensing his end, Nazimuddin considered requesting London for the Governor-General's recall. Apart from being unwell, Ghulam Muhammad was patently in league with the bureaucrats and the Commander-in-Chief. The Prime Minister still enjoyed the confidence of parliament and could conceivably turn the tables on his enemies. But Nazimuddin was not an intriguer. On 17 April 1953, he was summoned by the Governor-General along with his Cabinet and ordered to resign. Nazimuddin declined and had to be dismissed. Crestfallen by such a poor reward for his services, Nazimuddin tried appealing to Buckingham Palace only to discover that the overseas telegraph service was out of operation. Even the British High Commissioner thought it politic not to transmit the Prime Minister's telegram to the Queen. The Governor-General had acted under Section 10 of the adapted Government of India Act. Despite the constitutional gloss, he had, in fact, carried out a bureaucratic-military coup.[78]

The Munir Report, 1954

After the disturbances of 1953 had subsided and martial law withdrawn, a special Act was passed constituting a Court of Inquiry to investigate the causes of disturbances, the circumstances leading to the imposition of martial law, and the adequacy or otherwise of the measures taken to suppress the disturbances. It was to be a public inquiry and Justice Muhammad Munir, Chief Justice of the Lahore High Court at that time, was nominated as the President of the Committee and Justice Kayani as its member. The inquiry commenced on 1 May 1953 and the report was presented to the Government on 10 April 1954. The record of the inquiry was colossal—it consisted of 1600 pages of written statements, 2600 pages of evidence, 339 formally proved documents, numerous letters, some of which exceeded a 100 pages, and a host of books, pamphlets, journals, and newspapers. The report itself covers 387 closely printed pages. In the course of the inquiry, almost every conceivable subject was touched upon and the issues underlying the inquiry, which frequently emerged in all their directness and with all their implications, were very deep and fundamental to the new state of Pakistan.[79]

The committee examined the viewpoints of all leading *ulemas* in the country at that time. They included Maulana Abul Hasnat Sayyed; Muhammad Ahmad Qadri, President Jamiat-i-Ulema-i-Islam, West Pakistan; Maulana Abul Ala Maudoodi, founder and *Amir* of Jamaat-i-Islami, Pakistan; Mufti Mohammad Idris, Jamia Ashrafia Lahore and Member, Jamiatul Ulema-i-Pakistan; Maulana Daud Ghaznavi, President Jamiat-i-Ahl-i-Hadith, Maghrabi Pakistan; Maulana Abdul Haleem Qasimi, Jamiat-i-Ulema-i-Islam Punjab, and Ibrahim Ali Chishti. All the *ulema* were unanimous in their belief that the Ahmedis were *kafirs* (disbelievers) and anyone becoming an Ahmedi was liable to the death penalty because apostasy in an Islamic state was punishable by death.[80]

The committee also found from the interviews with leaders of various sects and schools of Islam that they could not stand one another and called each other *kafirs* as well. According to the Barelvi *ulema*, Deobandis and Wahabis were outside the pale of Islam and well liable to the death penalty if they fell within the definition of *murtad*, namely, if they had changed and not inherited their religious views. According to a *fatwa* of the Deobandis, all Asna Ashari Shias were *kafirs* and *murtad* for not believing in the *sahabiyyat* of Hazrat Siddiq-i-Akbar and *qazif* (deniers of the status) of Hazrat Aisha Siddiqa.[81]

The authors of the Report conclude:

'The net result of all this is that neither Shia nor Sunnis nor Deobandis nor Ahl-i-Hadith nor Barelvis are Muslims and any change from one view to the other must be accomplished in an Islamic state with the penalty of death if the government of the state is in the hands of the party which considers the other party to be *kafirs*. And it does not require much imagination to judge of the consequences of this doctrine when it is remembered that no two *ulema* have agreed before us as to the definition of a Muslim'.[82]

'Keeping in view the several definitions of a Muslim given by the *ulema*, need we make any comment except that no two learned divines are agreed on this fundamental. If we attempt our own definition as each learned divine has done and that definition differs from that given by all others, we unanimously go out of the fold of Islam. And if we adopt the definition given by any one of the *ulema*, we remain Muslims according to the view of that *alim* but *kafirs* according to the definition of every one else'.[83]

The Report ends with the following observations:

'And it is our deep conviction that if the Ahrar (the leading party) had been treated as a pure question of law and order, without any political considerations, one District Magistrate and one Superintendent of Police could have dealt with them. Consequently, we are prompted by something that they call a human conscience to inquire whether in our present state of political development, the administrative problems of law and order cannot be divorced from a democratic bed-fellow called a ministerial government which is so remorselessly haunted by political nightmares. But if democracy means the subordination of law and order to political ends—then Allah knoweth best and we end our report'.

The Muhammad Ali Formula

Compromise Formula on Federal Legislature

It has been discussed above that the second draft of the Basic Principles Committee, which was presented by Prime Minister Nazimuddin in 1952, came under severe criticism, especially from the Punjab. On the dismissal of Nazimuddin's government, Muhammad Ali Bogra was appointed Prime Minister who regarded it as one of his principal tasks to overcome the constitutional deadlock.

He was soon successful in achieving a compromise on the issue of representation between East and West Pakistan in the federal legislature. His formula, known as the 'Muhammad Ali Formula', was presented to the Constituent Assembly on 7 October 1953 and adopted by it on 6 October 1954.

The 'Muhammad Ali Formula' was as follows:

i. The federal legislature should be composed of two Houses—the House of Units and the House of the People.

The total strength of the House of Units would be fifty, to be equally divided among the five units which were constituted in the following manner:[84]

A. East Bengal;
B. Punjab;
C. North-West Frontier Province, Frontier States, and the tribal area;
D. Sindh and Khairpur.
E. Balochistan, Balochistan State Union, Capital of the Federation (Karachi) and the State of Bahawalpur.

The distribution of seats among the following 'Units' which consisted of more than one province or state was to be as under:

1.	North-West Frontier Province including Frontier States and the Tribal Area:	10
2.	Sindh and Khairpur.	10
3.	Balochistan including Balochistan States Union	3
4.	Capital of Federation (Karạchi)	3
5.	State of Bahawalpur.	4

The House of Units would be elected indirectly by the legislatures of the units, and where there was no legislature, the system of election was to be determined by an act of the federal legislature.

Apart from these seats, two additional seats were reserved for women.[85]

ii. The House of the People was to have a strength of three hundred to be divided among the five units as follows:[86]

A.	East Bengal	165
B.	Punjab	75
C1	North-West Frontier Province	13
C2	Frontier States and Tribal Areas	11
D1	Sindh	19
D2	State of Khairpur	1
E1	Balochistan	3
E2	Balochistan States Union	2
E3	Capital of Federation	4
E4	Bahawalpur State	7

iii. Equal powers were to be extended to both Houses. There was provision for a joint session of the two Houses for the election of the head of the state and for disposal of votes of confidence. Decisions were to be made by a simple majority, provided, however, that such a majority included at least 30 per cent of the members from each zone (East and West Pakistan).

iv. In case of a difference of opinion between the two Houses, a joint session of the two Houses would be called and the measure might then be passed by a majority vote, provided that the majority included thirty per cent of the members from each zone. If the difference could not be solved, the formula originally provided that the head of the state could dissolve the legislature but this clause was amended when the formula was adopted by the Constituent Assembly, seemingly producing a serious flaw in the formula. Similarly, the provision that the head of the state would be elected from a zone different from that to which the Prime Minister would belong was also amended, it being obvious that this provision might prove a serious handicap in the working of the Constitution. The formula, however, brought some improvement compared to the first and second drafts of the Basic Principles Committee; while it maintained the principle of parity between East and West Pakistan, it made a substantial departure from the parity clause of the second draft. The distribution of seats in the Upper House was made in accordance with the geographical facts of the country. As West Pakistan had the major part of the country's territory, it was given a clear majority in the House of Units. In the Lower House, East Pakistan, with the majority of the country's population, got a clear majority of seats in accordance with the democratic principle.

The distribution of seats in the two Houses was made in such a way as to ensure parity between East and West Pakistan. Each zone got 175 seats in the joint session of the two Houses and it was at the joint session that the more controversial issues were likely to be decided. By providing for a minimum vote of thirty per cent for each zone at the joint session, the formula sought to provide not only parity but the interdependence of the two. This provision may have proved a great hindrance in the smooth working of the Constitution, but it was a practical necessity to remove the fear of domination by either of the two zones. As explained by Muhammad Ali, no government could be formed or continue in office at the centre unless it had at least thirty per cent of members from each zone and no controversial measure could be passed unless it had at least 30 per cent of members present and voting from each zone.[87]

Critics of the formula, pointed out that it made a concession to provincial feelings by recognizing them in the Constitution instead of trying to eradicate them. The grant of equal powers to the Upper House which was to be elected indirectly was also regarded by the critics as 'undemocratic'. While the formula could be subjected to criticism, it can hardly be denied that it was a bold and sincere attempt to solve the constitutional deadlock. There was great enthusiasm when the formula was first published and it seemed to gather wide support as compared to the first and second drafts. But the enthusiasm soon died down and constitutional differences once again came to the surface. It is difficult to say wheather the new difficulties were due to an inherent defect in the formula. They seem rather to have originated in deliberate attempts by a group of politicians to perpetuate the deadlock to further their own selfish objectives.

An analysis of the problem of representation which was faced by constitution-makers in Pakistan reveals the feelings of mutual distrust, fear, and suspicion between the people of East and West Pakistan. This feeling had its origin in a number of factors, political, economic, cultural, linguistic, psychological, and others. The Muslims of undivided India were united in a unique way under the leadership of Muhammad Ali Jinnah and fought for Pakistan without any sense of distinction as Bengalis, Punjabis, Sindhis, and so on. But soon after the establishment of Pakistan, provincial and regional feelings began to manifest themselves. East Pakistanis felt that they did not have a fair and adequate share in the central government and administration. They felt that they had been neglected and were dominated by the West wing. This gave birth to the feelings of regionalism in East Pakistan, while provincialism was making a headway in West Pakistan. As a consequence, political issues often came to be judged on the basis of provincial interests. National unity and national feelings were considerably damaged and therein lay the root cause of the difficulty in finding a basis for representation in the legislature under the future Constitution. Each unit feared the domination of the other and, consequently, the framers of the Constitution had to evolve the formula of a government based on regional parity. The difficulties involved in such an arrangement were regarded as a painful necessity.[88]

Controversy over Provincial Autonomy and Strong Centre

The second issue in the controversy between East and West Pakistan was regarding the distribution of powers between the federal and the provincial governments. This problem was not peculiar to Pakistan; it is faced when framing any federal Constitution. An indispensable quality of the federal state lies in a distribution of powers between the federal authority and the federating units. A federal Constitution attempts to reconcile the claims of regional sovereignty and state sovereignty.

Geography and history alike demanded that Pakistan should have a federal government. While there was general agreement over this, conflicts developed, later between those who wanted maximum autonomy for the provinces with a weak centre and those who favoured a strong central government with provinces enjoying limited autonomy. The makers of the Constitution were at great pains to steer a course midway between these two conflicting aims. The problem was further complicated by the lack of understanding and mutual distrust between the people of the two wings. Disgruntled politicians in both wings wanted not only provincial autonomy but also a weak centre. The school demanding greater authority for the provinces claimed that in view of the geographical facts prevailing in Pakistan, the powers of the centre should be strictly enumerated and residuary powers should be vested in the provinces.[89]

It is rather strange that demands for maximum autonomy came first from the largest unit, namely East Pakistan, which should not have had any fear of domination. Unfortunately, this fear struck roots in East Pakistan. The people of that region felt they were neglected by the central government, and did not have a reasonable, fair, and adequate share in the central government and administration. They feared an increase in the power of the centre would mean a corresponding decrease in their power and influence. The national convention which was held in Dhaka on 4 and 5 November 1950, demanded that only three subjects namely, defence, foreign affairs, and currency, should be given to the centre and the rest should be vested in the provinces.[90] This demand for maximum autonomy in East Pakistan gained further impetus from a new political formation, the United Front, which secured an overwhelming victory in the provincial election in March 1954. There was popular opinion in favour of giving more powers to East Pakistan's provincial government because it had been felt over seven years that the province could best be administered in by the legislature in Dhaka rather than by the central legislature in Karachi.[91]

The school advocating greater authority for the centre used similar arguments in support of a strong national government. A.K. Brohi, former Minister for Parliamentary Affairs in Pakistan, said that if there had been geographical contiguity between East and West Pakistan, then the principles of decentralization of power might have been the basis of the Pakistan Constitution, but in order to overcome this mutual difficulty of the distance that separates the two wings, there was no alternative but to provide for a strong central government.[92]

The demand for a strong national government was supported by a majority of members of the first Constituent Assembly. It was felt that a such a government was necessary to fight provincialism which had so nearly succeeded in tearing the nation apart. They held that the only guarantee for a strong Pakistan was in a strong central government, but that in framing a Constitution they could not altogether ignore the demands for maximum provincial autonomy and decentralization.

After prolonged discussions, the Constituent Assembly arrived at a compromise relating to the distribution of powers that was somewhat different from two generally accepted methods of the distribution of powers in a federal state. The powers might be distributed in one of two ways: either the Constitution might provide what powers the federal authority could have and leave the remainder to the federating units (as in the USA) or it might state what powers the federating units could possess and leave the remainder to the federal authority (as in Canada). Neither of these two methods was acceptable in Pakistan. A third course was adopted, devised by the British experts when they distributed powers in the federal Constitution for undivided India under the Government of India Act, 1935. During the course of discussion which ultimately led to the promulgation of the Government of India Act of 1935, Muslims had demanded more powers for the provinces because in some provinces at least there was a preponderant Muslim majority where they felt that they would be able to capture power. The Hindus, on the other hand, demanded greater concentration of power in the Indian legislature. British constitutional experts devised a compromise by submitting two lists subjects over which the federation and the provinces respectively would have exclusive legislative jurisdiction and to enumerate in a third list the subjects on enumerating which they would have concurrent jurisdiction. Residual powers were vested neither in the centre nor in the provinces. The Governor-General, acting at his discretion, was empowered to allocate to the central authority or to the provinces, as he might see fit, the right to legislate on such subjects.[93]

The framers of the Pakistan Constitution found that the method devised by the British could be of great use in finding a compromise between those who demanded a strong centre and their opponents. In the final draft of 1954, they followed the method of preparing three lists of subjects, federal, provincial, and concurrent. The central government was given wide powers to manage defence, foreign affairs, currency and banking, communications, foreign commerce, and scores of other subjects. In all, there were sixty-six items in the federal list. The provincial list included forty-eight items comprising such matters as law and order, public health, education, agriculture, trade and commerce, and other subjects of local interest. The concurrent list was the smallest of the three lists and included relief and rehabilitation of refugees, broadcasting and television, criminal law, civil procedure, newspapers, welfare of labour, and others.[94] Residuary power, following the model of the 1935 Act, was vested in the head of the state who, in consultation with the provincial governments, might direct any specified subjects not mentioned in any of the lists to be classified as being a part of either the federal, the provincial, or the concurrent list. The federal legislature was given power to make laws for the whole or for any part of Pakistan for implementing any treaty, agreement, or convention with any other country or countries, or any decision made at an international conference, or by other international association or body (Section 151 of the proposed Constitution). If it should appear to the legislature or legislatures of one or more units to be desirable that any of the matters, with respect to which the federal legislature had no power to make laws for the unit or units, should be regulated in such unit or units by the federal legislature by law, and if resolution to that effect were passed by the unit legislature, the federal legislature could pass laws for regulating such matters. Similar provision could be found in the Government of India Act, 1935.

An analysis of the distribution of powers as adopted by the first Constituent Assembly shows that they were influenced by the need for a strong national government at the centre. While making concessions to natural and geographical factors in Pakistan, they made the central government sufficiently strong to meet any eventuality. With regard to subjects in the concurrent list, the predominance of federal legislation was provided for in case of conflict between the federal and provincial authorities. The superiority of the central government in the proposed Constitution as adopted by the first Constituent Assembly was equally ensured in the administrative sphere.

The Issue of National Language

The third issue in the controversy between East and West Pakistan was that of language. Pakistan is a multi-lingual state. There was a fundamental difference between East and West Pakistan regarding language. Bengali was spoken in the East, in the West there were a number of languages such as Punjabi, Sindhi, Pashto, and Balochi. Urdu was not the mother tongue in any area of West Pakistan but it was accepted as the common language of the whole region. The controversy was whether Pakistan should have a single state language, Urdu, or two state languages, Urdu and Bengali.

Among the cultural characteristics of nationality, language is and always has been, pre-eminent. The framers of the Constitution could see the importance of the issue and engaged themselves for months in working at an acceptable solution, but the task proved to be complex and difficult. In May 1954 they presented the following formula which was accepted by the Constituent Assembly:

1. The official languages of the Pakistan Republic should be Urdu and Bengali and such other languages as might be declared to be such by the head of the state on the recommendation of the provincial legislatures concerned;
2. Members of Parliament should have the right to speak in Urdu and Bengali in addition to English;
3. Notwithstanding anything in the above Article, for a period of twenty years from the commencement of the Constitution, the English language should continue to be used for all official purposes of the Republic for which it was being used immediately before such commencement;
4. For examinations of the central services, all provincial languages should be placed on an equal footing;
5. Provision should be made to teach Arabic, Urdu, and Bengali in secondary schools to enable students to study one or two of these in addition to the language used as the medium of instruction;

6. The state should take all measures for the development and growth of a common national language;
7. A commission should be appointed ten years after the commencement of the Constitution to make recommendations regarding the replacement of English; and
8. Notwithstanding anything in the foregoing Articles, the federal legislature might by law provide for the use, after the expiry of the period of twenty years from the commencement of the Constitution, of the English language for such purposes as might be specified in the law.[95]

It was clear from the day of its adoption that the formula could satisfy no one. While according equality of status to Urdu and Bengali as official languages and providing that the state should take all measures necessary for the development and growth of a common national language, it gave no indication what the common language should be. In the meantime, it was provided that English would continue to be used as the official language of the state for a period of twenty years. The Prime Minister, Muhammad Ali, explained that the formula attempted to reconcile the demands of all sections of the people. It tried to accede to the demand of the Bengalis and, at the same time, sought to maintain linguistic unity. In fact, the framers of the Constitution obviously wanted to postpone the issue for twenty years when they expected a better environment for a solution to the problem.

From the theoretical point of view, a multi-lingual state is not desirable as it raises many problems. But nations are made up of human beings whose deep feelings on questions of language are vitally important. No doubt, the adoption of one state language, if it were possible, would have been preferable from the standpoint of national unity, but it would have been unrealistic and unwise to ignore the demand of the people of East Bengal. The East Pakistanis insisted on Bengali as one of the state languages and to impose uniformity of language under such circumstances might have been detrimental to the national unity for which Jinnah had wanted one state language. The adoption of Bengali would have lead to stronger ties and better understanding between the peoples of the two wings. The multi-lingual solution, it would seem, was a pragmatic approach in the existing circumstances.[96]

Other Provisions

With the modifications made by the compromise formulae regarding the representation of provinces in the federal legislature, the allocation of subjects to the centre and the provinces, and the acceptance of national languages; other provisions of the second draft of the Constitution under the report of the Basic Principles Committee of 1952 were, by and large, retained in the report of the Basic Principles Committee as adopted by the Constituent Assembly on the 6 October 1954.

Elections in East Pakistan

Before the adoption of the draft Constitution on the report of Basic Principles Committee, provincial elections were held in East Bengal from 8 to 11 March 1954 resulting in an overwhelming victory for the United Front (Jugto Front), an alliance of parties opposed to the ruling Muslim League.

Out of 309 seats, the United Front (consisting of three Muslim parties—the Awami Muslim League, the Krishak Sramik Party and the Nizam-i-Islam) gained 2323 seats; the Muslim League, 10; Independents, 3; Khilafat-e-Rabani, 1; and minorities, 72.

The main items in the United Front's programme were as follows:

1. Recognition of Bengali as an official language at par with Urdu.
2. Rejection of the draft Constitution, the dissolution of the Constituent Assembly, and its replacement by a directly elected body.
3. Complete autonomy for East Pakistan in all matters except defence, foreign policy, and currency, which would be reserved for the central legislature.
4. Complete freedom from the centre with regard to export of jute.
5. Consultation between the centre and East Pakistan on the allocation of foreign exchange for imports.
6. Abolition of the Indo-Pakistani passport and visa system and of existing restrictions on trade between East and West Bengal. Devaluation of the Pakistani rupee.[97]

About 65 per cent of the electorate went to the polls, in which all five members of the outgoing Muslim League ministry lost their seats.

The defeat of the Muslim League in East Bengal which had 56 per cent of the total population of Pakistan, led to demands for the resignation of the central government and the dissolution of the Constituent Assembly as unrepresentative. These demands, were rejected by Muhammad Ali who stated: 'The task of framing the Constitution was not entrusted to the Muslim League as such, but to all members, Muslim or non-Muslim, specifically chosen for this purpose. There is no government party and no opposition in the Constituent Assembly'. For members from a particular province to resign merely because their party had gone out of office in that province would, he argued, create an unworkable precedent. Elections to one or other of the provincial legislatures would be held practically every year, and if the character of the central government changed whenever a new party came to power in one of the provinces, there would be no stability or continuity.

Following the Prime Minister's statement, the Working Committee of the Muslim League ordered its members from East Bengal in the Constituent Assembly not to resign their seats.

On 25 March 1954, Fazlul Haq (the leader of the Krishak Sramik Party), who had previously stated that he would make a point of preserving the best possible relations with Karachi provided that satisfaction was given on the issues of language, the Constitution, and provincial autonomy, announced that he was called upon to form a new government in East Bengal.[98]

Amending Acts of 1954

The Constituent Assembly, in the same session in which the Report of Basic Principles Committee was adopted, passed two important Bills. On the 20 of September 1954 it repealed the Public and Representative Offices (Disqualification) Act of 1949.[99] The Act, popularly known as 'PRODA', was passed while Liaquat Ali Khan was the Prime Minister and had been widely welcomed in the country as an effective and proper remedy against abuses of maladministration and corruption in public life. By this Act, complaints could be made to the Governor-General or to the Governors of provinces who, if satisfied with the substance of the allegations made, could order an inquiry to be conducted by judges of the High Court. If a person was found guilty, punishment would take the form of suspension of the right of holding public office for a specified number of years. The Act was applied on several occasions against ministers, including provincial Chief Ministers, and, in several cases, the inquiry went against ministers. Its hasty repeal by the first Constituent Assembly was unfortunate and considerably lowered the prestige of the Assembly in the estimation of the people. There was a suggestion in some quarters that the repeal had been effected in order to favour some members of the Constituent Assembly.

The second enactment was the amendment of sections 9, 10, 10A, and 10B of the Government of India Act, 1935, as adapted for Pakistan.[100] The net result of that amendment was to divest the Governor-General of his powers to dismiss his ministers who would no longer hold office during his pleasure but would instead be individually and collectively responsible to the federal legislature. Obviously, the Constituent Assembly did this to prevent the repetition of acts such as the dismissal of the Nazimuddin Cabinet in April 1953. It could be described as an important step towards the growth of parliamentary democracy in Pakistan, but the amendment was made in such haste that it could be termed a 'constitutional coup'.

Dissolution of the Constituent Assembly and Proclamation of a State of Emergency

With the constitutional issues at last settled and the drafting entrusted to experts working under a deadline of 1 January 1955, the Constituent Assembly was adjourned *sine die*. The Governor-General (Ghulam Muhammad), stung by the Assembly's action in curtailing his powers, struck back. On 24 October 1954, he dissolved the Constituent Assembly and announced an end to what he described as 'parliamentary bickering'.[101] He issued the following proclamation:

> The Governor-General having considered the political crisis with which the country is faced, has with deep regret come to the conclusion that the constitutional machinery has broken down. He therefore has decided to declare a state of emergency throughout Pakistan. The Constituent Assembly as at present constituted has lost the confidence of the people and can no longer function.

> The ultimate authority vests in the people who will decide all issues including constitutional issues through their representatives to be elected afresh. Elections will be held as early as possible. Until such time as elections are held, the administration of the country will be carried on by a reconstituted Cabinet. He has called upon the Prime Minister to reform the Cabinet with a view to giving the country a vigorous and stable administration. The invitation has been accepted.
>
> The security and stability of the country are of paramount importance. All personal, sectional and provincial interests must be subordinated to the supreme national interest.[102]

The significant thing in the proclamation was that it did not say in clear and specific terms that the Constituent Assembly was dissolved. It only said that the Constituent Assembly had 'lost the confidence of the people and can no longer function'. Another important omission was that it nowhere specified any provisions or sections of the Independence Act or Government of India Act, 1935 under which the proclamation was issued. Normally, whenever any order or proclamation is made the provision of law under which the power is exercised is indicated. The proclamation was the subject of lengthy legal disputes which will be discussed in the next chapter.

The two hasty enactments by the Constituent Assembly led to a new series of political manoeuvres and intrigue such as had charcterized Pakistani politics since the death of Jinnah and Liaquat. Compromises and formulas which had been widely proclaimed as the best contrivable solutions to certain problems were now being assailed. The dissolution of the Constituent Assembly threw the country into chaos and confusion by reviving old rivalries and reopening old controversies. It is true that the first Constituent Assembly had made undue delay in framing the Constitution. It is equally true that the East Pakistan elections of 1954 had demonstrated that it had lost the confidence of the people to a great extent, yet it is difficult to justify the Governor-General's action in abruptly dismissing the Constituent Assembly when it was about to finish its work. If it had been dissolved immediately after the election in East Pakistan, there might have been some justification but its dissolution after an attempt to curb the undemocratic and arbitrary powers of the Governor-General clearly indicates that the real motive of the Governor-General in dissolving the House was personal and were not based on any democratic principles or traditions. His subsequent attempt to give the country a Constitution through the decrees rather than by Constituent Assembly also substantiates the view that his motivation was purely personal.

Ghulam Muhammad instructed Muhammad Ali Bogra, the Prime Minister, to form a Cabinet without the benefit of parliament. Hastely, a Cabinet was put together which included Major-General Iskandar Mirza, Dr Khan Sahib, and General Muhammad Ayub Khan, who was the Commander-in-Chief of the Pakistan Army. This was the beginning of the army taking over civilian responsibilities as a Cabinet member, this time, as the Minister for Defence. This was also the beginning of the end of the supremacy of civilian over military power.

General Ayub graphically paints the picture of the happenings that immediately followed the proclamation of the Governor-General in the following words:[103]

Ghulam Muhammad was not the kind of man to take things lying down. Whatever else he might have lacked he certainly did not lack courage. He could fight anybody and stand up to anyone; the man was absolutely fearless. He was a sick man at that time and his speech was quite unintelligible. He must have said to himself, 'All right, if this is how you have treated me, I shall pay you back in the same coin.'

I went to the United States soon after this, with Prime Minister Muhammad Ali Bogra, Sir Zafarullah Khan, and Chaudhri Muhammad Ali. The Prime Minister got a message from the Governor-General to return home at once. I sensed trouble and realized that the old man was on the war-path and was going to dismiss him. The Prime Minister was also worried and cancelled his visit to Canada. We decided to return as quickly as possible. When we reached London we found that there was no eastbound flight that day, so we had to charter a plane to get back to Karachi.

At London Airport, there was a telephone call for me from the Governor-General. I could not understand what he was saying and gave the telephone to Iskander Mirza. All we could make out was that he wanted me to get back to Pakistan at once; he was not interested in the others. The Prime Minister was worried about what might happen to him on his return. It was with great difficulty that I persuaded him to accompany us back home. He kept asking me, 'Can you guarantee that I will not be put under arrest when I get back?' I could give him no guarantee but I assured him that such a thing could not possibly happen. He retorted, 'And supposing you are arrested too?' I replied, 'That will be fine. You will be in good company.'

On the way, I told Iskander Mirza and Chaudhri Muhammad Ali that it would be extremely unwise if the Prime Minister was taken to the Governor-General immediately on our arrival in Karachi; such a confrontation could lead to an ugly situation. The decision was that some of us should go to the Governor-General's house and persuade the old man to act with reason and come to some understanding with the Prime Minister. The Prime Minister should go to his own house and wait for a signal from us. Muhammad Ali Bogra put up a brave front but, I think, inwardly he was quite frightened. He had sent a message from London that he should be provided with army protection on arrival. I was deeply perturbed myself. Knowing the Governor-General's temperament, I was worried that he might do something desperate. The prestige of the country was involved and if some extreme measure was taken, it would bring her into disrepute. The only sensible course was to bring about a rapprochement between the Governor-General and the Prime Minister. Iskander Mirza, Chaudhri Muhammad Ali, and I went to the Governor-General's house while the Prime Minister, with some others, went to his own house.

The Governor-General was lying in his bedroom upstairs. He had very high blood pressure and an agonizing backache which compelled him to lie flat on hardboard. He was bursting with rage, emitting volleys of abuses, which, luckily, no one understood. Chaudhri Muhammad Ali ventured to say something and received a volley; then Iskander Mirza said something and got another. We were pleading with him to give another chance to Muhammed Ali. His only reply was angry growl, 'Go, off you go'. He kept on saying 'No, no'. All he wanted was to shoo us off.

We marched out of the bedroom in single file, Iskander Mirza at the head, Chaudhri Muhammad Ali following, and I bringing up the rear. I was about to step out of the room when the nurse attending the Governor-General tugged at my coat. I turned and found myself facing a different man. There he was, the sick old Governor-General, who a moment ago was insane with anger, now beaming with delight and bubbling with laughter. I said in my heart, 'You wicked old man!' He beckoned me with a peculiar glee in his eye. 'Sit down on the bed'. He then pulled out two documents from under his pillow. On one was written something to this effect: 'I, Ghulam Muhammad, so and so, because of this, that, and the other hand over such and such authority to General Ayub Khan and command him to produce a constitution within three months'. I looked at that paper and said to myself, 'Damn your soul. For the last eight years you have done damn all, and you expect me to produce a constitution in three months'. The other document was to the effect that I had accepted the offer, and for a brief moment I had those historic documents in my hand.

As I looked at these pieces of paper, everything within me cried 'NO'. I said: 'You are being reckless and you will do the country immense harm. I am engaged in building up the army. We have an enemy, an implacable enemy in India. We may not want to be India's enemy but she insists on treating us as one. I can serve this country better in my profession. I believe I can do something useful, and in your present frame of mind you are doing something which in the long run will only damage the country.' His answer was another volley of abuse. But he realized that I was not going to be a party to an act of recklessness.

While I was going through this, Muhammad Ali Bogra was engaged with his own advisers. They were telling him that the Governor-General could not possibly touch him. We found some difficulty in persuading Muhammad Ali Bogra to come to the Governor-General's house. The Governor-General and the Prime Minister finally came to some understanding and a kind of truce was arranged between them.

NOTES

1. Choudhry, G.W., *Constitutional Development in Pakistan*, 1969, Longman Group Ltd., London, pp. 31-2.
2. Williams, L.F. Rushbrook, *The State of Pakistan*, 1966, Faber and Faber, 24 Russell Square, London, pp. 139-40.
3. Quaid-e-Azam's speech at a public meeting at Dhaka, March 21 1948, *Speeches and Statements 1947-48*, 1989, published by Government of Pakistan, Ministry of Information and Broadcasting, Directorate of Films & Publications, Islamabad, pp. 180-81.
4. Williams, L.F. Rushbrook, *supra*, note 2, pp. 141-2.
5. Choudhry, G.W., *Documents and Speeches on the Constitution of Pakistan*, 1967 by Green Book House, Dhaka, pp. 29-30.
6. Ibid., pp. 32 to 33, reproducing the letter dated 7 September 1950 of Mr Tamizuddin Khan, Chairman, Basic Principles Committee to the Constituent Assembly submitting the Interim Report of the Basic Principles Committee.
7. Para 1, Part I, Annexure II of the Interim Report. *Constitutional Foundations of Pakistan* by Safdar Mahmood, 1990, Jang Publications, Lahore, pp. 52-83.
8. Paras 7, 8, 9 & 10 of Chapter I of Part III of the Interim Report.
9. Paras 17 & 18 of Chapter I of Part III of the Interim Report.
10. Para 23, Chapter II, Part II.
11. Para 30, Chapter II, Part III.
12. Para 39, Chapter II, Part III.
13. Para 36, Chapter II, Part III.
14. Para 38, Chapter II, Part III.
15. Paras 56, 58 & 59, Chapter I, Part IV.
16. Para 66, Chapter I, Part IV.
17. Paras 73, 74 & 77, Chapter I, Part IV.
18. Paras 45 & 88.
19. Para 120, Part IX.

20. *Supra*, note 1, p. 30.
21. *Pakistan Observer*, Dhaka, 15 October 1950.
22. *Supra*, note 1, pp. 72-3.
23. Choudhury, G.W., The First Constituent Assembly of Pakistan (1947-1954). His doctoral dissertation for the degree of Ph.D. at Columbia University Faculty of Political Science, 1956. pp. 116-117. This report is on pages 239 to 242 in *Constitutional Foundation of Pakistan*, compilation by Safdar Mahmood, 1990, Jang Publishers, Lahore.
24. Ibid., pp. 118-19. This Report is on also pages 243 to 245 of *Constitutional Foundations of Pakistan*, 1990, Jang Publishers, Lahore.
25. Ibid., p. 119.
26. Ibid., p. 120.
27. Ibid., p. 121.
28. Ayub Khan, Muhammad, *Friends Not Masters*, 1967, Oxford University Press, London, p. 49.
29. William, L.F. Rushbrook, *The State of Pakistan*, *supra*, note 2, p. 149.
30. Wolpert, Stanley, *Jinnah of Pakistan*, 1984, Oxford University Press, p. 360, quoting S.S.Pirzada 'The Last Days of Quaid-e-Azam', *The Pakistan Times*, 17 October 1979 that Jinnah called Liaquat 'mediocre' in his communication with M.A.Khuhro, the then Chief Minister of Sindh.
31. Bolitho, Hector, *Jinnah: Creator of Pakistan*. 1954. John Murray, London, pp. 104 to 106.
32. Khan, Mohammad Zafarullah. *The Forgotten Years: Memoirs of Sir Muhammad Zafrullah Khan*. Edited by A.H. Batalvi. Edition 1991, Vanguard Books, Lahore, p. 164.
33. Choudhry, G.W., *Constitutional Development in Pakistan*, *supra*, note 1, p. 73.
34. Para 13, Chapter I, Part III. Messrs S.C. Chattopadhyaya, Prem Hari Barma, B.K. Datta, and Begam Shah Nawaz on the Basic Principles Committee has recorded their dissent against this provision.
35. Paras 16 and 17, Chapter I, Part III. *Constitutional Foundations of Pakistan*, compilation by Safdar Mahmood, 1990, Jang Publications, Lahore, Report from pages 84 to 156.
36. Paras 28 and 30, Chapter I, Part III.
37. Para 38, Chapter II, Part III.
38. Para 43, Chapter II, Part III.
39. Para 46, Chapter II, Part III.
40. Para 43 (ii), Chapter II, Part III.
41. Schedule II to the Report.
42. Paras 81, 83 and 84, Chapter I, Part IV.
43. Para 89, Chapter I, Part IV.
44. Para 98, Chapter II, Part IV,
45. Para 92, Chapter I, Part IV.
46. Para 70, Chapter II, Part III.
47. Para 130, Chapter II, Part IV.
48. Para 58, Chapter II, Part III.
49. Para 111, Chapter II, Part IV.
50. Paras 161, 162 & 163 of Chapter I, Part X.
51. Para 164, Chapter I, Part X.
52. Para 170, Chapter I, Part X.
53. Para 175, Chapter I, Part X.
54. Para 176, Chapter I, Part X.
55. Paras 179 & 180, Chapter I, Part X.
56. Paras 182, 183 and 184, Chapter I, Part X.
57. Para 168, Chapter I, Part X.
58. Para 193, Chapter II, Part X.
59. Para 195, Chapter II, Part X.
60. Para 196, Chapter II, Part X.
61. Para 200, Chapter II, Part X.
62. Paras 202 & 203, Chapter II, Part X.

63. Para 204, Chapter II, Part X.
64. Para 207, Chapter II, Part X.
65. Para 224, Chapter I, Part XI.
66. Para 2, Chapter II, Part I.
67. Choudhry, G.W., *Constitutional Development in Pakistan, supra*, note 1, p. 74.
68. *Dawn*, Karachi, 31 December 1952.
69. Choudhry, G.W., *Constitutional Development in Pakistan, supra*, note 1, p. 75.
70. Jalal Ayesha, *The State of Martial Rule*, 1990, Cambridge University Press 1990, p. 148.
71. *Dawn*, 1 April 1951.
72. Jalal, Ayesha, *The State of Martial Rule*, *supra*, note 70, p. 151.
73. Ibid., p. 152.
74. Ibid., p. 153.
75. Ibid., p. 154.
76. Ibid., p. 173.
77. Ibid., p. 177.
78. Ibid., pp. 178-9.
79. Munir, Muhammad, *From Jinnah to Zia*, 1980, pp. 41-2, Vanguard Books Ltd., Lahore.
80. Ibid., p. 46.
81. Ibid.
82. Extract from Munir Report reproduced in Munir, Muhammad; *From Jinnah to Zia*, *supra*, note 81, pp. 46-7.
83. Page 218 of the Report, *supra*, note 81, p. 45.
84. Para 41 of Report of the Basic Principles Committee as adopted on 6 October 1954 by the Constituent Assembly. *Constitutional Foundations of Pakistan*, compilation by Safdar Mahmood. 1990, Jang Publishers, Lahore. The Report is from page 157 to 237.
85. Para 47(i).
86. Para 46.
87. *Constituent Assembly Debates*, Vol. XV, No. 2, p. 16.
88. Choudhry, G.W., *Constitutional Development in Pakistan, supra*, note 1, p. 78.
89. Ibid., pp. 78-9.
90. *Pakistan Observer*, Dhaka, 6 November 1950.
91. *Constituent Assembly Debâtes*, Vol. XVI, No.27, pp. 357-8.
92. Ibid., Vol. XV, No. 12, p. 349.
93. Choudhry, G.W., *Constitutional Development in Pakistan, supra*, note 1, p. 80.
94. Report of the Basic Principles Committee, adopted in October 1954 by the Constituent Assembly, Schedule I, List I (Federal), List II (Unit) and List III (Concurrent).
95. Ibid., para 276.
96. Choudhry, G.W., *Constitutional Development in Pakistan, supra*, note 1, pp. 82-3.
97. Keesing's Research Report, *Pakistan from 1947 to the Creation of Bangladesh*, 1973, Charles Scribner's Sons, New York, p. 31.
98. Ibid., p. 32.
99. *Public and Representative Offices (Disqualification) (Repeal) Act, 1954*. PLD 1954 Central Acts 173. See also PLD 1949 Central Acts, Ordinances, Orders & Notifications, page 177.
100. *Government of India (Fifth Amendment) Act, 1954*, PLD 1954 Central Acts and Notifications 172.
101. Wilcox, Wayne Ayres, *Pakistan: The Consolidation of a Nation*, 1963, Columbia University Press, New York, p. 179.
102. Ahmad, Syed Sami, *The Judgement that Brought Disaster*, 1991. Published by Justice Kayani Memorial Law Society, Karachi. The proclamation is reproduced on pages 5 & 6. It is also partly reproduced on page 251 of Federation of Pakistan v Moulvi Tamizuddin Khan, PLD 1955 Federal Court 240.
103. Ayub Khan, Muhammad, *Friends, Not Masters*, *supra*, note 29, pp. 51 to 53.

7

AN ERA OF LEGAL BATTLES

On the dissolution of the Constituent Assembly and the proclamation of emergency by the Governor-General, the focus of constitutional controversy shifted to the courts. The Federal Court of Pakistan, which was the apex court in Pakistan under the Government of India Act, 1935 as adapted in Pakistan, was called upon to give historic verdicts on fundamental constitutional issues. The judgments that followed raised more questions than were answered and echoes of these judgments can still be heard in current constitutional developments in Pakistan.

Moulvi Tamizuddin Khan's Case

The first challenge to the proclamation came from the President of the Constituent Assembly, the late Moulvi Tamizuddin Khan, a man of high repute and sincere convictions. He challenged the proclamation as 'unconstitutional, illegal, *ultra vires*, without jurisdiction, inoperative, and void' and asked for a writ of mandamus to restrain the government from interfering with the exercise of his functions as President of the Assembly and for a writ of *quo warranto* with a view to determining the validity of certain appointments to the Governor-General's Council of Ministers.[1]

The full bench of the Chief Court of Sindh decided unanimously in favour of Moulvi Tamizuddin Khan and allowed his writ petition.[2] The Court overruled the objection taken on behalf of the federal government that Section 223-A, Government of India Act, 1935, which invested the courts with the power to issue writs of *mandamus* and *quo warranto* had not received the assent of the Governor-General and was thus not a valid piece of legislation and no relief could thus be granted by the chief court thereunder. In the same way, the Court also overruled a similar objection against the new Section 10 which limited the discretion of the Governor-General in his choice of ministers. Interpreting the provision of the Indian Independence Act regarding assent of the Governor-General, the Court held that it did not provide that assent was necessary but only stated that if assent was necessary, then the Governor-General would have the full power. It was held that the Constituent Assembly had the sovereign power and supreme prerogative to amend and repeal existing laws and form and bring into force a new Constitution. The Court observed that when His Majesty's own intervention to give validity or force to the measures of the Constituent Assembly was not required, then how could the intervention of His Majesty's representative be required.

The Sindh Chief Court was indeed mindful of its previous ruling in which it had held that 'there is no limit imposed upon the legislative powers of the Constituent Assembly sitting as a constitution-making body'.[3] One of the judges on the Bench of Sindh Chief Court, Justice Mohammad Bakhsh, noted that while deciding two previous cases where statutes involved had not received the assent of the Governor-General, 'the Federal Court knew very well that no assent of the Governor-General had been obtained to this Act of the Constituent Assembly, and, therefore, it must be taken for granted that the Federal Court did not think that assent to be necessary'.[4]

On the power of the Governor-General to dissolve the Constituent Assembly, it was held that the Indian Independence Act did not contain any express provision for dissolution of the Assembly and, therefore, the Governor-General had no power of any kind to dissolve the Constituent Assembly. It was a sovereign body created for a special purpose and it was to function till that purpose was accomplished. The right to dissolve the legislature, it was observed, had ceased to be a prerogative in England and it was difficult to hold that the prerogative which had ceased in England was revived in Pakistan after 1947.

The Chief Court of Sindh thus issued quo-warranto to the ministers in the new Cabinet prohibiting them from exercising the office of minister and the writ of mandamus restoring Moulvi Tamizuddin Khan to the office as President of the Constituent Assembly was issued restraining respondents from interfering with his duties and from obstructing him in the exercise of his functions.

The Federal Court Judgment

An appeal to the Federal Court against the decision of the Sindh Court was filed by the government. By a majority of four to one the Federal Court, decided, on 21 March 1955, in favour of the government and rejected Moulvi Tamizuddin's petition challenging the proclamation of the Governor-General.[5] The most significant point in the Federal Court's judgment was that it did not go into the question of whether the Constituent Assembly was rightly dissolved by the Governor-General. It reversed the judgment of the Sindh Court on technical grounds namely, that Section 223A of the Government of India Act as adapted in Pakistan by virtue of which the Sindh Court issued the writ in favour of Tamizuddin Khan was 'not yet a law' because it had not received the assent of the Governor-General. The Court held that the enactments of the Constituent Assembly, whether it functioned as the central legislature or as the constitution-making body, required the assent of the Governor-General and since Section 223A of the Government of India Act had not received such assent, it was not yet law and, therefore, the Sindh Court had no power to issue the writs.

The majority in the Federal Court, interpreting the provision of the Indian Independence Act, 1947, concerning assent by the Governor-General[6] held that it made the Governor-General a constituent part of the legislature in as much as the right to give assent necessarily included in it the right to withhold assent. Every bill must, therefore, be presented to him to provide him an occasion to exercise that right and, unless a bill was so presented, a constituent part of the legislature did not function and the proposed legislation did not become law. The requirement of assent to the dominion legislation by the Crown, or its representative, was indispensible and had in no instance ever been dispensed with by the Crown.

> The legislation of the Constituent Assembly under sub-section (1) of Section 8 is a part of the government of the dominion within the meaning of section 5 and the whole Scheme of the Government of India Act proceeds on the assumption that the Governor-General represents the Crown when he assents in Her Majesty's name to the laws of the federal legislature.[7]

The position of the Constituent Assembly was held to be that of the legislature of the dominion when it made laws for the Constitution of the dominion and the federal legislature in its function was under the limitations imposed upon it by the Government of India Act, 1935.

Since the decision of the majority of the Federal Court was based on invalidity of section 223A of the Government of India Act, 1935 for want of assent of the Governor-General, therefore, the Court did not go into the other issues in the case.

Dissent of Justice A. R. Cornelius

Justice A. R. Cornelius wrote a strong dissenting opinion stating that there was no obligation that all laws made by the Constituent Assembly of a constitutional nature required the assent of the Governor-General for their validity and operation. His principal reasons for reaching such a conclusion were:

i. There were two precise acts of the Governor-General which could not be interpreted otherwise than as acts of denial of allegiance to the British sovereign. The first act was of the first Governor-General, Quaid-e-Azam Muhammad Ali Jinnah, who, while taking oath as Governor-General, refused to accept the earlier form which required the Governor-General to bear 'full faith and allegiance to His Majesty'. Thereupon, by agreement with the British sovereign, the oath that he took and which successors after him did take, required that he should bear true allegiance to the constitution and be faithful to His Majesty. The second act belonged to Governor-General Ghulam Muhammad. In deviation of the long- standing practice that on accession of a new British monarch, the royal styles and titles should require the assent 'as well of the Parliaments of the dominions as of the Parliament of the United Kingdom', no such matter was brought before the Constituent Assembly for its assent upon the accession to British throne of Queen Elizabeth II in June 1953. Hence, Her Majesty was indeed a mere symbol, although as Queen of Pakistan a more substantial position might perhaps have been claimed.

ii. The nature of freedom extended under the Indian Independence Act, 1947 resulted in making 'free peoples' in the dominions of Pakistan and India which necessarily meant that peoples of the dominions enjoyed the advantage of representative institutions according to British pattern.

iii. The extent of freedom accorded to the countries which, as dominions, were to replace the Indian empire, was in a very material degree greater than that which the older dominions had gained in 1931 under the Statute of Westminster 1931 that was the circumstance which could justify the application of the special description 'Independent Dominions' to the two new states which were brought into existence by means of this highly effective instrument, the Indian Independence Act, 1947.

iv. The argument that the Constituent Assembly derived power to make laws for the dominion under section 6(1) of the Indian Independence Act overlooked the fact that the Constituent Assembly was, as a body, not a creation of the British Parliament. It was a body created by a supra-legal power to discharge the supra-legal function of preparing a constitution for Pakistan. Its powers in this respect belonged to itself inherently by virtue of its being a body representative of the will of the people in relation to their future mode of government.

v. With respect to the necessity of assent by the Governor-General to laws of a constitutional nature passed by the Constituent Assembly, a serious doubt had arisen at a very early stage. The Law Ministry of the Government of Pakistan was of the opinion that such assent was essential but the Constituent Assembly had throughout maintained the view that assent was not necessary, and acting on that view, had made and promulgated a rule, bearing No. 62 in the rules of the Constituent Assembly to give formal expression to that view. This rule, as originally framed on the 24 February 1948 at a meeting presided over by the President, the Quaid-e-Azam Muhammad Ali Jinnah, merely provided that when a Bill had been passed by the Assembly, a copy of it should be signed by the President. As this was not followed by any provision for submission to the Governor-General for his assent, it was understood to provide a sufficient formal act to give validity as law to the Bill as passed, but apparently doubts were felt on this subject, and the rule was amended at a meeting presided over by the Deputy President, Tamizuddin Khan, and held on the 22 May 1948 to read as follows:

> When a Bill is passed by the Assembly, a copy thereof shall be signed by the President, and it shall become law on being published in the Official Gazette of Pakistan under authority of the President.
>
> The rule expressed very clearly the opinion of the Constituent Assembly on the subject and had been acted upon for nearly seven years and acquiesced in and accepted by the Executive, including the Governor-General.

vi. The Constituent Assembly was to be placed above the Governor-General, the chief executive of the state, for two reasons, firstly that the Constituent Assembly was a sovereign body, and secondly because the statutes under and in accordance with which the Governor-General was required to function, were within the competence of the Constituent Assembly to amend. The Executive Government of the federation had never, until after the event of 24 October 1954, shown any sign of doubt on this point.

vii. The Constituent Assembly being designed to be a sovereign body and to exercise sovereign power, including power to alter the constitution subject to which the Governor-General was intended to act, it would clearly be inconsistent with the design and purpose if the 'qualified negative' assent by the Governor-General were imposed upon its constitutional laws.

viii. It being within the complete power of the Constituent Assembly to determine the constitution of the 'Legislature of the Dominion', or Union Legislature, and to determine the scope of its legislative competency as well as the mode in which its laws should be enacted, the British Parliament could not affect to prescribe the requirement of assent, as an essential formality, in respect of the laws made by such a legislature. This would usurp the functions of the Constituent Assembly. To impose such a requirement upon laws of a constitutional nature made by the Constituent Assembly would be a direct affront to the position and authority of that body.

ix. There could be no possible doubt that neither the British sovereign nor the Governor-General, as such, was part of the Constituent Assembly.

Concluding Remarks

The judgment of the Federal Court in Tamizuddin Khan's case paved the way for future justifications by the judiciary of patently arbitrary, malicious, and capricious acts of the executive on hyper-technical grounds or self-serving theories or concepts. Much has been written on the motivation behind this majority judgment. The leading judgment was that of Chief Justice Muhammad Munir with which three other judges concurred. The ability and competence of Justice Munir is beyond any doubt. His motives have, however, been seriously criticized by many writers. He is accused of standing by his friend and fellow Kakkezai[8] Governor-General Ghulam Muhammad in his hour of need and bent the reasoning to justify his act which was patently and palpably *malafide*. Qudratullah Shahab, who was principal secretary to the Governor-General at the time, recounts in his Memoirs, *Shahabnama*, that one of his assistants used to disappear from the office in Karachi without his permission for days together around the time when Tamizuddin Khan's case was being heard by the Federal Court in Lahore. When Shahab called for explanations for absence without leave or permission, the man officially submitted his apology but orally stated that he was going on assignments to Lahore which were required to be kept secret. He used to deliver confidential messages in code words from the Governor-General to Chief Justice Munir.[9] After all, Ghulam Muhammad had acted in retaliation to the curtailment of his powers by the Constituent Assembly. It is unfortunate that such an action was taken only a few days after the Constituent Assembly had finally, after seven years of continuous struggle and deliberations, agreed on a Constitution. The loss of this colossal effort at Constitution-making in the early days of Pakistan cannot be overly lamented.

Justice Munir remained defensive and apologetic about his judgment in Tamizuddin Khan's case for the rest of his life.[10] He wrote and spoke on this point on various occasions. What he said in defence of his judgment at the time of his retirement as Chief Justice of the Supreme Court of Pakistan, in his reply to the address by the High Court Bar Association, Lahore on the 22 April 1960, is reproduced below:[11]

> On 7 November 1954 Mr Tamizuddin Khan, the deposed President of the Constituent Assembly, came to the Chief Court of Sindh with petition for writs of 'mandamus' and 'quo warranto' against the Federation of Pakistan, which meant the newly appointed Ministers of the Government. The Chief Court decided to issue the writs on 9 February 1955 *viz.*, some four months after the Government had been continuing in an established manner.
>
> The history of the litigation starting with the presentation of the petition for writs is a sad chapter in the history of Pakistan. In a country where the constitution is working in a normal manner, the work of a judge is mere routine, interspersed here and there with some case of more than ordinary importance. But in the aforesaid litigation the Federal Court was confronted more than once with a situation, unparalleled and unprecedented in the history of the world. The mental anguish caused to the judges by these cases is beyond description and I repeat that no judiciary anywhere in the world had to pass through what may be described as a judicial torture. Since in your address you have referred to my judgments in these cases, I propose to say a few words in their explanation.
>
> The basic point that is not to be overlooked for a moment in these cases was that a forcibly ejected ministry had come to a court of law for recognition of its right to remain in office and for obtaining from the court process for its restoration and the Court had issued enforceable writs against a *de facto* government. With all your experience and knowledge derived from textbooks and law reports can you recall to your mind anything even reminiscent of any such situation?
>
> May I, in this connection, refer to another occasion in our history in order to explain the point. Could any court having a discretion in the matter, issue an enforceable writ on the 8, 9 or 10 October against the government that had been brought into existence by the Proclamation of President Iskander Mirza? You will probably say that by 10 October, a revolution had come about but that on 9 February 1955 there was no revolution. And that is precisely the point I wish you to appreciate.
>
> The Federal Court could have said in April 1955 when it dismissed Moulvi Tamizuddin Khan's petition that no writ could issue against an established government, however illegally constituted the *de facto* government may be. That would have meant legal recognition of a revolution. But neither in that case nor in any of the subsequent cases did we say so.
>
> The Court found that for the action taken by the Governor-General a legal power in that behalf was to be found in the constitutional instrument itself. If the Court had upheld the enforceable writs, I am quite sure that there would have been chaos in the country and a revolution would have been formally enacted possibly by bloodshed, a far more serious situation than that created by the invalidation of a whole legal system which the new

Assembly promised by the Governor-General in his Proclamation could have easily validated.

Situations such as these are not for the courts to deal with unless the courts know for certain that their writs would be restored and enforced. But who could say that on 9 February, the coercive power of the state was at the service of the Court and not with the Governor-General? And if even a doubt arises as to where such power resides, a doubt must arise as to the very efficacy of the law, and the situation would be beyond the pale of judicial process. The writs being enforceable, who was to enforce them and was the Court itself in a position to punish the contempt committed by their disobedience?

The Chief Court had merely looked into the constitutional instrument and gathering the meaning thereof with the aid of some law reports had issued process, regardless of the events that had happened which made it impossible for the writs to be enforced.

At moments like these, public law is not to be found in the books; it lies elsewhere, *viz*., in the events that have happened. Where the enforcement of the law is opposed by the sovereign power the issue becomes political or military which has to be fought out by other means and the courts by espousing the cause of one party against the other merely prepare the ground for bloodshed. At a time like this, the very origin of the laws becomes uncertain, the law-giving agency being in a process of metamorphosis and the existing law struggling with some inchoate law neither of which the courts, so long as the state of uncertainty lasts, can recognize or define.

But as I have said, though the Court could dismiss the petition for writs on the ground that they were being asked for against a *de facto* government, it refrained from doing so and decided the case under the law of the land, finding that the Chief Court had no jurisdiction to issue them.

The above justification or explanation is hardly convincing. These appear to be the lame excuses of a guilty mind. It was Justice Munir's duty to apply the law and to decide correctly regardless of the consequences. The issuance of writ was his province and not its enforcement. Had Chief Justice Marshall been inhibited by considerations like these while issuing the writ in Marbury v Madison[12] the constitutional history of the USA would have been quite different. It is the bold decisions of courts that set the law on the right course. A timid and spineless judiciary leads to constitutional disaster.

The reasoning of Justice Munir revolves around his apprehensions about the consequences. He chided the Sindh Chief Court for proceeding in its decision without bothering about the consequences. He probably forgot what he had said earlier:[13]

> I am quite clear in my mind that we are not concerned with the consequences, however beneficial or disastrous they may be, if the undoubted legal position was that all legislation by the legislature of the dominion under sub-section (7) of section 8 needed the assent of the Governor-General. If the result is disaster, it will merely be another instance of how thoughtlessly the Constituent Assembly proceeded with its business and assuming for itself the position of an irrevocable legislature to what straits it has brought to the country. Unless any rule of estoppel requires us to pronounce merely purported legislation as complete and valid legislation, we have no option but to pronounce it to be void and to leave it to the relevant authorities under the constitution or to the country to set right the

> position in any way it may be open to them. The question raised involves the right of every citizen in Pakistan, and neither any rule of construction nor any rule of estoppel stands in the way of a clear pronouncement.

The above passage clearly demonstrates that he was fully conscious of the fact that the view he was taking in the matter was going to upset the entire constitutional and administrative machinery of the country. He was fully aware that, in consequence of his judgment, the ship of the state was going to be plunged into deep sea and further that, in that event, rescue operations will not be possible. Yet, he was not prepared to budge an inch from his preconceived notion that the Governor-General of Pakistan was as good as the King of England and that he had absolute power to exercise the King's prerogative.[14]

However, the most significant aspect of the judgment is that although it runs into 64 pages, there is no finding as to whether the Governor-General could dissolve the Constituent Assembly. There is a consensus of opinion that this judgment caused incalculable harm to the constitutional development of Pakistan and rocked the constitutional ship of the country in its infancy. This judgment irreparably undermined the image and credibility of the judiciary of Pakistan in the public eye.

The Usif Patel Case

As a result of the judgment of the Federal Court in Tamizuddin Khan's case, as many as forty-six Acts on the statute books became invalid. The country was faced with a legal vacuum. Six days after the judgment of the Federal Court, the Governor-General promulgated the Emergency Powers Ordinance IX of 1955 and assumed powers to:

1. Make provision for framing the Constitution of Pakistan;
2. Make provisions to constitute the province of West Pakistan;
3. Validate laws which had been passed by the Constituent Assembly but had not received the assent of the Governor-General;
4. Authenticate the Central Budget; and
5. Name East Bengal as East Pakistan.[15]

A 'state of grave emergency' was declared throughout Pakistan, presumably to prevent the breakdown of the constitutional machinery of the country, but the Governor-General's emergency powers were soon challenged before the Federal Court. A full bench of the Federal Court, presided over by Chief Justice Munir, declared on 13 April in another leading constitutional case of this period, *Usif Patel v The Crown*, that power to make provisions to the Constitution of the country could not be exercised by the Governor-General by means of an ordinance.[16] The court, therefore, held Section 2 of the ordinance promulgated by the Governor-General on 27 March 1955 (Ordinance No. IX of 1955) as *ultra vires*. Addressing the Advocate-General who was arguing for the Government, the Chief Justice was reported to have remarked, 'If you ride roughshod you will bring disaster in this country. You do not have a validating machinery nor do you intend to create one'. He further added, 'I do not know whether the Constituent Assembly was dissolved legally or not, but so far it does exist in law'.[17] It may be assumed that the Chief Justice implied the continuing legal entity of the Constituent Assembly. It was made clear by this latest judgment of the Federal Court that the power to make any provisions to the Constitution of the country was not conferred by law on anybody except the Constituent Assembly whose continuing legal status was recognized.

The Emergency Powers Ordinance, 1955 provided that every constitutional law specified in column one of the schedule to that ordinance should be deemed to have received the assent of the Governor-General on the date specified in column two of the schedule and to have had full legal force and effect from that date. One of the laws so specified was the Indian Independence (Amendment) Act, 1948. In the preamble as well as in Section 10 of the ordinance, the Governor-General was empowered to make 'by order such provisions as appear to him to be necessary or expedient for the purpose of making provision as to the constitution of Pakistan'.

Under Section 9 of the Indian Independence Act, the Governor-General had been empowered to make by order such provision as appeared to him to be necessary or expedient for bringing the provisions of that Act into effective operation and for making adaptations of the Government of India Act, 1935. This power by the terms of the section could not be exercised after 31 March 1948. By the Indian Independence (Amendment) Act, 1948, the Constituent Assembly had extended the period for the exercise of this power by one year till 31 March 1949. The Governor-General had thus added section 92 A to the Government of India Act, 1935, according to which, under certain circumstances, the Governor-General could issue a proclamation authorizing the Governor of a province to make laws for that province. The powers under section 92 A had been exercised by the Governor-General in respect of the province of Sindh and Governor of that province in exercise of the powers thus conferred on him had enacted a law called the Sindh Control of Goondas Act, 1952.

A person who had been declared to be a *goonda* (ruffian) under the Sindh Control of Goondas Act, challenged the Act as invalid because the 'Governor's' authority for that Act was a proclamation by the Governor-General under section 92 A of the Government of India Act, 1935, that the section was invalid because it was added to the Government of India Act after 31 March 1948, and that the extension by the Indian Independence (Amendment) Act, 1948, of the date of making orders under Section 9 of the Indian Independence Act from 31 March 1948 to 31 March 1949, was itself invalid, because the Amendment Act had not received the Governor-General's assent. The Federal Court, relying on the authority of Moulvi Tamizuddin Khan's case and Chief Justice Munir being the author judge, held that the power of the Governor-General to promulgate ordinances did not go beyond the federal legislature's powers to make laws, that since the Indian Independence (Amendment) Act, 1948, being a constitutional provision beyond the federal legislature's power to enact, had not received the Governor-General's assent, it was invalid and that because the Governor-General's subsequent attempt to validate it by the Emergency Powers Ordinance itself amounted to constitutional legislation, the attempted legislation was void for the reason that such legislation could only be passed by the Constituent Assembly, though with the assent of the Governor-General. The court explained the legal and constitutional position in the following paragraphs of its judgment:

> The rule hardly requires any explanation, much less emphasis, that a legislature cannot validate an invalid law if it does not possess the power to legislate on the subject to which the invalid law relates, the principle governing validation being that validation being itself legislation you cannot validate what you cannot legislate upon. Therefore, if the federal legislature, in the absence of a provision expressly authorizing it to do so, was incompetent to amend the Indian Independence Act or the Government of India Act, the Governor-General, possessing no larger powers than those of the federal legislature, was equally incompetent to amend either of those Acts by an ordinance. Under the Independence Act the authority competent to legislate on constitutional matters being the Constituent Assembly, it is that Assembly alone which can amend those Acts. The learned Advocate-General alleges that the Constituent Assembly has been dissolved and that therefore validating powers cannot be exercised by that Assembly. In Moulvi Tamizuddin Khan's case, we did not consider it necessary to decide the question whether Constituent Assembly was lawfully dissolved but assuming that it was, the effect of the dissolution can certainly not be the transfer of its powers to the Governor-General. The Governor-General can give or withhold his assent to the legislation of the Constituent Assembly but he himself is not the Constituent Assembly and on its disappearance he can neither claim powers which he never possessed nor claim to succeed to the powers of that Assembly.
>
> The judgment of this court in Moulvi Tamizuddin Khan's case attempted to put this position beyond doubt, as will appear from the observations on pages 41-43, 65 and 186-188. My own conclusion on this part of the case I stated in the form of the mathematical equation that the federal legislature is the Constituent Assembly plus the fetters to which it is subject under the Government of India Act, 1935. If that judgment was not understood as clearly laying down that the powers of the legislature of the dominion were exercisable in the first instance by the Constituent Assembly and that that Assembly when functioning as the federal legislature under proviso (e) to sub-section (2) of section 8 was to be deemed to have imposed limitations on its powers as the legislature of the dominion, the time and labour expended on that judgment have been merely wasted. So that we may now be understood more clearly, let me repeat that the power of the legislature of the dominion for the purpose of making provision as to the constitution of the dominion could under sub-section (1) of section 8 of the Indian Independence Act be exercised only by the Constituent Assembly and that that power could not be exercised by that Assembly when it functioned as the federal legislature within the limits imposed upon it by the Government of India Act, 1935. It is therefore not right to claim for the federal legislature the power of making provision as to the constitution of the dominion, a claim which is specifically negatived by sub-section (1) of section 8 of the Indian Independence Act. If the constitutional position were otherwise, the Governor-General could by an ordinance repeal the whole of the Indian Independence Act and the Government of India Act and assume to himself all powers of legislation. A more incongruous position in a democratic constitution is difficult to conceive, particularly when the legislature itself, which controls the Governor-General's action, is alleged to have been dissolved.
>
> This Court held in Moulvi Tamizuddin Khan's case that the Constituent Assembly was not a sovereign body. But that did not mean that if the Assembly was not a sovereign body,

the Governor-General was. We took pains to explain at length in that case that the position of the Governor-General in Pakistan is that of a constitutional head of state, namely, a position very similar to that occupied by the King in the United Kingdom. That position which was supported by Mr Diplock is now being repudiated by the learned Advocate-General and on the ground of emergency every kind of power is being claimed for the head of state. Let us say clearly if we omitted to say so in the previous case, that under the Constitution Acts the Governor-General is possessed of no more powers than those that are given to him by these Acts. One of these powers is to promulgate ordinances in cases of emergency but the limits within which and the restrictions subject to which he can exercise that power are clearly laid down in section 42 itself. On principle the power of the Governor-General to legislate by ordinance is always subject to the control of the federal legislature and he cannot remove these controls merely by asserting that no federal legislature in law or in fact is in existence. No such position is contemplated by the Indian Independence Act, or the Government of India Act, 1935. Any legislative provision that relates to a constitutional matter is solely within the powers of the Constituent Assembly and the Governor-General is under the Constitution Acts precluded from exercising those powers. The sooner this position is realized, the better. And if any one read anything to the contrary in the previous judgment of this court, all that I can say is that we were grievously misunderstood. If the position created by the judgment in the present case is that past constitutional legislation cannot be validated by the Governor-General but only by the legislature, it is for the Law Department of the Government to ponder over the resultant situation and to advise the Government accordingly. The seriousness of the implications of our judgment in the previous case should have been immediately realized and prompt steps taken to validate the invalid legislation.

For these reasons we are of the opinion that since the Amendment Act of 1948 was not presented to the Governor-General for his assent, it did not have the effect of extending the date from 31 March 1948 to 31 March 1949, and that since section 92 A was added to the Government of India Act, 1935, after the 31 March 1948, it never became a valid provision of that Act. Thus the Governor-General had no authority to act under section 92 A and the Governor derived no power to legislate from a Proclamation under that section. Accordingly the Sindh Control of Goondas Act was *ultra vires* and no action under it could have been taken against the appellant. That being so, the detention of the appellant is illegal.

The ordinance recites that the Governor-General had some other powers which enabled him not only to validate certain laws but also temporarily to abolish the federal legislature, to amend the provisions of the Government of India Act, 1935, relating to provinces and the High Courts and to make the future constitution. In the arguments before us, however, the learned Advocate-General did not rely on any such powers, his entire arguments having been confined to the powers of the Governor-General to promulgate ordinances under section 42.

For these reasons we accept the appeal and order the appellant to be set at liberty. One more observation before we conclude. During the course of arguments in Moulvi Tamizuddin Khan's case a question arose as to what the consequent constitutional position would be if the Constituent Assembly was validly dissolved or had ceased to function. The statement that Mr. Diplock made in reply to the questions on this subject is reproduced below from the transcript of court proceedings:

Mr Diplock: My Lords, it is important to note that in the proclamation of the Governor-General he has said that the election will be held as early as possible. Having taken the first step to avert the disaster by dissolving the existing Constituent Assembly, election will be held as early as possible. It was his intention, and I am instructed to inform Your Lordships that it is still his intention, to provide for the immediate election of fresh representatives to the Constituent Assembly by the Provincial Legislative Assemblies which was the method by which, Your Lordships would recall, the original members of the Constituent Assembly were elected. One hopes it would so act to provide as speedily as possible for direct elections. But nothing has been done by the existing Constituent Assembly to provide an election law or for the delimitation of constituencies for the election of the central legislature and such a provision for direct election would from the practical point of view take a minimum of 12 months or probably more.

Chief Justice: And for indirect elections?
Mr Diplock: Indirect election could be done within a period of a week or two. There are the Provincial Assemblies. They have got to be called together to select their representatives. Having regard to the fact about the practical difficulties for holding direct election, it may delay the matter.
In view of the delay as to the direct election, the Governor-General is anxious to adopt the quickest measures to have immediately an Assembly which could be as nearly perfectly representative of the people as could be obtained at the present moment through indirect election.
Chief Justice: So you agree that there is immediate need for a legislature?
Mr Diplock: Because the Governor-General has to act by Proclamation. He is acting on the advice of his Ministers but without the assistance of the representatives of the people.
Chief Justice: Will the proclamation have the force of law?
Mr Diplock: The Governor-General's intention is to get into operation as quickly as possible an Assembly which is as nearly representative of the wishes of the people as can be obtained immediately. That is a matter which will necessarily be within the Governor-General's discretion.
Mr Justice Rahman: Have you been formally instructed to this effect to inform us?
Mr Diplock: Yes, My Lord, I have been instructed to tell Your Lordships that it was the intention of the Governor-General while making this proclamation and still is his intention to summon a fresh Constituent Assembly elected so far as the provinces which have got Legislative Assemblies by members of those Assemblies.
As I said to Your Lordships, it was the Governor-General's intention at the time that the Proclamation was made that steps for the reconstitution of the Constituent Assembly should be taken at once. It may be that he took the view at that stage on the advice which was given to him that it was within his powers under the constitution to take the step which he has taken under the proclamation. I am only saying that it is not for us to say that we are right; it is for Your Lordships to decide whether it was right. In those circumstances, he thought it right, an immediate application having been made to the Sindh Chief Court, to wait unless the necessity become compelling, to wait until the court had said whether his interpretation of the law was right or not. My Lords, he took the view and I think whichever view is right as to construction; whether he is entitled to do under the Act, as I submit he is, or whether he is not entitled to do that—relying on the maxim *salus populi suprema lex*. He took the view that so far as possible, although representative institutions

are necessarily abrogated while he waited for the decision of the Court, it was undesirable that in addition to the abrogation of representative institutions which had already happened when the Constituent Assembly itself became unrepresentative, that it was undesirable to abrogate that other essential feature of the democratic constitution by the rule of force to prevent the matter coming before the courts. My Lords, it may be, indeed it would have been his duty, had circumstances so necessitated, to take those steps without regard to the writ which had been issued, because *salus populi suprema lex*; to go as far as that. Fortunately, it has not been necessary at present to do so...
As things stand at present it was his intention in October last to set up a new Constituent Assembly. That is action which he would have taken immediately after the 24 October had this litigation not started and that is his intention still. I hope Your Lordships will not press me to say anything more than I can necessarily say about the matter.

It might have been expected that, conformably with the attitude taken before us by responsible counsel for the Crown, the first concern of the government would have been to bring into existence another representative body to exercise the powers of the Constituent Assembly so that all invalid legislation could have been immediately validated by the new body. Such a course would have been consistent with constitutional practice in relation to such a situation as has arisen. Events, however, show that other counsels have since prevailed. The ordinance contains no reference to elections, and all that the learned Advocate General can say is that they are intended to be held.[18]

The decision of the Federal Court presented the country with a constitutional crisis of a greater magnitude than when the Governor-General had dissolved the Constituent Assembly. The central Law Minister, H. S. Suhrawardy, frankly stated the position when commenting on the decision of the Federal Court. He said: 'The country is faced with a grave situation.'[19] There was no federal legislature in existence competent to validate laws which were declared null and void by the Federal Court. Even provincial legislatures were deemed to have been illegal since the laws under which those bodies had been elected were illegal. In fact, the entire legal and administrative system was on the verge of collapse. The courts were flooded with cases challenging various actions of the government. The continued uncertainty about legal proprieties was bad for the government, for business, and for the organized life of the citizens.

Governor-General's Reference to the Federal Court

Important political developments followed the decision of the Federal Court rejecting the Governor-General's emergency powers. The Governor-General immediately summoned a 'Constituent Convention' to meet on 10 May. The government also announced that it would request the Federal Court to detail what interim steps should be taken to validate the laws which, by the Court's ruling, the Governor-General himself could not restore. Some steps were urgently needed to avoid a complete breakdown of the constitutional machinery. On 16 April the Governor-General assumed powers to validate thirty-five of these laws 'subject to any report from the

Federal Court' and until such time as the Constituent Convention could consider them. Two days later, the Federal Court restrained all other courts from interfering with this step pending its decision on matters referred by the Governor-General. The Court, suggested to the Governor-General that he could enlarge the terms of reference to include the basic question whether the Constituent Assembly had been rightly dissolved. The Court pointed out that the new Constituent Convention's validating powers might be challenged on the ground that the Convention was an illegal body. Unless it were decided whether the Constituent Assembly had been legally dissolved and the new one rightly constituted, there might be 'litigation of every sort'. The government accepted this suggestion and from 25 April the Court heard arguments on this enlarged reference.

The arguments before the Court and its judgment were almost an education in British and Commonwealth constitutional history, turning *inter alia* on the powers of the Crown represented by the Governor-General. As Sir Ivor Jennings pointed out, the litigation which followed the dissolution of the Constituent Assembly of Pakistan on 24 October 1954 dealt with the fundamental principles of constitutional law which was of interest throughout the Commonwealth because it was unique in the legal history.[20]

The questions referred to the Federal Court for its opinion by the Governor-General were:

1. What are the powers and responsibilities of the Governor-General in respect of the Government of the country before the new Constituent Convention passes the necessary legislation?
2. The Federal Court having held in Usif Patel's case that the laws listed in the Schedule to the Emergency Powers Ordinance could not be validated under section 42 of the Government of India Act, 1935, nor retrospective effect given to them, and no Legislature competent to validate such laws being in existence, is there any provision in the constitution or any rule of law applicable to the situation by which the Governor-General can by Order or otherwise declare that all orders made, decisions taken, and other acts done under these laws shall be valid and enforceable and those laws which cannot without danger to the state be removed from the existing legal system shall be treated as part of the law of the land until the question of their validation is determined by the new Constituent Convention?
3. Whether the Constituent Assembly was rightly dissolved by the Governor-General?
4. Whether the Constituent Convention proposed to be set up by the Governor-General will be competent to exercise the powers conferred by section 8 of the Indian Independence Act, 1947, on the Constituent Assembly?

In a lengthy opinion[21] by the full court consisting of five judges, these questions were answered by a majority of four to one as follows:

Answer to Question No.1. That this question was too general and need not be answered.

Answer to Question No. 2. That in the situation presented by the Reference the Governor-General has during the interim period the power under the common law of civil or state necessity of retrospectively validating the laws listed in the Schedule to the Emergency

Powers Ordinance, 1955, and all those laws, until the question of their validation is decided upon by the Constituent Assembly, are during the aforesaid period valid and enforceable in the same way as if they had been valid from the date on which they purported to come into force.

Answer to Question No. 3. That on the facts stated in the Reference, namely, (1) that the Constituent Assembly, though it functioned for more than 7 years, was unable to carry out the duty to frame a constitution for Pakistan to replace the transitional constitution provided by the Indian Independence Act, 1947, (2) that in view of the repeated representations from and resolutions passed by representative bodies throughout the country the Constituent Assembly, in the opinion the Governor-General, became in course of time wholly unrepresentative of the people of Pakistan and ceased to be responsible to them; (3) that for all practical purposes the Constituent Assembly assumed the form of a perpetual legislature; and (4) that throughout the period of its existence the Constituent Assembly asserted that the provisions made by it for the constitution of the dominion under sub-section (1) of section 8 of the Indian Independence Act were valid laws without the consent of the Governor-General, the Governor-General had under section 5 of the Indian Independence Act legal authority to dissolve the Constituent Assembly.

Answer to Question No. 4. That subject to this:

1. that the correct name of the Constituent Convention is Constituent Assembly;
2. that the Governor-General's right to dissolve the Assembly can only be derived from the Indian Independence Act;
3. that the arrangements for representation of states and tribal areas can, under the proviso to sub-section (3) of section 19 of the Indian Independence Act, be made only by the Constituent Assembly and not by the Governor-General; and
4. that the Governor-General's duty being to bring into existence a representative legislative institution he can only nominate the electorate and not members to the Constituent Assembly;

The new Assembly, constituted under the Constituent Convention Order, 1955,[22] as amended to date, would be competent to exercise all the powers conferred by the Indian Independence Act, 1947, on the Constituent Assembly, including those under section 8 of that Act.

Once again, the dissenting judge was Justice Cornelius who wrote his own lengthy opinion on these questions referred by the Governor-General. His answers to the questions were as under:

Answer to Question No. 1. The point had been placed beyond doubt in the leading Judgment in the case of Moulvi Tamizuddin Khan in the paragraph reproduced below:

'The Governor-General of Pakistan is appointed by the King or Queen and represents him or her for the purposes of the government of the dominion. The authority of the representative of the King extends to the exercise of the Royal prerogatives in so far as it is applicable to the internal affairs of the member State or Province, even without express delegation, subject to any contrary statutory or constitutional provisions.'

Answer to Question No. 2. The answer to this question was subservient to the answers to the Questions No. 3 and 4 and was answered at the end.

Answer to Question No. 3. In view of the decision of the majority of the judges in Moulvi Tamizuddin Khan's case, the Constituent Assembly as mentioned in the Indian Independence Act, 1947, is the 'legislature of the dominion' for the purposes of the government of the dominion. The majority of the judges have also held that the Governor-General is invested with all the Royal prerogatives, except where barred by express words or necessary intendment. The prerogative of dissolution of the legislature is recognized to exist in all representative institutions in the British Commonwealth of Nations and there are no words in the relevant instruments, taking away expressly or by necessary intendment, this prerogative power in relation to the 'legislature of the dominion'. Consequently, the Governor-General must be held to possess the prerogative to dissolve the Constituent Assembly.

The exercise of a prerogative power is not a justiciable matter. Therefore, the question whether the act of dissolution was 'rightly' performed does not arise within this court's jurisdiction, and the enquiry must be limited to the legality of this action.

Answer to Question No. 4. The powers coffered by section 8 of the Indian Independence Act, 1947, on the Constituent Assembly can only be exercised by a successor body, of the same name, summoned by the Governor-General, in the discharge of a duty so to do, which arises out of, and is complementary to, his order dissolving the Constituent Assembly. The duty of summoning does not involve, and cannot include, the exercise of any political initiative outside the constitutional instruments in force. It must be performed in accordance with the basic principles which were expressly followed in the setting up of the Constituent Assembly of 1947. These principles as stated with clarity in paragraph 18 of the Statement of the Cabinet Delegation and His Excellency the Viceroy and Governor-General of India, issued on the 16 May 1946.

Justice Cornelius returned to the answer to the Question No. 2 as under:

a. There is no provision in the Constitution and no rule of law applicable to the situation, by which the Governor-General can, in the light of this Court's decision in the case of Usif Patel, by Proclamation or otherwise, validate the laws enumerated in the Schedule to the Emergency Powers Ordinance, 1955, whether temporarily or permanently.
b. The expression 'laws which cannot without danger to the State be removed from the existing legal system' is altogether vague and, therefore, no answer can be offered to the second part of the question.

The legislative powers of the Governor-General under the existing constitution are confined within the terms of section 42, Government of India Act, 1935. Those powers are sufficient to enable the Governor-General to stay all proceedings in courts other than the Federal Court, in which legal provisions referred to are called in question, pending such action as the proposed Constituent Convention (Constitutional Assembly) may see fit to take in respect thereof.

Doctrine of Law of Necessity

It is thus noticeable that the Federal Court in 'Reference by HE the Governor-General' (*PLD 1955 FC 435*) had to fall back upon the doctrine of state necessity to take Pakistan out of the constitutional impasse it had led the country into by the judgments of the Moulvi Tamizuddin Khan case and Usif Patel case by validating the laws listed in the schedule to the Emergency Powers Ordinance, 1955 on the basis of such doctrine. One more case is worthy of mention, where the doctrine of state necessity was once again invoked by the Federal Court.[23]

In this case, two Acts of the Constituent Assembly, namely Privy Council (Abolition of Jurisdiction) Act, 1950 and Constituent Assembly for Pakistan (Increase and Redistribution of Seats) Act, 1949 came under scrutiny by the Federal Court for not having received the assent of the Governor-General. The majority of the Court (again led by Chief Justice Munir) held that although Privy Council (Abolition of Jurisdiction) Act, 1950 was not originally assented to by the Governor-General and although it could be supposed to have been declared invalid by the judgment of the Federal Court in Moulvi Tamizuddin Khan's case, still the Act having been validated temporarily and retrospectively by the Governor-General (as a result of Federal Court Judgment in Governor-General's Reference on the basis of the doctrine of necessity), it was at that time a valid law. Justice Cornelius arrived at the same main conclusion though by a different process of reasoning. He held that:

> The case of a law which does not provide a specific date for its commencement, and would, therefore, under the ordinary law be deemed to commence from the date on which assent is given is, however, distinguishable from the case of a law which itself fixes the date of its commencement. The Privy Council (Abolition of Jurisdiction) Act, 1950 does not fix the date of its commencement namely the 1st May 1950. This provision is part of the law as made by the Constituent Assembly and becomes valid upon the law receiving the assent of the Governor-General whenever that may be accorded.

It was argued that since the Constituent Assembly for Pakistan (Increase and Redistribution of Seats) Act, 1949 by which the Assembly added six members to its personnel, had not received such assent, therefore, the Privy Council (Abolition of Jurisdiction) Act, 1950 having been passed by an illegally constituted Assembly, was invalid and did not confer jurisdiction in the Federal Court to hear the appeal. On this proposition, there was marked difference in the opinion and the conclusion of the majority led by Chief Justice Munir on the one hand and Justice Cornelius on the other. The majority held:

> The general rule is that if legislature illegally adds to its members and the persons so added take part in discussion and voting, the laws passed by it are void. In the case of companies and statutory bodies, like municipal corporation, the rule is well-settled that the proceedings of such bodies are vitiated by strangers taking part in and voting at their meetings. Since the Privy Council (Abolition of Jurisdiction) Act, 1950 was passed not by the Constituent Assembly as defined by section 19(3)(b) (Indian Independence Act, 1947), but by that Assembly with six illegally added members, it was not a valid law, having been passed by an illegally constituted legislature of the dominion.

However, the Privy Council (Abolition of Jurisdiction) Act, 1950 was held valid on the ground of civil or state necessity, having been validated by Governor-General's proclamation of emergency of 16 April 1955. Justice Cornelius held the Acts of the Constituent Assembly valid notwithstanding the participation of those six newly included members on the basis of following reasons:

> As a juristic person, a Corporation is distinct from the Corporators, and certainly, it cannot be right to think that the acts of such a juristic person are vitiated *ex post facto* because of the discovery made subsequently that some of the Corporators, who participated in the acts of the Corporation perfectly bonafide, lacked the necessary qualifications or were either not validly appointed or included as Corporators. Where the defect is of subsequent discovery, and the inclusion and participation of the affected members is entirely bonafide, their presence cannot operate to vitiate either the constitution of the Corporation or the acts of such Corporation.

Justice Cornelius thus held the Act to be good and valid size. The Federal Court, thus, introduced the doctrine of necessity in the cases of Reference of the Governor-General and Ali Ahmad Husain Shah, which had a major impact on the constitutional cases to come later.

The Impact of Constitutional Cases

These constitutional cases left a major impact on the politics of the country. The entire constitutional and administrative set-up was shaken to its very foundation. The mischief caused by finding justification for an arbitrary, malicious, and capricious act of a Governor-General, who was neither mentally nor physically fit, had to be undone with enormous judicial jugglery and pedantic and abstract legal reasoning. The Federal Court had to import an alien concept of civil or state necessity to get out of the legal mess it had created without fully realizing the potential mischief of the doctrine for the future constitutional course of Pakistan. Chief Justice Munir, who was at the centre of this, cannot escape responsibility for setting the country on an uncertain constitutional and political course with attendant colossal losses in socio-politico-economic terms. The moral of the entire exercise is that one step taken in the wrong direction, for whatever reason, can hardly be corrected by the subsequent steps taken in the right direction because one such wrong step lets loose so much of negative energy and creates so much chaos and confusion that all its ramifications and consequences cannot be later curtailed, contained, or corrected. The corrective measures required are like putting the genie back into a bottle.

Justice Munir has tried to explain that his intentions were good and that he acted with promptness to correct the consequences that started to flow from the judgment in the case of Moulvi Tamizuddin Khan. He offered his defence in the following words:

The Judgment of the Federal Court in Tamizuddin Khan's case led the Governor-General to assume that he could no longer be saddled with a Constituent Assembly and could carry on without representative institutions. He, therefore, issued an Ordinance validating the laws which had been invalidated by the Federal Court and stating, *inter alia*, that he himself would give a constitution to the country, a claim the assertion of which was beyond the contemplation of the Federal Court in Tamizuddin Khan's case.

Therefore, when in a subsequent case before the Federal Court the question arose whether a law which had been validated by the Governor-General after the dissolution of the Assembly could have been validated by him, the Court denied that power to him on the ground that the Governor-General was still within the limitations of the constitution that he could not exercise the powers entrusted by the Indian Independence Act to the Constituent Assembly and that if he needed validation he was bound to call another Constituent Assembly because where representative institutions have been conferred by the Crown on a territory, the conference is absolute, unconditional, and irrevocable.

The Court thus held the Governor-General's action to be *ultra vires* but at the time the possibility of the Court's order not being obeyed was present in the mind of us all and each one of us was clear in his own mind that on any such contingency happening it would be for him to decide whether he would continue or resign.

Better counsels, however, prevailed. The Governor-General did not rely on the coercive power of the state. He reconstituted the Constituent Convention, and issued an ordinance validating the laws and asked for the Court's opinion whether in view of the action taken by him the validation was valid until the Constituent Convention was called, and whether the Constituent Convention was a legally constituted body. The Governor-General thus saved the country from a revolution by seeking to discover from the Federal Court the legal basis for his action. Subject to certain exceptions the Court recognized the validity of the Convention and thus a new Assembly took the place of the old one under the Indian Independence Act.[24]

Despite Munir's self-styled and self-serving justification, history and posterity may not see things the way he desired.

Second Constituent Assembly

The Federal Court's decision in the Reference by the Governor-General cleared the way for summoning the second Constituent Assembly. The verdict of the Federal Court in Usif Patel's case had put to an end the efforts of Ghulam Muhammad and his nominated Cabinet to make a Constitution by executive decrees.

The Federal Court unanimously declared that the task of framing a Constitution had to be performed by a Constituent Assembly. That decision was made on 13 April and two days later, the Governor-General, Ghulam Muhammad, by proclamation, summoned a sixty-member 'Constituent Convention' to meet on 10 May 1955. The Convention was to be elected from the existing provincial assemblies and its function would be to replace the first Constituent Assembly.[25]

The Convention, unless dissolved earlier, would stand dissolved at the expiry of six months and would be presided over by a person appointed by the Governor-

General. Of its sixty members, seven were to be reserved for non-Muslims in East Pakistan. The number of the seats were allocated as follows:

East Pakistan	30
Punjab	16
North-West Frontier Province	3
Sindh	4

The remaining seven would be nominated by the Governor-General on the basis of one each from Balochistan, Frontier States, Khairpur State, Bahawalpur State, and Karachi. The Tribal Areas had two representatives.

The proclamation of the Governor-General was amended by subsequent orders. Within fifteen days, two new orders were issued.[26] The first one related to the method of election to the Constituent Convention. It provided that the procedure for election would be the same as had been adopted for the Constituent Assembly elected in 1947 that is, by the method of proportional representation with a single transferable vote. The Governor-General issued a second amendment Order on 27 April under which the Convention would have eighty members and would also function as the federal legislature. The new Constituent Convention would now have all powers which were exercised by the first Constituent Assembly under the provisions of Section 8 of the Indian Independence Act. The composition now stood as follows:

East Pakistan	40 (9 for non-Muslims)
Punjab	21 (1 for non-Muslims)
NWFP	4
Sindh	5 (1 for non-Muslims)

The Governor-General would nominate ten members as follows:

Balochistan	1
Balochistan States Union	1
Frontier States	1
Tribal Areas	3
Khairpur State	1
Bahawalpur State	2
Karachi	1

The composition of the Convention was based on the principle of parity of representation between East and West Pakistan. In East Pakistan, the leader of the United Front, A.K. Fazlul Haq, was threatening to boycott the Constituent Convention on the ground that it did not give East Pakistan a majority of seats on the basis of population. Subsequently, as a result of a deal with the Prime Minister, Muhammad Ali, under which parliamentary institutions suspended since 1954 were restored in East Pakistan, the United Front agreed to accept parity of representation. The Awami League, under Law Minister Suhrawardy, had already accepted it.[27]

In the meantime, further steps to summon the Constituent Convention had to be postponed till the opinion of the Federal Court could be ascertained. The Federal

Court[28] declared on 10 May that the Governor-General had powers to summon a new Assembly but listed the following conditions before it could be regarded as legally constituted:

1. The correct name of the Constituent Convention should be Constituent Assembly;
2. The Governor-General's right to dissolve the Assembly could be derived only from the Indian Independence Act;
3. The arrangement for representation of states and tribal areas could be made only by the Constituent Assembly and not by the Governor-General; and
4. The Governor-General had no power to nominate any members of the proposed Convention (the Governor-General had planned to nominate ten members).

The Court held that the duty of summoning a new Constituent Assembly must be performed in accordance with the basic principles which were expressly followed in the setting up of the first Constituent Assembly in 1947. These basic principles were stated in paragraph 18 of the British Cabinet Mission plan of 16 May 1946.

In pursuance of the advice given by the Federal Court, it became necessary to supersede the earlier orders setting up a Constituent Convention. The Governor-General's Order No.12 of 1955 was issued to set up a Constituent Assembly and the name 'Constituent Convention' was dropped.[29] Now all the eighty members of the Constituent Assembly were to be elected and no provision was made for the nomination of some members by the Governor-General. In fact, the effect of the latest order was to set up a Constituent Assembly which was similar in structure to its predecessor. As with the first Assembly, the members were to be elected not directly but indirectly by members of the provincial legislature by the method of proportional representation with a single transferable vote. Special provision was made for elections in Balochistan and Karachi as there were no provincial legislatures in those units. Regarding the independent states and tribal areas, the arrangements for representation were left to the Constituent Assembly when summoned. The only novel element in the structure of the new Assembly was the principle of parity of representatives between East and West Pakistan. The Governor-General in his order asserted his power to summon, prorogue, and dissolve the proposed Assembly by virtue of his powers under the Indian Independence Act, 1947 under which the new Assembly was supposed to have been set up. The Governor-General also retained the right to nominate a Chairman of the Assembly till the President was elected.

Party positions in the second Assembly were very different. In the first Constituent Assembly, the Muslim League had an absolute majority, since it had captured almost all the Muslim seats. It was clear from the beginning that the Muslim League would not enjoy that position in the new Assembly. It was in East Pakistan that its position changed most radically. Out of 309 members in the East Pakistan provincial legislature, the League had only ten members and it could get only one seat from that province. In fact, it did not want to contest the election in East Pakistan but Prime Minister Muhammad Ali, who was also the President of the All-Pakistan Muslim League, persuaded it to give him a ticket from East Pakistan. The United Front and the Awami League shared between themselves the Muslim seats from East Pakistan. In West Pakistan, the League captured all the Muslim seats from Sindh and NWFP. In Punjab, however, internal divisions prevented it from having the monopoly. It lost three seats to the dissident group led by Malik Feroz Khan Noon, while Mian Iftikharuddin, the most vocal critic of the government in the first Assembly, retained his seat.

With twenty-five members in the house of eighty, the Muslim League was still the largest single party in the new Assembly but it had neither an absolute nor even a simple majority. The party position in the Assembly was as follows:

Muslim League	25
United Front	16
Awami League	12
Noon Group	3
Pakistan Congress	4
Scheduled Caste Federation	3
United Progressive Party	2
Independent Muslim	1
Others	6

Since no single party was in a position to command a majority, the various groups lost no time in seeking alliances. Seven out of fourteen members of Ghulam Muhammad's Cabinet either did not stand or failed to get elected to the new Assembly. A reshuffle of the Cabinet was therefore inevitable. A coalition of the Muslim League and the United Front was ultimately formed with Chaudhri Mohammad Ali, the former Finance Minister, as prime minister. Muhammad Ali Bogra quietly resumed his old assignment as Ambassador to the United States.

Chaudhri Mohammad Ali, as leader of the coalition party, contributed largely to the success of the new Assembly in framing a Constitution. Other prominent members of the new Assembly were H.S. Suhrawardy, leader of the Opposition who, from the very beginning, showed his talent as a great parliamentarian, and A.K. Fazlul Haq, the leader of the United Front, who assisted the prime minister greatly in arriving at a compromise over constitutional problems.

There was a complete absence of women from the second Assembly. In the first Assembly, there had been two women members and it was expected that the number would increase. Some leadng figures who had dominated the first Assembly, such as Khawaja Nazimuddin, Sardar Nishtar, Qayyum Khan, and Maulana Akram Khan, were not in the new Assembly. Like its predecessor, the second Constituent Assembly was elected indirectly.

The immediate task before the second Constituent Assembly was to revalidate those statutes which had become null and void as a result of the legal disputes that followed the dissolution of the first Assembly. The task was not too easy as it involved the delicate discussion of the merits of those statutes. The government, however, was successful in revalidating the statutes and the country was finally rescued from a critical legal predicament.

The Assembly first met on 7 July 1955 and immediately passed the Validation of Laws Act of 1955 which legitimized 38 Acts of the first Assembly. The Governor-General, Iskandar Mirza,[30] assented to these in October.[31]

West Pakistan Established as One Unit

The first important and highly controversial task performed by the second Constituent Assembly was the unification of West Pakistan. On 30 September 1955 the Assembly passed a bill merging 310,000 square miles into a single province. West Pakistan had formerly comprised three Governors' provinces, one Chief Commissioner's province, a number of States which had acceded to Pakistan, and the tribal areas. Geographically, they formed a homogeneous block with easy communications but with marked linguistic and ethnic distinctions. The result of the new Bill was to unify these various units into one province to be known as 'West Pakistan'.[32]

The Bill was hailed as a measure of administrative rationalization. It was claimed that the unification of West Pakistan would greatly simplify the federal structure of the proposed new Constitution. Now the task was to evolve a pattern in which the two provinces, East and West Pakistan, would be placed on a footing of equality. There was substance to the claim. The problem of representation of the various units in the proposed federal legislature had been a big hurdle in the way of making a Constitution. It was further claimed that the unification of West Pakistan would remove provincial rivalry and jealousy, in so far as it related to West Pakistan.

The merging of the entire West Pakistan was a big project. Some of the advantages claimed by its supporters are undeniable, but that mere abolition of provincial boundaries by an administrative act and tabooing the names, Punjab, Sindh, Pathan, Baloch, and so forth, could not automatically change a long established cultural identity. Provincialism could only change by a change in the outlook and policies of some politicians who fanned provincial feelings and prejudices to promote their narrow political interests.

While the One Unit scheme in West Pakistan could be supported on various grounds, the way in which it was established was not free from serious criticism. The original plan had been to introduce it by executive decrees. The decision of the government to introduce the One Unit scheme was first announced by the Prime Minister, Muhammad Ali, on 22 November. This was followed by the Governor-General's Order No. 8 of 1954 setting up a council for the administration of West Pakistan.[33] Then, in March 1955, the Governor-General assumed powers to constitute the new province of West Pakistan by an Order.[34]

The attempt to introduce the one-unit scheme by executive decrees was frustrated by the decision of the Federal Court in Usif Patel's case. Three provincial ministries, the Noon ministry in Punjab, the Rashid ministry in NWFP and the Pirzada ministry in Sindh, were dismissed by the central government on this issue. In similar circumstances, the ministry governing the State of Bahawalpur had been dismissed and the state legislature dissolved on 2 November 1954.

In Sindh, the Government dismissed Pirzada Abdus Sattar's ministry on 8 November on the grounds of 'maladministration' and appointed Khuhro as Chief Minister. Pirzada Abdus Sattar said that his dismissal was due to his stand in the Constituent Assembly against the merging of the West Pakistan provinces into a single unit, and claimed that his view reflected the 'unanimous will' of the people of Sindh against the One Unit proposal.[35]

In Bahawalpur, the Amir dismissed the state ministry on 2 November, dissolved the state legislature, and entrusted the administration to an adviser appointed by the central government. Major-General Mirza stated that the Amir had acted with the central government's approval, and that the ministry had been dissolved because of 'maladministration'.

In Khairpur, the State Assembly unanimously adopted a resolution on 10 November favouring the merger of the state in a single unit embracing the whole of West Pakistan. The government's proposals were subsequently endorsed by the various provincial assemblies and were generally welcomed throughout West Pakistan, although some opposition was expressed in Sindh and Karachi where student demonstrations took place. Resolutions approving the scheme were adopted by the legislative assembly of the NWFP unanimously on 25 November 1954 by the Punjab Legislative Assembly by a large majority on 30 November, by the Sindh Legislative Assembly on 11 December, and by the Shahi Jirga of Balochistan on 29 November. The Khan of Kalat expressed his support on 23 November and it was announced on 3 January 1955, that an agreement had been signed by the Khan and the other rulers of the states forming the Balochistan States Union for the merger of all these States (Kalat, Makran, Las Bela, and Kharan) into a unified West Pakistan.

Framing the Constitution

The second Constituent Assembly had also the advantage of profiting from the deliberations and work of its predecessor. It successfully utilized the groundwork done by the first Constituent Assembly and had no need to appoint various committees and sub-committees as had the first Constituent Assembly. Reports of committees and sub-committees were ready for the work of the second Constituent Assembly. In fact, most of 245 Articles in the draft Constitution reflected little change from those which had been rejected in October 1954 as coming from an Assembly 'unrepresentative of the people'.

But the difficulties of the second Constituent Assembly should not be ignored or minimized. Unlike the first Assembly, it had no party with an absolute majority. The ruling coalition party of the United Front and the Muslim League had within its fold several component groups holding diametrically opposite views on fundamental constitutional issues. The old issues of conflict such as the relation of the state and religion, a strong or weak centre; whether the electoral system should be joint or separate, and others were renewed and the various groups within the ruling party were sharply divided on these problems. The Hindu Congress and the United

Progressive Party threatened to sit on the opposition benches if joint electorate were not conceded while the Nizam-i-Islam and the Muslim League, two important groups of the coalition party, would have nothing to do with a joint electorate. Even as late as December 1955 there seemed to be little prospect of a compromise. During November and December, the Constituent Assembly was repeatedly adjourned because the coalition party could not resolve its differences, it seemed that the country had once again been brought to the verge of ruin. The different groups in the party resorted to pressure tactics to get their demands incorporated in the Constitution. As a result of these internal conflicts, the constitution which finally emerged was a poor product, judged by any criteria, based on compromises and expediency rather than on sound principles.

The draft Constitution published on 8 January 1956 was the product of four months labour by a committee of the ruling coalition party. The draft consisted of thirteen parts, covering 245 Articles. The Objectives Resolution which had been passed by the first Constituent Assembly in 1949 was included in its preamble with one new clause:

> Whereas the founder of Pakistan, Quaid-e-Azam Muhammad Ali Jinnah, declared that Pakistan would be a democratic state based on Islamic principles of social justice...

Part I of the draft defined the territories of Pakistan; Part II dealt with fundamental rights; Part III with directive principles of state policy; Part IV with the federal government and legislature; Part V with provinces and provincial governments, Part VI with relations between the federation and provinces; Part VII with property, contracts and suits, Part VIII with elections, part IX with the judiciary; Part X with the services of Pakistan; Part XI with emergency provisions; Part XII with general provisions; and Part XIII with temporary and transitional provisions. The draft was in many respects a replica of the draft Constitution made by the first Constituent Assembly. Pakistan was to be a federal republic consisting of East and West Pakistan and would be called the 'Islamic Republic of Pakistan'. It was based on the British parliamentary system. Though it provided for a President and a Vice President real power was vested in the parliament and its executive, the Cabinet.[36] But under the new draft, the powers of the President were enlarged as compared with those proposed in the draft of the first Constituent Assembly and it had subsequently to be amended. The draft envisaged a Constitution much simpler in structure, with a single chamber equally representative of the two wings instead of a complicated two-tier legislature with representation based on two principles. The unicameral legislature, to be called the National Assembly, would consist of three hundred members to be elected on the basis of parity between East and West Pakistan.

The draft provided for a strong centre. Its framers were guided by the principle that maximum autonomy should be granted to the provinces but this should be consistent with national integrity and solidarity. They recognized that a weak centre would bring disaster to the country and that while it need not be all-embracing, the centre must be sufficiently strong and effective to guide and control the provinces.

The same principle had been the guiding factor with the first Constituent Assembly. The provincial list under the new draft was larger, including Industries and Railways, residuary powers however were to be vested with the provinces, unlike in the previous draft.

In the Islamic provisions, some changes were made over the previous draft. They will be discussed while examining the Islamic character of the Constitution.

The draft had been prepared within the same set-up of political groupings with their various and sometimes complicating commitments, and with the same play and interplay of personal, group, and provincial ambitions. It was based on compromises. The drafters had adopted the device of setting up various commissions and councils such as the Economic Council, a National Finance Commission, an Islamic Research Organization while were expected to find solutions that the framers of the constitution themselves were unable to discover. There was wisdom in this method of 'cutting the Gordian Knot' because a deadlock was avoided.

The Law Minister, Chundrigar, claimed that the draft envisaged the establishment of an independent sovereign state consistent with the ideology for which Pakistan came into being. It was of a democratic and republican type, containing all that was necessary for a modern progressive state. The provisions in the draft would, he concluded, safeguard the unity, integrity, and solidarity of the country. The most encouraging feature of the draft from the national point of view was its firm rejection of a weak centre to which provinces might dictate their terms if armed with complete regional autonomy.

Political Reaction to the Draft Constitution

The publication of the new draft Constitution was met with mixed political reaction. The Muslim League, the United Front, the Nizam-i-Islam, and other political parties reacted favourably, although there was a demand for the amendment of several controversial Articles. It was only the Awami League and some Hindu and Leftist parties in East Pakistan that voiced an outright condemnation of the draft and demanded that it be scrapped. The Awami League insisted that it could not accept any constitutional scheme which failed to incorporate the famous 'Twenty-one Point' programme made at the time of the East Pakistan provincial elections in 1954. This manifesto of the United Front and the Awami League was a fundamental creed with the United Front at that time which conferred only three subjects on the centre: defence, currency, and foreign affairs. The practical difficulties of restricting the powers of the centre became immediately apparent and the United Front Party under its chief architect, Fazlul Haq, agreed to modify this unrealistic demand. The Awami League, had it been in power, would probably have come to the same realization. But its exclusion from power made it uncompromising and hence it continued to press for this stipulation. It organized a powerful campaign in East Pakistan against the draft. There were demonstrations, public meetings, a 'Resistance Day' strike and to crown it all, the chief of the Awami League in East Pakistan, Maulana Bhashani, was reported to have threatened secession. At a public meeting held in Dhaka on 15 January he said that if the centre did not right the wrong East Pakistan would have to think in terms of secession. Yet in 1956 when Suhrawardy became the prime minister, he had no hesitation in describing the Constitution as guaranteeing provincial autonomy up to 98 per cent.

Another prominent Awami Leaguer, Abul Mansur, declared in the Constituent Assembly that he did not find anything common between the two wings of the country except a common religion and the fact that they had achieved independence together from one platform. Otherwise, everything was different. He even spoke of the two wings as 'two countries' and 'two peoples'. In the Constituent Assembly, the Awami League Chief, Suhrawardy, condemned the talk of secession.

It is necessary to go a little deeper in order to appreciate the demands and feelings of the people of East Pakistan. It was the Muslims of Bengal who had given the most unflinching support to Jinnah in the movement for Pakistan. Of all the areas which now constitute Pakistan, Bengal had been the chief source of strength for the Muslim League in its struggle for Pakistan. Why had the Bengali Muslims now become reluctant to see a strong national government and why had East Pakistan become a fertile ground for political agitation? The problem in East Pakistan was largely economic. At the time of partition, Pakistan was a poor and under-developed country producing raw materials, with very little industry and not much control over commerce, and it was handicapped administratively and economically.[37] This was true of both East and West Pakistan, but East Pakistan was more drastically under developed as compared to West. It had been one of the worst neglected areas of undivided India; densely populated, the main occupation of the people being agriculture, still in a most primitive condition. The peasants of Bengal were one of the poorest in the world and they had been exploited by Hindu landlords and businessmen even before the British Raj. The Muslim peasants of Bengal had expected that after the achievement of Pakistan their economic condition would improve. Development was initiated but it was greatly hampered by political instability. The first Five-Year Plan of Pakistan, published by the central government in May 1956, admitted this fact in the statement 'East Pakistan has made appreciable progress since 1947... the rate of development, however, had not been as high as in West Pakistan.'

The economic malady of East Pakistan was further aggravated by the policies and actions of upper-class Hindus. They had dominated economic life before partition. When Pakistan came into being, some of them left while others who stayed followed a deliberate policy of ruining the economy of the province. Many of them had not yet reconciled to the creation of Pakistan and looked upon India as their real homeland and transferred their capital there by illegal methods.

The economic discontent in East Pakistan, reflected in repeated political agitation, had important bearings on constitution-making in Pakistan. The consequent apprehensions and misgivings in the eastern wing probably provide the basic explanation of East Pakistan's opposition to a strong national government.[38]

Final Approval by the Constituent Assembly

When the draft containing 245 Articles came up for detailed consideration by the Constituent Assembly, notices of as many as 670 amendments were given, mostly proposed by the members of the opposition party, the Awami League. The members of the ruling coalition party also brought a number of amendments. Out of 245 Articles of the draft, 179 were passed quickly; the remaining 66 Articles were regarded as being highly controversial, some of them being the subject of acute division within the ruling coalition party. Some of the important Articles in dispute related to: the powers of the President, particularly his right to dissolve the legislature at his discretion; emergency powers; the President's assent to Bills; the provision for a Vice-President; the relations between the Cabinet and the legislature; impeachment of the head of the state; the principle of the electorate; provisions relating to the Holy Quran and *sunnah*; the appointment of National Economic and Finance Commissions; the Federal Capital; the state language; and the title of the Constitution.

The coalition party arrived at a compromise over all these controversial issues except the principle of the electorate which it left to the decision of the National Assembly in consultation with the Provincial Assemblies. Thus the second Constituent Assembly was finally successful in fulfilling its mission of giving the country a Constitution. Its success demonstrated the fact that the real and greatest obstacle to constitution-making in Pakistan was internal power politics which, more than anything else, was responsible for the failure of the first Constituent Assembly. When the politicians realized that no further delay would be tolerated, they mended their ways and sought to solve all the complicated issues involved. In fact, the solutions agreed to in some of these controversial issues were not very different which had been offered as early as 1952; the parity of representation between East and West Pakistan, for instance, was suggested in 1952 and again in 1953 but all efforts to compromise were unsuccessful because of internal power politics.

Of greater importance was the fact that democratic institutions and the rule of law had been restored. To the credit of the government, it may be said that no attempt was made to evade the verdict of the highest judicial authority of the country. In this task of restoring democratic institutions and the rule of law the role of Moulvi Tamizuddin Khan deserves special mention. His bold and courageous step in bringing the constitutional crisis before the judiciary must be regarded as an important contribution to the cause of free institutions in Pakistan.

On 8 January 1956, the draft Constitution was presented to the country which, with certain changes and amendments, was finally adopted on 29 February 1956. Twenty-three days later, Pakistan was declared an Islamic Republic with a Constitution of its own and the legacy of the Government of India Act, 1935 was finally laid to rest.

NOTES

1. It is interesting to note that in the writ petition, Moulvi Tamizuddin Khan had arrayed Mr Muhammad Ali Bogra, the Prime Minister and members of his new Cabinet, namely, Iskandar Mirza, M.A.H Isphahani, Dr A.M. Malik, Dr Khan Sahib, General Muhammad Ayub Khan, Ghayasuddin Pathan, and Mir Ghulam Ali Talpur, as respondents. He, thus, challenged the formation of the new Cabinet and their being ministers in it.
2. Moulvi Tamizuddin Khan v Federation of Pakistan, PLD 1955 Sindh 96.
3. Muhammad Ayub Khuhro v Federation of Pakistan, PLD 1950 Sindh 49.
4. Reference was being made to Khan Iftikhar Husain Khan of Mamdot v Province of the Punjab, PLD 1950 F.C. 15 and Sarfraz Ali v The Crown, PLD 1951 F.C. 41.
5. Federation of Pakistan v Moulvi Tamizuddin Khan, PLD 1955 Federal Court 240. The dissenting judge was late Mr Justice A.R. Cornelius.
6. Section 6 sub-section (3).
7. Reference is to the Sections of Indian Independence Act, 1947.
8. Kakkezai is a *biradari* (brotherhood) to which both Justice Munir and Governor-General Ghulam Muhammad belonged. It is a small but well knit group or brotherhood and have throughout held important positions in Pakistan. There is a strong impression that the members of this group help and cooperate to advance one another's career.
9. Shahab, Qudratullah, *Shahabnama* 1992, Sang-e-Meel Publications, Lahore, p. 664.
10. He lived for about twenty-five years after this judgment.
11. Chaudhri, Nazir Husain, *Chief Justice Muhammad Munir: His Life, Writings and Judgments*, published in 1973, Research Society of Pakistan, University of the Punjab, Lahore, pp. 21-2.
12. I. Cranch 137, 2L. Ed. 60, 1803.
13. Pages 299-300 of the judgment. PLD 1955 F.C. 240.
14. Ahmad, Syed Sami, *The Judgment that Brought Disaster*, 1991, publication of Justice Kayani Memorial Law Society, Karachi, pp. 65-6.
15. Emergency Powers Ordinance 1955 (Ordinance IX of 1955). PLD 1955 Central Acts and Notifications.
16. Usif Patel v Crown, PLD 1955 F.C. 387.
17. *Dawn*, 14 April 1955.
18. These extracts are taken from Judgment in Usif Patel v Crown, PLD 1955 F.C. 387. These extracts are from pages 392, 395, 396, 397, 399, 400 and 401 of the Judgment.
19. *Dawn*, 15 April 1955.
20. Jennings, Sir Ivor, *Constitutional Problems in Pakistan*, published by Cambridge University Press, 1957.
21. Reference by His Excellency The Governor-General, PLD 1955 Federal Court 435.
22. Constituent Convention Order, 1955 (Governor-General's Order VIII of 1955). PLD 1955 Central Acts and Notifications 118.
23. The Federation of Pakistan v Ali Ahmad Husain Shah, PLD 1955 F.C. 522.
24. Chaudhri, Nazir Husain, *Chief Justice Muhammad Munir, supra*, note 11, pp. 22-23.
25. Constituent Convention Order, 1955. Governor-General's Order VIII of 1955. See PLD 1955 Central Acts and Notifications 118.
26. Constituent Convention (Amendment) Order, 1955. G.G's Order IX of 1955. PLD 1955 Central Acts and Notifications 138. Constituent Convention (Second Amendment) Order, 1955. G.G's Order X of 1955. PLD 1955 Central Acts and Notifications 142.
27. Choudhry, G.W., *Constitutional Development in Pakistan*, 1969, Longman Group Ltd., London, p. 91.
28. PLD 1955 Federal Court 435.
29. Constituent Assembly Order,, 1955. G.G's Order XII of 1955. PLD 1955 Central Acts and Notifications 161.

30. Who had in the meantime taken over from Ghulam Muhammad who had to quit because of very poor health.
31. Hayes, Louis D., *Politics in Pakistan: The Struggle for Legitimacy*, Edition 1984, p. 64. Westview Press/ Boulder and London.
32. Establishment of West Pakistan Act, 1955. See PLD 1955 Central Acts and Notifications 273.
33. The Pakistan (Establishment of Council for the Administration of West Pakistan Order, 1954. G.G's Order VIII of 1954. See PLD 1955 Central Acts and notifications 5.
34. West Pakistan (Establishment) Order, 1955. G.G's Order IV of 1955. See PLD 1955 Central Acts and Notifications 71.
35. Feldman, Herbert, *A Constitution for Pakistan*, Oxford University Press, 1955, p. 84.
36. The speech of Law Minister, Mr Chundrigar, introducing the draft in the Constituent Assembly, 1 January 1956.
37. Prime Minister Muhammad Ali's Speech in the Constituent Assembly, February 1956.
38. Choudhry, G.W., *Constitutional Developments in Pakistan, supra*, note 27, pp. 99-100.

8

THE CONSTITUTION OF 1956

After nine years of effort, Pakistan succeeded in framing a Constitution which became effective on 23 March 1956, proclaiming Pakistan as an Islamic Republic. In its general aspect, the 1956 Constitution was based on the pattern of the Government of India Act, 1935.

The 1956 Constitution was lengthy and detailed. It contained 234 Articles, divided into 13 parts and 6 schedules. On examination, we find several explanations for its length as stated below:

i. The Islamic character of the Consititution sought to base the Constitution on Islamic principles and provisions which occupied some length;
ii. It was a federal Constitution which is usually more complex, prescribing not only for the federation but also for the units;
iii. The relations between the federation and the provinces were complicated, necessitating considerable length;
iv. Special provisions had to be made for tribal areas and special areas;
v. Some matters which could have been dealt with by ordinary legislation, such as judicial organization, were included in the Constitution; the organization of the Federal Court and the judiciary of the provinces occupied as many as thirty-one Articles;
vi. There were other matters which the Constituent Assembly thought fit to include in the Constitution, relating to the public services, the languages of the federation, and the election commission, and others;
vii. It was found necessary to include emergency provisions covering Part IX of the Constitution; and
viii. Lastly, it was thought fit to include not only a lengthy Bill of Rights but also directive principles of state policy.

Lengthy constitutions are at times regarded as defective. The golden rule in constitution-making is 'never put in anything which can safely be left out'. A Constitution has to work not only in the environment of the time when it is drafted, but long after. It must, therefore, be flexible enough to adapt to new conditions as they arise. Every constitutional provision relating to an organization is a fetter limiting its action. What may be desirable in the present does not imply that it would be equally valid a century hence. The idea upon which a Constitution is based in one generation may be spurned as old-fashioned in the next. But the framers of the 1956 Constitution were not entirely free to choose whether they could make it short and flexible or lengthy and rigid. The interim Constitution, on which the new one was based so as to achieve continuity of tradition, had been the Government of India Act, 1935. In fact, many provisions of the 1956 Constitution were copied from that Act, which too was the lengthiest constitutional statute so far passed by the Parliament of the United Kingdom. Besides, the framers of the 1956 Constitution were confronted with a number of complicated issues which could not be safely ignored.[1]

Part I of the 1956 Constitution dealt with the Republic and its territories; Part II with Fundamental Rights; Part III with directive principles of state policy; Part IV with the federation; Part V with the provinces; Part VI with the relations between the federation and the provinces; Part VII with property, contracts, and suits; Part VIII with elections; Part IX with judiciary; and Part X with the services of Pakistan; Part XI dealt with emergency provisions; Part XII with general provisions; and Part XIII with temporary and transitional provisions. Of the six schedules, the first dealt with the election of the President; the second with oaths and affirmations; the third with powers of the Supreme Court and the remuneration of judges; the fourth with the remuneration and privileges of the President, the Speaker, the Deputy Speaker of the National Assembly and provincial assemblies, the members of the National Assembly and provincial assemblies, as well as the provincial governors; the fifth with the lists of subjects for which either the federation or the provinces, or both concurrently, would be competent to legislate; and the sixth with the election of the first President of the Republic.

Fundamental Rights

There was no Bill of Rights under the interim Constitution. The British constitutional experts who drafted the Government of India Act, 1935 were against the incorporation of such a Bill in the Act, but after independence, the preponderance of views in Pakistan as in other new democracies was in favour of a Bill of Rights being incorporated into the Constitution. Experience under the rule of law during British rule was not always happy because the British practice in their colonies differed from that in the United Kingdom. During the movement for freedom, the idea of a Bill of Rights, as incorporated in the Constitution of the United States of America and in many other modern constitutions, appealed very much to nationalist leaders. It was, therefore, natural that the nature and content of fundamental rights should have engaged the attention of the framers of the Pakistan Constitution from the very beginning of their assignment in 1947. A committee on the fundamental rights of the citizens and on matters relating to minorities was set up at the inaugural session of the first Constituent Assembly in August 1947. In fact, there were weighty arguments in favour of fundamental rights being defined and inserted in the proposed Constitution. In a country such as Pakistan where the English tradition of democratic practices was lacking and where public opinion was not yet articulate or powerful, the need for such a declaration was imperative. Further, since Pakistan had religious minorities, it was necessary to define and protect the rights of individuals, irrespective of caste, creed, or religion. The interim report of the Committee of Fundamental Rights was accepted in 1950 long before the adoption of any other laws of the Constitution. The single idea, in the interim report on Fundamental Rights, was to quote the words of Liaquat 'to respect the dignity of man'. The Fundamental Rights, as adopted by the first Constituent Assembly, included familiar liberties such as equality of status, of opportunity and before law; social, economic, and political justice; and freedom of thought, expression, belief, faith, worship, and association. Fundamental Rights were guaranteed to Muslim as well as to non-Muslim citizens, without any discrimination or distinction. No concept of 'second class citizens' could be found in the list of these rights which were to be enforced by the law courts.[2]

The second Constituent Assembly retained all these rights, liberties, and liberal principles and ideals behind them, but with improvement in the content of some. The 1956 Constitution laid great emphasis on fundamental rights by asserting that if any existing law or custom or usage having the force of law on Constitution day was inconsistent with any provision of fundamental rights, it would be void to the extent of such inconsistency and similarly no authority in Pakistan whether the federal government, the National Assembly, a provisional government or legislature, or any local authority, was competent to make any law, regulation, or any order which might be repugnant to any of the provisions of the fundamental rights and if any such law, regulation or order was made, it would to the extent of repugnancy be void.[3] Thus the democratic concept of limited government, that is, a government that rules by law is itself ruled by law, was established. The judiciary was given the power to enforce fundamental rights and the courts were to decide if a law was repugnant to any provisions of fundamental rights.

Familiar democratic rights and freedom such as freedom of speech and expression, of assembly and association, of movement and profession, were all provided for in the Constitution, with the usual qualifications. With regard to civil rights, familiar rights such as the right to life, liberty, and property were granted, again with the usual qualification and safeguards. Most of the constitutions which guaranteed such liberties have found it necessary to make qualifications regarding the exercise of such rights. An important provision from the standpoint of civil liberty was provided which laid down that a person arrested should not be detained in custody without being informed, 'as soon as may be' of the grounds for such arrest, and such person should not be denied the right of legal consultation and defence. Further, a person arrested or detained in custody was given the right to be produced before the nearest magistrate within a period of twenty-four hours and no further detention was allowed, except on the order of the magistrate.[4]

Such safeguards were, however, not applicable to an enemy alien, or anyone arrested or detained under a law providing for preventive detention. When the Constitution was in the process of being made, Security Acts regarding preventive detention were targets of severe criticism and attack from the opposition parties and also outside the legislature. The United Front in East Pakistan pledged itself to repeal any Security Act that may be in existence. The majority of the framers of the Constitution, including the members of the United Front felt that some safeguards against subversive, anti-state, and anti-social actions should be retained in the Constitution. They took sufficient steps to lessen the risk of such provisions being misused by limiting the powers of preventive detention to not more than three months, unless an advisory board appointed by the Chief Justice of Pakistan in the case of persons detained under a central Act and by the Chief Justice of the province in the case of people detained under a provincial Act, could certify that there was sufficient cause for such detention. The provision for review by a judicial body was undoubtedly an improvement which would act as a healthy check against abuses.[5]

During an emergency the President could, by an order, suspend the enforcement of fundamental rights guaranteed to the citizens under the Constitution. It is the right to move any court for the enforcement of the fundamental rights that could be suspended. Such an order was required 'as soon as may be' to be laid before the National Assembly.[6]

The principal fundamental rights guaranteed by the 1956 Constitution are briefly described below:

1. All citizens were equal before the law and entitled to equal protection of the law.[7]
2. No person could be deprived of life or liberty, save in accordance with the law.[8]
3. No person could be punished for an act which was not punishable when committed.[9]
4. The right to apply for a writ of habeas corpus could not be suspended, except in the case of an external or internal threat to the security of the state or other grave emergency.[10]
5. There should be no discrimination on grounds of religion, race, caste, sex, or place of birth with regard to access to places of public entertainment, recreation, welfare, or utility.[11]
6. All forms of slavery, servitude, forced labour, torture, or cruel or inhuman treatment or punishment were declared illegal.[12]
7. All duly qualified citizens were made eligible for appointment to the service of the state, irrespective of religion, race, caste, sex, descent or place of birth, provided that it should not be unlawful for the state to reserve posts in favour of any minority or backward section.[13]
8. No person could be deprived of his property without adequate compensation.[14]
9. All citizens were guaranteed (a) freedom of speech, expression, association, occupation, acquisition and disposal of property, and peaceful assembly; (b) the right to move freely throughout Pakistan and to reside in any part of the country.[15]
10. Freedom of conscience and the right to profess, practise, and propagate any religion, subject to public order and morality, were guaranteed.[16]
11. No one attending any educational institution could be required to receive religious instruction or to attend religious worship other than that of his own community or denomination. No religious community could be prevented from providing religious instruction to pupils of that community in any educational

institution which it maintained. No one could be compelled to pay any special taxes the proceeds of which were specifically appropriated for the propagation or maintenance of any religion other than his own.[17]

12. The notion of untouchability being inconsistent with human dignity, its practice was declared unlawful.[18]

These 'fundamental rights' contained a clear statement regarding the rights of individuals (whether *qua* individuals or members of a wider group like a community or a religious denomination), and these rights were fundamental not only in the sense that they had been mentioned in and guaranteed by the Constitution but were such as neither the legislature nor the executive could in any manner curtail or diminish. These rights limited legislative and executive powers and would be a clog on the 'temporary' will of the 'simple' majority in the legislature. They embodied a permanent and paramount law which could not be disturbed by the will of the legislature or of the executive. These fundamental rights would operate like a double-edged sword. They not only destroyed those portions of existing laws which were in conflict with these rights but also operated to render void any state action (whether in the legislative or executive field) which, after the coming into force of the Constitution, had the effect of taking away or abridging any of the fundamental rights.[19]

Directive Principles of State Policy

The Basic Principles Committee had recommended the inclusion of Directive Principles of State Policy. The following were included in the 1956 Constitution:

1. Steps should be taken to enable Muslims to order their lives in accordance with the Quran and the *sunnah*, *inter alia*, the compulsory teaching of the Quran, namely the prohibition of drinking, gambling, and prostitution, and the proper organization of mosques.[20]
2. The provision of food, clothing, housing, education, and medical relief should be made for citizens incapable of earning their livelihood owing to unemployment, sickness, or similar reasons.[21]
3. The improvement of living standards, the prevention of the concentration of wealth and means of production in the hands of a few, and the prevention of the exploitation of the workers and peasants.[22]
4. Abolition of illiteracy as rapidly as possible.[23]
5. Training and education for the population of different areas to enable them to participate fully in all forms of national activity and service.[24]
6. Discouragement of parochial, tribal, and racial feelings among Muslims.[25]
7. Strengthening of the bonds of unity between Muslim countries.[26]
8. Promotion of peace and goodwill among the peoples of the world.[27]
9. Separation of the judiciary from the executive, as soon as practicable.[28]
10. Protection of all legitimate rights and interests of non-Muslim communities.[29]

11. Protection of children, young people, and women against exploitation and employment in unsuitable occupations.[30]
12. To achieve parity in the representation of East Pakistan and West Pakistan in all spheres of federal administration.[31]
13. To eliminate *riba* as early as possible.[32]

The state was to be guided by these Directive Principles of State Policy in the formulation of its policies, but they were not enforceable in any court of law.[33] The provisions of the Constitution containing such principles constitute the manifesto of the policies and programmes of the state as they were to be administered and as they were visualized by the founding fathers and were required to be kept in view by subsequent generations so as to secure a continuity in the maintenance of a homogeneous and consistent policy in the matter of handling the affairs of the state.[34]

Parliamentary Form of Government

The first Constituent Assembly decided in favour of the parliamentary form of government, both at the centre and in the provinces. There were some who believed that parliamentary democracy was not suited to Pakistan. Their argument was that in the absence of two strong, stable, and responsible political parties, the parliamentary form of government, wherein the real executive authority is vested in a Cabinet responsible to the legislature, would become a farce and stable government a forlorn hope. They pointed out difficulties in the emergence of strong political parties in Pakistan, a probability that the legislature might be divided into small groups separated one from the other for personal or political reasons, thus making stable government impossible. Their main contention was that a new country like Pakistan required, more than anything else, a stable and strong government. Those who favoured a full-fledged Islamic state in Pakistan also considered that parliamentary government was not in accordance with the system which existed in the early days of Islam. Their intention was that the head of the Islamic state of Pakistan should be a Muslim and responsibility for the administration of the state should primarily be vested in the head of the state, although he might delegate part of his powers to any individual or body. The first Constituent Assembly, however, expressed faith in a parliamentary form of government in the hope that it would ensure a better relationship between the executive and the legislature.[35]

When the first Constituent Assembly was dissolved and attempts were made to introduce some sort of 'controlled democracy' with a 'Cabinet of talents', there was talk of strong government. Sir Ivor Jennings was asked to draft a Constitution in which, to quote his words, 'the American idea of an executive irremovable for four years was grafted on to a British system of representation'. He emphasized that there was no intention of introducing an undemocratic system. On the contrary, he continued, it was thought that a system in which the nature of the government was determined by bargains between the leaders of political groups, as in France, was likely to be less democratic and more corrupt than a system in which the government was given four years to carry out its policy.[36] Notwithstanding these doubts about the suitability of a parliamentary system, the second Constituent Assembly, like its predecessor, decided in its favour, both at the centre and in the provinces.

When the second Constituent Assembly met in 1955, the relationship between the executive and the legislature, particularly the powers and position of the head of the state, assumed great importance in view of certain controversial and undemocratic actions of the head of the state under the interim Constitution. The framers of the Constitution had before them vivid examples in the dismissal of a Cabinet enjoying the confidence of the legislature in 1953 and the dissolution of a legislature in 1954 when it sought to curb the powers which the head of the state had tried to exercise in an authoritarian way. They wanted to ensure that such actions would not be repeated. Hence, we find that the draft presented to the second Constituent Assembly in January 1956 had to be modified considerably regarding provisions relating to the powers and position of the head of the state. A parliamentary system was sought where real executive authority vested in a Cabinet responsible to the legislature would be guaranteed within the Constitution and not, as in Britain and in some Commonwealth countries, based on conventions alone. Countries having a parliamentary system have found it necessary to provide for a separate head of state who normally exercises only ceremonial and formal functions. In most important matters he acts on the advice of the Cabinet. Still, a separate head of the state seems to be necessary in a parliamentary system because a neutral constitutional official is needed to bridge the gap between outgoing and incoming ministries, not in taking over the government but in providing the decisions evolved in bringing a new government into office.

The President and the Cabinet

The executive authority of the federation in the 1956 Constitution was vested in the President and was to be exercised by him in accordance with that Constitution.[37] The President was to be a Muslim of not less than 40 years of age and qualified for election as a member of the National Assembly. He was to be elected by an Electoral College comprising members of the National Assembly and the Provincial Assemblies in accordance with provisions outlined in great detail in the first schedule appended to the Constitution.[38] He was to hold office for five years and no one could hold the office for more than two terms.[39] The President might resign or might, on a charge of violating the Constitution or of gross misconduct, be impeached by the National Assembly by an absolute majority.[40] He would not be allowed to hold any office of profit in the service of Pakistan but was not prevented from holding or managing any private property.[41]

The draft presented to the second Constituent Assembly originally provided for a Vice President but the proposal was not accepted and the Constitution provided that if the President was away from Pakistan or unable to perform his duties, the Speaker of the National Assembly would exercise the functions till the President resumed his duties or until a new President were elected.[42]

The Constitution provided for a Cabinet of ministers with the Prime Minister at its head 'to aid and advise' the President in the exercise of his functions. The President was required by the Constitution 'to act in accordance with the advice of the Cabinet' except in those matters in which he was empowered to act at his discretion. The Constitution strictly limited the discretionary powers of the President to the making of a few non-controversial appointments, such as the chairman and members of the Federal Public Service Commission, the Chief Election Commissioner, and other members of the Election Commission and the Chairman and Members of the Delimitation Commission. But the most important discretionary power of the President was to appoint from among the members of the National Assembly a Prime Minister who in his opinion was most likely to command the confidence of the majority of the members of the Assembly. While this may be a purely formal task in a clear cut two-party system, it becomes a function of great importance when the party situation is not clear. This discretionary power could very easily be misused. It was alleged that under the interim Constitution a head of the state had appointed somebody as Prime Minister who was not even a member of Parliament and 'who was flown from Washington without having any footing on the soil and planted as our Prime Minister'.[43] In the provinces too, several cases had occurred of chief ministers being nominated or imposed from outside. To ensure that the discretionary power was not misused, the Constitution provided a safeguard under Article 50 regarding the discretionary powers of the President and enjoined a ministry coming into power to call a session of the National Assembly within two months to demonstrate that it enjoyed the confidence of the legislature.

It was the duty of the Prime Minister to communicate to the President all decisions of the Cabinet and proposals for legislation and to furnish him with information as the President might call for.[44] The question whether any advice had been tendered by the Cabinet or a minister could not be enquired into by any court of law, nor was there any provision for countersignature by the Prime Minister or any other minister of an Act signed by the President.[45] This provision might have an effective safeguard to ensure the parliamentary nature of the executive. There was no remedy in the Constitution if the President disregarded the advice of the Cabinet except that it might resign in protest. But as the party system was not well developed, this remedy could not be an effective check on the powers of the President.

'The Prime Minister shall hold office during the pleasure of the President', such was the proposal in the provisional draft Constitution presented to the second Constituent Assembly in January 1956. But the proposal evoked great criticism and fears were expressed that this might lead to a repetition of the Cabinet dismissal of 1953. The second Constituent Assembly finally amended this as follows:

> The Prime Minister shall hold office during the pleasure of the President, but the President shall not exercise his powers unless he is satisfied that the Prime Minister does not command the confidence of the majority of the members of the National Assembly.

When the first Constituent Assembly presented its original draft in 1952, it was laid down that the ministers should hold office during the pleasure of the head of the state. When the draft was adopted by the first Constituent Assembly in 1954, the expression 'hold office during the pleasure' was significantly omitted and it was simply laid down that the Cabinet should be collectively responsible to the federal legislature. It is safe to assume that this significant change resulted from the dismissal of the Nazimuddin Cabinet in 1953. When the Constitution was redrafted in 1955–56, the tenure of the Cabinet and its relation to the President received close attention. On the one hand, the draft proposal was that the Prime Minister should hold office 'during the pleasure of the President' but, on the other hand, the opposition proposed that the Prime Minister should resign only following an adverse vote of Parliament. A compromise was finally made in the 1956 Constitution to the effect that the President should not exercise his powers unless he was satisfied that the Prime Minister did not command the confidence of the majority of the members of the National Assembly. However, this stipulation seemed to be dubious and hardly ensured the sanctity of the parliamentary system. It was the President alone who could decide whether the Prime Minister enjoyed the confidence of the National Assembly. The Constitution did not lay down any criterion or basis or rules by which the President would test whether the Prime Minister enjoyed the confidence of the National Assembly. Even if the National Assembly were to pass a vote of confidence in the Prime Minister, the President could still dismiss him. There was no remedy except that the new Prime Minister, whom the President would select, might be voted out by the National Assembly. This could have happened even if the term 'hold office during the pleasure' had been unqualified so that the sub-clause would seem to be ineffective as an additional safeguard. The most logical course would have been to lay down that the Prime Minister should quit office following an adverse vote of the National Assembly as was provided in the Constitution of the Fourth Republic in France. The removal of Suhrawardy from prime ministership by President Iskandar Mirza and the judicial decision of the Dhaka High Court regarding the dismissal of Chief Minister Abu Hussain Sarkar by the Governor, Hamid Ali, just a few minutes after his becoming Governor of East Pakistan substantiated the fact that the tenure of office of the Prime Minister or of a provincial Chief Minister under the 1956 Constitution was no safer than under the interim Constitution. The stability of the Cabinet and the sanctity of the parliamentary system depend not on the wording of the Constitution but on the growth of democratic conventions and the parliamentary spirit existing in England and in other Commonwealth countries.[46]

Unlike the position under the interim Constitution, the range of choice of a Prime Minister by the President was restricted to members of the National Assembly, except that, should the National Assembly stand dissolved, the President might select any one as Prime Minister. The appointment of a Prime Minister in 1953 and of provincial chief ministers, in some cases, of those not members of the legislature, had been criticized, hence this restriction to members of the legislature in the 1956 Constitution. Other ministers, who could be appointed and removed by the President on the advice of the Prime Minister, were not required to be members of the National Assembly at the time of their appointment but would have to become members of the National Assembly within six months. A Minister of State or Deputy Minister, however, had to be a member of the National Assembly.

The Cabinet was collectively responsible to the National Assembly.[47] Although the concept of collective responsibility of the Cabinet is based on convention under the British Constitution, yet it had been expressly included in the Constitutions of India, Sri Lanka, and the Irish Republic. The 1956 Constitution followed the example of these countries by expressly including it in the Constitution. When a Cabinet is formed by a single party, the collective responsibility can be easily accomplished. Similarly, under the leadership of a strong Prime Minister, it generally works to greater effect. In Pakistan, when Liaquat Ali Khan was Prime Minister, it operated reasonably well. Under the Nazimuddin Cabinet, solidarity suffered badly culminating in the so-called 'Cabinet of talents' of Ghulam Muhammad when Prime Minister Muhammad Ali and Law Minister Suhrawardy often made conflicting statements.[48] Cabinet solidarity proved not to be a pronounced success under the 1956 Constitution during a period of continuous coalition governments, sometimes drawn from divergent groups and parties. Conflicting public statements were not uncommon, although the legal requirement of collective responsibility to the National Assembly was maintained inasmuch as no minister voted against the decision or mandate of the Cabinet.

Functions and Powers of the President

The President, on the advice of the Cabinet, was entrusted with multifarious functions. Some of the key appointments, such as those of the Chief Justice of the Supreme Court and judges of the Supreme and High Courts, the Governors of the provinces, the Advocate-General, and the principal military officers, were made by the President on the advice of the Cabinet. He would constitute the National Economic Council, the National Finance Commission, the Inter-Provincial Council, the Commission for bringing the existing laws into conformity with the injunctions of Islam, and the Organization for Islamic Research and Instruction. He also had the power to issue proclamations of political or financial emergency and could suspend a provincial government. The supreme command of the Armed Forces was vested in the President and he was conferred the power to raise and maintain the naval, military, and air forces of Pakistan. The administration of the federal capital was vested in the President. He was also given powers to grant pardon and to remit, suspend, or commute a sentence passed by any tribunal.

Similarly, the President was given certain legislative functions to be exercised on the advice of the Cabinet. Thus he could summon, prorogue, and dissolve the National Assembly on their advice. In the draft Constitution of the second Constituent Assembly there was a provision that the President might at his discretion dissolve the National Assembly if he were satisfied that it had ceased to command the confidence of the majority of the electorate. This proposal raised strong protests both inside and outside the Assembly and consequently, the Constitution provided that the dissolution should take place on the advice of the Cabinet. But what would happen if the President should dismiss a Prime Minister, appoint a new one, and dissolve the Assembly on his advice? Was the President bound to accept advice for a dissolution if a Prime Minister who had been defeated in the National Assembly should advise the President to dissolve the Assembly? It was difficult to conceive that the President would accept such advice. In such a case, he could surely dismiss the defeated Prime Minister and appoint a new one. So occasion might have arisen when, under the Constitution, the President could force a dissolution or refuse advice for dissolution.

The President could address the National Assembly and send messages to it.[49] He would cause the budget to be laid before the National Assembly and no Bill imposing taxation or involving expenditure from the federal consolidated fund could be moved without the President's recommendation. He possessed a limited veto regarding laws made by the National Assembly.[50] When a Bill was passed by the National Assembly he could either assent to it or withhold his assent. In the latter case, if the National Assembly again passed the Bill, with or without amendment, by a majority of two-thirds of those present and voting, the President was bound to assent to it. He could also send a Bill for reconsideration and if such a Bill were passed again by a majority of the total members of the Assembly, it had to receive his assent.

When the National Assembly was not in session, the President possessed the positive power of making laws by ordinances which were to be laid before the National Assembly and would cease to operate at the expiry of six weeks from the next meeting of the National Assembly or at such time as a resolution of disapproval should be passed by the Assembly.[51] Should the National Assembly stand dissolved, the President might by ordinance authorize the expenditure from the federal consolidated fund (whether the expenditure was charged upon that fund or not), but such an ordinance was to be laid before the National Assembly 'as soon as may be' after reconstitution of the Assembly and the normal financial procedure[52] would have to be complied with not later than six weeks from that date.

An analysis of the relations between the President and his Cabinet, and between the President and the legislature under the 1956 Constitution, shows that the makers of the Constitution wanted to ensure the sanctity of the parliamentary system by statutes and were not prepared to leave it merely to rest on conventions, but some of the safeguards provided were dubious and problematic and were not effective in the actual operation of the Constitution. The net result was lacunae in the relationship between the President and the Cabinet, and the President and the legislature. An unscrupulous President could easily subvert the parliamentary system and reduce parliamentary democracy to a farce, both at the centre and in the provinces. There were several cases of such apparent misuse of powers by the President under that Constitution which will be discussed later when considering whether or not the parliamentary system was a failure in Pakistan.[53]

The Federal Government

Another basic feature was the federal form of the Constitution, following the decision in 1949. Although the solitary voice of the independent member, Fazlur Rahman, could be heard in the second Constituent Assembly in favour of a unitary form of government, the 1956 Constitution embodied all the characteristics of a federation: a written Constitution, dual polity, distribution of powers between the national and provincial governments, and a Supreme Court.

This federal structure was similar, in many respects, to that provided under the Government of India Act, 1935 which introduced a federal Constitution in undivided India. Federalism in Pakistan had to make room for self-expression and self-support for the units. The process of decentralization, therefore, was allowed under the 1956 Constitution to an extent which was unusual with other new federal constitutions. The federal Constitution of India, for instance, had a strong tendency towards centralization of authority and administration. A modern democratic government can hardly fulfil the wider objectives of social welfare services or full employment unless it has the power of legislation over the whole economic and fiscal field. Similarly, the nature of modern warfare is forcing a federal government to extend its sphere of operations.

In a complex modern society, the federal system could hardly be expected to work satisfactorily and smoothly without the process of centralization. Yet, the architects of the 1956 Constitution provided maximum room for decentralization in view of the number of powerful factors, political, economic, psychological, working towards demands for regional autonomy. Unless the demands were reasonably satisfied, the movement for secession which subversive elements were trying to create, might have been encouraged. On the other hand, the risk was that the decentralized structure of a weak federation might afford footholds for foreign intrigue and attack.

On closer scrutiny, the 1956 Constitution had granted what the Awami League leader, Suhrawardy, called '98 per cent of provincial autonomy' but it also provided for adequate safeguards to ensure the discharge of its responsibilities and duties by the national government. This was a commendable feature of the 1956 Constitution from the standpoint of national unity and solidarity.[54]

Turning to the distribution of legislative powers between the centre and the provinces, the powers were exhaustively enumerated in three lists—federal, provincial and concurrent, as in the Government of India Act, 1935. The extent of federal laws was extended to the whole or any part of Pakistan, including the power to make laws with extra-territorial operations. The power of a provincial legislature extended to the whole of that province or any part thereof.[55] Parliament was given exclusive power to make laws concerning thirty items in the federal list as against sixty-one under the Government of India Act, 1935, and sisty-six in the draft Constitution of the first Constituent Assembly. The subjects given to the centre included foreign affairs, comprising all matters which would bring Pakistan into relations with foreign countries; defence; currency; citizenship; foreign and inter-provincial trade and commerce; insurance and corporations set up by the federation; industries owned wholly or partially by the federation; posts and all forms of telecommunications; and minerals, oil, and gas.[56]

The provincial list was most comprehensive and included ninety-four items, as against fifty-five under the Government of India Act, 1935, and forty-eight in the draft Constitution of the first Constituent Assembly, which indicated the trend towards decentralization recognized by the second Constituent Assembly. The provincial list included, amongst others, public order, administration of justice, police, land, agriculture, local government, education, public health, sanitation, industries and corporations subject to the federal lists, factories, regulations of mines and mineral development subject to the federal and concurrent lists, forests, electricity, and other subjects of local interest.[57] The most important addition to the provincial list was railways which continued to be under central control at the time of the abrogation of the constitution in 1958.

The concurrent list was the smallest and included only nineteen items and was justified on the ground that there were certain matters which could not be given exclusively either to the centre or to the provinces since they might normally be dealt with by the provinces but occasions might arise when it would be desirable and necessary to deal with them on a national level. Again, the regulation of some matters by one unit might prejudice the interests of the other unit, or to secure legal and economic uniformity, federal jurisdiction might be necessary. The list dealt with such matters as civil and criminal law, scientific and industrial research, price control, economic and social planning, inter-provincial migration and quarantine, trade union, and other matters of common interest.[58]

With regard to subjects in the concurrent list, the precedence of federal legislation was guaranteed. So the Constitution had provided priority of federal legislative power over the provincial one applicable over the concurrent list, and the concurrent list had priority over the provincial, as had been provided for in the Government of India Act, 1935. In fact, the structure and content of Article 106 were identical with those of Section 100 of the Government of India Act, 1935.

The question whether residuary powers should be vested in the federal or in provincial authorities had produced lengthy discussions and controversies in the constituent Assemblies of Pakistan but under the 1956 Constitution residuary power was vested with the provincial legislatures which were to have exclusive power to make laws with respect to any matter not enumerated in the federal, provincial, or concurrent lists.[59]

The federal government was fully equipped for the conduct of international affairs. Parliament was authorized to implement treaties with laws which it might have no power otherwise to pass; a treaty could reach and control matters normally within the powers of the provinces. It was given power to make laws for implementing any treaty, agreement or convention or a decision taken by an international body even though it might deal with a matter enumerated in the provincial list, or a matter not enumerated in the provincial list, or a matter not enumerated in any of the three lists.[60]

The Chief Justice of Pakistan was assigned an important role in the settlement of disputes between the federal government and one or both provincial governments, or between the two provincial governments. He was to appoint a tribunal to settle such a dispute. The report of the tribunal was to be submitted to the Chief Justice who would forward it to the President who could make such orders as might be necessary to give effect to the report. This order must be made effective by the provinces and any action of the provincial legislature which might be repugnant to the President's order would be void.[61]

There was also provision for an inter-provincial council which the President could set up for the purpose of investigating and discussing subjects of common interest between the federation and one or both the provinces.[62] Neither a tribunal under Article 129 nor an inter-provincial council under Article 130 was set up in the duration of the 1956 Constitution.

There was no provision in the Constitution, as under the Indian Constitution, whereby the federal legislature could make laws in any provincial matters on the grounds of 'national interest'. There were, however, at least two processes which would enable the federal legislature to legislate even on a provincial subject. The first applied when a provincial legislature authorized parliament to make laws in any matter enumerated in the provincial list or any matter not enumerated in any of the three lists. An Act passed by the parliament in exercise of this power, in so far as it would affect a province could, however, be repealed by the provincial legislature.[63] In India, where similar power is given to the parliament, a federal law cannot be repealed. In Pakistan, the provision to repeal a federal law seemed to have been made to ensure the sanctity of provincial autonomy which the Constitution sought to preserve.

While legislation by the federal legislature under Article 107 was voluntary, the second process which would enable the federal government to intervene in provincial matters, was of far-reaching importance. This related to the power to issue a proclamation of emergency and while this was in operation, parliament was empowered to make laws for a province with respect to any matters not enumerated in the federal or concurrent lists.[64]

The Federal Legislature (The Parliament)

Unlike other federal constitutions of the time, the 1956 Constitution provided for a unicameral system. The first conflict relating to the federal structure in Pakistan was over the quantum of representation for the two wings of the country. After several years of acute controversy it was agreed that there should be parity of representation between East and West Pakistan. Under the draft Constitution made by the first Constituent Assembly there was provision for a second Chamber and parity of representation was provided for in the joint session of the two Houses. When the provinces and states in West Pakistan were amalgamated into a single unit by the second Constituent Assembly, the problem of representation in the federal legislature was made much simpler and it was, therefore, proposed that the legislature should have only one House in which parity of representation between East and West Pakistan could be maintained.

The reasons for, and the advantages of, having a second Chamber are, however, not confined to its utility as an instrument of representation of the units in a federation. From the standpoint of checks and balances, the Constitution suffered great defects in the absence of a second Chamber. Any political party with a simple majority in the legislature could upset the democratic structure of the government machinery.

The parliament of Pakistan under the 1956 Constitution consisted of the President and one House, the National Assembly.[65] The National Assembly was to consist of 300 members, half elected by constituencies in East and half by constituencies in West Pakistan. Ten additional seats were provided for women, five from East, and five from West Pakistan, for a period of ten years.[66] Hence, the female citizens of Pakistan were granted double franchise for at least ten years. Parliament might alter the numbers of the members of the National Assembly provided that the parity of representation between East and West Pakistan was maintained.

Members of the National Assembly were to be elected under an electoral system for which the second Constituent Assembly did not legislate, but left it to be decided by the National Assembly after consulting the provincial assemblies. In October 1956, the National Assembly, passed an electoral law amidst scenes of riot and confusion. The Bill was passed in great haste without giving the National Assembly or the country an opportunity to judge its merits. Debate over the system of electorate, whether it should be joint or separate, had a long history behind it and had been debated at great length. The Bill provided for a joint electorate in East and a separate electorate in West Pakistan.[67] It was the most ridiculous system ever to have been thought of and was the product of party alliances and groupings prevailing at the time. It apparently sought to satisfy the exponents of both joint and separate electorates and failed to satisfy either. Subsequently, electoral law was changed to joint electorates for the whole country,[68] but the issue was alive till the abrogation of the 1956 Constitution and it had a long-lasting impact on politics in Pakistan. The Awami League, in coalition with the Hindu Congress, advocated joint electorates while some of the Muslim parties were still opposed to it.

A person was entitled to vote for the National Assembly (as well as the provincial assemblies) if he were a citizen of Pakistan, not less than 21 years of age, not declared by a court to be of unsound mind, and had resided within the constituency for six months before the first day of the year in which the preparation of the roll should commence. Parliament could impose other qualifications in this respect.[69]

The candidate for election to the National Assembly was to be not less that 25 years of age and qualified to be a voter. The Election Commission, on reference from the Speaker of the National Assembly, could decide questions of disqualification of a member and its decision was final. No one could to be a member of the National Assembly for two or more constituencies, though a person could seek election from more than one constituency. A member of the National Assembly could lose his seat if he remained absent for sixty consecutive sitting days. No one could be a member simultaneously of the National Assembly and of a Provincial Assembly.[70] Under the interim Constitution, double membership was permitted and it caused much inconvenience and many complications.

The President, as noted earlier, was empowered to summon, prorogue, and dissolve the National Assembly on the advice of the Cabinet. There were to be at least two sessions of the National Assembly every year, and at least one session was to take place in Dhaka, the capital of East Pakistan. This was done to remove the feeling of neglect in East Pakistan. The Assembly was to be summoned within two months of the formation of a new Cabinet. Even a minister and the Attorney-General had the right to speak and take part in the proceedings of the National Assembly but not the right to vote unless he were a member. The President could address or send messages to the National Assembly.[71]

The National Assembly would choose the Speaker and Deputy Speaker from its own members. They could be removed by a resolution of the National Assembly, passed by a majority of the total membership. When the National Assembly stood dissolved, the Speaker would continue his office until the convening of the first meeting of the successor elected National Assembly.[72]

The National Assembly was to frame its own rules of procedure and the validity of any proceedings in the National Assembly could not be questioned in any court. The rules of procedure were based on the spirit and substance of those at Westminster. The usual procedure in the National Assembly was that a decision would be made by a majority of votes of the members present but in some specific cases, such as the impeachment of the President, the removal of judges of the Supreme Court, the overriding of the President's suspensive veto, and amendments to the Constitution, an absolute majority of the total membership was required. No member of the National Assembly could be made liable in any proceedings in any court regarding anything said or any vote given by him in the National Assembly or its committees. The privileges of the National Assembly, committees, the members thereof, and people entitled to speak therein could be determined by an Act of parliament.[73]

The procedure in financial matters was also largely based on the system existing in England and in Commonwealth countries. The tradition of parliamentary control over public money was largely maintained. No tax, for instance, could be levied for federal purposes, except by or under the authority of an Act of parliament,[74] custody of the federal consolidated fund including the payment of money into it and withdrawal of money from it and all matters connected with public money and public accounts, were to be regulated by an Act of parliament.[75] No proposal for the imposition of taxation or for appropriation of public revenues or for borrowing of money and similar matters could be made except with the recommendation of the President, that is, it could be made only with the approval and responsibility of the Cabinet.[76]

In the budget, the financial statement was divided into two parts: one showing the expenditure charged upon the consolidated fund—the expenditure which the National Assembly could discuss but not vote upon; the other part showing the sums required for the estimated expenditures of the various departments for the financial year. Expenditures charged upon the consolidated fund included; (a) remuneration and pension of the President, salaries of judges of the Supreme Court, members of the Federal Public Service Commission, the Speaker and the Deputy Speaker, the

Comptroller and Auditor-General, the Election Commissioners and members of the Delimitation Commission; (b) the administrative expenses of the Supreme Court, the Federal Public Service Commission, the department of the Comptroller and Auditor-General, the Election Commission; and (c) the debt charges binding on the federal government and sums required to satisfy any judgment, decree, or award against Pakistan by any court or tribunal and any other sum declared by the 1956 Constitution or by Act of Parliament.[77]

The National Assembly was given a normal life of five years but the President, on the advice of the Cabinet, could dissolve it earlier.[78] In the case of dissolution, fresh elections were to take place within six months and no by-election could be delayed beyond three months. These were to be healthy democratic checks against prolonged rule without a parliament or any attempt to avoid the expression of public opinion through by-elections. By-elections had often been unduly delayed or evaded altogether under the interim Constitution.

Provincial Governments and Legislatures

The provincial legislatures and executives were small replicas of the national legislature. Provincial Assemblies, like the National Assembly, were unicameral and were to be directly elected by the people through universal adult franchise under the same electoral law. The relationship between the provincial Governor, provincial Chief Minister, and the Provincial Assembly closely resembled that between the President, the Prime Minister, and the National Assembly. The Governor could appoint and dismiss the provincial Cabinet through a procedure similar to that of the President in exercising his powers at the centre. The provincial Cabinet was also collectively responsible to the provincial legislature which could be dissolved by the Governor on the advice of his Cabinet. Contrary to section 51(5) of the interim Constitution which laid down that in the exercise of his functions with respect to the choosing, summoning, and dismissal of ministers, the Governor would be guided under the general control and would comply with such particular directions as might be given, from time to time, by the Governor-General, there was no similar provision in the 1956 Constitution. Yet, in practice, the position was not different from that under the interim Constitution. The Governor continued to be an agent of the central government which could, and did, exercise pressure in provincial politics through the Governors.

Distribution of Powers between the Centre and the Provinces

In the distribution of legislative powers between the centre and the provinces the framers of the 1956 Constitution allowed a greater decentralization than under the Government of India Act, 1935. Administrative relations between the centre and the provinces, however, changed a little. The federal system showed, a marked tendency towards unified control and authority. It was the constitutional duty of the federal government to protect each province against external aggression and internal disturbance. Although the maintenance of law and order was a provincial subject, the federal government was vested with the ultimate responsibility of ensuring the peace and safety of the country, the primary duty which no national government can afford to neglect, be it under a unitary or a federal system. The federal government was also entrusted with the task of ensuring that the government of each province was carried on in accordance with the provisions of the Constitution.[79] A provincial government would not be allowed to flout the supreme law of the land, that is, the Constitution. A provincial government was obliged to exercise its executive authority in such a manner as to ensure compliance with the Acts of Parliament and existing laws applying to that province. The central government would make laws in the federal or concurrent lists which would apply to the provinces. Although these laws might be administered by the federal authority itself, yet the Constitution enjoined upon the provincial authorities the duty of giving due effect to the federal laws prevailing or applying to the provinces and not impeding or prejudicing the exercise of the executive authority of the federation. The federal government was entitled to give direction to a province with regard to the duties of the provincial authority and was further entitled to give directions to a province in the following matters:[80]

(a) the construction and maintenance of communications declared to be of national or military importance;
(b) the measures to be taken for the protection of railways within the province (although railways were included under the provincial list);
(c) the manner in which the executive authority of the province was to be exercised for the purpose of preventing any grave menace to the peace and tranquility or economic life of Pakistan or any part thereof;
(d) the carrying into execution in the provinces of any Act of parliament in Part II of the concurrent list, such as measures to combat corruption, or price control, and economic or social planning.

There was one important provision in the 1956 Constitution which would enable the federal government to delegate a provincial government as its agent. The President might, with the consent of a provincial government, entrust either conditionally or unconditionally to that government, or to its officers, functions regarding any matter to which the executive authority of the federation extended.[81] The practice of delegation to a provincial government or their servants the duty of executing orders of the federal government had been exercised under the interim Constitution. The federal government did not have sufficient number of officers in the provinces to execute its laws or orders, hence the necessity of such delegation. The framers of the Constitution allowed this process of delegation to provincial governments to continue, thus permitting the federal government to utilize provincial executive machinery for the enforcement of federal laws. Further, under Article 127(2), parliament might impose duties or confer powers on a province or its officers in a matter not within the jurisdiction of the federal legislature. In such cases, the federal government was obliged to pay the cost of administration which might be mutually settled or be determined by a tribunal appointed by the Chief Justice of Pakistan.

The 1956 Constitution made very little change regarding the distribution of financial resources between the centre and the provinces. The original distribution of financial resources under the Government of India Act, 1935 tipped heavily in favour of the centre and had been changed further to the advantage of the central government in Pakistan after independence. The result was that the provinces were left without adequate resources, particularly in East Pakistan which suffered greatly, and greater financial resources for the province were vigorously demanded in the Constituent Assembly by the members from East Pakistan. Notwithstanding this, the major sources of income under the 1956 Constitution were assigned to the centre which was given the power to levy custom duties, export duties, excise duties, corporation tax, taxes on income other than agricultural income, estate and succession duties regarding property other than agricultural land, tax on capital value of the assets exclusive of agricultural land, taxes on goods or passengers and taxes on minerals, oil, and natural gas. The principal source of income for the provinces were taxes on agricultural income, the capital value of agricultural land, taxes on land and buildings, taxes on mineral rights subject to the federal list, excise on alcohol and drugs, taxes on electricity, taxes on vehicles and advertisements, animals, boats, on professions and trades, and on luxuries.[82]

The Judiciary

Adequate provisions were made in the 1956 Constitution to ensure the independence of the judiciary so that 'justice could be dispensed in Pakistan in a real and unpolluted form'. The efficiency and independence of the judicial system depends to a great extent upon the method of appointment, tenure of service, and salary of the judges. The framers of the Constitution thought it desirable to include the organization of the judicial system and provisions relating to it were given in considerable length. The aim of such constitutional safeguards in the organization of the judiciary was to secure its independence as being fundamental to both the Islamic and the western concepts of justice.

Though the Supreme Court under the 1956 Constitution was the successor of the Federal Court, in the interim Constitution its jurisdiction was in some respects wider. Apart from expressed constitutional or statutory provisions there was no limit to its jurisdiction in matters decided by the High Courts.[83] The law which it would lay down was binding on all courts in Pakistan. As supreme tribunal, it was the sole judge of its jurisdiction and there was no judicial means of challenging its exercise. A judgment of the Supreme Court was binding on all courts in Pakistan; all executive and judicial authorities throughout the country also had to act in the aid of the Supreme Court and all directions, orders, decrees, or writs issued by that court were to be executed as if they were issued by the High Courts of the appropriate province.[84]

Like its predecessor, the Federal Court, the Supreme Court was entrusted with the task of interpreting the Constitution. It was specifically given the power to adjudicate in any dispute between:[85]

(a) the federal government and the government of one or both provinces, or
(b) the federal government and the government of a province on the one side and the government of the other province, or
(c) the governments of the provinces, if and in so far as the dispute should involve any:
    i. question of legal rights;
    ii. question relating to the interpretation of the Constitution.

The 1956 Constitution thus departed from the principle of parliamentary supremacy which exists in England and accepted the principle of judicial review found in the federal systems of Australia, Canada, and the United States of America. The Constitution was made the 'supreme law of the land' and the 'judiciary was made the guardian of the Constitution'. The position under the interim Constitution was similar when, after independence, the right of appeal to the Privy Council was abolished. In fact, in all the constitutional drafts which had been presented to the country from time to time there was hardly any difference of opinion as to the role and status of the judiciary.

The writ jurisdiction of the superior courts which was introduced in July 1954, was retained under the 1956 Constitution. Each High Court had the power throughout its territories to exercise jurisdiction to issue to any person or authority orders or writs including writs in the nature of habeas corpus, mandamus, prohibition, quo-warranto, and *certiorari* for the enforcement of any of the fundamental rights guaranteed under the Constitution or for any other purpose.[86] The writ jurisdiction of the superior courts in Pakistan constitute a perpetual reminder to the executive to exercise restraint and caution as imposed under the laws of the land. The courts exercised this power in a beneficial and befitting manner and thus earned the confidence and trust of the people.

The provisions regarding judiciary in the 1956 Constitution followed the pattern set under the Second Report of the Basic Principles Committee, 1952 which was more or less included *in toto* in the draft Constitution adopted by the first Constituent Assembly in October 1954. The Supreme Court consisted of the Chief Justice and not more than six judges, a number that could, be raised by the parliament under the Act.[87] The Chief Justice was to be appointed by the President and other judges were to be appointed by the President in consultation with the Chief Justice.[88] The qualification for appointment as a Judge of the Supreme Court was either five years standing as a Judge of a High Court or fifteen years standing as an advocate or pleader of a High Court.[89] The retirement age of a Supreme court Judge was fixed at sixty-five years and he was disqualified from pleading or acting before any Court or authority in Pakistan.

The provision regarding the removal of a Judge of the Supreme Court was similar to one provided under the Constitution of India.[90] A Judge could only be removed on the presentation of an address by the National Assembly by not less than one-third of the total number of members of the Assembly; by the President, if after due investigation and proof of misbehaviour, or infirmity of mind or body was established, with the National Assembly votes for his removal by two-thirds of its members present and voting (but not less than a majority of total membership) on the ground of misbehaviour, infirmity of mind or body.[91] There was also provision for the appointment of acting Chief Justice in the absence of the Chief Justice or when the office became vacant.[92] There were also provisions for acting judges and adhoc judges.[93]

The Constitution provided for two High Courts, one for the province of East Pakistan, and the other for the province of West Pakistan. Each High Court was to consist of a Chief Justice and such number of other judges that the President might determine.[94] The Chief Justice of a High Court was to be appointed by the President after consultation with the Chief Justice of Pakistan and the Governor of the province concerned. In case of appointment of other judges of the High Court, the President could appoint them in consultation with the aforesaid constitutional functionaries as well as the Chief Justice of the concerned High Court.[95] The retirement age was fixed at sixtee years. The qualification for appointment as a judge of a High Court included ten years standing as an advocate or pleader of a High Court, ten years standing as a member of the civil service of Pakistan including at least three years as a district judge, or holding of a judicial office in Pakistan for at least ten years.[96] Members of the civil service in India were not qualified for appointment as judges of High Courts.[97]

A High Court judge could not be removed from his office except by an order of the President made on the ground of misbehaviour or infirmity of mind or body, if the Supreme Court, on reference being made to it by the President, reported that the judge ought to be removed on any of those grounds.[98] There was provision for appointment of acting Chief Justice when the office of the Chief Justice became vacant or he was absent or unable to perform his duties.[99] However, transfer of judges from one High Court to another was made subject to the consent of the judge being transferred and subject to the consultation with the Chief Justice of Pakistan and the Chief Justice of the High Court of which he was a judge.[100] This procedure of transfer of a judge from one High Court to another could strengthen the judiciary and its independence and could pre-empt the interference of the executive with the judiciary.

As discussed above, the High Courts were given the power to issue writs of habeas corpus, mandamus, prohibition, quo-warranto, and *certiorari*. Similar powers were vested in the Supreme Court of Pakistan to issue all such writs for the enforcement of the fundamental rights guaranteed under the Constitution.[101] This provision was apparently borrowed from the Indian Constitution (enforced in 1950) wherein the Supreme Court was empowered to issue all such writs for the enforcement of fundamental rights.[102]

Islamic Provisions

According to the Constitution, Pakistan was declared as an 'Islamic Republic' wherein the principles of freedom, equality, tolerance, and social justice as enunciated by Islam should be fully observed.

The Islamic provisions were contained in the directive principles of state policy which were not enforceable in the law courts but were supposed to serve as a guide to state authorities in the formation of policies. According to the directive principles, steps were to be taken to enable the Muslims of Pakistan individually and collectively to order their life in accordance with the Holy Quran and *sunnah*.[103] Further, the state was to endeavour (a) to provide facilities whereby Muslims might be enabled to understand the meaning of life according to the Holy Quran and *sunnah*; (b) to promote amity and observance of Islamic moral standards, (c) to secure the proper organization of *zakat* and *waqf*. Article 24 provided that the state should endeavour to strengthen the bonds of unity among Muslim countries. The same Article enjoined Pakistan to foster friendly relations with all nations, Muslim and non-Muslim. Hence, it should not be interpreted as pan-Islamic.

The head of the state, the President, was to be a Muslim. The original proposal provided for a Vice President who should also be a Muslim, but the provision was not accepted. The Speaker of the National Assembly would exercise the functions of the President if he was absent from Pakistan or was unable to discharge the duties of his office owing to illness or any other cause. The Speaker might be a non-Muslim, so occasion might arise when the temporary head of the state could be a non-Muslim.

The argument for reserving the presidency for a Muslim was that Pakistan was founded on the basis of Islamic philosophy and it was, therefore, logical that the President as a symbolic head should be amongst those believing in the Muslim faith. It was further stated that as real power was vested in the parliament, therefore, reservation of the presidency for a Muslim would not reduce the non-Muslims to the position of second-class citizens. With the exception of this solitary clause there was no discrimination against any citizen on the grounds of religion, colour, race, or nationality. Moreover, adequate and generous provisions were made in the Constitution to safeguard the interests of non-Muslim minorities. Hence, there was no basis for apprehension that the introduction of an Islamic state in Pakistan would per se relegate non-Muslim citizens to an inferior status.

A more important Islamic provision laid down that 'no law shall be enacted which is repugnant to the injunctions of Islam as laid down in the Holy Quran and the *sunnah*' and that existing laws 'shall be brought into conformity with such injunctions'.[104] Whether a law was repugnant to Islam or not could only be decided by the National Assembly. Article 198 provided that the President should appoint within one year of the day of commencement of the Constitution a commission to make recommendations for bringing existing laws into conformity with the injunctions of Islam and to specify the stages by which the measures should be brought into effect. They were also to compile in a suitable form for the guidance of the National and provincial assemblies such injunctions of Islam as could be given legislative effect. The Commission was to submit its final report within five years of its appointment and might submit an interim report earlier. The report, whether interim or final, was to be laid before the National Assembly, and within six months of its receipt, the Assembly was to enact laws in respect thereof. It was made clear that nothing in this Article should affect the personal laws of non-Muslims or their status as citizens or any provision of the Constitution.

Emergency Provisions

The description of the federal structure under the 1956 Constitution would not be complete without a reference to the emergency provisions that is provided for as they greatly affected relations between the centre and the provinces. The Government of India Act, 1935 which introduced federation in the subcontinent for the first time made elaborate provisions for dealing with an emergency. Following this model, the 1950 Indian Constitution contained elaborate emergency provisions. The framers of the Pakistan Constitution also felt the need for such provisions. The draft Constitution made by the first Constituent Assembly contained detailed provisions for dealing with different types of emergencies. These were, however, subject to severe criticism from those political parties and groups which had described the first Constituent Assembly as 'unrepresentative of the people'. Curiously enough, the second Constituent Assembly in which those political groups had the opportunity to redraft the Constitution in Part IX (Articles 191–196) retained all these emergency provisions, making them even stronger in some respects.

Under Article 191, if the President was satisfied that a grave emergency existed in which the security or economic life of Pakistan or any part thereof was threatened by war or external aggression or by internal disturbance beyond the power of the provincial government to control, he could issue a proclamation of emergency which might also be issued before the actual occurrence of war or any such aggression if the President were satisfied that there was imminent danger thereof.

While this Article was being debated in the second Constituent Assembly, some of its members opposed its application to internal disturbance and wanted to restrict its application to war or armed rebellion. Another amendment sought to delete the words 'economic life of Pakistan'. The contention was that an emergency must be clearly defined, otherwise the powers would be misused. They stated that proclamation after proclamation had been made in Pakistan without sufficient cause. 'We understand threat of war, we understand external aggression, but we do not understand what is meant by internal disturbance. Anything may be internal disturbance. A movement against a particular measure of the government for the time being may be interpreted as internal disturbance'. Similarly, the term 'economic life of Pakistan' was stated to be vague. 'Anything might be considered as endangering the economic life of Pakistan'.[105] While the allegations that emergency provisions under the interim Constitution had been used on many occasions without sufficient cause contained substantial truth, this does not prove that emergency provisions to deal with internal disturbance are superfluous and a negation of democracy. Most existing federal systems grant such power to the central authority. The effects of a proclamation of emergency under Article 191 included:

(a) the power of the parliament to make laws for a province in matters which were not included in the federal or concurrent lists, that is, it would have power to legislate even in provincial matters;
(b) during a proclamation of emergency the federal executive authority had the power to give direction to a province regarding the manner in which the executive authority of the province was to be exercised;
(c) during a proclamation of emergency the President, might issue an order assuming himself, or directing the Governor of a province to assume on his behalf, all or any powers of the provincial government or any organ of the provincial government except the provincial legislature and judiciary. The President was also empowered to suspend in whole or in part the operation of any provision of the Constitution relating to any body or authority in the province except the High Court.

Clause 6 of Article 191 seemed to have granted the federal executive (the President) an undefined power to suspend democratic processes for an indefinite period, not only in the provinces but even at the centre. It provided that a proclamation of emergency should be placed before the National Assembly 'as soon as conditions make it practicable for the President to summon the Assembly'. Under the draft Constitution adopted by the first Constituent Assembly, a proclamation would cease to operate at the expiry of two months unless, before the expiration of that period it had been approved by a resolution of the federal legislature. A similar time limit is imposed under the emergency provision of the Indian Constitution which lays down that a proclamation shall cease to operate at the end of two months unless approved within the period by a resolution of both Houses of the Indian parliament.

Now the phrase 'as soon as it is practicable' for the President to summon the National Assembly was very vague. What would happen if the President did not find it practicable to summon the National Assembly but allowed the proclamation to continue for an indefinite period? While this Article was being debated in the Constituent Assembly, some members expressed apprehension about granting such unlimited powers to the President and amendments were moved to fix a time limit, but none of them were accepted. As a result, the 1956 Constitution had this lacuna which might have enabled the President on proclaiming an emergency, to rule the country for an indefinite period without the help of the National Assembly. It should be pointed out, however, that Article 51 provided that there should be at least two sessions of the National Assembly every year and six months should not intervene between the two sessions. There was no specific provision that while a proclamation was in operation, Article 51 should cease to operate, is had been expressly provided with regard to Article 50(1) which laid down that at least one session of the National Assembly should take place in Dhaka. This sub-clause could be suspended by an order of the President during an emergency period. It was not clear whether the

President could ignore Article 51 enjoining him to summon the National Assembly at least twice a year.

While emergency provisions of the type discussed above are common in existing federal systems, there was provision for another type of emergency, namely, the breakdown of constitutional machinery in a province, which was peculiar to the constitution of Pakistan. (The 1950 Indian Constitution, is also an exception). This unique feature had its origin in the Government of India Act, 1935 which elaborated provisions relating to an emergency due to a failure of the constitutional machinery, both at the centre and in the provinces.[106] There was no provision in the 1956 Constitution relating to the breakdown of constitutional machinery at the centre; it retained provisions to meet a constitutional crisis only in the provinces. Thus, under Article 193 of the 1956 Constitution, if the President, on the receipt of a report from the Governor of a province, was satisfied that a situation had arisen in which the government of the province could not be carried on in accordance with the provisions of the Constitution, he could, by proclamation, assume to himself, or direct the Governor to assume on his behalf, all or any of the functions or powers of the provincial government or any organ or body of the provincial government except the provincial legislature and judiciary and the National Assembly might be authorized to exercise the powers of the provincial legislature. The President could also suspend the operation of any provisions of the Constitution relating to any body or authority in the province except the High Court. The President, during a proclamation under this Article, was empowered to authorize expenditure from the provincial consolidated fund in anticipation of approval by the National Assembly.

The net effect of a proclamation under Article 193, as under 92A of the interim Constitution, would be to suspend parliamentary government in a province. This power of the central government to suspend democratic process in a province was the subject of severe criticism in many quarters and it appeared to many people that this power had previously been exercised by the central government not always with sufficient cause or justification, and seemingly abused on more than one occasion for party or sectional interests. It was an excellent weapon in the hand of the central government to put pressure and exert influence on provincial politics. When this Article came before the second Constituent Assembly it was under heavy fire from the exponents of provincial autonomy and provincial rights: 'We had a bitter experience of section 92A in Pakistan in the different provinces of Pakistan. During the last eight years of independence we have seen how this provision has been misused most undemocratically and for political ends. A misuse is likely to creep in and such misuse may arise when the provinces and the central government are not governed by the same political party; if the central government is of the opinion that the political party which is running the government in the province is to be suppressed it will not hesitate in the interest of good government to let it carry on purely for political motive, but it may bring about an influence to bear upon the President to suspend the democratic process in the province'.[107]

While the fears expressed by the members could not be dismissed easily, the provision relating to the breakdown of the constitutional machinery could be justified on the ground that it was the duty of the central government to ensure 'that the government of every province is carried on in accordance with the provisions of the constitution'. Occasions have arisen in different provinces in India since the adoption of the Constitution in 1950 by it, when no stable ministry could be formed in a province, and the central authority had to intervene. The 1956 Constitution, however, made definite improvement in one respect. Whereas under the Government of India Act, 1935 and under the 1950 Constitution of India, the provincial government might be suspended for as long as three years, the 1956 Constitution put a maximum limit of six months for such suspension of a provincial government. A proclamation under Article 193 could cease to operate after two months unless within that period it was approved by the National Assembly which might by resolution extend it for a total period of six months.

The type of emergency for which the 1956 Constitution made provisions related to the financial stability or credit of Pakistan. If the President were satisfied that a situation had arisen whereby the financial stability or credit of Pakistan or any part thereof was threatened, he could, after consultation with the provincial Governors or with the Governor of the province concerned, issue a proclamation of financial emergency. During the period of a financial emergency, the federal government could direct a province to observe such principles of financial propriety and any other direction required for restoring financial stability and credit, including a direction to reduce the salaries and allowances of government servants. Even the salaries of judges of the Supreme Court or the High Courts could be affected by such a regulation. A financial emergency could not extend for more than a total period of six months.

It is clear from the analysis of the emergency provisions of the 1956 Constitution that during a period of either political or financial emergency the federal character of the Constitution could be suspended and the country would be governed virtually as a unitary state.

The salient features of the 1956 Constitution, along with their historical perspective, have been discussed above. Other features included the composition of the Election Commission of Pakistan for holding periodic elections to the National Assembly and the Provincial Assemblies;[108] determination of conditions of service of persons in the service of Pakistan;[109] formation of All-Pakistan Services;[110] and establishment and composition of Public Service Commissions.[111] Urdu and Bengali were declared as the state languages.[112]

The 1956 Constitution or any of its provision could be amended by an Act of Parliament provided it was passed by a majority of the total number of members of the National Assembly and by the votes of not less than two-thirds of the members of that National Assembly present and voting. However, no amendment of a constitutional provision affecting the interest or composition of provinces or any of the provinces could be made unless such an amendment had been approved by a resolution of each Provincial Assembly, or, if it applied to one province only, of the Provincial Assembly of that province.[113] The condition of assent by the President appeared to be necessary for a constitutional amendment. However, no provision was made regarding the eventuality if the President withheld his assent or wanted the National Assembly to reconsider the amendment. It appears that the President could kill an Amendment Bill of the constitution by withholding his assent. This meant that the President had a veto power over Constitutional amendments and there was no way for the National Assembly to override it.

NOTES

1. Choudhry, G.W., *Constitutional Development in Pakistan*, 1969, Longman Group Ltd. London, p. 102-3.
2. Ibid., pp. 130-31.
3. Constitution of Islamic Republic of Pakistan 1956, Article 4.
4. Ibid., Article 7.
5. Choudhry, G.W., *Constitutional Development in Pakistan, supra*, note 1, p. 132.
6. Constitution of the Islamic Republic of Pakistan, Art. 192.
7. Ibid., Article 5(1).
8. Ibid., Article 5(2).
9. Ibid., Article 6.
10. Ibid., Article 22.
11. Ibid., Article 14.
12. Ibid., Article 16.
13. Ibid., Article 17.
14. Ibid., Article 15.
15. Ibid., Articles 8, 10, and 11.
16. Ibid., Article 18.
17. Ibid., Article 13.
18. Ibid., Article 20.
19. Brohi, A.K., *Fundamental Law of Pakistan*, 1958, Din Muhammad Press, Karachi, p. 309.
20. Ibid., Article 25.
21. Ibid., Article 28.
22. Ibid., Article 29.
23. Ibid., Article 28(b).
24. Ibid., Articles 28 & 29.
25. Ibid., Article 26.
26. Ibid., Article 24.
27. Ibid.
28. Ibid., Article 30.
29. Ibid., Article 27.
30. Ibid., Article 28(c).
31. Ibid., Article 31.
32. Ibid, Article 29(f).
33. In the matter of including Directive Principles of Policy, the Constitution of 1956 followed the example of Indian Constitution wherein also such Principles are provided under its Articles 36 to 51.
34. Brohi, A.K., *Fundamental Law in Pakistan, supra*, note 19, p. 313.
35. Chowdhry, G.W., *Constitutional Development in Pakistan, supra*, note 1, pp. 116.
36. Jennings, Sir Ivor, *Approach to Self-Government*, 1956, Cambridge University Press, pp. 18-19.
37. Constitution of Islamic Republic of Pakistan, 1956; Article 39.
38. Ibid., Article 32.
39. Ibid., Article 33.

40. Ibid., Article 35.
41. Ibid., Article 34.
42. Ibid., Article 36.
43. Referring to the appointment of Mr Muhammad Ali Bogra by Governor-General Ghulam Muhammad.
44. Constitution of Islamic Republic of Pakistan, 1956; Article 42.
45. Ibid., Article 37.
46. Choudhry, G.W., *Constitutional Development in Pakistan, supra*, note 1, pp. 120-21.
47. Constitution of Islamic Republic of Pakistan, 1956, Article 37(5).
48. When Constituent Assembly was dissolved by Ghulam Muhammad in 1954, he arbitrarily assembled a Cabinet under Muhammad Ali Bogra and described it as 'Cabinet of talents'.
49. Ibid., Article 52.
50. Ibid., Article 57.
51. Ibid., Article 69.
52. Ibid., Articles 63, 65, and 66.
53. Choudhry, G.W., *Constitutional Development in Pakistan, supra*, note 1, p. 124.
54. Ibid., p. 105-6.
55. Constitution of Islamic Republic of Pakistan, 1956, Article 105.
56. Ibid., Article 106(1), Fifth Schedule - Federal List.
57. Ibid., Article 106(3), Fifth Schedule - Provincial List.
58. Ibid., Article 106(2), Fifth Schedule - Concurrent List.
59. Ibid., Article 109.
60. Ibid., Article 108.
61. Ibid., Article 129.
62. Ibid., Article 130.
63. Ibid., Article 107.
64. Ibid., Article 193.
65. Ibid., Article 43.
66. Ibid., Article 44.
67. Electorate Act, 1956 (Act XXXVI of 1956). See PLD 1956 Central Acts and Notifications 482.
68. Electorate (Amendment) Act, 1957 (Act XIX of 1957). See PLD 1957 Central Statutes 276.
69. Constitution of Islamic Republic Pakistan, 1956, Article 143.
70. Ibid., Articles 45, 46, and 47.
71. Ibid., Articles 50, 51, 52, and 53.
72. Ibid., Article 54.
73. Ibid., Articles 55 & 56.
74. Ibid., Article 60.
75. Ibid., Articles 61, and 62.
76. Ibid., Article 59.
77. Ibid., Articles 60, and 61.
78. Ibid., Article 50.
79. Ibid., Article 125.
80. Ibid., Article 126.
81. Ibid., Article 127.
82. Choudhry, G.W., *Constitutional Development in Pakistan, supra*, note 1, p. 111.
83. Constitution of Islamic Republic of Pakistan, 1956, Articles 157, 158, and 159.
84. Ibid., Article 163.
85. Ibid., Article 156.
86. Ibid., Article 170.
87. Ibid., Article 148.
88. Ibid., Article 149(1).
89. Ibid., Article 149(2).

90. The Constitution of India, Article 124.
91. Constitution of Islamic Republic of Pakistan, Article 151.
92. Ibid., Article 152.
93. Ibid., Articles 153 and 154.
94. Ibid., Article 165.
95. Ibid., Article 166.
96. Ibid., Article 167.
97. The Constitution of India, Article 217.
98. Constitution of the Islamic Republic of Pakistan, 1956, Article 169.
99. Ibid., Article 168.
100. Ibid., Article 172.
101. Ibid., Article 22.
102. The Constitution of India, Article 32.
103. Constitution of the Islamic Republic of Pakistan, 1956, Article 23. See also preamble.
104. Ibid., Article 198.
105. Debates of the Constituent Assembly of Pakistan, 17 February 1956.
106. Sections 45 and 93 of the Government of India Act, 1935.
107. Debates of the Constituent Assembly of Pakistan, 9 February 1956.
108. Constitution of Islamic Republic Pakistan, 1956, Articles 137 and 138.
109. Ibid., Articles 179, 180, 181, and 182.
110. Ibid., Article 183.
111. Ibid., Articles 184, 185, 186, 187, 188, 189, and 190.
112. Ibid., Article 214.
113. Ibid., Article 216.

PART III

THE AYUB ERA: OCTOBER 1958 TO MARCH 1969

9

THE FIRST MARTIAL LAW

Unfortunately, the 1956 Constitution which was framed after nine years of effort did not last longer than two-and-a-half years. No general election was held under it.

Major-General Iskandar Mirza had taken over as Acting Governor-General in August 1955 when Ghulam Muhammad became too unwell to continue. Mirza was confirmed as Governor-General in October 1955. On the adoption of the Constitution on 23 March 1956, he assumed the office of the President under the new Constitution. He had publically voiced his conviction that religion and politics ought to be kept quite separate, and that some sort of 'controlled' democracy—an executive appointed for a fixed term and not dependent for its existence on a shifting and uncertain parliamentary majority—was the best form of polity to aim at.[1]

Muhammad Ali Bogra resigned as Prime Minister when he lost the support of the Muslim League Parliamentary Party. The League elected Chaudhri Mohammad Ali, a civil servant, who had, after some hesitation, taken the plunge into political life. Suhrawardy, an experienced politician, considered that he would be invited to form a government pledged to carry through the final stages of the unification of West Pakistan, but the Governor-General preferred Chaudhri Mohammad Ali who became Prime Minister in August 1955. Although he was a man of integrity with a reputation of working very hard, he did not possess the resilience to hold his own in the cut-throat game of politics.[2]

This was the political scenario at the time of the enforcement of the Constitution of 1956. The country expected great things from the combination of trained administrators in the highest positions and it was hoped that the influence of professional politicians would be lessened and more attention would be paid to the real needs of the people by suppressing corruption, undertaking agrarian reforms, and promoting economic development. Unfortunately, that was not to be. Chaudhri Mohammad Ali, who successfully unified West Pakistan and induced the Assembly to accept and ratify the draft Constitution of the Islamic Republic of Pakistan, found himself inadequate to meet the intrigues confronting him.

End of Chaudhri Mohammad Ali's Ministry

The bargaining and the deals necessary to reconcile the various interest groups into an acceptance of One Unit in West Pakistan and the adoption of the Constitution wore down the Prime Minister, Chaudhri Mohammad Ali. He proved a poor politician and failed to control his own party which led to his downfall. His greatest blunder was the selection of Dr Khan Sahib as Chief Minister of the unified province of West Pakistan against a section of the Muslim League which opposed his appointment.[3] Dr Khan Sahib was an old Congressman who had opposed the creation of Pakistan. The Muslim League thus opposed his appointment but he enjoyed the support of President Mirza. He cleverly manoeuvered to drop those Muslim Leaguers from his Cabinet who had opposed him and opted for those who supported him. By including dissident Muslim Leaguers and other supporters and, of course, with the blessings of President Mirza, he formed his own political party, the Republican Party.

Chaudhri Mohammad Ali, who was a Muslim Leaguer, found himself in a difficult position. On the one hand, he was the leader of a coalition at the centre of which the Republican Party formed a part and, on the other hand, his own party's parliamentary committee in West Pakistan was demanding Dr Khan Sahib's removal as Chief Minister. The Muslim League lost the game by sheer indiscipline. Had it been a united organization and had none of its followers deserted it to join the Republican Party, Dr Khan Sahib would have been forced to resign and most probably the Republican Party would not have come into existence. Moreover, the entire central government was working at this time against the Muslim League because Chaudhri Mohammad Ali was a politically weak man and real power lay with President Mirza who was an old friend of Dr Khan Sahib.

The central government could not remain unaffected in this situation. The Muslim League shared power in the centre as a major component of the coalition without being in office in any of the provinces. The Republican Party kept growing and in June 1956, it claimed itself to be the single largest party in the National Assembly with twenty-two members. But Khan Sahib continued to declare his full support to the Prime Minister and similarly, the Prime Minister persevered in his endorsement of the West Pakistan ministry. When pressed by Muslim League to act against the West Pakistan ministry, he took the stand that his actions as Prime Minister were governed by the good of the country and not by the resolution of any political party and that he was responsible only to the Cabinet and the parliament.[4] The Muslim League took this as a betrayal of the party and accused him of doing nothing to stop its disintegration in the National Assembly. When he called a meeting of the Coalition Parliamentary Party on 27 August 1956, Muslim Leaguers refused to attend, insisting that members who had joined the Republican Party at the centre should not be allowed to attend the meeting. Disgusted with this snip-snap, Chaudhri Mohammad Ali resigned on 8 September, resigning from his membership of the Muslim League as well.[5]

Chaudhri Mohammad Ali's resignation came at a time when he enjoyed the confidence of the National Assembly and commanded a clear majority in it. He had considered himself the leader of the coalition party as a whole rather than the leader of the Muslim League alone and, therefore, he had refused to side with one or the other group within the coalition party.[6] His decision to resign of his own accord while still commanding a majority in the Assembly is a unique example of political propriety in the history of Pakistan.

Suhrawardy's Ministry, September 1956–57

As the only Bengali of national stature who could claim a base of support in both the western and eastern wings, Suhrawardy's prime ministership might appear to have been a healthy departure from the norms of parliamentary government in Pakistan. All in all, the prospects for the polity 'looked much more hopeful' under Suhrawardy. President Iskandar Mirza had reconciled himself to having Suhrawardy as Prime Minister but he was planning to oust him through political intrigue. Suhrawardy had accepted three of Mirza's conditions: one, that he would not alter Pakistan's pro-western foreign policy; two, that he would not meddle with the army; and, three, that he would keep the left-wing Awami League led by Maulana Bhashani firmly in harness.[7]

A man of populist pretensions, Suhrawardy had slotted himself into office by forging an alliance with the oldest of the old guard.[8] As senior partners in the coalition, the Republican Party's heavyweight feudalists had no stomach for the Prime Minister's populism, much less for the mild palliatives he was wont to offer to keep the left-wingers in the Awami League in low swing. Suhrawardy's handling of the urgent political questions of the day established him as the reluctant mouthpiece of men who, having created the Republican Party on the ruins of the Muslim League in West Pakistan, needed some sort of a footing in the eastern wing to legitimize their claims to power at the centre. But, if being a Bengali was Suhrawardy's best credential, the Republican bosses and their backers within the presidency and the state bureaucracy were determined to miss no opportunity to convert the prime minister to the logic of central and, if possible, West Pakistan's imperatives.

And so, the one-time godfather of the Calcutta underworld began learning the captivating truths about prime ministerial office in Pakistan's state system. But for a remarkable reserve of political guile, a natural resilience, and an ambition matching that of the existing powerbrokers in Karachi, Suhrawardy may not have passed the initial tests of his new calling with such flying colours. However, with President Mirza acting *mufti*, there is reason to consider either the nature of the challenges or the response Suhrawardy was able to muster.

The controversy over the appropriate electoral system for Pakistan, whether joint or separate, revived almost as soon as Suhrawardy completed muttering the oath of office. A long-standing proponent of joint electorates, Suhrawardy became prime minister after the West Pakistan Assembly had plumped in favour of separate electorates by a joint Republican and Muslim League vote of 122 against ten cast by G. M. Syed's Sindhi Awami Mahaz and the Hindu MLAs. In West Pakistan, opposition to joint electorates bordered on the fanatical. According to the Muslim League and religious parties like the Jamaat-i-Islami, anyone espousing the cause was a traitor to Islam since the Hindu minority of East Pakistan wanted to do away with separate electorates in order to better exploit divisions among Muslims. The irony of a majority demanding electoral safeguards against a minority was completely lost on those champions of Islamic Pakistan.[9]

Attempts to link the electorate issue with Islam were embarrassing for the new Prime Minister. Not only his own party but a majority opinion in East Pakistan vehemently supported a joint electorate. On 1 October 1956, the East Pakistan Assembly pronounced overwhelmingly in favour of a joint electorate. This brought Mirza flying to Dhaka where the National Assembly was to meet to decide the matter. Presidential instructions were given to the Republicans; they were not to oppose the east wingers, much less question their fantastic proposal that the two parts of the country be allowed to choose different electoral systems. On 10 October, the Electorate Amendment Act recommending separate electorates for West Pakistan and joint electorates for East Pakistan was passed in the National Assembly by forty-eight to nineteen votes. The Prime Minister was left gasping at the President's nerve, but delighted in the privileged knowledge that joint electorates would eventually be enforced in both wings of the country. Saved by the presidential bell, Suhrawardy was temporarily beholden to the master. He realized that there were more advantages in keeping his fences with the President in good repair than pressing the Awami League's demands too insistently. The compromise distanced him from the party. This suited the central coterie since it left the Prime Minister with little choice except to harp their tunes unquestioningly.[10]

Opposition to One Unit is older than the system itself. In August 1956, six minor parties in the West Pakistan Assembly—the Sindhi Awami Mahaz, the Red Shirts, the Azad party, the Sindh Hari Committee, the Wrore Pakhtun, and the Ustaman Gal—formed the Pakistan National Party with the explicit purpose of abolishing One Unit and introducing radical agrarian reforms. It was the first-ever merger of parties in Pakistan's history. More significantly for the politics of West Pakistan, the PNP with its dozen or so votes in the Assembly held the balance between the Republican and the Muslim League. This acted as a spur to the anti-One Unit lobby at the centre. Suhrawardy hesitated before supporting One Unit more emphatically. The revelation weakened his hold over the rump of the Awami League in West Pakistan and foreclosed his joining the key anglers in the Muslim League and the Republican Party as they trawled for support in the smaller provinces. Under the laws governing the balance of power within the Pakistani state system, hanging on to prime ministerial office seemed to be inconsistent with enjoying the support of a popularly based party organization.

Not a man to let setbacks destroy his morale, Suhrawardy thought his political fortunes might change if he scored some successes on the economic front. By pandering to the demands of East Pakistani commercial and trading organizations, as well as alleviating the food shortage in the country, he thought he could outweigh the ill-effects of his lapses on domestic and foreign policy issues. On 18 November, at Suhrawardy's behest, Abul Mansur Ahmad, the Awami League Minister for Commerce and Industries, announced a series of concessions for small and medium-scale business groups in East Pakistan. These included parity in the allocation of foreign exchange between the two wings, and a review of the existing categories of importers to facilitate the entry of newcomers from East Pakistan, as well as from areas in West Pakistan which had hitherto been under-represented.[11] The move was hailed by East Pakistani commercial and trading groups. This landed Suhrawardy in deep trouble with the industrial magnates of Karachi. Already put off by the slackening of the government's aid to private industry programme, they were not about to accept cuts in their import quotas. Accusing the Awami League of provincialism, the President of the Federation of Chambers of Commerce and Industry lodged a strong protest with Mirza. This was one item in the charge-sheet which the West Pakistani business groups were to place on the President's desk just prior to Suhrawardy's fall.

The prime minister's efforts to find lasting solutions to the problem of food shortages never got off the ground, but they damaged whatever standing he had with the West Pakistani rural lords. He had given the food and agriculture portfolio to an Awami Leaguer with a view to alleviating the acute shortage of rice in East Pakistan. Since the food crisis in the country was linked with the need for major agrarian reforms, Suhrawardy encouraged his party to investigate the problem in a big way. In January 1957, an Awami League conference in Dhaka called for agrarian reforms and a constitutional amendment legalizing the state's confiscation of land without compensation. West Pakistan landlords protested against this un-Islamic (in their view) attitude towards private property. The reaction, however, was rooted in developments beyond the Awami League's paper proposal. During the summer of 1956, they had been startled by the sight of nearly 2000 tenants demonstrating in the streets of Lahore against illegal evictions. Instigated by the Awami Jamhoori Party, an extension of the Azad Party and the left wing of the Awami League, the march was a resounding success. Not only did it electrify populist parties and the main labour unions in the province but, and this was what worried the rural lords, the West Pakistan government actually conceded some of the demands in principle. Fearing that the Awami League's outlandish suggestions might set alight the Punjabi and Sindhi rural areas, they decided to set up the West Pakistan *zarai* (agricultural) Federation—an organization with no concern other than to ward off all threats to the existing agrarian structure. Its appearance on the scene was greeted warmly by the top Republican leaders, a clear hint of its pedigree.[12]

The prime minister had been issued a sharp warning. Not much more was heard of the Awami League's agrarian proposals. Hedging his bets, Suhrawardy took the easier—but for the state more expensive—route of allocating small sums of money to the agricultural sector. These bits of largesse were no substitute for the miracles Suhrawardy needed to refashion his public image. For one thing, unrest in the rural areas was comparatively more muted than the upsurge of organized labour activity in both wings of the country. Since the summer of 1956, striking workers had been demanding cost of living allowances, higher wages, and better terms of employment. But, with the West Pakistani industrialists planning how best to axe him, the Prime Minister dared not put his name to the mildest of labour reforms.

Suhrawardy's capitulations and the consequent dip in his popularity meant that President Mirza could become more dismissive of the Prime Minister. With no influence whatsoever on the Republican gaggle, Suhrawardy was reduced to rubber-stamping a series of presidential and gubernatorial edicts which, breathtaking though they were, served to discredit and eventually dismantle the tottering edifice of provincial politics in West Pakistan. By early 1957, the movement for the dismemberment of the One Unit had come to dominate politics in West Pakistan. Even the Republicans, already divided on the question of Khan Sahib's successor, had been affected. Facing an almost certain no-confidence motion on the issue, the Chief Minister succeeded in postponing a meeting of the Provincial Assembly until March when, short of presidential rule, there was no getting around legislative approval for the annual budget. But on 20 March, before the budget had been passed, thirty members of the Republican Party crossed over to the opposition benches. Having lost his majority, Khan Sahib called upon the centre to impose President's rule. Mirza obliged willingly.[13]

Constitutional propriety demanded that the governor should have called upon the Muslim League leader to form a new ministry, but this would have upset the coalition at the centre as well as the one unit arrangements so vital for the continued dominance of the bureaucratic-military axis. Suhrawardy's line that president rule was necessary to ratify the provincial budget, cut no ice with the national press who condemned this latest attempt to subvert the Constitution. His bluff called, President Mirza embarked upon a renewed attack on the British parliamentary system; saying that it was completely unsuited to Pakistani conditions and the sooner it was replaced by a modified version of the American system the better it would be for the country.[14] Khan Sahib had even more radical ideas. What Pakistan needed, he asserted, was the suspension of all political parties and the setting up of a revolutionary council to preside over the affairs of the state for a period of at least five years.[15]

In the meantime, Mirza—once again exceeding his presidential brief—began exploring the possibilities of bringing the Republicans back to power. Realizing that a Muslim League ministry in West Pakistan would mark the end of his term in office, Suhrawardy declared that a Republican ministry could be restored only if the President's 'party' was able to prove the support of at least 160 MLAs. Deeply worried about the fading magic of his tactical manoeuvre, Mirza ordered the Republicans to show their strength. They did so by means more foul than fair. In the first week of July 1957, a party which was incapable of winning power through the ballot box had conjured up support to form a ministry. Sardar Abdur Rashid was inducted to replace Khan Sahib as party leader and on 15 July, against a background of protest, a Republican ministry was returned to office.

On the face of it, Mirza's high-handedness had saved the Republican-Awami League coalition at the centre. But, in point of fact, the President had only secured the Republican position, Suhrawardy was now redundant. Developments in East Pakistan underlined his irrelevance. In early April, the East Pakistan Assembly had passed a resolution calling for full autonomy, especially in financial matters. This had been followed in quick succession by the left-wing of the Awami League demanding autonomy in all spheres except foreign affairs, defence, and currency. More disturbingly, some members of the Awami League ministry in East Pakistan were thought to be assisting their Hindu supporters in smuggling currency and gold, as well as rice and other consumer goods worth fifty to seventy crores of rupees each year across the 2000 mile long border with India.[16] The formation of the National

Awami Party in July 1957 underlined Suhrawardy's dispensability to the custodians of national imperatives. Consisting of Awami League dissidents led by Bhashani, the Ganatantri Dal, and the anti-One Unit PNP, the NAP's populist rhetoric and anti-American propaganda was a menace to the bureaucratic and military axis at the centre. NAP was equally dangerous for the Republicans. On 14 September, the West Pakistan Assembly was scheduled to meet to give a vote of confidence to the Republican ministry. Sensing defeat, the Republican stalwarts decided to negotiate an agreement with NAP. According to the terms, the Republicans would support the move to substitute One Unit with a zonal federation of linguistically and culturally autonomous units; in return, NAP would give its vote of confidence to the ministry. It was a typically Pakistani political accommodation, one devoid of any principles.

On 17 September 1957, the West Pakistan Assembly voted by 170 against four to abolish One Unit. A transparent ploy to keep the Republicans in office, the vote could not have been taken without a wink from Mirza. And indeed no sooner had the Assembly recorded its decision than Mirza and Suhrawardy publicly denounced the anti-One Unit resolution. This took away some of the bite from jubilant statements by NAP leaders and claims by some Awami Leaguers that the dismantling of One Unit would be accompanied by East Pakistan demanding representation in the National Assembly and in the services according to its population, as well as a larger share in the allocation of finances.[17]

Suhrawardy was now at the mercy of the central bureaucracy fighting to save One Unit. Seizing the moment, the Republicans informed Mirza of their decision to withdraw support for the coalition at the centre. With big business groups in Karachi lobbying against Suhrawardy's decision to distribute the better part of dollars 10 million of ICA (International Co-operation Administration Agency) aid to East Pakistan and to set up a national shipping corporation, President Mirza had absolutely no hesitation in demanding the Prime Minister's resignation. On 10 October 1957, after his request to seek a vote of confidence in the National Assembly was turned down and under threat of dismissal, Suhrawardy resigned.

Chundrigar's Ministry, October–December 1957

I. I. Chundrigar's ministry reserves a special place in Pakistan's history. Ousted before many had registered its existence, the ministry's brief stay in office was another episode in national politics. The leader of the Muslim League Party in the National Assembly, Chundrigar had served the state in various capacities. A close friend of Mirza with known sympathies for West Pakistani big business, Chundrigar qualified easily for the job of prime minister. Once Mirza invited him to form the government, the Republicans wisely dropped their claim to be the largest single party in the National Assembly and formed a coalition with the Muslim League. While refusing to accept Chundrigar's humiliating suggestion that they merge with the League, the Republican bosses agreed to support his party line on One Unit and separate electorates. With Chaudhri Mohammad Ali's Nizam-i-Islam and one faction of the Krishak Sramik pitching in, Chundrigar had no problems making his way into office.

Staying there was another matter. Seeing that his days might be numbered, Chundrigar lost no time in reversing Suhrawardy's decision on the allocation of the 10 million dollars of ICA aid; the creation of a national shipping corporation was also put into cold storage. The West Pakistani industrial magnates were understandably relieved. East Pakistani business circles reacted by giving unqualified support to the demands for provincial autonomy. The rift between the two wings of the country was now complete.

Under the circumstances, it was pure folly to revive the electorate controversy, but, with his party fighting street battles against the proponents of joint electorates, Chundrigar had to try and modify the Electoral Amendment Act. Declaring that his government would not be 'cowed down by the threats of bloodshed in the event of a change in the Electoral Law' was tantamount to equating the issue with a vote of confidence for the coalition ministry.[18] Called upon to ratify their understanding with the Muslim League, the Republicans dithered but finally refused to re-open the electorate issue. So, Chundrigar had to resign. However, President Mirza gave Chundrigar another chance to form a government. He failed because no major grouping in the National Assembly was prepared to form a coalition on the issue of separate electorates.[19]

Chundrigar's ministry was the shortest in the history of Pakistan—it lasted for only two months. Since the enforcement of the Constitution on 23 March 1956, a third ministry had been forced out in a little over a year-and-a-half. No wonder Nehru made that well-known remark that he did not know with whom to talk in Pakistan: 'Pakistan changes its prime ministers more often than I change my pyjamas'.

Noon's Ministry, December 1957–October 1958

Feroz Khan Noon was the last in the line of prime ministers called upon to stay the course of Pakistani politics. The leader of the twenty-one member Republican grouping in the National Assembly, Noon proved his majority by forging an alliance of convenience with as many as five different political groupings—the Awami League, the National Awami Party, the Krishak Sramik Party, the National Congress, and the Scheduled Caste Federation. A coalition dependent upon the support of a motley half-dozen parliamentary groups was not likely to create a stable government. The Awami League and the National Awami Party showed their contempt for the Republican-led coalition by refusing to join the Cabinet. This was a superb tactical move by Suhrawardy and the NAP leaders because until more Bengalis were brought in, the central government could not be considered representative, which was the best insurance that Noon would remain vulnerable to pressure from parties with bases of support in the eastern wing. By holding out a constant threat to withdraw support for the ruling coalition, Suhrawardy was able to re-assert himself as a national leader as well as prolong the tenure of the Awami League ministry in Dhaka. The NAP did the same, with twenty-nine votes in the 310-member East Pakistan assembly, it kept both the Republicans and the Awami League on tenterhooks.[20]

Times were changing. The centre's earlier success in manipulating provincial factions was losing its cutting edge; not because provincial politicians had found a way to parry central dictates, far from it. One result of the economic crises of the late fifties and the consequent polarization of social relations was that the splintered provincial groupings were most reluctant to toe the centre's line without first extracting concessions to improve their chances in the forthcoming general elections. These manoeuvres and the consequent impression of political instability had been inherent in the interim nature of the period between the passage of the Constitution and the holding of national elections. Although as hopelessly divided as ever, provincial politicians were now bidding for higher stakes, stirring just enough trouble to keep the centre perpetually off balance.[21]

Incessant bargaining between the centre and the provinces had dire implications for the administrative machinery. The imposition of One Unit, instead of easing administrative operations in West Pakistan, had accentuated tension between Punjabi and non-Punjabi civil servants. The policy of posting members of the old provincial cadres to different parts of the unified province was immensely unpopular, especially among Pathan and Sindhi civil servants who, unlike their Punjabi fellows, preferred to work in familiar surroundings. In East Pakistan, animosities between members of the provincial service and their mainly Punjabi superiors remained unmitigated. Riddled with regional and professional jealousies, the administrative structure was neither efficient nor reliable. Frequent use of the police to quash political opponents and the increasing concentration of power in bureaucratic hands—whether to issue licences, sanction government contracts, funnel chunks of foreign aid, or to supervise various development projects—had exposed the administration to malpractices once considered the exclusive preserve of the politicians. Since a rise in the cost of living had hit salaried groups hard, anyone not making extra rupees under the table found few sympathizers. With corruption rampant in the higher, middle, and lower echelons of the administrative machinery, the state's ability to counter the multiple challenges to its authority called for a chain of command quite different from the one in existence. The army's 'Operation Closed Door' in East Pakistan, so aptly named, was ominously hinting at the shape of things to come.

Realizing that the odds were against him, Noon began by throwing his weight behind the army's anti-smuggling operations in East Pakistan, but combined pressures from the Awami League, NAP, and the Hindu members of the National Assembly forced the government to accept a much watered down version of the anti-smuggling ordinance issued in December 1957.[22] Checkmated by his East Pakistani friends, Noon thought he might at least keep a semblance of control over his equally obstreperous supporters in West Pakistan. Heightened activity by the newly formed All-Pakistan Peasant Association with Bhashani at the helm had seen Lahore being flooded by evicted tenants and thousands of landless agricultural labourers demanding immediate government action. The Prime Minister's reassuring statement that his government would not tolerate any radical agrarian reform did nothing to assuage the landlords. Instead of burying their differences and rallying under the Republican umbrella, many landlords had begun gravitating towards the more extreme religious and communal groupings. Even if incapable of acquiring mass electoral support, these parties could at least be relied upon to support the status quo like the Republicans for whom power justified the most inglorious of compromises.

The overall situation in West Pakistan held out few hopes for a Republican victory at the polls. Even to make a respectable showing, the Republicans needed a chief minister with sufficient cunning to manipulate the administrative arrangements under One Unit during the elections. Sardar Abdur Rashid was considered too weak-kneed, so Mirza helped engineer his downfall, bringing in Muzaffar Ali Qizilbash, a Punjabi and Shia like the President, as chief minister. Once again denied the comforts of high office, the Muslim League launched a blistering campaign against Mirza. Qayyum Khan led the circus, enthralling his audience by dubbing the central coalition as 'employment exchange for unemployed politicians'.[23] The election campaign was now well and truly on its way.

Political Commotion

Developments in West Pakistan gave Mirza a good reason to dismiss any idea of forthcoming elections, thus the frequent postponement of the schedule and the downfall of four ministries in East Pakistan within six months, came as a welcome bonus. In March 1958, a reconciliation between the two factions of the Krishak Sramik Party under Sarkar's leadership spelt doom for Ataur Rahman's Awami League ministry. Ataur Rahman's request that the Assembly be prorogued was used as a pretext by the Governor, Fazlul Haq, to send the ministry packing. Haq, the founding father of the Krishak Sramik Party, contravened central advice and swore Sarkar in as the new chief minister. Suhrawardy responded by threatening to withdraw support from the coalition at the centre. So, within twelve hours of the news of the ministerial change reaching Karachi, Haq had been replaced with a new Governor who, predictably enough, dismissed Sarkar and brought back Ataur Rahman.

Encouraged by the events, a parliamentary board headed by Bhashani drew up a five-point programme which was to serve as the basis for NAP's future understanding with other parties. It included the demolition of One Unit, an independent foreign policy, early elections on the basis of joint electorates, and complete autonomy for all the provinces.[24] Suhrawardy's intervention prevented the provincial Awami League from accepting the NAP's stance on One Unit and foreign policy. On 18 June, Ataur Rahman's ministry was defeated because NAP members who held the balance in the Assembly opted to stay neutral. Two days later, Sarkar was back in office for seventy-two long hours. The provincial Awami League leaders now decided to ignore Suhrawardy's directives and came to terms with the NAP. Together, they defeated Sarkar's ministry. This time the centre reacted by proclaiming emergency under Article 193 of the Constitution and taking over power by the federal government in the province. It was not until 25 August that Ataur Rahman, not without help from

Suhrawardy at the centre, managed to form a new ministry. The Awami League again tried curtailing the Speaker's powers. On 20 September, Shahid Ali, the Deputy Speaker, made the fatal mistake of announcing that an Awami League motion declaring the Speaker to be of 'unsound mind' had been carried. Twenty hours after the event, the East Pakistan Assembly had been turned into a battlefield. Respectable members of the legislature gave vent to their frustration by hurling each other across the floor with the Deputy Speaker being a favourite catch, and while many were wounded, Shahid Ali never recovered. His death a few days later marked the beginning of the end of the parliamentary system, such as it existed, in Pakistan.

If it had been an isolated incident, the central government might have weathered the storm by simply extending the army's brief in the province, but the astonishing happenings in the Bengal Assembly were symptomatic of wider trends in Pakistani politics which, and this needs special emphasizing, reflected a crisis rooted in the nature of the state structure. As long as that structure was in the process of formation, appeals to the centres of the international system had allowed the ruling elite to partly neutralize Pakistan's political and economic crises. Now, contradictions within the structure of the state were constraining their room to manoeuvre. Impending elections had made the alleviation of centre-province tensions particularly urgent. To complicate matters, Pakistan was no longer seen by its patrons to be threatened by a communal hurricane. So the interplay of international and domestic compulsions was pointing to quite a different set of tactics and strategies to perpetuate the status quo than those which not so long ago had been deployed to give non-elected institutions a dominant role in state structure.[25]

It is true that on the eve of a long awaited general election, politics had become more chaotic. Given the deterioration of economic conditions in the country, it would have been remarkable if the various political groupings, whether in or out of office, had not tried to show a greater responsiveness to the disaffections of their prospective constituents by intensifying pressure on the centre for more financial support to the provinces. Yet, the centre, which for so long had dodged the issue of elections was unable to face them when its revenues were falling and defence and civil administration expenditures were rising. Barely able to remain solvent, the centre could meet the provinces half way only by slashing the budgets of the two institutions, the civil administration and defence, which were the best hope the state had for surviving assaults from below.[26]

By the summer of 1958, the central government was in dire straits. Drastic economic measures had led to cut-backs in industrial imports with the result that factories in Karachi were operating at a mere 35 per cent of their existing capacity. Despite the availability of thousands of acres of land in the Punjab and Sindh for cultivation, the government had been unable to finalize the allotments due to conflicting claims by refugee associations, local landlords, and the spokesmen of the indigenous peasantry, on the one hand, and of army personnel and members of the civil bureaucracy, on the other. Since it had also not been able to weed out the inveterate hoarders and the wily smugglers in the country, the food shortages had to be met by continuing to import heavily on government account. Towards the end of

June with the economy in shambles, the Finance Minister resorted to special pleading. Attributing the country's precarious foreign exchange position to recessionary trends in international markets, Amjad Ali called for 'a united effort at all levels—public, business, and official,'[27] but with the cost of living index soaring to new heights, partly as a result of the government's decision to abolish price controls, no one was moved by the Finance Minister's performance, least of all in East Pakistan where rice was selling at unaffordable prices.

As if to remind the central government that confessions about the state's economic dilemmas did not mean immunity from public accountability, labour unions in both the private and public sector had taken to orchestrating their demands more militantly. During May and June 1958, despite the state's Draconian labour laws, workers at a foreign oil concern in West Pakistan organized one of the most effective strikes in the country's history. It was followed by strikes by school teachers, telegraph workers union, and other government employees demanding better wages. Encouraged by the waves of unrest, student unions across the country sprang into action. Even the urban intelligentsia, accustomed to keeping their noses buried in the sand, were ready to take to the streets. People were in revolt; demanding early elections, a better quality of life, and a foreign policy meriting their respect.[28]

The political situation in East Pakistan, in the meanwhile, was becoming grim. A serious crises occurred on 31 March 1958, when Ataur Rahman Khan requested the Governor to prorogue the Provincial Assembly because the Cabinet had obtained a majority of only 15 votes in a debate on the Budget estimates, a request which Governor Haq refused. He subsequently dismissed the Ministry of Ataur Rahman Khan and immediately appointed Sarkar as chief minister, but Haq was dismissed later the same night by President Mirza, with the Chief Secretary of West Pakistan, Hamid Ali, being appointed as acting Governor. Within twelve hours of Ataur Rahman Khan's dismissal by Fazlul Haq, Sarkar, in turn, was dismissed by Hamid Ali, who reinstated the former Chief Minister, Ataur Rahman Khan and his entire Cabinet.

When the Provincial Assembly, which had been adjourned on 5 April, re-assembled on 12 June, a fresh crisis broke out, the National Awami Party ordered its thirty members in the Assembly 'not to lend any further support' to the Awami League coalition ministry headed by Ataur Rahman Khan unless the League was willing to sign the National Awami Party's five-point programme. Ataur Rahman Khan was, accordingly, defeated in the Assembly on June 19 by 138 votes to 126, the National Awami members abstaining. On the following day, Sarkar (Krishak Sramik Party) was sworn in as chief minister, but shortly before the swearing-in ceremony, the Awami League and the National Awami Party announced that they had concluded a coalition agreement and later the same day both parties decided to move a no-confidence motion against Sarkar, which was adopted.

In view of the situation, Governor's rule was imposed in East Pakistan and the Provincial Assembly was prorogued for a period of two months. On the expiry of this period, Ataur Rahman Khan was commissioned to form a new ministry. When the Provincial Assembly met again on 20 September 1958, a Muslim League member protested against the presence of six government supporters who had been disqualified by the Election Commission. [The Commission had ruled that the office of public prosecutor, which all these members held, was an office of profit, although a Bill was subsequently passed by the National Assembly making the holding of this office no longer a disqualification, it was not given retrospective effect and an ordinance had to be issued by the President for this purpose.] The Speaker, Abdul Hakim, reserved his ruling on this question, ruled out of order a motion of no-confidence in himself proposed by government supporters, and named several Awami League members for disorderly conduct. A fight then broke out. Government and opposition members attacked one another with chairs and steel microphone stands, the national flag was torn down and trampled on, and Hakim, who narrowly escaped serious injury, was forced to leave the Chamber.

On 21 and 22 September, the Assembly had to be adjourned as both sides had introduced hundreds of their supporters into the lobbies. On 23 September, the police excluded all outsiders from the premises, and also prevented Hakim from entering the Chamber. When Shahid Ali, the Deputy Speaker, tried to take the chair, opposition members pelted him with pieces of furniture, causing such serious injuries that he died two days later.[29] The police then entered the Chamber and forcibly expelled opposition members, two of whom were injured and taken to hospital. Several opposition members, including Sarkar, were arrested on 24 September and charged with the attempted murder of Shahid Ali but were released on bail. The provincial budget was passed on the same day in the absence of the opposition, who boycotted the House, and the Assembly was then adjourned.

Delay in General Elections and Declaration of Martial Law

Leading in eloquence was Qayyum Khan, the President of the Muslim League, demanding early elections and an independent foreign policy. He had kept the Muslim League out of the All-Parties Conference which agreed to postpone elections from November 1958 to February 1959. He threatened to launch 'direct action' if the government refused to announce a firm date for elections. The strong-arm tactics of the Muslim League's national guards were seen with favour by the military high command. On 20 September 1958, the central government's ban on all para-military organizations led to clashes between Muslim League workers and the police in Karachi.

It was evident that President Iskandar Mirza had lost control over the democratic forces in the country and was unable to influence the electoral process. Institutional pressure to seize power was increasing within the army, particularly by Lt.-General Musa (Army Chief of Staff), Major-General Yahya (Chief of General Staff, GHQ), Lt.-General Sheikh (Commanding Eighth Division, Quetta), Major-General Jilani (Commanding Army Staff College, Quetta), and Major-General Umrao (Commanding General, East Pakistan). General Ayub was also in favour of imposing Martial Law and taking over the affairs of the country by the summer of 1958, when the Muslim League leader, Ghazanfar Ali Khan, began inciting army officers in Lahore against him.[30]

During September 1958, Prime Minister Noon, in a last attempt to save his government, went in for a massive expansion of the central Cabinet, increasing the number of ministers from fourteen to twenty-six in order to satisfy Suhrawardy's Awami League. Within days, unhappy with their portfolios, the Awami League ministers resigned, and so ended this tragic experiment with parliamentary government. But not before the appearance of the army as the only reliable guarantor of the state's integrity. On 6 October, the Khan of Kalat reacted to the establishment of military bases in Balochistan by seceding from Pakistan. The revolt was scotched; the army had made its point loud and clear.

By the early morning hours of 8 October 1958, Ayub Khan with Mirza's connivance, had staged a successful coup. Before the news reached the citizens, the makers of the coup thought it politic to secure the blessings of Pakistan's foreign allies. Mirza summoned the American Ambassador and the British High Commissioner, along with a handful of other foreign dignitaries. Pakistan, he asserted in Ayub's presence, had been placed under martial law, but irrespective of changes at the domestic level, the new government 'would be even more pro-West than before'. Armed with the legitimacy they considered important, Mirza, at Ayub's behest, issued a proclamation abrogating the Constitution, dismissing the central and provincial governments, dissolving the three assemblies, banning all political parties, postponing elections indefinitely, and placing Noon, as well as other members of the central Cabinet, under house arrest. Not a shot was fired in protest against the imposition of martial law.[31]

Historians have shied away from interpreting the first military coup in Pakistan as a response to a crisis stemming in large part from the nature of the state structure. Focussing on the unseemly doings of politicians may be less controversial, even entertaining, but hopelessly inadequate if taken as the sole basis for an analysis of what actually prompted the October 1958 coup. Without a clear reading of the dialectic between state authority and the political process in the final months before military action, it is impossible to understand the failure of Pakistan's experiment with a parliamentary democracy, much less give it a decent burial.[32]

In his political biography, Ayub has described the change that took place in the month of October 1958 as follows:

> The hour had struck. The moment so long delayed had finally arrived. The responsibility could no longer be put off. For years we had all hoped that the political leaders of the country would wake up to their grave responsibilities. Among them were patriotic men, men of talent and ability, some close associates of the Quaid-i-Azam who had guided the struggle for Pakistan with great vision, statesmanship, and unfaltering fervour and determination. Later they had seen the cool, courageous, and tenacious manner in which Liaquat Ali Khan was trying to steer the ship of state through turbulent water. Each for a time managed to grab the central trapeze caught in the beams of giant arc-lights, but the next moment hurtled down into a dark net of intrigue and incompetence.[33]

This was the beginning of the recurring periods of martial law in Pakistan.

NOTES

1. Williams, L.F. Rushbrook, *The State of Pakistan*, 1962, pp.151-4, Faber and Faber, London.
2. Ibid., p. 156.
3. Ibid.
4. *Pakistan Observer*, 15 May 1956.
5. Aziz, K. K., *Party Politics in Pakistan: 1947-1958*. Published by National Commission on Historical and Cultural Research, Islamabad, 1976. pp. 33-5.
6. Ibid., pp. 35-6.
7. Jalal, Ayesha, *The State of Martial Rule*, 1990, p. 253, Cambridge University Press, Cambridge.
8. In September, 1956, there were seventy-seven members in the National Assembly, fifty-two in favour of the new coalition and twenty-five opposed. Of the government MLAs, a mere fourteen belonged to the Awami League. Even with the addition of one Ganatantri Dal member and seven Hindu MLAs from East Pakistan, the Republicans—twenty-seven of them from West Pakistan and three from East Pakistan, had a clear edge over Suhrawardy.
9. Jalal, Ayesha, *The State of Martial Rule*, *supra*, note 7, p. 254.
10. Ibid., p. 255.
11. *Dawn*, 19 November 1956.
12. Jalal, Ayesha, *The State of Martial Rule*, *supra*, note 7, p. 258-9.
13. Ibid., pp. 259-60.
14. See *Dawn*, 25 March 1957.
15. *The Pakistan Times*, 9 August 1957.
16. *Dawn*, 24 April 1957.
17. *Dawn*, 9 October 1957.
18. *Dawn*, 18 November 1957.
19. In December 1957, the party position in the National Assembly for the time being was as follows: Republicans 21, Awami League 13, National Awami Party 4, Krishak Sramik 6, Pakistan National Congress 4, Scheduled Caste Federation 2, Muslim League 15, Nizam-i-Islam 3, People's Progressive Party 1, and Independents 8. Total 77 (three seats were vacant).
20. Jalal, Ayesha, *The State of Martial Rule*, *supra*, note 7, pp. 263-4.
21. Ibid., p. 264.
22. *Dawn*, 5 January 1958.
23. *Morning News* (Karachi), 9 April 1958.
24. *Dawn*, 4 June 1958.
25. Jalal, Ayesha, *The State of Martial Rule*, *supra*, note 7, pp. 268-9.
26. Ibid., pp. 269-70.
27. *Morning News*, 26 June 1958.
28. Jalal, Ayesha., *The State of Martial Rules*, *supra*, note 7, p. 272.
29. A paperweight made of glass caught Shahid Ali in the head and perhaps proved fatal.
30. Jalal, Ayesha, *The State of Martial Rule*, *supra*, note 7, pp. 273-4.
31. Ibid., pp. 274-5.
32. Ibid., p. 270.
33. Ayub Khan, Muhammad, *Friends, Not Masters: A Political Autobiography*, 1967, p. 70, Oxford University Press, London.

10

AYUB'S BASIC DEMOCRACIES

The proclamation of martial law and the abrogation of the Constitution resulted in a complete void in the legal set-up. Therefore, three days after the imposition of martial law, on 10 October 1958, the Laws (Continuance in Force) Order was promulgated with a view to bringing about a new legal order. The general effect of this was the validation of laws, other than the last Constitution, that were in force before the promulgation of 7 October. It also restored the jurisdiction of all courts including the Supreme Court and the High Courts. The Order contained further direction that the government of Pakistan should act as nearly as might be in accordance with the late Constitution, and that the law declared by the Supreme Court should be binding on all the courts of Pakistan. The Supreme Court and the High Courts were also given the power to issue writs of *habeas corpus*, *mandamus*, *prohibition*, *quo warranto*, and *certiorari*. However, no writ could be issued against the Chief Martial Law Administrator or anyone exercising powers or jurisdiction under his authority. It was made clear that no court or person could call or permit to be called in question (i) the proclamation of 7 October, (ii) any order made in pursuance of the proclamation or any martial law order or martial law regulation, (iii) any finding, judgment or order of a Special Military Court or a Summary Military Court'. It was further provided that the powers of a provincial governor would be those that the President directed him to assume on his behalf under Article 193 of the late Constitution. The Governor was required to act under directions given to him by the President or by the Chief Martial Law Administrator (CMLA) or by a person having authority from the Martial Law Administrator.[1] The Laws (Continuance in Force) Order, 1958 seemed to have provided a legal framework to the state for the continuity of the legal system after the abrogation of the Constitution. The legal vacuum and the crisis which the country had faced after the dissolution of the first Constituent Assembly in 1954 were thereby avoided.

The expression used in the Order 'the Republic shall be governed as nearly as may be in accordance with the late constitution', was open to manoeuvres by the martial law government.[2] The government used it to mean those portions of the late Constitution which were necessary for the daily running of administration. Other provisions of the late constitution would apply according to the sweet will of the martial law regime to suit its convenience.

Ouster of President Iskandar Mirza

On the imposition of martial law, state power came into the hands of President Mirza and General Ayub Khan who had been appointed as Chief Martial Law Administrator (CMLA). The logical result of this sharing of power had to be a struggle between the two men, and it ensued soon thereafter. President Mirza tried to rationalize the power structure and the state framework by appointing Ayub Prime Minister on 24 October 1958. He formed a new Cabinet consisting entirely of non-political personalities.

This did not satisfy Ayub who had a stronger claim to power, being the Commander-in-Chief of the Army. President Mirza, nervous about his own future, tried to enlist the support of the Air Force and Ayub's rivals within the army. He allegedly made an unsuccessful attempt to order Air Commodore Rabb, the Chief of Staff of the Pakistan Air Force, to arrest four Generals close to Ayub, including Major-General Yahya Khan.[3]

On 27 October 1958, at a meeting with his Generals (Azam Khan, Burki, and Sheikh, all members of the central Cabinet) Ayub decided to rid himself of Mirza and assume complete control over the affairs of the state. Mirza was arrested and sent into exile to Great Britain where he later died, a sad end to an ambitious man who had ultimately fallen prey to his own intrigues. Ayub quickly set about proving to sceptics that he was not merely the army's 'front man' but 'absolute master' in Pakistan.

The Dosso Case

The validity of Laws (Continuance in Force) Order—in effect the validity and legitimacy of the imposition of martial law itself—was soon called into question before the Supreme Court of Pakistan. The question involved in this case was whether the writ issued by the Lahore High Court had abated under Clause (7) of Article I of the Laws (Continuance in Force) Order.

The Supreme Court, led once again by Chief Justice Munir, upheld the martial law and the Laws (Continuance in Force) Order.[4] In the leading judgment, Chief Justice Munir held that a victorious revolution or a successful *coup d'etat* is an internationally recognized legal method of changing a constitution. After a change of that character had taken place, the national legal order must for its validity depend upon the new law-creating organ. Even courts would lose their existing jurisdictions, and could function only to the extent and in the manner determined by the new Constitution. If the territory and the people remain substantially the same, there would be under the modern juristic doctrine no change in the corpus or international entity of the state. The revolutionary government and the new Constitution are, according to international law, the legitimate government and the valid Constitution of the state. Relying upon Hans Kelsen's *General Theory of Law and State*, the Supreme Court held that:

> Where a revolution is successful it satisfies the test of efficacy and becomes a basic law-creating fact. On that assumption the Laws (Continuance in Force) Order, however transitory or imperfect, was a new legal Order and it was in accordance with that Order that the validity of the laws and the correctness of judicial decisions had to be determined.

Chief Justice Munir also held that Article II of the Order provided that Pakistan was to be governed as nearly as might be in accordance with the late Constitution. This provision did not have the effect of restoring fundamental rights because reference to 'government' in this Article was to the structure and outline of government and not to the laws of the late Constitution which had been expressly abrogated by Article IV.

Justice A.R. Cornelius, agreeing with the resulting Order, did not accept the reasoning that prevailed with the majority. He did agree that the writs had abated and the *vires* of the laws had to be tested by reference to the Laws (Continuance in Force) Order, but regarding fundamental rights, he differed from the majority. He held that fundamental rights, as enumerated in Part II of the 1956 Constitution, did not derive their entire validity from the fact of having been formulated in words and enacted in that Constitution. A number of these rights, being essential human rights, inherently belonged to every citizen of a country governed in a civilized mode and that the view that they had ceased to exist involved a danger of denial of these elementary rights at a time when they were expressly assured by writing in the fundamental law of the country, merely because that writing was no longer of any force.

The judgment in Dosso's case, like that in Tamizuddin Khan's case, was a retrogressive one and set the clock back in the constitutional development and strengthening. The importation of a new and untried theory by an obscure scholar to justify martial law and military dictatorship is beyond explanation. There was evidently unnecessary haste on the part of the Supreme Court to legitimize the imposition of martial law. The cases before it could have been decided without entering into the question of the validity of Laws (Continuance in Force) Order. The appeals before the Supreme Court had been pending since long before the imposition of martial law and the validity of the Order was unnecessarily dragged into the controversy. These appeals were heard on 13 and 14 October and decided on 27 October 1958, only a few days after the imposition of martial law. Why could the Supreme Court not wait until somebody had directly challenged the *vires* of Laws (Continuance in Force) Order or the validity of martial law? In their unholy haste to legitimize the martial law, the Supreme Court Judges not only undid the writ jurisdiction of the High Courts but stripped the citizens of their fundamental rights, only to appease the new masters of the country.

Besides, Chief Justice Munir had adopted the legal logic applicable to a popular revolution such as the French, Russian, or Iranian revolutions to justify a *coup d'etat*, which can by no stretch of the imagination be described as a 'revolution'. He used the term 'revolution' even in his later writings to defend his reasoning[5] by posing a question: 'Could any court having a discretion in the matter, issue an enforceable writ on the 8, 9, or 10 October against the government that had been brought into existence by the Proclamation of President Iskandar Mirza?'[6] This argument also justified his verdict in Tamizuddin Khan's case. It was not for him to see if the verdict would be accepted. His sole duty was to stand for what was right and to decide each case on that basis alone, regardless of the enforceability of writs. A wrong verdict is not given only because a correct one might not be enforced. Had he risen above these evidently irrelevant considerations, the constitutional history of Pakistan might have been very different.[7]

Mehdi Ali Khan's Case

In the Mehdi Ali Khan case[8] which came up a few months later, the Supreme Court got an opportunity to review its decision in Dosso's case. The Dhaka High Court had issued *writs mandamus* directing the provincial government to withdraw the notifications by which they had acquired the *waqf* properties. The decision of the High Court was based on the fundamental right to manage one's religious institutions. The provincial government appealed to the Supreme Court but when the appeal came up for hearing, the Laws (Continuance in Force) Order, 1958 was in operation, Article 2(7) of which provided.... 'no writ or order for a writ issued or made after the Proclamation shall have effect unless it is provided for by this Order and all applications and proceedings in respect of any writ which is not so provided for shall abate forthwith'. The Supreme Court was faced with its previous decisions in Dosso's case wherein it had declared that fundamental rights 'are not a part of the law of the land and no writ can issue on their basis'.

It was, however, contended that by reason of Article 4 of the late Constitution, all laws inconsistent with the fundamental rights stood struck down when the Constitution came into force on 23 March 1956 and thus were not in force at the time of Proclamation of the Laws (Continuance in Force) Order, 1958. The Supreme Court followed its previous decision in Dosso's case and, by majority judgment, allowed the appeal. It held that the writ petitions giving rise to the appeals had all abated under Article 2(7) of the Laws (Continuance in Force) Order, 1958. In keeping with Dosso's judgment, the Supreme Court reiterated that after the abrogation of the Constitution, no law could be declared to be void merely because it came into conflict with a fundamental right and that all pending applications for writs in which a law by reason of fundamental rights had to be found to be void had abated. The laws which were in conflict with the fundamental rights but were 'in force' immediately and had not been struck down before being taken away, regained full efficiency.

Justice A.R. Cornelius wrote a dissenting opinion in which he held that the proceedings in the writs did not abate by the operation of Article 2(7) of the Laws (Continuance in Force) Order, 1958. The basic rights, according to him, remain valid not only within the framework of natural justice but also because they existed in the current legal order—modifying but not necessarily cancelling the 1956 Constitution. The difference was one of justiciability, not existence.

Justice Cornelius once again tried to secure fundamental rights in the military state to demonstrate the close relationship between justiciable rights and judicial powers.[9] The Supreme Court, led by Chief Justice Munir, let go the opportunity to undo or even modify its judgment in Dosso's case.

Action against Government Servants

Pakistan had always suffered at the hands of corrupt and incompetent public servants. Ayub's government embarked upon a drive against inefficiency and corruption. A thorough screening process was adopted against all government servants by conducting a close scrutiny of their service records. 'Misconduct' included bribery, corruption, jobbery, favouritism, nepotism, wilful maladministration, and wilful misapplication or diversion of public funds. Tribunals consisting of incumbent or retired judges of the Supreme Court or High Courts were created to try cases of misconduct against public servants.[10] The enquiries under this law were wide enough to include public servants or holders of public office on or after 15 August 1947. In addition to disciplinary actions such as dismissal, compulsory retirement, or reduction in rank, a public servant could be disqualified from holding any public office for up to fifteen years and could be made liable to make good any loss to the public revenue or property and to forfeit any gain for himself or another, found by the tribunal to have been caused by or to have resulted from his misconduct. The provisions of this law were in addition to and not in derogation of any law for the time being in force on the subject.

As a result, disciplinary action was taken by way of dismissal, compulsory retirement, and reduction in grade against about three thousand government servants, including 138 first class civil officers, 221 officers of the second class, and 1303 third class employees.[11] This shake-up immensely improved the morale of the hardworking officers who found themselves now empowered to set the tone for their departments. It also brought home to the subordinate ranks the reality of their responsibilities as public servants. The result was that government offices were now open at proper times; the officers attended to their duties diligently; and the clerks tried to be civil and helpful to the ordinary citizen. It was no longer necessary to give a bribe in order to make an appointment to see the right official. There was a notable cutting down of red tape; the transaction of official business was speeded up. The reaction of higher officials, who had striven so hard, and often so vainly, to hold the administration together was one of great relief. 'Thank goodness' one of them remarked, 'we can now get on with our job without interference from those wretched politicians.'[12]

Action against Politicians

As discussed above, the declaration of martial law had banned all political parties. A law was promulgated for disqualification of the politicians who, like public servants, had to be subjected to enquiry by tribunals to be appointed by the President or a Governor.[13] This law, Elective Bodies (Disqualification) Order, 1959 (popularly known as EBDO) defined misconduct of a politician as meaning any subversive activity, preaching of any doctrine or committing an act which contributed to political instability, bribery, corruption, or if he had a general or persistent reputation for favouritism, nepotism, wilful maladministration, wilful misapplication or diversion of public money and any other abuse of power or position. The reach of the law was very wide because elective bodies included any assembly, board, or committee of which the constituent members were chosen by means of election and included legislatures, municipal bodies, cantonment boards, district boards, and so on. Each tribunal to be formed for enquiry under this law had to be composed of three members with the presiding officer being an incumbent or retired judge of the Supreme Court, the Federal Court, or a High Court. A district and sessions judge, who was qualified for appointment as a High Court judge could also be appointed as the presiding officer of such a tribunal. A person could be disqualified for being a member of any elective body until 31 December 1966. An offer could be made to a politician to voluntarily retire from public life until 31 December 1966.

Under this evidently harsh law, several politicians like Suhrawardy, Qayyum Khan, and Ayub Khuhro were disqualified, or EBDO'd. The law, particularly its application, was severely criticized in legal and political circles throughout Pakistan. There is little doubt that in the application of the law and the proceedings of the tribunals, politicians of national standing and sound reputation were deliberately humiliated. The application of the law was not above personal grudges, score setting, and victimization. Suhrawardy and Qayyum Khan were treated shabbily in the proceedings before the tribunals. Ayub Khuhro suffered due to Ayub's personal dislike of him because it is said that Khuhro, as Defence Minister, used to make Ayub wait and cool his heels before seeing him. In any case, the date given for disqualification, 31 December 1966, was arbitrary and particularly unfair to politicians who were in their sixties or even late fifties. It deprived them of their rights and the country of their valuable experience and skill.

Land Reforms, 1959

Soon after taking over the affairs of the country, Ayub devoted his attention to the long standing question of land reforms in West Pakistan. Reforms had long been held as imperative for strengthening democracy. One of the chief obstacles to the working of free institutions in Pakistan had been the prevalence of an out-dated and rotten system of land tenure. About six thousand landlords owned immense tracts of land and thus exercised great political and economic domination. Ayub's land reforms put the maximum ceiling on land holding at 500 irrigated acres or one thousand unirrigated acres. Lands in excess of the ceiling were to be taken over by the government for distribution among deserving tenants, all *jagirs* were to be abolished without compensation (a *jagir* was the right enjoyed by certain landlords in the

Punjab to collect the land tax on commission); tenants were to be granted full ownership rights; and landlords were forbidden to increase rents without the permission of a revenue court.[14]

Ayub announced the reforms in a broadcast on 24 January 1959. Apart from the dictates of social justice, he described the reforms as 'an absolute necessity for the survival of the system and values which we cherish'. As a result of the special prestige which landlords enjoyed over large areas, political power was concentrated in the hands of a privileged few, hampering the free exercise of political rights by the people and stifling the growth of free institutions. The government's measures, he claimed, would go a long way towards breaking the monopoly of landed wealth in the hands of the landlords of West Pakistan, narrow down the existing inequalities of opportunity, and encourage a more intensive and productive use of the land by its actual tillers.[15]

The land reforms undertaken by Ayub could be described as a far more effective step towards the realization of free institutions in the country than any hasty and ill-conceived planting of western institutions on unprepared ground. Similarly, comprehensive measures for the rehabilitation of millions of refugees who had come from India during the riots of 1946–47 constituted another important move towards ultimately making the country stable and thus enabling it to sustain free institutions. Another fine job undertaken by Ayub's government was to set up a National Commission to look into the question of education. The Commission made a detailed report about the steps that were necessary to improve the quality of education and to spread it further among the people. No one who has carefully and objectively studied Ayub's socio-economic reforms would doubt his sincerity in endeavouring to lead Pakistan towards economic prosperity in keeping with the needs and requirements of an Asian country. However, regardless of the sincerity of purpose, these land reforms have been severely criticized as 'window dressing' or 'cosmetic', at worst, or 'inadequate' at best. Critics regard the limits fixed on ownership as very high. This was further stretched by using a measure determined on the basis of produce index units.[16] Influential landlords who had been in the government had their lands assessed at very low produce index units with the result that in certain areas, various land owners retained two to three thousand acres of cultivated land per head. Another lacuna left, maybe deliberately, was that the limit of land holding was fixed on an individual basis. Thus a family of six could easily retain from three to six thousand acres. In addition to holding of 500 acres of irrigated land, 1000 acres of unirrigated or 36,000 produce index units, a land owner was allowed one hundred and fifty acres as land under orchards.[17] Only those transfers of land that had taken place on or after 8 October 1958, which were in excess of the permissible limit of land, were declared void. Influential landlords, in connivance with the revenue staff, had their land holdings transferred ante-dated, to members of their family and, in this manner, most of these land holdings were saved. It is also alleged that the important land owners had been tipped in advance about the nature and extent of the land reforms and they had made adjustments to circumvent them. In fact, the land actually surrendered by the landlords or taken over at the conclusion of the operation was very little and mostly useless and barren. The land reforms, thus, did not create the socio-politico-economic impact that was intended and big landlords in West Pakistan continued to wield political influence.

These land reforms and subsequent land reforms in 1972 failed to break the hold of feudals over rural politics. They continue to be very powerful and generally win the rural constituencies particularly in interior Sindh, and in southern and western Punjab. About eighty feudal families in Pakistan have representation in the central or provincial legislatures where they have worked to protect their own interests in conflict with the national interest. These families have generally kept their area deprived of education so as to keep the people under their control. While several of the scions of these feudal families are well educated and have been to educational institutions of high repute in England and the United States, only a few have achieved the enlightenment to treat others as fellow humans. Their political machinations are as primitive, cruel, and offensive as those of their forebearers.

Basic Democracies Order, 1959

Ayub introduced a comprehensive scheme of local self-government popularly known as Basic Democracies. The scheme was enforced through a detailed law known as Basic Democracies Order, 1959 with effect from 27 October 1959.[18] While introducing it Ayub pointed out that western democracy could not be transplanted or imposed upon a soil that was not prepared for its healthy nourishment and growth. He further added that the choice before Pakistanis was a simple one as past experience revealed—to either wait for ideal conditions to prevail, or to study their own needs and work out a plan based on the realities of their own environment. In the words of Ayub:

> The scheme of Basic Democracies has been evolved by us after a careful study of the experience of other countries and of the special conditions prevailing in our own land. There is no need for us to imitate blindly the type of democracies to be found in other countries. We have to work according to the requirements of our own nation and the genius of our own people.[19]

Basic Democracies was a pyramidal plan enabling the people to elect directly to local councils the men they knew, who would in turn elect the upper tiers of the administration. There were altogether 80,000 Basic Democrats elected on the basis of adult franchise. Some of the important stipulations for it to work were: one, the system would not be foisted upon the people from above; instead, it would work from below gradually going to the top; two, the people would not have to go far from their neighbourhood to elect their representatives; and three, the system would be free from the curse of party intrigues and political pressures. The aim was to foster a spirit of cohesion and common effort in the people, the habit of depending on themselves, understanding responsibility, and how to exercise it.

Under the Basic Democracies system the following councils were constituted:

1. A Union Council for a number of contiguous villages in rural areas and a Town Committee for each town.
2. A *Thana* Council for each *Thana* (Sub-District) in East Pakistan and a *Tehsil* (Sub-Division) Council in West Pakistan.
3. District Council for a district excluding urban areas.
4. Municipal Committee for a city.
5. Divisional Council for a civil division.
6. Two Provincial Development Advisory Councils for East and West Pakistan respectively.

The most important administrative unit of the Basic Democracies was the Union Council covering a group of villages with a total population of ten to fifteen thousand people. A group of a thousand to fifteen hundred people were represented by one member, elected on the basis of adult franchise. A Union Council had a wide range of functions including promotion and development of the co-operative movement, village industries, forests, livestock, and fisheries; adoption of measures for increasing food production, the provision and maintenance of wells, water-pumps, tanks, and other works for the supply of water; the provision and maintenance of public streets; relief for widows, orphans, the poor and those in distress; the provision of first-aid centres and of libraries and reading rooms; aid in the promotion of education, and many other social and economic activities. The next tier of the Basic Democracies was the *Thana* or *Tehsil* Council. These bodies were to co-ordinate the activities of the Union Council and Town Committees in their respective areas and provide a forum for the discussion of mutual problems.

The third tier of the Basic Democracies was the District Council, the scope of which had been divided into two parts; functions which it would have to undertake compulsorily and those which it might perform voluntarily. The former included maintenance of primary schools, libraries, reading rooms; the adoption of measures for increased production of food and for improved breeds of cattle and promotion of village aid, the co-operative movement and village industry; the maintenance and improvement of roads, culverts, and bridges, and so on. Optional functions may likewise be summarized under the heads of education, social and economic welfare, and public works and health. The Council was free to undertake any extension of the above listed services.

The next tier was the Divisional Council. Its functions included the co-ordination of the work of local councils, municipal bodies, cantonment boards and the formulation of development schemes of importance to the Division; the review of progress and consideration of problems of importance to the Division in all branches of administration and the making of suggestions for development, improvement, and general advancement.

The fifth and last tier were the two high-powered Development Advisory Councils for East and West Pakistan. These provincial Advisory Councils, ceased to function with the introduction of the 1962 Constitution when provincial legislatures elected by the people through Basic Democracies came into existence.

The role of Basic Democracies did not stop at local self-government. It was later widened and extended to constituting an electoral college to elect the President and members of the National and Provincial Assemblies. This system was to disenfranchize directly the common citizen from electing their representatives to the legislatures and the universally accepted principle of adult franchise was rejected on the pretext of being unsuitable to the conditions in the country and the 'genius of the people'. For conditions suitable for western style democracy, Ayub said, we would have to wait for God knows how long.

Referendum/Presidential Elections

Ayub's Basic Democracies can be seen as the need of a martial law regime and its leader to find legitimacy since martial law is incompatible with any recognized form of modern governance. Such a government could not be subjected to universal suffrage, national mandate, or contentious elections. The Basic Democrats were turned into an electoral college, holding a referendum in order to seek a mandate from them to the effect that they reposed full confidence in Ayub not only to continue in office as President but also to authorize him to make a Constitution for the country.[20] However, referendum of even a limited electoral college has its risks. Given a chance, politicians, may even turn this into a political movement. Manzoor Qadir, Ayub's principal legal brain, was aware of this. He cleverly avoided collecting a large number of members of the electoral college at one place and ensured that voting remained a strictly localized affair.[21]

Under the President's Order 3 of 1960, Basic Democrats were required to vote by secret ballot on the question: 'Have you confidence in President Field Marshal Muhammad Ayub Khan, *Hilal-i-Jurat*?' If a majority of votes were in favour of the President, then Ayub would be deemed to have been given the authority to make a Constitution. He would also have been elected President of Pakistan to hold office for the first term under the Constitution to be drafted by him. The election/referendum was held on 14 February 1960 and naturally, in the absence of any alternative, 75283 Basic Democrats representing 95.6 per cent of the total, replied in the affirmative.[22] Thus, Ayub was not only elected President for five years but also got a mandate to give Pakistan a Constitution of his own choice.[23]

NOTES

1. President's Order (Post-Proclamation) No. I of 1958, Laws (Continuance in Force) Order, 1958. PLD 1958 Central Statutes 497.
2. There is an interesting story about the use of such vague expression in the Laws (Continuance in Force) Order. Both President Mirza and General Ayub, on being pointed out that the country was without any legal structure, summoned Mr Snelson, Federal Law Secretary, to the President House on 9 October 1958 and ordered him to produce some legal document reviving the legal structure in the country. He had not come prepared for the purpose and requested for time to draft a comprehensive document, which request was denied to him. He was not even allowed to go back to his office to draft such a document with the help of the books. He was asked to shut himself into a room in President House and to produce such a document forthwith. Mr Snelson is reported to have said that he could not produce any better document under the circumstances (of course without help of his books). It is interesting to note that the expression 'as nearly as may be' was used in Section 8 of the Indian Independence Act, 1947, though in a different context.
3. Khan, Asghar, *Generals in Politics: Pakistan 1958-82*, New Delhi, 1983, pp. 8-9.
4. The State v Dosso, PLD 1958 S.C. 533.
5. Munir, Mohammad, *Constitution of Islamic Republic of Pakistan*, 1965, All Pakistan Legal Decisions, Lahore, pp. 50-51.
6. Chaudhri, Nazir Husain, *Chief Justice Muhammad Munir: His life, writings and judgments,* 1983, Resurch Society of Pakistan, University of the Punjab, Lahore, p. 21.
7. Justice Cornelius, long after his retirement, once commented that Justice Munir lacked conviction and was very fond of saying that 'the law is an instrument for a Judge to use the way he pleases to do so in order to achieve the result that he intends to. Give me any case and I can write two judgments, one of conviction and the other of acquittal, and they will be equally convincing and legally correct.' No doubt, he had the ability to fiddle with the reasoning but the same ought to have been applied for achieving the results most beneficial for the country. Unfortunately, it was not to be. The author heard this from late Justice Cornelius himself.
8. Province of East Pakistan v Md. Mehdi Ali Khan, PLD 1959 S.C. 387.
9. Newberg, Paula R, *Judging the State—Courts and Constitutional Politics in Pakistan*, 1995, Cambridge University Press, Cambridge. p. 88.
10. Public Officers (Disqualification) Order, 1959. President's Order No. 3 of 1959 enforced from 25 March 1959. See PLD 1959 Central Statutes 152.
11. Williams, L.F. Rushbrook, *The State of Pakistan*, 1962. Faber and Faber, London, p. 189.
12. Ibid.
13. Elective Bodies (Disqualification) Order 1959. President's Order No. 13 of 1959 enforced from 7 August 1959. PLD 1959 Central Statutes 288.
14. West Pakistan Land Reforms Regulation, 1959. Martial Law Regulation No. 64. PLD 1959 Central Statutes 101.
15. *Speeches and Statements by Field Marshall Mohammad Ayub Khan*, Volume 1, October 1958-June 1959. Speech broadcast from Karachi on January 24, 1959, pp. 47-51.
16. Ibid., Para 9. A landlord was allowed to retain upto 36,000 produce index units or 500 acres of irrigated or 1000 acres of unirrigated land.
17. Ibid., Paras 8 and 9.
18. The Basic Democracies Order, 1959. President's Order No. 18 of 1959. See PLD 1959 Central Statutes 364.
19. President Ayub's speech of 2 September 1959 on the Scheme of Basic Democracies. See *Documents and Speeches on the Constitution of Pakistan*. Compilation by G.W. Choudhry. Green Book House, Dhaka, 1967. pp. 559-60.
20. Presidential (Election and Constitution) Order, 1960. President's Order No. 3 of 1960. PLD 1960 Central Statutes 30.

21. Gauhar, Altaf, *Ayub Khan—Pakistan's First Military Ruler*, 1994. Sang-e-Meel Publications Lahore, p. 169.
22. Ibid., pp. 169-70.
23. In the Preamble of the Constitution of 1962, it is stated as under:
'Now, therefore, I, Field Marshall Mohammad Ayub Khan, Hilal-i-Pakistan, Hilal-i-Jura'at, President of Pakistan, in exercise of the Mandate given to me on the Fourteenth day of February, one thousand nine hundred and sixty, by the people of Pakistan, do hereby enact this Constitution.'

11

THE CONSTITUTION COMMISSION AND ITS REPORT

Ayub wanted to enlist as broad a support for the Constitution as possible. Ostensibly at least, the masses would be invited to participate in the process and this was deemed to have been accomplished by the referendum of Basic Democrats on 14 February 1960. In addition, prominent citizens, political groups, and the bureaucracy would be involved so that few people would have the opportunity to complain that they had not been consulted.[1] It was also necessary, and desirable, to establish that parliamentary democracy had irretrievably failed in Pakistan and the Constitution of 1956 was unworkable so that Ayub could introduce a presidential form of government under a new Constitution. He wanted a prestigious and respected body of persons to arrive at this conclusion in a report formally to be submitted to him.

On 17 February 1960, Ayub appointed a Constitution Commission with the former Chief Justice of Pakistan, Justice Shahabuddin, as its Chairman to examine the causes of the failure of parliamentary government in Pakistan. The Commission was also to submit constitutional proposals aimed at giving the country a firm and stable government, effectively preventing undue influence or party consideration in the administration and the arbitrary exercise of power by the executive.

The terms of reference of the Commission were as under:

1. To examine the progressive failure of parliamentary government in Pakistan leading to the abrogation of the 1956 Constitution and to determine the cause and nature of the failure;
2. To consider how best the said or like causes may be identified and their recurrence prevented;
3. And, having further taken account of the genius of the people, the general standard of education, and of political judgment in the country, the existing state of a sense of nationhood, the prime need for sustained development, and the effect of the constitutional and administrative changes brought into being in the previous months, to submit constitutional proposals in the form of a report advising how best the following ends might be secured:
   - a democracy adaptable to changing circumstances and based on the Islamic principles of justice, equality, and tolerance;
   - the consolidation of national unity; and a firm and stable system of government.[2]

During the course of the enquiry, the Commission received the following additional term of reference:

> In the light of the social, economic, administrative, and political reforms which are being carried out by the present regime, particularly the introduction of the Basic Democracies, what would be the most appropriate timetable for the implementation of the proposals to be made by the Constitution Commission?[3]

Failure of the Parliamentary System

The Constitution Commission of 1960 made a detailed study of the parliamentary system in Pakistan upto the time that martial law was imposed.

The terms of reference of the Commission included, among others, the obligation 'to examine the progressive failure of parliamentary government in Pakistan leading to the abrogation of the Constitution of 1956 and to determine the cause and nature of the failure; to consider how best the said or like causes may be identified and their recurrence prevented'. The Commission came to the conclusion that the parliamentary form of government had proved a failure[4] and noted the following causes:

1. Lack of proper election procedure and defects in the late Constitution;
2. Undue interference by the head of the state in the ministries and political parties, and meddling by the central government in the functioning of the government of the provinces; and
3. Lack of of well-organized and disciplined parties and the general lack of character in the politicians.

According to the Commission, it was the last group of causes which were mainly responsible for the failure of parliamentary democracy in Pakistan. It was strongly contended by the politicians that the parliamentary system had not been given a trial in Pakistan and, therefore, the question of failure did not arise. The Commission was convinced that even if a general election had been held, the right type of leadership would not have emerged. So, lack of proper elections was not regarded as the main cause of the failure. The Commission referred to the election of 1954 in East Pakistan; whose result was that the parties were polarized and instead of one Muslim majority party many smaller groups emerged till a stage was reached when the Hindu minority bloc could hold the balance. In West Pakistan as well, the Commission noted that factional rivalries had erupted after provincial elections in the various units of West Pakistan.[5]

Regarding defects in the late Constitution which was also mentioned as one of the causes of its failure, the Commission remarked 'We do not see any that could have effectively prevented its being worked successfully'.[6] The Commission felt that notwithstanding its defects, the Constitution could be made workable if those who were entrusted with its implementation had been sincere. Regarding interference by the head of the state, the Commission took a lenient view of the role of the Governors-

General Ghulam Muhammad and Iskandar Mirza, who were regarded as the men mainly responsible for making parliamentary democracy unworkable. The Commission's contention was that they might have interfered, or been responsible for confusion in the political field, and might not have been free from personal or provincial considerations, but, according to the Commission, 'history shows that power passed effectively from the head of the state to the people's representatives only when the latter became disciplined and stood together to oppose autocracy. Till that stage was reached, the head of the state could always interfere with impunity; our not accepting the interference by the heads of the state as one of the real causes of the failure of the parliamentary form of government does not amount to their exoneration. What we should like to point out is that interference by these heads of the state would not have been possible if there had been discipline and solidarity in the parties in power'.[7]

While there cannot be any disagreement with the Commission's view that interference by the heads of state was made possible because of the lack of solidarity in political parties, it can be pointed out that Ghulam Muhammad and Iskandar Mirza actively contributed to it. Ghulam Muhammad's attempt to disrupt the Muslim League in 1953 to oust Nazimuddin's Cabinet and Iskandar Mirza's palpable encouragement of the formation of a dissident group, the Republican Party, among the Muslim Leaguers in 1956, are two glaring instances. Similarly, emergency provisions of the late Constitution were used by President Mirza seemingly for partisan gains and interests. As heads of state, it was the supreme duty on the part of Ghulam Muhammad and Iskandar Mirza to be loyal to the Constitution, but they seemed to have failed in discharging their highest obligation in the impartial manner expected from a constitutional head in a parliamentary system. The Constitution Commission failed to stress this aspect in assessing the causes of the unsatisfactory working of the parliamentary institutions in Pakistan.[8]

Lack of discipline and solidarity in political parties and the general lack of character in politicians, stressed by the Commission as the main factors for the alleged failure of the parliamentary system, were instanced by a number of specific cases of rivalry and intrigue in political parties. Referring to the dismissal of the Nazimuddin Ministry in 1953, the Commission observed 'in our opinion the Governor-General was able to appoint a new Prime Minister because of the lack of solidarity in the majority party in the Constituent Assembly'.[9] The subsequent endorsement of the Governor-General's action by the ruling Muslim League Party, and six members of the Nazimuddin Cabinet joining the new ministry headed by Muhammad Ali Bogra, were both cited as instances of the undisciplined nature of political parties in Pakistan. Similarly, the haste with which the 'constitutional coup' of 1954 was effected by the Constituent Assembly showed that those who sponsored it were not sure of the opinion of other party members.

The Commission again rightly pointed out that 'some of the members of the Muslim League passed a resolution in Sindh and the Punjab approving the action of the Governor-General which was welcomed by the parties other than the Muslim League'.[10] The Commission could have added that in East Pakistan, the Awami

League and the United Front seemed to have competed with each other in welcoming and garlanding the Governor-General at Dhaka Airport on his arrival in East Pakistan after his onslaught on the democratic process. This had clearly demonstrated how shaky and insecure the foundation of the democratic process in Pakistan was. If the head of state in any other parliamentary regime had ventured to take such drastic steps against parliamentary conventions and practices, he would surely have been discredited by all the parties and the people in general, but in Pakistan, apart from the solitary voice of Moulvi Tamizuddin Khan who challenged its legality in the law courts, there was hardly any popular uprising or condemnation by the political parties of the undemocratic action of the Governor-General.[11]

The Constitution Commission quoted Sir Winston Churchill's concept of the 'duties of a member of parliament' and noted with regret 'the members of the legislature in Pakistan, on an average, with a few honourable exceptions, did not regard any of these duties as binding on them.' They were, mainly concerned with furthering their individual interests. This was more evident in the former Punjab and Sindh provinces where changes took place within the same ministry in the early stages.[12]

Regarding undue interference by politicians in the administration, the Commission again cited a number of specific cases in the report. The East Bengal Police Committee, in its report of 1953, referred to an instance of interference with the workings of the police and the magistracy by a minister in a case of rioting and theft. The Commission also referred to the way in which military assistance in stopping smuggling of goods out of East Pakistan was interrupted by the Awami League ministry in 1957. The Commission added that criminal cases pending against some representatives of the people for misappropriation of public funds were withdrawn in East Pakistan by the Muslim League Cabinet on party considerations. Similarly, the United Front Ministry, the Commission alleged, threw the entire revenue administration out of gear 'with the motive of gaining political advantage'. A large sum of money, about two-and-a-half crores of rupees, due to the government from people who had taken loans, was written off.[13]

Turning to West Pakistan, the Commission noted: 'we have also before us information about the ministers granting favours to enlist support for their party. The instances range from granting route permits to waiving of interests due on *taccavi* loans, postponing the realization of land revenue arrears to favour a party, allotting government land to political supporters, and promoting a junior officer over the head of a senior in order to receive support from him through propaganda for the party'.[14] The Commission referred to the note of despair made by the Court of Inquiry appointed to look into disturbances in the Punjab in 1953. The Commission regretfully noted: 'most of the persons who stood for elections during the period under review regarded the money spent and effort put in by them as an investment from which they expected to draw dividends in the shape of benefits by putting pressure on the party in power. It is also clear from some of the statements made before us that the ministers were so busy helping their political supporters that they could not concentrate on questions of policies which were their main domain. They were so concerned with the consolidation of their position that they showed greater interest in administrative detail which, in advanced countries where the parliamentary system has been successful, is left to the experts and services'.[15]

The Commission referred rather casually to the interference by central government in provincial politics. It did not elaborate on this nor did it seem to have given much importance to this aspect of parliamentary democracy. It, however, said that 'such interference shows that the members of the party in power at the centre were more concerned with maintaining their own position than with working within the Constitution'.[16]

The Commission dismissed allegations that the services were also responsible for the unsatisfactory working of the parliamentary system. 'The services in general', the Commission observed, 'cannot be condemned as having contributed to the failure of parliamentary government, although it is admitted that there were cases of officers playing up to the ministers in order to exploit the situation to their advantage'.[17] A member of the Commission, Sardar Habibullah, stated, in a note of dissent:

> I am not in accord with the views expressed for services in Chapter I, where members of the services are altogether exonerated from all responsibility and a certificate of their achievement is given... They, in fact, in some cases acted as an instrument to the politicians for making and unmaking ministries or forcing the members to change their parties. The screening of a large number of higher and lower grade officers by the present regime speaks for itself.[18]

The defects that the Commission noted in the working of parliamentary democracy 'are but a reflection of the indiscipline, lack of sense of duty, and want of spirit of service and accommodation in an average member of society noticeable particularly in countries which have emerged into independence before attaining universal education and a minimum level of economic development'.[19] The Commission stressed the need for reforming the education system in order to create the basis of moral action and quoted Lord Bryce to substantiate the supreme importance of habit as the basis of moral action.

The Commission's conclusion that the parliamentary system of government had proved a failure in Pakistan was, however, challenged by the politicians. Chaudhri Mohammad Ali, the architect of the Constitution of 1956, in his replies to the questionnaire issued by the Constitution Commission, challenged the validity of the contention that the parliamentary system had failed. He said that the Constitution was abrogated by President Iskandar Mirza who, two-and-a-half years earlier had taken an oath to protect and defend it, and it was abrogated mainly because he found that however much he might juggle the various political groups, he had little chance of being re-elected. According to Mohammad Ali, President Mirza deliberately set out to discredit and destroy parliamentary democracy so that he could establish a lifelong dictatorship and at a suitable time even a kingship. He contributed, Mohammad Ali continued, more than anybody else to the creation of those conditions which were used in support of the alleged failure of the Constitution. Mohammad Ali, however, admitted that:

...the same lust for power that filled the breast of the President also inspired the activities of the great many political leaders and other higher politicians who in their scramble for power considered no means too ignoble. If they had power, they must retain it by hook or by crook, whether by corrupting legislature and political workers through favours granted at the expenses of the State or by demoralizing the administration or by any other means.'[20]

It seems that Chaudhri Mohammad Ali fully endorsed the findings of the Constitution Commission about the lack of character and parliamentary spirit among the politicians although, in his view, the head of state was the main culprit. Chaudhri Mohammad Ali thought that such a sad state of affairs could be avoided by suspending provincial Cabinets two months before the election and it was the duty of the President to hold the election in an impartial and fair way. As to the defects of the late Constitution, Chaudhri Mohammad Ali pointed out that a constitution, in order to be judged fairly, should be in operation for a considerable time. 'In a parliamentary democracy where free elections are of its essence, it is wholly unfair to judge a constitution after an experience of only two and a half years when not even one election had been held under it.' Chaudhri Mohammad Ali did not share the view that even after general elections political confusion would have remained. He listed a number of prerequisites for the successful working of democratic institutions and admitted that although these were not fully developed in Pakistan, it was through the process of free institutions and free elections that the people would acquire the essentials of a democratic system.[21]

The Awami League Leader, Ataur Rahman Khan, blamed the bureaucracy for the alleged failure of democracy.[22] He tried to show in his replies to the questionnaire of the Constitution Commission that 'a powerful clique in the bureaucracy did not want democracy to function in Pakistan and, therefore, did not want any opposition'. He chronicled the fall of successive ministries from Liaquat (first prime minister) to Malik Feroz Khan Noon (last prime minister) in an attempt 'to show that they had to go because they were very near framing a Constitution, or after its passage were trying to hold early elections'. The Constitution was abrogated, according to Rahman, because President Mirza did not foresee any chance of his becoming President for the second time.

The Dhaka Bar Association in its replies to the questionnaire, opined that democracy had been working smoothly until the death of Liaquat Ali Khan. With the ascendancy of the Governor-General Ghulam Muhammad and Iskandar Mirza, 'who had no political background or parliamentary tradition', parliamentary democracy was shattered.[23] The same view that the system of parliamentary government had never been given a fair and adequate trial because of Ghulam Muhammad and Iskandar Mirza was stated forcefully in the presidential address at the fifth annual session of the East Pakistan Lawyers' Association held in Dhaka on 25 June 1960.[24] The ex-Muslim League leader, Nurul Amin, also held the view that the parliamentary system had not been given a fair trial. In his deposition before the Constitution Commission on 26 June 1960, Nurul Amin stated 'to say that the parliamentary system of democracy had failed in Pakistan would be too hasty a verdict because the constitution was not given a fair trial'. Like other political leaders, Nurul Amin expressed the view that 'it is the action of the late Ghulam Muhammad and his successor more than anybody else which caused damage to the parliamentary system and did not allow it to function properly'.[25]

While the Constitution Commission blamed the politicians and the political parties, the politicians blamed Governors-General Ghulam Muhammad and Iskandar Mirza and a section of the permanent civil servants. But both the Commission and the politicians seem to agree on one thing: that the country suffered from extreme political instability, that parliamentary government in Pakistan had not worked as it does in Britain and other parts of the Commonwealth. If Governor-General Ghulam Muhammad was guilty of subverting the democratic process in 1953, no less guilty was the party which endorsed his actions. Similarly, if Iskandar Mirza was successful in ousting one Cabinet after another in order to perpetuate his position and in flouting constitutional provisions in July 1957 to bring his favourite party (Republican) in power, it was due to the support he received from the politicians and parties for such manoeuvring. As stated by the Constitution Commission, it could not have been possible for anyone to create a split unless the party in which the split was created was vulnerable and did not have the real interest of the country at heart.[26]

Despite the grim situation that presented itself, the Commission did not conclude that democracy should be discarded in Pakistan. The Commission observed 'incidents and tendencies noticed so far are no doubt distressing, but they can hardly be said to justify the view that we are not fit for any representative form of government and that we therefore need a benevolent head of state with unlimited powers'. The Commission added:

> the pessimists seem to forget that even the most successful democracies in the west had to pass through a phase in which we find ourselves, with only this difference that while they were fortunate enough to have, in the main, peace and security while developing themselves gradually, the Asian and African countries which emerged into independence before education could spread and the minimum level of economic development could be reached, and now they have to attain, in the shortest possible time, a standard which these developed countries reached in a process of evolution.

The Commission argued that the people of Pakistan have the right to designate the rulers of the country and to decide questions of national policy according to the requirements of the common good.[27] We may add 'the belief in democracy was interwoven with the drive for Pakistan and it would not be given up easily'. The Commission quoted with approval the sayings of Lord Acton that 'power tends to corrupt and absolute power corrupts absolutely' and it, therefore, categorically rejected any idea of an authoritarian system for Pakistan. It concluded that the form of government in the country 'cannot but be of a representative character'.[28]

Presidential Form of Government Recommended

Having come to the conclusion that the parliamentary system of government had proved a failure, the Commission inquired whether some modified form could be suitable for the country. The modifications suggested before the Commission were as follows:

(a) Control of political parties by restricting their numbers and requiring registration;
(b) Restriction on change of party affiliation by imposing an obligation to resign and stand for re-election;
(c) Incorporation in the constitution of conventions obtained in the United Kingdom;
(d) Statutory prohibition of interference by ministers and politicians in day-to-day administration and stringent laws for punishing them for misconduct; and
(e) Provision against interference by the President except during an emergency and for a few months preceding the elections when he should have the power to take over.[29]

The Commission examined each of these proposals and found that it was neither possible nor desirable to introduce them by statutes into the Constitution itself. For instance, the control of parties by law might not serve the purpose for which it would be intended. Similarly, statutory prohibition of ministerial interference with the day-to-day administration would create more difficulties than it would solve, nor did the Commission favour the idea of incorporating the conventions observed in England on the ground that these conventions were liable to change with circumstances and incorporation in the constitution would create new difficulties. Ultimately the safeguards for any democratic system depend on the sense of responsibility of ministers and the members of the legislatures, and mere statutory prohibition in the Constitution, the Commission felt, would not solve the problems facing the country.

The Commission recommended a form of government where there would be only one person at the helm of affairs, but with an effective restraint exercised on him by an independent legislature, members of which should not be in a position to interfere with administration by exercising political pressure for personal ends. The Commission concluded that such a system was available in the presidential form of government as found in the United States of America. The Commission's preference for the presidential system was influenced by the following factors operating under the presidential system:[30]

i. First, there is only one person at the head of affairs and not two (president and prime minister) and the collision of personalities that had marred Pakistan's politics since the death of Jinnah and Liaquat would be averted;
ii. Secondly, the opportunities and temptation open to an average member of the legislature to exploit his position to his advantage would be so restricted that persons who in the past had treated election to parliament as an investment would be discouraged from standing for election;

iii. Thirdly, there would be greater stability which was Pakistan's prime need; and
iv. Fourthly, administrators could be selected from among the ablest men available and not necessarily from among members of the Parliament.

While recommending the presidential form of governance, the commission stressed the importance and role of the legislature: 'if we want to have a democratic form of government, it [the legislature] should be in a sufficiently strong position to act as a check on the exercise by the executive of its extensive power without at the time affecting the firmness of the administration'.[31] Under the scheme proposed by the Commission, the legislature would control the public purse, legislate for the country, and could criticize the administration. The Commission dismissed the fear that the presidential system would deteriorate into a dictatorship like some Latin American countries. It pointed out: 'Our recommendation that the Presidential form of government may be adopted does not mean that we regard it as a fool-proof scheme which would avoid any constitutional breakdown in future. We recommend that form of government because, on a careful consideration of the possibilities and probabilities of the situation and experience we have been given during the past few years since independence, we consider that it is a safer form to be adopted in our present circumstances'.[32] The Commission's scheme of a presidential system was mainly modelled on the American pattern and proposed a comprehensive system of checks and balances.

Legislatures: Unicameral or Bicameral?

Turning to the details of the system, the Commission favoured a bicameral legislature consisting of a Lower House to be known as the House of the People and an Upper House to be known as the Senate. The Commission emphasized the need of an upper Chamber which would be able to check impetuosity of legislation by the Lower House and which would also exercise a healthy influence through its utterances, both on the legislature and the public. The Commission envisaged an Upper House as a body of elder statesmen selected from categories of people rather than of members elected on a territorial basis as in the American Senate.

This Senate would consist of forty-eight members; forty elected by an electoral college consisting of the Lower House at the centre and the two Provincial Houses on the basis of parity, that is, twenty from each province, from among meritorious personalities over fifty years of age, who were not members of any of the said legislatures. The remaining eight were to be nominated by the President. The Senators should be selected from among the following categories:[33]

i. Former presidents, governors, prime ministers, chief ministers and ministers of central or provincial governments;
ii. Retired judges of the Supreme Court and of the High Courts;
iii. Members of the recognized professions having a minimum standing of fifteen years;

iv. Retired government officers, not below the rank of secretaries of heads of departments of the central or provincial governments;
v. People who had made a notable contribution to any branch of learning or research; and
vi. Prominent citizens who had contributed to social welfare.

However, the Commission did not want to make the Senate as powerful as the American Senate. Its legislative powers were to be similar to those of the British House of Lords, but the Senate was to be given other powers, such as the approval of important appointments made by the President, including those of governors, ministers (central or provincial), and ambassadors, other than career diplomats. The memorandum submitted by the delegation of the government had opposed the system of approval by the Senate but the Commission felt: 'it is possible that he [the President] may be misguided or he may not be in possession of correct information about his nominees'. It pointed out further: 'in proposing provisions to be incorporated in the constitution it is our bounden duty to consider the question from the point of view of the institution and not personalities. We have to make provision for the possible contingency of a President lacking in experience of administration'. If there is no restraint at all on the powers of the President in the matter of appointments, the Commission felt, 'it is not likely that the Ministers and Governors would hesitate to disagree with his unlimited powers of appointment and dismissal. In such a case he will be deprived of disinterested advice and that would be a great disadvantage to him and to the country'.[34] The Senate was to be given the power of impeachment of the President, Vice President, governors, ministers (central and provincial), and Chief Justice and judges of the Supreme Court. It was also to have the right to participate in a joint session with the House of the People in matters of declaration of war and the ratification of treaties.[35]

The President and his Powers

As regards the proposed powers and duties of the President, the Commission enumerated them broadly as follows:[36]

1. Execution of laws;
2. Appointments of governors, central ministers, Auditor-General, Chief Election Commissioner, and ambassadors other than career diplomats with the consent of the Senate;
3. Appointments of judges of the Supreme Court and of the High Courts, Chairman and Members of the Public Service Commissions according to a procedure to be incorporated in the constitution;
4. Removal of governors, central ministers, and ambassadors (acting at his discretion) and of judges of the High Courts and other officers according to the rules and procedures elaborately provided in the report;
5. Receiving foreign envoys and ministers;

6. Making treaties subject to ratification by a majority of the members of the parliament attending a joint session;
7. Holding supreme command of the Army, Navy, and Air Forces;
8. Proclamations of emergency and calling for special sessions of the Parliament or of either House and issuing ordinances subject to certain conditions prescribed in the report;
9. Giving or withholding of assent in respect of Bills passed by the Parliament;
10. Granting of reprieves and pardons and
11. Nominating eight members to the Senate.

The Commission also favoured the idea of the President delivering messages to the legislature. In view of the wide range of functions and responsibilities conferred on the President, the Commission also recommended the office of Vice President.

In order to avoid a possible conflict between the President and the Vice President, the Commission favoured the American method of election of these two dignitaries, namely that the candidates for both the Presidency and the Vice Presidency would stand for election as 'running-mates', with the added condition that they should belong to the two different wings of Pakistan and that as far as the President was concerned, he should poll at least ten per cent of the votes in a province to which he did not belong. The term of the President would be fixed at four years and a person would not be eligible for election as president for more than two consecutive terms.

Those who opposed the Presidential system stressed the possibility of deadlock between the legislature and the executive over financial matters. The Commission recognized this possibility in the absence of democratic conventions and traditions through which the Constitution of the United States has worked successfully, and examined the issue in detail. It recognized the fact that the essence of the representative form of government is the people's participation and control over the public purse. It, therefore, tried to solve this problem in a way which would ensure the supremacy of the legislature over money matters, but at the same time devised means by which the President could overcome any temporary deadlock. The memorandum which was submitted by the official delegation to the Commission suggested that if a Money Bill was not agreed to by the Parliament or such a Bill were passed by Parliament in a form which the President could not approve, he should have the right to refer the Bill or any particular item in it for reconsideration with such amendment as he might wish to make. The Bill so referred back would become law unless two-thirds of the members of each House of Parliament should vote against it. The Commission could not accept the suggestion as it would seriously curtail the power of the legislature over money matters; the Commission stated: 'the proposal asks us to agree to an arrangement, whereby, while for passing a law with regard to a less important subject, say, the regulation of the cinema industry, at least a majority of the members sitting, which means about 51% of the persons attending the House would be the minimum majority required, in the case of an appropriation Bill when the President sends it back for reconsideration, only the support of about 34 persons out of hundred attending would do'.

The Commission recommended that the President should have the power of a partial veto regarding appropriation bills. He would also be able to give assent to those items that were passed according to his request or in substantial compliance with it. The legislature could cut down appropriation and, if the reduction were not substantial or the item reduced even substantially should be one introduced for the first time in the particular budget, the President should abide by the decision of the House of the People, even if the Senate should think otherwise. In case the reduction were substantial and the President should make a declaration to that effect giving the reason thereof, the matter should be considered by both the House of the People and the Senate and should the House of the People repeat their original decision, the President should then have the choice of either trying to carry on the administration with limitations imposed on the appropriation bill by Parliament or of continuing by ordinance the current year's appropriation, regarding the items concerned, for the following financial year. If he should take the latter step then he would have to pass such an ordinance which would have the force of an act of the legislature and would not require ratification. The Commission, however, did not propose this power of certification for an indefinite period. It was stated categorically that such a state of affairs would not be conducive to good government and a repetition of the certification of the budget for the following financial year should be avoided. It, therefore, suggested that the budget for the following financial year should be put before the House of the People six months before the end of the year for which an ordinance had been passed so that the attitude of the House might be known. Should the attitude of the House remain the same and the appropriation bill be again cut down substantially, the President would either try to manage with the appropriation so sanctioned or declare not later than a month thereafter that it was impossible to carry on the administration, in which case there should be a fresh election to the House of the People, and of the President and the Vice President. If no such declaration were made within the time fixed, the President would be bound by the appropriation Bill as passed. The Commission recognized the fact that such deadlocks had not arisen in the United States; that had obviously been due to strong public opinion which was a great corrective, but in Pakistan such public opinion was yet to be developed and the possibilities of deadlocks were there. The Commission, suggested the above remedy admitting 'the remedy we have suggested, drastic as it is, seemed to us to be the only one possible in the circumstances'.[37]

The official delegation had also recommended providing overriding powers to the President regarding a Bill relating to the security of Pakistan or the independence of the judiciary or the integrity of the civil and military services. The Commission did not favour any of these special powers, nor did it like the suggestion of the official delegation that the President should have any power in the matter of the adjournment or summoning of the legislature; the Senate and the House of the People should be independent of the executive in the sense that they would have their own programmes and rules regarding the conduct of business.

With regard to the President's special power during an emergency, the official delegation recommended, 'the President should be entitled to assume special powers in the event of a grave emergency on account of war or serious internal disturbance or financial instability'. This power, in the event of a war or serious internal disturbance, should include the suspension in whole or in part of the operation of any provision of the Constitution. The Constitution Commission, however, did not favour the granting of special powers, particularly to suspend some provisions of the constitution. 'We do not think it desirable that the power to suspend any of the provisions of the Constitution should be given for any emergency other than war and even that, we think, should be strictly subject to immediate ratification, by the House of the People if possible or at least by the Senate.'[38] Regarding internal disturbances, the Commission felt that it was not necessary to give any special power since the law of the land would make adequate provisions for such emergencies, and if for any reason military help was necessary, such help under ordinary law could be requisitioned. As for financial instability, the Commission recommended that the President should summon a special session of the Parliament and did not recommend any special power on this account. Thus we find that the Commission's recommendations envisaged much liberalization of the emergency provisions made in the late Constitution. It was really significant that an appointed Commission could make improvements over the enactments of an elected Constituent Assembly in the matter of liberalization of the Constitution.

From an analysis of the Commission's scheme for a presidential system, one thing emerges most significantly: in matters of legislation or of important appointments or in money matters, the Commission stressed the independence and importance of the legislature. This was a commendable feature since in a democratic form of government the legislature where the people's representatives sit must be supreme.

The Commission's preference for a presidential system was, however, not seen with favour by the political leaders who all preferred the parliamentary system. Chaudhri Mohammad Ali, for instance, said: 'In Pakistan if there is a truly independent legislature of the American type and not of those tame Parliaments conjured by contrivers of controlled democracy, it is a practical certainty that almost the entire legislature would be against the administration and its various sections would vie with each other in denouncing government proposals for expenditure and taxation as extravagant and burdensome'.[39] He felt that the presidential system would create deadlocks, particularly over the budget. The Awami League leader, Ataur Rahman Khan, pointed to the great distance between the two wings of Pakistan that made it impossible to have a presidential form of government viable. 'When a President is elected from one wing, the other wing will surely feel that its people have not been represented in the government. Active and effective participation by the people in the affairs of government is a *sine qua non* of an ideal pattern of government, that is only possible in a Parliamentary system of government and impossible in any form of Presidential government'.[40]

Federal Form of Government Recommended

The Commission discussed whether the form of government should be unitary or federal. It acknowledged the difficulties involved in arriving at an agreed solution to this problem affecting relations between East and West Pakistan. 'There is no part of the subject of our inquiry which seems to us to present greater difficulties than the question whether the form of government should be unitary or federal, as in the controversy feelings appear to run high'.[41] The Commission referred to the feeling at the time in East Pakistan 'of being treated as a colony'. It recorded that the people of East Pakistan who had worked wholeheartedly for the achievement of Pakistan felt betrayed 'as a result of neglect by the central government, their province, in spite of its superiority in numbers as well as its capacity to earn more foreign exchange, was far behind the other part of the country in the field of development'.[42] The Commission recognized the disparity in the industrial development between the two wings since independence, but contended that in West Pakistan industrial progress had been quicker than in the East where they had to make a start for the first time. The Commission gave figures of the central grants to East Pakistan over the years and pointed out that the amounts allocated to East Pakistan had not always been utilized. The official explanation was the delay in preparation of schemes coupled with the fact that the provincial ministers had not considered these schemes promptly. But the Commission also referred to the feeling in East Pakistan that the centre had delayed the financial sanction of these schemes in order to prevent the province's utilizing the allocations fully.

Having taken note of the prevalent feelings in the country, the Commission concluded: 'It is our considered opinion that if we impose a unitary form, ignoring the state of feeling in East and West Pakistan, we would be driving the average Muslims of East Pakistan into the arms of extremists and disruptive elements which are active in that province'.[43] This was wise counsel, and the Commission should be given credit for coming to the correct conclusion. The official delegation which appeared before the Constitution Commission had wrongly advocated the unitary form of government and, in doing so, pointed to the growing power of the provinces in opposition to the authority of the centre, resulting in administrative friction. The Commission rejected the view of the official delegation. Apart from the geographical position of the two wings of Pakistan which made a federal form inevitable, the Commission referred to other administrative difficulties involved under a unitary form of government. Under such a government there would be decentralization on an extensive scale without a provincial legislature to check on officials in order that they might not become autocratic. The official delegation made an alternative proposal that there should be one central parliament legislating for the entire country while sitting at the capital. It was conceded that provincial matters could be better dealt with by the province concerned and the suggestion was that power should be given to the provinces more or less on the lines of the late Constitution, subject to Railways and Industry being excluded from the provincial list and that the centre should be empowered to legislate regarding all subjects, including those of the provincial list. It was further suggested that instead of provincial legislatures, each half of the Parliament representing a province should act as a committee to deal with provincial affairs at the headquarters of the province and that the legislation passed by such a committee should receive the assent of the President and not of the Governor concerned. It was also said that this scheme would save 'time and expense' while it would retain the 'appearance of a unitary form of government'.

The Commission did not agree with the suggestion on the grounds that it would make members of Parliament parochial whereas it was essential to have a National Assembly with a broad national perspective. The Commission stated: 'if there be no Provincial Legislature where provincial matters can be discussed from a provincial angle, the Parliament itself would be converted into a Provincial Assembly and a member, who while sitting in the committee has approached the question from a provincial point of view and spoken in that connection with a provincial bias, would be inclined to do the same in the central Parliament, even with regard to a matter which concerns the entire country'.[44] As far as expense was concerned, the Commission rightly pointed out that 'a democratic form of government is certainly more expensive than an autocratic one and on the ground of expenditure alone we cannot refuse to have a legislature'.[45] Similarly, the Commission did not approve of the suggestion made by the official delegation that the centre should not have a list of subjects on which it could legislate, but that 'the Constitution should provide that it can legislate on every subject including those on the provincial list, as it would aggravate the suspicion and doubt already existing in East Pakistan which, as we have indicated above, it is extremely unwise if not hazardous to ignore'.[46] The Commission recommended that there should be three legislative lists—federal, concurrent, and provincial—as in the late constitution, favouring more or less the same distribution of power but making certain changes in favour of the central and concurrent lists.

The Commission rejected the view that the centre should have only three powers namely, defence, foreign affairs, and currency. It referred to tendencies in the existing federal system towards centralized control and power and expressed the view that neither East nor West Pakistan could develop without guidance and assistance from the central government. Apart from getting help from abroad, a strong central government alone, the Commission felt, could enable one province to share the resources available in the other where this would be advantageous to the country as a whole.

Although it recommended a strong national government, the Commission suggested that there should be a section of the Central Secretariat, stationed in Dhaka so that administrative delays might be avoided. It also recommended that the President, Vice-President, and central ministers should stay there for a longer period so that the 'feeling of isolation' prevailing in East Pakistan might be removed. It referred to a speech of Jinnah made in Dhaka on 1948 'I have only come here for a week or ten days this time but in order to discharge my duty as head of the state, I may have to come here and stay for days, for weeks and similarly Pakistan ministers must establish closer contact', the Commission went on to state that 'had he, Jinnah, lived longer he would not only have implemented them but would have brought about such a change of heart that the present feeling amongst the people of East Pakistan that their province was a colony of West Pakistan would not have arisen'.[47]

From an analysis of the Commission's approach to the problem of relations between East and West Pakistan, it appears that they perceived its magnitude and seriousness and although one might differ in certain respects from its recommendations, the Commission generally approached the whole problem with foresight and conviction.

Recommendations Relating to the Electorates

In a modern state, the electoral system is the 'basic structure' of a country's institutions. The electorate is, thus, treated as an important part of modern government.

Problems connected to the electoral system were debated at great length in both the first and second Constituent Assemblies of Pakistan. To organize an electorate on a sound basis is by no means an easy task, particularly in a country like Pakistan where the masses are illiterate and the means of communication are not yet properly developed, with a consequent lack of contact between voters and their representatives. While making the late Constitution (1947–56), the main problem considered by the Constituent Assembly regarding the electorate was whether it should be joint or separate. Under a separate electorates system, voters were to be divided on a religious basis, separate constituencies were to be carved out for Hindus and Muslims, and the voters belonging to either of these communities could vote only in the constituency reserved for their religious community. The system was the subject matter of acute controversy between the Hindus and the Muslims of undivided India. It also had considerable impact on the contemporary politics of Pakistan.

The framers of the new Constitution had two other important problems to consider: one, whether election of the President and the members of the legislature should be on a universal or a restricted franchise; and, two, whether it should be direct or indirect through an electoral college like the Basic Democracies.

The Constitution Commission discussed these three issues in detail. Regarding the question of a universal or a restricted franchise, the Commission began with an analysis of theories about the nature of suffrage and reached the conclusion that the right to vote is not inherent like the right to liberty, but is an office or function conferred only on those who are able to discharge its obligations. It further pointed out that in democratic countries like England and the United States of America, the existence of the franchise went hand in hand with education, with the result that the universal franchise followed universal education. But in Pakistan, the Commission pointed out, the percentage of literacy according to the census of 1961 was only 15 per cent. The Commission further noted that only a very small percentage of the people could read newspapers and kept themselves informed of affairs of state. It also referred to the low percentage of votes cast in the various provincial elections that had taken place on the basis of an adult franchise. The Commission noted the statement made before it by the Election Commission to the effect that 'in an election on adult franchise there is the danger of the public being easily misled into electing people not on a consideration of their programme but merely in an emotional state of mind created by inflaming passions by misinterpretation of facts', and cited the example of the election of 1954 in East Pakistan as a typical case.[48] The Commission reached the conclusion that 'we would be taking a grave risk if, in the matter of election of the President, the Vice-President, the House of the People, and Provincial Assemblies we adopt universal franchise in our present state of widespread illiteracy amongst the people whose passions can easily be inflamed'. They felt that the extension of the franchise should, as it did in England, go hand in hand with the spread of education and under the given circumstances recommended restricting the franchise to those citizens of Pakistan who (a) had attained a standard of literacy which would enable them to read and understand what was published about the candidates so that they might form their own judgment regarding their respective merits, or (b) possessed sufficient property or a stake in the country which would give rise to a keen desire in them to acquaint themselves with the antecedents and qualifications of the various candidates so that they might select proper representatives. They further recommended the immediate appointment of a Franchise Committee to submit its report within one year to determine the required standards.

Notwithstanding all these doubts and limitations, in the newly liberated countries of Asia, adult franchise had to be respected and adhered to if the ideals of democracy were to be upheld. Without the participation of the people there could be no true democracy and blame for the political chaos and confusion from which Pakistan suffered following the deaths of Jinnah and Liaquat could not be correctly placed on the electorate. In the 1946 election in undivided India and in that of 1954 in East Pakistan, the electorate followed the trends of public opinion as formulated by the intelligentsia. In any case, a system of restricted franchise was not in the spirit and notion of modern democracy.

The second issue, whether the system of election should be direct or indirect, acquired a special significance in Pakistan with General Ayub in power in 1958. As early as October 1958, he was thinking of possibilities of an electoral college where five hundred people might elect a person who in turn would choose an official. That was, according to him, one way to spread democracy in Pakistan. With the introduction of Basic Democracies, the suggestion was made that an electoral college should be developed for the election of the President and members of the legislature and the question continued to be debated widely. Hence, this problem of direct or indirect elections which has become more or less an academic issue in western democratic countries, assumed great importance at the time of making the new Constitution in Pakistan.

The Constitution Commission examined the problem with reference to Basic Democracies and came to the conclusion that in view of the wide responsibilities conferred on the President under the proposed Constitution, it was desirable that he should be elected by the people directly, on the basis of a restricted franchise. Similarly, the Commission recommended that members of the legislatures, both provincial and central, should be elected directly by the people. The Commission observed that the 'justification for an indirect election is that it eliminates the ignorance of a universal suffrage by restricting the ultimate choice to a body of select persons. This assumes that the electoral college, which is elected on universal franchise, should be of such a calibre that the ignorance of the average adult is successfully eliminated, but this standard cannot be said to be attained by an average Basic Democrat'.[49] The Commission opined, that the Basic Democracies scheme was very useful as far as local government was concerned. The system, in its opinion, would be of great help in educating the general mass of the people in the art of managing their own affairs by coordinated efforts. It regarded the Basic Democracy scheme as a more advanced system of local government than the former Union Boards in East Pakistan, because the Union Boards had insufficient financial resources and limited functions; but under the Basic Democracies scheme there was a close relationship between non-official members and officers of government of various grades both in development and non-development areas. The Commission, did not favour the idea of giving any judicial power to the Basic Democrats. It also noted the unfriendly attitude of some officers to the working of Basic Democracies.

Although the Commission recommended the system of direct election for both the President and members of the legislature, it suggested that in order to facilitate restoration of representative government before the end of 1960, the first election of the members of the central and provincial legislatures should be held by the Basic Democracies, as election on the basis of adult franchise would take two to three years and entail prolongation of martial law which the Commission considered undesirable. Similarly, as Ayub had already received a vote of confidence from the Basic Democrats, it recommended that he did not need to stand for election for the first term of three years when the legislatures would also be elected by Basic Democracies.

The last issue, whether the system of electorate should be joint or separate, was examined thoroughly by the Commission. It had started the discussion by pointing out that Islam was the main bond between the two wings of Pakistan. It raised the question of why religious minorities in Pakistan should want a joint electorate. In a country where people are basically religious, it argued, one would normally expect the minorities to ask for separate electorates, as had the Muslims in undivided India. When Pakistan was established, the minorities in West Pakistan asked for separate electorates and in East Pakistan too, a section of the scheduled caste favoured the system of separate electorates. Prime Minister Suhrawardy, when he introduced a joint electorate in Pakistan, explained the desire by the Hindus for a joint electorate 'due to a high sense of citizenship' and a 'keen desire to merge themselves in the majority'. The Commission, however, pointed out that the behaviour and the policies of caste Hindus in Pakistan had not proved any high sense of citizenship or any desire to merge with the majority. Rather, many of the upper class Hindus in East Pakistan preferred to keep their families in India and sent earnings to that country. They, therefore, could not dismiss the apprehension, stated by some witnesses before the Commission, that the demand of caste Hindus for a joint electorate might be based on a desire to influence the elections against the ideology of Pakistan. Given the political situation, the Commission stated, 'we are not prepared to say that this view is not amply justified. Their demand for a joint electorate seems clearly to be for some ulterior purpose other than the welfare of Pakistan'.[50]

As for the fact that there are joint electorates in other Muslim countries, the Commission stressed the fact that 'by the time a representative form of government requiring elections to be held came into force in those countries the minorities there had, for centuries, settled down as the nationals of those countries and had no reason to look for guidance from outside, but in Pakistan the tendency of the caste Hindus has been otherwise and till we can reasonably be certain that they have reconciled themselves to the continuance of Pakistan it does not appear safe to have a joint electorate.'[51] It also suggested that the Citizenship Act should be suitably amended to prevent non-Muslims in East Pakistan from keeping their families in India while remaining in Pakistan to earn money and remit it across the border: 'if a citizen of Pakistan feels that his family cannot be happy in Pakistan and has therefore to be left in India, he can hardly be trusted to be wholly loyal to Pakistan'.[52]

The Commission, therefore, recommended separate electorates for all of Pakistan. The Commission's conclusions can not be dismissed or regarded lightly, but if the Hindu minorities did not want a separate electorate, surely it was neither fair nor practical to impose it upon them.

Recommendations Regarding Revival of Political Parties

Another important issue closely connected with electoral politics was whether political parties were necessary and if they should be allowed to function. Democracy without political parties is unthinkable. The official delegation presenting the government's view before the Commission made the following proposal:

> All we need then to provide is that there should be no such thing as a political party demanding loyalty from its members. Of course, like-minded persons would get together and discuss political problems. They would find similarities in their approaches. They might associate with each other in exercise of their basic right of freedom of association. All that would need to be said would be that the election will not be held on a party basis with party tickets, but that the people will not be prohibited from associating with each other.[53]

The Constitution Commission had no hesitation in rejecting this proposal: 'We are unable to understand this proposal of banning political parties and allowing people who find similarities in their approach to exercise their basic rights of freedom of association. Are we to understand that they can assemble and discuss among themselves as to who should be preferred in their particular locality, but are not bound to act in accordance with that decision? If that is so, there will be no organized expression of opinion as in the absence of a party, there will be no preliminary selection of the candidates'.[54] The Commission referred to the role of parties in the process of discovering, sifting, testing, and choosing candidates and it admitted that in a country like Pakistan where a sense of political responsibility had yet to be fully developed, parties were formed not on principle but after a known personality. The Commission rightly pointed out that as long as a representative form of government had to be worked out, 'we fail to see how political parties can be avoided'. The Commission quoted with approval the remarks of Lord Bryce that political parties are far older than democracies; that they existed in nearly all countries and under all forms of government and that 'no one has yet shown how such government could get on without political parties'. The Commission reached the conclusion, 'if we want to have a democratic form of government our endeavour should be to create conditions in which a party based on principle can emerge'.[55]

Recommendations Relating to Islamic Provisions

In reaffirming that Pakistan was based on Islamic ideology, which was also the main bond between the two wings of the country, the Commission discussed the fundamental problems of the relationship between state and religion in Islam. It affirmed the view that Islam permeates the whole life of a Muslim and does not allow politics to be kept apart from ethics, as is the case in countries with a secular Constitution. Islam, it continued, is not merely incessant prayers and meditations but an active social life lived in accordance with the idea, which is why asceticism and mystical quietism have been discredited and the Quran emphasizes the deed rather than the idea. It is summed up in theism and virtuous life, the state being primarily an instrument to protect and promote good life. Emphasis throughout the Quran is laid on action for the obvious reason that a mere enunciation of belief unaccompanied by action in accordance with that belief, besides being hypocritical, does not contribute to progress either as an individual or as a member of society.[56] The problem of the relationship between state and religion produced a lot of discussion in Pakistan during the era of constitution-making (1947–1956). The Constitution Commission reaffirmed what the framers of the constitution, particularly at the time of the adoption of the Objectives Resolution in 1949, had enunciated. The Commission declared, 'we have thus an ideology which enables us to establish a model welfare state, and history shows that such a state had been established in the early days of Islam. If the modern generation doubts the efficacy of Islam, that is due to their lack of appreciation of the universal applicability of Quranic teaching and a lack of knowledge of Islamic history, the remedy lies in acquainting oneself with the principles of Islam and with Islamic history and not in discarding religion. Those who talk glibly of secularism in Pakistan overlook the fact that by a mere change of expression one's conduct does not change: if there is any chance of reforming ourselves it lies only in drawing inspiration from Islam'.[57]

The Commission also examined non-Muslims' objection to the idea of an Islamic state, but it felt that a Constitution based on the broad principles of Islam need not cause any apprehension to non-Muslim citizens of Pakistan. It pointed out that the treatment accorded to the minorities in a state depends on the ideals which the majority or those in power set before themselves. If the people are religious in the sense that they allow religion to permeate their practical lives, as is the case in most Asian countries, the ideals of the majority are coloured by the religion they follow. The Commission cited a number of shining examples of religious toleration under Islamic ideals and traditions.[58]

The Commission specifically raised the question of whether the preamble to the last Constitution, which declares the sovereignty of God and other provisions relating to the Islamic character of the Constitution, should be retained in the proposed constitution. It favoured the retention of the preamble and other Islamic provisions but suggested certain changes and improvements. With regard to the Islamic Research Institute, it recommended the retention of the Islamic Research Institute as provided under Article 197 of the last Constitution.[59]

The most important Islamic provision of the last Constitution was Article 198 which laid down that no law should be enacted which was in conflict with the injunctions of Islam and existing laws should be brought into conformity with the said injunctions. It further provided that a Commission should be appointed to make recommendations regarding the measures for bringing existing laws into conformity with the said injunctions and regardng the stages through which such measures should be brought into effect. The Commission examined the problems involved in detail in the provisions under Article 198 and noted that, in view of the diversity of opinion with regard to Islamic traditions, 'it appears to us necessary before taking any definite steps towards changing the general laws that are now in force to create a climate wherein different schools of thought could evolve unanimity with regard to the fundamentals of Islam as far as traditions are concerned'. 'Once this is done,' the Commission felt, 'it will be time enough for the next step to be taken, namely the drawing up of the principles which should be regarded as the standard to which the laws of the country should conform'.[60] The Constitution Commission recommended the appointment of another commission for this purpose and suggested that co-operation should be sought through diplomatic channels from other Muslim countries so that the proposed commission might work in collaboration with any similar commission in other Muslim countries. The proposed commission would advise whether instructions given by the Prophet (PBUH)with reference to local conditions should be followed literally, regardless of the local customs to which the people of various countries was accustomed, or whether only the principles should be adopted.

The Commission suggested, as a further step, a study of the basic values of Islam, and proper training and education of those who are entrusted with the task of preaching Islam. It recommended that a scheme be prepared under which only poeple trained for the purpose of teaching Islam, should be employed on a definite scale of pay, and entrusted with the duties of *Imam*. It further recommended that universities should open courses of religious studies, not only of the Quran, *Hadis*, and *Fiqah*, but also of modern sciences so that in the course of time there might be preachers in a position to present Islam to those of a western mind set.

Recommendations Regarding the Judiciary

The Constitution Commission, headed as it was by a former Chief Justice of Pakistan, reaffirmed the importance of the judiciary and suggested detailed provisions to secure its independence. The Commission began by stating, 'the judiciary is as important as the executive and the legislature, as it deals with the efficient administration of justice, not only between two men but also between the individual and the state. In countries with a written constitution it has also the task of interpreting the constitutional provisions and power to declare illegal executive or legislative acts which are in violation of those provisions'. The Commission referred to strict impartiality of the judiciary in the discharge of its duties as enjoined in the Quran: 'God doth command you to render back your Trust to those to whom they are due; and when ye judge between man and man, that ye judge with justice'.[61] It continued with a detailed examination of requirements for ensuring the independence of the judiciary and discussed salaries, tenure of office, method of appointment, and powers of the judges. As regards salary, the Commission noted that the existing scale for judges of the Supreme Court and High Courts was hardly adequate, the pension, particularly, being unsatisfactory; a Supreme Court judge received only 1600 rupees and a High Court judge 1200 rupees as pension at that time. The Commission, therefore, recommended an increase of at least the pensions if not the salaries of the judges.

The second inducement for the right type of man to accept judgeship was considered to be permanence of office. For this, the late Constitution had provided adequate safeguards. Under it a judge of the High Court, once appointed, would be entitled to continue in office till he reached his sixtieth year and he could be removed from office only by an order of the President issued on an adverse finding given by the Supreme Court after judicial investigation of the application made against him in a reference received from the President. As regards the Supreme Court, the provision in the late Constitution was that a judge would not be removed except by an order of the President made on an address presented to him by the National Assembly, supported by the majority of the total number of members of that Assembly by the votes of not less than two-thirds of the members present, voting for the removal of the judge on the grounds of proven misbehaviour or infirmity of mind or body. These provisions, the Commission pointed out, aimed at maintaining the independence of the judiciary by giving them security of tenure so that they did not hesitate to discharge their duties without fear or favour.

The Commission noted a proposal (though it did not mention the source) to the effect that the Chief Justice of Pakistan should hold office during the pleasure of the President and that if any allegations were made against him, they should be inquired into by the President himself. As regards puisne judges of the Supreme Court, the same proposal suggested that the Chief Justice should have the power to empanel a bench of three judges of that court to hold such an inquiry. The reason given for the suggestion was that, for a long time to come, the legislature would not have the requisite integrity and competency to sit in judgement over a superior judge. The

Commission did not agree with this proposal. According to the Commission 'to convert an office held during good behaviour into one held during the pleasure of the President is, in our opinion, a retrograde step which would seriously impair the independence of, and confidence of the people in, the highest court of the country'.[62] The Commission preferred a system of impeachment to remove the Chief Justice and other judges of the Supreme Court. The Commission prescribed a method for impeachment as follows:

The resolution for impeachment should be signed by not less than one-fourth of the total number of members of the House of the People. Fourteen days' notice thereof should be given before its being moved, and if the resolution were passed by a majority of the total number of that House, trial on the charges alleged in the resolution should be held by the Senate. The person impeached would then have to vacate his office should he be found guilty by two-thirds of the total number of the members of the Senate. The Commission prescribed the same procedure for impeachment of the President, Vice-President, Governors, and ministers (central and provincial). As for the removal of High Court judges, the Commission favoured the procedure adopted in the last Constitution under Article 169.

Regarding the appointment of Judges of the Supreme Court, the Commission agreed with the Law Commission that the recommendation for a judgeship of the Supreme Court should emanate from the Chief Justice after consultation with his colleagues and, as a matter of convention, the President should accept his recommendation. As regards the Chief Justice, the Law Commission suggested that a recommendation should be made by the retiring Chief Justice and if, on account of unforeseen circumstances, no such recommendation could be made, the President should select the Chief Justice from among the Supreme Court judges. While the Constitution Commission agreed that a recommendation should be made by the retiring Chief Justice, it added that the President should exercise his discretion in case the retiring Chief Justice should not recommend the next senior judge. The Commission noted that although seniority should not be the only consideration in making the appointment to the office of the Chief Justice, normally one would expect the senior judge to be appointed unless there were very strong reasons to the contrary, because if he were overlooked, the atmosphere of the court might be affected. Further, the Commission agreed that selection of the Chief Justice should not be confined to sitting judges of the Supreme Court but if an outsider should be appointed he should decidedly be of notable distinction. The Commission mentioned that a judge of the High Court should not be appointed as Chief Justice of the Supreme Court over the heads of the puisne judges of the said court. As for the Chief Justices of the High Courts, the Commission recommended that they too, should not ordinarily be preferred to the judges of the Supreme Court.[63] The Commission, however, made it clear that it did not wish to limit the discretion of the President in the matter as it could think of no alternative other than making the President responsible.

Regarding recruitment of judges of the High Courts, the Commission recommended that a provincial Chief Justice should, in consultation with his permanent judges, send his recommendation to the Governor and to the Chief Justice of Pakistan at the same time and they should express their opinion to the President. If the Chief Justice of Pakistan agreed with the provincial Chief Justice, the recommendation should be accepted unless the President, in consultation with the Governor of the province, should raise objections and give an opportunity to the justices to meet them. If the Chief Justices concerned should disagree in the matter, the case would be placed before the Supreme Court and the view of the majority should prevail unless the President and the Governor raised serious objections to the proposed appointment, in which case the Supreme Court should be given an opportunity to meet those objections. The Commission did not, however, elaborate what would happen if the Supreme Court were to make the same recommendation notwithstanding the objections.

As to the powers of the superior courts, the Commission favoured retention of the provisions of the last Constitution. It only referred to a proposal made by the official delegation with respect to the writ jurisdiction of the High Courts. The official delegation suggested that writs should not be issued against the government but could be issued against Secretaries to the government. The Commission did not favour this proposal. It observed, 'if it is to be laid down that writs can issue only against the Secretaries or the heads of the departments, those functionaries can successfully plead that the order by which the applicant is aggrieved was passed not by them but by the government and therefore, they could not possibly carry out the directions of the court. In other words, if the writs are to be confined to the Secretaries to the government, there could be no redress available to a party in respect of an order passed by the Cabinet'.[64] The Commission ended its discussion on the judiciary by laying emphasis on the fact that 'the independence of the judiciary should be maintained as has been the practice for a long time and any inroad into it that has been found necessary during the present authoritarian regime should not be treated in future as a precedence. Government should not take any step which is likely to affect the prestige of the court adversely. It must be realized that an independent judiciary adds to the strength of the administration and no effort should be spared to keep up its prestige and position. According to the Quran, the sayings of the Prophet, Islamic tradition, and the present-day canons of the democratic free world, an independent judiciary is a prerequisite for a just and good government'.[65]

Fundamental Rights and Directive Principles of Policy

The last Constitution, following the models of others, included a long list of fundamental rights and directive principles of state policy. The Commission inquired whether the provisions of the last Constitution regardng fundamental rights should be incorporated in the new one or if the assurance of such rights could safely be left, as in the United Kingdom, to the fundamental good sense of the legislature and operation of recognized principles through the wisdom and experience of the courts. The Commission noted that the preponderance of opinion expressed before it (98 to 39) was in favour of the first alternative and agreed that fundamental rights should be incorporated in the new Constitution and be enforceable by the courts. It observed, 'we do not think we can follow the example of England in this regard, because there the tradition that had grown and the genius of the people make it almost certain that the Parliament, though it is supreme in the sense that it can pass any law which the English courts have no power to declare as void, would not infringe the fundamental rights, except in grave emergency and that too only to the extent strictly necessary'.[66] The Commission maintained that in the absence of the traditions which guide the British people in the art of legislation and government, fundamental rights must be incorporated in the Constitution, and the power of the legislature has to be restricted as was done by Article 4 of the last Constitution to the effect that any law passed by it which would contravene any of the provisions enumerating fundamental rights, as well as any existing law which would be inconsistent with those provisions, could be declared void to the extent of inconsistency. The Commission favoured the retention of this provision.

Similarly, it favoured the retention of the directive principles of state policy as laid down in the last Constitution. It pointed out that although these directives were not enforceable in a law court, they had great effect on future legislation: 'It is the fundamental principle of any civilized government that its legislature should act within the sphere, and the limits, fixed by the Constitution under which they have been elected to office and although the Constitution would not, by merely enunciating the directive principles, make it obligatory on them to follow it, nevertheless the very fact that they are mentioned as principles to guide their deliberations, does have an effect on their minds; we would, therefore, incorporate them in the new constitution'.[67]

Note of Dissent

One of the members of the Constitution Commission, Sardar Habibullah, gave a note of dissent on certain points.[68] He was opposed to exonerating the services from their role in destabilizing parliamentary democracy in Pakistan. He disagreed with the recommendation for a federal form of government, and favoured the unitary form. He opposed the recommendation of qualified franchise based on literacy and property as it would deprive a large number of important sections of the population of their votes, particularly industrial and agricultural labour. He disagreed on the recommendation of direct elections and favoured indirect election by Basic Democrats elected on universal adult franchise. He also opposed a bicameral legislature at the centre and thought that the Upper House recommended by the Commission would be unnecessary in a presidential form of government. He was against the office of Vice-President recommended by the Commission because two elected people in power would soon develop rivalries and try to pull one another down. He opposed the recommendation of separate electorates because, according to him, it was the right of the minorities to ask for it and not for the majority to force it upon them.

Conclusion

The Commission was headed by the former Chief Justice of Pakistan, Justice Muhammad Shahabuddin, a man of integrity and honesty, held in high esteem and respected both in East and in West Pakistan.[69] He had been the Chief Justice of the Dhaka High Court and also Governor of East Pakistan. He was reluctant to accept the Chairmanship of the Commission but did so on the condition that the Commission would be unfettered in the due discharge of its functions and that its report would be published whether accepted or not. These terms were accepted and the personnel of the Commission were announced, but before the Commission could meet, Ayub and some of the ministers indicated what the Constitution would be. This resulted in a general impression that the Commission had been appointed only to endorse a plan already decided upon. At the first meeting, he made a statement clearly dispelling the impression. Ayub thereafter stated in a speech that it was the height of foolishness to suspect that the Commission could be used as a signing machine. Shahabuddin stated in a speech in the presence of some of the ministers that if he came across any pronouncements from them regarding the Constitution, he would resign. Thereafter, till the submission of the report, there were no further declarations regarding the Constitution.[70] G.W. Choudhry, who was closely associated with the Commission as an honorary adviser, has said that it enjoyed full freedom and powers in making its recommendations.[71]

Constitution-making was never an easy task in Pakistan. The framers of the 1956 Constitution had faced the following issues:

1. To determine the exact relationship between the state and religion. The problem, debated throughout the country with great enthusiasm and interest in the years preceding constitution-making (1947–56), was no longer a formidable problem before the Constitution Commission. The Islamic character of the proposed Constitution could no longer be a subject of controversy. Ayub had repeatedly given assurances that he would maintain Islamic provisions in the new Constitution. The Constituent Assemblies had already produced an admirable synthesis of modern needs and Islamic principles; the Constitution Commission made certain valuable contributions and suggestions in that direction.
2. The second group of problems was connected to the geographical features of the country, whether it should be a federal or unitary type of Constitution; what should be the basis for determining the quantum of representation of East and West Pakistan in the central legislature, and whether Pakistan should have a strong central government or if the provinces should be given full autonomy. The issues continued to be controversial and were of great significance to the Constitution Commission. As regards the form of government, the framers of the last Constitution had accepted a federal form as the 'dictate of geography' and it was more or less non-controversial. But, with the abrogation of the last Constitution, second thoughts were entertained; the official delegation,

representing the views of the government, favoured the unitary form but the majority opinion expressed before the Commission was in favour of the federal.

3. As regards the quantum of representation between East and West Pakistan in the central legislature, the principle of parity was agreed upon after years of deliberation. It was not expected that the Constitution Commission would depart from it. Curiously, however, the exponents of the unitary form of government also favoured parity. To demand parity in a unitary form was inconsistent. If there were to be a single government, how could the demand of East Pakistan for representation on the basis of population be ignored? Neither was the idea of preparing separate budgets for East and West Pakistan and a central budget for the entire country, as suggested by the official delegation, conceivable in a unitary system.
4. The distribution of legislative and financial powers between the centre and the provinces continued to be of great interest and significance. The Commission did not depart very much from the scheme of distribution made in the 1956 Constitution, but demand for self-rule or full autonomy for East Pakistan was still a major issue and a challenging factor to the emerging nationalism in Pakistan. The sooner the disparity in economic development between the two wings was removed, the better it would be for the ultimate unity and solidarity of the country. There was no greater problem in Pakistan than the relation between East and West Pakistan. There was still a great deal of good will and brotherly regard between the peoples of the two wings but, as later events showed, this store of good will was dissipated and wasted.
5. Relations between the executive and the legislature, and whether Pakistan should have a parliamentary or a presidential form of government, had acquired new significance and importance. The parliamentary form had been accepted in almost all the drafts of the Constitution since 1950; the main issue was to determine a system of powers and duties of the President, and there were divergent views on this. But with the abrogation of the last Constitution, parliamentary democracy of the Westminster variety, accepted in all other former British territories in Asia after attaining independence, was seriously challenged and it was contended that Pakistan was not suitable for this type of democracy. This issue was most thoroughly discussed and analysed by the Commission who, after careful analysis, favoured the presidential form of government as it exists in the United States, though with certain modifications. The Commission stressed the importance and role of an independent legislature which it regarded as the essence of any form of representative government.

There were problems and issues before the Constitution Commission which had not been faced by the framers of the last Constitution. For instance, whether the system of election should be direct or indirect; if political parties were necessary or should be banned; whether fundamental rights should be enforceable by the law courts. On all these issues, the recommendations of the Commission were welcomed in the country; its recommendation for restricted franchise was criticized, though it should be made clear that the Commission wanted not a permanently restricted franchise but a gradual and continuous extension, along with improvement in education and other socio-economic reforms. There was much to be said in favour of such an approach although any idea of a restricted franchise might be regarded out of tune with modern notions of a democratic form of government.[72]

In a nutshell, the Constitution Commission had done a commendable task of producing and finalizing a comprehensive report on 29 April 1961, encompassing various important issues of constitutional importance.

The recommendations of the Commission were generally balanced and well considered except for, perhaps, the adoption of separate electorates, in which case, the will of the majority of the Commission appears to have been carried. The Report still remains a document of considerable importance. Justice Shahabuddin did a great service to the nation by forcing the government to publish it, otherwise it might have gone the way many reports of commissions have gone over the years, unpublished and unheard of.[73]

NOTES

1. Karl von Vorys, *Political Development in Pakistan*, 1965, Princeton University Press, Princeton, New Jersey, p. 209.
2. Report of the Constitution Commission, 1961, Government of Pakistan, p. 1.
3. Ibid.
4. Ibid., Chapters I and II.
5. Ibid., p. 7.
6. Ibid.
7. Ibid,
8. Choudhry, G.W., *Constitutional Development in Pakistan*, 1969, Longman Group Ltd., London. p. 142.
9. Report of the Commission, p. 8.
10. Ibid.
11. Choudhry, G.W., *Constitutional Development in Pakistan*, *supra*, note 8, p. 143.
12. Report of the Constitution Commission, p. 10.
13. Ibid., p. 11.
14. Ibid., p. 12.
15. Ibid., p. 36.
16. Ibid., p. 9.
17. Ibid., p. 13.
18. Ibid., p. 140.
19. Ibid., p. 14.
20. Chaudhri Mohammad Ali's replies to the questionnaire issued by the Constitution Commission June 1960, quoted by G.W. Choudhry in *Constitutional Development in Pakistan*, *supra*, note 8, p. 146.
21. Ibid.
22. Ataur Rahman's replies to the questionnaire, June 1960, quoted by G.W. Choudhry, *Constitutional Development in Pakistan*, *supra*, note 30, p. 146.
23. *Pakistan Observer*, Dhaka, 27 June 1960.
24. Ibid., 26 June 1960.

25. Ibid., 27 June 1960.
26. Report of the Constitution Commission, p. 12-13.
27. Ibid., p. 17.
28. Ibid., p. 18.
29. Ibid., pp. 23-4.
30. Ibid., pp. 28-31.
31. Ibid., p. 28.
32. Ibid., p. 31.
33. Ibid., p. 47.
34. Ibid., pp. 59-60.
35. Ibid., p. 48.
36. Ibid., p. 85.
37. Ibid., p. 56-7.
38. Ibid., p. 62.
39. Chaudhri Mohammad Ali's replies to the questionnaire of the Constitution Commission, quoted by G.W. Choudhry, *Constitutional Development in Pakistan*, *supra*, note 30, p. 157.
40. Ataur Rahman's replies to the questionnaire, quoted by G.W. Choudhry, *Constitutional Development in Pakistan*, *supra*, note 30, p. 157.
41. Report of the Constitution Commission, p. 34.
42. Ibid., p. 35.
43. Ibid., p. 37.
44. Ibid., p. 41.
45. Ibid., p. 39.
46. Ibid., p. 42.
47. Ibid., p. 35.
48. Ibid., p. 67.
49. Ibid., p. 69.
50. Ibid., p. 76.
51. Ibid.
52. Ibid.
53. Ibid., p. 79.
54. Ibid.
55. Ibid., p. 80.
56. Ibid., p. 120.
57. Ibid., p. 121.
58. Ibid., pp. 116-20.
59. Ibid., p. 121.
60. Ibid., p. 124.
61. Ibid., p. 87.
62. Ibid., p. 89.
63. It appears that the lessons learnt about the appointment of Mr Justice Munir as Chief Justice of the Federal Court directly from Chief Justice of Lahore High Court was not lost on Mr Justice Shahabuddin. In 1954, when Chief Justice Mian Abdur Rashid retired as the Chief Justice of the Federal Court, then Governor-General Ghulam Muhammad, who was a close friend and a member of the *biradari* (Kakkezai) of Mr Justice Munir, wanted to appoint Mr Justice Munir as Chief Justice of the Federal Court directly. Munir was Chief Justice of Lahore High Court at that time and appointing him directly as Chief Justice of the Federal Court meant superseding all the incumbent Judges of the Federal Court at that time including Mr Justice A.S.M. Akram who was the senior-most among them. (Mr Justice Shahabuddin himself was next to him.) The Governor-General did not trust Justice Akram who was a Bengali. A proposal was floated to get a Law Lord from Britain for appointment as Chief Justice of the Federal Court, because at that time Pakistan had a Dominion status. When Justice Akram learnt about the proposal, he went to the Governor-

General and requested him not to do so. He said that bringing an Englishman as head of the Judiciary in Pakistan would be negation of the very struggle for independence waged by the Muslims in the subcontinent. He, however, offered to forego his claim for appointment in favour of any Pakistani Judge that the Governor-General was pleased to appoint. The Governor-General was perhaps waiting for such offer and immediately appointed Munir as Chief Justice.

64. Report of the Constitution Commission, p. 96.
65. Ibid., p. 100.
66. Ibid., p. 101.
67. Ibid., p. 105.
68. Ibid., pp. 140-2.
69. The members of the Commission were Azizuddin Ahmad, Muhammad Sharif, D.M. Barori, Tufailali A. Rahman, Abu Sayeed Chowdhary, Arbab Ahmad Ali Jan, Aftabuddin Ahmad, Sardar Habibullah, Obeidur Rahman Nizam, and Naseer A. Sheikh.
70. Shahabuddin, Late Mr Justice Muhammad, *Recollections and Reflections*, 1972. Published by the Supreme Court of Pakistan and printed by P.L.D. Publishers, Church Road, Lahore.
71. Choudhry, G.W., *Constitutional Development in Pakistan, supra*, note 8, p. 150.
72. Ibid., pp. 175-7.
73. Reference is made to Hamoodur Rahman Commission Report on the breakup of Pakistan which, despite its historical importance, has never seen the light of the day.

12

THE CONSTITUTION OF 1962

The report of the Constitution Commission was presented to Ayub on 6 May 1961.[1] It was examined by him and his Cabinet. A sub-committee of the Cabinet was appointed, with Manzoor Qadir, the Foreign Minister, as its chairman and Muhammad Shoaib, Zulfiqar Ali Bhutto, A.K. Khan, and Muhammad Ibrahim as its members. The sub-committee examined the report of the Constitution Commission and prepared a report of its own. It is alleged that the sub-committee was appointed and a report was obtained from it only in order to frustrate the report of the Constitution Commission. In this manner, Ayub could obtain alternate recommendations from two reports and had the option to choose those which were to his liking and inclination.[2] The 1962 Constitution was very different from the recommendations made by the Constitution Commission, Ayub favoured a presidential form of government which allowed the President to choose his own Cabinet, and also gave him the right to nominate provincial Governors.[3] Ayub disagreed with the recommendations of the Constitution Commission regarding restricted adult franchise; bicameral legislatures; creation of the office of the Vice-President; and procedure for resolving disagreements between the President and the legislature over the budget and money bills.[4] Ayub also received support for his views from a number of individuals, prominent among them were Mohammad Zafarullah Khan, Ghulam Ahmad Parvez, and Pir Ali Muhammad Rashdi. Zafarullah attacked the Constitution Commission's recommendations that political parties should be allowed to function but agreed with the Constitution Commission that there should be no sudden jump to universal adult franchise. He completely agreed with Ayub's electoral arrangement, and supported a presidential form of government. Parvez called the establishment of political parties a *shirk*. Rashdi went to the extent of suggesting a monarchy for Pakistan, with Ayub as the first monarch. Ayub was obviously pleased with such support.[5]

The two reports and their findings were examined by the Cabinet. The constitutional proposals were finally discussed at the Governors' Conference held in Rawalpindi from 24 to 31 October 1961. The Governors' Conference was attended by the provincial governors, central ministers, and senior officers. It was decided that the President would announce the outline of the constitution soon after the governors' Conference, but subsequently it was announced in its entirety in March 1962. While the Governors' conference was under way, Ayub declared in his speech on the third anniversary of 'Revolution Day' that the Constitution would be capable of producing a strong and stable government, with an emphasis on a strong executive.

Ayub was convinced that most of the politicians had not given up their old ways and were busy creating confusion in the public mind about the Constitution. Ayub did not realize that by using the Basic Democrats as an electoral college to get a vote of confidence for himself and then converting that vote into a mandate for assuming the office of the President, he had already defeated the purpose for which he had set up the Constitution Commission. It was with some impatience that Ayub decided he had had enough advice and the time had come for him to give a verdict on all contentious matters. With respect to the ideology of Islam, he decided that it should be left to the members of the legislature to interpret all questions relating to the Quran and *sunnah*. About the form of government, Ayub decided that the country needed a presidential form of government whereunder the centre should have powers over all subjects. He was convinced that he had given sufficient recognition to the principle of universal franchise by allowing the people to elect their representatives at the local level. He firmly opposed direct election of the President or members of the national and provincial legislatures. Ayub believed that whatever he was doing was in the interest of Pakistan. He was conscious of the difficulties of ordinary men and women, particularly in the rural areas, and wanted to alleviate their condition by all means at his disposal. But the people as the sovereign authority to whom he was answerable did not figure in his political plan. He viewed the populace as a collection of uneducated and inexperienced persons who needed help, guidance, and protection and thought it to be his duty and responsibility to provide it. In this he was encouraged by Manzoor Qadir and Bhutto. The former was convinced that the doctrine of the will of the people if not followed was inapplicable to the prevailing conditions in Pakistan, and the latter saw the people as useful pawns in a grand game of statecraft which could be moved and manipulated to serve any political purpose.[6]

The Governors' conference had appointed a drafting committee with Manzoor Qadir and the Law Secretary, Abdul Hamid, as members. The drafting committee was authorized to enlist, if necessary, the services of experts on constitutional law.[7] It took about four months to finally draft the Constitution which was announced in a broadcast to the nation by Ayub on 1 March 1962. In his speech, Ayub referred to the pledge given on 8 October 1958, to restore democracy in Pakistan and claimed that the new Constitution represented the fulfilment of that pledge.

Ayub thanked ex-Chief Justice Shahabuddin, the Chairman of the Constitution Commission, for producing an excellent report which had served as the working draft. He also expressed his gratitude to Manzoor Qadir for producing the final draft. He praised them both for their sincerity, integrity, and patriotism.[8] Ayub gave an outline and the salient features of the Constitution which included the powers and position of the President; composition of the National Assembly; powers and functions of the provincial Governors; Provincial Assemblies; principles of law-making; service rights; Basic Democracies, and the procedure of amendments to the Constitution.[9] It is pertinent to note that the Constitution Commission's recommendations relating to the system of election, fundamental rights, political parties, and the role of the judiciary, were not made part of the Constitution.

The 1962 Constitution contained 250 Articles divided into twelve parts and three schedules. It had a lengthy preamble, similar to the 1956 Constitution, based on the language of the Objectives Resolution. Significantly, the name initially given to Pakistan was 'The Republic of Pakistan',[10] which was a clear departure from the 1956 Constitution wherein Pakistan was named 'The Islamic Republic of Pakistan'.[11] This fact clearly demonstrates Ayub's secular mindset. Its most distinguished feature was the introduction of the presidential system of government.

Presidential Form of Government

The main emphasis of the 1962 Constitution of was a strong executive, expressed through the office of the President. The fundamentals of the system are enunciated below:

1. The President was elected independently of the legislature and had a direct mandate from the electors to perform the executive functions of government;
2. He was to hold office for a fixed term and could not be removed from office by an adverse vote in the legislature against any of his policies, but only by a special process of impeachment;
3. The legislature was elected independently and had a fixed term;
4. The legislature functioned independently of the executive and could not be dissolved by the executive or the President;
5. The legislature was the supreme law-making body of the country and no proposal could become law unless voted by this body;
6. The judiciary was responsible for the interpretation of laws and executive orders in the light of the principles embodied in the Constitution.

The Ayub government gave the following arguments in support of the presidential system: one, the presidential system had special advantages to offer to a nation which had recently emerged out of a colonial past and was embarking upon an ambitious programme of social reform and economic development political unity. Two, the presidential system, by giving executive authority to one individual with a mandate from the entire nation, could facilitate the growth of unity in the country.[12]

In introducing the 1962 Constitution, Ayub stated:

> We have adopted the presidential system as it is simpler to work, more akin to our genius and history, and less liable to lead to instability, a luxury that a developing country like ours cannot afford.[13]

Political leaders, however, continued to press for a parliamentary system. In a joint statement made by political leaders of different shades of opinion in East Pakistan, they reaffirmed their preference for the parliamentary system.

Powers of the President

Under the 1962 Constitution, the President was the repository of all powers. It was commonly said that the President under the Constitution was like the clock-tower of Faisalabad where all the bazaars converged.

The Constitution provided that there would be a President elected in accordance with the Constitution and the law.[14] The President was required be a Muslim, not less than 35 years of age, and qualified for election as a member of the National Assembly.[15] He was to be elected indirectly by an electoral college in accordance with the provisions outlined in the Constitution. The lower age limit for the President under the 1956 Constitution was 40 years, as against 35 years under the 1962 Constitution.

The system of election, that is, whether the President should be elected directly or indirectly, was discussed and examined in great detail by the Constitution Commission as well as by the people in general. The Constitution Commission favoured direct election on the basis of a restricted franchise. Ultimately, the system of indirect election through local government institutions was adopted. The President was to be elected by an electoral college formed by not less than 80,000 electors, equally distributed between the two provinces (East and West Pakistan). Each province was to be divided into not less than 40,000 territorial units to be known as electoral units.[16] Any citizen who was at least 21 years of age, of sound mind, and was a resident of or was deemed by law to be resident of an electoral unit would have the right to be enrolled. Those enrolled for an electoral unit would elect from amongst themselves a person of at least 25 years of age who would be an elector for that unit.[17] The electors thus elected in both the provinces formed the electoral college of Pakistan and this electoral college elected the President by a majority vote.[18]

The electoral college was to have other functions conferred upon them by law, particularly in relation to matters of local government. Thus, the electoral college was elected not simply for the election of the President and the legislatures but was also to act as the institution of local government. Critics of the system pointed out that, apart from the disadvantages of indirect election, it would wreck local government institutions by involving them in party politics. The argument put forward by the government was that if the electoral college was divorced from affairs of local government it would become a political forum and there was no means, specially for an unsophisticated electorate, to judge the members of the electoral college on the basis of their concern for public interest.[19]

When the constitution was implemented in 1962, Ayub became the first President of Pakistan in accordance with the result of the referendum held in February 1960. His term of office was three years,[20] since he had already served two years of his term from 1960.

Selection of Candidates for Election to the Office of President

If the number of candidates for election to the office of President exceeded three, the Speaker of the National Assembly was to convene a joint session of the members of the national and provincial assemblies to select three of the candidates for election, the remaining candidates thus becoming ineligible. This screening was not applicable to a person who was holding the office of the President, that is, if the incumbent President was also a candidate, the number of candidates could be four.[21]

The term of the President was fixed for five years. A person was not eligible for re-election if he had held the office of the President for a continuous period of more than eight years. However, with the approval of a joint sitting of the members of the national and provincial assemblies, such a person could be eligible for election of the President for more than two terms. In fact, with the approval of the legislatures there seemed to be no limit to the number of terms for which a person might be eligible for re-election as President.[22]

Impeachment and Removal of the President

The President could be impeached by the National Assembly on a charge of violating the Constitution, or for gross misconduct, in accordance with the following procedure:

One-third of the total members of the National Assembly had to give written notice to the Speaker for the removal of the President. The notice had to set out particulars of the charge and it was to be transmitted to the President by the Speaker. The resolution for removal of the President was not to be moved in the National Assembly earlier than fourteen days or later than thirty days after the notice of the resolution. The President had the right to appear or be represented before the National Assembly when it discussed the motion for impeachment. The President was to be removed from office if the resolution for impeachment was passed by votes of not less than three-fourths of the total members of the Assembly.[23]

A significant feature of the impeachment procedure was that if the resolution for removal of the President failed to obtain one-half of the total number of members of the National Assembly, the movers of the resolution would cease to be members of the National Assembly. A similar procedure had been provided for the removal of the President on the grounds of his physical or mental incapacity.[24]

The President was not allowed to hold any office of profit in the service of Pakistan but was not prevented from holding or managing private property. Protection of the President from legal proceedings while he was in office was provided.[25] Similar protection was provided in the 1956 Constitution.

Independence of the Executive Authority

The executive authority of the Republic was vested in the President to be exercised by him in accordance with the provisions of the Constitution and the laws.[26] The President was responsible for regulating the allocation and transaction of the business of the central government, and for establishing divisions of the government, he also had to specify the manner in which the orders and instruments made in pursuance of the authority vested in him should be expressed and authenticated.[27] The Constitution had conferred on the President adequate powers not only for the carrying out, or administration of laws, enacted by the legislature but also for the conduct of foreign affairs and of war; he had military and legislative powers and the limited judicial functions of granting pardons and reprieves.[28] He was the ceremonial head of state, chief of the executive, and also retained substantial power in law-making.

The President had the power to make all key appointments. He appointed the Governors, central ministers, Auditor-General, judges of the Supreme Court and the High Courts, the Election Commissioner, the Central Public Service Commission, the Council on Islamic Ideology, the National Finance Commission, the National Economic Council, the Attorney-General, among others.[29] The supreme command of the defence services was also vested in the President. He had the power (a) to raise and maintain the Defence Services of Pakistan, and (b) to grant commissions and to appoint chief commanders of those services and to determine their salaries and allowances.[30]

The list of powers granted to the President under the 1956 Constitution were also comprehensive but that constitution provided a parliamentary system in which the President was expected to exercise his extensive executive powers on the advice of the Prime Minister and the Cabinet who were responsible to the legislature. Under the 1962 Constitution, the President could exercise these powers independently. There was, no doubt, a council of ministers, but their advice was not binding on the President, nor were his ministers responsible to the legislature.

The President and his Cabinet

The President could appoint a council of ministers to assist him in the performance of his duties. The Constitution did not elaborate on the exact relationship between the President and his council of ministers. He was not bound by the advice of his ministers and the ministers held office at the pleasure of the President and could be removed from office any time, without the President having to assign any reason therefor.[31]

The President was empowered not only to dismiss a minister or a Governor, but also to disqualify him from public office for a period of five years on a charge of gross misconduct in relation to his duties. The Governors or ministers would have the option of agreeing to the disqualification or of having the matter referred to a tribunal for inquiry. In the case of a central minister, the tribunal was to consist of a Judge of the Supreme Court appointed by the President after consultation with the Chief

Justice.[32] The Constitution provided that if a member of the National Assembly should be appointed as a member of the President's council of ministers, he would lose his seat in the National Assembly,[33] but this provision was amended by the President within the first three months of the enforcement of the constitution.[34] The amendment would have greatly altered the character of the council of ministers. The ministers as members of the legislature would have some followers in the legislature and as such would exercise an influence unusual in a Presidential Cabinet. The strong sentiment among the politicians in favour of some form of parliamentary system in Pakistan would also consolidate and strengthen their position. As the President had to depend on the support of the legislature, it was not conceivable that a minister with a powerful backing in the legislature would be treated as a mere adviser.

It is generally believed that the need for the Presidential Order, enabling the ministers to retain their seats in the National Assembly, arose because of Muhammad Ali Bogra, who had been offered the office of Foreign Minister. Bogra had also been elected to the National Assembly from East Pakistan and he was not willing to lose his seat in the National Assembly on becoming a minister. The Presidential Order was declared by the Supreme Court of Pakistan as *ultra vires* upholding the earlier decision of the Dhaka High Court in this matter.[35] It was held that the amendment of Article 104(1) of the constitution by the Presidential Order so as to omit the word 'minister' from clause (1) of Article 104, with a view to enable ministers appointed from amongst members of the Assembly to retain their seats in the National Assembly after appointment was inoperative, because the Presidential Order was itself void and *ultra vires* the Constitution. The Supreme Court interpreted Article 224(3) of the constitution, which enabled the President to pass Orders for removing any difficulty that might arise within three months after the commencing day, so as to mean that the principal duty laid upon the President and those working with him was to bring the constitution and all its provisions into operation as an integral whole, without variation whatsoever. The responsibility, under Article 224(3), at the highest level was given to vary provisions in the constitution, not for the purpose of altering the constitution itself, but in order that the constitution as a whole should be brought into force. The provision of the constitution debarring the members of the council of ministers from continuing as members of the National Assembly had a very important purpose, namely, to bring into operation a Presidential form of government, in which the executive was to be completely separated from the legislature. The Court observed that instead of performing the major duty enjoined upon the President to bring these fundamental provisions into operation, they were altered in a fundamental way so as to change the form of government from the purely Presidential form to an anomalous parliamentary form.

Without second judging the wisdom of the Supreme Court in this case, the importance of a close and harmonious relationship between the executive and the legislature in a Presidential system could hardly be exaggerated. In the United States of America, the party machinery plays a considerable role in producing a close relationship. If the American President wishes something to be done by the legislature he can influence the legislature through the members of his party. Similarly, the American President has always been kept informed of the trends and tendencies in the legislature through the party machinery. In Pakistan, well-organized political parties were yet to emerge. Hence, the vacuum which in the United States of America was filled by the party machinery had to be filled through constitutional devices, such as the presence of ministers in the legislature, question-answer sessions, and adjournment motions.

Presidential Powers and the Legislature

The Presidential system is based on the theory of the separation of powers between the legislature and the executive. The executive usually not being an integral part of the legislature though retaining considerable power and influence in the legislative organ. Under the Parliamentary system, the executive and the legislature are united and the head of the state is an integral part of the Parliament. However, in the Presidential system adopted under the 1962 Constitution, the President was made an integral part of the central legislature which consisted of the President and one House, known as the National Assembly of Pakistan.[36]

The President could summon the legislature and prorogue it. The Speaker of the National Assembly could also summon the National Assembly at the request of not less than one-third of the total number of members of the National Assembly and when the Speaker had summoned the legislature, it was he who could prorogue it and not the President.[37]

The President was also empowered to dissolve the National Assembly at any time subject to the condition that in case of dissolution the President also had to quit office and there were to be fresh elections for both the President and the National Assembly.[38] This, no doubt, was a healthy check against arbitrary dissolutions of the National Assembly as the President himself would have to face the hazards of an election, and it was not likely that the President would exercise the power frequently or lightly. The idea of summoning, proroguing, and dissolving the legislature by the President seems again more in accord with a Parliamentary, rather than a Presidential form of government. As a further safeguard, the President was not given power to dissolve the National Assembly when it was to consider a resolution of impeachment against him under Article 13 or 14.[39]

In case of a difference of opinion between the President and the National Assembly, the President could call for a referendum on the matter to be conducted among the members of the electoral college. The matter to be referred to a referendum would be put in the form of a question capable of being answered either yes or no.[40]

The President had the right to address the National Assembly and to send messages to it. The members of the President's council of ministers and the Attorney-General had the right to speak and otherwise take part in the proceedings of the National Assembly or of any of its Committees, but were not entitled to vote.[41]

Certain categories of Bills could not be introduced or moved in the National Assembly without the previous consent of the President, for example, a Bill relating to preventive detention.[42]

The President had the right to veto Bills passed by the National Assembly. The American President also has veto power though not an absolute one since the Congress can override his veto if the Bill is passed again by a two-third vote in both Houses. The 1962 Constitution gave a more comprehensive and effective veto power. When a Bill had been passed by the National Assembly, the President could do one of the following:

(a) give assent to the Bill;
(b) withhold assent from the Bill; or
(c) return the Bill to the National Assembly with a message requesting that the Bill or a particular provision of the Bill be reconsidered and amendments suggested in his message be considered.

If the President did not take any of these three steps, the Bill would be deemed to have received his assent after the expiry of thirty days.[43]

If the President withheld assent from a Bill, the National Assembly could reconsider it and if the Bill was passed again by the votes of not less than two-thirds of the total number of members of the National Assembly, the Bill would again be presented to the President for assent. If the President returned the Bill for reconsideration and if the Bill was again passed by the National Assembly, without amendment or with amendment as suggested by the President in his message, by a simple majority vote, or if the Bill was passed by the National Assembly with amendments not suggested by the President by votes of two-thirds of the total members of the National Assembly, the Bill would be presented to the President for assent.

When the Bill was sent to the President for the second time for consideration, the President could do either of the following:

(a) give assent to the Bill;
(b) refer the Bill to a referendum under Article 24 in the form of a question whether the Bill should or should not receive assent.

If the Bill received majority votes of the total number of members of the electoral college, the President would be deemed to have assented to the Bill.[44] So, the veto power of the President under the constitution was very effective. If he withheld assent, it must receive an absolute majority vote of two-thirds of the National Assembly's members, even then the President could persist in refusing his assent and refer the matter to a referendum. Thus, the Presidential veto could be overcome only by an absolute majority vote in the legislature and the majority votes of the electoral College.

Legislative Powers of the President

The President had the power to make and promulgate ordinances which had the same force of law as Acts of the central legislature. The President could promulgate an ordinance when the National Assembly stood dissolved or was in session and he was satisfied that circumstances existed which necessitated immediate legislation. Such an ordinance, however, had to be laid before the National Assembly as soon as practicable. If the ordinance was approved by the National Assembly, it was deemed to have become an Act of the central legislature. In case of disapproval by the National Assembly, the ordinance ceased to have any effect after the expiry of the prescribed period. The power of the President to make laws by ordinance was restricted to matters with respect to which the central legislature had competence.[45] The power to legislate by ordinance was provided under both the interim and the 1956 Constitutions.

Presidential Control over the Budget

Critics of the Presidential system in Pakistan stressed again and again the possibilities of deadlocks between the President and the legislature over the budget in the absence of democratic traditions and conventions similar to those which have grown in the United States of America. Nobody could deny or dismiss altogether the validity of this apprehension. The Constitution Commission examined this issue in great detail and suggested a procedure by which the ultimate control of the public purse by the legislature was retained by providing the President with a limited power of certification for a period not exceeding one year. But if the deadlock continued for more than one year, both the President and the legislature would have to face election. When the proposals of the Constitution Commission were reviewed by the Cabinet sub-committee, the recommendation of the Constitution Commission in respect of budgetary matters was not accepted. The Cabinet sub-committee was supposed to have evolved a new formula under which no new taxation or increase in the existing taxation or in existing expenditure could take place unless the National Assembly approved.[46] Ayub while introducing the 1962 Constitution stated that in order to reduce the chances of conflict between the National Assembly and the President, and to prevent paralysis of the administration, and to ensure continuance of ongoing schemes, the constitution provided that a previously passed budget would not be altered without the permission of the President and new taxation would not be levied without the consent of the National Assembly. This, according to Ayub, was based on the theory that the President was finally responsible to the country for administration and members of the National Assembly represented the feeling of the people who had to pay taxes.[47]

The 1962 Constitution drew a distinction between recurring expenditure and non-recurring expenditure. While the National Assembly had the power to discuss, debate, and pass opinion on non-recurring expenditure, it would have no power to reject this item of the budget. It was only with regard to new expenditure and new taxation that the legislature had been given unqualified power.

Custody of the central consolidated fund, including payment of money into, and withdrawal of money from, that fund, and all matters connected with public money and public accounts were to be regulated by an Act of the central legislature or, subject to any such Act, by rules made by the President.[48] The President was to present the budget, and the annual financial statement before the National Assembly. The financial statement was divided into two parts. Part one showing the expenditures charged upon the consolidated fund, the expenditure which the National Assembly could discuss, but not vote upon.[49] Expenditures charged upon the consolidated fund included:

1. Remuneration of the President and other expenditures relating to his office.
2. Remuneration payable to:
   (a) Speaker and Deputy Speakers or other members of the National Assembly;
   (b) Judges of the Supreme Court;
   (c) members of the President's council of ministers;
   (d) the Chief Election Commission;
   (e) the Comptroller and Auditor-General;
   (f) members of the Advisory Council of Islamic Ideology.
   (g) Parliamentary Secretaries appointed by the President;
   (h) members of the Central Public Service Commission.

   It may be added here that under the 1956 Constitution, the salaries of ministers were not included under this category of expenditures.

3. Administrative expenses of the National Assembly, Supreme Court, Comptroller and Auditor-General, Chief Election Commission, any Election Commission, Advisory Council of Islamic Ideology, and the Central Public Service Commission.
4. Debt charges binding on the federal government.
5. Sums declared by the constitution or by an Act of the central legislature to be so charged.[50]

The new expenditure was explained as under:[51]

1. Where the expenditure for any particular project approved by the National Assembly under Article 42 exceeded by more than 10 per cent the approved expenditure for that year.
2. Any other expenditure which was not recurring expenditure.
3. Any recurring expenditure for which no provision was made as recurring expenditure in the previous financial year.
4. Any excesses by more than 10 per cent of a recurring expenditure.

The 'recurring expenditure' was defined as the kind of expenditure which was required from year to year. With respect to recurring expenditure, the National Assembly could discuss it, but had no right to vote upon it. It was only with respect to new expenditure, as defined under the 1962 Constitution that the National Assembly could vote.

As a further safeguard for continuation of the economic development projects it was provided that the financial statement might specify in relation to a project the sum required not for the current year but also for the subsequent years of the project. Once the National Assembly had approved the project, the expenditures for the subsequent years could be placed before the National Assembly, but it would have no right to reject them.[52] This particular provision regarding the development projects was suggested by the Administrative Committee which examined proposals before the 1962 Constitution was finally drafted. The argument in favour of this restriction on the powers of the legislature was that these projects were vital to the economic development of the country and as such they should not be left to the whims of the legislature. Once the National Assembly had approved them, it should be bound to grant money for the subsequent years. It was pointed out that in the past development projects were often subjected to partisan or sectional considerations and consequently had been hampered.[53]

All the innovations of recurring, new expenditure, and expenditure for projects extending over several years no doubt limited the powers of the legislature. The National Assembly thus had power to discuss, debate, and express opinion on recurring expenditure, but had no power to reject it. Only with regard to new expenditure and taxes it had unqualified powers. Thus, effective control of the legislature was limited to a small percentage of the total amount involved in the financial statement. Judged by the criteria of a western democratic constitution, this was no doubt a deviation from the accepted principles of the unqualified powers of the legislature over the public purse.

After consideration of the annual budget estimate by the National Assembly, the President had the responsibility of causing the schedule of authorized expenditures to be prepared showing (i) the sums to meet expenditures upon the central consolidated fund, (ii) sums granted or deemed to have been granted by the National Assembly under Article 41. No money was to be withdrawn from the central consolidated fund unless provided for in the schedule of authorized expenditures as authenticated by the President and laid before the National Assembly for information.[54]

Provisions for supplementary and excess budget estimates as well as provisions for unexpected expenditure had been provided in the 1962 Constitution.[55] If for any reason the schedule of authorized expenditure for a financial year could not be authenticated before the commencement of that year, the President could authorize withdrawal from the central consolidated fund of amounts to meet expenditures provided for in the annual budget estimates, but this was restricted to expenditures charged upon the central consolidated fund and recurring expenditures.[56]

No proposal relating to Money Bills, namely, no proposal for imposition of taxation, or for the appropriation of public revenues, or for borrowing of money and similar matters, could be made except with the recommendation of the President.[57] As regards taxation, Article 48 provided that no tax could be levied except by or under the authority of an Act of the central legislature.[58]

Emergency Powers of the President

If the President was satisfied that a grave emergency existed in which Pakistan or any part of Pakistan was threatened by war or external aggression or in which the security or economic life of Pakistan was threatened by internal disturbances beyond the power of a provincial government to control, the President could issue a proclamation of emergency. The proclamation of emergency had to be laid before the National Assembly 'as soon as it was practicable', there being no fixed time-limit. The President could revoke a proclamation when satisfied that the grounds on which it was issued had ceased to exist.[59]

During a time of emergency, the President was authorized to make and promulgate such ordinances as might appear to him to be necessary to meet the emergency. The President could exercise this extraordinary legislative power even when the National Assembly was in session.

With the revocation of the proclamation of emergency the ordinances made by the President ceased to have effect unless such ordinances had been approved by the National Assembly. One significant aspect of the emergency powers of the President was that the President's power to make laws by ordinance was again restricted within the legislative competence of the central legislature.

Although the constitution did not prescribe any time-limit, yet there was a safeguard under Article 109 which laid down that there should be at least two sessions of the National Assembly in a year and not more than 180 days should intervene between the last sitting of the National Assembly in one session and its first sitting in the next session. Since there was no provision that during an emergency the President would have any power to suspend any clause of the constitution, the National Assembly had to be summoned within 180 days of its last session, and this indirectly gave a time-limit during which President could rule without the aid of the National Assembly. It was indeed an improvement inasmuch as the emergency power under the constitution did not give the President the power to suspend any clause or Article of the constitution. The 1956 Constitution had given the President the power to suspend certain parts of the constitution and under Articles 191 and 193 of the 1956 Constitution, the President could suspend the operation of any provision of the constitution relating to any body or authority in the province except the High Court. However, no such power was available to him under the new 1962 Constitution.

A Centralized Federal System

After independence, a highly centralized federal system was established in Pakistan under the interim constitution. There were a number of factors responsible for the dominance of the centre over the provinces. The Government of India Act, 1935 as well as the 1956 Constitution provided for the centre's dominance over the provinces and most importantly political and financial controls of the centre over the provinces. If the centre had exercised this power in a broad national perspective, the dominance of the centre might have been an asset. Unfortunately, however, in the formative stages of Pakistan's nationalism, those in power at the centre during the political turmoil and instability in Pakistan of the 1950s could not inspire confidence among the people of East Pakistan and the result was a great sense of frustration and bitterness in East Pakistan against the centre. This is the reason why when the 1956 Constitution was framed, there were repeated demands for a weak centre in the second Constituent Assembly.

The political parties with predominant following in East Pakistan did not accept the 1956 Constitution as containing sufficient provincial autonomy. The fact was that even under the 1962 Constitution, the central government continued to dominate, and the provincial and regional feelings continued to grow, particularly over the economic development of the country.

Ayub, like Jinnah, wanted to rejuvenate Pakistani nationalism. He declared on numerous occasions that economic injustices suffered by East Pakistan in the past must be redressed. He was also in favour of a strong central government, believing that without it Pakistan could not make progress, but regional feelings in both wings had already become deep-rooted. It was not an easy task for the framers of the 1962 Constitution to arrive at an agreed formula relating to the federal structure.

The distribution of legislative powers under the Government of India Act, 1935 was unique in its character. It had three lists of powers. Following the model of the Government of India Act, all the constitutional drafts made in Pakistan and the 1956 Constitution also divided the lists of subjects into central, concurrent, and provincial. Similarly, in India, the same method of distribution on the basis of three lists had been followed. The 1962 Constitution, however, provided for a much simpler method of distribution of powers, under which there was only one list of subjects of national importance, all other subjects were left to the provinces.[60] The central government, however, was given overriding powers in matters concerning the security of the country, coordination between the provinces, and economic development. It was provided that the central legislature would have exclusive power to make laws (including laws having extra-territorial operation) for the whole or any part of Pakistan with respect to any matter enumerated in the third schedule of the constitution.[61] The subjects given to the centre included defence, external affairs, inter-provincial trade and commerce, national economic planning and national economic coordination, currency, foreign exchange, central banking, insurance, nuclear energy, mineral oil and natural gas, industry owned wholly or partly by the central government or by a corporation set up by the centre, preventive detention for reasons connected with defence, external affairs, and the security of Pakistan. There were in all forty-nine items in the central list as against thirty in the 1956 Constitution, sixty-one under the Government of India Act, 1935, and sixty-six under the draft constitution of the first Constituent Assembly.

A Unicameral Central Legislature

The 1962 Constitution, like the 1956 Constitution, provided for a unicameral system though most of the federal systems in the world have a bicameral system. The central legislature consisted of the President and one House known as the National Assembly of Pakistan.[62] It had 156 members on the basis of parity of representation between East and West Pakistan. There were 150 elected constituencies, half elected by constituencies in East and the other half by constituencies in West Pakistan. Six seats were reserved for women—three from East Pakistan, and three from West Pakistan.[63] Whereas, under the 1956 Constitution, the seats reserved for women were for a period of ten years, there was no such time-limit under the 1962 Constitution. Women could also contest general seats in the National Assembly. Thus, female citizens in Pakistan enjoyed a double franchise. The term of the National Assembly was fixed for five years unless it was sooner dissolved by the President.[64]

The members of the National Assembly were to be elected under the same system as was provided for election of the President, that is, indirectly by the members of the electoral college. A candidate for election to the National Assembly had to be at least 25 years of age and his name had to appear on the electoral roll for any electoral unit. The constitution specified the disqualification which could prevent a person from being elected as a member of the National Assembly.[65] A person could not, at the same time, be a candidate for election to more than one seat in any Assembly or to a seat in more than one Assembly. If a person who was a member of one Assembly was elected to another Assembly, then he would lose his seat in the previous Assembly, of which he was a member.[66]

The President could summon and prorogue the National Assembly. The Speaker could summon the National Assembly on the requisition of one-third of the members and when the Speaker summoned the National Assembly, only he could prorogue it. If the offices of the President, Speaker, and Deputy Speaker, were vacant at any time, the Chief Justice of the Supreme Court could summon the National Assembly.[67]

No member of the National Assembly was liable to any proceedings in any court in respect of anything said or any vote given by him in the National Assembly or any of its committees. The privileges of the National Assembly, its committees, the members thereof and a person entitled to speak therein could be determined by law.[68] It was provided that if a member of the National Assembly was elected as President or appointed as a Governor or minister or to any other office of profit in the services of Pakistan, he would cease to be a member of the Assembly.[69]

There were two interesting and novel provisions under the 1962 Constitution with regard to 'instruction in law-making' and 'conduct of members'. The Speaker of an Assembly was expected to make such arrangements as were necessary to ensure that the members of the Assembly understood the functions of the Assembly as an organ of the state and of their responsibilities as its members.[70] Similarly, it was provided that when the Speaker of an Assembly was satisfied that a member of the Assembly had committed a breach of the rules framed by the Assembly relating to the conduct of the members in such a way as to have been guilty of gross misconduct, he would refer the matter for inquiry to the Supreme Court (in case of the National Assembly) or to the High Court (in the case of a Provincial Assembly) and if the court was satisfied that the member had been guilty of gross misconduct, he ceased to be a member of the Assembly.[71] Such stringent provisions regarding the instruction and discipline of members seem to be a curious and anomalous phenomenon in any representative form of government. It could, however, be pointed out that incidents in the Assembly under the previous constitution, leading to the death of a Deputy Speaker and the beating of a Speaker, probably influenced the framers of the new constitution to impose such stringent measures.

Governors and Provincial Legislatures

The Provincial Legislatures and executives were smaller replicas of the national legislatuers and executives, subject to overriding control and supervision of the President over the provincial executives. The provincial executives under the constitution were directly subordinate to the President inasmuch as the provincial government, the head of the provincial executive was appointed by and held office during the pleasure of the President. The Governor was not merely a figurehead but the holder of the real executive authority in the province. The provincial Cabinet was responsible to the Governor who, however, could not appoint or remove a Provincial Minister without the concurrence of the President.[72] It was further provided that Governor of a province should, in the performance of his functions, be subject to the direction of the President.[73]

Relations between the provincial Cabinet and the Governor and the provincial executive and legislature were more or less the same as in the central government. The procedure for the dissolution of a Provincial Assembly was, however, different. In cases of conflict between the provincial government and the Provincial Assembly, the conflict could be referred to the National Assembly and if the National Assembly decided in favour of the Governor and if the President concurred, the Governor could dissolve the Provincial Assembly.[74]

The financial procedure in the provincial legislature resembled that of the central legislature and the powers of the provincial legislature in respect of money matters were similarly curtailed.

The provincial governments were structured in a manner similar to the central government. The Governor, like the President, was the chief executive of a Province and selected his council of ministers.[75] He could appoint Parliamentary Secretaries and the Advocate-General.[76] However, the Governor, being an appointee of the President, had to work under the direction and supervision of the President. Although several ideas under the 1962 Constitution were borrowed from the Constitution of the United States of America, yet there was major digression in the matter of appointment of Governors. The Governors of the states in the United States are elected like the President, for a fixed term and enjoy autonomy within their own sphere.

The provisions regarding Provincial Consolidated Funds and Public Moneys of provincial governments were similar to the provisions regarding Central Consolidated Fund and Public Moneys of the central government respectively. Financial procedure of the provinces was similar to the financial procedure of the centre.[77]

Relations between the Centre and the Provinces

A provincial legislature was given more power to make laws for the province or any part of the province with respect to any matter other than those enumerated in the central list.[78] The central legislature, however, could legislate on any matter connected with a provincial subject on the grounds of national interest in relation to the security of Pakistan, including the economic and financial stability of Pakistan, planning, co-ordination, or the achievement of uniformity in respect of any matters in different parts of Pakistan.[79] The central legislature could also legislate on a provincial subject when the provincial legislature authorized the central parliament to make any laws in a matter not enumerated in the third schedule. If a resolution to that effect was passed by the provincial legislature, the central legislature had the power to make laws in provincial matters but any law made in pursuance of this power could be amended or repealed by an Act of the provincial legislature.[80]

In case of conflict between the central and provincial laws the latter had to give way to the former to the extent of such repugnancy.[81] The 1962 Constitution, like the 1956 Constitution, had provided predominance of the central legislative powers over provincial powers. Such was the provision also under the Government of India Act, 1935 and the same is the case with the Indian Constitution.

Residuary power had been vested in the provincial legislatures which had an undefined residuum of power to make laws with respect to any matter not enumerated in the third schedule. The question whether residuary powers should be vested in the federal or provincial authorities produced lengthy discussion and controversy in the Constituent Assemblies of Pakistan. Those who wanted to make the centre strong naturally wanted this power to remain with the central authority, arguing that it should have as free a hand as possible to meet the changing needs and requirements of society. In the Indian Constitution, the residuary subjects are with the centre. The supporters of provincial autonomy in Pakistan were equally firm in demanding residuary powers for the provinces and ultimately the 1956 Constitution vested the residuary power in the provinces; this practice was retained under the 1962 Constitution.

Both the Government of India Act, 1935 and the 1956 Constitution contained detailed provisions relating to the administrative relation between the centre and the provinces. The 1962 Constitution, however, contained hardly any provision in this respect. It was provided that executive authority of the central government extended in all matters with respect to which the central legislature had exclusive power to make laws under clause (1) of Article 131.[82] Where a law was made by the central legislature on a provincial subject and if the law provided that such law was to be administered by the central government, the central executive authority might be extended to the execution of such law. The extent of the executive authority of the province was defined to include all matters over which the legislature of the province had power to make laws.[83] Other than these two Articles there is no further provision as to the administrative relation between the centre and the provinces.

The President could delegate with the consent of a provincial government functions in relation to any matter in which the executive authority of the central government extended.[84] Similar provision was provided under Article 127 of the 1956 Constitution. The practice of delegating to a provincial government or its officers the duty of executing the orders of the central government was also exercised under the Government of India Act, 1935. The central government had an insufficient number of officers in the provinces to execute its functions, hence the necessity of such delegation. The framers of the 1956 Constitution recognized this need and allowed this process of delegation to continue, thus permitting the federal government to utilize the provincial executive machinery for the enforcement of federal laws. A similar consideration perhaps had led the makers of the 1962 Constitution to retain the practice of delegation of powers to the provincial government.

Distribution of Financial Resources between the Centre and the Provinces

An analysis of the allocation of financial resources under the Government of India Act, 1935 proves that it was tipped in favour of the central government. The provinces, by no means, secured complete fiscal autonomy under the Government of India Act, 1935 and their revenues were comparatively inelastic.

Immediately after the creation of Pakistan, the original distribution of financial resources under the Government of India Act, 1935 was further amended to the advantage of the centre. This was done in view of the extraordinary expenditures on defence and rehabilitation of refugees which the central government of Pakistan had to face immediately after independence in 1947. Thus, sharing of income tax with the provinces was discontinued, the sales tax which was a provincial source of revenue was also taken over by the centre though 50 per cent of the net proceeds was allowed to the provinces subject to a guaranteed minimum for East Pakistan. The central government also took over the duty on agricultural land which had been a provincial source of revenue.

During the era of constitution-making, particularly in the second Constituent Assembly, the members from East Pakistan time and again demanded that the constitution should ensure a fair and equitable distribution of resources, in the absence of which provincial autonomy, it was feared, would become a farce.

The 1956 Constitution, however, did little in respect of financial autonomy for the provinces; the distribution of financial resources made under the Government of India Act, 1935 was allowed to continue with minor changes. The 1956 Constitution, however, provided a machinery for making recommendations as to the distribution between the federation and the provinces of the net proceeds of some important taxes such as the export duty on jute and cotton, taxes on income and on sales and purchases and any other specified tax; and as to the making of grants by the centre to the provinces. The recommendations were to include provision for regulation of borrowing powers of both the federal and provincial governments. The machinery was the National Finance Commission which was to be constituted by the President at intervals of not more than five years and was to consist of the central and provincial Finance Ministers and such other persons might have been appointed by the President on the recommendation of the provincial Governors. The National Finance Commission, however, was not constituted till 1958 and then dissolved with the abrogation of the constitution before it could make any recommendations. The Ayub government set up a committee in May 1961 to examine the question of allocation and apportionment of revenues between the central and provincial governments. It was a five-member committee with the Secretaries of the Ministries of Finance and Commerce of the central government and Finance Secretaries of East and West Pakistan.[85]

Under the 1962 Constitution, the allocation of the proceeds of the taxes and duties collected and administered by the central government to the provinces were as follows:

i. 50 per cent of the income tax including corporation tax, as compared to 50 per cent of income tax excluding corporation tax and taxes collected in Karachi under the previous arrangement.
ii. 60 per cent of the sales tax as against 50 per cent in the previous arrangement.
iii. 60 per cent of the excise duties on tobacco, tea, and betel nuts were allocated to the provinces as against 50 per cent under the previous arrangement.
iv. 100 per cent of the export duties on jute and cotton would go to the provinces as compared to 62.5 per cent of the export duties on jute allotted to East Pakistan under the previous arrangement. Under the new arrangement both East and West Pakistan would receive 100 per cent share from the joint pool of export duties on jute and cotton on the basis of population.

The basis of allocation had also been changed. According to the previous arrangement, income tax and excise duties were distributed broadly in the ratio of 55 per cent to West Pakistan and 45 per cent to East Pakistan and sales tax was distributed on the basis of collection. The new basis of allocation as regards sales tax was 70 per cent to be allocated on the basis of population and 30 per cent on the basis of incidence, that is, the point of collection, and as regards the remaining taxes, they were distributed on the basis of population.[86]

As regards the distribution of the power to tax between the centre and the provinces, the 1962 Constitution did not alter the scheme of distribution as given under the interim and the 1956 Constitutions. The centre was given power to levy customs duties (excluding export duties), excise duties including duties on salt but excluding duties on alcoholic liquor, corporation taxes and taxes on income other than agricultural income, state and succession duties, taxes on capital value of assets, taxes on sales and purchases, terminal taxes on goods or passengers carried by sea or air and taxes on mineral oil and natural gas. The sources of revenue for the centre were more or less similar as under the 1956 Constitution. The provincial sources of revenue had not been mentioned in the 1962 Constitution specifically because any other source which had not been specifically given to the centre was given to the provinces under the new arrangement.

The President, however, was to constitute a National Finance Commission consisting of the central Finance Minister and provincial Finance Ministers and such other persons as the President might appoint after consultation with the Governors of the provinces. The Commission was to make recommendations to the President as to the distribution between the central and the provincial governments of the proceeds of the following taxes:

i. taxes on income including corporation tax;
ii. taxes on sales and purchases;
iii. export duty on jute and cotton and such other export duties as might be specified by the President; and
iv. such excise duties imposed by the central government as might be specified by the President, and any other taxes that might be specified by the President.[87]

The National Finance Commission would also consider the grants-in-aid by the central government to the provincial governments.

On the recommendation of the National Finance Commission, the President would specify, by order, the share of the proceeds of the above-mentioned taxes which were to be allotted to each provincial government. The National Finance Commission's recommendations would be laid before the National Assembly and each of the Provincial Assemblies. As compared with its functions under the 1956 Constitution, the National Finance Commission, however, under the 1962 Constitution had been given an additional function, which was that it would make a report to the President as to the progress made, during a period of the economic development plan, to remove the disparity between the provinces and between different areas within the provinces; it had also to make recommendations as to the manner in which the disparity could be removed in the next succeeding plan. The recommendations were to be taken into consideration by the National Economic Council in formulating its plan.

The National Economic Council was to be appointed by the President by nominating its members.[88] The National Economic Council under the 1956 Constitution consisted of four ministers of the federal government, three ministers of each provincial government and the Prime Minister who was to be *ex-officio* chairman of the National Economic Council. The functions of the National Economic Council under the 1962 Constitution were to review the overall economic development of Pakistan. It was stressed that in formulating the plans, the National Economic Council was to ensure that disparities between the provinces, and between different areas within a province, in relation to income per capita should be removed and the resources of Pakistan, including resources in foreign exchange, be used and allocated in such a manner that disparities between the provinces should be removed in the shortest possible time. It was further stressed that the duty of each government should be to make the utmost endeavour to achieve this object of removing economic disparity between the provinces.

Further, the National Economic Council was to submit every year to the National Assembly a report on the results obtained and progress made in the achievement of removing disparity and a copy of that report was also to be laid before each Provincial Assembly. It was expected that discussion on the reports of the National Economic Council and of the National Finance Commission would give useful opportunities to the legislatures to discuss economic problems and grievances.

An Independent Judiciary

When Ayub decided to restore constitutional government and the 1962 Constitution was in process of being drafted, there was an almost universal demand for restoration of the full jurisdiction and powers of the courts and the incorporation of a Bill of Rights under the new constitution. The Shahabuddin Commission stressed and emphasized the fact that the independence of the judiciary should be maintained as had been the practice for a long time and any inroad into it, which had been found necessary during the martial law period, should not be treated as a precedent. The Shahabuddin Commission recommended all the safeguards to ensure the independence of the judiciary as recognized under the 1956 Constitution. The recommendations of the Shahabuddin Commission relating to the powers of the judiciary and fundamental rights were, however, modified by the cabinet sub-committee when giving final touches to the 1962 Constitution.

The security of tenure of office and other conditions which give trust and confidence to the judiciary were guaranteed in the 1962 Constitution. The method of removal of judges of the superior courts was, however, made different from that of the 1956 Constitution. Under that constitution, judges of the Supreme Court would hold office till the age of 65 years unless, of course, they were removed from office on the ground of misbehaviour or infirmity of mind or body by an Order of the President, following an address by the National Assembly praying for such a removal. Under the 1962 Constitution, the President was to appoint a council to be known as the Supreme Judicial Council, consisting of the Chief Justice and the two next senior judges of the Supreme Court, and the Chief Justice of each High Court.[89] If, on information received from the Supreme Judicial Council, or from other sources, the President was of the opinion that a judge of the Supreme Court or of a High Court might be incapable of performing the duties of his office by reason of physical or mental incapacity or might have been guilty of gross misconduct, he was to direct the Supreme Judicial Council to enquire further into the matter and remove the judge from office if need be. The method of removal of the judges under the 1962 Constitution was on the same lines as that recommended by the first Constituent Assembly in its draft constitution of 1954. The idea behind the new method was that legislatures in the country were not yet mature and competent enough to decide the issues relating to the removal of judges. It had indeed been suggested in some quarters that for some time to come, legislatures might not have the requisite integrity and competence to sit in judgment over a superior court judge.

As to the powers of the judiciary, the 1962 Constitution had made some changes in its jurisdiction. The 1962 Constitution had departed from the well-established system of umpiring the constitution through the judiciary. No law could be challenged in a court on the grounds that the legislature by which it was made lacked the necessary powers. This was an acceptance of the principle of parliamentary supremacy as it exists in England and it was a departure from the system of judicial review which exists in the United States of America. Under both the interim and the 1956 Constitutions, the judiciary had power to adjudicate upon the *vires* of legislative provisions.

It would be incorrect to say that the judiciary had no part in interpreting the constitution. The original power under the 1962 Constitution of the Supreme Court included jurisdiction in any dispute between the central government and a provincial government, or between two provincial governments. Similarly, the appellate jurisdiction of the Supreme Court provided that an appeal from a judgment, decree, order or a sentence, would lie as of right if the High Court should certify that the case involves a substantial question of law as to the interpretation of the constitution.[90] Thus, Articles 57 and 58 appeared to be in conflict with Article 133 which laid down that responsibility for deciding whether a legislature had power under the constitution to make a law was that of the legislature itself, and that the validity of a law would not be called in question on the ground that the legislature by which it was made had no power to make the law. How could the judiciary settle disputes between the central and a provincial government, or interpret the constitution, if it had no power to decide the constitutionality of enactments passed by any legislature?

The first amendment of the 1962 Constitution, made in 1963, however, greatly changed this position.[91] The judiciary was vested with full power to pass judgment over the *vires* of the legislature. Judicial control over the executive from the inception of the 1962 Constitution had been fully maintained. As to the judicial review of executive action, the 1962 Constitution had faithfully preserved the jurisdiction of the courts, on the lines of the common law of England. The substance of the former writ jurisdiction which were greatly valued and cherished in Pakistan had been preserved under the Constitution of 1962 though the latin names of *habeas corpus*, *mandamus*, *certiorari*, and *quo-warranto* had not been mentioned. The constitution laid down that a High Court of a province might, if it was satisfied that no other adequate remedy was provided by law:

(a) on application of any aggrieved party, make an order:

i. directing a person performing in the province functions in connection with the affairs of the centre, the province or a local authority to refrain from doing that which he is not permitted by law to do or to do that which he is required by law to do; or

ii. declaring that any act done or proceeding taken in the province by a person performing functions in connection with the affairs of the centre, the province, or a local authority, has been done or taken without lawful authority and is of no legal effect; or

(b) on the application of any person, make an order;

i. directing that a person in custody in the province be brought before the High Court so that the court may satisfy itself that he is not being held in custody without lawful authority or in unlawful manner; or
ii. requiring any person in the province holding or purporting to hold a public office to show under what authority of law he holds that office.[92]

This particular Article was an important provision under the constitution for the protection of individual rights and liberties and could be compared with section 223A of the interim constitution and Article 170 of the 1956 Constitution.

Other provisions relating to the Judiciary regarding appointment of the Chief Justice and judges of the Supreme Court; the Chief justices and judges of the High Courts; their retirement age; appointment of acting Chief Justice, acting judges and ad hoc judges of the Supreme Court; appointment of acting Chief Justice and Additional judges of the High Courts; transfer of judges; and their remuneration were identical or similar to the provisions of the 1956 Constitution.[93]

Elections through the Electoral College

As discussed above, the Constitution of 1962 introduced indirect elections not only for the President but also for the National as well as Provincial Assemblies. The Basic Democrats, that were elected, constituted the electoral college for the election of the President and the Assemblies. The Basic Democrat, who was elected for the local self government, was called elector and the electors in both provinces constituted the electoral college for five years. On the expiry of five years, the electoral college stood dissolved. However, the functions performed by these electors in relation to matters of local government would not be disturbed by the dissolution of the electoral college.[94] An electoral roll had to be maintained for each electoral unit.[95] The qualification for being elected as an elector was that he had not to be less than 25 years of age.[96]

The system of indirect election to the Assemblies, in particular, was quite unusual for a democratic constitution and created a strong possibility of political corruption and purchase and sale of votes. After all a member of the National Assembly was elected by about 500 to 550 electors on the average and a member of a Provincial Assembly was elected by half as many electors. Hence, the inherent possibility of purchase of votes in such a set-up. Furthermore, the members of the legislatures are representatives of the people at large in a democratic system and ought to be elected by the people through universal suffrage. In this system, as given by the new constitution, the representatives of the people were not elected by the people themselves.

Indirect election to the office of the President is not unusual in other countries. The constitutions of India, Germany, Italy and quite a few other countries provide for indirect elections for the Presidency based on an electoral college consisting of the central and provincial legislatures. But it must be borne in mind that in these countries, there is parliamentary form of government and the President is only a figure head. The real power rests with the Prime Minister and the cabinet. In the presidential system of government, the President has dual capacity of the head of state as well as the head of government. Thus, most of the constitutions providing for the presidential system require the President to be elected by the people of the country directly on the basis of adult franchise. The constitutions of France, Mexico, Brazil, and others provide for direct presidential election. In United States, the constitution provides for an electoral college, however, with the passage of time and the establishment of a two-party system and the growth of conventions in this behalf, the election to the office of the President has virtually become a direct one.

Islamic Character of the Constitution

The preamble, so far as the Islamic character of the constitution was concerned, was almost identical with that of the 1956 Constitution. In the first paragraph of the earlier preamble, the words 'authority to be exercised by the people of Pakistan within the limits prescribed by Him (Allah) is a sacred trust' occur. In the preamble of the 1962 Constitution there was no reference to the fact that people would exercise authority 'within the limits prescribed by God'. Presumably, this was done to avoid difficulties in determining the 'limits prescribed by God'. The question could arise as to what were those 'limits', who would decide those 'limits', and so forth. It may be added here that the Objectives Resolution of 1949 on which both preambles were based included additional wording: 'The sovereignty over the entire universe belongs to God Almighty alone and authority which He has delegated to the state of Pakistan through its people for being exercised within the limits prescribed by Him is a sacred trust.' The preamble followed the Objectives Resolution in laying emphasis on the principles of democracy, freedom, equality, tolerance, and social justice, with the qualification that these principles should be observed as enunciated by Islam.

Islamic provisions were continued, as in the 1956 Constitution, in the Directive Principles where according to the constitution, 'the Muslims of Pakistan should be enabled individually and collectively to order their lives in accordance with the fundamental principles and basic concepts of Islam and should be provided with the facilities whereby they may be able to understand the meaning of life according to those principles and concepts.[97] The relevant section of the 1956 Constitution read 'lives in accordance with the Holy Quran and *sunnah*', for which was substituted 'lives in accordance with the fundamental principles and basic concepts of Islam.'

Further, it was laid down in the Principles of Policy that (i) teaching of the Quran and Islamiat to the Muslims of Pakistan should be made compulsory—the word Islamiat was not included in the relevant Article of the former constitution; (ii) unity and observances of Islamic moral standards would be promoted among the Muslims of Pakistan; (iii) proper organization of *zakat*, *waqfs*, and *mosques* should be ensured.[98] It was provided that the bonds of unity among Muslim countries should be preserved and strengthened.[99] Similar provision was also made in the 1956 Constitution, but this was not meant to be Pan-Islamic as the same Article enjoined Pakistan to foster friendly relations among all nations, Muslim and non-Muslim.

The head of the state, the President, was to be, as in the 1956 Constitution, a Muslim.[100] Under the 1956 Constitution also the Presidency was reserved for the Muslims and the Constitution Commission favoured the retention of this clause.

Article 1 of the 1956 Constitution designated Pakistan an 'Islamic Republic'. It was laid down that 'Pakistan shall be a federal republic to be known as Islamic Republic of Pakistan'. The relevant clause of the new constitution laid down simply that the 'state of Pakistan shall be a republic under the name, the "Republic of Pakistan".'[101] The word 'Islamic' was dropped. When the National Assembly met in 1962, there was a demand that the word 'Islamic' should be reintroduced. There was justification for this demand. If Islamic provisions were to be maintained, there was no reason why the republic should not be designated an Islamic Republic. The first amendment, therefore, rectified the anomalous position.

The most important Islamic provision in the 1956 Constitution was Article 198 which laid down that no law should be enacted which would be repugnant to the injunctions of Islam as laid down in the Holy Quran and *sunnah* and that existing laws should be brought into conformity with such injunctions. In the draft constitution prepared by the first Constituent Assembly, the Supreme Court was given jurisdiction for determining whether or not a particular law would be so repugnant, every citizen of Pakistan being given the right to challenge the validity of any legislation on such grounds when a bench of not less than five judges of the Supreme Court would decide the matter. Under the 1956 Constitution, it was the National Assembly which would decide the issue of repugnancy. Article 198 provided that the President would appoint a commission to make recommendations as to the measures for bringing existing laws into conformity with the injunctions of Islam and as to the stages by which measures should be brought into effect and to compile in a suitable form for the guidance of National and Provincial Assemblies such injunctions of Islam as could be given legislative effect. But it was the legislature which was given the final authority to accept or reject the recommendations of the Islamic Commission. So, ultimately it was the National Assembly which would decide whether a particular law would be repugnant to the injunctions of Islam and would also decide how far and which or what existing laws should be brought into conformity with the Islamic injunctions.

The 1962 Constitution substituted Article 198 of the 1956 Constitution with a simple clause on the 'principles of law making' to the effect that 'no law should be repugnant to Islam'.[102] The responsibility of deciding whether a proposed law disregarded or violated Islam or was otherwise in accordance with the principles of law making was that of the legislature concerned. This provision was not enforceable in the law courts and it was one of the principles which the law makers had to bear in mind.

The 1962 Constitution provided for an Advisory Council of Islamic Ideology to be appointed by the President. It was to consist of not less than five or not more than twelve members who would be appointed on such terms and conditions as the President might determine. In selecting the members of the council, the President was to have regard to the persons' understanding and appreciation of Islam and of the economic, political, legal, and administrative problems of Pakistan. The members were to hold office for a period of three years. The President might remove a member from office if a resolution recommending his removal was passed by a majority of the total members of the council.[103]

The function of the council was to make recommendations to the governments, both central and provincial, as to the steps and means which would enable and encourage the Muslims of Pakistan to order their lives in accordance with the principles and concepts of Islam. A more important function of the council, however, was to advise the National Assembly, a Provincial Assembly, the President or a Governor, on any question referred to the council for advice as to whether a proposed law disregarded or violated or was otherwise not in accordance with the principles of law-making enumerated under Article 6 of the constitution.[104] When a question was referred either by a legislature or by the President, or by the Governor to the Council for advice, it was to give information within seven days regarding the period within which it would be able to furnish the advice. If the Assembly or the President or the Governor, as the case may be, considered that in the public interest the proposed law should be made without waiting for the advice, the law could be made before the advice was furnished.

Hence, the advice of the council was not binding on the legislature or the President or the Governor. The responsibility of deciding whether a proposed law did or did not disregard any of the principles of law-making was that of the legislature concerned. The council was given only an advisory power and the legislature itself was the final arbitrator.

The Islamic Research Institute which was provided for under Article 197 of the late constitution, was retained under the new constitution. It was provided that there would be an institution to be known as the Islamic Research Institute which was to be established by the President.[105] The function of the Institute was to include Islamic research and instruction in Islam which would help in reconstituting the society on a truly Islamic basis.

The principal objections to the 1962 Constitution were the Presidential system, the indirect franchise, and the non-justiciability of fundamental rights. Ayub was not willing to consider the preference of the East Pakistanis for parliamentary form of government. He felt very strongly about the state structure he had created under the 1962 Constitution and removal of any vital element from the constitution, in his opinion, would cause the whole edifice to collapse. He was convinced that only a

Presidential form of government could ensure Pakistan's unity and hence, there could be no tempering with this feature of the constitution. He felt that all the powers of state should be concentrated in the hands of the President who alone could guarantee unity, integrity, and solidarity of the state of Pakistan.

NOTES

1. President Ayub's Broadcast of 1 March 1962, *Speeches and Statements of F.M. Mohammad Ayub Khan*, Vol. IV, p. 170.
2. Ayub was well aware of the views of Manzoor Qadir and Bhutto who had already written articles in support of Ayub's ideas on future constitution. A document drafted by Manzoor Qadir on 26 May 1960 and the other titled 'Thoughts on constitution' by Bhutto on 10 October 1959 had already voiced what Ayub desired in the future Constitution by way of limited and indirect franchise, centralized structure and very powerful presidency. Altaf Gauhar in his biography of Ayub, at page 176, has referred to his Personal Papers in regard to these documents.
3. Ayub Khan, Mohammad, *Friends, Not Masters*, 1967, pp. 205-206, Oxford University Press, London.
4. Ibid., pp. 212-16.
5. Gauhar, Altaf, *Ayub Khan—Pakistan's First Military Ruler*, 1994, Sang-e-Meel Publications, pp. 179-81 and 184-6.
6. Ibid., pp. 190-91.
7. Choudhry, G.W., *Constitutional Development in Pakistan*, 1969, p. 178, Longman Group Ltd., London.
8. *Speeches and Statements of F.M. Mohammad Ayub Khan*, Vol. IV, P. 170.
9. Ibid., pp. 170-79.
10. The Constitution of the Republic of Pakistan, Part I Article 1. PLD 1962 Central Statutes 143.
11. The Constitution of the Islamic Republic of Pakistan, Part I, Article 1. PLD 1956 Central Acts and Notifications 54.
12. A Pledge Redeemed—a pamphlet circulated by the Government of Pakistan in March 1962, explaining and justifying the Constitution. Quoted by G.W. Choudhry, *Constitutional Development in Pakistan, supra*, note 7 P. 190.
13. *Speeches and Statements of F.M. Mohammad Ayub Khan*, Volume IV, p. 170.
14. The Constitution of 1962, Article 9.
15. Ibid., Article 10.
16. Ibid., Article 155.
17. Ibid., Articles 156, 157, and 158.
18. Ibid., Article 165.
19. A Pledge Redeemed, *supra*, note 12.
20. The Constitution of 1962, Article 226.
21. Ibid., Article 167.
22. Ibid., Articles 165 and 166.
23. Ibid., Article 13.
24. Ibid., Article 14.
25. Ibid., Article 116.
26. Ibid., Article 31.
27. Ibid., Article 32.
28. Ibid., Article 18.
29. Ibid., Articles 33, 36, 50, 66, 92, 144, 145, 147, 182, 191, and 201.
30. Ibid., Article 17.

31. Ibid., Article 118.
32. Ibid., Article 121.
33. Ibid., Articles 103 and 104.
34. Removal of Difficulties (Appointment of Ministers) Order, 1962. President's Order No. 34 of 1962. PLD 1962 Central Statutes 647.
35. Fazlul Quadir Chowdhry v Mohammad Abdul Haque, PLD 1963 S.C. 486, upholding the Judgment of the Dhaka High Court in Mohammad Abdul Haque v Fazlul Quadir Chowdhry, etc., PLD 1963 Dhaka 669.
36. The Constitution of 1962, Article 19.
37. Ibid., Article 22.
38. Ibid., Article 23.
39. Ibid.
40. Ibid., Article 24.
41. Ibid., Article 25.
42. Ibid., Article 26.
43. Ibid., Article 27.
44. Ibid., Article 29.
45. Ibid., Article 29.
46. Choudhury, G.W., *Constitutional Development in Pakistan, supra*, note 7, p. 203.
47. *Speeches and Statements of F.M. Mohammad Ayub Khan*, Vol. IV, p. 173.
48. The Constitution of Pakistan, 1962, Article 38.
49. Ibid., Article 41.
50. Ibid., Article 39.
51. Ibid., Article 41.
52. Ibid., Article 42.
53. Choudhry, G.W., *Constitutional Development in Pakistan, supra*, note 7, pp. 204-205.
54. Ibid., Article 43.
55. Ibid., Articles 44 and 45.
56. Ibid., Article 46.
57. Ibid., Article 47.
58. Ibid., Article 48.
59. Ibid., Article 30.
60. Ibid., Third Schedule to the Constitution.
61. Ibid., Article 131.
62. Ibid., Article 19.
63. Ibid., Article 20.
64. Ibid., Article 21.
65. Ibid., Article 103.
66. Ibid., Article 105.
67. Ibid., Article 22.
68. Ibid., Article 111.
69. Ibid., Article 104.
70. Ibid., Article 112.
71. Ibid., Article 113.
72. Ibid., Article 82.
73. Ibid., Article 66.
74. Ibid., Article 74.
75. Ibid., Article 82.
76. Ibid., Articles 84 and 85.
77. Ibid., Articles 86, 87, 88, and 89.
78. Ibid., Article 132.
79. Ibid., Article 131(2).

80. Ibid., Article 131(3).
81. Ibid., Article 134.
82. Ibid., Article 135.
83. Ibid., Article 136.
84. Ibid., Article 143.
85. Choudhry, G.W., *Constitutional Development in Pakistan*, *supra*, note 7, p. 226.
86. Ibid., pp. 227-8.
87. The Constitution of 1962, Article 144.
88. Ibid., Article 145.
89. Ibid., Article 128.
90. Ibid., Article 58.
91. Constitution (First Amendment) Act, 1963. Act I of 1964. PLD 1964 Central Statutes 33.
92. The Constitution of 1962, Article 98.
93. Ibid., Articles 49, 50, 52, 53, 54, 55, 92, 94, 95, 96, 99, and 124.
94. Ibid., Article 158.
95. Ibid., Article 156.
96. Ibid., Article 158(1).
97. Ibid., Principles of Policy, Para 1.
98. Ibid.
99. Ibid., Para 21.
100. Ibid., Article 10.
101. Ibid., Article 1.
102. Principles of Law Making, Para 1.
103. Ibid., Articles 199, 200, 201, 202, and 203.
104. Ibid., Article 204.
105. Ibid., Article 207.

13

AYUB'S CIVILIAN FACE

On the promulgation of the 1962 Constitution, the three-and-a-half year martial law era of Ayub came to an end and a civilian constitutional government under Ayub replaced his previous military regime.

Under Article 225 of the 1962 Constitution, the Presidential Proclamation made on 7 October 1958, imposing martial law throughout the country, was revoked with effect from the convening day. The Laws (Continuance in Force) Order, 1958 and certain other President's Orders were also replaced. All martial law regulations, except five, including the West Pakistan Land Reforms Regulation and Scrutiny of Claims (Evacuee Property) Regulation, were replaced. The saved martial law regulations were to become Acts of the central legislature from the dates given against them.[1] All the laws existing on the commencing day continued to remain in force so far as applicable and with necessary adaptations until altered, repealed, or amended by the appropriate legislature. The President was, however, empowered to make, by order, such adaptations which he deemed necessary or expedient, in any provision of the existing laws in order to bring it in accord with the provisions of the Constitution. This power could be exercised by the President within two years of the commencing day. The President could also authorize a Governor to exercise such power in relation to his province. The day when the Constitution it was to come into force was also when the first meeting of the National Assembly was be to held.[2] However, for the purpose of holding elections to the assemblies, the constitution was to be deemed to have taken effect from the date of its election.[3] The President was given the power to make an Order for the removal of difficulties within three months of the commencing day by which the constitution would be subject to such adaptations, whether by way of modification, addition, or omission, as may be deemed necessary or expedient for the removal of difficulties.[4] When in exercise of such power, Ayub made the Removal of Difficulties (Appointment of Ministers) Order, 1962 by which members of the National Assembly were made eligible for appointment as ministers without losing their seats in the Assembly, the Supreme Court, upholding the judgment of Dhaka High Court, declared the President's Order as *ultra vires* being in excess of his power under the Article 224(3).[5]

The pending proceedings before any special military court or a summary military court on the commencing day stood transferred to the criminal courts which had the jurisdiction to try the offence constituted by the facts of that case under ordinary law.[6] The pending petitions for review of sentences awarded by military courts were to be disposed of by the Commander-in-Chief of the Pakistan Army or Commander of Corps, depending upon the length and gravity of the sentences.[7] Similarly, these authorities could entertain petitions for annulment and commutation of sentences already awarded by the military courts.[8] All sentences passed during martial law by a martial law authority were deemed to have been passed lawfully and would be carried into execution according to their tenure.[9] Complete protection was given to all actions done and proceedings taken during the period by any martial law authority and none of these actions or proceedings could be called into question.[10] Complete indemnity was also provided to all actions and proceedings in connection with the administration of martial law.[11] All martial law orders made or issued by any martial law authority stood repealed on the commencing day.[12]

Revival of Political Parties

As discussed earlier, Ayub was personally opposed to political parties and accused them of causing instability and uncertainty in the country. He issued an ordinance on 10 May 1962, banning the revival of organizations for political purposes until the National Assembly had had time to examine the question of political parties 'after full and public discussion', and had legislated upon it. The Order prohibited the setting up of political organizations, as well as the collection of funds for them, and the acquisition or ownership of property by such organizations. It was also provided that no association of persons, with or without an organizational structure, could call itself by any of the former party names.[13]

When the new National Assembly met for the first time on 8 June 1962, Ayub (who was sworn in during the session as the first President of Pakistan under the new Constitution), addressing the session, stressed that martial law had been lifted with the enforcement of the Constitution and that the country was governed by the normal law of the land.

There were a number of political parties at the time of the imposition of martial law in October 1958. The Muslim League was the oldest one amongst them and had enjoyed the longest spell of power. The manifesto of the party for the aborted elections of 1959 was full of promises too good to be true. It promised homes for the homeless, refuge for refugees, schools for the illiterate, hospitals for the sick, social security for the workers, land to the landless, nationalization of key industries, efficient administration, safeguarding the rights of the minorities, and the pursuit of an independent foreign policy. But, in fact, the party had fallen prey to the feudal interests in West Pakistan and had no will to enforce its social agenda. Daultana, Khuhro, and Qayyum, who were still the key figures in West Pakistan, had not carried out a radical re-adjustment of property in their respective provinces when they were in power and no land reforms could be expected from them.

The second major party was the Awami League. It was initially an offshoot of the Muslim League and was named Jinnah Awami Muslim League when it was announced in a convention held in Lahore in December 1952 under the leadership of Suhrawardy. In West Pakistan, it had a very small following but for a few turncoats like Nawab Mamdot. It attained a high degree of organization and cohesion in East Pakistan and successfully exploited the feelings of discontent in East Pakistan over provincial issues like regional autonomy, nationalization of jute and tea industries, and recognition of Bengali as a state language. It was a major partner in the United Front that swept the polls in East Pakistan in 1954. Its members in the National Assembly did not sign the Constitution which, in their view, had not conceded the party's basic demand for regional autonomy. It was also opposed to One Unit in West Pakistan and Pakistan's membership in military alliances like SEATO and CENTO.[14] The party came into power at the centre during Suhrawardy and its performance in office was at variance with its political stance. This *volte face* brought Suhrawardy in conflict with Maulana Bhashani, the president of the East Wing Awami League, who withdrew from the party and joined the National Awami Party.

The National Awami Party was a party of those who opposed the Muslim League. It was led by nationalists like Ghaffar Khan, G.M. Syed and Abdus Samad Achakzai who had struggled for unity with India and, after independence, championed provincial autonomy. Maulana Bhashani became their ally after the split within the Awami League. It was formed at the Convention of Democratic Workers held in Dhaka in July 1957 with a leftist programme which included opposition to military pacts and alliances, nationalization of industrial enterprises, securing the rights of the working classes, abolition of landlordism and its substitution with peasant proprietorship, and opposition to One Unit in West Pakistan. The leaders of the party were mainly concerned with the setting up of autonomous provinces and the radical programme was only adopted for securing countrywide support.

The Krishak Sramik Party was the revived form of an old organization founded by A.K. Fazlul Haq in 1927. It was formed in 1953 under this name, once again under the leadership of Fazlul Haq who led the United Front to victory in East Pakistan in the elections of 1954 and became chief minister. The party was involved in manoeuvring for office and no attention was given to organizational aspects. Consequently, it had no existence in West Pakistan. Its programme for the establishment of socialism, abolition of *zamindari* and *jagirdari* without compensation, nationalization of the jute and cotton trade, and the betterment of the lot of peasants and workers was never seriously pursued.

The Republican Party gained its notoriety due to power gimmicks. The Party owed its origin and existence to Dr Khan Sahib, its founder, who created it when he was in power as the chief minister of West Pakistan. It gained its strength due to the weakening of major parties and widespread demoralization in the Muslim League. It proclaimed to be wedded to the democratic form of government and opposed to martial regimes. The party functioned mainly within the four walls of the parliament and its policies in power clearly showed its bias towards the land owning class from where its main leadership was drawn. It had virtually no existence in East Pakistan. Out of the 2000 delegates who attended its second convention on 28 and 29 September 1958, only twelve were from East Pakistan.[15] The Republican Party was opposed to land reforms and had no appeal for the common man even in West Pakistan.

The Nizam-i-Islam Party was originally a component of the United Front. It stood for the establishment of a religious polity based on Islamic teachings without any specific programme for the formulation of state policies. It broke with the United Front as it believed in separate electorates. It had a limited following in East Pakistan with no presence in West Pakistan.

The Jamaat-i-Islami claimed to be a movement which stood for Islamic ideology embracing Pakistan polity. It was formed in 1941 in Lahore. Initially, it was opposed to the establishment of Pakistan but later found it congenial soil for transforming religious ideology into a political creed. It was in the election to the Karachi Municipal Corporation in 1958 that the Jamaat entered the electoral arena for the first time in a big way and captured more than a dozen seats. But the Jamaat was not a party for the masses. Like totalitarian parties, it demanded strict discipline and loyalty from its members and no deviation from its doctrines. Membership was, therefore, given by a selective process and the entrant had to demonstrate that he lived according to the tenets of Islam and could carry out the duties assigned to him by the party by sacrificing time and money. The total membership of the party in 1957 was only 1271 members.[16] Even associate members had to fulfil obligations not required of the regular members of other parties. The Jamaat started establishing adult education centres, libraries, and dispensaries for free medical aid to build its popularity among the masses, and infiltrated student unions through its ancillary organization, the Islami Jamiat-e-Tulaba. The party believed in the sanctity of private property and no limit on individual ownership provided the acquisition was legal. It argued against making economic power an instrument of political power and was opposed to state enterprise. It was in the moral and spiritual realm that the Jamaat advocated state intervention. In Maulana Maudoodi it had not only a political but also an intellectual leader whose prolific writings on a wide variety of subjects like the constitution, economics, political theory, and ethics were a source of inspiration to the party. The Jamaat had accepted the democratic system temporarily to be discarded after its objective of achieving state power was accomplished.

Political Situation at the Time of the 1962 Constitution

The National Assembly met on 8 June 1962 in Rawalpindi in a building named Ayub Hall. The Constitution came into effect on that date.[17] Ayub addressed the assembly and announced that martial law had been terminated and after forty-four months, a civilian government had been restored. He emphasized that he would support all efforts aimed at ensuring the stability and development of the country but that he would deal harshly with those who sought to disrupt the polity by undermining the people's confidence in the government. In order to facilitate the operation of the National Assembly, seventeen Parliamentary Secretaries (drawn from the membership) and one Chief Parliamentary Secretary and Chief Whip were appointed who were to maintain a close liaison between all members of the National Assembly (MNAs), the Minister-in-Charge of Divisions, and their administrative secretaries. Essentially, they were to assist the ministers in parliamentary activities. The Parliamentary Secretaries were also entrusted with public relations duties for their respective divisions. Thus, like the basic democracies which were linked to and dominated by the bureaucracy, the legislators were brought under administrative influence.

The central and provincial government secretariats were reorganized in this period. In addition, many of the heretofore centrally directed activities were provincialized. The railways[18] and the Industrial Development Corporation[19] were bifurcated, and agricultural development corporations were established in each province. Each provincial government was given its own Planning and Development and Basic Democracies departments while the central government promised funds for new projects. The Second Five Year Plan initiated in 1960 was suddenly everyone's responsibility. With the President acting as Chairman of the Central Planning Commission and the National Economic Council, it was apparent that a concerted effort would be made at energizing the development programme and accelerating economic progress. The Central Planning Board which was set up in 1953 and was responsible for drafting Pakistan's First Five Year Plan (1955–60), was converted into the Planning Commission and Development Boards in the provinces. By 1961, the President assumed the chairmanship of the Planning Commission and the Deputy Chairman, a high-ranking CSP officer, was given the status of a central minister. At the same time, the Commission was given the status of a Division in the President's Secretariat, and the scope of its functions and powers was enhanced by the inclusion of responsibility for implementation and review as well as the formulation of national plans. The delegation of planning to the provinces followed after the promulgation of the Constitution. Similarly, the Rural Works Programme, which was launched in East Pakistan as a pilot project in 1961, became a countrywide operation by 1963.

The President's Cabinet underwent some major changes in this period. The new advisory group reflected the political climate which suddenly enveloped the country. Manzoor Qadir retired from public life and resumed legal practice in Lahore. Some people believe he was simply exhausted and had requested the President to relieve him. Others thought his role as chief draftsman of the Constitution made it necessary for him to step down. Rumours circulated that he disagreed with the President's intention to politicize the administration and yield to pressure to reinstate the political parties.[20] The Cabinet included a number of politicians. The former prime minister, Muhammad Ali (Bogra), succeeded Manzoor Qadir as Foreign Minister. Similarly, Abdul Monem Khan (replaced Ghulam Faruque as Governor of East Pakistan), Wahiduzzaman, Abdul Sobur Khan, A.K.M. Fazlul Quadir Chowdhry, Shaikh Khurshid Ahmad, Abdullah-al-Mahmood, Abdul Waheed Khan, and Al Haj Abd-Allah Zaheer-ud-Din (Lal Mia) were selected from among the victorious members of the National Assembly to fill the ministerial positions.

The President's tactics were obvious but unconstitutional. Article 104 of the new Constitution specifically prevented a minister from serving in the National Assembly. The President ignored this section and proceeded to issue Order 37 which allowed the ministers to keep their legislative positions. When the President's action was challenged in the High Court of East Pakistan, it was ruled unconstitutional and the ruling was later sustained by the Supreme Court.[21]

The inability of the President to modify the Constitution was partly due to the expanding influence of the political opposition, and partly due to the judiciary under the leadership of Chief Justice A.R. Cornelius. The judiciary enjoyed a high level of independence during the period and the Court owed much to the integrity, independence, learning, and leadership of the late Justice Cornelius.

The ban on political parties continued by proscribing anyone from holding out as a member of a political party and by making such conduct punishable by law.[22] This condition was later relaxed in an election to the electoral college.[23] This prohibition was virtually removed by the Political Parties Act, 1962 and anyone could hold out at an election as a member of, or candidate having the support of, a political party.

The absence of political parties meant there could be no responsible organizational programmes for the electors to consider. It also meant the legislators would have great difficulty in organizing their affairs once the assemblies convened. This latter dilemma was especially evident when the Speakers and Deputy Speakers of the legislatures had to be elected. The initial impulse was to organize along provincial lines, and members from East and West Pakistan huddled in separate caucuses to work out their respective strategies. This was certainly not what the President desired, and the fear that a continuation of the ban on political parties would only lead to deepening cleavages and more intense conflicts between the East and West Pakistani contingents compelled him to reconsider his position. Hence, Ayub decided to lessen his hostility towards the political parties.

Political Parties Act, 1962

The political activity that followed the enforcement of the Constitution focused on the Constitution. Those in the opposition condemned it as autocratic and undemocratic. The banning of political parties, the continuation of restrictions on the EBDO'd politicians and those convicted under the Security of Pakistan Act, the forced detention of other political figures, the indirect process of elections, and the non-justiciability of fundamental rights were offered as grounds. The silence of the President on these expressions of political disfavour encouraged some of the more vocal members to seek legislation in the Assembly for the legalization of political parties. In point of fact, the National Awami Party (NAP), Muslim League, Jamaat-i-Islami, Awami League, and Krishak Sramik Party were already operating with impunity outside the legislatures. On 4 July 1962, a bill providing for the formation and regulation of political parties was drafted by the government and referred to a select committee of the Assembly.

The select committee was composed of people representing different shades of opinion, and three days later they returned it to the floor of the Assembly citing their inability to agree on a *modus operandi.* Nevertheless, on 14 July the draft bill was put up to a vote and passed virtually unmodified. The next day, the National Assembly passed another bill liberalizing the Preventive Detention Laws. The President gave his assent on 16 July and the Political Parties Bill became law.[24] Despite many controversial features making it difficult for the opposition in the National Assembly to associate itself with the new law [i.e., the law prevented the disqualified under the Elective Bodies Disqualification Order, 1959 from participating in political activities, and it gave the government authority to declare others ineligible should they engage in activities considered detrimental to the health and security of the nation],[25] political parties were quick to legitimize their operations after its enactment.

Revival of the Political Parties and Political Activity

Within a few days, the Jamaat-i-Islami announced that it was back in business. In August, the Nizam-i-Islam Party revealed its intention to engage in political activity. Although Ayub acknowledged that he was a prisoner of events and hence was forced to accept the reinstatement of political parties, he was convinced that the country would be better off without them. Nonetheless, on 20 July, accepting the *fait accompli*, he made a fervent plea for a broad-based nationalist political party which could unify the nation and direct its energies towards constructive endeavours. At the time, it did not seem that he would consider joining any political party. He emphasized his concern that a party organized and led by him would receive the opprobrium of the people in that it would be considered a 'King's Party'.[26] However, Ayub urged his followers to get on with the job of building a party that would represent the government in the assemblies, and it was known that he urged government members to take the name of the defunct Muslim League. The President was criticized for using the name of the Muslim League, but no one disputed the fact that it was important as a political symbol to the party in power which still sought to legitimize itself.

The Muslim League, on its revival, was split into three factions. The 'conventionists',[27] who favoured the party's revival on a broad basis supported Ayub's government, while the other two, the 'council group' and the 'non-revivalists', who maintained that the party could not be re-established pending the restoration of full democracy, allied with other opposition parties in demanding the democratization of the new Constitution.

Two leaders of the former Awami League (Ataur Rahman Khan and Sheikh Mujibur Rehman) said likewise that the question of a revival of that party did not arise. A similar statement was issued by the leaders of the former Krishak Sramik Party. Both statements alleged that the political climate in Pakistan was still unsuitable for the working of democratic organizations.

Meanwhile, the formation of the 'Democratic Group had been announced in June', a section of the East Pakistan members of the National Assembly claiming the support of more than forty out of the seventy-eight members from East Pakistan. The formation of an opposition group of East Pakistani members in the National Assembly, under the name of the People's Democratic Group, was announced in August.

In October 1962, the 'National Democratic Front' was formed to press for, *inter alia*, the introduction of adult franchise, the justiciability of fundamental rights, and a parliamentary system of government. The Front was supported by the 'Council' Muslim League, the Awami League, the National Awami Party, the Krishak Sramik Party, and the Nizam-i-Islam Party, as well as sections of the Republican Party and the Jamaat-i-Islami. The EBDO'd politicians were too shrewd to be defeated so easily. Since they could not become members or hold office of any political party, they therefore rallied around the National Democratic Front, which was termed a movement, not a political party.[28] A demand that the President should hold a round-table conference with prominent politicians to discuss amendments to the Constitution was rejected by the President on the grounds that such a procedure would be unconstitutional.[29]

All the resources of the government were placed at the disposal of pro-government politicians in the legislatures. In effect, a political party was formed in reverse order. On 4 September 1962, the Muslim League (Conventionists) became the official government party. The Conventionists comprised the ministers, a majority of members of the Assembly, and other followers of the government. Almost all of then were relatively new to politics and had not held posts in the pre-1958 Muslim League. Of the older, more seasoned Muslim Leaguers, those who were allowed to participate in politics formed their own Muslim League, which was distinguished by the term 'Councillors'. The Councillors derived their name from the Muslim League Council, which refused to accept the Conventionists as genuine Muslim Leaguers.

Abdul Qayyum Khan, the last president of the Muslim League before the imposition of martial law, was imprisoned by the authorities a few days after the passage of the Political Parties Bill. He did not rejoin the Council Muslim League until February 1967 when his EBDO term expired. Therefore, the Muslim League Councillors selected former Prime Minister Khawaja Nazimuddin to lead them. When he died in 1964, Nurul Amin took control of the party. Nurul Amin was also made leader of the National Democratic Front after the death of Suhrawardy in 1963. He was leader of the opposition in the National Assembly and helped form the Pakistan Democratic Movement. He led the Democratic Action Committee, a coalition of eight opposition parties which sought to displace Ayub Khan.

The Conventionists had as their chief organizer, Chaudhri Khaliquzzaman, president of the Muslim League after the death of Muhammad Ali Jinnah, but he was too old and weak a figure to lead the party. On 15 December 1962, the only obvious choice for a leader was identified, and Ayub was requested to assume the post. In being asked to take the assignment he was reminded that not only Jinnah but Liaquat, the first Prime Minister, had held the presidency of the party while simultaneously administering the affairs of state. The President agreed to consider the proposal but laid stress on the need for the party to restructure itself; to lay down the guidelines that it intended to follow.

He finally joined the Conventionists in May 1963 and proceeded to list the following objectives for the party:[30]

1. To take such steps in religious, educational, social, economic, and other fields that would bring about unity of thought and action amongst people and to make them feel pride in their homeland and its achievements and to bring self-respect, self-reliance, and a sense of responsibility and discipline.
2. To build a society with spiritual, moral, and civic sense capable of keeping pace with the modern age.
3. To encourage such activities as would enable the nation to enter the age of science and technology within the shortest possible time.
4. To encourage industrialization to the maximum extent possible and to modernize agriculture so as to get the maximum benefit from the lands and to remove economic disparities wherever possible.
5. To take such measures as would enable the benefits of development to be shared by as many people as possible.
6. In order to do that, to take steps to see that while private enterprise would be encouraged, undue accumulation of wealth did not take place in a few hands.
7. To establish Islamic political ideology, social justice, and economic order and to move in the direction of a welfare state in accordance with the resources of the country.
8. Meanwhile, to encourage people to regulate charities on a local, collective, and national basis so as to take care of the needy and deserving.
9. To stand by the solemn promise to assist the people of Jammu and Kashmir to attain their freedom.
10. To conduct foreign relations in a manner that would gain Pakistan friends and to ensure maximum security and development of the country.

Seven months later on 24 December 1963, Ayub accepted the unanimous vote of the Pakistan Muslim League and became its President. Despite his aversion to politics, particularly party politics, he had to become a part of it.

From the moment the political parties were permitted to operate, Ayub was on the defensive. Overtures were made to both Khawaja Nazimuddin and H.S. Suhrawardy to cease their criticism and join with the Conventionist Muslim League in the forging of a strong national party. Both men chose to rebuff the invitations. However, Suhrawardy was arrested on 30 January 1962, under the Security of Pakistan Act, and his imprisonment without trial disturbed his followers as well as the volatile student community. Demonstrations erupted in and around Dhaka and some of the other municipalities of East Pakistan in defiance of martial law which resulted in the imprisonment of a number of political leaders. When he was finally released from prison on 19 August 1962, Suhrawardy not only refused to accept Chaudhri Khaliquzzaman's invitation to join the Conventionists (an interesting invitation in view of Suhrawardy's EBDO status) but started organizing the entire opposition against Ayub. In order to do this, he severed his ties with the Awami League and formed the National Democratic Front (NDF). The NDF, according to Suhrawardy, was not a political party and therefore he was able to skirt the disqualification bar. He was to toil in its behalf until illness forced him to seek medical attention in

Beirut, where he died on 5 December 1963. There was widespread and persistent speculation in Pakistan that Ayub had poisoned him so that he could no longer threaten his authority. In point of fact, Suhrawardy had been ailing for many years and his multifarious activities, both political and social, simply took their final toll. But there was no convincing those who loved Suhrawardy and despised Ayub. Suhrawardy was an extremely talented man, and a politician of much integrity. It is a pity that his talent and experience could not be constructively used only because the politics of Pakistan was so bedeviled by intrigues between bureaucratic and feudal interests.

Nazimuddin refused to join the Conventionists for virtually the same reasons as Suhrawardy. Despite having been decorated by the President in the year following the *coup d'etat*, Nazimuddin grew disenchanted with Ayub's handling of the affairs of state. He was especially critical of the new Constitution and the presidential form of government, which he felt gave far too much power to the executive. And as for the Conventionists, he could not accept them as fellow Muslim Leaguers. Instead, he agreed to accept the leadership of the Council Muslim League. Nazimuddin joined both Suhrawardy's NDF and, at the outset of the electoral campaign in 1964, the Combined Opposition Parties (COP). In 1964, he was considered the possible COP leader for the presidency before it was decided to adopt Miss Fatima Jinnah as the presidential candidate. In October 1964, he died suddenly. In Nazimuddin's death, Pakistan lost one of its political sages, an extremely honest man, perhaps too decent for the rough politics of Pakistan. He had no stomach for intrigue and the way his government was dismissed was one of the most shameful episodes in Pakistan's political history. He was one of the principal lieutenants of Jinnah and had unflinching faith in the creation of Pakistan and great devotion for the country. Nazimuddin was indeed one of the very few men of honour in the politics of Pakistan.

The only other personality who might have tested Ayub's power was Tamizuddin Khan, Speaker of the National Assembly, but his sudden death in 1963 also removed his name from contention. It was no wonder, then, that the COP in looking for someone to stand against Ayub was compelled to request the assistance of Miss Fatima Jinnah.

Franchise Commission and its Report

Having given in to the demand to reinstate political parties, Ayub let it be believed that he would yield on other major issues as well. In his question and answer session with the press on 1 March 1962, Ayub disclosed that he would appoint a Franchise Commission to investigate all aspects of the issue surrounding direct or indirect elections. This had also been recommended by the Constitution Committee. Addressing the criticism of the electoral college with its power to elect the President and the members of the national and provincial legislatures, Ayub stated that he would welcome a better system than the one he had designed. Commenting at the time he said:[31]

> They can produce two more qualifications and say that anyone who is educated beyond a certain level, or anyone who owns property beyond a certain level or pays taxes beyond a certain level, might be given the right to vote. What else can they say? Very well, as soon as you do that, you are going to create a tremendous imbalance between your city population and your rural population. You are going to disenfranchise 80 per cent of your people. You are going to set them at a disadvantage straightaway. One may well say that this is not an insurmountable problem because if a constituency has 500 voters, shall we say, by a certain criteria to elect one man and another constituency has 5000 or 50,000 voters on the same criteria, it does not make that much difference. But then how are you going to select your President on that basis? Can you make certain that the number of voters in East and West Pakistan would be equal? Can you say that East and West Pakistan are going to be at par with each other in so far as the numerical strength of votes is concerned, and if they are not thus at par, then can you say that 100 East Pakistanis will count as eighty West Pakistanis? The position would obviously be absurd. But I am going to set up a Commission and I will be interested to see what they bring up but I beg of you please to get it into your head that direct universal franchise in Pakistan, other than on the basis of which I am suggesting, is not a practical proposition for the present at least.

Despite his firm conviction that the process of indirect elections was the only one presently suited to Pakistani society, Ayub gave in to the pressure of the intelligentsia. On 30 July 1962, he appointed a five-member Franchise Commission to investigate alternative propositions.

Akhtar Husain, the Chairman of the Commission, and his associates, were requested to address themselves to two principal questions:

1. Whether the system of election of the President and members of the assemblies through Basic Democracies was [an] efficacious and appropriate instrument for a realistic representation of the people; and
2. If the Commission recommended universal suffrage, whether any qualifications should be imposed upon the electors.

The Commission submitted its report on 12 February 1963, with two members, including the Chairman, dissenting. It was an embarrassing moment for Ayub. The majority report, like the Constitution Commission before it, ruled against indirect elections and insisted that only universal adult franchise should be the basis of election for the President and members of the assemblies. The minority report was in keeping with Ayub's ideas, however. With opinions of the members of the Commission divided (three to two), the Law Ministry was ordered by Ayub to appoint a special committee to examine all recommendations dispassionately 'keeping in view the socio-economic and administrative requirements of the country'.[32] Later, when the special committee submitted its report, no one was surprised to find it in favour of the minority view that the system of indirect elections should continue. 'Until such time as a majority of the people become literate, any election based on direct voting would be an unreliable index of responsible public opinion and will provide an opportunity to unpatriotic and hostile elements to create confusion and arrest the progress of the country'.[33]

To this, five opposition members on the special committee courageously contributed a note of dissent which read in part: 'We are finally of the opinion that the present system is a denial of the rights of the people and that it would only perpetuate a thinly veiled dictatorship in the country'.[34] Not everyone would go so far as to use the language that Maulvi Farid Ahmad employed in his personal note of dissent, but it illustrated the disillusionment and frustration of the opposition in this fretful exercise: 'It is, perhaps, unique and unheard of in the annals of running the government and the appointment of commissions that a commission, the child of its own creation, has been neglected and consigned ingloriously to the gutters. This is a matter which the country should not fail to notice except with the gravest concern'.[35]

It is open to question whether Ayub was wise in appointing the Franchise Commission. While he wished to show his honest intentions, he was unprepared from the outset to listen to and accept recommendations running counter to his own judgments. Also, with the Constitution already in force and with Basic Democracies being given increasing consideration, it was already too late to consider a new approach, that is, unless a drastic revision of the political structure was contemplated. A somewhat independent but apologetic analysis of the Ayub Constitution concluded that:

> While the present Constitution has rightly taken steps against the political and economic instability as experienced in Pakistan in the past, it may be necessary in the course of the working of the constitution, to provide some additional safeguards against the danger of arbitrary government. With a sincere and well meaning President such as the present President of Pakistan, there may not be any such risk.[36]

In the end, however, Ayub only added fuel to the fire set by his detractors, who now felt all the more justified in accusing him of dictatorial acts. If anything was gained from the episode it was that the President was successful in having things done his way; but opposition to his ideas and policies was clearly on the upswing.

The First Amendment

Fundamental Rights in the Constitution Made Justiciable

When the new Constitution was in the process of being framed, the demand for the incorporation of a Bill of Rights like the one under the 1956 Constitution was almost unanimous. The Constitution Commission found that preponderance of opinion (98.39 per cent) was in favour of a Bill of Rights being incorporated into the new Constitution. The Constitution Commission discussed in great detail two aspects of fundamental rights: whether they could be incorporated in the Constitution, or if the courts were to be entrusted with the responsibility of seeing that no law was enforced that was contrary to the basic rights of citizens. In both cases, the Commission gave an affirmative answer. When the report of the Commission was examined by the

Cabinet Sub-committee, it was suggested that the substance of fundamental rights should be laid down within the Constitution as a 'principles of law-making', but that they should not be enforceable by the courts. Ultimately, this suggestion won the approval of those who finally drafted the Constitution. The 'principles of law-making' sought to maintain most of the fundamental rights guaranteed under the 1956 Constitution such as freedom of speech and expression, of assembly and association, of movement and profession subject to the usual safeguards; but these were merely pious declarations and no remedy was provided should principles be violated. It was meaningless to formulate and declare a long list of rights without a machinery to enforce them. It has been said very rightly that, from the standpoint of the science of jurisprudence, nothing is a 'right' unless it is enforceable in the courts of law.

The framers of the Constitution tried to justify the new method by citing the case of Britain where Parliament is the custodian of these rights, but in the absence of the great English tradition, this was not reliable for protecting the basic rights of citizens. It was because of this realization that the first and the second Constituent Assemblies, as well as the Constitution Commission strongly recommended the powers of the courts to enforce basic rights. The authors of the 1962 Constitution referred to the alleged defects of judicial review in the United States and put the issue in the form of a choice between a judge and the people's interpretation of the Constitution.

As soon as the Constitution was published, there was vehement criticism of the curtailment of the powers of courts in protecting the fundamental rights of citizens. The issue created a storm of controversy and insistent demands were made on behalf of the people to make these 'principles of law-making' enforceable by courts.

The elections to the National Assembly in 1962 brought in a large number of politicians from amongst opposition parties which apparently forced Ayub to accept Moulvi Tamizuddin Khan as Speaker of the National Assembly and Muhammad Ali Bogra, a former prime minister, as his foreign minister. The elections thus strengthened the democratic forces in the country, demanding the introduction of fundamental rights in the Constitution.

Ayub responded to the people's wishes and the changes were made.[37] A Bill on fundamental rights was introduced in the National Assembly during its Dhaka session in March 1963 which made these rights justiciable. The effect of the proposed amendment was to convert the 'principles of law-making' in the Constitution into constitutional restrictions on the power of a legislature, so that the decision of whether the legislature safeguarded fundamental rights would be vested in law courts. If any legislature should pass a law repugnant to or inconsistent with any of the fundamental rights enumerated in 'principles of law-making', the courts would have the power to declare any such law void. This would give the courts the same power as Article 4 of the 1956 Constitution which put an embargo on the legislature against passing any Bill violating fundamental rights. Thus the amendment sought to make the courts rather than the legislature the custodian of fundamental rights. The Law Minister claimed that it would virtually incorporate a Bill of Rights into the Constitution and enlarge the jurisdiction of the courts which would be entrusted with the task of enforcement of rights.[38]

By the First Amendment,[39] the Constitution was greatly democratized and liberalized. The rule of law was fully restored in Pakistan. While Article 98 of the Constitution gave power to the judiciary to act as guardian over executive actions in Pakistan, the new amendment made the judicial review over the legislative Acts competent. No legislature in Pakistan could pass a Bill which was inconsistent with the fundamental rights as laid down in the Constitution and the judiciary was empowered to scrutinize and pass judgment upon the validity of any enactment, either of the executive or of the legislature. Many actions of the head of the state could be declared *ultra vires* by the judiciary in Pakistan.

The first amendment was provided with a 'qualifying clause' with the aim of protecting some of the laws and reforms made during the martial law regime as also a number of ordinances and regulations through which socio-economic reforms, such as land reforms and family law ordinance, were made. The qualifying clause which was popularly known as the 'rider clause' in the first amendment was criticized by the members of the opposition in the National Assembly on the grounds that it meant an encroachment on the rights provided under the Constitution. Undoubtedly, some acts and regulations were put outside the scope of the first amendment as a result of this qualifying clause but it was justified on the ground that the reforms and the laws made during the martial law period had to be validated and protected. Ayub attached great importance to the reforms undertaken by him during the martial law period and he was not prepared to sacrifice them to the plea of civil liberties or rights. It was an encouraging development that the government through the first amendment of the Constitution had made the fundamental rights justiciable. It met, to a large extent, the demands of the public who wanted to make the Constitution more democratic and liberal. It also showed Ayub's concern to restore the powers to the people in a peaceful and constitutional manner.

The fundamental rights enumerated under the first amendment were nearly the same as were embodied in Chapter 1 of Part II of the Constitution originally as Principles of Law-Making. This chapter was completely substituted under the first amendment. The fundamental rights were essentially the same as enumerated under the 1956 Constitution which included equality before law, freedom of speech and expression, freedom of association, freedom of movement, freedom to acquire property, freedom of profession and trade, freedom of religion, safeguards against arrest and detention, protection against retrospective punishment, protection against forced labour, access to public places, protection of languages and cultures, protection against slavery and the practice of untouchability. The first amendment added to these fundamental rights the right to the security of person, safeguards against taxation for purposes of any particular religion, safeguards as to educational institutions in respect of religion, and safeguards against discrimination in services. It is of interest to note that unlike the 1956 Constitution and other constitutions like the Indian Constitution, the various fundamental rights were not numbered as separate Articles of the Constitution, but were enumerated under the heading of 'The Rights' following Article 6. It did not matter as long as these fundamental rights had been made justiciable.

Another significant change brought about by the first amendment was the renaming of the Republic as the 'Islamic Republic of Pakistan'. Ayub, whose actions signify secular tendencies, was brought under pressure by the religious parties, political or otherwise. He succumbed to this demand and agreed to introduce the word 'Islamic' before 'Republic of Pakistan'. The opposition parties had also joined into the demand because it appeared to them as a rallying point to embarrass Ayub and his political party.

The Second Amendment

The Second Amendment to the Constitution was quite a comprehensive one.[40] It added or amended ten Articles. Important changes or modifications brought about by this amendment included the extension of the period to hold office by the President beyond the expiry of his term until his successor entered upon office; modification of the provision that the President would cease to hold office until his successor entered upon office if he dissolved the National Assembly prior to the expiry of its full term of five years; elections to the National Assembly to be held within 120 days of its dissolution by the President before the expiry of its term; the election to the office of the President to be held in 120 days in case he dies before the expiry of his term of office; and conferring of power in the President to make special provision for representation of tribal areas in the electoral college.

This amendment was primarily designed to remove the difficulties felt during the first two years of the enforcement of the Constitution. The amendment came into effect on 8 July 1964. Its most creditable act was the curtailment of the discretionary power of the President to dissolve the National Assembly who would lose office if he dissolved the Assembly before the expiry of its term. This provision was a serious check on the President against using such power arbitrarily, wantonly, or capriciously. Nevertheless, correspondingly with this provision, the President was allowed to continue in office until his successor entered upon office despite the expiry of his term. This meant that if he dissolved the National Assembly prematurely, he would continue in office till his successor was elected. The process of the election of the successor was spread over 120 days and so was the process of the election to the National Assembly after its dissolution. So, he exercised the powers of his office despite having ceased to hold office during the period when the election to the new National Assembly was to take place. He could continue to command influence and power while new elections to the National Assembly were taking place. Coupled with this was the provision that the dissolution of the National Assembly did not prevent the President from seeking re-election as President.[41] All these provisions read together made the position of the President far more powerful as compared to the National Assembly.

Supreme Court's Judgment in Maudoodi's Case: Jamaat-i-Islami Banned

Although the Constitution had been enforced in June 1962 and a civilian government had been installed, military dictatorship did not change. Opposition parties were looked at with great suspicion and their meetings were monitored by the intelligence agencies. Eight leading opposition leaders, Z.H. Lari, Mahmoodul Haq Usmani, Sheikh Abdul Majeed, Mian Mahmood Ali Kasuri, Tufail Muhammad, Maulana Abdus Sattar Niazi, Khawaja Muhammad Rafiq, and Nawabzada Nasrullah Khan, were arrested on charges of sedition for holding a meeting at the Karachi residence of Suhrawardy in May 1963 and for passing a resolution criticizing the prevailing political situation, Ayub's methods of administration, and calling for a united opposition against his government. This resolution was officially interpreted as an attempt to provoke contempt for the government and was, therefore, regarded as seditious.[42]

Another attack on the opposition was directed against the Jamaat-i-Islami. The Home Minister accused the Jamaat of creating a sense of frustration and despondency by unwarranted criticism of government policies. He also attacked one of its members, Amir Maulana Abul Ala Maudoodi, as a foreign agent. There were student disturbances in November 1963, primarily directed against an ordinance that restricted student union activities and gave unbridled power to the authorities to expel students or even annul degrees awarded to them.[43] Student unrest spread to the cities of Lahore, Rawalpindi, and Faisalabad. Ayub blamed the Jamaat for fomenting trouble against him and the obvious reason for such an accusation was that the leaders of the student unrest were mostly drawn from Islami Jamiat-e-Tulaba, the student wing of the Jamaat. There is little doubt that the Jamaat was pursuing an active campaign of criticism against the Ayub government. The government thus struck on 6 January 1964. Both the provincial governments, on the same day, declared the Jamaat-i-Islami to be an 'unlawful association' under section 16 of the Criminal Law Amendment Act, 1908 as amended by Ordinance XXI of 1960.

These notifications were challenged before the West Pakistan High Court by Maudoodi and the Dhaka High Court in exercise of writ jurisdiction. The petition filed before the High Court in Lahore was dismissed, but the one presented to the High Court in Dhaka succeeded and it was held that the notifications issued by the East Pakistan government had no binding effect and should be rescinded, cancelled, or withdrawn.[44] Appeals against both decisions were made to the Supreme Court and were heard together.

The Supreme Court, by a unanimous verdict, accepted the appeal of Maudoodi and dismissed that appeal of the government of East Pakistan.[45] The Court held that the declaration by the provincial governments of the association as unlawful would be an administrative act open to judicial review by the courts. The principle of natural justice (show cause notice, and opportunity of hearing) were applicable to all administrative proceedings including the proceedings to declare any association of people 'unlawful'. Since the action taken against the Jamaat was without notice and without affording the opportunity of a hearing before or after taking action, it therefore, was unlawful and void. The Criminal Law Amendment Act of 1908 was held repugnant to the seventh fundamental right of 'freedom of association' and its provisions were held not to fall within the scope of 'reasonable restrictions' contemplated by that right. The provision of the Act of 1908 giving provincial governments arbitrary and unqualified power to declare an association unlawful was found to be an unconstitutional interference with the right of 'freedom of association' because the making of such declaration depended upon the subjective satisfaction of such governments. The notifications of 6 January 1964 of both the provincial governments were thus held illegal and void for violation of the fundamental right of 'freedom of association' under the Constitution and for other reasons set out in the judgment, and the governments were directed to cancel and withdraw these notifications.

This judgment is one of the most important ones in the constitutional law of Pakistan upholding the fundamental right of 'freedom of association'. It gave protection to the political parties against the government that was using its power arbitrarily to ban them and to stifle their activities.

NOTES

1. The 1962 Constitution, Article 225. Land Reforms Regulation was deemed tobe an Act with effect from 7 February 1959 and Scrutiny of Claims Regulation with effect from 23 August 1961.
2. The Constitution of 1962, Articles 224(i) and 242. The first meeting of the National Assembly was held on 8 June 1962, which was the commencing day.
3. Ibid., Article 224(2). The date of enactment was 1 March 1962.
4. Ibid., Article 224(3).
5. See Fazlul Quadir Chowdhry v Muhammad Abdul Haque PLD 1963 S.C. 486 and Muhammad Abdul Haque v Fazlul Quadir Chowdhry PLD 1963 Dhaka 669.
6. Martial Law (Pending Proceedings and Protection) Order, 1962. President's Order No. 26 of 1962, Art. 3. PLD 1962 Central Statutes 623.
7. Ibid., Article 4.
8. Ibid., Article 5.
9. Ibid., Article 6.
10. Ibid., Article 7.
11. Ibid., Article 8.
12. The commencing day of the Constitution was 8 June 1962, the day on which the first meeting of the National Assembly was held. Only five Martial Law Regulations including Land Reforms Regulations, were saved under Article 225 of the Constitution. Martial Law Orders (Repeal) Order 1962. President's Order No. 29 of 1962. PLD 1962 Central Statutes 627.
13. Political Organizations (Prohibition of Unregulated Activity) Ordinance, 1962. Ordinance XVIII of 1962. PLD 1962 Central Statutes 228.
14. Ahmad, Mushtaq, *Government and Politics in Pakistan*. 1959. Pakistan Publishing House, Karachi, p. 164.
15. Ibid., p. 171.
16. Ibid., p. 182.
17. The Constitution of 1962, Articles 224 and 242.

18. Transfer of Railways Order, 1962. President's Order No. 33 of 1962. PLD 1962 Central Statutes 641.
19. Industrial Corporations (Dissolution) Ordinance, 1962 (Ordinance XXXVI of 1962). PLD 1962 Central Statutes 551. Provincial Industrial Development Corporation (East Pakistan) Ordinance, 1962 (Ordinance XXXVII of 1962). PLD 1962 Central Statutes 553. Provincial Industrial Development Corporation (West Pakistan) Ordinance, 1962 (Ordinance XXXVIII of 1962). PLD 1962 Central Statutes 581.
20. Ziring, Lawrence, *The Ayub Khan Era*. 1971, Syracuse University Press, p. 31.
21. PLD 1963 S.C. 486 and PLD 1963 Dhaka 669.
22. The Constitution of 1962, Article 173.
23. Ibid., explanation to Article 173. This explanation was added by the Constitution (Second Amendment) Act, 1964 (Act VI of 1964), Section 10. PLD 1964 Central Statutes 195.
24. Political Parties Act, 1962 (Act III of 1962). PLD 1962 Central Statutes 698.
25. Ibid., Section 5.
26. *Dawn*, July 31, 1962.
27. It is interesting to note that 'Convention Muslim League' got its name from a convention of Muslim Leaguers called by some minor and obscure leaders. This Convention was not attended by any Muslim League leader of standing or fame.
28. Afzal, M. Rafique, *Political Parties in Pakistan 1958-69*, Vol. II, 1987, p. 39. Published by National Institute of Historical and Cultural Research, Islamabad.
29. Keesing's Research Report, *Pakistan—From 1947 to the Creation of Bangla Desh*, 1973, Keesings' Publications, Longman Group Ltd. New York, pp. 81-2.
30. *Dawn*, May 23, 1963.
31. Ziring, Lawrence, *The Ayub Khan Era*, *supra*, note 20, p. 36.
32. Mahajan, V.D, *The Constitution of Pakistan*, 1965, Munawar Book Depot, Lahore, p. 113.
33. Ibid., p. 115.
34. Ibid., p. 116.
35. Ibid.
36. Choudhry, G.W., *Democracy in Pakistan*, 1963, Green Book House, Dhaka, p. 220.
37. Author learnt from late Malik Aslam Hayat, a former President of Lahore District Bar Association, who had led a delegation of lawyers from Lahore to see Ayub at the Governor House, Lahore demanding inclusion of fundamental rights in the Constitution, that Ayub did not even have the concept of such rights. He asked rather naively as to which rights they were talking about. When these rights were enumerated before him, he asked with surprise as to who was preventing them from exercising such rights.
38. At the time of introduction of the Bill for the amendment of the Constitution in order to make the fundamental rights thereunder justiciable, retired Chief Justice Muhammad Munir was the Law Minister. He, in his later writings, had greatly credited himself for piloting this Bill and, for this reason, he claimed that he had joined the Cabinet of Ayub.
39. Constitution (First Amendment) Act, 1963. Act I of 1964. PLD 1964 Central Statutes 33.
40. Constitution (Second Amendment) Act, 1964. (Act VI of 1964). PLD 1964 Central Statutes 195.
41. The Constitution of 1962, Article 23(5).
42. Feldman, Herbert, *From Crisis to Crisis: Pakistan 1962-1969*, 1972, Oxford University Press, London, pp. 63-4.
43. West Pakistan Universities (Amendment) Ordinance, 1962. (Ordinance XL of 1962). PLD 1962 West Pakistan Statutes 354.
44. Tamizuddin Ahmad v The Government of East Pakistan. PLD 1964 Dhaka 795.
45. Abul Ala Maudoodi v Government of West Pakistan, PLD 1964 Supreme Court 673.

14

PRESIDENTIAL ELECTIONS, 1965

Under the constitution, a Presidential election was to be held within 120 days before the expiry of the incumbent's term of five years. Since the first term of Ayub as President was to expire on 14 February 1965 (having been deemed to have begun on 14 February 1960), the presidential election was fixed for 2 January 1965. Ayub was adopted as Presidential candidate for re-election by the Convention Muslim League. He was, however, anxious to know whom the opposition would bring forward to oppose him.

The Opposition Announces its Candidate

The principal opposition parties in the National Assembly had already joined forces to oust Ayub from power, under the banner of the Combined Opposition Parties (COP). This group included the Council Muslim League, led by Khawaja Nazimuddin and Mian Mumtaz Khan Daultana; the Awami League, led by Sheikh Mujibur Rehman; the National Awami Party, led by Maulana Bhashani; the North-West Frontier group of the National Awami Party, led by Wali Khan, son of the famous Abdul Ghaffar Khan; the Nizam-i-Islam Party, led by Chaudhri Mohammad Ali and Farid Ahmed; and the Jamaat-i-Islami, led by Maudoodi. To these were added other prominent political personalities who were determined to oust Ayub.

On 16 September 1964, it was announced, after much confabulation, that the Combined Opposition Parties had invited Miss Fatima Jinnah, the Quaid's sister, to be their candidate, an invitation she accepted although she had been virtually inactive in politics since her brother's death. It was, nevertheless, well-known that Miss Jinnah was decidedly opposed to Ayub. In regular public pronouncements published on occasions such as *Eid-ul-Fitr*, the anniversary of her distinguished brother's death or his birthday, the undertone of criticism was notably indignant even in the days when Ayub was treated, or treated himself, as beyond criticism. Of course, as sister of Jinnah and one who had stood firmly by his side during all the years of endeavour to win Pakistan, Miss Jinnah was in a special position. There was not a great deal that Ayub could do to her.[1]

At that time, the selection of Miss Jinnah was generally interpreted as having been more or less forced upon the COP among whom diversity of feeling and purpose prevented agreement on a mutually acceptable candidate. The selection was also interpreted as an attempt to influence the electorate simply by evoking the magic of

Pakistan's most famous name and there were many who considered that Miss Jinnah should not have allowed herself to be made a party to such exploitation.

Even the proposal to invite Miss Jinnah, with its obvious advantages, had equally obvious dangers of which the first one was the problem of her own personality. She was by no means young, and although her character was firm and indomitable, the flesh might prove weaker than the spirit. She was, moreover, a difficult person to deal with, having a powerful will and a sharp, imperious temper. After her brother's death, her own political hopes were disappointed and she had pursued a life of retirement, a blighting experience after the activity and prominence she had known for many years. None of this had done anything to sweeten or appease her nature and were she to have been elected President, those who served under her as ministers might well have found life difficult.

She was not equally acceptable to all the parties and groups which formed the combined opposition. There were some, particularly from East Pakistan, who had resented Miss Jinnah's attitude to Suhrawardy, particularly at the time of his death. On a rather different plane, there was the difficulty that others felt about a woman candidate and a woman President, were she to have been elected. For those who belonged to parties wedded to religious orthodoxy, for instance the Jamaat-i-Islami, this prospect raised grave questions of law and conscience. In fact, this point became an issue. A gathering of *ulema* produced a *fatwa* declaring that in Islam a woman could not be a head of state. In reply to this, Maudoodi, the head of the Jamaat-i-Islami, announced that Islam permitted a woman to be a head of state though it was not desirable.[2] The *Pir* of Dewal Sharif went considerably further. He claimed that in the course of meditation, the Almighty had favoured him with a communication which indicated divine displeasure with the COP. An indignant public, which had shown no great concern with the question of the legality in Islam of Miss Jinnah's candidature, claimed that the *Pir* was criticizing Miss Jinnah, the sister of the Quaid-e-Azam and this the *Pir* promptly denied.[3] It is clear that such renderings of the so-called *ulema* and *Pirs* had no substantial influence on the candidature of Miss Jinnah, who enjoyed wide public support throughout Pakistan during her election campaign.

The announcement of Miss Jinnah as the candidate came as a shock for the Ayub government. The two provincial Governors, who had maintained law and order with an iron hand and snuffed out all dissent, were bewildered by the ecstatic manner in which the people celebrated Miss Jinnah's decision to fight their hero, the soldier statesman Ayub. She had no experience of government, no knowledge of administration, and no contact with world leaders. Nevertheless, she was the idol of the people and thousands of people would gather only to catch a glimpse of her. She could hardly speak any of the national languages, but her charisma was irresistible. She was seen by the crowds as the only person who could bring down Ayub's authoritarian rule and restore the democratic rights of the people.[4]

In addition to the two prominent figures, Ayub and Miss Jinnah, there were two minor candidates, K. M. Kamal and Mian Bashir Ahmad. The purpose of these two unknowns in seeking nomination is obscure and many stories were current at the time. It seems that there was no real purpose in their standing for election except, perhaps, to gain a little notoriety. There may also have been interest in the sum of money which, under the Constitution, each candidate could obtain from the government to cover election expenses, but even this was done away with in November 1964. Still, the appearance of these two candidates, whose nomination papers were in order and had been accepted, drew attention to a serious constitutional problem. Had both Ayub and Miss Jinnah died on election day, would it have followed automatically that one of the other two would be deemed to have been elected? There was no provision in the constitution for eventuality of death of a candidate during the election campaign.

Elections to the Electoral College

It should be remembered that before there could be an election of a new President, the constitution required the election of members for a new electoral college, comprising 80,000 Basic Democrats to be chosen, in equal numbers, by each of the two provinces. Thus, the initial battle would be fought at this level and Ayub hoped to ensure that as many persons as possible favourable to himself would be so elected. He might well expect to be successful in this since the election of the Basic Democrats would take place while he was still President and while his party had clear majorities in the National and Provincial Assemblies. His party members would use their influence in the constituencies they represented and would extract promises of support from the candidates they helped. This, as has previously been explained, was the purpose of the controversial second amendment to the constitution, enacted in June 1964. Although it was prima-facie desirable that as many members of the electoral college as possible should be known to be favourable to Ayub in order to facilitate, if not to ensure, his re-election, it has also been said that it did not really matter who was sent to the electoral college since it would be easy to corrupt these people afterwards, with the help of Assembly members and bureaucracy. This may appear too cynical a view but such fears, prompted by a general awareness of existing political corruption, caused the country to reject this particular part of Ayub's constitutional structure.

Thus the programme was that elections to the electoral college would take place in November 1964. The Presidential election would follow and after that elections for new Assemblies, National and Provincial, would be held. In all this, the key election was for the office of President.

The electoral college that came to be formed, as a result of elections in 1964, was evidently favourable to the Ayub regime. Of the total number of 80,000 voters, 3282 (about 4.5%) were tribals and about 32,000 (about 40%) were sitting Basic Democrats.[5] Both these categories were favourably disposed to the ruling party. The tribals were selected by the political agents of the government. For the old Basic Democrats, it would suffice to say that they, already having enjoyed a term of power and prestige, had developed a stake in the continuance of the Basic Democrats system and, therefore, of the Ayub regime.

The electoral college, moreover, was considerably susceptible to manoeuvrability. This was not so much because of its limited number of 80,000 members as due to lack of any fast and binding political commitments on their part. Although the elections to the electoral college were contested very keenly, these contests did not take place on rigid party lines. The PML had not officially sponsored its candidates but had banked upon the course of 'owning' the victorious ones. The COP, on the one hand, due to its internal contradictions, was compelled to propose more than one candidate for a single electoral unit at many places, and on the other hand, because of its fragile organizational base, it was unable to put up any candidate at other places. Hence, the overwhelmingly large number of contests in the elections to the electoral college were triangular[6] and the majority of candidates elected were independent. That the parties in the election arena did not have a firm grip over the candidates participating in the above elections is further revealed by the fact that a large number of seats went uncontested due to behind-the-scenes bargaining between the rival candidates.[7] It is indeed surprising to discover that there should have occurred as many as over 6000 unopposed elections in West Pakistan[8] and 2462 in East Pakistan[9] at the fundamental level of electoral college polls.

The behaviour of an electoral college of the above type, which lacks in strong political commitments, is liable to be more amenable to pressures, propaganda, and inducements. Even if the ruling party's claim of not having resorted to practices like intimidation and bribery to fetch votes in the Presidential elections was true,[10] the fact remains that even with other means, the electoral college of fluid loyalties could be more remunerative to the Ayub regime. With more resources at its command, it was in a better position to influence the electoral choice. A comparative analysis of the respective funds of the party in power and the COP shows that while, for example, the former was able to collect in Karachi alone from the industrialists and businessmen five crores of rupees in a few weeks time,[11] the latter had from time to time to issue appeals to the masses at large to contribute whatever little they could. Again, while the ruling party was able to buy 1000 new jeeps for its campaign, the COP could purchase only 27.[12]

Opposition's Crisis of Confidence

The opposition parties from the very outset had been apprehensive that the general election would not be fair and free. They alleged that the previous few by-elections had been marred by uninhibited official interference and hence there was no basis for them to believe that this interference would not be resorted to by the ruling party in the coming elections. They, therefore, demanded that various measures of political control like the Press and Publications Ordinance, the Loudspeaker Ordinance, and the Public Safety Acts should be withdrawn, all political prisoners should be released, steps be taken to ensure that section 144 of the Penal Code would not be enforced during the election campaign to curb their political activity and that the official machinery would not be misused to their detriment.[13]

At one stage of the election campaign Miss Jinnah went to the extent of demanding the installation of a caretaker government to supervise the election to ensure its free character.[14] Though most of these demands were rejected by the ruling party, it instructed all the government servants to refrain from misusing their influence in favour of any candidate in the election.[15] It also time and again, reiterated its intention to hold an impartial and fair election. Despite such instructions, the bureaucracy throughout the country interfered with the electoral process with predisposition to help Ayub win the elections. But for such interference, the results of the elections might have been different.

But the opposition parties could not be assured by these promises. In fact, as the election campaign gathered momentum, charges of various kinds were levelled by them against the government. In retrospect, the opposition's fears, allegations, and insinuations regarding the malafide intentions and actions of the ruling party in the general election, look very formidable. When considered cumulatively, these apprehensions amounted to a virtual distrust on its part in the elections as a mechanism of constitutional change of government. It was believed that it was difficult to dislodge an unconstitutional government by constitutional means. There was a strong opinion in certain quarters of the opposition after the conclusion of the Presidential polls that in the existing political conditions when the ruling party was bent upon resorting to all possible malpractices to register its victory, the elections to the National and Provincial Assemblies should be boycotted.[16]

Gerrymandering of Constituencies

To begin with, the COP charged that the delimitation of constituencies for elections to the electoral college had not always been done on the basis of the provisions laid down in the Electoral College Act, 1964. It was alleged that principles like 'territorial contiguity' and the population limit of 1072 voters for each unit were often flouted by the Election Commission authorities in order to bestow special advantages to some persons with utter disregard to the convenience of people. Constitutional petitions were filed in the High Courts and statements were issued to the Press in which specific instances of breach of the provisions of the Electoral College Act were cited.[17]

The total number of objections and suggestions received by the Election Commission on the delimitation work was over 10,000, the total number of units delimited was 80,000, of which 7000 were filed in East Pakistan and 3000 in West Pakistan.[18] It was argued by the Election Commission authorities that this was not a very high number because first, the number of units delimited was very large; secondly, most of the objections and suggestions received were of a minor nature; and lastly, in a large number of cases objections were filed in duplicate for the same electoral units.

The doubts about fairness in the work of delimitation of constituencies, however, continued to persist in the opposition's mind. The apprehensions that faulty delimitation of electoral units would turn the ensuing election into a farce was frequently expressed by it. No less a person than Miss Jinnah charged:

> Again, in the framing of the rules and the demarcation of constituencies even the legitimate opportunities of the people have been denied and thus in their own system every step is being taken to see that the legitimate representatives of the people are not allowed to be elected.[19]

Faulty Voters' Lists

The opposition was of the view that the registration of voters had also been done with malafide considerations. It charged that the names of persons who had been thought to be antagonistic to the party in power had been omitted from the voters' lists whereas fictitious names had been included in them to enable bogus voting in favour of the ruling party.[20]

In fact, the draft voters' lists published by the Election Commission contained some gross errors. For instance, the total number of voters in Karachi district in the draft lists was 1,086,641, whereas the number of objections and claims filed in connection with electoral rolls was 125,822.[21] In Lahore also, as disclosed by the Chairman of the West Pakistan Election Authority, Mr Afzal Agha, the number of objections and claims exceeded one hundred thousand.[22] There were many inexplicable omissions and surprising additions; names of many dead and even non-existing persons had been included in lists whereas the names of many VIPs and government officials were missing from them. It was also found that several Union Committees were not observing government instructions so far as the timings and proper display of the preliminary lists were concerned.

The opposition was also critical of the procedures laid down for the preparation of electoral rolls. Chaudhri Mohammad Ali charged that the time-period of one month was insufficient for the preparation of accurate voters' lists. Khawaja Nazimuddin demanded that the electoral rolls should be printed and sold to the public in order to permit their widest possible circulation and rectification.[23]

When the draft electoral rolls were released, the opposition lost no time in branding them as faulty and unreliable. Khawaja Nazimuddin in a telegram to the Chief Election Commission described them as beyond rectification and therefore useless. He demanded drafting of fresh lists of voters to ensure fair elections. However, the demand for the extension of time for the filing of claims and objections was eventually complied with by the Election Commission when it pushed ahead the last date for filing objections and claims by six days. But the opposition remained discontented. It alleged that six days were insufficient to rectify errors in the electoral rolls.[24] The opposition's demand for a further extension of time was, however, not accepted by the Election Commission on the grounds that sufficient time had already been given. But about one-and-a-half months later, at a time when the elections to the electoral college were around the corner, an ordinance was promulgated on 14 October 1964, which by an amendment to the Electoral College Act, 1964, empowered the Chief Election Commission to include in the electoral rolls the names of those who had been omitted from them but were otherwise eligible to vote.[25] Instead of welcoming this move, the opposition charged that the government, prompted by ulterior motives, was trying to load the electoral rolls with its own supporters.[26]

It was also alleged in East Pakistan that many intending voters, who went to the registration office in Dhaka during the week following the day the Electoral College Act, 1964 was amended, were told that no instruction had been received by the East Pakistan Election Authority for further inclusion of names in the electoral rolls from the Chief Election Commission. The officials concerned, therefore, refused to register their names. The more hard hit among the sufferers were those who wanted to file their nominations for the elections to the electoral college but could not do so since their names had been omitted from the voters' lists.[27]

Bogus Voting

Yet another source of grievance to the opposition parties was the practice of bogus voting during the electoral college polls. It was alleged that the procedure laid down for the electoral college elections was not fool-proof. The procedure suffered from certain built-in loopholes permitting large scale bogus voting and all manners of corrupt practices.[28] Firstly, it was not required of the voter to sign his name or give his thumb impression before receiving his ballot paper from the presiding officer; and secondly, the identity of the voter was testified by a polling agent of any of the candidates after which he was accepted as a prima-facie voter in the unit. Although the identity of a voter could be challenged by another agent, the challenged vote, however, was taken into account for the purpose of counting.

Due to these shortcomings the practice of bogus voting had assumed a huge proportion. *The Pakistan Observer* commented:

> Bogus voting by hired professionals was complained of. In fact, batches are believed to have gone round in urban localities day after day from one station to another to vote in the name of different persons at the same station. Women from red light areas were used to impersonate ladies' votes.[29]

Moreover, it was alleged that bogus voting had been refined to perfection. For example, at some places certain candidates and their associates had compiled separate lists of voters, who were either out of station or who were not likely to come to the polling stations during a particular period of time in order to facilitate their impersonation. Thus it was found that the latecomers consisting mainly of gazetted officers and members of the intelligentsia had generally become the target of bogus voting.[30]

The charges of the opposition were, however, not without substance and a lot of bogus voting did not take place in the elections to the electoral college.

Unfair Rules for Presidential Poll and Pakistan Election Commission

Such being the magnitude of the alleged malpractices prevalent in the electoral college elections, the COP lost no time in demanding an immediate judicial inquiry conducted by a judge of the Supreme Court to investigate into them. Believing that these did not speak well of the shape of things to come in the Presidential election, it became frantic in demanding rectification of the errors of omission and commission in the rules for the Presidential polls. First, to safeguard against bogus voting, it demanded that instead of having one attested photograph of the holder of the card, his photograph should also be kept by the returning officer so that at the time of polling no room was left for impersonation. Moreover, since there were rumours that in certain cases duplicate cards were being issued, the COP demanded that they should be issued by the District Judges.[31] It was further necessary to ensure against the polling of forged ballot papers, the COP said, to allow polling agents to sign or affix their seal on the back of ballot papers in the morning of the polling day.[32]

Secondly, to ensure freedom from official pressure at the polling stations, the COP urged that the presiding officers should invariably be drawn from the civil judges who were under the control of provincial High Courts instead of from the broad spectrum of what were called judicial officers which normally included even tehsildars and magistrates and, therefore, liable to be under official pressure of the executive directly.[33]

Thirdly, taking exception to the Election Commission's decision to arrange polling in West and East Pakistan on two different days, the COP urged that the same day should be fixed for polling throughout the country lest the party in power after knowing the election results in one wing of the country try to influence polling in the other wing.[34]

Lastly, objecting to the provision of a large number of polling stations (certain stations served units of just 50 and at some places even 18 voters), it demanded that the number of polling stations should be reduced so that each of them catered to at least 200 voters.[35]

Only one of the above demands, namely, fixing of one date for polling in both the wings, was accepted by the Election Commission. The opposition was, however, not satisfied by the arguments given by the Election Commission against the acceptance of the rest of its demands.[36] The Steering Committee of the COP recalled the entire attitude of the Election Commission towards them, after the declaration of the defeat of their Presidential candidate, and ruefully noted:

> The refusal of the Election Commission to agree to our basic demands for ensuring fairness of polls presented to us with so grave a problem that we thought at one time of boycotting the polls, particularly, since no appeal to any tribunal lay against election however unfairly conducted. But we decided to go forward with the election in the face of most adverse circumstances.[37]

The opposition parties thus alleged that the Election Commission was working in close complicity with the party in power. As an instance of this complicity, the opposition pointed out that the dates for filing the nominations by the Presidential candidates and for holding the Presidential polls were fixed by the Election Commission after consultation with the ruling party. Otherwise how was it possible that the Central Communications Minister, Khan A. Sabur could disclose to the press the date of the presidential polls earlier than the official announcement by the Election Commission?[38] The opposition pointed out that the registration officer of the electoral unit where the COP candidate was enrolled was not available throughout the day on 23 November to certify that Miss Jinnah was a voter in that unit.[39] Thus, deliberate attempts were made to restrain the COP candidate from filing nomination papers in time and Miss Jinnah termed the entire behaviour of the Election Commission in this respect as a great injustice to the opposition.

So high were the feelings of the opposition on this alleged collusion between the ruling party and the Election Commission that at her first projection meeting, Miss Jinnah registered a protest in a vitriolic tone against the ruling party and the Election Commission:

> This is the first confrontation meeting arranged by the Election Commission to enable the Presidential candidates to explain their policy and programme to you. I was looking forward to meeting you but the arrangements for the meeting have been so defective and so many obstructions have been placed that my faith in the whole process has been shaken... I have been treated in a discourteous manner... The administration and the Convention League have conspired to defeat the purpose for which we stand... I have decided as a mark of protest not to deliver my address at this meeting. The proper thing is that the programme for future meetings should be arranged by mutual consultation.[40]

In the Presidential elections, according to the COP, the presiding officers openly marked the ballot papers in favour of the ruling party candidate.[41] The COP, as a matter of fact, held the misbehaviour of the presiding officers as one of the major causes of their defeat in the Presidential elections. Its press release, issued on 4 January 1965 after the declaration of the election results, bemoaned:

> Despite repeated and strenuous representations by the COP Steering Committee to appoint judicial officers under the administrative control of the High Court and not officers of the executive as presiding officers, the Election Commission chose to appoint the bulk of presiding and polling officers from amongst the very class of executive officers who had made themselves the instruments of the ruling party for intimidating MECs. While there have been few serious irregularities in the major cities, the manner in which the presiding officers have behaved in most rural areas has confirmed our worst fears. There has been neither freedom nor secrecy of poll. With no one to supervise their doing and with all the powers the Election Commission had delegated to them, presiding officers felt free to do as they liked.[42]

Misuse of Official Machinery and Public Money

The COP further charged that the official machinery was being employed by the ruling party for furtherance of its election campaign. As Miss Jinnah in her message to voters of East Pakistan on the eve of the electoral college elections remarked:

> The most unfortunate aspect of the present conditions is that the administrative machinery of the country is being identified with Mr Ayub Khan's election campaign.[43]

It was pointed out that radio, television, and other government-controlled agencies were used as a propaganda media of the ruling party's campaign. Radio Pakistan was functioning as a mouthpiece of the party in power and was blocking out the opposition's viewpoint. The officials at the behest of the party in power, continued the COP, indulged in nefarious acts like intimidation, indoctrination, coercion, harassment, and victimization of the supporters of the opposition candidate in order to wean them away from its influence. In fact, the real motive of the ruling party in keeping a gap of about two months between the elections to the electoral college and that to the Presidency was to provide it with ample time to influence voters in its favour with the help of the official machinery.[44] The police and the CID men went around questioning Basic Democrats about their party affiliation, status, and means of livelihood, and sent the information thus collected to the ruling party in order to facilitate its election manipulations.[45] At certain places the Deputy Commissioners arranged meetings in which they canvassed for the ruling party.[46]

The COP also alleged that public money and resources were also misutilized by the party in power to promote its election campaign. The governors, ministers, and parliamentary secretaries, both central and provincial, drew money from the public exchequer as travel allowances to meet the expenses of their campaign tours,[47] during which they also grossly abused public resources like official transport, such as aeroplanes, launches, cars, and saloons.[48]

Even in Karachi, which was a stronghold of Miss Jinnah, every effort was made to influence the results.[49] High police officials had locked up hundreds of members of the electoral college in official residence for about two weeks prior to the elections in order to deliver their votes to Ayub.[50] The state of bureaucratic and official interference with the conduct of elections in order, particularly in West Pakistan, to ensure victory for Ayub was evident. Nawab Amir Muhammad Khan, Governor of West Pakistan, was in complete control of the official machinery in the province to give a landslide victory to his friend and benefactor, Ayub.

Election Campaign and Results

There was an intense election campaign throughout the country in which the people of Pakistan fully participated. Miss Jinnah addressed large gatherings and rallies. Ayub's supporters, with the help of the government machinery and huge funds collected particularly from business interests, also managed to have large gatherings for him to address. Barring a few instances, the election campaign was largely peaceful. Both the major candidates and their principal supporters made appeals through the press and otherwise, for tolerance, for law and order, and an abstention from mud-slinging.

Clear-cut issues were presented to the electorate although, as the campaigning went on, it became more and more evident that the dominating issue was Ayub's own personality and conduct. The general attack on his record was focused on the form of the constitution he had given to the nation. It was considered dictatorial, having concentrated unlimited and uncontrolled power in his hands. The system of indirect election was severely criticized and resented. The Basic Democracies system was described as corrupt. His economic policies were criticized and he was accused of having loaded Pakistan with foreign debt that would burden the country for years to come. The Indus Waters Treaty, signed with India, was the subject of a heavy onslaught and the exchange of polemics on this became acrimonious.

Ayub's reply was that he had given the country some seven years of stable and orderly government. Pakistan's economic progress had been the object of much praise in many parts of the world and, for the first time in the country's history, planning had not only been explicit, but had been implemented. The social and economic benefits of the land reforms were emphasized and also the social reforms brought by his family laws legislation. He claimed that since his coming to office, Pakistan's stature had been raised in the eyes of the world. He accused those who criticized him and desired his fall as enemies of Pakistan who, for their own interests, sought a return to the bad old days. Above all, with the threat from India hanging over them, an India armed to the teeth by the Soviet Union, the United Kingdom, and the United States, the country required a firm hand at the helm and a person capable of understanding what was involved in the problems of defence. This was one reason why his constitution provided that the Minister of Defence must be a person holding, or who at least had held, the rank of Lieutenant-General (or the equivalent in the Navy or Air Force).[51]

But, as has so often and so unfortunately been the case in Pakistan, the election was fought less with reference to the political and economic programmes offered by the contending parties, than with personalities, and in particular that of Ayub. Was he corrupt? Was he a dictator? Was he guilty of nepotism and favouritism? Had he teamed up with the nation's great capitalists? These were the questions that almost exclusively preoccupied most electors' minds. In saying this, we must remember that the electors comprised 80,000 Basic Democrats, not the mass of the people, but the interest of the masses was reflected in the part they could play in influencing the men they had voted for the Basic Democrats themselves.

In relation to Ayub's personality and conduct, one of the most publicized questions was that of the considerable fortune said to have been accumulated by his son, Captain Gohar Ayub, who had retired from the army after a few years' service and had entered the world of business in a very substantial way, in association with his father-in-law, Lieutenant-General Habibullah Khan Khattak. Vexed with this allegation, Ayub made a long and prevaricating statement in which he avoided the real issue. The issue was not that Gohar Ayub had gone into business and had made money, but that he had used his father's position and influence to do so. He had obtained access to financial resources which no young man, army officer or other, without substantial property or business experience, could ever hope to secure. The question was not whether the business had been acquired (substantially it consisted of the General Motors Corporation assembly plant located at Karachi) through wealth corruptly gained or whether the business itself was being badly or dishonestly conducted. The question was that of improper use of influence to which Ayub had lent himself or, at any rate, had done nothing to prevent. His reply was not satisfactory and the case of Gohar Ayub continued to be pressed against him.

The election was held on 2 January 1965 and the result of the election announced on 3 January. Ayub had polled 49,951 votes and Miss Fatima Jinnah 28,691. The minor candidates, K. M. Kamal and Mian Bashir Ahmad, had polled 183 and 65 votes respectively. In West Pakistan, Ayub's votes were 28,939 against Miss Jinnah's 10,257 and in East Pakistan, Ayub had obtained 21,012 against Miss Jinnah's 18,434. Miss Jinnah had a lead over Ayub in Dhaka Division (5986 against 5861), Chittagong Division (5779 against 4794) and Karachi Division (1061 against 907). In all, over the administrative divisions, Ayub Khan had a huge lead over Miss Jinnah.

Factors Responsible for Ayub's Victory

Apart from allegations of massive rigging, for which there was strong evidence, there were some real factors that could be attributed to the success of Ayub. There was always a widespread feeling throughout the campaign that Miss Jinnah's defeat under the existing electoral system was a foregone conclusion. The system worked against the opposition in a number of ways.

In the first place, the COP's campaign for the restoration of the parliamentary form of government based upon direct elections and universal franchise amounted to demanding from the Basic Democrats to give up their exclusive electoral rights, which had bestowed upon them power, privilege, and status in the society. Thus, they had a vested interest in perpetuating the existing electoral system and the COP was virtually asking them to sign their own death warrants. On the other hand, the prospects of the Basic Democrats system was linked up closely with Ayub's success.

Secondly, Ayub had an initial advantage of more than 3000 votes from the tribal areas who were nominees of the administration. Out of 3282 members of the electoral college from the tribal areas, Ayub secured 92.5 per cent, while his support from the tribal areas of the former NWFP was 95 per cent.

The third and very important factor was the weakness of the COP itself, which was a mixture of strange political bedfellows. There was lack of discipline among its ranks. Its unity was a mere hotch potch of antagonistic ideologies and political programmes beneath which was the surging waves of inter-party ambitions, suspicions, and misgivings. These parties quarrelled *inter se* over the allocation of tickets for the elections to the electoral college. The acrimonious bickerings between them sometimes characterized even their election campaign. While in West Pakistan, the Council Muslim League complained that the National Awami Party did not share the platform with it during Miss Jinnah's tour of the former North-West Frontier Province, in East Pakistan the National Awami Party and the Awami League, the two traditional rivals, could at times be seen jostling with each other on the stage for a better seat or an earlier say at the mike. These dissensions in the COP were there for all to see. The restoration of democracy was all right, many might have reasoned, but democracy under whose dispensation, they might have asked. In fact, the questions as to whether and how Miss Jinnah would be able to control the contradictory conglomeration of quarrelsome politicians who had discredited themselves in the past and were still fighting amongst themselves even in her own presence, were publicly put to her. She had a stock reply which meant: 'Wait and see'. On one occasion replying to a questioner who wanted to know about her ability to preserve unity in the opposition ranks, she remarked that the five parties had joined hands to restore democracy and that, 'You need not worry, *Inshallah* (God willing) we shall win *Ganatantri* (Democracy)'.[52] The question 'After democracy what', however, could not be dismissed easily. It must have weighed heavily in the minds of many of the admirers of democracy and compelled them to have second thoughts regarding their Presidential choice.

Fourthly, Miss Jinnah lost votes, particularly in the North-West Frontier, on account of Abdul Ghaffar Khan whose attitude to Pakistan and the question of a separate Pakhtoonistan was only too well-known. His son Wali Khan was leader of a section of the National Awami Party and a prominent member of the COP high command.

The next factor was the superior resources available with Ayub being an incumbent President. There was no doubt that Ayub's party coffers were full. It soon became known that at least two of his ministers, those whose portfolios brought greater contact with the business community, had been charged with the collection of funds. It appears that a regular tariff was fixed, based on the nature of the business. Traders who held import licence quotas contributed proportionately to the nominal value of the quota. In the case of jute, cotton, and wool textile mills, the levy was based on the number of looms and spindles installed. Years afterwards, in 1969, the *Weekly Mail of Karachi*,[53] published facsimiles of the two secret letters dated 6 and 12 November 1964 circulated by the All Pakistan Textile Mills Association to its members, asking them to pay their contributions to the funds of the Pakistan (Convention) Muslim League on the basis of Rs 2 per installed spindle and Rs 25 per installed loom. On the basis that 37,340 cotton looms and 2,952,580 spindles were in use at the time, the contribution to Ayub's party chest from this source alone would have been in the order of Rs 15 million.

Another factor that had been attributed to the victory of Ayub was the strange and to some extent dubious role of Maulana Bhashani. It is stated that when the COP decided to unite for the purpose of selecting a candidate whom they would all support, it was agreed that such a candidate must be the object of a unanimous agreement amongst all the constituent parties. To this, Bhashani is said to have added a further condition, that no one who had been associated with the martial law administration which had assumed power in 1958 could possibly be acceptable. The reasonableness of this suggestion was difficult to refute among political parties so firmly opposed to Ayub's methods of governance and so firmly wedded to the democratic ideal. The effect, however, was to eliminate the possibility of candidature of Lieutenant-General Azam Khan. Azam was one of Ayub's military colleagues associated with the declaration of martial law in 1958. Later, however, they quarrelled and Azam came out in political opposition. As an election rival, he might well have proved formidable. Previously, he had been Governor of East Pakistan until his differences with Ayub, and there he had been extremely popular; so popular that he might well have reckoned on carrying that province in an election. In West Pakistan, those opposed to Ayub might also have voted for him, in which case he might have gained an overall majority. However, his chances were nullified by Bhashani's stratagem, engineered by Ayub's Foreign Minister, Zulfikar Ali Bhutto, working through his friend, Masihur Rahman, who happened to be a confidant of Bhashani.[54] Although Bhashani was one of the staunch supporters for the candidacy of Miss Jinnah, he remained inactive in East Pakistan and did nothing to advance her prospects of success. There was a strong rumour circulating in the last days before the election that Bhashani had been won over by Ayub and a deal had been worked out between them. A transaction of 20 million rupees was also mentioned.

Election Results Disputed

The magnitude and gravity of the allegations levelled by the COP against the manner in which the elections had been conducted created an impression that it suffered from a lack of faith in the entire election process. This crisis of confidence was amply reflected in the COP's instantaneous refusal to accept the poll results. While the steering committee of the COP branded the elections as a farce, Miss Jinnah charged that 'these elections have been rigged. I am sure that the so-called victory of Mr Ayub Khan is his greatest defeat'.[55]

More than anything else, the indirect system of electing the President was responsible for the COP's crisis of confidence in the electoral process. It pointed out that it was in fact this system which permitted all sorts of malpractices to occur. It allowed the manipulation of voters because their numbers were small. The use of official machinery in the elections, the corruption of voters by bribery and their intimidation, became easier and uninhibited. And during this process, the COP charged, the popular will became distorted and the electoral system produced a result which was 'directly contrary to the will of the people'.[56] The government based upon the consensus achieved through these processes, the COP reasoned, could neither be democratic, nor entitled to claim any legitimacy. The outcome of these elections, the COP further maintained, was incapable of conferring legitimacy to the constitution, as was claimed by Ayub, its architect.

The election results have remained disputed ever since which affected the legitimacy of the government of Ayub from January 1965 onwards. When the public finally turned against him, after November 1968, this question was often voiced. Several people, notably Air-Marshal Asghar Khan, claimed that the Presidential election had not been as clean as many people assumed. Mr J.A. Rahim, the Acting Chairman of Bhutto's Pakistan Peoples' Party bluntly said the election had been corruptly managed. Some people, notably among Bhutto's opponents, thought that J.A. Rahim ought to know!

Aftermath of the Presidential Election

On the evening of 2 January 1965, Ayub broadcast his thanks to the nation. There were the customary assurances of fresh dedication to the service of Pakistan and he did not fail to observe that the nation had given him a clear mandate to pursue 'my internal and external policies'. He made a call for national unity and expressed goodwill to all, including Miss Jinnah, and he urged that 'no trace of malice, nor of revenge should inhibit us from rejoicing in the glory of the people'. He added: 'Together let us build, together let us accomplish; so that Pakistan may endure and prosper.' Unfortunately, things did not work out that way.

The morning of 4 January revealed Captain Gohar Ayub, standing in a jeep, apparently firing pistols into the air in unrestrained paroxyms of delight, and leading a procession of trucks through the streets of Karachi. These were all driven by Pakhtoons since most of Karachi's trucking business was in their hands. It seemed as if every three-tonner in the city had been mobilized for what appeared to be a show of force and a reminder to Karachi that although it had voted for Miss Jinnah and not for Ayub, there need be no doubt as to the outcome of the election. The procession not only caused a great deal of inconvenience but also raised the question of whether this was a breach of section 144 which was in force in Karachi at that time, and if so, whether an exemption from the effect of the order had been granted by the Commissioner, Roedad Khan, who happened to be a Peshawar man. Further, people were asking themselves whether the exemption, if any, had been granted before or after the procession. It appeared improbable that Gohar Ayub would be troubled by such niceties and it did not seem that the Commissioner was the kind of man to insist on their observance.

In the circumstances, it may not appear that any of this was of much importance, and certainly nothing more would have been heard of it had not worse soon followed. That night, the Pakhtoon henchmen went down into those areas, including Liaquatabad, known to have been solidly opposed to Ayub and there wrought vengeance. Huts and dwelling-places were burnt down and people were fired upon. Those attacked promptly defended themselves and a night-long battle ensued. The injured were taken to hospitals with bullet-wounds and when order was restored the visible damage indicated the anger and determination with which the contending factions had fought and defended themselves.[57] The army was called out and on 5 January was patrolling the streets in the areas which had been a witness to these grim scenes. In such circumstances, there was little prospect of renewed fighting but there was danger that the attacked might sally out during the night looking for revenge.

According to the newspapers that appeared the following day, six people died in the affair. Later, a figure of twenty was mentioned, but it was generally believed that the number of lives lost was much greater than the official admission. Loss of lives and property were not the only consequences; Karachi became irrevocably opposed to Ayub and the ground was laid for a feud between Pathans and the refugee communities from India which endured for a very long time and in the months that followed January 1965 sporadic acts of vengeance occurred. This feud has only aggravated over a period of time and the unfortunate clashes between Muhajirs and Pakhtoons in Karachi in the late eighties are a continuation of this feud, claiming thousands of lives and billions of rupees worth of property.

The government covered up the incident and dropped the inquiry ordered in this behalf. Roedad Khan, who was Commissioner of Karachi at that time, has narrated the unfortunate episode in the following words:[58]

> The morning after the election, I was sitting out on the lawn when at about 10.30 a.m., the telephone rang and somebody, not an official, informed me that a victory truck procession led by Captain (retd.) Gohar Ayub, the President's son, had run into trouble with the residents of the area through which the procession was passing and that there had been some stone-throwing. I had no knowledge of this procession. I tried to contact the District Magistrate and the Police Chief. Both were unavailable, so I contacted police control who confirmed the incidents and told me that the police were escorting the procession. Police control kept me informed of the progress of the procession. Very soon, reports of more serious incidents started pouring in. By about midday, I finally succeeded in establishing contact with the DIG at his residence. He told me later that he was very tired and had, before going to bed, unplugged the telephone in his bedroom, giving strict instructions that he was not to be disturbed. Together, we toured the area. By this time, armed clashes had taken place between the processionists and the residents of the area, resulting in heavy loss of life and property. Several houses and shops were reduced to ashes. The army had to be called in to restore law and order. The District Magistrate told me that he had authorized the procession and the route it had to follow, but some unauthorized deviation had taken place. The record maintained at the police control room seemed to confirm this. The inquiry ordered by the government made no headway and was subsequently dropped. Mr Ghulam Nabi Memon, Law Minister, Government of West Pakistan, came down to Karachi to assess the situation. In his railway saloon, he met the DIG Police, the District Magistrate Karachi, and myself. Mr Abdul Qadir Sheikh, a future judge of the Supreme Court of Pakistan, then assistant Advocate-General was also present. One of the sinister suggestions made was that the record kept by the police control should be suitably altered and, if necessary, destroyed altogether. For this, my concurrence was necessary. I refused point-blank and told Ghulam Nabi Memon and others present that this could only be done over my dead body. The matter ended there. The inquiry was dropped, ostensibly due to non-cooperation from the opposition. Soon thereafter, I got my marching orders to Quetta as Commissioner. I have no hesitation in saying that, regardless of who was at fault, as the head of the administration, I had failed to protect the lives and property of the people of Karachi. This was certainly not my finest hour and it has haunted me ever since.

The reasons for going into details of the Presidential election of 1965 are two-fold: in the first place, it was the only contested Presidential election in a Presidential form of government in Pakistan, and secondly, it was first election of its kind which was manipulated by the government in power to retain power by using all possible governmental and other resources. Though rigging had also been alleged in some earlier elections, there was nothing of this scale, particularly the way government machinery was used and the money was spent in the elections to influence the results. It was also the beginning of the end of Ayub's regime because a large population of Pakistan had been mobilized against him in the elections and felt cheated by the election results. The methods used in this election by the party in power did cast a shadow on the coming events. These were adopted and used by the party in power in the elections to come to achieve the desired results. This election was also one of the causes of alienation of East Pakistan and was used for the purpose by those interested in widening the gulf between the two wings.

Ayub asked for detailed analysis of the election campaign and its results from the central information secretary. The analysis showed that the demand for democracy had been Miss Jinnah's main source of popularity, and had won her the support of the intelligentsia. The government had suffered because of allegations of corruption, and it was widely known that the administrative machinery had been used to swing the members of the electoral college in Ayub's favour. The analysis brought out the deep feelings of alienation among the people who had been denied any meaningful participation in the affairs of the state since independence. The Basic Democrats system had further increased the isolation of the people. The ruling party was seen as a haven for opportunists and time-servers dominated by Ayub's minions and stooges.[59]

The analysis was put on the agenda of the Governors' Conference a few weeks after the election. By then, the ruling party had convinced Ayub that he had scored a convincing victory and the opposition had been thoroughly trounced. The ruling party had obviously learnt no lesson from the opposition campaign or from the results of the election.[60]

NOTES

1. Miss Jinnah died on 11 July 1967. She was buried at Karachi and the crowd that followed her bier was estimated at about half a million. The opportunity was taken to raise slogans against Ayub and there was some rioting in which members of the Jamaat-i-Islami and left-wing groups were involved. The police had to recourse to tear-gas and rifle fire. The dead were variously estimated between two and twelve.
2. The word used was *'bid'at'*, which can be translated as bad precedent.
3. The Pir of Dewal Sharif, at that time, was a comparatively youthful man. He was well-educated and made a great impression on many people in West Pakistan. At one time it was widely believed that Ayub was one of his devotees but this has remained uncertain. He, however, wielded a lot of influence on account of this general impression during the Ayub era.
4. Gauhar, Altaf, *Ayub Khan—Pakistan's First Military Ruler*. 1993. Sang-e-Meel Publications, Lahore. p. 275.

5. Misra, K.P. *Pakistan's Search for Constitutional Consensus*, 1967, Impex India, New Delhi, p. 194, citing Sharif-al-Mujahid, 'Pakistan's First Presidential Elections', *Asian Survey*, June 1965, Vol. 5, No. 6, p. 293.
6. While in West Pakistan, it was estimated that one hundred thousand candidates were in the run for thirty thousand contested seats, the figures of East Pakistan showed that about one hundred and thirty thousand candidates were in the field for thirty seven thousand contested seats. Whereas on an average three candidates were contesting for each unit, in some cases the number of candidates varied from four to seven. *The Pakistan Times*, 1 & 8 November 1964. The above position of triangular contests not only characterized the rural areas where the political parties did not have any organization worth the name but also in the politically sophisticated urban areas where they were comparatively better organized. Hence, the figures for places like Dhaka city and Karachi city read no different from the overall figures for the country as a whole. While in the former, there were 1376 candidates for 441 seats, in the latter there were 5448 for 1561. Ibid. 31 October 8 November 1964.
7. The extent of this bargaining can be gauged by the large number of withdrawals from the contest. In East Pakistan, for example, as a result of these withdrawals the number of uncontested seats increased from 626 as on 24 October 1964 to 1073 on 25 October 1964 *The Pakistan Observer*, 25 & 26 October 1964. By 10 November 1964 this figure touched the mark of 2462. In West Pakistan, the number of withdrawals were higher since more seats in that wing went unopposed. *Dawn*, 11 11 November 964.
8. *The Pakistan Times*, 2 November 1964.
9. *Dawn*, 11 November 1964.
10. There were some independent political observers who alleged that Ayub regime had resorted to such practices. For example, Rawl Knox of *Daily Telegraph* said that many pledged to vote for Miss Jinnah were scared because of whispering campaign that Government would punish those who voted for her. Quoted in *Pakistan Observer*, 14 January 1965.
11. Ralph Joseph, 'Pakistan's First General Elections', *Eastern World*, February 1965, Vol. XIX No. 2, p. 10.
12. Ibid.
13. 'The resolution of the Working Committee of the Pakistan Council Muslim League', *The Pakistan Times*, 6 June 1964.
14. Ibid., 22 October 1964.
15. *Dawn*, 28 June 1964.
16. For details see *Pakistan Observer*, 18 to 27 January 1965; *Dawn*, 22 January 1956 and *The Pakistan Times*, 24 and 25 January 1965.
17. For some interesting examples, see *Pakistan Observer*, 13 and 18 August 1964.
18. *Dawn*, 4 August 1964.
19. *Dawn*, 21 October 1964.
20. *The Pakistan Times*, 21 November 1964.
21. *Dawn*, 18 September 1964.
22. *Dawn*, 16 September 1964.
23. *Dawn*, 6 July 1964. The argument for not printing the voters' lists as given by the Chief Election Commissioner, was that this was economically not feasible. Khawaja Nazimuddin contesting the above argument remarked that this was a false pretext since the need for fair and free elections was of foremost importance.
24. One Mr Salahuddin Abbasi, an Awami Leaguer, in a letter to the editor of *Dawn*, complained: 'Though the date of claims and objections was extended till 25 August it has been observed that about 50 per cent eligible voters have been left out'. *Dawn*, 28 August 1964.
25. *Pakistan Observer*, 17 October 1964.
26. *Dawn*, 30 October 1964.
27. *Pakistan Observer*, 21 October 1964.
28. Ibid., 7 November 1964.
29. Ibid., 12 November 1964.

30. Ibid., 6 November 1964.
31. See the statement of Mahmoodul Haq Usmani, a member of the COP Steering Committee, *Dawn*, 9 December 1964.
32. See the statement of Mian Mahmud Ali Kasuri, a COP leader, Ibid., 11 December 1964 and also the statement of the COP Steering Committee, *Dawn*, 28 December 1964.
33. *Pakistan Observer*, 21 December 1964.
34. See the statement of Mian Tufail Mohammad, Secretary-General of the Jamaat-i-Islami, *Pakistan Times*, 26 November 1964.
35. *Pakistan Times*, 19 December 1964 and Pakistan Observer, 21 December 1964.
36. See the statement of Chaudhri Mohammad Ali, the Chief of the Nizam-i-Islam Party, *Dawn*, 2 January 1965.
37. Ibid., 5 January 1965.
38. Even a senior member of the Election Commission, Mr Justice Iqbal, was constrained to say that it was not proper that somebody should issue statements to the Press anticipating decisions made by the Commission. See his statement before the Rawalpindi Projection Meeting, *The Pakistan Times*, 9 December 1964.
39. *The Pakistan Times*, 24 November 1964.
40. *Pakistan Observer*, 9 December 1964.
41. West Pakistan COP's Press release, *Pakistan Observer*, 4 January 1965.
42. *Dawn*, 5 January 1965.
43. See Miss Jinnah's statement, ibid., 7 December 1964.
44. The statements of Khwaja Mohammad Safdar and Lt.-General Azam Khan appearing in *Dawn*, 30 July 1964 and *Pakistan Observer*, 16 November 1964 respectively.
45. See the Press statements of Z.H. Lari, President of the Karachi Zonal Council Muslim League and Sardar Mohammad Zafarullah, ibid., 14 and 15 November 1964.
46. Ibid., 28 December 1964.
47. The Provincial Committee of the W.P. COP estimated that the amount of money so misused ran into lakhs of rupees, *Dawn*, 1 November 1964.
48. See the Press statement of Farid Ahmad, Chairman of the E.P. COP, *Pakistan Observer*, 15 December 1964.
49. The Deputy Commissioner of Karachi at the time of the election has narrated instances where the members of the Electoral College were made to disappear or frightened into staying home and in their place bogus voting was arranged. The bogus votes were generally obtained from the Pathans living in Karachi area. In one instance, a Pakhtoon Pathan came to vote in the Presidential election and with great difficulty read out his name as Saqlain Husain Jaffri. Pakhtoons /Pathans generally do not have such names. Author learnt this from Sh. Amjad Ahad, who was Deputy Commissioner of Karachi at that time and was later sacked by Yahya Khan as one of 303 Officers removed from service.
50. The D.I.G., Bahawalpur, Mr Allah Nawaz Tarin, around 20 December 1964 had a number of B.D members locked in and around his residence. Later on, he was richly rewarded by Ayub through grant of business and industrial licences and permits.
51. The Constitution of 1962, Article 238.
52. Miss Jinnah at the Chittagong Projection Meeting, *Dawn*, 20 December 1964.
53. 5 December 1969.
54. Feldman, Herbert, *From Crisis to Crisis: Pakistan 1962-1969,* 1972, Oxford University Press, London, p. 71.
55. *The Pakistan Times*, 4 January 1965.
56. The Press Release of the COP, *Dawn*, 5 January 1965.
57. Herbert Feldman claimed to have visited the area shortly afterwards and found it extremely devastated. See his book titled *From Crisis to Crisis. supra*, note 54, p. 81.
58. Khan, Roedad. *Pakistan: A Dream Gone Sour*, 1998, Oxford University Press, Karachi, pp. 20-21.
59. Gauhar, Altaf *Ayub Khan—Pakistan's First Military Ruler. supra*, note 4, pp. 286-7.
60. Ibid., p. 288.

15

WAR WITH INDIA AND RIFTS WITHIN

The elections to the national and provincial assemblies that followed, on 21 March 1965 and 16 May 1965 respectively, were clearly lopsided and in favour of the Convention Muslim League. The COP which was in great disarray and demoralized after losing the presidential elections, did not contest the elections seriously and vigorously, which were again indirect, voting being confined to the Basic Democrats. Knowing that Ayub had returned to power for five more years, there was little reason for Basic Democrats to annoy him and his political party. Miss Jinnah, after losing the presidential election, did not take part in active politics again. The result was that the Convention Muslim League won hands down in the elections to the national and provincial Assemblies. The defeat of opposition parties in the elections to the Provincial Assembly of West Pakistan was so complete that only one candidate from the opposition was returned and that too from Karachi.[1] Ultimately, the strength of the opposition in the West Pakistan Assembly (of 156 members) grew to five. The results of the National Assembly elections were as under:

Muslim League (Conventionist)	126
Combined Opposition Parties	13
Independent Group	10
Other Independents	6

The National Assembly elected in 1965 was very different from the one elected in 1962 which had a large number of members from the opposition. The results of the 1965 election are also indicative of massive interference by the administration with the electoral process, thus ensuring that the party in power was returned with an overwhelming majority.

Third, Fourth, and Fifth Amendments to the Constitution

With the political party of Ayub having won an overwhelming majority in the new National Assembly, it was no problem for him to have the Constitution amended the way he desired, for which only a majority of two-thirds of the total number of members of the National Assembly was required[2] and Convention Muslim League had many more than that number. The Constitution (Third Amendment) Act, 1965[3] added the Fifth Schedule to the Constitution in which a number of offices or appointments were mentioned which did not disqualify a person from being elected as a member of the National and the Provincial Assemblies.

The Constitution (Fourth Amendment) Act, 1965[4] empowered the government, after consulting the Public Service Commission, to retire in the public interest any person below 55 years of age who had completed 25 years of qualifying service or, subject to rules, any person who had reached the age of 55.

The Constitution (Fifth Amendment) Act 1965[5] empowered the President, during a Proclamation of Emergency, to suspend a number of fundamental rights, namely freedom of movement, freedom of assembly, freedom of association, freedom of trade and business, freedom of speech and provisions as to property. The President was also empowered to suspend the right to move any court for the enforcement of any of the fundamental rights and to suspend any pending proceedings before a court regarding the enforcement of fundamental rights during the Proclamation of Emergency. This amendment further enlarged the powers of the President to restrict the liberties of the citizens and curtailed the powers of the courts.

The root of the objection to the Fifth Amendment was not that it had withdrawn any fundamental rights, but that it had rendered them ineffectual and enabled the government to contravene them as it chose without risk of challenge. Furthermore, this remained the position for more than three years.

It was the continuance of the state of emergency and the power that it placed in Ayub's hands which created much discontent, and in the years that followed he was frequently taxed with it. An attempt was made in the National Assembly to withdraw the declaration of emergency or, at any rate, to strongly condemn, but this was easily and successfully resisted.

Indo-Pakistan War, 1965

The number of clashes between the Indian and Pakistani forces on the cease-fire line in Kashmir had greatly increased during 1964, and increased during the first half of 1965. In April and May 1965, there were serious skirmishes between the armed forces of India and Pakistan in the region known as the Rann of Kutch. Pakistan's armed forces gave a good account of themselves which might have given rise to misplaced confidence in the mind of the military leadership that it could take on India militarily.

Finally, a serious crisis in Indo-Pakistani relations precipitated on 5 August 1965 when armed freedom fighters from Azad Kashmir began entering Indian occupied Kashmir in an unsuccessful attempt to foment revolt. Further parties of freedom fighters entered on 18 August. India protested against what it called 'infiltration', but such protestations were rejected by Pakistan.

The number of skirmishes on the cease-fire line in Kashmir increased in May and June. However, this number declined after the signing of the Rann of Kutch cease-fire agreement. Exchanges of fire all along the line once again erupted on 8 August and on 16 August Indian troops crossed the border and occupied Pakistani border posts. In early September, Pakistani forces advanced into the Indian sector, capturing a key post on 5 September. On the same day, the Indian Defence Ministry accused a Pakistani aircraft of attacking an Indian Air Force ground unit near Amritsar, without causing any damage. This was the first incident reported outside Kashmir. On the following day Indian troops launched an offensive across the Punjab frontier into West Pakistan. The Indian Defence Minister claimed as justification for crossing international borders that the Indian attack had been launched in order to pre-empt an attack by Pakistan on Indian Punjab.

When India attacked Pakistan, the man most surprised was Ayub. His surprise was shared by the Commander-in-Chief of the Pakistan Army. They had been assured by Bhutto, Foreign Minister, and Aziz Ahmad, Foreign Secretary, that India would not cross international borders to attack Pakistan. They had even suppressed a message from the Pakistan High Commissioner in New Delhi sent through the Turkish Embassy to the Foreign Office in Islamabad, that India was planning to launch an attack on Pakistani territory on 6 September. Ayub was woken up at four o'clock in the morning on 6 September and given the news of the Indian advance towards Lahore. He telephoned General Musa, Commander-in-Chief of the Pakistan Army, who said he had also heard the news but was waiting for confirmation.[6] All this badly exposed the military genius of Ayub and his army chief.

In a broadcast on 6 September, Ayub declared 'We are at war', and proclaimed a state of emergency, although an Indian government spokesman commented: 'India is not at war with Pakistan or the Pakistani people. India's operations are intended to destroy Pakistan military bases from where they attacked India.' On 11 September, the Khem Karan counter-offensive ran aground and with that collapsed Pakistan's entire military strategy. For Pakistan, the war was over.[7]

Fighting continued on all fronts until 23 September. The UN Security Council adopted a resolution which stated *inter alia*:

> The Security Council... demands that a cease-fire should take effect on Wednesday, 22 September 1965 at 0700 hours GMT, and calls upon both governments to issue orders for a cease-fire at that moment and a subsequent withdrawal of all armed personnel back to the positions held by them before 5 August 1965.

At Pakistan's request, a special meeting of the Security Council was held in the early hours of 22 September at which Bhutto announced Pakistan's decision to order a cease-fire but warned the Council that if it did not bring about a settlement of the Kashmir question within a limited period of time, Pakistan would quit the United Nations.

The cease-fire came into effect as ordered, but was jeopardized by a series of violations by both sides and by their refusal to withdraw from the positions they held in each other's territories. The Indian government alleged that after the cease-fire, Pakistani forces had intruded into the Fazilka area and many border areas of Rajasthan which they had not previously occupied, and a number of engagements took place in both sectors.

An emergency meeting of the Security Council on 27 September adopted a resolution demanding that both India and Pakistan 'urgently honour their commitments to the council', and calling upon them 'promptly to withdraw all armed personnel'. Both sides, however, continued to accuse each other of violations of the cease-fire, particularly in Kashmir and in the Fazilka and Rajasthan sectors.

The cease-fire took place at 3:00 a.m. on 23 September 1965, both sides having intimated their agreement on the previous day. On the evening of 22 September, Ayub addressed the nation in which he expressed gratitude to China, Indonesia, Iran, Turkey, Saudi Arabia, Jordan, and Syria, in that order. He insisted that India had been guilty of 'blatant and unprovoked aggression' which had a 'history of eighteen years behind it', and added 'We have informed the Security Council that the United Nations are faced with a grave responsibility and are on trial. If they wish to bring about lasting peace in this area, they must address themselves urgently to evolving an honourable solution of the Kashmir dispute. If they fail in this, this continent will be engulfed in a much wider conflict.'

The tone of the Security Council proceedings was characteristic of most, if not all, debates on the Kashmir question. The parties to the dispute came with different premises, to which they resolutely adhered. The Indians said that, in conformity with the Security Council resolution, Pakistan must vacate Azad Kashmir first. Thereafter, the question of the plebiscite could be considered. Pakistan said that all this was unsatisfactory, in that it offered no assurance that India would not then occupy Azad Kashmir and retain its grip permanently. All that was necessary, according to Pakistan, was a plebiscite by the Kashmiris to decide what they wanted to do with their future.

Not until 6 December 1965 did General Marambio, U Thant's representative, arrive in Pakistan to arrange troop withdrawals, by which time Ayub and Lal Bahadur Shastri had agreed to meet at Tashkent in the Soviet Union.

The Tashkent Declaration and Student Protests

The President of Pakistan and the Prime Minister of India began discussions on 4 January 1966, in Tashkent, following the Soviet government's offer in November 1965 of its good offices in helping to resolve the dispute. The Soviet Prime Minister, Alexei Kosygin, was in Tashkent throughout the six day negotiations and played a vital part in their eventual successful termination, after it had seemed at one point that they would end in deadlock. Largely as a result of Kosygin's mediatory efforts, talks ended on 10 January with the signing of the Tashkent Declaration, under which India and Pakistan agreed to renounce the use of force in the settlement of their disputes and to withdraw their troops to the position existing on 5 August 1965, before the outbreak of hostilities between the two countries. The main provisions were:

1. The Prime Minister of India and the President of Pakistan agree that both sides will exert all efforts to create good-neighbourly relations between India and Pakistan in accordance with the UN Charters.

They reaffirm their obligation under the Charter not to have recourse to force and to settle their disputes through peaceful means. They considered that the interests of peace in their region and particularly in the Indo-Pakistan subcontinent and, indeed, the interests of the peoples of India and Pakistan, were not served by the continuance of tension between the two countries.

It was against this background that Jammu and Kashmir was discussed, and each of the sides set forth its respective position.

2. All armed personnel of the two countries would be withdrawn not later than 25 Febuary 1966, to the positions they held prior to 5 August 1965, and both sides would observe the cease-fire terms on the cease-fire line.
3. Relations between India and Pakistan would be based on the principle of non-interference in the internal affairs of each other.
4. Both sides would discourage any propaganda directed against the other country.
5. The normal functioning of diplomatic missions of both countries would be restored, and the High Commissioners of both countries would return to their posts.
6. Measures towards the restoration of economic and trade relations, communications, and cultural exchanges would be considered, and steps taken to implement the existing agreements between India and Pakistan.
7. Prisoners of war would be repatriated.
8. Discussions would continue relating to the problems of refugees and evictions of illegal immigrants. Both sides will create conditions which will prevent the exodus of the people.
9. The Prime Minister of India and the President of Pakistan have agreed that the sides will continue meetings both at the highest and at other levels on matters of direct concern to both countries. Both sides have recognized the need to setup joint Indo-Pakistan bodies which will report to their governments in order to decide what further steps should be taken.

Within a few hours of the signing of the Indo-Pak Declaration, Shastri, who was sixty-one, died suddenly in the early hours of 11 January 1966.

Following unsuccessful talks at the ministerial level (in accordance with the Tashkent Declaration) held in Rawalpindi on 1 and 2 March, diplomatic exchanges continued throughout the spring and summer. These led to no result, as Pakistan maintained that the most important issue to be discussed was that of Kashmir, whereas the Indian government continued to uphold its view that Kashmir was an integral part of India.

The euphoria built up during the 1965 war had led to public perception in West Pakistan, nurtured by the government, that Pakistan was winning the war. The government propaganda machinery made people believe that Pakistan could have taken Kashmir by force while defending its international borders, had it not been forced to accept the cease-fire. This belief was misconceived. In fact, the war had resulted in a stalemate. Pakistan had to accept the cease-fire as it was running out of ammunition and supplies and was in no position to continue fighting or to take on India again in a second round.

News of the agreement in Tashkent shocked Pakistanis who had expected something quite different. Virtually everyone believed the talks would fail, and preparations were underway to welcome Ayub back to Pakistan as a hero of the people, but when the news was relayed in the evening over Radio Pakistan there was only surprise and dismay. The following morning, when it was learnt that the Indian Prime Minister had suffered a heart attack and died shortly after the signing ceremony, public attention was still riveted on the agreement. Had Pakistan made so great a sacrifice only to accept the restoration of the *status quo ante*? When Ayub finally returned to Rawalpindi there were no celebrations, no press conferences, and no high-level meetings. Ayub did not seem inclined to explain why he chose to sign the agreement and went into immediate seclusion. The reasons for the President's silence are not known, but it may be conjectured that he was deeply affected by the sudden passing of Shastri. Undoubtedly, he also wondered how Shastri's death would affect the agreement he had just signed. Bhutto, likewise, refused to comment, and went directly to his ancestral home in Sindh. Ayub's reluctance to explain his reasons for accepting the Tashkent Declaration was more than what the aroused Pakistanis could tolerate. Hence, after an impatient pause of almost forty-eight hours, demonstrations erupted in several areas of West Pakistan. Not unexpectedly, the student community stood in the forefront of this activity and public peace was shattered.

The most serious riots occurred in Lahore, the celebrated city of the seventeen-day war. Section 144 of the Code of Criminal Procedure was in force in Lahore as in other parts of West Pakistan, making it a violation to take out processions or hold public meetings of more than five people. Nevertheless, students from Punjab University and other local colleges moved out of their campuses defying the order, and proceeded to march on the downtown area. Earlier a band of students, dressed in black and carrying banners calling upon the government to reconsider the position taken at Tashkent, camped outside the main gate leading to the Governor's residence. Efforts to persuade the students to leave proved futile and police reinforcements arrived to bolster the detachment already on the scene.

Rioting began some time after noon. The police ordered a halt to the marchers converging on the city, many of whom were joined by veiled women who carried children alleged to be the dependents of men killed in the war. Shouts of 'Give us back our husbands, fathers, and brothers' pierced the air, and the crowds became more difficult to manage. From Regal Chowk and Charing Cross, the students marched towards Government House, several hundred yards down the Mall Road, where they sought to petition the Governor. It was at this juncture that the police asserted itself.

All attempts to stop the students were answered with increased resistance and rowdiness. Soon, the brick-throwing began, and the police were ordered to counter-attack by using tear gas. The battle raged for several hours but damage to public utilities was not extensive, though a double-decker omnibus of the West Pakistan Road Transport Corporation was attacked, its windows smashed, and an attempt made to set it afire. Fluorescent tubes lighting the downtown area and traffic lights were also easy targets. Disorder spread around the city colleges where the police resorted to shooting. An official government announcement stated that the first victim was a policeman, but the struggle grew as a result.

Rioting in Lahore continued into the night and when it was finally brought under control, four people were dead, many were injured, and several hundred were in jail. Punjab University, local colleges, and schools were ordered to be closed for an indefinite period; parts of the city were littered with debris and hastily scrawled obscenities were to be seen in a number of localities. One theme explained everything. The President, according to the demonstrators, had 'sold Kashmir' to the Hindu 'babus' and 'warlords'. Many people were outraged, more were quietly bitter, but hardly a person could be found who was not prepared to voice his displeasure with the unexpected turn of events in Tashkent. Popular sympathy was with the students, who reflected the feelings of West Pakistan's urban population.[8]

Concerned with the violent reaction to the Tashkent Declaration and urged by his advisers to lay the matter before the people, Ayub broke his self-imposed silence with a mid-day radio address to the nation on 14 January. Speaking in Urdu, he explained that the Tashkent Declaration had in no way detracted from or damaged the country's position on Kashmir. 'The Kashmiris' right to choose their future remained inviolable', he reiterated.[9] Ayub declared that once the withdrawal of the armed forces had taken place, Pakistan would be in a position to request the Security Council to mediate the dispute. This was in keeping with the resolution of 20 September 1965, he explained. But no matter what happens in the future, he continued, Pakistan would never abandon the Kashmiris and the country would never enter a no-war pact with India 'unless the Jammu and Kashmir dispute was settled honourably and equitably'.

Taking note of the sentiment aroused against his policies, Ayub remarked: 'There may be some amongst us who will take advantage of your feelings and will try to mislead you. They are not more patriotic, perhaps, than you or me. The ordeal is not yet over'. Clearly, Ayub held to the view that the demonstrations were the work of his political antagonists. It was the judgment of most impartial observers, however, that he had failed to gauge the temper of the population that, in fact, violent reaction was a predictable response and was absolutely spontaneous. Politicians had reacted much more slowly to Tashkent and, though they had not created the disturbances, they sought to reap some advantages from them.

After the President's broadcast, *The Pakistan Times*[10] ran a headline declaring: 'All Misgivings Dispelled' and followed with the comment that the 'people left their radio sets with a sense of relief, satisfied when they heard their President declare that the Declaration had in no way harmed our view-point on the Jammu and Kashmir issue'. Despite these pronouncements by the government press, it was obvious that everyone was not 'relieved' and that popular misgivings were the rule rather than the exception.

In order to understand the intensity of this feeling, it is necessary to realize that the people of Pakistan, especially those in the Punjabi-speaking areas of West Pakistan, held it as an article of faith that India had no intention of coming to a settlement over Kashmir; that the attack on Pakistan was simply the precursor to its destruction, and that in the hostilities which followed that attack, the Pakistan Army and Air Force inflicted such destructive defeats on the Indian forces that they, the Pakistanis, were actually poised for a decisive advance. They believed that Ayub should in such circumstances, have submitted tamely to the provisions of the Tashkent Declaration. Feelings against him were harsh, particularly in the armed forces and among those who had lost men not in the fighting. It was the government's propaganda that had given the impression that Pakistan had an upper hand in the war. The truth was otherwise, but Pakistanis were kept in the dark.

The injury caused to Ayub's image by the Tashkent Declaration cannot be doubted. He was obliged to launch a special, countrywide campaign in order to exonerate himself, although it is unlikely that he ever gave the real reasons for signing it. Zulfikar Ali Bhutto, who must have known a good deal of the actual situation even if his military judgment was untutored, was opposed to the Tashkent Declaration, and a few months later he quarrelled with Ayub over it and was dropped from the government. Bhutto had always claimed that the whole truth about Tashkent had never been stated and, at various times, had threatened to expose everything. Whether this related to the possibility of carrying on the war with prospects of success, or to the course of the negotiations has never been made clear.

Reaction of Politicians to the Tashkent Declaration

The reaction of political parties to the Tashkent Declaration was edifying. There were those like Chaudhri Mohammad Ali (Nizam-i-Islam), and Shaukat Hayat Khan (Council Muslim League), who condemned every feature of the agreement; there were others like Mujib (East Pakistan Awami League), and Bhashani (National Awami Party), who refrained from criticism. Bhashani's NAP seldom argued the cause of Kashmir, and consistent with its previous stand, avoided taking sides in this clash. Maudoodi's Jamaat-i-Islami vehemently criticized the Tashkent Agreement. Although his party was extremely well-organized, it never captured the popular imagination nor harnessed the sentiments of important and articulate interest groups. Whereas the more conservative West Pakistani opposition emphasized the limited objective of removing Ayub, it remained divided on questions of organization and programme. The forces led by Bhashani, like those which rallied around Mujib in East Pakistan, were represented by contrasting radical interests. For them, Ayub was only a preliminary target.

Both the NAP and Awami League sought comprehensive changes in Pakistan's political organization. They refused to be associated with the anti-Tashkent agitation since it was too limited an objective.

Undaunted by dissension in their ranks, rightist political parties refused to alter their course. Tashkent seemed to be an issue worth exploiting and they diligently set about their task. Their tactics were simple and conventional. In spite of government directives imposing section 144 in all the major urban centres of West Pakistan, politicians held public meetings and offered themselves for arrest when the police appeared. It is doubtful whether this tactic had more than symbolic or sentimental importance. All the same, members of the Council Muslim League, Nizam-i-Islam,

Jamaat-i-Islami, and West Pakistan Awami League pursued their original plans. Having violated section 144, they went to prison one by one.

In Dhaka, Nurul Amin, a moderate, former chief minister of East Pakistan, convener of the National Democratic Front (NDF), and leader of the opposition in the National Assembly, called upon the authorities to end the state of emergency proclaimed during the war under which politicians in West Pakistan were being arrested. While seeking the release of all political prisoners and the rescinding of section 144, he avoided condoning the anti-Tashkent agitation. Nurul Amin intimated that the Tashkent Declaration was in the best interest of the country but he deplored the government's action denying the right of dissent to those who opposed it. Still another opposition leader who sympathized with the dissenters while supporting the agreement was Z.H. Lari, President of the Karachi Zonal Council Muslim League. Like Nurul Amin he condemned the government for preventing public expression on a vital issue. Apparently, Lari was not speaking for all the party members and was soon expelled from his party. Fatima Jinnah was silent on Tashkent. Farid Ahmad, General Secretary of the Nizam-i-Islam, came out in favour of the agreement, but both agreed with Nurul Amin and Lari that the government should avoid using repressive tactics.[11]

Frustrated by the government and their own inability to agree on important issues, West Pakistani leaders announced that a national conference would be held in Lahore on 5 and 6 February 1966 to thrash out differences. But before the conference convened it was announced that the central issue would be the Tashkent Declaration. On learning this, East Pakistanis, with the exception of a small contingent led by Mujib, declined the invitation. The NAP insisted that they were never invited, but the West Pakistani president of the Awami League (who went to East Pakistan in an effort to gather support for the meeting) said they had flatly refused to join. In fact, the working committee of the NAP in the Punjab and Bahawalpur passed a resolution condemning the Lahore meeting, noting that not only would it disrupt the solidarity of the country but that it would also 'further the sinister interests of the imperialists'. The clash between right-wing and left-wing parties was clearly defined. The moderate East Pakistani opposition may have declined the invitation to join in the protest movement because the Kashmir issue was too remote. They did not want to risk going to prison for a cause they could not fully support.

The Jamaat-i-Islami, Nizam-i-Islam, Council Muslim League of West Pakistan, and Awami League of West Pakistan sponsored the meeting, maintaining their individual identities throughout the proceedings. As anticipated, Nurul Amin's NDF and the NAP boycotted the conference. Even Chaudhri Mohammad Ali's request that they send observers went unheeded. With the absence of these 'antagonists' it would have been expected that the convention would agree on a common programme but this was not the case. The only East Pakistanis to turn up in Lahore were those led by Mujib, and their demands were enough to fracture what little unity the conference could muster.[12] Mujib made a lengthy speech in which he highlighted the manner in which the defence of East Pakistan had been ignored. He said that there was less than one military division of troops[13] in all of East Pakistan, and that was inadequately equipped. According to him, there were only six aircrafts and four tanks with the

Pakistan Army in East Pakistan and if India had chosen to attack, East Pakistan was a sitting duck for them. During the course of his speech, he gave detailed proposals for the autonomy and defence of East Pakistan, which included separate foreign trade, foreign exchange reserves, and an East Pakistan militia. These proposals later attained great notoriety as the 'Six Points Programme' of Mujib.[14] When the meeting was finally called to order, more than 700 delegates were present with only twenty-one from East Pakistan.

From the outset, there was bickering and indecision. Each delegation's leader harangued the government and condemned it for resorting to 'undemocratic practices'; all the arguments had been heard before, and their impact was negligible. The publication of these speeches was banned by the government and thus they had little effect on the population at large.

The national conference ended in two days. From most standpoints, it failed to attain any of the objectives for which it had been organized. A proposal for launching a civil disobedience movement aimed at gaining the revocation of the Tashkent Declaration was presented by some members of the West Pakistan Council Muslim League and West Pakistan Awami League, but it was not taken up for want of consensus. Some young firebrands held the view that the matter should be pressed with deliberate force, but senior politicians were unimpressed and indicated a desire to pursue their objectives through constitutional means. Later, the conference passed resolutions condemning the Tashkent Agreement and urged the government to abrogate it. Mujib, having met with stiff opposition on his own proposals demanding more autonomy for East Pakistan, not only rejected these resolutions but marched his small delegation out of the conference and returned to his native province. For all intents and purposes, the meeting was a dismal failure. Its historical significance lies in the launching of the Six Point Programme by Mujib and the beginning of the end of Pakistan's unity.

With the conference over and the opposition hopelessly divided, the government moved to silence some of the West Pakistani dissidents. On 17 February, the government arrested three West Pakistan Awami League and two West Pakistan Council Muslim League leaders in Lahore. The politicians were taken in custody under Rule 32 of the Defence of Pakistan Rules (1965) for what was called 'persistently indulging in activities which were highly prejudicial to the maintenance of public order'. The leaders were: Nawabzada Nasrullah Khan, President of the All-Pakistan Awami League; Sardar Shaukat Hayat Khan, General Secretary of the Council Muslim League; Malik Ghulam Jilani, a former member of the National Assembly, and Khawaja Muhammad Rafiq, both members of the central working committee of the Awami League; and Sardar Mohammad Zafarullah, President of the Lahore branch of the Council Muslim League.

On hearing of the arrests, virtually all political parties issued a strong condemnation of the government but even this did not bring them together.

The Sixth and Seventh Amendments of 1966

The Sixth Amendment[15] to the Constitution was an extension of the Fourth Amendment. A government servant could be retired, in the public interest, on completion of twenty-five years of service. The retirement age was fixed at fifty-five years. The requirement to consult the Public Service Commission could be dispensed with in specific cases or the matter could be referred to some other authority for consultation.

The Constitution (Seventh Amendment) Act, 1966[16] amended the provisions relating to the ordinance-making powers of the President and the Governors, and the ordinance-making power of the President during emergency. The amendment did not make any significant change in these provisions which were already very stringent. However, the method of converting an ordinance into an Act of the central legislature or a provincial legislature was further simplified. An ordinance could become an Act on the passing of a resolution by the concerned legislature. Even if the resolution had modified the ordinance, it could still become an Act if assented to by the President or a Governor, as the case may be. The ordinance-making power of the President during an emergency was unfettered under the Constitution and it could not be disapproved by the National Assembly. However, the Seventh Amendment allowed the National Assembly to convert such an ordinance into an Act of the central legislature by passing a resolution of approval. Even if a resolution had made an amendment in the ordinance, it could become an Act if assented to by the President.

It is noticeable that through various amendments to the Constitution, the powers of the President or his nominated Governors, which were already enormous, were further expanded and extended, particularly as far as the control on bureaucracy or law-making institutions were concerned. A lot of legislation was done through ordinance-making which was later rubber stamped by the assemblies. This was the beginning of the tendency on the part of the legislatures to abdicate the law-making functions in favour of the executive, and the ordinances framed by the law ministries of the central and provincial governments eventually became Acts of legislature without going through the requirements of successive readings of the Bills and without the benefit of meaningful discussion in the legislatures. When ordinances were placed before the assemblies, their approval without any amendment by the concerned legislature was deemed to be a matter of prestige for the government and was hustled through the legislature with the help of brute majorities commanded by the government. Any objection or suggestion by an individual member, particularly if he was from the opposition, was brushed aside with contempt regardless of how useful or weighty it might be.

These amendments made the following changes:

a. Terms and conditions of public servants were changed with special reference to the age of retirement and the discretionary power of the President to direct the retirement of civil servants was further extended.

b. Other minor changes in terms and conditions of service were changed including change in the definition of certain categories of public servants.
c. Changes were made in Articles 29 and 30 with respect to the President's power of legislation by ordinance during emergency and otherwise.

Of all these, the most important group, as far as its practical effect and the power it gave Ayub to manipulate the public administration was concerned, belonged to the first category listed above. Ayub's intention was to get rid of public officials whom he did not like and to retain those whom he liked long after the prescribed age of retirement. It may be said that these were necessary powers. It should be possible for any public administration to disembarrass itself of incompetent or otherwise undesirable public servants. The issue was the undermining of all institutions of governance and the overbearing powers of the President.

The Sixth Amendment, enacted on 31 March 1966, was an elaboration of the Fourth Amendment, enacted on 11 August 1965, seven months earlier. The Fourth Amendment made it possible to direct the retirement of civil servants in the central and provincial governments at fifty-five instead of at the age of sixty, as had been established by Ayub in December 1962. The reasons for adopting a retirement age of sixty have been explained, but thirty-four months after giving effect to this policy, Ayub evidently concluded that fifty-five was the right age after all. The Fourth Amendment gave effect to this conclusion but the manner in which it did so apparently did not suffice and, seven months later, it was decided that this arrangement required elaboration so that the President (or a Governor) could not only direct retirement at the age of fifty-five, or after completion of twenty-five years of pension-qualifying service, but could also allow an extension of service beyond the official retirement age, at his discretion, on such terms as he might decide.

Here a number of interesting questions arise. The advancement of the age of retirement to sixty was provided for by a simple Finance Ministry notification. Why could the new arrangement for retirement at fifty-five with possible retention after that age not have been made in precisely the same way? Why was it necessary to import the new arrangements into the Constitution, when the previous arrangement could had been carried out by a simple administrative act? It could well be that having decided on the new arrangement, Ayub wanted to make it as unchallengeable as possible.

It may further be asked why the elaboration contained in the Sixth Amendment was thought necessary so soon after the Fourth Amendment was enacted. Why was the entire change, lowering of the retirement age and the right to retain people after retirement not made in one amendment? Two explanations are possible. Either, when preparing the Fourth Amendment, the clause authorizing retention after retirement age was not thought about, or it was considered that the public, more particularly the civil services, should not be asked to swallow too much at once. It must be remembered that these changes affected many peoples's lives, favourably or unfavourably and the reduction of the retirement age, so soon after its advancement to sixty, was far from a popular measure with the powerful bureaucracy.

Ayub could not totally ignore the growing opposition to the continued application of Article 30.[17] It was, therefore, changed in the Seventh Amendment, dated 20 December 1966, so as to extend, very slightly, the power of the National Assembly to participate in legislation by ordinance which was part of the presidential prerogative. Thus this amendment was principally concerned with clause (6) of Article 30.

As originally drafted, clause (6) provided that the National Assembly had no power to disapprove of any ordinance promulgated under Article 30 but that it could, by resolution, approve of it, in which case the ordinance would be deemed to have become an Act of the National Assembly. If the Assembly did not confer its formal approval in this way, the ordinance would cease to have effect if and when the state of emergency ended. This arrangement was changed by the Seventh Amendment which replaced the existing clause (6) by clauses (6) and (6A). While disapproval of an ordinance promulgated under Article 30 would still remain outside the authority of the National Assembly, it could, by resolution, approve of the ordinance with or without amendment. The power to amend was thus introduced and under the new arrangement an ordinance approved by the Assembly would become an act of the central legislature provided the amendments it had proposed received presidential assent. This extension of the Assembly's authority was clearly minimal and did nothing to moderate or clip the powers which Ayub exercised for so long after the emergency was first proclaimed. Nevertheless, a chorus of acclaim came from his supporters to these changes as a great and important addition to the National Assembly's powers.

Whatever else may be said of these amendments, they certainly concentrated all power in the President. They indicated that Ayub had no intention of withdrawing the state of emergency, and so long as that continued such legislative powers as the national and provincial assemblies possessed were nullified. Therefore, dissatisfaction remained and this group of amendments laid the foundation for fresh discontent. A number of senior and, in some cases, very capable civil servants were compulsorily retired from service and a number of others were rapidly advanced to high places in the bureaucracy.

Political Developments in East Pakistan: February 1966–November 1968

Following the partition of Bengal, Nazimuddin was elected leader of the Parliamentary Party and took over as Chief Minister of East Pakistan. In the contest, Nazimuddin was supported against Suhrawardy by the Central Muslim League, which distrusted the latter because of his involvement with the independent Bengal movement, and his association with Gandhi to bring about communal harmony in India. Suhrawardy was not treated well by the government of East Pakistan, not allowed to address public meetings, and was externed from the province in June 1948.[18] Earlier, on 18 May, he was deprived of his membership of the Constituent Assembly because the Assembly amended its Rules of Procedure whereby a person not resident in Pakistan ceased to be a member of the Assembly.[19] Suhrawardy was hit very hard by this because he had stayed back in Calcutta for some time after independence.

In February 1948, the restructuring of the Pakistan Muslim League was undertaken which proved divisive and led to widespread splits in all the provinces. In East Pakistan, the appointment of Maulana Akram Khan as the provincial organizer led Bhashani and his supporters to break away from the Muslim League. In a convention of political workers on 24 June 1949, attended by Bhashani, Fazlul Haq, and other League leaders, a new party called East Pakistan Awami Muslim League was formed, with Bhashani as President. So important was the support of students even to veteran political leaders that Mujib, a student leader at that time in jail, was appointed Joint Secretary of the party. Suhrawardy, whose supporters had joined the Awami Muslim League, tried to bring it within the framework of a national party. In March 1950, he called a convention of political workers at which a new party called the All Pakistan Awami Muslim League was formed with himself as the President and chief organizer.[20] The manifesto of the party included provincial issues like nationalization of the jute trade, Bengali as the state language, and the holding of general elections on the basis of adult franchise. The differences within this national organization arose because the conditions in the two wings were completely different. Suhrawardy's attempt to synthesize the politics of the two wings through an indigenous national organization reflecting post-independence realities, failed.

In East Pakistan, the Awami League had emerged as a well organized and disciplined opposition party. In 1953, its council approved the party manifesto and unanimously elected Bhashani as President and Mujib as General Secretary. On top of the list in the manifesto was provincial autonomy, leaving only defence, foreign affairs, and currency to the centre, and Bengali as the state language.[21]

During the first decade of independence, there were three main areas of conflict in the East-West relationship. They were the status of Bengali, constitution-making, and economic centralism. The status of Bengali was resolved in the first 1956 Constitution but, in the process, the controversy left permanent scars on the national polity. Some understanding was reached on constitutional issues like joint electorate and parity of representation between the two wings in the central legislature, but no consensus could ever be reached on economic issues which led to the demand for complete provincial autonomy. The undemocratic regime of Ayub only aggravated the grievances of East Pakistanis who felt more and more negated particularly in economic activities.

There was also a hue and cry from various sections of East Pakistan's population about inequities and disparities they were allegedly suffering from at the hands of the central bureaucracy and military. They alleged that there was dominance of West Pakistan in these services. It was one of the avowed objects of the 1956 and 1962 Constitutions to bring about parity between the two provinces in economy and in the services. Despite this, the gulf only kept widening. Some efforts were made in Ayub's period to bridge the gap, particularly in the economic sphere. But the gulf between the two provinces in the field of economics was not being abridged to the satisfaction of the people of East Pakistan. In the central services, the gulf was widening and East Pakistan was seriously under-represented.

It is true that clause (4) of Article 145 stated that 'a primary object of the [National Economic] Council . . . shall be to ensure that disparities between the two provinces and between different areas within a province, in relation to income per capita are removed...', but it was felt in East Pakistan that the prevailing circumstances were quite adverse to all such efforts, however genuine. Of all the organizations set up to deal with development and growth, particularly financial resources and the allocation thereof, there was not one which maintained its head office in East Pakistan. These included the Pakistan Industrial Credit and Investment Corporation, the Investment Development Bank of Pakistan, the House-Building Finance Corporation, the Agricultural Development Bank of Pakistan and later, the National Investment Trust Ltd. and the Investment Corporation of Pakistan. Why, it was asked, should all these important institutions have their centres of gravity in the western province and be more susceptible to West Pakistani influence?

The extent of this influence can be judged from the prominent place of West Pakistani personnel among class I civil servants in the various ministries and departments of the central government. In 1966, the position was as follows:[22]

	East Pakistan %	West Pakistan %
President's Secretariat	19	81
President's Personal Section	nil	100
Commerce Ministry	36.4	63.6
Defence Ministry	8.4	91.6
Industries Division.	25.6	74.4
National Resources Divsion	24.7	75.3
Rehabilitation and Works Divsion	17.4	82.6
Home and Kashmir Affairs Divsion	22.5	77.5
Education	33.3	66.7
Health, Labour, and Social Welfare	19.0	81.0
Foreign Ministry	22.2	77.8
Law and Parliamentary	35.0	65.0
Communications	17.8	82.2
Finance	24.4	75.6

The numerical distribution of all employees of the central government was:

East Pakistan		West Pakistan	
Gazetted	Non-Gazetted	Gazetted	Non-Gazetted
1338	26,310	3708	82,944

These and other inequities to which were added charges such as under-recruitment of East Pakistanis into the public services and, particularly, into the armed forces, had been long standing grievances and by the time Ayub relinquished office in 1969, it was maintained that nothing had been done to address these. It was pointed out that the economic gap between the two provinces was far from closed, although the country's principal earner of foreign exchange since 1947 had been East Pakistan. It was all very well for Ayub to boast of the rapid advance in the export of manufactured goods, thus vindicating his economic planning, but the value of exported jute goods from East Pakistan was greater than that of all other manufactured goods put together. It was probable that the total value of raw jute and jute manufactures exported from East Pakistan was equal to about half of the country's export earnings, but did this money benefit East Pakistan? The East Pakistanis did not think so.[23]

There were several factors that caused the widening of the gulf between East and West Pakistan and all of it was not attributable to Ayub, but their aggravation during his regime cannot be ignored. These factors included the death in 1963 of Suhrawardy. It robbed the eastern province, as well as the entire country, of one of its ablest men. Despite some flaws of character injurious to his personal image and despite a much-thwarted political career in Pakistan, Suhrawardy was a man of undoubted capability and, notwithstanding his advancing years and his opposition to Ayub, he might well have made an important contribution to the solution of the political impasse between the two wings. His death left Khawaja Nazimuddin in charge, a man respected more for the piety of his character than for his political ability. He however, also passed away in September 1964. His brother, Khawaja Shahabuddin, was not really a part of the political scene and Nurul Amin, also in opposition, had evidently lost much of his former vigour. Thus, in East Pakistan, political leadership fell more and more into the hands of men such as Bhashani, also in advancing years but with extraordinary vitality, and Mujib, one of Suhrawardy's lieutenants.

When Ayub launched his presidential system, East Pakistani leaders argued that the real mischief lay in Pakistan's political structure which did not represent the intentions of the Pakistan Resolution as proposed by the *Sher-i-Bengal* ('Lion of Bengal') A.K.M. Fazlul Haq passed in Lahore on 23 March 1940. This suggestion appeared to strike at the roots of the country's existence and was played down in West Pakistan, but it could not be totally suppressed, especially as Ayub went on amending his Constitution in the face of protests.

It was during Ayub's administration that East Pakistan's movement towards autonomy acquired a more definite form. It was during his administration that the word secession became not only utterable but printable. Eventually, it was Ayub who expressed the liberal view that the only link between the two provinces lay in the fact that the Governor of each of them was appointed by the centre. 'Remove him (the Governor) and you have two countries straight away.'[24] He was deeply worried about relations between East and West Pakistan. What disturbed him most was that Bengali Muslims saw little benefit in living together with West Pakistanis. He sensed separation to be inevitable.[25]

Ayub failed as much in East Pakistan, as in West Pakistan, because his regime became more oppressive and more corrupt without providing any material benefits to the deprived masses. It is quite possible that these evils were felt more in East Pakistan than in West Pakistan, not only because of the existence of greater poverty but by reason of the methods adopted by Monem Khan, Governor of East Pakistan. He enlisted the support of the Basic Democrats by entrusting them with such functions as the distribution of food grains, clothing, and other necessities in times of shortage or disaster. The management of the Rural Works Programme was largely in their hands and many other forms of patronage allied to the exercise of minor administrative functions, enabled these people to oppress the poor, to secure all kinds of unfair advantage, and, of course, to enrich themselves. It is for this reason that when trouble became rife in the cold weather of 1968–9, violence took a specific turn in East Pakistan against these village masters, some of whom were brutally murdered.

Mujib's Six Points

As discussed earlier, opposition parties saw the Tashkent Declaration as a chance to embarrass Ayub and a conference was called at the house of Chaudhri Mohammad Ali to which Mujib was invited. Ostensibly, the purpose was to pressure Ayub. Mujib went to Lahore with the intention of collaborating but he also raised the question of East Pakistan's grievances and produced the Six Points Programme as they had been originally drafted. This was waived aside on the ground that the only purpose of the conference was to discuss Tashkent and Mujib's proposals could be discussed on another occasion. Sensing in this a repetition of the indifferent attitude towards East Pakistan, Mujib went back to his province, announced his support for the Tashkent Declaration, and proceeded to publish the Six Points which, he said, were essential if East Pakistan was to survive and prosper.

As originally drafted, this (four-point) programme said:

1. The Constitution should provide for a federation of Pakistan in its true sense on the basis of the Lahore Resolution and parliamentary form of government with the supremacy of the legislatures elected on the basis of universal adult franchise and direct voting.
2. The federal government should deal with two subjects—defence and foreign affairs; all other residuary subjects should vest in the federating states.

3. Regarding currency, either of the two following suggestions should be considered;
   (a) Two separate, freely convertible currencies or
   (b) One currency for the whole country with effective constitutional provisions to stop the flight of capital from East to West Pakistan. A separate banking reserve was also to be made for East Pakistan.
4. Separate fiscal and monetary policies were to be adopted for East Pakistan.

Mujib was not the author of these extreme suggestions. He was no profound political theoretician. His ability and skills lay in political organization for which talent Suhrawardy often spoke warmly about Mujib.[26] Mujib also possessed a gift for powerful oratory, with an appeal to emotions unfortunately with an undertone of violence. Armed with this programme, he now began to stump the countryside, preaching a new gospel of autonomy within the parameters of the Lahore (Pakistan) Resolution and through the Six Points.

The original draft which was the work of a group of East Pakistani intellectuals who were dissatisfied with the attitude of the central government, and with the evident advantages that West Pakistan, justly or unjustly, enjoyed. The draft was first presented to Nurul Amin who realized that a demand for secession could be read into it. He delayed his reply and the authors showed the draft to Mujib, who was about to attend the conference on the Tashkent Declaration in Lahore. Seeing in the draft a crystallization of what he wanted but had not been able to enunciate so precisely, Mujib seized it and carried the proposals to Lahore. After their adoption by Mujib's party, the draft was amended and clarified to present six clear issues. They read as follows:

1. A federal Constitution for Pakistan.
2 Central government portfolios to be limited to Defence and Foreign Affairs only.
3. The two provinces to have separate currencies or, alternatively, restrictions on the movement of capital funds from one province to the other.
4. All taxes to vest in the province of collection.
5. All foreign exchange earned by East Pakistan to be at the disposal of East Pakistan.
6. An East Pakistan militia to be formed.

The movement gathered in pace and strength and Bhashani, sensing the change of atmosphere, decided to jump aboard the autonomy bandwagon. Following the example of Mujib he, too, made speeches declaring that full provincial autonomy was the only means of ensuring a viable, durable, united Pakistan. However, he did not speak in favour of the Six Point Programme and, significantly enough, incurred no visible, official displeasure. So far as Ayub's government went, Bhashani stayed out of trouble. For that matter, his contribution was negligible and enigmatic. In West Pakistan, in line with the customary practice of ignoring or omitting to report anything that had unpleasant or uncongenial implications, the situation in East Pakistan was vaguely reported and details of the Six Points were kept out of newspaper columns. Instead, there was some writing about secession and in March 1966, Ayub made reference to the dangers of slogans about autonomy. At about the same time, Bhutto, still Ayub's Foreign Minister, challenged Mujib to a public debate on the Six Points. This contest in dialectics never took place, each intending disputant adroitly sidestepping the other without actually appearing to do so. This must be regarded as fortunate since, had there been any public meeting for this purpose, the result would certainly have been uproar and possibly bloodshed.

Instead, in April Mujib demanded a nationwide referendum on the Six Point issue and stepped up the campaign with virulent attacks on those in power and on those who had been in power. He claimed that East Pakistan was being despoiled and robbed of its due share in the gross national product in order to feed West Pakistan. On 19 April, he was arrested in Jessore under the Defence of Pakistan Rules and was promptly released on bail, which did not suit the government. On 23 April, he was again arrested under the Defence of Pakistan Rules and under the East Pakistan Safety Ordinance, but this time on a non-bailable warrant. He was removed to Sylhet, conveniently distant from Dhaka by train and on the way he was greeted by demonstrators at various stations. His trial began on 7 May, in Sylhet Jail, for making seditious speeches and other such offences. Thus began his two-year odyssey from one prison to another, terminating at the cantonment where, in 1968, he was among the accused of the Agartala Conspiracy Trial.

Mujib's arrest did nothing to sweeten the temper of East Pakistan and its people. The movement continued to gather strength. In August, Ayub visited the province and made threatening reference to the idea of secession: 'If the trouble goes on, other measures will be necessary'. During this visit, he also addressed a meeting of the members of the National and Provincial Assemblies in which he dealt with 'the secession issue', as he termed it, in undisguised language. In his words, there were discernible indications that West Pakistan was becoming weary of East Pakistan's constantly reiterated complaints, grievances, and insinuations.[27]

For some time, negotiations were held between the representatives of Ayub and Mujib and his lieutenants but the attempt did not succeed. Ayub concluded that the arrest of Mujib, an energetic and aggressive personality, had blunted the edge of the movement. In December 1966, he again visited East Pakistan where, it is said, he succeeded in weaning away some of Mujib's supporters and in cutting the Six Point movement down to manageable proportions by a lavish distribution of import licences and other money-spinning favours.

Despite this, the movement continued and on New Year's Day, 1967, it was announced that on 13 February, a Six Point Programme Day would be observed. Encouraged by Ayub's effective steps of the preceding December, the Press in Pakistan, notably *Dawn*, in an editorial which appeared on the day, described the movement as a fiasco, but the *Dacca Weekly Holiday*, in an issue dated 21 February, said that the popular observance of Six Point Programme Day amounted to an 'uprising'. The event was significant enough to take Ayub to East Pakistan yet again, in the month of March. During this visit, Ayub said that demands for autonomy would divide the country, involving dangers for East Pakistan. Later, on his return to Lahore, he also said that the demand for automony was a 'camouflage for separation'. It was evident at the time that his visit had not been as successful as the earlier one, but the official view claimed that the Six Point Movement was losing its appeal. Meanwhile, more and more East Pakistanis were accepting this programme as minimal. So the word warfare went on until, some months later, events took another and much more dramatic turn.

The Agartala Conspiracy Case

On 2 January 1968, the daily newspapers reported details taken from a statement issued by the government in Islamabad that the activities of 'anti-national elements' had attracted notice and there was reference to arrests 'recently made'.[28]

On 7 January, it was made public that twenty-eight people had been taken into custody on serious charges. All of them belonged to the eastern province and included officers and men of the armed forces as well as three members of the civil service of Pakistan.[29] It was also stated that the office of the Deputy High Commissioner for India was implicated and that the Pakistan government had asked for P.N. Ojha, a First Secretary, to be withdrawn. This request was complied with and the Indian government retaliated by expelling M.M. Ahmad, Counsellor at the Pakistan High Commission in Delhi, alleging that he had distributed arms and money to subversive groups in India. A few days later, it was announced that Mujib, at that time in jail, was involved and would stand trial along with those already under arrest. Excitement rose steadily with the news that some of the conspirators had visited Agartala in India to make plans by which, with Indian help, an independent East Bengal could be established. Hence the Agartala conspiracy case.

After the arrests and the excitement associated therewith, little was heard of the matter until 22 April 1968, when an ordinance appeared by which a Special Tribunal could be set up to try the conspirators. Entitled the Criminal Law Amendment (Special Tribunals) Ordinance 1968,[30] it was promulgated by Ayub under Article 30 of the Constitution, relating to the President's powers in an emergency (which had been declared in September 1965) and other provisions. The ordinance is an interesting piece of legislation because it did not purport to set up a single, special tribunal to deal with the Agartala case, but made it possible for a special tribunal, at any time, to try any case relating to offences concerned with conspiracy, mutiny in the armed forces, or inciting or seducing a member of the armed forces against or from his allegiance or duty. Thus, under this ordinance, the government could, whenever it chose, put together a special tribunal to deal with the alleged offences. The ordinance contained a section which overrode all laws for the time being including the Evidence Act, and the provisions of the ordinance could not be questioned in any court including the Supreme Court. What was meant by the omnibus clause to do with overriding effect is not clear. Mainly, it was aimed at the Evidence Act so that the tribunal should not be bound by the existing law on the subject which might make certain evidence inadmissible and so preclude the possibility of conviction. But the section went further and could be interpreted to mean that the tribunal could make its own law as it went along. There appeared to be no provision by which those convicted by any such tribunal, could appeal.

The intention of the government was clear that if Mujib was convicted and sentenced to a substantial term of imprisonment, he could be safely silenced for a long time without the constitutional complications inherent in any sole reliance upon the Defence of Pakistan Rules and without the legal difficulties involved in sedition cases before the ordinary courts.

On 19 June 1968, the trial opened and was conducted in Dhaka cantonment where the accused were kept in custody. Eleven peoeple associated with the affair had made full confessions and were pardoned. Four of the accused made judicial confessions. All these confessions formed, of course, the testimony of accomplices and even if they corroborated one another, as accomplice-testimony this evidence was clearly tainted. The amount of direct evidence, as it came out in the Court, was limited. During the proceedings, there was some confusion over identification and one prosecution witness was declared hostile and, therefore, made liable to cross-examination by the prosecution. The evidence was extensively reported and provided people with plenty to talk about and discuss, especially in East Pakistan where, in offices and factories, the day's work started with a thorough discussion of the morning's newspaper report.

On behalf of Mujib, a British lawyer, T. Williams, QC, appeared before the Dhaka High Court with a petition that raised a number of weighty and pertinent constitutional issues relating to the validity of the ordinance under which the trial was proceeding. The High Court heard Williams, but the petition was adjourned for further hearing, subject to the condition that the trial would go on. As it turned out, the petition was rendered infructuous by the government's own action in withdrawing the Agartala case and nothing more was heard of Williams' legal ingenuity.[31]

The accused elected not to give sworn evidence in the witness-box. Instead, each of them submitted a written and signed statement to the Court. The burden of all these statements, taken together, was that:[32]

(a) None of them had conspired against the state.
(b) During interrogation, they had been subjected to inhuman treatment, including various specified forms of physical torture, in order to extract a confession.
(c) Those accused who were members of the armed forces or the civil services had taken no part in politics and did not know the political people implicated in the case.
(d) At least one of the accused, Ahmed Fazlur Rahman, said he had been falsely implicated out of spite. As a Deputy Secretary in the Ministry of Finance of the central government, he had made it his business to conduct his work equitably between the two provinces and had opposed measures which were unfair to East Pakistan or wasteful of the nation's resources. For these reasons, he claimed that he had incurred the dislike of his superiors who happened to belong to West Pakistan.

(e) Mujib made a statement in writing giving details of the preceding two years during which he had been moved from one jail to another, the inference being that a man in jail ought to find it difficult to conspire with others outside in order to plan an insurrection. He declared his innocence and mentioned that he had supported the Tashkent Declaration.

And so the trial wore on and before any outcome, it was overtaken by political events in the country. Demonstrations, political and otherwise, paralyzed the administration and Ayub was forced into a total withdrawal of the Agartala case. The proceedings came to an abrupt end and all the accused were released unconditionally.[33] This outcome was marred by the death of one of the accused when he was shot and bayoneted 'attempting to escape', as the official version had it. Apart from this tragic incident, all the armed forces personnel were reinstated with arrears of pay. The three members of the CSP, however, were compulsorily retired, with pension rights, by an order made by Ayub's successor, Yahya.

The withdrawal of the Agartala case was a political event of great significance. Of all the reversals that Ayub suffered in the course of his ten years' administration, this was the most serious and the most humiliating. It was inflicted by East Pakistan and it was the outcome of his duel with Mujib. The fact of withdrawal and the circumstances which compelled it bear implications of a most serious nature. Either the accused were guilty, that there was a true bill against them, in which case Ayub was evidently bent on saving his own skin irrespective of the nation's interests, or they were not guilty in which case the prosecution should never have been instituted.

Political Developments in West Pakistan: February 1966–November 1968

It may be said in defence of Ayub that his political failure in East Pakistan was due to some extenuating circumstances not of his making. But there is little to offer in his defence for his political failures in West Pakistan, the languages, culture, and way of life of the people he largely knew. Ayub and his Governor, the Nawab of Kalabagh, had adopted a policy of violence or conniving at violence, as a method of government. They sought to keep together the constituent parts of the province which formed the One Unit in West Pakistan. The creation of One Unit in 1955 and its political fall-out until October 1958 has already been discussed. Some factors that caused political complications in West Pakistan later due to the One Unit are discussed below.

The people of the projected new province were not homogeneous in language, culture, or way of life. They were all Muslim and, for the most part, of the Sunni section, but the language of the North-West Frontier, Pashto, is as different from Punjabi as the language of East Pakistan, Bengali. Punjabi-speaking people would experience real difficulty in understanding a Sindhi or a Baloch and might well not understand him at all. Theoretically, of course, everyone in West Pakistan had to learn Urdu at school but this assumed that everyone would be going to school and that ideal was far from achieved.

A more significant objection in the minds of those who opposed the One Unit was that more than half the population of the projected One Unit would be Punjabi-speaking and this group might well exercise major influence in the new province. Punjabis were not only more numerous but could reasonably claim to be better educated, harder working, and more enterprising than their provincial compatriots, apart from some small, well-known commercial communities (Memons, Khojas, Bohras, Hindus, and Parsees) which are numerically tiny but politically insignificant. Again, by reason of numbers and a generally higher educational standard, Punjabi-speaking people dominated the armed forces and the public services, although in the professions and in business they were fewer. The Punjabis, particularly those from Chiniot, were also well represented in industry and trade.

The Punjabi-speaking community claimed that in so far as they bore this responsibility, they had discharged it. They pointed out that in the newly created National Assembly, after the 1956 Constitution, they had given up some seats to which they were otherwise entitled on the basis of linguistic representation. This had been done partly in pursuance of the principle of parity as between the two provinces of East and West Pakistan and partly as a concession to their other partners in the western province. Clearly enough, the Punjabi-speaking community was guilty of a short-sightedness which, as the years went by, became more and more apparent. In particular, those in the public administration did not display impartiality, and as time went on the very evils that the minority communities feared became more and more apparent. They affected the choice of personnel for desirable appointments, promotion, and seniority, the allotment of permits to establish industries, and the award of valuable contracts. Ultimately, this gave rise to sinister intrigues.

These things had taken root before Ayub assumed power in 1958 and for this reason he cannot be entirely blamed for the eventual decision to dissolve the One Unit and revert to separate linguistic administrative units in West Pakistan. Ayub's particular failure lies in the fact that, armed as he was with exceptional powers, he did nothing to ameliorate a situation of whose existence he must certainly have been aware, in particular the sense of injustice that existed and was finding expression. He adopted methods more repressive than his predecessors by hounding political rivals from one jail to another; closing all newspapers opposed to him and suppressing public discussion by the abuse of section 144; and police excesses which were never subject to enquiry. He appeared unable or unwilling to recognize that there might be a case for administrative reform which, while retaining the advantages that the One Unit offered, would redress the grievances of the people living in non-Punjabi speaking areas which had been merged into the province of West Pakistan.

It has been said earlier that opposition to the One Unit persisted from the time it was first made and was never, at any moment, entirely dissipated. Indeed, evidence of reaction was by no means wanting, some of it in entirely legal and even commendable form. Of this the Sindhi Adabi Board is a good example. A scholarly organization with its headquarters in Hyderabad, it set about publishing books on the language, history, and culture of Sindh. This work had little about it that was political or controversial but the underlying motive was plain enough. At a different level, pamphlets appeared in profusion setting forth the miseries, injustices, and oppressions suffered by the people in whose language these various polemics were written. These publications came out regularly and were just as regularly proscribed.[34] Local newspapers also participated in this undercurrent of opposition and, in July 1968 the West Pakistan government issued an order to newspapers that they were not to publish information that might create ill-feeling among Muslim sects.[35]

In Balochistan there was more actual, physical resistance to the integration than anywhere else and, at one time, it almost appeared as if Balochistan had seceded *de facto* if not *de jure* by the open defiance of authority which prevailed there. But Sindh, with which Karachi is for the present purpose included, was the greater problem and the government was more concerned with the growth of opposition and unrest in Sindh than elsewhere. There were three reasons for this. Sindh was much more politically sophisticated, and in Karachi Ayub lost the election of 1965. It was economically more important, and its territory lay astride the vital communications, road and rail, that connected Karachi with the north.

A habit of the administration which developed notably during the period of Ayub's government was that of ignoring unpleasant realities and, by not reporting them or by discouraging or suppressing all report of them, to create an illusion of their non-existence. This happened more than once, with the inevitable consequence that when, ultimately, truth could no longer be stifled or withheld, its effect upon the public mind was magnified so much more.

This attitude was very true of the opposition to One Unit, but the fact of its existence could not be disguised totally and as early as 1965, the Governor of West Pakistan was making speeches on the essential unity of the province. The meaning was not lost on anyone, but not until 1967 did Ayub's administration realize that the movement against One Unit had attained meaningful proportions. Ayub's response to this discovery was to suggest that those speaking against One Unit would be well advised not to waste their breath. This airy dismissal implies that he and his advisers, while realizing that such a movement existed, were confident that it could be contained and whittled away. After all, to this end the jails were open, and amenable men could be won to the side of the government by grants of land and similar methods of persuasion which had proved very successful on other occasions.

This was an error of judgment. By 1967, the agitation against One Unit had assumed a clear and fixed direction. More and more people were coming to support it or, at any rate, to recognize the need for reform. The causes of the agitation had crystallized and grievances were being openly canvassed. Particularly among the Pathans, but also among the Punjabis, money and favours were distributed in the form of licences and permits for trade and for setting up industry. This was done openly and in pursuit of government policy to ensure a more equitable distribution of wealth. Whether or not other people in West Pakistan were getting their share of these valuable advantages, the fact was that the permits and licences awarded were, as often as not, carried to Karachi where they found their way into the hands of established businessmen and industrialists.

But, it was also said, that with the cash thus acquired, the Punjabi-speaking population was able to enter Sindh and acquire agricultural land to the disadvantage of the Sindhis. The unfair distribution of barrage land caused bitter condemnation. Land was distributed on the basis of political favour and members of the bureaucracy, even those with no ancestral roots in the area, helped themselves liberally to it. The claims of the local people were ignored and the poor, uninfluential, landless peasants found themselves excluded.

By the middle of 1967, it was made public that in Balochistan the state of law and order had degenerated to the level where recourse to the armed forces was necessary and aerial bombing was resorted to. In some areas, the writ of the government no longer ran but rather that of the local *sardar* who, as likely as not, was detained in jail, thus confounding the confusion. In particular, the method of distribution of Guddu Barrage land, guided as it was by political motives and bureaucratic greed, caused much ill-feeling not only against the government but also between the Baloch tribes. It was possibly a goverment tactic to break their unity.

Until November 1968, when all restraint disappeared, debate on One Unit tended to be reserved. The topic was still sacrosanct and any adverse mention of it could carry a charge of sedition. After November 1968, however, all who disliked One Unit cast aside their reserve and came out openly in its condemnation. Among those who had much to say on this topic were leaders from East Pakistan, notably Mujib, who declared that One Unit had to go. Since the people of East Pakistan had not endured any of the misery or oppression which had fallen upon people in West Pakistan as a result of this consolidation, it is worth considering why Mujib and other East Pakistani leaders were so emphatic about its disappearance.

. Out of the dissolution of One Unit, valuable political advantages could accrue to East Pakistan. The reappearance of the old provinces that made up West Pakistan would greatly simplify the possibility of forming some kind of alliance with, for example, Sindhi-speaking members of the National Assembly. Such an alliance would certainly make it possible for East Pakistan to dominate that chamber. The weight of this political fact is incontestable and had all along been a powerful element in the thinking of everyone concerned with One Unit and its future.

It is an undoubted disaster for West Pakistan that Ayub's period of administration led to these results. One Unit consolidation had its political, financial, economic, and cultural difficulties but the logic of the idea can scarcely be contested. If so, the logic of those who led or rallied to the agitation against it must be conceded, but it was a case that pointed to reform. It is difficult to see why, with a realizable scheme of regional councils, it would not have been possible to remedy grievances and, at the same time, retain the advantages which a single provincial legislature and administration offered.

Apart from the factors discussed above, there were others that added to the political turmoil and widening of the gulf between the two wings of the country. These factors included enrichment of a few families at the expense of all others and the dominance of the bureaucracy. Even inter-marriages between leading industrialist families and bureaucrats' families became commonplace, being mutually enriching.

The Power of Twenty-two Families

Unequal distribution of wealth is a natural consequence of the process of industrialization in any country. So it was in Pakistan during Ayub's era. This concentration was not the result of industrialization alone and had much to do with government patronage which was favouring a few cronies by granting licences to do business in lucrative areas or sectors of the economy or by granting permits to install industrial units likely to yield guaranteed profits.

To cap it all was the allegation of the enrichment of Ayub's own family. The soldier-turned-industrialist-cum businessman, Gohar Ayub, was benefitting enormously by government patronage. Ayub appeared to be either actively involved or passively condoning the activities of his sons who appeared to be doing wonders in commerce and industry.[36]

There was another political angle to this lopsided enrichment. It was seen in East Pakistan as the machination of West Pakistan to control the entire wealth of the country. Nearly all the twenty or twenty-two families belonged to West Pakistan, whatever scarce industry was installed in East Pakistan, particularly the jute mills, was mostly owned by industrialist families from West Pakistan like the Adamjee's and the Dawood's.

This unjust distribution of wealth also helped the politicians to play on the sentiments of the common man, who felt ignored and alienated, and to make leftist and socialist programmes. It was in these circumstances that the semi-socialist manifestos of Bhutto's Peoples Party, which called for the nationalization of major industries and banks, caught the imagination of the people of West Pakistan.

The Dominance of Bureaucrats

Ayub's term of office was the golden era for the bureaucracy which exercised its powers unbridled by any political interference. Ayub, had a great mistrust of politicians and felt at home with servile bureaucrats. CSP officers were having the time of their life. They were the true bosses and the dominant class in the country who held all the key positions and jealously guarded their powers and privilege. They would not let any other person rise to the position of the central secretaries or even deputy secretaries. Commissioners and Deputy Commissioners in the administrative divisions and districts were the real power yielders and reported directly to the Governor from whom they took instructions. They cared little for the ministers or members of the National and Provincial Assemblies. They had become so drunk with power that in 1967, Ghulam Yazdani Malik, Commissioner of Bahawalpur Division, openly abused and slapped a member of the West Pakistan Assembly from

Bahawalpur who had circulated a pamphlet against him for his excesses and injustices, in the premises of the West Pakistan Assembly. It is of importance to note that despite his outrageous conduct, he was shielded by his fellow CSP officers for quite some time.

There was another unfortunate angle to this preponderance of the bureaucracy. Since most of the members of the CSP were drawn from West Pakistan, particularly from the Punjab, their acts and conduct created a further wedge between East and West Pakistan and between various areas within West Pakistan, particularly in Sindh. The officers continued to be trained on the pattern of colonial civil servants of British times. They were instructed to stay away from the common people, live like rulers, and shirk the ruled. They were fully trained in snobbery and in the concept of the colonial administrative class of British colonialists. They were given senior administrative appointments soon after completion of their training at the administrative academy in their middle or late twenties. With little experience in life and faulty training, they became a class unto themselves without the faintest idea of the public service they were required to render for the country. They were as patrician and obnoxious in their behaviour in the former areas of Punjab as they were in other parts of the country, but since they were mostly Punjabis, their attitude and conduct was seen with hatred in the areas outside Punjab. So much was their conceit and false sense of superiority that officers who were posted to East Pakistan did not bother to learn Bengali, which was a national language anyway. As the CSP officers were wielding absolute power they turned exceedingly corrupt. The stories of their corruption, graft, and bribery could put to shame those of Byzantine rulers or The Komintine regime in China.[37]

It was in East Pakistan that these officers did the most damage. They were seen by the people of East Pakistan as vintages of colonial British rulers who cared little for the people. Their unfortunate attitude and conduct was a significant factor behind the demand of the people for autonomy in Sindh, Balochistan, and NWFP.[38]

Leading Constitutional Cases

During this period, there were a number of constitutional cases of significance. None of these were of the importance of cases like those of Abul Ala Maudoodi or Fazlul Quadir Chowdhry, where basic constitutional and political issues had to be addressed. However, under the able leadership of Chief Justice A.R. Cornelius, the judiciary continued to liberalize the law in favour of the citizens through its judgments. Jurisdiction of the courts was extended, the expression 'without lawful authority', used in Article 98 was given a wide meaning to signify more than 'jurisdiction'.[39]

It has been discussed above that after the Tashkent Declaration, a number of political leaders including Malik Ghulam Jilani, Nawabzada Nasrullah Khan, and Sardar Shaukat Hayat Khan, were placed under detention under the Defence of Pakistan Rules and Defence of Pakistan Ordinance, 1965. All of them filed writ petitions before the West Pakistan High Court in Lahore and, in keeping with its dubious tradition of upholding most of the actions of the government, the Lahore High Court dismissed their petitions, holding the detention orders passed against them as bonafide. The High Court judgment was challenged in an appeal before the Supreme Court which accepted the appeals of Nawabzada Nasrullah Khan and declared his detention as void *ab initio*, but dismissed appeals of Sardar Shaukat Hayat Khan and Malik Ghulam Jilani.[40] The Supreme Court, in its detailed judgment, laid down some broad and liberal principles and guidelines for the cases of political detenus. The Court held that 'reasonable belief' did not mean 'suspicion'. The 'satisfaction' of the detaining authority about the acts and activities of the detenus should be based upon reasonable grounds and objective criteria and considerations. The Court held that all orders of preventive detention passed by executive authorities were open to judicial review.

Shorish Kashmiri, a political journalist and public orator, was detained under the Defence of Pakistan Rules, 1965. The High Court of West Pakistan accepted the writ petition against his detention. In appeal, the Supreme Court, upholding the judgment of the High Court, gave the finding that Article 2 of the 1962 Constitution requiring 'every person to be dealt with in accordance with law' was as comprehensive as the American 'due process' clause. In exercise of judicial review, the High Court could decide whether there were reasonable grounds upon which a reasonable person would have formed the same opinion as that framed by the detaining authority. It was held that the High Court had all the power to go into the reasonableness and sufficiency of grounds even if the statute did not require the authority to act upon reasonable grounds and the authority was left to act upon his own subjective satisfaction.[41] The Supreme Court thus introduced the test of reasonableness in the cases of preventive detention while adjudicating upon the grounds of detention.

Mir Abdul Baqi Baloch, a politician from Balochistan, was active in opposition to Ayub. He was placed under preventive detention under the order dated 11 August 1966 of the Deputy Commissioner, Karachi, alleging that he was inciting people in Karachi to lawlessness, disaffection, and violence, thus disturbing and endangering public peace. His writ petition was dismissed by the Karachi Bench of the West Pakistan High Court and he filed an appeal before the Supreme Court. The Supreme Court allowed his appeal and remanded the writ petition to the High Court to decide it afresh in accordance with the principles enunciated in Ghulam Jilani's case.[42] It was held by the Supreme Court that the High Court, in exercise of their constitutional jurisdiction of judicial review of administrative acts, could insist on disclosure of materials on which executive authority had acted. Not only the jurisdiction of executive authority to make the order of detention, but the manner of exercising jurisdiction could be subject to judicial review. The High Court, it was held, should have examined the grounds of detention in order to test their reasonableness. However, the Supreme Court did not go into the pleas that the grounds on which the President proclaimed an emergency had ceased to exist and the Constitution required it to be revoked. This was held to be a purely political question outside the competence of the courts to decide. The Court could not substitute its satisfaction for the satisfaction of the President.

When some students of Dhaka University were expelled by its syndicate without any show cause notice, the Dhaka High Court accepted their writ petitions. The Supreme Court, upholding the judgment of the Dhaka High Court, held that the expelled students had the right to be heard before the passing of the expulsion orders on the grounds of alleged misconduct and indiscipline. In all proceedings held by whomsoever, whether judicial or administrative, the principles of natural justice have to be observed if the proceedings were to result in consequences affecting 'the person or property or other right of the parties concerned.' In order to ensure the elementary and essential principles of justice as a matter of necessary implication, the person to be affected should be made aware of the nature of allegations against him (or her) and should be given a fair opportunity to defend himself (or herself) against such allegations.[43]

Similar decisions were made in other cases, holding the principle that 'no one can be condemned unheard' should be read into every law unless its application was excluded by express words and that every administrative tribunal is under a duty to act fairly and justly and with due regard to the principles of natural justice.[44]

When a member of the National Assembly resigned in a letter addressed to the President, he wrote a letter to the Speaker of the National Assembly stating that he had resigned from the membership of the Muslim League Assembly (Party) and not from the membership of the Assembly. He also sent telegrams to the Speaker in which he strongly repudiated any intention to resign from the Assembly. However, the Speaker notified that he had resigned his seat in the National Assembly within the meaning of Article 107 of the Constitution. The High Court of West Pakistan accepted his writ petition and held that his resignation had not taken effect. The Speaker went in appeal before the Supreme Court which was dismissed. The Court rejected the plea of the Speaker that the matter was not justiciable in view of the bar of jurisdiction under Article 111 of the Constitution on the ground that the matter did not concern the proceedings of the National Assembly and that the jurisdiction of the High Court was not barred to determine any matter relating to the Constitution of the National Assembly. It was held that the communication of resignation to the Speaker was necessary and since the resignation was not addressed to the Speaker, therefore, it did not take effect. It was observed that even if the member had addressed the letter of resignation to the Speaker, he had the right to withdraw it before it was brought to the notice of the Speaker and the latter had taken the decisive step to notify it.[45]

Where a preventive detention law did not provide for communication of grounds of detention to the detenue, the Supreme Court held it to be repugnant to Para 5 of fundamental rights granted to the citizens as its provisions amounted to unreasonable restriction on the right of freedom of movement of a citizen inside Pakistan. It was also held that the detaining authority should particularize the nature of activities prejudicial to the stability or integrity of the country in the grounds of detention. Vague and indefinite grounds were held to be unconstitutional. The detaining authority was also required to specify the period of detention and the order of detention 'till further orders' was held defective and illegal.[46]

It is noticeable that the Supreme Court under the leadership of Chief Justice A.R. Cornelius, established its independence and gave landmark rulings which gave meaning to the fundamental rights and civil liberties of citizens. These rulings set in motion the trend towards judicial activism which was later checked by dictatorial regimes and pliable judges. Nevertheless, a sound foundation was laid for liberal constitutional interpretation, particularly by promoting and strengthening concepts like 'judicial review' and 'due process of law'.

NOTES

1. He was M. H. Sayyid, a former Secretary to the Quaid-e-Azam and was closely associated with Ms Jinnah during the election of 1965.
2. Article 209.
3. Act IV of 1965, PLD 1965 Central Statutes 165.
4. Act XV of 1965. PLD 1966 Central Statutes 5.
5. Act XVII of 1965. PLD 1966 Central Statutes 76.
6. Gauhar, Altaf, *Ayub Khan—Pakistan's First Military Ruler,* 1993, Sang-e-Meel Publications, Lahore, pp. 335-6.
7. Ibid., p. 343.
8. Author participated in these students' demonstrations being the Secretary of the Punjab University Students' Union at that time.
9. All the President's speeches were now delivered in Urdu. On the day the Indians attacked West Pakistan, the President spoke to the nation in English, but a few days later the government decided that all future addresses would be in Urdu. It is also noteworthy that English-language news reports were eliminated from television programming and a few weeks later Radio Pakistan announced that English news programmes would be reduced to two each day. By contrast, at the beginning of the hostilities there were English news programmes almost every two hours.
10. 15 January 1966.
11. Ziring, Lawrence, *The Ayub Khan Era—Politics in Pakistan 1958-1969*, 1971, pp. 75, 77 and 78, Syracuse University Press, New York.
12. Author was present during two of the sessions of the Conference, particularly the one in which Mujib spoke. The Conference was held at the residence of Chaudhri Mohammad Ali.
13. A military division in Pakistan consists of approximately 15,000 troops and is commanded by a Major-General.
14. In fact, Mujib did not announce any six point programme while addressing the Conference. It was the government and its minions and government sponsored press in West Pakistan that named his speech as his six point programme. All this was done with the purpose to discredit the political opposition in the country as disloyal and unpatriotic. Little did they realize that they were doing incalculable harm to the polity in Pakistan and in the process, built Mujib into Bengali nationalist leader with a nationalist programme which historical opportunity he fully availed to the destruction of the unity and integrity of Pakistan.
15. Constitution (Sixth Amendment) Act, 1966. Act II of 1966. PLD 1966 Central Statutes 147.
16. Act XXI of 1966. PLD 1967 Central Statutes 65.
17. Ordinance-making power of the President during the currency of proclamation of emergency.
18. Zaheer, Hassan, *The Separation of East Pakistan*, 1994. Oxford University Press, Karachi, pp. 13, 18.
19. Constituent Assembly of Pakistan Debates. Vol. III, No. 2 (18 May 1948).
20. Ibid., p. 19.

21. *Dawn*, 10 July 1953.
22. Information supplied by the Government in reply to a question in the National Assembly. National Assembly Debates, 23 June 1966.
23. It is probable that by the end of Ayub's administration, the position of jute had become less favourable to East Pakistan's case. In 1957-8 the total export of manufactured and miscellaneous goods amounted to Rs 227.51 million, of which jute manufacturers accounted for Rs 105.94 million. In 1966-7, the total had grown to Rs 1429.43 million of which jute manufactures accounted for Rs 581.04 million, a relative decline from 46 per cent to 40 per cent. Comparing the value of the export of raw jute and jute goods combined against total exports for the same years, the results are even more revealing. In 1957-8 total exports amounted to Rs 1421.65 million of which raw jute and jute goods provided Rs 959.50 million. In 1966-7 total exports amount to Rs 2871.00 million of which jute and jute goods provided 1451.23 million, a relative decline from 67 per cent to 50.54 per cent. These figures are taken from Herbert Feldman, *From Crisis to Crisis*, Edition 1972, Oxford University Press, London, P. 170.
24. Television interview in Rawalpindi on 14 August 1967, reported in *Dawn*, 16 August 1967.
25. Ayub said to Altaf Gauhar in 1968: 'Listen, my dear fellow, I gave them the second capital because they are going to need it one day. They are not going to remain with us'. See Altaf Gauhar's *Ayub Khan—Pakistan's First Military Ruler*, pp. 410-11.
26. An interesting instance of this gift occurred when Martial Law was declared in 1958 and when all political parties were abolished. At that time, Mujib was chief executive, in East Pakistan, of the Alpha Insurance Co. Ltd. He, therefore, recruited into that Company as many of his partymen as possible. In this way he not only provided them with incomes, but kept them together and provided a convenient cover for such meetings as they desired to hold. The trick is not new but it takes an organizer to think of it and execute it.
27. This speech was reported verbatim in *Dawn*, 21 August 1966.
28. From petitions later presented to the High Court on behalf of some of the arrested men, it became known that some, if not all, had been taken into custody on or about 23 December 1967.
29. One of them, Ahmed Fazlur Rahman, had been known to Herbert Feldman, when he was stationed in Karachi, and was very outspoken on the subject of East Pakistan's grievances. Although this has no bearing on the question of guilt or innocence with respect to the Agartala Trial, his indiscretions may have contributed to his arrest. See Herbert Feldman, *From Crisis to Crisis*, 1972, Oxford University Press, London, pp. 184.
30. Ordinance VI of 1968. PLD 1968 Central Statutes 96.
31. Feldman, Herbert, *From Crisis to Crisis*, 1972, Oxford University Press, London, pp. 187-8.
32. Ibid., p. 188.
33. The Court was mobbed by the people in Dhaka and the presiding Officer, Mr Justice (Retd.) S. A. Rahman, a former Chief Justice of Pakistan, barely escaped the mob from the back door and that also said to be without his shoes on.
34. Examples are: *Disposal of Guddu Barrage State Lands*, to do with scandals relating to the allotment of land brought under irrigation with the opening of the Guddu Barrage, and *Balochistan Zindabad*, in Sindhi, by Hyder Bakhsh Jatoi. The title, meaning Long Live Balochistan, speaks for itself. Both were proscribed.
35. This could also refer to ill-feeling between Sunnis, Shias, etc., especially at the time of Moharram when Sunni-Shia antipathy is apt to heighten.
36. At the end of July 1968, Gohar Ayub was Chairman of three companies, namely Arusa Investments Limited, Arusa Industries Ltd., Hashimi Can Company Ltd; he was Managing Director of Gandhara Industries Ltd. and Gohar Habib Ltd. and Director in two other big companies. He and his family held 268,030 shares in Gandhara Industries, 65,250 in Gandhara Industries through Arusa Investments Ltd., and 204,533 shares in Hashmi Can co. Ltd. directly or through Arusa Investments Ltd. His interests in Gandhara Industries and Hashmi Can Co. Ltd. came to approximately 16 million rupees or US$ 3,346,560.00 at the official rate of exchange. It was estimated that the total wealth of the family of Ayub was between U.S.$ 10 million and $ 20 million around 1969 which,

during the ten years of Ayub in power the Gandhara Industries Ltd. (incorporated in 1963) and other companies or business in which the family of Ayub had interest, were the creation of 1960s. These figures have been taken from Appendix B to the book of Herbet Feldman *From Crisis to Crisis*, *supra*, note 31, pp. 305-306, who claimed to have obtained the same from the office of Joint Registrar of Joint Stock Companies, Karachi.

37. Commissioner of Rawalpindi, in 1968, had his daughter married. The stories that took round about the luxury, waste, and graft during the marriage were simply astounding and speak volumes about those times. It is rumoured that he had the entire Inter Continental, Rawalpindi, booked for his guests for four days, where they resided and the receptions went on for many days. The gifts given to the bride included eight cars, 125 refrigerators and 60 television sets. The extravagant Nawabs and Rajas of erstwhile princely India could not dream of extravaganza of senior bureaucrat earning (at that time) about Rs 2000/- per month as salary and allowances (equivalent to US$ 400 at that time).
38. It may be of interest to reproduce a joke that circulated about the CSP officers during the period of agitation against Ayub from November 1968 to March 1969. During this period, persons from nearly all walks of life took out processions and were often *lathi* charged by the police. No procession was, of course, taken out by the CSP officers. The joke was that if they took out a procession, they would not be *lathi* charged by the police but the public was most likely to *lathi* charge them. Such was the alienation and the gulf between the bureaucracy and the poeple of Pakistan.
39. Jamal Shah v Member Election Commission, PLD 1966 S.C. 1.
40. Malik Ghulam Jilani v The Government of West Pakistan, PLD 1967 S.C. 373.
41. Government of West Pakistan v Begam Shorish Kashmiri, PLD 1969 S.C. 14.
42. Abdul Baqi Baloch v The Government of Pakistan, PLD 1968 S.C. 313.
43. University of Dhaka v Zakir Ahmad, PLD 1965 S.C. 90.
44. Abdus Saboor Khan v Karachi University, PLD 1966 S.C. 536. See also Murlidar v University of Karachi, PLD 1966 S.C. 841.
45. A.K. Fazlul Quadir Chowdhry v Shah Nawaz, PLD 1966 S.C. 105.
46. Government of East Pakistan v Rowshan Bijia Shaukat, PLD 1966 S.C. 286.

16

THE FALL OF AYUB

In 1968, Ayub's government decided to celebrate a decade of progress, designed to highlight the achievements of Ayub's regime over the previous ten years and to prepare the people of Pakistan for another five-year presidency in 1969. This was to prove counterproductive and became one of the immediate causes of Ayub's fall. Nevertheless, the achievements of his government in agriculture and the industry were substantial.

Ayub's creative emphasis lay in economic development. Agriculture, along with industry and commerce, made significant strides during his tenure. A traditional subsistence agrarian economy was restructured during the Second Five-Year Plan (1960–65). The 3.4 per cent annual growth rate for agriculture over the plan period compared favourably with the annual rate of 1.3 per cent in the earlier period following independence. Foodgrain output increased 27 per cent and per capita income was up 14 per cent. The Third Five-Year Plan (1965–70) sought to sustain this momentum and aimed at five per cent growth rate. Although the Indo-Pak war and major droughts in 1965 and 1966 threatened agricultural objectives, the introduction of new wheat and rice varieties brought crop yields almost in line with projected goals. Statistically, the country was making progress, and the administration was not modest about its achievements.[1]

Private initiative was stimulated and positive payoffs created incentives for further investment. The most surprising result in the early 1960s was the proliferation of private tube wells throughout West Pakistan.[2] With the government providing major infrastructure, credit, subsidies, price stabilization, and demonstration and extension services, agricultural development was entering a revolutionary phase. The Commission on International Development listed these striking statistics:[3]

Rates of Growth in Agriculture:

West Pakistan	1949–50/1959–60	1959–60/1967–68
Wheat	1.1	4.0
All major crops	2.3	5.0
East Pakistan		
Rice	0.3	2.4
All major crops	0.5	2.6

While referring to accomplishments and identifying agricultural breakthroughs, it may be mentioned that there were shortcomings too. Though agriculture accounted for 48.2 percent of the GNP (1964–65) and carried the burden of the nation's foreign exchange earnings, yields remained among the lowest in the world. The average farm holding was a mere 6.8 acres which, coupled with the rapid increase in population (approximately 3 per cent per annum), made it difficult to be sanguine. Even with food production exceeding population increase, prospects were not propitious for the majority and, only a very small portion of Pakistan's population genuinely prospered.

Manufacturing accelerated during the Ayub decade. Liberal tax concessions were granted, and credit facilities were extended through the establishment of the Industrial Development Bank and the Pakistan Industrial Credit and Investment Corporation (PICIC). In general, the government permitted greater freedom for private investors by shifting from direct to indirect controls. As a consequence of the stress on industrialization and the apparent ease with which profits could be made, landlords, professionals, traders, civil servants, and retired military officers 'increasingly clamoured for permits that would let them in on an obviously good thing'.[4] Thus, as Papanek relates, the growing ranks of prestigious private industrial entrepreneurs was exceptionally rapid and the result of deliberate government policy.[5]

Pakistan was making significant gains in all economic sectors, but precious little advantage was filtering down to poor urban and rural people. Concentration of capital was justified on the grounds that profits were being plowed back into the economy;[6] but only twenty-four economic units controlled almost half of all private industrial assets. In addition, the resources, experience, and contacts of the leading private families made them strong contenders for ownership when semi-governmental corporations put their plants on the open market. It is estimated that over two-thirds of the assets thus sold were bought by the leading families.[7] This accumulation of wealth and power was naturally viewed with rising indignation.

Amid the squalor and wretched poverty of the Pakistani masses, a new elite now flaunted its prowess and privilege. Those who possessed wealth were perceived as having gotten it illegally, and Ayub was accused of filling his personal coffers. In contrast with the situation of the privileged few, the knowledge that industrial wages were stationary or declining, per capita income among the lowest in the world, food prices skyrocketing, and little being done to provide adequate urban housing, health, or welfare services, exacerbated the situation.

Given the unchanging misery of the multitude of poor peasants, the decade of development began to look like something less than a statistical success. When the Speaker of the National Assembly, Jabbar Khan, suggested that Ayub be given a life-presidency so that economic development might continue uninterrupted, more grist was provided for the mills of the discontented. It is not surprising to note, that the disturbances which eventually forced Ayub from office were precipitated by the government's elaborate festivities saluting the ten years of economic progress. Government propaganda could hardly be expected to placate those who did not share in the overly publicized economic revolution. As matters stood, it was to prove extremely abrasive. Celebrations spread over a four-week period in October 1968.

Estimated expenditures for the festivities are put at 150 million rupees (30 million dollars).

The seemingly interminable repetition of slogans and grandiloquent speeches were more than the dissident urban population, particularly the students, could tolerate and toward the end of the month the disturbances began. Once the students expressed their displeasure, opposition politicians began holding public meetings to condemn the government for its lavish spending. The administration answered with the imposition of section 144, making it unlawful to congregate in public places, but the politicians would not be silenced and were actually encouraged when the former Chief of the Pakistani Air Forces, Muhammad Asghar Khan, joined their growing ranks. The chorus of dissent reached a new pitch as members of the bar, journalists, teachers, doctors, and the articulate urban lower middle classes joined in.

Even Ayub realized that the publicity was not going in his favour. He remarked on 16 December 1968 to his Information Secretary: 'Is the *tamasha* about the decade of reforms still going on? They tell me it is not doing us much good'.[8]

If the campaign failed there could be two causes. The first was that actual grievances could not be removed by a public relations effort. Pangs of hunger are not assuaged by widely circulated reports of a breakthrough in agriculture.

The second cause was that those who planned and executed the campaign had no realization of the depth of public discontent, for they, like Ayub, had come to believe in the publicity in which the country was arowned. It is certain, that not until the very last moment did it occur to them that dislike for Ayub might be smouldering beneath an apparent acquiescence. When rebellion finally surged forth, their startled surprise was perfectly genuine, but much too late.

Latent dissatisfaction with Ayub's regime increased from 1966 to 1968, when demands for democratic rights in West Pakistan and autonomy for East Pakistan led to a gradual breakdown of law and order. In a matter of only five months (from November 1968 to March 1969), country-wide agitation brought down the edifice of Ayub's regime built over a period of ten years.

Student Protests and Political Agitation in West Pakistan

A major political crisis developed in West Pakistan in October 1968 when students began agitating for educational reforms, demanding the repeal of the University Ordinance, which, *inter alia*, restricted student political activity and provided for the forfeiture of the degrees of graduates accused of subversive activities, the reduction of tuition fees, and changes in the examination system. Their agitation, which began with sporadic strikes at Karachi University, was at first peaceful but became increasingly violent as it merged with a propaganda campaign against the regime led by Zulfiqar Ali Bhutto, who was making a tour of West Pakistan at the time. Bhutto had been Foreign Minister in 1963 but had disagreed with Ayub and subsequently left the government in 1966, denouncing Ayub's rule as 'a dictatorship under the label of democracy'. Bhutto consequently formed his own party, the left-wing People's

Party. When Ayub arrived for a visit to Peshawar on 9 November 1968, police had to use strong measures to disperse students demonstrating against him and at a public meeting on the following day, a young student fired two shots close to the platform on which Ayub was sitting, but no one was hit.

Bhutto was arrested under the emergency regulations on 13 November 1968 on a charge of inciting the students to violence and rioting broke out in many cities of West Pakistan following this arrest. Fourteen others were arrested at the same time, including seven members of the People's Party and five members of the left-wing National Awami Party. More clashes between police and students ensued but, by 15 November, the trouble had temporarily subsided, a number of student and opposition leaders were arrested and all colleges and schools were temporarily closed.

The anti-government agitation revived on 25 November 1968, when protests and demonstrations against the arrests of the opposition leaders took place in Karachi, Lahore, Rawalpindi, and Peshawar, organized by the Pakistan Democratic Movement (PDM), an alliance of five opposition parties, the Awami League (which was moderately socialist in outlook), the Council Muslim League (the faction of the Muslim League which had gone into opposition after the revival of political parties in 1962), the Nizam-i-Islam (the liberal Islamic party), the ultra-orthodox Jamaat-i-Islami, and the East Pakistan National Democratic Front.

Undoubtedly, Bhutto shared responsibility for the student disorders. Not only had he refused to aid the government in restoring law and order, but had urged his young supporters to continue the fight until Ayub was forced out of office. His standard reply to those wanting an end to the turbulence was 'how can I do that when they are fighting against tyranny'. It is possible that Bhutto wanted the government to arrest him. He had been unsuccessful in uniting the political factions opposing Ayub and in that volatile situation a stint in jail might have provided him with the needed leverage. What the government lost in the way of prestige, Bhutto gained.

Repression and Breakdown

By 15 November 1968, forty-five politicians had been incarcerated. Unlike 1966, those seized represented Pakistan's leftist parties, particularly People's Party and the National Awami Party (NAP). According to the government, these groups pursued policies detrimental to the unity of the country. The NAP, for example, had resurrected its old demand that West Pakistan be broken up into its pre-1955 provinces.

With many of the prominent politicians in government custody, a new personality now entered the arena. On 17 November 1968, the former Chief of the Pakistan Air Force, Air Marshall Muhammad Asghar Khan, announced that he would actively support the political opposition. Charging the Ayub regime with corruption, nepotism, graft, and administrative incompetence, the airman said he would begin a nation-wide tour 'to mobilize public opinion for the solution of problems facing the country'. Although long in retirement, even though only forty-nine years of age, Asghar was the highest ranking military officer ever to come out in opposition to Ayub. Asghar condemned the suppression of freedom of the press and speech generally and noted that the administration could remain in power only so long as it enjoyed the capacity to coerce. Obliquely, he called upon his fellow officers to recognize the plight of the country, the unpopularity of Ayub, and the need for them to remain neutral at this difficult moment. There could be no mistaking his strategy. In the circumstances, Ayub could not govern without the direct support of the military.

With Asghar in the field, student ranks were swelled by other groups previously uncommitted but sympathetic to the cause. The jailing of political leaders was a last desperate act of a quickly declining administration, but it did more to accelerate the movement than to slow it down. Rebellious youth were in no need of leadership for their objective was the destruction of the old system. What would follow did not seem to matter. With national leaders removed from the scene, the crowds became more, not less, truculent.

In the agony of a country no longer governable it is impossible to distinguish the guilty from the innocent who usually perish together. Throughout Pakistan, property was damaged and the semblance of whatever civilized order was left was rapidly deteriorating. While the PDM was considering a boycott of the 1969–70 elections in order to dramatize their dissatisfaction with the government's repressive tactics, Pakistani society appeared to be coming apart. No one led the urban crowds and certainly no one controlled them. Hence, no one could really speak for them either. The explosive fury of the people had reached a point of spontaneous destruction.

Some preferred to interpret the chaos in a favourable light; the country was passing through a catharsis; after the storm, a new beginning could be anticipated. It is possible that this view was what compelled S.M. Murshed, a former Chief Justice of the East Pakistan High Court, to enter politics. East Pakistan needed political representation in this uncertain period. Murshed reflected the pious belief that the prevailing anarchy would somehow cleanse Pakistani society. He declared that the time was at hand for the creation of 'a truly advanced society'.[9] Political amateurs like Asghar and Murshed kept opposition hopes alive but, like their predecessors, they refused to come to grips with the realities of the nation's life-style.

Ayub made some low-key attempts to put his house in order. Early in December, he offered the olive branch to the rampaging students. Major concessions were announced in an effort to redress long standing grievances. A seven-year-old ordinance which permitted the government to withdraw college degrees from students engaged in actions determined to be anti-administration was repealed. Minimum qualification grades were lowered and students in the lowest academic ranking were to given another chance to improve their standing. Ayub defended the government's prerogative to arrest anyone performing an unlawful act. This, he reiterated, meant politicians who directly or indirectly inflame public passions. In reference to the accusations that his regime was corrupt and undemocratic, he called the former 'an incurable disease' and said the latter charge was completely unfounded. 'Political parties are free to present their programme to the people. There is only one condition; these political differences should not assume the shape of lawlessness, violence, force, and terrorism'.[10]

Ayub's sense of frustration was at its peak. He was convinced that Pakistan had made considerable progress during his ten years in office. It was impossible for him to understand the depth of popular dissatisfaction. 'If in the face of evidence anyone shuts his eyes and says that he sees no progress at all; that no development has taken place; that, in fact, conditions are worsening, then there is no cure for the malady'.[11] Ayub pulled out all the stops. He made references to the external threat and how Pakistan's enemies could make capital of Pakistan's disunity, but he sounded unconvincing. Even his defiant response that he would not stand by idly and watch the efforts of the preceding ten years be destroyed sounded hollow.

In December, the demonstrations which were at first confined to West Pakistan spread to the eastern province. Precipitated by the appearance of Asghar, they were soon exploited by NAP and NDF members. Speaking in Dhaka's central mosque, Asghar called upon Ayub to resign and his audience responded with wild cries of 'Down with Ayub'. But East Pakistan politicians did not want Asghar leading their movement. Neither he nor Bhutto were acceptable substitutes for Ayub. They shared a common determination but the relationship was ephemeral. After all, Asghar was a West Pakistani and a military figure. These were both attributes that the East Pakistanis had to weigh carefully. Asghar afforded them an opportunity to gain leverage with dissident groups within the bureaucracy and the armed forces, which, was to their advantage, but too much success could undermine East Pakistan's separatist goals. Certainly, it would make it less possible for Bengalis like Nurul Amin, S.M. Murshed, and Mujib to compete for high office. Thus the decision was made to take advantage of, but not to directly support, Asghar's campaign.

Ayub was in East Pakistan at that time. He seldom ventured forth from Government House, and there were rumours that he was seriously contemplating retirement. His problem essentially revolved around the choice of a successor. Ayub trusted no one in the opposition. His contempt for the politicians was undiminished. Their activities in the previous few months confirmed his worst fears concerning their destructive propensities. The more he pondered the consequences of his retirement, the more his mind turned towards a military solution.

The violence that erupted in West Pakistan in late October 1968, continued into 1969. In mid-January, it spread and intensified. Student demonstrations resulted in numerous deaths in Dhaka and a general strike paralyzed the city. Angry young people dominated the streets; their battle cry demanded Ayub's resignation. In the tumult, newspaper offices belonging to the government's National Press Trust were burned, government installations were attacked, and the National Assembly (which was in session at the time) was surrounded. In Karachi, Lahore, Rawalpindi, Chittagong, and elsewhere, the story was the same. Crowds were running excitedly through the streets, taunting, burning, and destroying, effigies of Ayub were burned in dozens of places in both wings of the country. The fires that blazed in the battered cities and towns were often fed by gleeful students who took special delight in destroying the President's newly published autobiography, *Friends, Not Masters*.

Curfews were imposed in the major metropolitan areas in an effort to stem the rising tide of death and destruction, but to no avail. By this time, law enforcement was on the verge of collapse. The administrators and the police sensed that the government had lost control of the situation and they began retreating in a desperate effort to preserve themselves. There was failure on the part of local officials to face up to their responsibilities. Ayub dispatched his personal confidant and adviser, Fida Hasan, to East Pakistan to investigate the continuing strife. He was also charged with the futile task of trying to rally the demoralized and beleaguered civil and police services. A career officer, it was thought he could inspire the administrators and possibly help in restoring their confidence. Fida Hasan explained that the President had decided to make new concessions, the reforms were to be in keeping with the demands of the rebellious public, but the situation was beyond recall. Rebellion, not reform, was the order of the day. Disillusioned government officers found themselves sympathizing with the opposition.

Toward the end of January, part of the Pakistan Army moved into Karachi, Lahore, Peshawar, Dhaka, and Khulna, which were scenes of more serious disturbances. More newspaper offices had been damaged and foreign installations assaulted. The authorities by this time had arrested thousands of people and while no accurate figure could be given for the number of dead, the estimated toll ranged in hundreds. The mobs had turned on Ayub's supporters with the Muslim League offices being prime targets. A number of party workers were slain and others seriously wounded. Martial law was put into effect in the heavily populated regions. Not since October 1958 had the military been asked to pacify so many areas at the same time.

The Opposition Organizes Itself

With the rioting unabated, the opposition organized an ad hoc coalition called the Democratic Action Committee (DAC), comprising eight parties. The DAC quickly drafted a programme of joint demands and presented them to Ayub. Only Mujib's East Pakistan Awami League and the NAP declined to cooperate with DAC, but even these parties did not disagree with the purpose of the programme. Above all, the DAC insisted on the restitution of the federal parliamentary system and direct adult franchise. Under pressure from his advisers Ayub agreed, if reluctantly, to examine the committee's proposals. His reply, however, was indirect and came in the form of an editorial in the daily *The Pakistan Times*. In it, Ayub said he was willing to meet with the politicians but hedged where the specific proposals were concerned. Pakistan required a stable political system and to Ayub, anything less than a strong Presidency would mean anarchy, not democracy. The DAC had no need to compromise, however. They had already announced publicly that their demands were non-negotiable. Hence Ayub's apparent willingness to discuss 'constitutional issues' was interpreted as a tactic to buy time and possibly get the opposition leaders to reduce the level of hostility. But they certainly had no intention of playing into Ayub's hands and repeated their all-or-nothing proposals.

The new found semi-unity and determination of the opposition paid quick dividends. In another broadcast to the nation on 1 February Ayub stated he would put aside his 'personal pride' and meet with his political detractors on their terms. He said: 'I have on previous occasions expressed my views on amending the constitution. The constitution is not the word of God. It can be changed'. Commenting on the necessity of holding consultations with the representatives of 'responsible political parties' he added: 'We shall have no hesitation in agreeing to any settlement that is arrived at through mutual discussions'. In a letter sent to Nawabzada Nasrullah Khan, convener of the DAC, all political leaders were invited to a meeting to be held in Rawalpindi on 17 February. The tone of this letter was in sharp contrast to Ayub's earlier remarks condemning the same individuals for their anti-social and anti-state activities.

As a precondition for the talks the opposition now insisted that the state of emergency be lifted and all political leaders be released from custody. This was necessary in order to clear the atmosphere, to make it more conducive to what was expected to be hard bargaining. At this point, Ayub again pulled up short. He was convinced that many of those detained were guilty of criminal acts. In disgust he exclaimed: 'How can you release them in a hurry?' But there was also little reason to believe he could long refuse to satisfy these demands.

With the invitations extended, Ayub flew to East Pakistan for a meeting of his Muslim League Party. Seeking to restore confidence and calm the fears of the membership he said he would not remove himself from the political wars, and thus allowed himself to be re-elected for another term as president of the organization. It was a last symbolic gesture at maintaining the solidarity of his political following and it appeared to be ample proof that he had not yet decided to step down. Many Muslim Leaguers were unimpressed with Ayub's performance, however. Defection mounted with each new disturbance. In the absence of bureaucratic and military support Ayub's politicians could only think of running. The situation was now critical.

Ayub Decides to Retire

On 18 February the Ayub government capitulated and lifted the three year old state of emergency. The announcement came one hour before Bhutto was scheduled to begin a hunger strike in protest against the same regulation. With the termination of the emergency, a ludicrous act in view of the turmoil that was opening society at the seams, Bhutto and other political detainees were set free. It was hoped these leaders, especially Bhutto, would now take advantage of Ayub's invitation for a round-table conference.

But even these developments did not end the civil disobedience. The Hyderabad bazaar was set afire, demonstrators were tear-gassed and beaten in Lahore, and Karachi was a virtual no man's land. In East Pakistan two more newspapers were put to the torch and labour strife began in earnest. Business and public transportation were at a standstill in both provinces and total paralysis was beginning to set in. The period was one of uncontrolled passion. Bhutto's return to the political arena spurred his supporters to expand their activities. Thousands assembled in Larkana to celebrate their leader's freedom and vindication. Some days later, while riding in a triumphant motorcade through Karachi, Bhutto was implored not to negotiate with Ayub. When elements loyal to the government tried to disrupt the festivities a melee followed. Undaunted, Bhutto proceeded to Jinnah's tomb where he made another of his emotionally charged speeches. If Ayub thought Bhutto would sit down and discuss their differences, he was badly misinformed. The former Foreign Minister made it clear he would not accommodate his once-revered leader.

In Lahore, Bhutto's wife led one of the two large processions which again reminded the politicians that they should not be trapped into talking with Ayub. All the while Ayub remained secluded in his residence in Rawalpindi awaiting an official response from the DAC. When it finally came it was decidedly less than what he had hoped for. The DAC, with some members pushing for and others opposing the conference, was forced to compromise. It was finally agreed that only Nasrullah Khan would attend. As for Bhutto, he and six other opposition leaders declared they wanted no part of any negotiations and would boycott the talks. Bhutto was quoted as saying Ayub could not be trusted. He was playing 'a yes-and-no game, a cat-and-mouse game'. Bhutto refused to give Ayub the satisfaction of outfoxing his antagonists. Nothing was to be done which would enable Ayub to regain his respectability. Ayub was still a power to be reckoned with, and only by sustaining societal turmoil would the opposition politicians be in a position to loosen his grip. Bhutto knew exactly what he wanted. Once committed to demolishing Ayub, he could not relent. Reforms were totally unacceptable. In this he shared a common bond with the demonstrators who had already gone beyond the point of no return.

On 21 February the first significant impact of the disturbances rolled over a dazed Pakistani nation. Ayub dramatically and without prior warning spoke to his disenchanted and frightened people. In a calm voice but betraying anguish he declared: 'I shall not be a candidate in the next election. This decision is final and irrevocable. All doubts, suspicions, and misgivings must end with this announcement'.[12] But he obviously was not yet about to bow out of the picture. Again the President was attempting to buy time. Alluding to the reluctance of the opposition to accept his invitation for a round-table conference, he offered the thought that 'I shall have only one course open to me and that will be to place before you my constitutional proposals.... As required by the constitution, these proposals would then go to the National Assembly for approval'. He concluded his speech with a flourish, exclaiming 'offices and power are things transient. Pakistan will hold for ever.'

Parleys with the Opposition Fail

Ayub's decision to retire with the expiration of his term in January 1970 galvanized the opposition into a feverish activity. It was now agreed that nothing would be lost by meeting Ayub. Not only had he agreed to step aside in the forthcoming elections but he had also ordered the release of Mujib and the other defendants of the Agartala trial. The release of Mujib however added another dimension to the political confusion. While the rioting in the streets continued, the leading politicians scurried around trying to shore up their ruptured organizations. None among them commanded a national following. Each suspected the other of deviousness. Hence an acceptable replacement for Ayub would not be a simple matter.

Nasrullah Khan had minimum support in West Pakistan and none in East Bengal. Daultana, Chaudhri Mohammad Ali, and Maudoodi, though different, had something in common. Each had passed that moment in time when they could have commanded a wide following. None were acceptable to the Bengalis. While Bhutto and Asghar attracted much public attention, and perhaps were instrumental in forcing Ayub to retire, their capacity for leading a coalition government was questionable. Among the East Pakistani politicians, Bhashani was too old and certainly too radical for the more orthodox leaders. This left only Mujib, and his protestations down through the years made his name anathema in many circles. The exit of Ayub was about to leave a political vacuum which would heighten the emphasis given to vice-regal politics in Pakistan. It also explains why the military-bureaucratic nexus succeeded in perpetuating itself.

Mujib's first public address upon being released emphasized East Pakistan's desire for proportionate representation and genuine autonomy. There was no question but that most articulate East Pakistanis felt this was the ideal moment to press their major objectives. There is also little doubt that this is exactly what the rioting students and workers wanted their leaders to do. Ayub's power may have eroded but there was still no indication that West Pakistan's hold on East Pakistan had weakened. If East Pakistan tempered its demands, West Pakistan would refuse to make concessions. The Bengalis wanted one of their own to succeed Ayub. Hence the new importance was given to Mujib's possible candidacy.

The postponed round-table talks were finally held in Rawalpindi toward the end of February. After four days of deliberation, Ayub capitulated and agreed to dispense with the indirect elections (the electoral college of Basic Democrats). Direct election based on universal franchise was to be written into law and put into practice in the forthcoming campaign. Moreover, the Presidential system would be modified and the parliamentary institution resurrected. Mujib expressed dissatisfaction with the outcome of the talks, however. The question of autonomy for East Pakistan remained unanswered. Furthermore, the new federal structure failed to spell out the fact of the One Unit. Was West Pakistan to remain a single administrative province or was it to be divided into its pre-1955 components? Mujib made it clear where he stood while the West Pakistani leadership vacillated. As a result, Mujib announced he was removing his party from the DAC and made another of his celebrated withdrawals. Asghar was reasonably satisfied with the decisions taken at the meeting and sensing that the moment had arrived to become actively committed to the political struggles revealed that he would create a new political organization which would be 'truly national in character'. It would be called the Justice Party.

Bhutto had boycotted the talks. When they were terminated, he lost no time in registering his displeasure. Apparently in an effort to woo the East Pakistanis he called upon Ayub to submit his resignation and allow for the immediate formation of a national caretaker government. The caretaker government would arrange to hold the elections and also guide the elected representatives in the drafting of a new constitution. As he envisioned the new political system, East Pakistan would be given its autonomy within a federal structure. The federal structure, he noted, would also necessitate relative autonomy for the newly reconstituted provinces of Sindh, Balochistan, the North-West Frontier, and the Punjab. Bhutto's plan reserved a place for an elected President but, given the emphasis on federalism and parliamentary government, executive authority had to be shared. The Prime Minister would be responsible to the parliament but must be an East Pakistani if the President was from the West, or vice versa. The central legislature would be bicameral with each province having the same number of representatives in the upper chamber. The lower house, it was assumed, would be organized on the basis of population. Although the Bhutto plan reflected the objectives sought by East Pakistanis in the period 1947–56 it was greeted with considerable suspicion. In West Pakistan, there was apprehension.

Bhashani also absented himself from the Rawalpindi discussions. He indicated relative satisfaction but cautioned that 'political freedom is meaningless without economic independence'. The NAP still wanted an end to alliance commitments and the nationalization of all private business, both foreign and domestic.

Ayub was left with two bitter alternatives: one, to stay in office and observe his erstwhile enemies fight over the carcass of his defunct system, or, two, to resign and give the military a free hand. Only the latter option promised him a return to stable rule. It was also the only way to provide for continuity and preserve a semblance of the old order. Enervated and disillusioned, Ayub opted for the latter alternative.

The DAC was dissolved with the conclusion of the round-table conference. Nasrullah Khan, Nurul Amin, Daultana, Chaudhri Mohammad Ali, Maudoodi, Khawaja Khairuddin, and Hamidul Haq Chowdhury met with the President before returning to their homes. Representing the moderates and determined to bring peace to their ruptured country, they believed Ayub when he told them every effort would be made to hold the elections on schedule. Ayub noted that once the new parliament had been organized the remaining demands could be thrashed out. While the politicians appeared satisfied with Ayub's assurance, they were apprehensive over the intransigence shown by Mujib, Bhutto, and Bhashani. The situation in East Pakistan was deteriorating steadily and none of these politicos seemed concerned with the consequences. The moderates wanted to consolidate their newfound gains and this meant restoring the social order. If they did not concentrate on the latter they knew the military would have to, but the extremists were blinded by their success and their attitude remained defiant.

The All-Pakistan Student Action Committee meeting in Dhaka endorsed a demand for a general strike. Bhashani announced he would organize a convention of his party on 30 March. He explained that the President's declaration was insufficient and the peasants and workers of the Krishak Sramik should be afforded the opportunity to express their views concerning the future course of action. In the meantime, Mujib, who would listen to no one (including Bhutto and Asghar), presented his own draft of constitutional reforms to Ayub in which he rejected any form of incrementalism. Thus East Pakistani affairs were in sharp contract with those of West Pakistan. In the latter, turbulence had subsided appreciably. In the former, the storm continued to rage.

All of West Pakistan was the enemy of the eastern province. 'Awake Bengal, Arise Bengal' became a war cry. Ayub's collapse, it was hoped, heralded the end of West Pakistan domination. In the districts of Dinajpur, Dhaka, Mymensingh, and Bogra, the police were in retreat, and as the law enforcement agency crumbled, Ayub's supporters were exposed to the fury of the mob. A miniature civil war spread in the rural areas of these districts but the human toll can only be guessed at. Doubtless, the extent of the carnage will never be known, but no one can deny that indiscriminate killing had occurred.

On 21 March in a surprise manoeuvre, Ayub replaced General Musa with Yusuf Haroon as Governor of West Pakistan. Almost simultaneously, he selected M. N. Huda to succeed Monem Khan, who fled to the more friendly confines of Rawalpindi. Haroon, a leading industrialist, and Huda a professor of economics and East Pakistan Minister of Finance, represented different philosophies and backgrounds and in a more settled time might have made successful administrators in their respective provinces. In the given circumstances, however, neither had a chance, nor were they to be given one. Their selection at this late hour merely stands as evidence of Ayub's desire to cling to power.

East Pakistan was now in chaos. Train service in Chittagong, Khulna, Mymensingh, and Dhaka districts was suspended as a result of a continuing strike. Student delegations besieged the provincial government with demands. Gazetted and non-gazetted staff of the East Pakistan Cooperative Directorate left their posts to march in the streets. *Mujahids* organized as militia were in armed revolt, and rumours circulated that they had linked forces with the National Awami Party. Factory workers had seized their managerial staffs and in numerous instances forced them to increase their salaries. One of Pakistan's leading industrialists, G. M. Adamjee, was coerced into increasing the wages of mill workers by a total of approximately six million rupees after his executive officer had been threatened with bodily harm. As a consequence of the strike, jute production was cut almost in half and industry throughout the province was coming to a standstill.

Still another dimension of the struggle in East Pakistan lay in the conflict between the NAP and the Jamaat-i-Islami. With the future uncertain, the Jamaat feared a communist take-over in East Pakistan. Processions taken out in Kushtia, Barisal, Jessore, Chittagong, and several rural areas by the Jamaat attempted to warn the populace about the threat. 'Down with the Communists', 'Long Live Religion', and 'Make Pakistan an Islamic State' were typical slogans. The leader of the Jamaat-i-Islami, Maudoodi, was reported in an Indian newspaper as saying the 'tongues of those who speak of communism will be torn out'. In reply, Bhashani is supposed to have said: 'The house of religious fanatics would be burned'.[13] In this conflict, Mujib was cast in the role of a moderate. Though outwardly neutral, he appeared to favour the Jamaat rather than the NAP. Maudoodi was no threat and with the NAP in difficulty, Mujib's Awami League could be expected to carry the field. But Mujib had misread Ayub's intentions.

Ayub had studied the Awami Leaguer's draft of amendments to reform the constitution and was convinced that he should not be given an opportunity to gain political office. He concluded that Mujib would eventually win control of the province and with such leverage perhaps the country as well. Mujib wanted to shift the capital to East Pakistan, give East Pakistan a majority in the parliament, and establish a separate and independent budget. Denied these changes, he might well be inclined to mobilize Bengali sentiment behind a movement to create an independent state.

The indiscriminate slaughter of lower government functionaries, particularly those affiliated with the Basic Democracies and Ayub's party, was cause for exceptional concern. Ayub did not hide the fact that 'mob rule is the order of the day', and declared that he dare not hesitate in bringing it under control. Public executions began to mount and rural police officials, tax collectors, and Basic Democrats were the principal victims. The general intimidation of local officials was emphasized when student dissidents demanded the resignation of all those associated with the Basic Democracies. Nor were the killings confined to administration supporters. Attacks on authority were a convenient cover for local feuds which now escalated into violent acts of individual, premeditated murder. While the enlarging death toll was of immediate concern, the frenzied destruction of crops and property could not go unnoticed either.

The outnumbered, poorly trained and equipped police detachments were in no position to restore equilibrium. In most instances, they chose not to interfere and desertions were commonplace. Left to defend themselves from known and unknown enemies, many preferred to flee from their homes. Others whose lives were spared were brought before 'people's courts' and summarily forced to sacrifice their property. In the cities, the story was the same. Governor Monem Khan remained secluded in his residence until 19 March when he flew secretly to West Pakistan. With the government's power gone, strikes paralysed the economy, murder and arson went unchecked, prices for scarce food-stuffs soared, and administrative services were at a standstill. East Pakistan had been brought to the brink of anarchy. Even the events of 1958 were eclipsed by those now convulsing the province.

On 25 March 1969, Ayub, frustrated by the politicians, abandoned by the bureaucrats and police, and no longer commanding the loyalty of the armed forces, resigned the office he had held for ten years and five months. Army Commander-in-Chief General Agha Muhammad Yahya Khan took up the reins and immediately reimposed martial law throughout the country. As in 1958, the constitution was abrogated, the national and provincial legislatures dissolved, and all political parties banned. Members of the President's Cabinet and the two newly appointed provincial Governors ceased to hold their offices under the proclamation. Yahya announced that his first objective was the restoration of 'sanity' in the country. The air would be cleansed, authority re-established, and political stability guaranteed before making any attempt to redress societal grievances.

In the circumstances, it is remarkable how smoothly the transfer of power was accomplished. Ayub had justified his rule on the need for political stability. When it became clear he could no longer perform his task, he was compelled to pass his responsibility to those who could. From his vantage point, the politicians were in no position to govern the country. In his last address to the nation, he commented that to accept the opposition programmes would spell 'the liquidation of Pakistan'.

I have always told you that Pakistan's salvation lay in a strong centre. I accepted the parliamentary system because in this way also there was a possibility of preserving a strong centre.
But now it is being said that the country be divided into two parts. The centre should be rendered ineffective and a powerless institution. The defence services should be crippled, and the political entity of West Pakistan be done away with.

It is impossible for me to preside over the destruction of our country. It hurts me deeply to say that the situation now is no longer under the control of the Government. All government institutions have become victims of coercion, fear, and intimidation... Except for the Armed Forces there is no constitutional and effective way to meet the situation.'[14]

In a letter to Yahya, Ayub expressed his contempt for the politicians who, in his judgment, had placed their individual desire for power above the national interest:

It is most tragic that while we were well on our way to a happy and prosperous future, we were plunged into an abyss of senseless agitation. Whatever name may have been used to glorify it, time will show that this turmoil was deliberately created . . . I have exhausted all possible civil and constitutional means to resolve the present crisis. I offered to meet all those regarded as the leaders of the people. Many of them came to a conference recently but only after I had fulfilled all preconditions. Some declined to come for reasons best known to them. I asked these people to evolve an agreed formula. They failed to do so in spite of days of deliberations.[15]

Having provided the politicians what he considered ample opportunity to help him in restructuring the political system, Ayub's patience had evaporated. Humiliated by the politicians, he now took his revenge. Ayub transferred authority to his brother-in-arms and the politicians once more retired to their individual retreats. The demonstrations and rioting, which had rocked the foundations of the state for more than four months, suddenly ceased. Once more, an artificial calm covered the land.

Thus ended the decade of Ayub's rule. He left Pakistan more divided and chaotic than he found it in October 1958.

The 'Benevolent Dictator' in Retrospect

Ayub's ten years in power are regarded by many people as a period of stability in the history of Pakistan. Nobody can dispute his role as a dictator but his apologists would like to call him a 'benevolent dictator'. His assumption of power was initially welcomed by a large segment of population as the only way out of the mess created by the politicians in the first eleven years of Pakistan's existence. In retrospect, his accession to power through force appears to be totally unjustified. He left the country in a greater mess than he found it in and only aggravated the divisions within the country by adopting a dismissive attitude towards the real problems facing the polity.

It can be said to his credit that he was a modern leader who wanted to take Pakistan into an era of development. He focussed on policies that made an impact on improvement in agriculture and industry. His thinking was progressive and he had the courage to stand up to obscurantist forces in the country. Ayub's Muslim Family Laws Ordinance 1961 was indeed one of the most progressive legislation attempted in Pakistan. Other progressive measures like land and bureaucratic reforms were also greatly welcomed. Ayub pursued an independent foreign policy by moving out of the shadow of the United States and building a lasting relationship with China, and by normalizing Pakistan's relationship with the Soviet Union.

All these steps, although in the right direction, were destined to fail because his state structure was a castle built on sand and fell when put to the test in the popular discontent of 1968–69. He failed to realize that real progress could not be achieved without the participation of people, based on the principles of equality and interdependence. Under his highly centralized system, people in the provinces never had the feeling of equality nor were they bound together in a network of collective self-reliance.[16]

Ayub was an epitome of self-righteousness and self-indulgence. He lived in the delusion of being a saviour and the content, tenor, and style of his political autobiography *Friends, Not Masters* amply depict his frame of mind. He ignored the reports of constitution and franchise commissions in favour of his own ideas. Those who differed with him were, in his estimation, miscreants, trouble makers, and traitors. He, therefore, snuffed out all criticism and dissent and was ultimately surrounded by sycophants and courtiers. Ayub was so isolated and divorced from reality that when it dawned upon him, he was left wondering: 'How did it all go wrong?[17]

Ayub allowed his sons to become industrial tycoons overnight, of course under government patronage. His family became rich during the course of his regime. He refused to submit to any system of accountability and used corrupt and coercive means through the bureaucracy to get himself re-elected as President in 1965.

Even his economic policies were not as resounding a success as claimed by him and his supporters. His politics were lopsided and benefitted only those whom he favoured through government patronage of licences and permits. They led to the concentration of wealth in very few hands, some say twenty or twenty-two families, which caused widespread despondency in the populace, thus opening ways for demagogues like Bhutto and Mujib. Industrialization was concentrated towards common goods and basic industries like steel mills and chemicals were ignored. The obvious result was that industrialization was without sound foundation.

Whatever achievements had been made in the economic field were largely nullified by his own misadventure of the war with India in 1965. It was a disaster in the military, economic, and in the diplomatic sense. It exposed his poor military acumen. He misread the sentiments of Kashmiris and launched an ill-thought, half-baked, and mis-advised adventure for the liberation of Kashmir which backfired. This further widened the gulf between the two wings of the country and deepened the feelings amongst the people of East Pakistan that they had been abandoned and neglected.

Even his much trumpeted land reforms proved to be only a window dressing. These were so loose ended and full of loopholes that they did not make any real impact on land distribution in the country. The ceiling on the individual land holding was so high and flexible that the land reforms failed to accomplish their primary purpose of liquidation of feudalism and feudal structure which continue unabated to dominate the politics of Pakistan.

At the end, one is forced to conclude that his regime proved to be 'much ado about nothing'. Its facade was big but its content was little. Its claims were high sounding but its achievements were modest. Ayub impressed the world but failed to impress his own people. Ayub was so right when he said towards the end 'We managed to bluff the world but our own people called the bluff'.[18]

NOTES

1. Report of the Commission on International Development, Partners in Development, New York, Preger, 1969, pp. 307-9.
2. E. H. Clark and M. Ghafoor, 'An Analysis of Private Tubewell Costs', Research Report No. 79, Pakistan Institute of Development Economics, March 1969.
3. Report of the Commission on International Development, *supra*, note 1, p. 309.
4. Papanek Gustov, F., *Pakistan, Development, Social Goals and Private Incentives*, 1967, Harvard University Press, Cambridge, Mass. p. 71.
5. Ibid., p. 72.
6. Report of Commission for International Development, *supra*, note 1, p. 310.
7. Papanek, Gustov F., *supra*, note 4, p. 67.
8. Gauhar, Altaf, *Ayub Khan—Pakistan's First Military Ruler*. 1993, Sang-e-Meel Publications, Lahore, p. 431.
9. *The New York Times*, 29 November 1968, p. 161.
10. President Ayub's broadcast to the nation, 1 December 1968.
11. Ibid.
12. Gauhar, Altaf, *Ayub Khan—Pakistan's First Military Rule*, *supra*, note 8, p. 455.
13. *The Statesman* (Calcutta), 24 March 1969.
14. *Dawn*, 26 March 1969.
15. Ibid.
16. Gauhar, Altaf, *Ayub Khan—Pakistan's First Military Ruler*, *supra*, note 8, p. 486.
17. Ibid., p. 474.
18. Ibid., p. 490.

PART IV

THE YAHYA REGIME: MARCH 1969 TO DECEMBER 1971

17

YAHYA'S MARTIAL LAW

When Ayub stepped down as President of Pakistan on 25 March 1969 he handed over the reins of power to Army Chief General Yahya who placed the country under martial law with immediate effect. He announced the abrogation of the Constitution and the dissolution of the National Assembly and the two provincial assemblies. Members of the President's Council of Ministers and the two provincial Governors ceased to hold their offices under the proclamation. Yahya assumed the office of Chief Martial Law Administrator (CMLA) and appointed deputy army chief, air force chief, and naval chief as Deputy CMLAs. Twenty-five martial law regulations were issued on the same day listing offences, punishments, and trial procedures.

In his broadcast to the nation on 26 March 1969, Yahya called for the return of sanity and conditions conducive to Constitutional government. He promised direct elections based on universal adult franchise and a Constitution that would be framed by the elected representatives of the people. On the question of administrative shortcomings which had figured so prominently during the previous months of agitation, he took a firm stand: 'We have had enough administrative laxity and chaos and I shall see to it that this is not repeated in any form or manner'. He continued with assurances to students, labourers, and peasants. 'I am conscious of the genuine difficulties and pressing needs of various sections of our society... Let me assure you that my administration will make every endeavour to resolve these difficulties'. He concluded by saying that the martial law administration would not tolerate agitation or destruction and appealed to everyone to 'do his bit to repair the damage caused to the economy and well-being of Pakistan.'[1]

In both provinces, the declaration of martial law was received by most people without serious demur, although in Dhaka there were street demonstration. A common feeling was that at the very moment when East Pakistan was on the threshold of securing the acceptance of its just constitutional and economic claims, martial law thwarted them. The resentment thus created was in no way assuaged by arrests but it sufficed to restore and maintain order. What was to come thereafter no one ventured to guess.

On 1 April, Yahya assumed the office of President of Pakistan. On 4 April, an order was issued that, with immediate effect, photographs of Ayub in government offices were to be taken down and replaced by those of Yahya. It could thus be said that Ayub's disappearance from public life was complete. Shortly after he relinquished the office of President, it was announced that Ayub would proceed to Swat, there to spend some time with the ruler of that state[2] to whose son Ayub's daughter was married. With an escort of a single jeep, he travelled north, crossing almost unnoticed the boundary that divided Swat from Pakistan's settled areas.

In his broadcast of 26 March 1969, Yahya had denied any personal ambition and said that he wanted to create conditions conducive to the establishment of constitutional government. The sole aim of martial law, according to him, was to protect the life and property of the people and to put the administration back on track.

The proclamation of martial law, notwithstanding the abrogation of the Constitution and subject to regulations and orders made by the CMLA, allowed all laws (including Acts, ordinances, notifications) in force immediately before the abrogation of the Constitution to continue in force and all courts and tribunals were allowed to continue and exercise all their powers and jurisdiction which they exercised before the abrogation. However, no court could call in question any martial law regulation or order or any judgment of a military court. No writ or any other order could issue against the CMLA and anyone exercising power under his authority. All the judges of the Supreme Court and the High Courts, and other constitutional office holders like the Comptroller and Auditor-General, the Attorney-General, and Advocates-General and those in the service of Pakistan, were to continue in office. All other officers and authorities under the Constitution were to continue. However, this was subject to the discretion of the CMLA.[3]

Provisional Constitution Order

On 4 April 1969, a Provisional Constitution Order was promulgated by the CMLA wherein it was provided that, notwithstanding the abrogation of the Constitution, the state of Pakistan would be governed as nearly as may be possible with the last Constitution. The CMLA was to be the President of Pakistan and would perform all functions assigned to the President under the last Constitution or any other law. However, all fundamental rights, except for security of person, prohibition against slavery, and forced labour, freedom of religion, access to public places, and abolition of untouchability, were abrogated and all pending proceedings in regard to their enforcement abated.

No judgment, decree, writ, order, or process could be made or issued by any court or tribunal against the CMLA or a Deputy CMLA or any authority exercising powers or jurisdiction under them. Ordinances by the President or a Governor were not subject to time limits. No court or tribunal could call or permit to be called in question the proclamation, any order in pursuance of the proclamation, or any martial law regulation or order, or any sentence or order of special or summary military courts. Appeals to the Supreme Court could only lie against any judgment, final order, or sentence of a High Court that had awarded death sentence or transportation for life, reviewing an order of acquittal, or had convicted a person after holding trial, or had certified a case for involving substantial questions of law, or had imposed punishment for contempt of court. Subject to this, the jurisdiction of the Supreme

Court, a High Court, and all other courts and tribunals were allowed the powers and jurisdiction they had before the proclamation. The President, by order, could make such provisions, including constitutional provisions, as he deemed fit for the administration of the affairs of the state.[4] Yahya assumed the office of President with effect from 25 March 1969 through a notification dated 31 March 1969 gazetted on 4 April 1969.[5]

Action against Senior Civil Servants

The hold on power and consequential arrogance of senior civil servants increased manifold during the Ayub regime as they had been given a free hand in the administration of the country. There was thus considerable resentment against them and it was demanded at various public forums that action be taken against them. General Yahya, obviously in order to gain popularity, made a move against senior civil servants under the Martial Law Regulation No. 58[6] under which regulation, the President or a Governor could dismiss, remove, reduce in rank or prematurely retire any person in the civil service of the centre or a province, as the case may be, if in his opinion, such a person was inefficient, guilty of misconduct, or could be considered corrupt. A person could be deemed to be corrupt if he or his dependents had property or pecuniary resources which he could not account for, or had a style of living beyond his ostensible means, or had persistent reputation of being corrupt. However, a tribunal was to be appointed for giving show cause notice and opportunity of hearing to the person concerned before any final order was passed against him. Action under this regulation did not protect a government servant from any action under any other law and his ill-gotten property and wealth could also be forfeited.

Action was initiated against a large number of people, notoriously known by the number 303, and orders of dismissal, removal, and premature retirement were made against them. Action against most of them was acclaimed by the public as correct and well deserved. There were some cases of extreme corruption and misuse of powers. One M.H. Shah, Commissioner of Rawalpindi Division in 1968, had arranged such a fabulous marriage for his daughter that the entire Inter Continental Hotel in Rawalpindi was booked for a number of days. His daughter was reported to have received bridal gifts which included a number of brand new cars, refrigerators, and television sets. The resources of the officer could not justify such luxury, or even if he could, it was against all norms of decency and proper conduct which a public servant was required to observe. He was one of these notorious 303 cases. Mr Altaf Gauhar, who was very close to Ayub throughout his regime and was considered his favourite, was also removed from service though he was not known to be either corrupt or inefficient. He was indeed one of the few men reputed for their intellect in the civil service.

Curtailment of Jurisdiction of Courts

The judiciary is often the most likely candidate run afoul of martial law regimes because the orders and regulations of martial law authorities are at times challenged before the superior courts, even if there is an embargo on their jurisdiction. Such a situation led Yahya to make a presidential order removing doubts about the jurisdiction of the Supreme Court and High Courts *vis-à-vis* special or summary military courts.[7] This order reiterated what was stated in the Provisional Constitution Order about the jurisdiction of the superior courts in relation to special or summary military courts. It was clarified that any court decision given, judgment passed, writ ordered, notice or process issued or made in such case were ineffective. All matters of correctness, legality, or propriety of the exercise of any powers or jurisdiction by a military court or a martial law authority were to be referred to the CMLA whose decision thereon had to be final. All questions regarding the interpretation of any martial law regulation or martial law order had to be referred to the martial law authority issuing it and its decision could not be challenged before any court or tribunal including the High Court or the Supreme Court.

As if to cut the judiciary to size, a presidential order was passed for the judges of the superior courts, requiring them to declare their assets.[8] Every judge was to submit to the Supreme Judicial Council a statement of his properties and assets on a prescribed form. Such a statement had to include the properties and assets that stood in the name of the judge's parents, wife, or children or any other person. Upon receiving the statement of assets from a judge, the Council was to make enquiries about the correctness of the statement and propriety of acquisition of the assets declared and submit a report to the President setting out its findings and recommendations. It was under this presidential order that enquiries were held into the financial affairs of the judges by the Supreme Judicial Council and some judges were found delinquent. One of them resigned while full-fledged proceedings for misconduct were held against another who was found guilty and his removal from office was recommended.[9]

The Mir Hassan Case

What appears to have prompted the CMLA to make Jurisdiction of Courts (Removal of Doubts) Order, 1969 was the case of Mir Hassan. Malik Mir Hassan and others were summoned to stand trial before the special judge (central), Rawalpindi. They filed petitions for quashment before the West Pakistan High Court on the ground that allegations against them did not constitute an offence. While the matter was pending before a single judge, orders were passed by the martial law administrator transferring these cases from the special judge to a special military court. It was urged before the High Court that the cases could not be transferred to the special military court. The single judge requested the Chief Justice to refer the case to a larger bench. A full bench of three judges of the High Court, in one of the most courageous judgments, upheld the contention of the petitioners by giving the ruling that the order of transfer of the cases was defective and without jurisdiction.[10] It was also held that the promulgation of Martial Law Regulation No. 42 had not in any manner whittled down the power or curbed the jurisdiction of the High Court, as the provisional Constitution Order could not be subjected to martial law regulations or orders, and the jurisdiction of the superior courts of the country had been recognized by Article 6 of the Provisional Constitution Order. It was further held that as Article 2 of the 1962 Constitution still held therefore, any direction or order of any authority including a martial law authority, would be invalid if it did not have the backing of a constitutional provision. A few passages from the judgment deserve mention verbatim:

> Martial law arises from State necessity, and is justified as the common law by necessity, and by necessity alone, *quod necessit as cogit, defendit*, (what necessity forces, it justifies), where the case is a case of riot rather than a case of rebellion, as the necessity is less, so the discretion of these concerned is limited.
>
> Where the courts are sitting, there is no doubt that (i) it is a time of peace, (ii) they are sitting in their own right, and (iii) not merely as licensees of the military power. The jurisdiction of the ordinary courts, therefore, continues to vest in them and the same cannot and has not been taken away by the proclamation of martial law.
>
> The Provisional Constitution Order is in addition to the provisions of the proclamation and neither in derogation of it nor subject to it. It can, therefore, be amended not by a martial law regulation or order but by amendment of Provisional Constitution Order itself. Whether the President and Chief Martial Law Administrator, who is himself not above the law, can now at all amend it is a question which will be answered when the time comes to do so.
>
> A general and recognized rule of law is 'the jurisdiction of superior courts is not taken away except by express words or necessary implication and that such jurisdiction cannot be excluded unless there is clear language in the statute which is said to have that effect'. It is, therefore, not open to anyone to argue that such jurisdiction can be affected as if it were by a side wind, by a statute containing no express words to that effect in it. Unless, therefore, it could be shown that a martial law regulation exists which deprives the ordinary courts of jurisdiction to try offences under the ordinary law, such jurisdiction would exist in its full force.

It was no coincidence that the judgment in Mir Hassan's case and Jurisdiction of Courts (Removal of Doubts) Order 1969 came on the same date, 30 June 1969.

Constitutional Changes: Dissolution of One Unit

In a nation-wide broadcast on 28 November 1969, Yahya announced far-reaching constitutional developments, outlining the legal framework for the restoration of a federal parliamentary system; the holding of general elections on 5 October 1970 on the basis of 'one man, one vote'; the task of framing the Constitutions for the newly elected National Assembly which would have to be completed within 120 days, failing which the Assembly would be dissolved and a new National Assembly elected; the conferment of maximum autonomy on the provinces, consistent with the maintenance of a strong federation; the dissolution of the One Unit in West Pakistan and the restoration of its separate provinces; and permission for the resumption of unrestricted political activity from 1 January 1970.

In preparation for the resumption of political activities, a regulation was promulgated in December 1969 by the CMLA laying down rules and guidance for the conduct of political campaigning.[11] According to this regulation, 'no political party shall propagate opinions or act in a manner prejudicial to the ideology, integrity, or security of Pakistan'; the interests of the common man would be protected against the acquisition of political power through the use of money, force, or coercion; freedom of the Press would be fully protected; and any action which might amount to causing obstruction in the way of holding general elections would constitute an offence under the regulation.

In conformity with the reforms announced in November 1969, full-scale political activity in Pakistan, including the lifting of all restrictions on public meetings and processions, resumed from 1 January 1970, but general elections had to be postponed to December because of the disruption caused by exceptionally severe floods in East Pakistan, which had claimed about a hundred lives and rendered hundreds of thousands of people homeless.

The two decisions taken by Yahya of dispensation with the principle of parity between the two wings of the country ending One Unit in West Pakistan were hurried and unilateral. He had no mandate to make these basic constitutional changes which went to the roots of the understanding between the two wings of the country were made by one of the wings of the country, West Pakistan. The principle of parity in representation in the central legislature was the result of a protracted and exhaustive constitutional debate in the first Constituent Assembly and had been duly incorporated in both the 1956 and the 1962 Constitutions. It was a sacred pact between the two parts of the country which no General, no matter how powerful could undo. No less than a new Constituent Assembly or a Constitution Convention could change this pact. This step was certainly a factor that contributed to the country's disintegration. Had the parity in representation of the two wings been maintained, Mujib and his party would not have had an absolute majority in the new National Assembly with the unfortunate consequences that followed.

Much could be said against the creation of One Unit in West Pakistan by an unpopular Governor-General in 1955, yet this was adopted as a constitutional measure by the second Constituent Assembly[12] and was incorporated in the first 1956 Constitution of Pakistan. In fact, One Unit and parity between the two wings of Pakistan were the basic cornerstones of constitution-making and were more or less wedded to one another. West Pakistan, as one province with 46 per cent of the population and 85 per cent of the land area, and East Pakistan, with 54 per cent of the population and 15 per cent of the land area, somehow balanced one another and parity between the two provinces a natural and reasonable arrangement. It is true that the principle of parity was accepted in an overall sense; not only in representation but also in the economy, services, military, and so on, which had not been not been adhered to. The answer was not in dispensing with the principle but in taking affirmative steps to achieve true and effective parity. In any case, the fate of One Unit was sealed by a military dictator, Yahya, whose role was purely transitional. He had no mandate whatsoever to tinker with the One Unit, leave alone of dissolving it altogether.

After the announcement, Yahya made a presidential order for the dissolution of the province of West Pakistan.[13] Four provinces: namely Balochistan, the NWFP, the Punjab, and Sindh, were carved out of West Pakistan, keeping the Islamabad capital territory and the centrally administered tribal areas out of these reconstituted provinces. Pakistan Western Railway, running through all four provinces, was vested in the President. West Pakistan Water and Power Development Authority (WAPDA) continued as before. Certain corporations set up under the West Pakistan laws and administered by the West Pakistan government were not divided and were allowed to continue, with the President exercising the powers of the provincial government in relation to these corporations. However, the High Court of West Pakistan had to be split into separate High Courts, one each for the four provinces, leaving more than one province sharing a common High Court. By another presidential order, separate High Courts for the provinces of the Punjab and the NWFP and a common High Court for the provinces of Sindh and Balochistan were established.[14] A separate Public Service Commission for each province was to be established. Civil servants belonging to provincial services were to be allocated to the new provinces. The existing laws of the West Pakistan province were to continue and duly adapted by the new provinces. Territories assigned to each new reconstituted province were described in the schedule to the dissolution order.

Legal Framework Order, 1970

In a broadcast on 28 March 1970, Yahya announced that the Legal Framework Order, 1970, gazetted on 30 March, would lay down the basic principles for the future Constitution of Pakistan; that the One Unit system would end by 1 July in West Pakistan; that the National Assembly would consist of 313 members, of which 13 seats would be reserved for women; and the provincial elections would be held not later than 22 October 1970. 'The main objective that I have placed before myself', Yahya declared, 'is the peaceful transfer of power to the people.'

The Legal Framework Order, 1970, in laying down the fundamental principles which would be incorporated in the new Constitution, stated *inter alia*:[15]

1. The National Assembly would consist of 313 members, of whom 300 would be elected to fill general seats and 13 to fill seats reserved for women. East Pakistan was allocated 162 general seats and 7 women seats. The Punjab was allocated 82 general seats and 3 women seats, Sindh 27 general seats and 1 women seat, the NWFP 18 general seats and 1 women seat, and Balochistan 4 general seats and 1 women seat. The tribal areas were allocated 7 general seats.[16]

2. There would be a Provincial Assembly for each province, consisting of a number of members elected to fill general seats and a number to fill seats reserved for women. East Pakistan would again hold the largest number of seats. The seats were allocated as under:[17]

	General	Women
East Pakistan	300	10
The Punjab	180	6
Sindh	60	2
Balochistan	20	1
The NWFP	40	2

3. Polling for election to the National Assembly would commence on 5 October 1970, and for the Provincial Assemblies not later than 22 October 1970.
4. The Constitution would be so framed as to embody the following fundamental principles:
   i. Pakistan should be a federal republic to be known as the Islamic Republic of Pakistan.
   ii. (a) Islamic theology, which is the basis for the creation of Pakistan, would be preserved.
       (b) The head of state would be a Muslim.
   iii. (a) Adherence to fundamental principles of democracy would be ensured by providing direct and free periodical elections to the federal and provincial legislatures on the basis of population and adult franchise.
       (b) The fundamental rights of the citizens would be laid down and guaranteed.
       (c) The independence of the judiciary would be secured.
   iv. All powers, including legislative, administrative and financial, would be so distributed between the federal government and the provinces that the provinces would have maximum autonomy, with maximum legislative, administrative and financial powers; but the federal government would also have adequate powers, including legislative, administrative and financial powers, to discharge its responsibilities in relation to external and internal affairs and to preserve the independence and territorial integrity of the country.
   v. It would be ensured that:
       (a) people of all areas in Pakistan would be enabled to participate fully in all forms of national activities; and
       (b) within a specified period, economic and all other disparities between the provinces and between different areas in a province would be removed by the adoption of statutory and other measures.
   vi. The Constitution would contain in its preamble an affirmation that:

(a) The Muslims of Pakistan would be enabled, individually and collectively, to order their lives in accordance with the teachings of Islam as set out in the Holy Quran and *Sunnah*; and

(b) The minorities would be free to profess their religions freely, and to enjoy all rights, privileges, and protection due to them as citizens of Pakistan.

vii. The Constitution would provide that:

(a) The National Assembly, constituted under the order, would:

(1) be the first legislature of the federation for the full term if the legislature of the federation consisted of one House; and

(2) be the first Lower House of the legislature of the federation for the full term if the legislature of the federation consisted of two Houses.

(b) the provincial assemblies elected in accordance with this order should be the first legislatures of the respective provinces for the full term.

viii. The National Assembly would frame the Constitution in the form of a Bill to be called the Constitution Bill within a period of 120 days from the date of its first meeting, and on its failure to do so would stand dissolved.

5. Provisions were made regarding the summoning of the National Assembly after elections, its Speaker and Deputy Speaker, privileges of its members were also made.
6. Provisions regarding qualifications and disqualifications for being a member of the National Assembly had also been made.

Political parties contesting the forthcoming elections were required to contest the elections within the limits of the Legal Framework Order, accepting the pre-conditions laid down in it. It necessarily followed that such political parties had to make their manifestos within the four corners of this law and not in contravention of it. A political party that did not accept the broad outlines, structure, and conditions of this law had to stay out of the forthcoming elections which would be held under this law.

Mr Justice Abdus Sattar of the Supreme Court was appointed Chief Election Commissioner to prepare for and hold elections to the National and the Provincial Assemblies.

Political Alliances and Free Electioneering

As discussed above, political activity was free from 1 January 1970, and all the parties were allowed electioneering. Around twenty-four political parties or groups were in the contest. Since no one quite knew about voters' preferences, each group believed that it had a chance. Yahya tried to persuade some of the smaller groups to join together but the advice fell on deaf ears.

It was, however, discernable that Mujib in East Pakistan and Bhutto in West Pakistan would emerge as leading political leaders. Both were good orators and took full advantage of the radio and television to put forward their programmes. They were both vocal about the concentration of wealth in a few hands and in advocating the nationalization of basic industries. Unlike Mujib, Bhutto laid considerable stress upon foreign policy in his speeches. He was critical of the USA, friendly towards China, and espoused Kashmir's cause of self determination. His campaign was orderly and was conducted with skill. He promised semi-socialist reforms. Both leaders faced, in their respective wings, numerous political opponents who had small political parties, confused programmes, and were utterly divided. This gave them greater advantage over their opponents. Unfortunately, neither one of them took any interest in the elections in the other wing. Bhutto's Peoples Party did not nominate a single candidate in East Pakistan. Mujib's Awami League did nominate seven candidates (out of 138 constituencies) in West Pakistan but they were wholly on their own. This was an omen of the widening political gulf between the two wings.

Mujib's platform was his indictment of West Pakistan for everything that was wrong in East Pakistan. In his first election speech, he declared that the Bengalis had made a mistake in accepting parity in the 1956 Constitution.[18] The central government, he thundered, was a mere tool in the hands of West Pakistani exploiters who had robbed East Pakistan of her capital, her economic potential, her foreign exchange, her sons' right to job in the administrative and defence services, and of participation in the conduct of national and local affairs and in the profitable industries built up in West Pakistan on the fruits of this colonial style spoliation. He had collected around himself a band of able academicians who supplied him with carefully selected facts and figures to support his contentions. After the flood and cyclone disasters of 1970, his rhetoric sank to the level of a vitriolic smear campaign against West Pakistan. He campaigned on the basis of his Six Points which he called the charter which would secure the rights of East Pakistanis. He did not utter a word about the exploitation of Muslim Bengal by Hindu interests based in Calcutta which had done their utmost to hinder the development of the substructure of Muslim expertise and experience which could have guaranteed economic progress. Nevertheless, the ruling classes and bureaucrats in West Pakistan had their share of the blame for the misery of East Pakistan which was extremely over-populated and under-developed.

Critics of the Awami League and its political opponents found it impossible to voice their views in public because the Awami League supporters or their hired hoodlums broke up the meetings of other parties, particularly Council Muslim League and the Jamaat-i-Islami, and their workers were beaten up. All potential political rivals were silenced and terrorized by these strong-arm tactics of the Awami League who had a campaign of intimidation in full swing by the time elections were announced. When the Jamaat-i-Islami held its first election rally at the Paltan Maidan, Dhaka, it turned into a melee. Bloody clashes took place and the Jamaat blamed the Awami League for them because the battlefield was resounding with *Joi Bangla* (Long Live Bangla) slogans. Two people were killed and fifty injured, twenty-five of them seriously. The party Amir, Maulana Maudoodi, who had flown from Lahore specially to address the meeting had to return from the venue of the meeting. The Jamaat emerged from the skirmish not only as the aggrieved but also as a disabled party.[19]

It is beyond comprehension why the martial law administration remained a silent and helpless spectator in the face of this grave situation where one political party used the most reprehensible intimidatory tactics to drive out and demoralize their political opponents. Furthermore, the Six Point Programme was anathema to the principles and guidelines laid down in the Legal Framework Order, under which the elections were being held. Why did the martial law administration not take timely action to enforce its own law?

It should not be lost sight of that in his pre-election pronouncements, Mujib did not, at any occasion, demand or even hint at secession. One of his main appeals to moderate voters was that the Six Points would strengthen Pakistan by bringing the western and eastern regions to a new understanding with each other. The Awami League's campaign was an expensive one, with thousands of paid supporters and with its leaders travelling extensively throughout East Pakistan. No one quite knew where the funds came from. Mujib's campaign of 'full rights for East Pakistan and the Six Points' made enormous appeal not only to East Pakistanis but to all those who were ethnic Bengalis. He became a popular hero, a position which should have made him a responsible statesman, but he lost balance and restraint in his utterances.

There was, however, a militant element in the Awami League which believed in socialism as the solution to the poverty in East Pakistan and which argued that only in an independent East Bengal or Bangladesh would it be possible to set up a socialist order. The nucleus of this group was formed in 1962 in Dhaka University and it obtained control of the East Pakistan Students League (EPSL) which, along with the pro-Beijing East Pakistan Students Union (EPSU), played a leading role in the presidential elections of 1965 and in the agitation against Ayub in 1969. Until the emergence of Bangladesh, it posed as an integral, though radical, part of the Awami League. Other leftists gave priority to a revolutionary class struggle of the masses whose interests, they argued, were being jeopardized by promoting the secession of East Pakistan under bourgeois leadership. They eventually chose to boycott the poles but the radicals in the Awami League regarded elections as a step towards the final goal of independence and threw themselves wholeheartedly into the campaign under a bourgeois leadership. The election campaign enabled them to organize a party cadre of thousands of urban educated youth for mass contact in the villages. By 6 June 1970, their group had drafted a declaration of independence and prepared the design for a new national flag. On 12 August, six months prior to the elections, the Central Committee of the EPSL adopted a resolution for a *Swadhin Samajtantrik* Bangladesh (Independent Socialist Bangladesh).[20]

General Elections, December 1970, and their Results

The general elections held on 7 December 1970, were the first ever throughout Pakistan held on the basis of 'one man, one vote' and resulted in an overwhelming victory for Mujib's Awami League in East Pakistan and a large majority for Bhutto's Pakistan People's Party in West Pakistan. Out of a total of 291 seats, the Awami

League gained 151 and the Pakistan People's Party 81. In all, twenty-three parties put forward 1237 candidates for the 291 seats, and there were also 391 independent candidates. Over 60 candidates in East Pakistan withdrew on the eve of the elections, ostensibly as a protest against the government's handling of relief operations in the Ganges Delta after the cyclone disaster of November 1970. They were generally believed to have done in order to avoid a humiliating defeat at the hands of the Awami League.

In a broadcast before the elections on 3 December 1970, Yahya had reminded the electorate that Martial Law was still in force and that the army would ensure that order was maintained. Apart from a few incidents, however, the election campaign and the voting took place in a peaceful atmosphere and all parties, including those that were defeated, agreed that the elections were both free and fair. In nine constituencies in East Pakistan, voting had been postponed until 17 January 1971 due to the effects of the cyclone, and all of these were taken by the Awami League. In East Pakistan, only 57 per cent of the registered voters cast their votes as against 69 per cent in the Punjab, 60 per cent in Sindh, 48 per cent in the NWFP, and 40 per cent in Balochistan.[21] Of the 57 per cent of the electorate who voted in East Pakistan, the Awami League gained 75 per cent; so that in fact it owed its massive victory, which eventually gave it 167 out of 169 seats allocated to the East Pakistan in a National Assembly of 313, to only 41 per cent of the East Pakistan electorate. Why the turnout was so poor in East Pakistan is not clear, but it is conjectured that this was due to the strong-arm tactics of the hired hoodlums of the Awami League.

The results of 1970 general elections for the National Assembly held on 7 December 1970, in tabulated form, are given below:

	East Pakistan	Punjab	Sindh	NWFP	Balochistan	Total
Awami League	151 (153)	- (2)	- (2)	- (2)	- (1)	151 (160)
Pakistan People's Party	- (-)	62 (77)	18 (25)	1 (16)	- (1)	81 (119)
Council Muslim League	- (50)	7 (50)	- (12)	- (5)	- (2)	7 (119)
Ahle Sunnat	- (-)	4 (39)	3 (8)	- (-)	- (1)	7 (48)
Jamaat-i-Islami	- (69)	1 (43)	2 (19)	1 (15)	- (2)	4 (148)
Qayyum Muslim League	- (65)	1 (34)	1 (12)	7 (17)	- (4)	9 (132)
Convention Muslim League	- (93)	2 (24)	- (6)	- (1)	- (-)	2 (124)
Pakistan Democratic Party	1 (81)	- (21)	- (3)	- (2)	- (1)	1 (108)
National Awami Party (Wali Group)	- (39)	- (-)	- (6)	3 (16)	3 (3)	6 (64)
Jamiatul Ulema-i-Pakistan (Hazarvi Group)	- (13)	- (47)	- (20)	6 (19)	1 (4)	7 (103)
Independents	1 (109)	5 (114)	3 (46)	7 (45)	- (5)	16 (319)
	153	82	27	25	4	291

Note: The figures in parentheses indicate the number of candidates put up by the party.

Mujib thanked the people, his party workers, students, labourers, and other admirers who went to see him. The poll results were a clear verdict in favour of his party's programme, as he pointed out.[22] Bhutto said that his party would give all help in framing a Constitution which would not concentrate wealth in the hands of twenty-two families alone but would guarantee fundamental basic rights for the twelve crore people of the country.[23]

Elections to the provincial assemblies were held on 17 December 1970. As expected, Mujib's Awami League swept the polls in East Pakistan. It bagged 266 of the 279 contested seats. Elections to 21 remaining seats were scheduled for 17 January 1971 due to the cyclone.[24] These seats were also won later on by the Awami League. In the Punjab, the People's Party (PPP) won 113 seats out of 180; the remainder divided between no fewer than eight splinter groups, with 28 independents. In Sindh, the PPP had a bare majority, 32 seats out of 60; again the remaining seats fell to splinter groups. In the NWFP, the PPP could secure only 3 out of 40 seats; the largest group, the Wali Khan section of the National Awami Party (NAP) won 12 seats, followed closely by the Qayyum Muslim League with 10 seats. In Balochistan, the Wali Khan section of the NAP led with 8 seats out of 20, splinter groups and independents shared the remainder.[25] A high proportion of the newly-elected members, both of the National and the provincial assemblies entered politics for the first time, and it was notable that unknown candidates bearing party endorsements of the PPP defeated the 'Old Guard', men who had taken part in politics from the time that Pakistan came into existence. It was clear that in the western wing, as in the eastern wing, electors were seeking a 'new deal'.

NOTES

1. *Dawn*, 27 March 1969.
2. Swat was later merged into NWFP and became a district of the Malakand Division.
3. Proclamation of Martial Law, Paragraph 5. PLD 1969 Central Statutes 42.
4. Provisional Constitution Order. PLD 1969 Central Statutes 41.
5. PLD 1969 Central Statutes 41.
6. Removal from Service (Special Provisions) Regulation, 1969. PLD 1970 Central Statutes 170.
7. Jurisdiction of Courts (Removal of Doubts) Order, 1969. President's Order 3 of 1969. PLD 1969 Central Statutes 119.
8. Judges (Declaration of Assets) Order, 1969. President's Order 4 of 1969. PLD 1969 Central Statutes 120.
9. Mr Justice Fazle Ghani Khan of Lahore High Court resigned and started his law practice in Karachi. Mr Justice Shaukat Ali was held guilty of misconduct and was removed on the recommendation of the Council. President v Justice Shaukat Ali, PLD 1971 S.C. 585.
10. Mir Hassan v The State. PLD 1969 Lahore 786.
11. Political Activities Regulation, Martial Law Regulation No. 60, PLD 1970 Central Statutes 173.
12. Establishment of West Pakistan Act, 1955. PLD 1955 Central Acts and Notifications 273.
13. Province of West Pakistan (Dissolution) Order, 1970. President's Order 1 of 1970. PLD 1970 Central Statutes 218.
14. High Courts (Establishment) Order, 1970. President's Order 8 of 1970. PLD 1970 Central Statutes 250.

15. Legal Framework Order, 1970. President's Order No. 2 of 1970. PLD 1970 Central Statutes 229.
16. Ibid., Schedule I.
17. Ibid., Schedule II.
18. *The Pakistan Observer*, Dhaka, 12 January 1970.
19. Salik, Siddique, *Witness to Surrender*, 1977, Oxford University Press, Karachi, p. 5.
20. Zaheer, Hassan, *The Separation of East Pakistan—The Rise and Realization of Bengali Muslim Nationalism*, 1994. Oxford University Press, Karachi, p. 126. He has quoted Lawrence Lifschultz, *Bangladesh: The Unfinished Revolution* (London: Zed Press, 1979), 27-9.
21. Williams, L.F. Rushbrook, *The East Pakistan Tragedy*, 1972, Tom Stacey Ltd., London, p. 44.
22. *Dawn*, 9 December 1970.
23. Ibid.
24. *Dawn*, 19 December 1970.
25. Ibid.

18

CONSTITUTIONAL BREAKDOWN

In the new circumstances created by the results of the elections, the danger of a confrontation between the Eastern and the Western wings in the National Assembly was obvious, and it was one which all patriotic Pakistanis wished to avoid. In East Pakistan, the Awami League and its leader were all-powerful. They commanded a majority in the National Assembly, apart from any support that they might expect to receive from small groups opposed to the PPP. How did they propose to use their newly-acquired power? There were some hopeful signs. Mujib had won the elections on a platform where the main plank was maximum provincial autonomy. He had repeatedly declared that this autonomy, would strengthen, not weaken, the country as a whole. He had also stated that his Six Points were negotiable. It was known that Bhutto also favoured maximum provincial autonomy and was ready to discuss the Six Points. Now that Mujib was assured the prime ministership of Pakistan, along with control over the central government, would his intention to reduce the position of the Centre to the barest minimum, remain as strong as ever? Like all other political leaders, he had accepted the Legal Framework Order as the basis of the elections and this laid down clearly that the central government must enjoy the powers necessary for the preservation of the integrity of Pakistan.

Yahya had high hopes that an agreement between the main parties over the general principles under which the National Assembly would operate could be achieved and for this purpose he strongly advised the respective party leaders to use the interval between the elections and the meeting of the Assembly for preliminary discussions which could result in a working understanding between them.[1] In order to give time for this, he thought it wiser to allow a couple of months before the session opened. He was steering a middle course which he hoped would strike everyone as fair. Mujib was pressing for an early meeting, while Bhutto and most of the West wing political leaders thought that more time should be allowed for preliminary consultations and exchange of views if the National Assembly was not to find itself stultified by sterile debates on points which ought to have been agreed before it met upon. Mujib began the New Year with a speech in Dhaka on 3 January in which he showed not the slightest spirit of accommodation. Indeed, all Awami League members of the National and provincial assemblies were required to take an oath that they would support the party programme for provincial autonomy, although the terms of the oath did not actually mention the Six Points.[2]

The post-election scene witnessed the accentuation of nationalist fervour in East Pakistan. Election results were seen not as the success of a single party but as the victory of Bengali nationalism. Bhashani, who seemed to have been bypassed by the overwhelming success of the Awami League and the segmentation of NAP, raised the demand for a sovereign independent East Pakistan in January 1971. He regarded the Awami League victory as the people's verdict for a separate East Pakistan and threatened to start a mass movement if the Awami League resiled from it.[3]

The centre of political interest shifted to Dhaka, where the western party leaders were meeting Mujib and his colleagues. In the course of these exchanges, Yahya acclaimed Mujib as the future prime minister of Pakistan, a title which the Awami League leader did not disavow.[4]

In his meetings with Mujib in January 1971, Yahya tried to persuade him to meet Bhutto who had won a majority of seats in the National Assembly in West Pakistan. Mujib refused to do so saying that just as other West Pakistani leaders had come to see him so could Bhutto. Yahya advised Mujib to modify his Six Point Programme so that he could carry the West Pakistani leaders with him. Mujib asked Yahya to call the meeting of the National Assembly on 15 February and claimed that he would not only obtain a simple majority but a two-thirds majority. He, promised that he would not ignore the interests of West Pakistan and that he would seek the co-operation of the Peoples' Party as well as the other parties of West Pakistan. These meetings did not resolve the differences. Mujib was non-committal about any compromise on the Six Points and only talked in general terms, and insisted on calling the Assembly session.[5]

The Awami League, flushed by its electoral triumph, was in a militant mood. Whether this mood affected the leader or whether it was inspired by him, remains uncertain. What is on record is that the tone and temper of his public pronouncements over the six points completely changed. Instead of repeating that they were negotiable, now that the interests of East Pakistan were adequately protected by the dominant position which the Awami League had won in the National Assembly, he asserted that each point must be embodied in the new Constitution, and these who did not agree with him could do what they liked.[6] Instead of repeating that he stood not for secession but for regional autonomy, he said that the majority of Pakistanis living as they did in '*Bangladesh*' could not 'secede', but that they had the right to autonomy and economic and social freedom. There was no more talk about strengthening and preserving the state's unity.

Yahya also held discussions with Bhutto in Larkana who cleverly tried to drag the army into the situation as the third party in addition to the Awami League and the Peoples' Party. Bhutto raised his concern about the implication of the six points. He indicated the possibility of an agreement if Mujib compromised on two points, foreign trade and foreign aid as well as taxation. As they stood, he thought the Six Points were bound to lead to secession. Bhutto's articulation of the dangers arising from them to the country and to army must have created a deep impression on the Generals. He gave an impression to Yahya that the army was with him on this issue. This meeting between Bhutto and Yahya and his Generals, particularly in the hometown of Bhutto in a relaxed atmosphere, must have created suspicions in Bengali minds of the army and Bhutto trying to deprive East Pakistanis of their electoral victory.

Bhutto and his delegation did visit Dhaka at the end of January and held a series of meetings with Mujib. He conveyed to Mujib that the general impression of the people of West Pakistan was that the Six Points spelt the end of Pakistan. He offered to go as far as possible to meet the essential demands. On the date of summoning the meeting of the Assembly, the two of them differed. Mujib wanted the earliest possible session of the National Assembly, not later than 15 February, Bhutto wanted more time. On his return, Bhutto informed Yahya that the Awami League had already prepared its draft of the Constitution which it would no doubt get passed by the Assembly. He assumed, without sufficient evidence, that the Awami League sought to impose constitutional obligations of intolerable financial burdens on the West Pakistan provinces to compensate East Pakistan for past inequalities. He advised Yahya not to call the Assembly session until he had made one more attempt to negotiate a settlement with Mujib.[7]

Postponement of the National Assembly Session

Mujib grew more and more adamant over the Six Points, and it became painfully clear that he had lost interest in anything but the future of East Pakistan. He consistently referred to the East Wing as 'Bangladesh' and refused to visit West Pakistan or to meet Yahya for further talks, sending him a message to the effect that if the Six Points were not accepted in their entirety, 'rivers of blood will flow'. Meanwhile, the political leaders of the western wing who had been elected to the National Assembly became more and more uneasy at the uncompromising attitude of Mujib. Yahya finally decided on 13 February to summon the National Assembly to meet in Dhaka on 3 March to which Bhutto announced on 15 February that the PPP would not attend the National Assembly session[8] if Awami League was not flexible. He demanded an adjustment on the Six Points. Mujib again reiterated that the Constitution would be based on the Six Points because such a mandate was given to him by the people.[9] Wali Khan announced the participation of NAP in the National Assembly session because, he said, constitution-making should be above party politics. Mujib made some conciliatory overtures and said that although there was to be no adjustment, some 'arrangement' was possible. He said that the Awami League would not impose the Six Points on the West wing and additional powers to the centre could be given if the units so desired.[10] Awami League prepared a draft Constitution incorporating the Six Points which was adopted by the parliamentary committee of the Awami League on 27 February 1971. The West wing was left to choose its own kind of autonomy.[11] The salient features of the draft constitutional principles were as under:[12]

i. The country would be named the Federal Republic of Pakistan.
ii. East Pakistan would be named Bangladesh and NWFP would be called Pakhtoonistan.
iii. There would be two seats of federal government, a winter seat in Dhaka and a summer seat in Islamabad.

iv. War or emergency would not be declared without the consent of the National Assembly.
v. Either the army headquarters would be in Bangladesh or the Navy and the Air Force.
vi. Foreign Affairs, Defence, and Currency would be central subjects.
vii. Two Reserve Banks for the two wings would be provided.
viii. Foreign loans would be paid by the provinces according to the proportion of utilization.
ix. The centre would have no taxation power.
x. The federal government would raise revenues through levy on the units on the basis of per capita income, expenditure, and according to the following percentage:

Bangladesh	..	27
Punjab	..	37
Sindh	..	21
Balochistan	..	8
Pakhtoonistan	..	7

After a meeting between Yahya and Bhutto, the latter turned bellicose. Bhutto demanded a postponement of the session of the National Assembly. He threatened a mass movement from 'Khyber to Karachi' and called for a general strike on 2 March. He threatened to take action against those members of the National Assembly (not from the PPP) from West Pakistan who went to attend the session of National Assembly in Dhaka. He said that if any member of his party attended the session, would liquidate him.[13] The actual words he is said to have used were: 'If any member of his party attended the session of National Assembly in Dhaka, his legs will be broken'. These words were ominous and set the stage for the breakup of Pakistan. In response to this demand, Yahya made the fateful mistake on 1 March 1971, of postponing the National Assembly session giving more time to the parties to reach a consensus on Constitution-making. Mujib deplored the postponement and called for a strike throughout East Pakistan on 3 March 1971.[14]

The Awami League in Revolt

The announcement of the postponement of the National Assembly session was received in East Pakistan with fierce resentment. The conclusions formed in East Pakistan were (a) the army was determined to frustrate all effective moves towards a democratic transfer of power, and (b) there was collusion between Yahya and Bhutto.[15] In West Pakistan, public reactions were mainly gloomy. It was said openly that each time the military interfered in politics, the result was worse.

On 1 March, Awami League militants looted and burned many shops and houses and raided the Narayanganj Rifle Club for arms. Almost all the students of Dhaka University, except committed militants, went home. Iqbal Hall and Jagannath Hall were used as centres from which armed gangs went out to collect arms, vehicles, and money. On 2 March, two firearms shops were looted and taken to an arsenal in Jagannath Hall. Practice firing was heard all day in the University grounds. On the previous night, there had been looting and arson. Encouraged by the fact that the troops were confined to the barracks on the orders of the Governor, mobs armed with firearms, staves, and iron bars raided business premises in Jinnah Avenue and Baitul Mukarram. The Shalimar Hotel and Gulistan Cinema were attacked and set on fire. Police officers reported that they could no longer trust their rank and file to deal with the mobs and asked for the assistance of the military. This was granted, and a curfew was imposed. An army unit was attacked at Sadarghat and six rioters were killed in the firing. There was extensive defiance of the curfew, and inspite of the efforts of the military, arson and looting continued throughout the night. On 3 March, mob violence spread to other parts of Dhaka, particularly Islampur, Patnakhali Bazar, and Nawabpur. Shops, private houses belonging to non-supporters of the Awami League, and business premises were looted and set on fire. In the disturbances, five people were killed and sixty-two wounded. Mujib announced the launching of a campaign of complete civil disobedience and ordered the closing of schools and colleges so that all students, except hard-core militants who had not yet left for home, proceeded to do so. Violent intimidation continued against all these who were not active supporters of the Awami League. Radio and TV stations in Dhaka were compelled to play the new national anthem of 'Bangladesh'. Raiding of arms' shops and looting continued to take place. On 5 March, telephone and telegraph employees ceased work and ordinary communications between East Pakistan and the outside world and between Dhaka and other parts of East Pakistan came to an end. On the night of 5 and 6 March, militant students tried to set fire to the British Council premises but troops arrived in time to drive them off. On 6 March, there was a jail-break of 341 prisoners from Central Prison. During the escape, seven prisoners were killed when the wardens opened fire. A sergeant and six wardens were wounded. The escaped prisoners joined Awami Leaguers and activist students and paraded through the streets of Dhaka shouting anti-Pakistan slogans. The Government Science Laboratory in Dhaka was seized and all available explosive chemicals were taken, but a raid on the Polytechnic was foiled when troops arrived to disperse the mob.

Whenever the troops went into action, a minimum of force was used. They did not interfere with peaceful processions or political meetings but only with mobs engaged in looting and arson. The fact is that there were far too few of them to maintain order effectively in an enormous city like Dhaka with the virtual breakdown of the machinery of civil government because of the campaign of non-co-operation. The situation, both in the capital and in many other parts of East Pakistan, became completely chaotic. It was widely believed that nothing could break the hold of Mujib and the Awami League over the country and that the army, scattered as it was in small groups except for larger bodies stationed clear of the Indian frontier, would be helpless in the face of the Awami League's determination to take full control. Moreover, as was pointed out by responsible foreign correspondents, the army's Eastern Command consisted of only one division of fifteen battalions of which nine were from West Pakistan. The remaining six were sections of the East Bengal Regiment who were almost exclusively Bengali by race in rank and file. Also, in the commissioned ranks, except for a sprinkling of West Pakistanis mostly in junior positions, the majority were Bengalis. There were 3000 men in the East Bengal Regimental Centre in Chittagong alone; while the East Pakistan Rifles numbered 14,000 fully armed and trained men. In addition, the para-military force of Ansars who guarded the frontier in pursuance of the long-standing policy of keeping the regulars well back to minimize border clashes, numbered about 100,000. Among these bodies of men, too, Mujib's propaganda had made great headway and in addition to their own equipment of mortars, recoilless rifles, heavy and light machine guns, and full transport, there was a steady supply of rifles, ammunition, and plastic explosives from across the Indian border, the Indian and foreign markings of which spoke for themselves.

By 5 March, Mujib was effectively running a parallel government and life in the province was ordered in compliance with his directives.[16] So much so, that the banks opened and operated according to Mujib's diretives, as did the markets. All activity in East Pakistan was organized in accordance with Mujib's orders. He was firmly in the saddle and the army had been withdrawn to the barracks.

Mujib must thus have felt completely secure even if it came to a clash of arms, with the support of the police, most of whom were with him. So Mujib could count on some 176,000 armed Bengalis as against only 10,000 soldiers from West Pakistan. Moreover with the ban on over-flying Mujib was confident that, there would be no reinforcements coming from West Pakistan. Accordingly on 7 March he announced plans for setting up a parallel government of his own. These included the complete closure of all educational institutions, government offices and courts; the stoppage of any remittances to West Pakistan; and the organization of revolutionary councils in every union, *mohalla*, *thana*, sub-division and district who were to take over the administration under the direction of local Awami League units. Later, the original directive to pay no taxes to the western wing was modified to ensure that taxes were collected but paid into two private banks. Detailed directives were issued to the Press and to the radio and TV stations ensuring that nothing went out which did not conform to the liking of the Awami League. In the days that followed, the Awami League and their supporters, reinforced by the lawless elements which readily take advantage of such situations, raged unchecked through the streets of Dhaka, terrorizing and molesting the persons and properties of non-Bengalis. Many peaceful citizens, including those in high positions, left in fear of their lives and of the lives of their families. These riots were not confined to Dhaka. In many places in East Pakistan, frightful atrocities were committed by Awami League ruffians on non-Bengalis and on those who were not supporters of Mujib. There seems to have been little trace of religious intolerance about the killings, beatings, and burnings. The criterion was political, and Muslims suffered as much as Hindus. The Particularly serious rioting took place in Chittagong on 3 March and in Khulna on 5 March resulting in hundreds of casualties. To add to the growing anarchy, the East Bengal Regiment, the East Pakistan Rifles, and the bulk of the para-military frontier security guards, far from using their strength to restore law and order, expressed their sympathy with the local Awami League.[17]

Nothing seemed to cool down or reverse the situation in East Pakistan. Even the announcement by Yahya Khan on 6 March to hold the session of National Assembly on 25 March 1971, went unheeded by East Pakistan.[18] It was too little too late. The situation had already gone out of everybody's hand, even perhaps, out of Mujib's hands. The extremists in the Awami League were having a field day. It must go to the credit of Mujib that contrary to expectations, he did not make a unilateral declaration of independence and refused to unfurl the national flag of independent 'Bangladesh' when he addressed a large public meeting at the Race Course Maidan.[19] He blamed Bhutto for ending the dialogue. He stated that Awami League would attend the National Assembly session if his demands were accepted, which were:

(a) Immediate withdrawal of martial law.
(b) Transfer of power to the elected representatives of the people.
(c) Immediate withdrawal of all military personnel to the barracks.
(d) Immediate cessation of the military build up and the heavy inflow of military personnel from the western wing.
(e) Immediate cessation of firing upon civilians.
(f) Non-interference by the military authorities in the different branches of government functioning in Bangladesh and directions from the Centre to desist from victimization of government officers and employees.
(g) Maintenance of law and order to be left exclusively to the police and the Bengal EPR assisted, wherever necessary, by Awami League volunteers.[20]

It appears that Mujib's strategy was to put forward demands which, would either make the central government lose face by yielding to them, or to take the blame for forcing him into unilateral action. He continued to rule East Pakistan by decrees that he issued from time to time.

Hijacking of an Indian Aircraft

Another very important incident that took place around this time, was the hijacking of an Indian aircraft. Seen in the perspective of the political situation at the time, this incident clearly points to a conspiracy to break up Pakistan.

On 30 January, a Fokker aircraft of the Indian Airlines Corporation made an unscheduled landing at Lahore Airport. Enquiries revealed that two of the passengers, claiming to be 'Kashmiri Freedom Fighters', had hijacked the plane as a protest against the externment of opposition leaders by the Indian-supported Kashmir government prior to the Indian general elections. Feelings against the Indian government were already running strong in the Punjab, and when news of the hijacking became known, there was great public enthusiasm. The Pakistan government was in an awkward situation. Under international convention, the hijackers had to be arrested, but they refused to leave the plane. With great difficulty, they were persuaded to release the passengers and the crew, who were taken to the best hotel in Lahore, provided with clothing and other necessities, and given full VIP treatment before being taken to the Indian frontier. Several of them later thanked the Pakistan authorities for the care and consideration which had been shown to them. The Indian High Commission was informed and assured of the efforts of the Pakistan government to return the plane safely. The High Commission was also invited to send a representative to the spot if it so wished. Meanwhile, the two hijackers were acclaimed as popular heroes. They addressed a press conference, one of them remained on the plane and asked for political asylum. Since the Pakistan government has consistently refused to acknowledge India's occupation of part of Kashmir holding that Kashmiris are not Indian nationals, the request was granted.

This action, and the reasons for taking it, hit India on a sensitive spot. The reaction by the Indian press and public opinion was immediate and bitter. Pakistan was accused of engineering the incident. Threats were made to the lives of the Pakistani High Commissioner and his staff in New Delhi, and there were ugly mob demonstrations against Pakistan. The excitement in India increased when, in the middle of the efforts of the Pakistan authorities to persuade the two hijackers to leave the plane so that it could be returned to India, it blew up. The Indian government announced that it held Pakistan responsible for the blowing up of the plane, neglecting the contention that the hijackers were neither Indian nor Pakistan nationals and thus not Pakistan's responsibility, and demanded compensation for the plane. Without giving the Pakistan government time to reply, India unilaterally suspended all flights by Pakistani aircrafts, civil and military, across Indian territory between East and West Pakistan. The Pakistan government protested strongly at what it regarded as a serious breach of international convention, and declined to give up the two hijackers to a country to which, in their view, the two men did not belong. They offered to settle the incident in a reasonable spirit of compromise. India did not agree. Hostile demonstrations against Pakistani nationals persisted, and the ban on over-flying was not lifted. Anti-Muslim riots broke out in Allahabad and Baroda, and relations between the two countries became very strained.

Nothing could have suited Mujib better than the imposition of this embargo upon the communication line between West and East Pakistan when the Awami League was working for a drastic reduction in the power of the central government. The journey between Karachi and Dhaka, customarily taking less than three hours, stretched to nearly seven hours, making it one of the longest non-stop flights anywhere in the world. It was well within the capacity of the long range high-ceiling Boeings which PIA possessed, but the strain upon both cockpit and cabin crews was enormous.

Public opinion in West Pakistan began to speculate whether the hijacking of the plane and the ban on over-flying which followed were as 'spontaneous' as they seemed. Weight was lent to these rumours by the publication of a letter from Sheikh Abdullah, one of the externals and perhaps the best known of all Kashmiri leaders, to the Indian humanist Mr Jaya Prakash Narayan, published by the *Indian Express* of New Delhi on 15 February 1971. Sheikh Abdullah roundly accused the principal hijacker, Hashim, of being an Indian agent whose plan to seize the plane and create an international incident was known to the authorities in Srinagar and New Delhi. In order to ascertain if these statements were correct, Yahya appointed a Judicial Enquiry Commission under Mr Justice Noorul Arfin of the High Court of Sindh and Balochistan. The enquiry took considerable time as it had to examine the reports and statements of the hijackers and of a number of witnesses. Its report was presented on 15 April 1971, after taking all the available evidence. The Commission concluded that the Pakistani authorities had done everything in their power to release the crew and passengers of the aircraft and to secure the safety of the aircraft in order to return it to India, but that when the hijackers realized that this would isolate them completely they blew up the aircraft. The Commission found Hashim, the principal hijacker, in close contact with, and under the supervision of, Indian intelligence agencies, without whose co-operation he could not have entered the aircraft. Moreover, the revolver and the hand grenade carried by the hijackers were later found to be dummies, no doubt to ensure that the lives of the Indian crew and passengers were never in any real danger. The commission concluded that the incident had been engineered by India with the objective of providing a pretext to ban flights over Indian territory, disrupting communications between the eastern and the western wings at a time when parleys between the Awami League and the Pakistan People's Party were being held in Dhaka.[21]

Bhutto did not help matters. In a show of bravado, he went to visit the hijackers in the plane and photographed himself with them. He extended unnecessary encouragement and legitimacy to people of suspect origin and doubtful motivation.

Negotiations for Political Settlement

Despite the complete breakup of law and order in East Pakistan, army units were ordered to use minimum force, and these orders were so strictly obeyed that Mujib and his followers thought that the army was powerless. The second of his four-point demand had long been complied with in the sense that the military had never attempted to occupy Dhaka and other cities. In fact they only emerged from their barracks when a serious outbreak of arson and looting had to be checked. For the rest of the time, they were not seen in the streets at all. Yahya was determined to arrange a meeting of the National Assembly and did not want to give Mujib any pretext to claim that political negotiations were being conducted under the threat of force.

Yahya made some efforts to resolve the impasse caused by Mujib's 'take it or leave it' attitude. Since Mujib would not come to see him, he went to Dhaka on 15 March to see him. There followed some ten days of complicated discussions in which Yahya tried to prevent a breach between the eastern and western political leaders. On 17 March, his advisers met an Awami League team and drafted a regulation to set up a Council of Ministers drawn from the elected members to advise the Governor of each province and to withdraw martial law gradually. Further, the third of Mujib's four points was met by Yahya's offer to set up a commission to enquire into the circumstances in which the army acted in aid of civil power. This was to be headed by a judge of the High Court of East Pakistan to be selected by the Chief Justice. Its members were to consist of men drawn from the civil service, the police, the army, and the East Pakistan Rifles. The next day, 18 March, Mujib rejected the commission on the grounds that the appointment would be made under a martial law order and the report would be made to the martial law authorities. In view of the fact that the country had been under martial law since 1969, this objection appeared to lack substance, and established Mujib's reluctance to co-operate. His next step, on 19 March, was to insist that the draft martial law regulation framed on 17 March should invest the National and Provincial Assemblies with legislative powers, accompanied by representative government in both areas, and that there should be complete withdrawal of martial law.

Yahya and his advisers clung to the argument that if the proclamation of martial law on 25 March 1969 was revoked, there would be no validity to the central and provincial governments. Awami League representatives urged that the issues were really political, not legal, and should be resolved in a political manner. Yahya felt uneasy about this, but agreed that his advisers should draft another martial law regulation in an endeavour to meet the Awami League's wishes. This draft regulation provided for the setting up of central and provincial Cabinets, for investing the National and Provincial Assemblies with the powers that they enjoyed under the dormant 1962 Constitution; abolishing martial law administrators and military courts, but retaining the presidential function of CMLA to avoid the risk of a legal vacuum. Yahya was hopeful that progress was being made, and asked three West Pakistan leaders representing the Council Muslim League and the Jamiat-i-Ulema-i-Islam to meet him in Dhaka. Even very serious provocations by the Awami League rowdies in Chittagong and Joudevpur, where the normal unloading of army supplies from a ship was obstructed in one case and a convoy was attacked in the other, did not interrupt the negotiations, although it was proof of the contemptuous attitude which Mujib's followers had against the army and all constituted authority.[22]

When Yahya met Mujib and his principal lieutenants on 20 March, he made it clear that his agreement to hand over power depended upon its acceptance by all political leaders. He further stated that the legal validity of the proposed proclamation would have to be examined by experts. Yahya's advisers were doubtful about this point, but the Awami League representatives promised to produce their own legal expert, Mr A.K. Brohi, in support of their views. This fundamental question was set aside for the moment; and a set of objectives was drawn up for examination by both sides. The first objective was the lifting of martial law; the second was the setting up of central and provincial Cabinets; the third, investing of central and Provincial Assemblies with legislative powers; the fourth that East Pakistan, in view of its geographical situation, should enjoy a greater degree of provincial autonomy than other provinces; the fifth, that further discussions should take place about the exact way in which all these objectives could be achieved. It was pointed out to Mujib that until the National Assembly, to be summoned on 25 March, ratified the proclamation for achieving them, martial law had to continue. He did not agree. But in order not to hold matters up, a number of salient points which the proposed proclamation would have to cover were drawn up. On 21 March, an ominous note was introduced into the discussions. In an unscheduled meeting with Yahya, Mujib stated that he no longer wanted the setting up of a central Cabinet. At this juncture, Bhutto reached Dhaka at Yahya's invitation. In spite of Mujib's publicly announced refusal to meet the PPP leader, Yahya persuaded the two men to hold a joint meeting with him on 22 March. At this meeting, according to the official record, another unexpected development occurred; Mujib requested the withdrawal of the presidential order summoning the National Assembly on 25 March. He refused a suggestion that it should be summoned on 2 April to give legal cover to the proposed proclamation. It seemed an appropriate sequel to his attitude that on that same evening the Central Students' Action Committee should announce that 23 March customarily celebrated as Pakistan Day throughout the country, would in East Pakistan be observed as 'Resistance Day'.[23]

The amended draft proclamation had been handed over to Bhutto and to Tajuddin Ahmad of the Awami League for discussion. The PPP held that after martial law was lifted and before it was ratified by the National Assembly, the proposed proclamation should either be endorsed by the National Assembly or, if published, it should not take effect until after such endorsement. As an alternative, they thought Yahya might continue as CMLA to provide legal cover until the National Assembly acted so. They further suggested that a clause should be added providing that no law or Constitution could be presented to the National Assembly unless it was approved by a majority of members of each Wing. They were also anxious to know if the Legal Framework Order would be protected.

Although on 23 March there were armed rallies and demonstrations and the 'Bangladesh' flag was hoisted, the constitutional discussions continued. The Awami League refused to work on the draft proclamation which until then had been the working-paper, and produced one of their own. In this new draft, which did not seem to take account of the legal difficulties already under discussion, several novel proposals were put forward. It was proposed that members of the National Assembly elected 'from the state of Bangladesh' and the states of West Pakistan were to be sworn and set up separately to frame Constitutions for the 'state of Bangladesh' and for the states of West Pakistan. There was an alteration in the oath of office laid down in the Legal Framework Order. More revealing still, was the suggestion that the National Assembly should proceed to frame a Constitution of the 'Confederation of Pakistan', an expression applicable only to an agreement between independent sovereign states to join together for certain purposes. This, along with other provisions which would have left the central government a mere ghost without taxation-powers to raise funds even for the shadowy functions allowed to it, ran clearly contrary both to the Legal Framework Order and even to Mujib's own Six Points, one of which provided that Pakistan should be a federal republic. The serious implication of a proclamation of this kind which intended to serve the purpose of an interim Constitution, were pointed out both by Yahya's advisers and by the representatives of the West wing political parties, but the Awami League representatives refused to modify even a single point. Tajuddin Ahmad went so far as to say that even this proclamation would be redundant if it was not issued within the following forty-eight hours. It was in vain that a number of distinguished political leaders called upon Mujib in the hope that he would adopt an attitude which would have room for the views of other people. They found him completely inflexible, elevated in spirit by a vast procession of armed volunteers parading past his house. It was on the evening of 24 March that Yahya held his last meeting with the Awami League leaders. They declined to alter their stand as set out in their own draft proclamation, and in a subsequent news conference Tajuddin Ahmad announced: 'From our side there is no need for further meetings'. In other words, their proclamation was their ultimatum.[24]

Political Impasse between the Centre and the Eastern Wing

While political negotiations were going on in Dhaka, the situation both in the capital and in the outlying cities and districts of East Pakistan was deteriorating rapidly because of the Awami League's persistent defiance of lawful authority and determination to establish its own system of government. Supporters of 'Bangladesh' were now claiming that Mujib's followers maintained perfect order, better order than was customary under Yahya's administration. The record does not support this claim. On the contrary, the most serious mob violence took place in Chittagong, Khulna, Jessore, Rangpur, Dinajpur, Comilla, Saidpur (where the mob was bold enough to fire upon troops in the cantonment), Bogra, Mymensingh, and other places. Under Yahya's direct orders, the army was only permitted to intervene in extreme circumstances. For example, it is known that in the rioting by large mobs in the first week of March, only twenty-three people were killed and twenty-six wounded by army firing while the total casualties amounted to 172 killed and 358 injured. This policy of restraint allowed the Awami League to take over the machinery of administration virtually unchallenged and to direct mob violence against its antagonists in an almost scientific manner. Moreover, the League came to believe that it was all-powerful, that nothing could disturb its grip upon the province, and that it could act as it pleased, without any risk of its actions being challenged by any other authority. The mood of Mujib's supporters might be gathered not only from the speeches of their leaders but also from the mass of inflammatory printed and cyclostyled leaflets and pamphlets distributed widely throughout the towns and countryside. They announced that the National Liberation Movement was in progress and incited the people to take up arms, liquidate the 'enemy troops', arm themselves with any weapon that they could find, destroy roads and bridges, and keep bombs and Molotov cocktails in every house. If attacked, a bloody resistance was to be offered, and an armed struggle of long duration was to be prepared for.[25]

On 24 and 25 March, circumstances were combining to make Yahya's policy of cautious restraint in the face of intense provocation more and more difficult. On 24 March, while the cyclostyled and printed incitements to violence were circulating, serious arson occurred at Golahat, North Saidpur. Moreover, a mob armed with *lathis* and lethal weapons, numbering around eight thousand, converged on Saidpur to attack non-Bengali residents, and fifty houses were set on fire. The violence continued the next day as well. Golhat was attacked, Saidpur cantonment ransacked, and the troops were fired at. Systematic effort was made to block communication between the port and the city of Chittagong, important not only as East Pakistan's main deep-water port but as the headquarters of the East Bengal Regiment. Huge barricades were set up to prevent supplies reaching the cantonment where some West Pakistani troops were stationed. In Dhaka, barricades sprang up in many parts of the city, and, as it became clear later, Iqbal and Jagannath Halls of Dhaka University were put under seige.

In the light of the evidence which later became available, it seems impossible to doubt that a systematic armed uprising was planned. Mujib had begun to make military appointments. An ex-Colonel, Usmani, was named as Commander-in-Chief of the Revolutionary Forces responsible directly to him, while Major-General (Retd.) Majeed and Lieutenant-Commander (Retd.) Moazzam were deputed to enlist ex-servicemen, lists of whom had been prepared in the Awami League headquarters. The acquisition of arms seems to have presented little difficulty. In addition to those which were coming in substantial quantities from across the Indian border, stocks had been piled up by looting arms shops. The Awami League knew that it could rely upon the bulk of the East Bengal Regiment, the East Pakistan Rifles, and many of the Border Guards, all of whom had their own weapons. So far as Dhaka itself was concerned, there would be little difficulty in obtaining the 15,000 rifles and ammunition kept at Police Headquarters. Further, the East Pakistan Rifles and the East Bengal Regiment had their service-type wireless transmitters, so that instructions could be passed quickly. In contrast, perhaps, to the expectation of the rank-and-file of 'Bangladesh' partisans who had been warned to prepare for a long-drawn out guerilla struggle it looked to the outside observer as though the Highcommand of the Awami League was banking upon a quick takeover which would confront the Pakistan government and the outside world with the *fait accompli* of a 'Bangladesh', independent, with its own government and its own armed forces capable of dealing with any internal resistance or with any attack from the outside.[26]

No information has so far been published about the precise moment when the plans for a *coup d'etat* based on armed violence came to the notice of the authorities, but it is evident that right up to the last moment, Yahya was hoping to arrive at an understanding with the Awami League which would stop the uprising before it began. He failed, and on 24 March, negotiations broke down and a political impasse was reached. Bhutto met Yahya the same day. Both of them agreed that the Awami League had progressively raised its stakes from provincial autonomy to the constitutional break up of Pakistan. Whatever course of action they might have contemplated or decided upon, it was announced that the talks were still continuing. Tajuddin Ahmad, General Secretary of the Awami League, declared in the evening, that his party 'had submitted its final proposals and had nothing to add or negotiate'.[27]

West Pakistani politicians, experts, and advisers, including Bhutto's aides, started flying back to Karachi, sensing what was coming. Some of the Awami League advisers were surprised at the breakdown of negotiations. On being asked if some hope was still left after the confederation proposal had been made, it was said that

that was where the miscalculation was made only because the Awami League sources inside the government confirmed that the army was giving in and so they pressed on.[28]

On 26 March, in a nation-wide broadcast which echoed his own deep disappointment, Yahya gave an account of his efforts to transfer power by peaceful means and of the reasons why these efforts came to nothing. He assured the nation that his firm intention of transferring powers to constitutionally chosen governments, central and provincial, remained unaltered but that in view of the very grave situation that had developed, he had called upon the armed forces to restore order, banned political activity, and banned the Awami League as a political party, and had imposed Press censorship.

According to another viewpoint, the negotiations held by Yahya with Mujib were a farce and were never meant to succeed. The talks were just a stratagem to give Tikka Khan and the army additional time to bring in reinforcements from the western wing. Mujib's last press release said 'we have reached agreement on the transfer of power and I hope the President will now make the announcement'. A notable feature of the negotiations was that they never really broke down and the end came with the military action on the night of 25 March.[29] This view does not inspire confidence. Reading the events from 15 March to 25 March, it appears that talks between Yahya and Mujib were held in right earnest. Their failure was due to the fast deteriorating political and law and order situation over which both of them seemed to have little control. They were both captives in the hands of their own hawks. Yahya was advised by his Generals who wanted military solution, and Bhutto did not want the negotiations to succeed. Mujib, meanwhile, was in the hands of his rabid, young lieutenants who, due to their extremist object of secession of East Pakistan, were making things difficult by the day.

While the happenings in East Pakistan were leading to deep political turmoil, Bhutto, the majority leader in West Pakistan, was doing nothing to help matters. He actually aggravated the widening gulf between the two wings of the country when he voiced a strange and unreasonable demand for transfer of power to the Awami League in East Pakistan and to the People's Party in West Pakistan. His strange logic was that although he strongly advocated 'One Pakistan', his demand was in accord with the democratic principles applicable to a country divided into two parts.[30] No wonder that he made the statement on 26 March 1971 in Karachi, after the military action had commenced on 25 March, that 'Pakistan has at last been saved'.[31] This statement must have haunted him for the rest of his life.

This view finds support from Sardar Shaukat Hayat Khan's book *The Nation that Lost its Soul*.[32] He has argued that Mujib was a patriot. Dismayed at the unexpected failure of the Muslim League in the Punjab because he had hoped to use the strength of the Muslim League as a leverage to persuade certain elements in his party to ease up on the Six Points, Mujib also worried at the success of some young extremists in his party.[33] Bhutto, on the other hand, came out suspect in Shaukat Hayat Khan's view. He has regarded Bhutto as a pawn in the hands of the Generals who had little interest in constitutional solutions. Bhutto's attitude is described as unreasonable because he insisted on a prior agreement between the two major parties before the

Assembly could be convened. Qayyum Khan, who was an ally of Bhutto at that time, had clearly told Shaukat Hayat that East Pakistan had nothing in common with West Pakistan, that it was a liability, and it was best to let it go.[34] Yahya also does not come out any better in Shaukat Hayat's estimation. General Umar, a close confidant and colleague of Yahya, had told him that East Pakistan was turning into a liability and that it should best be rid of and that Yahya's mind was made up on it. That is why Yahya and his advisers had deliberately prolonged the negotiations, forcing Awami League to take more rigid stands under public pressure. Meanwhile, final touches were being given to a Turkish style of Constitution in which the Army could become its sole guardian.[35] During the negotiations, fresh troops were arriving from West Pakistan and the Awami League was quick to appreciate that East Pakistan leaders was being occupied in unnecessary parleys with the Generals while they in fact, were preparing to crush them by force.[36] Shaukat Hayat compliments Mujib by reproducing the following extract from his last telephone conversation with Shaukat Hayat:

> Shaukat Bhai, we may not meet in this world, but we are sure to be together in the next as we had been together in the creation of our homeland Pakistan.[37]

It is obvious that during the negotiations Bhutto's role was anything but positive. He was applying all methods to stall a settlement. He sent back his party leaders on 24 March.[38] He and his remaining colleagues in the PPP booked their seats for the morning of 26 March without waiting for a meaningful settlement. He agreed with Yahya and Tikka Khan's 'final solution' to the Bangladesh 'problem', and like them, he obviously considered Mujib's Awami League demand and the hoisting of Bangladesh flags atop buildings all over Dhaka a 'nightmare of fascism'.[39]

Yahya-Bhutto Military Axis

The decision to postpone the National Assembly meeting was regretted in retrospect by West Pakistani intelligentsia as a tragic decision which led to the break up of Pakistan. A considerable body of opinion holds Bhutto responsible for it. Two aspects of the situation, as it had emerged in the last week of February, need to be highlighted to put the controversy in its proper perspective. It may also be mentioned in passing that at the time these momentous decisions were taken they were not criticized by the Press or the intelligentsia of West Pakistan in the manner in which they are now, with the acquired wisdom of hindsight. In fact, most of the vocal classes and forums welcomed the army action taken in the last week of March. The opposition to Yahya came from Admiral Ahsan and the Generals serving in East Pakistan who were more realistic than the Generals in Rawalpindi. In their courageous stands they got no support from any quarter and in West Pakistan they were even condemned as traitors for pleading peace and harmony between the two wings of the country.

The first aspect relates to the consultative process by which Yahya arrived at the decision to postpone the Assembly session *sine die*. Yahya was initially dismayed at the election results and the post-election behaviour of Mujib, but after his discussion with the Awami League leader in Dhaka in the second week of January, he regained his confidence. In a buoyant press conference immediately after these meetings, he called Mujib—the only time he did so—the future Prime Minister of Pakistan. He saw no harm in the Six Points, but in Larkana, Yahya faced the combination of the political and military leadership of West Pakistan who thought differently. Mujib's failure to tone down his public statements on the Six Points, his rejection of the repeated invitations to come to Rawalpindi, and the unwillingness to show the Awami League draft Constitution which he had promised before the elections, weakened Yahya's credibility. He could no longer overrule or ignore his advisers' latent suspicions. He spoke more frequently of 'saving' West Pakistan. The sequence of events immediately before the decision to postpone the Assembly indicates a pattern. In early February, after receiving a report of his meetings with Awami League leaders from Bhutto, Yahya invited Mujib to Rawalpindi. Mujib refused. Yahya was furious and asked Ahsan to read and then hand over the following message to Mujib in the presence of the MLA. 'Convey to Mujib that I am very dissatisfied with his refusal to accept my invitation to visit Rawalpindi. If he does not arrange to come to Rawalpindi as soon as possible, he will be entirely responsible for the serious consequences which will follow.' Although Yahya agreed to withdraw the message on Ahsan's persuasion, it does show the degree of estrangement between the principal spokesmen of the two wings.

On the other hand, there was complete harmony between Yahya and Bhutto. Bhutto checked with Yahya before demanding the postponement of the National Assembly session and raised such a demand after confirmation from Yahya. The link between the five-and-a-half hour Bhutto-Yahya meeting on 19 February and the amendment in the LFO[40] on 20 February which enabled Bhutto to strengthen his control over his recalcitrant party-men, is too obvious to be missed. During the Governor's Conference two days later, Ahsan found the atmosphere in Rawalpindi one of crisis and imminent military intervention. Yahya's ideas had started changing after the Larkana meeting. The pressures exerted by Bhutto and the hawkish Generals and the continued truculence demonstrated by Mujib, led Yahya to seriously consider the re-imposition of martial law to regain control over the situation. It is alleged that there was an understanding between Bhutto and the central army leadership to prevent the Awami League from implementing the Six Points, which it would have done if the National Assembly had been allowed to meet. The course of political affairs after the Larkana meeting lends credence to the belief that the army's perceptions merged with Bhutto's.[41]

Six Points and West Pakistan

The second aspect pertains to the substantive question whether the martial law regime was prepared to accept the new financial, economic, and administrative structure envisaged by the Six Points. It may be assumed that the Constitution framed by the Assembly would have been based on the Six Points as far as East Pakistan was concerned. The Awami League's original manifesto had envisaged Pakistan 'as a federation granting full autonomy on the basis of the Six-Point formula to each of the federating units'. However, in the post-election discussions, it was conceded by the Awami League that West Pakistan provinces might follow different constitutional arrangements. The analysis of the Six Points that follows is, therefore, with reference to East-West relations.

Point number one, relating to the federal parliamentary system based on direct adult franchise and representation on population basis in the federal legislature, had already been conceded. The remaining five points envisaged a fundamental change in the centre-provinces relationship. Point number two restricted the federal government only to foreign affairs, defence, and currency; the latter two, in turn, were circumscribed by the conditions set forth in the other four points. Even under foreign affairs, foreign economic relations were sought to be provincialized. Point number three provided either separate currencies for the two wings or a single currency with separate federal reserve systems for each wing. The single currency under the proposed arrangements was only symbolic; the procedure in each case was to prevent free movement of capital between the two wings. The Bengali grievance that West Pakistani capitalists were taking the profits away to West Pakistan had a basis but for the enterprise of non-Bengalis, there would have been very little industrialization in East Pakistan, and internal and foreign trade would have continued to remain in the hands of Calcutta capitalists. In the industrial sector alone, six non-Bengali industrialists with assets in East Pakistan (Adamjee, Dawood, Bawany, Ispahani, Amin, and Karim) controlled over 40 per cent of the total assets, 32 per cent of the production in the large manufacturing sector, and 81.5 per cent of the jute industry of the country. Three houses (Adamjee, Ispahani, and Amin) accounted for 69.1 per cent of the total jute manufacture, Adamjee alone holding the major share of 49 per cent. Out of the six industrial houses, four had their entire holdings in East Pakistan in 1961. Each of the other two houses (Adamjee and Dawood) had about 50 per cent of their total net assets located in East Pakistan. A comparative study of 1961 and 1970 shows that, except for a few changes in relative rankings in terms of value of assets and dispersal of holdings, the top houses remained the same over the decade.[42] The heavy stakes of non-Bengali capitalists in East Pakistan no doubt emerged from the windfall profits they made but the growth in their assets showed that most of these earnings were being ploughed back into East Pakistan. The big business houses, the degree of concentration of wealth in them, and the kind of windfall profits which enabled them to increase their capital assets were the same in both the wings. Reforms were needed at the national level. Point number three only sought to regionalize monopoly capitalism by subjecting non-Bengali capitalists to such conditions as were applicable to foreign investors. Point number four entrusted all taxation powers to the provinces, the federal government was to be provided with 'requisite revenue resources for meeting the requirements of defence and foreign affairs... on the basis of a ratio to be determined by the procedure laid down in the constitution'. This revenue assignment was to be consistent 'with the objective of ensuring control over the fiscal policy by the governments of the federating units'. The defence budget would thus be subject to the fiscal policy of East Pakistan, which was bound to be at variance with the security threat perceptions of the West-dominated army. Point number five sought separate accounts of the foreign exchange earnings of each federating unit under the control of the respective province; the requirements of the federal government were to be met by the federating units on the basis of a formula incorporated in the Constitution. This Point also gave powers to the regional government to negotiate foreign aid and trade within the framework of the foreign policy of the federal government. With no consensus on foreign policy, it was difficult to conceive a coherent foreign aid and trade approach by the two wings. The substantial defence requirements of foreign exchange were likely to be subjected to the same scrutiny by the East Pakistan government as the total budget before agreeing to any contribution. Point number six empowered East Pakistan to maintain a militia or para-military forces under the control of its government. This provision would enable East Pakistan to become self-sufficient in defence in terms of its own perceptions of threats from across the borders. The East Pakistan government was not, therefore, likely to be responsive in financial terms to the competitive state of preparedness with India that was always demanded by the Pakistan Army. The Bengalis, in general, were not deeply committed to the Kashmir problem and the Awami League was inclined towards good relations with India. They had always had serious reservations, particularly after the 1965 War, about the army's strategy of defending East Pakistan not on their own soil but by powerful thrusts on the western borders of India. Points three to six would have necessitated a fundamental restructuring of foreign and defence policies of a kind which no West Pakistani leadership drawing its strength from the Punjab, and least of all a Punjab-dominated military regime, could possibly accept.

The Six Points were never referred for official examination to bring out their full implications and to develop alternative proposals to accommodate Bengali demands within a viable federal structure. This had become necessary after the elections when they had become the official policy of the majority party. Yahya did not clinch the issue when the Awami League leaders made a presentation of the Six Points to him in January. He had not been briefed to ask the Bengali leaders informed and intelligent questions about the shape of the federation that would emerge from the implementation of their formula. Indeed, a day before these meetings, according to Ahsan Peerzada,[43] he was searching for a copy of the Six Points. The Awami League, backed by professional economists, had issued detailed explanations of its programme from time to time and made light of the dangers perceived in West Pakistan to the integrity of the country through complete regional autonomy. In the party literature on the subject, Six-Point autonomy was justified with reference to the concept of regional autonomy of the British Cabinet Mission Plan of 1946 and the autonomy envisaged in the Lahore Resolution of 1940. The West Pakistan media and academic circles regarded the Six Points as just a dangerous slogan. There appeared to be little realization of the emergence of new political forces which required a re-ordering of the established system and a new national compact among the major federating units.

According to the rules of procedure, the Planning Commission or the Ministry of Finance could initiate formal examination of a sensitive political issue like the Six Points only under instructions from the President, and not on their own. M.M. Ahmad confirms that the 'Six Points were never examined in depth at the official level. They were not taken seriously before the elections, as Mujib had given an understanding to Yahya that they were merely bargaining points.'[44]

Who Lost East Pakistan?

From the above analysis of the February situation, Bhutto, in opposing Mujib and the Six Points, emerges as a member of the West Pakistan's establishment who was really articulating their stand. His refusal to go to the National Assembly had the full support of Yahya and the Rawalpindi Generals. However, it would not be fair to blame Bhutto alone for the postponement of the National Assembly session unless it is conceded that the Six Points were acceptable to the army, to the establishment, and to West Pakistan in general. If the Six Points were acceptable to Yahya, then he need not have postponed the Assembly session. The army could have easily ensured the security and attendance of such West Pakistani members as were willing to attend the session, Bhutto's threat of dire consequences notwithstanding. But Yahya gave no assurance of security to the elected members of the National Assembly who intended to attend the session. In fact, Yahya seems to have used Bhutto to get out of the situation created by his thoughtless decisions. Bhutto, on the other hand, used Yahya to build himself up as the sole leader of West Pakistan and earned the permanent odium of forcing the postponement of the assembly, leading to the secession of East Pakistan. Bhutto could have as effectively adopted the democratic path of attending the session and using the Assembly floor for whatever he wanted to project. In the last resort, he could have walked out after showing that he had exhausted all constitutional means to maintain the integrity of Pakistan.[45]

Bhutto was an extremely ambitious politician. It was difficult for him to wait to get into power. Playing the opposition card in the National Assembly was fraught with risk and uncertainties. It was only logical for him to force the issue, the outcome of which was the separation of the two wings. He had, after all, Yahya and the military leadership with him to achieve his purpose and used them to the maximum to achieve his ends, though at the cost of Pakistan.[46] His statement on 26 March 1971 that: 'Pakistan has been saved' was not without meaning. What he meant was that West Pakistan had been saved for him to rule.

Yahya and the military leadership at that time cannot escape the blame either. They deliberately let the situation drift out of their hands and allowed events to take their own course. They did nothing while East Pakistan slided into anarchy and chaos. Their last attempt at negotiations was 'too little too late' and thus their acts and intentions are not above doubt and suspicion.

No doubt, that political situation in East Pakistan in 1970–71 was not due to Yahya and Bhutto only, it had its roots in 1947 when India was divided, but their acts and omissions only aggravated the process of estrangement between the two wings of the country.

The press and public opinion in West Pakistan in 1971 are also no less to blame for creating conditions that led to the break up of the country. There was such mass hysteria created in West Pakistan about the Six Points that there was nobody seriously ready to look at them and evolve an acceptable constitutional formula incorporating the Six Points. There was so much fervour against handing over power to the Awami League that the military action was met with support and enthusiasm in West Pakistan. Asghar Khan, who tried to make a tour of the Punjab to mould public opinion in favour of accommodation with the Awami League was attacked, brickbatted, and prevented from speaking.[47] Such manifestation of public outrage against Mujib and East Pakistan ultimately led Yahya to take the fatal step of military action. Politicians in West Pakistan, too, were in no less degree responsible for the situation. They did not show courage and speak their mind. They were scared and over-awed by the hysteria worked up in West Pakistan by Bhutto and his minions and thus decided to bury their faces in the sand. Though later, some politicians like Sardar Shaukat Hayat,[48] claimed that they spoke out against this madness the record does not support their claim. They cannot escape the responsibility for their inaction particularly when they held more than fifty seats in the National Assembly elected in December 1970.

Thus the press, politicians, and public opinion in West Pakistan are jointly responsible for the bitter harvest of the secession of East Pakistan and they will always stand accountable to history for failing to speak when the truth was necessary, and failing to act when action was imperative.

NOTES

1. *Dawn*, 19 January 1971.
2. Feldman, Herbert, *The End and the Beginning—Pakistan 1969-71*, 1975. Oxford University Press, London, p. 101.
3. Zaheer, Hassan, *The Separation of East Pakistan—The Rise and Realization of Bengali Muslim Nationalism*, 1994. Oxford University Press, Karachi. p. 131.
4. *Dawn*, 15 January 1971.
5. Zaheer, Hassan, *The Separation of East Pakistan*, *supra*, note 3, pp. 132-5.
6. *Dawn*, 10 February 4, 5, 12, and 25 January 1971.
7. Ibid., pp. 136-9.
8. *Dawn*, 14 February 1971.
9. *Dawn*, 16 February 1971.
10. *Dawn*, 25 February 1971.
11. *Dawn*, 28 February 1971.
12. Mahmood, Safdar, *Pakistan Divided*, 1984, Ferozsons Ltd., Lahore, p. 113.

13. *Dawn*, 1 March 1971.
14. *Dawn*, 2 March 1971.
15. Feldman, Herbert, *The End and the Beginning*, *supra*, note 2, p. 114.
16. These directives are in the White Paper, *The Crises in East Pakistan*, 1971, pp. 37-46.
17. Williams, L.F. Rushbrook, *The East Pakistan Tragedy*, 1972. Tom Stacey Ltd., London, pp. 53-6.
18. *Dawn*, 7 March 1971.
19. Salik, Siddique. *Witness to Surrender*. Edition 1977. Oxford University Press, Karachi. p. 54.
20. *Dawn*, 8 March 1971.
21. Williams, L.F. Rushbrook, *The East Pakistan Tragedy*, *supra*, note 17, pp. 49-52.
22. Ibid., pp. 60-61.
23. Ibid., pp. 61-2.
24. Ibid., pp. 62-3.
25. Ibid., pp. 64-5.
26. Ibid., pp. 66-7.
27. *The Pakistan Observer*, Dhaka, 25 March 1971.
28. Salik, Siddique, *Witness to Surrender*, *supra*, note 19, p. 68.
29. Mascarenhas, Anthony, *The Rape of Bangla Desh*. 1971. Vikas Publications, Delhi, p. 108.
30. *Dawn*, 15 March 1971.
31. *Dawn*, 27 March 1971.
32. Khan, Sardar Shaukat Hayat, *The Nation that Lost its Soul*, 1995. Jang Publishers, Lahore.
33. Ibid., p. 296.
34. Ibid., p. 302.
35. Ibid., p. 309.
36. Ibid., p. 313.
37. Ibid., p. 315.
38. Wolpert, Stanley, *Zulfi Bhutto of Pakistan: His life and Times*, 1993, Oxford University Press, New York, p. 154.
39. Ibid., p. 155.
40. Legal Framework (Amendment) Order 1971. President's Order 1 of 1971. PLD 1971 Central Statutes 118.
41. Zaheer, Hassan, *The Separation of East Pakistan*, *supra*, note 3, p. 143.
42. Amjad, Rashid, 'Industrial Concentration and Economic Power' an article in *Pakistan: The Unstable State*' edited by Hasan Gardezi and Jamil Rashid, 1983. Vanguard Books Ltd., Lahore, pp. 178 & 179.
43. Peerzada was principal staff officer of Yahya.
44. Zaheer, Hassan, *The Separation of East Pakistan*, *supra*, note 3, pp. 143-7.
45. 45. Ibid., p. 147.
46. The author was told by one of the close associates of Bhutto that during this period, his associates asked him why was he cooperating with Yahya and his military junta. He told them in reply that he could not cross two bridges at the same time. With the help of Yahya and military leadership, he would first confront and after Mujib was out of his way, he would confront Yahya and military.
47. Khan, Muhammad Asghar, *Generals in Politics: Pakistan 1958-1982*, 1983. Vikas Publishing House, New Delhi, pp. 31-2.
48. See his book *The Nation that Lost its Soul*, *supra*, note 32.

19

THE BIRTH OF BANGLADESH

Late on the evening of 25 March 1971, the voice of Mujibur Rehman came faintly on a wavelength close to that of the official Pakistan Radio. In what must have been a pre-recorded message, Mujib proclaimed East Pakistan to be the People's Republic of Bangladesh. The full text of the proclamation has been published in the Bangladesh documents released by the Indian Foreign Ministry. It said, 'This may be my last message. From today, Bangladesh is independent. I call upon the people of Bangladesh, wherever you are and with what you have, to resist the army of occupation to the last. Your fight must go on until the last soldier of the Pakistan occupation army is expelled from the soil of Bangladesh and final victory is achieved.'[1]

Military Action in East Pakistan

With the final and irreversible breakdown of political negotiations on 25 March, Yahya ordered military action to suppress the revolt of the Awami League. Political activity was prohibited throughout the country and Awami League was banned as a political party. Censorship was clamped on the press. Yahya said, 'Let me assure you that my main aim remains the same, namely, transfer of power to the elected representatives of the people. As soon as the situation permits, I will take fresh steps towards the achievement of this objective'.[2]

In Dhaka, the headquarters of the rebellion, fighting was soon over. Attempts had been made to isolate the forces in the cantonment from the city by the erection of numerous barricades. No fewer than fifty barricades had been erected between the Intercontinental Hotel in the centre of the residential quarter and Dhaka airport. These barricades presented little difficulty to the highly-trained troops, whose main object was to remove them with minimum loss of life. Accurate gun fire soon drove off those who manned barricades and snipers' nests in surrounding huts were cleared by the use of tracer bullets which set fire to inflammable materials and obliged the occupants to escape to safety. The main streets were thus quickly cleared. The only serious resistance which the army encountered was from the well-armed men of the East Bengal Regiment and the police, who manned a number of strong points. These were systematically reduced. The army never opened fire until it was first fired upon. When this happened, it reacted sharply. In an operation of this kind, some civilian casualties are inevitable as innocent people are caught in the cross-fire, but the army never fired upon civilians as such, only upon those who resisted it with arms. Many people of the middle and upper class families had already left the city to escape violence at the hands of the Awami League operatives; college and university students had gone home, partly because of the approaching vacation and partly because of the closure of educational institutions by Mujib's decree. Iqbal Hall and Jagannath Hall of Dhaka University which had been turned into an arsenal and strong-point manned by members of the students' branch of the Awami League, were razed to the groumd during the military action. Iqbal Hall was hit by two rockets and Jagannath Hall by four. The rooms were mostly charred but intact. A few dozen half-burnt rifles and stray papers were still smouldering. The damage was grave. There were mass graves in the university with three pits of five to fifteen metres diameter each. The foreign press alleged several thousand deaths (in the university area) while army officers placed the figure at around a hundred. Officially, only forty deaths were admitted.[3]

Mujib was arrested at 1:30 a.m. on the morning of 26 March, but a number of his lieutenants fled from Dhaka to those parts of East Pakistan which were under Awami League control. Mujib was kept overnight at the Adamjee School. Next day, he was shifted to Flag Staff House from where he was flown to Karachi three days later.[4] Kamal Hossain surrendered the following day. Except for these two, the entire Awami League leadership left for India, either from fear or by design. It was a major failure of the military action that the elected leaders, students, and political activists went over to India. It would have been different if the elected leadership had remained available and not lost their political freedom of action by escaping to India. Within a few weeks, overt resistance had been overcome by the army. However, the fleeing members of the National Assembly from Awami League were successful in announcing a government in exile for Bangladesh in India.

Immediately before his call upon the army to take action against the planned rebellion fixed for the small hours of 26 March, Yahya ordered the expulsion of foreign journalists from East Pakistan. Many of them had been in Dhaka for some time covering first the cyclone and then the activities of the Awami League. They had been carefully cultivated by Mujib and his followers. Some of them had become enthusiastic supporters of 'Bangladesh' whose emergence as an independent state they were hourly expecting. This latter group had succeeded in conveying to the outside world an impression that West Pakistan was hostile to the legitimate aspirations of the people of East Pakistan. Some of the journalists accused the military in East Pakistan of 'genocide'.[5] The true facts may never be known. Emotions still run so high on the subject that it is difficult to make an objective analysis. Both the contending parties had set their propaganda machines in motion and they were issuing conflicting versions of the facts and figures. The figures were so exaggerated about the atrocities committed by the other side that they are not in any way reliable.

Nevertheless, it appears that,[6] as long as General Tikka Khan was in command, the troops were kept under control and they did what was strictly necessary in the military sense. There might have been some instances of excesses but that was not the policy. General Tikka had strictly advised the army contingent to stay away from the local population and only to interfere when there was a serious breach of law and order or a threat to human life and property. When he was replaced by Lieutenant-General Niazi, things changed for the worse. The new General was known to be a debauch who indulged in wine and women. What was worse, he encouraged men under his command to indulge in excesses such as the rape of women and the theft of valuables. It was under him that certain shameful excesses took place which were magnified manifold by the Indian and other foreign media. These also brought a bad name to the Pakistan Army and its morale suffered. It made the army look like an occupation force and became the target of hatred by even those who otherwise did not support the Awami League.

Meanwhile, a large number of people crossed over to India, first due to the atrocities of the Awami League operatives and later as a result of the military action. The estimate of refugees vary widely. The Indian propaganda machine gave the figure as high as 3.5 million but a more moderate estimate put it at 800,000. The refugee problem provided India with a pretext to intervene in East Pakistan, an excuse they were looking for all the time. They were already training and arming the rebels who called themselves *'Mukti Bahni'*.

Reaction in West Pakistan

Unfortunately, political parties in West Pakistan actively or tacitly supported the military action in East Pakistan. The press in West Pakistan was jingoistic and supported statements of Yahya that aggravated the sad situation in East Pakistan. His bellicose statements directed against India and other foreign powers did not help matters. The politicians and the press in West Pakistan tried to create war hysteria and certain impudent zealots tried to launch what was called the 'Crush India' campaign. It was indeed a major failure on the part of political parties in West Pakistan because they failed to understand and appreciate the gravity of the situation and the consequences that were likely to follow. They meekly and willingly submitted to the short-sighted military solution being offered by the military government and made little effort to put their weight on the side of a political solution to solve the crises.

Only a handful of journalists and politicians in West Pakistan raised their voice against the military action. The daily *Azad* from Lahore persuaded about fifty prominent citizens of Lahore to sign a public statement opposing military operations in East Pakistan and called for a political settlement. No other newspaper except *Azad* dared to carry this statement. A public meeting was held at the premises owned by former Air Force Chief and former Punjab Governor, Air Marshall Nur Khan, where military operations were denounced. Abdullah Malik, one of the editors of *Azad*, had used the expression 'Bangladesh' in his speech at the Engineering University and had expressed sympathy for the people of East Pakistan. He was tried by a military court and sentenced to one year's imprisonment.[7]

Attempts at Reconstitution

It was plain that after the pre-emptive military action on 25 and 26 March, contemporaneously with the neutralization of insurgents and the pacification of the countryside, Yahya's immediate tasks were to: (a) win back the confidence of East Pakistan; (b) revitalize belief in the prospect of an acceptable Constitution; (c) counter Indian propaganda and restore Pakistan's world image; (d) repair the damaged economy. To embark on these tasks implied, of course, that the old Pakistan could hold together, a belief flowing from the decision to pre-empt secession. Moreover, the doctrine that the Awami League (as distinguished from the people of East Pakistan) and India were in complicity was based on the idea that the people of East Pakistan desired unity despite all that had happened and was still happening. Criticism of India as a base for insurgents and rebels justified the doctrine that once these marauders had been killed or captured, tranquility would return.

Some people considered the pre-emptive strike unwise and the coup a failure which had left the two wings irretrievably sundered. It is doubtful whether East and West Pakistan were indeed irretrievably sundered, but the difficulty was to resolve the visible contradictions. Was it possible to win back East Pakistan's confidence when the army was roving the countryside seeking to destroy the self-proclaimed liberation forces, challenging the loyalty of any person it suspected, and making use of courts organized in terms of Martial Law Regulation No. 88? Was not the very scope of these military operations a measure of the prevailing disaffection? Could confidence be restored among a people, a million of whom lived in exile in India with scarcely a family where a death or destruction had not been recorded? Had not Mujib, East Pakistan's hero, been removed to West Pakistan, there to stand trial in secret for being a traitor and rebel by the same president who was now appealing for faith and goodwill?

Judged by any standards, the task of reconciliation was formidable, but Yahya believed it could be accomplished. He had around him a panel of advisers in whose ability he had great faith. He had distributed political and administrative responsibilities amongst them. The caucus, after 25 March 1971, comprised:

(a) General Abdul Hamid Khan and Major-General Gul Hasan, handling the army.
(b) Lieutenant-General S.G.M.M. Peerzada whose political responsibilities had special reference to the Pakistan People's Party and the National Awami Party, both groups.
(c) Major-General Ghulam Umar whose political responsibilities had special reference to Jamaat-i-Islami and the three Muslim Leagues whose unification he laboured to bring about. This concern with rightist parties showed itself particularly in East Pakistan after 25 March, and it brought him into collision with the People's Party which served him ill when Bhutto became President.
(d) Lieutenant-General A.O. Mitha, an old regimental comrade, dealing with the civil service.
(e) Major-General M. Akbar, Director of Military Intelligence, who supervised intelligence affairs generally.

(f) Brigadier Karim, an East Pakistani on the staff of the Chief Martial Law Administrator, to supervise and advise on East Pakistan affairs.
(g) Brigadier Abdul Karim, on the staff of the Chief Martial Law Administrative, to supervise civil affairs. He later became Chief of the General Staff in Bhutto's administration.
(h) Lieutenant-Colonel M.A. Hasan, legal and constitutional adviser. He was a prominent member of the prosecution in the Agartala trial.

In addition, mention should be made of the Commander-in-Chief of the Air Force, Air-Marshall Rahim Khan who, although not a soldier, enjoyed a good personal equation with Yahya and was in constant touch with him on military matters, in contrast with the Commander-in-Chief of the Navy who was completely ignored.[8]

For three months the position after 25 March was studied by these men and, on 28 June, Yahya addressed the nation stating what was, in fact, the outcome of their study. He said that:
(a) he re-affirmed his aim to restore democratic government;
(b) declared that East Pakistan had voted for provincial autonomy and not for secession;
(c) accused Sheikh Mujib and the Awami League of defiance, obduracy, and of seeking secession;
(d) declared his conclusion that the framing of a Constitution by an assembly was not feasible;
(e) considered that there was no alternative but to have a Constitution prepared by a 'group of experts' (afterwards spoken of as the 'Constitution Committee') whom he had, as it appeared, already selected;
(f) the 'martial law cover' would remain 'for some time';
(g) political parties must be 'national' and he had already recommended to the Constitution Committee that 'it would be a good thing if we ban any party which is not national in the practical sense' and that 'we must eschew the habit of sub-parties';
(h) his proposed Constitution could be amended by the National Assembly by means of machinery to be provided by the Constitution itself;
(i) the Legal Framework Order would be amended to suit the new arrangements;
(j) by-elections would be held to fill vacant seats in the assemblies.[9]

This address raised a host of questions and doubts. Quite apart from the hostility with which these proposals were greeted in East Pakistan, there was much in them which provoked disapproval in West Pakistan too. It was noted with bitterness that Yahya had discovered, but only after much bloodshed and at the risk of losing East Pakistan, that it would have been wiser for him in the first place to have offered a draft Constitution to the National Assembly for its consideration. It was noted that the names of the constitutional experts were not disclosed, but that they had already been appointed. It was noted that amendments to the proposed Constitution would depend on the mechanics provided in the Constitution itself and on that point no one had the least information. Further, what was meant by 'national parties'? A party with a trifling representation in both wings of the country might claim to be 'national' whereas a party such as Bhutto's with a large representation in the National Assembly, but from one wing only, might be termed 'regional'. In short, it appeared that in creating these stipulations, Yahya's administration was trying to reserve the powers of manipulation comparable with those which had made the Legal Framework Order suspect and which would make the transfer of power, when it came, illusory.

In September, Yahya made it known that the National Assembly would have ninety days after receiving the draft Constitution, in which to propose amendments. These amendments would, however, require his assent. Moreover, before the Assembly could meet, by-elections would be necessary. In August, a list of eighty-eight East Pakistan Assembly members was issued stating that they were clear of all adverse allegations and that they retained their seats. This left seventy-nine East Pakistani members who were called upon to answer charges, failing which they would have to vacate their seats in the Assembly. In particular, the seats held by Mujib and Dr Kamal Hossain were declared vacant although, so far as anyone knew, Mujib's trial, which began in August, had not yet concluded and his guilt or innocence was still unpronounced. Shortly afterwards, the public was informed that by-elections would be held during the period 25 November–9 December 1971.

It was said that the miniature general election in East Pakistan would afford excellent opportunities to create a National Assembly which would fit in well with the policies that Yahya and his group desired to promote, and evidence of a plan to that end soon emerged. As early as 15 October, out of seventy-nine seats declared vacant in East Pakistan, fifteen had already acquired National Assembly representation because the candidates were declared to have been elected unopposed, although elections were not due until the fortnight 25 November–9 December. The political complexion of these successful members was unmistakable, comprising, as they did:[10]

Pakistan Democratic Front	5
Jamaat-i-Islami	5
(Convention) Muslim League	2
Qayum Muslim League	1
Nizam-i-Islam Party	2

These unopposed results disclosed several things. First of all, that there would again be a confusing multiplicity of parties in the House, creating plenty of room for contention although with a general drift as to outlook. Much more important was the fact that this number of unopposed returns so early in the day spoke of an indifference in East Pakistan to the by-elections.

It was said in Dhaka that some intending candidates were being warned by District Magistrates, acting on the instructions of the martial law authorities, not to oppose certain candidates already nominated in some constituencies.[11] It was further reported that others were being dissuaded from standing for election either by physical force at the hands of the military or by the threat of it, and it was significant that the Governor of East Pakistan, Dr A.M. Malik, made reference to 'not entirely satisfactory elections'.

This was a bold statement for Dr Malik to make seeing that he was the appointee of the martial law administration. His appointment was clearly intended to placate sentiment in East Pakistan by giving to that province a civilian Governor born on its own soil, but the idea was a nullity at the outset. Not only was the purpose as transparent as it was disingenuous, but Dr Malik's past associations with the central government over the years robbed him of whatever credibility he might otherwise have had. Moreover, a martial law administrator remained, the only change being that General Tikka Khan returned to military duty and was replaced by Lieutenant-General A.A.K. Niazi. But this was not all; if the eastern province was deserving of a civilian Governor after everything that had happened there, why not the western provinces where there had been no rebellion and no secessionist moves? This discrimination simply underlined the truth of Dr Malik's appointment, a sop to East Pakistan, without sacrificing an iota of control. To make matters even worse, Monem Khan, Ayub's ex-Governor of East Pakistan, a heartily detested figure, was actually invited to Malik's swearing-in ceremony.[12]

The proposed elections were never held as they were overtaken by war with India.

The Draft Constitution

It has been mentioned above that the elections in December 1970 were held to elect a Constituent Assembly which was required to frame a Constitution for Pakistan within 120 days. After having framed such a Constitution, the Assembly would have become the central legislature and would have transferred power to the elected Prime Minister and the Cabinet amongst them and would have acted as Parliament in a parliamentary form of government. Unfortunately, all this did not come about. While East Pakistan was in turmoil and under military action, Yahya promised a constitution in his address to the nation on 28 June 1971. A draft Constitution was already prepared and circulated.

The draft Constitution gave a presidential form of government. It was based on the 1962 Constitution with the following departures

i. The office of Vice-President for Pakistan was provided for.
ii. There was to be a bicameral legislative at the Centre, two Houses to be called the Senate and the National Assembly.
iii. The Senate was to be the Upper House with fifteen members (out of a total membership of sixty-five) to be nominated by the President. The Senate was to be a permanent House not subject to dissolution. Half of its membership was to change every two years.
iv. The number of seats in the National Assembly was to be 313, with 264 as general seats, 13 seats reserved for women, 17 for the scheduled castes, 15 for caste Hindus, 1 for Buddhists, and 3 for Christians and others. East Pakistan was allocated 169 seats out of which 130 were to be general seats, the remaining seats being allocated to women and minorities.

v. There were provisions for the joint sitting of the two Houses of the Parliament to iron out differences between the two Houses on legislation.

vi. The power of taxation and the subjects for taxation by the central legislature were specifically spelled out in the main body of the draft Constitution.

vii. A chapter of the draft Constitution was devoted to political parties. The aims and purposes that a political party could have were clearly laid down which included, amongst others, true faith and allegiance to Pakistan to preserve its integrity and sovereignty as an Islamic Republic; to observe the principles of democracy within its own organization; not to be a foreign aided party; and to adopt exclusively constitutional methods to bring about a change in the Constitution or the law of Pakistan. There were also provisions for the registration of the political parties. These provisions were apparently necessitated by the experience with the Awami League.

viii. There was a provision for the imposition of martial law in whole or any part of Pakistan but only in compelling circumstances which were defined as attack or invasion by a foreign power or its imminent danger; law and order within the country being in grave jeopardy; and a serious problem affecting the whole, or any substantial part of the country or any province. Martial law was to be declared by the Commander-in-Chief of the Pakistan Army at the request of the President or of his own motion. The declaration of martial law could only be revoked by the Commander-in-Chief after consultation with the President.

Except for these features and some other minor ones, the draft Constitution was a reproduction of the 1962 Constitution. This draft Constitution was never promulgated. Nevertheless, it appears to have been used as a working paper for the interim Constitution of 1972 and, later, the permanent 1973 Constitution, particularly the provision regarding the Senate and the joint sittings of the two Houses of Parliament.[13]

International Responses

On 19 July, Yahya declared that Mujib would be tried by a military court in camera and the allegations were such that he could be awarded the death sentence. On 3 September, Dr A.M. Malik and General Niazi were appointed Governor and Martial Law Administrator of East Pakistan, respectively.

The first step taken by Dr A.M. Malik's government was to announce general amnesty for those alleged to have committed crimes in East Pakistan since March. This decision resulted in the release of a large number of prisoners. Meanwhile, Dr Malik had established contact with the Awami League leaders in exile and had come to the conclusion that they were frustrated with the Indian government because it did not support their movement out of sympathy for the Bengali Muslims, but was motivated by the desire to dismember Pakistan. He, therefore, made repeated appeals to the refugees to come back home, but it did not have any impact because the

Awami League leaders were kept under constant vigilance by the Indian authorities[14] and it was no longer possible for them to return even if they so desired. The guerrilla activities and sabotage campaign of the *Mukti Bahini* had assumed alarming proportions and, by October, East Pakistan seemed to be in the midst of civil war.

As for international developments, the Indian government tried to put diplomatic pressure on Islamabad for an immediate political solution, but the government of Pakistan resisted it on the plea that it was an internal matter. Pakistan insisted on her sovereignty and refused to accept the representatives of international agencies. By the middle of April, Pakistan was able to secure general approval of the international community regarding the political position. Some countries, including China, extended complete support to Pakistan in the campaign to convince the international community that what had happened in East Pakistan was purely an internal problem. By the beginning of May, normalcy had returned to East Pakistan to a great extent and the general situation permitted Islamabad to allow the United Nations to begin relief and rehabilitation activities.

Meanwhile, India began to undermine Pakistan's position by exploiting the refugees who were called freedom fighters and, with the help of an organized propaganda machinery, insisted on becoming a party to the East Pakistan situation. The Indian government refused to return the refugees and turned down the United Nations' offers for providing assistance at the borders. India was supported by the exiled Bengali leaders in her campaign to condemn the UN efforts.

In June, India launched a monsoon offensive against Pakistan which was aimed at disrupting communications by blasting bridges and terrorising the public. Yahya made half-hearted attempts to win over moderate Bengalis by promising the restoration of political life. Since he had no organized campaign or clear programme and also suffered from a credibility gap, these efforts were doomed to failure.

In July, U Thant proposed the appointment of UN representatives on both sides of the East Pakistan border to facilitate the return of refugees and placed this suggestion before the Security Council. Yahya immediately accepted the proposal but the Indian government rejected it. By then, a significant change in Sino-American relations was taking place as a result of Kissinger's visit to Peking, with the announcement by President Nixon in July to visit China the following year. This development led India to realize the difficulty of supporting the Bangladesh liberation movement without the support of a superpower. During this period, the USSR had decided, for various reasons, to establish closer relations with India.

After the signing of the Indo-Soviet Treaty in August 1971, the government of the USSR adopted a hostile attitude towards Pakistan and made it clear that it would frustrate every attempt to involve the US in the East Pakistan crisis. Soviet commitment also encouraged India to intensify the activities of the *Mukti Bahini*. During September and October, the Soviet Union tried, for the last time, for a political solution of the East Pakistan crisis and pressurized India to limit her commitment to the Bangladesh movement. However, Yahya's broadcast on 12 October convinced the Soviet Union that Pakistan was not yet prepared for any such settlement by accepting confederation between the two wings of Pakistan. After October, Soviet military assistance to India assumed larger proportions and war seemed imminent. Pakistan depended too much on the UN and the world powers for intervention in the prospective war. It was, perhaps, because of this that Pakistan decided to widen the circle of war by opening a front on the western border on 3 December. By then, it was too late.

By November, the Pakistani nation had been shaken and demoralized due to regional polarization. A majority of East Pakistanis had turned hostile towards the army because of the military action and the subsequent failure of the military authorities to restore the people's confidence in the government. The army's morale had also been affected because the *jawans* had been in the trenches for several months without rest and proper food. Even otherwise, the army was not as disciplined as it was in 1965. Yahya had concentrated his attention more on promotions in the higher cadres than on its equipment and training. Moreover, Yahya's position was unstable as compared to Ayub because the *junta* on which he depended was itself a divided house.

Conditions within East Pakistan were depressing. The economic fabric had been shattered because of the virtual closure of industry since March. The monsoon offensive of the *Mukti Bahini* had not only done great damage to the communication system, roads, and bridges but had also created uncertainty and terror. The Indian propaganda presenting events in Bangladesh as a liberation movement and Pakistan as a colonial country had moulded international public opinion against the latter. Circumstances were thus favourable for an Indian offensive against Pakistan.

Indo-Pak War and the Fall of Dhaka

Having realized that the *Mukti Bahini* could not achieve the objective, India decided to launch an attack on the eastern front. Although full-scale war started on 22 November, yet 'unimpeachable Indian military sources said that, in spite of official denials, Indian troops crossed the borders into East Pakistan' in the first week of November.[15] This was the 'first confirmation that Indian soldiers had operated inside East Pakistan in the current crisis'.[16] The *New York Times* also carried a similar report on 13 November 1971.

As soon as Dr Malik came to know about the Indian attack, he left for Islamabad on 26 November to advise the President to avert the war, either by seeking UN intervention or by making political settlement with the Awami League leaders. He knew that in case of an all-out war, East Pakistan would be lost. He returned to Dhaka on 1 December and expressed dissatisfaction about his talks with Yahya.

Although Jessore had been captured by the Indian Army on 6 December, Yahya was not conveyed this news till 8 December. Moreover, the unrealistic attitude adopted by Pakistan's representative at the Security Council was an indication to Dr Malik that the correct military position of East Pakistan was not being communicated to Yahya. He, therefore, addressed a letter to Yahya appreciating the valour of the Pakistan Army and painting a discouraging but realistic picture of the lack of military and civil supplies, breakdown of law and order, large scale murders of Pakistan supporters, and requested for physical intervention within forty-eight hours. He made it clear that if no help came, the problem should be solved through negotiations so that power was transferred peacefully and millions of human lives were were not put at stake. It is obvious that help from foreign friends was assured by Islamabad to Dr Malik and General Niazi. As the situation became critical, both Niazi and Dr Malik badgered Islamabad for the promised help. General Niazi even went to the US Consul-General in Dhaka to ask 'if US military assistance was to be provided'.[17] Yahya's response to Dr Malik's letter was precise and self-explanatory. He replied: 'we are praying for you'. It is difficult to say if the problem could have been settled politically at this stage as proposed by Dr Malik when the Indian Army was racing towards Dhaka. However, there is no doubt that Yahya did not make any serious effort for political settlement before the war although he knew that Pakistan's position was weaker and India had made preparations for inflicting a military defeat on Pakistan.

Siddiq Salik reproduced the desperation at the Government House on 7 December in the following words:

> Governor Malik, General Niazi, and two other senior officers sat in a comfortable room at Government House. They did not talk much. Every few minutes, silence overtook the conversation. The Governor did most of the talking, and that too, in general terms. The crux of his discourse was: 'Things never remain the same. Good situations give way to bad situations and vice versa. Similarly, there are fluctuations in the career of a General. At one time, glory magnifies him while at another defeat demolishes his dignity.' As Dr Malik uttered the last part of his statement, the burly figure of General Niazi quaked and he broke into tears. He hid his face into his hands and started sobbing like a child. The Governor stretched out his elderly arm to General Niazi and, consoling him, said: 'I know, General Sahib, there are hard days in a commander's life. But don't lose heart. God is Great'.[18]

On 9 and 10 December, General Niazi sent messages to the Chief of General Staff informing him that a regrouping of troops and the re-adjustment of battle positions was not possible due to intense enemy air activity and the hostility of the local population. He stated that air fields, bridges, and heavy weapons had been seriously damaged. He requested for reinforcement by airborne troops to protect Dhaka. General Niazi's message clearly stated that the situation was critical and the resistance of the Pakistan Army was likely to last only a few more days.

On 10 December, Dr Malik sent another message to Yahya requesting him to arrange an immediate cease-fire and negotiate a political settlement. In response, Yahya authorized the Governor of East Pakistan to take suitable decisions as required by the circumstances because the East-West Pakistan link had been severed. He said that he would approve all measures taken by him. At the same time, Yahya directed General Niazi to follow the decisions taken by the Governor. After the receipt of this message, Dr Malik contacted the Assistant Secretary-General of the United Nations, and delivered a message demanding a peaceful transfer of power to the people's representatives through the United Nations after the cease-fire and the withdrawal of the Indian Army. Facilities for the repatriation of the Pakistan Army and protection of the non-Bengali population were also demanded. The message made it clear that there was no question of surrender.

Yahya buried the message as soon as he came to know of it and an official spokesman denied its despatch. On 11 December, Pakistan invoked its understanding with friendly powers to come to its assistance. Dhaka was told that help was expected from friends, which never arrived, and the war continued. By 15 December, Indian forces had reached the outskirts of Dhaka. On 14 December, the Governor's House was rocketed by Indian planes as a result of which the Governor and his Cabinet resigned and sought protection from the Red Cross. General Niazi again met the American Consul-General and requested him to arrange for an immediate cease-fire. On 16 December, the instrument of surrender was signed by General Niazi and General Jagjit Singh Aurora, Commander-in-Chief, Indian Army, and Dhaka fell.

Role of the United Nations

Several attempts, most of them half-hearted, were made in the United Nations to stop the war between Pakistan and India. Full-fledged war started on the eastern front on 22 November and spread to West Pakistan on 3 December, yet the United Nations remained unperturbed till 4 December 1971 when Argentina, supported by seven other members of the Security Council, requested an emergency session of the Security Council. At this session, the United States sponsored a draft resolution calling for a cease-fire and for the withdrawal of troops. The resolution also proposed posting UN observers on the borders. It was vetoed by the USSR.[19]

On 4 December, the USSR sponsored a draft resolution calling for 'political settlement in East Pakistan which would inevitably result in cessation of hostilities'.[20] The resolution was supported by Poland but the other twelve members of the Security Council abstained from voting. If accepted by Pakistan, this resolution would have led to a cease-fire and political settlement in East Pakistan which Pakistan needed desperately. After October 1971, Pakistan also favoured a political settlement or, at least, paid lip service to the idea under American pressure. Negotiations through American diplomats had started with the Bangladesh government in exile, so there was nothing objectionable from Pakistan's point of view and the resolution, if accepted, would have saved Pakistan from unprecedented humiliation. But the resolution was vetoed by China, with of course, the prior approval of Islamabad. Pakistan, therefore, missed a good opportunity to achieve peace which was the greatest need of the hour.

One fails to understand why Pakistan did not approach the United Nations. It should be recalled that Bhutto had advised Pakistan not to approach the Security Council in case of war with India.[21] He did not spell out the logic behind this advice. Later on, opposition parties in Pakistan criticized Bhutto's statement and held him responsible for delayed action in the United Nations. After Bhutto's removal from the prime ministership in 1977, Yahya also alleged that Bhutto acted against the advice of the government, but the question is who stopped Yahya from accepting the Russian resolution when he knew about Pakistan's military position in East Pakistan better than anyone else.

It has remained a mystery why the Polish Resolution was not accepted either. Bhutto spoke in the United Nations, tore up this resolution, and walked out of the Security Council session. This act is without explanation except the worst. It feeds on the allegation that he did not want help from any quarter and wanted the army to surrender and let 'Bangladesh' become an irreversible fact. Bhutto knew that as long as Pakistan remained united, he had very little chance of becoming its president or prime minister.

China had also sponsored a resolution which was subsequently withdrawn. Another resolution sponsored by Argentina and supported by seven other countries on the same day was vetoed by the USSR. The resolution contained proposals similar to the American one. Yet another resolution was submitted by the USSR calling 'for cease-fire and effective action by the Pakistan government towards a political settlement giving immediate recognition to the will of the East Pakistan population as expressed in the December 1970 elections'.[22] This presented a way of extricating the Pakistan Army but Pakistan did not show interest in it and consequently it was not voted upon. If Pakistan had pressed for its acceptance, there were chances that the resolution would have been passed and implemented under Soviet pressure.

Then the matter was transferred to the General Assembly under 'The Uniting for Peace Procedure'. A thirty-four member revised resolution on which debate began on 7 December, demanded a cease-fire immediately and 'withdrawal of forces on the territory of the other to their own side of the border'.[23] The resolution was passed with an overwhelming majority of 104. Only eleven countries voted against it. Pakistan accepted the resolution, but India kept it pending for three days. Then India laid down Pakistan's withdrawal of forces from East Pakistan as a pre-condition for the acceptance. This was in fact a tactic to gain time. Yet another resolution was sponsored by the United States in the Security Council calling 'upon the government of India forthwith to accept a cease-fire and withdrawal of armed forces as set forth in the General Assembly Resolution'.[24] The resolution was again vetoed by the USSR.

The second resolution, otherwise the eighth, was sponsored by Poland on 15 December, after the arrival of Z.A. Bhutto in the United Nations. The resolution called for the transfer of power 'to the lawfully elected representatives of the people' and with the beginning of this process 'military action in all the areas will be ceased and an initial cease-fire will start for a period of 72 hours'.[25] The resolution also demanded the evacuation of armed forces, West Pakistani civilians, and other persons 'from the eastern theatre of conflict'. Although Indian forces were threatening to enter Dhaka, Pakistan did not show any interest in the draft resolution and preferred to negotiate for surrender with India. 'The resolution was never voted upon, but if Pakistan had shown any interest in having it passed, it could have been discussed and passed.'[26]

Bhutto, who knew that the war had been lost, made a lengthy speech in the Security Council on 15 December. He said; 'I find it disgraceful to my country and to my person to remain here...legalize aggression, legalize occupation...I will not be a party to...we will go back and fight. The object of the UN had been to permit the fall of Dhaka.... Why should I waste my time here? I will go back to my country and fight'. But he remained in New York until 18 December, when he was asked by Yahya to return to Pakistan to take over.[27]

It is obvious that the Security Council had been dragging its feet till the fall of Dhaka. It is also true that Pakistan neither evinced interest in the proceedings of the United Nations nor made serious efforts for a cease-fire. In fact, Pakistan missed quite a few opportunities, without any cogent reason, of achieving peace and saving herself from humiliation. An impression is gained that the *junta's* plan was to surrender East and to continue army rule in West Pakistan. Perhaps, they did not fully visualize the consequences of surrender.

The Breakup of Pakistan: An Analysis

Mr G.W. Choudhry, in his personal account of the last days of united Pakistan, considers a secret deal between Bhutto and Lieutenant-General Peerzada as an important factor in the army coup against Ayub.[28] This understanding, according to him, also played an important part in the developments leading up to the disintegration of Pakistan in December 1971. Both men had been sacked by Ayub, one as foreign minister and the other as his military secretary, and they were drawn together by their common hostility to him.[29]

Pakistan under Yahya showed that it could carry out a peaceful transfer of power from a military to a democratic regime. Yahya intended to have a genuine political settlement between the two parts of Pakistan by giving the Bengalis, who formed a majority of the population, a real share in the decision making process within a loose federal or confederal system. He believed that the East Pakistanis had not had their fair share in any sphere of national life and that this should be rectified. That is why in his speech on 28 November 1969, he announced the dissolution of One Unit in West Pakistan and an end to the principle of parity in representation between the two parts of the country in the central legislature.

Yahya's plan conceded all the demands put forward by Mujib: elections on the basis of one man, one vote, a single-chamber central legislature, and the abolition of the amalgamation of West Pakistan into 'One Unit'. Although the Bengalis of the East 'wing' formed a majority in undivided Pakistan, their representation in the federal legislature had always been equal to that of the West 'wing'. They accepted this parity of representation in 1955 on condition that it should also apply in the allocation of funds for economic development, representation in the armed services, and in every other sphere. But in practice, there had been no parity except in the electoral representation of the two 'wings', the Bengalis demanded to be released from their side of the bargain. They were also opposed to a bicameral system for the central legislature because they feared that what they gained by being represented on a 'one man, one vote' basis in one chamber would be lost if a second chamber, constituted on a territorial basis, had a majority of West Pakistani seats.

The most important constitutional issue of all, however, was the relationship between the centre and the provinces. Paradoxically, the Bengalis, who as a majority should have had no fear of domination, were anxious to secure the maximum degree of autonomy for their province, particularly in economic and financial matters. Yahya made no attempt to tackle this crucial issue. Instead, he left it to the decision of the new National Assembly which was to draw up a Constitution, at the same time strongly supporting the Bengali claim for maximum autonomy. Naturally, Mujib had no objection to leaving this issue to the new assembly in which there would be a clear Bengali majority.

Many questions can be asked about a plan which aroused such strong expectations. Did the army really want to hand over power at all? Did Mujib want a settlement on the basis of a united Pakistan or did he only intend to use the elections to establish his credentials as the sole leader of an emerging Bangladesh? What were the aims of Bhutto? Was he bent on capturing power, no matter whether in a united or a truncated Pakistan?

One thing that was soon apparent was that the army Generals and the West Pakistani political leaders thought that Yahya had gone too far in trying to placate the Bengalis at the cost of the 'national interest', as they interpreted it. In order to protect the country against a Bengali-dominated assembly, they put forward two particular demands. First, that the constitutional document which (since the country had no Constitution) had to be promulgated before elections could be legally held and that it must contain a definition of the limits of provincial autonomy; and second, in the new assembly, constitutional matters must be decided not by a simple majority but by a two-thirds vote, or 60 per cent of the total membership. It was argued that there was no reason why Yahya should not take a definite decision on the extent of provincial autonomy, just as he had decided on the basis of representation and the break up of 'One-Unit'. The non-Awami League leaders from East Pakistan took this line as well as the West Pakistani leaders and the military *junta*.

The matter was thrashed out at a series of meetings of the 'inner Cabinet' which was composed of Yahya; his principal staff officer, General Peerzada; the Chief of Staff, General Hamid, who began to entertain hopes of succeeding Yahya as the country's third military President; two military provincial Governors and the two deputy (provincial) martial law administrators of East and West Pakistan. Mr G.W. Choudhry was the only civilian present and he attended not as a Cabinet Minister but as a constitutional expert. Eventually, it was decided that the demand for a two-thirds majority on constitutional matters and the extent of provincial autonomy in the constitutional document or 'Legal Framework Order 1970' (popularly known as LFO) could be accepted, but Mujib made it clear through the Governor of East Pakistan, Admiral Ahsan, that to do so would mean the end of negotiations and the beginning of an armed confrontation.

Yahya was in a real dilemma. The Generals seemed to prefer to have a confrontation before elections before Mujib could consolidate his position in East Pakistan. But Ahsan, the only member of the *junta* who understood the political realities in the east 'wing', assured Yahya that a united Pakistan would not survive a confrontation with Mujib. In an attempt to find a way out of the impasse, Mr Choudhry proposed at a meeting of the inner Cabinet in January 1970 that instead of trying to define the extent of provincial autonomy, the LFO should define the minimum requirements that were essential for the existence of one Pakistan. This proposal surprised Yahya and angered the hawks among the Generals, but it was strongly supported by Ahsan, and he was allowed to elaborate upon it. Surprisingly, and to the great relief of Yahya, Ahsan, and Choudhry, it was eventually accepted by the Generals. Although the crisis seemed to be over, subsequent events showed that it had only been postponed for a year.

The LFO, which was at last published on 31 March 1970, contained five points or principles which were regarded as the minimum requirements for a united Pakistan. (1) Pakistan must be based on Islamic ideology. (2) The country must have a democratic Constitution providing free and fair elections. (3) Pakistan's territorial integrity must be upheld in the Constitution. (4) The disparity between the 'wings', particularly in economic development, must be eliminated by statutory provisions to be guaranteed in the Constitution. (5) The distribution of power must be made in such a way that the provinces enjoyed the maximum degree of autonomy consistent with giving the central government sufficient power to discharge its federal responsibilities, including the maintenance of the country's territorial integrity. No doubt, the intention was to set up a conventional federal system, but since the wording of this stipulation was deliberately vague, it was capable of more than one interpretation. It allowed Mujib to base his election campaign on the Six Points.

The LFO was criticized, particularly in East Pakistan, as a retreat from the plan put forward by Yahya in November 1969. In a sense, this was true, but those who knew the inside story of how the document had been drawn up realized that some compromise was essential and were not dissatisfied with the outcome. Mujib, who learned what had gone on from Ahsan, accepted the outcome, and when the Awami League council demanded that he should boycott the elections because of the 'new restrictions' in the LFO, he did not agree. He was reported to have told his 'inner Cabinet' that his sole aim was to win the elections by capturing 99 per cent of the Bengali seats. Who could then, he was said to have argued, ignore his plan for Bangladesh? He was also reported to have predicted support from 'outside sources'.

Elections were originally fixed for October 1970, but after disastrous floods in East Pakistan in August, they were postponed for two months. In November, East Bengal was devastated by a cyclone and there were demands for a further postponement of elections. Mujib, however, threatened to revolt if the elections were delayed any longer, and Yahya agreed that they should go ahead. This decision finally destroyed Mujib's doubts about Yahya's sincerity and made the relationship between them even more cordial. In November 1970, they had three secret meetings and Yahya cheerfully said that the new Pakistan Constitution would combine Mujib's Six Points and the five principles laid down in the LFO. He had just completed his triangular tour of Moscow (June), Washington (October), and Peking (November), and it was widely believed that he had already reached an understanding with Mujib that he should continue as President while Mujib became Prime Minister.

Meanwhile, in West Pakistan where right-wing parties had always been strong, Bhutto was winning more and more support. The main theme of his election campaign was a 'thousand years' war with India to restore the national honour which Ayub was alleged to have sacrificed at the Tashkent Conference in 1966 under pressure from the Soviet Union. More significant, and ominous, were Bhutto's growing links with the Generals. They turned to him to protect the so-called 'national interests' because they realized that they had been deprived of their confrontation with Mujib. Far from rejecting the LFO, he now seemed to have a better understanding than ever with Yahya on constitutional issues. Moreover, it was clear that Mujib was going to win at the polls and that his victory would be all the greater because the highly emotional Bengalis were furious with the central government for its alleged failure to deal adequately with the cyclone disaster.

The elections held on 7 December 1970, were completely free and fair. As expected, Mujib had a landslide victory in East Pakistan, gaining an absolute majority in the National Assembly by capturing 167 out of the 169 seats allotted to the East 'wing'. He enjoyed a similar success in the provincial assembly in Dhaka. What was surprising about the election results was the total defeat of right-wing and orthodox parties in the West 'wing' and the emergence of a non-Punjabi, Bhutto, as the leader of the West Pakistan, or, more precisely, of the Punjab.

Bhutto's success boded ill for the future of a united Pakistan. There was no love lost between him and Mujib. On the contrary, they shared a mutual distrust and dislike, if not hatred for each other. More importantly, neither possessed any broad perspective or vision. Unlike such Congress leaders as Gandhi and Nehru, or Muslim League leaders like Jinnah, neither Mujib nor Bhutto possessed any of the qualities of a leader whose aim is to achieve his objectives at a minimum cost in terms of human suffering and loss to society. In a sense, both were products of Ayub's authoritarian regime. Both flourished on negative appeals to the illiterate voters of Pakistan, one by whipping up regional feelings against Punjabi domination and the other by whipping up militant national feeling against India. Neither had any constructive or positive approach. The third party in the political equation, the army, unlike the British authorities in 1946–47, also seems to have been insincere, bent on retaining the absolute power which it had enjoyed for the past eleven years. Only Yahya, Ahsan and a few other Generals, particularly among the younger group in the Pakistan Army, seemed to want a genuine political settlement. But their standing was weakened after the election when the country began to drift inexorably towards a confrontation.

In the LFO, Yahya had provided that the new National Assembly must complete its task of framing a new Constitution within 120 days. This time limit was accepted by all political leaders. It had taken two Constituent Assemblies nine years to frame a Constitution for Pakistan between 1947 to 1956, and everyone wanted to prevent a repetition of this tragic delay. It was also agreed that the majority group or group responsible for producing a Constitution would show the draft to the President before formally presenting it to the Assembly. Mujib had already solemnly promised Yahya during their secret talks in November to show him the Awami League's draft constitution.

Yahya, who was anxious to begin talks with the newly elected leaders as soon as possible, invited Mujib to come to Rawalpindi. Mujib declined, but invited him to come to Dhaka instead. Yahya accepted and asked Mr Choudhry to go with him so that he could have expert advice on Mujib's draft Constitution. The two leaders met on 12 January and talked for more than three hours. But Yahya emerged from the meeting a bitter and frustrated man. Mujib, he complained, had gone back on his word and refused to show him his draft Constitution on the grounds that, as leader of the majority party, he alone was responsible for the new Constitution. Mujib also demanded the immediate summoning of the Assembly, threatening dire consequences otherwise. It seemed plain that the confrontation, which had been avoided with such difficulty in 1970, could no longer be averted.

Yahya went on from Dhaka to hold talks with Bhutto in his home town, Larkana. Bhutto had also begun to show signs of intransigence. He started to issue press statements declaring that the 'Punjab was the bastion of power' and could not be ignored in any future government or in the making of the Constitution. He also made it clear that he would 'not play the role of a loyal opposition leader', and that since the Awami League victory was confined to one region (East Pakistan), 'two majority groups' must be recognized and 'two Prime Ministers' might be necessary. An impartial reading of Bhutto's utterances, together with his active lobbying of the hawks in the Pakistan Army, would lead one to conclude that if he had to make a choice between two 'Ps', Power or Pakistan, he would choose the former.

In Larkana, Yahya and prominent members of the *junta*, including General Peerzada and General Hamid, enjoyed Bhutto's hospitality and held long conferences with him. Mr Choudhry was not present at these talks but he learned about them later from reliable sources. It seems that they were fatal for the prospects of a united Pakistan. Bhutto exploited to the full the sense of frustration left by Yahya after his meeting with Mujib in Dhaka. He was strongly supported by his old friend, Peerzada, who enjoyed Yahya's unlimited trust and confidence. The result was that while still in Larkana the *junta*, ignoring Bhutto's provocative utterances, decided to prepare a contingency plan in case Mujib persisted 'in his uncompromising attitude'. At a meeting on 14 February, it decided to dissolve the Pakistan Cabinet, apparently because the Bengali ministers and one non-Bengali minister (who was a close friend of Mujib) were working hard to find a compromise. At the same meeting, it was also decided that Admiral Ahsan (who had in fact expressed a wish to resign) should be replaced as Governor of East Pakistan by a hawk, General Tikka Khan.

In the meantime, India had stopped all flights between East and West Pakistan because of the alleged hijacking of an Indian plane by Pakistanis. While negotiations over the incident were still going on between the Indian and Pakistani governments, Mujib publicly described it as a 'conspiracy' to postpone the transfer of power, while Bhutto declared that the so-called hijackers were 'national heroes'. Mujib's remarks were resented by the Generals, who began to describe him as an 'Indian agent'. At a farewell party given for members of the Cabinet, General Hamid told Mr Choudhry that his 'boys' (meaning his soldiers) were 'getting restless for action'. When he pointed out the dangers of such a course of action, he retorted: 'I could fix it up in seventy-two hours'.

On 1 March, the National Assembly session due to convene two days later, was indefinitely postponed after Bhutto threatened to boycott it unless Mujib came to terms with him. By now, their mutual suspicion and hatred made this impossible. In East Pakistan, there was a violent reaction to the postponement. Mujib described it as non-cooperation; not the Gandhian type of non-violent non-cooperation but an open revolt which amounted to a unilateral declaration of independence for Bangladesh. Cries of *Joy Bangla* (victory for Bengal) were heard everywhere, and what was almost a parallel government began to function under Mujib's instructions. Between 3 and 25 March, the central government's writ did not run in East Pakistan.

The explosive situation was created mainly by Bhutto's boycott of the assembly. Many people still feel that if it had not been postponed, Mujib might have been able to produce a Constitution with the help of West Pakistani deputies who did not belong to Bhutto's party, and who had already arrived in Dhaka for the opening of the assembly. But Bhutto was by now the *junta's* most influential adviser. He was even reported to have prepared Yahya's various statements, including the decision to postpone the session.

Even at this late stage, Yahya and Mujib were still talking to each other on the telephone and seemed anxious to negotiate. Mujib appeared to be getting nervous about the activities of his own extremists, while Yahya still hoped to go down in history as the man responsible for a voluntary transfer of power from a military to a civilian regime. On 15 March, he went to Dhaka and the next day began a crucial series of talks with Mujib. The negotiations were carried on at two levels: at a summit level between Yahya and Mujib, with Bhutto joining in later; and at an expert level between three teams, Yahya's advisers, led by his former Law Minister (now Law Adviser), Justice Cornelius, and General Peerzada;[30] the Awami League team, led by Tajuddin (who subsequently acted as Prime Minister of Bangladesh before Mujib's return from detention in West Pakistan) and Dr Kamal Hossain (later Bangladesh's Law Minister); and Bhutto's team, consisting of members of his party secretly advised by senior Punjabi bureaucrats.

By 20 March, the press was reporting that a compromised constitutional formula incorporating most of the fundamentals of Mujib's Six Points had been agreed upon. The reports turned out to be too good to be true. The next day, Mujib rejected the compromise formula and on 23 March a new formula, drawn up by the Awami League team, was presented by Dr Hossain. There was as Dr Hossain himself was reported to have said, very little difference between the two drafts. Both preserved the unity of Pakistan and both restricted the powers of the centre, as far as East Pakistan was concerned. All the same, the Dhaka talks broke down, and on 25 March the Pakistan Army took matters in its own hands. The resort to force was bound to destroy a united Pakistan and the end came with the entry of a triumphant Indian Army into Dhaka on 16 December 1971.

Since both drafts envisaged one Pakistan, why did the army and Bhutto reject the Awami League's Constitution? And since both conceded the Bengalis' demand for autonomy on the basis of the Six Points, why did Mujib and the Awami League reject Yahya's draft? During two visits to Pakistan in 1971, Mr Choudhry sought the answers to those two crucial questions, but failed to provide a satisfactory or definite explanation. Perhaps the break up of Pakistan was made inevitable by the growing tension, suspicion, and even hatred between the ruling elite of West Pakistan and the Bengali intelligentsia. It came as a great shock to many people, like Choudhry, who had cherished the ideals behind the Muslims' demand for a separate state in the 1940s. Could the terrible bloodshed connected with the emergence of Bangladesh have been avoided? Gandhi and Nehru committed themselves to full independence for India, yet they showed great statesmanship in accepting dominion status and even a British Governor-General so that a smooth and quick transfer of power could take place. Could Mujib have shown the same wisdom and prevented the killing of (according to his estimate) three million Bengalis? Could he have avoided a situation which led inevitably to the introduction of foreign (Indian) troops and the destruction of the country's economic infrastructure and of its social fabric?

What happened at the final Dhaka talks in March 1971 is not fully known, but Choudhry speculates that when Yahya went to Dhaka in January, he was prepared to accept Mujib's Six Points without reservation. Choudhry was asked to prepare a formula on the relationship between the centre and the provinces. He drafted a plan for a confederal solution on the basis of the Six Points, which he knew was the only way to preserve a united Pakistan. Yahya wrote on the draft: 'What is the difference between your scheme and the Six Points?' Yet he accepted it and took it with him to Dhaka in January. Mujib's mistake was his refusal at that meeting to honour his pledge to show Yahya the draft Constitution. But the story is incomplete without a reference to Bhutto and his friends in the army like Peerzada and Hamid. When the full story of Pakistan's dismemberment can be told, they may well be found to have the prime responsibility for the failure of the final Dhaka talks and their tragic consequences.

Conclusion

The analysis of Choudhry inspires confidence because he had an insider's knowledge of the events. His integrity is generally believed to be beyond doubt and there is no question of his sincere belief in a united Pakistan. His analysis of the role of Mujib and Bhutto appears to be accurate. They were indeed men driven by blind personal ambition and national interest was of little importance to them. But his defence of Yahya is a bit too generous. Although it may be correct that Yahya's intentions were right and his motives were above board, he still made certain crucial mistakes. He is not to be blamed for all the ills that divided East from West Pakistan but certain steps taken by him accelerated the process of disintegration and escalated the differences between the two parts of Pakistan into an open confrontation. Those fatal steps can be described as under:

(a) He should not have taken the unilateral decision of dissolving One Unit in West Pakistan and ought to have left it to the Constituent Assembly.
(b) He should not have dispensed with the principle of parity between the two parts of Pakistan in the matter of representation. This was a basic constitutional agreement voluntarily arrived at by the Constituent Assembly that made the 1956 Constitution. Such a constitutional understanding could only be changed, modified, or varied by another Constituent Assembly. In any case, Yahya had no mandate to make such fundamental changes in the constitution. By his own violation, he was a temporary repository of power to restore law and order in the country, hold peaceful elections, and hand over power to the elected representatives. He could not extend his functions to make fundamental constitutional changes.
(c) He should not have allowed Mujib to campaign on the Six Point Programme and should have enforced the LFO. Having allowed them to do so, it was too difficult and too late to stop Mujib after the elections.
(d) He should have contained Awami League excesses against other parties during the election campaign in East Pakistan. It was his duty to protect other political parties and to give them a fair chance to reach the voters with their programmes. It was also a demand of fair and impartial democratic elections that all political parties could participate in them without any fear or favour.
(e) He should not have been bullied by Bhutto and should, in no case, have postponed the session of the National Assembly which triggered the unfortunate situation.
(f) He should not have taken the decision of a military crackdown and should have followed the path of political settlement.

The dismemberment of Pakistan is a scar which loyalists feel deep in their heart. It was specially painful for those people (like the present writer) who had been born after independence and found themselves in a united Pakistan. For them, it was as shocking as a divorce between one's parents.[31] How tragic and ironic that Bengalis seceded from the union of Pakistan which they had done the most to achieve. Muslims in Bengal had participated in the freedom movement far more actively than any province or any part of the provinces that formed West Pakistan. They were indeed true Pakistanis. The arrogant military and bureaucratic establishments in Pakistan, coupled with self-centred and short-sighted politicians from West Pakistan, alienated them and ultimately pushed them into the arms of a demagogue like Mujib.

Bhutto's role in the break up of Pakistan is major and G.W. Choudhry has correctly laid a lot of blame on his shoulders. As an extremely ambitious man, he could not wait any longer to take over the reigns of power. He knew that in a united Pakistan he could not become the head of government by democratic means. His party had no presence in East Pakistan which held the majority of the seats in the central legislature. That is why he came up with the incongruous demand for transfer of power to Mujib in East Pakistan and to himself in West Pakistan. In one of his most often quoted remarks, addressing Mujib publicly soon after the elections of December 1970, he said '*Udhar tum, Idhar hum*, you there, me here'. He would rather have Pakistan dismantled than give Mujib power in a united Pakistan. He later tried to justify his role in the whole tragedy, but with little conviction.[32] His role in the break up of Pakistan will always remain under a cloud.

Nevertheless, except for Yahya, the main characters in the drama that led to the formation of Bangladesh, suffered unnatural and violent deaths. Mujib was killed mercilessly in 1975 along with several members of his family by his own military units. His killers have gone unpunished. Bhutto was hanged in April 1979 on the orders of the courts for having committed murder. Mrs Indira Gandhi, who was Prime Minister of India and responsible for the invasion of East Pakistan, was assassinated by her own bodyguards in October 1984.

NOTES

1. Salik, Siddique, *Witness to Surrender*, 1977, Oxford University Press, Karachi, p. 75.
2. *Dawn*, 27 March 1971.
3. Salik, Siddique, *Witness to Surrender. supra*, No. 1, p. 77.
4. Ibid., p. 76.
5. Mascarenhas, Anthony, *The Rape of Bangla Desh*, 1971. Vikas Publications, Delhi, pp. 111-20.
6. The present writer interviewed a number of prisoners of war involved in military action who commonly gave this version.
7. Author is grateful to Mr I. A. Rahman, Director, Human Rights Commission of Pakistan, for providing him with this information, which has not otherwise appeared anywhere else in print.
8. Feldman, Herbert, *The End and the Beginning: Pakistan 1969-71*, 1975, Oxford University Press, London. pp. 145-8.
9. Ibid., p. 149.
10. Ibid., pp. 153-4.
11. Notably in the case of the Jamaat-i-Islami leader Chaudhry Ghulam Azam.
12. Feldman, Herbert, *The End and the Beginning. supra*, note 8, pp. 154-5.
13. This draft Constitution was prepared by Chief Justice (Retired) A. R. Cornelius who was then in 1971, the Central Law Minister. The present writer has a copy of this draft Constitution which he received from Late Cornelins.
14. Article of Major-General Rao Farman Ali, *Jang*, Rawalpindi, 20 December 1977.
15. *The Times*, London, 8 November 1971.
16. Ibid.
17. Mahmood, Safdar, *Pakistan Divided.* 1984, Ferozsons Ltd., Lahore, p. 194. He cites Kuldip Nayyar's *Distant Neighbours*, Vikas Publishing House, Delhi, 1972, p. 189 and Wayne Wilcox's *The Emergence of Bangladesh,* American Enterprise Institute for Public Policy Research, Washington, 1973, p. 50.
18. Salik, Siddique, *Witness to Surrender. supra*, note 1, pp. 193-4.
19. UN Security Council Draft Resolution (S/10416).
20. UN Security Council Draft Resolution (S/10418).
21. *Dawn*, 24 November 1971.
22. Security Council Resolution (S/10428).
23. UN General Assembly Resolution (2793 XXVI).
24. Security Council Draft Resolution (S/10446, Rev. 1)
25. Security Council Draft Resolution (S/10453 Rev.1)
26. *The Outlook* (Weekly), Karachi, 25 November 1974, p. 10.

27. Mahmood, Safdar, *Pakistan Divided*, *supra*, note 17, p. 207.
28. Mr G. W. Choudhry had been head of Research Division of the Ministry of Foreign Affairs. He joined the Cabinet of Yahya Khan in November 1969.
29. Choudhry, G.W., The Last Days of United Pakistan. A personal account. An article Published in 49 International Affairs (1973), pp. 229-39.
30. Yahya asked Mr Choudhry to take part, first as an official adviser and then as a private citizen. He declined both offers because it seemed to him that neither side was prepared to compromise and, therefore, the talks were a futile exercise. But he was very well-briefed on what happened by Justice Cornelius.
31. The day Dhaka fell was indeed one of the loneliest and saddest days in the life of the author who, at that time, was in the United States in connection with his higher studies.
32. *The Great Tragedy* by Zulfiqar Ali Bhutto. A Pakistan People's Party Publication, Vision Publications Ltd., Karachi. 1971.

PART V

THE BHUTTO REGIME: DECEMBER 1971 TO JULY 1977

20

CIVILIAN MARTIAL LAW

In a broadcast on 16 December 1971, Yahya admitted defeat in East Pakistan and went on to declare that the war would go on: 'We will continue to fight the enemy on every front, and also continue our efforts to form a representative government in the country which the enemy, by launching an attack, tried to set aside. According to the programme, the Constitution will be announced on 20 December. This guarantees the maximum autonomy to East Pakistan on the basis of one Pakistan, for whose establishment and protection the people of both wings of the country sacrificed so much. A central government will be formed after this, and subsequently provincial governments will come into being...'

Shortly afterwards, Mrs Gandhi under pressure from the United States, announced that she had ordered a unilateral cease-fire on the western front from 8:00 p.m. on 17 December. She declared that 'India has no territorial ambitions'. She went on to add that since the Pakistani forces had surrendered and Bangladesh had gained freedom, 'it is pointless in our view to continue the present conflict'. After this decision was communicated to Yahya through the Swiss Embassy, he announced that he had also ordered a cease-fire to come into force at the same time.

A UN resolution put forward by Japan, Argentina, and other countries, called for strict observance of the cease-fire in all the areas of conflict, and asked for the withdrawal of all armed forces as soon as practicable to their respective territories and to positions which fully respected the cease-fire line in Kashmir. The resolution also called on all countries to refrain from actions which might complicate the situation in the subcontinent. It also called on all those concerned to observe the Geneva Conventions of 1949 on the protection of the wounded and sick prisoners of war and the civilian population. It called for international assistance in the relief of refugees and their return in safety to their homes, and authorized the Secretary-General to appoint, if necessary, a special representative to lend his good offices for the solution of humanitarian problems. This resolution was adopted by thirteen votes to none, with Poland and the Soviet Union abstaining. The Chinese delegation, while voting for the resolution, expressed dissatisfaction with it.

Meanwhile, violent demonstrations began on 18 December, against the military regime in West Pakistan, followed by a vocal revolt by army officers in GHQ, Rawalpindi on 19 December,[1] which led to Yahya's resignation. Bhutto was subsequently sworn in as Pakistan's new President on 20 December 1971.

The United States had announced the cancellation of all outstanding licences of shipment of military equipment to India on 3 December 1971, and all US economic aid to India was suspended on 6 December. A State Department spokesman said that 'the United States will not make a contribution to the Indian economy which will make it easier for the Indian government to sustain its military effort', and that the question of similar action against Pakistan did not arise because all the aid in the pipeline was earmarked for humanitarian relief in East Pakistan.

In its aggression against Pakistan, India had invoked Article 9 of the Indo-Soviet Treaty of Peace, Friendship, and Co-operation, which had been signed on 9 August 1971, for an initial period of twenty years and which provided for consultations in the event of an attack or threatened attack upon either party. The Soviet government attributed the responsibility for the war to Pakistan in a statement issued by the official Tass agency on 5 December and warned other governments to avoid becoming involved in the conflict. Chinese official statements attributed the entire responsibility for the war to India, and accused the Soviet Union of encouraging Indian 'aggression'.

Bangladesh Government Established in Dhaka

The city of Dhaka was in a state of virtual anarchy after the surrender of the Pakistan Army. Elements of the *Mukti Bahini* used the opportunity to take revenge on 'collaborators', especially the *razakars*. Violence was provoked by the massacres reported to have been carried out by Pakistani soldiers and the *razakars* from March 1971 till the time of surrender. The mutilated bodies of 20 leading Bengali intellectuals were found on 18 December, and over a hundred others in the next three days. Subsequent investigation established that a massacre of intellectuals, technicians, and professionals had taken place during the last stages of the war. Evidence of other massacres involving many thousands of people was discovered in the next few weeks.

Members of the Bangladesh government in exile finally arrived in the city on 22 December 1977, the delay in their return being due to the Indian Army's wish to restore order before a civilian government took over. The Cabinet was reshuffled and a list of measures were drawn up to deal with immediate tasks.

Mujib, who had been arrested on the night of 25–26 March 1971, and had been held ever since in West Pakistan, was released on 8 January 1972. He flew to London, where he revealed that he had been sentenced to death in West Pakistan. On his return to Dhaka on 10 January, he was given a tumultuous welcome. Two days later, he resigned the presidency and became Prime Minister whilst Justice Abu Sayeed Chowdhury was sworn in as the new President of Bangladesh.

Bhutto Takes Over

Despite the political and military disaster in East Pakistan, Yahya was stuck with the notion that in spite of everything he could carry on as President. At the GHQ, a strong current of opinion was against him. However, on the question of his successor, there was a distinct difference of opinion. Some favoured Asghar Khan, who had contributed to the departure of Ayub and had built a political following. Others, considered this a mistake. The introduction of yet another armed forces man as President might well provoke stiff opposition in a nation which had no reason to have any confidence in the political skill of men in uniform. Moreover, in the election of 1970, Asghar Khan had been soundly defeated in a Rawalpindi constituency which was the veritable home of the armed forces by a People's Party candidate of no great prominence. Thus, Asghar Khan was not a member of the National Assembly, nor was anyone else from his Tehrik-i-Istiqlal Party.

The second school of thought favoured Bhutto as Yahya's successor. His qualifications were that (a) he was not an armed forces man; (b) he was an elected member of the National Assembly; (c) his party had a majority in the assembly since Mujib's Awami League had been unseated; (d) it was evident that Bhutto had emerged, in West Pakistan at least, as a popular leader; and (e) he was already Deputy Prime Minister. It is evident that before leaving New York, and perhaps in Rome too, Bhutto received information from his close political colleagues that events in Pakistan were taking an unpredictable course and that he should return as soon as possible.

There still remained the question of Yahya's intentions and, on 17 December Gul Hasan, along with Rahim Khan, went to the President House to confront Yahya. On arrival, they found Yahya still busy with his radio address. At the meeting at which General Abdul Hameed Khan was present, Gul Hasan and Rahim Khan informed Yahya that nothing remained but for him to go. At first, Yahya resisted this suggestion, but when they pressed him more firmly, he agreed and added that he would then go back to the army as Commander-in-Chief. This, Gul Hasan and Rahim Khan treated as absurd and insisted that Yahya must go altogether. In the face of this pressure, it seems that Yahya obliquely suggested that Gul Hasan might become President and, more explicitly perhaps, that Abdul Hameed Khan might become the Commander-in-Chief. At about this time, or somewhat later, so much is obscure, Gul Hasan realized that the broadcast of Yahya's address had begun and, at once, ordered it to be stopped.

To the proposal that he become Commander-in-Chief, Abdul Hameed Khan demurred and said he would not accept any such proposal unless he first met the officers at the GHQ to obtain their reaction to the idea. He, therefore, called a meeting of senior officers which included those with ranks of Lieutenant-Colonels and above, at the GHQ, on 20 December. Shortly afterwards, it was announced that all officers at the GHQ would attend and some thirty minutes before the meeting was held all officers of the Rawalpindi garrison were required to be present. The circumstances which led to this significant expansion of Abdul Hameed Khan's audience are unclear and it may have been Gul Hasan who, as Chief of the General Staff, had these orders issued through the Staff Duties Directorate. It is believed that Gul Hasan advised some officers who had consulted him, not to withhold their opinions or mince their words. The meeting was a stormy one in which strong language was used and Abdul Hameed Khan was unable to satisfy his audience.

From 18 to 20 December, the country was virtually without a government and Yahya was more or less a prisoner. His coterie of political Generals had been rendered impotent and the only person exercising authority was Gul Hasan. On his arrival in Rawalpindi, Bhutto was met by Gul Hasan and Rahim Khan and, with them, he went straight to the President's House where he took over office from Yahya.

An impression may be formed here that Bhutto was simply a military nominee but this would not do him justice. It is true that, in politics, the final arbiter is the man with the pistol in his pocket (and political maturity can be measured by the ability to dispense with so drastic a recourse). Nevertheless, Bhutto had electoral success behind him which was very much a personal achievement. Bhutto was as necessary to the army as the army's sanction was to him. It should be added that Bhutto gave some account of these events in his address on 20 December 1971. The words he used were 'summoned by the nation'.[2]

Meanwhile, Pakistan's forces in the eastern province had surrendered, the independence of Bangladesh had become a reality, and India, having announced a unilateral ceasefire, held its positions on the west front. In the new Pakistan, it remained only for Bhutto to enter upon the task of restoring the country's shattered fortunes.[3]

Bhutto: His Background to Political Ascendancy

After the fall of Dhaka and the emergence of Bangladesh, there was no justification left for Yahya to continue in power. His own military colleagues prevailed upon him to hand over power to Bhutto, whose party, the PPP, had emerged as the majority party in the erstwhile West Pakistan. Thus, Bhutto was summoned from the United States where he was staying after tearing up the Polish Resolution as Foreign Minister of Pakistan. Before leaving for Pakistan, he met President Nixon in Washington D.C. He reached Pakistan on 20 December 1971 and, as stated above, was handed over power as President and Chief Martial Law Administrator. He thus had the dubious distinction of being a civilian CMLA, a rare occurrence indeed. He decided to continue martial law because he wanted to implement some of the programmes promised in his 1970 election manifesto under the protection of martial law.

Delving into Zulfiqar Ali Bhutto's history and his rise in the political arena it can be said that he came into prominence when he was taken into the first Martial Law Cabinet on 8 October 1958. He was a recommendee of President Iskandar Mirza[4] but was retained in the Cabinet by Ayub despite the ouster of Iskandar Mirza. He was a bright young man of about 31 years of age at that time, having studied in California and England where he had been called to the Bar. He had a strong political background, being the son of Shahnawaz Bhutto of Larkana. His father had been the President of the District Board of Larkana and was awarded the title of Khan Bahadur in 1921, and Companion of the Indian Empire in 1925. In 1930, Shahnawaz was knighted in the New Year's Honours list, the citation reading:[5]

> He is the most influential zamindar in Sind, he has constantly and effectively exercised influence in support of the government.

Shahnawaz also served as a Minister of Local Government in the Bombay Cabinet in 1934. It is to the credit of Shahnawaz Bhutto that he struggled hard, and successfully, for the separation of Sindh from the old Bombay Presidency, a demand which was accepted under the Government of India Act, 1935. He was, however, defeated in the elections of 1937 after which he retired from politics. He later served on the Public Service Commission in Bombay and in 1947, was appointed *divan*[6] of the State of Junagarh. It has already been noted that on the creation of Pakistan, Junagarh, with a Muslim ruler and a predominantly Hindu population, had acceded to Pakistan. However, agitation by the pro-Congress population stymied this attempt and forced the ruler to abdicate from the state in 1947. Faced with a real possibility of bloodshed and civil disruption, Shahnawaz made the controversial decision to invite the Indian Dominion to take over and, on the 8 November 1947, left for Pakistan with his family.[7] He died in 1957 at the age of 69.

Bhutto inherited a large tract of land from his father. Before the 1959 Land Reforms, the Bhutto clan reportedly held around forty to sixty thousand acres of extremely productive land in Larkana, Jacobabad, Thatta, and Sukkur.[8]

Zulfiqar Ali Bhutto returned to Pakistan in 1954 after completing his education in the West and settled into a law practice in Karachi. He taught part time at the Sindh Muslim Law College as well. In Ayub's Cabinet, he served for nearly eight years and was one of his most trusted lieutenants. He held various portfolios in Ayub's Cabinet, becoming Foreign Minister in 1963 on the demise of Mr Muhammad Ali Bogra. In this position, he got opportunities of national exposure which ultimately built him into a national leader. He ran into serious differences with Ayub on the Tashkent Declaration and finally left his Cabinet as a disillusioned young man. Initially, he maintained strict silence. Later, however, he voiced his opinion on various political issues. Looking at Ayub's Muslim League Party in 1966, he thought it could be revitalized only if a 'forward bloc' were created within the organization. The bloc comprised those individuals who possessed revolutionary ideas and were willing to initiate unorthodox programmes. The 'forward bloc' was not a new device in the subcontinent's politics. Usually employed by disenchanted elements within a party, it historically heralded the breaking away from the parent organization. Bhutto's call for a 'forward bloc' was nothing less than an attack upon Ayub. Although first insisting that he stood with his old leader, he later changed his position and remarked that it was only Ayub's election manifesto (which he had probably helped to draft) and the welfare state idea that he really supported.

On a visit to East Pakistan in November 1966, Bhutto openly attacked Ayub's policies and expressed his support for the Six Point Programme of Mujib. Only a few months earlier, as Foreign Minister, he had condemned Mujib and volunteered to debate the Six Point Programme with him. But soon after throwing this challenge, Bhutto excused himself saying that he had more pressing matters to attend to. Now that he was no longer a member of the Ayub Cabinet, Bhutto publicly defied Ayub by coming out in support of a programme which Ayub had labelled parochial, divisive, and aimed at the destruction of Pakistan. Returning to West Pakistan, Bhutto declared that he would reserve the option to join another party or form a new one if the Muslim League failed to fulfill its pledge to the people. He noted, however, that there was still scope for a 'forward bloc' in the Ayub Muslim League.

On 10 December, Malik Khuda Bakhsh Bucha, then President of the West Pakistan Muslim League, took note of Bhutto's demand and declared emphatically that 'there was no place for any "forward or backward" bloc in the Muslim League'.[9] He said that 'fissiparous tendencies in the Muslim League were noticeable at certain places' and they had the effect of dissipating party vigour and strength. He called upon the discontented to close ranks and offered his good offices in an effort to resolve the outstanding differences. The party could not be dominated by any particular individual or group of personalities. Moreover, the Muslim League, said Bucha, refused to engage in political sloganeering: 'Gone are the days when a political party was meant only for electioneering and seeking votes'. Now the most urgent political work involved the social and economic betterment of the people. Bhutto was put on his guard; he had to either accept the view that the Muslim League was an instrument for mobilizing the masses for the development work or to quit the organization.

In the spring of 1967, Bhutto toured West Pakistan and spoke out against the government on both domestic and international matters. It may be noted that a number of EBDO'd politicians celebrated the termination of their restrictions at a lavish dinner in Karachi's Hotel Intercontinental on the evening of 31 December 1966. Although Bhutto was in the dining room, few politicians felt it wise to spend too much time at his table. While he failed in his attempt to form a forward bloc within the Pakistan Muslim League, Bhutto was not prevented from launching his own People's Party. Prior to this event, in July 1967, the government sought to discredit him by publishing documents which purported to show that the former Foreign Minister considered himself a citizen of India at least up to the year 1958. The Bhutto family at one time possessed land which after partition was located in India. Bhutto, like so many other Pakistanis, registered applications with the Indian government in connection with the eventual restitution of this property. The legal transactions were handled through the office of the Custodian of Evacuee Property. In this proceeding, it was alleged that Bhutto declared that he had always been an Indian citizen. It was only in 1958 after he became Ayub's Minister of Commerce that he filed a petition with the Supreme Court of India withdrawing his appeal against the Custodian's decision.

The question of Bhutto's citizenship became a heated issue and the opposition asked why, if this information was known in 1965, was Bhutto allowed to remain in office for still another year. To this, the central government's Information Minister Khwaja Shahabuddin responded that the details were not clearly known at the time. When prodded by the opposition to debate the matter with Bhutto personally, and also to agree to the holding of an inquiry into the antecedents of other ministers, Shahabuddin backed away.

Bhutto later denied the principal allegation, but admitted that he had travelled to the United States on an Indian passport in 1947. He added that a Pakistani passport was issued to him in Karachi on 12 July 1949. Bhutto also verified that he had laid claim to ancestral holdings in India. He however, emphatically rejected the allegation that he did so as an Indian citizen. Furthermore, he reported, that the Pakistan government had been kept informed of the negotiations. Later, under advice from his lawyer, he had withdrawn his case altogether.

It was three months after Bhutto's exchange with the administration that he chose to create his own political party. With a political organization in tow, Bhutto began looking for recruits over and above his eager student supporters. At a press conference in Karachi in October 1967, he said that he intended to develop a programme which would look like a socialist manifesto. Its main plank would be the nationalization of banks, insurance companies, heavy industry, and all public utilities. In the matter of foreign policy, Bhutto said his party would be independent and he would insist on Pakistan's withdrawal from both SEATO and CENTO. Moreover, closer links would be forged with Afro-Asia, especially with other Muslim states.

According to Bhutto, none of the existing opposition parties measured up to his criteria in leadership or in programmes. With elections scheduled for late 1969, there was little time to get his new organization in high gear, but he expected students and professionals to assist him in cultivating the opposition. As for the opposition, the Awami League and the National Awami Party had split, Mian Mumtaz Daultana was unable to broaden the base of the Council Muslim League, and Chaudhri Mohammad Ali's Nizam-i-Islam had no appeal for the rural population. Only Maudoodi's Jamaat-i-Islami presented an organized front. Unfortunately, however, the latter's programme had little appeal for the Pakistani masses. Even the Pakistan Democratic Movement comprising the Council Muslim League, Jamaat-i-Islami, Awami League, and Nizam-i-Islam had far too limited objectives in Bhutto's estimation.

Even if these diverse parties were capable of working together for a time, their basic differences were enough to impede the building of a coherent political base, and without a stable foundation, the restructuring of Pakistani society was impossible. Hence Bhutto's decision to forge ahead with an entirely new party and his determination to face Ayub at the ballot box.

Bhutto's challenge could not be taken lightly. In an oblique reference to the former foreign minister, Central Communications Minister Khan A. Sobur rejected Bhutto's call for a socialist state. According to Sobur, socialism had failed to develop in India and it was unrealistic to assume it could work in Pakistan. Asserting that Bhutto was a charlatan and an opportunist, though with a fertile mind, he reminded his East Pakistani brethren that this was the same man who had condemned the Six Point Programme, suggested that Pakistan should be a one party state, and assisted in operationalizing the 1962 Constitution. Over and over again, Ayub, his Cabinet ministers, and party officials reminded their listeners that dissidents like Bhutto concealed their nefarious motives and that such men preached the cult of parochialism, provincialism, and division and were to be rejected lest the country be torn apart. Interestingly, the parochialism to which Bhutto and others like him appealed were not considered dangerous by the public. The more the government sought to undermine their attractiveness the greater their strength grew amongst the people.[10]

When Bhutto took over the affairs of Pakistan on 20 December 1971, all around him was defeat and despair. The country had been ripped apart. Six thousand square miles of territory was under Indian occupation and nearly 90,000 prisoners of war were in Indian camps. The army was demoralized and disgraced and the economy was ravaged. It goes to Bhutto's credit that he took to the task of re-building Pakistan with courage and determination. He inspired confidence among those around him and among the people at large. He made an emotional appeal to the nation in his first address on radio and television and asked for help and co-operation. He said that the nation had repeatedly been failed by its leadership and that he wanted to put things right. He promised not to fail the people of Pakistan.

Civilian Martial Law and Bhutto's Reforms

It has been discussed earlier that at the time of taking over power, Bhutto assumed unto himself the dual capacity of the President and the CMLA. Chief Justice Hamood-ur Rahman was appointed to probe into the military debacle in East Pakistan. As CMLA, Bhutto issued orders and pronouncements covering a whole range of subjects. The passports of Pakistan's leading industrialists and their families were seized and they were barred from going abroad. He began to set up para-military and intelligence organizations in order to monitor his opponents, ambitious army officers, and even his own party men. He appointed some notorious police officers to the Federal Intelligence Bureau. He started victimizing his old antagonists like industrialist Habibullah Khattak, banker S.U. Durrani, and ex-Naval Chief A.R. Khan, who were imprisoned without adequate reason. He had Altaf Gauhar, the editor of *Dawn*, arrested for criticizing him. He retired a number of military Generals and appointed General Gul Hasan as Army Chief. Whilst all this was happening, Yahya was put under house arrest.

Release of Mujib

The manner in which Bhutto released Mujib speaks volumes for his style and intentions. While addressing a huge public meeting in Karachi on 3 January 1972, he asked about Mujib: 'Shall I let him go? I want the people's will to prevail. Shall I release him? If you say no, I won't, but if you want me to release him, I will. Raise your hands, all those who want me to release him.' The hands shot up, and he thanked them 'for having given him permission to release Mujib.'[11] Obviously, all this was a gimmick meant to befool the simple souls in the crowd. The decision had already been taken because Mujib's release was necessary for him to bring the sad chapter of the dismemberment of Pakistan to its logical end and to establish the State of Bangladesh once and for all. Mujib, after many meetings with Bhutto, the details of which were kept secret, was released on 8 January 1972 and was flown to London before he returned to Dhaka. Although there was no point in keeping Mujib under detention, his release could have been made subject to the repatriation of Pakistan's prisoners of war. In this way, an important lever for the release of prisoners of war was given away, apparently for nothing.

Nationalization of Basic Industries: Economic Reforms Order, 1972

Bhutto announced on 2 January 1972 that ten categories of basic industries were being taken over by the state 'for the benefit of the people of Pakistan'.[12] The industries included iron and steel foundries; basic metal, heavy engineering, heavy electrical, assembly and manufacturing of motor vehicles; tractor plants, assembly and manufacture; heavy and basic chemicals; petro chemicals, cement; public utilities, like electricity generation, transmission and distribution; gas, and oil refineries. In pursuance of this announcement, the Economic Reforms Order, 1972[13] was issued as a President's Order on 3 January 1972. All establishments that fell under any of the above categories were taken over by the central government by appointment of a Managing Director for each such establishment. Employees of these establishments were to continue in service. No court, including the Supreme Court and the High Courts, could call in question any provision of this Order or of any rule or order made or anything done or any action taken or purporting to be made, done or taken thereunder. Similarly, no court could grant any injunction against anything done under this Order. The central government and the managing directors of these establishments were indemnified for anything done in good faith.

It can be said in favour of this step that it was part of the manifesto of the People's Party which it was duty bound to enforce. However, this step could have been taken in a more organized manner and national loss could have been avoided. There was unprecedented theft and pilferage in these establishments during the process of taking over by the managing directors. Raw materials worth millions of rupees just disappeared from inventories of the industrial units that were nationalized. The managing directors that were appointed were mostly bureaucrats with no practical experience of managing industrial units. They were generally corrupt and cared little about the health and profitability of these units. The cost of production in these units sky rocketed, with the result that most of the nationalized establishments suffered heavy losses. It is necessary before the nationalization of industries, to prepare a cadre which is duly trained and motivated and able to run them in the national interest. According to Wali Khan, 'it was not nationalization but bureaucratization of industry'. With the advantage of hindsight, it can be said that this nationalization, in fact, hampered the process of industrialization and resulted in the flight of capital and entrepreunial skill abroad. It is also said that had this nationalization not taken place, a lot of foreign capital could have entered Pakistan, particularly around 1973 to 1974 during the period of the Arab oil embargo against the West. With Arab money, Pakistan could have developed economically and thus a great opportunity was lost. In any case, the experiment of nationalization of industries is an admitted failure.

Even Bhutto's daughter, Benazir, had to admit it and initiate the process of denationalization and privatization of these industries.

Land Reforms

On 11 March 1972, the Land Reforms Regulation was introduced as an edict of martial law.[14] The land reforms envisaged under it were an improvement over those of Ayub in 1959. The maximum ceiling of agricultural land was reduced from 500 to 150 acres for irrigated land, and from 36,000 to 15,000 produce index units. All transfers in excess of this limit made on or before 20 December 1971 were declared void. However, alienations made prior to 20 December 1971 in favour of heirs including wife, sons, daughters, father, mother, and sons and daughters of a deceased son or daughter of the owner of the land, were declared valid. Transactions of land in excess of the limit given between 1 March 1967 and 20 December 1971 were to be considered void unless the Land Commission that was to be constituted under the regulation found any such transaction to be valid. Another important step under this regulation was the grant of land vesting in government, as a result of surrender of land in excess of the maximum limit or through resumption, to the tenants tilling such land free of charge. A tenant was given the first right of pre-emption in respect of the land in his tenancy which was a progressive step long overdue.

The jurisdiction of courts was barred regarding challenge to the provisions of the regulation itself and no court could issue an injunction in relation to anything done or intended to be done by the Land Commission or any of its officers. The government or anyone else acting thereunder was indemnified regarding anything done or intended to be done under the regulation in good faith. Certain restrictions were placed on partition of joint holding or alienation of holdings with the objective that the land holdings should not be allowed to go down below economic or subsistence levels.

This regulation, though progressive in nature, did not really achieve the purpose for which it was ostensibly made. There were too many loopholes which were made use of by influential and powerful land owners, including the Bhuttos, to defeat and frustrate the land reforms. Some of the common methods used were:

(a) Since the regulation exempted the transactions in excess of the permissible limits before 20 December 1971 if made in favour of kin, powerful landlords, in connivance with corrupt land revenue administration officials, got fake sales entered into the records prior to 20 December 1971 in favour of their heirs. Entire land revenue registers of old estates were replaced with new and fake ones showing oral sales or gifts by the land owners in favour of their sons, daughters, mothers, and fathers.

(b) Where, despite fake transfers to the heirs, the entire land holding had not been saved, then similar fake oral sale transactions by the land owners in favour of their other near relatives were entered into these fake and forged records, prior to 20 December 1971. Such transactions had to be proved bonafide before the Land Commission which could easily be done for lack of adversary. Revenue officials were the real beneficiary of this operation. They enriched themselves through bribery and graft while poor landless tillers for whom these land reforms were apparently made got little out of them.

(c) The maximum ceiling by way of 150 acres of irrigated land or 300 acres of un-irrigated land was easily undone by the alternative provision of produce index units (maximum being 15,000). It is common knowledge that the record of produce index units in various districts was not accurate. In the districts of Sindh and the Punjab where there were large land holdings, the land was generally assessed to low produce index units, again through the connivance of and in collusion with corrupt land revenue staff. Thus in districts like Multan, Muzaffargarh, Rahim Yar Khan, Sukkur, Larkana, and Nawabshah, 15,000 produce index units could cover up to seven or eight hundred acres of very fertile and irrigated agricultural land.

Consequently, even Bhutto's land reforms failed to break the stranglehold of the feudals and big landlords in Sindh and the Punjab, particularly over the politics and economics in their respective regions. After all, Bhutto himself was one of them.

Colleges and Schools Taken Over

Another reform introduced by Bhutto was taking over the management of private colleges and schools under a martial law regulation[15] gazetted on 1 April 1972. The rationale behind this reform was to put an end to the exploitation of the teaching staff at the hands of private owners of educational institutions. There were, of course, many instances of such exploitation. In the first place the minimum pay scales prescribed by the government for the teachers, both in the private and public sectors, were being defeated. In many cases teachers receiving low salaries were forced to give the school owners receipts for larger amounts. The owners of private schools were defrauding the treasury by evading income tax. This problem however was not all that pervasive. There were also a number of high quality educational institutions run by credible and prestigious bodies like the Anjuman-e-Himayat-ul-Islam, Presbyterian Church, Catholic Church, and so on which were managing their educational institutions very well and were paying their teaching staff and other employees according to pay scales prescribed by the government, if not better.

Also, according to the above-mentioned regulation, the management of all privately managed colleges was taken over by the central government if they were situated in the Islamabad capital territory and by a provincial government if they were situated in a province, with effect from 1 September 1972. The central government, in the case of a school situated in Islamabad, and the provincial government in any other case, could by notification on or after 1 October 1972 take over the management of such schools. All teachers of privately managed colleges and schools which were taken over by the government were made entitled to the same scales of pay and other conditions of service as had been allowed to teachers of colleges and schools maintained by the government. The jurisdiction of the courts, including the Supreme Court and a High Court, to question the regulation or any rule, order, or notification made or issued thereunder, was completely ousted and courts could issue no injunction in this behalf. Central government or provincial governments and persons acting on their behalf were given complete indemnity if they acted in good faith.

This regulation did a lot of damage to the educational set-up in the country. Certain leading educational institutions like Forman Christian College, Kinnaird College for Women, Gordon College, Rawalpindi, and Islamia Colleges run by the Anjuman-e-Himayat-ul-Islam were taken over by the government and virtually destroyed. Their reputation for imparting high quality education and for maintaining high standards was ruined. Educational institutions run by missionary organizations provided opportunities for education and employment to the native Christians who were otherwise a depressed minority. They were deprived of this opportunity. These educational institutions fell prey to violent student organizations who were actually student wings of political parties and these institutions were turned into bastions of violence and lawlessness. The employees of institutions, in their greed to take over the property of the owners under these institutions, misconstrued the regulation to mean that the title of properties thereunder had also been transferred to the government. The Supreme Court ultimately put an end to this controversy by holding that taking over of educational institutions did not mean transfer of ownership of the properties under these institutions to the government.[16]

The net result of this exercise was that the taken over colleges and schools suffered a decline in their standards and reputation. Instead of establishing new institutions of excellence, the government got bogged down in the management of the colleges and schools taken over by it with obviously negative results.

Screening of Government Servants

Bhutto also moved against corrupt and inefficient government servants to secure their removal. Under a martial law regulation[17] that came into force on 10 March 1972, the competent authority (as defined in the regulation) could proceed against any person in government service who was corrupt or known to be corrupt, guilty of misconduct, inefficient, or engaged in subversive activity. The competent authority, even without giving any show cause notice, could dismiss, remove, reduce in rank, or retire prematurely any such person. No action taken, order passed, thing done, or power exercised under the regulation could be called into question by or before any court including the Supreme Court or a High Court.

The central and the provincial governments carried out extensive scrutiny under this regulation and disciplinary action resulting in any one of the above penalties was taken against as many as 1300 government servants. It was a major shake-up in the services, especially amongst the senior ranks.

Political Manoeuvres till the Interim Constitution

The continuation of martial law, even though it had a civilian face, was disturbing to the political and democratic forces in Pakistan. The matter of framing a Constitution was also in limbo. Initially, the government announced that there would be no interim Constitution because, in the words of the then Law Minister, Mian Mahmood Ali Kasuri, 'it would amount to giving a Constitution by one man. The country had very unpleasant experience of a one man Constitution and, therefore, it would not be proper to repeat it'.[18] Wali Khan, President of the National Awami Party (NAP), criticized Bhutto for continuing martial law and opposed the plan for 'phased democracy'.[19] On 30 January, Bhutto took the decision of Pakistan's withdrawal from the Commonwealth. It was an unjustified and impulsive decision. The reason given was that Britain joined the European Common Market,[20] but it makes no sense. It caused enormous inconvenience to a large number of Pakistanis living in the United Kingdom who were suddenly deprived of the status of belonging to a Commonwealth country and were left high and dry. There was no benefit occurring to Pakistan in any way from this irresponsible decision.

The Governor of Sindh, Mr Mumtaz Ali Bhutto, a cousin of Bhutto, and the Governor of Punjab, Mr Ghulam Mustafa Khar, appointed Advisers to run the provincial governments of Sindh and Punjab. On 6 February 1972, Wali Khan gave the ultimatum to lift martial law or lose the co-operation of NAP. He even threatened to launch a mass movement for the restoration of democracy.[21] The demand was soon joined in by other political parties. Bhutto promised to announce a time table to lift martial law and return to democracy 'for all times to come', once certain basic reforms had been introduced.[22]

On 3 March, Bhutto suddenly announced a shake-up of the Command of the Armed Forces. He sacked Lieutenant-General Gul Hasan as Commander-in-Chief of the Pakistan Army and replaced him with General Tikka Khan. Air Marshal A. Rahim Khan was replaced by Air Marshal Zafar Chaudhry as Chief of Pakistan Air Force. The reason he gave for these sudden removals was to wipe out the Bonapartist influence on the Armed Forces which had resulted in turning professional army commanders into professional political leaders.[23] By moving swiftly, Bhutto removed the threat, if any, brewing in the armed forces against him.

Ultimately, Bhutto reached an accord with Wali Khan and Jamiat-i-Ulema-i-Islam led by Mufti Mahmood. It was agreed that martial law be lifted on 14 August 1972, and that majority parties in NWFP and Balochistan would be allowed to form governments and an interim Constitution would be given by 17 April 1972.[24] The National Assembly session was called on 14 April 1972. Bhutto received a unanimous vote of confidence and was elected as the National Assembly President. He made a dramatic announcement in the National Assembly that martial law would be lifted on 21 April, instead of 14 August, if the Interim Constitution was passed by 17 April.[25] On 21 April 1972, martial law came to an end, the interim Constitution having been adopted by the National Assembly a day earlier. Bhutto was sworn in as President under the Interim Constitution on 21 April 1972. After some further negotiations on the PPP and NAP/JUI accord of 6 March (certain difficulties had arisen in the meantime), the nominees of NAP/JUI, namely Mir Ghaus Bakhsh Bizenjo, and Arbab Sikandar Khan Khalil, were appointed Governors of Balochistan and NWFP respectively on 29 April 1972.

The Asma Jilani Case

Malik Ghulam Jilani, a politician from Lahore, and Altaf Husain Gauhar, Editor-in-Chief, *Dawn*, Karachi were arrested and placed under preventive detention under the Defence of Pakistan Rules and Martial Law Regulation No. 78. The Constitution petition against the detention of Malik Ghulam Jilani was dismissed by the Lahore High Court, relying on the decision of the Supreme Court in the case of *State v Dosso*[26] holding the Jurisdiction of Courts (Removal of Doubts) Order 1969 as valid, and ousting the jurisdiction of the courts. The Constitution petition against the detention of Altaf Gauhar also failed because the Sindh High Court held that it had no jurisdiction to grant relief against martial law orders for substantially the same reasons as given by the Lahore High Court in the case of Malik Ghulam Jilani. Both appealed to the Supreme Court.

The precise question before the Supreme Court was whether the High Courts had jurisdiction under the 1962 Constitution to enquire into the validity of detention under Martial Law Regulation No. 78 of 1971 in view of the bar created by the provisions of the Jurisdiction of Courts (Removal of Doubts) Order, 1969. Another question was whether the doctrine enunciated in the case of *State v Dosso* was correct and applicable. The Supreme Court observed that in laying down a novel juristic principle of such far-reaching importance, the Chief Justice in Dosso's case proceeded on certain assumptions, namely:

1. That the basic doctrines of legal positivism, which he was accepting, were such firmly and universally accepted doctrines that the whole science of modern jurisprudence rested upon them;
2. that any 'abrupt political change not within the contemplation of the Constitution' constitutes a revolution, no matter how temporary or transitory the change, if no one has taken any step to oppose it; and
3. that the rule of international law with regard to the recognition of states can determine the validity also of the states' internal sovereignty.

The Supreme Court held that these assumptions were not justified. Kelsen's theory was by no means a universally accepted one, nor was it a theory that could claim to have become a basic doctrine of the science of modern jurisprudence, nor did Kelsen even attempt to formulate any theory which 'favours totalitarianism'.[27] The Court further held that the observation in Dosso's case, that if the territory and the people remain substantially the same, there is 'no change in the corpus or international entity of the state and the revolutionary government and the new state are, according to international law, the legitimate government and the valid constitution of the state;' does not find support from any principle of international law.

The Court held that the *grund-norm*[28] of Pakistan was contained in the Objectives Resolution which postulates that legal sovereignty belongs to Almighty Allah alone, and the authority exercisable by the people within the limits prescribed by Him is a sacred trust. It is under this system that the functional head of the state is chosen by the community and has to be assisted by a council which must hold its meetings in public view and remain accountable to the public and only then would the government become a government of laws and not of men. Thus, the principle enunciated in Dosso's case could not be treated as good law either as a precedent or even otherwise.

The Supreme Court traced the history of events from 24 March 1969, and observed that Ayub had no power under the Constitution of 1962 to hand over power to anybody. He could have resigned and the Speaker of the National Assembly could have taken over as acting President. After a thorough discussion on the legal interpretation of martial law, the Court came to the conclusion that it is not correct to say that the proclamation of martial law must necessarily give the commander of the armed forces the power to abrogate the Constitution, which he is bound by oath to defend.

After making a detailed examination of the events and circumstances leading to the handing over of power to Yahya, the Court came to the conclusion that Yahya did not allow the constitutional machinery to come into effect. Instead, he usurped the functions of government and started issuing all kinds of martial law regulations, presidential orders and even ordinances. There was thus no question that the military rule sought to be imposed upon the country by Yahya was entirely illegal. The presidential order barring the jurisdiction of the courts, being sub-constitutional legislation, could not curtail the jurisdiction given to the High Courts and the Supreme Court under the Constitution of 1962, for that jurisdiction was preserved even by the Provisional Constitution Order. Martial Law Regulation No. 78 was struck down as having been made by an incompetent authority and, therefore, lacked the attribute of legitimacy.

After having held Yahya as an usurper and all laws enacted during his regime as illegal, the Supreme Court took recourse to the doctrine of necessity because ignoring it would result in disastrous consequences to the body politic and upset the social order. After having come to the conclusion that the acts of the usurper were illegal and illegitimate, the question arose as to how many of his acts, legislative or otherwise, should be condoned or maintained, notwithstanding their illegality, in the wider public interest. Applying this test, the Court condoned,

1. All transactions which were past and closed, (for no useful purpose could be served by re-opening them);
2. All acts and legislative measures which were in accordance with, or could have been made under, the abrogated Constitution or previous legal orders;
3. All acts which tended to advance or promote the good of the people; and

4. All acts required to be done for the ordinary orderly running of the state and all such measures as would establish or lead to the establishment of the objectives mentioned in the Objectives Resolution of 1949.

The judgment in Asma Jilani's case was certainly a departure from the past, particularly the Dosso case. The judgment was widely appreciated. It was also criticized because it was given after the overthrow of the usurper. The real test of independence of the Supreme Court would have been if the judgment had been made while Yahya was still in power. However, Asma Jilani's case was an important milestone in the judicial history of Pakistan.

NOTES

1. Khan, Lt.-Gen. Gul Hasan, *Memoirs*, 1993, Oxford University Press, Karachi, pp. 339-40. He describes the meetings of army officers which the COS General Hamid addressed on 19 December. He was continuously interrupted by a near-rebellious audience. Once or twice, the COS left the stage and went out to collect himself, and then resumed his talk. Such performance by a disciplined body of men had never been seen before, Lt.-Gen. Gul Hasan states.
2. Feldman, Herbert, *The End and the Beginning–Pakistan 1969-1971*, 1975. Oxford University Press, London. pp. 187-9.
3. The removal of Yahya has been described as a 'mini-coup' and the part played by Gul Hasan and Rahim Khan as king-breakers and king-makers is not easy to assess. It is noteworthy that about three months after Bhutto became President, both these men resigned and afterwards went abroad in ambassadorial appointments. Gul Hasan in his book *Memoirs* denies any direct role in inducting Bhutto as President, writes that it was Bhutto who summoned and prevailed upon him to become Commander-in-Chief of Army which he accepted subject to certain conditions. See pp. 346-50.
4. President Mirza and Bhutto had wives of Iranian origin which appears to be common ground between the two.
5. Taseer, Salmaan, *Bhutto: A political biography*, 1980, Vikas Publishing House, New Delhi, p. 16.
6. *Divan* was the title given to the Prime Minister of the State in certain Princely States in British India.
7. Taseer, Salmaan, *Bhutto: A political biography. supra*, note 5, p. 20.
8. Ibid., p. 13.
9. *The Pakistan Times*, 11 December 1966.
10. Ziring, Lawrence, *The Ayub Khan Era*, pp. 94-7.
11. *Dawn*. 4 January 1972.
12. *Dawn*. 3 January 1972.
13. President's Order I of 1972. PLD 1972 Central Statutes 86.
14. Martial Law Regulation No. 115. PLD 1972 Central Statutes 388.
15. Martial Law Regulation No. 118. PLD 1972 Central Statutes 441.
16. Board of Foreign Missions of Presbyterian Church v Government of the Punjab, PLJ 1987 S.C. 464.
17. Removal from Service (Special Provisions) Regulation, 1972. Martial Law Regulation No. 114. PLD 1972 Central Statutes 387.
18. *Dawn*, 16 January 1972.
19. *Dawn*, 25 January 1972.
20. *Dawn*, 31 January 1972.
21. *Dawn*, 7 February 1972 and 12 February 1972.
22. *Dawn*, 19 February 1972.

23. *Dawn*, 4 March 1972. Gul Hasan writes in his book *Memoirs* that he voluntarily offered to resign because he no longer could work with Bhutto. However, the resignations from him and Air Marshall Rahim were presented with separate files, in which their respective resignations had already been typed out, to sign. See pp. 367-9.
24. *Dawn*, 7 March 1972.
25. *Dawn*, 15 April 1972.
26. PLD 1958 S.C. 533.
27. Asma Jilani v Government of the Punjab, PLD 1972 S.C. 139.
28. *Grund-norm* is a German expression which means 'basic principle'.

21

THE INTERIM CONSTITUTION OF 1972

The Interim Constitution that came into force on 21 April 1972 on the withdrawal of martial law, was adopted by the National Assembly that had been elected in December 1970 on an all-Pakistan basis. It is true that this was to be a Constituent Assembly and enjoyed a mandate to give a new Constitution to what remained of Pakistan after the war in December 1971. Due to the formation of Bangladesh, this Assembly lost its efficacy and mandate and the members elected from West Pakistan could not act and form a Constituent Assembly of their own. It would have been appropriate to hold fresh elections in West Pakistan for a Constituent Assembly on the basis of the changed constitutional and political realities so that this assembly could have had a fresh mandate to give a new Constitution to the remainder of the country.

It is, indeed, strange why new elections were not called for immediately after December 1971 and why a truncated assembly was rejuvenated into the role of a Constituent Assembly. In former East Pakistan (now Bangladesh), fresh elections were held soon after December 1971 and a Constituent Assembly was elected under the new political circumstances. Why was this not done in Pakistan? Perhaps Bhutto, head of the majority party in the truncated National Assembly, did not wish to face fresh elections in which his role in the East Pakistan crisis would have certainly been questioned and he was by no means certain that his party would have been returned in the same strength in a new National Assembly.

Political parties in the opposition were equally responsible for not unitedly demanding fresh elections. Perhaps they were not sure of themselves after the drubbing they had received in the general elections of December 1970 from the People's Party. They were demoralized and thus contented themselves with the seats they had obtained.

In order to assemble the members of the National Assembly elected in December 1970 from West Pakistan and two members[1] elected from the East Pakistan, on the ticket of parties other than the Awami League, Bhutto issued a presidential order, National Assembly (Short Session) Order 1972[2] on 23 March 1972. Under this order, the National Assembly was to be the one provided for in the Legal Framework Order, 1970. The business of the assembly was restricted to a vote of confidence in the President of Pakistan; continuance of martial law till 14 August 1972; framing of the Interim Constitution of Pakistan; and appointment of a committee of the assembly to prepare a draft of the permanent Constitution of Pakistan not later than 1 August 1972 for submission to the National Assembly. It was under this order that the remnants of the assembly elected in December 1970 (being 146 in all, 144 from West

Pakistan and two from East Pakistan) were assembled in the name of the National Assembly of Pakistan with the power to adopt an Interim Constitution, to draft a permanent Constitution, and to prolong its own life. It was this assembly that adopted the Interim Constitution of Pakistan in April 1972.

Salient Features

It has been discussed above that for detailed provisions of the Constitutions, particularly pertaining to financial procedures, the procedure for passing of bills in assemblies and the structuring of Courts, the Government of India Act, 1935 has been used as a model. The 1956 Constitution became a working paper for future constitutional documents such as the 1962 Constitution, the Interim Constitution of 1972 and the permanent Constitution of 1973. These Constitutions have differed on basic provisions like the form of government, distribution of subjects, relations between the centre and the provinces, and other subjects. The fundamental rights and the principles of policies, as written down in, the 1956 Constitution, were reproduced more or less in the same form and language in the 1962 Constitution, the Interim Constitution of 1972, and the 1973 Constitution. Provisions regarding Chief Election Commissioner, electoral laws, the conduct of elections, Islamic institutions like the Advisory Council of Islamic Ideology, the Islamic Research Institute, the Auditor-General of Pakistan, the Service of Pakistan, and so on, were the same as those in the 1962 Constitution. The distinguishing features of the Interim Constitution are discussed below:

1. Presidential Form of Government

The Interim Constitution provided for a presidential form of government. The President was to be the head of the state as well as the head of government. The President had to be a Muslim, at least 40 years of age, and otherwise qualified to be elected as a member of the National Assembly.[3] Under the 1962 Constitution, the age requirement for the President was only 35 years.[4] Under the 1956 Constitution, the minimum age for the President was fixed at 40 years.[5] (Subsequently, in the 1973 Constitution, the minimum age for the President was fixed at 45 years.[6]) Although the minimum age of 40 appears to be appropriate for the office of President, yet it could not be forty-five under the 1972 Interim Constitution because Bhutto was 44 years of age at that time. He turned 45 when the Constitution of 1973 was enacted. The President's term of office was fixed at five years. The Constitution was silent about the mode of election to the office of the President. However, in the case of a vacancy in the office of the President, the successor was to be elected by the National Assembly in the manner provided under the third schedule to the Interim Constitution. Thus, the person elected as President by the National Assembly under the National Assembly (Short Session) Order 1972 was deemed to be the President of Pakistan under the Interim Constitution[7] The provisions of the order of 1972 were somehow contradictory. On the one hand, it provided that one of the main businesses of the assembly was to pass a vote of confidence in the President of Pakistan and, on the other hand, the procedure for the election of the President was given under the schedule. There is a great deal of difference between an election and a vote of confidence. For a vote of confidence, one has to hold the office before such a vote is taken.

To avoid controversy, it was clarified that the President was the Supreme Commander of the Defence Services of Pakistan and had the authority to appoint Chiefs of Staff of the three Armed Forces namely, the Army, the Navy, and the Air Force.[8] The President also had the legislative power to make and promulgate ordinances when the National Assembly was not in session or had been dissolved.[9]

2. The Vice-President

The Interim Constitution provided for the office of a Vice-President with the same qualifications as for the President. The Vice-President was to be elected by the National Assembly according to the procedure provided under the third schedule.[10] His term of office was fixed at five years. He was to act as President in the absence of the President and, in the event of the death of the President, he was to take over his functions until a new President was elected and had entered office.[11] The Vice-President was a member of the President's council of ministers though he took precedence over other members.[12] Otherwise, his functions were such as might be assigned to him by the President from time to time.[13] The Office of Vice-President finds mention only in the Interim Constitution of 1972. All other constitutions, including the later one of 1973, did not provide for this office. Its absence from the 1962 Constitution was very conspicuous because the office of Vice-President is generally provided in the presidential system. This omission in the 1962 Constitution was seriously felt in 1967 during the illness of Ayub, and again during the political agitation of 1968–69 against him. A Vice-President, who in all probability would have been from the East Pakistan, could have played an important role in resolving the political crises by being a compromise choice between the party in power and the opposition parties for a settlement of political issues. The reason for this obvious omission was perhaps the lingering fear on the part of Ayub that a Vice-President, through intrigue, might undermine his position. This was not the case with the Interim Constitution because it was only transitory. Besides, this provision was made to accommodate Mr Nurul Amin, who stood against the Awami League for a united Pakistan and also to give a semblance of representation to East Pakistan as well.

3. Unicameral Legislature

The Interim Constitution provided for a unicameral legislature, that is, one House consisting of the National Assembly as the federal legislature. The National Assembly had the power to legislate on all subjects mentioned in the Federal and Concurrent Legislative lists given under the fourth schedule. The National Assembly could also legislate for a province on the subjects enumerated in the Provincial Legislative List during the Proclamation of Emergency by the President.[14] The President could withold assent from any Bill passed by the National Assembly and could return it for reconsideration with his recommendations for amendments. The National Assembly, after reconsideration, could pass the Bill once again without any amendment and the President was bound to give his assent, provided the number of members voting for such a Bill, on reconsideration was not less than seventy-five[15] which meant an absolute majority of the assembly at that time. The procedure for financial matters was the same as provided under the previous Constitutions.

4. The Federal Government

The President was the head of government and he worked with the aid and advice of a council of ministers.[16] A minister had to be a member of the National Assembly and if he ceased to be so for a period of twelve consecutive months, then he ceased to be a minister.[17] It was in this manner that certain aspects of the parliamentary form of government were included in the interim constitution. All orders and other instruments made and executed in the name of the President had to be authenticated in the matter provided by him.[18]

5. The Provincial Governments

The parliamentary form of government was introduced under the Interim Constitution at the provincial level. Governors were appointees of the President and served at his pleasure.[19] The executive authority in a province was to be exercised by the Governor, either directly or through officers subordinate to him.[20] For the administration of provincial affairs, there was to be a council of ministers, headed by the Chief Minister, to aid and advise the governor in the exercise of his functions.[21] The Governor was to appoint as chief minister a person who commanded the confidence of the majority of the total members of the Provincial Assembly. The council of ministers was collectively responsible to the Provincial Assembly and the ministers could be appointed and removed from office by the Governor on the advice of the Chief Minister.[22] The Chief Minister held office during the pleasure of the Governor who could not remove him until he was satisfied that the Chief Minister did not command the majority of the total number of the members of the Provincial Assembly, to ascertain which, the Governor could ask the Chief Minister to obtain a vote of confidence from the Provincial Assembly.[23] The Chief Minister could be removed by a vote of no confidence in the Provincial Assembly but it was required that in the motion for a vote of no confidence, the name of another member of the Provincial Assembly had to be given as his successor so that when such a motion was passed, the Governor had to ask the successor named in the motion to take over as the Chief Minister.[24]

The division of functions between the Governor and the Chief Minister was quite strange. Normally, the Chief Minister is the head of government in a province and the Governor is a figurehead and an agent of the federal government, but these provisions were unclear about the respective role of these two key functionaries. It appears that in the Interim Constitution of 1972, the Governor had the real executive authority and the Chief Minister had a subordinate position. The Chief Minister had all the burdens of the office without its powers. It is difficult to understand what was intended by such ambiguous provisions.

6. The Provincial Legislatures

The provincial legislatures were also unicameral. The Provincial Assemblies, required to be summoned under the Provincial Assemblies (Summons and Powers) Order, 1972,[25] were to be the first under the Interim Constitution. The President's order had already defined the Provincial Assemblies as provided for in the Legal Framework Order, 1970. These assemblies were to meet on 21 April 1972. In this way, the Provincial Assemblies elected in December 1970 became the Provincial Assemblies under the interim constitution. This was the key to the compromise between the government and the opposition. The opposition had the majority in two Provincial Assemblies, those of NWFP and Balochistan, and was to be given power in these two provinces. In exchange, the opposition was not to demand fresh polls for the Constituent Assembly.

The Provincial Assembly had the power to make laws on subjects enumerated in the 'Provincial Legislative List' and the 'Concurrent Legislative List' under the fourth schedule. However, in case of repugnancy between a federal law and a provincial law on the same subject included in the 'Concurrent Legislative List', the federal law was to prevail.[26] The provisions regarding assent of the Governor to the Bills passed by the Provincial Assembly were similar to those applicable to the Bills passed by the National Assembly.

7. Administrative Relations between the Federation and the Provinces

Administrative relations between the centre and the provinces were regulated by provisions similar to those of the 1962 Constitution. A National Economic Council was to be constituted to review the overall economic position of Pakistan and formulate policies for its economic development.[27] The President could appoint a commission to resolve a dispute over the distribution of water supplies between the provinces.[28] He could also establish a council for inter-provincial co-ordination for resolving disputes between the federation and a province or between the provinces, to discuss subjects of common interest, and to make recommendations for the better co-ordination and uniformity of policy.[29]

8. The Courts

The provisions regarding the judicature in the Interim Constitution were similar to the Constitution of 1962, except that all provisions regarding the Supreme Court and the High Courts were given together under one part of the Constitution. New provisions relating to the judicature in the Interim Constitution, as distinguished from the 1962 Constitution, were:

i. the permanent seat of the Supreme Court was to be in Islamabad;
ii. a common High Court for Sindh and Balochistan was to be established under the Constitution;
iii. the minimum age for a judge of a High Court was fixed at 40 years for the first time; and
iv. the age of retirement for a judge of a High Court was raised from 60 to 62 years.

All other provisions relating to the judicature including those of the Supreme Judicial Council were the same as provided under the 1962 Constitution.

9. Validation of Laws

All existing laws were continued in force with necessary adaptations. All martial law regulations and martial law orders, except those specified in the seventh schedule, stood repealed with effect from the commencing day of the Interim Constitution.[30] The specified martial law regulations and martial law orders were deemed to have become Acts of the appropriate legislature and with the necessary adaptations, had effect as such.[31] All proclamations, President's orders, martial law regulations, martial law orders, and all other laws made as from the 25 March 1969, were declared valid notwithstanding any judgment of any court and were not called in question in any court. All orders made, proceedings taken, and acts done by any authority or persons under any of the above mentioned laws were deemed to have been validly made, taken, or done and no suit or other legal proceedings would lie in any court against any such authority or person.[32]

These provisions were challenged before the courts and the courts determined the parameters of the validation clause which are discussed later in this chapter.

The Simla Agreement

The opening of peace negotiations between India and Pakistan was delayed for some months partly because of difficulties arising from Pakistan's refusal to recognize Bangladesh and partly because the leaders of both countries made a number of visits to foreign countries in the first half of 1972 to obtain support for their respective positions. Talks were held in the hill station Murree, near Rawalpindi, from 26 to 29

April 1972, attended by special emissaries from India and Pakistan, and a joint statement issued on 30 April said that they had settled the modalities for a meeting between Bhutto and Mrs Gandhi towards the end of May or the beginning of June.

The summit conference between Bhutto and Mrs Gandhi opened on 28 June 1972, in Simla, which was selected in preference to New Delhi because of a heatwave in the Indian capital. In the absence of an agreement (the main stumbling block being Kashmir) the talks, which had been due to end on 1 July were extended for another day. An agreement was finally arrived at on 2 July and was signed shortly after midnight.

The agreement contained the elements of earlier Indian drafts, but the wording was considerably modified to make it acceptable to Pakistan. In particular, the clause referring to the ceasefire line in Kashmir was rephrased to read: 'The line of control resulting from the cease-fire of 17 December 1971, shall be respected by both sides without prejudice to the recognized position of either side.'

The main text of the agreement was as follows:

(i) The Government of India and the Government of Pakistan are resolved that the two countries put an end to the conflict and confrontation that have hitherto marred their relations and work for the promotion of friendly and harmonious relations and the establishment of durable peace in the subcontinent, so that both countries may henceforth devote their resources and energies to the pressing task of advancing the welfare of their peoples.

In order to achieve this objective, the Government of India and the Government of Pakistan have agreed as follows:

1. That the principles and purposes of the charter of the United Nations shall govern the relations between the two countries.
2. That the two countries are resolved to settle their differences by peaceful means through bilateral negotiations or by any other peaceful means mutually agreed upon between them. Pending the final settlement of any of the problems between the two countries, neither side shall unilaterally alter the situation and both shall prevent the organization, assistance, or encouragement of any acts detrimental to the maintenance of peaceful and harmonious relations.
3. That the prerequisite for reconciliation, good neighbourliness, and durable peace between them is a commitment by both countries to peaceful coexistence, respect for each other's territorial integrity and sovereignty, and non-interference in each other's internal affairs, on the basis of equality and mutual benefit.
4. That the basic issues and causes of conflict which have bedeviled the relations between the two countries for the past twenty-five years shall be resolved by peaceful means.
5. That they shall always respect each other's national unity, territorial integrity, political independence, and sovereign equality.
6. That, in accordance with the charter of the United Nations, they will refrain from the threat or use of force against the territorial integrity or political independence of each other.

(ii) Both governments will take all steps within their power to prevent hostile propaganda directed against each other. Both countries will encourage dissemination of such information as would promote the development of friendly relations between them.

(iii) In order to progressively restore and normalize relations between the two countries step by step, it was agreed that:

1. Steps shall be taken to resume communications—postal, telegraphic, sea, land, including border posts, and air links including overflights.
2. Appropriate steps shall be taken to promote travel facilities for the nationals of the other country.
3. Trade and cooperation in economic and other agreed fields will be resumed as far as possible.
4. Exchanges in the fields of science and culture will be promoted. In this connection, delegations from the two countries will meet from time to time to work out the necessary details.

(iv) In order to initiate the process of the establishment of durable peace, both governments agreed that:

1. Indian and Pakistan forces shall be withdrawn to their side of the international border.
2. In Jammu and Kashmir the line of control resulting from the ceasefire of 17 December 1971, shall be respected by both sides without prejudice to the recognized position of either side. Neither side shall seek to alter it unilaterally, irrespective of mutual differences and legal interpretations. Both sides further undertake to refrain from the threat or use of force in violation of this line.
3. The withdrawals shall commence upon the entry into force of this agreement, and shall be completed within a period of thirty days thereafter.

(v) This agreement will be subject to ratification by both countries in accordance with their respective constitutional procedures and will come into force with effect from the date on which the instruments of ratification are exchanged.

(vi) Both governments agree that their respective heads will meet again at a mutually convenient time in the future and that, in the meantime, representatives of the two sides will meet to discuss further the modalities and arrangements for the establishment of durable peace and normalization of relations, including the questions of repatriation of prisoners of war and civilian internees, a final settlement of Jammu and Kashmir, and the resumption of diplomatic relations.

The effect of the clauses relating to the withdrawal of forces and the ceasefire line in Kashmir was that Indian troops would be withdrawn from 5139 square miles of Pakistani territory in the Punjab and Sindh occupied during the war, and Pakistani troops from 69 square miles of Indian territory in the Punjab and Rajasthan. In Kashmir, India would retain 480 square miles of territory west and north of the former ceasefire line in the Poonch, Tithwal, and Kargil sectors, and Pakistan 52 square miles east of the line in the Chhamb sector.

Following the ratification by Pakistan on 15 July and by India on 3 August, the agreement came into effect on 4 August 1972.

Detention of Journalists and Political Opponents

Soon after taking over power, Bhutto came down heavily on political opponents and the editors and journalists who wrote against him. Muhammad Mukhtar Rana, a member of the National Assembly from Faisalabad, who belonged to the People's Party, fell out with Bhutto soon after his assumption of power. He was charged with criminal offences under martial law regulations in February 1972 and sent for trial before a special military court. Altaf Husain Qureshi, editor, and his brother Dr Ijaz Husain Qureshi, printer and publisher of the monthly *Urdu Digest* and Mujib-ur-Rahman Shami, editor of the weekly *Zindagi* were arrested and detained under martial law regulations in April 1972 for writing against Bhutto and his policies. Similarly, Husain Naqi and Muzaffar Qadir, editor/publisher and the printer of the weekly *Punjab Punch* respectively, were also arrested and detained under martial law regulations. All these men, were sentenced to various terms of imprisonment by special military courts under various martial law regulations. However, writ petitions filed by them or by their friends or relatives before the Lahore High Court challenged their detention and subsequent conviction. These writ petitions were allowed by a Full Bench of the Lahore High Court on 6 July 1972.

The Ziaur Rahman Case

The judgment of the Lahore High Court in these cases was challenged by the government before the Supreme Court in various appeals which were all heard together and decided on 8 January 1973.[33] It was argued by the Attorney-General on behalf of the government that the judiciary could, in no way, be concerned with the question of policy, nor could it exercise the power to strike down any provision of the Constitution on the basis of any other document, however important or sanctified it may be.[34] The Constitution, he urged, being a fundamental and supreme organic law of the country from which all functionaries of the State derived their existence and powers, its substantive provisions could not be controlled by its preamble or even the Objectives Resolution. He argued that the position of the Objectives Resolution in a system in which a Constitution had been subsequently framed, was no more than what it described itself to be, namely, an enunciation or declaration of the goals sought to be attained by the people, an expression of their aspirations and the ideal sought to be achieved. Its position was no better than that of a preamble to a statute and that it could serve no higher purpose. He urged that the Constitution once framed and adopted had become the organic law of the state and there was no power or authority that could exist outside the Constitution. The judiciary, like other organs of the state, was a creature of the Constitution and had to submit, like all other organs of the state, to the limitations placed upon its jurisdiction.

The Supreme Court accepted this contention and held that it never claimed to be above the Constitution or had the power to strike down any provision of the Constitution. The Court accepted its position that it derived its powers and jurisdiction from the Constitution and that it had to confine itself within the set limits by which it had taken oath to protect and preserve. It had, however, the right to interpret the Constitution and could declare any legislation as unconstitutional and void. This power did not mean that judicial power was superior in degree or dignity to legislative power but that the Constitution itself had vested it with this power. It was held that the judiciary could not claim to declare any provision of the Constitution as *ultra vires* or void under its power of interpretation.

The Supreme Court repelled the contention that it had already declared the Objectives Resolution as '*grund norm*' for Pakistan in Asma Jilani's case[35] and in this way held that it stood above even the Interim Constitution or any Constitution that might be framed in the future. The Court observed that it did not say that the Objectives Resolution was the '*grund norm*' but that the *grund norm* being the doctrine of legal sovereignty accepted by the people of Pakistan, consequences would flow from it.

It was also argued before the High Court and the Supreme Court that the Interim Constitution itself was not a valid document because it had not been framed by a competent body as the majority of its members, 160 out of 300 elected from East Pakistan, had not participated in its proceedings. It was also contended that in view of the judgment in Asma Jilani's case, the 1962 Constitution still held the field. These contentions were considered untenable. It was held that the National Assembly had the framing of the Constitution as its first purpose and it had performed its first function in accordance with the mandate given to it by the people. It was not for the courts to question the mandate of the people. The court held that the National Assembly was validly constituted and that it had ratified the Interim Constitution and the assumption of power by the President.

The Supreme Court also considered the effect of the Validation Clause under the Interim Constitution as laid down in Articles 280 and 281. The government had taken the position that these Articles of the Constitution had ousted the jurisdiction of the courts and they could not look into the orders made and proceedings taken that had been validated under those Articles of the Interim Constitution. The Court did not accept this blanket interpretation sought to be put on these provisions by the government and held that the validity given by clause (2) of Article 281 of the Interim Constitution to acts done or purported to be done in exercise of the powers given by martial law regulations and orders had since been repealed or that even in the purported exercise of those powers, their provisions did not have the effect of validating acts done *coram non judice* or without jurisdiction or malafide.

The State v Ziaur Rahman case brought rationalized some of the findings and observations made by the Supreme Court in Asma Jilani's case thus bringing the law within the limitations of the recognized legal and constitutional confines. The judgment put in place the role and the constitutional position of the Objectives Resolution and upheld the Interim Constitution, thus saving the country from constitutional anarchy. It also placed a progressive construction on the Validation Clause thus opening the way for the courts to examine and review those orders and proceedings which were malafide, *coram non judice,* or without jurisdiction and thus widened the scope of the judicial review.

The autocratic style of Bhutto and his remorseless pursuit of power soon brought him into conflict with other political leaders. Bhutto's government became increasingly harsh with dissidents and opponents. It victimized politicians, political workers, journalists, students, and workers and jailed their leaders. It shut down numerous newspapers and periodicals and arrested their editors. Coercive methods were used, such as the withholding of newspaper advertising, and the breaking up of public meetings (particularly those of Asghar Khan and Wali Khan) by PPP toughs. The opposition was given no access to the media, and newspapers and broadcasting organizations only propagated the government stand.

Dismissal of the Provincial Government in Balochistan and Resignation of the Provincial Government in NWFP

It has been mentioned above that Bhutto reached an accord with the NAP-JUI leaders in February 1972 under which he agreed to appoint NAP nominees, Arbab Sikandar Khalil and Ghaus Bakhsh Bizenjo, as Governors of NWFP and Balochistan respectively. The accord also allowed NAP-JUI governments to be formed in these provinces. In return, NAP-JUI agreed not only to the continuation of martial law until 14 August 1972 but also to vote in favour of a motion of confidence in Bhutto as President when the matter came up in the National Assembly, and agreed not to oppose the central government's emergency powers.

This three-party agreement, as it was called, ran into trouble within days of its conclusion. It seems that Wali Khan and his colleagues in the NAP developed serious misgivings about the continuance of Martial Law when Bhutto removed hundreds of public officials without giving them access to courts. Martial law had been used to restrict fundamental rights, judicial authority, and the due process of law. In so far as many of the dismissed civil servants belonged to the provincial governments, Bhutto's move could also be construed as an invasion of provincial authority. In view of these considerations, Wali Khan announced that his party would not vote for the continuance of martial law in the National Assembly and that the NAP-JUI government would review the cases of provincial civil servants removed under martial law regulation 114.[36]

Wali Khan's change of stance, however well-intentioned, amounted to a violation of the three-party agreement. Bhutto treated it accordingly and withheld the appointment of the NAP nominees as Governors of NWFP and Balochistan. Following an exchange of letters between him and Wali Khan in which suitable explanations were provided Bhutto and his colleagues went to Peshawar to confer with the NAP-JUI leaders on 8 April 1972. After a morning session, with the understanding that they would meet again in the evening, Bhutto went to have lunch with Abdul Qayyum Khan and accepted his offer of an alliance as a result of which his party, the Qayyum Muslim League (QML), agreed to support the PPP in the National Assembly and the NWFP Assembly and, in return, Bhutto agreed to take Qayyum Khan as minister for interior in his Cabinet.[37] Bhutto's meeting with the NAP-JUI leaders in the evening failed to resolve their disagreement but it seems he had already decided to withdraw martial law. At the National Assembly session on 14 April, he announced this and, in return, received the assembly's approval of a provisional Constitution and a unanimous vote of confidence in his government. On 28 April 1972, the NAP nominees assumed office as Governors in NWFP and Balochistan and, on 1 May the NAP-JUI governments were sworn in.[38]

The NAP-JUI leaders spoke of traditional democratic values. They were interested in stability, tranquility, respect for individual rights, and the rule of law. They said they would treat all citizens equally well and work for complete harmony between the provincial and the central governments. Mufti Mahmood, the new Chief Minister of NWFP, appealed to all citizens to remain within the bounds of law. He called upon landlords to stop ejecting tenants forthwith and asked the latter to pay the landlord his share of the crop. The NAP-JUI governments invited investment in their provinces and assured prospective investors that their properties would be fully protected. Ataullah Mengal, the Chief Minister of Balochistan, told newsmen that he and his colleagues were working 'day and night' to make his province a 'shining example of good government'. None of the NAP or JUI leaders had held high public office before. They embarked upon their new careers with considerable enthusiasm but they were not allowed to continue for long.

Bhutto encouraged rival political forces in NWFP and Balochistan to disrupt the NAP-JUI governments. He did not really need Qayyum Khan's support but took him as his Interior Minister probably because the latter had been a foe of the NAP leaders for twenty-five years and could be relied upon to use the resources of his office to harass the NAP-JUI governments. Hayat Mohammad Khan Sherpao, minister for water and power in the central government, became the leader of the opposition in the NWFP Assembly. As a central minister, he could deny the province funds and co-operation and, as leader of the opposition in the Provincial Assembly, he could denounce the NAP-JUI government for its failure or tardiness in solving the people's problems.[39] Militant socialists in the PPP camp were eager to create class conflict in NWFP and Balochistan and thus worked in aid of Qayyum Khan's mission to destabilize the NAP-JUI governments.

Within weeks of his return from Simla, Bhutto began accusing the NAP-JUI government in NWFP of seeking a confrontation with the central government. Qayyum Khan and other central ministers branded the NAP leaders as traitors, foreign agents, puppets of capitalists and industrialists, and exploiters of the Pakistani workers and peasants. Meraj Muhammad Khan urged the peasants in NWFP to spill the landlord's blood and seize his lands. In some instances federal ministers harboured individuals against whom the provincial governments in NWFP and Balochistan had issued warrants of arrest. At the same time, they condemned the NAP-JUI governments for failing to maintain public order.[40]

Some disruption of the public order also took place in Balochistan. First, the new NAP-JUI government resolved to return to the provinces of their origin several thousand non-Balochi public servants to make room for the local aspirants. The Bhutto regime denounced this plan as narrow parochialism that would set one Pakistani group against the other. Later, in 1972, Marri tribesmen raided Punjabi settlements in the Pat Feeder area and killed several men. The Balochistan Students Organization (BSO), an affiliate of the NAP at that time, kidnapped federal railway officials in Quetta and interfered with the movement of trains. Bhutto and his colleagues alleged that the Balochi NAP leaders, notably the Mengal and Marri *sardars*, opposed the central government's efforts to bring modernization to the province, roads, electricity, schools, clinics, irrigation, industry, rule of law, and impersonal administration, because they wanted to hold their tribesmen as serfs.[41] They also asserted that the NAP leaders were still secessionists at heart and that they had been smuggling weapons into the province to equip a secessionist force. Reports appeared in pro-government newspapers that Sher Muhammad Marri was training 20,000 Baloch guerrillas somewhere in Afghanistan. On 12 February, the police in Islamabad forced its way into the Iraqi embassy and seized more than 60 crates of weapons which, the government said, had been intended for the NAP secessionists in Balochistan.

In December 1972, the NAP-JUI government arrested the leaders of the Jamote tribe in Lasbela. The Jamotes, who had long been rivals of the Mengals, responded with an uprising. Pleading insufficiency of regular police forces in the province, Ataullah Mengal, the Chief Minister, raised a private force, *lashkar*, supplied it from government armouries, and despatched it to subdue the Jamotes. In the central government's version, this *lashkar* killed 42 Jamotes, besieged 8000 of them in the adjoining hills, and proceeded to starve them by cutting off their supplies. On 31 January 1973, the central government called upon Mengal to halt his operation and, on 9 February it ordered federal troops into Lasbela to disarm his *lashkar* and to relieve the Jamotes. Governor Bizenjo and Chief Minister Mengal opposed the use of federal troops in their province and, on the night of 14 February, Bhutto dismissed them.[42] The NAP-JUI government in NWFP resigned in protest. A few months later, on 16 August, the central government arrested Ghaus Bakhsh Bizenjo, Ataullah Mengal, and Khair Bakhsh Marri and sent them to jail. These events brought on a mini civil war in Balochistan which went on for more than four years and resulted in thousands of casualties.[43]

The NAP leaders disputed the central government's version. They claimed that they were patriotic Pakistanis and that they were wholly committed to the nation's territorial integrity. They disowned Sher Muhammad Marri and repudiated the suggestion that the arms found in the Iraqi embassy were destined for them. They pointed out that the BSO kidnappers and the Marri invaders of Punjabi villages had been arrested and jailed. They said that eight Jamotes, not forty-two, had been killed, and that no one had been besieged or starved. Above all, they charged that the Bhutto regime had engineered the Jamote rebellion and other acts of violence in the province to destabilize the NAP-JUI government. Khair Bakhsh Marri told a newsman in May

1973 that Bhutto wished to coerce the NAP leaders into obeying his 'commands', despite the fact that their coalition, and not his party, enjoyed majority support in the provincial legislature. He had sent the army into Balochistan to wipe out the support base of the unyielding Mengal and Marri tribal leaders.[44]

Most opposition leaders rejected Bhutto's accusations against the NAP leaders. They asserted that Bhutto had provoked an insurgency in Balochistan and condemned his dismissal of the NAP-JUI government as a design to bring the province under his control through undemocratic means.[45] They demanded the reinstatement of the NAP-JUI government and the army's return to the barracks. Some of them were severely critical of the army's role. Speaking in the National Assembly, Sher Baz Mazari said the army had been shooting people down in Balochistan as if they were dogs, and Mahmood Ali Kasuri charged that its bombings and strafings had killed more than one thousand people.[46]

Bhutto's desire to enlarge his domain moved him to destabilise and then dismiss the government in Balochistan, but it is noteworthy that political rivalries and the balance of forces in this province, as well as in the NWFP, worked to his advantage. The Balochi NAP leaders, Marri, Mengal, and Bizenjo, were the leaders of their respective tribes. Of these, the Marri and Mengal are major tribes. The Bugtis are another large tribe of which Nawab Akbar Khan was the leader. Sardar Doda Khan and Nabi Bakhsh were the leaders, respectively, of the Zarakzai and the Zehri tribes. Nabi Bakhsh Zehri and his brother, Qadir Bakhsh, were multi-millionaires as a result of operating coal and marble mines on which they held long-term leases from the provincial government. They belonged to the Qayyum Muslim League, and they had been rivals of the Mengals and the Bizenjos for many years.

In November 1972, the NAP-JUI government issued a series of ordinances enabling it to cancel the leaseholders' mining concessions, and to operate the mines through a government agency or a public corporation. The ordinances, if implemented, would have ruined the Zehris. On 4 December 1972, the government arrested Nabi Bakhsh's son-in-law, Zafar Iqbal Zehri, on the charge of killing a worker. The Zehris, thereupon, joined forces with Bhutto in his developing conflict with the NAP leaders. They also sought Qayyum Khan's protection. The NAP leaders later charged that the Zehris and their allies, the Zarakzais, had instigated and funded the afore mentioned Jamote uprising in Lasbela.[47]

Nawab Akbar Bugti did not belong to the NAP but had supported its election campaign in 1970. He believed that, in proper gratitude for his earlier assistance, the NAP leaders should have consulted him before making a settlement with Bhutto. Instead, they drove a wedge between him and his younger brother, Ahmad Nawaz, by appointing him minister for finance and mineral resources in their government. Nabi Bakhsh Zehri, whose daughter was married to Akbar's son, Salim, also visited the nawab in London. His plea, and Bhutto's reassurances, persuaded Bugti to return to Pakistan.[48] He supported Bhutto allegations against the NAP leaders. He claimed that he, too, had been a party to their secessionist conspiracy but that he had learned better and abandoned it. Thus, he strengthened Bhutto's case for dismissing the NAP-JUI government. In return, Bhutto appointed him to succeed Bizenjo as

Governor of Balochistan.[49] Bhutto stated that he knew Bugti and the NAP leaders had been 'birds of the same feather', that they had become opponents for tribal reasons and that he had taken advantage of their recent rivalry.[50]

Even after the formation of the NAP-JUI government in the NWFP, Pakhtoon grievances relating to the pre-empting of all the lucrative sources of revenue by the central government and its alleged unwillingness to make amends for this through generous allocation of central revenues to the province continued. Regional disparities were further heightened by the way the central government had allowed industrialists to exploit the resources of Balochistan and the NWFP for the benefit of Punjab and Sindh. Voicing his indignation at such injustices, Wali Khan pointed out:

> The natural gas of Balochistan while providing power to Karachi and the Punjab, has hardly lit any of the dwellings of the common people of the province or brought them other minimum comfort and amenities. The NWFP, which is the biggest producer of raw tobacco, has no cigarette producing plants or factories. The bulk of its hydro-electric power is used for the benefit of others. In keeping with these trends, it is no surprise that the Pathans are used as an easily available pool of cheap migrant labour in Pakistan and elsewhere.[51]

The Federal Government in reply to such charges, pointed out that the distribution of powers of taxation between the centre and the provinces had not changed significantly from 1966 to 1972 and that the Bhutto government under the new Constitution was making payments to the provincial governments of Balochistan and the NWFP from the revenues that they had realized from natural gas in Balochistan and the generation of hydro-electric power in the NWFP.[52]

Because Wali Khan had made such statements abroad, he was accused by the government spokesmen of being unpatriotic and disloyal to the concept of Pakistan. The federal government did not realize that this acrimonious debate did not contribute to national unity and, above all, it was not coming to grips with the fundamental problem. The smaller provinces had certain legitimate grievances that were likely to be further accentuated by the fact that after February 1973, these provinces were no longer functioning under their own popularly elected governments.[53]

The Language Crisis in Sindh

When the PPP established its governement in Sindh headed by Mumtaz Bhutto, a cousin of Bhutto's, the proponents of Sindhi language moved to advance their case armed with the confidence that a Sindhi prime minister was in power at the centre. In March 1972, a procession of two thousand men marched to the Governor's mansion in Karachi demanding that Sindhi be accepted as one of the national languages of Pakistan and that 90 per cent of the radio and television programmes broadcast in the province be in that language. Rasool Bakhsh Talpur, the Governor, assured the group that Sindhi would soon be declared the official language of the province[54] even though the *muhajirs* were bound to resent this decision.

In a speech in Sanghar on 31 March, Bhutto urged a 'logical and reasonable' settlement. He declared that the question of national language would be decided by the National Assembly. He deprecated the banning of Urdu newspapers and assured the *muhajirs* that they were entitled to equal rights and opportunities as citizens of Pakistan. He asked the *muhajirs* to treat Sindh, where they had been living for the last twenty-five years, as their homeland and to learn to live with Sindhis in a spirit of brotherly accommodation, but, at the same time, he regretted that there were places in Sindh where *muhajirs* had become the majority and had reduced the local population to a minority. He warned that the natives of Sindh must not be made to accept the fate that had befallen the 'Red Indians' in America and that history had not forgiven America for doing that.[55] This comparison encouraged the protagonists of Sindhi language to stand firm, and Mumtaz Bhutto, the Chief Minister of Sindh, declared that a Bill designating Sindhi as the official language would soon be moved in the assembly. By June, official forms were being printed in English and Sindhi but not in Urdu, and meetings in the government secretariat were conducted in Sindhi.[56] Students at the Liaquat Medical College and Sindh University in Jamshoro harassed the *muhajir* members of faculty and, in some cases, assaulted them, invaded their homes and took their property. *Muhajir* students at a polytechnic institute treated the Sindhi faculty in a similar manner and killed one of them.[57]

As the summer of 1972 approached, the trend towards violence increased. In Bhutto's hometown, Larkana, young men armed with sticks, knives, and axes ordered shopkeepers to remove their Urdu nameplates, signboards, posters, and calendars. In other towns, *muhajir* stores and Urdu newspaper establishments were attacked. Bhutto condemned this behaviour as gangsterism and said it would be suppressed. He pleaded that the struggle in Pakistan must be one between the oppressor and the oppressed and not between the provinces and their cultures. *Muhajirs* and Sindhis were all Pakistanis, and they must all have justice. Turning then to the *muhajirs*, he told them that it would be the height of injustice if the Sindhis were reduced to the status of a minority in their own province.[58]

The central committee of the PPP counselled restraint to the provincial government but Mumtaz Bhutto, professing readiness to lay down his life rather than betray Sindhi interests, announced that a Language Bill would be presented to the Provincial Assembly on 7 July. Copies of the proposed bill were distributed to members on the morning of 5 July. The *muhajir* group submitted amendments later the same day, but it also called for a general strike in the province on 7 July to demonstrate its opposition to the Bill. As the assembly met for discussion on the Bill, the speaker disallowed the amendments. As the Speaker disallowed the amendments, the members of the assembly demanding Urdu as an official language along with Sindhi tore the Bill into bits, walked out and abstained from the rest of the proceedings while the Bill was put through the process of clause-wise reading and voting. Out of the eighteen members of the opposition, eleven walked out of the House, while seven (Sindhi speaking) voted for the Bill. Two members from the PPP, who were Urdu speaking, also joined the walk-out. A member from the PPP, Haji Zahid Ali, proposed to refer the language issue to Bhutto for arbitration. His proposal was shot down by the Law Minister,

Syed Qaim Ali Shah. In all, fifty members of the House (including seven from the opposition) passed the Bill.[59]

The Bill and its passage resulted in widepread agitation and protests in Karachi and other urban centres of Sindh. The agitation took on a violent turn and curfew had to be imposed in certain areas of Karachi like Liaqatabad, Nazimabad, and Pak Colony. Curfew was also imposed in Hyderabad, Tando Jam, Hala, and other urban centres in Sindh.[60] Over the next few days of agitation, *muhajirs*, Sindhis, Jiye Sindh and Sindhu Desh militants, plain gangsters, and the police battled one another, burnt standing crops, plundered and destroyed homes and stores, stole cattle, and killed a large number of people.[61]

In a radio speech on 7 July Bhutto told the nation that he had instructed the Governor of Sindh to postpone the signing of the Bill that the assembly had passed. At the same time, he invited the two groups to talks in Rawalpindi. The *muhajir* delegation included I. H. Qureshi, Husain Imam, Professor A. B. Haleem, Professor Ghafoor Ahmad, G. A. Madani and several other dignitaries. The Sindhi team consisted of Sheikh Ayaz (a famous Sindhi poet and intellectual), Qazi Faiz Muhammad, Ali Bakhsh Talpur, Muhammad Khan Soomro, and two Sindh government ministers, namely, Qaim Ali Shah (Law) and Dur Mohammad Usto (Education). After a preliminary meeting on 10 July at which the two sides set forth their respective positions, Bhutto appointed a committee to consult with the two delegations. It included Abdul Hafiz Pirzada, Hayat Mohammad Sherpao, Meraj Muhammad Khan, all of them central ministers, and Malik Meraj Khalid, the Chief Minister of the Punjab. Pirzada was a Sindhi, Sherpao a Pathan, and Meraj Muhammad Khan an Urdu-speaking *muhajir* from Karachi. It was, thus, a well-chosen committee. The two delegations submitted their demands, and their accusations against each other, to the committee the next day. The *muhajir* delegation asked that:[62]

1. Urdu and Sindhi, both be named the official languages of Sindh;
2. Either the Governor or the Chief Minister, half of the ministers in the provincial Cabinet, and half of the members of the public service commission be 'new Sindhis' (meaning *muhajirs* or other non-Sindhi speaking residents);
3. 40 per cent of the posts in the provincial government be reserved for the new Sindhis, an equal number for old Sindhis, with the remaining 20 per cent to be filled on merit;
4. 50 per cent of all higher officials in the provincial government, secretaries to the government, department heads, directors, be new Sindhis;
5. Either the deputy commissioner or the superintendent of police in each district be a new Sindhi;
6. The existing technical and professional colleges in the city of Karachi be reserved for new Sindhis;
7. Karachi's quota of jobs in the central government be merged with that of Sindh (with the result that the more competitive *muhajirs* may obtain jobs reserved for the native Sindhis);

8. The city government of Karachi be given additional powers and functions, made autonomous, and placed under an elected mayor.

The old Sindhi's demands, equally extravagant, were as follows:[63]

1. Sindhi should not only be the official language of Sindh but one of the national languages of Pakistan;
2. Sindhi inscriptions should appear on currency notes and coins, office buildings, and street signs;
3. The peoples of the four provinces of Pakistan should be recognized as four nations living in a confederation;
4. A militia consisting only of the old Sindhis should be raised and maintained in the province;
5. All secretaries to the government, deputy secretaries, department heads, commissioners, deputy commissioners, superintendents, and deputy superintendents of police in the province should be old Sindhis;
6. Land allotted to non-Sindhi military and civil officials in Sindh should be taken back;
7. The railways, posts and telegraphs, radio, television, organizations concerned with the development of industry, water and power, and the civil service of Pakistan should be provincialized;
8. Sindh's share of the Indus waters should be increased to the level agreed to in an inter-provincial compact in 1945;
9. No refugees from Bangladesh should be settled in Sindh.

The government negotiators used delay as a tactic for tiring out the *muhajir* delegation. At their meetings on 13 and 14 July, Pirzada proposed to let the Sindh Governor sign the Bill that the Sindh Assembly had passed and, at the same time, issue an ordinance incorporating such *muhajir* demands as were found to be appropriate. The *muhajir* delegation insisted upon the acceptance of Urdu as an official language along with Sindhi, and when Dr Qureshi warned that the *muhajir* community would react most unfavourably to the exclusion of Urdu, Pirzada responded that his government was not without experience in handling strong reactions. He added that the old Sindhis, too, were ready to take on the *muhajirs*.[64]

On 15 July, student leaders affiliated with the Jamaat-i-Islami, organized a large procession and public meeting in Lahore to voice support for Urdu. There were signs of mounting resentment in other towns of the Punjab against the happenings in Sindh. Not only were the Punjabis strongly pro-Urdu, they were greatly disturbed by the news of attacks on Punjabi settlers, and molesting of Punjabi women, in interior Sindh. The Punjab was the bastion of the PPP's strength, and it was well understood that the party could ill afford to lose ground there. Malik Meraj Khalid, the Punjab Chief Minister, emphasized these considerations to his colleagues on the government team and pressed for some meaningful concession to the *muhajir* group.[65]

The government then softened its position and an agreement was reached. It provided that Sindhi would become the official language of Sindh, that Urdu would be honoured and promoted as the national language, and that for a period of twelve years no one would be disadvantaged in public employment or transactions on the ground that he did not know Sindhi. Bhutto called upon the Sindh government to take a lenient view of those detained during the language riots. He promised to compensate those who suffered during the disturbances.[66]

The *muhajirs* had evidently failed in their mission. They had only received a respite of twelve years during which they must learn Sindhi well enough to compete with its native speakers. They and the migrants from the Punjab and NWFP had worked hard to bring about the industrial development and commercial growth in Karachi and in other towns of Sindh. They felt they were entitled to compete on an equal basis for the jobs and benefits the public authority provided in the province of their adoption. Equal opportunity would preserve their dominance which the native Sindhis were no longer willing to accept. Sindhi-speaking people had their own point of view which was not invalid. They were indeed host to immigrants that came from India, whether they were Urdu-speaking, Punjabi-speaking, or others. Had the Sindhis been hostile and not accommodating in their attitude, it would not have been possible for other ethnic groups to settle in Sindh in such large numbers. Their apprehension that they were being reduced to a minority in their own province was not without justification. Living predominantly in rural areas, the Sindhis rightly felt that they were not given their due and that resources had been diverted to urban areas where non-Sindhi-speaking people were in majority.

Thus, the struggle between the old and the new Sindhis was not a struggle between right and wrong. It was a contest between two sets of claims neither of which could be dismissed as unworthy. It was a contest between two rights, the kind that is often the most difficult to resolve.

Bhutto and the PPP government in Sindh did not acknowledge the complexity that characterized the conflict. They spoke and acted from a spirit of simple partisanship. During a tour of Sindh towards the end of July 1972, Bhutto preached peace and assured justice to all but he made no effort to heal the wounds the riots had caused. He insisted that the Sindh Assembly had acted reasonably in passing the Language Bill, and that the riots had been instigated by the 'reactionaries' (meaning the Islamic parties), who had been trying to dislodge his government since its inception. He said he commanded the power of the state and knew how to use it, and that he would crush those who conspired against his government. Bhutto, being a Sindhi, might have been convinced that the Sindhi case had more reason behind it than the *muhajir* assertions. But his partisanship should also be viewed in the context of his party's base in Sindh. The support for the PPP in Sindh in the 1970 election had come largely from the Sindhi-speaking voters. The *muhajirs* in Karachi and Hyderabad ignored the PPP candidates for the National Assembly. In the Provincial Assembly election a few days later, the bulk of the *muhajir* vote went to the Islamic parties and against the PPP. Concessions to the *muhajirs* on the language issue would not necessarily dispose them to favour the PPP in the next election. They might regard these concessions as something to which they were entitled, if not as a sign of diffidence on the part of Sindhis and the PPP government.[67]

Of the sixty-three members in the Sindh Assembly, the PPP commanded the support of forty-three, including four *muhajirs*. But initially, when the election results were announced in December 1970, it had won only twenty-eight seats. Others joined its ranks when they saw that it was likely to form the government. Given these 'opportunists' in its ranks, the party's majority in the assembly in the summer of 1972 could not be considered entirely secure. It had to mend fences and enlarge its support base. The Sindhi 'nationalist' organizations stood ready to denounce Bhutto and the PPP as agents of the Punjab and as traitors to the Sindhi cause. Thus, the party could not afford to ignore the claims of Sindhis.

In order to build his own support base in the province, and also to lift himself from the subordinate station in which Bhutto wished to keep him, Mumtaz Bhutto chose to project himself as a great Sindhi patriot. He befriended Sindhi nationalists and gave them jobs in his administration. Pro-Sindhu Desh publications, which had numbered only a half-dozen before 1972, rose to more than thirty during his tenure as Chief Minister. The PPP's own Sindhi language newspaper, *Hilal-e-Pakistan*, employed journalists belonging to the Jiye Sindh school of thought and published their separatist thinking.[68] Regardless of how popular Bhutto might have been in the Punjab, he could not ignore his political base in Sindh or lose it to Mumtaz Bhutto. The Sindhis who had voted for the PPP looked to him to protect their rights and to restore their honour. It would not do for him to oppose the advancing tide of Sindhi self assertion.

There was rioting that resulted in death and destruction. Neither Bhutto nor his lieutenants in the government of Sindh acted promptly to prevent the violence. In handling rioters, they were inclined to treat the *muhajirs* more sternly. Being partisans of the Sindhi cause, they might have believed that the *muhajirs* must be defeated in street warfare before they would yield to the Sindhi point of view. The rioting eventually stopped and, in that sense, the crisis ended for the time being. But it should be noted that in all of this, no kind words were spoken to the *muhajirs* and no effort was made to engage them in a reasoned dialogue.

It cannot be denied that the crisis in the growing estrangement between the ethnic communities living in Sindh, far from being resolved, was aggravated. It remained suppressed for a time but, fourteen years later, it would reappear with an incredible ferocity. Meanwhile, Bhutto and the PPP earned the *muhajirs*' abiding hostility. This explains the continuing crises between *muhajirs* and Sindhis throughout the province of Sindh, particularly after *muhajirs* formed a semi-militant organization named the Muhajir Qaumi Movement (MQM) which has swept all polls in Karachi and Hyderabad, the stronghold of *muhajirs*, since the general elections of 1988.

Bhutto's Repression of Opposition Politicians

With the passage of time, Bhutto became more intolerant and the PPP regime became increasingly violent and repressive. Meetings of opposition politicians were broken up by hoodlums hired by the party in power. Asghar Khan, who was hounded the most, made a statement that the PPP government was a fascist regime.[69] A large number of opponents in the political parties, amongst journalists, student leaders, and labour leaders were arrested and detained. Some of the notables amongst those arrested and detained in the years 1972 and 1973 are:[70]

Year	Persons Arrested	Allegations/Remarks
1972	S. U. Durrani (bankers)	Offensive to Bhutto during the the Yahya regime
	Mahmood-ul-Haq Usmani Nawab Muzaffar Usman Kennedy (opposition politicians in Sindh)	Complicity in language riots
	Altaf Gauhar (editor of *Dawn*)	Endangering national security and critical of Bhutto
	Bawar Khan Usman Baluch Habib-ur-Rahman Tikka Khan Shabbar Khan (labour leaders in Karachi)	Inciting labour unrest
	Rang Ali Khokhar Malik Ataullah Mrs Khurshid Ahmad Muhammad Nisar (labour leaders in the Punjab)	Inciting labour unrest
	Javed Hashmi Altaf Parvez Ahmad Bilal (pro-Jamaat-i-Islami student leaders in the Punjab)	Inciting student unrest
	Ali Mukhtar Rizvi Amir Hyder Kazmi (pro-NAP student leaders in Sindh)	Inciting student unrest
	Maulana Ehsan Ilahi Zaheer (religious leader)	Preventive detention

Year	Name	Charge
	Jam Saqi Lal Rind (Sindh NAP leaders)	Preventive detention
	Mukhtar Rana (PPP dissident)	Incitement to murder
	Abdul Hamid Jatoi (PPP dissident MNA from Sindh)	Abduction and suspicion of murder
	Sher Baz Mazari (opposition MNA from Dera Ghazi Khan)	Gun-running
	Altaf Husain Qureshi Ijaz Husain Mujib-ur-Rahman Shami (pro-Jamaat-i-Islami editors of *Zindagi* and *Urdu Digest*) Husain Naqi and Muzaffar Qadir (editor/publisher and printer of *Punjab Punch*)	Preventive detention
1973	Ghulam Jilani (retired Major-General and NAP leader)	Inciting armed revolt
	Ghaus Bakhsh Bizenjo Khair Bakhsh Marri Abdul Hayee Baluch (MNAs) Ataullah Mengal Ahmad Nawaz Bugti (MPAs) Muhammad Aziz Kurd Zamurrad Husain Zulfiqar Ali Jamote (Senators) plus numerous pro-NAP student leaders in Balochistan	Charges against Bizenjo included murder and robbery
	Khalifo Amin Fakir Mir Muhammad Wassan Muhammad Aqil (Sindh MPAs)	Attending a 'seditious' meeting

Ghulam Mustafa Owais (a sessions judge in Sindh who granted bail to those arrested and five lawyers who often appeared for political prisoners)	Preventive detention
Mian Tufail Muhammad (Amir, Jamaat-i-Islami)	Preventive detention
Malik Muhammad Qasim (Convention Muslim League)	Preventive detention
150 NAP and Pakhtoon Zalme workers	Preventive detention
Muhammad Salah-ud-Din (editor of *Jasarat*, Karachi)	Preventive detention (critical editorials)

Some of the people named above were subjected to physical torture and personal humiliation. In a petition filed at the Lahore High Court, Ghulam Jilani alleged that he had been lodged in a filthy cell in the Lahore Fort, kept awake and interrogated for thirty-six hours, and denied medicine for his angina pains because he would not agree to testify that the arms seized in the Iraqi embassy in February 1973 were intended for the Pakhtoon Zalme.[71] Mian Tufail Muhammad was allegedly assaulted in a Lahore jail. Malik Muhammad Qasim told the Lahore High Court that while he was in a cell at a Lahore police station, two constables made him lie on his stomach, jumped on his legs and back, and injured his spine. Wali Khan charged that four attempts had been made on his life and that the Bhutto regime had instigated them. Abdul Sadiq Kansi, an opposition politician in Balochistan, was killed in April 1972. Opposition leaders asserted that the PPP government had ordered the murder of Dr Nazir Ahmad, a Jamaat-i-Islami leader in Dera Ghazi Khan, in June 1972 and that of Khawaja Rafiq in Lahore in December that year. The assailant of Dr Nazir Ahmad was arrested but later released for lack of sufficient evidence in spite of the fact that several witnesses had seen and identified him. The men who killed Kansi and Rafiq were never found.

The Soomro family in Sindh was persecuted because Maula Bux (MNA) and Rahim Bux (MPA), who had won their seats in the 1970 election as independent candidates, would not join the PPP. Two textile mills and a 7-Up bottling plant in Shikarpur belonging to the family were forcibly closed in June 1972 and thirty friends and relatives of the Soomros faced prosecution on various charges. Rahim Bux and Maula Bux's son, Ilahi Bux, were charged with attempted murder (attacking a group of workers, none of whom were hurt).[72]

Sher Baz Mazari, an independent MNA from Dera Ghazi Khan, and a friend of the NAP leaders as well as a critic of Bhutto's anti-NAP moves in Balochistan, rejected the regime's invitations to join the PPP and even declined the Prime Minister's invitation to accompany him to the United States in September 1973. His chastisement was therefore considered necessary. A nephew of his, Farhat Aziz, his estate manager and servants, and 47 men belonging to his tribe were arrested. Some of them, were made to walk the city streets in handcuffs while a 'mob of gangsters' hurled insults at them. PPP workers encouraged his tenants to seize the harvested and standing crops on his lands. The police in distant Rahimyar Khan registered a case of armed robbery involving a sum of 45 rupees (less than five dollars) against his son.[73]

Shah Mardan Shah, popularly known as the Pir of Pagaro, was one of the biggest landlords in Sindh and the spiritual guide (*pir*) of several hundred-thousand fiercely loyal *hurs* (fighters for freedom). The *Pir* had never thought much of Bhutto. Indeed, his *mureeds* (followers) had disrupted Bhutto's meetings and might have been among those who fired at him and his party in Sanghar on 31 March 1970. His immense following made it much too risky to arrest him or to harm him physically. The regime adopted the strategy of harassing his associates and *mureeds* in the hope of weakening him by showing that he was incapable of protecting them.[74] In May 1973 Syed Zulfiqar Ali Jamote, a Senator, and Khalifo Amin Fakir, Mir Muhammad Wassan, and Muhammad Aqil (MPAs), all supporters of the *Pir*, were arrested for attending a UDF meeting which the government called 'seditious'. More arrests were made in August when the UDF decided to launch a movement for the 'restoration of democracy'.

On 5 October 1973, Ali Bakhsh Junejo, a Pagaro *mureed* who had defected to the PPP was murdered probably by the headman of a fishing village whom he had insulted earlier in the day. The administration imposed a curfew in Sanghar and arrested four hundred men, many of them Pagaro's *mureeds*, under the Defence of Pakistan Rules. The police raided Mir Wassan's house in Shahdadpur and arrested all members of his family, including the women. Eighty thousand pounds of cotton were allegedly carted away from his ginning factory, crops on his lands were destroyed, and his cattle were taken. Six of Pagaro's *mureeds* were brought to a police station and asked to confess not only to Junejo's murder but to a conspiracy to overthrow the government. They refused, two of them died under torture, and the other four were carried to a lonely spot by the Mathrao canal and shot dead. The police later claimed that all of them had been killed while resisting arrest. Crops, cattle, and agricultural machinery belonging to Faiz Muhammad Rajar, another *mureed,* were seized and his house was razed to the ground. A factory owned by Dhani Bakhsh Nizamani was shut down, Senator Jamote's lands were flooded, and his crops destroyed. Khalifo Amin Fakir went to see Jam Sadiq Ali, a provincial minister, and then disappeared.

The public meeting organized and held by United Democratic Front (UDF) at the Liaquat Bagh, Rawalpindi, on 23 March 1973, was fired upon by the PPP operatives. At least nine people were killed in heavy firing and seventy-five were taken to hospital with serious injuries. Thirteen buses were also burnt.[75] Most of the people who were killed belonged to the NAP from NWFP. It goes to the credit of Wali Khan that he did not make it a provincial or parochial issue. There was extreme tension in the air in Peshawar and in other places of NWFP amongst the Pakhtoons, particularly against the Punjabis, when the dead bodies were brought to Peshawar and the other cities of NWFP. Wali Khan went to all lengths to assuage the feelings of the people of the province by saying that it was not the work of the Punjabis but that of Bhutto and his political party. Anybody who harboured suspicions about the loyalty of Wali Khan to Pakistan should have rested his doubts after this incident. Nevertheless, this brutal and violent incident at the hands of PPP has always remained a blot on its name. It could have caused a civil war with all kinds of dangerous possibilities.

The opposition leaders, for their part, were no models of civility. They attempted to destabilize Bhutto's government by making accusations calculated to bring him into public contempt and hatred. There are a number of examples of their denunciations of Bhutto. At a press conference in Lahore on 27 April 1973, Asghar Khan called Bhutto 'foolish, mentally sick, insane, thoroughly evil, a fascist and, above all, a *goonda* (gangster)'. On other occasions, he alleged that Bhutto had engineered the army action in East Pakistan to force it out of the union; that he had instigated the language riots in Sindh; had secret agreements with India; that he saw all signs of life and movement in the country as threats to his rule; that he had rigged by-elections and closed all avenues of democratic action; that he intended to establish the 'worst imaginable' fascist regime in Pakistan; that he had broken all his promises to God and man and cut the throat of each one of his benefactors; that he had given the nation nothing but poverty and despair; and that he not only drank liquor but bathed in it. Asghar Khan also said that he did not recognize Bhutto's government as legitimate and that he intended to organize a mass movement to oust it.[76]

Mian Tufail Muhammad (Jamaat-i-Islami) asserted that Bhutto was among those upon whose advice Yahya had ordered the Pakistani commander in Dhaka to surrender; that he had requested the Indian government to keep the Pakistani POWs and thus prevent them from revealing his responsibility for the dismemberment of Pakistan; that he had been humiliating the Pakistan Army with the purpose of weakening it; and that he meant to bring dishonour to the nation by recognizing Bangladesh.[77] Professor Ghafoor Ahmad, and Maudoodi made similar statements[78] but that of the Jamaat-i-Islami spokesman, Dr Nazir Ahmad, was the most extravagant. He made personal attacks on Bhutto and called him a drunkard, a womanizer, a tyrant, and a corrupt and morally bankrupt person, as well as a traitor and an Indian agent. He did not even spare his wife and family.[79]

Chaudhry Zahur Ilahi was not to be left behind. Speaking at a UDF meeting in Hyderabad (Sindh) on 9 May 1973, he held Bhutto responsible for the murders of Dr Nazir Ahmad and Khawaja Rafiq and called him 'insane, cruel, shameless, honourless, a drunkard, and plunderer'. Lesser politicians in the opposition, referred to the modest social origins of Bhutto's mother and wondered aloud in their public meetings about the identity of his 'real' father.

Bhutto might not have personally ordered the repression and its specifics in each case but there can be little doubt that he knew who was being suppressed and how. He did not put an end to it and he must, therefore, bear the ultimate responsibility for it. He also knew that repression had a way of spreading. Public officials who broke the law to harass those who had displeased Bhutto did the same to their own opponents. The entire regime, Bhutto and his ministers, the bureaucracy, the security forces, legislators, and party functionaries at all levels became involved in repression. Thousands of tyrants filled the land.

Constitutional Amendments

The Interim Constitution had vested powers in the President to make by order such provisions as appeared to him necessary or expedient to bring the Constitution into effective operation for meeting difficulties and for making omissions from, additions to, modification of, and amendments in the Constitution.[80] This power could not be exercised after 31 March 1973. It was quite extraordinary to give the President the power to amend the Constitution. There was no provision otherwise for amendments. Perhaps the idea was that the Interim Constitution would not last for more than a year, therefore, instead of providing for an elaborate procedure to make these amendments, the President was empowered to make appropriate amendments in this interim period. Besides, the power was to come to an end within one year of the Interim Constitution becoming operational after which no amendments could be made, thus making it imperative to enact a permanent Constitution.

This power, though available for a limited period of time, was exercised liberally and frequently and as many as thirteen amendment orders were passed within a year. These amendment orders did not make material changes in the Interim Constitution and mostly pertained to addition, omission, substitution, or alteration of the provisions under the schedules to the Interim Constitution. However, the important amendments are discussed as under:

1. A provision was made prohibiting provincial legislatures or provincial governments from making any laws, taking executive actions, or imposing any tax which would cause any restriction on the inter-provincial trade.[81]
2. Article 281, the Validation Clause, was amended inserting the expression 'notwithstanding any judgment of any court'. This was apparently done to undo the effect of the judgments of the Supreme Court and the Lahore High Court in Ziaur Rahman's case. It was never tested in the courts and might have been struck down as malafide.[82]
3. The Governors were given power to prepare an Annual Budget Statement and a schedule of authorized expenditure when the Provincial Assembly was not in session.[83] This was apparently done to meet the situation created by the dismissal of the provincial government of Balochistan.

Eight amendments, Constitution Sixth Amendment Order 1973 to the Constitution Thirteenth Amendment Order 1973, were made after 31 March 1973, which was clearly repugnant to Clause (2) of Article 279 of the Constitution. The President, under this clause, had no power to make any amendment to the Interim Constitution by order after 31 March 1973. Hence, these amendments, if challenged, could have been declared *ultra vires* by the courts.

Constitution-making: The Initial Difficulties

Following the overthrow of Ayub and the constitution Bhutto had imposed, a national consensus developed in favour of a parliamentary system of government, universal adult franchise, and direct elections to the central and provincial legislatures. Politicians in West Pakistan had come to recognize that the next Constitution would have to allow substantial autonomy to the provinces in a federal union. Determining the place of Islam in the Constitution had been a vexing issue since the founding of the state in 1947. The Islamist parties, and others friendly to their persuasion, had been insisting that since Pakistan was established in the name of Islam it could be preserved only if it became an Islamic state. Provincial autonomy, the role of Islam, and the enlargement of democratic principles were thus major issues the National Assembly had to address in framing a new Constitution.[84]

Bhutto had pledged to restore democracy but he now felt that the government should be able to restrain, even suppress, its opponents. He was a Muslim but he had no desire to allow the *ulema* an interventionist, much less directing, role in the affairs of state. He would, if he could, leave it to individuals to practise Islam according to their own convictions, schism, or school of jurisprudence. He had written against a strong centre and advocated provincial autonomy when he did not hold office. Now that he was head of the central government, he would rather enlarge than diminish its domain.

The more notable of the opposition groups in the National Assembly were the two Muslim League factions, the three Islamist parties, and the National Awami Party (NAP). The Muslim League had always favoured a reasonably strong central government and had been content with symbolic concessions to Islamic sentiment. The Islamic parties had lived on their advocacy of an Islamic state but they looked to an energetic central government to implement their goal. The NAP had been urging decentralization and provincial autonomy since the mid-1950s and it was secular in its outlook. These differences of orientation and emphasis within the opposition provided Bhutto his opportunity to gain approval for a Constitution that answered his needs and preferences to a considerable extent.

Bhutto's own party would follow his lead and so would others who had joined his camp. They were numerous enough, 110 in a house of 146 at that time, to pass a Constitution with an impressive majority, but Bhutto wanted wider support. In his controversy with Mujib in early 1971, he had argued that a Constitution should be acceptable to all provinces and that it should not be imposed upon the country by the 'brute' majority in one of them. Others could make the same argument now. The PPP had lost the 1970 election in the NWFP and in Balochistan, the two provinces where the movement for provincial autonomy had been strong. A Constitution rejected by them would then not be satisfactory.

On 17 April 1972, Bhutto appointed a committee of twenty-five members of the National Assembly, including six from the opposition, to prepare a draft Constitution. After a few meetings during which the main directions to be taken were settled, the committee asked its chairman, Mahmood Ali Kasuri, to present a draft for discussion. In the meantime, some differences were brewing within the PPP on constitutional issues. Bhutto reiterated that he wanted a parliamentary system for the country not necessarily of the Westminster type but suited to Pakistan's peculiar conditions and in accord once with the people's aspirations.[85] There were speculations in the press that Bhutto wanted tthe French system which had become predominantly presidential in 1958 on the adoption of the Constitution of the Fifth Republic. Under this system the president is all powerful particularly in matters of defence and foreign affairs, and the prime minister is in a subordinate capacity. Mahmood Ali Kasuri, the Law Minister, had submitted his resignation on some point of difference in September 1972 which had not been initially accepted by Bhutto. However, he started working again on 29 September 1972 and made a press statement that all such speculations were wrong and the ultimate decision on the future Constitution would lie with the National Assembly.[86] Bhutto further stated that the PPP was irrevocably committed to giving the country a federal parliamentary Constitution enshrining two pivotal principles, first, that the provinces would enjoy autonomy consistent with the integrity and solidarity of Pakistan and, second, that the system would be parliamentary ensuring that the executive would be responsible to the legislature. The Punjab Governor, Ghulam Mustafa Khar, attacked Kasuri for his resignation and called him a 'political non-entity' and threatened him with '*gherao*' by political workers. Kasuri reacted sharply to such a statement and said that he had never been over-awed by anybody, including Ayub and his Governor Amir Muhammad of Kalabagh.[87] However, ultimately Kasuri resigned as Law Minister, Deputy Leader of the PPP Assembly Party, and Chairman of the Constitution Committee. He retained his seat in the National Assembly. He gave the reasons for his resignation which included disagreement on constitutional pattern; difference of opinion on dismissal of civil servants under martial law regulation No. 114; economic depression; the existing law and order situation; and continuation of emergency.[88]

Constitutional Accord

Abdul Hafeez Pirzada succeeded Kasuri as the Law Minister and Chairman of the Constitution Committee. The members of the opposition in the Constitution Committee boycotted the meetings of the Committee. Bhutto invited leaders of parliamentary parties in the National Assembly for discussions on constitutional issues on 17 October.[89] After four days of hard bargaining, an accord was reached on 20 October 1972 where the following decisions were taken unanimously:[90]

1. There would be a federal parliamentary system of government answerable to the National Assembly.

2. All actions would be taken in the name of the President but the chief executive would be the Prime Minister. The President would act on the advice of the Prime Minister on all matters which would be binding on him in all respects.
3. The National Assembly would elect one of its members to be the Prime Minister who would be called upon by the President to form the government.
4. It would be the right of the Prime Minister to seek the dissolution of the National Assembly at any time, even during the pendency of a motion for a vote of no-confidence against him.
5. In order to ensure stability in the country, the following provisions would be incorporated in the Constitution, and they should apply *mutatis mutandis* (with due alteration of details) to the provincial legislatures:
   (a) A vote of no confidence could not be moved unless by the same resolution, the name of another member of the assembly was proposed as his successor.
   (b) A vote of no-confidence could not be moved during the Budget Session.
   (c) Once a vote of no-confidence was defeated, a subsequent vote of no-confidence could not be moved for a period of at least six months.
   (d) For a period of fifteen years, or three general elections thereafter, whichever was longer, a vote of no-confidence could be deemed to have failed unless passed by a majority of not less than two-thirds of the total membership of the National Assembly.
6. The Prime Minister should be a member of the National Assembly. Other ministers might be from either the National Assembly or the Senate, provided that the number of ministers from the Senate did not exceed one-fourth of the total number of the members of the Cabinet.
7. The parliament would consist of two Houses, namely, the National Assembly (the Lower House) and the Senate (the Upper House).
8. The National Assembly would consist of 200 members elected on the basis of direct adult franchise. In addition, for a period of ten years, there would be ten seats reserved for women to be elected by the members of the National Assembly from their respective provinces.
9. Allocation of seats in the National Assembly to the provinces, the centrally administered tribal areas, and the federal capital area should be on population basis, and would regulated by an organic federal law.
10. (a) The Senate would consist of sixty members. Each province should be allocated fourteen seats to the Senate. Two seats should be allocated to the federal capital area and two seats to the centrally administered tribal areas.
    (b) The members of the Senate would be elected —
       i. from the four provinces by the members of the provincial legislature of that province, exercising a single transferable vote, so as to ensure proportionate representation in the Senate of the parties in the respective Provincial Assemblies;
       ii. from the centrally administered tribal areas by the members of the National Assembly from those areas; and

   iii. from the federal capital area in a manner, to be prescribed by the President, acting on the advice of the Prime Minister.
11. There would be two legislative lists,[91] namely the federal list and the concurrent list.
12. Residuary powers of legislation would, vest in the provinces.
13. The subjects to form part of the federal and the concurrent lists were finalized and listed.

This accord was finalized by Bhutto and his important ministers, including the Attorney-General, Yahya Bakhtiar, with Qayyum Khan of QML; Arbab Sikandar Khalil (NAP); Mir Ghaus Bakhsh Bizenjo (NAP), Ghulam Farooq (NAP); Mufti Mahmood (JUI); Sardar Sikandar Hayat (CML); Major-General (Retd.) Jamal Dar, MNA, Tribal Areas; Shah Ahmad Noorani (JUP); Professor Ghafoor Ahmad (JI); and Sher Baz Mazari, MNA (Independent).[92]

In addition to the main features of the Constitution above mentioned, Bhutto agreed to designate Islam as the state religion of Pakistan, something which had not been done before. In addition, he consented to the proposed oaths of office for the President and the Prime Minister (which provided for them to be Muslim), the establishment of a council to propose the Islamization of laws, and the deletion of references to Islamic socialism in the draft Constitution. As a concession to the provincial autonomists, he agreed to the creation of a 'Council of Common Interests' to redress provincial grievances over the distribution of river waters, revenues from the sale of natural gas and electricity, and industrial development. In return, the opposition leaders accepted a larger federal jurisdiction than the one allowed in the 1956 Constitution and about as large as that envisaged in the Government of India Act of 1935. They also agreed that for the next fifteen years, a two-thirds majority vote in the National Assembly would be required to pass a motion of no confidence against the prime minister, and that he could dissolve the assembly even while such a motion was in debate. They accepted a Senate with virtually no powers of its own. As they came out of the meeting, they smiled, hugged one another, and seemed pleased with the agreement they had just signed, even though they had got much less than they had been demanding. Perhaps they had expected even less. The political realities and strategies which brought about this accord were the same as those which produced virtually unanimous support for the Constitution adopted in April 1973.

Permanent Constitution Adopted

The government moved a Constitution Bill in the National Assembly on 30 December 1972, and the opposition found that it did not fully correspond with the accord they had signed in October. They proposed amendments but these got nowhere because the PPP and its allies in the assembly would not accept them. On 13 March 1973, after two weeks of discussion, the opposition parties came together in an alliance called the United Democratic Front (UDF) to press for a more Islamic and democratic

Constitution. They wanted to strengthen its Islamic provisions, reduce the government's preventive detention and emergency powers, allow the superior courts to review the decisions of special tribunals, soften the requirements for passing a no-confidence motion against the Prime Minister, lower the voting age to 18 years, make the Election Commission autonomous, rationalize the constitutional protection to be given to laws made during the operation of martial law, and provide job security to civil servants.[93] On 16 March, they sent their proposals to Bhutto and beginning 24 March they boycotted the National Assembly's consideration of the draft Constitution.

Bhutto and his associates held meetings with the UDF leaders on 9 April, continued their negotiations the next morning, and reached agreement minutes before the National Assembly met on 10 April. The opposition members, led by Wali Khan, returned to the assembly, and Abdul Hafeez Pirzada moved to adopt the agreed changes in the provisions that had been in dispute. The assembly then passed the constitution without any dissenting votes and with only a few abstentions. It is interesting to note how major controversial issues were settled before interpreting how the accord on 20 October 1972 and the consensus on 10 April 1973 were obtained.

The Constitution did not concede much to the autonomists in the allocation of governmental powers and functions. In addition to defence, foreign affairs, currency, and communications, the functions they would assign the federal government, it placed more than sixty subjects on an exclusive federal list and fourty-seven on a concurrent list with respect to which the federal law was to prevail over the provincial law. The residuary functions and powers were left to the provinces. The federal list included most revenue sources, banking and insurance, economic planning and co-ordination, air transport, regulation of corporations, industrial development, inter-provincial trade, preventive detention in connection with national security, railways, oil and gas, nuclear energy, elections, and the higher judiciary among others. The concurrent list allowed the federal government overriding jurisdiction with regard to criminal law, criminal procedure, civil procedure, and labour relations along with numerous other subjects.

The Constitution provided potentially significant safeguards for provincial interests. Balochi politicians had laid claim to the revenues obtained from the extraction of minerals and the sale of natural gas piped out of their province; politicians in the NWFP had made a similar claim concerning the electricity generated there and distributed to other provinces. Sindh and the NWFP had worried over the distribution of the Indus waters. The Constitution called for a Council of Common Interests composed of the four provincial chief ministers and an equal number of federal officials to formulate policies regarding the industrial development, water, power, and the railways, and to supervize the related establishments. Its decisions were to be made by majority vote but a dissatisfied province could appeal to a joint session of parliament whose determination would be final. A National Economic Council, including provincial representatives, was appointed to make plans 'in respect of financial, commercial, social, and economic policies', and a National Finance

Commission, with provincial representation, was set up to make recommendations concerning federal grants-in-aid and sharing of the net proceeds of certain federal taxes between the federation and the provinces.

The framers of the new Constitution retained the Islamic provisions contained in the two previous Constitutions and added some of their own. Article 2 designated Islam as the state religion. The President and the Prime Minister had to be Muslim and their oath of office required them to affirm their belief in the unity of God, the finality of prophethood of Muhammad (PBUH), the Quran as the last of the holy books, and the day of judgment. This oath had the effect of excluding members of the Ahmedi sect from holding either one of these offices. Article 228 provided for a Council of Islamic Ideology and Article 230 required the legislature to consider the validity of any law that had been referred to the Council which it had found to be repugnant to Islam. It also provided for the Council to submit, within seven years of its appointment, its final report on the Islamization of existing laws and asked parliament and the provincial legislatures to consider the report and 'enact laws in respect thereof' within a period of two years.

The constitution gave the government nine years before the Islamization of laws came into effect. It did not follow that parliament would have to accept the Council's recommendations as submitted. An obligation to do so would have made the Council supreme over the parliament. Once the Council's report was placed before the legislatures, public pressure for its acceptance might be generated but there were also ways of frustrating the Council. It had to consist of persons who had 'knowledge of the principles and philosophy of Islam . . . or understanding of the economic, political, legal, or administrative problems of Pakistan' (Article 227). It would necessarily include the various schools of Islamic thought. The prospect of a consensus among its members might, then, be limited and political manipulation by the government of the day could reduce it further.

These concessions to Islamic sentiment were matched by a touch of socialist flavour. Article 3 promised to create a polity that took 'from each according to his ability' and gave to each 'according to his work'. Article 38 committed the state to promoting general welfare by preventing the concentration of the 'means of production and distribution in the hands of a few... and by ensuring equitable adjustment of rights between employers and employees, and landlords and tenants'. More important, Article 253 authorized parliament to limit private property of any and all kinds, and to designate businesses and industries that might be placed in the public sector to the partial or complete exclusion of private owners. The *ulema* and their allies in the National Assembly accepted these provisions, even Article 34, which required the state to ensure the 'full participation' of women in all spheres of national life.

Under the 1956 Constitution, the executive authority of the federation was vested in the President, and the Prime Minister served during his 'pleasure'. Bhutto expected to be the Prime Minister under the new Constitution but, given his political standing in the country, he would not countenance an interfering President. Accordingly, Article 90 of the Constitution named the Prime Minister as the chief executive of the federation, and Article 48 made the President wholly dependent upon his advice. The

Constitution also secured the Prime Minister against his opponents in the assembly. Article 96 stated that a resolution calling for a vote of no confidence against the Prime Minister must, simultaneously, include the name of a successor, and that it must have the support of a majority of the total member of the assembly to be passed.

The Constitution appeared to guarantee fundamental rights to citizens but in several instances it made the right subject to 'reasonable restrictions' in the public interest. The power of preventive detention and the authority to declare a state of emergency, during which the fundamental rights could be suspended, were retained.

Why did the opposition accept this constitution, and the earlier accord in October 1972, which left much to be desired? It should first be noted that the opposition was not without divisions and mutual suspicions within its ranks. Ghaus Bakhsh Bizenjo cautioned his colleagues in the NAP councils that the 'rightists', such as those in the Jamaat-i-Islami, would 'stab us in the back' when the 'crunch' came. He also thought the NAP had more in common with the PPP than it did with the Islamist parties or the Muslim League.[94] Mir Mardan Khan Jamali, a Muslim League leader from Balochistan, believed that the PPP was a lesser evil than the NAP. Zahid Sarfraz, another Muslim League leader, shared this view. Maulana Ghulam Ghaus Hazarvi of the Jamiat-i-Ulema-i-Islam (JUI) was openly pro-PPP and critical of the NAP and the Jamaat-i-Islami. Maulana Abdul Haq (JUI) and Maulana Zafar Ahmad Ansari felt free to have their own separate negotiations with the regime during the critical days preceding the adoption of the Constitution. Some members of the Jamiatul-Ulema-i-Pakistan (JUP) did not honour the UDF's boycott of the Assembly.[95] But above all, the opposition knew that, at best, it commanded only thirty-six votes against the government's 110 in the assembly.

Bhutto employed the stick and the carrot to tempt, harass, intimidate, and exhaust the opposition. His government and party directed their moves primarily against the Jamaat-i-Islami and the NAP. Leftist columnists and editorial writers who abounded in the government-controlled media intensified their long-standing campaign against Maudoodi, the founder of the Jamaat-i-Islami. They recalled his pre-independence denunciations of the Muslim League leaders and his opposition to the idea of Pakistan. They suggested that he and his party did not regard the country as worth preserving because it would not accept and follow their 'obscurantist' notions. The intense questioning of the party's patriotism weakened its posture.

A similar campaign was launched against the NAP. Pro-government commentators pointed out that Wali Khan, his father, and others in the NAP, had once opposed the establishment of Pakistan and alleged that they had not reconciled to its continuance. The NAP leaders' denials of separatist intent and their declarations of patriotism were drowned in the noise of government propaganda against them. The NAP, like the Jamaat-i-Islami, was put on the defensive.

NAP-JUI coalitions governed the NWFP and Balochistan when the constitutional accord was negotiated in October 1972. This was the first time in their careers that any of the NAP or JUI leaders had tasted the fruit of power, and it seems they liked it. Wali Khan, the president of NAP, was deeply suspicious of Bhutto's intentions but he was away in London when the accord was singed. Bizenjo, who deputized for him, reasoned that the NAP had not prospered as an organization when its leaders and workers dwelt in jail and that it was important for the party to remain in power to renew and expand its support base.[96]

The Jamaat-i-Islami accepted the proverbial half-loaf in October 1972, presumably reserving the right to demand the remaining half at a more opportune time in the future. The JUI was content with the proposed Islamic provisions of the Constitution, and it did not want to fight for greater provincial autonomy. The NAP did not wish to be alone in contending with the Bhutto regime. The principal opposition leaders, each for their own reasons, were thus ready to make a settlement. Bhutto, on his part, seemed to have concluded that concessions to the Islamist parties would cost him less in terms of his ruling authority than concessions to the provincial autonomists.

In February 1973, Bhutto dismissed the NAP-JUI government in Balochistan and, reacting impetuously, the NAP-JUI government in NWFP resigned in protest, probably to his great relief. On 23 March, PPP workers, aided by the Punjab police, opened fire at a UDF public meeting in Rawalpindi, killing several NAP workers among others. One might have expected that the opposition leaders would now refuse to have anything further to do with the Bhutto regime. Actually, they exercised remarkable self-restraint. Two weeks later, they were once again ready to join Bhutto at the conference table, and the NAP representatives did not demand greater provincial autonomy. Two considerations might have weighed with them. Bhutto had caused the impression in NAP-JUI circles that their governments in Balochistan and in the NWFP might be restored.[97] They did not want to jeopardize this prospect by annoying him. Secondly, Wali Khan and his party hoped to shed their regional image and gain support in the Punjab and in Sindh. But in the wake of East Pakistan's secession, provincial autonomy, in the sense of limiting the central government to a few functions, was anathema to the Punjab. If Wali Khan wanted to be a national leader, and if the NAP was to be a national party, they would have to soften their traditional stand on provincial autonomy.

The passage of the 1973 Constitution is generally acknowledged to have been one of Bhutto's more significant accomplishments. In the years following his ouster from power, even some of his bitter opponents longed for the restoration of this Constitution. They considered it a great national asset because, unlike the two previous Constitutions, it represented a broad national consensus. Bhutto's bargaining skills had a part in producing this consensus, but the opposition's willingness to be reasonable and realistic also had a role. They had all made concessions, and they had all made gains.

Bhutto had reasons to be pleased that the central government, of which he was to be the head, had suffered no significant loss of jurisdiction, and that his own office had become more secure and powerful than ever before. The Islamist parties could take satisfaction from having placed the National Assembly under an obligation to move in the direction of Islamizing the country's laws. The autonomists had not been able to reduce the central government, but they could look to the Council of Common Interests and the National Finance Commission for a redressal of provincial grievances. The government of the day might obstruct the working of these bodies and thwart their ends but it could not do so without inviting odium. The institutions established by the Constitution might, over time, develop their own drives for survival and self-assertion, aided by friendly political forces and public opinion.

Presidential Reference on Bangladesh

It has been discussed earlier that Bhutto's role in the events of 1971 that led to the breakup of Pakistan, was pivotal. It was only reasonable that he wanted to recognize Bangladesh and close the most unfortunate chapter in Pakistan's history but recognition of Bangladesh was not without its inherent political risks. He had to prepare the nation so that this bitter bill could be swallowed. He wanted to shift the burden of this decision to the National Assembly and the Supreme Court. He, therefore, decided that the government should move a resolution which would express the opinion of the National Assembly that the government of Pakistan might accord formal recognition to Bangladesh at a time when, in the judgment of the government, such recognition would be in the best national interest of the country and would provide for a fraternal relationship between the two Muslim communities of the subcontinent. The resolution was to seek a firm assurance from the National Assembly to take all legal and constitutional measures necessary to this end.

In order to preclude any questions about the validity of the proposed resolution, a reference was made to the Supreme Court for its opinion on the validity of such a resolution envisaging such constitutional measures as might be necessary before the according of formal recognition.

The Supreme Court unanimously held that there was no legal bar to the National Assembly considering or adopting such a resolution. However, it was observed that no opinion was being expressed at that stage about the constitutionality or the validity of the measures, legislative or executive, that might be taken before the according of formal recognition. It was also made clear that adoption of such a resolution would not pre-empt the parliament, present or future, from considering any legislative meaures or any constitutional amendment brought before it uninhibited any assurance that it might have given earlier. No legislature could legally abrogate its sovereign right to legislate as and when a legislative measure was brought before it in the light of its own provisions. The legislature could not be bound by any previous promise or assurance to legislate in a particular manner. Such a promise or assurance would neither be legally binding nor enforcible.[98]

NOTES

1. They were Nurul Amin and Raja Tridev Rai.
2. President's Order 11 of 1972. PLD 1972 Central Statutes 434.
3. Article 50 of the Interim Constitution.
4. Article 10 of the Constitution of 1962. This appears to be modelled on the United States Constitution which also provides thirty-five as minimum age for the President under Section 1 of Article II.
5. Article 32 of the 1956 Constitution.
6. Article 41 of the 1973 Constitution.
7. Article 282.
8. Articles 55 and 56.
9. Article 94.
10. Article 57.
11. Articles 59 and 60.
12. Article 58.
13. Article 60.
14. Articles 137, 138, and 139.
15. Article 81.
16. Article 62.
17. Article 63.
18. Article 66.
19. Article 100.
20. Article 102.
21. Article 103.
22. Article 104.
23. Ibid.
24. Ibid.
25. President's Order 12 of 1972. PLD 1972 Central Statutes 440.
26. Article 143.
27. Article 151.
28. Articles 153 and 154.
29. Article 156.
30. Article 280.
31. The Martial Law Regulations specified in the Seventh Schedule were mostly those which were made by Bhutto during the Civilian Martial Law, including Land Reforms Regulation, Removal from Service Regulation, Schools and Colleges (Taking Over) Regulation.
32. Article 281.
33. The State v Ziaur Rahman. PLD 1973 Supreme Court 49.
34. This argument was probably necessitated because one of the Judges of the Lahore High Court sitting in Full Bench held the Objectives Resolution as '*supra*-Constitutional Instrument which is unalterable and immutable and that the present National Assembly has no power to enact any Constitution or law which either directly or indirectly contravenes any of the provisions of the said Resolution', and further that 'the Courts in Pakistan being the repository of judicial power, as trustees of the people and the Almighty shall not, and have no jurisdiction to accept any tinkering with it by anybody including any Assembly'. Another Judge of the Lahore High Court, a member of the Full Bench, held it 'to be transcendental part of the Constitution'.
35. PLD 1972 S.C. 139.
36. *Outlook*, 8 April 1972 pp. 9-11 and *Outlook*, 13 May 1972 pp. 3-4.
37. Syed, Anwar H, *The Discourse and Politics of Zulfiqar Ali Bhutto*, first published in 1992. The Macmillan Press Ltd., Hong Kong. p. 182.
38. *Jang*, 29 April and 2 May 1972.

39. Askar Ali Shah, 'The Coalition's Anxiety', *Outlook*, 19 August 1972, p. 5.
40. *Zindagi*, 14 September and 14 October 1972, Askar Ali Shah's report in *Outlook*, 1 July and 19 August 1972, *Outlook*, 29 April 1972, p. 5; 16 September 1972, p. 7; and 4 June, and 6 and 23 May 1972.
41. Government of Pakistan, White Paper on Balochistan (Rawalpindi October 1974), p. 5.
42. Ibid., pp. 18-23.
43. Harrison, Selig, Nightmare in Balochistan, *Foreign Policy*, Fall 1978 p. 139.
44. Statements of Ataullah Mengal and Khair Bakhsh Marri, made in Lahore High Court, *The Pakistan Times*, 1 and 4 December 1974. Khair Bakhsh Marri's interview in *Zindagi*, 27 May 1973.
45. Statements made by Prof. Ghafoor Ahmad and Mian Tufail Mohammad of Jamaat-i-Islami, *Nawae Waqt*, 27 April and 8 June 1974; Asghar Khan, *Nawae Waqt*, 10 June 1974; Chaudhry Zahur Ilahi and Mufti Mahmood, *Pakistan Times*, 15 February 1974.
46. *Nawae Waqt*, 31 March and 28 June 1974.
47. Muslim Qureshi's report in *Zindagi*, 27 November 1972 and Aqil Khan's report in *Outlook*, 9 December 1972.
48. Aqil Khan, Ibid.
49. *Zindagi*, 7 January 1973, pp. 21-2.
50. *Pakistan Times*, 15 February 1974.
51. Letter from Wali Khan, 'Pakistan Under Strain: The Politics of Divide and Rule?' *Manchester Guardian*, 20 May 1974.
52. The federal government's rejoinder was to the charges of Wali Khan in his Written Statement in the Supreme Court of Pakistan. PLD 1976 S.C. 57.
53. Sayeed, Khalid B., *Politics in Pakistan: The Nature and Direction of Change*, 1980, Praeger Publishers USA pp. 128-9.
54. Jamil-ud-Din Aali's column in *Jang*, 29 March 1972.
55. *Dawn*, 1 April 1972.
56. *Outlook*, 15 July 1972, p. 4.
57. *Jang*, 8 May 1972 and *Zindagi*, 28 August 1972, pp. 10, 20.
58. *Jang*, 3 April and 30 May 1972.
59. *Dawn*, 8 July 1972.
60. *Dawn*, 10 July 1972, 11 July 1972.
61. *Dawn*, 10 July 1972 reports that three-day death toll during the agitation reached 22. *Zindagi*, 24 July 1972, raised the figure to 55. Also see Abu Tahir Sirhindi's report in the same journal dated December 31, 1972. Sirhindi wrote that of the 55 persons killed, most of them in police firing, 15 were Sindhis and 40 were *muhajirs*.
62. *Zindagi*, 17 July 1972, p. 5.
63. Ibid.
64. *Zindagi*, 24 July 1972, pp. 10-11.
65. Regarding the Punjab factor, see Zafrullah Poshni's report in Outlook, August 12, 1972.
66. *Dawn*, 16 July 1972.
67. Syed, Anwar H., *The Discourse and Politics of Zulfiqar Ali Bhutto*, *supra*, note 37, p. 196.
68. See Abu Ijaz's report in *Zindagi*, 8 October 1973 and Zaheer Ahmad's report in the same journal dated 20 November 1972.
69. One of the author's acquaintances narrated that when he was a Magistrate in Lyallpur (now Faisalabad) in 1973, he was assigned the task along with other members of the District administration to fail the public meetings called by Asghar Khan. He, being a hefty man, was told to stay near Asghar Khan and to keep pushing him physically away from the stage which he did quite successfully while the PPP operatives brokeup the meeting violently and uprooted the stage. During this incident, Asghar Khan told him to quit as Magistrate and open a 'wrestling club' to which he replied 'Sir, whatever you may say but I will not let you reach the stage'.
70. The list is taken from the book of Anwar H. Syed, *The Discourse and Politics of Zulfiqar Ali Bhutto*, *supra*, note 37, pp. 215-17. He prepared this list from these sources: *Outlook*, 16 December

1972, 24 March 25 August and 1 September 1973; *Zindagi*, 14 October 1972 and 11 March 1973; *Jang*, 6 May and 22, 1972.

71. *Outlook*, 24 March 1973, p. 5.
72. *Outlook*, 1 July 1972, pp. 7-8.
73. *Outlook*, 3 November 1973, pp. 5-6.
74. *Zindagi*, 21 September 1972, p. 4; 22 October 1973, pp. 7-10; M. H. Shah, 'Sanghar, A Study in Tyranny', *Outlook*, 22 June 1974, p. 6.
75. *Dawn*, 25 March 1973.
76. *Zindagi*, 27 May 1973, p. 17.
77. *Zindagi*, 17 December 1972.
78. *Zindagi*, 11 March and 29 April 1973.
79. *Zindagi*, 29 April 1973, pp. 27-32 and 15 May 1973, p. 21.
80. Article 279 of the Interim Constitution.
81. Constitution Fourth Amendment Order, 1973. President's Order 1 of 1973, adding Article 157-A to the Interim Constitution. PLD 1973 Central Statutes 298.
82. Constitution Sixth Amendment Order, 1973. President's Order 3 of 1973. PLD 1973 Central Statutes 418.
83. Constitution Tenth Amendment Order, 1973. President's Order 14 of 1973. PLD 1973 Central Statutes 58.
84. Bhutto promised parliamentary set-up, fundamental rights, and maximum autonomy to the provinces while speaking at the annual dinner of the High Court Bar Association, Karachi, on 31 August 1972. *Dawn*, 1 September 1972.
85. *Dawn*, 16 September 1972.
86. *Dawn*, 30 September 1972.
87. *Dawn*, 1 October 1972.
88. *Dawn*, 8 October 1972. Kasuri narrated the story of his resignation to a number of persons, particularly from the Bar, including the author, according to which he had differences with Bhutto on the form of government under the new constitution. Bhutto favoured presidential form of government, based upon the French model, but did not want to make a public statement to this effect. He wanted Kasuri to propose it, to work for it, and to prepare ground for it, but Kasuri refused to do so. He admitted that at one stage he said in the presence of Bhutto that he preferred presidential system over the parliamentary one which led Bhutto to ask him to convass for that. He refused because, according to him, the PPP was committed to the nation to give a parliamentary system and could not go against this mandate of the people. The difference on this issue became so acute that he resigned and became a very vocal member of the opposition in the National Assembly. The attack on him by Khar was on the asking of Bhutto, he said, because Bhutto wanted to humiliate him.
89. *Dawn*, 15 October 1972.
90. *Dawn*, 21 October 1972.
91. Ibid.
92. Ibid.
93. Ghafoor Ahmad, *Phir Marshal Law Aa Gaya* (There comes the Martial Law again), Urdu, Lahore: Jang Publishers, 1988, pp. 37-8, 43.
94. Correspondent's report in *Outlook*, 21 April 1973, pp. 4-5.
95. Mukhtar Hasan's report in *Zindagi*, 11 March 1973, pp. 5-7; and Zafar Awan's report in the same journal, 22 April 1973, pp. 12-13.
96. Ibid.
97. Mukhtar Hasan's report in *Zindagi*, 11 March and 22 April 1973.
98. In re: Special Reference under Article 187 of the Interim Constitution of the Islamic Republic of Pakistan by President Zulfiqar Ali Bhutto, (Special Reference 1 of 1973), PLD 1973 S.C. 563.

22

THE CONSTITUTION OF 1973

It has been discussed earlier that the 1973 Constitution was adopted with the consensus of all the political parties in the National Assembly. Undoubtedly, no constitutional document can be described as perfect. It is always a product of compromises amongst various political parties and forces present within the constitution-making body. Nevertheless, the 1973 Constitution embodied the best possible arrangement to accommodate the various political parties, political issues and demands, economic interests, parties' manifestos, and so on. Pakistan People's Party (PPP), the majority party in the National Assembly, had promised in the general elections of 1970 to introduce an egalitarian set-up in Pakistan. The National Awami Party (NAP) was the main opposition party in the National Assembly, with a strong presence in the assemblies of the NWFP and Balochistan. It championed the cause of provincial autonomy. NAP also had the support of another party in these provinces, Jamiat-i-Ulema-i-Islam (JUI). Hence a formula had to be devised which could strike a balance between the conflicting demands of provincial autonomy and a strong centre.

It was also necessary to reach a compromise between the Islamic and the socialist concept. The PPP had landed itself in difficulty by raising three apparently irreconcilable slogans: Islam is our faith, democracy is our politics, and socialism is our economy. The Islamic and socialist ethos were satisfied through Articles 2 and 3 of the Constitution respectively. Article 2 declared Islam as the state religion of Pakistan and Article 3 provided for the elimination of all forms of exploitation and equitable distribution of economic resources in keeping with the ability and work put in by individuals.

Another sticky point was the distribution of powers between the president and the Prime Minister, since a national consensus had been arrived at (at least it was so perceived) on the rejection of the presidential form of government (as introduced in the 1962 Constitution) and introduce a federal parliamentary form of government (as was done in the 1956 Constitution). There can be no cavil with the proposition that in a parliamentary set-up, real powers rest with the cabinet headed by the prime minister, and the president is only a figurehead. Nevertheless, the president does become, in certain parliamentary democracies, a repository of power in difficult emergency conditions and thus plays a vital role by exercising the real powers of the state. It is beyond doubt that exercise of such functions by the President is vital in certain circumstances like national emergencies, constitutional breakdowns, and so on. But Pakistan has bitter experience of Governor-Generals' and Presidents' meddling in politics to advance their own personal political interests and objectives. This issue was resolved in a lopsided manner, reducing the president to a rubber-stamp and making the prime minister all powerful. The orders of the President had to be countersigned by the prime minister to be valid. An unusual expression, particularly in constitutional jargon, was used to describe the prime minister as the chief executive of the federation.[1] Hence, it was made amply clear that the executive powers of the federation would vest in the prime minister.

But for a few Articles pertaining to constitutional matters, the framers of the 1973 Constitution followed the pattern of the earlier Constitutions of 1956 and 1962. Even the language used in the earlier Constitutions was retained in a majority of the Articles.

This Constitution, like the earlier ones, was lengthy and detailed. It contained 280 Articles divided into twelve parts and six schedules. Part I dealt with the Republic and its territories and other introductory matters; Part II with fundamental rights and directive principles of policy; Part III with the federation; Part IV with the provinces; Part V with relations between the federation and the provinces; Part VI with property, contracts, and suits; Part VII with judicature; Part VIII with elections; Part IX with the Islamic provisions; Part X with emergency provisions; Part XI with amendment of constitution; and Part XII with miscellaneous, temporary, and transitional provisions. Of the six schedules, the first one dealt with the laws constitutionally protected; the second with election of the President; the third with oaths and affirmations; the fourth with legislative lists; the fifth with powers of the Supreme Court and the remuneration of judges; and the sixth with the laws altered, repealed, or amended without the previous sanction of the President.

Fundamental Rights

Like the previous Constitutions of 1956 and 1962, the new Constitution provided for the fundamental rights of the citizens. It laid great emphasis on these rights by asserting that if any existing law or custom or usage having the force of law was inconsistent with any provision of fundamental rights, it would be void to the extent of inconsistency and that no authority in Pakistan, whether the federal government, the National Assembly, a provincial government, or legislature, or any local authority, was competent to make any law, regulation, or any order which might be repugnant to any provisions of the fundamental rights. If any such law, regulation, or order was made, it would, to the extent of repugnancy be void.[2] The judiciary was given the power to enforce fundamental rights and the courts were to decide if a law was repugnant to any of their provisions.

The familiar democratic rights and freedoms such as freedom of speech and expression, of assembly and association, of movement and profession were all provided for in the constitution, with the usual qualifications. Regarding civil rights, familiar rights such as rights to life, liberty, and property were granted, again with the usual qualifications and safeguards. An important provision from the standpoint of civic liberty laid down that if a person were arrested he/she could not be detained in custody without being informed, 'as soon as may be' of the grounds for such arrest, and he or she could not be denied the right of legal consultation and defence. Further, a person arrested or detained was given the right to be produced before the nearest magistrate within a period of twenty-four hours and no further detention was allowed except on an order of the magistrate. Serious restrictions were laid down regarding laws relating to preventive detention. No law could authorize the detention of a person beyond one month unless the appropriate Review Board headed by a Supreme Court judge in case of a federal law, and by a High Court judge in case of a provincial law, after affording opportunity to the *detenu*, came to the conclusion before the expiry of such period that there was sufficient cause for such detention. It was also provided that the detaining authority should communicate to the *detenu*, within one week, the grounds of his detention so that he could have representation against such order. It was also provided that no detention under a law for preventive detention could exceed eight months in a span of two years for acting in a manner prejudicial to the public order and twelve months in any other case.[3] Such safeguards were, however, not applicable to any person arrested or detained for anti-national activities under any law providing for preventive detention.

During an emergency, the President could, by an order, suspend the enforcement of some of the fundamental rights guaranteed to the citizens under the Constitution. The right to move any court for the enforcement of fundamental rights could also be suspended.[4]

The principal fundamental rights guaranteed by the 1973 Constitution are briefly described below:

1. All citizens are equal before the law and entitled to equal protection of laws.[5]
2. No person should be deprived of life or liberty save in accordance with the law.[6]
3. No person should be punished for an act which was not punishable when it was committed.[7]
4. There should be no discrimination on grounds of religion, race, caste, sex, or place of birth with regard to access to places of public entertainment, recreation, welfare, or utility.[8]
5. All forms of slavery, servitude, forced labour, torture, or cruel or inhuman treatment or punishment were declared illegal.[9]
6. All duly qualified citizens were made eligible for appointment in the service of the state, irrespective of religion, race, caste, sex, descent, or place of birth, provided that for an initial period of ten years it would not be unlawful for the state to reserve posts in favour of members of any sex or class or residents of any area to secure their adequate representation in the service of Pakistan.[10]
7. Every person was guaranteed a right to acquire, hold and dispose of property in any part of Pakistan subject to reasonable restrictions and public interest under the law.[11] No person should be deprived of his property save in accordance with the law. The right to property was subject to a number of constitutional restrictions including acquisition of enemy property; acquisition of property for providing housing, education; maintenance of sick, old, and infirm; acquisition of property acquired through unfair means and in an illegal

manner; or acquisition of property in excess of the maximum limit provided under a law for land reforms. However, the new constitution did not specifically provide for fair compensation. Adequacy of compensation provided under any law relating to compensation for acquisition of property, could not be called in question in any court.[12]

8. All citizens were guaranteed (a) freedom of speech, expression, and press; (b) freedom to assemble peacefully; (c) freedom of association; and (d) the right to move freely throughout Pakistan and to reside in any part of the country.[13]
9. Freedom of conscience and the right to profess, practise, and propagate any religion, subject to public order and morality, were guaranteed. Every religious association and every sect thereof was guaranteed the right to establish, manage, and maintain its religious institutions.[14]
10. No person attending any educational institution should be required to receive religious instruction or to attend religious worship other than that of his own community or denomination. No religious community should be prevented from providing religious instruction for pupils of that community in any educational institution which it maintained. No person should be compelled to pay any special taxes, the proceeds of which were specifically appropriated for the propagation or maintenance of any religion other than his own.[15]
11. The dignity of man and the privacy of home were declared inviolable. Procuring evidence through torture was prohibited.[16]
12. Protection was provided against double punishment and self incrimination.[17]
13. Every citizen was guaranteed the freedom to enter upon any lawful profession or occupation or to conduct any lawful trade or business. However, this freedom was subjected to such qualifications as might be prescribed by law.[18]
14. Other fundamental rights granted by the constitution included as under:
    (a) Safeguards against discrimination in services on the ground only of race, religion, caste, sex, residence, or place of birth. This right was, however, subjected to regional quotas for some time.[19]
    (b) Non-discrimination in respect of access to places of public entertainment or resort. However, special provisions could be made for women and children.[20]
    (c) Right to preserve and promote distinct language, script, and culture.[21]

Directive Principles of State Policy

Like the earlier Constitutions, the new Constitution also included Directive Principles of Policy. It was made the responsibility of each organ and authority of the state and those performing functions under them to act in accordance with these principles.[22]

These principles are enumerated as under:

1. Steps to be taken to enable Muslims to order their lives in accordance with the Holy Quran and the *sunnah*. The state should endeavour to facilitate learning

of Arabic, to promote observance of Islamic moral standards, and to secure the proper organization of *zakat*, *auqaf* and mosques.[23]

2. Securing the well-being of the people, prevention of the concentration of wealth and means of production in the hands of a few, providing of basic necessities of life, reducing disparity of income, provision of food, clothing, housing, education, and medical relief for citizens incapable of earning their livelihood owing to unemployment, sickness, or similar reasons.[24]
3. Promotion of social justice by removing illiteracy; providing of free and compulsory secondary education; ensuring inexpensive and expeditious justice; making provisions for securing just and humane conditions of work; enabling the people of different areas to participate fully in all forms of national activities; preventing prostitution, gambling, alcoholic liquors, drugs, etc.[25]
4. Discouragement of parochial, tribal, and racial feelings among Muslims.[26]
5. Strengthening of the bonds of unity between Muslim countries and promotion of peace and goodwill among the peoples of the world.[27]
6. Protection for all legitimate rights and interests of the non-Muslim minorities.[28]
7. Protection of marriage, the family, the mother, and the child.[29]
8. To ensure full participation of women in all spheres of law.[30]
9. To promote local government institutions.[31]
10. To eliminate *riba* as early as possible.[32]
11. To enable people from all parts of Pakistan to participate in the armed forces of Pakistan.[33]

It is interesting to note that in the new Constitution, separation of the judiciary from the executive was not relegated to the chapter of the principles of policy. This principle was, instead, included in the operative part of the Constitution. It became a dictate of the Constitution and the separation was required to take place within three years.[34]

Parliamentary Form of Government

After the sad experience of the presidential form of government under the 1962 Constitution, Pakistan was ready to revert to the parliamentary form on the pattern of the 1956 Constitution. As discussed earlier, serious resistance had come from Bhutto to the re-introduction of the parliamentary system, resulting in the resignation of a law minister. Nevertheless, Bhutto finally succumbed to the pressure in favour of the parliamentary form primarily because his party had committed itself to it in the general elections of 1970. However, the political happenings and bargainings prior to the adoption of the Constitution were not without impact on the ultimate shape of the parliamentary set-up under the new Constitution. Bhutto succeeded in introducing some basic changes in the parliamentary system as it had been known in the subcontinent. The changes thus introduced tried to address the following fears rooted in the constitutional and political experience in Pakistan:

i. The parliamentary system is vulnerable to frequent changes in government with the resultant instability, insecurity, and uncertainty.
ii. Presidents, under the parliamentary system, try to increase their powers and influence by indulging in partisan politics, thus weakening and undermining the governments.
iii. The political oppositions act with irresponsibility and indulge in Byzantine intrigues, thus rendering the government in power weak and ineffective. Often, the opposition collaborates with the President or uses the provision for vote of no-confidence as a constant sword hanging over the head of the government in power.
iv. A powerful bureaucracy in cohorts with the President, army, and/or the opposition could undermine a government.
v. All these factors are aggravated especially when the party in power does not command a clear majority and is dependent upon smaller parties or groups to keep itself in power. This situation is ideal for manipulations and intrigues, whether they are launched by the President, army, opposition, bureaucracy, or small political parties or groups.

In brief, the primary concern before Bhutto and other constitution-makers was: how to ensure a stable government under the parliamentary system? This concern was addressed in the new Constitution by introducing the following changes:

(a) The office of the Prime Minister was made extremely powerful and the office of the President was made correspondingly weak, ineffective, and dependent. The Prime Minister was more than the sum of the Cabinet put together and the President was less than a figurehead. The Prime Minister became the Chief Executive of the federation.[35] The President could not exercise his option to appoint a member of the National Assembly as Prime Minister, of course subject to his obtaining a vote of confidence later on. The Prime Minister had to be elected immediately after the election of Speaker and Deputy Speaker by the National Assembly with the votes of the majority of its membership.[36] The President's veto over legislation was completely done away with. He had only seven days to give his assent to a Bill passed by the parliament and if he failed to do so within such a period, the Bill would become law.[37] The President was required to act on the advice of the Prime Minister which was binding on him. Such advice was made non-justiciable.[38] The President was also without power to dissolve the National Assembly which could only be dissolved on the advice of the Prime Minister. In case he failed to act on the advice, the National Assembly would automatically stand dissolved on the expiration of forty-eight hours from such advice.[39]

(b) The procedure for a vote of no-confidence against the Prime Minister was made difficult and cumbersome. A resolution for a vote of no-confidence could not be moved in the National Assembly unless, in that very resolution, the name of another member of the assembly was put forward as the successor. If the resolution was by a majority of the total membership of the assembly then the President had to call upon the person named in the resolution as successor to assume office as Prime Minister. However, for the first ten years, a provision was made in order to prevent floor crossing to the effect that the vote of a member, elected to the National Assembly as candidate or nominee of a political party, in favour of the resolution would be disregarded if the majority of the members of that political party in the National Assembly had cast its votes against such a resolution.[40] However, on the failure of such a resolution, no further resolution for a vote of no-confidence could be moved in the National Assembly for a period of six months.

The main thrust of this provision was to ensure a stable government and to prevent frequent blackmail by the threat of a vote of no-confidence. The provision of naming a successor in the resolution for a vote of no-confidence was unique, particularly in the subcontinent. It was apparently borrowed from the German Constitution[41] and was designed to prevent irresponsible motions of no-confidence and to guarantee continuity through immediate succession. Thus members of the assembly were virtually voting on the dismissal of one government and the election of its successor. This provision allowed the members to exercise their votes with clarity as they knew whom they were electing as the successor. It also avoided any interregnum or void and precluded the pains of succession and transfer of power.

The President and the Cabinet

As discussed above, the President was reduced to merely a figurehead under the new Constitution. The executive authority of the federation was to be exercised in the name of the President by the federal government consisting of the Prime Minister and the federal ministers.[42] The qualifications of being elected as President were that he was required to be a Muslim of not less than forty-five years of age and qualified to be elected as a member of the National Assembly.[43] The President was to be elected by an electoral college comprising members of the parliament in joint sitting in accordance with provisions of the second schedule.[44] His term of office was five years and no one could hold the office for more than two consecutive terms.[45] The President could resign or might, on charges of violating the Constitution or gross misconduct or on the ground of physical or mental incapacity, be removed by the parliament in a joint sitting by a two-thirds majority of the total membership of the parliament.[46] The President was required to act on and in accordance with the advice of the Prime Minister which was binding on him.[47] However, the Prime Minister was supposed to keep the President informed on matters of internal and foreign policy and on all legislative proposals that the federal government intended to bring before the parliament.[48]

The Prime Minister and the federal ministers were collectively responsible to the National Assembly.[49] Federal ministers and ministers of state were to be taken from the parliament and were appointed by the Prime Minister. No more than one-fourth of such federal ministers and ministers of state could be taken from the upper House, the Senate.[50] It is noticeable that in the new Constitution, the word 'Cabinet' was carefully avoided. In its place, expressions like 'federal government' or 'the Prime Minister and the federal ministers' were used. Theoretically, the parliamentary system postulates Cabinet and the joint responsibility of the Cabinet. The Prime Minister is part and parcel of the Cabinet and not separate or different from it. He is regarded as first amongst equal members of the Cabinet. But in the new Constitution, the Prime Minister's position, powers, and responsibilities were separately and expressly described. He was clearly the boss of the federal ministers and Chief Executive of the federal government. Another departure from the peculiarities of the parliamentary system was the appointment of the ministers by the Prime Minister and not by the President. Generally, in parliamentary democracies, ministers are appointed by the President though on the recommendation and nomination of the Prime Minister. These provisions, however, established the office of a super prime minister to befit the concept, personality, and the ambitions of Bhutto.

The President, subject to the advice of the Prime Minister, was entrusted with multifarious functions. Some of the key appointments, such as those of the Chief Justices and judges of the Supreme Court and the High Courts, the Governors of the provinces, the Attorney-General and the Chiefs of Staff of the Armed Forces, the Chief Election Commissioner, Auditor-General, and the Chairman and members of the Islamic Ideology Council were to be made by the President.[51] He could constitute the National Economic Council, the National Finance Commission, the Council of Common Interests, and the Islamic Ideology Commission for bringing the existing laws into conformity with the injunctions of Islam.[52] He also had the power to issue proclamations of political or financial emergency and could suspend a provincial government.[53] The President was empowered to raise and maintain the naval, military, and air forces of Pakistan.[54] He was also given powers to grant pardon and reprieve, and to remit, suspend or commute a sentence passed by any court, tribunal, or any other authority.[55] All these powers were exercisable on the advice of the Prime Minister.

Similarly, the President was given certain legislative functions to be exercised on the advice of the Prime Minister. He could summon, prorogue, and dissolve the Parliament on his advice.[56] The President could address the National Assembly and send messages to it.[57] When a Bill was passed by the National Assembly, he could not withhold his assent for more than seven days. After the expiry of seven days, the Bill would automatically become an Act of Parliament.[58] When the National Assembly was not in session, the President possessed the positive power of making laws by ordinances which were to be laid before the National Assembly and would cease to operate at the expiration of four months from its promulgation, or at such time as a resolution of disapproval was passed by either House of the Parliament.[59]

The Federal Government

Another basic feature of the new Constitution was the federal form of the government like the previous Constitutions. A clear distribution of powers between the national and provincial governments was provided and the principle of decentralization was accepted.

As for the distribution of legislative powers between the centre and the provinces, the powers were enumerated in two lists, federal and concurrent.[60] The extent of the federal laws was extended to the whole or any part of Pakistan, including the power to make laws having extra-territorial operations.[61] The power of a provincial legislature extended to the whole of that province or any part thereof.[62] The subjects given to the centre included foreign affairs comprising all matters which would bring Pakistan into relation with any foreign country, defence, currency, citizenship, foreign and inter-provincial trade and commerce, census, leisure, taxes and duties of excise and customs, copyright, trade mark, designs, maritime shipping and navigation, central bank, postal and all forms of telecommunications, minerals, oil and gas, and others. The federal legislative list consisted of two parts. Part I had fifty-nine items and Part II eight items.

The concurrent list comprised forty-seven items and was justified on the grounds that there were certain matters which could not be given exclusively either to the centre or to the provinces because, although such matters might normally be dealt with by the provinces, an occasion might arise when it would be desirable and necessary to deal with these matters on a national level. The list dealt with such matters as civil and criminal law, marriage and divorce, adoption, bankruptcy, arbitration, trusts, transfer of property and registration, preventive detention, arms and explosives, drugs, population planning, electricity, tourism, trade union, and other matters of common interest. With regard to subjects in the concurrent list, the precedence of federal legislation over the provincial legislation was guaranteed. A provincial law, to the extent of repugnancy with the federal law on the same subject, was to be void.[63]

The Constitution did not provide for a separate provincial legislative list and Provincial Assemblies were extended power to make laws on the residuary subjects, that is, matters not enumerated in either the federal or in the concurrent list.[64]

The Chief Justice of Pakistan was assigned an important role in the settlement of disputes between the federal government and a provincial government under a federal law conferring powers on provincial governments. He was to appoint an arbitrator to settle such a dispute[65] and was empowered to appoint an arbitrator to settle disputes between the federal government and a provincial government arising out of refusal by the federal government to entrust functions to a provincial government regarding broadcasting and telecasting or due to any conditions imposed by the federal government in this behalf.[66]

There was also provision for a Council of Common Interests which the President could set up in relation to matters enumerated in Part II of the Federal Legislative List or the Concurrent Legislative List or regarding exercise of supervision and control over related matters.[67] This was meant to be an important body for the provinces to air their grievances against the federation or other provinces and for redressal of such grievances. If the federal government or a provincial government was dissatisfied with the decision of the Council, it could refer the matter to parliament in joint sitting, whose decision would be final.[68]

There was provision in the Constitution whereby the federal legislature could make laws on any provincial matter. There were, however, two processes which would enable the parliament to legislate on a provincial subject. The first applied when a provincial legislature would authorize parliament to make laws in any matter within its competence. An Act passed by the parliament in exercise of this power, in so far as it would affect a province could, however, be repealed by the provincial legislature.[69] While legislation by the federal legislature under this provision was voluntary, the second process which would enable the federal government to intervene in provincial matters, was of far-reaching importance. While a proclamation of emergency was in operation, parliament was empowered to make laws for a province concerning any matter not enumerated in the federal or in the concurrent lists.[70]

The Federal Legislature (The Parliament)

Unlike the Constitutions of 1956 and 1962, the 1973 Constitution provided for a bicameral system. As discussed earlier, under the draft constitution made by the first Constituent Assembly, there was provision for a second chamber. The reasons for and the advantages of having a second chamber are, however, not confined to its utility as an instrument of representation of the units in a federation. From the standpoint of checks and balances, the second chamber is considered very useful and has a restraining as well as a sobering effect on the other chamber.

The 1973 Constitution is distinguishable from the earlier Constitutions particularly in two respects: the federation now had four provinces or federating units rather than the earlier two, and the principle of parity had ceased to be effective. Thus, in the chamber of the people (the National Assembly), where the representation is made on population basis, the small provinces like Balochistan would be meagrely represented. Therefore, the Upper House or House of States/Provinces would be meant for checks and balances. By allowing equal representation to all the provinces in the Upper House, regardless of their size and population, the smaller provinces were given a greater voice and larger role in the national affairs. The Upper House thus becomes a bulwark for the protection of smaller provinces against the brute majority commanded by the larger provinces in the Lower House. This situation is all the more pronounced in Pakistan (or what is left of Pakistan) where one province, the Punjab, holds an absolute majority of the population and the other three provinces put together are in minority. Thus, the unicameral system would necessarily result in the dominance of the Punjab. The bicameral system had, therefore, become a necessity and the Upper House, called the Senate, was introduced in the Constitution of 1973.

Members of the National Assembly were to be elected under an electoral system to be provided for by the parliament. The matters to be decided regarding elections included allocation of seats, delimitation of constituencies, preparation of electoral rolls, the conduct of elections and election petitions, matters relating to corrupt practices in the elections, and so on.[71] In the electoral laws that followed, the system of joint electorate was enforced.

A person was entitled to vote for the National Assembly (as well as a Provincial Assembly), if he was a citizen of Pakistan, not less than 18 years old, had not been declared by a court to be of unsound mind and his name had appeared in an electoral roll.[72]

A candidate for election to the National Assembly had to be at least 25 years of age and had to be qualified to vote. The Election Commission, on reference from the Speaker of the National Assembly, could decide questions of disqualification of a member and its decision was to be final.[73] No one was to be allowed to be a member of the National Assembly from more than one constituency, though a person could seek election from as many seats as he wished.[74] A member of the National Assembly could lose his seat if he remained absent for forty consecutive sitting days without leave of the House.[75] No one was allowed to be a member simultaneously of the National Assembly and of the Senate (of a federal house) and a Provincial Assembly.[76] The National Assembly would elect its Speaker and Deputy Speaker from amongst its members in its first meeting.[77] The term of the National Assembly was fixed at five years, on the expiration of which it would stand dissolved, if not dissolved earlier.

The Senate was to consist of sixty-three members, of whom fourteen were to be elected from each province by the members of the Provincial Assembly of that province in accordance with the system of proportional representation by means of a single transferable vote. Five members were to be elected by the National Assembly members from the Federally Administered Tribal Areas, and two were to be chosen from the Federal Capital in a manner prescribed by the President. The Senate was meant to be a permanent House not subject to dissolution. The term of office of its members was to be four years, half of them retiring every two years. However, the term of office of a person elected or chosen to fill a casual vacancy was to be the unexpired term of the member whose vacancy he had filled.[78] Like the National Assembly, the Senate also had to elect its Chairman and Deputy Chairman at its first session, from amongst its own members. However, the term of the office of Chairman or the Deputy Chairman was to be two years from the date of assumption of office.[79]

As discussed above, the 1973 Constitution introduced bicameral legislation for the first time in Pakistan. The federal legislature was given the name of Parliament and its two Houses were to be known as the National Assembly and the Senate.[80] The President was empowered to summon and prorogue the parliament.[81] There were to be at least two sessions of the National Assembly each year and not more than one hundred-and-twenty days were to intervene between any two sessions.[82] There was a similar provision for the Senate.[83] Every federal minister and minister of state and the Attorney-General had the right to speak and take part in the proceedings of either

House of the Parliament but not the right to vote unless he were a member of that House.[84]

Either House of the Parliament was empowered to frame its own rules of procedure and the conduct of its business.[85] No member of the National Assembly could be made liable in any proceedings in court regarding anything said or any vote given by him in the assembly or its committees.[86] The privileges of the National Assembly, committees, the members thereof, and persons entitled to speak therein could be determined by an Act of Parliament.[87] In keeping with the principle of separation of powers, no court could enquire into the proceedings of Parliament.[88] Correspondingly, no discussion could take place in Parliament concerning the conduct of any judge of the Supreme Court or of a High Court in the discharge of his duties.[89]

The financial procedure provided by the Constitution was similar to that of the previous ones. No tax, for instance, could be levied for federal purposes except by or under the authority of an Act of Parliament.[90]

In the budget, the financial statement was divided into two parts; one showing the expenditure charged upon the consolidated fund, the expenditure which the National Assembly could discuss but not vote upon; the other part showing the sums required for the estimated expenditures of the various departments for the ensuing financial year. Expenditures charged upon the consolidated fund included; (a) remuneration and pension of the President, salaries of judges of the Supreme Court, members of the Federal Public Service Commission, the Speaker and the Deputy Speaker, the Attorney General, the Chief Election Commissioner, Chairman and Deputy Chairman of the Senate, and (b) the administrative expenses of the Supreme Court, the Federal Public Service Commission, the department of the Auditor-General, the office of the Election Commission, the Senate and the National Assembly; and (c) the debt charges binding on the federal government and sums required to satisfy any judgment, decree, or award against Pakistan by any court or tribunal, and any other sum declared by the Constitution or by Act of Parliament.[91]

The introduction of bicameral legislature at the centre had its effect on the legislative procedure. It has been discussed earlier that the competence of the parliament to make laws was extended to the federal and concurrent legislative lists. The federal legislative list, as stated before, was divided into two parts: Part I and Part II. The scheme of this division appears to be that the subjects enumerated in Part I were purely federal subjects and the subjects enumerated in Part II were subjects in which the provinces had special interest like the railways; minerals, oil and natural gas; Council of Common Interests, and others. The subjects enumerated in the concurrent list were, of course, of common interest and importance for the federation and the provinces. This being the case, it became imperative that the Senate, being a House of provinces, should be given greater role and voice in legislation on the subjects enumerated in Part II of the federal legislative list ànd the concurrent legislative list. Thus, different legislative procedures were given in the constitution for legislation on the subjects enumerated in Part I of the federal legislative list on the one hand and the subjects enumerated in Part II of the federal legislative list on the other.

A Bill relating to matters in Part I of the federal list could only originate in the National Assembly and if it was passed, it was transmitted to the Senate for consideration. If the Senate passed it without amendment or did not reject it or amend it within ninety days of transmission to it, then it would be deemed to have been passed. However, if the Senate rejected the Bill or passed it with amendment, then it would be presented to the National Assembly for reconsideration and if after such reconsideration, the National Assembly passed it again, with or without amendments proposed by the Senate, it would be deemed to have been passed and presented to the President for his assent.[92] A Bill relating to matters in Part II of the federal list or the concurrent list could originate in either House and if it was passed by one House, it would be transmitted to the other House. If the Bill was passed by the other House without amendment, it was presented to the President for his assent. In case the other House rejected it or passed it with amendment, the Bill, at the request of the House where it originated, had to be considered in a joint sitting of the two Houses of the Parliament which the President would summon.[93] If the Bill was passed by the votes of the majority of the total membership of the two Houses, then the same would be presented to the President for assent.

The purpose of different legislative procedures for the passing of the Bill relating to Part II of the federal list and the concurrent list was to give greater weightage to the Senate which could exercise a temporary veto against a Bill passed by the National Assembly on any such matters. Nevertheless, the National Assembly could override such a veto in a joint sitting because it initially had 210 members compared to sixty-three in the Senate and a majority in the joint sitting meant 137 votes which the National Assembly alone could procure.

The Money Bills could only originate in the National Assembly and, if passed, they would be presented to the President for assent, without transmission to the Senate. If a question arose as to whether a Bill was a Money Bill or not, the decision of the Speaker of the National Assembly thereon should be final.[94]

Provincial Governments and Legislatures

The provincial legislatures and executives were small replicas of the institutions at the national level. The provincial legislature remained unicameral and directly elected by the people through universal adult franchise under the electoral laws common for the federal and provincial legislatures. The relationship between the provincial Governor, provincial Chief Minister and the Provincial Assembly closely resembled that between the President, the Prime Minister, and the Parliament. A Chief Minister was to be elected by the Provincial Assembly in the same manner in which the Prime Minister was to be elected by the National Assembly.[95] The Chief Minister and the provincial ministers were to be collectively responsible to the Provincial Assembly concerned which could only be dissolved by the Governor on the advice of the Chief Minister. The procedure of vote of no-confidence against a Chief Minister was the same as that for the Prime Minister, meaning thereby that a successor had to be named in a resolution for a vote of no-confidence.[96] The Governor did not have any power to veto any Bill passed by the Provincial Assembly and had to assent to it within seven days, otherwise it would be deemed to have been assented.[97] Governors could dissolve Provincial Assemblies but only on the advice of the Chief Ministers.[98] Various provisions relating to the Parliament or a House thereof were to apply to the Provincial Assemblies with appropriate adjustment of reference to the relevant authorities.[99] The Governor continued to be an appointee of the President and an agent of the central government which could exercise pressure in the provincial politics through the Governors.[100]

Distribution of Powers and Relations between the Centre and the Provinces

Administrative relations between the centre and the provinces were on the same lines as provided under the previous Constitutions. The federal system showed a marked tendency towards centralized control and authority. It was the constitutional duty of the federal government to protect each province against external aggression and internal disturbance and to ensure that the government of each province was carried on in accordance with the provisions of the Constitution.[101] A provincial government was obliged to exercise its executive authority in such a way as to ensure compliance with the Acts of Parliament and existing laws applying to that province.[102] The federal government was entitled to give direction to a province with regard to the duties of the provincial authority and was further entitled to give directions to a province in the following matters:[103]

(a) as to the construction and maintenance of communications declared to be of national or strategic importance;

(b) as to the manner in which the executive authority of the province was to be exercised for the purpose of preventing any grave menace to the peace and tranquility or economic life of Pakistan or any part thereof.

There was one important provision in the Constitution which would enable the federal government to delegate power to the provincial governments as its agents. The federal government might, with the consent of a provincial government, entrust either conditionally or unconditionally to that government, or to its officers, functions relating to any matter to which the executive authority of the federation extended.[104] Similarly, a provincial government, with the consent of the federal government, was also empowered to entrust, either conditionally or unconditionally, some of its executive functions to the federal government or to its officers.[105]

The new Constitution made no material changes regarding the distribution of financial resources between the centre and the provinces. The centre was given the power to levy custom duties, export duties, excise duties, corporation tax, taxes on income other than agricultural income, estate and succession duties regarding property other than agricultural land, tax on capital value of the assets exclusive of agricultural land, taxes on goods or passengers, and taxes on mineral, oil, and natural gas. The principal source of income for the provinces were land revenue and taxes on agricultural income, the capital value of agricultural land, taxes on land and buildings, taxes on mineral rights subject to the federal list, excise on alcohol and drugs, taxes on electricity, taxes on vehicles and advertisements, animals, boats, on professions and trades, and on luxuries.[106]

The Judiciary

In the new Constitution provisions relating to the judiciary were on the same lines as those in the previous Constitution. However, an effort was made to regulate and confine the powers and jurisdiction of the superior courts. It was clearly stated that no court should have any jurisdiction except that which was conferred or would be conferred in future, on it by the Constitution or by or under any law.[107] Thus, the courts could not assume unto themselves any jurisdiction or powers which were not expressly conferred on them by the Constitution or a law. This provision was clearly meant to whittle down the concept of inherent powers and jurisdiction of the superior courts.

The Supreme Court continued to be the apex court in the land. The law which it would lay down was binding on all courts in Pakistan.[108] All executive and judicial authorities throughout the country would act in aid of the Supreme Court and all directions, orders, decrees or writs issued by that Court were to be executed as if they were issued by the High Courts of the appropriate province.[109] The Supreme Court was entrusted with the task of interpreting the Constitution. It was specifically given the power to adjudicate in any dispute between any two or more 'governments', which term included the federal government and the provincial government.[110] The Supreme Court had appellate jurisdiction, both criminal as well as civil, over the judgments, decrees, final orders, and sentences passed by the High Courts. The Supreme Court could also hear an appeal from any judgment, decree, order, or sentence of a High Court on grant of leave.[111] The Supreme Court also had advisory jurisdiction on any question of law that the President might consider of public importance and refer it to the Supreme Court.[112] The Supreme Court was conferred with original jurisdiction to make orders on a question of public importance with reference to the enforcement of any fundamental rights.[113] The Constitution of 1973 for the first time provided for administrative courts and tribunals to be set up for the civil servants in relation to the matters of their terms and conditions including disciplinary matters. Appeals against the orders or judgments of such courts or tribunals would lie directly to the Supreme Court and that also on grant of leave to appeal on a substantial question of law of public importance.[114]

The writ jurisdiction of the superior courts which was conferred under the previous Constitutions was retained under the new Constitution. Each of the High Courts was conferred power throughout the territories regarding which it could exercise jurisdiction to issue to any person or authority, orders in the nature of *habeas corpus*, mandamus, prohibition, quo-warranto and *certiorari*. The High Courts were also empowered to issue orders for the enforcement of any of the fundamental rights guaranteed under the constitution.[115]

The Supreme Court was to consist of the Chief Justice and as many other judges as might be determined by an Act of Parliament or until so determined, as might be fixed by the President.[116] The Chief Justice was to be appointed by the President and other judges were to be appointed by the President in consultation with the Chief Justice.[117] The qualification for appointment as a judge of the Supreme Court was either five years standing as a judge of a High Court or fifteen years standing as an advocate of a High Court.[118] The retirement age of a Supreme Court judge was fixed at 65 years and he was disqualified from pleading or acting before any court or authority in Pakistan.[119]

A judge could only be removed by the President on the report of the Supreme Judicial Council to the effect that he was incapable of performing the duties of his office or had been guilty of misconduct. Such a report could only be made after due inquiry and affording opportunity to the judge concerned to defend himself.[120] The Supreme Judicial Council would consist of the Chief Justice of Pakistan, two next senior-most judges of the Supreme Court and the two most senior Chief Justices of the High Courts. There was also provision for the appointment of an Acting Chief Justice in the absence of the Chief Justice or when the office of the Chief Justice had become vacant.[121] There were also provisions for acting judges and adhoc judges for the Supreme Court.[122] The seat of the Supreme Court was to be at Islamabad but until such time it was so established, it was to be at a place appointed by the President.[123]

The Constitution provided for three High Courts, initially, one for the province of the Punjab, one for the province of NWFP and a common High Court for the provinces of Sindh and Balochistan.[124] Each High Court was to consist of a Chief Justice and such number of other judges that the President might determine.[125] The Chief Justice of a High Court was to be appointed by the President after consultation with the Chief Justice of Pakistan and the Governor of the province concerned. In case of appointment of other judges of a High Court, the President would appoint them in consultation with the aforesaid constitutional functionaries as well as the Chief Justice of that High Court.[126] The retirement age was fixed at 62 years.[127] The qualification for appointment as a judge of a High Court included ten years standing as an advocate of a High Court, ten years service as a member of the civil service of Pakistan including at least three years as a district judge, or holding of a judicial office in Pakistan for at least ten years.[128]

A judge of a High Court could not be removed from his office except by an order of the President made on the grounds of misbehaviour or infirmity of mind or body, if the Supreme Judicial Council, on reference being made to it by the President, reported that the judge ought to be removed on any of those grounds.[129] There was provision for the appointment of an Acting Chief Justice when the office of the Chief Justice became vacant or he was absent or unable to perform his duties.[130] The President had no option in the matter of appointment of Acting Chief Justice. He could only appoint the most senior of the other judges of the High Court to act as Chief Justice. However, transfer of judges from one High Court to another was made subject to the consent of the judge being transferred and subject to consultation with the Chief Justice of Pakistan and both the Chief Justices of the High Court of which he was a judge and to which he was being transferred.[131] The decision of a High Court on a question of law would be binding on all courts subordinate to it,[132] and which each High Court was empowered to supervise and control.[133]

Islamic Provisions

Islam was declared the state religion of Pakistan.[134] The Islamic way of life was to be promoted including steps like the organization of *zakat*, *auqaf,* and the mosques.[135] Strengthening of bonds with the Muslim world was another principle of policy under the Constitution.[136] The Head of the State, the President, was to be a Muslim.[137] The Prime Minister was also required to be a Muslim member of the National Assembly.[138]

An important Islamic provision declared that 'no law shall be enacted which is repugnant to the injunctions of Islam as laid down in the Holy Quran and the *sunnah*' and that existing laws 'shall be brought into conformity with injunctions of Islam as laid down in the Holy Quran and *sunnah*'.[139] The President would appoint within ninety days of the commencement of the Constitution a Council of Islamic Ideology to make recommendations to Parliament and the Provincial Assemblies for bringing the existing laws into conformity with the injunctions of Islam and as to the stages by which such measures should be brought into effect.[140] The Council was also to compile in a suitable form for the guidance of Parliament and the Provincial Assemblies such injunctions of Islam as could be given legislative effect. The Commission was to submit its final report within seven years of its appointment and might submit any interim report earlier. The report, whether interim or final, was to be laid before the Parliament and each Provincial Assembly within six months of its receipt and its legislatures, after considering the report, were to enact laws in respect thereof within a period of two years of the final report.[141]

Emergency Provisions

Under Article 232, if the President was satisfied that a grave emergency existed in which the security of Pakistan or any part thereof was threatened by war or external aggression or by internal disturbances beyond the power of the provincial government to control, he could issue a proclamation of emergency. The effects of a proclamation of emergency under Article 232 are as under:

(a) the parliament has the power to make laws for a province on those subjects which were not included in the federal or concurrent lists, that is, the Parliament would have power to legislate even in provincial matters.

(b) the federal executive authority has power to give direction to a province as to the manner in which the executive authority of the province would be exercised.

(c) the federal government might issue an order assuming unto itself, or directing the Governor of a province to assume on its behalf, all or any powers of the provincial government or any function of the provincial government except that of the Provincial Assembly. The federal government is also empowered to suspend in whole or in part the operation of any provision of the Constitution relating to any body or authority in the Province.[142]

There was also provision for the proclamation of emergency due to the breakdown of constitutional machinery in a province. If the President, on receipt of a report from the Governor of a province, was satisfied that a situation had arisen in which the government of the province could not be carried on in accordance with the provisions of the Constitution he could, by proclamation, assume to himself, or direct the Governor to assume on his behalf, all or any of the functions or powers of the provincial government or any organ or body of the provincial government except the Provincial Assembly, and the Parliament might be authorized to exercise the powers of the Provincial Assembly. The President could also suspend the operation of any provisions of the Constitution relating to any body or authority in the province. The President, during a proclamation under this Article, was empowered to authorize expenditure from the provincial consolidated fund in anticipation of approval by the Parliament in the joint sitting.[143] The President, on the advice of the Prime Minister, has the discretion to make such a proclamation but, on the resolution of the two Houses, is under compulsion to make such a proclamation.

Another type of emergency for which the Constitution made provisions related to the financial stability or credit of Pakistan. If the President was satisfied that a situation had arisen whereby the financial stability or credit of Pakistan or any part thereof was threatened, he could, after consultation with the provincial Governors or with the Governor of the province concerned, issue a proclamation of financial emergency. During the period of financial emergency the federal government could direct a province to observe such principles of financial propriety and any other direction required for restoring financial stability and credit, including a direction to reduce the salaries and allowances of government servants or any other class of people serving in connection with the affairs of the federation.[144]

During the period of emergency, the operation of certain fundamental rights like freedom of movement, freedom of assembly, freedom of association, freedom of trade and business, freedom of speech, and property rights, could be suspended. The President could declare by order that the enforcement of fundamental rights during the period of emergency would remain suspended.[145] A proclamation of emergency could be varied or revoked by a subsequent proclamation.[146] The Parliament could enact laws of indemnity for those people in government service or otherwise regarding any act done in connection with the maintenance or restoration of order in any area in Pakistan.[147]

Other Features

Other features of the Constitution included the composition of the Election Commission of Pakistan for holding periodic elections to Parliament and the Provincial Assemblies,[148] determination of the conditions of employment of people in the service of Pakistan,[149] and the establishment and composition of the Public Service Commission.[150] The terms and conditions of service of civil servants were no longer protected under the Constitution but were made subject to ordinary law. Administrative courts and tribunals were to be set up under ordinary law for adjudication of questions arising from the terms and conditions of government servants, including disciplinary matters.[151]

The Constitution, or any of its provisions, could be amended by an Act of Parliament provided it originated and was passed by the votes of not less than two-thirds of the total number of members of the National Assembly and by the votes of a majority of the total membership of the Senate. However, no amendment of a constitutional provision affecting the limits of a province could be made unless such amendment had been approved by a resolution of its Provincial Assembly by not less than two-thirds of the total membership of that assembly.[152] However, the President can not withhold his assent to the amendment beyond seven days of the presentation of the Bill, after the expiry of which period, he would be deemed to have assented. If the Amendment Bill was not passed within ninety days of its receipt by the Senate, it would be deemed to have been rejected. An interesting aspect of this provision was that the Senate had complete veto power over the amendment of the Constitution. There was no provision for sending the Bill for consideration to the two Houses of the Parliament in the joint sitting. Thus, any two provinces could successfully thwart any effort to amend the Constitution to their dislike or disadvantage.

Another important provision was the validation of all laws including all proclamations, President's orders, martial law regulations, and martial law orders during the civilian martial law of Bhutto. All orders, proceedings taken, and acts done by any authority or person during the period of civilian martial law under the aforesaid laws were validated and those passing such orders, holding such proceedings, and performing such acts were indemnified.[153] All existing laws, subject to the Constitution, were continued in force so far as applicable and with necessary adaptations until altered, repealed, or amended by the appropriate legislature.[154]

Urdu was declared the national language of Pakistan. Steps were to be taken to bring it in use as the official language within fifteen years of the commencement of the Constitution and until such time, the English language might be used for official purposes.[155] The President, the Prime Minister, governors, chief ministers, federal ministers, ministers of state, and provincial ministers were granted immunity from court action for any act done in exercise of their powers or in performance of their functions.[156]

The Proclamation of Emergency on 23 November 1971 was deemed to be a Proclamation of Emergency under Article 232 and all laws, rules or orders made in pursuance of that proclamation would be deemed to have been validly made.[157]

NOTES

1. Constitution of Islamic Republic Pakistan, 1973, Article 90.
2. Ibid., Article 8.
3. Ibid., Article 10.
4. Ibid., Article 233.
5. Ibid., Article 25.
6. Ibid., Article 9.
7. Ibid., Article 12.
8. Ibid., Article 26.
9. Ibid., Article 11.
10. Ibid., Article 27.
11. Ibid., Article 23.
12. Ibid., Article 24.
13. Ibid., Articles 15, 16, 17, and 19.
14. Ibid., Article 20.
15. Ibid., Articles 21 and 22.
16. Ibid., Article 14.
17. Ibid., Article 13.
18. Ibid., Article 18.
19. Ibid., Article 27.
20. Ibid., Article 26.
21. Ibid., Article 28.
22. Ibid., Articles 29 and 30.
23. Ibid., Article 31.
24. Ibid., Article 38.
25. Ibid., Article 37.
26. Ibid., Article 33.
27. Ibid., Article 40.
28. Ibid., Article 36.
29. Ibid., Article 35.
30. Ibid., Article 34.
31. Ibid., Article 32.
32. Ibid., Article 38(f).
33. Ibid., Article 39.
34. Ibid., Article 175(3).
35. Ibid., Article 90(1).
36. Ibid., Article 91.
37. Ibid., Article 75.
38. Ibid., Article 48.
39. Ibid., Article 58.
40. Ibid., Article 96.
41. Article 67 of the Grundgesetz (the Basic Law) for the Federal Republic of Germany adopted in 1949.
42. Constitution of Islamic Republic of Pakistan, 1973; Article 90.
43. Ibid., Article 41.
44. Ibid.
45. Ibid., Article 44.
46. Ibid., Article 47.
47. Ibid., Article 48.
48. Ibid., Article 46.

49. Ibid., Article 90.
50. Ibid., Article 92.
51. Ibid., Articles 100, 101, 168, 177, 193, 213, 228, and 243.
52. Ibid., Articles 153, 156, 160, and 238.
53. Ibid., Articles 232, 234, 235, and 236.
54. Ibid., Article 243.
55. Ibid., Article 45.
56. Ibid., Articles 54 and 58.
57. Ibid., Article 56.
58. Ibid., Article 75.
59. Ibid., Article 89.
60. Ibid., Fourth Schedule.
61. Ibid., Article 141.
62. Ibid.
63. Ibid., Article 143.
64. Ibid., Article 142.
65. Ibid., Article 146.
66. Ibid., Article 159.
67. Ibid., Articles 153 and 154.
68. Ibid., Article 154.
69. Ibid., Article 144.
70. Ibid., Article 234.
71. Ibid., Article 222.
72. Ibid., Article 51.
73. Ibid., Article 63.
74. Ibid., Article 223.
75. Ibid., Article 64.
76. Ibid., Article 223.
77. Ibid., Article 53.
78. Ibid., Article 59.
79. Ibid., Article 60.
80. Ibid., Article 50.
81. Ibid., Article 54.
82. Ibid., Article 54.
83. Ibid., Article 61.
84. Ibid., Article 57.
85. Ibid., Article 67.
86. Ibid., Article 66.
87. Ibid.
88. Ibid., Article 69.
89. Ibid., Article 68.
90. Ibid., Article 77.
91. Ibid., Article 81.
92. Ibid., Article 70.
93. Ibid., Article 71.
94. Ibid., Article 73.
95. Ibid., Article 131.
96. Ibid., Article 136.
97. Ibid., Article 116.
98. Ibid., Article 112.
99. Ibid., Article 127.
100. Ibid., Article 145.

101. Ibid., Article 148.
102. Ibid.
103. Ibid., Article 149.
104. Ibid., Article 146.
105. Ibid., Article 147.
106. Ibid., Fourth Schedule.
107. Ibid., Article 175(2).
108. Ibid., Article 189.
109. Ibid., Articles 187 and 190.
110. Ibid., Article 184.
111. Ibid., Article 185.
112. Ibid., Article 186.
113. Ibid., Article 184(3).
114. Ibid., Article 212.
115. Ibid., Article 199.
116. Ibid., Article 176.
117. Ibid., Article 177.
118. Ibid.
119. Ibid., Articles 179 and 207.
120. Ibid., Article 209.
121. Ibid., Article 180.
122. Ibid., Articles 181 and 182.
123. Ibid., Article 183.
124. Ibid., Article 192.
125. Ibid.
126. Ibid., Article 193.
127. Ibid., Article 195.
128. Ibid., Article 193.
129. Ibid., Article 209.
130. Ibid., Article 196.
131. Ibid., Article 200.
132. Ibid., Article 201.
133. Ibid., Article 203.
134 Ibid., Article 2.
135. Ibid., Article 31.
136. Ibid., Article 40.
137. Ibid., Article 41.
138. Ibid., Article 91.
139. Ibid., Article 227.
140. Ibid., Articles 228 and 230.
141. Ibid.
142. Ibid., Article 232.
143. Ibid., Article 234.
144. Ibid., Article 235.
145. Ibid., Article 233.
146. Ibid., Article 236.
147. Ibid., Article 237.
148. Ibid., Articles 213, 215, 218, 219, and 220.
149. Ibid., Article 240.
150. Ibid., Article 242.
151. Ibid., Article 212.
152. Ibid., Articles 238 and 239.

153. Ibid., Article 269.
154. Ibid., Article 268.
155. Ibid., Article 251.
156. Ibid., Article 248.
157. Ibid., Article 280.

23

BHUTTO'S DEMOCRACY

Although the Constitution Bill had been passed and authenticated by the National Assembly on 16 April 1973, its day of commencement was the twenty-sixth anniversary of the independence of Pakistan. However, a number of steps had to be taken before the Constitution was enforced, such as the election to the Senate, election of the President, election of the Chairman and Deputy Chairman of the Senate, election of the Speaker and Deputy Speaker of the National Assembly, and, finally, the election of the Prime Minister. Once again, no new elections were to take place and the National Assembly in existence under the Interim Constitution (elected in December 1970), was to be the first under the Constitution of Pakistan and would continue, unless dissolved, till 14 August 1977.[1] Hence, the assembly elected on an all-Pakistan basis in December 1970, whose number had been reduced to 146 from 313, was to continue for another four years after having served for one-and-a-half year. This was inherently unfair because the assembly was extending its life under the Constitution. The provincial assemblies were also to continue till 14 August 1977 in like manner.[2]

Elections to the Senate and the Offices of the President and the Prime Minister

The number of seats in the Senate had been fixed at sixty-three; fourteen from each province, five from the Federally Administered Tribal Areas (FATA), and two from the federal capital.[3] However, for the first Senate, the total membership had been reduced to forty-five; ten from each province, three from the FATA, and two from the federal capital.[4] The members elected to the first Senate had to be divided into two groups by drawing of lots, the first group consisting of five members from each province, two members from the FATA, one member from the federal capital, and the remaining were to fall in the second group. The term of office of the first group was to be two years and that of the second group four years. After the first elections to the National Assembly under the Constitution, additional eighteen members of the Senate were to be elected; four from each province and two from the FATA.

Elections to the Senate were completed in stages during July 1973 with each Provincial Assembly meeting to elect its ten members to the Senate on the basis of a single transferable vote. The National Assembly met to elect three members from FATA and two from the federal capital. The Senate held its inaugural session on 6

August 1973 and elected Khan Habibullah Khan as Chairman and Mirza Tahir Muhammad Khan as Deputy Chairman.[5]

The 1973 Constitution had given a federal parliamentary system to the country in which the President was a mere figurehead, hence Bhutto's decision to become Prime Minister under this Constitution. Moreover, special pains were taken in this Constitution to ensure that the office of the President was totally ineffective. The election to the office of the President was called for on 10 August 1973. On 9 August, the National Assembly elected Sahibzada Farooq Ali a PPP nominee, unopposed as Speaker of the National Assembly. On 10 August, Chaudhry Fazal Elahi, previous Speaker of the National Assembly, was elected President under the new Constitution. He was a nominee of the PPP and defeated the candidate of the opposition parties, namely Amirzada Khan.[6]

On 12 August 1973, the National Assembly met to elect Bhutto as the Prime Minister. In a House of 146 members, Bhutto secured 108 votes and the joint opposition candidate, Maulana Shah Ahmad Noorani of JUP, received 28 votes.[7] Upon his election, Bhutto reiterated his party's determination to establish democratic traditions and to see democracy function in the country for all times to come. Wali Khan, the leader of the opposition in the National Assembly, offered full co-operation for the rule of law.

Constitution Enforced on 14 August 1973

The Constitution formally came into force on 14 August 1973 which was referred to as the 'commencing day'.[8] Chaudhry Fazal Elahi was sworn in as President and Bhutto was sworn in as Prime Minister. Thus came into existence and force, the third permanent Constitution of Pakistan within twenty-six years of its independence. If we add the provisional/interim constitutions of Pakistan, then it was the sixth document which served as the Constitution of the country. Speaking on the occasion, Bhutto said that the days of palace intrigues and coups were ended and that venom and violence in politics must stop.[9] He, however, warned the opposition against confrontation.

Old habits die hard, and soon Bhutto was at his game again. Two days after the enforcement of the new Constitution, Bhutto flouted his own rules. Ghaus Bakhsh Bizenjo, former Governor of Balochistan, Sardar Khair Bakhsh Marri, former Chief Minister of Balochistan, and Sardar Ataullah Mengal, an MNA from Balochistan, were arrested on 16 August on various charges of corruption, malpractices, and seditious activities. The confrontation with the opposition was initiated in a big way. It would go on for many years, indeed till Bhutto's ouster.

Administrative Reforms

Pakistan inherited its bureaucratic set-up from the British who ruled India with an iron hand through bureaucrats who were completely loyal to them, regardless of the political currents in the country or the sentiments of the people. This institution developed its own internal unity, fraternity, and coherence, often described as a steel frame. At times, it acted in concert against other institutions and people, including the politicians. It was due to its internal organization, cohesion and unity that Pakistan's history was chequered by frequent interference from the bureaucrats in its early days when the bureaucracy became so powerful and confident that it completely undermined the political process in the country and took over the task of governing the country itself.[10] Several bureaucrats turned into successful politicians and from among their ranks emerged two of Pakistan's Governors-General, Ghulam Muhammad and Iskandar Mirza (who also became the first President of Pakistan under the 1956 Constitution), and one Prime Minister, Chaudhri Mohammad Ali.

Few people can dispute the incalculable harm done to the constitutional, legal, and political institutions and practices in Pakistan by the aforesaid Governors-General. Ghulam Muhammad created the first constitutional crisis in Pakistan by dismissing the first Constituent Assembly in 1954, thus leading to court battles which culminated in the judgments of the Federal Court in the cases of Moulvi Tamizuddin Khan, Usif Patel, and Governor-General's reference. Iskandar Mirza freely meddled with parliamentary politics by getting involved in political intrigues, thus destabilizing successive governments to serve his own interest and position. As if all that was not enough for him, he abrogated the first Constitution of Pakistan in October 1958 and imposed martial law throughout the country. This led to another court battle. The Supreme Court upheld the martial law in State v Dosso on the rationale that a victorious revolution or a successful *coup d'etat* was a recognized legal method of changing a constitution.

During the martial law years of 1958 to 1962, the bureaucracy gained further powers as it was not accountable to the people. The martial law administration was totally dependent upon the civil bureaucracy for its day-to-day business of running the country and the citizens fell completely into the merciless clutches of a bureaucracy unfettered by any political checks and balances. The 1962 Constitution hardly brought any change in the situation and the bureaucracy continued to grow more powerful, arrogant, and indifferent to the needs of the common man. To put it in the words of Bhutto, the bureaucracy became 'a class of Brahmans or Mandarins unrivalled in its snobbery and arrogance, insulated from the life of the people and incapable of identifying itself with them'.[11] It was only obvious that there would be an outcry from the people against this institution. The political agitation against Ayub's regime from November 1968 to March 1969 brought to the forefront public resentment against the bureaucrats.

In the general elections of December 1970, Bhutto, as leader of the People's Party, included in his election manifesto bureaucratic and administrative reforms, including measures to cut down the powers and privileges of the bureaucray. In his first speech as President delivered to the nation on 20 December 1971, he deprecated the bureaucracy as having been 'nursed and brought up on the traditions and concepts of colonialism'. He stressed the need for a bureaucracy 'with a liberal outlook, dynamic in its working, and motivated with a desire to serve the nation'.[12] A high powered committee was appointed to address itself to the task of overhauling the administration. The committee was required to take stock of the existing position, to review the recommendations of various experts, commissions and committees made from time to time and to chalk out a programme of administrative reforms in the light of new requirements. This committee submitted its recommendations after examining various issues, such as the revision of the service structure, the eradication of corruption, creation of a more scientific and effective machinery, and the establishment of sound and rational training programmes.[13] The recommendations accepted by the government were:

i. Constitutional safeguards and guarantees were to be abolished and terms and conditions of service of the civil servants were to be brought under the control of legislatures through ordinary legislation;
ii. Administrative tribunals were to be set up as fora where government officials could get their grievances redressed;
iii. All the services and cadres were to be merged into a unified grading structure with equality of opportunity for all who entered the service at any stage, based on the required professional and specialized competence necessary for each job;
iv. All 'classes' amongst government servants were to be abolished and replaced by a unified grading structure: a peon or equivalent at the bottom and a secretary or departmental head at the top. The existing classification of the services into Class I to Class IV would no longer operate. The road to the top would be open to all on merit;
v. The use of service labels like CSP, PSP, etc. were to be discontinued immediately;
vi. The unified structure would enable promotions to the highest jobs throughout the range of public service and for horizontal movements from one cadre to another including the movement of the technical personnel to the cadre of general management. There would also be scope for out-of-turn promotion to exceptionally able officers;
vii. The correct grading for each post would be determined by job evaluation;
viii. There would be provision for entry into government service for talented individuals from the private sector in fields such as banking, insurance, industry, and trade.

In keeping with the aforementioned recommendations of the Committee, the 1973 Constitution made a clear departure from all the previous constitutions in respect of the provisions regarding guarantees to the civil servants against arbitrary and wrongful dismissal or removal from service or reduction in rank. The Constitution made no mention of any guarantees extended to government servants under the previous constitutions and the matter of determination of their conditions of service was relegated to the realm of ordinary laws as enacted from time to time by the parliament or the provincial assemblies, as the case may be.[14]

The parliament and the provincial assemblies were empowered to enact laws for the establishment of one or more administrative courts or tribunals to exercise exclusive jurisdiction in respect of the following matters:[15]

(a) Terms and conditions of persons in the service of Pakistan, including disciplinary matters;
(b) Claims arising from tortious acts of government or its servants while acting in exercise of their duties, or of any local or other authority empowered to levy any tax or cess; or
(c) the acquisition, administration, and disposal of enemy property under any law.

The jurisdiction of such administrative courts and tribunals was made entirely exclusive and, on their establishment, no other court could grant an injunction, make any order, or entertain any proceedings regarding matters within their jurisdiction. Provisions of clause (2) of Article 212 were not applicable to an administrative court and tribunal established under an Act of the Provincial Assembly unless at the request of that assembly made in the form of a resolution. Parliament by law extended these provisions to such a court or tribunal. On the request of the provincial assemblies of the North-West Frontier Province, the Punjab, and Sindh, the parliament, by statute, extended the provisions of Article 212(2) of the Constitution with effect from 6 May 1974, to the Service Tribunals established by the three provinces.[16] Similarly, on the request of the Provincial Assembly of Balochistan, the Parliament by statute extended the provisions of Article 212(2) of the constitution with effect from 19 May 1976 to the service tribunal established for Balochistan.[17] Appeal was provided to the Supreme Court against the decisions of the administrative courts or tribunals only in case the Supreme Court grants leave to appeal on a substantial question of law of public importance.

The Bhutto regime initiated a programme of 'lateral entry' into the public service. Over a three-year-period, 514 men and women holding mid-career positions in government, business, industry, universities, and the professions were appointed to middle management and higher positions in the central and provincial governments.[18] Appointments were made upon a scrutiny of the candidates' credentials in the Establishment Division, a written examination, an oral examination, or a combination of all of them. Waqar Ahmad, the establishment secretary at the time, maintained that 95 per cent of the 'political element' had been eliminated in these appointments and that Bhutto himself had rejected the recommendations of some of his ministers because the persons concerned were not worthy enough. Even if Waqar Ahmad had understated the number of political appointees, it seems that most of the lateral entrants were professionally competent.

The new appointees filled the vacancies created by the departure of Bengali officials following the separation of East Pakistan, especially in the foreign office, and those created by the retirements and dismissals ordered under martial law regulation number 114. Bhutto maintained that, in the first place, these large number of vacancies could not have been promptly filled through the usual entry level competitive examinations. Secondly, these appointments served to break open the CSP's fortress of special preserves. A lateral entrant placed as a permanent secretary or additional secretary in a ministry could be supervizing CSP officers who had already put in twenty years of service. Thirdly, the new entrants were doubtless aware that they owed their positions to the Bhutto regime and had reason to be loyal to it. They could thus be counted upon to serve as a counterpoise to the conventionally established higher civil servants, particularly the CSP.

The government hoped that these measures would enable it to pursue 'scientific career planning'on the basis of equality and professional competence, undertake more effective performance ratings, and stress merit in promotions. The road to top positions would be open to all. Theoretically, a messenger boy or a janitor in grade 2 could some day become a central government secretary in grade 22. The government also expected to bring in, through lateral entry, scientists, engineers, economists, accountants, statisticians, and other professionals to manage the industries it had nationalized and implement the reforms it was undertaking. But there were other, stated and undeclared concerns that underlay the administrative restructuring described above.

It cannot be said that the administrative reforms were in vain. The abolition of service labels and classes, discarding of reservation of key posts for the CSP, equality of opportunity for the specialist with the generalist, simplification of the position classification system, emphasis on merit in promotion were all sound and progressive ideas supported by the scholarly opinion as well as the common man.

First Amendment and the Recognition of Bangladesh

Ever since the secession of East Pakistan in December 1971, the question of recognition of Bangladesh was a sensitive political issue in Pakistan. Opposition parties were resisting the recognition of Bangladesh. Although Bhutto appeared to be inclined towards recognition and perhaps had released Mujib for the purpose, he was not confident enough to take a definite step in this difficult and sensitive matter particularly when his own role in the breakup of Pakistan was far from clear. He was under constant accusation for masterminding the breakup of Pakistan. He was looking for ways and means to resolve this issue without appearing too keen to recognize Bangladesh. Bhutto referred the matter for the opinion of the Supreme Court and some hearings were held but the matter was still pending when the 1973 Constitution was enforced.

The Constitution also kept the matter open. While describing the territories of Pakistan, East Pakistan was omitted, but it was laid down that the Constitution would be appropriately amended so as to enable the people of East Pakistan, as and when foreign aggression in that province and its effects were eliminated, to be represented in the affairs of the federation.[19] Finally, the opportunity to recognize Bangladesh presented itself in February 1974. The Second Islamic Summit Conference was going to be held at Lahore. The absence of representation from Bangladesh, the second most populated Muslim country, would have been seriously felt. On this occasion, Bhutto, under the blessings of King Faisal of Saudi Arabia, Qaddafi of Libya, and others heads of state from Muslim countries attending the conference, invited Mujib to attend the conference. Mujib was not willing to come unless he was treated as head of the government of a Muslim country and that his country was recognized as a separate national entity. Keeping this difficulty in view, Pakistan recognized Bangladesh and this issue was put to an end once and for all. Whatever the role of Bhutto in the East Pakistan crisis, it can be said with all fairness to him that there was no justification to keep this matter pending endlessly, particularly when the creation of Bangladesh was a reality, howsoever bitter it might be. The recognition of Bangladesh was a recognition of reality.

Consequent to the recognition of Bangladesh, Article 1 of the Constitution was amended under the First Amendment, thus deleting Clause (2) from it which provided for representation of East Pakistan in the federation of Pakistan after the effect of foreign aggression over them were eliminated.[20]

Other important amendments to the Constitution brought about by the First Amendment were as under:

1. Article 17 pertaining to the freedom of association was amended providing for reasonable restriction on this freedom to form associations imposed by law in the interest of sovereignty or integrity of Pakistan. Such law was also to provide that where the federal government declared that any political party had been formed or was operating in a manner prejudicial to the sovereignty or integrity of Pakistan, the federal government should, within fifteen days of such declaration, refer the matter to the Supreme Court whose decision on such reference would be final. In keeping with this constitutional amendment, Political Parties Act, 1962 was also amended to the same effect and in addition to provide that on such declaration by the federal government, the political party, against which the declaration was made, would stand dissolved and all its properties and funds forfeited to the federal government.[21] It was under these provisions of the amended constitution and Political Parties Act that NAP was later dissolved in 1975 with the matter referred to the Supreme Court.
2. The maximum period intervening the two successive sessions of the Senate, the National Assembly, and the Provincial Assemblies, was reduced from 130 days to 90 days.
3. Chief Justice of a High Court could require a judge of another High Court to attend the sittings of his court provided the judge so asked consented to it and the President approved the same after consultation with the Chief Justice of Pakistan and the Chief Justice of the High Court of which he was the judge.
4. On the establishment of a service tribunal, all proceedings pending before any court, in relation to the terms and conditions of service of employees to which the jurisdiction of such tribunal extended, would abate.

Second Amendment: Ahmedis Declared Non-Muslims

It has been discussed above that an anti-Ahmediya movement started by the Ahrar party in the early 1950s in Punjab turned into a rebellion against the state and martial law was imposed in the city of Lahore in March 1953 to control the riots. This anti-

Ahmediya agitation brought down the government of Mian Mumtaz Muhammad Khan Daultana in the province and severely shook the government of Prime Minister Nazimuddin at the Centre. Another such agitation erupted in 1974 and seriously threatened the Bhutto regime.

On 22 May, a group of 160 students from Multan boarded a train to Peshawar. As the train stopped at Rabwah, a predominantly Ahmedi town that housed the community's spiritual and organizational headquarters, it was alleged that hundreds of them came out and shouted slurs and offensive slogans. Upon their return from Peshawar on 29 May, they stopped at Rabwah again. This time, the Ahmedis were ready. Hundreds of them, armed with knives and sticks, fell upon the students and injured more than thirty of them. News of this event infuriated the Muslim community throughout the country. The Punjab government promptly arrested seventy-one men in Rabwah and appointed Mr Justice K.M.A. Samadani, a judge of the Lahore High Court, to investigate the incident and submit his findings. Hanif Ramay, the Chief Minister, appealed for calm and asked the people not to make this breach of public order into a sectarian issue.[22]

But calm was not to be had. Nor would the opposition parties and leaders forgo the opportunity of embarrassing Bhutto. Islamist parties, like the Jamaat-i-Islami, Majlis-e-Ahrar, the Khaksars, student groups, and prayer leaders in mosques demanded the dismissal of Ahmedis from key posts in government, the disarming of their youth organizations, and the making of Rabwah, which they alleged had become a 'state within a state', into an 'open city'. Violent demonstrations began and continued for a week in all major cities of the Punjab. Enraged crowds burnt down the houses of Ahmedis and their shops, gas stations, and factories. The leaders of the agitation called for a countrywide general strike on 14 June to protest the government's tardiness in meeting their demands which now included the designation of Ahmedis as a non-Muslim minority.[23]

The agitation slowed down and became essentially non-violent after a week. This improvement resulted partly from the way Bhutto reasoned out the issue with the people in his statements and speeches, and partly from the provincial government's readiness to use force to discourage violence. The government imposed partial censorship to prevent commentaries on the subject from becoming inflammatory and arrested hundreds of demonstrators (most of whom were subsequently released).

Bhutto and other official spokesmen stated repeatedly that the government would protect the life and property of all citizens regardless of their religious affiliation and, to this end, they would use the army if necessary. In addition, Bhutto suggested that an Indo-Soviet 'lobby' had inspired the anti-Ahmediya disturbances to weaken Pakistan. In a statement to the press on 31 May, Bhutto asked: 'Is our response to India's atomic blast to be that we shall quarrel among ourselves and attempt to tear ourselves apart?'[24] Speaking in the National Assembly on 3 June, he opposed discussion of the Ahmediya question in the House until after public order had been restored. Those in the opposition who wanted immediate discussion wished only to intensify the agitation and ruin the country, he declared.

Bhutto maintained that there was no need for an agitation because the government, the opposition, and the people at large had the same belief on the issues. He asked the nation to consider the Ahmediya question at the appropriate time and do so calmly and sensibly, without hatred and bigotry. Bhutto addressed the nation on radio and television on 13 June. He urged patience, peaceableness, and civility. The Ahmediya question, he said, had been in the public domain for ninety years and it could not be resolved in a day. It must be settled with due regard to the feelings of the people and considerations of national solidarity. He assured his listeners that he would place the issue before the National Assembly which would then discuss it. He maintained that the issue had already been settled in the 1973 Constitution but went on to suggest that the assembly might nevertheless refer it to the Advisory Council of Islamic Ideology. He added that the members of his own party in the assembly would be free to vote on the subject according to their conscience.[25]

As one might have expected, the *ulema* and their associates did not find Bhutto's assurances satisfactory. Mufti Mahmood, head of the JUI, suspected that Bhutto did not intend to honour the Muslim nation's demand and that he meant to put it in 'cold storage'. The 'Action Committee' of an organization dedicated to preserving the belief in the finality of prophethood of Muhammad (PBUH), '*Tahaffuz-e-Khatm-e-Nabuwat*', asserted that it would not be enough for the assembly to pass a mere resolution or to refer the matter to the Advisory Council of Islamic Ideology; it must pass a Bill declaring the Ahmedis a non-Muslim minority. Leaders of the Islami Jamiat-e-Tulaba took the same position, demanded quick action, and warned that Bhutto would not remain in power if he continued his 'double talk' on the Ahmediya question.[26] Opposition members in the Punjab Assembly spoke to the same effect, and so did Mian Tufail, '*amir*' of the Jamaat-i-Islami, and Nawabzada Nasrullah Khan, president of the Pakistan Democratic Party (PDP). It seemed the issue would not go away, and violence could begin again. Finally, Bhutto relented and took the issue to the National Assembly which, after extended considerations, passed the Second Amendment to the Constitution in September 1974.[27]

Clause (3) was added to Article 260 explaining thereunder who is a non-Muslim. This Article pertains to definitions under the Constitution. The new clause stated that 'a person who does not believe in the absolute and unqualified finality of the Prophethood of Muhammad (PBUH) as the last of the Prophets or claims to be a Prophet, in any sense of the word or of any description whatsoever, after Muhammad (PBUH), or recognizes such a claimant as a Prophet or a religious reformer, is not a Muslim for the purposes of the constitution or law'. Still this definition or explanation did not specifically refer to the Ahmedis, therefore, Article 106, which pertains to the formation of provincial assemblies and distribution of the seats within such assemblies was also amended to make mention of Ahmedis amongst the non-Muslim faiths described in the Article for the purpose of reservation of special seats for them. They were referred to as 'persons of the Quadiani group or the Lahori Group (who call themselves 'Ahmedis')'.[28]

Bhutto and his government calmed the situation for the time being by acceding to the demand of the religious parties who had worked up a frenzy in the country but did not realize the long term implications, legal as well as constitutional, of this move. It may be important to examine the deep rooted resentment of the Muslims against the Ahmediya community and the events and circumstances that immediately preceded the events of 1974.

The Ahmediya Question and its Background

Mirza Ghulam Ahmad, the founder of the Ahmediya sect, was born in village Qadian, District Gurdaspur, in the part of Punjab which is now included in India. There is controversy about the year of his birth which ranges from 1831 to 1839 according to different versions. He was born in a family of landowners who were loyal to the East India Company and to the British rulers. His father, Ghulam Murtaza, is said to have supplied fifty horses and fifty recruits to the British during the war of independence of 1857 to crush the revolt of the Indians against the rule of East India Company.[29] Mirza Sahib had some religious education and a modest education otherwise.

Beginning with 1870s, Mirza Sahib started claiming that he received *Ilham* (revelations about future events or hidden knowledge about things). He claimed to be an ardent follower of Prophet Muhammad (PBUH), so much so, that he had developed into a *zil* (shadow) of the Holy Prophet. This is where Mirza Sahib's claim as prophet appears to emerge because the shadow would also have the attributes of its personage. It was argued by his followers that in this age of sin, such a reformer was like a messenger. He also claimed to be the second coming or rebirth of Messiah (being referred to as *Masih-i-Mau'd,* the promised Messiah). It is believed by Muslims that Jesus was not actually crucified but raised to the heavens alive and would come back again to the world to eliminate the evils that have spread all over the world. The Christians believe that Jesus was crucified but was later resurrected and then raised to the heavens. They also believe in the second coming of Jesus. This difficulty was resolved by making an attempt to prove that Christ had travelled to and died in Kashmir[30] (not far from Gurdaspur). Thus, it was argued by his followers that the second coming of the Messiah in the physical sense was impossible and Mirza Sahib was the *maseel* (likeness of) Messiah and had to fulfil the prophesy about the second coming of Messiah.

In addition to being the *zil* of Holy Prophet (PBUH) and *maseel* Messiah, Mirza Sahib has also been described as and called '*mehdi*'. This is based on a popular belief amongst Muslims that when the affairs of the Muslims are in great distress, the *mehdi* will come to the earth to reform them. This belief has led many over the centuries to claim themselves as *mehdis*. In fact, '*mehdis*' keep coming up from time to time and from place to place, throughout the Muslim world.

Mirza Sahib wrote a number of books and pamphlets for the guidance of his followers. They also contained a large number of revelations he claimed to have received from time to time. With the passage of time, Mirza Sahib's claim of being a shadow of the Holy Prophet (PBUH) developed into being a *nabi* (Prophet) himself but one who was subordinate to an actual *rasool* (Messenger), meaning thereby that he was without any *shariah* of his own and, ultimately, around 1900–1901, he declared himself to be a prophet with *shariah.* One of the principal doctrines of his *shariah* was the renunciation of *jehad* (holy war). This suited the British very much who were wary of unrest amongst Muslims of India and the slogan for *jehad* against the alien non-Muslim British rulers. Mirza Sahib's doctrine would put an end to this issue once and for all.

Mirza Sahib died in the year 1908. At the time of his death, all his followers believed in him as prophet. In 1914, one of his followers, Muhammad Ali, seceded from the main body of Ahmedis and formed his own group known as Lahoris because it was based in Lahore. The Lahori group renounced Mirza Sahib as a prophet but regarded him as a saint or a religious reformer. On the partitioning of Punjab in 1947, Qadian being in district Gurdaspur went to India and Ahmedis there migrated to Pakistan and established their new centre at Rabwah, near River Chenab in the district of Jhang.

The doctrine of Ahmedis does not appear to be very persuasive or even much coherent, but faith is faith. Everyone is entitled to believe in anything or anybody they choose to. The occurrence of latter day saints is not unusual or unique to Islam. Other religions, particularly Christianity and Buddhism, have experienced similar apostasy. Actually, a close parallel can be drawn between the Ahmedis in Islam and the Mormons in Christianity. A young man named Joseph Smith Jr. from upstate New York, proclaimed himself as prophet in 1827. He claimed to have received from an angel Moroni, golden plates from which he translated the *Book of Mormons.*[31] These plates were written in an old Egyptian language and translated into English by his spiritual knowledge and power. The *Book of Mormons* was meant to be the second part of the Bible, according to Joseph Smith Jr. He soon had followers who started growing in number. Christians on the eastern coast of the United States started feeling alarmed and called him an imposter. He and his followers were chased out of New York state. Joseph Smith and his followers started moving west looking for a safe haven but in 1844 he was ultimately overtaken in Illinois near river Mississippi and murdered by Illinois militiamen. However, some of his followers succeeded in crossing the Mississippi to safety and led by his principal disciple, Brigham Young, established their base far into the west near Great Salt Lake, Utah, in the city known as Salt Lake City. The Mormons remained persecuted for some time in the USA but have now settled down with full rights as citizens. They remain a relatively small community with most of their temples in Salt Lake City and a few elsewhere in the USA.

Thus, latter-day saints and reformers have come into every religion. They lose their appeal after some time and the strength of their followers starts dwindling. Such religious factions generally fade out after some time and their followers join the main-stream of the religion. But it is said that most religious beliefs have been saved by their persecutors. It appears to be the case here as well. The persecution of Ahmedis has become their main strength. It has built resolve amongst the followers of this faction who have fled to different parts of the world seeking political asylum. A large number of them have actually been granted asylum by different countries in the West. This development has led them to cultivate their missions in a large number of countries and has extended unity and cohesion to the whole community. It has also made them prosperous in trade and business. Bigoted political leaders and political parties, by victimizing and persecuting the Ahmedis in Pakistan for their narrow political ends, have only tarnished the image of Pakistan internationally and have involved the country in a non-issue which has no bearing on the real political issues facing the country.

The anti-Ahmediya agitation of the early fifties had shaken the community. However, the martial law of 1953 succeeded in restoring law and order in the Punjab. This agitation gave the Ahmedis an inner strength. They became a close community, helping out one another everywhere. They got an opportunity during Ayub's regime to occupy key positions in the civil and the military bureaucracy. A few Generals belonging to this community did well in the Indo-Pakistan war in 1965 and were decorated. Around the beginning of the seventies, they established themselves in the leadership of the armed forces and quietly promoted members of their community to higher ranks.[32]

Ahmedis had made deep inroads and held key positions in the civil bureaucracy as well. Mr M.M. Ahmad, a prominent Ahmedi, was very close to Ayub and remained Deputy Chairman of the Planning Commission for a long time. He helped his community to several important positions in the administration. He was later taken in a senior position at the World Bank in the early seventies.

All these developments over nearly two decades, instilled confidence in the members of the community. It also, correspondingly, generated fear and resentment against them amongst the bigoted political leaders who used to further their narrow political interest at their expense. It was widely believed amongst Muslims that the Ahmedis were not true Muslims and therefore did not interact with them. Zafarullah Khan, Pakistan's first Foreign Minister, belonged to the Ahmediya community and was always chastized for not participating in the funeral prayers of Jinnah. Some Ahmedis, in their exuberance and over confidence, had also started doing things which rubbed the ordinary Muslim the wrong way and made him susceptible to the bigots.[33]

The Second Amendment was the beginning of the process of legal victimization and persecution of the Ahmediya community in Pakistan, followed by Draconian laws and adverse judicial pronouncements against religious minorities in general. Members of the community have been pushed against the wall and are a constant target of threats and hyperbole on the part of political and religious bigots. Succeeding governments have failed to stem the tide of victimization and have, at times, succumbed to the pressure. It is always an easy and convenient path for an incumbent government to gain cheap popularity and to appease the bigots by conceding to their unreasonable demands without realizing that political blackmail never ends.[34] When the Ahmedis appealed to the courts for protection, they found themselves in the hands of judges who were not only totally unsympathetic to them but gave strong judgments against them, further restricting their religious freedom and civil rights.[35]

An Aborted Coup Attempt and F.B. Ali's Case

On 30 March 1973, the ministry of defence announced that a small group of military officers had conspired to seize power. The alleged conspirators were tried before a special military court presided over by a little known Major-General, Muhammad Ziaul Haq. Two of the persons being tried, Brigadier (Retd.) F.B. Ali and Colonel (Retd.) Abdul Aleem Afridi, challenged their trial before the military court in the Lahore High Court in writ jurisdiction. The Lahore High Court dismissed their petitions and the matter finally came up before the Supreme Court. The following points were raised by them before the Supreme Court:[36]

(a) Since they had been retired from the army, therefore, they were no longer subject to the Pakistan Army Act and they could not be tried by a general court martial.

(b) That the amendment of the Army Act by Ordinances III and IV of 1967, making persons other than serving personnel of armed forces as subject to the jurisdiction of the military courts, was unconstitutional being violative of the fundamental rights of security of person and equality of citizens before law under the 1962 Constitution.

(c) That the amendments in the Army Act, subjecting non-military or retired military personnel under its jurisdiction, were not laws because they purported to unreasonably deprive a citizen of even the norms of a judicial trial.

The Supreme Court repelled all these contentions. It held that the retired personnel from the armed forces and even civilians fell within the ambit of the Army Act if they were accused of seducing or attempting to seduce any person subject to the Act from his duty or allegiance to the government or had committed an offence under the Official Secrets Act in relation to the armed forces.

The Ordinances III and IV of 1967, bringing about the aforesaid amendment in the Army Act, were held to be valid pieces of legislation particularly as they had subsequently been approved by the National Assembly. The Court observed that the prevention of the subversion of loyalty of a member of the defence services of Pakistan was as essential as the provision of arms and ammunition to the defence services or their training. It was held that the said ordinances fell within the meaning of law because, according to majority of the bench of five, the 'law' under the 1962 Constitution would, in its generally accepted connotation, mean positive law, that is to say, a formal pronouncement of the will of the competent lawgiver and that there was no condition that a law must, in order to qualify as such, also be based on reason or morality. Thus, it was observed, the Court could not strike down a law on any higher ethical notions nor could courts act on the basis of philosophical concepts of law. In the dissenting opinion on this point only, it was held that the term 'law', in addition to positive law, must be construed to also include the judicial principles laid down from time to time by the superior courts and the accepted forms of legal process and juridical norms obtaining in Pakistan.[37]

The Supreme Court did not hold Ordinances III and IV of 1967 as violative of the 'equality before law' and 'equal protection of laws' clauses under the Fundamental Right Number 15 of the 1962 Constitution because the legislation in question, though it applied only to a certain group of people and not to others, had the effect of treating alike persons concerned under similar circumstances which was a constitutionally permissible classification. The Supreme Court held that the ordinary courts should not interfere with the court martial in the exercise of their power of judicial review merely on the ground that some rule of procedure was not followed but that there would be no bar of jurisdiction where action was without jurisdiction, *coram non judice* or malafide.

Hence the appeal of F.B. Ali and his co-appellant failed before the Supreme Court. He, and other conspirators, were found guilty by the special military court and were sentenced to heavy terms of imprisonment. These trials afforded an opportunity to Ziaul Haq to attract the attention of Bhutto. He worked closely with Bhutto who personally examined the relevant trial papers and intelligence reports.[38]

Third Amendment: Victimization of Political Opponents

It has been discussed above that the Bhutto's government was becoming increasingly intolerant and repressive towards its political opponents who were being arrested and detained. These political opponents were forced to knock the doors of the judiciary which did not have too high a morale. The judgments were mostly in favour of the government and, once in a while, some relief was allowed to political opponents. Even this limited judicial interference in his dealing with political opponents was not seen with favour by Bhutto and his colleagues. A policy for the curtailment of powers and jurisdiction of courts, including a general plan to demoralize the judiciary, was adopted. An amendment was introduced in the Code of Criminal Procedure prohibiting the courts from granting bail before arrest to a person unless a case was registered and that an order of bail would be effective only regarding the case that stood registered against him and specified in the order.[39] Previously, the courts had allowed blanket bail before arrest to political opponents in cases registered and to be registered as part of the process of such victimization.[40]

A constitutional amendment was introduced to curtail the rights of a *detenu* detained under a law for preventive detention, extending the powers of the detaining authority. Article 10 of the Constitution which provided for certain safeguards against preventive detention was amended in February 1975 under the Constitution (Third Amendment) Act, 1975[41] to the following effect:

(a) The period of preventive detention for a *detenu* was originally fixed at one month, beyond which period no law for preventive detention could authorize preventive detention unless the appropriate Review Board,[42] after affording the *detenu* an opportunity of being heard in person, reviewed his case and reported that, in its opinion, there was sufficient cause for continuation of detention beyond one month. This initial period of detention was extended from one month to three months under the third amendment.

(b) Under the constitution originally, it was required that a *detenu* held under a law for preventive detention should be communicated the grounds of his detention not later than one week of such detention so that he could make representations against the order of detention at the earliest. The Third amendment extended this period from one week to fifteen days.

(c) The constitution limited the total period of preventive detention to the maximum of twelve months within a period of twenty-four months. However, an exception to this limitation was for a person who was employed by, or worked for, or acted on instructions received from the enemy. Such person could be detained indefinitely. This exception was extended under the third amendment to include any person 'who is acting or attempting to act in a manner prejudicial to the integrity, security or defence of Pakistan or any part thereof or who commits or attempts to commit any act which amounts to an anti-national activity as defined in a federal law or is a member of any association which has for its objects, or which indulges in, any such anti-national activity'.

It is obvious that the Third Amendment curtailed the rights of political *detenus* and correspondingly enhanced the powers of the government. It also enabled the government to put political opponents under detention for an indefinite period after accusing them of indulging in anti-State activities. By the time the Third Amendment was passed, action against the NAP had already been taken and this amendment enhance of the powers of the government to deal with a political opponent firmly and to put its leadership under indefinite detention.

The Third Amendment also extended the period of Emergency proclaimed by the President. Under the Constitution in its original form, the period of such Emergency could be six months at the most and that also by the resolution of a joint sitting of the two Houses of the Parliament.[43] The Third Amendment provided that the Emergency would continue indefinitely until a resolution disapproving the proclamation was passed by the votes of the majority of the total membership of the Houses in joint sitting. This amendment was also retrogressive in nature, extending the powers and period of emergency, particularly in view of the fact that Pakistan remained under Emergency for more than twenty years, for political rather than national reasons.

Fourth Amendment: Jurisdiction of Courts Curtailed

The Bhutto government's decision to curtail the powers and jurisdiction of the courts preventing them from granting relief to political opponents, particularly in exercise of constitutional jurisdiction under Article 199, came about under the Fourth Amendment to the Constitution.[44] High Courts were forbidden from prohibiting the making of an order for preventive detention of a person or to grant bail to any one so detained. This was a major curtailment of constitutional jurisdiction of High Courts denying them jurisdiction to come to the aid of political victims or even to grant such people bail during their detention.

The constitutional jurisdiction of the High Courts was also curtailed in the matter of stay of recovery, assessment, or collection of public revenues. Any stay order granted in such a matter would cease to have effect on the expiry of sixty days unless the matter was finally decided by the Court within such time. All such interim orders made by a High Court before the fourth amendment would also cease to have effect on the expiry of sixty days.

The only redeeming feature of this amendment was the allocation of six special seats to the minorities in the National Assembly and an increase in the number of seats for the minorities in the provincial assembly of the Punjab from three to five.

This amendment was passed in a very unfortunate manner. Members of the opposition in the National Assembly wanted to have a debate particularly regarding the curtailment of the powers of the High Courts. They were denied the opportunity to speak and were physically thrown out of the National Assembly by the security staff led by Sergeant-at-arms. A vote on this amendment was then rushed through in the absence of the opposition.[45] It is indeed true that Bhutto had more than the requisite two-third majority in the National Assembly to push through any constitutional amendment but it was against all norms of decent democratic behaviour to gag the voice of the opposition in the assembly and to subject the members of the opposition to the humiliation of being physically maltreated and pushed and thrown out of the assembly.

National Awami Party (NAP) Banned and the Supreme Court Judgment

The Bhutto regime had projected the NAP-JUI governments as incapable of maintaining law and order, but the state of public order did not improve after their dismissal. An insurgency raged in Balochistan. In 1974 and later, several bomb explosions occurred in the NWFP. Bhutto, his ministers, and the pro-government media charged that the NAP leaders, had planned these explosions to spread chaos in the country and to damage its unity and integrity in collaboration with the government of Afghanistan. On 8 February 1975, an explosion killed Hayat Mohammad Sherpao[46] as he rose to address a gathering of students at Peshawar University. A few days later, the central government declared the NAP to be an unlawful organization, closed down its offices, and arrested many of its leaders in the NWFP and in Balochistan, including Wali Khan. Members of the National Assembly and the provincial assemblies of NWFP and Balochistan belonging to the NAP and unwilling to change their affiliation were removed, enabling pro-Bhutto groups to establish secure legislative majorities in these provinces.

The background of this swift and sweeping action against NAP and Wali Khan was the continuing rivalry between the PPP and the NAP and the underlying conflict between the personalities of Bhutto and Wali Khan who had emerged as a principal opponent at the national level having been designated as leader of the opposition in the National Assembly. One could see that, during the 1970s, for any political party to capture power at the national level it had to build bases of support in more than one province. Just as Bhutto had built majority support in Sindh and Punjab and was planning to develop similar support in the NWFP and Balochistan, it seemed that the opposition leader, Wali Khan, had started thinking along the same lines. Starting with his base in the NWFP, he wanted to mobilize political support in the Punjab. In the beginning of 1974, he toured Punjab and it seemed that his meetings were attracting large crowds. He felt that perhaps in another six months he would be able to take on Bhutto and the PPP in the Punjab. According to Wali Khan, Bhutto got so worried by such developments that he had to imprison him under some pretext.[47] Even if this version is somewhat exaggerated, there is a considerable amount of plausibility in it. In any case, a government committed to Pakistan's national integration should have allowed Wali Khan to move out of his parochial or ethnic moorings and transform himself into a truly national leader.

In his lust for power and without any consideration for national unity and consensus, Bhutto, used every means possible to keep Wali Khan out because he feared the alternative could be his own eventual overthrow. He not only imprisoned Wali Khan by charging him with high treason but went about publicizing this factor while overlooking the damage that this could cause to Pakistan. Dubbing national leaders as traitors can undermine the confidence of the average Pakistani in the depth and strength of his country's leadership. To publicly designate a leader identified with Pakhtoon nationalism as a traitor was to inflame further provincial and ethnic animosities between the Punjabis and the Pakhtoons.

By a notification issued on 10 February 1975, the federal government declared that the NAP was operating 'in a manner prejudicial to the sovereignty and integrity of Pakistan' and by another notification of the same date, the federal government also declared that as a result of the first mentioned notification, the NAP 'stands dissolved, properties and funds are forfeited to the federal government'. Thereafter, as required by Section 4 of the Political Parties Act, 1962, the federal government made reference to the Supreme Court on 24 February 1975.

Notices were issued by the Supreme Court on the detained leaders of the NAP and on 24 May 1975, a consolidated written statement on behalf of the party was filed in the Court. Thereafter, on 14 June, Messrs Wali Khan, Arbab Sikandar Khan Khalil, Sardar Khair Bakhsh Marri, Mir Ghaus Bakhsh Bizenjo, and Sardar Ataullah Mengal also filed separate written statements. An application was made before the Court that the federal government be directed to provide funds for conducting the defence of the case and for permission for the *detenus* to be present in the Court during the hearing of the reference. On this application, the Court directed the government to pay certain amounts for the defence of the reference. On the matter of personal presence, the Court only allowed Wali Khan to remain present in the Court throughout the proceedings of the reference, subject to the conditions that he would only speak through his counsel and would not give any interview to any member of the Press in the precincts of the court.

Wali Khan appeared before the Supreme Court on 19 June 1975. He wanted to speak but was forbidden to do so, except through his counsel. He, therefore, discharged his counsel and claimed the right to appear in person. He objected to the presence of Justices Muhammad Gul and Muhammad Afzal Cheema on the Bench.[48] These judges were consulted and they both said that they were, in no way, embarrassed by sitting on the Bench as constituted for they had done nothing from which any inference of bias on their part could legitimately be drawn, nor were they in any way, biased or prejudiced against the dissolved party or any of its leaders. The objection was, therefore, overruled. At this stage, Wali Khan announced that in the circumstances, he would not be prepared to participate in the proceedings and walked out of the court room.

The Court considered the objection against the two judges in the absence of the defence and rejected it in categorical terms. Chief Justice Hamoodur Rahman authored the opinion of the Court and held on the point of bias that the mere fact that Mr Justice Cheema was Law Secretary at the time when the Law Minister had publicly stated that the question of banning the party was under examination for a period of two to three years, did not disqualify him or even form the basis of the objection which was rejected as vague and nebulous. Mere suspicion of bias, even if it was not unreasonable, was not sufficient to disqualify a judge and held that in that case even the suspicion was unreasonable because it did not necessarily follow that it was the ministry of law which had examined the question of banning the party or that the secretary of the ministry had of necessity to deal with this question. The learned Chief Justice also relied on the affidavit of the witnesses of the government stating that the question of banning the party was done mainly by the ministry of interior and not by the ministry of law.[49] With due respect to the learned judge, the reasoning on this point is not very convincing. Any reasonable and prudent man can infer that when the question of banning a political party is under consideration by the government, its Law Secretary in certainly involved and his opinion must to have been sought. Who can believe that a matter of such constitutional and legal importance was mainly dealt with by the ministry of interior and not by the ministry of law? If it was factually so, then it speaks volumes against the manner and methodology of the government. In such a case, there was no need of proving the bias but a strong inference should have been enough because not only should justice actually be done but it should appear to have been done.

In the matter of the other judge, Mr Justice Muhammad Gul, the Court went even further. The learned judge offered to withdraw from the case on the ground that he had already dealt with the material which formed the basis for banning the party in his capacity as Chairman of the Advisory Board,[50] on the continuance of the detention of Wali Khan, and some other leaders of the NAP. However, the Chief Justice turned down this offer as untenable because, in the absence of any constitutional or statutory bar, a judge is not disqualified from sitting at a trial of a person merely because he had previously participated in other legal proceedings against the same person, whether in the capacity of a judge or of an administrative tribunal or official. It was further observed that the mere fact that the detention of some of the persons concerned was extended on the advice of a judge did not mean that he had also taken the decision regarding to the banning of the party. Such an inference could be neither factually nor legally correct. The opinion that Mr Justice Gul might have formed as the Chairman of the Advisory Board did not affect the case in hand because there was no allegation against him of any personal animosity, ill-will, or personal interest. The Chief Justice thus reduced the legal concept of bias to its bare minimum and his reasoning is not the least convincing. Although Wali Khan's decision to boycott the proceedings appeared to be rash, in light of these findings it seems justified.

The Court rejected the plea of the Attorney-General that the function of the Court in the reference was no more than that of judicial review and that it could only pronounce upon the propriety of the executive action. The Court held that it could lay down its own rules for the proceedings before it and, after the First Amendment, the Constitution itself guaranteed that unless such a decision was given by the highest judicial authority in the country, a political party should not be dissolved. The decision of the Court, therefore, was not merely confined to judicial review and affirmation of an executive act but had to be in the nature of judicial determination of the question whether the party was or was not acting in a manner prejudicial to the sovereignty and integrity of Pakistan. The Court also held that the government's action in forfeiting the assets of the party was legally incorrect because the decision of the Supreme Court was a condition precedent for the dissolution of an offending political party and for the forfeiture of its assets. The constitution of NAP as a political party thus remained unaffected during the proceedings and till the final decision of the Court. The dissolution of the party was, however, treated by the Court as interim suspension of the party.

On merit, the Court held that the NAP was acting in a manner prejudicial to the sovereignty and integrity of Pakistan. It adopted a novel reasoning under which a political party was held not to be a corporate body having separate corporate existence apart from its members. The Court elaborated that though the acts of one or two individual members of the party, however important they might be, can not necessarily be considered the acts of the party, when a fairly substantial segment of members were shown to be acting or behaving in a particular manner without any objection from any of the other members of the party or its controlling body, it might well be presumed that the individuals concerned were speaking for or acting on behalf of the party and to that extent, therefore, their acts would also be treated as the acts of the party. Hence, insofar as the party consistently failed to repudiate the utterances or actions of its leadership or failed to dissociate itself from such actions or utterances, it must be held that the party itself subscribed to the same view.

The Court did not accept the source or intelligence reports to be admissible in evidence but allowed the referring authority to draw upon the source report only to the extent that it had received corroboration from the happening of the events mentioned in the report, if those events could be established independently by reliable evidence. Newspaper reports of contemporaneous events were held admissible, particularly when they happened to be events of local interest or of such public nature as would generally be known throughout the community and where testimony of an eye witness is not readily available. If a person did not avail the opportunity to contradict or question the truthfulness of the statement attributed to him and duly published in newspapers, he could not complain if that publication was used against him. Such an issue would not be hit by the rule of hearsay.[51] Transcripts of speeches personally made by officers of the Special Branch or the Intelligence Bureau were accepted as admissible evidence if proved by the person hearing the speech and making notes of it contemporaneously. Tape-records of speeches were admitted in evidence if the officers who recorded such speeches could identify the voice of person speaking. Reports of foreign broadcasts were also accepted as authentic if the officer monitoring such broadcasts described them in detail.

The Court observed that to say that Pakistan did not consist of one 'nation' but several 'nationalities' each having ethnic, cultural, social, and political differences, was to deny the very basis of Pakistan and if, along with it the right of self determination for each nationality was demanded, then it amounted a demand for the breakup of Pakistan, destroying its integrity and setting up several independent states within Pakistan. The concept of nationalities, it was observed, was opposed to the fundamentals of Islam which preached that the entire Muslim *Millat* was one nation under one *Khalifa*.

The Supreme Court held the following acts of the offending party (NAP) as prejudicial to the sovereignty and integrity of Pakistan:

(a) Contention of the NAP and its leaders that they were no longer bound by the constitution as the ruling party had itself violated the Tripartite Accord[52] and the constitution both in its letter and spirit. This, according to the Court, was subversion of the constitution.

(b) The claim of the NAP and its leaders that the Pakhtoonistan movement was merely seeking renaming of two provinces was held to be wholly untenable. Actually, it was observed, they were demanding secession in the name of autonomy by carving out a new province and demanding complete self-government with only three subjects left to the centre.

(c) The sovereignty includes external sovereignty and a political party that talks of shifting international boundary from one place to another vitally affects sovereignty of the country.

(d) When the tribal areas opted for Pakistan, the right of self determination was exercised and no such question could further arise. Seeking the right of self determination in the existing circumstances would amount to a breakup of the existing structure of the country and achievement of this goal by force, if necessary, amounted to operating in a manner prejudicial to the sovereignty and integrity of the country.

(e) That the characterization of the two-nation theory as a spurious slogan raised to seek partition of India, and the suggestion that once the objective had been attained, the theory ceased to be of any validity, and the standpoint that the founder of the country had recounted his views about polity in the country and desired it to be a secular state were all complete distortion of facts.

The judgment of the Supreme Court in the NAP case suffers from several weaknesses:

i. It was an *ex-parte* judgment based on *ex-parte* proceedings. The defence did not get any opportunity to rebut the case made out by the government in the reference.
ii. The objection to the two judges on the Bench was not without force and substance and they should have voluntarily withdrawn from the case rather than create the unpleasant situation of forcing one-sided proceedings. After all, it was not an ordinary case and should not have been dealt with according to the principles used in ordinary cases regarding the bias of a judge. Dissolution of a political party is made once in decades. It infringes upon a very important fundamental right, the right to freedom of association, which the constitution has itself safeguarded by making it subject to the decision of the Supreme Court on reference. The Court should have been all the more careful and cautious because no appeal could lie from its decision.
iii. The manner in which the objection was disposed of and the reasoning adopted give the impression of an unfriendly, if not hostile, attitude of the Court towards the respondent party and its leaders.
iv. The conclusions reached by the Court against the NAP and its leadership were harsh and based upon inherently inadmissible evidence. The Court ought to have been careful in appreciating the evidence before it particularly when the defence was not represented and the witnesses could not be cross-examined in the way it is done in adversary proceedings.
v. The applications of certain politicians and political parties for being impleaded in the proceedings were summarily dismissed. There was no harm if other politicians or political parties had been allowed to participate in the proceedings which were to have an impact on the entire political situation in Pakistan. The proceedings should have been treated less formally as such reference is in the nature of an open-ended enquiry by the highest judicial forum in the country.

It was indeed the last major judgment given by Mr Justice Hamoodur Rahman who retired soon after its announcement. He had been a good judge and wrote some outstanding opinions. This judgment and the proceedings on which it was based were certainly a disappointment.

Fifth Amendment: Chastizing the Judiciary

The State of the Judiciary in 1976

Pakistan inherited a fairly good judicial structure with judges known for their competence and integrity. The first Chief Justice of Pakistan, Mr Justice Abdur Rashid, was known to be extremely discreet. He strictly followed the tradition of remaining aloof and avoided going to public functions. He was a man of unimpeachable character and reputation. His successor, Mr Justice Muhammad Munir, though a learned and competent man, proved to be controversial. He was responsible for certain disastrous judgments, which have been discussed above, that rocked the boat of Constitution during Pakistan's formative years. He was also known for having favourites amongst judges and lawyers, one of whom was Sardar Muhammad Iqbal. Mr Justice Munir was succeeded by Mr Justice Shahabuddin and Mr Justice A. R. Cornelius who were both men of character, integrity, and competence.

When Munir became Law Minister in 1962, he appointed Sardar Iqbal as a judge of the West Pakistan High Court. Along with him was appointed Maulvi Mushtaq Husain. They were both said to be only 40 years old with Sardar Iqbal being a few months older. They both appeared to have understated their age, particularly Maulvi Mushtaq Husain, who always looked much older. Both of them were fairly competent but their competence had no comparison to their bloated egos and unsatiated ambitions. They soon became rivals and, in the process, extended their rivalry amongst judges in the West Pakistan High Court and amongst the members of the Bar. They caused the judges and the lawyers to be divided into factions led by either one of them. Each faction of judges was known to be pre-disposed and exceedingly accommodating to its own faction of lawyers and hostile to the rival faction. Fortunes in law practice changed for bettter or for worse as one faction gained more power than the other. Sardar Iqbal was certainly more shrewd, being adept at public relationing, while Maulvi Mushtaq was a short-fused character with vindictiveness as his main weapon.[53]

Matters became worse when Sardar Iqbal was appointed as Chief Justice of the Lahore High Court in 1972 on the elevation of Chief Justice Anwarul Haq to the Supreme Court. It was a consistent practice and tradition of the court in Pakistan and India that Chief Justices of High Courts were elevated to the Supreme Court and they accepted such elevation with grace and gratitude. In defiance of this practice, Sardar Iqbal decided to crown himself as the judicial king of the Punjab by staying put as Chief Justice of the Lahore High Court until his retirement age, which was more than eleven years away. It was his sweet will not to accept elevation as a judge of the Supreme Court which he regarded as an inferior office. As Chief Justice, he was to administer the huge judicial set-up in the province of Punjab with hundreds of civil judges and scores of district judges under him. He would hold a *darbar* where his favourite judicial officers and lawyers would assemble to nod favourably to his inexhaustible and unlimited harangue studied with references to his incomparable generosity, intellect, and experience. He let his juniors be elevated as judges of the Supreme Court.

Maulvi Mushtaq was no novice at this game. He had the patience, persistence, and perseverance of an undaunted opponent. He also decided not to accept the elevation to the Supreme Court and stayed on as Senior Puisne Judge of the Lahore High Court, thus breathing down the neck of his opponent and looking for an opportunity to undo his grandiose plans. They were wary of one another and the grouping and factionalism amongst judges and lawyers further intensified and polluted the environment at the Bench and the Bar. In the meantime, a number of judges of the Lahore High Court junior to both of them were elevated to the Supreme Court.[54]

The method and manner of appointment of judges were affected by considerations of political patronage, nepotism, and favouritism, particularly under Ayub. He appointed a brother of a politician from NWFP who had helped him in the Presidential election of 1965 as a judge of the West Pakistan High Court.[55] He also held interviews for the recommendees and made appointments for political considerations or personal reasons which were highly subjective and whimsical.[56]

Another unfavourable practice that developed amongst members of the judiciary was based on nepotism. The chief justices started promoting their own sons and sons-in-law or those of their colleagues on the Bench obliging one another for mutual benefit of their kith and kin. Whenever a son returned from abroad, with or without a foreign law degree, or started law practice, he was widely introduced by his judge father to his uncle judges with the understanding that he should be looked after. Naturally, law practice of the sons and sons-in-law of the judges flourished overnight to the chagrin and frustration of the less privileged members of the Bar. They were engaged on fabulous fees with the expectation that they would obtain relief due to political reasons, which they actually did in many cases. Besides, they carried awe for the members of subordinate judiciary whom they easily frightened with their overbearing attitudes and arrogance. Those who did not make it in the law practice despite all advantages and benefits got appointed as law officers and were eventually elevated to the Bench.

It was no surprise that the pent up feelings of the lawyers against such practices found expression through their representatives in 1975. Sheikh Shaukat Ali, President of Lahore High Court Bar Association, had his axe to grind against the judiciary because he had been humiliatingly dismissed as a judge of the Lahore High Court in 1971 on the recommendation of the Supreme Judicial Council. He exploited these feelings and targetted Chief Justice Sardar Iqbal to settle old scores. The secretary of the Bar and a very close friend of his targetted Maulvi Mushtaq due to some personal domestic dispute. For a change, the two of them had a common cause. There were also reports in the press about malpractices of the relatives of the judges. The judges decided to strike back and with their favourite weapon, the law of contempt of court. Contempt of court notices were sent to the president of the Bar, Sheikh Shaukat Ali, in two cases. He submitted an unqualified apology in both cases. A full bench of the Lahore High Court held Sheikh Shaukat Ali as contemner and imposed upon him a fine of five thousand rupees.[57] In the other case of contempt, a division bench of Lahore High Court took a lenient view and admonished him and directed him to pay two thousand rupees.[58] This lenient view was taken because he had submitted an unqualified apology and had resigned as the President of the High Court Bar Association.

The editor and printer of the weekly *Lail-o-Nihar*, wherein report of the malpractices of the relatives of the judges was published, were found guilty and convicted for contempt of court and sentenced to six months in prison. The Secretary of the Bar Association was also issued a contempt notice for having published an advertisement in a number of newspapers reproducing a resolution of the Bar Association taking exception to the initiation of contempt proceedings against the President of the Bar, Sheikh Shaukat Ali. This advertisement was taken by the Court as an expression of opinion in a matter subjudice before the Court and the Secretary was convicted for contempt of court and sentenced to simple imprisonment of six months and a fine of Rs 2000. On the release of the Secretary, on bail granted by the Supreme Court, a procession was taken out by the lawyers holding placards with inscriptions against the law of contempt of court and against nepotism, corruption, and malpractices. Sheikh Shaukat Ali and three other lawyers, including the aforesaid Secretary of the High Court Bar and President of Lahore District Bar Association, were served with contempt notices for taking out of the procession and the placards and for raising slogans against the judiciary. In this case also, Sheikh Shaukat Ali tendered an unqualified apology and a lenient view was taken and he was sentenced to a fine of one thousand rupees. Each of the other three respondents, who did not tender an apology, were sentenced to simple imprisonment for a period of four months and a fine of one thousand rupees.[59] These three advocates served their sentences for a few days before the Supreme Court suspended them on appeal. However, the Supreme Court dismissed the appeal of these three advocates and directed that they should serve out the remaining period of their sentences.[60] However, they did not serve the remainder of their sentences because, before they could be sent to jail, they were granted pardon by the President and their sentences were remitted. This was humiliating for the judiciary because the verdicts of the Supreme Court and the Lahore High Court were frustrated and negated by the decree of the executive.

Such was the state of judiciary when the Constitution (Fifth Amendment) Bill was moved before the parliament.

Debate on the Fifth Amendment Bill

Constitution (Fifth Amendment) Bill was introduced in the National Assembly on 1 September 1976 providing for the establishment of separate High Courts for Balochistan and Sindh, extending the period of separation of judiciary from the executive, fixed terms of the Chief Justices of the Supreme Court and the High Courts, compulsory transfer of judges from one High Court to another, powers of punishment for contempt of court, and restriction of jurisdiction of the High Court to grant interim bail.[61] During the debate on the amendment Bill in the National Assembly, the judiciary came under severe criticism. Federal Education Minister, Mr Abdul Hafiz Pirzada, in his speech on the Bill said that the judiciary had been trying to encroach upon the functions of the legislature and the executive. He said that if the judges were not happy with their positions, then they should quit their office and contest elections to occupy seats in the parliament.[62] He said that the judiciary was the creation of the Constitution and drew powers from it to impart justice within the given jurisdiction. Any action outside the jurisdiction conferred by the Constitution would tantamount to subversion and high treason. He also said that there was an unfortunate confusion over the limits of the powers of the judiciary and it was the duty of the legislature to remove it. He defended the fixing of tenures of the Chief Justices of the Supreme Court and the High Courts because all other state positions like the President, the Prime Minister, and members of parliament had a fixed term of office. He said that in the present position, one could visualize the frustration of the other judges if the incumbent Chief Justice continued for fifteen years or more. According to him the appointment of a Supreme Court judge was given to the best talent and it was justified to retire a judge of the High Court if he did not accept appointment as Supreme Court judge.

He also justified the transfer of judges from one High Court to another on the basis that there was already a precedent in this regard and that Balochistan had meagre resources and could not afford a full High Court. Referring to the amendment concerning contempt of the superior courts, Pirzada said that there was consensus all over Pakistan that the interpretations placed by superior courts about their own powers regarding contempt were too harsh. He referred to a resolution of the Pakistan Bar Council, the highest body of lawyers, urging the National Assembly to amend the Constitution to provide for relief. He said that, according to the principles of justice and rule of law, anyone who was biased could not sit in judgment in his own case. He said the power of passing interim orders for bail was being taken away because reasons for the order were not given as required by the Constitution. The courts, he said, were not passing 'speaking orders' while passing interim orders and the government was being condemned unheard. By the exercise of interim power, he said, actions and functioning of the government was being frustrated. He criticized the courts for passing interim orders while hundred of thousands of cases were piling up and pending before them.[63]

The views expressed in Pirzada's speech represented the views of the ruling party seeking amendment to the Constitution. One of the members of the opposition, Maulana Abdul Mustafa Al Azhari, said that a unanimously adopted Constitution was being made controversial and disputed by the amendments.[64]

Winding up the debate on the Fifth Amendment Bill, Bhutto said that his government wanted 'harmonious co-existence' of all three organs of the state, legislature, executive, and the judiciary with none of them transgressing into the orbit of the other. He stressed that independence of the judiciary did not mean the supremacy or sovereignty of the judiciary. In a parliamentary system, he said, sovereignty belonged to the legislature elected by the people. Bhutto emphasized that the fundamentals of the Constitution were not being touched upon though the parliament was empowered to change the Constitution, amend it, or even scrap it if it so liked. He endorsed Pirzada's speech and said that the judiciary had to be subordinate to the law. It could not become a parallel legislature or executive. He said that the Fifth Constitutional Amendment had been necessitated by repeated decisions of the judiciary trespassing into the field of the executive.[65]

The Constitution (Fifth Amendment) Bill was passed by the National Assembly on 5 September 1976 by 111 votes. The opposition staged a walk out during the second reading of the Bill.[66] The Bill was passed by the Senate on 8 September 1976 and became an Act on 15 September 1976 on receiving the assent of the President.[67]

Constitution (Fifth Amendment) Act, 1976

The Fifth Amendment brought about the following major changes in the Constitution:

(a) The Governor of a province was not to be a permanent resident of that province.

(b) The period for separation of the judiciary from the executive was enhanced from three years to five years.

(c) The Chief Justice of the Supreme Court, unless he retired earlier on attaining the age of sixty-five, would hold office for a period of five years.

(d) In the same manner, the Chief Justice of a High Court would hold office for a period of four years.

(e) On the completion of the term of office as the Chief Justice of the Supreme Court or a High Court, as the case may be, he would have either of the two options, to retire from his office and receive the pension to which he would have been entitled had he retired from office on attaining the age of retirement; or to assume the office of the most senior of the judges of the court concerned and to continue to receive the same salary which he was receiving while holding the office of Chief Justice.

(f) A Chief Justice, who continued after the completion of his term of office as senior most judge, could not even be appointed as acting Chief Justice in the absence of the Chief Justice or when vacancy occurs in the office of Chief Justice.

(g) The term of office of the Chief Justice was to apply to those Chief Justices too who were appointed prior to the enactment of the Fifth Amendment.

(h) The power of the Supreme Court to issue directions, orders, or decrees was made subject to the Article 175(2) of the constitution, which states that 'No court shall have any jurisdiction save as is or may be conferred on it by the constitution or by or under any law'. Thus the Supreme Court's jurisdiction was restricted to what was expressly granted under the constitution or a law.

(i) The common High Court of Sindh and Balochistan was dissolved and separate High Courts for these two provinces were to be established.

(j) The Supreme Court and the High Court were forbidden from making any order under Article 199 prohibiting the making, or suspending the operation, of an order for the detention of any person under any law providing for preventive detention; releasing on bail any person detained under any law providing for preventive detention; releasing on bail, or suspending the operation of an order for the custody, of any person against whom a report or complaint had been made before any court or tribunal, or against whom a case had been registered at any police station, in respect of any offence, or who had been convicted by any court of tribunal; prohibiting the registration of a case at a police station, or the making of a report or complaint before any court or tribunal, in respect of an offence; or granting interim relief to any person referred to above.

(k) All the orders, whether made by the Supreme Court or a High Court, making of which was being forbidden under the Fifth Amendment, were to become ineffective after the commencement of the Fifth Amendment and all applications for such orders were to abate.

(l) A judge of a High Court could be transferred to another High Court for a period upto one year without his consent and without the consultation of the Chief Justices concerned.

(m) Article 204, regarding contempt of court, was amended and the power of the High Courts to punish a person for contempt of court was made subject to ordinary law.

(n) A judge of a High Court who refused to accept appointment as a judge of the Supreme Court would be deemed to have retired from his office.

It is obvious that the predominant focus of the Fifth Amendment was the judiciary whose powers and jurisdiction were curtailed and its members made insecure, having been exposed to the threat of transfer. It took away the option of the Chief Justice or other judges of High Courts to refuse elevation to the Supreme Court. One could only do so at the cost of immediate retirement. The judiciary was snubbed and its powers to punish for contempt of Court and constitutional provisions in this regard were withdrawn. The judiciary was thus fully chastized. One of the immediate consequences was that Sardar Iqbal was obliged to quit as Chief Justice of the Lahore High Court and to retire on completion of his term of four years in October 1976. His dream to continue as Chief Justice of the court for another eight years was shattered. Chief Justice Ghulam Safdar Shah of the Peshawar High Court was also forced into retirement as he had completed a period of four years in service.

The Fifth Amendment was widely criticized by lawyers and in political circles as it greatly undermined and harmed the judiciary as an independent organ of the state. For the members of the judiciary there was little sentiment in their favour, especially amongst the lawyers, since judges had been repeatedly convicting and sentencing lawyers for contempt of court.

New Law for Contempt of Court

A positive development of the lawyers' endeavours against the law of contempt was that a new law on the subject came at the end of 1976. The Contempt of Court Act, 1976[68] was progressive compared to the previous Act of 1926. The earlier law was rather stringent and was made all the more so by its liberal application by the judiciary.[69] The law had been used by the judges as a shield against criticism and they had gone to the point of using it when they were not even acting in their judicial capacity. It was in this environment that malpractices by the relatives, friends, and proteges of judges were spreading and the name of the judiciary was being dragged in the mud. By the use of this law, the judges tried to gag the lawyers who spoke in criticism. Little did they realize that at least some of the criticism was genuine and they ought to have taken it constructively in order to review their attitudes.

The new law provided for criticism by way of fair comments about the general working of courts and the merits of a decision of a court. It also allowed the publication of a fair and accurate report of any judicial proceedings, of making true averments for initiation of action for, or in the course of disciplinary proceedings, against a judge, or reasoning a plea of truth as defence in proceedings for contempt of court. However, all this was allowed subject to the condition that it was in good faith and expressed in temperate language. The law also provided for appeals and transfer of proceedings from one judge or Bench to any other. In cases involving personal scandalization of a judge, he could not sit in judgment over the matter and the trial was to be held by another judge or a Bench of judges.

Nationalization of Banks and Small Industries

It has been discussed above that one of the first reforms brought about by Bhutto was the nationalization of basic industries like steel, chemicals, and cement in 1972 during the civilian Martial Law under the Economic Reforms Order, 1972. This was justified on the ground that the PPP had made a promise in its 1970 election manifesto that it would nationalize the basic industries. The measure was carried out in a haphazard manner and with gross incompetence and corruption, resulting in a heavy loss to the government and a serious setback to industrialization. Within a short time, productive industrial units were turned into sick units by the bureaucrats installed to run them.

The process of nationalization did not stop there. Next came the turn of the vegetable oil industry. The ownership and management of hydrogenated vegetable oil mills were taken over by the federal government through an ordinance in September 1973.[70] The ordinance was followed by an Act of parliament on the same terms.[71] The vegetable oil mills so nationalized were small industrial units and not many workers were employed in them. They were run by small or medium size entrepreneurs who were suddenly deprived of their main assets and activity in life. These units had been generally run efficiently by their owners and were profitable. When these industrial units fell into the hands of government-picked bureaucrats, they ran up high costs of operation due to inexperienced and bureaucratic management with several overheads. These industrial units also ran into heavy losses and the price of vegetable oils, shot up instead of getting reduced. Further expansion of the industry also slackened and there were shortages and rationing of vegetable oil. This unnecessary nationalization had a depressing effect on the industrial environment and investment climate in the country leading to further flight of capital.

Then came the major step of nationalization of banks in March 1974. All banking companies registered under the Company Law in Pakistan were nationalized and the ownership, management, and control of all banks stood transferred to and vested in the federal government.[72] The federal government or a corporation wholly owned or controlled by the federal government, got the exclusive right to establish a bank. The compensation provided to the shareholders of the nationalized banks was neither adequate nor prompt. Like the previous nationalizations of the Bhutto era, it was also virtually expropriation of the assets of others. A Pakistan Banking Council was constituted to make policy recommendations to the federal government, formulate policy guidelines for banks, evaluate their performance, determine the area of co-ordination between them, and to assist them in the management of banks. The timing of nationalization of banks could not be worse. It came at a time when the Arab countries were in confrontation with the West due to Arab-Israel war of October 1973 and had cut off or reduced the supply of oil to western countries. This was an opportunity for Pakistan to encourage Arab countries to invest in banks in Pakistan or to establish their own banks. The Arab petro-dollars could have come in a big way into Pakistan if the matter was attended to and tackled properly. By nationalizing the banks, the Arabs were driven away. They even withdrew the deposits lying in Pakistani banks. Mr Hassan Abidi, an enterprising banker and head of the United Bank Limited, was forced out of Pakistan. Abidi, with the patronage of Arabs, established an international bank by the name of Bank of Credit and Commerce International (BCCI) and attracted substantial petro-dollars which could have otherwise come to Pakistan and could have been made available for the development of the country.

Last in the series of nationalization was the most shocking of all. In July 1976, through three ordinances, flour mills, rice mills, and cotton ginning factories throughout the country were nationalized.[73] These ordinances were followed by identical Acts of the parliament on these subjects in September 1976.[74] The factories or nationalized units were generally very small, run by a few people or at times by the members of single family. Many of them were small businesses which could not even be described as industrial units. Many families were deprived of their only source of income and were even displaced and made homeless by the cruel and callous bureaucrats who took over these units, particularly where a family had its residential quarters within the premises of the unit. Thus, a large number of small businessmen and traders in small towns were ruined, displaced, rendered unemployed and homeless, and driven to extreme privation. It was not possible for the government to run these small agrarian based units profitably and the stocks of cotton, rice, and wheat or flour lying in their premises were either pilfered or wasted. Wrong inventories were prepared. The banks, which had given loans for the running of these seasonal units, were suddenly deprived of their securities and suffered heavy losses because the loans became non-performing. In the ultimate analysis, this nationalization caused colossal loss to the national treasury and the people of Pakistan.

The question is why did Bhutto do all this? The nationalization of banks and heavy industry could be justified on an ideological plane, the PPP had socialist pretensions, but the nationalization of small seasonal industrial units like vegetable oil units, rice mills, flour mills, and cotton ginning factories could not be justified on any ground whatsoever. There was no mention in the PPP manifesto of the nationalization of these small industrial units the Party had clearly exceeded its mandate which caused the country incalculable loss and irreparable economic setback. A theory is advanced to the effect that these nationalizations were an impulsive act of Bhutto who wanted to get even with the small traders and businessmen specially of *mandi* (market) towns in the Punjab because they were presenting stiff resistance and opposition to PPP candidates in the by-elections held from 1973 to 1976. God knows if there is any truth to this theory, but whatever the reason this senseless nationalization did cost the country heavily and Bhutto and his party also paid dearly for it. These deprived and dejected traders, businessmen, and industrialists became the standard bearers, financers, and front-liners of the PNA movement of 1977 because they were fighting for their survival and wanted to settle the issue with Bhutto and his party once and for all. They also became staunch supporters of the martial law regime of Ziaul Haq and co-operated with him in resisting the PPP's return to power.

Sixth Amendment to the Constitution

The Sixth Amendment to the Constitution was passed rather quickly and overnight. While the National Assembly was having its last session before its dissolution prior to fresh elections, the Constitution (Sixth Amendment) Bill was placed before the parliament and was passed. The main provision of the Sixth Amendment was extending the term of the Chief Justices of the Supreme Court and the High Courts beyond the age of retirement. It was provided that the Chief Justice of the Supreme Court who had attained the retirement age of sixty-five, and a Chief Justice of a High Court, who had attained the retirement age of sixty-two and had not completed their term of office of five years and four years, respectively, would continue to hold office until the completion of their respective term of office, as the case may be.[75] Other provisions of the Sixth Amendment were minor.

This amendment is another instance of the arbitrary style of working of the Bhutto government. On the one hand, by fixing a term of office for the Chief Justices, they were forced to retire before reaching the retirement age and, on the other hand, they were allowed to continue, under the Sixth Amendment, even after the age of retirement to complete their term of office. This Amendment was brought about in the Constitution to favour the then Chief Justice of the Supreme Court, Yakub Ali, who was due to retire in the middle of 1977 after serving for less than two years as Chief Justice. He had been very close to Bhutto and prevailed over the latter by persistent requests to allow him to remain Chief Justice for more than three years after his retirement age, even if it meant an amendment to the Constitution. Bhutto thus had the Constitution amended to accommodate a friend.

Further Land Reforms

Days before the dissolution of the National Assembly, another set of land reforms were introduced through an ordinance,[76] soon followed by an Act of parliament in the same terms.[77]

The main features of these land reforms were as under:

(a) No person should own or possess more than one hundred acres of irrigated or two hundred acres of unirrigated land or an area equivalent to eight thousand produce index units of land, whichever would be greater.
(b) Any transfers of land made by a person holding more than the ceiling fixed, before he had relinquished the excess land, should be void.
(c) Compensation was to be paid for the surrendered land at the rate of Rs 30 per produce index unit and that also through negotiable bonds, redeemable in ten years and carrying interest from July 1977.
(d) Land resumed by the government, unless required for public purpose, would be granted free of charge to tenants in cultivating possession.
(e) Land not granted to the tenants in cultivating possession was to be granted to other landless tenants or persons owning less than twelve acres.

These land reforms were never acted upon due to the political conditions that ensued, and even the operation of land reforms of 1972 was not completed.

Important Constitutional Cases

Apart from the case of F. B. Ali that has been discussed above, there were some other important constitutional cases that were decided during this period. It has also been discussed above that the Supreme Court held in State v Ziaur Rahman',[78] while discussing the validation clause of the interim Constitution of 1973 with ouster of jurisdiction clause that in its writ jurisdiction the High Courts were not precluded from scrutinizing the orders, proceedings, and acts made, taken, or done without jurisdiction, with malafide or which were *coram non judice*. This principle was once again upheld and reiterated in another case coming before the Supreme Court after the enforcement of the 1973 Constitution while discussing the validation clause thereunder and the clause ousting the jurisdiction of the superior courts.[79] The Supreme Court elaborated the concept of 'malafides' in this judgment and held that 'malafides' literally means 'in bad faith'. Action taken in bad faith is usually action taken maliciously, that is to say, in which the person taking the action does so out of personal motives either to hurt the person against whom the action is taken or to benefit oneself. Action taken in colourable exercise of powers, that is to say, for collateral purposes not authorized by the law under which the action is taken is a fraud on the law and is also malafide.

There was dispute over the genuineness or voluntariness of a resignation of a member of an assembly submitted to its Speaker. The High Court, in writ jurisdiction, held that 'no duty is cast on the Speaker to satisfy himself about the genuineness, proper execution, or legal effect of a resignation, or to determine a dispute concerning it'. The matter finally came up before the Supreme Court which held as under:[80]

1. It is the duty of the Speaker to decide the genuineness or validity of a resignation for resignation cannot be equated with disqualification suffered by a member under Article 63 of the constitution.
2. A Speaker is under a duty to enquire into the validity of a resignation to take effect, for the provision giving automatic effect to resignation once it reaches the Speaker implies that the resignation is genuine and voluntary.

On the death of the Chief Justice of Sindh and Balochistan High Court, Mr Justice Tufail Ali Abdur Rahman, on 16 January 1975, Mr Justice Abdul Kadir Shaikh, a permanent judge of the Supreme Court, was appointed as Chief Justice of that Court with the added term and condition that he would 'continue to retain his lien on the office of, and seniority as, judge of the Supreme Court'. This appointment was challenged by a member of the Bar in Karachi by filing a *quo warranto* writ petition requiring Mr Justice Abdul Kadir Shaikh to show under what authority of law he claimed to hold the office of Chief Justice. The plea taken was that, as a permanent Chief Justice of a High Court, he could not have retained lien and seniority as a judge of the Supreme Court. The Sindh High Court dismissed the writ petition holding that the petitioner as a member of the Bar had no *locus standi* to challenge the seniority of the Supreme Court. The High Court also found the writ petition not maintainable as the High Court would not issue a writ against one of its judges.

The Supreme Court on appeal held that the appointment as Chief Justice was unexceptional though he could not hold simultaneously the judgeship of the Supreme Court. On the question of maintainability of the writ petition against a judge of a superior court, the Bench of four judges was divided equally. Two judges, Chief Justice Yakub Ali and Mr Justice Anwarul Haq held the writ petition not maintainable because 'High Court' is not a 'person' within the meaning of Article 199 and that the Chief Justice (and for that matter, any judge) was a part of the High Court and not a separate entity from the High Court. Another reason given for non-maintainability was the ground of high degree of comity among the judges of the superior courts. The other judges, namely Mr Justice Salahuddin Ahmad and Mr Justice Muhammad Gul, held that such writ petition was maintainable. They held that a 'judge of a High Court' and 'a High Court' are not always synonymous, interchangeable, or convertible. Further, comity among the members of superior judiciary is not a rule of law and certainly cannot outweigh the imperative necessity of correctly interpreting the constitution.[81]

Since the judges on the Bench were equally divided, the appeal was dismissed. The net gain of the judgment was the finding that a person cannot hold two permanent constitutional judicial appointments. Abdul Kadir Shaikh had to forego his lien and seniority on the Supreme Court. When he was again appointed to the Supreme Court, he became junior to so many other judges appointed after his first stint as Supreme Court judge that he did not become the Chief Justice of Pakistan.

As far as the finding on the maintainability of writ petition against a judge is concerned, the latter development of law in Pakistan, India and other countries clearly supports the view that such a writ petition is maintainable.[82]

Preventive Detentions and the Courts

Changing political winds were reflected in the breach of personal liberties of the citizen by the State. For the courts, this meant frequent habeas corpus petitions, challenges to preventive detention and censorship,[83] resistance to the continued use of Ayub Khan's war-era laws, and accusations of official mistreatment and torture in prisons. As open fora, the courts were unwitting accomplices to these disputes when the government and its opponents brandished litigation as a weapon of politics. Government efforts to silence critics often provoked legal challenges which led to renewed repression and further litigation. Circularity did not mean substantive equality before the law, for the power of the state far exceeded that of the individual. By 1977, the government had lodged hundreds of cases against politicians and party members (as well as their families and other non-combatants) on matters sometimes only distantly related to politics.

As the law varied under which emergency detentions were enforced, so did the capacity of the courts to redress grievances. It was easier to uphold individual rights under the 1960 West Pakistan Maintenance of Public Order Ordinance than under the Defence of Pakistan Rules, which explicitly restricted available remedies. Nonetheless, in its 1973 cases, the Karachi High Court supported citizen's rights even when it could not offer relief. Taking up petitions filed after language riots in Sindh in 1972, the High Court reminded the government that 'an infringement of the rights of liberties of the citizens should be strictly construed,' and suggested that statutory interpretation should, whenever possible, favour the citizen.[84] Judging a group of sixteen habeas corpus petitions from the same period, Justice Agha Ali Hyder reminded the government that 'in Jilani's case, the *detenu* would have been disqualified for exercising his political rights but for the judgment of the court.'[85] In matters concerning its own powers, the Supreme Court cautioned the government that 'the jurisdiction conferred on the Supreme Court by clear terms of the constitution itself cannot be whittled down on considerations of policy or convenience'.[86] Clearest in its judgment against the government's use of emergency provisions, however, was the Peshawar High Court. In a warning that soon resonated in cases against many Frontier opposition leaders, Justice Shah Zaman Babar stated:

> It is a misconception to think that either under the Defence of Pakistan Ordinance or the rules framed thereunder any arbitrary, unguided, uncontrolled, or naked power has been given to any authority. These provisions only confer a power which is coupled with a duty. The power can only be exercised after the duty has been discharged in accordance with the guidelines provided in the statute and the rules.[87]

This judgment released an unlawfully detained prisoner in June 1973. Later that year, NAP leaders were less fortunate.

The Lahore Court also relied on the letter of the constitution to transmit the spirit of law and order when it ruled on government transgression of rights and rules. Justice Sardar Muhammad Iqbal reminded the government that preventive detention was allowed under the Constitution only when used with discretion.[88] Ruling on the detention of a Jamiatul Ulema-i-Pakistan (JUP) politician, the Court noted that 'the law is...extremely chary of the deprivation of the liberty of a citizen at the hands of the investigation agencies.' As it would do increasingly, it reminded the government of due process rights, including the right of the accused to be informed of charges against him and the responsibility of the police to act expeditiously.[89] The Supreme Court later noted that 'even during the Proclamation of Emergency, the executive is precluded from taking any action which is not covered by the authority of law.[90]

The Lahore Court interpreted the citizen rights broadly. Ruling on a writ petition challenging a required monetary deposit to publish a newspaper, the Court submitted that 'the concept of freedom of expression would imply that every citizen is free to say or publish what he wants, provided that he does not trample upon the rights of others.'[91] With time, its language became more insistent. When it heard one of the dozens of writ petitions filed by opposition politician Chaudhry Zahur Ilahi (against whom the government filed dozens more), the Court decided that the 1971 Defence of Pakistan Ordinance included certain rights protections.[92] 'The word 'liberty',' said Justice Ataullah Sajjad, 'carries with it a wider meaning of a citizen following fully his course of action in matters of his private life... The mere existence of a law enabling the public functionaries to impose restraints on the liberty of a citizen is not enough to justify the action taken thereunder... There is a duty cast on the public functionary... to act impartially and reasonably.' He responded to government immunity claims by defending judicial review, writing that 'it is the duty of the superior judiciary to review the actions of the executive, otherwise the constitutional guarantees given to the citizens would be vain and illusory'.

From the time he assumed office, Bhutto held military and civil power concurrently. By extending the dual executive capacity in Emergency proclamations, he prompted frequent jurisdictional questions. Bars to civil court jurisdiction in the Defence of Pakistan Ordinance and Rules meant that tribunals established under those laws frequently usurped otherwise normal judicial duties. At the least, remedies provided by those tribunals had to be exhausted before the civil judiciary could begin to exercise any authority.[93]

A serious challenge to the intersection of civil-military conflicts in law came within a year of the passage of the 1973 Constitution. Retired military officers accused of fomenting a conspiracy against the state filed a writ petition in the Lahore High Court challenging court martial proceedings against them. Overruling their objections, a court martial in Attock Fort convicted the officers while they awaited judgment on their writs, provoking further petitions contesting the validity of the Army Act in proceedings against civilians and the validity of extended emergency provisions invoked against them. The High Court dismissed the writs in *F. B. Ali* v *The State*

(PLD 1975 Lahore 999), holding that a challenge to laws on the basis of conflicts with rights was equivalent to an attempt to enforce fundamental rights, an action that was barred during an Emergency. It also ruled that the first constitutional amendment ousted High Court writ jurisdiction,[94] that court martial jurisdiction under the Army Act covered civilian offences, and that legislative extensions of the state of emergency were valid.

Internal Politics of the PPP and Factionalism

Ideological differences, property and class differentiations, caste distinctions, ancestral rivalries, clashes of personal ambition and interest, and even certain frivolous and fanciful reasons generated factionalism within the PPP. In March 1972, a faction disrupted Prime Minister Bhutto's public meeting at the Qaddafi Stadium in Lahore to discredit those (the Ramay group) who had been in charge of the arrangements Another factional fight disrupted a 'tea party' at the Shalimar Gardens (Lahore) in honour of the newly appointed Chief Minister of the Punjab, Malik Meraj Khalid. In May 1972, rival groups fought and broke up furniture in the party office in a small town near Wazirabad. A few days later, a factional fight occurred in the nearby district town of Gujranwala, in which fists and kicks were freely exchanged until the police came to restore order. Many similar incidents were subsequently reported in the press.

During the 1970 election campaign, Sheikh Rashid, president of the Punjab PPP at the time, had done much organizational work and gained the loyalty of a large number of party workers in the province. Ghulam Mustafa Khar, Bhutto's friend and confidant, was the secretary-general. Before long, the two men, Rashid and Khar, became rivals.[95] During 1972 and the first half of 1973, many pro-Rashid elements were harassed, intimidated, and/or thrown out of the party hierarchy throughout the province. Only one branch organization in the city of Lahore, the one in Baghbanpura, was said to have any pro-Rashid functionaries. Khar was able to take these measures because as Governor he controlled not only government patronage but the police as well. In the summer of 1973, Mian Muhammad Afzal Wattoo, a Khar supporter who had lost the 1970 election in a Bahawalpur constituency, replaced Sheikh Rashid as president of the Punjab PPP. His appointment meant that Khar would now be the effective head of both the party and the government in the Punjab. During 1972 there were many bloody clashes between peasants and landlords for protection from the full impact of Bhutto's land reforms. He suppressed the 'extremists', dissidents, and opponents within and without the PPP with a ferocity reminiscent of Kalabagh's rule in the 1960s. That some of his ministers, notably Mian Iftikhar Tari, were widely alleged to have underworld connections damaged the regime's legitimacy. Mumtaz Bhutto's government in Sindh operated in like fashion.[96] By the fall of 1973, Bhutto concluded that he must dissociate himself from their heavy handed political style. Towards the end of January 1974, as reports circulated in PPP drawing-rooms that Khar might soon be dismissed, forty Punjab Provincial Assembly members (MPAs) submitted a petition to Bhutto alleging numerous cases of corruption and other malfeasance on Khar's part. In early February five MPAs attacked him on the assembly floor and engaged in a free exchange of colourful Punjabi vocabulary with some of his supporters.[97]

Khar, who was now the Chief Minister, resigned from his post on 10 March 1974, and Bhutto designated Haneef Ramay, the outspoken painter and former journalist, to succeed him. Khar appeared to accept his ouster with good grace, professing infinite loyalty to Bhutto, and suggested that he might withdraw from politics. On his part, Bhutto tried to soften the blow by indicating that he still valued Khar's friendship. He took him to Al-Murtaza, his home in Larkana, and stayed at Khar's house during visits to Lahore. Ramay accommodated two Khar supporters, Abdul Khaliq and Mian Afzal Wattoo, in his cabinet.

Khar soon abandoned any thought of retirement he might have had and decided to fight it out with Ramay to show the party Chairman who really mattered in the Punjab. He toured the province to meet and organize his supporters in the party. He began to criticize the Ramay government, claiming that he, not Ramay, commanded majority support in the assembly. The Ramay government, unsure of Bhutto's mind on the subject, did not wish to treat Khar with the harshness customarily reserved for political opponents. There were some factional disruptions of his meetings and a moderate amount of police harassment during his tour of the province. A provincial minister accused him of fomenting labour and student unrest. Sheikh Rashid alleged that Khar had bought a restaurant in London worth 100,000 pounds with funds illegally transferred abroad. Other charges of corruption and misconduct were made and some local PPP organizations demanded his expulsion from the party.

At this point, Khar decided to challenge the Prime Minister himself. He made contact with the opposition parties and PPP dissidents outside the Punjab. He kept in 'constant touch' with the NAP leaders, entertained the Talpur brothers at his Clifton residence in Karachi, and visited Meraj Muhammad Khan. He claimed to know of Bhutto's lapses that were much worse than anything Ayub might have done at Tashkent. At the same time, he was reported to be seeking a meeting with the Prime Minister who was in Lahore. Before seeing Khar, Bhutto dissolved the Punjab PPP and appointed Malik Meraj Khalid, one of Khar's opponents, as president with a mandate to re-organize the party in the province. On 22 May, he met Khar and, after two extended meetings, a 'reconciliation' was announced.

Factionalism in the PPP was a complex phenomenon. Bhutto stood above the internal divisions and rivalries. Party notables often declared that they were his creatures, owing their legislative and ministerial roles to his personal popularity with the electorate. Factionalism involved competition for a higher rating in the order of merit and precedence with the Party chief. Legislators and party officials at the district and local levels made estimates of where contending dignitaries stood in Bhutto's esteem and shifted their support accordingly.

Announcements were made periodically of an impending reorganization of the Punjab PPP for the purpose of cleansing it. During Afzal Wattoo's presidentship, a purge of the corrupt elements was to be completed by the end of March 1974, but actually only a few *tehsil*-level presidents were removed. The president of the Multan district PPP, M.A. Goher, lost his post but gained a position on the party's provincial committee.[98]

Malik Meraj Khalid replaced Mian Wattoo in May 1974 and prepared to embark upon another reorganization. He said that Bhutto had directed him to rid the party of self-seekers, opportunists, luxury-loving big spenders, and gangsters, and to bring in the *shurafa* (decent folks). The people had begun to hate the PPP, he said, because of the corruption, violence, and high-handedness that its functionaries had practised.[99] Reorganization committees, one for each division, would screen divisional and district level presidents and secretaries and replace the ones found wanting.[100] The party leadership called upon government agents at the *tehsil* level (*tehsildars*) to submit lists of respectable people in their areas who might then be persuaded to join the party. One of Bhutto's special assistants, Khuda Bakhsh Bucha, toured the Punjab countryside to spread the word that the PPP wanted to improve its image, that the *shurafa* would have a role in it, and that their dignity and honour would be preserved.[101] But the planned reorganization did not take place, and Malik Meraj Khalid, himself a model of decency, had to abandon the reformation he wanted to undertake.

Bhutto did some reorganizing of his own. In March 1975, he appointed Khar as Governor of the Punjab again and Khar had to resign his assembly seat to accept that post. Ramay was still the Chief Minister and, as before, the two men could not work together. In July, Bhutto dismissed both of them and persuaded Ramay to resign his assembly seat in return for the promise of a seat in the federal Senate. Both Khar and Ramay were thus cast out of the Punjab government and its legislative politics. Khar tried to return to the assembly by contesting a by-election for the seat Ramay had vacated but Bhutto denied him the party nomination and police was used to fire upon a Khar election meeting. At that point, Khar broke with the party and, surprisingly, so did Ramay. After they were rebuffed by Asghar Khan's Tehrik-i-Istiqlal, the two men found places in the Pagaro faction of the Pakistan Muslim League in November 1975.

In June 1974, Bhutto dismissed J.A. Rahim as a federal minister and as Secretary-General of the party because of his 'misbehaviour' at a dinner party at the Prime Minister's House. Not only that, Saeed Ahmad Khan, Chief of Security at the Prime Minister's House, along with members of the Federal Security Force, went to the house of Mr Rahim and gave him a physical thrashing. This was the unfortunate reward given to an old man who was Bhutto's mentor and the mind behind the creation, concept, and manifesto of the PPP.

Khurshid Hasan Meer resigned later in the year because Bhutto would not stop Maulana Kausar Niazi (Information Minister) from hounding Meer in the press and denouncing him as a communist. Mubashir Hasan, the Finance Minister, was sent away to be the party's Secretary-General in place of Rahim, but he performed no function in that post because Bhutto assigned him none. By 1976, the balance of influence within the PPP had tilted heavily in favour of the conservatives as the provincial governments were placed under *nawabs* and landed aristocrats. The Nawab of Bahawalpur came out of retirement to become Governor of Punjab and Nawab Sadiq Hussain Qureshi became the Chief Minister. Dilawar Khanji, son of the former Nawab of Junagadh, was appointed Governor of Sindh, and the former Nawab of

Kalat was appointed as Governor of Balochistan. Ghulam Mustafa Jatoi, a big landlord, and Jam Ghulam Qadir, once the ruler of Lasbela, were the chief ministers respectively, in Sindh and Balochistan. As another general election approached, landlords, opportunists, and self-seekers, the kind Malik Meraj Khalid had hoped to expel, flooded the party once again.

Bhutto knew of the corruption, factionalism, and violence in the PPP. The files in his secretariat revealed also that, from time to time, he recommended civility and moderation to his associates. For instance, a note to Mumtaz Bhutto (20 May 1973) regarding the Sindh government's plan to import four hundred buses cautioned: 'Please see that no hanky-panky takes place and that everything is done above board'. Complaining to his Finance Minister about corruption in a government lending institution (3 July 1973), he said: 'The loans must go to genuine persons and the genuine persons must be the poor people'. Many other notes on file contained the statement: 'I will not tolerate this corruption'. A letter from Senator Agha Ghulam Nabi Pathan (dated 22 November 1973) informed him that the party's involvement with ration depots and the associated black marketing and smuggling, had lowered its standing so that most party workers could not face the public or do their political work. Noting that 'for quite some time I have been receiving similar complaints', Bhutto circulated Pathan's letter to members of the central committee eliciting their views and suggestions.[102]

Bhutto had likewise been aware of violence and gangsterism in the party. A note to Mumtaz Bhutto (27 December 1972) referred to a report he had received of 'utter lawlessness' and the 'reign of terror' that gangsters patronized by the party had unleashed in Shikarpur. A memo to Governor Khar (16 August 1973) opened with the following observations: 'Pistols to the right of us, pistols to the left of us, pistols all around us. This seems to be the motto of the party. For the most trivial of things pistols are drawn and flashed'. Bhutto went on to say that the gangsters who did this sort of thing must feel they 'have protection, because this was not their brave habit before we assumed office. How are we going to end if this becomes the order of the day?'

Why these suggestions, appeals, and gentle remonstrances? Were stronger measures not available? Like many other politicians, Bhutto probably believed that in his craft, as practised in Pakistan, a certain amount of factionalism, graft, and arm-twisting were unavoidable. In addition, he did not fully control the government and the party. Even though his associates and lieutenants insisted that they respected his word as law, it was a 'law' they often neglected to implement. His files contained many notes to ministers, provincial governors, and chief ministers, even civil servants, reminding them of things he had asked them to do and which they had not done. He urged them in the name of Pakistan's toiling masses, recalled the pledges made in the party's election manifesto, and reminded them that 'men of conscience' must be answerable to the electorate, warning them of the consequences of the party's falling popularity.[103]

But another perspective is also relevant. His exhortations did not have effect because he did not follow them in his own conduct. He was not averse to the use of violence against his own opponents. He might have tolerated corruption in the belief that it worked as a cement to keep men together in a party. He made no serious effort to eradicate factionalism. He might indeed, have even intensified it. Instead of valuing internal coherence, Bhutto was inclined to maintain a balance between contending factions within the party to create what he called a 'Napoleonic order'.[104] He placed opposites together. He must have known that Sheikh Rashid, a serious socialist, and Khar, a pragmatic pursuer and user of power, could not work together as president and secretary-general, respectively, of the Punjab PPP. Again, when he made Malik Meraj Khalid, a moderate man who had come up from modest beginnings, president of the Punjab PPP, he appointed Nasir Rizvi, a landed aristocrat, as the secretary-general. There was no way this team could pull together. Rizvi thought of Meraj Khalid as a weakling.[105] These appointments only guaranteed that issues would not be settled at the provincial level and would have to be submitted to Bhutto for resolution.

In a note to Mumtaz Bhutto, Bhutto explained his thinking on the difficult art of maintaining a balance between warring factions, in this case the Lunds and the Mehars in Sindh.[106] He advised Mumtaz Bhutto to consider which faction wielded more influence in its region and was, thus, more capable of helping or hurting the PPP and its government in Sindh. Bhutto went on to suggest that Mumtaz Bhutto should weigh the antecedents, associations, and basic loyalties of each faction as well as the price it demanded for its support.

All of this might be sensible, but it is clear that the balancing game could be played only if the political landscape was occupied by contending forces. If the overlord was given to playing this game and there were no warring factions to be balanced one against the other, he might create them so that the game could be played.

Preparations for General Elections

The general elections had to be held under the Constitution before 14 August 1977. Bhutto was busy making preparations. In 1976, he announced centenary celebrations commemorating the hundredth birthday of Jinnah in December that year. In this way, he wanted to identify himself and the PPP closely with Jinnah, the founder of Pakistan. As part of his party's pre-election propaganda battle plan, thousands of little red-cover books called 'Bhutto says', modelled on the little red books of Chairman Mao's sayings, were distributed widely in Karachi, Lahore, and Rawalpindi. He encouraged all segments of the population to join his party. All the feudals, whom his party had defeated in 1970, joined the party in 1976 with a lot of fanfare. Every day, newspapers were full of names of people joining the PPP with thousands of their supporters.[107]

He even sought support from orthodox Islamists, both internally and externally, during the early months of 1976. By bolstering the long-standing central pillar of his foreign policy, Sino-Pakistan friendship, and pushing his nuclear weapons programme, Bhutto felt more confident about holding elections in early 1977. He wanted to be sure of winning at least two-thirds majority required for changing the Constitution to return Pakistan to a presidential system, rather than having to appear before the National Assembly every month or so to justify virtually every step he took. He had hired an academic expert on constitutional government, Professor Leslie Wolf-Phillips of the London School of Economics and Political Science, who was busy preparing the new presidential constitution that year in London, working for the Pakistan Embassy there, devising his own 'secret codes' and deceptive use of 'appendices' to draft a document that no one could read or understand until Bhutto himself was ready to spring it on his unsuspecting nation.[108]

It is, by all accounts, certain that Bhutto was dissatisfied with the parliamentary system which, in his words, was the system that protected the privileges of the few at the expense of the rights of the many'. He was unhappy with the 1973 Constitution and the constraints that it imposed on the executive. He thought that the opposition was using its provisions and was responsible for Pakistan's economic and social backwardness. He made speeches to this effect throughout 1976 at various places in Pakistan. His message was loud and clear. Bhutto was going back to the people to seek a mandate for bringing about a change in the country's political and constitutional structure.[109]

NOTES

1. Article 271 of the Constitution of 1973.
2. Article 273.
3. Article 59.
4. Article 272.
5. *Dawn*, 7 August 1973.
6. *Dawn*, 11 August 1973.
7. *Dawn*, 13 August 1973.
8. The Constitution of Islamic Republic of Pakistan, 1973, Article 265.
9. *Dawn*, 15 August 1973.
10. Khan, Hamid, *Administrative Tribunals for Civil Servants in Pakistan*. 1990, Progressive Publishers, Lahore, p. 19.
11. Address of Bhutto, Prime Minister of Pakistan, to the Nation on Television and Radio on 20 August, 1973. Text of the speech is reproduced on pages 5 and 8 of daily *Dawn* in its issue of 21 August, 1973.
12. Ibid.
13. Ibid.
14. Article 240.
15. Article 212.
16. Provincial Service Tribunals (Extension of Provisions of the Constitution) Act, 1974 (Act XXXII of 1974).
17. Provincial Service Tribunals (Extention of Provisions of the Constitution) (Amendment) Act, 1976 (Act XXXIV of 1976), amending Act XXXII of 1974.
18. Kennedy, Charles H., *Bureaucracy in Pakistan*, 1987, Oxford University Press, Karachi. p. 131.
19. Article 1 of the 1973 Constitution Clause (2) had provided for the contingency of representation to East Pakistan.
20. Constitution (First Amendment) Act, 1974, Act XXXIII of 1974. PLD 1974 Central Statutes 252.
21. Political Parties (Amendment) Act, 1975 (Act XXI of 1975), substituting Section 6 of the Act. PLD 1975 Central Statutes 107.
22. *Nawae Waqt*, 31 May 1974.
23. Ibid., 1 June and 10 June 1974.
24. *The Pakistan Times*, 1 June 1974.

25. Ibid., 14 June 1974.
26. *Nawae Waqt*, 14 and 17 June 1974.
27. Constitution (Second Amendment) Act, 1974 (Act XLIX of 1974) PLD 1974 Central Statutes 425.
28. Ahmedis are referred to by the Muslim community in general in pejorative sense as 'Qadianis', in reference to Qadian, a place in the district of Gurdaspur now in India, which was their earlier centre or as 'Mirzais' in reference to their spiritual leader, Mirza Ghulam Ahmad. Lahories are a faction which split with the main body in Qadian and later in Rabwah and established their headquarters in Lahore.
29. Mujibur Rehman v Federal Government of Pakistan, PLD 1985 Federal Shariat Court 9 (p.32). In this judgment, the circumstances of the life of Mirza Ghulam Ahmad are given in detail and are fairly well researched. The author has relied on this judgment for the facts regarding Mirza Sahib.
30. Chaudhry Mohammad Zafarullah Khan, one of the the most prominent and respected personalities amongst Ahmedis, wrote a pamphlet in which he discussed in detail about the death of Jesus Christ in Kashmir and his grave is also shown to be there. Zafarullah Khan was a very accomplished person. He served as member of the executive council of the Viceroy from 1935 to 1941 and served as a judge of Federal Court of India from 1942 to 1947. He served as Foreign Minister of Pakistan during the first seven years of its existence. He was chosen for this office by Quaid-e-Azam himself. He rendered invaluable services to Pakistan during the freedom movement and after the creation of Pakistan. He was later elected as a Judge of International Court of Justice (ICJ) and served as such for twelve years. Out of this period, he was Vice President of ICJ for three years and President of the Court for another three years.
31. *The New Encyclopaedia Britannica*, Vol. 12, 1974, p. 442.
32. There is a story about a Brigadier, who was military secretary in the late sixties and was an ambitious man. Fearing that his promotion as Major-General may not be aborted by the Ahmedi *junta*, he got entered a document into his personal file declaring himself an Ahmedi. He was nevertheless promoted as a Major-General. Later on, when the Ahmedis were ousted in the mid seventies from the leadership of armed forces, he using his clout in the military secretary branch, got this document taken out of his personal file. Whatever the worth of this story but one thing is clear that the Ahmedi generals in the army mattered a lot at that time and subordinates feared discrimination at their hands in the matter of promotion and other conditions of service.
33. Air Marshal Zafar Chaudhry, an Ahmedi and Chief of Air Staff from 1972 to 1974 (a very gentle and genial character) is rumoured to have ordered the Air Force planes to fly low over Rabwah during the annual meeting of the Ahmedis in order to show respect to the congregation below. The incident at the Rabwah Railway station on 30 May 1974 was also a manifestation of their over confidence which ultimately proved to be their undoing.
34. Zia introduced a very Draconian law called Anti-Islamic Activities of Qadiani Group, Lahori Group and Ahmedis (Prohibition and Punishment) Ordinance, 1984 (Ordinance XX of 1984), PLD 1984 Central Statutes 102, virtually denying them the use of their religious places.
35. See Mujibur Rehman v Federal Government, PLD 1985 FSC 8.
36. F.B. Ali v The State, PLD 1975 S.C. 506.
37. The dissenting opinion was that of Mr Justice Anwar-ul-Haq.
38. Taseer, Salman, *Bhutto: A political biography*, 1980, Vikas Publishing House (Pvt) Ltd., New Delhi, p. 150.
39. Code of Criminal Procedure (Amendment) Ordinance, 1975, PLD 1976 Central Statutes 57. Code of Criminal Procedure (Amendment) Act 1976 (Act XIII of 1976) PLD 1976 Central Statutes 175. Section 498-A was added to the Code of Criminal Procedure.
40. In the mid-sixties, Chaudhry Zahur Ilahi, a politician from Gujrat, was under constant political victimization from the then Governor of West Pakistan, Nawab Amir Muhammad Khan of Kalabagh. The Lahore High Court granted him bail in all the cases registered and to be registered against him as part of such victimization.
41. Act XXII of 1975, PLD 1975 Central Statutes 109.

42. In case of detention under a federal law, the Review Board was to consist of three incumbent or former judges of Supreme Court or a High Court, and in case of detention under a Provincial Law, such Board was to consist of three incumbent or former judges of a High Court.
43. Article 232 of the Constitution.
44. Constitution (Fourth Amendment) Act, 1975. Act LXXI of 1975. PLD 1975 Central Statutes 337.
45. *Dawn*, 15 November 1975. The members of the opposition who were forcibly removed from the National Assembly by the security staff were Chaudhry Zahur Ilahi, Mahmood Ali Kasuri, Malik Suleman, Mufti Mahmood, Professor Ghafoor Ahmad, Ahmad Raza Kasuri, Dr Ghulam Husain, and Zulfiqar Ali Bajwa.
46. Hayat Mohammad Sherpao was a close associate of Bhutto and had served as a member of his cabinet. At the time of the explosion, he was senior minister in the cabinet of NWFP.
47. Sayeed, Khalid B., *Politics in Pakistan*, 1980, Praeger Publishers, New York, p. 135.
48. These judges had served as federal law secretaries at different points in time and there was suspicion that they had dealt with the file of NAP and its leaders in such capacity, which of course they did being part of the executive at that time.
49. Islamic Republic of Pakistan v Abdul Wali Khan, PLD 1976 S.C. 57.
50. This Board is constituted under Article 10 to consider the continuation of preventive detention of a person.
51. This is indeed a dangerous precedent set by the Court. Newspaper reports are universally known to be of doubtful veracity because of the views and partisan interests of the owners of such newspapers. Wrong statements are attributed for their own reasons and denials are not correctly printed. The onus should not be placed on persons to whom statements are attributed.
52. This refers to the Accord reached between the PPP on the one hand and the NAP-JUI alliance on the other hand before the Constitution became effective.
53. A story is worth mentioning in this behalf. It was alleged that Sardar Iqbal, around the time of his appointment as a judge in 1962, through one of his assistants caused some interpolation in a certified copy of a judgment in order to save period of limitation that had expired due to oversight or negligence. It is said that he was saved from the consequences by the Law Minister Munir by having him elevated to the Bench and his assistant was made the scapegoat who was later lightly punished. The file of this case assumed great importance around 1971, when Sardar Iqbal was next in line to become the Chief Justice of the Lahore High Court. While being the senior judge (in the absence of Chief Justice Anwar-ul-Haq), he ordered listing of the case during the summer vacations before a judge belonging to his faction in order to get over the matter once and for all. The judge, before whom the case was fixed, locked the file in his Court almirah. Maulvi Mushtaq, who monitored the whole affair, immediately reported the matter to the Chief Justice Anwar-ul-Haq, who was on vacations at that time. The Chief Justice ordered the cancellation of the case from the list and directed a court official to take the file into his custody. On learning that the file had already been locked up, the court official was ordered to break open the locker and take over the custody of the file which he did. Mr Justice Cheema gave the Registrar a notice for contempt of Court. However, the Chief Justice came to the rescue of the Registrar. A Bench of judges was formed to hear the contempt matter and the Registrar was discharged by the Bench. The judge concerned, Mr Justice Afzal Cheema, wrote a note on the file that a case having been assigned to him could not have been withdrawn or transferred even by the Chief Justice. Nevertheless, the Chief Justice ordered the Registrar for the withdrawal of the file from Mr Justice Cheema. The poor Registrar of the Court, Mr Mohammad Hassan Sindhar, later suffered at the hands of Sardar Iqbal, when he became Chief Justice, who saw to it that he was superseded in the elevation to the High Court. He later became a judge of Lahore High Court when Maulvi Mushtaq Husain was Chief Justice. He was not given oath under Provisional Constitution Order in 1981 and was retired unceremoniously.
54. These included Mr Justice Muhammad Gul, Mr Justice Muhammad Afzal Cheema and Mr Justice Muhammad Akram.

55. The story is that the politician wanted his brother to be appointed as a civil judge or may be a sessions judge because he had not appeared as an advocate before the High Court. Ayub appointed him to the High Court because, as the story goes, he did not know that courts existed below the High Courts. Another judge was appointed because a *pir* of Ayub had recommended him.
56. One of the candidates was not appointed because the shoes he had on were rather gaudy and did not go with the suit he was wearing. Another was rejected because he had dropped egg on his collar while eating boiled eggs for breakfast before going for the interview. A candidate from Lahore was only asked if he was a typical Lahori which he candidly admitted that he was. It cannot be said if he liked the answer but the poor candidate was not appointed. A candidate was appointed because he hailed from Rawalpindi district and members of the National and Provincial Assemblies from the district met Ayub and requested for his appointment as a representative from the Rawalpindi district.
57. Habibul Wahab Elkheri v Sheikh Shaukat Ali, PLD 1976 Lahore 373.
58. State v Shaukat Ali, Advocate. PLD 1976 Lahore 714.
59. The State v Sheikh Shaukat Ali Advocate and three others. PLD 1976 Lahore 355.
60. Hakam Qureshi and two others v Judges of the Lahore High Court, PLD 1976 S.C. 713.
61. *Dawn*, 2 September 1976.
62. *Dawn*, 4 September 1976.
63. Ibid.
64. Ibid.
65. *Dawn*, 5 September 1976.
66. *Dawn*, 6 September 1976.
67. Constitution (Fifth Amendment) Act, 1976. Act LXII of 1976. PLD 1976 Central Statutes 538.
68. Act LXIV of 1976. PLD 1977 Central Statutes 18.
69. The Supreme Court had previously taken very strict view of any shade of contempt by punishing even bonafide comments made about functioning of the judiciary, publication of articles, or comments regarding a pending case or even making comment on a question of law in such pending case. See Sir Edward Snelson v The Judges of the High Court of West Pakistan, PLD 1961 S.C. 237. The judicial philosophy in respect of the law of contempt of court perhaps best reflected in the following observation of Kaikaus, in M.H. Khondkar v The State (PLD 1966 S.C. 140)
'It is essential for the administration of justice that judges of superior Courts be absolutely protected from attack for otherwise it would be difficult for them to function at all.'
70. Hydrogenated Vegetable Oil Industry (Control and Development) Ordinance, 1973. Ordinance XIX of 1973. PLD 1973 Central Statutes 635.
71. Hydrogenated Vegetable Oil Industry (Control and Development) Act, 1973. Act LXV of 1973. PLD 1974 Central Statutes 7.
72. Banks (Nationalization) Act, 1974. Act XIX of 1974. PLD 1974 Central Statutes 196.
73. Flour Milling Control and Development Ordinance. Ordinance XXIV of 1976. PLD 1976 Central Statutes 423. Rice Milling Control and Development Ordinance, 1976. Ordinance XXV of 1976. PLD 1976 Central Statutes 431. Cotton Ginning Control and Development Ordinance 1976. Ordinance XXVI of 1976. PLD 1976 Central Statutes 439.
74. Flour Milling Control and Development Act, 1976 (Act LVII of 1976). PLD 1976 Central Statutes 489. Rice Milling Control and Development Act, 1976 (Act LVIII of 1976). PLD 1976 Central Statutes 497. Cotton Ginning Control and Development Act, 1976 (Act LIX of 1976). PLD 1976 Central Statutes 505.
75. Constitution (Sixth Amendment) Act, 1976. Act LXXXIV of 1976. PLD 1977 Central Statutes 46.
76. Land Reforms Ordinance, 1977 (Ordinance II of 1977) effective from 5 January 1977. PLD 1977 Central Statutes 101.
77. Land Reforms Act, 1977 (Act II of 1977) effective from 9th January 1977. PLD 1977 Central Statutes 126.
78. PLD 1973 S.C. 49.
79. Federation of Pakistan v Saeed Ahmad Khan, PLD 1974 S.C. 151.

80. Tahir Beg v Kausar Ali Shah, PLD 1976 S.C. 504.
81. Abrar Hassan v Government of Pakistan, PLD 1976 S.C. 315.
82. See Al-Jehad Trust v Federation of Pakistan, PLD 1996 S.C.324. Also Supreme Court Advocates-on-Record Association v Union of India. AIR 1994 S.C. 268.
83. For example, State v Yusuf Lodhi, PLD 1973 Peshawar 25, and Fakhare Alam v The State and another, PLD 1973 Supreme Court 525, Maulana Musahib Ali v The State, PLD 1975 Karachi 909; Kanayalal v The State, PLD 1977 Karachi 675.
84. Liaqat Ali v Government of Sind through Secretary, Home Department, PLD 1973 Karachi 78.
85. Zafar Iqbal v Province of Sindh and two others, PLD 1973 Karachi 316. See Also Abdul Hamid Khan v The District Magistrate, Larkana and two others, PLD 1973 Karachi 344.
86. Khan Muhammad Yusuf Khan Khattack v S. M. Ayub and two others, PLD 1973 Supreme Court 160.
87. Fida Muhammad v Province of NWFP through Home Secretary, Peshawar, PLD 1973 Peshawar 156.
88. Begum Nazir Abdul Hamid v Pakistan (Federal Government) through Secretary Interior, PLD 1974 Lahore 7.
89. Maulana Abdus Sattar Khan Niazi v The State, PLD 1974 Lahore 324. Due process matters were also considered in Nawab Begum v Home Secretary, Government of Punjab, Lahore, PLD 1974 Lahore 344; Mrs Habiba Jilani v The Federation of Pakistan through Secretary, Interior Ministry, PLD 1974 Lahore 153; Kh. Mohammad Safdar v The State and another, PLD 1974 Lahore 200.
90. Federation of Pakistan v Ch. Manzoor Elahi, PLD 1976 Supreme Court 430.
91. Muzaffar Qadir v The District Magistrate, Lahore, PLD 1975 Lahore 1198.
92. Chaudhry Zahur Ilahi v Secretary to Government of Pakistan, Ministry of Home and Kashmir Affairs, PLD 1975 Lahore 499.
93. For example, Indo-Pakistan Corporation Ltd., Lahore v Government of Pakistan through Secretary, Ministry of Political Affairs, PLD 1975 Lahore 1058.
94. Justice K. E. Chauhan cited Abdul Ghani Khan v Government of West Pakistan and others, PLD 1968 Lahore 1244, on the fundamental rights question. The court limited the ouster of writ jurisdiction in amended Article 199. 'If a case does not fall within the four corners of the jurisdiction-ousting conditions, then writs therein can be issued by this Court.'
95. *Jang*, 15 and 22 May 1972.
96. A number of political analysts have attributed Khar's political repression to his feudal ethos. In an interview on 20 August 1974 Ghulam Mustafa Jatoi, who succeeded Mumtaz Bhutto as the Chief minister of Sindh, observed that Mumtaz followed the Kalabagh model of repressive rule because it suited his personal inclinations. Yousuf Hasan, a PPP ward leader in the Korangi-Landhi area of Karachi, stated that the PPP government's use of the police and gangsters to deal with its political opponents had lowered the party in public esteem. The feudal style and nature of Khar has been explicitly and graphically represented by his former wife, Tehmina Khar in her book *My Feudal Lord*, published by Vanguard Books, Lahore, Edition 1996.
97. Syed, Anwar H., *The Discourse and Politics of Zulfiqar Ali Bhutto*, 1992, The Macmillan Press Ltd. Hong Kong, p. 209.
98. *Pakistan Times*, 17 and 27 January, 1974, *Nawae Waqt*, 17 January 1974.
99. *Nawae Waqt*, 3 July 1974.
100. *Nawae Waqt*, 3 July 1974.
101. *Nawae Waqt*, 23 May 1974.
102. Syed, Anwar H., *The Discourse and Politics of Zulfiqar Ali Bhutto*, *supra*. note 97, p. 212.
103. Ibid., p. 213.
104. Bhutto's interview with a correspondent of Le Monde reprinted in the overseas weekly *Dawn*, 26 October 1975.
105. Interview of Mr Anwar H. Syed with Taj Mohammad Langah and Nasir Rizvi on 1 and 2 August 1974 respectively. In his interview with Bhutto on 18 August 1974, he confirmed that these appointments were designed to balance contending elements within the party.
106. Note dated 16 August 1974 in the prime minister's file.

107. There was a joke making rounds at that time that if the newspaper reports were believed, then the number of people who were said to have joined the PPP in 1976 would outnumber the total population in the country.
108. Wolpert, Stanley, *Zulfi Bhutto of Pakistan—His Life and Times*, 1993, Oxford University Press, New York, p. 267.
109. Burki, Shahid Javed, *Pakistan under Bhutto, 1971-1977*, 1988, Macmillan Press, Hong Kong, pp. 182-3.

24

GENERAL ELECTIONS, MARCH 1977

On 7 January 1977, Bhutto announced that general elections would be held in March and assured the nation that they would be fair.[1] The President of Pakistan then dissolved the assemblies, and the Election Commission appointed 7 and 10 March as the polling dates, respectively, for elections to the National Assembly and to the four provincial assemblies. On 21 January, nine opposition parties came together in an electoral coalition called the Pakistan National Alliance (PNA), to oppose the PPP. The PNA launched a vigorous campaign and its public meetings drew large crowds. It seemed that the contest would be lively, to say the least, and that the PPP would have to work hard to win.

Bhutto was still popular and many people thought he was the fittest person among the available politicians to 'hold the reins of government', but his party was as sick with corruption and factional strife in 1976 as it had been during the preceding four years.[2] Bhutto's advisors told him that party workers were more despised than corrupt public officials and that party leaders were ineffective and colourless.[3] Commenting on the state of the party in the Punjab, Rao Abdul Rashid, a police officer who worked as a 'special secretary' in the Prime Minister's secretariat, reported that the Chief Minister, Nawab Sadiq Hussain Qureshi, was not much of a politician, had no mass following, and had alienated his Cabinet colleagues and the PPP legislators; that the party lacked public speakers who could hold a crowd and sway the audience, and that neither the ministers nor the MPAs were thinking of the party and its interests.[4] Writing again in February 1977, Rao Rashid stated that the party notables who had failed to get the nomination ('ticket') for the coming election were ready to oppose party nominees, and that many of the latter believed it was now the provincial government's task to help them win.[5]

It is not surprising then that the PPP as an organization played only a peripheral role in the election. Its 'parliamentary boards' did recommend candidates for the award of party tickets but Bhutto made the actual selection, considering the assessments which district officers and intelligence agencies had submitted regarding each aspirant's financial position, local standing, *biradri* connections, character, and reputation. He tried to strike a balance between the party faithful and the new entrants.[6]

That the party was in disarray is not to be taken to mean that its nominees were going to lose. Many of them would win because of their individual standing, connections, and resources. Others were likely to win because the voters did not like the PNA candidates. Some of the central and provincial ministers whose corruption and high-handedness had angered constituents were likely to lose in a fair fight.

Those with limited funds would need help. Busy with his official duties, Bhutto was not free to campaign for party candidates on the scale of the 1970 elections. His campaign managers thus concluded that the party needed the administration's friendly intervention in the forthcoming elections.

Putting together the assessments of PPP's electoral prospects, which the district officers and intelligence agencies submitted periodically, it appeared that the party could win between 95 to 120 of the 192 general seats in the National Assembly.[7] After gaining the allegiance of most of the eight tribal members and six minority representatives who had generally sided with the larger party, and after taking its share of the ten seats reserved for women, the party could have a comfortable, though not an overwhelming, majority in a house of 216. On 4 March, three days before the election, the Central Intelligence Bureau predicted that the PPP would easily win 55 of the 116 National Assembly seats in the Punjab,[8] and noted that it 'should be able to win' 16 more seats from amongst those for which the contest was likely to be hard. Thus, the PPP might win as many as 71 National Assembly seats from the Punjab. After consulting his field officers, the chief secretary to the Punjab government provided a similar estimate: the PPP would win 70 seats.[9] But the actual results, as they came out on the evening of 7 March and during the day on 8 March, showed the PPP to have won 155 of the 192 general seats, including 108 of the 116 seats from the Punjab. This was a victory beyond all expectations. Rao Abdul Rashid recalls that its size startled and then alarmed Bhutto.[10]

The PPP won nearly four-fifths of the National Assembly seats. The PNA managed to win less than one-fifth, while the remainder went to the independents. In fact, the PPP's success was even more impressive than the table suggests, since the eight independents from the 'tribal areas' were all quasi-PPP candidates. Following a tradition that went back to the British Raj when electoral politics was first introduced into this part of British India, tribal leaders, while not accepting party labels, were expected to side with the ruling party. Counting the independents with the PPP gave the party 81.5 per cent of the National Assembly seats.

Party Positions in the 1977 Elections

	PPP		PNA		Independent*		
Province	seats won	% of total	seats won	% of total	seats won	% of total	Total
Punjab	107	93.0	8	7.0	–	–	115
Sindh	32	74.4	11	25.6	–	–	43
NWFP	8	30.8	17	65.4	1	3.8	26
Balochistan	7	100.0	–	–	–	–	7
Islamabad	1	100.0	–	–	–	–	1
Tribal Areas	–	–	–	–	–	100	8
Total	155	77.5	36	18.0	9	4.5	200

* Independents include one seat won by Qayyum Muslim League in NWFP.

The PPP's popular support, in terms of the total number of votes cast for its candidates was less overwhelming. It received 58 per cent of the vote against 35 per cent for the PNA. This was not as impressive as its performance in the election of 1970 when, in a field crowded with twelve major political parties, it obtained 39 per cent of the total votes cast.[11] But this wide margin between the number of seats won and popular support is not unusual in parliamentary elections. According to a survey carried out by the government-owned Associated Press of Pakistan (APP), about seventeen million people, or about 55 per cent of the registered voters, cast their ballot. Out of this, the PPP polled about ten million votes and the PNA about six million (59 per cent and 36 per cent respectively).[12]

The results surprised all parties. The PNA lost in three of the four provinces. It won a majority of seats in only one major city, Karachi, but was roundly beaten in Lahore, Faisalabad, Hyderabad, Multan, and Rawalpindi. The PPP's success in the Punjab, where it won 93 per cent of the seats, surprised even the party leader.

Allegations of Rigging the Polls

The PNA alleged that the election had been rigged on a massive scale, rejected the results, boycotted the Provincial Assembly elections scheduled for 10 March, and launched a mass movement to secure Bhutto's resignation and new elections under impartial auspices. General Ziaul Haq, Chief of the Army staff, overthrew the government on the morning of 5 July 1977 and dissolved the newly elected assemblies. Since the election thus became infructuous, discussion of the party manifestos and the campaign may be unnecessary. Instead, the accusations of the PNA need examination.

The PNA's allegation, referred to above, meant that the Bhutto governemnt had resorted to all manners of malpractice, including corruption, coercion, violence, and fraud, to win. There were indeed instances of bogus voting at numerous polling stations in Sindh where the voter turnout had equalled, or even exceeded, the total number of registered voters.[13] Upon preliminary investigation, the Election Commission found that the election in at least a half-dozen National Assembly constituencies in the Punjab had been rigged.[14] The PPP had won 15 seats unopposed in Sindh, and of the remaining 28 seats, the PNA won 11. In the NWFP, the PNA won more than twice as many seats as the PPP and in Balochistan it did not contest. Its charge of rigging was then more pertinent to the PPP's lop-sided victory in the Punjab.

Zia's regime later published a White Paper, consisting of 405 pages of text and 1032 pages of 'documents', to establish that Bhutto had rigged the election. It includes photocopies of a few notes Bhutto sent to his associates and officials, many more notes and memoranda which the latter addressed to him, official reports, and miscellaneous material. It also included statements of public servants who had a role in the conduct of the election which the martial law authorities obtained after Bhutto's ouster. These officials, some of them in jail and others under suspension or threat of dismissal, were pressured to implicate Bhutto in wrongdoing, but the pressure did not work in all cases. The text in the White Paper is malevolent. The notes and memoranda addressed to the Prime Minister and his notations on the margins appear to be genuine, but selective faking cannot be ruled out, and its contents should be approached with considerable caution.[15]

The White Paper opens with an account of a master plan, called the 'Larkana Plan', which Bhutto is alleged to have prepared in April 1976 as a model to be followed in all districts of the country. It would require the civil and police administration at all levels to monitor the election campaign in each constituency from day to day, mobilize the voters in favour of the PPP candidate, and deliver the vote for him on election day. In his rejoinder to the White Paper, written from his prison cell, Bhutto stated that a Sindhi politician had brought this plan to him and that he signed and sent it along to his officials without even reading it.[16] The document is not written in Bhutto's own style, but what is even more important is that it was never implemented. Rao Rashid claims, along with other district officials, that they had never even heard of it.[17] The 'Larkana Plan' may then be disregarded.

The campaign was 'rigged' in other ways. Several high-ranking civil servants assisted with planning and executing the ruling party's election strategy. Rao Rashid headed the election 'cell' in the Prime Minister's Secretariat. Correspondence regarding the election campaign addressed to the Prime Minister passed through his secretary, Afzal Said Khan. Vaqar Ahmad, the Cabinet Secretary, took it upon himself to give advice on matters relating to the election. Nasim Ahmad, Secretary to the Ministry of Information, guided the PPP's publicity campaign. Deputy Commissioners and superintendents of police in the field submitted data on the demographic composition, families and clans, alliances and rivalries, likely candidates and their reputations, in each constituency. The intelligence agencies assessed the relative strength and weakness of PPP candidates and suggested ways of maximizing the party's victories. One million rupees, taken from a secret fund in the Ministry of Information, were placed in a separate account and disbursed to party officials for helping needy candidates.[18] Money out of the secret funds in the Prime Minister's Secretariat and in the provincial governments may also have been used to the ruling party's advantage. Buses, jeeps, and cars belonging to government departments, nationalized banks, and other public authorities were loaned to PPP candidates for use during the election campaign. It is likely that district officers had a role in taking rival candidates out of the race in at least some of the fifteen constituencies in Sindh where the PPP nominees won unopposed.[19]

But were field officers in the districts, from the Deputy Commissioners down to the *naib tehsildar*, and from the police superintendent to the sub-inspector in charge of a local police station, asked to employ unlawful means to enhance the PPP's vote on election day? The 'evidence' presented in the White Paper is problematic. Three provincial chief secretaries, Brigadier Muzaffar Ahmad in the Punjab, Syed Munir Hussain in NWFP, and Nasrum Minallah in Balochistan, asserted in their statements to the martial law authorities that their political superiors had not asked them, and they did not ask any of their subordinates, to rig the election. In the Punjab, where the PPP's victory was amazingly large and where rigging might have taken place more than in any other province, the statements of a few Punjabi field officers included in the White Paper may be considered.

Muhammad Asghar Khan, the Deputy Inspector-General of Police (DIG) in Multan at the time, asserts that, at a meeting concerning elections, the chief secretary named the PPP candidates who must be enabled to win 'at all costs' and the opposition candidates who must be defeated. In another meeting, the Chief Minister of the Punjab told the DIG that the Prime Minister would be 'very annoyed' if the PPP lost both the National Assembly seats in Multan. Asghar Khan claims to have rebuffed the Chief Minister, saying that any interference by the administration would result in a disturbance of the public order. He goes on to say that the Deputy Commissioner and the police superintendent at the district headquarters had 'obviously' agreed to rig the election for the regime. A few paragraphs later in his statement, Asghar Khan changes his mind and observes that 'the police had hardly any role to play in rigging the election'.[20]

Shortly before the election, Naved Asif, Deputy Commissioner of Faisalabad, met Fazal-e-Haq, the Interior Secretary in the central government, who said that he heard Bhutto tell the provincial chief ministers at a recent conference that they must not do anything on election day 'which he may have to explain later on for five years'. But contrary to this address a group of civil servants on the subject of elections, the Punjab Chief Minister, observed that 'he who has a conscience would have to put it to sleep'. In any case, Naved Asif did not receive instructions from his superiors 'to ignore any flagrant violation of the law by the PPP candidates or their supporters', and in actual fact he did order the police to register cases against PPP notables and workers when they broke the law.[21]

Naved Asif notes that the PPP leaders in the area demanded the district administration's help during the campaign, but they were told that none would be forthcoming. On the evening before election day, Mian Ataullah, a federal minister and the PPP candidate for a National Assembly seat from Faisalabad, visited the Deputy Commissioner to inquire if his plans for 'fixing' the election were ready. He hurled 'filthy abuses' at the officer, and threatened to 'fix him up' when told that no such plans had been, or would be, made.[22] On election day Mian Ataullah's men confronted the PNA's supporters at a polling station, opened fire, and killed one person. They were subsequently arrested. The supporters of another PPP candidate, Malik Ghulam Nabi, beat up an official at a polling station in Samundri, and a case was registered against them. This is not to say that the PPP candidates were stopped from doing anything illegal. Four of them organized mobile armed gangs that went to remote polling stations in the district, made a show of force, drove voters away, intimidated the polling staff, and put bogus votes in the ballot boxes. Naved Asif says he reported these incidents to his superiors, and no one asked him to overlook them. In fact, the Divisional Commissioner urged him to take prompt action against the culprits, and the chief secretary told him to do his duty under the law.

A quick reference may now be made to the statements of Syed Sarfraz Hussain and Syed Muhammad Baqir Ali, Deputy Commissioner and Superintendent of Police, respectively, in the district of Gujrat.[23] They say the chief secretary told them in

January 1977 that 'the Prime Minister does not want to win the election in a manner that he wins it in the country but loses it internationally'.[24] In other words, the Prime Minister wanted his party's victory to be credible. Sarfraz Hussain and Baqir Ali understood the chief secretary to mean that the PPP should not win more than 80 per cent, or less than 60 per cent, of the National Assembly seats. They allege that the Divisional Commissioner told them that the PPP candidates in the district 'were to be supported at all costs', and that at a meeting in February 1977 he proposed that ballot boxes filled with favourable votes might be taken to polling stations where the PPP candidates were weak. Upon hearing the Commissioner speak thus, they 'got upset' and said 'this will not be done'. The Commissioner then suggested that the PPP candidates could be given a free hand to ensure their own success and that the administration could leave their gangsters free to do their work. The two officers decided not to get involved in the Commissioner's wicked plan![25]

The police superintendent adds that the PPP candidates in the district were all well-connected and the lower field staff were 'at their beck and call'. They had arranged the rigging of polls, wherever it occurred, due to their hold on the local administration.[26] Naved Asif, the Deputy Commissioner of Faisalabad, made a similar observation that deserves to be quoted:

> Although there did not appear to be a central plan or directive for universally rigging the polls, some of the ministers and candidates appeared to have determined, on their own, to commit serious irregularities. Wherever they could overawe or persuade the administration to join them in this nefarious design they were able to [implement] it with ease. At other places, including Faisalabad, where the administration refused to succumb to their threats or pressures, they chose to bypass the administration and commit irregularities (anyway).... The logistical support available to the district administration was extremely inadequate.... Each polling station had one or two regular and four or five irregular security persons.... There were 1000 polling stations scattered all over the district. Once the polling staff and the security staff had been instructed and sent to their outposts, there was very little that officers at the headquarters could do to... ensure that they would or could do their duties according to their instructions.[27]

The testimony in the White Paper is inconclusive. Some district officers allege that their superiors had asked them to rig the election but that they did not do so. Others say that they were not even asked. The Chief Secrętary of the Punjab government, the district officers in Gujrat, and the Deputy Commissioner of Faisalabad, agree on one point: any rigging that actually took place was done by the candidates themselves, and they were probably helped 'by those local officials whose postings they had been able to arrange through political channels'.[28]

A word should also be said about this matter of postings. Beyond the civil and police officers and their role in the districts, to which reference has already been made, thousands of recruits were needed to conduct the actual voting, safeguard the ballot boxes, take them to the appropriate 'returning officer', count the votes, and announce the results. Tens of thousands of polling stations and several hundred thousand officials were involved. Many of them were school and college teachers, middle-ranking officials in banks or public corporations, and government servants. The provincial government, with help from the district administration, prepared lists of people available for election duty and sent them on to the Election Commission which made the appointments. The Prime Minister's advisors wanted to ensure that people with an anti-PPP bias were not appointed. His notations on their memoranda show that he shared their concern, but we can also see that the advisors wanted to do more than exclude 'bias'. In his notes on the subject, Rao Abdul Rashid emphasized the need for 'absolutely reliable and dependable' persons. In one of these notes, dated 13 July 1976, he comes close to revealing his mind. Speaking about Balochistan, he writes that *tehsildars* and *naib tehsildars* would play a vital role in the election. In selecting them for election duty, considerations of efficiency and honesty would have to be set aside. 'Officers have to be found who are resourceful and who would be fully co-operative. In other words, who can deliver the goods.'[29] The Prime Minister wrote nothing on the margin alongside this paragraph in Rao Rashid's hand.

There was certainly indication from the central leadership a few days before the poll to the candidates to do something for themselves to secure their position in the elections. Some reliable returning officers and presiding officers in the elections were also approached and informed that they should be pre-disposed to help the PPP candidates.[30]

That the elections held on 7 March 1977 were rigged to some extent is beyond doubt, but two aspects of the matter deserve further attention: the extent of rigging, and Bhutto's responsibility for it. It should first be noted that the PNA leaders, encouraged by large and apparently enthusiastic crowds at their meetings, had seen fit to declare that the election would be rigged if it did not produce a victory for them. Asghar Khan, the Tehrik-i-Istiqlal leader, got carried away. He not only predicted victory but vowed to hang Bhutto at the Kohala Bridge on the Jhelum River. Thus, even before the election was held, the PNA leaders had decided to allege rigging in case they did not win. The Zia regime subsequently charged that more than a hundred contests had been rigged, but this statement can be dismissed as a self-serving exaggeration. Professor Ghafoor Ahmad, deputy chief of the Jamaat-i-Islami and a prominent PNA leader, has recently stated that the PPP would have won a 'clear majority' in a fair election.[31] Many observers at the time expected the PPP to win approximately 120 seats. The assessment provided by the Central Intelligence Bureau on 4 March, showed the PPP as a likely winner in ninety-nine constituencies and as a possible winner in another twenty-three. Even if one is cautious and allows the PPP victory in no more than one half of the twenty-three hard contests, it would still have ended up with 110 seats nationwide. The PPP was declared to have won 155 seats, thus it can be said that the election in perhaps as many as forty-five constituencies was rigged. In a conversation with Bhutto shortly after the election, his Finance Minister, Abdul Hafiz Pirzada, placed the number of such constituencies somewhere between thirty to forty.[32]

In a rejoinder to the White Paper referred to earlier, Bhutto said that he had not rigged the election and that he could not be held responsible for the statements and actions of other people. This may be true, but only to an extent. He had assigned certain civil servants and government agencies roles and responsibilities connected to the election. He authorized the disbursement of the government's 'secret funds' to the PPP. It follows that in these particulars, at least, he did, personally and directly, commit malpractices. He might not have ordered the detention of opposition candidates to prevent them from filing their nomination papers but he knew of these happenings and did not move to stop them. At the same time, there is no direct evidence anywhere in the White Paper to show that he ordered the use of violence or fraudulence at polling stations.

Bhutto did say on several occasions that the election must be honest and fair, but many candidates, even civil servants, assumed that malpractices would be allowed. If public officials could be asked, as they had been under all regimes, to fabricate false criminal cases against the government's political adversaries, they would surely be expected to overlook bogus voting to ensure the regime's victory in an election. Bhutto had a role in encouraging this frame of mind. The district administration in his home town, Larkana, arrested his opponent, Jan Muhammad Abbasi, on 18 January 1977 and kept him at an undisclosed location until after the date for filing nomination papers (19 January) had passed. The Prime Minister was, thus, declared to have been elected unopposed. He could have intervened to allow Abbasi an opportunity to file his nomination papers, but he did not do so and, by all accounts, this was a blunder. Bhutto was immensely popular in Larkana, and his victory was certain. Had he come to Abbasi's rescue, his own standing and credibility would have been enhanced. Even if Bhutto did not order Abbasi's arrest, it is difficult to believe that he did not know about it. Following his example, each one of the four provincial chief ministers secured unopposed election to the Provincial Assembly. These developments strengthened the belief among PPP candidates, and the fear in other quarters, that the election would be rigged.[33] These blatant incidents of high-handedness destroyed public confidence in the electoral process from the very beginning and every accusation, true or false, seemed credible to the people.

Another consideration cannot be ignored. Several hundred thousand polling staff were essentially local people. Some of them were related to one or another candidate by family ties, clan, caste, sect, or neighbourhood. The government agencies simply did not have the capacity to undertake a screening so thorough as to ensure that only 'neutral' or pro-PPP persons would be appointed to election duty. Inevitably those siding with the opposition were included. Moreover, the polling staff and even the bureaucracy partook of the polarization existing in society. Many of them liked Bhutto and may have wanted to help the candidate he had nominated, but many other despised him and did what they could to deny his nominee any unfair advantage. There was rigging, yes, but not as much as the PNA alleged. Nor is the probability to be overlooked that the PNA also resorted to malpractices where it could, notably in the city of Karachi.

Before concluding, one cannot ignore a subsequent statement of Justice Sajjad Ahmad Jan, the Chief Election Commissioner, that the elections were a hoax. He said that there was no defect in the ground rules that were prepared by the Election Commission nor was any effort spared to conduct the election fairly and honestly.

The failure of the electoral process was, by and large, due to the candidates of the ruling party who exploited their position and succeeded in hoaxing the officials in charge of the elections, thus destroying the sanctity of the ballot box.[34]

Political Agitation and Cases Pertaining to Election Rigging

As discussed above, the PNA refused to accept the results, charged that the elections were rigged by the government, and boycotted the provincial assemblies election.[35] The central council of the PNA met on 9 March 1977, and made the following decisions:[36]

(a) The elections to the provincial assemblies were to be boycotted.
(b) PNA's nominees declared elected were to resign from the National Assembly.
(c) Immediate resignation of the Chief Election Commissioner was demanded.
(d) A call was given to the people to stage a peaceful country-wide strike on March 11.
(e) Fresh elections were demanded 'under the supervision of the judiciary and the army'.

The boycott of the PNA in the elections to the provincial assemblies on 10 March 1977 was effective and very few voters were seen at the polling stations. The PNA's strike call for 11 March produced a massive response in many of the major cities. In Karachi and Lahore, work stopped completely. Even taxis and privately owned public transport were off the road. Strikers also tried to obstruct rail traffic at many places and the army had to be called in to remove protesting squatters from the railway track.[37]

Encouraged by the response of the people during the Provincial Assembly elections and the strike, on 12 March 1977 the PNA council resolved to launch a mass movement to secure Bhutto's resignation, dismissal of the newly elected assemblies, and holding of new elections under the supervision of the judiciary and the army. Thousands of city-dwellers, spirited, determined, and incensed by the news of electoral fraud, answered the PNA's call. Neither the police *lathi*-charges and tear gas, nor the imposition of martial law in the cities of Lahore, Hyderabad, and Karachi, could subdue the agitation. In April, it spread to smaller towns and by the time the PNA called it off in the first week of June, several hundred people had been killed, many more injured, and tens of thousands jailed. Property worth hundreds of millions of rupees was destroyed and businesses slumped.

Bhutto tried to enter into dialogue with the PNA leader. He wrote a letter to the PNA Chief, Mufti Mahmood, on 13 March in which he invited him for dialogue which would be 'open and sincere'.[38]

The PNA declined to enter into any dialogue with Bhutto. In his broadcast on 12 March 1977 over radio and television, Bhutto said that the National Assembly elections were a settled matter but that he was ready to talk about 'other things'. He said that not only was he prepared to listen to the complaints of the opposition but was also willing to find remedies.[39] Thus, Bhutto was willing to hold the elections to the provincial assemblies again. Later, he indicated that he could negotiate on 24 seats to the National Assembly, in which he said that some of his ministers and partymen had indulged in malpractices during the elections.

In keeping with the above offer, the Election Commission was invested with powers to hold a summary inquiry into a contested election in any constituency if the Commission was satisfied on valid proof that such an election was vitiated by grave illegalities. An ordinance was accordingly promulgated amending the Representation of the Peoples Act, 1976.[40] This remedy was in addition to those which could be obtained under the existing law by way of election petitions. The Election Commission commenced proceedings against a number of newly elected members of the National Assembly which included some former federal ministers, namely Hafizullah Cheema and Malik Akhtar. After summary proceedings, the Election Commission declared the election of a number of members of the National Assembly (belonging to the PPP) as void.[41]

Despite these proceedings before the Election Commission and the unseating of a number of members of the National Assembly, the leader of the PNA and its supporters were not appeased. They were not interested in the few seats in the National Assembly that Bhutto was offering them on a platter. The PNA knew that the PPP would still retain a two-thirds majority after conceding 20 to 24 seats and, knowing the vindictiveness of Bhutto, they realized that he would strike at them with a vengeance as and when he had the opportunity to do so.

In a speech in the National Assembly on 28 April, Bhutto asserted that agencies of the United States government, presumably the CIA and the American Embassy in Islamabad, had instigated and funded the PNA movement. In a subsequent statement he alleged that a 'foreign power', meaning the United States, had recruited Mian Tufail Muhammad (head of the Jamaat-i-Islami) and General Ziaul Haq (Chief of Staff of the Pakistan Army) in a conspiracy to overthrow his government. Bhutto reviled a plot between the Americans, Mian Tufail, and General Zia that, in the event of losing the election, the PNA would accuse Bhutto of rigging it and launch a protest movement; Zia would then seize the government at an appropriate moment and remove Bhutto from the PNA's path; and the succeeding regime would abandon Bhutto's project of acquiring a nuclear reprocessing plant for Pakistan. He alleged that Mian Tufail and even Zia had received money from the Americans. Mian Tufail Muhammad, Bhutto wrote, disbursed some of this money to the heads of other parties in the PNA without giving them a full account of his bargain with the Americans. Similarly, Ziaul Haq did not tell the other Generals all he knew.[42] Bhutto wrote that, after taking over power and upon the urging of Mian Tufail Muhammad, Ziaul Haq destroyed the evidence of the American involvement which his government had collected and which Aziz Ahmad had presented to Cyrus Vance, the American Secretary of State, when the two men met in Paris in May 1977. He was, therefore, not able to substantiate his charge.

Known cases of American intervention in the domestic politics of other countries are far too numerous and frequent to dismiss Bhutto's allegations as simply false, but what could be inferred from it? Bhutto's friends would say that without American help, the PNA movement would not have gathered the momentum that it did, that the government would have controlled it easily. These inferences are infirm. It should first be noted that powerful, even irresistible, mass movements have been launched in Pakistan without American instigation or funding. There was, for instance, the anti-Ahmediya movement in 1953–4, and the anti-Ayub movement in 1968–9. It cannot be assumed that without American support the PNA movement would have failed. Secondly, it cannot be accepted that the American involvement had made Bhutto helpless. He could have thwarted Zia had he acted more expeditiously in making a settlement with the PNA. Thirdly, the Jamaat-i-Islami spokesmen in the PNA did not favour a military coup to oust Bhutto.

The door to negotiations remained shut during the month of April, but other noteworthy developments took place: seven members of the National Assembly and six members of the Punjab Provincial Assembly, elected on the PPP ticket, resigned from their seats; Dr Mubashir Hasan walked away from his post as the party's secretary-general; Khurshid Hasan Meer, a former federal minister, and Taj Langah, once the deputy secretary-general of the party in the Punjab, supported the demand for new elections.[43] Seven PPP members of the National Assembly met Bhutto on 16 April to urge a new election. These desertions made Bhutto appear weak.[44]

While the top, and even the second-ranking, PNA leaders were in jail, their movement was guided by the *imams* in mosques and other spokesmen of the Islamist establishment, who added the demand to Islamize society to the PNA's cluster of demands relating to the elections. On 17 April, Bhutto, in an attempt to dislodge them, banned drinking and gambling, shut down night-clubs and race-courses, and reconstituted the Islamic Advisory Council with the mandate to propose measures for Islamizing the country's laws within six months.[45] But the mass movement against his regime would not stop. Curfews had already been imposed in the cities of Karachi, Lahore, Faisalabad, and Hyderabad.

Partial Martial Law and the Lahore High Court Verdict

On 26 April 1977, martial law was imposed in Karachi, Lahore, and Hyderabad, under Article 245 of the Constitution. It was made clear that this martial law had no parallel with the two previous martial laws of Ayub and Yahya, and was imposed by the federal government under the powers it enjoyed under the Constitution.[46] The imposition of martial law was challenged before the Lahore High Court and a full bench of the Court accepted the writ petition and declared the martial law unconstitutional.[47] The Court took notice of the fact that Article 196 of the 1956 Constitution, Article 223-A of the 1962 Constitution, Article 278 of the Interim Constitution of 1972, Article 237 of the 1973 Constitution and Article 34 of the Indian Constitution all related to the powers of the Parliament to make laws of indemnity. The Court found it noteworthy that while the word 'martial law' occurs in all the aforesaid relevant provisions of the previous constitutions of Pakistan and

Article 34 of the Indian Constitution, it was conspicuous in its absence in Articles 234 and 245 of the 1973 Constitution. This clearly showed, the Court held, that the framers of the 1973 Constitution intended to bury martial law as was evident in the speech of the Prime Minister on 21 April 1972. Apart from this, the Court noticed that the Articles of other constitutions provided not only for passing laws indemnifying acts done by the concerned persons (including army officers) during the period of martial law, but also provided for making laws validating any sentence passed, punishment inflicted, and forfeiture ordered during the period. But Article 237 of the 1973 Constitution does not provide for making laws validating any sentence passed, punishment inflicted, and forfeiture ordered by them (the military courts). This glaring difference clearly indicates, the Court held, that the 1973 Constitution neither envisages the imposition of martial law nor the exercise by the armed forces of any judicial functions. The Court concluded that the operation being carried out by the armed forces in the district of Lahore was not 'martial law' in any of the recognized meanings of the term.

Seventh Amendment to the Constitution

In the early days of May 1977, there were contacts between Bhutto and his assistants in the PPP with the PNA leader which were mostly confined to Sihala near Rawalpindi. Bhutto's offer of dialogue and settlement was discussed by PNA leaders and a comprehensive response was given to the offer. The PNA demanded the immediate lifting of emergency, martial law, and section 144 of the Code of Criminal Procedure, the release of all political prisoners, dissolution of special courts and tribunals, removal of Press curbs, dissolution of National and Provincial Assemblies not later than seven days after an agreement was reached, holding of general elections to the National and Provincial Assemblies simultaneously within a period of thirty days after their dissolution, the appointment of a new Chief Election Commissioner, and the constitution of a new Election Commission with mutual consent, appointments of Governors of all four provinces with mutual consent, and changes in certain key appointments with mutual agreement to ensure free and fair polls.[48]

It is noticeable that the PNA leader dropped the basic demand of Bhutto's resignation which shows a shift in their thinking and that they were disposed to dialogue and settlement. Bhutto asked the PNA leader to stop issuing calls for further demonstrations and to reduce their charter of demand if they were sincerely interested in a meaningful dialogue with the ruling party. He asked four or five of his ministers to have preliminary discussions with the PNA leader in Sihala.[49] There was also Saudi Arabia's effort to mediate between the PPP and the PNA. Bhutto met the PNA Chief, Mufti Mahmood, in Sihala on 12 May and expressed the hope of a settlement. The PNA, in its press release on 12 May, said that it was sticking to its basic three demands and that there would be no compromise on them.[50]

At this point, contacts between the PPP and the PNA were temporarily suspended. Bhutto informed the National Assembly about the opposition's final 'no' to two months efforts to start a dialogue. He said that fresh elections to the National Assembly, in the conditions prevailing, would be disastrous for the nation because of the threat of foreign intervention[51] and grave internal problems. He said that since he had been made the central figure of the opposition's campaign, he had decided to put the matter in the hands of the people through a referendum.[52] He proposed that a joint session of Parliament would pass a temporary amendment to the Constitution to provide for a referendum. Accordingly, the Seventh Amendment to the Constitution was passed and became effective on 16 May 1977.

The Seventh Amendment provided for a referendum to demonstrate confidence in the Prime Minister.[53] The referendum was to be held in accordance with a law made by Parliament. A Referendum Commission was set up to hold the referendum, count the votes, and declare its result. If, on the final count of the votes cast at the referendum, the Prime Minister failed to obtain a majority of the total votes cast, he would be deemed to have resigned from office. Another provision of the Seventh Amendment barred High Courts from exercising jurisdiction under Article 199 in relation to any area in which the armed forces were acting in aid of the civil power in pursuance of Article 245. However, the proceedings pending before the High Courts were saved.

The Seventh Amendment was not only a novel but a rather unusual constitutional provision and was inherently repugnant to the parliamentary system. A vote of confidence is to be obtained from the Parliament in a parliamentary system and not through a referendum. If a prime minister is obliged to go to the people for a vote of confidence, then he owes nothing to the parliament and should not be answerable to it. It tantamounts to a presidential system and the prime minister literally assumes the attributes of a president after winning any such referendum since referendum is conceptionally a part of the presidential system.

Why was the proposal of holding a referendum made and enacted? Why was it not pursued after the constitutional amendment? The answer to the first question is rather simple. At that point in time, the prospects of dialogue and settlement with the opposition had become more or less negligible. Both the PPP and the PNA had taken an uncompromising stance on the three basic demands of the dissolution of the National Assembly, holding of new elections, and removal of the Chief Election Commissioner. The answer to the second question is rather difficult and complex. Nothing was heard of the referendum soon after the passing of the Seventh Amendment and no law was enacted by Parliament for the constitution of the Referendum Commission. One speculation which appears to carry weight is that the armed forces leader indicated to Bhutto to negotiate with the opposition and forget about any referendum. This speculation has a ring of truth about it because Bhutto, at one stage, had asked the chiefs of the armed forces to share power with him and had thus accepted the role of the armed forces. He also appointed General (Retd.) Tikka Khan as Defence Adviser to liaise with army generals.

Parleys for Political Settlement

On 18 May 1977, Bhutto visited Mufti Mahmood at the Sihala 'rest' house (a jail for dignitaries near Rawalpindi), reiterated his willingness to hold a new election, and once again invited the PNA to talks. Negotiations began on 3 June. Abdul Hafiz Pirzada and Kausar Niazi, both federal ministers, assisted Bhutto while Mufti Mahmood, Nawabzada Nasrullah Khan, and Professor Ghafoor Ahmad spoke for the PNA. The meetings took place in the Cabinet Room of the Prime Minister's Secretariat, often in the evenings, and proceeded in a pleasant environment. Each time the PNA spokesmen arrived at the Secretariat, the Prime Minister came out and greeted them at the steps of the main building. On a few occasions at least, he entertained them to a meal and ordered special desserts for Mufti Mahmood who was known to have a weakness for sweets. There were times when the two sides appeared deadlocked, and Bhutto broke spells of awkward silence by engaging Mufti Mahmood in light chit-chat. The PNA representatives had withdrawn their demand for Bhutto's resignation and while they were firm on most other issues, they yielded on matters of detail. Bhutto, too, was conciliatory.

A word now to introduce the actors beyond the conference table who influenced the negotiations and their outcome. The PNA spokesmen at the table were not plenipotentiaries. Any agreement they negotiated required the unanimous approval of the PNA council which consisted of two representatives for each of its nine constituent parties. Four of them did not really desire an agreement with the government and preferred that the army oust Bhutto, take over the government, and then hold an election. They were Asghar Khan (Tehrik-i-Istiqlal), Sher Baz Mazari, Begum Nasim Wali Khan (National Democratic Party), and Maulana Shah Ahmad Noorani (Jamiatul Ulema-i-Pakistan). Asghar Khan tried, more than once, to assure the PNA council that the army would hold new elections within ninety days of taking power. It is noteworthy that, as early as 4 May 1977, he had addressed a message to the armed forces in which he invited them to destroy the Bhutto government which, he said, was illegal:

> As men of honour [it is for you] to do your duty and the call of duty in these trying circumstances is not blind obedience to unlawful commands. There comes a time in the lives of nations when each man has to ask himself whether he is doing the right thing. For you that time has come. Answer this call honestly and save Pakistan.[54]

Bhutto also had a part, unwittingly, of course, in encouraging the idea of military intervention. He involved the generals in devising his responses to the PNA agitation, discussed the political situation with them as it developed from one week to the next, invited them to Cabinet meetings, kept them posted on the progress of his negotiations with the PNA, and solicited their reactions to its proposals. Twice in these meetings the possibility of a military coup was mentioned. On 31 May, Kausar Niazi referred to it as one of the possible ways of ending the current crisis. On 14 June, Bhutto lectured the Generals on the possibility of a coup, making the rather unconvincing argument that governing a conntry was 'no bed of roses'. On both occasions, General Zia stood up, pledged loyalty to the Prime Minister, and assured him that he and his colleagues had no thought of taking power.[55] In April, Zia had advised the imposition of martial law in certain cities, but in May the corps commanders protested that the army should not be asked to shoot down people. They professed to be praying for the success of the negotiations with the PNA, while erecting a barrier to that success by vetoing two of the PNA's critical demands: the army's return to the barracks in Balochistan, and the disbandment of a special tribunal that was trying Wali Khan and other NAP leaders in Hyderabad jail. Begum Nasim Wali Khan and Sher Baz Mazari were not likely to accept an agreement that did not meet these two conditions, and the Generals knew it.

Some of Bhutto's ministers and party notables, too, opposed a settlement on the PNA's terms. Abdul Hafiz Pirzada acted the part of a tough negotiator. In his advice to Bhutto, he exaggerated the latter's support within the army and among the masses, understated the PNA's influence, and berated its motives and credentials. The ministers who had won the last election by rigging it, and who feared an honest one, voted against concessions to the PNA. Still others wished to appear as intensely loyal to Bhutto and, therefore, wholly unyielding to his enemies.

What was the substance of the negotiations? At their ninth meeting on 15 June, the two sides reached an agreement on all the basic issues, new elections and the dates on which these would be held, a new election commission with enhanced authority, the release of political prisoners, and the establishment of an 'Implementation Council' to supervise the proposed elections. Ghafoor Ahmad and Pirzada were asked to fill in the details. Then, without prior notice to the PNA, Bhutto proceeded on a quick tour of neighbouring Muslim countries on 17 June. In his absence, Pirzada and Ghafoor Ahmad made no progress in their mission because they could not work together. The PNA team now prepared a revised draft agreement, including additional specifics about the constitutional status, composition, authority and powers of the Implementation Council, and presented it to Bhutto upon his return to Pakistan on 23 June. At their eleventh meeting on 25 June, the two teams examined each clause in this revised draft. Bhutto accepted most of it, suggested minor changes of a scheduling nature, proposed to postpone consideration of a few items, and asked that the Implementation Council limit itself to matters relevant to the holding of new elections.

Instead of picking up the thread of negotiations where it had been left on 25 June, the PNA prepared still another, and this time 'final' draft. The council approved it on 27 June and authorized Mufti Mahmood to sign an accord with the Prime Minister if he accepted the draft but insisted that any changes he might suggest, howsoever inconsequential, must be brought back to the council. The presentation of this draft as an 'ultimatum' caused the government some irritation, but Mufti Mahmood and Bhutto were able to overcome it in talks on 29 June.

The two sides began their twelfth negotiating session at eight o'clock in the evening on 1 July and when they rose at 6:30 the next morning, ten-and-a-half hours later, they had reached agreement on all issues, large and small. Both sides made concessions and, as a result, the PNA's 'final' draft had undergone some change. The more important provisions of this agreement are reproduced below to have a measure of the concessions Bhutto made to his opponents:[56]

1. The assemblies elected on 7 and 10 March 1977 would be dissolved on 15 July; new elections to the National and Provincial Assemblies would be held on 8 and 10 October respectively, and 'President's rule' would prevail in the provinces until then.
2. An Implementation Council, composed equally of the government and of PNA representatives, chaired by the Prime Minister, and by Mufti Mahmood in his absence, would ensure the holding of free and fair elections, and to this end it would:
   (a) exercise the powers of the President of Pakistan and those of the federal government in relation to the provincial governors and administrators;
   (b) proceed against government officials accused or suspected of obstructing the holding of free and fair elections;
   (c) approve appointments to all key posts in the central and provincial administrations;
   (d) no law, ordinance, or regulation relating to elections or to the work of the Council, would be made without its prior authorization;
   (e) in case of disagreement between the government and PNA representatives in the Council, the issue would be referred to the Supreme Court which must settle it within 72 hours;
   (f) the Prime Minister would secure the implementation of the Council's decisions.
3. New provincial governors would be appointed with the PNA's approval.
4. The government would lift the ongoing state of emergency, restore fundamental rights, release all political prisoners, and disband all special tribunals except the one trying the NAP leaders in Hyderabad jail.
5. The chairman and members of a new Election Commission would be named with the PNA's approval, and the Commission would have the administrative and financial authority necessary for holding fair elections, including the authority to summon the armed forces for assistance.
6. The army would cease its operations in Balochistan within forty-five days of the signing of the accord.
7. All amendments to the 1973 Constitution which had the effect of limiting the rights of citizens or the authority of judges would be repealed.
8. The government would secure the passage of laws necessary for putting this accord into effect.

The PNA council had decided not to insist upon the dissolution of the Hyderabad tribunal and its negotiators withdrew the demand for a temporary constitutional amendment that would protect the Implementation Council from legal challenges to its existence and authority. It is clear that Bhutto made far-reaching and, in some instances, even radical concessions. In agreeing to the Implementation Council the PNA wanted, he accepted an authority that would override him and his Cabinet.

This agreement needed the PNA council's approval. Its negotiators had believed that the changes in their 'final' draft, which they had accepted, were minor and that the council would not hesitate to approve them. In the words of Ghafoor Ahmad, this was 'a comprehensive and an exemplary accord which two rival parties had concluded through negotiations in the best interest of the nation.'[57] But when the council met on the evening of 2 July, Asghar Khan, Sher Baz Mazari, and Begum Nasim Wali Khan condemned the negotiators for entertaining Bhutto's proposed changes. After further discussion, and consultation with its legal advisers, the council produced nine additional 'points' with the instruction to Mufti Mahmood to sign the accord if the Prime Minister accepted them. The more important of these points were as follows:[58]

1. The Implementation Council must have constitutional protection.
2. Provincial Governors would not be changed without the PNA's consent.
3. The Federal Security Force would be placed under the authority of the Army General Headquarters (GHQ), and not under the Ministry of Defence as Bhutto had wanted.
4. Special tribunals would follow the ordinary courtroom procedure.
5. The President of Pakistan must sign and promulgate any ordinances the Implementation Council might send him to remove such difficulties as had arisen in the way of its mission.

Political Impasse and Imposition of Martial Law

The PNA spokesmen took these 'points' to Bhutto at 10:00 p.m. on 3 July 1977. They said that they regretted having to introduce changes at this stage but, as he knew, their acceptance of his draft had been contingent upon the council's approval. Mufti Mahmood and Nawabzada Nasrullah Khan argued that their new points, being essentially of a technical nature, did not materially affect the accord they had reached the day before. That was not entirely true, for the demand regarding special tribunals would, in effect, disestablish the Hyderabad tribunal, which was something the generals still opposed. According to Kausar Niazi, the Mufti and the Nawabzada also reported that some members of their council were expecting the generals to intervene and impose martial law. Bhutto consulted his team in an adjoining room. Niazi favoured acceptance, but Pirzada insisted that the talk of military intervention was a mere bluff, that the generals were loyal to Bhutto, and that the PNA should be made to bend. Bhutto then told Mufti Mahmood that he needed more time to respond. Upon hearing this, the three PNA representatives left visibly anguished.[59]

The dominant view at a Cabinet meeting later the same evening, opposed further concessions to the PNA. Zia, who was also present, stood up once again, both hands on his chest, to assure Bhutto of his 'complete support', adding 'please rely on us, we are your strong arm.'[60] Bhutto then told newsmen that the PNA had gone back on the agreement it had made, presented new demands, and that he would now have to consult his associates. The newspapers on 4 July carried the report that the government and the PNA had once again hit an impasse.

Bhutto held his last Cabinet meeting on the evening of Monday, 4 July 1977. The minutes of this meeting show that he had second thoughts during the day. He observed that the continuing conflict with the PNA would damage the country's inner stability and international standing. If the PNA revived its agitation, and even if the government were able to control it, negotiations with its leaders would have to be held again. Mere restoration of 'law and order would not solve the problem'. The armed forces had stood by the government, he said, but 'they would be out to a severe strain' in case of another agitation.[61] Kausar Niazi recalls that, when the Cabinet rose, Zia had a private meeting with Bhutto, after which the General left hurriedly, unsmiling.

It appears that on the evening of 4 July, apprehensive of a military coup, Bhutto was ready to make a settlement with the PNA. He consulted further with Abdul Hafiz Pirzada, Ghulam Mustafa Jatoi (the Chief Minister of Sindh), and Mumtaz Bhutto. Pirzada still opposed concessions to the PNA, but Jatoi and Mumtaz Bhutto counselled acceptance of its latest demands. At a press conference held at 11:30 p.m. Bhutto announced his intention to accept the PNA's terms, saying; 'The PNA negotiating team had brought in ten new points; they did so apologetically, saying they were helpless; perhaps they were; but I am not helpless, and so I shall sign the accord tomorrow'.[62] But before the 'tomorrow' of Bhutto's declared intention could dawn, Zia had struck and overthrown him and martial law was declared throughout the country on the night between 4 and 5 July.

The version of the evening of 4 July although given by Kausar Niazi, a close associate of Bhutto, is not free from doubt. If Bhutto was really keen to sign the accord, there was nothing to stop him from doing so on the evening of 4 July. All of the PNA leadership was available in Sihala.

The Fall of Bhutto: An Assessment

Elections in Pakistan had been rigged before, notably the presidential election in 1965 and the Provincial Assembly elections in the early 1950s, but rigging in these instances did not arouse the mass anger it did in 1977. The people of Pakistan were evidently not of the same mind now as they were in those earlier periods. Bhutto had changed them, polarized them. Those who disapproved of him did so with a passion. Perceiving his party's victory as dishonest, they were determined to undo it. His supporters, on the other hand, had become the 'silent majority'. The party that might have mobilized them on his behalf lacked the organizational capacity to undertake such a task. In June 1977 when Bhutto asked Ghulam Hussain, the PPP secretary-general, to call party conventions presumably to make a show of strength, the one held in Multan disintegrated as rival factions threw furniture at one another.[63] The cardinal fact about Bhutto's negotiations with the PNA, is that he bargained from a position of political weakness and the relevant forces in the country, including the generals, knew this to be the case.

Zia knew that Bhutto was about to make a settlement with the PNA.[64] Yet he moved to forestall it. Why? An obvious explanation may be that, at this point, he simply did not want the government-PNA negotiations to succeed. He saw that Bhutto had weakened. His own arrangements were all made, and the call to power, which had been ringing loud and insistent in his ear, had now become irresistible. But the preparations for a coup are not made in a day. It is probable that Zia had resolved to oust Bhutto as early as April 1977, when he and the corps commanders advised the imposition of martial law in Lahore, Hyderabad, and Karachi. The General was not only a 'pious' man in terms of traditional Islamic observances, he was also favourably disposed toward the Jamaat-i-Islami. Bhutto was known to be 'sinful', and his regime had not only persecuted but insulted the Jamaat-i-Islami leaders. It stands to reason, then, that Zia did not regard Bhutto as a fit ruler for Muslim Pakistan. His remarkable capacity for duplicity kept his disapproval of Bhutto, and his own design, hidden.

But had Bhutto promptly settled matters with the PNA, Zia might not have found the opportunity to execute his plans. No regime in Pakistan, or perhaps even elsewhere, submits to an agitation as soon as it begins. Its first impulse is to exhaust or suppress the agitators. Bhutto should have known from his own experience of the mass movement which overthrew Ayub that concessions can come too late to save a regime. Negotiations with the PNA had been made by the end of April. Its demand for Bhutto's resignation was admittedly irritating, but if instead of wielding the stick once again and sending the PNA leaders back to jail, he had offered to hold new elections under credible safeguards, the PNA would probably have withdrawn this demand as, indeed, it later did.

Bhutto was unusually forthcoming once he sat down with the PNA spokesmen at the conference table, but he was late in arriving there, having wasted the entire month of May, and he allowed a week in June to be frittered away after the negotiations had begun to move forward. He did sense a threat to his political survival but, deceived by Zia's repeated professions of loyalty, he did not realize how imminent it was. He thought he had the time for a little more of the traditional diplomacy. This was a miscalculation, but in saying this we do, of course, have the advantage of hindsight.

It is difficult to understand how Asghar Khan, Sher Baz Mazari, and Begum Nasim Wali Khan, were persuaded that the army would seize power only to let them have it. One could say they were simply naive, or that their hatred of Bhutto blinded them. But in an important respect their inclination was similar to Bhutto's. Instead of employing political means to deal with his opponents, Bhutto had increasingly relied upon the bureaucracy and the security forces to counter them. He found that to be easier. The PNA 'hardliners' were doing the same. They looked to the army to remove their formidable foe from the scene and clear the road to power for them. Bhutto paid for neglecting his craft, which was 'politics of the people', first by losing his office and then his life. The PNA leaders, including Asghar Khan and his friends, had to endure oblivion, some of it in prison, for the next eight years while Zia ruled Pakistan under Martial Law. Meanwhile, the nation suffered political decay.

To the amazement of his opponents, Bhutto retained an unswerving following among the Pakistani masses. The repeated attempts to discredit him by the army *junta*, the media, and his political opponents failed to dull his appeal. The embers of the fires he lit could not easily be extinguished. Throughout his political crusade, he appealed directly to the poor, reiterating that they were the 'fountain of power'. His economic policies although wasteful, were re-distributive, and did to some extent improve the lot of the common man, at least to the extent of his self respect. During his tenure, Bhutto increasingly toured the remotest corners of Pakistan carrying his message: 'Zulfiqar Ali Bhutto is the friend and saviour of the poor'. And in Pakistan, that message was widely believed.

Another interesting argument put forward by Shahid Javed Burki in his book *Pakistan under Bhutto, 1971-1977*,[65] is that the election Bhutto called in March 1977 could not have averted the crises that developed in the spring of that year, because by then Bhutto had lost the support of the bulk of the politically articulate electorate, the middle class. It was the political know-how of this class, combined with the mass support that Bhutto had been able to build for himself, that had assured him victory in the elections of 1970. Elections as a device for political selection are a device that the middle class use and understand. They are not so used or understood by the large mass of people who are at the fringes of the political arena. Elections can, therefore, lead to political succession only when these two classes, the middle and the lower, work together to achieve reconcilable goals.

In 1946, the Muslim League's remarkable and unexpected victory in all parts of Muslim India was the product of such a coalition between the two classes. Jinnah's demand for the revival of Islam in the Indian subcontinent and the creation of a new Muslim state in the area were popular with the masses. The masses supported not only the Muslim League but helped the middle class that dominated the party to achieve its objectives within the legal and constitutional framework of the day. A similar coalition of the two classes of people made it possible for Bhutto and the PPP in West Pakistan and Mujib and the Awami League in East Pakistan to use elections held within Yahya's 'legal framework' order. In fact, the coalition was powerful enough to establish an independent Bengali state in East Pakistan and the establishment of popular civilian rule in West Pakistan despite all odds.

But because of the fundamental changes that had occurred in Pakistan's polity and economy since the assumption of political control by Bhutto and the PPP in 1971, elections could not be expected to produce the results that either Bhutto or his opponents hoped for. No matter what the results of the elections had been, political tension was inevitable. The fact that the tension generated by the elections surprised Bhutto suggests that he had not fully understood the political dynamics that he had helped unleash. His continuing popularity with large segments of the population did get him votes in the elections and win him seats in the central and provincial legislatures, but they did not win him the power that he needed to introduce changes in the political and economic order. These were the changes that threatened the middle class.

Bhutto did not fully anticipate the extent of the middle classes' disillusionment with the way his economic and political programmes had evolved. He seems not to have comprehended their anger and their sense of humiliation at what they saw as a deliberate attack on their interests and system of values. What gave the middle classes tremendous political power was the remarkable change that had occurred in the social composition of the armed forces.

Why did Bhutto, credited as he has always been with a remarkable knowledge and sense of history and historical movements, lead himself toward such a tragic end? The answer probably lies in his background, his character, and in his disposition. He was a rural aristocrat who had developed a deep empathy for the poor. He was at home in two very different worlds: the world occupied by Pakistan's elite and the world in which lived the majority of Pakistan's under-privileged people. But he was not comfortable with the ground that lay in-between; the growing space occupied by the middle classes. He did not understand their value system, did not appreciate their economic interests, and did not comprehend the power they had begun to wield. He abandoned them and they allowed him to go to the gallows.

Burki's analysis focuses on the importance of the role of middle classes in society because they man all the important centres of power in the country: the armed forces, the bureaucracy, the judiciary, and the professions. Alienating them would deprive any party, even if backed by working classes, from effective administration and meaningful government. If these centres of power become hostile, then they can lead to the fate Bhutto met with, despite his popularity with the common man and his ability to win elections on the basis of universal adult franchise.

NOTES

1. *Dawn*. 8 January 1977.
2. Government of Pakistan, White Paper on the Conduct of the General Elections in March 1977 (Rawalpindi, July 1978). Rao Rashid's secret note to the Prime Minister dated 29 July 1976, pp. A. 212-16 (Annexures).
3. Ali Muhammad Rashdi's note to the Prime Minister and Rao Rashid's note dated 25 June 1976 in the White Paper, pp. A 25, A 203.
4. Rao Rashid's note to the Prime Minister dated 4 May 1976 in the White Paper, pp. A 473-4.
5. Rao Rashid's note to the Prime Minister dated 1 February 1977 in the White Paper, p. A 502.
6. Bhutto's notations on Rao Rashid's note of 4 May 1976 and his notes dated 21 October and 13 November 1976 in the White Paper, pp. A 470-72 and pp. A 570-78.
7. See the Intelligence Bureau's estimates dated 19 February and 4 March 1977 (and one undated) in the White Paper, pp. A 517, 576, 578, 581 and a detailed analysis for each Constituency at pp. A 584-633.
8. White Paper, p. A 517.
9. Statement of Punjab Chief Secretary to the Martial Law Authorities in the White Paper, p. A 762.
10. Abdur Rashid, Rao, *Jo Main ne Dekha* (*That Which I saw*), Urdu (Lahore, Atishfishan Publications, 1985), pp. 224-5.
11. Burki, Shahid Javed, *Pakistan under Bhutto, 1971-1977*, 1988, Macmillan Press, Hong Kong, pp. 196-7.
12. Rashid, Akhtar, *Elections '77 and Aftermath: A Political Appraisal*, 1981. P.R.A.A.A.S. Publishers, Islamabad, p. 9.
13. Burney, I. H., 'The March 1977 Elections: An Analysis', *Pakistan Economist*, 23 July 1977, pp. 13-22.
14. Ibid., p.18.

15. Syed, Anwar H., *The Discourse and Politics of Zulfiqar Ali Bhutto*, 1992, The Macmillan Press Ltd., Hong Kong, p. 226-7.
16. Bhutto, Zulfiqar Ali, *If I am Assassinated*, 1979, Vikas Publishing House Pvt Ltd., New Delhi, pp. 69-70.
17. Abdur Rashid, Rao, *That Which I Saw*, *supra*, note 10, p. 226.
18. Correspondence between Afzal Said Khan (Prime Minister's secretary) and Nasim Ahmad (information secretary) in the White Paper, pp. A 327-30.
19. The statement of Mohammad Khan Junejo (Home Secretary of Sindh) in the White Paper, pp. A 255-6.
20. White Paper, pp. A 901-903, 907, 909.
21. White Paper, pp. 913, 915-16.
22. White Paper, p. A 920.
23. The statements of these two officers appear in the White Paper at A 785-91, 792-6.
24. Syed Sarfraz Hussain's statement in the White Paper, p. A 787.
25. White Paper, pp. 788-9, 793-4.
26. White Paper, p. A 795.
27. White Paper, p. A 924.
28. Statement of Chief Secretary of the Punjab in the White Paper, p. A 762.
29. Rao Rashid's note to the Prime Minister in the White Paper, pp. A 267-8.
30. The author learnt this from the presiding officers in a constituency of National Assembly from Sargodha. The author also learnt from a PPP candidate for a Provincial Assembly seat in Lahore that he and other candidates were instructed by the party leadership to meet and have communication with the presiding officers in their constituencies. What was the purpose of this was not indicated.
31. Ahmad, Professor Ghafoor, *Phir Marshall Law Aa Gaya* (Again Comes the Martial Law), 1988, *Jang* Publishers, Lahore, pp. 95, 100-101.
32. Niazi, Kausar, *Aur Line Kut Gayee* (And the Telephone Line was Cut), 1987, *Jang* Publications, Lahore, p. 41.
33. Syed, Anwar H., *The Discourse and Politics of Zulfiqar Ali Bhutto*, *supra*, note 15, pp. 232-3.
34. *Dawn*, 29 November 1977.
35. Press Conference of Asghar Khan of 8 March 1977. *Dawn*, 9 March 1977,
36. Press Conference of Secretary General of the PNA, Rafique Bajwa on 9 March 1977. *Dawn*, 10 March 1977.
37. Rashid, Akhtar, *Election '77 and Aftermath*, *supra*, note 12, p. 12.
38. *Dawn*, 21 March 1977. It reproduced the contents of the letter of Bhutto dated 13 March letter in reply of 14 March from Mufti Mahmood and another letter of Bhutto to Mufti Mahmood on 15 March 1977.
39. *Dawn*, 13 March 1977.
40. Representation of the People (Second Amendment) Ordinance, 1977. Ordinance XV of 1977. PLD 1977 Central Statutes 212. Representation of the People (Third Amendment) Ordinance, 1977 (Ordinance XVI of 1977) PLD 1977 Central Statutes 213.
41. In re: Complaint of Malpractices in Constituency No. NA-57, Sargodha v PLD 1977 Journal 164. In re: Complaint regarding the malpractices committed during the election to Constituency No. NA-80, Lyallpur-XIII, PLD 1977 Journal 187. In re: Complaint of malpractices in the election to Constituency No. NA-76, Lyallpur-IX, PLD 1977 Journal 190. In re: Malpractices committed in the election to Constituency No. NA-89, Kasur-I, PLD 1977 Journal 198. Ziauddin v Rai Hafizullah Khan Tariq, PLD 1977 Journal 215.
42. Bhutto, Zulfiqar Ali, *If I am Assassinated*, *supra*, note 16, Chapter II.
43. *Dawn*, 17 April 1977.
44. Syed, Anwar H., *The Discourse and Politics of Zulfiqar Ali Bhutto*, *supra*, note 15, pp. 226.
45. *Dawn*, 18 April 1977.
46. *Dawn*, 27 April 1977.
47. Darvesh M. Arbey, Advocate v Federation of Pakistan, PLD 1977 Lahore 846.

48. *Dawn*, 6 May 1977.
49. *Dawn*, 9 May 1977.
50. *Dawn*, 13 May 1977.
51. By 'foreign intervention', he meant US intervention against him.
52. *Dawn*, 14 May 1977.
53. Constitution (Seventh Amendment) Act, 1977. Act XXIII of 1977. PLD 1977 Central Statutes 304.
54. Text of Asghar Khan's message may be seen in Professor Ghafoor Ahmad's book, *Phir Marshall Law Aa Gaya*, *supra*, note 31, pp. 29-30.
55. Niazi, Kausar, *Aur Line Kut Gayee*, *supra*, note 32, pp. 177, 184, 195-6.
56. See the text in Professor Ghafoor Ahmad's book, *Phir Marshall Law Aa Gaya*, *supra*, note 31, pp. 234-8, A 74-80.
57. Ibid., p. 239.
58. Ibid., pp. 245-6.
59. Niazi, Kausar, *Aur Line Kut Gayee*, *supra*, note 32, pp. 177, 184, 195-6.
60. Ahmad, Professor Ghafoor, *Phir Marshall Law Aa Gaya*. *supra*, note 31, p. 249.
61. Minutes of the meeting, prepared by the Cabinet Deputy Secretary, may be seen in the White Paper, pp. A 1026-7.
62. Niazi, Kausar, *Aur Line Kut Gayee*, *supra*, note 32, pp. 200, 202.
63. Ibid., p. 179.
64. The minutes of the Cabinet meeting on 4 July 1977 do not list General Ziaul Haq among those present. The minutes were prepared after his coup, and the omission of his name may have been deliberate. But as we have seen above, Kausar Niazi recalls that the general was present.
65. Burki, Shahid Javed, *Pakistan under Bhutto, 1971-1977*, *supra*, note 11, pp. 200-201.

PART VI

THE ZIA ERA:
JULY 1977 TO AUGUST 1988

25

ZIA'S 'OPERATION FAIRPLAY'

During the night between 4 and 5 July, the armed forces led by Army Chief General Muhammad Ziaul Haq, took over the administration of the country. Bhutto, his Cabinet colleagues, and top PNA leaders were placed under 'protective custody'. The National and Provincial Assemblies were dissolved, and martial law was imposed throughout the country. In his broadcast to the nation over radio and television on 5 July, Zia said that he had faith in democracy and that elections would be held in ninety days and power would be transferred to the elected representatives of the people. However, all political activities were banned till further orders.

Having assumed the office of Chief Martial Law Administrator (CMLA), Zia announced that he wanted to make it 'absolutely clear' that he neither had any political ambitions nor did the army want to be detracted from the profession of soldiering. He said that he was obliged to step in to fill the vacuum created by the political leaders and accepted this challenge as a true 'soldier of Islam'.[1] He promised free and fair polls and transfer of power to the elected representatives of the people. 'In the next three months, my total attention will be concentrated on holding the elections and I would not like to dissipate my powers and energies as Chief Martial Law Administrator on anything else.' He said that the tension created during the political confrontation in the country and the mutual distrust between the PPP and the PNA had made the prospects of political compromise impossible. At the end of his address, he said what was to become his justification to remain in power in the years to come:

> To conclude, I must say that the spirit of Islam demonstrated during the recent movement was commendable. It proves that Pakistan, which was created in the name of Islam, will continue to survive only if it sticks to Islam. That is why, I consider the introduction of the Islamic system as an essential pre-requisite for the country.[2]

The operation of taking over the country by the armed forces was code-named 'Operation Fairplay'. President Chaudhry Fazal Elahi whose term was to expire in August 1978, was allowed to continue after Zia had a meeting with him on 5 July. He also met the Chief Justice of Pakistan, Mr Justice Yakub Ali. He appeared to be satisfied with his talks with the President and the Chief Justice. The Governors of the provinces had also ceased to hold office and, in their place, the Chief Justices of the four provinces were taken as acting Governors of their respective provinces.

Constitution Suspended and Laws (Continuance in Force) Order, 1977, Promulgated

Unlike the previous two proclamations of martial law, the Constitution was not abrogated but was only held in abeyance.[3] However, like the 1958 martial law, Laws (Continuance in Force) Order 1977, was promulgated to administer the affairs of the country.[4] It repeated the expression used in the Laws (Continuance in Force) Order 1958 and Provisional Constitution Order, 1969 that 'Pakistan shall, subject to this order and any order made by the President and any regulation made by the Chief Martial Law Administrator (CMLA) be governed as nearly as may be, in accordance with the constitution'. The courts were allowed to function but the powers of the Supreme Court and the High Courts to issue writs under Article 199 were taken away and all proceedings pending in these courts in exercise of writ jurisdiction were suspended. This was a sweeping denial of jurisdiction to the superior courts and would have caused enormous alarm and inconvenience if it was not corrected after two days by CMLA Order 2 of 1977 which provided that the Supreme Court and the High Courts would continue to have writ jurisdiction except against the CMLA or an MLA or any person exercising powers or jurisdiction under the authority of either.[5]

The fundamental rights under the 1973 Constitution and all proceedings pending in the courts regarding their enforcement were suspended. No court, tribunal, or other authority could call or permit to be called in question of the proclamation of martial law or any order, ordinance, martial law regulation, or martial law order made in pursuance thereof and no judgment, decree, writ, order, or process could be passed or issued in this behalf. Subject to the order or ordinances of the President and regulations by the CMLA, all laws, other than the Constitution, all ordinances, orders-in-council, orders made by the President, rules, by-laws, regulations, notifications, and other legal instruments in force in Pakistan or any part thereof were continued in force. Ordinances made by the President or by a Governor would not be subject to the limitation as to its duration prescribed in the Constitution. All persons who were in the service of Pakistan or were in office as judges of the Supreme Court or a High Court, Auditor-General or Advocate-General on the proclamation of martial law were allowed to continue on the same terms and conditions and to enjoy the same privileges, if any. The provisions related to the Review Board regarding preventive detention were rendered ineffective.

Zia's Differences with Bhutto

It appears that, in the beginning, Zia was not hostile towards Bhutto. In fact, was so closely associated with Bhutto that some leaders of the PNA suspected that the imposition of martial law might be Bhutto's move to frustrate the PNA movement and to back out of the settlement reached with them. After all, Zia had every reason to be beholden to Bhutto because he had been appointed Army Chief of Staff superseding seven or eight senior Lieutenant Generals. Earlier utterances by Zia soon after the imposition of martial law also reflected his respect and admiration for Bhutto. While addressing a press conference on 14 July 1977, he referred to his three telephonic conversations with Bhutto since 5 July and said that he was 'quite happy and enjoying life'.[6] He also said that he would be releasing Bhutto and other PPP leaders soon and that he would meet him before then. He reiterated that he had limited aims before him and would stay for ninety days of which eight had already passed. The Military Council, he said, had decided not to take any action against politicians even if there was certainty about their misdeeds. He said it was for the people's representatives to decide about such action against anyone.

Uptil this point in time, it appears that Zia held no malice towards Bhutto and wanted to be even-handed. This appreciation is nevertheless subject to enormous doubts because his later conduct showed him in a different light, a man full of hypocrisy and deceit. On 15 July, he visited Bhutto and Mufti Mahmood in Murree.[7] It seems that this meeting changed the relationship between the two. Nothing is recorded about what transpired between during this meeting but there are several speculations about the discussion between the two. It is rumoured that Bhutto told Zia that he had committed high treason by imposing martial law and that he could be tried under Article 6 of the Constitution. It is also believed that Bhutto was rude and insulting in that meeting which shook the latter very much and he returned sour and worried. The official photograph of the occasion also shows Bhutto in an angry mood and Zia sitting before him like a scared lamb.

It is difficult to understand why Bhutto did not want to deal with Zia who now held the power. After all, he had successfully manipulated Yahya on many occasions in 1971.[8] He should have dealt with Zia in the same manner and should have encouraged him to hold elections, paving the way for his return to power. Afterwards, he could have dealt with Zia the way he pleased. The explanation generally given is that Bhutto had very little respect for Zia whom he regarded as a sycophant and his own creation.[9] He could not humble his pride before a man he had favoured out of the way by promoting him over the heads of senior Generals. He had surely fallen into a trap by the outward humility and servility of the man.

The of murder of Nawab Muhammad Ahmad Khan happened on the night of 10 November 1974, Ahmad Raza Kasuri, a member of the National Assembly who was elected on the PPP ticket but had later fallen out with him and had become his bitter opponent, was driving home from a wedding reception with his father, Nawab Muhammad Ahmad Khan, sitting by his side. Soon after he left the house, a volley of shots burst out. Ahmad Raza accelerated away when he heard two more bursts. A bullet hit the dynamo of his Toyota car so that the lights went out making him a difficult target in the dark. After driving on till he felt safe, he turned to his father and found him soaked in blood. Ahmad Raza took his father to a hospital but he did not survive. He dictated his version of the entire incident in the First Information Report (FIR) to the police official present, alleging that he was the target and his father had been shot by mistake. When asked the name of the culprit, he said, 'Zulfiqar Ali Bhutto'. On the insistence of Ahmad Raza, the police and wrote Bhutto's name as the murderer in the FIR.[10]

On 28 July 1977, Bhutto, Mufti Mahmood, and other leaders in 'protective custody' were released. On 29 July, Bhutto addressing party workers in Islamabad said that he would work within the bounds of the existing laws and martial law regulations in the larger interest of the country.[11] Limited political activity had been allowed from 1 August and on 2 August 1977, the date for elections to the national and provincial assemblies was announced to be 18 October. Bhutto launched the election campaign of the PPP and toured Multan, Lahore, Karachi, and Peshawar. Everywhere, he was received by large enthusiastic crowds. His mass popularity was leading towards an inevitable showdown with the military *junta*. With every passing day, and emboldened by swelling crowds at his receptions, he started making speeches confronting the military *junta*. His popularity coupled with his bellicose speeches created panic in the members of the military *junta* who started planning to contain him somehow. After the imposition of martial law, the family members of Ahmad Raza had revived the murder case of Nawab Muhammad Ahmad Khan that took place in 1974. They lodged a criminal complaint, hearing of which was being held by an Additional Sessions Judge in Lahore. The murder complaint was transferred to the Lahore High Court on 27 August and the Court was informed that the State would present a *challan* against Bhutto by 29 August.[12] Now the martial law regime had come out openly against Bhutto.

On 3 September 1977, Bhutto was arrested from his residence in Karachi, flown to Lahore, and remanded to police custody in Lahore on charges relating to the murder of Ahmad Raza's father.[13] His bail application was moved before the High Court which was admitted for regular hearing on 6 September. On 13 September, Bhutto was granted bail by the order of Justice K.M.A. Samdani of the Lahore High Court on the ground that from the material produced before the court, there was only circumstantial evidence indicating his possible involvement and that further evidence was yet to be collected.[14]

After grant of bail Bhutto went to Leghari House[15] in Lahore, where he addressed party workers. He made an extremely belligerent and bellicose speech against the military *junta*, using threatening words against Zia and his military colleagues.[16] It appears that his success in obtaining bail lured him into further confrontation with the military and he was clearly carried away by the favourable response from the crowd present at the occasion. His words intimidated and frightened the already scared members of the military *junta* who decided to get rid of him once and for all. Bhutto was arrested again on 17 September this time under a martial law order.[17]

Election Campaign and Postponement of Elections

It has been mentioned earlier that political activities were allowed from 1 August 1977, after which full fledged political activities and election campaign started. The election campaigns intensified during the month of August and became direct contest between the PPP and the PNA, largely on the pattern of the March elections. The PNA realized that Bhutto was not yet undone, but was a potential danger as long as the elections loomed large on the horizon. Meanwhile, the martial law government felt constrained to stop Bhutto's eventual return to power. It seemed that elections could only help Bhutto. The only way out for the martial law regime was to bar the PPP leader from participating in the elections.

The PNA was in disarray and was taking a long time in deciding and finalizing their list of candidates for the National and Provincial Assemblies. There were differences amongst the PNA leader about the organizational base of the PNA. Mufti Mahmood, Professor Ghafoor, and Haneef Ramay favoured a merger of the political parties in the PNA.[18] Asghar Khan, on the other hand, said that Tehrik-i-Istiqlal was not willing.[19] No wonder, Bhutto made a statement that the PNA was a toy of clay which could be smashed with a blow.[20] Chaudhry Zahur Ilahi also contributed to the cracking of the fragile unity of the PNA by insisting that he would contest in Lahore from the constituency in which Bhutto was contesting.[21] This constituency had previously been assigned to a nominee of Asghar Khan who withdrew in favour of Chaudhry Zahur Ilahi, but after considerable controversy, acrimony, and bitterness.

The division within the PNA further widened on the issue of holding elections on time. While Asghar Khan was ready to countenance the postponement of elections in the interest of accountability, and also in the hope that it might disqualify Bhutto from participation, Mufti Mahmood and the NWFP's PNA leader in general favoured the electoral path to defeat Bhutto.[22] On 3 September, Zia declared that he would be willing to postpone the elections if the parties so desired; that the presidential system was in keeping with Islam's principles; that the Islamic Ideology Council would be reconstituted; that the flour mills and rice husking units previously taken over were to be de-nationalized, and that ex-servicemen were to be arrested only by the military authorities, unless permitted otherwise.[23] These measures indicated that the contours of the martial law regime were being shaped around Islamic ideology as the source of legitimacy, concentration of power in the hands of the head of state with small businessmen as a social support group, and the military including its retired personnel, as the core constituency. Bhutto was arrested the same day. On 7 September, Martial Law Regulation 21 was issued for inquiry into the assets of the members of the National and Provincial Assemblies under the PPP regime, with the express purpose of disqualifying them from participation in the elections.[24]

Thus, the stage was set for the postponement of general elections as the confrontation between Bhutto and military *junta* was coming to a head. Bhutto's habeas corpus petition was admitted by the Supreme Court as a result of which Chief Justice Yakub Ali had to lose office and was replaced by Justice Anwar-ul-Haq. Pir Pagaro, who had always claimed to be GHQ's man, cabled for the accountability of Bhutto and his colleagues and the settlement of law and order in the country before elections were held.[25] Asghar Khan and Noorani also cabled for accountability first.[26] On 29 September Zia announced that the decision on postponement of elections would be taken by 10 October and a White Paper on the PPP government would be published by the end of October.[27] On 30 September, the PNA chief, Mufti Mahmood, also urged accountability before the polls.[28] This meant that the PNA had become demoralized by seeing that the PPP, now led by Nusrat Bhutto, was attracting large crowds in their election rallies. The PNA leadership rushed into the arms of Zia and the military *junta* seeking the postponement of elections. The announcement thus was only a formality carried out by Zia on 1 October, banning all political activities.[29]

Withdrawal of the Fifth and Sixth Amendments

Since Zia and his *junta* had decided to stay in power and postpone elections by the third week of September, they needed to exercise wide and sweeping powers. Nusrat Bhutto had moved the Supreme Court against the detention of Bhutto in its original jurisdiction for enforcement of fundamental rights under the constitution.[30] The matter came up for hearing for the first time on 20 September 1977, when Justice Muhammad Yakub Ali, as the Chief Justice, presided over the Court. Yahya Bakhtiar, former Attorney-General and now counsel for Bhutto, presented his petition. He also distributed copies to journalists and foreign reporters sitting in the Court.[31] The Court ordered the admission of the petition and the immediate transfer of Bhutto and other accused to Rawalpindi and adjourned the case to 25 September 1977. The other judges of the Court obviously concurred with the decision. The military *junta* must have sensed that the Chief Justice was not going to play their game. Zia retaliated through CMLA's Order Number 6 of 1977 issued on 22 September, which amended Article 2 of Laws (Continuance in Force) Order 1977, the effect of which was that the term 'constitution' was to be construed as if Articles 179, 195, and 199 of the Constitution had not been amended by any of the Acts amending it.[32] It was also provided that an incumbent in any office who would have retired from office in the absence of an amendment to the Constitution, would cease to hold office forthwith. In other words, by a CMLA's order, the Constitution was amended so that the Fifth and Sixth amendments incorporated therein were withdrawn and the provision for a Chief Justice to serve his term of office after reaching the age of retirement was set at nought. The net result of this amendment was that Chief Justice Yakub Ali, who had crossed the age of retirement, ceased to hold office. Justice Anwar-ul-Haq assumed office in his place.

This was the first act on the part of the CMLA to amend the 1973 Constitution, while it was still being held in abeyance, to accomplish his immediate objective. The effect was the removal of the Chief Justice of Pakistan and when his successor took office as a result of the CMLA order and the Supreme Court accepted this transition, not only was the immediate goal of getting rid of Justice Yakub Ali achieved but the Supreme Court's submission to the power of the CMLA was also established. How could a court which accepts such change and re-constitution of the law later turn around to state that the law maker had no power to make such a law? The Supreme Court actually welcomed this step and stressed that Justice Anwar-ul-Haq had been arbitrarily denied office of the Chief Justice for six months already. The change brought about and the appointment of Justice Anwar-ul-Haq was taken as a divine dictation because 'Till day before yesterday, none of us had the slightest idea that the injustice done to your lordship would be so readily undone'.[33] The military *junta* now had a different Chief Justice to preside over the Supreme Court which was to commence the hearing of Nusrat Bhutto's case on 25 September.

The Supreme Court had landed itself in a predicament which found appropriate expression in an extract from the judgment of Justice Qaiser Khan in Begum Nusrat Bhutto's case.[34] The extract is reproduced verbatim as under:

> If we hold that on the basis of legality the legal order was no order, then this Court would be signing its own death warrant for then there could be no government at all. For argument sake, if the Judges do not rely on the new norms then what norms are available for them to proceed with? In a revolutionary situation like the present one, they have either to quit or to accept the new norms.

The Nusrat Bhutto Case

When the Supreme Court re-assembled on 25 September, Justice Anwar-ul-Haq had taken over as Chief Justice. The order passed on 20 September 1977, according to which Bhutto and others were to be transferred to Rawalpindi was, of course, never complied with. The case was heard by a full Bench of the Supreme Court of Pakistan or, rather, a full court consisting of nine judges.[35] The hearing ended on 1 November 1977. Yahya Bakhtiar, counsel for the petitioner, Begum Nusrat Bhutto, relied mainly on Asma Jilani's case and contended that Zia, Chief of the Army Staff, had no authority under the 1973 Constitution to impose martial law in the country; that this intervention amounted to an act of treason in terms of Article 6 of the Constitution; that as a consequence, the proclamation of martial law dated 5 July 1977 was without lawful authority, the Laws (Continuance in Force) Order 1977 as well as Martial Law Order Number 12 under which Bhutto and his colleagues were detained, were illegal and without lawful authority. He further argued that even if all or any of these acts or actions could be justified in the name of the 'doctrine of necessity', the arrest and detention of the top leader of Pakistan People's Party was highly discriminatory and malafide, intended solely for the purpose of keeping the PPP out of the forthcoming elections. It was also argued that the Chief of the Army Staff could not place himself beyond the reach of the courts by relying on an order promulgated by himself because the 1973 Constitution continued to be the supreme legal instrument of the country, especially when the Chief of the Army Staff had declared that this Constitution was not being abrogated but only certain parts of it were being held in abeyance for the time being in order to create a peaceful atmosphere for the holding of elections and restoration of democratic institutions. Yahya Bakhtiar further argued that the orders of detention had resulted in flagrant violation of the *detenus*' fundamental rights as enshrined in the Constitution.

A.K. Brohi, counsel for the federation of Pakistan, raised two preliminary objections to the maintainability of the petition. He contended that the writ was directed against the Chief of the Army Staff, whereas the order of detention had been passed by the Chief Martial Law Administrator; and that the petitioner was not an aggrieved person in terms of Article 184 (3) of the Constitution read with Article 199 thereof, as she had not alleged any violation of her own fundamental rights, but only those of the *detenus*. He further submitted that the Supreme Court had no jurisdiction to grant any relief in the matter owing to the prohibition contained in the Laws (Continuance in Force) Order, 1977, which clearly contemplated that no court, including the High Court and the Supreme Court, could question the validity of any martial law order or regulation or any other order made thereunder by a martial law authority. He argued that under the Laws (Continuance in Force) Order, the right to enforce fundamental rights was suspended and for that reason too the petition was not maintainable.

As to the legal character of the new regime, and the validity of the Laws (Continuance in Force) Order, 1977 and various martial law regulations and orders issued by the CMLA and the President under his authority, Brohi submitted that up to 5 July 1977, Pakistan was being governed under the 1973 Constitution, but on that day a new legal order came into force by virtue of the proclamation issued by the Chief Martial Law Administrator and this legal order had displaced, although temporarily, with the old legal order. According to him, the validity or legality of any action which took place after 5 July 1977 could only be tested against the guidelines provided by the new legal order. He submitted that the *grundnorm* of the old legal order, as provided by the 1973 Constitution, had given way to a new *grundnorm* provided by the proclamation of martial law and the Laws (Continuance in Force) Order, and to that extent the jurisdiction of the superior courts had been altered. He submitted that, as the change from the old legal order to the new legal order had not been brought about by any means recognized or contemplated by the 1973 Constitution, therefore, it constituted a meta-legal or extra-constitutional fact attracting the doctrine of revolutionary legality. According to Brohi, whenever a Constitution and national legal order under it were disrupted by an abrupt political change not within the contemplation of the Constitution, such a change was called a revolution, which also included *coup d' etat*. In such a situation, the court had to determine certain facts which might be termed as constitutional and which related to the existence of the legal order within the framework of which the court itself existed and functioned. If it found that all the institutions of state power had, as a matter of fact, accepted the existence of the new legal order which had thus become effective, then all questions of legality or illegality were to be determined within the framework the of new legal order. According to him, a viable alternative could be found between two extreme positions adopted by the Supreme Court of Pakistan earlier in Dosso's case[36] and in Asma Jilani's case.[37] The earlier judgment had held that every revolution, once successful, was legal and the other one held that revolution as such was illegal. He contended that the view taken by the Supreme Court in Asma Jilani's case left several questions unanswered by rejecting Kelson's pure theory of law because it did not provide any guidelines to what the law courts ought to apply in case a revolution had become effective by suppressing or destroying the old legal order. Brohi, therefore, suggested that the Court should lean in favour of holding that a new legal order had effectively emerged in Pakistan by means of this meta-legal or extra-constitutional change and, for the time being, this was a legal framework according to which all questions coming before the Court must be decided. In his view, it was not necessary for the Court nor was it a concomitant of judicial power to either side with the revolution or to act as a counter-revolutionary by giving a seal of approval to the military intervention or to condemn it by describing it as illegal. Judicial restraint required that the court should only take judicial notice of events which had transpired in the country and decide as a constitutional fact whether the new legal order had become effective or not.

As to the necessity for the imposition of martial law on 5 July 1977, Brohi stated that the events leading thereto fell into two categories. The first one related to the unconstitutional and illegal governance of the country by the *detenus* and their associates, which terminated on the eve of the imposition of martial law; and the second category related to the preparations which were being made by the *detenus* and their associates for fomenting civil war within the country to frustrate and prevent the holding of free and fair elections and thereby to consolidate their illegal tenure of office.

Brohi then referred to the massive rigging of election held on 7 March 1977 which, according to him, was based up on a master plan conceived, directed, and implemented by the then Prime Minister Bhutto. He further said that the dialogues between Bhutto and the leader of the PNA were deliberately prolonged in a malafide manner so events took a critical tern and the spectre of civil war loomed ahead. It became clear beyond doubt that there was no possibility of a free and fair election being held as long as the levers of power were in Bhutto's hands. According to him, martial law was imposed not in order to displace a constitutional authority, but in order to provide a bridge to enable the country to return to the path of constitutional rule.

Sharifuddin Pirzada, the newly appointed Attorney-General of the military regime, appearing as 'law officer' of the court had supported Brohi's submissions that the change which had taken place in Pakistan on 5 July 1977 did not amount to the usurpation of state power by the Chief of the Army Staff but was, in fact, intended to oust the usurper who had illegally assumed power as a result of massive rigging of election results on 7 March 1977. It was, he argued, also intended to displace the illegally constituted legislative assemblies, both at the centre and in the provinces, as a majority of the members had succeeded by corrupt and criminal practices and that the present situation was not covered by the dicta of the Supreme Court in the well known cases of Dosso and Asma Jilani, for the reasons that the circumstances were radically different where change brought about by military intervention was of a permanent nature, whereas the purpose of the present CMLA was to remain in power only for a limited period so as to hold fair election for the restoration of the democratic institutions.[38]

Sharifuddin Pirzada continued that, although he would generally support Brohi's submission as to the legal character of an effective revolution, he did not wish to adopt a position contrary to the one he had taken up while appearing as *amicus curiae* in Asma Jilani's case regarding the validity and applicability of Kelson's pure theory of law relating to the meta-legal character of the change and the birth of a new *grundnorm*. He submitted that there were several renowned jurists who did not fully subscribe to Kelson's view and considered that its effectiveness alone to the exclusion of all considerations of morality and justice could not be made a condition of the validity of the new legal order. He further submitted that the circumstances culminating in the imposition of martial law on 5 July 1977 fully attracted the doctrine of 'state necessity' and of '*salus populi est suprema lex*' with the result that the action taken by the CMLA ought to be regarded as valid and the Laws (Continuance in Force) Order 1977 ought to be treated as being a super-constitutional instrument now regulating the governance of the country. He continued that the doctrine of necessity was not only a part of the legal systems of several European countries, including Britain, but was also recognized by the Holy Quran. Consequently, all actions taken by the CMLA to meet the exigencies of the situation and to prepare the country for further elections with a view to restoring democratic institutions must be accepted by the courts as valid and there could be no question of condonation which would apply only in the case of the acts of a usurper. Pirzada concluded that the Court could not, accordingly, grant any relief to the *detenus* under the 1973 Constitution as the fundamental rights stood suspended by the Laws (Continuance in Force) Order, 1977.

In response to Brohi's arguments, a detailed statement was submitted in the Supreme Court on behalf of Bhutto. It was alleged that the Chief of the Army Staff had conspired against him, that a foreign power was behind him, and that there was massive foreign interference in the internal affairs of the country. The CMLA was condemned for postponing the elections on the pretext of accountability. As far as the process of accountability was concerned, Bhutto asserted that only an accountable government answerable to the people, could hold accountability. He accused the CMLA of bad faith and of having reneged on his promise to the country and before the General Assembly of the United Nations on 28 September, to hold election on 18 October 1977 and to transfer power to the elected representatives. In reply to the allegation of malafide in prolonging the dialogue between the PPP and the PNA, Bhutto stated that the dialogue had come to a successful conclusion and a formal agreement would have been released to the public on 5 July if the Chief of Army Staff had not intervened through 'Operation Fairplay', which was actually 'Operation Foulplay'. Bhutto also chided Brohi for relying upon Kelson and insisted that the people alone could take accountability and that the silence of the people should not be taken as their acquiesence.[39]

After considering the arguments of the parties, the Chief Justice delivered the leading judgment of the court.[40] He referred to the six periods of martial law which had been imposed in Pakistan since independence, and then went on to discuss the two earlier cases of the Supreme Court, namely Dosso's case and Asma Jilani's case. The Chief Justice noted that in Asma Jilani's case, Sharifuddin Pirzada (Attorney-General) and A.K. Brohi, learned counsel for the Federation of Pakistan, had appeared as *amicus curiae*[41] and had vehemently opposed the decision of the Supreme Court in Dosso's case by contending that a system of government in which power was regulated and derived not from law but from force could not claim to be a legal system of government and that in Pakistan no single person could be the sole repository of state power because it would be repugnant to the *grundnorm* of Pakistan, namely, the Objectives Resolution. The Court wondered how Brohi was now pleading that Dosso's case had laid the correct law and should be followed by the Court. The submissions of Brohi with reference to Dosso's case were not accepted.

The Chief Justice held that the controversy in the case must proceed on the assumption that the 1973 Constitution had been validly framed and was in force when the Chief of the Army Staff proclaimed martial law on 5 July 1977. The Chief Justice further observed that the theory of revolutionary legality as propounded by Brohi had no application or relevance to a situation where the breach of legal continuity is admitted or declared to be of a purely temporary nature and for a specified limited purpose. Such a phenomenon could more appropriately be described as one of constitutional deviation rather than of revolution. It would indeed be highly inappropriate to apply Kelson's theory to such a transient and limited change in the legal or constitutional continuity. Accordingly, no justification had been made for resurrecting Dosso's case in supersession of the view adopted by the Court in Asma Jilani's case regarding the application of Kelson's theory of revolutionary legality in the circumstances obtained in Pakistan. The Chief Justice went on to say that he would rather prefer the view advocated by Brohi in Asma Jilani's case to the one which was being canvassed by him in the present case, which sought to rob the present political change of its moral content and also left its legal character uncertain and undecided. The Chief Justice then took note of all the statements and counter-statements made in the proceedings and observed that the Court was not called upon to establish the factual correctness or otherwise of the several allegations and counter-allegations made by the parties against each other. The Court, according to him, was primarily concerned with ascertaining the broad trends and circumstances which culminated in the overthrow of the government of Bhutto. The Chief Justice took judicial notice of the following facts:

1. That from the evening of 7 March 1977, there were wide-spread allegations of massive official interference with the sanctity of the ballot in favour of candidates of the Pakistan People's Party;
2. That these allegations, amounting almost to widespread belief among the people, generated a national wave of resentment and gave birth to a protest agitation which soon spread from Karachi to Khyber and assumed serious proportions;
3. That the disturbances resulting from this movement were beyond the control of the civil armed forces;
4. That the disturbances resulted in heavy loss of life and property throughout the country;
5. That even the calling out of the troops under Article 245 of the Constitution by the federal government and the consequent imposition of the local martial law in several important cities of Pakistan and the calling out of troops by the local authorities under the provisions of the Code of Criminal Procedure in smaller cities and towns did not have the desired effect, and the agitation continued unabated;

6. That the allegations of rigging and official interference with elections in favour of candidates of the ruling party were established by judicial decisions in at least four cases which displayed a general pattern of official interference;
7. That public statements made by the then Chief Election Commissioner confirmed the widespread allegations made by the opposition regarding official interference with the elections and endorsed the demand for fresh elections;
8. That, in the circumstances, Bhutto felt compelled to offer himself to a referendum under the Seventh Amendment to the Constitution but the offer did not have any impact at all on the course of the agitation and the demand for his resignation and for fresh elections continued unabated with the result that the referendum plan had to be cancelled;
9. That in spite of Bhutto's dialogue with the leaders of the Pakistan National Alliance (PNA), and the temporary suspension of the movement against the government, officials charged with maintaining law and order were apprehensive that in the event of the failure of the talks there would be a terrible explosion beyond the control of the civilian authorities;
10. That although the talks between Bhutto and the PNA leader had commenced on 3 June 1977 on the basis of his offer for holding fresh elections to the National and Provincial Assemblies, they had dragged on for various reasons, and as late as 4 July 1977, PNA leader was insisting that nine or ten points remained to be resolved while Bhutto was also saying that his side would similarly put forward another ten points if the General Council of PNA did not ratify the accord on the morning of 3 July 1977.
11. That during the crucial days of the deadlock between Bhutto and the PNA leader the Punjab government sanctioned the distribution of fire-arm licences on a vast scale to its party members, and provocative statements were deliberately made by the prime minister's special assistant, G.M. Khar, who had patched up his differences with the prime minister and secured this appointment as late as 16 June 1977; and
12. That as a result of the agitation, all normal economic, social, and educational activities in the country stood seriously disrupted, with incalculable damage to the nation and the country.

The Chief Justice concluded that the extra-constitutional step taken by the armed forces of Pakistan was justified by requirements of State necessity and welfare of the people. The legal consequences and true legal position that emerged was stated as under:

i. That the 1973 Constitution still remained the supreme law of the land subject to the condition that certain parts thereof had been held in abeyance on account of state necessity;
ii. That the President of Pakistan and the superior courts continued to function under the Constitution. The mere fact that the judges of the Superior Courts had taken a new oath after the proclamation of martial law did not in any manner derogate from its position as the courts had been originally established

under the 1973 Constitution and continued in their functions in spite of the proclamation of martial law;

iii. That the CMLA, having validly assumed power by means of an extra constitutional step, in the interest of the state and for the welfare of the people, was entitled to perform all such acts and promulgate all legislative instruments as falling within the scope of the law of necessity, namely:
   (a) All acts or legislative measures which were in accordance with, or could have been made under the 1973 Constitution, including the power to amend it;[42]
   (b) All acts which would advance or promote the good of the people;
   (c) All acts required to be done for the ordinary orderly running of the State; and
   (d) All such measures as would establish or lead to the establishment of the declared objectives of the proclamation of martial law, namely restoration of law and order, and normalcy in the country and the earliest possible holding of free and fair elections for the purpose of restoration of democratic institutions under the 1973 Constitution;

iv. That these acts, or any of them, may be performed or carried out by means of presidential orders, ordinances, martial law regulations, or orders as the occasion may require; and

v. That the superior courts continue to have the power of judicial review to judge the validity of any act or action of the martial law authorities, if challenged, in the light of the principles underlying the law of necessity as stated above. Their powers under Article 199 of the Constitution thus remain available to their full extent, and may be exercised as heretofore, notwithstanding anything to the contrary contained in any martial law regulation or order, presidential order or ordinance.'

Before concluding, the Chief Justice referred to the assurance given to the Court by Brohi as well as Sharifuddin Pirzada, the Attorney-General, with regard to the elections. The Chief Justice observed:

> Before parting with this judgment, it is necessary to refer to certain misgivings and apprehensions expressed by Mr Yahya Bakhtiar, learned counsel for the petitioner, to the effect that the postponement of the elections scheduled to be held on 18 October 1977, has cast a shadow on the declared objectives of the Chief Martial Law Administrator. After seeking instructions from his client, Mr A. K. Brohi has informed the Court that the Chief Martial Law Administrator intends to hold elections as soon as the process of the accountability of the holders of public offices is completed, and the time factor depends upon the speed with which these cases are disposed of by the civil courts concerned. The learned Attorney-General has stated at the Bar that, in his opinion, a period of about six months is needed for this purpose, and thereafter it will be possible to hold the elections within two months.

The Chief Justice concluded by emphasizing that:

> While the Court does not consider it appropriate to issue any directions, as suggested by Mr Yahya Bakhtiar, as to a definite time-table for the holding of elections, the Court would like to state in clear terms that it has found it possible to validate the extra-constitutional action of the Chief Martial Law Administrator not only for the reason that he stepped in to save the country at a time of grave national crisis and constitutional breakdown, but also because of the solemn pledge given by him that the period of constitutional deviation shall be of as short a duration as possible, and that during this period all his energies shall be directed towards creating conditions conducive to the holding of free and fair elections, leading to the restoration of democratic rule in accordance with the dictates of the constitution. The Court, therefore, expects the Chief Martial Law Administrator to redeem this pledge, which must be construed in the nature of a mandate from the people of Pakistan, who have by and large, willingly accepted his administration as the interim government of Pakistan.

Waheeduddin Ahmad, Dorab Patel, Muhammad Haleem, and G. Safdar Shah, concurred with the Chief Justice. Muhammad Afzal Cheema, Muhammad Akram Qaiser Khan and Nasim Hasan Shah while concurring with the Chief Justice also wrote separate short judgments. Justice Muhammad Afzal Cheema, supported the line of arguments of the Chief Justice and observed that the doctrine of necessity was not a western jurists' concept but was of Islamic origin having been based on and deduced from various verses of the Holy Quran. He cited a number of verses of the Holy Quran in support thereof. Justice Muhammad Akram, discussed at length Kelson's pure theory of law and demolished it. He came to the conclusion that the principles of state necessity and the arguments of the maxim '*Salus populi suprema lex*' were fully attracted to the peculiar facts and circumstances of the case, as validating factor. Justice Qaiser Khan, however, was fairly straightforward and direct. While agreeing with the Chief Justice, he observed that the Supreme Court derived its jurisdiction from the Laws (Continuance in Force) Order and it had to accept and enforce the laws of 'de facto government' for the time being. According to him, the Courts had to ensure that the conflict between the Court and State was always avoided, even if the government was a de facto one.

As a consequence of this unanimous verdict of the Supreme Court, the act of the Chief of the Army Staff, General Zia, ousting Bhutto from power was declared to be valid in the name of 'state necessity'. Begum Nusrat Bhutto's petition challenging the detention of Bhutto and others under Martial Law Order 12 was dismissed as incompetent. The judgment was delivered on 10 November 1977. The *detenus* were, however, allowed to move the High Court concerned under Article 199 of the Constitution.

There is controversy about the words 'including the power to amend it' in the leading judgment of the Chief Justice.[43] It is because of these words that Zia was given a free hand to amend the 1973 Constitution which he mostly abused, defacing the Constitution and introducing basic changes which had not the remotest connection with the doctrine of state necessity. There is a viewpoint that the aforesaid words were not included in the typed draft of the judgment circulated amongst other members of the Supreme Court Bench and they were later added by Justice Anwar-ul-Haq.[44]

The doctrine of necessity expounded by the Supreme Court in Nusrat Bhutto's case was read narrowly by the High Courts. When it was challenged before the Peshawar High Court that military courts did not meet the criteria of necessity, the Court responded as under:[45]

> To say that it is the duty of this Court to judge in exercise of its constitutional jurisdiction, the political implications of this or that action will be an argument to which we cannot subscribe. All that we have to ensure is whether an impugned action reasonably falls within any of the categories enunciated in Begam Nusrat Bhutto's case.

However, the Sindh High Court, in a similar case, construed the Nusrat Bhutto case more liberally holding that detention without trial on the instructions of the executive would virtually be making the same authority both the prosecution as well as the judge, and such an anomalous state of affairs inherently tended to arbitrariness.[46]

The Sindh High Court entertained a petition challenging Zia's constitutional amendments, restricting the powers and jurisdiction of the High Courts under Article 199 to pass orders, injunctions, and process against martial law regulations and orders of CMLA or MLA or anything done, or action taken, or intended to be taken, or done thereunder. Under this amendment, the High Courts were also prohibited from making any order relating to the validity or effect of any judgment or effect of any judgment or sentence passed by a military court or tribunal or pass any injunction, make any order or entertain any proceedings in respect of any matter to which the jurisdiction of a military court or tribunal extended or of which cognizance had been taken by a military court or tribunal.[47]

A majority of the Bench of five judges in the Sindh High Court upheld the constitutional amendment as valid. The dissenting judges found the amendment unreasonable and invalid, violating the power of judicial review vested in the superior courts in Nusrat Bhutto's case. Justice Zafar Husain Mirza, a dissenting judge, observed that the majority misread Nusrat Bhutto's case and on no principle of necessity could the power of judicial review vested in the superior courts under the 1973 Constitution be taken away. According to him, the martial law regime could not promulgate 'in the shape of constitutional amendment a permanent constitutional measure to outlive itself resulting in perpetuation of military dispensation of justice after restoration of democracy'.[48]

NOTES

1. *Dawn*, 6 July 1977.
2. Ibid. The text of General Zia's address is on page 8.
3. Proclamation of Martial Law, 5 July 1977, PLD 1977 Central Statutes 326.
4. Chief Martial Law Administrator's Order 1 of 1977. PLD 1977 Central Statutes 327.
5. Laws (Continuance in Force) (Amendment) Order, 1977. PLD 1977 Central Statutes 325.

6. *Dawn*, 15 July 1977.
7. *Dawn*, 16 July 1977.
8. One of Bhutto's close associates told the author that when he complained to Bhutto in 1971 as to why he was cooperating with Yahya, he said that he could not cross two bridges at the same time. He would cross the bridge of Mujib with the help of Yahya and then he would take him on.
9. Bhutto often made Zia the butt of public ridicule, shouting at him from the head of the dinner table, 'Where is my monkey-general? Come over here, Monkey!' He would pretend to pull Zia towards himself on an invisible string and then introduce him to a distinguished guest, quickly dismissing him, even before Zia finished bowing, ever smiling. Sometimes, Bhutto 'joked' about how funny 'Zia's teeth looked', humiliating the man he had singled out for such high and powerful distinction. Zia apparently never took umbrage at such 'jests', always smiling, bowing, even 'thanking' his Prime Minister for 'your such kind attentions, Sir!' And like Bhutto, Zia forgot no insult, no social slight, no attack upon his *izzat*, no challenge to his faith, his God, or himself. See Wolpert, Stanley. *Zulfi Bhutto of Pakistan — His life and times*, 1993, Oxford University Press, New York, p. 263.
10. Taseer, Salmaan, *Bhutto: A political biography*, 1980, Vikas Publishing House, New Delhi, pp. 177-8.
11. *Dawn*, 30 July 1977.
12. *Dawn*, 28 August 1977. It may be explained that a complaint case is prosecuted by the complainant himself with the help of his witnesses. But a challan case is prosecuted by the prosecution branch of provincial government after investigation by the police. In such a case, it is State's responsibility to adduce the best evidence to obtain conviction of the accused.
13. *Dawn*, 4 September 1977.
14. Zulfiqar Ali Bhutto v State, PLJ 1978 Criminal Cases (Lahore) 9.
15. Leghari House belonged to Sardar Farooq Ahmad Khan Leghari who later became the President of Pakistan.
16. As reported by some workers of the PPP on the occasion he referred to Zia saying that on his return to power he would pull out his (Zia's) moustache and would use it as his shoe laces. He is also reported to have said that he would make the members of the military *junta* clean toilets.
17. *Dawn*, 18 September 1977.
18. *Dawn*, 20 and 23 August 1977.
19. *Dawn*, 24 August 1977.
20. *Dawn*, 26 August 1977.
21. Chaudhry Zahur Ilahi had boasted that he could spend eight million rupees to defeat Bhutto.
22. Waseem, Mohammad, *Politics and the State in Pakistan*, 1989, Progressive Publishers, Lahore. p. 367.
23. *Pakistan Times*, 4 September 1977.
24. *The Pakistan Times*, 4 September 1977.
25. *Dawn*, 21 September 1977.
26. *Dawn*, 27 September 1977.
27. *Dawn*, 30 September 1977.
28. *Dawn*, 1 October 1977.
29. *Dawn*, 2 October 1977.
30. Article 184(3).
31. Mahmood, M. Dilawar, *The Judiciary and Politics in Pakistan*, 1992, Idara Mutalia-e-Tareekh, Lahore. p. 48.
32. Laws (Continuance in Force) (Fifth Amendment) Order, 1977. PLD 1977 Central Statutes 441.
33. Address of Mr Justice Muhammad Afzal Cheema as Senior Judge of the Supreme Court welcoming the new Chief Justice on his own and on behalf of other Judges in the Full Court Reference held in the honour of the incoming Chief Justice. PLD 1977 Journal 257.
34. PLD 1977 S.C. 657 at p. 746.

35. The judges namely S. Anwar-ul-Haq CJ, Waheeduddin Ahmad, Muhammad Afzal Cheema, Muhammad Akram, Dorab Patel, Qaiser Khan, Muhammad Haleem, G. Safdar Shah and Nasim Hasan Shah, JJ.
36. PLD 1958 S.C. 533.
37. PLD 1972 S.C. 139.
38. It may be recalled that the military regime of Yahya did not last even for three years.
39. The contents of Bhutto's statement have been taken from the book of M. Dilawar Mahmood, *The Judiciary and Politics in Pakistan* which has produced extracts from his statement on p. 53 to 57.
40. Begum Nusrat Bhutto v Chief of Army Staff and Federation of Pakistan. PLD 1977 S.C. 657.
41. He is a person, generally a member of the Bar present in Court and heard by leave of the Court to assist it in the case already before it. He is not engaged by any of the parties but may instruct, inform, or move the Court on the matter of which the Court may take judicial cognizance.
42. Emphasis is supplied.
43. PLD 1977 S.C. 657 at p. 716.
44. One of the Judges on the Bench, Mr Justice Dorab Patel told the author that he did not remember reading these words in the draft circulated by the Chief Justice.
45. Nasirullah Khan Babar v Chief of Army Staff, PLD 1979 Peshawar 23.
46. Mumtaz Ali Bhutto v The Deputy Martial Law Administrator, PLD 1979 Karachi 307.
47. Constitution (Amendment) Order, 1980. President's Order 1 of 1980, PLJ 1980 Federal Statutes 137.
48. Yaqoob Ali v Presiding Officer, Summary Military Court, PLD 1985 Karachi 243.

26

BHUTTO'S TRIAL AND EXECUTION

The trial of Bhutto and the judgments of the Courts as a result are not, strictly speaking, a constitutional case. Since the trial was held by the High Court, it was not supposed to be a political trial or a military verdict. Nevertheless, the trial, appeal, and eventual execution of Bhutto have left a deep and everlasting effect on the political scene of Pakistan. The verdict has created international as well as political controversy, the judiciary has laboured under its cloud ever since. The trial and the appeal of Bhutto, therefore, deserve detailed narration and appreciation in the present work.

The Background

Justice Maulvi Mushtaq Husain has been discussed earlier mainly in the context of his strong rivalry with Chief Justice Sardar Muhammad Iqbal. Maulvi Mushtaq was known to be a man of strong likes and dislikes with a propensity towards vindictiveness. But for these weaknesses, he was a learned man with a potential of being a good and courageous judge, attributes which he manifested in a number of cases, Mir Hassan's case[1] was one which goes to his credit. His reputation of being strong-headed was known to all the governments under whom he served, a quality that did not endear him to them because governments in Pakistan generally looked for weak and pliable judges for appointment to key judicial offices like the Chief Justices of the Supreme Court and the High Courts so that the governments could manipulate political situations through them.

It has been mentioned above that Sardar Iqbal was prematurely retired as Chief Justice of the Lahore High Court in October 1976 as a result of the Fifth Amendment to the Constitution. Maulvi Mushtaq was next to him in the Lahore High Court and had been waiting for a long time for the coveted office of Chief Justice. He had previously declined elevation to the Supreme Court and allowed his juniors to be so elevated. Now the moment had come for which he had been waiting for a long time, but the Bhutto government was silent about the successor to Sardar Iqbal, keeping everyone concerned in anxiety and suspense. Finally, the suspense was broken and Mr Justice Aslam Riaz Husain, eight years junior to Maulvi Mushtaq Husain in the Court, was appointed as the Chief justice. Justice Aslam had superseded as many as seven senior judges of the Lahore High Court. The considerations behind his appointment appear to be all negative. He was not known to be a bright judge and had no significant judgment to his credit. He was known to be weak and ineffectual, attributes that the PPP government was looking for. He was believed to be a friend of Yahya Bakhtiar, the Attorney-General at that time. They had studied together for the Bar examination in the United Kingdom and perhaps Bakhtiar had assured Bhutto of his dependability. The PPP government apparently did not want to risk a strong Chief Justice like Maulvi Mushtaq in the Lahore High Court for four years.

There was widespread resentment against this appointment and the injustice done to Maulvi Mushtaq amongst members of the judiciary and the Bar. The PPP government soon found to its disappointment that weak people are of little utility to the government and cannot be loyal to any one. For example, in the mini martial law case of 1977 when a full Bench of the Lahore High Court presided over by Chief Justice Aslam Riaz declared the mini martial law imposed by the PPP government was unconstitutional.[2] Aslam Riaz CJ was the author of the judgment which although based on correct reasoning was poorly written. Maulvi Mushtaq was not going to forget the way Bhutto slighted him. He did not resign but became disheartened and showed little interest in his work.

When Zia imposed martial law in July 1977, he knew that Maulvi Mushtaq was aggrieved and that perhaps held a grudge against Bhutto. He started favouring him. Maulvi Mushtaq was first appointed as Chief Election Commissioner and later as acting Chief Justice of the Lahore High Court, while he was also the acting Governor of the Punjab. Thus, he came in a position where he could get even with Bhutto.

Detention and Cancellation of Bail for Bhutto

An incomplete *challan* had been presented by the prosecution before a magistrate in Lahore against Bhutto on 11 September 1977, charging him of the murder of Nawab Muhammad Ahmad, father of Ahmad Raza Kasuri, in November 1974. The magistrate concerned sent this *challan* to the court of sessions. On that day, the state moved an application in the High Court the transfer of the case to the High Court. Maulvi Mushtaq, as acting Chief Justice, passed the order transferring the case to the Lahore High Court for trial, without any notice to Bhutto.[3]

It is mentioned earlier that Bhutto was allowed bail on 13 September 1977 under the order of Justice K.M.A. Samdani. The bail order had clearly displeased Zia and the military *junta* who arrested Bhutto again on 17 September from his residence in Karachi under Martial Law Order Number 12 which empowered the CMLA to order the detention of anyone preventing him from acting in any manner prejudicial to the purpose for which martial law had been proclaimed. Zia justified the detention of Bhutto and his ten colleagues by saying that enquiries had unearthed 'a plethora of evidence' to show that during the Bhutto regime all civil institutions in the country were systematically destroyed, and that the civil services were politicized and rendered ineffective and insecure. It was alleged that the public funds were used for personal luxury and party benefits; the life, property, and honour of law-abiding citizens were made unsafe; and inhuman and barbaric methods were employed to crush all dissidents and political opponents. He also alleged the Bhutto's government had rigged elections on a massive scale in March 1977 and government funds, transport, means of communications, and government agencies were used in support of the PPP's candidates.[4]

It appears that after the High Court granted bail to Bhutto, Zia lost faith in the High Court and ordinary courts in handling Bhutto's case the way he wanted. Therefore, an announcement was made that he would be tried by a special military court presided over by a Brigadier or a Major-General in Lahore.[5] It is belived that Zia was advised that a military trial would bring bad name and international embarrassment to his government and he that should allow ordinary civilian courts to try him. This explanation carried weight but Zia was not going to be dissuaded merely by the fear of international censure because, by that time, he had already gone too far in his confrontation with Bhutto and could not take the risk of Bhutto being released. He needed iron-clad assurances and guarantees that this would not happen and these guarantees must have come from somewhere. The object of speculation can only be Maulvi Mushtaq, especially in view of the events that unveiled soon thereafter.

Maulvi Mushtaq formed a full Bench of five judges for Bhutto's trial with himself at the head of the Bench. He took care that Justice K.M.A. Samdani, who had granted bail to Bhutto, was kept out of the Bench. A petition for cancellation of the bail was entertained and admitted to regular hearing on 21 September by the same full Bench of five judges. This was clearly against the established practice of the High Courts that the petition for cancellation of bail is fixed before the same judge who granted it in the first place or before a Bench of which he is a member. The cancellation of bail, though academic because Bhutto was already under detention, was a clear harbinger of events to come at the trial. It was no surprise when the full Bench cancelled Bhutto's bail by its order dated 9 October 1977. In the detailed order, the full Bench held that on the basis of all the material produced before them, 'there appears reasonable ground for believing that the respondent has been guilty of an offence punishable with death or imprisonment for life'. The judges also observed that there was evidence of motive on the part of Bhutto who had been threatening Ahmad Raza on the floor of the National Assembly. They also referred to the evidence of the approver Masood Mahmood, connecting Bhutto directly with the abetment.[6]

The judgment in the case for cancellation of bail was a forebearer of what to expect at the trial and must have satisfied Zia and his *junta* that things were on the right track. It was announced by the full Bench that trial proceedings would commence on 10 October. No wonder, the trial by special military court was heard of no more.

The Trial of Bhutto

Bhutto was tried before a full Bench of five judges consisting of the acting Chief Justice Maulvi Mushtaq Husâin, Zakiuddin Pal, M.S.H. Qureshi, Aftab Husain, and Gulbaz Khan, JJ; Maulvi Mushtaq had made the selection of the Bench rather carefully. Zakiuddin Pal was an old Muslim Leaguer known to be hostile to Bhutto.

Aftab Husain was a protege of Maulvi Mushtaq and would go along with him. The other two were not known for writing dissenting judgments and were quite manageable. There were four others accused with Bhutto, Mian Muhammad Abbas, a senior official of the Federal Security Forces (FSF), and three junior officials of the FSF.

At the commencement of the trial, all the accused had pleaded not guilty but later on the three junior officials of the FSF, Ghulam Mustafa, Arshad Iqbal, and Rana Iftikhar Ahmad, made confessional statements saying that they acted under orders. Initially, trial proceedings were open to the public but after 25 January 1978, the proceedings were held in camera. Bhutto boycotted the proceedings of the trial and withdrew the power of attorney of his counsel after his application dated 18 December 1977 for transfer of the case and 22 December 1977 (requesting for hearing of the application of 18 December 1977) were dismissed by the Court in chambers. In his statement, recorded as an accused person he stated that he would not be offering his defence as he was boycotting the proceedings of the trial. He added further that he would confine his statement mainly to two issues, namely, his lack of confidence in the fairness of the trial and the why this case had been fabricated against him. The High Court *vide* its judgment dated 18 March, 1978 convicted all the accused for criminal conspiracy and murder and sentenced them to death.[7] The accused were given seven days' mandatory period for filing an appeal in the Supreme Court against their sentence and conviction. The statement of Bhutto had not been reproduced in the judgment of the High Court.

Was the Trial Fair?

It has been argued in the years preceding the trial that Bhutto never got a fair trial. If the apprehension and pleadings of the accused are any criterion, then Bhutto's transfer application moved in the High Court as well as in the Supreme Court bear ample testimony to the fact that he did not get a fair trial. In the application moved in the Lahore High Court, Bhutto levelled a number of allegations of substance with regard to the trial of the case by the Full Bench presided over by the acting Chief Justice (Mushtaq Husain). In order to appreciate the contention in this application it may be kept in mind that the learned acting Chief Justice was also functioning as the Chief Election Commissioner at the time. (He was confirmed as the Chief Justice during the hearing of this case). The application is reproduced below:

1. That the central executive of the Pakistan People's Party at its meeting held in Karachi on 3 August 1977 under the chairmanship of the petitioner expressed in clear and unambiguous terms that Mr Justice Mushtaq Husain, the Chief Election Commissioner was prejudicial and partial against the Pakistan Peoples Party. The central executive put the view on public record in his statement published in the newspapers on 4 August 1977 and, *inter alia*, stated that:

(i) Combining the office of the Chief Election Commissioner with that of the Chief Justice of the largest High Court in the country is a travesty of justice.

(ii) The Chief Election Commissioner who was superseded by the People's Party government has already betrayed his bias and prejudice against the party in his recent television press conference. He has made irrelevant, fortuitous, and baseless remarks thereby shown his partisan attitude....

2. That a Press Note in reply issued by the Election Commission of Pakistan (Published in the Newspapers on 5 August 1977), *inter alia*, stated:

   The Election Commission of Pakistan today considered the allegations of partisanship and bias made by the Chairman of Pakistan People's Party (PPP) in respect of the observations of the Chief Election Commissioner in his television press conference. Though the allegations were incorrect as the observations of the Chief Election Commissioner are supported by the records of the Commission, it was decided to ignore the allegations as the Commission had no intention to start a dialogue but it would always welcome and act upon the constructive suggestions from whichever quarter they emanate.

3. That in the early hours of 3 September 1977, a large contingent of army commandos, FIA men, and the police armed to the teeth raided the residence of the petitioner, broke open the house and arrested him. It was subsequently announced that the arrest had been made under sections 302/307/120-B/109 PPC on the basis of an FIR lodged with the Lahore Police on 11 November 1974 by Mr Ahmad Raza Kasuri soon after the death of his father caused by fire arms injuries. After the arrest in Karachi the petitioner was brought to Lahore and put under army custody in a house somewhere in the army cantonment. Later he was confined in Kot Lakhpat jail. A bail application was moved on his behalf and on 13 September 1977 Mr Justice K.M.A. Samdani of this Honourable court was pleased to order his release. Three days later, that is, on 16 September 1977 he was again arrested from his residence in Larkana under martial law order number 12 and put in solitary confinement, first in Sukkur and then in Karachi and finally on 22 September 1977 again in Kot Lakhpat Jail, Lahore.

4. That prior to that a Division Bench of this Court consisting of Mr Justice K.M.A. Samdani and Mr Justice Mazharul Haq was already enquiring into a private complaint of Mr Ahmad Raza Kasuri about the same incident as mentioned in his FIR of 11 November 1974. While the High Court Division Bench was conducting enquiry into the said complaint and Mr Justice Samdani was hearing the bail application, an incomplete *challan* on the basis of the said FIR of 11 November 1974 was submitted in the court of a magistrate in Lahore which was immediately forwarded to the sessions judge, Lahore.

5. That apprehension of the petitioner about the partiality and prejudice of Mr Justice Mushtaq Husain, the acting Chief Justice, expressed a month earlier and before the institution of these cases, was substantiated by his order transferring the above mentioned *challan* case from the lower court to the High Court. On the same day the petitioner was enlarged on bail by Mr Justice K.M.A. Samdani, even before a complete *challan* was submitted to the trial court.

6. That again the order passed on the same day, i.e., 13 September 1977 by Mr Justice Mushtaq Husain constituting a special Bench of five judges presided over by himself for the trial of the *challan* case, which the private complaint with regard to the same matter was already being inquired into by the said Division Bench of the High Court caused further apprehension in the mind of the petitioner about not getting a fair trial.

As already submitted that on that date even though the complete *challan* had not been filed, yet 24 September 1977 was fixed for the trial of the case.

7. That withdrawal of the *challan* case from lower court without hearing the petitioner has caused prejudice to him and deprived him of his valuable rights including those of appeal/revision to the High Court.

8. That at the first hearing of the *challan* case on 24 September 1977, the petitioner requested for three weeks adjournment as all his senior counsels were appearing at that time in the Supreme Court in Rawalpindi in Begum Nusrat Bhutto's constitutional petition questioning the validity of the detention of the petitioner and some other prominent PPP leaders under MLO number 12. The Bench, however, only adjourned the case for seven days, as required by law, assuring the petitioner that further adjournment would be considered if his counsel needed it after seven days. On this a junior advocate, Mr Aftab Gul intervened and requested for more time. The Court took amiss Mr Aftab Gul's sudden intervention, therefore, the petitioner rose to stop him and stated that he had confidence in the court clearly implying thereby that he was satisfied with the seven days of adjournment on the assurance of the Court that if needed, a further adjournment to the date of commencement of the trial would be granted. This incident was not reported in the Press the next day i.e., on the 25 September 1977. However, on that date i.e., on 25 September 1977 a report appeared that a petition for Leave to Appeal had been moved in the Supreme Court on behalf of the petitioner, *inter alia*, alleging partiality and bias against Mr Justice Mushtaq Husain. It was further reported that the same had been dismissed by the Supreme Court on the ground that the points may be raised in the first instance before the High Court itself. This was done as mentioned in the following paragraph. Thereafter on 26 September 1977 a news report appeared in the *Pakistan Times* and other newspapers that the counsel for the petitioner had misstated the position before the Supreme Court and that the petitioner had the 'fullest confidence' in the Bench presided over by Mr Justice Mushtaq Husain. This inspired and misleading report came as a complete surprise to the petitioner.

When the petitioner was brought before the Bench again on 27 September, 1977 he availed the very first opportunity to point out the misleading report and explained that at the previous hearing, the question pertained only to fixing the next date of hearing of the *challan* case about which he had expressed his satisfaction and confidence in that limited context and not 'fullest confidence' generally in the Bench. It was inconceivable for the petitioner to specifically instruct his counsel to move the Supreme Court against the prejudice and partiality of Mr Justice Mushtaq Husain and yet on the same day and at about the same time to express his 'fullest confidence' in the Bench presided over by him. The fact that the Bench did not dispute the explanation of the petitioner at that time clearly shows that the inspired newspaper reports were made deliberately with the purpose of misleading the public and casting a reflection on the petitioner.

9. That the objections mentioned in the foregoing paragraphs were raised before this Honourable court by Miscellaneous Application No. 933-M/1977 dated 4 October 1977 along with Miscellaneous Application No. 932-M/1977 dated 4 October 1977. These miscellaneous applications were heard on 4, 5, and 8 October 1977 and summarily dismissed on 9 October 1977 by the Bench of five judges presided over by Mr Justice Mushtaq Husain.

10. That as a result of the bail granted to the petitioner by Mr Justice K.M.A. Samdani on 13 September 1977, the authorities were greatly disturbed is clear from the records of the Supreme Court in the constitutional petition of Begum Nusrat Bhutto. However, on 21 September 1977 the Bench presided over by the acting Chief Justice on the application of special public prosecutor, issued a show cause notice to the petitioner as to why the bail granted to him on 13 September 1977 by Mr Justice K.M.A. Samdani be not cancelled? The petitioner was at that time already confined in Karachi jail under MLO number 12. This fact was within the knowledge of the learned acting Chief Justice and other members of the Bench. This notwithstanding the Court ordered immediate service of this show cause notice for 24 September 1977 which was taken by a special messenger to Karachi the same day and served at about midnight on the petitioner in Karachi Jail. The petitioner failed to understand the haste and urgency in serving this show cause notice on him when he was already in jail and in solitary confinement? However, subsequently, the records of the Supreme Court referred to above, threw light on these unusual and extraordinary measures.
11. That while counsel for the petitioner Mr Ghulam Ali Memon was arguing Cr. Misc. No. 932 1977, the petitioner rose on two or three occasions to intervene on certain points. On the first occasion he wanted to clarify a point after some observation from the Bench not directly related to the submissions of his counsel. Similarly, on the second and third occasions the petitioner rose and stated that he wanted to supplement the submissions of his counsel on the points which were being argued and on which the counsel was questioned by the Bench. On each occasion the petitioner was categorically assured that he would be given sufficient opportunity to address the Court after conclusion of his counsel's submissions. On the second occasion the learned acting Chief Justice promised to give the petitioner time to make submissions for 'hours and hours'. This assurance was repeated again in open court and was heard by every one present in Court. However, at the conclusion of the arguments of the petitioner's counsel on 8 October 1977, before the petitioner could rise to make his submission as promised to him, the learned acting Chief Justice, to the utter surprise of the petitioner and those present in Court, observed with obvious vehemence, that the petitioner would not be permitted to address the Court but, if he wanted, he could submit in writing his views for which services of a stenographer would be made available to him in the Court premises by the Court. The Court further announced that the orders on these applications and on the application for cancellation of bail which had been argued earlier by the special public prosecutor and the petitioner's counsel, Mr Muhammad Hayat Junejo, would be announced on the following day.
12. That after the Court rose the petitioner politely declined the 'kind' offer of the Court to make submissions in writing and brought the fact on record that he had not been given the promised opportunity to address the Court.
13. Before the commencement of trial, when the petition for cancellation of bail was being argued, with the passage of a night, a dock was specially put in the court and the petitioner was directed to be seated before it. The petitioner was made to sit behind that specially erected dock with a senior intelligence officer on his right and senior police officer seated on his left. This seating arrangement is being continued at each hearing. This arrangement deprives the petitioner to give instructions in confidence to his lawyers in court out of hearing of these officers. In addition, this dock has been specially devised and put into use to cage and humiliate the petitioner. Many accused had been tried in this High Court on its original side over the years, but this is the first

time that such a dock has been made to humiliate the petitioner on the one hand and to make it impossible for him to give instructions to his counsel on the other. The object is also to devalue the importance and stature of the petitioner and to psychologically prepare public opinion for a biased and prejudicial decision. Otherwise there is no reason to add insult to injury in this manner.

14. That in the course of the trial of the case the learned acting Chief Justice thought it proper to give an interview to the correspondent of BBC (British Broadcasting Corporation) and another foreign newspaper journalist with the object of impressing the world that the petitioner was getting fair trial according to Common Law traditions and that special arrangements had been made like tape-recording the proceedings. This interview was broadcast by the BBC and reported in newspapers including the *Pakistan Times* of Lahore. It is the submission of the petitioner that it is not normal for judges claiming to follow Common Law traditions to give press interviews about the manner and conduct of trial whilst the trial is in progress. It clearly indicated that the learned acting Chief Judge felt that general impression inside and outside the country was that the petitioner was not getting a fair trial, and the learned Chief Justice was at pains to dispel this impression in the said interviews.

15. After reading the interview in the *Pakistan Times* the petitioner submitted an application to the Court protesting against the observations of the learned acting Chief Justice but the said application was directed to be 'filed'.

16. That in the course of trial the petitioner got seriously indisposed. He was running a temperature of up to 103° and under the advice of the doctors could not attend the Court for several days. The learned acting Chief Justice by way of 'favour' adjourned the case for two days at the most and told the counsel for the petitioner that thereafter he would proceed with the trial in the absence of the petitioner. The request of the counsel that he was severely handicapped in cross-examination of the witnesses in the absence of the petitioner as he would not be available to give instructions in the course of cross-examination was not accepted by the Court. Thus the examination and cross-examination of witnesses was conducted for about three weeks in the absence of the petitioner, to his great prejudice.

17. That the petitioner preferred a petition for special leave to appeal before the Supreme Court but the said petition in so far as it concerned the bias in the trial Bench was withdrawn on the assurance that the petitioner would be at liberty to raise this question after the trial, and if necessary, even earlier.

18. That for reasons stated above and more so from the manner and conduct of the trial by the Bench presided over by Mr Justice Mushtaq Husain, the petitioner is convinced beyond doubt that he is not getting a fair trial. The objections and requests of the defence counsel are often rejected without being recorded. Similarly, relevant questions put to prosecution witnesses are either disallowed without being recorded or the question and answers are recorded after significant discussions between the counsel for defence, special public prosecutors, and the Bench in the presence of the witnesses thus defeating the very purpose of cross-examination. Important documents of benefit to the defence are at times not allowed to be put to the witnesses or to come on record. Similarly, other documents which the defence wants to prove through prosecution witnesses are not brought on record. Some of the important documentary evidence in possession of the prosecution or government departments is not made available to the defence or is made available only after repeated requests and protestations. Counsel for the defence have been insulted, ridiculed and brow-beaten in open court on several

> occasions by the Bench. The petitioner has also been subjected to insults from time to time. It has been noticed that the evidence dictated in Court and typed is recast and re-typed later and copies of the re-typed record are supplied to the parties and the press. So far the petitioner has patiently exercised exemplary restraint in the face of repeated provocations only to show to the people of Pakistan that he is being subjected to a naked and unparalleled witch hunt for no other reason except for political considerations.[8]

The application continues and gives instances of uncalled for remarks by Maulvi Mushtaq about or against Bhutto during the proceedings which included reference to his supersession as Chief Justice and the civilian martial law. Several instances of the insulting attitude of the acting Chief Justice towards the defence counsel were also mentioned in the application at length. It was alleged that he frequently lost his temper at the defence counsel and instances were mentioned therein. It was alleged that the record of the proceedings was being incorrectly prepared deliberately. Several instances were mentioned which included:

- answers to relevant questions pertaining to the veracity of important witnesses were not recorded;
- many relevant questions put to prosecution witnesses by the defence counsel were disallowed and overruled;
- answers of the prosecution witnesses to the questions in the cross examination were misrecorded in a way that would advance the case of the prosecution;
- Court interjected whenever an answer favourable to the defence was given by a prosecution witness and suggested an answer to the witness which was favourable to the prosecution case;
- Special public prosecutors were allowed to put all types of questions, relevant or irrelevant, admissible or inadmissible including leading ones to their own witnesses and the objections taken by the defence were ignored with contempt or overruled summarily;
- Changes in the record of the Court were made subsequent to the recording of statements of the witnesses in the Court;
- Carbon copies of the statements of the witnesses were not supplied to the defence on that day and after two or three days, photocopies of the statements were given to the defence implying thereby that transcripts of the evidence recorded were changed or improved in the meanwhile;
- Very often the evidence of the prosecution witnesses was tailored, polished, tightened, and improved upon by questionable means to help the prosecution;
- The proceedings were being tape recorded but no tapes were supplied to the defence despite requests in this behalf and the defence was also not allowed to place its own tape recorder despite application made for the purpose;
- The acting Chief Justice or a member of the Bench would put his hand on the microphone when a remark was made by him to avoid it being tape-recorded and subsequently a microphone was installed with an automatic switch controlled by the ACJ and he could stop the recording as and when he desired; and

> Instance of unpleasant exchange between Bhutto and Maulvi Mushtaq were given which were used to bar Bhutto from being present in the Court and for proceeding with the trial in absentia.

This application was dismissed in Chambers by the Bench after which Bhutto refused to offer any defence in the proceedings and boycotted the trial altogether.

The trial proceedings, after a certain stage, were ordered to be held in camera. The justification was that Bhutto refused to enter upon his defence and tried to turn the Court into a political forum. The Court justified the proceedings in camera and *ex parte* proceedings in the judgment in the following words:

> Mr D. M. Awan[9] addressed arguments on the questions of maintainability of the petition. He did not argue the points which had already been decided. He also did not address on matters on which rulings had been given after giving full hearing and which could only be urged in appeal. The other new points were sheer calumnies which he made no effort to justify. During the course of the hearing the principal accused tried to interrupt and interfere in the proceedings, but he was informed that he would be given an opportunity to supplement the arguments of his counsel on merits. After finishing his arguments, Mr D. M. Awan requested to be allowed to withdraw from the case. This request was not granted since there appeared to be no ground for allowing him to withdraw from the prosecution of the defence. He then prayed that the accused might also be given a chance to make some submissions on merits. The accused was allowed to argue on merits although he had no right to address the Court in person when he was represented and his counsel had already been given a full hearing. Instead of making any contribution towards the merits of his petition, he started a political speech which was absolutely irrelevant. He was warned several times and asked to be relevant in his submissions but he finished his submission by saying that if he was not allowed to say what he wanted to say, he would not address the Court any further. The petition for transfer was then dismissed.
>
> When the Bench assembled in the court room for recording the evidence of Ghulam Hussain, approver (P.W.31) who had already been cross-examined at length by Mr Ehsan Qadir on behalf of the principal accused, the learned counsel stated that he had no more question to ask since his client had instructed him to do so.
>
> Later, Mr D. M. Awan stated at the Bar that his client had withdrawn the powers of attorney of all his counsel. He also placed on record a writing by the principal accused that he did not want to defend in view of what had happened that day. The reference was obviously to the hearing of his petition for transfer in Chamber, its dismissal, and the fact that the said accused had to be ordered to take a seat since the Court was not inclined to hear irrelevant arguments or a political speech in a trial which is to be conducted under the provisions of the Evidence Act.
>
> Mr Ehsan Qadir and Mr D. M. Awan were directed to conduct the defence at State expenses, Mr Ehsan Qadir appeared before the Bench after the Court rose for the day and requested to be relieved since he had other professional business at Sargodha where he usually practices. Next day Mr D. M. Awan also requested to be relieved on the ground that the above mentioned accused refused to give him any instructions.
>
> The High Court rules make provisions for arranging a counsel in a sessions Court for an unrepresented person accused of an offence punishable with capital sentence in case he is indigent. Where the case is tried by the High Court on its original side Rule 2 Chapter 4-E

of Volume V of the *High Court Rules and Orders* vests the Court with a discretion to arrange representation even for the defence of an accused who is not a pauper and can afford to engage a counsel. It was in exercise of this discretion in favour of the accused that the Court had asked the counsel who had defended him so long, to continue defending him at state expense. Since the accused appeared bent upon thwarting this attempt to arrange for his defence at state expense and refused to cooperate with the counsel, the court relieved Mr D. M. Awan and directed the accused to conduct the case himself.

This was the only course open to the Court since it has no authority under the above rule to force upon the accused the services of a counsel if he is unwilling to accept them. As observed by a Division Bench of the Lahore High Court in PLD 1954 Lahore 547 (*Iftikhar-ud-Din v State*) if the accused contumaciously refused to accept the offer of legal advice made to him and is not willing to accept the representation arranged by the Court, he must be left to conduct his case himself.

The accused refused to cross examine other witnesses who were formal. Mr Qurban Sadiq Ikram, learned counsel for Mian Muhammad Abbas, accused, however, cross-examined them in detail on all relevant points. He brought on record and proved through the prosecution witness most of these statements under sections 161 and 164 Cr.P.C. made by witnesses for the prosecution with which the counsel for the principal accused had tried to confront them. This was done presumably because the defence of the two accused appears to be identical.

When the first question was put to the said accused in his examination under section 342 Cr.P.C., he stated that since he was boycotting the proceedings, he would not be offering any defence. He would, however, make a statement only about the reasons why the present case was fabricated against him and why he apprehended that he would not get fair trial and justice in this Court.

A reference to the last point was entirely uncalled for since the accused had already submitted a number of petitions making false, baseless, and scandalous allegations against the Court which had been disposed of. These allegations were not at all relevant to the statement under section 342 Cr.P.C. Yet if the accused considered it necessary to harp on the same tune, it must be only with the intention that his calumnious and slanderous statement may receive publicity in open court as well as in the Press. This was the object with which he wanted the last petition for transfer to be heard in Court.

Now no court, much less a superior court, can allow a litigant to challenge before it its fairness, integrity, and impartiality, or to scandalize it, and to go on repeating with impunity, scandalous and libelous attacks on judges which are calculated to lower the authority of the judges and to malign them. If this is allowed, it would shake the public confidence in the administration of justice. In exercise of the discretion vested in the courts by the proviso to section 352 Cr. P.C., the proceedings were, therefore, directed to be held in camera.

Next day, when the Court assembled, the principal accused showed surprise that the Press and the public had been excluded from the Court. He emphasized that it should be an open trial. His attention was drawn to section 352 of the Criminal Procedure Code which confers a discretion upon the Court to order at any stage of any particular case if it thinks fit that the public generally or any particular person shall not have access to or be or remain in the room or building used by it. The accused stated that he would consult his lawyers on the question whether the proceedings could be held in camera, it was pointed out to him that he had already given up his lawyers. The next questions under section 342

Cr.P.C. (Question No.54) was then put to him. Instead of answering the question, he dictated a statement covering more than nine pages in which he, amongst other things, attacked the Court's impartiality and the legality of the order holding the trial in camera.

At the end of this irrelevant address, the Chief Justice advised him to answer the questions since it was in his own interest to do so and assured him that in case he agreed to make a statement, all questions would be put to him again. He requested for time to consult Mr Yahya Bakhtiar and Mr D. M. Awan. The case was, therefore, adjourned to the 28th of January, 1978 to enable the accused to seek legal advice.

The accused met his counsel, Mr Yahya Bakhtiar, for 3-1/2 hours on 25 January 1978. He again met his counsel in jail on the next two days. However, he submitted an application for copy of the order for holding the proceedings in camera and copies of his statements recorded on 24 and 25 January 1978. The copies of the order as well as his statement made on 24 January 1978 were supplied to him on 28 January 1978. The copy of the statement made on 25 January 1978 could not, however, be supplied to him since it contained scandalous and scurrilous remarks against the Court. On 28 January 1978 the accused again requested for further time to consult his counsel on the question whether the proceedings could be held in camera. It was pointed out to him that he was given an opportunity to see his counsel only on the question whether he would like to make statement under Section 342 Cr. P.C. The Court, however, agreed to give him five minutes for this purpose.

The Court re-assembled after about half an hour. The accused stated that his counsel had by then hardly read a few questions out of the statement made on the 24 January 1978, and the time given to him was insufficient for advice. The Court did not agree to any further adjournment since the reading of his earlier statement under Section 342 Cr. P.C. was not material for tendering advice on the question whether he should answer questions particularly when My Lord the Chief Justice had assured him that all the questions will be put to him again in case he agreed to answer them. When the next question was put to the witness, he again dictated a statement almost repeating what he had already stated on the 25 January 1978. This statement covers more than eleven pages. Thereafter, he did not answer any question put to him.

After his statement was recorded, the said accused was asked to sign it, but he refused to do so. He was asked to read the statement. On his inquiry whether he could correct the typographical or grammatical errors, he was told to make any correction so long as the substance of the statement was not changed. He wrote certain uncalled for and incorrect remarks that the statement might not have been complete.

Thereafter, the accused sent an application through the superintendent jail, in which he alleged that his statement was not correctly and completely recorded. This application was dismissed since the statement had been typed on the dictation of the accused himself, and the allegations levelled in the petition were absolutely false.

On 25 January 1978, a few supporters of the principal accused demonstrated against the holding of the Court in camera and created disturbances inside the Chambers of My Lord the Chief Justice. In view of the possibility of such disturbances occurring in future, it was ordered that the proceedings of the trial should continue in camera.

On 7 February 1978, after the defence evidence had been recorded, the accused was asked whether he would like to cross-examine D.W.4 who had been produced on behalf of the three confessing accused. The accused stated that he would not cross examine him but make a statement on his statement. He was allowed to do so although he had no right to make such a statement after the close of his statement under section 342 Cr.P.C. He dictated more than eleven pages to the typist and repeated all that had been said by him on 25 and 28 January 1978 and also attacked the order to continue all further proceedings in camera. Thereafter, he refused to even read or sign the statement.[10]

At the end of every day during the in-camera proceedings, the Court released a summary of the proceedings for publication in the Press.[11]

From the contents of above paragraphs of the judgment, the tension between the Court and the accused and his counsel is evident. Whatever the justification offered by the Court in its judgment, it is clear that the accused party had lost all faith in the Court and was refusing to co-operate. This situation, particularly the environment of the Court, could not be considered conducive to the dispensation of justice. The Court and the accused had become adversaries and the trial had become ineffectual, rather a farce.

Bhutto vigorously challenged the trial by the full Bench on grounds of bias and pleaded that for the trial proceedings were vitiated. While boycotting the proceedings, Bhutto confined his statement to lack of confidence in the fairness of the trial and the reason why this case had been fabricated against him.

Mr Irshad Qureshi, counsel for the three co-accused with Bhutto, Ghulam Mustafa, Arshad Iqbal, and Rana Iftikhar Ahmad, made a press statement in 1996 that Bhutto's trial was unfair and part of a conspiracy to which he himself was a party to remove him from the political scene. This statement should not be accepted without doubts to his veracity because it has been made after eighteen years of the conclusion of the trial and it was made during the government of Benazir Bhutto. The possibility of an effort to please the government and to get personal benefits cannot be overlooked.

The Judgment of the High Court

The judgment dated 18 March 1978, authored by Justice Aftab Husain, was a lengthy and detailed one, discussing various points and principles relating to criminal law.[12] However, the principles discussed or laid down in the judgment have generally not been followed or even referred to by the courts in Pakistan. Generally, the abettors to a murder are not awarded capital punishment, and this judgment stands out unique in this respect. All the five accused, including the three who had confessed, were sentenced to death. Apart from being judged about criminal culpability, the Court also took pains to judge each man as a good Muslim. Bhutto's belief in Islam and commitment to Islamic ideology was questioned. He was held incapable of being elected to the high office of the Prime Minister nor was he considered true to his oath because he had used the Constitution and the law as the handmaiden of his polity.

The remarks about his faith or his disrespectful attitude towards the Constitution had apparently no relevance to the offence he was charged with. They only reveal the mindset of the judges and betray their innate dislike for Bhutto and his style of governance.

Constitution of the High Court Bench Challenged

The order of the Lahore High Court, cancelling Bhutto's bail was challenged before the Supreme Court and the main grounds taken therein were as under:

(a) That the Chief Justice of Lahore High Court (Aslam Riaz Husain) on taking over as the Governor of Punjab, had ceased to be the Chief Justice and in the absence of the Chief Justice, the High Court was not properly constituted; and

(b) That one person could not combine in himself two constitutional offices like acting Chief Justice and Chief Election Commissioner, as Maulvi Mushtaq had done.

For these reasons, it was contended that the trial being held by the High Court was vitiated and the order of the Court cancelling his bail on 9 October 1977 was illegal.

The Supreme Court held that the constitution and continuity of the High Court is not affected by a temporary vacancy in the office of the Chief Justice or of any of the judges from among the prescribed strength of the High Court. It would be affected only if the office of the Chief Justice were to be abolished and only in that case could it be said that the High Court has ceased to be properly constituted in terms of the Constitution.[13] Temporary appointment of the Chief Justice of the High Court as acting Governor of the province did not amount to the vacation of office of Chief Justice by the incumbent of that office.

On the other matter, the Supreme Court held the disability of the Chief Election Commissioner to perform judicial functions as a serving judge of the Supreme Court or of a High Court only applied to one holding the permanent appointment and not to an acting appointment. Hence, the acting Chief Justice Mushtaq Husain did not suffer from any disability, disqualification, and prohibition in performing his judicial duties because his appointment as Chief Election Commissioner was in the nature of a temporary and ad hoc appointment for the limited purpose of holding forthcoming elections.

The reasoning adopted by the Supreme Court was highly pedantic and unconvincing. A Chief Election Commissioner, temporary or permanent for three years, is performing duties of this constitutional office and so long as he does it, the bar of not performing other judicial functions applied to him because otherwise the simultaneous performance of functions as Chief Election Commission and a judge could be contradictory and conflicting. There is every likelihood that a decision made by the Chief Election Commissioner is challenged before a High Court in writ jurisdiction and then the acting Chief Justice, in exercise of his other constitutional position, would be either hearing the petition himself against his own decision or assigning it to some other judge of his choice for decision. How would that be conducive to the administration of justice? There has been an unfortunate practice by the members of the judiciary to hold more than one office at the same time and this has never been seen with favour by the lawyer community or the public at large. Furthermore, the decision in this case is clearly repugnant to the findings given by the Supreme Court in an earlier judgment in a similar case of a judge holding two constitutional positions. It was observed that appointment of a permanent judge of the Supreme Court as Chief Justice of a High Court was not beneficial to the interests of the judiciary or to the people at large and should not be regarded as a healthy precedent.[14]

While disposing of the case (*Zulfiqar Ali Bhutto v The State*), Justice Anwar-ul-Haq, took the opportunity to further expand the doctrine of necessity in the following words:

> Once an extra-Constitutional action or intervention is validated on ground of state or civil necessity, then, as a logical corollary, it follows that the new regime or administration must interpret and be permitted, in the public interest, not only to run the day-to-day affairs of the country, but also to work toward the achievement of the objectives or the basis on which its intervention has earned validation.

The Chief Justice thus gave Zia greater authority than he had received in the Nusrat Bhutto case. At the same time, the Supreme Court narrowed the scope of judicial review in the following words:

> It must be clearly understood that in judging whether an action taken by the President or the CMLA is valid under the law of necessity, the court is not to sit in appeal over the executive or legislative authority. The responsibility for the relevant action, its methodology and procedural details, must rest on that authority. In exercising its power of judicial review, the court is concerned with examining whether the impugned action reasonably falls within any of the categories enumerated by the Supreme Court in Nusrat Bhutto's case.

Appeal before the Supreme Court

Bhutto filed an appeal against his conviction before the Supreme Court which was argued for months before a Bench of nine judges presided over by the Chief Justice. Bhutto took the plea of bias and unfair trial before the Supreme Court. He filed a concise statement in the Supreme Court, the relevant extracts of which are reproduced as follows:

> It is indeed a mockery for this regime to pontificate on the independent character of the Chief Election Commissioner when it has brazenly merged the office of the Chief Election Commissioner and the Chief Justice of Lahore High Court, under the control of the man who is known to be after my blood. The Chief Election Commissioner's prejudice against me is, by now, accepted internationally. It is an axiomatic fact beyond reach of denial.
>
> Against a background of much hostility, Maulvi Mushtaq Husain was pleased to hear my detention petition virtually 'in camera' inside the prison walls of Lahore camp jail. This was in January 1969. However, it was not he who released me from detention, but the government which withdrew the detention order, in view of the prevailing circumstances.

With the change in the situation, Maulvi Mushtaq Husain met me in the Punjab House in Rawalpindi soon after I became President of Pakistan. He gave blatant indications of his ambitions, suggesting that, at this critical juncture in the history of Pakistan, the new President would need a trustworthy man in control of the judiciary. He was gravely dejected when his expectations were not met, when a few months later Sardar Muhammad Iqbal was appointed the Chief Justice of the Lahore High Court by my government.

He did not conceal his anger. He displayed his resentment in many ways, both in his official capacity and otherwise. In sheer desperation, he suggested to Ghulam Mustafa Khar, the former Governor and Chief Minister of the Punjab to have me 'shot through the head'. When, following the constitutional amendment, Mr Justice Aslam Riaz Husain was appointed the Chief Justice of Lahore High Court, he interpreted this second supersession to be an intolerable insult, to the extent that he gave vent to his pent up anger on the very first day of the murder trial, by pointedly referring to his supersession as 'a hypothetical case'.

Earlier, in the fall of 1975, he had an unpleasant and unmentionable altercation with Mr Abdul Hafiz Pirzada, a senior Federal Minister. After his second supersession he did not seriously attend to his official functions, spending most of his time brooding away in his Chamber. On the slightest pretext he would fly off to Europe to sublimate. He was in Europe when the *coup d'etat* of 5 July 1977, took place. He was summoned to Pakistan by the ringleaders of the coup to become a member of the inner circle. He responded to the invitation with the enthusiasm of a fanatic.

In anticipation of the meritorious services he was to render, he was immediately rewarded with the office of the acting Chief Justice of Lahore High Court. He was confirmed as Chief Justice during the course of my trial for murder. Simultaneously with his appointment as Acting Chief Justice of Lahore High Court, he was appointed as Chief Election Commissioner. He baptised the appointment with a vicious attack on the Pakistan People's Party's government in an interview which was heard on the radio and television.[15]

An application alleging bias against the Chief Justice of Supreme Court, Justice S. Anwar-ul-Haq, was also moved. The main contentions of this application have been reproduced in the following manner by the Chief Justice himself:[16]

i. that I resented the constitution sixth amendment made by the parliament under the appellant's leadership of the House, whereby my predecessor got an extension in the term of his office, and my promotion to the office of Chief Justice of Pakistan got consequently delayed;
ii. that in the judgment of the Court in Begum Nusrat Bhutto's case, while holding that the 1973 Constitution is still the supreme law of the land, I have given arbitrary powers to General Ziaul Haq to rule the country for an indefinite period, including the powers to amend the constitution, which I found necessary to do, as he had nullified the sixth amendment to pave the way for my appointment as Chief Justice;
iii. that before my appointment as Chief Justice, judges of the Supreme Court had declined to take the oath as prescribed by the Chief Martial Law Administrator, but on my assumption of office all the judges immediately agreed to take the new oath ordered by the General;
iv. that I have been critical of his administration for making amendments in the constitution, thus showing my deep resentment against him, as evidenced by my

speeches at the time of the Full Court References on the assumption of my present office, on the occasion of the Fourth Jurists Conference held in Lahore in December 1977, and while addressing the District and High Court Bar Associations of Karachi on 23 and 24 January 1978;

v. that I and Mr Justice Mushtaq Husain, the Chief Justice of the Lahore High Court, have been close friends for many years, and both are zealously collaborating with the martial law regime; and

vi. that while his appeal was pending before the Supreme Court, I did not consider it indiscreet or embarrassing to accept General Ziaul Haq's offer to appoint me as the acting President of Pakistan, thus actively identifying myself fully with the executive, and merging albeit temporarily, the executive and the judicial organs of the state.

Chief Justice Anwar-ul-Haq dismissed the application of Bhutto as untenable after quoting Lord Hewart: 'that it is of fundamental importance that justice should not only be done but should manifestly be seen to be done' and went on to hold that he could do justice without fear or favour. Bhutto's plea of bias was rejected.

With regard to the allegation of bias against the acting Chief Justice of Lahore High Court, Chief Justice Anwar-ul-Haq observed:

> ...I have reached the conclusion that although some of the orders made by the trial Bench in the day to day conduct of the case may not have been correct on a strict view of the law; and some others may not have been fully called for in the fact and circumstances of the case, yet these were all matters within the discretion of the Court, and mere error therein cannot amount to proof of bias. The appellant was unfortunately misled into thinking from the very start of the case that the learned acting Chief Justice was biased against him. There were, in fact, no factual basis for such an apprehension. In any case, there was no such apprehension in respect of any of the other four learned Judges constituting the Bench.[17]

Accordingly, Bhutto's contention that the trial was vitiated by reason of bias on the part of the presiding judge of the Bench was rejected.

It is submitted with respect that the view of the learned Chief Justice was not correct. Enough material was brought on the record by Bhutto which legitimately laid the foundation for bias. Various factual allegations made with regard to bias were not controverted by the state nor by the Chief Justice. Bhutto succeeded in casting substantial shadow of suspicion on the trial. In an interview which appeared in a monthly magazine[18] on 18 April 1984, Mushtaq Husain was asked why he did not go to the Supreme Court of Pakistan, although he was elevated to the highest Court of the country on more than one occasion. His reply was as follows:

> On one and two occasions I was asked to go to the Supreme Court of Pakistan but I declined. My elevation to the Supreme Court was particularly insisted upon when Mr Aslam Riaz Husain was made Chief Justice of the Lahore High Court. I opted to stay in the High Court as senior puisne judge and I wanted to retire as a judge of the Lahore High Court. Wife of Mr Anwar-ul-Haq, who at that time was the senior judge of the Supreme Court of Pakistan, requested me that I should accept my elevation to the Supreme Court.

> On my refusal she asked me the reason for this persistence, I replied 'In the heart of my hearts I know that if I stayed in the High Court, Mr Bhutto would appear before me in some case and I am waiting for that 'supreme moment' and as you know this 'supreme moment' came sooner than I had expected.[19]

Thus Bhutto was tried by a Bench which was presided over by the Chief Justice cum the Chief Election Commissioner, and that Chief Justice was waiting for the 'supreme moment' when Bhutto would be hauled up before him for him to get even with him. Need one say more about the partiality of the Chief Justice?[20]

Retirement of Members of the Bench

Yahya Bakhtiar, who was counsel for Bhutto in the Supreme Court, took a long time arguing the case in appeal. He could have concluded the arguments in two to three weeks if he wanted to, but he went on for months on end with a long-winded approach full of repetition, irrelevant submissions, and digressions like reference to poetry in Urdu. This approach proved to be fatal for Bhutto. Due to the flux of time, two judges on the Bench seemingly favourable towards the acquittal, dropped from the Bench of nine, reducing its strength to only seven. Mr Justice Qaiser Khan, from his remarks in the open court during the hearing of the appeal, seemed inclined towards acquittal, particularly on the point of bias and want of fair trial against the accused. He remarked at one stage that if any party before him stated that he did not want him to hear his case, he would throw the file on to his (objector's) face and would tell him to take it to some other Judge he had confidence in.[21] This loud thinking on his part was a clear message to the two Chief Justices (of the Lahore High Court and the Supreme Court) against their insistence on holding the trial and hearing the appeal. He said in his address on his retirement:

> It is common knowledge that people do not care much for the ability of a Judge but they care very much about his integrity. If people have confidence in the integrity of a judge then they do not mind even if their cases are decided against them. But if they doubt the integrity of a judge then, however learned he may be, they are not satisfied with his judgment.[22]

It would have been only appropriate that Justice Qaiser Khan should have been allowed to continue to sit as ad hoc judge for the hearing of this appeal because he retired (on 30 July 1978) while the appeal was being heard. Since his remarks had touched wrong chords in the hearts of the people who mattered, they felt relieved on his retirement and did not let him continue as an ad hoc judge to risk his judgment.

Another judge on the Bench was Justice Waheeduddin Ahmad, who was an ad hoc judge of the Supreme Court at that time. He fell seriously ill around the end of the year 1978. He even requested the Chief Justice to postpone the hearing of the appeal for four to six weeks to enable him to join the Bench after his recovery, but such a reasonable request was not acceded to and the hearings of the appeal continued in his absence by the remaining seven judges on the Bench.[23] This judgment is also against the established practice of the Supreme Court. If a judge, who is member of a Bench, retires, dies, or is incapacitated, then proceedings before the remaining members of the Bench are not continued in a part-heard case. The Chief Justice, in such a case, constitutes another Bench which hears the case afresh from the very beginning.

Why did Bhutto's counsel take so long? Why did he not sense that early disposal of the appeal by nine judges were likely to favour his client? This question has been put to Yahya Bakhtiar many times and he explained that this was because of instructions from Bhutto who thought that time would run in his favour and that there would be a public outrage against the trial and the masses would force the martial law government through demonstration or otherwise to free him. He also thought that international pressure would mount on Zia to set him at liberty. All this proved to be a figment of his imagination. No doubt, Bhutto had support from a large segment of the population but they were not in a position to launch and sustain a nation-wide movement against a martial law government determined to use brutal force against them. No doubt, several governments of friendly countries approached Zia and requested him not to execute Bhutto but these requests fell on the deaf ears of a man who was power hungry and desperate to remove his nemesis from the scene.

The Judgment in Appeal

Lengthy arguments in appeal, spanning nearly a year finally culminated into a lengthy judgment dated 6 February 1979. Everyone was surprised to learn that it was a divided verdict: four to three, divided at the seams. Four judges, all hailing from Punjab, upholding the conviction and three judges, from other provinces, writing dissenting judgments in support of Bhutto's acquittal.[24] On the question of bias, the Supreme Court held that there was no factual basis for any apprehension of bias. The majority view held the statements of dead men admissible but the minority view was that such statements are hearsay and inadmissible. The majority considered the evidence on conspiracy admissible but the minority held it to be inadmissible. The majority view regarding approver was that even if he did not disclose all the facts before a magistrate his statement before the trial court containing more details could still be relied upon. The minority thought that such a statement could not be relied upon.

On the question of proceeding with the trial in the absence, due to illness, of the accused, the majority held that the Court could proceed in the absence of the accused by dispensing with his personal attendance so that the trial of the other co-accused was not delayed. The minority view was that the Court should exercise its discretion in such a matter judiciously because illness is beyond the control of the accused. The view of the majority on this point is clearly repugnant to the general principle and practice of law that a trial of a person should be held in his presence and trials in absentia have always been seen with disfavour under the recognized principles of criminal jurisprudence.

On the question of reliability and credibility of the statement of an approver/ accomplice, the majority view was that he should be judged as any other witness without introducing an artificial requirement of corroboration of his evidence. The minority held that the evidence of an accomplice required corroboration without which it should not be accepted. The minority view is based upon the settled principle of law as applied for more than a century in the Indo-Pakistan subcontinent. The majority held that motive is relevant as an aid in appreciation of evidence in criminal cases but the minority view was that evidence of motive is always a weak form of corroborative evidence. The majority view on motive was that Bhutto had strong motive to do away with the complainant but the minority firmly held that the prosecution had failed to establish its case on motive.

The majority held that the prosecution had fully established the existence of conspiracy, identity of the conspirators, and the death of the deceased being a probable consequence of such conspiracy and, therefore, the accused was rightly convicted. The minority, after an extensive and thorough appreciation of evidence, reached the conclusion that the prosecution failed to establish the case against Bhutto beyond doubt and, therefore, he should be acquitted. The appeals of Bhutto and Mian Abbas were dismissed by the majority of four to three, but the appeals of the confessing three appellants were dismissed unanimously.

Review Application and its Dismissal

A petition was filed on behalf of Bhutto before the Supreme Court for review of the judgment. The review petition was dismissed on 24 March 1979 unanimously by all the seven judges.[25] They all agreed that the sentence could not be altered in review, as prayed for by Yahya Bakhtiar in the alternative, from the death sentence to life imprisonment. However, all the seven judges felt that the grounds relied upon by Yahya Bakhtiar for mitigation of sentence were relevant for consideration by the executive authorities in the exercise of their prerogative of clemency. In this way, even the four judges, who up held the conviction and death sentence of Bhutto, seemed inclined to the commutation of death sentence to life imprisonment but it was too much to expect from the executive to commute Bhutto's sentence to life imprisonment. Zia and his military *junta* were keenly waiting for the verdict.

Controversy over the Supreme Court Verdict

This Supreme Court judgment has also been a subject of controversy within and outside Pakistan. The retirement of one judge during the course of the hearing of the appeal and incapacitation of another, has given rise to debate, controversy and speculation. It has been said that Justice Qaiser Khan should have continued on the Bench as an ad hoc judge for the hearing of the case. The constitution permitted this. The reason for not doing so was because he had clearly expressed his view against the conduct of the trial while hearing the appeal. It is also alleged that Justice Waheeduddin was not allowed to continue to sit on the Bench after his illness despite his request because the Chief Justice sensed that he would vote in favour of Bhutto's acquittal. All this led to the speculation that if all the nine judges originally on the Bench were to decide the case, the verdict would have gone in Bhutto's favour by five to four.

Another unfortunate aspect was the division of the judges on provincial lines, all four judges from the Punjab standing in favour of the conviction and the three judges from the other provinces standing in favour of an acquittal. So, the proponents of provincialism allege that it was a conspiracy of the Punjabis against a Sindhi Prime Minister, the High Court of the Punjab holding the trial and sentencing him to death and the Punjabi judges on the Supreme Court upholding the verdict. This further strengthens the speculation that since the two judges who were prevented from continuing the hearing of the appeal come from outside the Punjab, the verdict would have gone in favour of Bhutto's acquittal.

The controversy will go on. However, a recent interview of Justice Nasim Hasan Shah, who was a member of the Bench of the Supreme Court, has shed some light on the thinking of the Court and the underlying factors.[26] He said that Justice Maulvi Mushtaq had personal differences with Bhutto, particularly on account of his supercession as Chief Justice, and should not have heard the case. He also said that the judges hearing the appeal were inclined in favour of a lesser punishment (of life imprisonment), but the counsel for Bhutto did not seek it. He indicated that there was immense personal pressure on the judges, giving the example of Justice Muhammad Haleem who was afraid for the life and safety of his only son who was living in Karachi at that time.

It is, however, difficult to accept this argument since the award of punishment in a criminal case is not dependent upon the pleadings and request of the counsel but it is for the Court to decide in the light of the evidence as to what should be the appropriate punishment.

The Execution of Bhutto

Despite reference to clemency by the Supreme Court in its judgment on the review application, no mercy was shown by Zia or his military *junta*. Kurt Waldheim, Secretary-General of the United Nations, President Jimmy Carter of the USA, Helmut Schmidt, Chancellor of West Germany, President Giscard d'Estange of France, Prime Minister Trudeau of Canada, and Prime Minister James Callaghan of the United Kingdom, were amongst the western statesmen who urged clemency. Soviet and Chinese heads of state also requested for mercy. Every Muslim and Arab state, without exception, pleaded for Bhutto's life.[27]

> Zia told me 'It's either his neck or mine', Roedad Khan recalled. 'He said, "I have not convicted him, and if they hold him guilty, by God, I am not going to let him off!"' Then

Secretary-General of the Ministry of Interior, Roedad was responsible for digesting many mercy petitions and pleas that came to Pakistan from heads of states the world over. These appeals were summarized so that they could be submitted to Zia in only a few pages, permitting him to 'read' them more easily, but that boiling-down process took a 'lot of time', or so it seemed to Zia, who was 'impatient to get the hanging over and done'.[28]

In his last days, Bhutto had become very weak and frail. He was pessimistic and knew well that he could expect no mercy from Zia. He had an infection of the gums which were full of pus and bleeding. His mouth was swollen. Even his dentist was unsuccessful at relieving the acute periodontal pain whose 'source' may have been 'pancreatic' or 'liver disease' that had plagued Bhutto's last years.[29]

On 4 April 1979, Zulfiqar Ali Bhutto was hanged at 2:00 a.m. in the morning at Rawalpindi Central Jail. Contrary to the usual practice of hanging prisoners at dawn, the authorities thought it prudent to accomplish it in the dead of the night so that his body could be flown to Larkana and be buried by the time the news broke among the population. At 4:00 a.m., Bhutto's body was flown from Chaklala airport to Larkana and was buried in his ancestral graveyard at Garhi Khuda Bakhsh in the presence of his first wife Sheerin, Mumtaz Bhutto, and Bhutto's relatives and servants, next to the grave of his father, Sir Shahnawaz. Neither Begum Nusrat nor Benazir had been informed in time to fly down to witness the burial.[30] Benazir wrote: 'Yet, not until yesterday (3 April 1979) had I allowed myself to believe that General Zia would actually assassinate my father'.[31] Such was the delusion and complacency in the minds of the members of Bhutto's family.

It is a pity that a man as brilliant as Bhutto was wasted like this. He had great potential and promise but unfortunately his arrogance, impulsiveness, over-arching ambition, and intolerance took the better of him and he left the world as an extremely controversial man, passionately loved by some and intensely hated by others.

Zulfiqar Ali Bhutto: A Political Legacy

The confluence of events that brought Zulfiqar Ali Bhutto to political power offered him an opportunity to reshape Pakistan, to turn it from being a bureaucratic state into a nation with a common purpose. He could have given the country political institutions which it had failed to develop. In particular, a Constitution that could not be subverted to fit the aspirations of powerful interest groups, and a political party that would be capable of aggregating and synthesizing the interests of many diverse groups. Under Bhutto, circumstances were favourable enough to help Pakistan graduate from the ranks of poor nations and move into those of middle income countries. Bhutto had the mandate from the people to develop the mechanisms for ensuring that the under-privileged segments of the population gained access to basic human needs. Bhutto could have evolved an administrative structure not beholden to a few interest groups but commited to achieving the nation's purpose.

The moment was right when Bhutto was put into office for achieving all this and much more. But Bhutto failed. His legacy was a country divided by provincialism, sectarianism, and growing ethnicity. The political institutions he helped create did not fulfil their early promise. The Pakistan People's Party, instead of housing a number of different groups, was able to accommodate only a few of the more powerful interest groups. The economy, instead of picking up the momentum of development generated during the years of Ayub Khan, faltered and went into a recession unprecedented in Pakistan's history. The administrative structure, shaped and reshaped many times, lost its sense of purpose. Bhutto, upon assuming power, had managed to rally behind him a nation that had been extremely demoralized by the events of 1969–71. In the summer of 1973, when he gave Pakistan its third Constitution, a confident nation looked to the future with considerable expectation. Much of that confidence was dissipated in the period following the promulgation of the Constitution on 14 August 1973. It appears that Bhutto could provide leadership only during periods of crisis and there were several of those between 1971 and 1973. But he did not prove himself to be a leader for all seasons. He lost control when the ship of state left turbulent waters and entered a placid stretch. He left the shipadrift.

With such an indifferent record of performance why does Bhutto remain important in Pakistan's politics? To answer this question, we must recall for a moment the analysis of social group dynamics presented earlier. It was argued that the PPP success in the elections of 1970 and the popularity of its chairman from 1969, when the party was founded, to 1974, when Bhutto brought about a fundamental reorientation in his programme, was the result of a remarkable coalition that represented all classes of the Pakistani society. From 1974 onwards the middle classes began to drift away from the PPP coalition and a segment went to the religious parties, in particular the Jamaat-i-Islami. At the same time, an influential section of Pakistan's elite classes consolidated its hold over the party. When Bhutto was deposed and executed, what remained behind was not a political party with a shared purpose but a series of impressions and interpretations of what Bhutto would have accomplished had he survived. These interpretations and impressions constitute the meaning of 'Bhuttoism'.

The under-privileged segments of society continue to believe that the middle classes resisted Bhutto's effort to alleviate poverty, to provide the poor with basic human needs, and to arrange for a better participation of the poor in the social and political life of the country. The gains they made as a result of the remittances from the Middle East are attributed to the policies of the PPP government and the untiring efforts of its chairman. But not all the benefits promised in the election manifesto of 1970 were realized. For the poor, therefore, Bhuttoism means the promise to achieve these objectives.

For most of the middle classes, Bhuttoism has a negative connotation. It means an attack on the values that the middle class (the *shurafaa*) holds dear. It also means recklessness in the way the affairs of the country are managed. However, for some members of the middle class, in particular the urban intelligentsia, Bhuttoism also means non-alignment in foreign policy; the freedom to follow Pakistan's own diplomatic objectives rather than those of the United States. The elites have yet another interpretation of Bhuttoism. For them, Bhuttoism means a political and economic arrangement that wins the support of the landless poor, the industrial workers, the urban labour, without major economic sacrifices being made by the propertied classes.

It is obvious that these four different interpretations of Bhuttoism cannot be reconciled in one economic programme. It is the failure to achieve a synthesis which explains the Pakistan People's Party's difficulty in coming up with a manifesto that would have as broad an appeal as the document which won the party victory at the 1970 polls. Therefore, while Bhutto lives on in the shape of at least four 'Bhuttoisms', his legacy to his own party has not been an easy one.[32]

Partnership between the Military and the Judiciary

From the very beginning, the military *junta* that took power on 5 July 1977, involved the judiciary with it. Zia met Chief Justice Yakub Ali on 5 July. The the Chief Justices of the High Courts of the four provinces were appointed acting Governors of their respective provinces. The four chief justices readily accepted this appointment although they had little executive power which was actually vested in martial law administrators of the provinces. It is shocking the way the judiciary fell into the lap and ultimately the trap of the martial law government and accepted various assignments given to them without demur. The military *junta* must have immediately sensed the weakness of the members of the judiciary for offices and thin perks and privileges from the manner and the haste with which they were accepted.

But the early honeymoon was not without its difficulties. Zia and his coterie were wary of the judges because they had to obtain a verdict of legitimacy from them and feared that the judges might pose some difficulty in this regard. In addition to governorship, the judges were appeased by restoring their writ jurisdiction on 7 July, two days after withdrawing the jurisdiction under Laws (Continuance in Force) Order 1977.[33] However, by this time, the military *junta* had an adviser who was a past master on fixing the judiciary, Sharifuddin Pirzada, who was made Attorney-General soon after the imposition of martial law, evidently advised them that apart from obliging and appeasing the judges, they should be put through an acid test to ally them with the martial law regime. He must have comforted the members of the ruling *junta* and alleviated their fears by assuring them that he knew the judges too well and that they were so culpable that they would not risk losing favour with Zia. So the *junta* decided to go along with his advice.

First came the High Court judges. A President's order was passed on 7 July 1977 requiring all High Court judges to take oath in the form set out in the schedule thereof where[34] significant and material alterations and omissions were made compared to the form of the oath set out in the third schedule of the 1973 Constitution. These were:

(a) From the sentence 'I will discharge my duties, and perform my functions, honestly, to the best of my ability and faithfully in accordance with the Constitution of the Islamic Republic of Pakistan and the Law' in the third schedule, the words 'the Constitution of the Islamic Republic of Pakistan and' were omitted.
(b) The entire sentence 'That I will preserve, protect, and defend the Constitution of the Islamic Republic of Pakistan' was totally omitted.

Despite this order, the martial law regime was cautious and did not immediately impose this oath on High Courts judges waiting for an appropriate time. In the order, there was no requirement to make the oath immediately and it was left to the Governor of the province concerned to put a schedule to this. In spite of the open-ended provision and the fact that Governors of provinces were Chief Justices who could have stalled such oath taking, all the judges of the High Courts of Sindh, Peshawar, and Balochistan took oath under the said order. In the Lahore High Court, twenty-two out of the thirty-two judges took oath.[35] Thus they stood up to the test.

However, things came to a head on 20 September 1977 when the petition of Begum Nusrat Bhutto against the detention of Bhutto was admitted directly by the Supreme Court in the exercise of its original jurisdiction. The military *junta* was rattled and its legitimacy was under serious question. The marriage between the military and the judiciary was on the rocks. The *junta* had to move quickly to remove the threat and bring the judiciary in line. It took the step of withdrawing the Fifth and Sixth Amendments to the Constitution on 22 September. The office of Chief Justice of the Supreme Court became vacant as a result and Justice Anwar-ul-Haq was appointed to the office who took over. The entire Supreme Court accepted it and the transition went smoothly. Having achieved this the martial law regime felt confidant that the judiciary could be made to fall in line. The order regarding oath of High Court judges was amended on 22 September, and High Court judges who had not already taken the oath were required to take it within twenty-four hours. It was provided that in case a judge failed to do so, he would cease to hold office.[36] On the same day a similar president's order was passed for the Supreme Court judges to take the oath.[37] It was similar to the one taken by the High Court judges. The requirement to discharge duties and perform functions according to the Constitution and the duty to preserve, protect, and defend the Constitution were all dispensed with.

The *junta* had the Constitution amended and the judiciary accepted it and made the transition under it. All the High Court judges of Sindh, Balochistan, and NWFP and a majority of the judges of the Lahore High Court had already taken the oath. All the judges of the Supreme Court took oath on 22 September before the President of Pakistan in Rawalpindi and the remaining ten judges of the Lahore High Court also took the oath on the same day.[38]

The judiciary went along with the martial law in weeding out those judges who had been appointed after 1 January 1977 under the President's order for scrutiny of High Court judges who had been appointed between 1 January and 5 July 1977.[39] The Supreme Judicial Council (which included Chief Justice Anwar-ul-Haq and acting

Chief Justice Maulvi Mushtaq) was vested with the power to scrutinize the appointments. The Council started its proceedings and forced three judges of the Lahore High Court and two judges of the Sindh High Court to resign. One judge of the Lahore High Court was relegated to the position of a sessions judge.

The judges also suffered the ignominy of sitting on tribunals with Brigadiers for cases of disqualification of politicians. These disqualification tribunals were the most manifest demonstration of partnership between the military and the judiciary and their working in cohort.

Aftermath of the Nusrat Bhutto Case

The judiciary did the ultimate favour to the martial law regime by legitimizing it in Nusrat Bhutto's case, giving power to the CMLA to amend the Constitution and without setting any date or deadline for holding the general elections. In return, the judiciary assumed to itself the power of judicial review over the acts and orders passed by the martial law authorities. By the verdict in Bhutto's case, the judiciary further obliged the regime and strengthened it by getting rid of its arch enemy.

The two chief justices, Anwar-ul-Haq and Maulvi Mushtaq, thought that they were the benefactors of the regime and that they could get anything done. Maulvi Mushtaq, in association with Anwar-ul-Haq, made a number of appointments to the Lahore High Court, in two batches of nine each in 1978 and 1979. Most of these were unknown lawyers who had been favourites of Maulvi Mushtaq over the years. He started demanding more and more favours, which he and Anwar-ul-Haq thought were their exclusive right. Anwar-ul-Haq was obliged by being made acting President during the foreign trips of Zia, a favour he must have been very happy about. They did not realize that they had served out their utility for the martial law regime and that they could make demands up to a point. They learnt this the hard way.

Regarding the exercise of power of judicial review, the judiciary was cautious. Martial law regulations and orders were not generally touched in exercise of judicial review. The judges did interfere with the sentence of the military courts, detention cases under the martial law regulations, or where military officers asserted their authority in matters of purely civil nature. Even here, the judges were extremely cautious. They did not strike down those sentences of the military courts where there was some inquiry made by the court, evidence of some independent witness was recorded, or some procedure was followed. Only in those cases where there was either no evidence or evidence of independent nature was not there, that the judges interfered. Similarly, in detention cases, the courts only interfered where there was no material available for the order of detention or if it was totally extraneous. Where there was some material, however inadequate, the detention orders were not set aside. In a nutshell, the standards applied by the superior courts in reviewing the sentences and detention cases under martial law were not the same that they would have applied to the procedures adopted or sentences passed by the ordinary courts or in detention cases by civilian authorities. It is generally believed that relief was granted in about 10 per cent of the cases brought before the superior courts. The judges were careful not to annoy the military regime.

Even such limited and selective interference by the superior courts was an irritant for the martial law authorities who did not want any check on their powers. The military establishment wanted to put to an end to this interference. Ultimately, the step was taken and the power of judicial review of the acts and orders of the martial law authorities was put to an end by adding Article 212-A to the constitution through an amendment.[40] The honeymoon between the judiciary and the martial law government was finally over.

All Political Activity Banned

It has been mentioned above that general elections scheduled for 18 October 1977 were postponed on 1 October. All political activities in the country were banned. Zia announced that the process of accountability would be completed first and then a new date for polls would be fixed.[41] Although the PNA leaders accepted the postponement of elections after having been shaken-up by the popularity of Bhutto, they did not like the drastic step of a ban on all political activities. All they wanted was that the PPP should be banned but that they should be allowed to continue their political activities. They voiced their concern and Zia met the PNA leaders on 13 October. He assured them that political activities would be restored at an early date. He pleaded for time to complete the process of accountability which, in his reckoning, could take not less than six months. He thus made it clear that elections would not be held before the following year and, according to the official announcement, the PNA leaders agreed to postponement till March 1978. He offered the PNA to form a council for running the affairs of the country in which representatives of the PNA and the PPP could sit together. The PNA leaders also urged the CMLA for the withdrawal of cases against those facing trial before the Hyderabad Tribunal[42] and, according to Mufti Mahmood, they were assured that the matter would receive due consideration.[43]

There were rumours circulating about disunity in the ranks of the PNA. Asghar Khan of Tehrik-i-Istiqlal was getting impatient with other PNA leaders. He laboured under the illusion that he was the only one amongst the nine party leaders with the stature of a national leader to challenge, Bhutto and the other PNA leaders were only a drag on him. He thought that the PNA's popularity and appeal among the people was due to his personality and charisma. Bickering amongst the PNA parties also convinced him that the alliance would not hold much longer and he must find his own way. The way he was overruled by the PNA Council in the matter of nomination of Zahur Ilahi to the Lahore seat for opposing Bhutto, a seat which was initially assigned to his party, left him feeling very bitter. He indicated that his party would review the feasibility of maintaining the unity of the PNA once the process of accountability against the PPP Chairman and his party colleagues was over.[44] Hence, cracks in the PNA had come out in the public which strengthened the argument of the

PPP and its supporters that the PNA was a house of cards and that voting for it would be voting for chaos.

It did not come as a surprise when Asghar Khan announced on 11 November 1977 that the Tehrik-i-Istiqlal was withdrawing from the PNA due to its faulty policies and indefinite programme. He accused the PNA of being a reactionary group. He also alleged that the PNA lacked the capability of fulfilling the aspirations of the people and forming a government that would be stable and competent.[45] Other parties and their leaders in the PNA condemned Asghar Khan for deserting them and reiterated their resolve to stick together so that the PNA remained a political force. The response of the PPP was interesting. On the one hand, the PPP central executive committee accused the PNA of being the creation of a foreign power and, on the other, it said that a split in the PNA would serve extra-national needs.[46] The PPP executive also called for polls as soon as possible by December 1977.[47] Mufti Mahmood, the PNA Chief, called for elections in March 1978.[48]

Wali Khan and fourteen other leaders, including Marri and Bizenjo, were granted bail by the Hyderabad Special Tribunal,[49] which was clearly done on the direction of Zia who wanted to have good relations with all anti-Bhutto forces in the country. On his release, Wali Khan said that there was no reason to doubt the sincerity of the CMLA in his resolve to hold elections. He said that free and fair elections could only be held when Bhuttoism was completely eliminated from politics.[50] He requested for a general amnesty in Balochistan so that a congenial atmosphere could be created to let the people of that province participate in the elections without fear. The Hyderabad Tribunal was finally dissolved and cases against all fifty-two accused persons were withdrawn.[51] Zia explained the process of accountability in three stages. After the completion of enquiries, a committee of martial law would review cases and decide whether the people involved should be allowed to continue in politics or not. At the same time, the committee would decide whether the cases of those selected for action were to be referred to the judiciary.[52] Hence, the process of accountability was made lengthy and complicated so that Zia could continue in power indefinitely. However, he did state for the sake of the media and to placate the demands of political parties that polls would be held within 1978.[53] Wali Khan took a direct approach to the problem but was making no demands for elections. He made repeated statements that the myth of Bhuttoism should be shattered and the process of accountability be completed first before the question of elections could be taken up.[54]

The process of accountability was given an ostensible beginning by appointing twelve special courts for the purpose, each headed by a judge of a High Court. These tribunals were assigned cases of various public functionaries like the president, prime minister, federal ministers, ministers of state, chief ministers, provincial ministers, parliamentary secretaries, members of National and Provincial Assemblies and others. A special court consisting of Justice Shafiur Rehman, was to hear cases against Bhutto.[55] A number of cases were filed before it and the charges included rigging of polls, misuse of funds, evasion of Customs Duty and Sales Tax, and so on.[56] Cases of eighty-nine other politicians were sent to the other tribunals. They included two former Governors, one former Speaker, ten former federal ministers, and nine former

Sindh ministers. Begum Nusrat Bhutto was included in this list.[57] These special courts got nowhere with the cases because the main purpose of the exercise was achieved by the execution of Bhutto. It is interesting to note that except for the special court for the cases against Bhutto consisting of Justice Shafiur Rehman, the other eleven Special Courts were changed and in their place, eleven disqualification tribunals were created each having a High Court judge and a Brigadier on it. Thus, Zia was not prepared to leave the process of accountability and disqualification to judges alone and ensured a watch on them by putting a Brigadier on each of the tribunals with them.[58] A number of PPP leaders were disqualified including Sadiq Hussain Qureshi, a former Governor and Chief Minister, and Sheikh Rashid, a former federal minister.

Zia Backs Out of Holding Elections

By this time Zia had started reneging on his promise to hold elections without saying it in so many words. He said that before elections could be held, not only the process of accountability and purge of politicians had to be completed, but the country had also to be put on a sound economic base.[59] He came out with his actual designs when he said in unequivocal terms that elections in the country would be held only when he and his colleagues were convinced of 'positive results'.[60] The expression 'positive results' was repeated by him several times in the years to come in order to justify the indefinite postponement of general elections. Later on, he retracted slightly and renewed his pledge to hold elections and transfer power to the elected representatives of the people, subject to the condition that there would be no instability and negation of the objection for which martial law was imposed.[61] He then turned around and said that the presidential form of government was more suitable for the country as it reflected the thinking and psyche of the Muslims.[62] It was clear by February 1978 that Zia and his colleagues in the military *junta* had decided to continue their rule and avoid elections on one pretext or the other. They had also been legitimized by the Supreme Court. They had gone the whole hog against Bhutto and the PPP and had also found that the PNA was weak and divided and greatly dependent on them. Thus they saw no reason to give up power.

Internal dissensions started weakening the PNA further after the withdrawal of Tehrik-i-Istiqlal. More internal bickering was witnessed. Jamiatul Ulema-i-Pakistan was unhappy with the other parties in the alliance and its chief, Shah Ahmad Noorani, demanded the resignation of Mufti Mahmood as President of the PNA. The only thing that was keeping these parties together in a weak alliance was their collective fear of Bhutto. The leaders of the PNA were no longer interested in the elections as they thought they could not face Bhutto and the PPP at the polls. Their popular support had dwindled over only a few months because of their internal bickering and strife and many of their erstwhile supporters now looked up to Zia to protect them from Bhutto and his party. PNA leaders had reached the decision that the martial law government should disqualify Bhutto and his party from contesting elections. Only then should elections be held in which they could participate among themselves or against one another.

In these circumstances, the PNA leadership was ready and willing to share whatever little power the martial law government was ready to give them. They jumped at the offer of negotiations for the formation of a so called 'national government'. Ghafoor Ahmad, Secretary-General of the PNA, said that their participation in the national government had been decided in the greater national interest.[63] He, opposed the participation of those PPP leaders in the proposed national government who had taken undue advantage of their official position while in power. He was referring to the efforts of Kausar Niazi who had broken ranks with the PPP (apparently on the nod of Zia) and wanted to join the proposed national government. Niazi said that the PPP was divided into two factions, one which comprised an 'overwhelming majority' believed that the atmosphere of confrontation and bitterness should be cleared.[64] Even Asghar Khan said that his party was not against the formation of a national government but insisted on in the country by October or November 1978.[65]

However, the formation of a national government was not easy even, though there was constant contact between Zia and the PNA leader they could not see eye to eye on everything. After meeting Zia Asghar Khan, declared that his party would not join the government with the representatives of the PNA. However, the meeting of the PNA negotiating team with the CMLA remained inconclusive. Mufti Mahmood said that the PNA felt committed to extend co-operation to the martial law government either by joining the proposed civilian government or by supporting it from outside to enable it to discharge the responsibilities it had undertaken on 5 July 1977 for holding elections. Both these proposals were placed by the PNA leaders before the CMLA.[66] However, Zia did not want any more of all this and announced that a federal Cabinet would be formed on 5 July 1978 and the idea of a national government had been abandoned. He also indicated that provincial governments would be formed.[67]

Pakistan Muslim League, led by the Pir of Pagaro, took the first step in agreeing to join the new Cabinet proposed by Zia. This step was taken on its own without consultation with the PNA. There were dissentions within the PML ranks but the majority favoured joining the civilian government.[68] Kausar Niazi, Chairman of the PPP splinter group, announced after meeting with the CMLA that his men would also like to join the government. However, in the Cabinet announced by Zia on 5 July nobody was taken from the splinter PPP group. Most of the ministers were either bureaucrats or military Generals, and some ministers were taken from Pagaro Muslim League, including Chaudhry Zahur Ilahi and Khawaja Safdar.[69] Another constituent party of the PNA, Jamaat-i-Islami expressed its opinion in favour of joining the Cabinet and asked the PNA to negotiate its inclusim in the government.[70] National Democratic Party, another constituent party, demanded the ouster of Muslim League from the PNA for failure to follow the discipline. Detailed discussions and negotiations took place between Zia and, Mufti Mahmood. Finally, the PNA decided on 6 August 1978 to join Zia's military government.

The PNA claimed to have three avowed objectives in participating in the government, first, to hold general elections in the country 'as early as possible';

second, to maintain close contact with people and seek immediate solutions to their problems; and, initiate measures for introduction of *Nizam-e-Mustafa* (Islamic system) in the country.[71] However, this step cost the PNA another constituent party. The National Democratic Party (NDP) severed its ties with the PNA.[72] In all, three major parties in the PNA, Tehrik-i-Istiqlal, Jamiatul Ulema-i-Pakistan (JUP), and the National Democratic Party (NDP) broke away from the PNA, leaving it with six parties out of which only three, Jamiat-i-Ulema-i-Islam (JUI), Jamaat-i-Islami, and Muslim League, had some following and the remaining three were political parties only in name. Consequent to the PNA's agreement with Zia to join the government, a federal Cabinet was sworn in consisting of twenty-one federal ministers, thirteen of whom were from the PNA parties. The main objectives were general elections by October 1979, implementation of the Islamic system, and economic stability in the country.[73] Restricted political activities were allowed from the day the new federal Cabinet was sworn in.

In the meantime, the martial law government continued to tighten the screws on Bhutto and the PPP. A White Paper was issued on 23 July, regarding the rigging of general elections held in March 1977. The White Paper has been widely quoted above for instances of rigging in various constituencies. Another White Paper was issued on 27 August 1978 regarding Bhutto's misuse of the media and intolerance of the free press; tight control on press, radio and TV for government propoganda; and misuse of public funds to project his personality cult.[74] It was alleged that Bhutto used distribution of newsprint and government advertisements to gag the press. Independent, opposition papers were victimized. The PPP party newspaper *Musawat*, it was alleged, received advertisements worth millions from the government treasury at spurious and inflated advertisement rates. The opposition was totally ignored by the state controlled media, and the Radio and Television were used to unleash a barrage of propaganda against the opposition parties.

Another significant development was the retirement of President Chaudhry Fazal Elahi on 16 September 1978. President Chaudhry had already completed his five year term as President on the 14 August 1978. He is said to have relinquished office at his own request.[75] Zia assumed office as President of Pakistan in addition to being the CMLA and the Chief of Army Staff. Zia was sworn in as President on 14 September 1978.[76] The whole thing was anomalous, particularly the holding of the office of the President and the Chief of Army Staff. The Defence Minister is supposed to be superior of the Army Chief but a subordinate of the President. Nevertheless, Zia understood that his real base of power was his being the Army Chief which he could not leave at any cost.

The partnership between PNA and Zia came to an end soon after the execution of Bhutto. The PNA decided to quit the government on 16 April 1979 and Zia, after some efforts to make the PNA change its mind, agreed to relieve the PNA ministers. A new federal Cabinet was sworn in on 21 April without the PNA ministers. This alliance of the PNA and Zia was a mutual need and a marriage of convenience. Zia needed PNA's political support to do away with Bhutto. The PNA wanted Zia to execute Bhutto so that only non-PPP politicians could take part in the general elections to be held on 17 November 1979. As soon as Bhutto was executed, the PNA withdrew its ministers so that it could contest elections while being out of the government. The PNA leaders did not realize that Zia had little use for them now and could continue without them. The PNA had, in any case, lost its credibility by entering into a partnership with the martial law government. Entering into partnership with the martial law government, had lost its political standing and credibility.

Constitutional Amendments

Superior Courts Empowered to Declare Any Law Un-Islamic

On 7 February 1979, a constitutional amendment was made through a President's order conferring jurisdiction on the High Courts to examine and decide the question whether or not any law or provision of law was repugnant to the injunctions of Islam as laid down in the Holy Quran and the *sunnah*.[77] If so, then it had to give reasons for such an opinion, state the extent to which such law or provision was so repugnant, and specify the day on which the decision should take effect. The President, in case of a federal law, and Governors in case of provincial laws, were to take steps to amend the law or to bring such law or provision into conformity with the injunctions of Islam according to the opinion of the High Court.

Every High Court was required to constitute a Bench of three Muslim judges, to be called the Shariat Bench for exercise of jurisdiction being conferred under this constitutional amendment.[78] Appeal would lie to the Supreme Court against decisions of the High Courts in exercise of this jurisdiction. For the purpose of hearing and deciding such appeals, the Supreme Court was to constitute a Bench of three Muslim judges of the Supreme Court, to be called the Shariat Appellate Bench. The pending proceedings under the law, which might be declared as repugnant to the injunctions of Islam were saved and allowed to continue.

This constitutional amendment was the first step taken by Zia towards his programme of Islamization.

Hudood Laws Introduced

Soon after the constitutional amendment mentioned above, another major step in the Islamization of laws was taken by Zia. On 9 February, three ordinances and one President's order[79] were issued prescribing *hadd* punishments.[80] These laws, according to Zia, formed a package introducing Islamic laws in Pakistan.

Under the prohibition law, manufacture, import, export, transport, bottling, selling, or serving of any intoxicant was made an offence punishable by whipping and imprisonment. Drinking of intoxicating liquor was made punishable by *hadd* punishment (eighty lashes). However, very strict proof of two male witnesses, who are credible according to the high standards of Islamic law of evidence, is required for administering the *hadd* punishment. Lighter punishment of up to three years imprisonment or whipping up to thirty stripes can be administered in case the quality of proof did not meet the requirement of *hadd*.

In case of theft or robbery, *hadd* punishment for amputation of the right hand from the joint of the wrist, for the first theft, and amputation of left foot up to the ankle for the second theft, was provided. In case of theft for the third time, life imprisonment was provided. However, for *hadd* punishment in case of theft, the same strict standard of proof was required as in the case of drinking. In case of theft not liable to *hadd*, lighter punishment of imprisonment was provided.

The third law pertained to the offence of *zina*.[81] In case of adultery, the punishment provided was stoning to death and in case of fornication,[82] to whipping, at a public place, numbering one hundred stripes. The proof for *hadd* in *zina* cases is extremely strict which is four adult male witnesses, meeting the high standard of credibility under Islam, giving evidence as eye-witnesses to the act of copulation. In case such standard of proof was not available, then lighter punishment of imprisonment up to ten years and whipping numbering thirty stripes could be awarded. In *zina-bil-jabr* (rape), the same punishment and standard of proof was provided (the victim is not to be punished). However, for rape the lighter punishment is very severe, which is imprisonment for up to twenty-five years and thirty stripes.

The fourth law pertained to false testimony or false accusation of *zina*. The *hadd* punishment is whipping eighty strips. This is subject to strict proof of two adult male witnesses. Lighter punishment could be imprisonment upto two years and whipping not exceeding forty stripes.

These laws generated a lot of controversy in the country. The proponents of these laws say that since they derive their origin from the Holy Quran and *sunnah*, they are permanent. There is no doubt that these laws have been abused to embarrass an opponent or by the police to blackmail others. However, the courts have generally been cautious in the application of these laws and *hadd* punishments have been awarded rather rarely. Despite fifteen years of introduction of these laws, no one has been stoned to death and no amputation of hand or foot has taken place.

Another step in the process of Islamization by Zia was the setting up of an organization for the assessment, collection, and disbursement of *zakat* and *ushr*.[83] Under this law, *zakat* was made compulsory and was to be forcibly collected from the savings accounts of the people, something which is inherently opposed to the concept of *zakat* in Islam which is required to be a voluntary act of the Muslims.

NOTES

1. PLD 1969 Lahore 786.
2. PLD 1977 Lahore 846.
3. Mahmood, M. Dilawar, *The Judiciary and Politics in Pakistan*. 1992, Idra Mutalia-e-Tareekh, Lahore, p. 76.
4. *Dawn*, 18 September 1977.
5. *Dawn*, 19 September 1977.

6. State v Zulfiqar Ali Bhutto, PLJ 1978 Cr.C. (Lahore) 1.
7. State v Zulfiqar Ali Bhutto and others. PLD 1978 Lahore 523.
8. The extracts of the application have been taken from the book of M. Dilawar Mahmood. *The Judiciary and Politics in Pakistan*, *supra*, note 3, pp. 80-87.
9. Counsel for Bhutto before the trial court (Lahore High Court).
10. Paragraphs 293 to 310 of the Judgment, PLD 1978 Lahore 523.
11. (Bhutto - the truth about his rule and his trial), p. 22. It is a booklet which does not mention the name of author or publisher. It was apparently published by the Zia government anonymously and circulated to justify government's prosecution of Bhutto and conduct of trial against him.
12. PLD 1978 Lahore 523.
13. Zulfiqar Ali Bhutto v The State, PLD 1978 S.C. 40.
14. Abrar Hassan v Government of Pakistan, PLD 1976 S.C. 315.
15. This extract is taken from the book of M. Dilawar Mahmood, *The Judiciary and Politics in Pakistan*. *supra*, note 3, pp. 117-19.
16. Zulfiqar Ali Bhutto v The State. PLD 1978 S.C. 125 on p. 128.
17. Zulfiqar Ali Bhutto v State, PLD 1979 S.C.53 at p. 387.
18. *Moon Digest*, April 1984 issue.
19. Translation by M. Dilawar Mahmood.
20. Mahmood, M. Dilawar, *The Judiciary and Politics in Pakistan*, *supra*, note 3, p. 122. Mr Dilawar Mahmood was one of the closest associates of Maulvi Mushtaq. He was appointed judge of Lahore High Court during the Chief Justiceship of Maulvi Mushtaq in the year 1978. His performance as a Judge was commendable and he gave some good judgments particularly in the matter of civil liberties and human rights. He also struck down orders and acts of Martial Law Regime. He was ultimately ousted from the High Court in 1980, again due to his close association with Maulvi Mushtaq who at that time had fallen from favour with the Zia regime. There are few persons as qualified to comment on Maulvi Mushtaq as Dilawar Mahmood who was regarded as the former's understudy and protege.
21. This remark was made by Justice Qaiser Khan in open court which was heard by all the lawyers present in the court and has been widely discussed amongst the lawyer circles.
22. Address of Mr Justice Qaiser Khan at the Full Court Reference on the eve of his retirement. See PLD 1978 Journal 117.
23. Zulfiqar Ali Bhutto v The State. PLD 1979 S.C. 38.
24. Zulfiqar Ali Bhutto v The State. PLD 1979 S.C. 53.
25. Zulfiqar Ali Bhutto v State, PLD 1979 S.C. 741.
26. Interview of Chief Justice (Retd) Dr Nasim Hasan Shah, *Jang*, Sunday Magazine of 25 August 1996.
27. Salman, Taseer, *Bhutto: A Political Biography*, 1980. Vikas Publishing House, New Delhi, pp. 188-9.
28. Wolpert, Stanley, *Zulfiqar Ali Bhutto of Pakistan—His life and times*, Edition 1993, Oxford University Press, New York, p. 327.
29. Ibid., p. 328.
30. Ibid., pp. 328-9.
31. Bhutto, Benazir, *Daughter of the East*, 1988, Hamish Hamilton, London. p. 5
32. Burki, Shahid Javed, *Pakistan Under Bhutto, 1971-1977*, 1988, Macmillan Press, London, pp. 237-9.
33. The writ jurisdiction was restored through Laws (Continuance in Force) (Amendment) Order 1977. CMLA Order No. 2 of 1977. However, no writ jurisdiction was available against CMLA or any MLA or any person acting under their authority.
34. High Court Judges (Oath of Office) Order, 1977. President's Order (Post Proclamation) 1 of 1977. PLD 1977 Central Statutes 325.
35. *Dawn*, 24 September 1977.
36. High Court Judges (Oath of Office) (Amendment) Order, 1977. President's (Post Proclamation) Order 10 of 1977. PLD 1977 Central Statutes 437.

37. Supreme Court Judges (Oath of Office) Order, 1977. President's (Post Proclamation) Order 9 of 1977. PLD 1977 Central Statutes 436.
38. Two judges of the Lahore High Court, Mr Justice K.M.A. Samdani and Mr Justice A.S. Salam, seriously considered not taking the oath but other judges prevailed over them and they also went along.
39. High Court Judges (Scrutiny of Appointment) Order, 1977. President's (Post Proclamation) Order No. 13 of 1977. PLD 1977 Central Statutes 455.
40. Constitution (Second Amendment) Order, 1979. President's Order 21 of 1979. PLD 1979 Central Statutes 567.
41. *Dawn*, 2 October 1977.
42. Abdul Wali Khan and other leaders of the banned NAP.
43. *Dawn*, 14 October 1977.
44. *Dawn*, 15 October 1977.
45. *Dawn*, 12 November 1977.
46. *Dawn*, 14 November 1977.
47. *Dawn*, 16 November 1977.
48. *Dawn*, 1 December 1977.
49. *Dawn*, 7 December 1977.
50. *Dawn*, 15 December 1977.
51. *Dawn*, 2 January 1978.
52. Ibid.
53. *Dawn*, 12 January 1978.
54. *Dawn*, 9 January 1978 and January 10, 1978.
55. *Dawn*, 17 January 1978.
56. *Dawn*, 3 February 1978 and February 5, 1978.
57. *Dawn*, 4 February 1978.
58. Ibid.
59. *Dawn*, 17 February 1978.
60. *Dawn*, 24 February 1978.
61. *Dawn*, 15 March 1978.
62. *Dawn*, 28 March 1978.
63. *Dawn*, 25 April 1978.
64. *Dawn*, 23 April 1978.
65. *Dawn*, 27 April 1978.
66. *Dawn*, 23 June 1978.
67. *Dawn*, 26 June 1978.
68. *Dawn*, 2 July 1978.
69. *Dawn*, 6 July 1978.
70. *Dawn*, 13 July 1978.
71. *Dawn*, 7 August 1978.
72. *Dawn*, 17 August 1978.
73. *Dawn*, 24 August 1978.
74. *Dawn*, 28 August 1978.
75. *Dawn*, 15 September 1978.
76. *Dawn*, 17 September 1978.
77. Constitution (Amendment) Order, 1979. President's Order 3 of 1979. PLD 1979 Central Statutes 31.
78. The draft of this constitutional amendment was circulated by Chief Justice of the Lahore High Court, Justice Maulvi Mushtaq, amongst the judges for soliciting their opinions. He in particular solicited support to the effect that Shariat Benches in the High Courts should be constituted by the Chief Justice concerned and not, as provided in the original draft, be left to the discretion of the President. Most of the judges present in the meeting obviously supported him. One of the judges, who narrated this story to the author, took exception to the draft being discussed at all because,

according to him, the same might be challenged before the High Court after it became a law. By discussing the draft, he argued, the High Court judges might just be pre-empting themselves from examining it on the judicial side. However, in the final outcome, the legislation left it open as to who could constitute Shariat Benches and obviously in such circumstances, the Chief Justice came into the position to do so.

79. Offences against Property (Enforcement of Hudood) Ordinance 1979, Ordinance VI of 1979. PLD 1979 Central Statutes 44. Offence of Zina (Enforcement of Hudood) Ordinance, 1979. Ordinance VII of 1979. PLD 1979 Central Statutes 51. Offence of Qazf (Enforcement of Hadd) Ordinance, 1979. Ordinance VIII of 1979. PLD 1979 Central Statutes 56. Prohibition (Enforcement of Hadd) Order 1979. President's Order 4 of 1979. PLD 1979 Central Statutes 33.
80. *Hadd* means punishment ordained by the Holy Quran or Sunnah.
81. *Zina* means wilful sexual intercourse between a man and a woman without being validly married to each other.
82. Offenders being unmarried.
83. *Zakat* and *Ushr* (Organization) Ordinance, 1979. Ordinance XXIX of 1979. PLD 1979 Central Statutes 277.

27

HOUNDING THE JUDICIARY

In February 1979, Zia announced general elections for 17 November 1979. This was apparently in keeping with the promise made with the PNA parties which were in government. After the execution of Bhutto in April, Zia and the PNA had gone their separate ways, the PNA having withdrawn from government. From the events that followed, it was obvious that Zia and his military coterie had no intention of giving up power, particularly after having removed the main hurdle in their way—Bhutto. It is understandable that the military government had not executed Bhutto to hand over power to the PNA—particularly after the PNA splintered into many groups and no longer enjoyed wide public support.

Zia decided to postpone the general elections fixed for 17 November 1979 by declaring that local bodies' elections would take place first. All preparations were made to hold these elections on 28 September 1979 which were held on non-party basis. The reason was that Zia did not want any party to show its strength in these elections and the people elected on non-party basis would be obliged to him. It was from amongst these people that he wanted to create a political cadre for himself. Local bodies elections were also likely reveal the strength and weakness of Zia's opponents. Regarding general elections, Zia had already made up his mind that these would not be held. He indicated that the method of elections was totally un-Islamic and that there was no concept of political parties in Islam. He also said that it was necessary to complete the introduction of *Nizam-e-Islam* before the elections. Some of the factors he indicated were:

(a) the bitter experience of the results of past elections;
(b) the tradition of negative politics in the country; and
(c) the tendency towards violence and agitation.[1]

He made extensive amendments to the Political Parties Act, 1962 laying down stringent conditions for the political parties. This was done to make it difficult for them to participate in the elections, thus paving the way for him to postpone the elections. These amendments included the requirements that:

(a) every political party should register with the Election Commission;
(b) a party's registration might be cancelled if it acted in any manner prejudicial to the ideology of Pakistan, the maintenance of public order or the integrity or independence of the judiciary, or had spread disaffection against the Armed Forces;

(c) every political party would hold annual elections at every level; and
(d) all political parties would submit their accounts for audit, indicating their sources of income to the Election Commission which could declare any party ineligible for participating in the elections if it was found to have received foreign aid.

In case a political party failed to meet any of these requirements, it could not participate in an election to a seat in a House of Parliament or a Provincial Assembly or to nominate or put up a candidate at any such election.[2]

The conditions laid for registration or for cancellation were reasonable except for condition (b) which was amenable to all kinds of mischievous interpretation and could be used to keep any political party from participating in the elections. The political parties could not meet the other conditions either, since the structure had always remained weak in Pakistan. Some of the parties were small and could hardly maintain accounts or afford an establishment of any kind. Even the larger parties at the national level like the PPP had either very poor internal structures or none at all. Generally, no internal elections were held and persons were nominated to various party offices from the party leadership. Thus the parties which talked so much about democracy did not have a democratic internal set-up. This created dissatisfaction amongst party workers, a weakness that Zia understood very well and wanted to use to disqualify all major political parties, especially the PPP, from participating in the general elections. Political parties also did not maintain proper accounts which could be used as a ground to disqualify them.

The major political parties, the PPP and the PNA, did not apply for registration within the time limit but both of them applied for election symbols. Other parties like Tehrik-i-Istiqlal (TI) and Jamiatul Ulema-i-Pakistan (JUP), applied for registration in time. The Jamiat-e-Islami (JI), a component of the PNA, violated the unanimous decision of the PNA to keep out of the polls unless the registration clause was withdrawn and applied formally for registration and the award of an election symbol.[3] Thus JI opted out of the PNA, leaving it virtually ineffective without any political party of consequence except JUI. In this way, sixteen parties including JI, TI and JUP were registered and others including the PNA, the PPP, and the NDP (National Democratic Party) stayed out.[4] Thus, the main purpose of Zia behind this exercise was accomplished. Despite this, the PNA did not ask for the postponement of the polls and urged Zia to hold elections as promised on 17 November.[5] However, after lengthy negotiations between Zia and Mufti Mahmood, further amendments were made in the Political Parties Act to the effect that those political parties which had submitted their accounts but had not applied for registration could still participate in the forthcoming elections if they replied to the questionnaire to be published by the Election Commission.[6] This was a compromise worked out to satisfy the PNA which was averse to the use of the word 'registration'. Nomination papers could be submitted by 13 October 1979 but the date of polling was placed under doubt because according to the official press note: 'The polling date may have to be re-adjusted to hold elections within 1979.'[7] Despite this announcement, no fresh schedule with a definite date for polling was giving. Political parties started clamouring for either keeping 17 November as the polling date or giving a definite date with a schedule as promised 'within 1979'. Silence was maintained by the government and restrictions on political activities continued despite repeated demands of the political parties to lift them.

This silence was finally broken on 16 October 1979 by Zia and the ambitions he had been nurturing for a long time came out in the open. He was not to give up power in any event. In his address to the nation[8] he announced the postponement of elections indefinitely; all political parties were dissolved and all political activities banned, newspapers and journals said to be involved in anti-national activities were closed; press censorship was imposed; the right to strike by workers and the right to lock out by factory owners was rescinded; criminal cases being heard in Martial Law courts could not be challenged in civil courts; and the process of Islamisation was to be speeded up. He blamed the PNA for putting party interest above national interest and not filing nomination papers by the fixed date. He said that these parties were fighting shy of the elections but wanted to shift the responsibility for the postponement of elections to the government.

He also came down heavily on the courts in the country calling the structure of civil laws and judicial procedures complex and prone to delays. The result, he said, was that judgments given by military courts were rendered ineffective by challenging them in civil courts. While announcing the draconian measures of a ban on all political activity and press censorship, he said that 'martial law will now be run like martial law'.

This was the end to the acts of political jugglery that the nation had witnessed for more than two years. Zia continued in power on one pretext or the other but kept promising elections. It was also an end to his courtship with the PNA which he used to his own benefit. This sordid affair was a time-proven reminder that democratic parties cannot share power with dictators. If they do so, they only strengthen the dictators and lose their own political capital and are left high and dry. This was what happened to the PNA which, after this announcement, practically ceased to exist. In its dealing with Zia, the PNA leadership followed the strategy of using Zia to get rid of Bhutto but eventually they found that the results were the other way around. It was Zia's strategy of using the PNA to absorb the political shock of Bhutto's execution. At the end of the day, Zia was firmly in the saddle as dictator and the PNA was a helpless combination of political parties which were constantly fighting with one another and dropping out of the PNA. Neither the PNA as an alliance, nor the political parties that dropped out of it separately, were left with a substantial political clout, credibility, or following. They had simply been turned into a laughing stock by Zia and he abandoned them in that condition.

Introduction of Separate Electorates

It has been discussed above that Muslims in India during the British Raj demanded separate electorates in order to ensure adequate representation in the legislature.

Separate electorates enabled the Muslim League to make a strong showing in the constituencies for Muslim seats in the general elections of 1946, which ultimately paved the way for the creation of Pakistan.

After independence, the Muslims now in a predominant majority, no longer needed separate electorates. It could only be the minorities that could now demand separate electorates for their own protection, but no such demand was ever made. Thus, all the Constitutions and election laws made thereunder provided for joint electorates.

However, the politics of electorate came to a head in 1977 when the opposition PNA composed of some religious parties felt that it was at a disadvantage in the system of joint electorate. It was felt that the voters belonging to the minorities generally sided with the PPP, primarily because of its liberal views and stance. The PPP candidate received votes from the minorities which was at times a deciding factor in very close races. Religious parties like Jamaat-i-Islami, Jamiatul Ulema-i-Pakistan, and Jamiat-i-Ulema-i-Islam, felt that disenfranchising members of the minorities from the general seats would go to their advantage and, correspondingly, to the detriment of the PPP.

Ziaul Haq, who feared the resurgence of the PPP and would take any step to undermine its power and popularity, bought the idea. He introduced separate electorates through an amendment in the Representation of the Peoples Act 1976.[9] Election to the seats reserved for non-Muslims was made through a direct vote by electors enrolled on the electoral rolls for non-Muslims. Consequently, provisions were made for separate electoral rolls for non-Muslims for national and provincial assemblies and for carving out new constituencies for the non-Muslims in these Assemblies. Consequently, the electoral rolls for general seats in the national and provincial assemblies would only bear the names of Muslims.

Ultimately, separate electorates also found their way into the Constitution through Revival of the Constitution of 1973 Order, 1985 Clause (4-A) of Article 51 and Clause (5) of Article 106 were substituted providing for election of members of the national and provincial assemblies respectively belonging to minorities on the basis of separate electorate. This was indeed unfortunate, particularly in view of the fact that there was no demand by the minorities in Pakistan for separate electorates and the decision was imposed by the majority on an unwilling minority.

Military Courts Established under the Constitution

It has been mentioned above that martial law was re-invigorated in full force on 16 October 1979, political activity was banned, and the press muzzled. It was also announced that the decisions of the military courts could not be challenged or reviewed by the civil courts which was clearly against the dictum of the Supreme Court in Nusrat Bhutto's case. During the period when superior courts actively exercised judicial review of the acts and orders of military courts in contests between the state and civil society, the burden of proof was on the citizen rather than the state. When the courts questioned military judgments and occasionally overturned military convictions, that is, when they acted like real courts rather than puppet tribunals, the regime reacted by severely restricting their purview to only the most neutral cases.[10]

Consequent to this announcement, a constitutional amendment was made adding Article 212-A to the Constitution establishing military courts or tribunals in the country.[11] The CMLA could, by a martial law order, establish military courts or tribunals for trial of offences punishable under the martial law regulations or martial law orders or any other law, including a special law. Any case could be transferred from a civilian court to any military court. Once any military court or tribunal was established, no other court, including a High Court, could grant an injunction, make an order, or entertain any proceedings in respect of any matter to which the jurisdiction of the military court or tribunal extended or where a case had been transferred to such court or tribunal or that such court or tribunal had taken cognizance of any matter. By this amendment, the military courts or tribunals which existed and functioned under the Army Act had suddenly been clothed with constitutional recognition.

In pursuance of this amendment, more than one hundred military courts and tribunals were set up in all the four provinces of the country. There were also large-scale arrests and detentions of political workers and journalists under martial law regulation. Hundreds of people were sentenced to imprisonment and flogging merely for participating in normal political activity banned under martial law. By this amendment, the powers of judicial review, reserved for the superior courts by the Supreme Court in the judgment of Nusrat Bhutto's case, were completely nullified. This, of course, was a challenge to the Courts which had extended legitimacy to the martial law regime. Zia justified this step by saying that this amendment was introduced after consultation with the heads of the judiciary. He obviously referred to Chief Justices Anwar-ul-Haq and Maulvi Mushtaq.[12]

Challenge to the Amendment

This constitutional amendment and martial law regulation number 48 banning all political parties were challenged before the Supreme Court directly by the Tehrik-i-Istiqlal under Article 184(3) of the Consitition, urging that it was against the fundamental right of freedom of association. This petition came up for hearing before a Bench of six judges of the Supreme Court on 4 November 1979. Before the case could be heard on merit, two applications were filled by the counsel for the petititoners, Mr Mahmood Ali Kasuri, raising the following points:[13]

(a) that the matter should be heard by the same Bench which had decided the case of Begum Nusrat Bhutto v The Chief of the Army Staff, PLD 1977 S.C.657, as the petition in effect sought review of that judgment;

(b) that even otherwise it would be inappropriate for the Bench of six judges to hear the petition as all of them were drawn from one province (the Punjab), and the matter in issue concerned the entire federation; and

(c) that Mr Sharifuddin Pirzada, the Attorney-General, had disqualified himself from appearing in the case as an Advocate on behalf of the federal government or even in his capacity as Attorney-General because;
   i. he was holding another political office under the government, namely, Minister for Law and Parliamentary Affairs, in which capacity he could not appear before the courts of law;
   ii. three of the judges on the Bench were appointed to the Supreme Court during his tenure as Law Minister and, therefore, it was not appropriate that he should appear before them as an Advocate; and
   iii. in his capacity as Law Minister, he was in a position to initiate disciplinary proceedings against the judges of the Supreme Court, and for this reason as well, it was not proper for him to appear in the case before the Court.

All these valid objections were rejected in the strongest terms with Chief Justice Anwar-ul-Haq writing the judgment. Very strong words like 'regrettable', 'mischievous', 'condemned' and 'deprecated' were unnecessarily used, betraying his temper. At the end, he passed strictures on Qasuri for having cast unwarranted reflections on the independence, impartiality, and competence of the Bench and the competence of Pirzada to appear as Attorney-General. In fact, it was the Chief Justice himself who became very upset and rude with Qasuri during the course of the arguments on these applications. Instead of dealing with the objections in right earnest, he took them as an affront to himself and conducted himself in the Court as if he had been insulted.

However, at the end of the arguments, Qasuri withdrew the main petition to pursue similar petitions before the High Courts. A full Bench of the Lahore High Court, presided over by Chief Justice Maulvi Mushtaq, admitted to regular hearing of the writ petition filed by Asghar Khan challenging the dissolution of his party, Tehrik-i-Istiqlal.[14] This writ petition was argued before a full Bench of the Lahore High Court at length. The proceedings went on for months together and were studded with Maulvi Mushtaq's tantrums and demands for various explanations from the federal government which only delayed the proceedings. He also made some unwarranted and threatening remarks against the federal government. These remarks must have raised alarm in high government circles. It is difficult to understand what he wanted to accomplish by such remarks. Even after the conclusion of the arguments, he sat on the judgment for quite some time for some inexplicable reason.

Exorcizing the Judiciary

The martial law government reacted quickly and strongly to the rumour that the Lahore High Court was going to pronounce a verdict against it in Asghar Khan's case and before the Full Bench headed by Chief Justice Maulvi Mushtaq could deliver a judgment, a constitutional amendment was promulgated on 27 May 1980 barring the High Courts from making any Order relating to the validity of martial law regulations.[15] It restricted the 'writ jurisidiction' of the High Courts and barred them from making an Order relating to the validity or effect of any Martial Law Regulation or any martial law order or anything done, or action taken, or intended to be done or taken thereunder. It also prohibited the High Courts from reviewing the judgments or sentences passed by military courts or tribunals, or from taking any action against anyone acting with the authority of the Martial Law administrators. It also stated that the superior Courts' jurisdiction had been curtailed retrospectively. It then went on to declare the 1977 military takeover to be legal, with all subsequent orders passed by the military authorities as valid. These included President's Orders and CMLA Orders and Regulations.

The purpose of this constitutional amendment was to deprive the superior judiciary of its powers to review the decisions of military courts, the legality of martial law or any orders issued by any Martial Law authority. The High Courts could no longer grant relief by way of grant of bail or review any sentence unjustly awarded by a military court to a political person. Martial Law Order Number 72,[16] setting out the jurisdiction of military courts was substituted by Martial Law Order Number 77, further extending the jurisdiction of the military courts at the expense of civilian courts.[17] Military courts were given exclusive jurisdiction over cases of treason subversion, sedition, sabotage, activity prejudicial to martial law, and seducing of the members of the Armed Forces. These courts were also empowered to try any 'contravention of any martial law order or martial law regulation', and all offences under the Pakistan Penal Code.

Along with this amendment, very severe action was taken against Chief Justice Maulvi Mushtaq on 26 May 1980. He was summarily removed and despatched to the Supreme Court as an Acting Judge.[18] His chamber and office in the Lahore High Court were locked up by Army personnel and he was virtually locked out. To add insult to injury, his arch rival, Mr Justice Shamim Hussain Qadri, was appointed Acting Chief Justice of the Lahore High Court in his place.[19] A member of the full Bench that had tried and sentenced Bhutto, Mr Justice Aftab Husain[20] was banished to the newly created Federal Shariat Court.

The martial law government had reached the conclusion that it had had enough of these judges and that they should be cut down to size. Although they had served the regime exceptionally well by legitimizing it and by getting rid of Bhutto by a judicial verdict, Zia had little use for them now. The judges, particularly those who were making demands on him because of their past services, were a source of irritation to him and his *junta*. He, therefore, decided that he should rule with the help of military justice. It was also decided that any order of injunction passed by a civilian court against the execution of a military court order should be ignored.

The Hamid Baloch Case

The case of Hamid Baloch was one of several instances in which superior courts were by-passed. The Balochistan High Court had stayed death sentences handed down by martial law tribunals (manned by military officers) operating in this huge, remote province of Pakistan. The questions which were being debated in the High Court in Quetta were of a most serious nature, of fundamental importance, and related to the rights and prerogatives of the superior judiciary in the country, seeking to define the relationship between the Constitution and the existence of martial law. The provincial military governor, Lieutenant-General Rahimuddin Khan, stated in October 1979 that the sentences awarded by military tribunals in cases of murder would soon be executed. The constitution of these military courts had already been assailed before the High Court on a number of grounds. It was alleged that the procedure of these tribunals was without adequate safeguards for a fair trial and that the military courts themselves had no authority in law. The High Court thus stayed the execution of sentences. On 25 October 1979, a day after the governor's statement, the lawyers of those convicts who were in jail following conviction by military courts appeared before the High Court and submitted that their clients were about to be hanged despite repeated High Court orders forbidding the execution. The Chief Justice of the Balochistan High Court, Mir Khuda Bakhsh Marri, immediately issued fresh stay orders commanding prison authorities to desist from carrying out the sentences and to obey all previous orders of the High Court passsed in this regard.

According to the legal circles in Quetta, the provincial militiary authorities ordered the prison authorities to carry out the death sentences. However, the High Court reminded the jail officers that any execution would be illegal and would also amount to contempt of Court. Officials in jail then, reportedly, informed the provincial martial law authorities that if the military wished to execute anyone, they should come to the prison and do so themselves, but that the jail authorities did not wish to attract the charge of violating the order of the High Court nor would they like to risk eventually being arrested for having hanged a man without lawful authority.

Military officers in the province were also told that if any army officer or soldier carried out the sentence against the order of the High Court, all those who carried out the sentence and those who gave the orders would not only be held guilty of contempt of Court but at a subsequent date all those concerned could be arrested on charges of pre-meditated murder. The Chief Justice of Balochistan High Court and his colleagues stood firm. Militiary authorities did not move to carry out the sentences.[21]

It goes to the credit of the Balochistan High Court that despite the constitutional amendment of May 1980, it continued to hear cases in which the *vires* of Articles 212-A had been challenged. A full Bench of the Balochistan High Court formulated the following questions:

1. whether Article 212-A is *intra vires*;
2. if the above question is answered in the affirmative, then what is the effect of:

   (a) Article 212-A and MLO-4, as amended by MLO-72, on the powers of judicial review under Article 199; and
   (b) of Article 212-A on cases finally decided by military courts and tribunals and cases pending before them.

The full Bench decided in its judgment dated 12 July 1980, that the amendments of the Constitution by way of introduction of Article 212-A and Clauses 3-A, 3-B and 3-C in Article 199 were *ultra vires* of the powers of the Chief Martial Law Administrator, though he acted as President while promulgating such amendments. These amendments were held to have failed to come up to the test of necessity laid down in Nusrat Bhutto's case. As the first question had been answered in the negative, the second question was not required to be answered.[22]

The Balochistan High Court had earlier been showing courage in the face of martial law. A divisional Bench of the Court held that an ordinary citizen could not be tried by a military court for offences created by ordinary laws, provided such offence was not committed by way of resistance to martial law itself.[23] The government went in appeal against the said judgment before the Supreme Court of Pakistan. The Supreme Court, however, did not answer the question. It merely observed that the proposition and observations made by the High Court of Balochistan were too wide and open to exception and would require careful examination in a proper case. No decision on merit was given because the provincial government had decided to try the respondent under ordinary law applicable to the case and the appeal had been rendered infructuous. This judgment was delivered by the Supreme Court on 24 June 1979. Unfortunately, however, the proposition laid down by the High Court had not been examined in the case nor in any of the large number of other cases involving similar questions of law which were pending in the Supreme Court. Decisions on these questions was tactfully avoided.[24]

But for the Balochistan High Court, the rest of the judiciary was put under a leash after the amendment of May 1980. Nothing more was heard of the case of Asghar Khan challenging Article 212-A or MLR-48. The new Acting Chief Justice of the Lahore High Court had made sure that it was not re-listed or re-heard. Perhaps that was important for his own survival.

The Federal Shariat Court

Hard times for the judiciary were not yet over. Another major blow was dealt to the superior courts by the withdrawal of powers to examine any law or any provision of a law if it was in accordance with Islamic injunctions. The Federal Shariat Court was set up with powers to declare invalid any law or provision of a law as repugnant to the injunctions of Islam as laid down in the Holy Quran and the *sunnah* of the Holy Prophet (PBUH).[25] In a nutshell, the powers that had been conferred only a year earlier on the Shariat Benches of the High Courts under Constitution (Amendment) Order 1979, were withdrawn and vested in a new and parallel court, the Federal Shariat Court. This was another show of lack of confidence by Zia in the superior courts.

The Federal Shariat Court was to consist of five members, including the Chairman, who was to be appointed by the President. The chairman was to be a person who was, or had been, or was qualified to be, a judge of the Supreme Court. A member was to be a person who was, or had been, or was qualified to be, a judge of a High

Court.[26] The chairman or a member was to hold office for a period not exceeding three years but could be appointed for a further term. A judge of a High Court who refused to accept appointment as a member would be deemed to have retired from his office. Appeal was provided to the Supreme Court Bench called the Shariat Appellate Bench consisting of three Muslim judges of the Supreme Court.

Subsequently, appellate powers against the conviction and sentences under the *Hadood* laws were also conferred in this Court. This was apparently done to give more work to and to strengthen the Court which was otherwise dealing with abstract and academic controversies and questions. But correspondingly, the appellate jurisdiction of the High Courts in criminal cases was curtailed. The judiciary that had colluded with martial law for nearly three years now fell under its weight.

The Federal Shariat Court, a manipulative creation of Zia, soon ran foul of him and started creating serious embarrasments. In a case in which the sentence of *Rajm* (stoning to death) for *zina* was challenged as repugnant to Islam, the Court, with a majority of 4 to 1, held in its judgment of 21 March 1981 that the provisions of sentence of *Rajm* as *Hadd* in section 5 and 6 of the Offence of *Zina* (Enforcement of Hudood) Ordinance 1979, were repugnant to the injunctions of Islam and that the only *Hadd* was one hundred stripes and that necessary amendments be made in these sections by 31 July 1981.[27] This judgment, when it came to light, raised a big furore in religious circles and the judges of the Federal Shariat Court were condemned for their lack of knowledge of Islam and for being western-educated and West-oriented. There was an outcry that *ulema* should be introduced into the Court, a demand to which Zia succumbed to appease the *mullahs*. A constitutional amendment was made for introducing three *ulema* into the Court in addition to five judges, including the Chairman. The *ulema* members were to be chosen from a panel of *ulema* to be drawn by the President in consultation with the Chairman of the Court.[28] As a face-saving device, the Court was empowered to review its decisions.

In this way the Federal Shariat Court was invaded by the so-called *ulema*. Finally, the judgment on *Rajm* in Hazoor Bakhsh's case was reviewed on the application of the federal government in 1982, with the *ulema* sitting on the Bench of five. Only one judge amongst the original five, Aftab Husain, who had become Chief Justice by then, sat on the review Bench. The review application was accepted and the earlier judgment was set aside and the punishment of *Rajm* was accepted as valid under the injunctions of Islam.[29] These events exposed the inherent weakness of the newly established Federal Shariat Court—there was lack of personal independence on the part of its judges. It was also established that the Court was vulnerable to manipulation in order to reach politically desired results.

In April 1978, communists in the armed forces of Afghanistan deposed and killed President Daud and assumed the power of the state. A known veteran, Noor Muhammad Taraki, was made the President of the new communist state. This violent takeover was not accepted by the people of Afghanistan who are largely conservative and religious. Thus, resistance started within Afghanistan against the government. The communist government itself suffered from serious internal dissensions and factionalism. Finally, in an internal feud in October 1979, Prime Minister Hafizullah

Amin had President Taraki shot to death in a meeting of the Communist Party and assumed the office of the President. Hafizullah Amin's hold on power was weak and he started making overtures to the West which displeased the Soviet Union. In any case, he was losing ground to the rebel Islamic groups within Afghanistan trying to overthrow the communist government.

In these circumstances, the Soviet Union intervened directly and more than one hundred thousand Soviet troops invaded Afghanistan. Hafizullah Amin was removed and killed, and, in his place, a puppet government headed by Babrak Karmal was installed. This development provided Zia with an opportunity. He decided that it was in his interest to help the Afghans resist communism. It was a risky venture but it worked for him and his regime because the United States and other western powers, China, and the Arab States were attracted towards Zia and extended financial and military assistance to his government, forgetting altogether that he was a military dictator. That gave him international stature and exposure, and stabilized his regime. Zia's bold adventure in Afghanistan was one of the main causes of his longevity in power.

Creation of Permanent Benches of the High Courts

In January 1981, permanent Benches of the Lahore High Court were created at Bahawalpur, Multan, and Rawalpindi under High Courts (Establishment) Order (Punjab Amendment) Ordinance, 1981.[30] The reason given for these Benches was that justice was being taken to the doorsteps of the people. In fact, the motive was different. After the postponement of general elections by Zia, and banning of political activities in the country, the lawyer community was offering serious resistance to the martial law regime and demanding restoration of the 1973 Constitution, restoration of the powers of the judiciary, holding of general elections, and the lifting of Martial Law. The hub of their activities was Lahore where lawyer conventions were being held by the premier Bar of the country, the Lahore High Court Bar Association. The Permanent Benches in Punjab were obviously created to punish the lawyers of Lahore by dispersing them throughout the province and by undermining their premier bar association.

There was, in any case, no justification for creating these permanent Benches. One circuit Bench was already functioning in Bahawalpur. There was demand for a circuit Bench in Rawalpindi which was fully justified as the Principal Seat of the Supreme Court had already been established in Rawalpindi in 1974. All that was needed to be done was to establish a circuit Bench in Rawalpindi. The permanent Bench in Multan was not justified because a circuit Bench was already functioning in Bahawalpur, at a distance of about 100 kilometers.

The manner in which the shifting of the personnel of the Lahore High Court to the Permanent Benches took place speaks volumes of the contempt in which the martial law regime held the judiciary. There were no facilities at these places of Permanent Benches, except in Bahawalpur, for holding of Court and for the residence of judges.

Acting Chief Justice Qadri ordered the functioning of these Permanent Benches in Lahore till such time that appropriate facilities were provided at these places. Martial Law authorities did not like this order and the Governor directed the Acting Chief Justice to transfer the record of the cases from the areas assigned to these Benches to the respective Benches and to ask the judges to go to these Benches and hold court there. All this was required to be done within forty-eight hours.[31] Qadri, who was a very weak person, succumbed to this unreasonable demand and withdrew his earlier order. He made a mess of the move. The judges were stranded, there was no accommodation for them or premises to hold Court. The files were misplaced and the Court staff was in a spin. The Lahore High Court had been treated in a most humiliating manner and the judiciary faced further ignominy at the hands of the military government.

The Permanent Benches of the High Courts were given a semi-constitutional position under the Provisional Constitution Order 1981,which provided for Permanent Benches of:

i. the Lahore High Court at Bahawalpur, Multan, and Rawalpindi;
ii. the High Court of Sindh at Sukkur;
ii. the Peshawar High Court at Abbotabad and Dera Ismail Khan; and
iv. the High Court of Balochistan at Sibi.

Movement for the Restoration of Democracy (MRD)

After the final break between Zia and the PNA in October 1979, nearly all the political parties in the country were arrayed against Zia. There was still a segment of the population and political workers who supported Zia for either the fear of return of the People's Party to power or for their narrow personal political objectives. The Muslim League, led by Pir Pagaro, continued to support Zia and his regime as he had admitted on more than one occasion that he was an agent of General Headquarters (GHQ) of the armed forces. He believed in sharing power, not wresting it from the army. He and his party had little following and his followers were looked down upon as 'collaborators' or 'lackeys'.

Despite antagonism with Zia, the PNA parties and those that broke from the alliance did not find it easy to come to terms with the leader of the PPP. There was the recent history of great hostility towards the PPP, including co-operation with the military *junta* for the execution of Bhutto. The PPP leader took time to overcome the shock of Bhutto's execution. Their immediate reaction to the execution was dealt with a heavy hand with protesters sentenced to imprisonment and lashes, which were instantly administered. The student wing of the Jamaat-i-Islami also helped the government in controlling the beating up of agitators under the protection and patronage of the police. Thus what divided the PPP from other political forces in the country was blood rather than political differences. The PPP leader, the mother and daughter of Bhutto, Nusrat and Benazir, were under house arrest. Some of the more vocal opponents from other parties, like Asghar Khan,[32] were also under house arrest.

Finally, political forces in the country rose from their slumber and decided to put their differences aside for the time being and face the military dictatorship by uniting against it. The political parties opposed to the PPP thought that the real damage had come from Zia and not the PPP, particularly after the death of Bhutto. The PPP leadership also realized that they had to put the execution behind them and act under the political logic and compulsion of the situation and reach for the erstwhile political opponents for waging a collective struggle against the military dictator. After years in the political wilderness and exploitation of their political differences by the military regime, the PPP and most of the parties in the defunct PNA, decided to sit together on a table.

On 6 February 1981, the PPP and several smaller parties who had never been or were no longer associated with the PNA, formed a group named the Movement for the Restoration of Democracy (MRD) that would work both for putting an end to Martial Law and for holding free elections in accordance with the suspended 1973 Constitution.[33] The MRD included Jamiat-i-Ulema-i-Islam (JUI), headed by Mufti Mahmood, and Tehrik-i-Istiqlal (TI), headed by Asghar Khan. Jamaat-i-Islami stayed away from MRD because, according to its leadership, the gulf between the Jamaat and the PPP was unbridgeable. The Jamaat continued to support Zia. The fact that Jamaat was led by Mian Tufail Muhammad, also an Arain from Jullundhur like Zia and with a similar social and economic background, was obviously a factor in the context. It was widely known that Mian Tufail was related to Zia – an uncle perhaps. This suggestion was later denied by Mian Tufail.[34]

For some time, Zia's government was in trouble due to agitation in various cities by students, doctors, and others. But the hijacking in 1981 of a Pakistan International Airlines (PIA) plane by Al-Zulfikar an organization led by one of Z.A. Bhutto's sons, from Karachi first to Kabul and then to Damascus, deflected people's attention. The hijackers killed a young army officer while the plane was in Kabul and the incident created reaction amongst the people against the PPP once again. Zia arrested a large number of people and held them under preventive detention. He was thus able to ride the storm.

Al-Zulfikar, whose origin and organization were shrouded in mystery, brought a bad name to the PPP in particular and to the MRD in general. This organization was said to have been formed abroad with India's encouragement to promote terrorism in Pakistan with the purpose of destablizing Zia's government. It was allegedly headed by Murtaza Bhutto, the elder son of Bhutto. A number of acts of terrorism were carried out in Pakistan, including bombing public places and the murder of Chaudhry Zahur Ilahi in September 1981. Maulvi Mushtaq was also in the car with Zahur Ilahi when he was killed but he was lucky to escape without injury despite a barrage of bullets fired at the car and a grenade that fell into his lap that did not explode. Al-Zulfikar was supported by the Soviet government and its puppet regime in Afghanistan and its activities were sponsored and controlled from Kabul. Murtaza was reported to have travelled to Kabul several times in connection with terrorist activities. The activities of Al-Zulfikar were a constant political embarrassment to the PPP and MRD and Zia's government tried to blame every act of terrorism in Pakistan on Al-

Zulfikar, thus raising and reviving the fears of Pakistanis, particularly from the middle classes, against the PPP. Thus, Al-Zulfikar indirectly helped Zia to remain in power.

NOTES

1. Address to the nation by General Ziaul Haq on 30 August 1979 published the Ministry of Information, Government of Pakistan, Islamabad.
2. Political Parties (Amendment) Ordinance, 1979. Ordinance XIII of 1979. PLD 1979 Central Statues 466.
3. *Dawn*, 2 October 1979.
4. *Dawn*, 3 October 1979.
5. *Dawn*, 6 October 1979.
6. Political Parties (Third Amendment) Ordinance 1979, Ordinance LIII of 1979. PLD 1979 Central Statues 555.
7. *Dawn*, 8 October 1979.
8. 'President Ends Political Uncertainty'. President Ziaul Haq's address to the Nation, 16 October 1979, published by Ministry of Information, Islamabad.
9. Representation of the Peoples (Amendment) Ordinance 1979. Ordinance L of 1979. PLD 1979 Central Statues 532, Section 47-A.
10. Newberg, Paula R., *Judging the State: Courts and Constitutional Politics in Pakistan.* 1995, Cambridge University Press, Cambridge, U.K. p. 174.
11. Constitution (Second Amendment) Order 1979. President's Order 21 of 1979. PLD 1979 Central statues 567.
12. Zia told a delegation of lawyers that the draft of Article 212-A had been vetted by Chief Justices, Anwar-ul-Haq and Maulvi Mushtaq.
13. Hamid Sarfraz v Federation of Pakistan. PLD 1979 S.C. 991.
14. *Dawn*, 12 November 1979.
15. Constitution (Amendment) Order, 1980. President's Order 1 of 1980. PLD Central Statutes 89.
16. CMLA order number 72, 20 October 1979. PLD 1979 Central Statutes 568.
17. CMLA order number 77, 2 June 1980. PLD 1980 Central Statutes 152.
18. Appointment of Acting Judge of the Supreme Court is made under Article 181 of the Constitution. He is not permanent Judge.
19. Mr Justice Qadri had all the furniture from the chamber and office of the Chief Justice removed and had then got the same fully washed and cleaned before the furniture was put back to set up the office again. Mr Justice Qadri said that, before starting his work in the office, he wanted to exorcie the place which had been subjected to some satanic acts previously. It is said that Qadri, when Bhutto was in power, had taken two black goats to him to win favour of and impress upon him that these goats should be sacrificed so that the bad dream he had seen about Bhutto might not come true.
20. He authored the trial Court Judgment in Bhutto's murder case.
21. Mahmood, M. Dilawar, *The Judiciary and Politics in Pakistan*, 1992, Idara Mutalia-e-Tareekh, Lahore, pp. 129-31.
22. Suleman v President, Special Military Court. Full text of the Judgment is available on p. 96 to 120 of the book of Mir Khuda Bakhsh Marri (former Chief Justice of Balochistan and head of the full Bench rendering the Judgment), *A Judge May Speak*, Ferozsons (Pvt) Ltd., Lahore, 1990.
23. Muhammad Niaz v Martial Law Administrator, PLD 1979 Quetta 179.
24. Martial Law Administrator v Muhammad Niaz. PLD 1979 S.C. 921.
25. Constitution (Amendment) Order, 1980. President's Order 1 of 1980. PLD 1980 Cenral Statues 89.
26. Article 203-C.
27. Hazoor Bakhsh v Federation of Pakistan. PLD 1981 F.S.C. 145.

28. Constitution (Amendment) Order, 1981. President's Order 5 of 1981. PLD 1981 Central Statutes 251.
29. Federation of Pakistan v Hazoor Bakhsh. PLD 1983 F.S.C. 255.
30. Ordinance I of 1981. PLD 1981 Punjab Statues 1.
31. It is said that Governor, Lieutenant-General Ghulam Jilani Khan, a dubious and sneaky character, told the Acting Chief Justice that if the Army could move battalions of thousands of troops in a few days, then why could not a few judges and few thousand files be moved.
32. Asghar Khan, while addressing Peshawar High Court Bar Association, had called Zia as the 'biggest hypocrite in the history of Pakistan'.
33. Burki, Shahid Javed and Baxter, Craig, *Pakistan Under the Military – Eleven Years of Zia-ul-Haq*, 1991, Westview Press, Boulder, Colorado, p. 34.
34. *Herald*, Karachi, April 1987, 'Personality Interview: Mian Tufail Muhammad'.

28

THE PROVISIONAL CONSTITUTION ORDER, 1981

Zia was quick to take full advantage of the aversion of the general public to the hijacking of a PIA plane in March 1981. The night between 24 and 25 March 1981, the Provisional Constitution Order (PCO) was enforced[1] which was to serve as the constitution of Pakistan for years to come. It was the CMLA's order, meant to make adequate provisions for governing Pakistan and 'for effectively meeting the threat to the integrity and sovereignty of Pakistan and its Islamic ideology.' It restated that the 1973 Constitution was held in abeyance, while adopting 138 Articles of the Constitution of 1973. These Articles related to the daily working of government, both federal and provincial.

Other important features of the PCO were as under:

1. All fundamental rights under the 1973 Constitution and the provisions for their enforceability were taken out.
2. The office of Vice President was created. The CMLA could appoint one or more Vice Presidents of Pakistan who would serve at the pleasure of the CMLA and would perform functions assigned by the CMLA.
3. A Federal Council (*Majlis-e-Shoora*) would be set up consisting of people selected by the President. The Council would perform functions as specified in an order made by the President.
4. A number of provisions relating to the judiciary were excluded from the PCO and they were replaced by new provisions, the important ones being:
   (a) The Supreme Court could transfer cases from one High Court to another.
   (b) Principal seats and permanent Benches of the High Courts were determined and the permanent Benches that had been formed under provincial laws were made part of the constitutional document.
   (c) Provision regarding the acting Chief Justice of a High Court gave the President the power to appoint any judge of the High Court concerned or even a judge of the Supreme Court to be the acting Chief Justice in the absence of the Chief Justice or when the office of the Chief Justice was vacant.
   (d) The writ jurisdiction of the High Courts, with a number of restraints and exceptions, was however retained. Martial law authorities and military courts and their acts and orders were placed beyond the pale of the writ jurisdiction of High Courts.

(e) A High Court judge could be transferred from one High Court to another for a period of up to two years without his consent and without consultation with the Chief Justices of the High Courts concerned.
(f) A retired judge was not to hold an office of profit in the service of Pakistan within two years of his retirement.
(g) Jurisdiction of the Supreme Court, the High Courts, or any other court or tribunal was barred in the cases of those civil servants who had been retired after completion of twenty-five years of service.

5. Only those political parties would be allowed to function, whenever political activity was restored, which had registered themselves with the Election Commission by 11 October 1979. All other political parties stood dissolved and their funds forfeited to the federal government. No new political party could be formed except with the previous permission in writing of the Chief Election Commissioner.
6. The Proclamation of 5 July 1977, President's Orders, CMLA's Orders, including those amending the Constitution, all Martial Law regulations and orders, and all other laws made on or after 5 July 1977, were declared valid notwithstanding any judgment of any court. All orders made, proceedings taken, and acts done or purported to have been made, taken or done under the aforesaid laws or notifications thereunder were also declared valid. Any execution of any order made or sentence passed was deemed to be and would always be deemed to have been validly made, taken or done and could not be called in question in any court on any ground whatsoever. The courts were barred from granting any injunction against the acts and orders of any martial law authority or a military court or tribunal. The superior Courts could not even issue any process against the CMLA, the MLA, or people acting under their authority. All orders, injunctions, or processes issued or to be issued were declared null and void.
7. The President and the CMLA would have and would be deemed always to have the power to amend the Constitution.
8. All judges of the Supreme Court, the High Courts, and the Federal Shariat Court, including the Chief Justices, were required to take an oath under the PCO. However, the taking of oath was not left to the choice of the judges alone; the President had the option not to give oath to any judge. Those judges who did not take the oath or were not given the oath were to cease to hold office.
9. Judges, who took the oath under the PCO, were to be bound by the provisions of the PCO and could not call into question or even permit to be called into question the validity of its provisions.

Hence, the PCO fell heavy on the judiciary and drastically curtailed its powers and position. The judiciary had already been under fire for more than a year but whatever little independence was left was finally done away with under the PCO. Zia and his *junta* were confident that they had been able to subdue and neutralize whatever little political resistance existed in the country. It was made sure that even a remote chance of a challenge to its unlawful authority from the judiciary was completely neutralized. The provision regarding the Vice President was never acted upon and the office remained vacant. It was speculated at one stage that Chief Justice Anwar-ul-Haq might be accommodated into this office, but it seems that due to resistance within the government, led by Attorney-General Sharifuddin Pirzada, this possibility did not materialize.

Public Humiliation of the Judiciary

The Zia government believed that merely stripping the judges of their powers and jurisdiction was not enough and that they should also be subjected to humiliation, particularly in the public eye. The judiciary was so demoralized that no judge could entertain the thought of defying the martial law government.

Since it was the option of the President to give or not to give oath to any judge, lists were prepared on the morning of 25 March of those judges who had to be administered oath. Even the Chief Justices of the Supreme Court and the High Courts were not consulted in the process and the lists were kept confidential. All of the judges were in a quandary as to whether to take the oath or not, and whether or not it would be given. They requested their respective Chief Justices for guidance, but found them equally blank. The Chief Justices of the High Courts tried to establish communication with the Governors of their respective provinces to find out what was going on.

The matter of taking the oath was discussed amongst the judges of the Supreme Court and there were two points of view. Justice Dorab Patel, who was the senior most judge after the Chief Justice, wanted the Supreme Court to take a clear stand against the oath taking. Justice Fakharuddin Ibrahim, who was only an ad hoc judge, was with him. Justice Maulvi Mushtaq argued strongly in favour of taking the oath. A predominant majority of the judges favoured taking the oath. Thus, the decision was in favour of taking the oath.[2] When Zia spoke to Anwar-ul-Haq, he asked him and the other judges of the Supreme Court to take the oath before him but advised him not to bring Maulvi Mushtaq because he was not to be included. Anwar urged Zia to give oath to Mushtaq, for old times sake, and must have referred to his services, but Zia did not agree. Even when Anwar threatened that he would not be taking the oath if Mushtaq was not given it, Zia did not budge from his position. Thus, Anwar-ul-Haq was cornered into not taking the oath. Consequently, Anwar-ul-Haq, Dorab Patel, and Fakharuddin Ibrahim did not take the oath and Maulvi Mushtaq was not given it. In this way, two leading benefactors of Zia in the judiciary, Anwar-ul-Haq and Maulvi Mushtaq, met a sad and ignominious end to their careers at the hands of their own principal beneficiary. They learnt the hard way the abject lesson of history that those who twist principles for their immediate interests and betray their fellows must ultimately come to a sad end.

The remaining six judges of the Supreme Court took the oath without their Chief Justice. Justice Muhammad Haleem,[3] who was the most senior amongst the remaining judges, took oath as the acting Chief Justice of the Supreme Court. It was a matter of exceptional courage on the part of Dorab Patel not to take the oath, particularly when he was the senior-most judge and could have certainly been made the Chief Justice, a position he would have held for eight or nine years. He sacrificed office for his principles, a courage very few judges in Pakistan have shown.

The Balochistan High Court had only three judges, a Chief Justice and two judges at that time. Chief Justice Marri and Justice M. A. Rashid did not take the oath and only one judge was left in Quetta, Abdul Qadeer Chaudhry, who took the oath. Justice Zakaullah Lodhi of the Balochistan High Court, who was at that time a judge of the Federal Shariat Court, was brought to Quetta and administered the oath as acting Chief Justice of the Balochistan High Court. It must be said about the Balochistan High Court that its judges proved to be the most independent amongst the four High Courts, particularly since the Chief Justice and the senior most judge refused to take oath.

The Chief Justice and five judges of the Peshawar High Court took their oath in Peshawar before the Governor of the NWFP, Lieutenant-General Fazle Haq. One of the judges of the Peshawar High Court, Justice Muhammad Daud Khan, who at that time was the Chairman of the Federal Service Tribunal, was not given the oath.

All the Sindh High Court judges decided to take the oath but two of them, Justice Abdul Hafiz Memon and Justice Ghulam Muhammad Shah Syed, were not given the oath because they were regarded as being close to the leader of the People's Party.

The scene in the Lahore High Court was the most confused. The judges did not know what to do and acting Chief Justice Qadri was too weak and confused to offer leadership in making a collective decision. A few of them argued that they should not take the oath because it required total loyalty to the government. Others were in favour of taking the oath. It was not clear who would be given the oath. Two permanent judges, Zakiuddin Pal and K. M. A. Samdani, and three additional judges, Aamer Raza, Aftab Farrukh, and Habibullah, had decided not to take the oath. Samdani was persuaded by another judge, M.S.H. Qureshi, to take oath and went with him to the Governor House for the purpose. The three additional judges named above went to see acting Chief Justice Qadri to seek his guidance in making up their minds but were not allowed in because the acting Chief Justice was in a meeting with a Deputy Attorney-General.[4] These poor fellows, after waiting a while, left and did not take the oath. One of the judges left his courtroom after packing up his personal belongings and bidding goodbye to his staff with the obvious intention of not taking the oath. Subsequently, he took the oath on the persuasion of Qadri. Another judge, who was reportedly not being given oath but was keen to take it, went with Qadri to the Governor House to remove any misunderstanding with the government. He was a favourite of Qadri's who wanted him to stay as judge and ultimately prevailed upon the Governor.[5] A judge, who had gone for inspection of the courts in Sialkot district, was summoned on a wireless and told to reach Lahore for the oath-taking. He rushed to Lahore with his driver breaking all speed limits, but when he went to the Governor

House for taking the oath he was told that he was not one of the chosen few. At the Governor House, three judges, K.M.A. Samdani, Khalil-ur-Rahman, and one additional judge, Khurshid Ahmad, were returned because they were not to be given oath. Other judges present, including the acting Chief Justice, did not take any stand for the three colleagues who were being so blatantly insulted and humiliated. Everyone was busy saving his own office and did not care what he had to pay in terms of self-respect to retain it. Justice K. M. A. Samdani had allowed bail to Bhutto in September 1977 and later on as Law Secretary taken a stand at a meeting of the federal secretaries with the CMLA. All this had added against him, and was enough for the military regime to deny him the oath of office. He was contacted by the Governor on the following day to come and take the oath but he refused to do so. Out of the two High Court judges in Multan, Justice Muhammad Hassan Sindhar, who was known to be personally close to Maulvi Mushtaq, was not given the oath.

The episode is a very unfortunate chapter in the constitutional and judicial history of Pakistan. As an organ of the state, the judiciary was insulted and humiliated by a military government who had no respect for the rule of law and institutions under the Constitution.[6]

The Generals could not be entirely blamed for this unfortunate episode. Judges were equally responsible because they had submitted themselves to such humiliation. Had there been unity amongst them, they would not have seen such a day. But, unfortunately, they were not made of the mettle that judges should be made of. They sacrificed the prestige and honour of the institution of the judiciary at the altar of their personal ambitions and career. By their actions, they reduced an organ of the state to a mere department of the government. They behaved as if they were not members of an independent institution but only government servants who would serve on any terms and conditions, howsoever humiliating. By their conduct, they let down and undermined the judicial organ of the State and caused irreparable damage to its prestige. Former Chief Justice A. R. Cornelius, commenting on the unfortunate episode, called it 'the rape of the judiciary'.[7]

The Provisional Constitution Order (PCO) Upheld

It did not take long for the judiciary to uphold the PCO as valid. In keeping with its dubious tradition, the Lahore High Court applied its seal of approval to the PCO soon thereafter. A retired army general who was convicted and sentenced by a Field General Court Martial, challenged the PCO on the ground that during the subsistence of the 1973 Constitution, the PCO could not be issued, nor could the CMLA, an army officer under oath to defend the Constitution of 1973, give such a provisional Constitution in its supersession. These contentions were repelled by a divisional Bench of the Lahore High Court as under:[8]

i. The PCO appeared to be a misnomer. It was not a compact and self contained constitutional document but derived its existence, strength, and validity from the judicially recognized proclamation of 5 July 1977 read with Laws

(Continuance in Force) Order, 1977, and could not be of a superior or a higher status than its ancestor. The PCO, therefore, was just another order of the CMLA and did not lay down or give a new legal order.

ii. The effect of the PCO as regards the powers of the High Court and terms and conditions of the superior judiciary was to relegate the two to substantially the same position as it was after the Fifth Amendment to the Constitution. If the CMLA could amend the Constitution to remove the effect of the Fifth Amendment, he could also withdraw his own enactment even if its effect was to curtail the powers of the High Court.

iii. Since the Supreme Court had conceded to the CMLA the power to amend the Constitution, the PCO could not be said to be in excess of or *ultra vires* to the power of the CMLA.

iv. The courts would neither be pleased with more powers nor dismayed with less. The judges had never criticized any law on the ground of it being harsh or unjust and did not refer to the administration for amending any law for the reason that it did not provide just or full relief. The judges, being themselves a creation of the law, ought to be indifferent as to the state of law which would be a pure political question.

The reasoning adopted by the High Court to validate the PCO was clearly complex, laboured, and faulty. The judges carefully avoided examination of the PCO on the touchstone of Nusrat Bhutto's case. Who can deny that the extra-constitutional step of martial law was validated by the Supreme Court, subject to the condition that superior courts would exercise the power of judicial review against acts and orders of the martial law authorities. This power of judicial review was completely taken away by the PCO. In any case, it could not be expected from judges who had taken a humiliating oath under the PCO to invalidate the same.

PCO-II—Reinstatement Orders of Civil Servants Nullified

It has been mentioned earlier while discussing General Zia's regime, that 303 senior officers in the civil services of Pakistan were dismissed, removed, or retired from service under Martial Law Regulation number 58 in 1969 and 1970. Many of them challenged the orders before the High Court in writ jurisdiction. These petitions were pending when service tribunals were established at the federal as well as the provincial level under Article 212 of the Constitution. Therefore, petitions pending before the High Courts abated. These cases were then filed as appeals before the Federal Service Tribunal in the case of federal civil servants and before the appropriate provincial service tribunal in the case of provincial civil servants. The Federal Service Tribunal, in which a predominant majority of such appeals were pending, dismissed all of them for the reason that it had no jurisdiction to determine and adjudicate upon such cases. This judgment was challenged before the Supreme Court which reversed the decision of the tribunal, holding that jurisdiction was vested in it in such cases and that all the appeals were remanded to the tribunal for hearing on merit.[9] This decision was taken by the Supreme Court in 1980 by which time the fate of these men had hung in the balance for more than ten years and many of them had already crossed the age of superannuation.

The Federal Service Tribunal heard these appeals on merit after remand from the Supreme Court and accepted a number of appeals and ordered reinstatement of the successful appellants.[10] The federal government, instead of complying with these orders or filing appeals against them before the Supreme Court, nullified all such decisions and validated the orders that had been set aside by the Service Tribunal by means of an amendment in the Provisional Constitution Order.[11] All proceedings pending before any tribunal or court arising out of MLR 58 of 1970 were held to have been abated. The matter did not end here. Those members of the tribunal who had ordered reinstatement came under fire and were removed. In this way, the process of law for these ill-fated people came to nothing after legal proceedings of more than ten years.

The Federal Council (*Majlis-e-Shoora*)

It was provided under the PCO that the President could constitute a Federal Council (*Majlis-e-Shoora*) to perform functions that were to be assigned to it by the President. This was a step taken to create a political lobby for Zia and his cronies and to groom these people in future for election to the assemblies in addition to the people elected to the local bodies who owed allegiance to Zia. Nominees to the Federal Council were carefully selected by the Governors of the provinces on the basis of reports of bureaucrats and the intelligence agencies. Their chances of getting elected to the assemblies in the future based on their family background was given due weight. In this way, scions of feudal families got generous representation in this Council.

After this selection had been finalized by the end of 1981, Zia issued a President's Order for setting up the Federal Council.[12] The purpose of the council given thereunder was that pending restoration of democracy and representative institutions, it was deemed necessary to make an interim arrangement for association and consultation regarding the affairs of the state. Hence, the Federal Council was an interim arrangement made by the martial law government and the nominees thereto were expected to serve as the political arm of the military regime.

The President could nominate up to 350 members to the Federal Council. Due representation was to be given to *ulema*, *mashaikh*, women, farmers, professionals, labourers, and minorities. The Council would have a chairman and four vice chairmen, one from each province, all to be appointed by the President and to hold office at his pleasure. The Council could recommend to the President the enactment of a law, or the amendment of an existing law. It could discuss the Five Year Development Plan and make recommendations. It could also discuss the annual budget but could not vote on any of its items. The quorum of the Council was one-fourth of its total strength and decisions of the Council were to be taken by consensus of the members present. It could not discuss the conduct of judges. Its members were immune from any prosecution or proceedings in any court for anything said or any opinion expressed in the Council. The President could dissolve it at any time and it would be automatically dissolved upon the establishment of permanent representative institutions.

After the nomination of its members, the Federal Council met in February 1982 and Zia addressed the first session. Khawaja Muhammad Safdar from Sialkot, an old Muslim Leaguer, was nominated as its Chairman. The Council held its sessions from time to time. It clearly had no powers and, of course, deserved none. It was a fake parliament holding mock discussions. It was a window dressing, an insult to the intelligence of the people of Pakistan and a reminder to them of their helplessness in the face of an unashamed dictator backed only by brute force bent upon usurping the power of the state and trying to fool the people and the world with such gimmicks. Everybody took a sigh of relief when the Sham Council met its end on the holding of general elections in February 1985.

The Office of the Ombudsman (*Wafaqi Mohtasib*)

Since Zia did not want to restore the Constitution and democratic institutions, he kept experimenting with various ideas that could strengthen and validate his govenment. At the same time he wanted to show to the United States and western powers that institutions similar to theirs were functioning in Pakistan. One such idea was to establish the office of Ombudsman on the lines of such an institution in Sweden and other Scandinavian countries. He toyed around with the idea for a long time and ultimately promulgated a President's Order establishing the office of *Wafaqi Mohtasib* (Ombudsman).[13]

The jurisdiction of the Ombudsman was extended to all departments of the federal government and statutory corporations or other institutions established or controlled by the federal government. He could hear cases of 'maladministration' which included a decision, process, recommendation, act of omission or commission which was:

(a) contrary to law, rules, or regulations or was a departure from established practice or procedure, unless the same was bonafide and for valid reasons; or
(b) perverse, arbitrary or unreasonable, unjust, biased, oppressive, or discriminatory; or
(c) based on irrelevant grounds; or
(d) involved the exercise of powers, or the failure or refusal to do so, for corrupt or improper motives, such as bribery, jobbery, favouritism, nepotism, and administrative excuses.

Acts and omissions that caused neglect, inattention, delay, incompetence, inefficiency, and ineptitude in the administration or discharge of duties and responsibilities would also constitute 'maladministration'.[14]

The Ombudsman was to be appointed by the President for a term of four years and his terms and conditions of service and remunerations were to be determined by the President. He could recommend action in any case of maladministration, after due inquiry, but could not enforce his decision. If any agency did not implement his recommendations, he could write to the President who might, at his discretion, direct the agency concerned to implement the recommendation. No appeal was provided against his decision but a representation could be filed with the President within thirty days of his decision or order.

The idea of an 'ombudsman' in Pakistan and its statute are not conceptually clear. It appears that, at that time, due to lack of representative institutions in the country, a machinery for the redress of grievances was provided against the misuse and abuse of power and authority by the federal bureaucracy. It is certainly different to the concept of 'ombudsman' as understood in the Scandinavian countries, where he is independent and carries a lot of clout due to support from the legislatures of these countries. It is also very different to the concept of a 'Parliamentary Commissioner' as it exists in the United Kingdom, where it is meant to assist the parliament in controlling the excesses of the executive by digging into the questionable acts of government departments and by submitting reports to the parliament periodically for taking action or for amending the laws to overcome the difficulties noticed by him. In Pakistan, the office of 'Ombudsman' is dependent on the President (and now the Prime Minister), who is the head of the government.

The experience with the office of 'Ombudsman' over more than ten years does not indicate any positive results. It has failed to check the bureaucratic strangulation of the people of Pakistan. The first Ombudsman, Sardar Iqbal, made tall claims in his reports, but a majority of these claims were of form rather than substance. The fact remains that the citizens cannot say what tangible benefit they have derived from this office for the establishment of which hundreds of millions of rupees have been sunk. It would have been much better if the money spent on this office was given to the judiciary to resolve some of the endemic problems faced by judges like shortage of judges, lack of proper court rooms, and poor residential facilities for judges of subordinate courts in the big cities.

Zia's Constitutional Plan

Zia and his military coterie were carrying on the affairs of government by repressing political parties in the country and by denying all political activities. The media was under complete control of the government and press censorship of the worst kind had been imposed. It was not possible for the newspapers to print any news about political parties. Any statement which contained the slightest criticism of an act of the government was not allowed to be published. The scissors of government officials from the government's Department of Information, assigned the task of censorship, worked extensively to cut off all independent news.

Under these circumstances, lawyers and their associations did what political parties were supposed to do. They stood up to the martial law government demanding, consistently and repeatedly, restoration of the Constitution, abolition of military courts and restoration of full powers and jurisdiction to the courts under the Constitution and the law, release of all political prisoners, and holding of general elections for transfer of power to the representatives of the people at the earliest. They held national conventions of lawyers, mostly in Lahore, where those political leaders who were also lawyers got an opportunity to raise their voice. The lawyers who actively participated in the movement for the restoration of the rule of law suffered through detention and withdrawal of all benefits originating from any government source. The martial law government declared war on lawyers and the creation of permanent Benches of the High Courts was part of the scheme to divide, disperse, and demoralize them.

The MRD also tried to launch an agitation against Zia but for one reason or the other, it fizzled out. In 1983, the MRD agitation was undone by a speech of Indira Gandhi in the Indian Parliament supporting the objectives of the opposition in Pakistan. This created a reaction in Pakistan, particularly in the Punjab. In Sindh, the MRD was able to sustain the agitation for quite some time but it unfortunately degenerated into lawlessness and wanton acts of violence and killing.

Apart from the internal pressures, Zia was also being pressurized by the USA and other western powers supporting him in the struggle against Soviet Union in Afghanistan. They were embarrassed by the criticism that they were supporting a military dictator who had sapped democracy, fundamental rights, and civil liberties in his own country. They impressed upon Zia the need to create a semblance of democracy that would give his regime some appearance of legitimacy. Zia capitulated to the pressure from the donor countries and decided to work out a framework of civilian government while continuing as President with most of his powers intact.

Addressing the *Majlis-e-Shoora* (Federal Council) in Islamabad on 12 August 1983, Zia gave his own constitutional plan. As was habitual with him, the address was lengthy and repetitive. He severely criticized the parliamentary form of government and held it responsible for the political crisis of 1977 which, according to him, had brought the country to the brink of civil war, caused setbacks to the national economy, and disruption of normal life in the country. He quoted a personal notebook of Jinnah (the authenticity of which is doubtful) to the effect that Jinnah considered the presidential form of government more suitable for Pakistan and that the parliamentary form of government had only worked satisfactorily in England and nowhere else.

Zia discussed three alternatives available to him at that time: one, to restore the 1973 Constitution as it was; two, to abrogate the Constitution, frame a new one, and seek its endorsement by the people; and three, to promulgate the 1973 Constitution with necessary amendments.

He ultimately chose the last alternative and decided to make elaborate and fundamental changes to the 1973 Constitution in the following manner:

1. The 1973 Constitution was to be restored, but a balance was to be brought about between the powers of the President and the Prime Minister and the Constitution was to be harmonized with Islamic principles. In adopting these amendments, due consideration was to be given to the opinion of the members of the *Majlis-e-Shoora* and the recommendations of the Ansari Commission.
2. There was a lot of controversy regarding the role of the armed forces. Zia wanted to end this. The armed forces would have no new constitutional role. The accepted position then in this matter was to be maintained.
3. Elections would be held on the basis of adult suffrage.
4. The Prime Minister would be appointed by the President, but the person appointed must, in the President's view, command a majority support in the National Assembly. The Prime Minister, within two months of assumption of office, would be required to obtain a vote of confidence from the National Assembly.
5. When the President felt that a need had arisen for seeking a fresh mandate of the electorate, he could dissolve the National Assembly, but in such an event, fresh elections would have to be held within seventy-five days.
6. The President would have the powers to return for consideration to the National Assembly and the Senate a Bill which had already been passed.
7. The President would be the Supreme Commander of the armed forces. He would appoint the Chairman of the Joint Chiefs of Staff Committee and the Chiefs of Staff of the three armed services and determine the terms and conditions of their appointments.
8. The appointment of the Chief Election Commissioner and members of the Commission would also be made by the President in consultation with the Chief Justice of Pakistan.
9. The provincial Governor would also be appointed by the President.
10. Additionally, a National Security Council would be established. The government of the day would not be able to declare an emergency without the advice of the Council. The composition and duties of the National Security Council would be announced later.
11. In order to improve the economic conditions of the country, the private sector would be encouraged and protected.
12. For representation of minorities, separate electorates would be introduced both at the national as well as provincial level.

He expressed reservations about holding elections and thought that it would be better if the process of Islamization was continued without election. Nevertheless, he expressed his willingness to hold elections in the following words:

> So far as elections are concerned, you are aware, I have never denied their need and usefulness. It has always been my view that in the present-day world there is no alternative to elections. So elections will have to be held some day or the other. Had conditions permitted I would have held elections a long time ago. Twice I had resolved to hold elections and each time they had to be postponed. I gave the nation the reasons for the

postponement and pointed out that I was not responsible for it but there were others. I would not like to dilate on this issue all over again.

This time contradictory views have been received on the issue of holding elections. Some people have advanced the opinion that we should forget about elections altogether, and instead concentrate on Islamization, rehabilitation of the economy, and other good work. Another section is of the view that elections must be held but at an appropriate time, for holding elections now will be tantamount to jeopardizing the security of the country. Still another school of thought advocates the immediate holding of elections and it wants us to hand over power and quit. If you were to ask my personal opinion I would say that this third group is right to some extent, maybe to the extent of fifty percent, the remaining fifty percent is my own concern. But I am being very honest when I say that had it been in my power I would have acquitted myself of this task a long time ago. But I cannot, just for the sake of elections, allow anyone to play with the fate of the country. I am alive to the fact that it is not in the interest of this country to keep the democratic process suspended for a long period. But what you have to take into account is whether there is greater risk in holding the elections immediately or putting them off for a further period. In my view holding elections at an inappropriate time is far more harmful than holding delayed elections because elections merely for the sake of elections is a meaningless slogan. The crux of the matter is that the results of the elections must at all costs be positive. That is why we have decided to hold elections in two stages. But at each stage it will be mandatory to observe certain principles and rules and regulations. The following will have to be observed for purposes of elections:

1. The criterion for the nomination of candidates will be the candidates' personal character and not their affluence or the influence that their families exercise.
2. It will be compulsory for voters to be in possession of the national identity card while casting vote.
3. The duration of the election campaign will be brief and the contact between the candidates and the voters must be strictly in accordance with the Islamic standards. In this connection, you should bear in mind that self-canvassing is not permissible in Islam.
4. Local bodies will not be used as an electoral college.
5. The rights of women will be fully protected and they will have the same right of franchise as men. Their quota in the assemblies will be maintained.
6. Minorities in Islam are not an oppressed and persecuted lot but a privileged section of society. In fact, in an Islamic polity their rights exceed those of the Muslim population. Under an Islamic system of government their rights are fully safeguarded. There will be separate electorate system for them so that like their fellow countrymen they may elect their own representatives freely.
7. Representation will be given to workers, peasants, technocrats, other professional classes, and the *ulema*. I hope some day the Pakistani society will positively be transformed into an Islamic society.

I also strongly believe that, Allah willing, elections will be held and held soon. And those motivated by Islam will sit in this House and work for the further edification of the country, the nation, and Islam. We, however, cannot altogether ignore other members of the society. As such we propose to benefit in this House from the services of the *ulema*, the religious scholars, educationists, scientists, technocrats, workers, and peasants. If we were to scrupulously abide by the Islamic procedures even then perhaps it might not be possible for people from these special groups to be elected either on their own initiative or at the behest of others. That is why we have decided to reserve seats in each House for these special groups.

Keeping in mind these factors, elections will be held in two stages. In the first stage (about to begin) local bodies elections will be held. Their dates have either been announced or are about to be announced by the provincial governments. These elections, Allah willing, will be completed during the current year.

You will recall, four years ago when local bodies elections were held after an interval of fifteen years the political parties had opposed them. Notwithstanding this opposition we held these elections and established these institutions. The last four years' experience has proved that this decision was timely and correct. We are happy that the next elections to the local bodies are being held on the scheduled time and the enthusiasm and fervour being demonstrated by the common people for the election these days is a measure of the popularity and importance of these elections. I hope the candidature of those contesting these elections will have the support of good, sincere, and virtuous people. I also hope that our masses will elect good, sincere, and pious people for this is a basic requirement of an Islamic democracy and to my mind local bodies constitute an important base. If they are sound then the structure that will be erected on such a base will be strong. If the base is weak then the structure so erected will also be weak.

These elections, too, will be held on a non-party basis as previously. I hope that those who are elected will fully devote themselves to the development of their people.

In the second stage, we will hold elections to the Provincial and National Assemblies and the Senate and this stage will, Allah willing, be completed by 23 March 1985.

There are about eighteen months intervening between today, 12 August, and 23 March 1985. Compare these eighteen months with the previous thirty-seven years. May Allah bless our efforts with success. This period will be for federal level elections to the National Assembly and the Senate. After the elections to the National Assembly and the Senate and after the elections to the Provincial Assemblies, provincial governments will be formed and the elections to the National Assembly will be followed by the formation of a federal government. When these stage-wise elections are over and the democratic process is restored, the martial law will be lifted.

I want to make it clear to my countrymen, colleagues, friends, and admirers that the measures that I have announced today will be completed under my supervision. We do not want that the country should drift once again to chaos, confusion, disorder, and destruction. By the grace of Allah Almighty, we will ensure a peaceful, orderly, and smooth transfer of power so that the country is not deprived of the continuity that it needs.

Mr Chairman, under this programme martial law will not be lifted as long as the democratic process is not restored. We shall proceed in accordance with a definite and settled programme; you may treat this programme as the manifesto of the present government during the interim period.[15]

This constitutional plan formed the basis of Revival of the Constitution of 1973 Order 1985 (RCO) which was promulgated immediately after the general elections of February 1985, and later got incorporated into the Constitution with some modifications as the Eighth Amendment to the Constitution. In a nutshell, Zia promised elections on a non-party basis within eighteen months. Some people wondered if, with a promise to hold elections within ninety days, he could hang on to power for more than six years, how were eighteen months to be measured along that scale.

The Referendum, December 1984

The problem of Zia's continuation as President under a civilian set-up was yet to be resolved. He did not want to face a national election and risk mobilization of people against him by the political parties. He knew that he could not be elected in a fair election. Rigging an election at that level was also not easy and not without its many risks and dangers. So an ingenious scheme was made by his brilliant and contriving advisers. A referendum was to be held for a vote of endorsement to the process of Islamization which was started by him. Who would vote against Islam? The affirmative vote was deemed to have given him a term of five years as President.

The Referendum Order, 1984[16] was passed, putting a complex question to the citizens but, in essence, seeking endorsement of the process initiated by Zia for Islamization in Pakistan. The question read as follows:

'Whether the people of Pakistan endorse the process initiated by General Muhammad Zia-ul-Haq, the President of Pakistan, for bringing the laws of Pakistan in conformity with the injunctions of Islam as laid down in the Holy Quran and *sunnah* of the Holy Prophet (PBUH) and for the preservation of the ideology of Pakistan, for the continuation and consolidation of that process, and for the smooth and orderly transfer of power to the elected representatives of the people.'

The question, by all standards, was very complex and complicated, particularly for the simple people of Pakistan. It was a loaded question couched in such a language that it could not be answered in the negative in all its aspects. An affirmative vote, it was stated in the order, was to result in a five-year term for Zia as President of Pakistan. The MRD boycotted the referendum. The referendum that was held on 19 December 1984, left very little doubt in anybody's mind in Pakistan that it was a total hoax. Very few people went to the polling stations to cast their votes. All the polling stations gave a deserted look and the government staff on duty stuffed the ballot boxes with affirmative votes. All government servants were strictly instructed to cast their ballots in the referendum, of course, in the affirmative, failing which they could be hauled up for disciplinary action against them. A few who ventured to the polling stations found their ballots already cast.[17]

Fully aware of the fraud being played on the nation, it was announced by the Chief Election Commissioner that the polling was fair and orderly and out of 34,992,425 registered voters, 21,750,901 (about 62%) had cast their ballots. Out of them, 21,253,757 (97.7% of the total polled) answered in the affirmative to the question put to them, while 316,918 answered in the negative. 180,226 ballots were found to be invalid.[18] One of the glaring proofs of the hoax and cooked up results is that the results of such far-flung areas as Kohlu, Sibi, and Kalat were declared before those of Lahore, Peshawar, Rawalpindi, Quetta, and Karachi.[19]

General Elections, February 1985

After the referendum, Zia announced elections to the National Assembly for 25 February 1985 and elections to the Provincial Assemblies for 28 February 1985. The opposition parties (the MRD) boycotted the elections for the reasons that their demands for party based elections and restoration of the 1973 Constitution *in toto* were not met. On the contrary, Zia insisted that political parties should not take part in the elections and, as an additional precaution, detained almost all the opposition's leaders for the period of the elections.

The successful boycott of the referendum of December 1984 led the MRD to miscalculate their next confrontation with the government. Relatively confident of public support, they chose to boycott the general elections. The voters, faced with the opportunity of voting in national and provincial elections for the first time in more than seven years, turned out in large numbers at the polls. The consequence was doubly disadvantageous. Popular support of the electoral process and the later stages of democratization undermined the MRD's very *raison d'etre* and the MRD politicians were effectively isolated from any positive role in subsequent developments.[20]

The general elections to the National and Provincial Assemblies were held peacefully and unlike the referendum, the people participated in large numbers. This was largely because the candidates persuaded the voters particularly in the Punjab. Total turn-out of the voters for the National Assembly elections was 53.69%; in the Punjab 60.14%; in the NWFP 40.63%; in Sindh 44.38%, and in Balochistan 37.42%.[21] In the Provincial Assemblies elections, where the constituencies were smaller and the contests were even harder, the turn-out of the voters was even better. It was 57.37% nationwide, 62.34% in the Punjab, 48.20% in NWFP, 50.15% in Sindh and 46.86% in Balochistan.[22]

Since the elections were on non-party basis, therefore, no party position emerged, but the voters strongly rejected most people who were closely associated with Zia. All but one of his federal ministers lost in their bid for elections to the National Assembly. The people sent an indirect message to Zia. Jamaat-i-Islami was the only political party which was allowed to participate as a political organization in the elections but it lost miserably except in a couple of constituencies in Lahore. Jamaat's notorious association with Zia was an important factor in its poor showing at the polls, particularly so when it had no political organization opposing it.

Constitutional Amendments during Zia's Rule

Zia could amend and alter the Constitution at will and he kept making amendments to the Constitution every now and then. In some cases, such amendments were made through the CMLA's orders and others through President's orders. It was after all his sweet will as to when, how, and in what manner, he made such amendments. Some of the important amendments are discussed below:

1. By amendment in the Provisional Constitution Order (PCO), he introduced the definitions of 'Muslim' and 'non-Muslim' as under:[23]
   (a) 'Muslim' means a person who believes in the Unity and Oneness of Almighty Allah, in the absolute and unqualified finality of the Prophethood of Muhammad (PBUH) the last of the prophets, and does not believe in, or recognize as, a prophet or religious reformer, any person who claimed or claims to be a prophet, in any sense of the word or of any description whatsoever, after Muhammad (peace be upon him), and
   (b) 'Non-Muslim' means a person who is not a Muslim and includes a person belonging to the Christian, Hindu, Sikh, Buddhist, or Parsee community, a person of the Quadiani group or the Lahori group (who call themselves 'Ahmedis' or by any other name), or a Bahai and a person belonging to any of the scheduled castes.

   This amendment was made apparently to clarify and determine the status of Ahmedis as 'non-Muslims'. The second amendment of 1974 only gave definition of 'non-Muslim' but not of 'Muslim'. Even in the definition of 'non-Muslim' there was no specific reference to Ahmedis.
2. By another amendment,[24] the Federal Shariat Court was given revisional jurisdiction over the criminal courts trying cases of *hudood*. The Supreme Court was vested with appellate jurisdiction over the judgments, final orders or sentences of the Federal Shariat Court in *hudood* cases. The decisions of the Federal Shariat Court were made binding on the High Courts. Thus, the revisional jurisdiction of the High Courts in criminal cases was further curtailed. The status of the High Courts was reduced and subordinated to the Federal Shariat Court.
3. The nomenclature of the 'Chairman' and 'members' of the Federal Shariat Court were changed to 'Chief Justice' and 'judges' respectively.[25]
4. A major change was brought about in the Shariat Appellate Bench of the Supreme Court which previously consisted of three Muslim judges. It was extended to five: three Muslim judges of the Supreme Court and two *ulema* to be appointed by the President to sit on the Bench as ad hoc members.[26] Thus, the *ulema* who had sneaked into the Federal Shariat Court after the judgment in the '*rajm*' case, now found their way into the Shariat Appellate Bench of the Supreme Court. It was a harbinger of things to come which were to disturb the settled laws in a big way, particularly in relation to pre-emption and land reforms.
5. The decisions of the Federal Shariat Court striking down a law or a provision of a law as repugnant to the injunctions of Islam would not take effect before the expiration of the period within which an appeal might be preferred to the Supreme Court or, where an appeal was so preferred, before the disposal of the appeal.[27]

Further Steps towards Islamization

The process of Islamization that was started in February 1979 with the promulgation of *hudood* laws was continued during this period, from March 1981 to February 1985. Major steps in this regard were as under:

Profit and Loss Sharing Accounts in the Banks

With effect from 1 January 1981, all the banks in the country were asked to open non-interest bearing accounts. The name given was 'profit and loss sharing accounts'. Theoretically, these accounts were supposed to be in the nature of partnership between banks and depositors. The customers were to share the profit or loss, as the case may be, that resulted from the investment made by the banks of their deposits, but, in reality, it was the same thing as a savings account. No bank, including those owned and controlled by the government, could dare announce any loss on its depositors' money. So what was previously interest was now announced as profit on these deposits. Zia was well aware of what was happening but he believed in form rather than in substance.

Ehtram-e-Ramzan Ordinance, 1981

In June 1981, Zia promulgated what he called '*Ehtram-e-Ramzan*' Ordinance (Reverence of Ramadan Ordinance) as part of the process of Islamization initiated by him.[28] There was complete prohibition of eating, drinking, and smoking in a public place and anyone found contravening that was punishable with imprisonment and a fine. All cinema houses and theatres were to remain closed at sunset, the time for breaking the fast.

This ordinance is a rank example of Zia's insult to the people. Muslims have always observed great respect and reverence for Ramadan, fasting during this month being one of the five basic tenets of Islam. Muslims in Pakistan have always observed fasting during the holy month of Ramadan long before Zia came into power and would continue to do so after he was gone. They did not need an ordinance from him to do what they were obliged to do as an article of their faith. It was a reprehensible attempt on his part to make political capital out of a religious practice. Even before this ordinance, nobody, even a non-Muslim, ate, drank, or smoked publicly. Eating places that were open during the fasting hours, were always fully covered so that nobody from outside could see anyone cooking or eating. All cinema houses used to hold recess for the audience to enable them to break their fast and to say their prayers.

This ordinance only gave an additional handle in the hands of the police and the magistracy to harass the people to extract additional money for *Eid-ul-Fitr* which was celebrated at the end of the month of Ramadan.

Curb on the Religious Activities of Ahmedis

It has been discussed above that the Ahmedis had been ostracized from Islam under the Second Amendment to the Constitution in 1974. They were declared to be outside the definition of 'Muslim'. Later on, the definition of 'non-Muslim' was also introduced in the Constitution according to which they were clearly included, regardless of whether they belonged to the Qadiani or the Lahori group. More was to come by way of Ordinance XX in 1984.[29]

Under this ordinance, the Ahmedis were prohibited from using any of the epithets, descriptions, or titles reserved for holy personages or places in Islam. They were forbidden from calling their place of worship '*Masjid*'. Anyone contravening this provision was liable to punishment of imprisonment and fine. An Ahmedi found calling himself a Muslim or preaching or propagating his faith was liable to punishment of imprisonment and fine. They were forbidden from reciting the '*azan*'.

The Ahmedis were thus prevented from practising, preaching, and propagating their faith and were made liable to harassment and prosecution for any of their religious practices. They had, however, the audacity to challenge this ordinance before the Federal Shariat Court which upheld it as valid and constitutional.[30] An Ahmedi who got some common Muslim religious expressions printed on the invitation card to the marriage of his daughter, landed in jail and languished there for quite some time. Even the High Court did not enlarge him on bail.[31] He was eventually bailed out by the Supreme Court.[32]

In 1989, the Ahmedis wanted to hold centenary celebrations of their faith at Rabwah, District Jhang, but this was banned by the order of the provincial Home Secretary, Punjab on 21 March 1989 under Section 144 of the Code of Criminal Procedure. The Ahmedis were directed to remove ceremonial gates, banners, and illuminations and they were forbidden from any further writings on the walls. This order of ban was challenged before the Lahore High Court in a writ jurisdiction and was upheld.[33] The Court held that there was no meeting point between the Ahmedis and the Muslims as the latter believed in the finality of Prophethood while the Ahmedis believe in Mirza Ghulam Ahmad as a new prophet. It was held that the reasons of public policy, public good, and in the interests of the ordinary people of the country, the celebrations could be banned because activities of Ahmedis and the propagation of their faith is resisted by the Muslim *ummah* to keep the mainstream faith pure and unpolluted and also to maintain the integrity of the *ummah*. This judgment was upheld by the Supreme Court.[34]

The Ordinance XX of 1984 and the judgments that followed, discussed above, are apparently based on the premise that Ahmedis constitute a threat to Islam and to the Muslim *ummah*. This premise, with due respect, is incorrect and rather misconceived. It has blown the importance and strength of Ahmedis beyond all proportions. What threat can be posed by a miniscule minority in the population of Pakistan and a negligible number compared to the entire Muslim *ummah*? What danger can a handful of followers of Mirza Ghulam Ahmad constitute for the universal faith of Islam? Actually, a non-issue has been blown into a big issue by those who evidently want to make political capital out of it. Persecution of any community for whatever reason is unhealthy and brutalizes the society in which it is practised.

Islamization of the Law of Evidence

The law of evidence in Pakistan and India has been regulated under a statute, the Evidence Act, 1872. This statute proved to be a very successful law and was applied by the courts in the subcontinent for more than a century with very few amendments. Zia ordered its Islamization and, as a result, a President's Order, namely the *Qanoon-e-Shahadat*, 1984 was promulgated and enforced in October 1984.[35] It was nothing but a repetition of the Evidence Act of 1872 with some amendments/ alterations/ variations in four sections of the Act and some additions in four Sections. The Sections in the Evidence Act were re-numbered as Articles in the *Qanoon-e-Shahadat*, putting the courts and the lawyers to a great deal of inconvenience as they were called upon to consult the comparative table frequently. They generally remembered the section of the old Act on their finger tips.

The only significant changes made by the new law are as under:

(a) The courts have been given the power to determine the competence of a witness in accordance with the qualifications prescribed by the injunctions of Islam.[36]

(b) In matters pertaining to financial or future obligations, if reduced in writing, the instrument is required to be attested by two men, or one man and two women, so that one may remind the other.[37]

(c) The courts can decide a claim on oath provided all the parties agree to do so.[38]

(d) The court can allow any evidence to be produced that might be obtained or made available because of modern devices or techniques.[39]

All these alterations or additions could have been made by just amending the Evidence Act of 1872. Zia and his advisers knew well that there was no justification for a new law and that, in any case, very few changes were being made in the old law. It was another example of his preferring the form to the substance and his endeavour to gain some political mileage by giving an Islamic name to an old law and claiming it as an advance towards the Islamization of laws.

Introduction of Islamic Banking

At the end of 1984, two ordinances[40] were promulgated and enforced with the purpose of introducing Islamic banking in the country. The change again was more in form rather than in substance. The word 'loan' was substituted by the word 'finance'. 'Interest' was forbidden for banks and, in its place, the concept of participation in profit and loss, mark-up or mark-down in price, hire purchase, lease, rent sharing, licensing, charge or fee of any kind, purchase and sale of property and actionable claims, *musharika* and *modaraba* certificates, were introduced. Banking tribunals were established to decide cases arising out of disputes from the Islamic mode of banking.

In reality, very little change has come about in the banking practice in Pakistan. The banks, instead of charging interest, now charge mark-up at a pre-determined rate which is generally much higher than the previous rates of interest. The cost of obtaining loans from the banks has become much higher and more oppressive than the previous mode of banking which was interest based. Now the banks are obliged to take immediate court action against a party that has defaulted in repayment and cannot give accommodation because the mark-up stops running at the expiry of a certain period.

NOTES

1. Provisional Constitution Order, 1981. CMLA's Order 1 of 1981. PLD 1981 Central Statutes 183.
2. The present author learnt this from Mr Justice Dorab Patel.
3. He was one of the three dissenting judges in the judgment in appeal in the murder case of Bhutto.
4. Deputy Attorney-General is a middle level law officer. Perhaps this particular law officer was given importance because he was believed to be very close to an important general in the Army.
5. It is reported by witnesses present that he bowed and begged before the then Governor, Lt.-General Ghulam Jilani, who took pity on him and recommended to the President to allow him to take the oath. The request was granted.
6. It is learnt on good authority that these generals later in a meeting, giggled and laughed at the way these judges ran to them, falling on their faces and stepping over one another, begging them to give them oath.
7. A couple of days after the PCO, the author found Cornelius sitting with his head down and looking sad. He had learnt all that had happened. He remarked, sadly but so aptly, 'see, how the judiciary has been raped.'
8. Tajjamal Husain Malik v Federal Government of Pakistan, PLD 1981 Lahore 462.
9. M. Yamin Qureshi v Islamic Republic of Pakistan, PLD 1980 S.C. 22.
10. W.A. Sheikh v Pakistan, 1981 PLC (C.S) 363; Qazi Mohammad Anwar Barlas v Secretary Establishment Division, 1981 PLC (C.S) 330; M.H.Shamim v Secretary Establishment Division, 1981 PLC (C.S) 337.
11. Provisional Constitution (Second Amendment) Order, 1982. CMLA Order No.3 of 1982. PLD 1982 Central Statutes 349.
12. Federal Council (*Majlis-e-Shoora*) Order, 1981. President's Order No.15 of 1981. PLD 1982 Central Statutes 123.
13. Establishment of the Office of *Wafaqi Mohtasib* (Ombudsman) Order, 1983. President's Order 1 of 1983. PLD 1983 Central Statutes 17.
14. Ibid., section 2.
15. The speech was in Urdu. Translation in English is taken from *Dawn*, 13 August 1983.
16. President's Order 11 of 1984 (1 December 1984). PLD 1985 Central Statutes 449.
17. A lawyer from Lahore, who took exception to his ballot having been cast before he went, was explained by the staff that since he had not shown up till the afternoon, therefore, they thought he was not going to cast his vote and they did it for him. Anyway, to compensate him, they offered him to cast two ballots (of course somebody else's) instead of one.
18. *The Muslim*, 21 December 1984.
19. Ibid. See Editorial.

20. Baxter, Craig & Wasti, Syed Razi, *Pakistan — Authoritarianism in 1980s*, 1991, Vanguard Books, Lahore. p. 79.
21. *Report on the General Elections 1985*, Volume II, published by Election Commission of Pakistan, Islamabad, p. 73.
22. Ibid., p. 205.
23. Provisional Constitution (Amendment) Order, 1981. CMLA Order No.2 of 1981. PLD 1981 Central Statutes 310.
24. Constitution (Second Amendment) Order, 1982. President's Order 5 of 1982. PLD 1982 Central Statutes 155.
25. Provisional Constitution (Amendment) Order, 1982. CMLA's Order 1 of 1982. PLD 1982 Central Statutes 153.
26. Constitution (Third Amendment) Order, 1982. President's Order No.12 of 1982. PLD 1982 Central Statutes 344.
27. Constitution (Amendment) Order, 1984. President's Order 1 of 1984. PLD 1984 Central Statutes 86.
28. *Ehtram-e-Ramzan* Ordinance, 1981. Ordinance XXIII of 1981. PLD 1981 Central Statutes 278.
29. Anti-Islamic Activities of Qadiani Group, Lahori Group and Ahmedis (Prohibition and Punishment) Ordinance, 1984. PLD 1984 Central Statutes 102.
30. Mujibur Rehman v Federal Government of Pakistan. PLD 1985 F.S.C. 8.
31. Nasir Ahmed v The State, PLJ 1992 Cr.C (Lahore) 427.
32. Nasir Ahmed v The State, PLJ 1993 S.C. 1.
33. Khurshid Ahmad v Government of Punjab. PLD 1992 Lahore 1.
34. Zaheeruddin v The State, PLJ 1994 S.C. 1.
35. President's Order 10 of 1984. PLD 1985 Central Statutes 14.
36. Article 3.
37. Article 17.
38. Article 163.
39. Article 164.
40. Banking and Financial Services (Amendment of Laws) Ordinance, 1984 (Ordinance LVII of 1984). PLD 1985 Central Statutes 498; Banking Tribunals Ordinance, 1984 (Ordinance LVIII) of 1984). PLD 1985 Central Statutes 507.

29

THE EIGHTH AMENDMENT

It has been discussed above that general elections to the National and Provincial Assemblies were held in February 1985 on a non-party basis. No political party was allowed to nominate candidates in the elections. Before the parliament could meet on 23 March 1985, the Constitution was comprehensively amended through a President's Order, known as Revival of the Constitution of 1973 Order (RCO), on 2 March 1985.[1] The RCO made fundamental alterations in the Constitution and made significant departures from its original premises and concepts. As many as sixty-five Articles were amended/substituted/added/modified/varied/deleted/omitted. RCO can be regarded with justification as part of the Eighth Amendment without which the significance and importance of the Eighth Amendment cannot be fully comprehended, appreciated, or analysed.

Main Features

Important changes brought about by the RCO are briefly enumerated below:

1. Article 2A was inserted, making the Objectives Resolution of 1949 a substantive and effective part of the Constitution. The Resolution, with some modifications, had already been adopted as a preamble to the constitutions of 1956, 1962, and 1973. Now the resolution was reproduced as an annex and made an operative part, with a significant change. The sixth paragraph of the Objectives Resolution in its original form read as follows:

   > Wherein adequate provision shall be made for the minorities freely to profess and practise their religions and develop their culture.

   While reproducing the above paragraph in the Annex, the word 'freely' was omitted.
2. The electoral college for election to the office of the President was modified so as to comprise both Houses of Parliament and all four provincial assemblies (with equal weightage given in terms of votes to each Provincial Assembly).
3. The President was supposed to act on the advice of the Cabinet, the Prime Minister, or the appropriate minister, but he could require the Cabinet to re-consider such advice.

4. The President was empowered to dissolve the National Assembly at his discretion where, in his opinion, appeal to the electorate was necessary. On such dissolution, elections were to be called within a hundred days.
5. On the dissolution of the National Assembly, the President could ask the Prime Minister to continue in office until his successor entered the office of Prime Minister. This apparently applied to the Prime Minister in the event of either his resignation from office or where the National Assembly was dissolved on his advice. Where the National Assembly was dissolved at the discretion of the President, a caretaker Cabinet would be appointed till such time that the election of the Prime Minister had taken place on the reconstitution of the National Assembly after the general elections.
6. The seats reserved for women in the National Assembly were increased from ten to twenty. These special seats for women were only available until the holding of third general elections to the National Assembly under the Constitution.
7. The number of members in the Senate was raised from sixty-three to eighty-seven, with five seats from each province reserved for technocrats, *ulema,* or professionals. The number of seats for federally administered areas was increased from five to eight. Seats for the federal capital were increased from two to three.
8. The period of time provided for the President to give assent to the Bills passed by Parliament was increased from seven to forty-five days. The President could return a Bill (other than a Money Bill) within forty-five days for reconsideration. This gave the President a power to veto a Bill, but this could be overridden by passing the same Bill again by a majority of the members, present and voting, of both Houses of parliament in a joint session.
9. The President could, at his discretion, appoint any member of the National Assembly as Prime Minister who, in his opinion, could command the confidence of a majority of the members of the National Assembly. However, a Prime Minister so appointed had to obtain a vote of confidence from the National Assembly within sixty days. The Prime Minister was to hold office during the pleasure of the President, but the President could not remove him unless he was satisfied that the Prime Minister did not command the confidence of the majority of the members of the National Assembly.
10. Federal ministers and ministers of state were to be appointed by the President on the advice of the Prime Minister.
11. Procedure for passing the motion of vote of no-confidence against the Prime Minister was altered and the requirement of giving the name of an alternative candidate in such a motion was omitted.
12. The provision for amendment to the Constitution was modified and under the new provision, an amendment to the Constitution could only be passed by a majority of two-thirds of the total members in the National Assembly and the Senate and by an absolute majority in all four Provincial Assemblies. The procedure for amendment to the Constitution was further modified under

President's Order 20 of 1985, and the requirement of laying the Amendment Bill before the Provincial Assemblies was dispensed with except where such amendment had the effect of altering the limits of a province. In such a case, the Provincial Assembly of the concerned province had to pass the amendment by two-thirds of its total membership.[2]

13. The Governor was supposed to act on the advice of the Cabinet or the Chief Minister, or appropriate minister, but he could require the Cabinet to reconsider such advice.
14. The period of time provided for the Governor to give assent to the Bills passed by the Provincial Assembly was increased from seven to forty-five days. The Governor could return a Bill (other than a Money Bill) within forty-five days for reconsideration. This gave the Governor power to veto a Bill but it could be overridden by passing the same Bill again by the votes of the majority of the total membership of the Provincial Assembly.
15. The Governor could appoint a member of the Provincial Assembly as Chief Minister who, in his opinion, could command the confidence of the majority of the members of the Provincial Assembly. However, a Chief Minister so appointed had to obtain a vote of confidence from the Provincial Assembly within sixty days. The Chief Minister was to hold office during the pleasure of the Governor but the Governor could not remove him unless he was satisfied that the Chief Minister did not command the confidence of the majority of the members of the Provincial Assembly.
16. Provincial ministers were to be appointed by the Governor from amongst the members of the Provincial Assembly on the advice of the Chief Minister.
17. Procedure for passing the motion of vote of no-confidence against a Chief Minister was altered and the requirement of giving the name of an alternative candidate was omitted.
18. The number of general constituencies (for Muslims) of the National Assembly was raised from 200 to 207. In addition to that, ten seats for minorities were reserved. Previously, under the Fourth Amendment, six seats were provided for non-Muslim minorities. However, previously the elections to the minority seats were held in the National Assembly itself, based on proportional representation with a single transferable vote. The RCO provided ten seats for minorities, four for Hindus and scheduled castes, one for Sikhs, Buddhists, and Parsee communities and other non-Muslims, and one for Ahmedis. These members were to be elected simultaneously with members from general constituencies, on the basis of separate electorates.
19. The seats in the Provincial Assemblies of Balochistan, the NWFP, the Punjab, and Sindh for minorities were raised from one to three, one to three, five to eight and two to nine, respectively. Their allocation to various non-Muslim communities was as under:

Province	Christians	Hindus and others belonging to the scheduled castes	Sikh, Budhists and Parsi communi--ties, and other non-Muslims	Those others belonging to the Qadiani group or the Lahori group (who call themselves Ahmedis)
Balochistan	1	1	1	-
The North-West Frontier Province	1	-	1	1
The Punjab	5	1	1	1
Sindh	2	5	1	1

These members were to be elected, simultaneously with members from general constituencies, on the basis of separate electorates.

20. Separate electorates for minorities were given constitutional recognition for the first time in Pakistan. Zia had previously introduced separate electorates for minorities in 1979 by amendment to the Representation of the People Act, 1976.[3] The RCO, however, gave constitutional status to the separate electorates.
21. There was, however, a strange contradiction in Articles providing seats in the National and Provincial Assemblies. In Article 51, providing seats in the National Assembly, it is stated that there would be 207 Muslim members in the National Assembly (which were previously known to be general seats representing constituencies on territorial and population basis). On the other hand, Article 106, providing for seats in the Provincial Assemblies, made no specific mention of general seats belonging to Muslims only.
22. One of the most striking changes brought about by the RCO was a large number of additions to the qualifications and disqualifications for membership to the parliament. Originally, the Constitution provided for a few qualifications which included requirements of citizenship and minimum age. The disqualifications provided originally in the Constitution were also few, which included insanity, insolvency, termination of citizenship, and holding of office of profit in the service of Pakistan. The RCO made wholesale additions to these qualifications and disqualifications.

The qualifications added under Article 62 require a candidate for the parliament to be someone:

(a) of good character and not commonly known as one who violates Islamic injunctions;

(b) with adequate knowledge of Islamic teachings and practices and obligatory duties prescribed by Islam as well as abstaining from major sins;
(c) sagacious, righteous, non-profligate, honest and *ameen*;
(d) with no criminal conviction involving moral turpitude or for giving false evidence; and
(e) after the establishment of Pakistan, never to have worked against the integrity of the country or opposed the ideology of Pakistan.

The disqualifications added under Article 63 require a candidate for the parliament not to:
(a) be propagating any opinion, or acting in any manner prejudicial to the ideology of Pakistan, or the sovereignty, integrity, or security of Pakistan, or the maintenance of public order, or the integrity or independence of the judiciary of Pakistan, or which defames or brings into ridicule the judiciary or the armed forces of Pakistan; or
(b) have been, on conviction for any offence which in the opinion of the Chief Election Commissioner involves moral turpitude, sentenced to imprisonment for a term of not less than two years, unless a period of five years has elapsed since his release; or
(c) have been dismissed from the service of Pakistan on the ground of misconduct, unless a period of five years has elapsed since his dismissal; or
(d) have been removed or been compulsorily retired from the service of Pakistan on the ground of misconduct unless a period of three years has elapsed since his removal or compulsory retirement; or
(e) have been in the service of Pakistan or of any statutory body or any body which is owned or controlled by the government or in which the government has a controlling share or interest, unless a period of two years has elapsed since he ceased to be in such service; or
(f) have been found guilty of a corrupt or illegal practice under any law for the time being in force, unless a period of five years has elapsed from the date on which that order takes effect; or
(g) have been convicted under Section 7 of the Political Parties Act, 1962 (III of 1962), unless a period of five years has elapsed from the date of such conviction; or
(h) have, whether by himself or by any person or body of persons in trust for him or for his benefit or on his account or as a member of a Hindu undivided family, any share or interest in a contract, not being a contract between a co-operative society and government, for the supply of goods to, or for the execution of any contract or for the performance of any service undertaken by, government.

It is noticeable that some of the qualifications and disqualifications are specific and can be adjudicated upon while others are so general that if they are strictly applied, hardly anyone would qualify.

23. The RCO also introduced the office of Adviser to the Prime Minister. The President could appoint up to five Advisers to the Prime Minister, on the advice of the Prime Minister. However, these Advisers could not participate in the proceedings of either House of the Parliament.
24. The executive authority of the federation would vest in the President which should be exercised by him, either directly or through officers subordinate to him, in accordance with the Constitution. This was a clear departure from the original scheme of the Constitution which provided that the executive authority of the federation should be exercised in the name of the President by the federal government consisting of the Prime Minister and the federal ministers which should act through the Prime Minister who was the chief executive of the federation. Thus, the President was given a preponderant position over the Prime Minister.

A similar provision was made regarding the relationship between a Governor and the Chief Minister of a province.

25. The Supreme Court was empowered to transfer any case pending before any High Court to any other High Court.
26. It was provided for the first time that the President could request one of the judges of the Supreme Court to act as Chief Justice of a High Court. This provision of the RCO has been grossly abused ever since. At various points in time, at least five judges of the Supreme Court have been asked to be acting Chief Justices of the Lahore High Court and the Sindh High Court for extended periods of time running into several years. This provision caused great harm to the independence of the judiciary.
27. The permanent Benches of the High Courts, which were mentioned in the PCO, were incorporated in the Constitution and thus their establishment was made part of the permanent Constitution. An effort was also made to establish divisional courts and there was specific mention for their establishment.[4] Fortunately, they were never established, otherwise it could have further undermined the position and prestige of the High Courts.
28. The President was conferred with the discretionary power to appoint the Chairman, Joint Chiefs of Staff Committee, and Chiefs of Army, Naval, and Air Staff. This was a very important power given to the President by the PCO.
29. All martial law regulations, martial law orders, laws framed during the martial law regime, and acts and orders made thereunder were validated under Article 270-A. Complete indemnity against suits and prosecution was extended to all people or authorities for or on account of or in respect of any order made, proceedings taken, or act done under such regulations, orders, laws, notifications and so on.
30. Appointment of the Governor of a province was left to the discretion of the President.
31. A National Security Council was to be constituted under Article 152-A which was to include the President, the Prime Minister, the Chairman of the Senate,

the Chairman of the Joint Chiefs of Staff Committee, and the Chiefs of the three armed forces.

Revival of the Constitution Order

Zia thus made sweeping changes in the Constitution before reviving it. The amendment was made immediately after the general elections and before nominating the Prime Minister and prior to the formation of a civilian government. These amendments were based on his constitutional plan which he announced on 12 August 1983. The balance of power had clearly shifted in favour of the President after the RCO and the office of the Prime Minister was relegated to a subservient and subordinate position. Zia held that the powers of the President were enhanced without reducing the authority of the Prime Minister and a balance was struck between the two. He thought that the lacunae discovered in 1977 in the powers of the President had been removed according to the constitutional and political requirements of Pakistan.[5] He referred to the Constitution of India and said that the provisions being incorporated through the RCO regarding the powers of the President were the same as contained in the Indian Constitution. He was of the opinion that the expression used in the 1973 Constitution 'the President will act on the advice of the Prime Minister and such an advice shall be binding on him' was an insulting manner of giving powers to the President. He said that his aim was not to enjoy maximum power. When asked under what conditions he would consider it necessary to exercise the right to dissolve the National Assembly, he replied when the government, the Prime Minister, and the National Assembly lose the confidence of the people. This would mean that a situation had arisen wherein the people and the Assembly were thinking along different lines and the President could adjudge the right time to dissolve the assembly and hold fresh elections. It would be only then, he said, that he would use his discretion.[6] His explanation of the use of discretionary power of the President to dissolve the National Assembly was very different from the way in which it was actually exercised by him after three years.

Although the RCO brought some basic changes in the structure of the Constitution[7] which were to create constitutional and political crises in the country later on, it was a step towards the restoration of civilian government under the 1973 Constitution, even though greatly defaced. It was certainly some progress over what the people had experienced during the previous eight years. At least, with the introduction of the RCO, the reprehensible PCO had come to an end.

Civilian Government Formed under Martial Law

On 10 March, Zia promulgated a new order enforcing all but 27 Articles of the amended Constitution. Twenty-one of the Articles which were left suspended, related to the fundamental rights and writ jurisdiction of the High Courts. Also unenforced, was Article 6 which described the abrogation or subversion of the Constitution as high treason punishable under the law.[8] Elections were held to the Senate on 12 March and Pakistan finally had a parliament.

Under the RCO, the President was given the authority to nominate and appoint the Prime Minister at his discretion from amongst members of the National Assembly. Similarly, the provincial Governors were vested with the power to appoint Chief Ministers of their respective provinces from amongst the members of the Provincial Assemblies. This power of the President and the Governors was qualified to the effect that the Prime Minister and the Chief Ministers being so appointed should command the confidence of the majority of the National Assembly and the Provincial Assemblies respectively. In the party-less assemblies, there was no question of any one commanding the confidence of the majority and, therefore, appointment by the President and the Governors (to whom all the members of these assemblies looked up to) was sufficient for them to obtain a vote of confidence. That was exactly what Zia wanted; divided and dependent assemblies, with all power gravitating in his own hand and in the hands of his nominated Governors.

Zia nominated a veteran politician from Sindh, Muhammad Khan Junejo, as Prime Minister on 23 March 1985. The next day, Junejo won a unanimous vote of confidence from the National Assembly. Addressing the National Assembly, Junejo said that a civilian government could not co-exist with martial law for a long time and that the transitional arrangement should end at the earliest.[9] In the contest of Speakership of the National Assembly, the hand-picked Chairman of the erstwhile *Majlis-e-Shoora*, Khawaja Safdar, lost to a young MNA from Southern Punjab, Fakhar Imam. The defeat of Khawaja Safdar could be attributed to his close association with Zia.

While handing over power to Junejo and his government, Zia made it clear that it was not a transfer of power from a military to a civilian government. It was at best the sharing of some of the powers by the military with the newly formed civilian government. He had the audacity to state that the plant of democracy could grow under the tree of martial law. Zia envisaged a servile and subordinate civilian government working under the umbrella of the military with him being the ultimate repository of power. Thus the concept was not the establishment of a civilian government, rather it was the introduction of 'civilianized' government under military hegemony. However, as we learnt later, Junejo had other ideas.

In the provinces, the Governors appointed the Chief Ministers. In the largest province, the Punjab, a young man in his thirties who came from an industrialist family of Lahore, Mian Nawaz Sharif, was appointed Chief Minister by the military Governor, Lieutenant-General Ghulam Jilani Khan, who is reported to have had business connections and dealings with the family. The most unlikely appointment was made in Sindh. A judge of the Sindh High Court, Ghaus Ali Shah, who was still serving and not a member of the Provincial Assembly of Sindh, was appointed Chief Minister. It was only afterwards that he resigned as a judge and was elected as a member of the Sindh Provincial Assembly in a by-election. All the chief ministers easily obtained a vote of confidence from their respective provincial assemblies.

Zia was soon to discover that Prime Minister Junejo had a will of his own. The main divergence was on the party system. The new Prime Minister revived the Muslim League and other registered parties were allowed to function and participate in the elections. The stringent restrictions imposed on political parties by amendments made to the Political Parties Act of 1962 were not acceptable to the PPP and its allies in the Movement for Restoration of Democracy and they refused to comply with the registration process.

During 1985, Prime Minister Junejo enhanced his prestige and power. He was elected president of the All Pakistan Muslim League and also the leader of the Muslim League Parliamentary Party. His popularity increased when he lifted the emergency and restored fundamental rights. A vast majority of the members of the National Assembly joined the Muslim League, further strengthening the Prime Minister. Under the rules of business, the Prime Minister was the final authority in the daily administration of the State. The Prime Minister controlled the purse strings and enjoyed the privilege of appointing and transferring officials except for the chiefs of staffs of the armed forces, who were appointed by the President at his discretion.

The process of elections and the formation of a civilian government gave prominence and credibility to many individuals who were at best minor players in earlier political dramas in Pakistan. The major events that brought the newly elected members of the National and Provincial Assemblies into prominence were the local bodies elections in 1979 and 1983, and the appointment of the *Majlis-e-Shoora*. These measures provided both exposure and experience to them and they became the new political elite.

Eighth Amendment: Compromising the Constitution

As has been discussed earlier, the civilian government was running the day-to-day affairs of the state. There was evidently no justification for the continuation of martial law. Junejo had promised the nation he would lift martial law and restore the Constitution of 1973. This was not easy to come by. Zia, by then, had been elected President for five years as a result of the referendum of 1984 and was in no hurry to lift martial law, certainly not without iron clad guarantees that he would continue to enjoy a preponderant position and sweeping powers, and that all the laws, regulations, and orders of martial law were protected and validated. In a nutshell, Zia wanted the National Assembly and the civilian government formed under Junejo to accept his constitutional package of the RCO.[10]

It was in these circumstances that the Constitution (Eighth Amendment) Bill was moved. The Eighth Amendment did not make extensive changes like the RCO, it modified some of the alterations already made under the RCO. Eighteen Articles in all were amended, added, modified, varied, or omitted. Their cumulative effect was to reduce the powers of the President a little bit and to correspondingly extend the powers of the Prime Minister and the Cabinet. While the powers of the President were not curtailed in material terms, the enactment of the Eighth Amendment led the way to the lifting of martial law.

Modifications Made in the RCO

Although the parliament was forced to accept most of the constitutional package of the RCO, certain material modifications were brought about by the Eighth Amendment which are discussed below:[11]

1. The President was required to act on the advice of the Prime Minister or Cabinet (but not the appropriate minister). The President could, however, require the Prime Minister or the Cabinet to reconsider such advice.
2. The period for giving assent by the President to the Bills passed by the Parliament, was reduced from forty-five to thirty days, but the rest of the provisions of the RCO remained the same.
3. The President retained the power to dissolve the National Assembly at his discretion, but this power was conditional. He could dissolve the National Assembly provided that, in his opinion, the government could not be carried on in accordance with the provisions of the Constitution and an appeal to the electorate became necessary. However, the period for holding elections after the dissolution of the National Assembly was reduced from 100 to ninety days.
4. The President retained the power to appoint, at his discretion, Chiefs of armed forces and the Chief Election Commissioner.
5. The power of the President to appoint the Prime Minister was limited to a period of five years, that is, until 20 March 1990 after which date, the President was required to invite that member of the National Assembly who commanded the confidence of the majority of its members, as ascertained in a session of the assembly summoned for the purpose, to assume the office of the Prime Minister. In other words, the procedure for the election of the Prime Minister by majority of total membership of the National Assembly was restored.
6. The President retained the power to appoint, at his discretion, Governors of the provinces but in consultation with the Prime Minister.
7. The power of the Governor to appoint the Chief Minister was limited to three years, that is, until 20 March 1988 after which date, the Governor was required to invite that member of the Provincial Assembly to be the Chief Minister, who commanded the confidence of the majority of the members of the Provincial Assembly as ascertained in a session of the assembly summoned for the purpose. In other words, the election of the Chief Minister by majority of total membership of the Provincial Assembly was restored.
8. The Governor could also dissolve the Provincial Assembly at his discretion, but subject to the previous approval of the President where, in his opinion:
   (a) a vote of no-confidence having been passed against the Chief Minister, no other member of the Provincial Assembly is likely to command the confidence of the majority of the members of the Provincial Assembly in

accordance with the provisions of the Constitution, as ascertained in a session of the Provincial Assembly summoned for the purpose; or

(b) a situation has arisen in which the government of the province cannot be carried on in accordance with the provisions of the Constitution and an appeal to the electorate is necessary.

9. Article 152-A, regarding the Constitution and establishment of the National Security Council, was omitted.
10. Article 270-A, regarding validation of the laws, acts, and orders of martial law regime was extended to cover more cases. The word 'validation' was substituted by the word 'affirmation'. In addition to the President's order, ordinances, martial law regulations, martial law orders, Referendum Order, 1984, the RCO and other constitutional amendments by Zia from time to time were affirmed and validated. Article 270-A has the dubious distinction of including the name of Zia (as General Muhammad Ziaul Haq) and affirming him as President as a result of the referendum held on 19 December 1984. Thus, this Article covered up the fraud played by Zia on the nation in the name of referendum.

The Eighth Amendment was clearly a capitulation, or at least a compromise, on the part of the newly formed civilian government to get martial law lifted. Zia and his Generals, realizing the vulnerable position of the fledgling government of Junejo, took full advantage of it and forced them to make maximum concessions to the military regime. Despite getting iron clad guarantees by way of affirmation of all acts and orders of martial law and indemnity for all its functionaries, Zia ensured his preponderant position as President by reserving unto himself the power to dissolve the National Assembly at his discretion and to appoint a caretaker government. For a change, he was true to his word, though for self-serving reasons, when he said that he was not transferring power to the civilian government but was only sharing some of his power with it. To quote the daily, *The Muslim*:

> When the dictator realized that the time had come for him to lift the curse of martial law, he used his assembly, composed mostly of individuals without any conscience, to destroy the 1973 Constitution. He employed some of the most diabolical legal tricksters to draft what was called the eighth amendment. It was this document which the military dictator used as a bargaining lever to perpetrate his personal rule under the screen of a constitutional arrangement. Threats, blackmail, bribery, and every evil stratagem, was used to convert the members of the Assembly to the General's point of view. It was this perfidious alliance between a military dictator and a supine assembly which drove the country into the quagmire of the eighth amendment.[12]

Zia's unscrupulous tampering with and the addition of his commandments to the 1973 Constitution changed the entire complexion of the supreme law of the land. While retaining elements of both the parliamentary and the presidential forms of government, the Eighth Amendment tilted the balance of power in the latter's favour. While making the office of the President the fulcrum of power, the Eighth Amendment reduced the status of the Prime Minister, making him subservient to the desires of the former. Removing the 'excessive' powers of the Prime Minister in the original 1973 Constitution, the amendment grafted presidential 'discretion' without the protection of a system of checks and balances.

The 'balance' that Zia struck between the powers of the Prime Minister and the President began to tell immediately on the new political system. Popular will had been flouted and national politics had changed from parliamentary democracy to military dictatorship. Zia's main obsession was to retain power at any cost, even if this meant the negation of constitutional democracy, national integrity and national institutions. He deliberately contrived constitutional devices in which he, as life-long President of the country, was above the parameters of the Constitution and unaccountable to the people.[13]

Defection Clause in the Political Parties Act

The Junejo government was weak because it did not come into power as a result of party politics. Junejo first became Prime Minister and then formed a political party and had members of Parliament join his party. The loyalties of the members thus formed are generally suspect. In order to ensure the stability of his government, Junejo had the Political Parties Act amended to provide for a defection clause.[14] It stipulated that if a member of the House (of Parliament or a Provincial Assembly), having been elected as a candidate or a nominee of a political party or having become a member of a political party after such election, defected, or withdrew himself from the political party, he would stand disqualified from being member of the House for the unexpired period of his term. The question of disqualification would be determined by the Election Commission on a reference by the leader of the parliamentary party to which he belonged.

This law in itself was healthy because it discouraged defection and horse-trading in the assemblies which had always been a source of instability of governments. It was meant to keep the erstwhile independent members who had joined the Muslim League in line with the party and under its control.

Longest Ever Martial Law Lifted

After having made a deal with the parliament and the civilian government by way of the Eighth Amendment, and after having secured ultimate powers and validating all martial law regulations and orders with actions taken thereunder, General Zia lifted martial law on 30 December 1985.[15] It had continued for eight-and-a-half years, the longest martial law in the history of Pakistan.

All martial law regulations and martial law orders by the CMLA and MLAs stood cancelled on 30 December 1985.[16] However, nine martial law orders and four martial law regulations issued by the CMLA and specified in the schedule to the MLO 107 were saved with some modifications and would continue as law of the land and their contravention would continue to be punishable. The cancellation of martial law regulations and martial law orders would not affect the previous operation thereof and anything done, action taken, or liability incurred, or punishment suffered, or proceedings commenced would be deemed to have been properly and validly done, taken, incurred, or commenced, as the case may be. Cases pending before special or summary military courts stood transferred to competent criminal courts. The President and the Governors retained power in regard to cases decided and disposed of by the special and summary military courts but were awaiting confirmation. They also retained the powers of review of sentences passed by such military courts before 30 December 1985.

NOTES

1. Revival of the Constitution of 1973 Order, 1985. President's Order 14 of 1985. PLD 1985 Central Statutes 456.
2. Constitution (Second Amendment) Order, 1985. President's Order 20 of 1985. PLD 1985 Central Statutes 582.
3. Representation of the People (Amendment) Ordinance, 1979. Ordinance L of 1979. PLD 1979 Central Statutes 532. Section 47-A was added for the purpose.
4. Article 198(2).
5. Interview with General Mohammad Ziaul Haq by a panel of editors of national newspapers in Islamabad on 3 March 1985. Published by Ministry of Information, Government of Pakistan, Islamabad.
6. Ibid.
7. Even an old friend of Zia, former Chief Justice Anwar-ul-Haq, said that the RCO had changed the basic structure of the Constitution, *The Muslim,* 8 March 1985.
8. *The Muslim*, 11 March 1985.
9. *The Muslim*, 25 March 1985.
10. Khan, Hamid, *Eighth Amendment: Constitutional and Political Crisis in Pakistan*, 1994, Wajidalis Ltd., Lahore, p. 47.
11. Constitution (Eighth Amendment) Act, 1985. Act XVIII of 1985. PLD 1986 Central Statutes 1.
12. *The Muslim*, Islamabad, 2 March 1993, editorial.
13. Maluka, Zulfikar Khalid, *The Myth of Constitutionalism in Pakistan*, 1995, Oxford University Press Karachi, p. 272.
14. Political Parties (Amendment) Act, 1985. Act XXII of 1985. PLD 1986 Central Statutes 18.
15. Proclamation of Withdrawal of Martial Law. PLD 1986 Central Statutes 9.
16. Martial Law Order by CMLA No. 107. PLD 1986 Central Statutes 9.

30

PARTIAL DEMOCRACY AND THE DEATH OF ZIA

While installing Junejo in power, Zia had made it clear that it was not a transfer of power but a sharing of power. It had been communicated in no uncertain terms that the military would still call the shots through the President who had the discretionary power to dissolve the National Assembly and thus dismiss the federal government. The President retained the power to appoint the Chairman of the Joint Chiefs of Staff Committee and Chiefs of Staff of the Army, the Navy, and the Air Force. Hence, democracy was at the sufferance of the military. It was said by the dictator that the sapling of democracy would grow under the tree of martial law, which was an inherent contradiction in terms.

Junejo tried to pursue an independent course on several occasions but in the public eye his government was never respected for its autonomy. Junejo could not ignore the fact that his government had been planted by a military dictator, owed its existence to him, and was thus duty bound to obey and appease him.

Benazir Bhutto Returns in April 1986

Ms Benazir Bhutto and her mother, Mrs Nusrat Bhutto, who had been under confinement for a long time during Zia's martial law, particularly from 1979 to 1984, were both allowed to go abroad in 1984, ostensibly for medical treatment.[1] They were thus relieved of the agony that they had undergone during the Zia regime, particularly after the execution of Bhutto. However, the family suffered another tragedy in 1985 when the youngest brother of Benazir, Shah Nawaz, was found dead in his apartment in Cannes, France, apparently as a result of an overdose of drugs. His death has remained a mystery. His body was flown to Pakistan and buried in the family graveyard in Larkana.

After the lifting of martial law on 30 December 1985, Benazir felt secure enough to return to Pakistan and take over the leadership of the PPP as an heir to Zulfiqar Ali Bhutto. A guarantee of her freedom and security was said to have been given to a friendly foreign power. After Bhutto's death, Nusrat had been accepted by the PPP as the chairperson. However, in order to give the reins to Benazir, Nusrat had her made the party co-chairperson. In this capacity, Benazir returned to Pakistan on 10 April 1986 to a tumultuous welcome in Lahore by a very large gathering of her supporters. She led a procession of hundreds of thousands through the city and addressed a very large crowd. Soon afterwards, she visited other towns in the Punjab and was received by similarly enthusiastic crowds. Her confidence grew, and she boasted that she could take over the Governor House and the government buildings in Lahore that day, if she wanted.

However, Benazir soon found that her popularity was not sufficient to oust the government which was backed by the military and the establishment. Her call for agitation and demonstration against the government in the streets in August 1986 was not successful and the government easily crushed the protest that took place. Through this, Benazir Bhutto must have learnt that a government in power could not be brought down by agitation alone and that it could easily crush all opposition if it enjoyed the support of the centres of power in the country like the military, the judiciary, and the business community. Her father had learnt this lesson the hard way. Despite his widespread support throughout the country, he could not escape execution.

The Afghan War Settlement

Zia's gamble in supporting the *mujahideen* in Afghanistan in their struggle against the Soviet invasion paid him huge dividends. Soviet forces suffered heavily in terms of men and material. The Afghan war effort proved very costly to even a world power like the Soviet Union. In the beginning, the Soviet army was successful in occupying and controlling Afghanistan. It has always been said about Afghanistan that it can be invaded and occupied easily but it is very difficult to hold and control power there. Afghans have a history of resisting foreign invaders. The British imperial power failed in three attempts to occupy and hold Afghanistan.[2] The Soviets were to learn the same lesson for themselves. The turning point in the war came when the *mujahideen* were supplied with Stinger missiles by the United States. Till then, the Soviet forces had been successful in controlling guerilla activity by using helicopter gunships in the mountains and in the deserts. The *mujahideen* suffered enormous casualties being out-gunned and overwhelmed by the extraordinary force of a super-power which was operating easily from the air through helicopters, bombers, and other aircraft. Stinger missiles changed all this. It was a very accurate weapon against air operations, particularly to target helicopters from the ground. These missiles were simple to operate. Just two men could easily handle and operate them.

Other than the problems faced due to the Afghan war effort, the Soviet empire was breaking apart at the seams. Its size and commitments had grown too big for its resources and its economy was in shambles. The Baltic states of Latvia, Lithuania, and Estonia were in revolt and were demanding independence. The Central Asian states and states between the Black Sea and the Caspian Sea were suffering from serious internal dissensions and ethnic problems. Communism in the Soviet Union was under a great strain and challenge. The new Soviet leader, Gorbachev,[3] promised economic reforms and 'restructuring'[4] and 'openness'[5] of the media and the society. All these factors led the Soviet leadership to seek peace in Afghanistan.

The offer of negotiations on Afghanistan was accepted by the Junejo government which entered into dialogue with the Soviet government and its puppet regime in Afghanistan. Junejo took the opposition parties into confidence, this being a national issue. A national conference was held and it was attended by the leaders of most of the political parties in the country, including Benazir.[6] As a result of negotiations, the Geneva Accord was signed on 14 April 1988[7] under which the Soviet Union agreed to withdraw its forces in two instalments; the first half by 15 May 1988, the date the Accord came into force, and the remaining by the end of May 1989.[8] The Soviet government lived up to its commitment of withdrawal of forces according to the agreed timetable.

Still, the victory in Afghanistan was achieved at a very great cost to Pakistan. It had to look after and feed more than three million Afghan refugees that crossed over to Pakistan. The refugees, apart from being an economic burden, caused enormous problems of crowding in the cities of NWFP. They came into conflict with the local population in these cities and are generally blamed for the spreading of contraband drugs. The Afghan war also caused gun running in the country. Afghan freedom fighters would sell guns in the market and get another one free from foreign arms suppliers. Pakistan was glutted with automatic weapons which landed into the wrong hands and contributed to the increase in crime and terrorism in the cities. The Kalashnikov, an assault rifle of Russian make, later copied and manufactured in China and Pakistan, became a household word in Pakistan. Dangerous drugs like heroin also came into common use in Pakistan.

Long after the Afghan settlement, most of the refugees are still in Pakistan and refuse to go back to their country, for as yet there is no peace in Afghanistan. The Soviet forces have left and the puppet government has fallen, yet peace has not returned as various *mujahideen* groups are bitterly fighting one another for dominance. Kabul has been destroyed in the battles between the rival power-hungry warlords. Afghanistan is virtually without a government, and there appears to be no end to this unfortunate situation. Pakistan continues to suffer from the legacy of the Afghan war such as refugees, drugs, guns, crime, and terrorism.

Benazir Bhutto's Case—Requirement for Registration Waived

It has been discussed earlier that through an amending ordinance in 1979,[9] the Political Parties Act had been amended and sections 3-A, 3-B, and 3-C were added to it. In brief, these provisions required all the political parties to submit their accounts to the Election Commission and apply to it for registration. A political party which failed to do so could not conduct any political activity. It could not participate in any election or nominate its candidates. Later, the requirement of registration was relaxed[10] after negotiations between Zia and Mufti Mahmood and, instead of registration, the Election Commission could satisfy itself by circulating a questionnaire to the political parties and receiving their replies to it. However, a number of political parties remained unregistered, including the PPP, and only a few minor parties were registered. Zia's purpose was to keep the PPP out of the general elections proposed to be held in 1979. However, general elections were indefinitely postponed by Zia.

Further amendments were made to the Political Parties Act, 1962 in January 1985, before the general elections of February 1985. These elections were to be held on a non-party basis but Zia feared that important leaders of the PPP might decide to contest the elections in their individual capacity and get elected. The presence of such persons in the National Assembly could cause difficulties and problems to him. Also, these elected members, Zia feared, might try to thwart his constitutional plan. He wanted a pliant, docile, and servile parliament elected on a non-party basis which could agree to any of his terms and conditions for the transfer (rather sharing) of power and the lifting of martial law.

The amendments to the Political Parties Act[11] provided that any person who had at any time after 1 December 1971, been an office bearer or even a member of the executive committee at the national or provincial set-up of a political party which had neither been registered nor declared eligible to participate in elections by the Election Commission by 11 October 1979, would not be qualified for a period of seven years to be elected or chosen as a member of Parliament or a Provincial Assembly. However, the members of the Federal Council (hand picked by Zia and his underlings) were not to be hit by the aforesaid disqualification. It was further provided that any person who had been a federal minister, or minister of state, an advisor or provincial minister, at any time between 1 December 1971 and 5 July 1977 (during Bhutto's regime), would not be qualified for a period of seven years to be elected as a member of Parliament or a Provincial Assembly. These provisions clearly and manifestly ensured that the entire leadership of the PPP was disqualified from being elected to the parliament or the provincial assemblies.

In the capacity of co-chairperson of the PPP, Benazir challenged all such offending provisions of the Political Parties Act as unconstitutional and violative of the fundamental right of freedom of association under the Constitution. A constitutional petition was filed directly before the Supreme Court in its original jurisdiction under Article 184(3) of the Constitution. The following points were urged in support of the petition:

i. Article 17(2) of the Constitution provides firstly the imposition of 'reasonable restrictions' by law in the interest of the sovereignty and integrity of Pakistan, and secondly that a political party is required to account for the source of its funds in accordance with law. Therefore, requirements in the Political Parties Act which were extraneous to these conditions were void.

ii. That the requirement for a party to submit its finances and accounts to audit by a person or authority authorized by the Election Commission was a highly unreasonable restriction and void as being beyond the scope of Article 17.

iii. While the requirement of registration of political parties might not be *per se* unconstitutional, the giving of untrammelled power to the Election Commission to allow or not to allow a political party to function was on the face of it arbitrary, unreasonable, and unconstitutional.

iv. The Election Commission was given unfettered power to cancel the registration of a political party and the same was final and could not be challenged in appeal. This subjected the political parties to double jeopardy as there were provisions in addition to this for dissolution of a political party.
v. The provisions regarding the participation of political parties in the elections were discriminatory, the object being to allow certain parties in the former PNA to participate in the elections indirectly, though they had not applied for registration directly.
vi. The provision regarding the removal of disqualification for a member of the Federal Council was discriminatory and arbitrary. The absolute discretion of the President to remove the disqualification without any guidelines was also unreasonable and discriminatory.
vii. The Freedom of Association Order 1978,[12] applying restrictions on the freedom of association beyond the ambit of Article 17, stood repealed by implication by the Revival of Constitution Order, 1985 (the RCO) and its provisions, being sub-constitutional, could not override Article 17, which had been revived.
viii. The amendment made in the Political Parties Act between 5 July 1977 and 11 November 1985, though validated under the Eighth Amendment, had the status of ordinary law and could be struck down as unconstitutional if found to be violative of the fundamental rights under the Constitution.

The case was heard by the Supreme Court consisting, at that time, of eleven judges including the Chief Justice. Chief Justice Muhammad Haleem wrote the opinion of the Court which was concurred by five judges, namely Aslam Riaz Husain, Javed Iqbal, Saad Saood Jan, Ali Husain Qazilbash, and Usman Ali Shah. The remaining five judges, namely Muhammad Afzal Zullah, Nasim Hasan Shah, Abdul Kadir Shaikh, Shafiur Rehman, and Zaffar Husain Mirza, also concurred with the Chief Justice but each of them added his separate concurring note.[13]

The Supreme Court accepted the constitutional petition of Benazir and repelled the two objections taken by the federal government, firstly, that Benazir was not an aggrieved party as no act detrimental to her had been taken under the provisions of the laws being challenged; and secondly, that she should have approached the High Courts first, particularly when similar petitions were already pending in some of the High Courts. The Court held on the first objection that an enactment might immediately on coming into force take away or abridge the fundamental rights of a person by its very terms and without any further overt act being done. In such a case, the infringement of the fundamental right would be complete instantly on the passing of the enactment and, therefore, there could be no reason why the person so prejudicially affected by the law should not be entitled immediately to avail himself of the constitutional remedy. The Court went on to hold that a political party could also be an 'aggrieved party'. Regarding the second objection, the court held that as to the choice of the forum, ordinarily the forum of the court in the lower hierarchy should be invoked but that principle would not be inviolable and genuine exception could exist to take it out of that practice. The exception was applied in favour of the case in hand because, the Court observed, too rigid an adherence to precedent might lead to injustice in a particular case and also unduly restrict the proper development of the law.

Regarding validation of the laws under Article 270-A, the Court held that this Article did not give protection to existing laws which were violative of fundamental rights. The Political Parties Act, 1962 had not been given validity against constitutional violations because it did not find mention in the seventh schedule to the Constitution wherein the laws mentioned had been given constitutional protection. If a legal measure was not itself in existence (being unconstitutional), the Court observed, how could it operate prospectively. The Freedom of Association Order, 1978 being an ordinary law itself, could not give any protection to the provisions of Political Parties Act, 1962 as against fundamental right under Article 17 and its remaining on the statute book would be of no effect.

The Court held in no uncertain terms that the constitutional guarantees to every citizen (if not in the service of Pakistan), including the right to form a political party, could only be subject to reasonable restrictions imposed by the law in the interest of the sovereignty or integrity of Pakistan. The right to form associations is not an absolute or uncontrolled one, but the restrictions thereto under the Constitution (as stated in Article 17(2)) should be construed as exhaustive and liable to strict construction.

On the question of rendering of accounts by a political party for audit, the Court held that it could not be regarded as an unreasonable restriction or outside the ambit of Article 17(3). This contention of the petitioner was thus rejected.

Regarding inclusion of the expression 'security of Pakistan' in addition to other expressions used in the Political Parties Act, it was held that inclusion of this expression was a constraint on the 'freedom of association' beyond the scope of Article 17. This expression was not used in Article 17 and, therefore, its inclusion in the Act was violative of Article 17 and hence void.

Compulsory registration of political parties was also declared by the Court as violative of Article 17 as it placed unreasonable restrictions on the exercise of a right by superimposing itself on the fundamental right since it was not simply registration, but was accompanied by penal consequences. It was also observed that the power of cancellation of registration, which was vested in the Election Commission, was without any safeguards and was entirely discretionary to the Election Commission and no remedy had been provided against its decision. Hence, the Court concluded that it constituted an unreasonable restriction on the right to form associations.

The Supreme Court declared and held to be void the following provisions of the Political Parties Act, 1962 (to the extent stated) being inconsistent with the fundamental right of freedom of association as enshrined in Article 17 of the Constitution:

1. Section 3(1) in so far as it relates to and includes therein the disability regarding 'security of Pakistan' was void. The remaining part of section 3 was upheld.

2. Section 3-A (regarding rendition of accounts by a political party) was upheld but the penalty under section 6(1) arising therefrom by its insertion therein was declared void.
3. Section 3-B (regarding registration of a political party) was declared void in its entirety.
4. Section 3-C (regarding circulation of a questionnaire) was held to have outlived its purpose.
5. Section 6(1) in so far as it related to and included therein the references to 'security of Pakistan' and 'the contravention of the provisions of Section 3-A' was held void. However, the inclusion of the expressions 'Islamic ideology', 'morality', and 'maintenance of public order' used in section 6(1) was upheld for the reason that these expressions formed part of and were thus inherently included in the expressions 'sovereignty' and 'integrity' of Pakistan used in Article 17 of the constitution.
6. The remaining parts of section 6 including sub-section (2) thereof was upheld.
7. Regarding sections 7 and 8, it was observed that in view of the decision in respect of other provisions of the Act, it was for the legislature to amend them.

This judgment was announced by the Supreme Court on 20 June 1988 while Zia was still alive. It was a clear rebuff to Zia who had dissolved the National Assembly on 29 May 1988, dismissed Junejos government, and announced that elections would be held on a non-party basis. It is, of course, one of the very few judgments given against Zia while he was still in power and for this reason, this judgment stands out. It also had the effect of reviving the political party system which Zia had tried hard to suppress for eleven years. This judgment paved the way for party-based elections in November 1988. It was also the first judgment that whittled down the Validation Clause under Article 270-A which was included as a result of the Eighth Amendment to the Constitution.

Mustafa Khar's Case and Validation Clause under the Eighth Amendment

The RCO introduced Article 270-A in the Constitution validating all martial law regulations, martial law orders, President's orders, and other laws passed between 5 July 1977 and the RCO. This Article also saved all orders passed, proceedings taken, and acts done during the said period. The Eighth Amendment modified this Article and extended its scope to affirm the results of the referendum of 1984, election of the President, the Constitution (Second Amendment) Order, 1985 (P.O. No. 20 of 1985) and the Constitution (Third Amendment) order, 1985 (P.O. No. 24 of 1985). These two amendment orders were passed by the President after the RCO and before the first meeting of the Parliament, that is, between 2 and 23 March 1985. P.O. No. 20 of 1985 amended Article 239 of the Constitution modifying the procedure of amendment to the Constitution.[14] P.O. 24 of 1985 made amendments in certain provisions relating to the High Courts and Federal Shariat Court.

A significant modification was made by the Eighth Amendment in Article 270A and the word 'validation' used in the RCO was substituted by the word 'affirmation'. All the laws, regulations, orders, proclamations etc. stood 'affirmed, adopted and declared' under this Article. The expressions 'affirmed' and 'affirmation' were apparently used to avoid judicial review of such laws, regulations, or orders and/or Acts, orders or proceedings thereunder, under the dictum of '*State v Zia-ur-Rehman*'.[15]

Despite the effort and intention to pre-empt any challenge to Article 270-A, it became the subject-matter of a number of cases. In such cases, the Lahore High Court held that:[16]

i. All legal measures mentioned in clause (1) of Article 270-A of the constitution, having been validated, cannot be subjected to judicial review.
ii. As regards the orders passed, proceedings taken, and acts done in exercise of the powers derived from said legal measures, the jurisdiction of High Courts is limited to *coram non judice*, without jurisdiction, malice in law and violation of the constitutional provisions.
iii. Article 270-A cannot be struck down on the assumption that the parliament was not sovereign.

Article 270-A then came up for interpretation before the Supreme Court of Pakistan.[17] The Court held that by enacting clauses (2) and (5), Parliament had not intended to validate such acts, actions, or proceedings or to put them beyond the reach of courts or to deprive persons who had suffered thereunder of any remedy or relief whatsoever. The Court observed that during martial law, when fundamental rights stood suspended, Article 4 furnished the only guarantee or assurance to the citizens that no action detrimental to the life, liberty, body, reputation, or property of any person would be taken except in accordance with law.[18] Acts, actions, or proceedings which suffered from excess or lack of jurisdiction or were *coram non judice* or malafide, could hardly be treated as those in accordance with law. Such acts, actions, or proceedings, it was observed, were bad even under the system which was validated by Parliament under Article 270-A on account of violation of the guarantee of due process of law given by Article 4. The Court repelled the argument that by enacting clauses (2) and (5), Parliament had intended to validate such acts, actions or proceedings or to put them beyond the reach of the courts or to deprive the persons who had suffered thereunder of any remedy or relief whatsoever. There is always a legal presumption that legislature does not perpetuate inequity or injustice and there is no reason why such a presumption should not be invoked while interpreting clauses (2) and (5) of Article 270-A.

The Supreme Court thus held that there is no clog on the jurisdiction of the courts to exercise their power of judicial review in respect of the acts, actions, and proceedings made, taken or held by those authorities which suffered from defect of jurisdiction or were *coram non judice* or were malafide. The protection under Article

270-A could not be used for defending an order which, ex facie, was without jurisdiction.[19] The Supreme Court held that constitutional validity given by Article 270-A(1) is retroactive and is of a character of a curative or validating statute[20] and must be understood and be operative in that context. However, it was observed that the provision of Article 270-A(1) has not given protection to the existing laws which are violative of fundamental rights. The Political Parties Act, thus, has not been given validity against constitutional violations.

Conflict between Civilian and Military Authorities

It has been discussed above that the Afghan war effort provided strength to Zia's government due to American support. Although Pakistan was flooded with 3.5 million refugees from Afghanistan with the attendant problems of gun running, drugs, smuggling, and an increase in crimes throughout Pakistan, yet the Afghan war stabilized the Zia government. The government, particularly the Inter Services Intelligence (ISI), was a conduit for the supply of arms and ammunition to Afghan freedom fighters. This afforded an opportunity to some of the generals involved in this effort to help themselves to handsome money by selling some of the arms to Iran, particularly missiles for use in the Iran-Iraq war. It is therefore no wonder that some generals have become rich beyond belief.

It cannot be said with any certainty whether it was to cover up such unauthorized sales of weaponry that an explosion occured at Ojheri camp, or if the explosion on 10 April 1988 took place accidentally. Ojheri was an ordinance depot situated near the twin cities of Islamabad and Rawalpindi and when it exploded, missiles, rockets and other weapons flew in different directions in the two cities, killing hundreds of people and injuring many others. About 100 people died within the first hour, most of them instantly, while many more were maimed permanently and quite a few succumbed to injuries later in the following days and weeks.[21] There was also substantial damage to property. One of the federal ministers[22] was also killed because his car was struck by a missile flying from Ojheri. There were clear attempts on the part of the military establishment to cover up the matter and not to give out accurate and adequate information to the public. The press and the Parliament clamoured for truth and demanded an exhaustive and impartial enquiry into the Ojheri incident. It was under this pressure that Junejo agreed to a thorough enquiry and punishment of those responsible for the grim tragedy which had brought so much misery and suffering to the common people of the federal capital and Rawalpindi.

The decision to hold an enquiry into the Ojheri incident was not seen favourably by military authorities. The Generals saw it as blatant interference in their military affairs and Zia was asked to come to their aid. The enquiry could have exposed the misdeeds of many a general and would have embarrassed the military *junta*. The conflict between the civilian and military authorities on the Ojheri incident became a major reason for the parting of ways between Zia and Junejo.

There were other irritants too. Junejo was becoming too assertive and independent for Zia and his generals to bear. He was forgetting that he had been inducted as Prime Minister in a subordinate role. He did not spare the military high-ups. He ordered a spartan style of government by ordering federal secretaries and military generals to give up big staff cars in favour of small Suzuki cars. He also used the expression 'putting Generals into Suzukis' while addressing Parliament. The generals, who had become used to unbridled power and unparalleled perks and privileges, took this as an insult to them. A few of them even protested in the press that they had been belittled.

The Afghanistan war settlement was yet another irritant in relations between Zia and Junejo. Junejo had taken major initiatives independent of Zia in settling the dispute directly with the Soviet Union in the negotiations at Geneva. He had invited leaders of all the political parties, including Benazir, which could not possibly be with Zia's blessing. He signed an accord with the Soviet Union on 14 April 1988 over the withdrawal of Soviet forces from Afghanistan which, it is rumoured, did not find favour with Zia and his military colleagues.

After the lifting of martial law in December 1985, battles over protocol and personnel started in earnest between the Prime Minister and the President. These included differences over the appointments of Ambassadors and Secretaries, and even on such petty issues like the use of the 'Falcon' aircraft. For instance, Zia advised the Foreign Office to prepare a summary for a proposed visit to Africa, but this was shot down by Junejo since he felt that being Prime Minister, he should be making all the foreign tours. Concurrently, there were two consistent refrains in Junejo's public pronouncements; first, taking 'credit' for lifting martial law and restoring democracy and secondly, blaming the country's ills on prolonged military rule.

The first serious problem surfaced in February 1986 over ties with India. In his December 1985 visit to New Delhi, Zia had initiated a process of normalization of relations between the two countries. One of its important components was discussions on trade and economic co-operation which Dr Mehbubul Haq pursued with enthusiasm and vigour. By passing a strongly worded resolution on Kashmir and later ousting Dr Mehbubul Haq as Finance Minister, Junejo managed to reverse this process. Later, other factors came into play from the Indian side that thwarted this attempt.

In July 1986, Junejo embarked on a state visit to the United States which proved a watershed in the relationship between the President and the Prime Minister. Junejo came back so excited from his American sojourn that Zia remarked to one of his confidants, 'I hope this visit does not go to his head'. Junejo felt that after having received a 'pat on the back' from Reagan, he had been politically strengthened within Pakistan. His first act of bravado was to remove Major-General Agha Nek Muhammad as head of the Intelligence Bureau without clearing this decision in advance with Zia. Junejo felt that Zia was trying to undermine him by playing the 'Jatoi card'. It was then, in August 1986, that Ghulam Mustafa Jatoi launched his political party with great fanfare and the covert blessings of Zia.

By late 1986, the relationship between Zia and Junejo was marked by increasing suspicion and mutual distrust. Basically, Zia had started suspecting Junejo on two counts. First, he felt that Junejo, in some form or the other, was hobnobbing with Benazir Bhutto by giving her a free hand to abuse Zia without anyone in the government willing to defend him. In fact, he felt that Junejo and Benazir had reached some sort of an 'understanding' whereby, in return for the freedom given to her, Benazir would not attack Junejo. That she somehow refrained from criticizing Junejo added to Zia's suspicions. The second, perhaps more important suspicion was that Junejo was trying to undermine his position as Chief of Army Staff by encouraging criticism of his wearing 'dual hats' (as President and COAS). Zia felt that General K.M. Arif's much-talked-about 'Presidential looks' were being encouraged by Junejo with the purpose of putting pressure on him from within the army.

Beneath these suspicions, there were other factors as well. Deep down, Zia felt that Junejo was a modest provincial politician whom he had elevated to an august position but, in return, he was not only 'ungrateful' and 'disloyal' but also behaved in a manner that was unbecoming of his position as Prime Minister. Zia had expected Junejo to be perhaps like the Prime Minister of, say, South Korea, Egypt, Nepal, or Sri Lanka. Much to his surprise and chagrin, Junejo seemed determined to nibble at the Presidential authority at every available opportunity. For instance, once Zia responding to a question from newsmen said that such and such decision would be taken at the Cabinet meeting to be held on a particular date that he mentioned. Just to prove him wrong, the date of the Cabinet meeting was changed. For his part, Junejo saw his model in the late Zulfiqar Ali Bhutto. Junejo felt he carried the same title as Bhutto; came from the same province and the same social background, lived in the same residence as Bhutto, flew in the same plane as Bhutto, and was entitled to the same perks and privileges that Bhutto did while he was Prime Minister.

Zia also felt that all his 'men' were either being purged by Junejo or their authority considerably pruned. Junejo consciously cut Zia's 'three doctors' down to size: Dr Mehbubul Haq, Dr Asad, and Dr Attiya Enayatullah. However, the countdown to the 29 May operation began in November 1987 with the easing out of Sahabzada Yaqub Khan as Foreign Minister. Yaqub's exit was followed by an informal instruction by the Prime Minister that henceforth no file from the Foreign Office would be sent to the President. Zia not only felt that he was losing control over his favourite area, foreign affairs, but that there was a design on Junejo's part to exclude him from the domain of foreign policy and that too in a period when the crucial Afghan issue seemed to be reaching a conclusion. Privately, Zia had started expressing his 'disgust' with Junejo and the civilian set-up, and by the time things started moving on the Afghan issue in 1988, the only question in Zia's mind was not whether he should get rid of Junejo but the right moment when he should embark on this fateful surgical operation.[23]

To be fair to Junejo, he consulted Zia frequently and gave him his due respect. Their mutual uneasiness emerged out of the power sharing process. Zia frequently wrote directives to the ministers and his staff pestered them for a quick response.

Under the rules of business, the ministers were required to route their replies to the President through the Prime Minister's Secretariat. The delay annoyed Zia. His crafty staff blamed Junejo for the delay and the gap between the two, created by suspicions, kept widening. Junejo requested Zia to address all the directives to him directly and promised their speedy implementation. This was in conflict with Zia's style, the direct personal approach. Such incidents created bitterness between the two men which was exploited by Zia's close advisers. They advocated pre-emptive action before Junejo could cause grievous political damage to Zia.[24]

Zia was informed by his advisers that Junejo had secretly connived to get a resolution passed by the National Assembly calling upon Zia to seek retirement from the army and the appointment of a full time Chief of Army Staff. The aim was to put Zia under moral pressure and to remove him from his power base. Junejo had his own story. He denied the existence of any proposal to pass such a resolution but maintained that, despite the petty irritations and mischief caused by the President's staff, his relations with Zia were normal. He could never stoop so low, he said, as to commit such treachery. This was a figment of the imagination of General Akhtar Abdur Rahman who was extremely apprehensive after the Ojheri Camp fire incident and felt that the disciplinary axe would fall on him. Since General Akhtar had selected that arms depot in the middle of a populated area and had failed to shift it despite the passage of many years, he saw the noose tightening around his neck. Before he could be blamed and punished, he concocted stories, filled Zia's ears with falsehood, and pushed him into an unconstitutional act. He also held Lientenant-General Syed Rafaqat, the President's Chief of Staff, responsible for the dismissal of Junejo's government.[25]

Other minor incidents occurred to put a strain on the civilian-military relationship. This included a car accident involving a member of the Punjab Assembly and an army colonel which took an ugly turn till the reports reached the very top. Yet other minor incidents in which military personnel were involved were seen as a humiliation of the military at the hands of civilian authorities. However, the Ojheri incident proved to be the last straw that broke the camel's back. The military leadership decided to assert itself and undo its own democratic experiment. Ultimately, the democratic sapling had to die its natural death under the shade of the martial law tree.

Dissolution of Assemblies and the Dismissal of Junejo's Government

Zia knew that his real constituency was the armed forces. It was due to their support that he had survived for eleven years in power. That was the reason that despite being President, he did not shed his uniform and clung so dearly to the office of Chief of Army Staff. He knew that the office of Army Chief was his real power base and ceding this office to anyone (even to a close associate) would make him vulnerable.

Having come under pressure from the military leadership, particularly after the Ojheri incident, Zia decided to act in order to please, or maybe protect, his generals. On 29 May 1988, he dissolved the National Assembly and dismissed Junejo's government. This was followed by the dissolution of the Provincial Assemblies by the Governors. On 30 May 1988, addressing the nation on television and radio, Zia levelled the following allegations against the Junejo government:

1. The government remained ineffective despite enjoying full powers during its three-year tenure.
2. The National Assembly, which was elected on a non-party basis, was converted into a party-based body because of political compulsions of the former Prime Minister.
3. Plots and permits were used as political bribes, besides financial benefits to gain political support. 'Nepotism was at its peak', he remarked in the speech.
4. About the amount provided for the members of the assemblies for development projects, Zia said 'every one of us knows how it was spent and where. If corruption is patronized at the highest level, how can it be stopped at the lowest level?' he asked. The funds provided to MNAs and MPAs in the name of development were misappropriated.
5. The economy was crippled. The government was depending, both internally and externally, on loans, and the economy was in the grip of a crisis as a result of faulty economic policies. Bribery and nepotism were well entrenched.
6. The state of affairs in the country over the three-and-a-quarter years compelled him to take this step, as he could not remain a silent spectator to this situation. He said that he had been informing the Prime Minister, in private conversations with him and in public speeches, that the conditions were not satisfactory but no heed was paid to his advice.
7. The life, property, and honour of the citizens were no longer secure.
8. Linguistic, regional, and ethnic differences assumed enormous proportions.
9. In-fighting between Muslims was being waged in some parts of the country.

Zia also announced the following measures to be taken by him:

1. A caretaker Cabinet would be announced within the next few days.
2. The constitutional requirements in that regard would be fulfilled.
3. The process for Islamization would be stepped up.
4. Measures would be taken to accelerate the process of providing speedy and inexpensive justice to the people.
5. The law and order situation would be improved to guarantee an absolute sense of security to the people.
6. Criminals, offenders, and murderers would be given deterrent punishment.
7. The foreign policy being pursued was successful and was to remain unchanged.
8. Due priority would be given for establishing an Islamic democratic system in the country, strengthening democratic institutions, and inducting an elected government.

Thus the priorities announced by Zia included acceleration of the process of Islamization; dispensation of speedy and inexpensive justice; restoration of law and order and stabilization of the country's faltering economy.[26]

Zia also announced a caretaker government but without a Prime Minister. The ensuing elections would be partyless once again, and elections to the National Assembly would be held on 17 November 1988. He thus committed a breach of the provisions of the Constitution[27] which required him to hold general elections within ninety days of the dissolution of the National Assembly by the President at his discretion under Article 58(2)(b). He deliberately fixed a date 172 days after the dissolution of the National Assembly. This speaks volumes for his lack of respect for the Constitution which he believed more in breaching than in complying.

Performance of Junejo's Government Reviewed

Junejo was nominated by Zia as Prime Minister on the specific understanding that his nomination was not a transfer of power but only a sharing of power. These were the conditions under which Junejo had to work till the end of December 1985 when martial law was finally lifted. Before he was nominated, the RCO was enforced by Zia. Junejo's position was weak and vulnerable as he had to labour under the amendments made in the Constitution from July 1977 onwards which made the position of the President paramount and that of the Prime Minister subordinate. Junejo promised the nation that he would lift martial law and civilian government would be restored at the earliest. He did carry out his promise but at the price of the Eighth Amendment, validating the RCO and previous amendments in the Constitution with slight modifications. To be fair to him, it cannot be denied that he had no real option but to relent under the pressure of the military regime that had brought him into power. These were the circumstances in which the Eighth Amendment was passed by the Parliament.

After the lifting of martial law, Junejo tried to take a course independent of Zia. He annoyed military generals by withdrawing big staff cars from them and replacing them with small cars. He tried to conduct an independent foreign policy, particularly on Afghanistan, by taking into confidence and consulting leaders of other political parties, including Benazir, the leader of the PPP. His government even tried to probe into the military bungling and fiasco at the Ojheri Camp near Islamabad on 10 April 1988, which resulted in the death of and serious injuries to a large number of civilians. This probe perhaps became the immediate cause for the dismissal of his government by Zia on 29 May 1988 in exercise of his power under Article 58(2)(b).

Although Junejo had no claim of his own to power and he was beholden to Zia for being appointed prime minister, his performance was commendable. With limited options and Zia breathing down his neck, he did what was possible for him. He restored the fundamental rights of citizens under the Constitution which had been denied to them for a very long time. He tried to put the country on the course of development and some progress was made, particularly in the area of construction of roads in rural areas and the electrification of villages. Keeping in view the conduct and character of contemporary political leaders in Pakistan, he was an honest man. He is faulted for introducing political corruption by allowing each member of

Parliament five million rupees every year for development programmes in his constituency when everyone knew that these funds would be misappropriated. But for a sugar mill in his native village, Sindhri, which he installed in association with some other partners, there is no other blemish on him personally. He was a polite and low-key political personage; traits which are not easy to find in political leaders today.

Caretaker Government without a Prime Minister

Following Junejo's dismissal on 29 May 1988, Zia was required under Article 48(5)(b) to appoint a caretaker cabinet. There can be no concept of a Cabinet without a prime minister but Zia, who cared little for constitutional provisions, defied them once again by appointing a caretaker Cabinet. Most of the members of the Junejo Cabinet were retained. Only those people were excluded who were known to be close to Junejo personally and loyal to him. In the provinces, Zia retained those chief ministers who had his confidence. Nawaz Sharif, who was known to be closer to Zia than to Junejo, was retained. He was even encouraged by Zia and his henchmen to take on Junejo within the Muslim League. At a stormy meeting of the Muslim League in July/August 1988, the two factions headed by Junejo and Nawaz openly collided and there were scenes of pandemonium. Junejo was declared to have lost.

The prime minister, even in a caretaker government, is essential under the Constitution despite the Eighth Amendment. He is head of the cabinet and the president is required to act in accordance with the advice of the cabinet or the prime minister.[28] Even the advice of the cabinet is conveyed to the president through the prime minister. It is not always possible to call a cabinet meeting for every matter concerning the federal government and the day-to-day business of the government is run on the advice of the prime minister. Technically, cabinet meetings cannot be held without the prime minister calling them. Hence, the business of the government after 29 May 1986 was not being run according to the Constitution and the failure to appoint a caretaker prime minister was clearly unconstitutional.

The Shariah Ordinance, 1988

The dissolution of the National Assembly and the dismissal of Junejo's government had left Zia more vulnerable than ever before. He was suddenly left alone and exposed. Martial law had been lifted and he had to run the government under the constitutional umbrella, which he was not used to. He had done to death the civilian government and the assembly which he had himself created. The dismissal of Junejo's government was a clear admission on his part of the failure of the constitutional plan he had proudly announced on 12 August 1983. He was left once again to survive by his wits. Zia was still the Chief of Army Staff. In order to give new life and legitimacy to his regime, he once again fell back on political exploitation of Islam. He promulgated an ordinance on 15 June 1988 for the enforcement of *shariah* in Pakistan.[29]

Shariah, defined as the injunctions of Islam as laid down in the Holy Quran and *sunnah*, was declared the supreme source of law in Pakistan and the *grundnorm* for policy-making by the courts in the country. They were required to refer all questions of repugnancy of any law or provision of law to *shariah* in the Federal Shariat Court. The questions relating to Muslim personal law, any fiscal law, or any law relating to the levy and collection of taxes and fees, or banking or insurance practice and procedure were to be referred to the High Court which were to be heard and decided by a Bench of not less than three judges. The implementation of the decision of the High Court in the above matters, subject to appeal to the Supreme Court, would not take effect until at least six months from the date of the decision. However, the High Court had no powers to stay proceedings before any court or tribunal functioning under the law under challenge before it.

It was provided that experienced and qualified *ulema* would be eligible for appointment as judges of courts subordinate to the High Courts. Similarly, such *ulema* from reputable institutions of Islamic learning and *deeni madaris* in Pakistan or abroad would be eligible to appear before any court in matters of interpretation of the *shariah*. Persons holding graduate and post-graduate degrees in law and *shariah* from the universities or the International Islamic University, Islamabad would be eligible as advocates, notwithstanding provisions of the law relating to legal practitioners and the Bar Councils. Provision was also made for appointment of *muftis* for assistance to the Supreme Court, the High Courts, and the Federal Shariat Court. A *mufti* had the right of audience before the Supreme Court and the High Courts while exercising jurisdiction under this Ordinance and the Federal Shariat Court. However, *muftis* were prohibited from pleading on behalf of any party. They could only address the courts on the interpretation of *shariah*. A *mufti* could be entitled to the remuneration of a Deputy Attorney-General of Pakistan.

There was also a provision for the Islamization of the economy for which a commission was to be appointed to undertake an examination of fiscal laws and determine whether they were repugnant to the *shariah*. A similar commission was to be appointed for the Islamization of education. Steps were to be taken for the promotion of Islam's values through the mass media. All laws were to be interpreted in the light of the *shariah*. The Council of Islamic Ideology was to undertake expeditious codification of Islamic laws. However, the financial obligations incurred or to be incurred and contracts made or to be made between a national institution and a foreign agency would remain valid, binding, and operative and no court could pass any order or make any decision about any such obligation or contract.

From the above provisions, it is evident that the *shariah* ordinance was nothing but window dressing and another last step by Zia to legitimize and perpetuate himself in power in the name of Islam. It was meant to cover up his unconstitutional and malafide act of dissolving the National Assembly and dismissing Junejo's government. The only practical aspect of the ordinance was to usher in a class of so-called *ulema* for appointment as *muftis*, advocates, and judges, so that this class could serve as the vanguard of his political support and become a rival of lawyers who were disturbed and agitated by his unconstitutional and impetuous acts. Zia wanted to create a class of his supporters within the judiciary and the Bar but his sordid designs were not to succeed. Providence intervened to rescue Pakistan from his stranglehold.

Zia's Death, August 1988, and a Review of his Regime

Zia was killed in an air crash on 17 August 1988 near Bahawalpur on his way back from a demonstration of tanks. He was in uniform and was accompanied by a number of generals, including the Chairman, Joint Chiefs of Staff Committee, Chief of General Staff, and other high military officials. He was also accompanied by the US Ambassador to Pakistan and his Military Attaché. The two American diplomats also died with him in the crash. The Vice Chief of Army Staff, General Mirza Aslam Beg was also present at the tank demonstration but he did not accompany Zia in the C-130 plane which crashed. He later admitted to having flown in his own military plane over the crash site and seen the plane burning. He did not stop but flew directly to Islamabad where the question of succession to Zia had to be decided.

On the confirmation of Zia's death, a meeting was held in Islamabad to decide the question of succession. Some of the participants like General Fazle Haq, Chief Minister of NWFP, were in favour of the imposition of martial law. However, the military chiefs present there, including Mirza Aslam Beg, did not support the idea and allowed transition to take place constitutionally. Under the Constitution,[30] when the office of President becomes vacant by reason of death, resignation, or removal of the President, the chairman of the Senate acts as President until a new President is elected under the Constitution. Ghulam Ishaq Khan, chairman of the Senate, took over as acting President. One of his first acts was to appoint Mirza Aslam Beg as Chief of the Army Staff. He was thus immediately rewarded for his support to the peaceful transition of power in a constitutional manner.

Zia was initially seen as an unassuming and 'reluctant coup-maker'. He was constantly underestimated by his friends and foes. Most people saw him as a transitional figure. There were few expectations attached to him and the earlier years allowed him to grow in office, particularly because of the exclusive attention that was devoted to the Bhutto trial.

Zia came from the middle class. His hallmark was humility. His double handshake and triple embrace as the style of greeting became a legend, together with his routine opening of car doors for his visitors and waiting in the driveway till the visitor departed.[31] He was patient and never in a hurry. In fact, he was slow to the extent that for him indecision, by design or by default, was almost an instrument of policy, probably in the belief that if a problem was allowed to drag on interminably then it would eventually go away.[32] He had a relaxed and stable relationship with his colleagues. He relied on them and had a *de facto* number two in General Arif for almost seven years although most of his colleagues were eased out by Zia with a 'golden handshake'.[33] Though outwardly a cool man, he had a very good memory and would give a blow or two to his opponents at a time of his own convenience.

Zia was pragmatic in his approach, a fact reflected in his choice of such diverse friends as the communists of China, the capitalists of America, the marxists of Zimbabwe, the socialists of Turkey, and the theocrats of Saudi Arabia. He did what suited him and institutionalized ad hocism as a policy. He could back down or make a compromise during crises as he did during 1980 *shia* agitation or the 1981 hijacking. To his credit are the continuation of Pakistan's nuclear programme and the avoidance of conflict with India, despite the fact that he fuelled the Sikh agitation for Khalistan in India.

Zia was a lucky man and rode his luck for too long. Events somehow favoured Zia. Whether it was the timing of the Islamic revolution in Iran which led to the ouster of the Shah, one of Bhutto's closest supporters, or the fact that Bhutto's hanging was followed three days later by the hanging of the former Iranian Prime Minister, Hoveida, the international impact of Bhutto's hanging was nullified. A large number of people resented Bhutto's death but were too engaged in the dynamics unleashed by the boom in the Middle East to undertake any serious attack on Zia.[34] The Soviet military intervention which aroused western interest in Pakistan, or the PIA hijacking which effectively scuttled the newly formed MRD's agitation in its infancy, or even the timing of Mrs Gandhi's assassination just when she was planning a military strike against Pakistan, were all developments that somehow came to Zia's rescue.

In many ways, he was an enigmatic, authoritarian military leader, who could not easily be slotted in the category of classic third world tinpot despots or military dictators. He presided over Pakistan's longest period of military rule but then himself lifted martial law to begin a unique power-sharing experience with civilian politicians. His rule was one of Pakistan's worst periods of human rights abuses, which included for the first time in the country's history the whipping of journalists, lawyers, and political workers. But he also tolerated a reasonably lively and free press, uncharacteristic of third world military rulers. He had his predecessor, Bhutto, executed but then went ahead to appoint as Chief Justice of the Supreme Court one of the three judges who had sought Bhutto's acquittal. During his rule, he continued to lead and strengthen Pakistan's one organized institution, the army, but, at the same time, he ensured the weakening of all other institutions, the civil bureaucracy, the judiciary, the political parties and, of course, the Constitution. He loved to be in the limelight and to call the shots, but also consciously avoided a personality cult, unlike his predecessors. Despite his abiding pro-Americanism, he defied Washington on the nuclear issue and built a close rapport with Iran.

If one word can describe his rule, it would be 'ad hocism'. There were no long term, well thought-out policies for specific sectors like industry, agriculture, education, or health. He followed a cautious, moment to moment, reactive, one-step-at-a-time approach that was guided more by his instinct for political survival rather than by a well-defined vision for Pakistan.

However, he was clear on the basics, as he saw them. For instance, soon after overthrowing Bhutto, there was little doubt about what Zia had in mind regarding the fate of his predecessor. A month after the coup, in August 1977, Zia went to Multan to address army officers where he was asked about Bhutto. Till then, no charge had been pressed against the former prime minister and he was not under arrest on the charges of having conspired to murder one of his political opponents. Zia responded to this question with a wide grin and looked at two of his staff officers, Brigadier Mian Afzaal and Brigadier Ilyas, who were standing close by: 'Why should I kill Afzaal myself when I can make Ilyas do it' he asked. The long-drawn judicial process which began in September 1977 with the arrest of Bhutto ended in April 1979, eighteen months later with his execution under a split Supreme Court verdict. Some time later, in July 1978, when Zia was told that the Supreme Court might acquit Bhutto (the two judges of the Supreme Court, allegedly sympathetic to Bhutto, had not retired), he responded: 'If the Supreme Court releases him, I will have the bastard tried by a military court and hung'.[35]

If Zia was clear on the fate of Bhutto, he was equally clear on the question of his own relationship with power which was more like a 'catholic marriage' in which there could be no divorce. He wanted to rule with the exclusion of political parties or politicians of stature. Genuine power-sharing was out, as the dismissal of Junejo exemplified. He wanted to maintain the status quo as far as possible; no 'rocking of the boat' was permissible. Finally, all through this, he knew that the army was his primary constituency.[36]

Zia successfully created for himself an image of a pious and devout Muslim, but his brand of Islam created fear even among the deeply religious people of Pakistan. Zia also managed to attain a reputation as an honest man, despite the fact that he developed a habit of dishonouring his own promises, due to which some people interpreted his official title CMLA as not 'Chief Martial Law Administrator', but 'Cancel My Last Announcement'. He is alleged to have been involved in underhand deals for the sale of Stinger missiles to Iran during the Iran-Iraq war from where he is alleged to have made a lot of money. There were about half a dozen bungalows owned by Zia or his near relatives in various places, including Islamabad.[37] So much for his honesty. He also fostered his image as a very friendly, direct, and simple man, unlike a typical military dictator, but his actions proved otherwise and even his 'friends' could never predict what his next move would be.[38]

History's judgment on Zia's rule will probably be harsh. He built no political institution that could outlast him. The old Constitution was not preserved nor was anything new put in its place. Even when he spawned a new political order through non-party polls in 1985, he demolished it himself three years later. His rule turned out to be a running battle between him and the political forces, with him usually holding the initiative. He, alternately, tried to use the political forces, repress them, confuse them, and confront them, combining the military techniques of surprise and deception. Towards the end of his rule, they were all getting together against him. Politicians were always suspicious of him as if waiting to be 'ambushed' by his next move. For his part, he defied predictions about his 'imminent fall', particularly in crisis situations like 1979 after Bhutto's hanging, in 1981 after the PIA hijacking, in 1983 during MRD agitation, in 1984 with the failed referendum, and in 1986 after Benazir's return.

He had little respect for state institutions. The judiciary met with rough treatment at his hands. He appointed and dismissed judges at his sweet will. He treated the Constitution no better than a scrap of paper which he could keep amending to his convenience. He made basic changes in the constitutional structure as it stood originally and succeeded in changing the face of the Constitution beyond recognition.

Zia's emphasis on Islam helped him create a constituency based on the support of the Islamic ethos among Pakistan's clergy, sections of the middle-class, and other conservative segments of society. He was not above exploitation of religious sentiment for his narrow political ends. Zia spent eleven years trying to legitimize his position and, in this endeavour, changed the face of the Constitution, destroyed and debased institutions like the judiciary, created divisions that did not exist before, and aggravated the divisions that already existed in society. The Muhajir Qaumi Movement (MQM) is his gift and legacy to the nation. The country was already burdened with the frictions of four nationalities and he helped create a fifth one. His objective was temporary and narrow, to create a balancing political force against the PPP in the province of Sindh, but the mischief that he helped create has opened the wounds of the nation. He caused the escalation of conflict between *shias* and *sunnis* which was dormant before him. His policies caused schisms within the *sunnis*, with militant wings belonging to different *sunni* schools, going for each other's throat. Various religious groups were encouraged to demand that their rival groups be declared non-Muslim. Thus, a disgusting trail of *fatwas* and demands, like the *Anjuman-e-Sipah-e-Sahaba*, a self-styled representative of the *sunni* sect demanding declaration of the *shia* sect as non-Muslim, and the Deobandi sect clamouring for *zikris*, *Ismailis*, etc. to be declared *kafirs*, surfaced in the already strife-ridden political permutations of Pakistan. Hiding his guile and brutality under the mask of humility and ostentatious religiosity, Zia relied on two powerful pillars of authoritarianism, military force and obscurantism. These were recklessly employed to suppress every legitimate demand for human rights, constitutionalism, and federalism in the country.[39]

The Afghan war and its debilitating consequences for Pakistan are Zia's most dangerous legacy. Pakistan was burdened with the support of more than three million Afghan *mohajirs*. Due to Pakistan's deep involvement in the Afghan war effort, Pakistan became a target for gun running and drugs. The Klashnikov culture and escalation in crime throughout Pakistan are a consequence of the Afghan war. The heroin culture, unknown to Pakistan before him at such a scale, has taken root. The internal conflicts of Afghanistan and their spillover into in Pakistan are constant sources of worry, anxiety, and tension.

In his quest for legitimacy, Zia let loose retrogressive forces in Pakistan which continue to bedevil any attempt towards progress. In order to build his constituencies, he mobilized a class of so-called '*ulema*' and tried to create courts for them in the name of *Kazi* courts. He succeeded in creating a parallel court structure in the name of Islam by establishing the Federal Shariat Court which has clearly undermined the institution of the judiciary. His Islamization of laws was nothing but window dressing. The Islamization of banking laws has only changed the name of 'interest' to 'mark-up' and made it all the more atrocious. The law of evidence was only given an

Islamic name without any material change in its content. By re-arranging the chapters and sections of the Evidence Act of 1872, he called it '*Qanoon-e-Shahadat*' and thus delivered on his promise to Islamize the law of evidence. He believed in the form rather than in the spirit of Islam. All this proved his innate and inherent hypocrisy. He had no qualms about lying publicly and kept on making false promises to the nation to hold elections. Zia could recite from or refer to the Holy Quran and tell a lie in the same breath.

The army remained his primary power base and he headed it for over twelve years, the longest in the history of Pakistan. Three characteristics made Zia somewhat different both as Chief of Army Staff and as President. One was his relationship with his '*rufaqa*' (colleagues), which was defined by a close camaraderie and a relaxed bond. The other was the degree of trust and delegation of authority to his *de facto* number two, General Arif, for a long period of almost seven years. Another important difference between Zia and his military predecessor was in his being probably the first representative of a new generation of 'native' Generals. He was unlike the Sandhurst trained, stiff upper-lipped Anglicized Generals of Ayub's times. Deep religiosity apart, he was also the first of his type who spoke Urdu without an English accent! Zia and his colleagues were mostly the product of Short Service Commission given by the British during the last years of World War II and therefore, lacked the requisite training of a soldier in having a sense of honour to keep his word.

With his sudden death on 17 August 1988, Zia left Pakistan in the same state of uncertainty and fear of the future that existed eleven years earlier when he seized power in a military coup.

It has been mentioned earlier that after the sudden death of Zia, the transition to democracy took place constitutionally. Ghulam Ishaq Khan, who was chairman of the Senate at that time, stepped in as acting President. He announced that the general elections fixed by Zia for 16 and 19 November for National and Provincial Assemblies respectively, would be held on schedule. He also promised to hold free, fair, and impartial elections.

Any attempt on the part of the army leaders to take over the control of the country and reimpose martial law after Zia's death could have been counter-productive. Recent examples in other Asian countries, namely the Philippines and South Korea, also manifested dangers of continuing dictatorship, particularly when people were eagerly expecting democratic revival. Also, there were signs of dissent in the armed forces after Zia's death. Any action taken hurriedly could have been costly for the military. Under the circumstances, General Beg's decision appeared to be the only sensible option available to him at the time.[40]

Dissolution of National Assembly Challenged

The major constitutional issue arising out of the RCO as modified by the Eighth Amendment was the exercise of discretionary powers by the President to dissolve the National Assembly before the expiry of the term for which it was elected. It emerged as the leading problem causing constitutional crises no less than four times within a period of eight years. The exercise of this power led to serious conflicts between two top constitutional functionaries, the President and the Prime Minister. As a result, none of the National Assemblies (elected in the years 1985, 1988, 1990, and 1993) could complete their full term of five years and all of them were dissolved prematurely. Each time the dissolution of the National Assembly was challenged before the superior courts but with different results.

Order of Dissolution of National Assembly

This discretionary power was exercised for the first time after the lifting of the last martial law on 29 May 1988, by General Zia. In exercise of his power under Article 58(2)(b) of the Constitution, Zia, through a short order, dissolved the National Assembly and as a consequence, the Junejo government was dismissed. The order of dissolution said:

> WHEREAS the objects and purposes for which the National Assembly was elected have not been fulfilled;
> AND WHEREAS the law and order in the country have broken down to an alarming extent resulting in tragic loss of innumerable valuable lives as well as loss of property;
> AND WHEREAS the life, property, honour and security of the citizens of Pakistan have been rendered totally unsafe and the integrity and ideology of Pakistan have been seriously endangered;
> AND WHEREAS public morality has deteriorated to unprecedented level;
> AND WHEREAS in my opinion a situation has arisen in which the government of the federation cannot be carried on in accordance with the provisions of the Constitution and an appeal to the electorate is necessary.
> NOW THEREFORE, I, General Muhammad Zia-ul-Haq, President of Pakistan in exercise of the powers conferred on me by clause (2)(b) of Article 58 of the Constitution of the Islamic Republic of Pakistan hereby dissolve the National Assembly with immediate effect and in consequence thereof the Cabinet also stands dissolved forthwith.[41]

Challenge before the Lahore High Court

This order of the President was challenged before the Lahore High Court as unconstitutional and without lawful authority and of no legal effect, in a Constitution petition which was finally decided by a full Bench of the Lahore High Court in the case titled '*Muhammad Sharif v Federation of Pakistan*'.[42] The Lahore High Court held in this case that a perusal of the grounds mentioned would make it quite clear that these could be urged any time for dissolving the National Assembly. The Court observed that such draconian discretion was not envisaged by the Constitution which provided for a free people. The Court noticed that on 25 May 1988, the President had called for the session of the National Assembly, and then only four days later, on 29

May, he ordered its dissolution. What had happened within these four days the Court asked. It was held that in these circumstances, it was not possible to sustain the order of dissolution.

The next question for determination by the Court was: what relief could be granted after holding the order of dissolution as unsustainable? The Court declined to grant any relief on the rationale that the dissolution meant the death of the assembly and that what had been done to death could not be brought back to life. Thus, no declaration could bring the dead to life. Other factors that were taken note of and perhaps weighed heavily with the Court while declining relief, were that, (i) the assembly was elected by excluding political parties from participating in the process of elections; (ii) all the political parties were, at the time, demanding fresh elections; (iii) the concerned parties had accepted the fact of dissolution; (iv) no responsible person, such as the Leader of the House or the Speaker of the National Assembly, had challenged the action; and (v) the entire nation was looking forward to the ensuing general elections including the leading members of the dissolved assembly.

When the counsels in the case were asked if they could cite any example from anywhere in the world where a dissolved assembly had been restored by a court, they failed to cite any such example. The Court, therefore, considered proper not to frustrate the will of the people who were all geared to go to the polls. It was held that it would be a very unwise and unjudicious exercise of discretion to restore the assembly and, for these reasons, the Court declined the request for the restoration of the Assembly and the Cabinet.

Appeal before the Supreme Court

The judgment of the Lahore High Court was challenged before the Supreme Court of Pakistan which finally decided the matter in the case titled '*Federation of Pakistan v Haji Muhammad Saifullah Khan*'.[43] The Supreme Court held that the exercise of the discretionary power by the President in dissolving the National Assembly could be called into question before the Court and the Court could examine whether such discretionary power was exercised reasonably, fairly, and in terms of the statute and its spirit. If it was not so exercised, the Court could pass an appropriate judgment striking down the exercise of such power for being unreasonable and unfair. It was also held that the discretion conceded to the President by Article 58(2)(b) of the Constitution could not be regarded as absolute but was to be deemed to be qualified in the sense that it was to be exercised in consonance with the objects of the law that conferred it. The mere fact that the circumstances about the impugned action had political over-tones, it was observed, would not prevent the Court from interfering with it provided it was shown that the action taken was violative of the Constitution. It was also held that the superior courts in the country have an inherent duty together with the appurtenant power in any case coming before them to ascertain and enforce the provisions of the Constitution and as this duty is derived from the express provisions of the Constitution itself, therefore, the Court would not be deterred from performing its constitutional duty merely because the action impugned had political implications. Thus, the Supreme Court upheld the judgment of the Lahore High Court and found that the prerequisite prescribed for the exercise of the powers in this behalf did not exist and, therefore, the action of dissolution was not justified in law.

On the question of relief, the Supreme Court upheld the judgment of the Lahore High Court and denied the relief of restoration of the National Assembly and the Cabinet.

A major gain from these judgments was that the action of the President in dissolving the National Assembly at his discretion was subjected to judicial review by the superior courts. The order of the President was struck down as unjustified and unreasonable. These judgments, however, came after the death of Zia on 17 August 1988. One of his sons had the audacity to boast publicly that no such judgments would have come had his father been alive. Nevertheless, it cannot be denied that a healthy beginning had been made by the superior courts to build on later on.

Law Denying Election Symbols to Political Parties Struck Down

Election symbols allocated to political parties play an invaluable role in a predominantly illiterate society by helping the voter to identify the political parties, their candidates, and the issues involved, and in facilitating the casting of votes.[44] Although a provision of the law on election to the National and Provincial Assemblies allowed allocation of prescribed symbols to each contesting candidate, there was no specific provision in the law for allocation of a symbol to a political party.[45] This provision of law was challenged as invalid by Benazir before the Supreme Court being violative of the fundamental rights of freedom of association under Article 17 of the Constitution. It was contended that the citizens of Pakistan enjoyed the fundamental right of not only forming a political party but also of its functioning as such. This right necessarily extended to its participation at all stages of the constitutional process of elections, culminating in the formation of the government in a parliamentary system. It was thus contended that the provision of allocation of election symbols to candidates and not political parties fielding candidates in the elections, was violative of Article 17 of the Constitution. It was further argued that denial of the election symbol to a political party or to a combination of political parties, was frustrating the dictum of the Supreme Court in *Benazir Bhutto v Federation of Pakistan*[46] upholding the right of citizens to form and run political parties.

The Supreme Court accepted the petition, holding that the provisions of section 21(1)(b) of the Representation of the People Act, 1976 were violative of the fundamental right enshrined in Article 17(2) of the Constitution insofar as they failed to recognize the existence and participation of political parties in the process of elections, particularly in the matter of allocation of symbols and, for that reason, would be void to that extent.[47] In the words of Dr Nasim Hasan Shah J.

Section 21, as it now stands, is neither cognizant of existence of political party, which alone can enable it to effectively participate in the process of elections, renders nugatory the right to form a political party and accomplish its objectives, namely, to organize and fight an election with a view to capture political power.

Party-based General Elections, 1988

The elections to the National and Provincial Assemblies in Pakistan were held in a more or less peaceful atmosphere on 16 and 19 November 1988 respectively. They appeared, by and large, to be free and impartial as is evident from the almost universal acceptance of the verdict by all the political parties. There was some resentment on the condition of identity cards being made mandatory for voters and allegations of rigging in some areas. Compared to the 1977 polls when Bhutto's Pakistan People's Party (PPP) blatantly resorted to rigging that led to violent agitations and eventually resulted in the overthrow of Bhutto's government, these elections appeared to be peaceful and impartial.

One noteworthy aspect of the elections was that the percentage of voting was rather low—less than 50 per cent. This was in contrast to the earlier elections of 1970 (58 per cent), 1977 (55 per cent), and 1985 (53 per cent), the last being held on a non-party basis. It showed a declining trend in voters' participation. The reasons could be general public apathy towards politicians and the political process, the gradual withdrawal of womenfolk, at least among the uneducated, to their shells, or the strict implementation of the condition to produce the identity card at the time of casting one's vote.

The results of the National Assembly elections confirmed earlier fears that no party would be in a position to command an absolute majority in the Parliament. Determined campaigns were launched by the two political tendencies, one spearheaded by the PPP of the Bhuttos and the other by the Islamic Democratic Alliance or the Islami Jamhoori Ittehad (IJI), led by the ruling Pakistan Muslim League. In fact, pre-poll assessments had pointed to such a possibility. The PPP assessment wing comprising eminent party men and a few US experts, had predicted in early November that it would get about 101 seats in the National Assembly elections which was eight short of an absolute majority. (Incidently, the assessment had predicted the sure defeat of IJI leader and former Prime Minister Muhammad Khan Junejo.)

A poll survey conducted by the mass circulation Urdu daily *Jang* had concluded that a coalition government was likely to be formed after the elections surico. According to the survey, the PPP was expected to get 82 and the IJI 61 seats only, far short of a comfortable majority.

However, when the votes were counted, the PPP turned out to be the largest single party, having 93 seats out of the 205 seats for which polling was held, followed by IJI that won 55 seats. More than 80 per cent of the latter's strength came from the Punjab. However, the PPP's popularity was balanced at the national level, the populous Punjab contributing 52 seats, followed by Sindh with 31 seats. The PPP's national image was further reinforced as the IJI failed to muster even a single seat from Sindh whereas the PPP improved its position in the NWFP and registered its presence in Balochistan. The voting pattern in provincial elections held three days later was more or less a repetition of the national elections except for improvements by the IJI in the province of the Punjab and in the NWFP. While the PPP maintained its two-thirds majority in Sindh, in the Punjab it was relegated to second position unlike the National Assembly elections. In the NWFP, too, the PPP slid down. In Balochistan there was no change. However, in the overall tally of Provincial Assembly seats, the PPP had 187 seats and remained ahead of the IJI which had 146 seats. In other words, the PPP had vindicated its position as the largest national political party in the country. This became all the more significant in view of the fact that the other political force, the IJI, was an alliance of nine disparate political parties or groups, the main constituents being the Pakistan Muslim League (PML) led by Junejo, the Jamaat-i-Islami (JI) led by Qazi Hussain Ahmad, the National People's Party (NPP) of Ghulam Mustafa Jatoi, and the Independent Parliamentary Group (IPG) of Fakhar Imam.

Pakistan: National Assembly Elections, 16 November 1988
Results—Party Position

	Punjab	Sindh	NWFP	Balochistan	FATA	Islamabad	Total
No.of seats	115	46	26	11	8	1	205
PPP	52	31	9	1	-	-	93
IJI	45	-	8	2	-	-	55
JUI(FR)	-	-	3	4	-	-	7
JUI(D)	-	-	1	-	-	-	1
PAI	3	-	-	-	-	-	3
PDP	1	-	-	-	-	-	1
ANP	-	-	2	-	-	-	2
NPP(K)	1	-	-	-	-	-	1
MQM	-	13	-	-	-	-	13
BNA	-	-	-	2	-	-	2
Independents	12	2	3	2	8	1	27

Pakistan: Provincial Assembly Elections, 19 November 1988
Results—Party Position

Parties	Punjab	Sindh	NWFP	Balochistan
IJI	108	1	28	8
PPP	94	67	22	4
PAI	2	-	-	-
PDP	2	-	-	-
JUI(FR)	1	-	2	11
NPP(K)	1	-	-	-
PPI	-	1	-	-
BNA	-	-	-	10
PNP	-	-	-	2
Watan	-	-	-	1
ANP	-	-	13	-
Independents	32	31*	15	4
Total	240	100	80	40

* included 26 MQM

The Muhajir Qaumi Movement's (MQM) success stands out, perhaps, as the most significant, yet not a surprising development, in the 1988 general elections. The MQM is essentially an ethnic political movement of Urdu-speaking Muslim immigrants from northern and central India who settled in the Sindh province when Pakistan was carved out of the Indian subcontinent and was developed and encouraged by Zia to counteract the popularity of the PPP in Sindh.

NOTES

1. Ms Benazir Bhutto was said to be suffering from some ear ailment and Mrs Nusrat Bhutto was said to be suffering from malignancy.
2. In the first Afghan War (1839–1845), the British forces did occupy Afghanistan and removed its King, Amir Dost Mohammad Khan, but could not hold it for long and had to leave it after heavy loss of men. Their attempts to do so in Second Afghan War (1879–80) and in 1919–20, during King Amanullah's regime, failed.
3. He became Secretary-General of the Communist Party in March 1985 on the death of Chernenkov.
4. Perestroika.
5. Glasnost.
6. It is said that Benazir had agreed to participate in the political leaders conference on the condition that Zia would not come or even be seen around the conference area.
7. The signing of the Geneva Accord was delayed as a result of Zia's disagreement with Junejo.
8. Baxter, Craig & Wasti, Syed Razi, *Pakistan—Authoritarianism in the 1980s*, Vanguard Books, Lahore. 1991, pp. 61-2.
9. Ordinance No. XLII of 1979.
10. Ordinance No. LIII of 1979.
11. Political Parties (Amendment) Ordinance, 1985. Ordinance III of 1985. PLD 1985 Central Statutes 567.

12. President's Order 20 of 1978. PLD 1978 Central Statutes 171.
13. Benazir Bhutto v Federation of Pakistan. PLD 1988 S.C. 416.
14. Under the 1973 Constitution originally, an Amendment Bill in the Constitution could only originate in the National Assembly and could be passed by a two-thirds majority of the total membership of the National Assembly and a majority of the total membership of the Senate. The RCO substituted Article 239 (relating to Constitution Amendment Bill) and allowed a Constitutional Amendment Bill to originate in any House and both the Houses are required to pass the Amendment Bill by two-third majority of their total membership. It was also provided that after the Bill was passed by the Parliament, the same was to be transmitted to the Provincial Assemblies each of which was to pass it by a majority of the total number of its members present and voting. P.O.20 of 1985 deleted the role of the Provincial Assemblies in the Amendment procedure except in case of alteration in the limits of a province.
15. PLD 1973 S.C. 49.
16. Ghulam Mustafa Khar v Pakistan, PLD 1988 Lahore 49.
17. Federation of Pakistan v Ghulam Mustafa Khar, PLD 1989 S.C. 26.
18. Article 4 of the Constitution embodies 'due process clause'.
19. National Bank of Pakistan v Wafaqi Mohtasib (Ombudsman), PLD 1992 Karachi 339.
20. Benazir Bhutto v Federation of Pakistan, PLD 1988 S.C. 416.
21. Joshi, V.T., *Pakistan: Zia to Benazir*, 1995, Konark Publishers, New Delhi, p. 77.
22. Namely, Khakan Abbasi.
23. Husain, Mushahid, *Pakistan's Politics—The Zia Years*, 1990, Progressive Publishers, Ichhra, Lahore. pp. 245-7.
24. Arif, General Khalid Mahmud, *Working with Zia: Pakistan's Power Politics, 1977-1988* 1995, Oxford University Press, Karachi, p. 392.
25. Ibid., pp. 394, 395 and 396.
26. *The Nation*, 31 May 1988.
27. Article 48(5).
28. Article 48(1).
29. Enforcement of Shariah Ordinance, 1988. (Ordinance I of 1988) PLD 1988 Central Statutes 29.
30. Article 49(1).
31. Husain, Mushahid, *Pakistan's Politics—The Zia Years*, 1990, Progressive Publishers, Ichhra, Lahore, p. 134.
32. Ibid., p. 132.
33. He offered his parting colleagues diplomatic offices like Ambassadorships etc. He also gave them commercial and residential plots of very high value so that they could retire in comfort.
34. Burki, Shahid Javed and Baxter, Craig, *Pakistan Under the Military*, 1991, Westview Press, Boulder, Colorado, p. 20.
35. Husain, Mushahid, *Pakistan's Politics—The Zia Years*, *supra*, note 31, p. 266.
36. Ibid.
37. Joshi, V.T., *Pakistan: Zia to Benazir*, *supra*, note 21, p. 55.
38. Hymen, Anthony, *Pakistan: Zia and After*, 1989, Abhinav Publications, New Delhi. p. 105.
39. Maluka, Zulfiqar Khalid, *The Myth of Constitutionalism in Pakistan*, 1995, Oxford University Press, Karachi. p. 276.
40. Hyman, Anthony, *Pakistan: Zia and After*, 1989, Abhinav Publications, New Delhi. p. 120.
41. Reproduced on pp. 756-7 in PLD 1988 Lahore 725.
42. PLD 1988 Lahore 725.
43. PLD 1989 S.C. 166.
44. Chaudhry, Barrister A.G., *The Leading Cases in Constitutional Law*, 1995, Sehar Publishers, Lahore. p. 258.
45. The Representation of the People Act, 1976, Section 21(1)(b).
46. PLD 1988 S.C. 416.
47. Benazir Bhutto v The Federation of Pakistan, PLD 1989 S.C. 66.

PART VII

THE POST-ZIA PERIOD: AUGUST 1988 ONWARDS

31

BENAZIR'S FIRST TERM: A DIVIDED HOUSE

It is apparent from the earlier chapter that the discussion polls gave a divided verdict between the PPP and the IJI. In the National Assembly, with 207 general seats,[1] the PPP did not get a majority but emerged as the largest single party with 93 seats, followed by 55 seats taken by the IJI. The PPP still required 11 seats to form a majority. The independents had secured 27 seats which was a very important factor because they could tip the balance either way and each one of them was free to make his or her own choice. Another important factor was the MQM which secured 13 seats in the National Assembly, all from the urban areas of Karachi and Hyderabad. Other political parties did not fare well at the national polls. Only JUI (Fazlur Rahman Group) secured 7 seats, 3 from NWFP and 4 from the Pakhtoon areas of Balochistan.

The PPP, headed by Benazir Bhutto, faced the task of forming alliances with other political parties or independents to be able to show its majority in the National Assembly so as to be invited to form the government. Nawaz Sharif, head of the IJI, made an announcement on the day following the national polls that the IJI would form the new government. It was difficult to see how, with 55 seats out of 207, the IJI could form a government or obtain a vote of confidence. Nawaz Sharif was apparently relying on acting President Ghulam Ishaq to manoeuvre things in his favour. He had been helped in the planning of the elections by the establishment, particularly by the ISI and as the results proved, the number of seats the IJI had won were much above its expectations.

Benazir Nominated Prime Minister

The crucial factor in the power equation was the presidential power to nominate the prime minister. Under the original scheme of the Constitution, the prime minister was to be elected by the National Assembly in its first session immediately after the election of the Speaker and the Deputy Speaker. The RCO amended the Constitution and the president was empowered to appoint, at his discretion, any member of the National Assembly as prime minister who, in his opinion, could command the confidence of the majority of the National Assembly.[2] This provision was modified by the Eighth Amendment and this power of the President was limited to five years, that is, until 20 March 1990, after which date the President had to invite that member of the National Assembly who commanded the confidence of the majority of its members in a poll held for the purpose, to take over as prime minister.[3]

Thus, in 1988, the president had the discretionary power to appoint the prime minister, an unfettered power particularly in the event of a divided verdict where no party had an absolute majority. No doubt, the person appointed as prime minister had to obtain a vote of confidence from the National Assembly within a period of sixty days,[4] but this could be managed by those who held the reins of power. The independents, in particular, were likely to go with whoever was nominated by the president and thus had been brought into power. Understandably, the IJI was counting on this presidential power. If the president had nominated someone from the IJI, he would have time (sixty days), to win over fifty other members to form a majority and to obtain a vote of confidence. But Ishaq, a consummate bureaucrat who had survived under all governments in Pakistan and had served in nearly every important administrative position, had other ideas. He was, after all, only an acting president and was aspiring for a full five-year term of his own. The IJI was in his pocket because it was a creation of the establishment that he headed. Ishaq had good rapport with the chiefs of the armed forces, so he found his options open. He could obtain the votes of the IJI and the others that the establishment could deliver to him. The only opposition that he could face was from the PPP. Ishaq could make a deal with the PPP by appointing Benazir Prime Minister. With the help of the establishment, he had already delivered a majority in the Provincial Assembly of the Punjab to the IJI, guaranteeing Chief Ministership to Nawaz Sharif who could be used to contain Benazir Bhutto at the centre.

Benazir had her own reasons to seek power. She received two sets of advice. Perhaps the more rational one was not to make a compromise and not to seek the office of prime minister at a price. She was only thirty-five-years-old and could bide her time. With a hostile government in the Punjab under the protection of the establishment and the President, and the establishment breathing down her neck, she could not succeed and would fall into the trap of those who wanted to prove that she was not up to the mark. The other advice was that she should not miss the opportunity to take power. A majority of members of her party had suffered for eleven years at the hands of Zia and his *junta* and they were desperate to get into power regardless of the terms and conditions being offered to them. Another factor was Benazir's family. She had been married a year earlier into the family of Zardaris of Nawabshah who had suspect credentials. Asif Zardari had not married her to do opposition politics. He had his own agenda and wanted immediate power. Benazir went for the second option and embarked upon the course to seek the office of prime minister. Her first step was to forge alliances with the MQM and the JUI (FR). These alliances gave her a clear majority in the National Assembly. Some of the independents were also won over.

However, the most important move was the deal with Ishaq Khan who was offered full support of the PPP in the forthcoming presidential election. This eventually resulted in Benazir's appointment as Prime Minister of Pakistan on 1 December 1988.

Z.A. Bhutto's Political Heir

Benazir, the eldest child of Zulfiqar Ali Bhutto, was born on 21 June 1953. An aristocrat by birth and heir to the large land holdings of Bhutto, she studied at the Radcliffe College at Harvard University. As a student, she was a Pakistani projecting her country's case about Kashmir by highlighting India's hegemonistic designs on Pakistan and in pleading for the right of self determination for the Kashmiris. She spent four years at Oxford University, the first three devoted to a gruelling graduate course in politics, philosophy, and economics. In the last year she took a post-graduate course in international law and diplomacy. At Oxford, Benazir had three months tenure as president of the prestigious Oxford Union, beginning in January 1977.[5]

Benazir wanted to apply to the foreign service of Pakistan but her father's execution drove her to a political career marked by struggle and torment. She remained in solitary confinement in Sukkur Jail in 1981 and was then confined in Karachi Central Jail. She was then moved to Al-Murtaza, the family residence in Larkana, which was declared a sub-jail. She spent two years in this sub-jail which was far better than the solitary confinement she had suffered earlier. In 1984, Benazir was allowed to travel, ostensibly for the treatment of an infection in her ears.

After the lifting of martial law in December 1985, Benazir returned home in April 1986 with a crowd of half a million receiving her at the Lahore airport. Her tour of the country drew huge crowds everywhere and her popularity indicated the potential to win a national election. In 1987, Benazir married Asif Zardari, of the Zardari family of Nawabshah, who had the reputation of being a playboy. His father, Hakim Ali Zardari, was a member of the NAP with a dubious reputation. She gave birth to a son in 1988, who was named Bilawal. Although Benazir's success in the general elections was primarily the sympathy vote elicited after her father's execution, as a young, attractive, and educated woman, she had a charisma of her own, which must have also contributed to her success.

Benazir had been groomed by her father from the very beginning to be his successor, which is why he asked her to study political science and economics at Harvard and Oxford and took her with him to Simla in 1972 with a view to exposing her to international diplomacy. Even in his death cell, he wrote several letters to Benazir designed to educate her in history, government, and diplomacy. One of his letters to her dated 21 June 1978, written from a death cell in the District Jail of Rawalpindi, was highly educative, full of examples of international diplomacy, and modern-day problems faced by governments, particularly in the third world.

At the end, Bhutto recalls his shooting of a wild parrot in 1957 and goes on to give the following compliments and message to Benazir and to his other children:[6]

> When the parrot fell to the ground near the terrace, you cried your eyes out. You had it buried in your presence. You cried and cried. You refused to have your meals. A dead parrot in the winter of 1957 in Larkana made a little girl weep in sorrow. Twenty-one years later, that little girl has grown into a young lady with nerves of steel to valorously confront the terror of the longest night of tyranny. Truly, you have proved beyond doubt that the blood of warriors runs in your veins.

> What I write is full of infirmities. I have been in solitary confinement for twelve months and in a death cell for three months, deprived of all facilities. I have written much of this by resting the paper on my thigh in unbearable heat. I have no reference material or library. I have rarely seen the blue sky. The quotations are from the few books I was permitted to read and from the journals and newspapers you and your mother bring once a week during your visits to my suffocating cell. I am not making excuses for my deficiencies but it is very difficult to rely on a fading memory in such physical and mental conditions.
>
> I am fifty years old and you are exactly half my age. By the time you reach my age, you must accomplish twice as much as I have achieved for the people. Mir Ghulam Murtaza, my son and heir, is not with me. Nor are Shah Nawaz and Sanam-Seema. This message has to be shared with them as a part of my heritage. Mir Sain is a close friend of the son of Robert Kennedy. That youthful leader of America wrote:
>
> 'Every generation has its central concern, whether to end war, erase racial injustice, or improve the condition of the working man. Today's young people appear to have chosen for their concern the dignity of the individual human being, they demand a limitation upon excessive power. They demand a government that speaks directly and honestly to its citizens. The possibilities are too great, the stakes too high, to bequeath to the coming generation only the prophetic lament of Tennyson:
>
> Ah, what shall I be at fifty, should nature keep me alive, if I find the world so bitter, when I am but twenty-five?'

Ishaq Elected President

According to the consummation of the deal between Ishaq and Benazir, the PPP voted for Ishaq. Ishaq had also been adopted as the candidate of the IJI. Other candidates, of whom Nawabzada Nasrullah was the most prominent, were ignored. Nawabzada's party was a constituent of the MRD which had fought alongside the PPP against Zia for the restoration of democracy. The PPP ignored its old ally in favour of an old bureaucrat who used his position to make a deal.

Ishaq won the election with an overwhelming majority. Four candidates, including Ishaq, Nawabzada Nasrullah Khan, Ahmad E.H. Jaffar, and Muhammad Nauroz Malik, took part in the polls. The votes they received were counted according to the procedure laid down in the Constitution. The results were:[7]

1. Ahmad E.H. Jaffar	6 votes
2. Ghulam Ishaq Khan	603 votes
3. Muhammad Nauroz Khan Malik	3 votes
4. Nawabzada Nasrullah Khan	140 votes

Despite the fact that Ishaq hailed from NWFP, the Awami National Party (ANP) decided to support the Nawabzada from the Punjab. This was done apparently because ANP beleved in the political credentials of Nawabzada Nasrullah instead of Ishaq's whom they called a technocrat and a staunch supporter of the legacy of Zia. Similarly,

Jamiat-i-Ulema-i-Islam (JUI) declared its support for Nawabzada as a more suitable candidate. The JUI believed that Ishaq being a one-time comrade of Zia should not be supported because he could prove dangerous to the prospects of democracy in Pakistan.

Provincial Governments Formed

In Sindh, the PPP had won 67 out of a 100 general seats in the Provincial Assembly. Out of 31 independents elected to the Sindh Assembly, 26 belonged to the MQM. They had not used the party ticket but the voters in Karachi and Hyderabad knew that though independent, they represented the MQM. Hence, the PPP had no difficulty in forming a government. In any case, the Chief Ministers were not to be appointed by the Governors but were to be elected by the respective provincial assemblies. The period until the Governors could appoint chief ministers had lapsed on 20 March 1988.[8] Hence, Qaim Ali Shah, a nominee of the PPP, was easily elected as the Chief Minister of Sindh.

In the NWFP, the situation was complex. No one political party had won an absolute majority in the Provincial Assembly. Out of 80 general seats, the IJI had won the highest number of seats, 28, followed by the PPP which won 22, and the ANP which won 13 seats. As many as 15 independents had been elected. In this situation, IJI and ANP could form the government. Benazir approached Wali Khan, head of the ANP, to form a coalition government and the offer was accepted. Hence, the PPP, in coalition with ANP, by winning over a number of independents, formed the government with Aftab Sherpao as the Chief Minister. The coalition between the PPP and ANP did not last very long in the NWFP and after some bickering, the ANP withdrew from the government. However, Sherpao held on as Chief Minister with a paper thin majority by holding on to the independents and by making some dents in the opposition.

The situation in the Punjab was the most difficult for the PPP. Despite winning more seats in the Punjab in the National Assembly as against the IJI (52 to 45), the situation reversed in the Provincial Assembly. The IJI got 108 seats as against 94 seats won by the PPP. With the help of most of the independents (32 in number), the IJI was able to form a government in the Punjab with Nawaz Sharif as the Chief Minister. The PPP did everything within its power to prevent this from happening but failed. The IJI had support from the President and the establishment who were interested in keeping Benazir in check by having a government of the opposition installed in the Punjab.

In Balochistan, the situation was even more complex. Out of 40 general seats, 11 went to JUI (FR), 10 to Balochistan National Alliance (BNA), 8 to IJI, 4 to the PPP, and the remaining seven to minor political parties and independents. It was difficult to form a government, particularly when the two largest parties, JUI and BNA, did not see eye to eye with one another. The Provincial Assembly met on 2 December 1988 to elect the Speaker and the Deputy Speaker of the assembly and, after that, to elect the Chief Minister of the province. Out of a total of 44 members of the assembly, the Speaker and 42 members were present. Mir Zafarullah Khan Jamali was proposed as Chief Minister. He received 21 votes in favour and 21 votes against him. The Speaker issued a certificate declaring him elected by securing 22 votes including the casting vote of the Speaker. In this way, he formed a very fragile government in the first week of December 1988.

Dissolution of the Balochistan Provincial Assembly

The Balochistan Chief Minister, Jamali was in a vulnerable position and he was in fear of losing his office on a vote of no-confidence at any time. On 15 December 1988, he advised the Governor to dissolve the Assembly. The dissolution was challenged on the ground that Jamali had not obtained the majority vote of the Provincial Assembly, which meant that he had not obtained a vote of confidence and, therefore, he was not empowered to advise the dissolution of the Assembly.

A full Bench of the Balochistan High Court accepted this contention, thus holding that unless the Chief Minister had obtained a vote of confidence from a majority of the total members of the assembly (not merely a majority of those present and voting), he could not advise the Governor to dissolve the Provincial Assembly as he was not a Chief Minister within the meaning of Article 112 of the Constitution.[9]

This judgment opened the door to challenge an order of dissolution of a Provincial Assembly even where it was done on the advice of the Chief Minister. Prior to this case, it was generally believed that dissolution of an assembly, National or Provincial, if based on the advice of the Prime Minister or a Chief Minister (as the case may be), could not be subject to judicial review by the courts.

The Haji Saifullah Case

After the Junejo government was dismissed by Zia in May 1988, Zia chose to appoint a caretaker government without a prime minister. Thus, Pakistan was without a prime minister for more than six months till Benazir was sworn in in December 1988. This led to a serious constitutional question as to whether the federal government was functioning legally and constitutionally during this period and whether the actions taken and the orders passed during this period could be regarded as valid. The Supreme Court considered this matter in '*Federation of Pakistan v Muhammad Saifullah Khan*'[10] and held that the office of the prime minister was necessary at all times for running the affairs of the country and that the President should have appointed a prime minister to head a caretaker cabinet. It was also observed that the absence of the prime minister from a caretaker cabinet altered the character of the Constitution from a parliamentary democracy to a presidential system of government and was tantamount to violation and breach of the essential features of the Constitution which the courts could neither countenance nor condone. However, the legal consequences of the individual acts done or actions already taken and suffered were left to be decided in individual cases when they were brought before the court.

This judgment led the federal government to conclude that all appointments, including judicial ones, were invalid during the period when there was no prime minister. A press note to this effect was issued by the Law Ministry. As a result, more than thirty judges of the superior courts appointed during the said period did not function for about a week. This matter was resolved in a review petition[11] in which the Supreme Court held that a portion of the press note did not appear to reflect accurately the judgment of the Supreme Court insofar as it stated the consequences of the judgment to the effect that actions taken, orders passed, or appointments made between 29 May 1988 and 2 December 1988 by the President, which were required to be taken, passed, or made on the advice of the Prime Minister were illegal and required regularization and re-affirmation awaiting which the appointees should suspend the performance of their official duties. The Court held that such relief was in fact requested from the Court but was not granted.[12] The findings, it was observed, on all matters in controversy were recorded to remove all doubts and ambiguities with regard to distribution of functions and powers under the constitution for guidance in the future.

Motion of 'No-Confidence' against Benazir

As already noted, it did not take long for Benazir and the PPP to fall out with their allies. The alliance with the MQM did not last long and the latter abrogated its eleven-month old accord with the PPP alleging that the PPP had failed to implement even a single clause. It entered into a secret agreement with the IJI which was signed in September 1989.[13] The Awami National Party (ANP) of Wali Khan, though ideologically close to the PPP, also fell out with the PPP due to the latter's style of governance. The government in Punjab led by Nawaz Sharif of the IJI was already hostile and, with the support of the MQM and the ANP, the common front calling itself Combined Opposition Parties (COP), gained strength and moved a motion of no-confidence against the Benazir government.

On 23 October 1989, the COP handed over to the Secretary of the National Assembly a notice for a no-confidence resolution against Benazir. It claimed the support of 129 to 135 MNAs (out of a total of 237) including 14 MQM members.[14] However, the leading members of the PPP expressed confidence that the opposition's no-confidence motion would be defeated.[15] Nevertheless, the notice submitted for the vote of no-confidence was signed by 86 MNAs belonging to all the constituents of the COP, including some independents.[16] On 24 October, the resolution was formally submitted to the National Assembly and 98 opposition members stood up in its support. The Speaker granted leave to move the resolution and 1 November was fixed for voting on it.[17]

The no-confidence motion set the stage for a showdown between the government and the opposition. The opposition, with the tacit support of the President and the resources of the provincial government of the Punjab under IJI chief Nawaz Sharif, embarked upon an endeavour to win over an adequate number of members to carry the motion. The government of Balochistan, headed by Nawab Muhammad Akbar Khan Bugti, threw in its lot in favour of the no-confidence motion. The government took steps to ensure that there were no dissensions in its ranks and that some members of the opposition were induced to switch their allegiance. There were allegations that the government physically prevented members of the opposition from attending the session of the National Assembly during the vote on the no-confidence motion. The opposition even sought the support of the army to protect its MNAs and approached the President who assured them of the maintenance of law and order. Meanwhile, more than 100 MNAs from the PPP were taken to Mingora and kept there so that they were beyond the reach of the opposition.[18]

On 1 November 1989, the no-confidence motion was debated and put to vote. The debate was initiated by the leader of the opposition in the National Assembly, Ghulam Mustafa Jatoi, who accused the government of failure to maintain law and order, and for being inefficient and corrupt. After a couple of speeches, Benazir spoke with passion and eloquence and defended her government of eleven months. The motion was then put to vote and defeated. Only 107 members present in the National Assembly voted for the motion and 124 members present in the Assembly opposed the motion. Five members, including Wali Khan, were absent. There were six defections from the ranks of the opposition and three from the government.[19] Some of the defecting members of the opposition were later rewarded by being inducted into the Cabinet and by the award of soft loans from nationalized banks.

Conflict over Division of Powers between the President and the Prime Minister

Article 94 of the Constitution, in its original form, allowed the prime minister to continue in office along with his cabinet on the dissolution of the National Assembly till such time that a successor was elected by the National Assembly, after the ensuing general elections. Since, under the original scheme, the dissolution of the National Assembly was only possible on the advice of the prime minister, the president could not appoint a caretaker government for the period till the election of a new prime minister. However, the RCO as modified by the Eighth Amendment, empowered the President to dissolve the National Assembly at his discretion and also to appoint a caretaker Cabinet. Even when the National Assembly was dissolved on the advice of the prime minister, the continuation of the incumbent prime minister in office was no longer guaranteed. Under Article 94, as replaced by the RCO and the Eighth Amendment, it is the option of the president to ask the prime minister to continue to hold office until his successor. This can also mean that the president might not ask the prime minister to continue in office and might appoint a caretaker prime minister and cabinet in such a situation.

These provisions again made the office of the president very powerful. He had the discretion to appoint a caretaker cabinet of his choice not only at the centre but also in the provinces. This power had the effect of influencing and affecting the future course of events, in particular the conduct and results of the ensuing elections. Caretaker governments could be key actors in the manipulation of the election machinery with obvious effects on the results.

There were other areas under the Constitution, as amended by the RCO and the Eighth Amendment, where the president was given clear ascendancy; for instance, the appointment of chiefs of the armed forces and the chief election commissioner. These appointments could be made by the president at his discretion without the advice of or even consultation with the prime minister. Even in the appointment of governors, the president had the final say. He was only required to consult with the prime minister. There was no requirement to act on his advice.[20] Even if the president was required to act on the advice of the prime minister or the cabinet in other matters, he could still send back the matter to the prime minister or the cabinet, as the case may be, for reconsideration of the advice.[21]

It did not thus take long before the President and the Prime Minister ran into conflict with one another. Ishaq was obviously supporting Nawaz Sharif in his opposition to Benazir and was making life difficult for her. He sat on a number of matters referred to him by her. He was constantly asserting his powers and position and avoided making appointments on her advice. Consequently, there was widespread frustration in the federal government. Some of the President's stalling actions were not without justification because recommendations made to him were often irresponsible and outrageous. still, the dictates of the Constitution had to be obeyed and the Prime Minister and the Cabinet were to allowed to perform their constitutional functions.

The conflict between the President and the Prime Minister was particularly sharp in two areas: the appointment of military chiefs and superior court judges. When, at the end of 1989, the term of office of the Chairman of the Joint Chiefs of Staff and Chiefs of Naval and Air Staff was nearing expiry, it was given out from the prime ministerial circles that Benazir wanted to have a say in the appointment of their successors. Ishaq refused to have any of this because these appointments were within his discretionary domain. This caused enormous tension in relations between the top constitutional functionaries. The other major irritant was the appointment of judges of the superior courts. Even in this area, the President asserted himself and sat on the appointments advised by the Prime Minister.

Conflict over the Appointment of Judges

On the face of it, it appears that appointments to the superior courts were required to be made on the advice of the prime minister, if Articles 177 and 193 were read in conformity with Article 48. Articles 177 and 193 do not state that the appointments of judges of the Supreme Court and High Courts could be made by the president at his discretion. Therefore, the obvious construction that can be placed on these Articles is that such appointments should be made on the advice of the prime minister as envisaged under Article 48. This matter was once tested before the courts, but it was still in a state of uncertainty. The Lahore High Court in '*M.D. Tahir v Federal Government*',[22] observed that the prime minister did not find mention in Article 193 amongst the persons with whom the president was required to consult before appointing the judges. The argument concerning advice of the prime minister under Article 48 was brushed aside with the observation that since Article 193 specifically dealt with appointments of High Court judges and Article 48 ordains generally that, in exercise of his functions, the president should act in accordance with the advice of the cabinet or the prime minister, therefore, under the rules of statutory interpretation, where there are two provisions, one of which is specific in character and the other of a general nature, then the specific provision ought to be applied unfettered by the general one.

This judgment was belatedly challenged by the federal government before the Supreme Court and the case was argued at length before a full Bench of the Supreme Court consisting of eleven judges. During the course of the hearing the judges on the Bench were sharply divided on the issue. This was obvious from observations they made openly during the hearing which clearly ran contrary to one another.[23] However, after lengthy arguments spread over a number of weeks, the federal government, apparently under the pressure of the President, withdrew the petition for leave to appeal purportedly on the basis of mutual agreement reached between the President and the Prime Minister. No final decision on this question could, therefore, be rendered by the Supreme Court. The Supreme Court,[24] excised a para of the judgment of the Lahore High Court in which the aforesaid reasoning was given. The question, thus, remained unresolved. It would only be appropriate that the provision of Article 48 regarding advice of the prime minister be read in consonance with Articles 177 and 193, meaning thereby that the appointment of the judges of the Superior Courts be made on the advice of the prime minister.

The aforesaid mutual agreement contained a detailed procedure about the guiding principles for the exercise of presidential constitutional functions and the procedure regarding the appointment of judges of the High Courts, Chief Justices of the High Courts, judges of the Supreme Court, and the Chief Justice of the Supreme Court, which reads as follows:[25]

> Mutually agreed guiding principles for the exercise of the president's constitutional functions were:
>
> 1. Discretion. The President should normally and, as far as possible, exercise his discretion after taking the Prime Minister into confidence by prior information.
> 2. Where word President simpliciter is used, the President shall accept the advice of the Prime Minister subject to requirement for reconsideration. The reconsidered advice should be tendered by the Prime Minister normally and as far as possible accommodating the views of the President.

3. Where the advice of the Prime Minister is incorporated in the Article itself then it is the advice which shall be accepted by the President without requirement of reconsideration.
4. Consultation, satisfaction, opinion, thinks fit, considers, subject to detailed examination of the individual Articles of the constitution, in principle decision will be based on consultations and as mutually agreed in one or more than one meetings. The Prime Minister will tender advice to the President reflecting the consensus/agreement reached with will be approved by the President accordingly.

Appointment of judges of the High Courts.

1. On his own initiative or on receipt of information from the Law and Justice Division (verbal or written), a panel of three names against each vacancy is forwarded by the Chief Justice of the concerned High Court to the Governor of the province. A copy of the communication is sent to the Federal Law Secretary.
2. From the Governor, the file goes to the Chief Minister of the province. The Chief Minister through office file makes recommendations or his comments on each nominee of the Chief Justice to the Governor.
3. The Governor sends a DO letter to the Federal Law Secretary containing his opinion on each nominee in the Chief Justice's panel based on the recommendations/ comments of the Chief Minister.
4. Copies of the DO letters of the Provincial Chief Justice and the Government are sent by the Federal Law Secretary to the Chief Justice of Pakistan for his comments.
5. Based on the recommendations/comments/opinions of the Provincial Chief Justice, Governor of the Province, and the Chief Justice of Pakistan, the Law and Justice Division submits a summary to the Prime Minister together with the recommendations of the Chief Justice and Governors. The Law and Justice Minister approves the submission of the summary.
6. On receipt of the summary, the Prime Minister calls for report from the DI.B and DG ISI.
7. After completion of the above formalities, the Prime Minister and the President hold consultations in the light of recommendations, comments, opinions, and intelligence reports etc.
8. Based on such consultations and as agreed in one or in more than one meetings, the Prime Minister tenders advice on the summary to the President reflecting the agreement reached which is approved accordingly.

Appointment of the Chief Justice of a High Court.

1. Chief Justice of Pakistan sends his recommendation to the Federal Law Secretary.
2. Law and Justice Division obtains the views of the Governor of the concerned province. Views of the Governor, based on the opinion of the Chief Minister of the province, are communicated to the Law and Justice Division.
3. In the matter of appointment of the Chief Justice of a High Court, due weight is given to the recommendation of the Chief Justice of Pakistan.
4. Preference is given to the senior-most puisne Judge of the High Court for appointment as Chief Justice.
5. The senior-most judge would be superseded only if there is anything adverse on record against him. In that case consultation would be held between the President and the Prime Minister in order to determine the question of supersession. If it is agreed that on the basis of record the supersession of the most senior judge is not justified, then the next most senior judge of the High Court will be appointed Chief Justice.

Appointment of the judges of the Supreme Court.

1. At the request of the Law and Justice Division or on his own initiative, the Chief Justice of Pakistan sends a panel to the Federal Law Secretary to fill available vacancies.
2. On the basis of the recommendations of the Chief Justice of Pakistan, a summary (submission authorized by the Law and Justice Minister) is submitted by the Law and Justice Division to the Prime Minister.
3. Based on such recommendations and as agreed in one or in more than one meetings, the Prime Minister tenders advice on the summary to the President reflecting the agreement reached with is approved accordingly.
4. Following has been the consistent practice so far in the appointment of Supreme Court judges:-
   (i) On recommendation of the Chief Justice of Pakistan, Supreme Court judges have been appointed from amongst the nominees of the Chief Justice of Pakistan.
   (ii) Nominees were judges of the High Court.
   (iii) Representation of the various High Courts was kept in view.
5. Above practice would continue to be followed in future also.

Appointment of the Chief Justice of Pakistan

1. On occurrence of a vacancy of Chief Justice of Pakistan, a Summary is submitted by the Law and Justice Division to the Prime Minister. Submission of the summary is authorized by the Law and Justice Minister.
2. Preference is given to the senior most judge of the Supreme Court for appointment as Chief Justice. The senior judge would be superseded only in case there is anything adverse on record against him.
3. Decision in principle would be made in the light of item 2 of Mutual Arrangements.

Dissolution of Assemblies

The conflict between the President and the Prime Minister had its drop scene on 6 August 1990 when the President applied *coup de grace* by issuing an order under Article 58(2)(b) of the Constitution, thereby dissolving the National Assembly of Pakistan. In consequence thereof, the Prime Minister and the Cabinet ceased to hold office forthwith. The order passed by the President reads as follows:

> The President having considered the situation in the country, the events that have taken place and the circumstances, and among others for the reasons mentioned below is of the opinion that the government of the federation cannot be carried on in accordance with the provisions of the Constitution and an appeal to the electorate is necessary:
>
> (a) The utility and efficacy of the National Assembly as a representative institution elected by the people under the Constitution, and its mandate, is defeated by internal dissensions and frictions, persistent and scandalous 'horse-trading' for political gain, and furtherance of personal interests, corrupt practices and inducement, in contravention of the Constitution and the law, and by failure to discharge substantive legislative functions other than the adoption of the Finance Bill, and further the National Assembly has lost the confidence of the people.

(b) The Constitution envisages the federation and the provinces working within the spheres respectively assigned to them with clearly delineated executive and legislative authority, and with a view to safeguarding the structure of the Federation also contains special provisions of mandatory nature to ensure and protect the authority granted to the provinces, by creating specific constitutional institutions consisting of federal and provincial representatives, but the government of the federation has wilfully undermined and impaired the working of the constitutional arrangements and usurped the authority of the provinces and of such institutions resulting in discord, confrontation, and deadlock, adversely affecting the integrity, solidarity, and well-being of Pakistan, in that, *inter alia*:

  i. The Council of Common interests under Article 153, which is responsible only to Parliament, has not been allowed to discharge its constitutional functions and exercise its powers despite persistent demands of the provinces, and Parliament has also not been allowed to function in this regard as required by Articles 153 and 154, and in relation to Articles 155 and 161.

  ii. The National Finance Commission under Article 160 has never been called to meet and allowed to function, thus blocking mandatory constitutional processes in the matter of allocation of shares of revenues to the provinces despite their persistent demands.

  iii. Constitutional powers and functions of the provinces have been deliberately frustrated and extension of executive authority of the federation to the provinces in violation of Article 97 and by the general manner of implementation of the people's programme.

  iv. The Senate, which is representative of the federating units under Article 59 and is an integral part of Parliament, has been ridiculed and its constitutional role has been eroded.

(c) Corruption and nepotism in the federal government, its functionaries and authorities, and agencies, statutory and other corporations including banks, working under its supervision and control and the holders of representative offices has reached such proportions, that the orderly functioning of the government in accordance with the provisions of the constitution including the requirements of the oath(s) prescribed therein, and the law, does no longer carry public faith and credibility and despite being subject to wide public condemnation, the government has failed to take appropriate action in this behalf.

(d) The federal government has failed in its duty under Article 148(3) of the Constitution to protect the province of Sindh against internal disturbances and to ensure that the government of that province is carried on in accordance with the provisions of the Constitution, despite the heavy loss of life and property, the rule of terror in urban and rural areas, riots, arson, dacoities, kidnapping for ransom, politics of violence among citizens and widely condemned failure of the provincial government and its law-enforcing agencies, and also, in this behalf, failed to act under appropriate provisions of the Constitution.

(e) The government of the federation has violated the provisions of the Constitution and the law in that:

  i. The superior judiciary has been publicly ridiculed and its integrity attacked and attempts made to impair its independence.

ii. Authority, resources. and agencies of the government of the federation including statutory corporations, authorities, and banks have been misused for political ends and purposes, and for personal gains.
iii. The Civil Services of Pakistan have been undermined by disregarding the provisions of Articles 240 and 242.
iv. The powers under Article 45 have been exercised by the government without prior approval of the President.

Now, therefore, I, Ghulam Ishaq Khan, President of the Islamic Republic of Pakistan in exercise of the powers conferred on me by clause (2)(b) of Article 58 of the Constitution of the Islamic Republic of Pakistan dissolve the National Assembly with immediate effect; and the Prime Minister and the Cabinet cease to hold office forthwith.[26]

The order of dissolution of the National Assembly was soon followed by the dissolution of the provincial assemblies. The chief ministers of Balochistan and the Punjab advised their respective provincial governors to dissolve their respective provincial assemblies. These provinces did not have PPP governments. In the PPP ruled provinces of Sindh and the NWFP, the governors had to exercise their discretionary powers under Article 112 to dissolve their respective provincial assemblies.

Benazir's First Term Reviewed

After eleven long years of the rule of Zia and his military *junta*, the induction of Benazir, a young and well-educated woman as Prime Minister appeared to be a pleasant change. The people of Pakistan had pinned their hopes and expectations on her. Unfortunately, they were deeply disappointed. Benazir had no economic programme, no future plans, and no clear idea about how to govern. Her claim to power and political ascendancy was purely hereditary, her political capital being the suffering inflicted on the family from the execution of her father by Zia and her confinement after his execution.[27] She wasted her political capital and got bogged down in unnecessary and wasteful confrontation with the provincial government of Punjab headed by Nawaz Sharif. Her main concern appeared to be to benefit the members of her party who claimed to have suffered for her. At times, Benazir gave the impression of being not the prime minister of the country but only head of her political party.[28]

One of her first acts on assuming office was to grant clemency under Article 45 of the Constitution, including commutation of all death sentences awarded by the military or other courts upto 6 December 1988, to life imprisonment. There was obviously no justification for the commutation of death sentences awarded by ordinary courts. Some of the most hardened offenders were spared execution for no reason whatsoever. This order is reminiscent of the times of monarchy when a King or Queen, upon ascending the throne, would remit or commute sentences of the prisoners as a mark of celebration on being crowned. This order was challenged before the Lahore High

Court. The Court held the order of clemency as repugnant to Article 2-A. It was also held that the cases in which death sentences had been awarded, the President had no power to commute, remit, or pardon because, under Islam, pardon in such cases is only vested with the heirs of the deceased.[29] On appeal, the Supreme Court reversed the judgment of the High Court.[30] It was observed that if the Court found that Article 45 of the Constitution contravenes the injunctions of Islam in some respects, it had to bring the transgression to the notice of Parliament which alone was competent to amend the Constitution, so that it could initiate remedial legislation to bring the impugned provision in conformity with the injunctions of Islam.

Benazir Bhutto's foreign policy was without any direction. She had no control over foreign policy and did not even have the option to appoint the Foreign Minister.[31] Her policy on Afghanistan was clearly a failure. Her government was seriously embarrassed by her husband, Asif Ali Zardari, who, it is generally alleged, went on a rampage of corruption, graft, bribery, blackmail, high handedness, and even acts of terrorism.[32] Although these allegations might be difficult to prove against him in a court of law for want of evidence, yet there was little doubt in the perception of the people that many of the rumours circulating about him were true. Benazir appeared to be helpless in curbing her husband and his father from causing enormous embarrassment to her government. Several of her ministers were known to be inept and corrupt. Many of them were in a hurry to make a quick buck as if they knew that the government was not going to last long and that the honeymoon would be over soon.

Not only that, Benazir also involved herself in disputes and confrontation with the President and military, particularly in the matter of appointment of the military chiefs and judges of superior courts. She was accused of political horse trading, particularly at the time of voting on the resolution for no confidence against her. She showered political favours on her partymen in the form of government jobs and plots of land in Islamabad.[33] Some political leaders of her party obtained loans at favourable terms from government banks. The law and order situation in the province of Sindh, where PPP was in power, went completely out of hand. Kidnapping for ransom was a daily occurrence and several leading men from her party, including her husband, were rumoured to have been involved. Her government took no action against the culprits and the only time it was attempted, it was a partisan act directed against the Muhajir Qaumi Movement[34] (MQM) outside Pucca Qila in Hyderabad.

When her government was ultimately dismissed on 6 August 1990 by the President under Article 58(2)(b), there were few who could defend its performance. It was a sorry end to the high hopes held and the great confidence reposed by the people of Pakistan in Benazir Bhutto.

The Caretaker Government of Jatoi

When Benazir's government was dismissed in August 1990, the President's power to appoint a caretaker cabinet at the federal as well as provincial levels, was abused to the maximum. Instead of appointing neutral and non-partisan caretaker cabinets, all the people who were in opposition and were known to be openly hostile to the dismissed government were appointed in the caretaker cabinets at the federal as well as at the provincial levels. The leader of the opposition in the erstwhile National Assembly, Ghulam Mustafa Jatoi, was appointed as the caretaker Prime Minister. Similarly, the chief ministers, particularly from Sindh and the Punjab, were taken from the opposition, especially from amongst those people who were openly hostile to the PPP. The caretaker Chief Minister of the Punjab, Ghulam Haider Wyne, was a hand-picked nominee of Nawaz Sharif. Wyne openly campaigned with Nawaz throughout the Punjab and made available to him all the resources of the provincial government. He was rewarded after the general elections by being elected chief minister of the Punjab in the IJI government.

The caretakers, under the guidance and support of the President, were to ensure that the PPP would not return to power and the favourites of the President would get themselves installed as prime minister of Pakistan and chief ministers of the provinces.[35] The desired results were eventually achieved with Nawaz Sharif elected prime minister and all provincial governments hostile to the PPP. Even in Sindh, where PPP emerged as the largest party in the Provincial Assembly, although not in a majority, it was not allowed to form the government and was kept out of power through clever manoeuvering by an extremely unscrupulous character, Jam Sadiq Ali, who later became the Chief Minister of Sindh.

Order of Dissolution of National Assembly Challenged and Court Verdicts

The order of dissolution of the National Assembly was challenged before the Lahore High Court and the Sindh High Court. A full Bench of the Lahore High Court decided the writ petition upholding the order of dissolution passed by the President.[36] The Court, in its judgment, took notice of the no-confidence motion moved against the Prime Minister and observed that the federal government and the provincial governments had been pitched against one another contrary to the wider national interest, and that there was no escape from self destruction if policies of confrontation were not avoided. The Court observed that the conduct of the members of the assembly utterly disappointed the nation and attracted public censure. It was observed that the members of the National Assembly who had been elected to solve the country's problems indulged in misuse of national assets for their own political gains unmindful of their responsibilities and had engaged in conspiracies disastrous to the country at public expense. It was also observed that the President had appealed through the press and otherwise, time and again, calling upon the government to perform its constitutional role to save the country, and, as it appeared, the federal government had paid no heed to the timely advice of the President. It was also held that the members of the dissolved National Assembly could claim no vested right to enjoy the full term of five years when they had lost the confidence of the people on account of their performance and conduct in the National Assembly. It was also observed that if the action taken by the President in dissolving the National Assembly was incorrect in their estimation, then the electorate, as the political sovereign and final arbiter, would re-elect them with a thumping majority.

The Court thus felt that the President was justified in forming the opinion that the government of the federation could not be carried on in accordance with the provisions of the Constitution and an appeal to the electorate had become necessary. This opinion could reasonably be formed from, amongst others, the following acts or omissions of the federal government:

i. No substantial legislative work had been and could be carried on by the government in the National Assembly *inter alia* for the reason that the government had virtually no representation in the Senate. During its twenty-months' tenure, out of fifty Ordinances/Bills presented before the National Assembly, only fifteen could be passed by Parliament while the remaining thirty-five were not processed and were allowed to lapse.
ii. The federal government had miserably failed to perform its obligations under Article 148(3) of the Constitution in protecting the province of Sindh against internal disturbances which continued unabated and assumed serious proportions beyond the control of the provincial government. Despite repeated advice of the President, clear view expressed by the Governor of Sindh, and opinion of the then Attorney-General, resort to the provision of Article 245 of the Constitution was not taken resulting in the colossal loss of life and property, thereby endangering the integrity and solidarity of Pakistan.
iii. The Constitution envisaged Pakistan as an Islamic Federal Republic wherein the federal government and the federating units had well-defined powers and sphere of operation. A mechanism had been provided in the Constitution to resolve disputes between the federation and its units and between the units *inter se*. Inaction on the part of the federation in resolving such disputes could endanger the federal structure of the state. In this regard, one of the important institutions, the Council of Common Interests constituted under Article 153 of the Constitution, was meant to formulate and regulate policies in relation to matters in Part II of the Federal Legislative List and Entry 34 (Electricity) in the Concurrent List (reference Article 154). The Council supervises and controls the related institutions and is also required to determine the rates at which net profits are to be calculated in terms of Article 161. The documents on record revealed that the federal government, despite repeated demands by three out of four federating units, and a unanimous resolution of the Senate, failed to call a meeting of the Council of Common Interests resulting in polarization and confrontation between the federation and two federating units which eventually obliged them to file a suit against the federation in the Supreme Court of Pakistan.
iv. The formation of the National Finance Commission, another important institution, required to be setup under Article 160 of the Constitution for distribution of revenues between the federation and the provinces, was

unnecessarily delayed with the result that not a single meeting could be convened, thereby depriving the federating units redress of their grievances.

v. The provincial autonomy guaranteed by the Constitution was eroded by launching the Peoples' Works Programme in a manner contrary to Article 97 without any legislative backing.

vi. Article 14 of the Constitution guaranteed that the dignity of man and, subject to law, the privacy of home would be inviolable. This fundamental right was flagrantly violated and disregarded by tapping the telephones of highly respected peoples, including dignitaries like the Chairman of the Senate and Speaker of the National Assembly. Even members of the government were not spared. The petitioner was one of those whose telephones were tapped.

vii. Important constitutional organs of the state like the Senate and superior judiciary were publicly ridiculed and brought into disrespect. Even the legal existence and validity of the Senate was disputed by the federal government.

viii. There was misuse by the federal government of secret service funds running into crores of rupees and unauthorized use of aircraft belonging to PAF and PIA for transporting MNAs at the time of the no-confidence motion.

ix. Wholesale and indiscriminate appointments were made in the civil services of Pakistan and the services under the statutory corporations which was clearly in violation of the law.

x. The federal government, in not giving effect to the judgment of the Supreme Court by legislating on the subject of *qisas* and *diyat*, had failed to carry on government in accordance with the provisions of the Constitution. The federal government did not present any legislation to give effect to the judgment of the Supreme Court and showed its resistance by dubbing the punishment under the Islamic Laws as impracticable and cruel.

The Court thus held that the President of Pakistan had validly passed the order of dissolution of the National Assembly because the government of the federation could not be carried on in accordance with the provisions of the Constitution and that appeal to the electorate had become necessary. The Court also held that the grounds which weighed with the President for passing the impugned order had direct nexus with the preconditions described under Article 58(2)(b) of the Constitution. The Court repelled the argument that if one of the grounds for the dissolution of the National Assembly was proved to be non-existent, the entire order for the dissolution of the National Assembly would fall.

Challenge before the Sindh High Court

A full Bench of the Sindh High Court also upheld the order of the President in terms similar to those of the Lahore High Court.[37] The Court held that if the several reasons and grounds given by the President in the order of dissolution are severable and independent, and the order of the President could be justified independently on some such grounds, the Court would uphold the order rather than strike it down as unconstitutional on account of the presence of other irrelevant and insignificant independent reasons in the order.

The Court examined the grounds given in the order of the President and found them specific, pinpointing the provisions of the Constitution which had been violated. The Court took specific notice of the speech made by the President in the joint meeting of the two Houses of Parliament on 2 December 1989, in which he made reference to the failure of the National Assembly as a legislative body, scandalous horse trading, conflict between the federal government and two provincial governments, non-convening of meetings of the Council of Common Interests and the National Finance Commission, and failure to maintain public order in Sindh. The Court felt persuaded from the material produced before it that it could be reasonably concluded that political horse-trading was resorted to at the time of the motion for vote of no confidence; that the meeting of two important constitutional institutions, namely the Council of Common Interests (CCI) and the National Finance Commission (NFC) were not convened, disregarding the wishes of the provinces, the Senate, and the President; that Peoples' Programme had no backing of law and its implementation amounted to over-stepping by the federation into the provincial sphere; that large number of ad hoc appointments were made in the service of the federation and its statutory corporations in flagrant violation of service rules and the law; that 'Pucca Qila Operations' in Hyderabad proved the breakdown of law and order and that the Senate was not shown the respect and importance due to the Upper House.

Appeal before the Supreme Court

The judgment of the Lahore High Court was challenged before the Supreme Court of Pakistan in *Khawaja Ahmad Tariq Rahim v the Federation of Pakistan*.[38] The Supreme Court, upheld the judgment of the Lahore High Court by a majority. The Court, after examining the grounds for the dissolution of the National Assembly and the material produced by the federal government in support of the grounds, came to the conclusion that the dissolution order of the President was justified. It was noticed that persistent requests had been made by the provinces to make constitutional institutions like the Council of Common Interests, and the National Finance Commission, functional with a view to sorting out disputes over various claims and policy matters concerning the federation and the federating units. The Court felt that despite the intercession of the President, no heed was paid and constitutional obligations were not discharged, thereby jeopardizing the very existence of the federation.

(a) The Opinion of the Majority

The Supreme Court, in its leading judgment by Justice Shafiur Rehman, took very serious view of defections of elected members of the National Assembly (called 'horse trading' in the order for dissolution by the President') for the following reasons:

i. If a member has been elected on the basis of a manifesto of a political party, or on account of his particular stand on a question of public importance, his defection amounts to a clear breach of confidence reposed in him by the electorate.
ii. The political sovereign, that is the elector, is rendered helpless by such betrayal by his own representative. The elector has to wait, till new elections take place, to repudiate such a person but, in the meantime, the defector flourishes and continues to enjoy worldly gains.
iii. The defection destroys the normative moorings of the Constitution of the Islamic State. It is nothing but mockery of the democratic constitutional process.

The term 'government' was held to have wide meanings and connotations which include legislative, judicial, and executive functions and hence the argument that Article 58(2)(b) talk of 'government' and not of 'national assembly' was repelled. Although the grounds like (c), e(ii), and e(iii) might not be independently sufficient to warrant such an action, yet the Court held, they could be invoked, referred to, and made use of along with grounds more relevant like (a) and (b) which by themselves were sufficient to justify the action taken.

(b) The Dissenting View

However, Justice Abdul Shakoor Salam, in his strong dissent, held that the discretionary power to dissolve the Assembly was exclusive to Zia, and that such power perished with his demise. The learned judge further held that such power could not be deemed to have devolved on his successor. If, according to him, divine will did not permit the late President to complete his mission or tenure, then nobody could step into his shoes. He further held that it was not advisable to continue the discretionary power of dissolution because that would strike at the very root of the parliamentary system of government established under the Constitution after much trial and error and after loss of half of the country. The learned judge also examined the grounds given in support of the order of dissolution and held that, notwithstanding the dissatisfaction of the president with the functioning of the prime minister or Parliament, the reasons for dissolving the National Assembly were not good enough under the Constitution and the principles previously laid down by the highest courts in the land. It was remarked that it could not be lost sight of that if the national and provincial assemblies were reckoned to be so bad by the President so as to be dissolved, then it was these assemblies that had not long before elected him as the President. So, he questioned, how could what was good then have become so bad now? How could a creature condemning the creator sound well?

Another dissenting opinion came from Justice Sajjad Ali Shah. He was of the view that the impugned order of dissolution suffered inherently from malafides, primarily because the unavoidable object behind it was not only that the government of the time be toppled, but that the image of the People's Party be tarnished in the eyes of the people so that it could be routed in the ensuing general elections. The learned judge, held the order of dissolution as not sustainable under the provisions of the Constitution and the law. However, he was of the view that relief for restoration of the National Assembly could not be granted (as held in the Haji Saifullah case) because after the dissolution of the Assembly, elections had taken place with the full participation of all political parties, including the deposed Prime Minister and her party.

Dissolution of Provincial Assemblies Challenged and Court Verdicts

Aftab Ahmad Khan Sherpao, the ousted chief minister of NWFP, challenged the order of dissolution of the Provincial Assembly before the Peshawar High Court. The order of dissolution dated 6 August 1990 read as below:

> No. Legis: 4(1) of 1977:-
>
> WHEREAS a situation has arisen in which the Government of the North West Frontier Province cannot be carried on in accordance with the provisions of the Constitution and an appeal to the electorate is necessary;
>
> NOW, THEREFORE, in exercise of the powers conferred by Sub-Clause (b) of Clause (2) of Article 112 of the Constitution of the Islamic Republic of Pakistan, I, Amir Gulistan Janjua, Governor of the North West Frontier Province, in my discretion and with the previous approval of the President, hereby dissolve the Provincial Assembly with immediate effect, and consequently, the Provincial Cabinet shall also stand dissolved.[39]

A full Bench of the Peshawar High Court, by a majority of four to one, accepted the Constitution petition and declared the impugned order of dissolution of the NWFP Assembly and the dismissal of the provincial Cabinet thereby as *ultra vires* of the Constitution, without lawful authority and, therefore, of no legal effect. The Court directed that the NWFP Assembly and the Cabinet would stand restored.[40]

The Court held that the grounds forming the opinion of the governor for the exercise of the said discretion should be objective and not vague, general, or devoid of particulars. On the matter of prior approval of the president, the Court held that was subject to the advice of the cabinet or the prime minister and that such approval could not be given by the president independently. It was held that the expression 'cannot be carried on' meant the breakdown of the constitutional mechanism, a stalemate or a deadlock in ensuring the observance of the provisions of the Constitution and the Court found no material indicating such breakdown, stalemate, or deadlock. On the contrary, the Court observed, the budget had been unanimously passed. The order of dissolution was thus held to be arbitrary, totally bereft of the reasons necessitating the dissolution of the Assembly, and without the objective conditions relatable to the grounds laid down in the Constitution. The Court did not deem it necessary to wait for and hear the Attorney-General (who was busy at that time before the other courts defending the order of dissolution of the National Assembly) and regarded the association of Advocate-General of the province in this case as adequate. To the plea that the relief of restoration of the Assembly and the Cabinet should not be granted, the Court held that the High Court, in exercise of its discretion to grant relief in its constitutional jurisdiction, was not bound by any precedent and relief could be granted or refused according to the objective conditions of each case.

Verdict of the Supreme Court

The judgment of the Peshawar High Court was landmark in the sense that, for the first time, restoration of an Assembly or a Cabinet had been ordered by a Court. However, this judgment was never given effect and was soon suspended.[41] The President was clearly offended by this judgment and the judges on the Bench had to face dire consequences for rendering such judgment.[42] This judgment was set aside by the Supreme Court by a majority judgment primarily on the ground that the judgment of the Peshawar High Court was vitiated because the mandatory requirement of notice to the Attorney-General of Pakistan before deciding substantial questions as to the interpretation of constitutional law had not been complied with.[43] In the majority judgment, it was observed that since there was no direct challenge to want of approval by the President nor to the lack of advice of the caretaker Prime Minister, therefore the High Court should not have proceeded to examine these facts on its own and a constitutional power reserved for the Governor and the President ought not to have been interfered with by raising a doubt. On merits, it was held that in view of large-scale defections in the province, the representative character of the renegades and the democratic character of the provincial government had become open to serious doubt and, thus, the provincial government was not functioning in accordance with the provisions of the Constitution.

Justice A.S. Salam, in his dissenting opinion, once more held that notwithstanding the absence of a formal notice, the Attorney-General had notice of the proceedings in the High Court and could have appeared or sought accommodation if he intended to appear. The learned judge was of the opinion that non-issuance of a formal notice in the circumstances could not annul the proceedings dealing with such high constitutional issues. On merits, he held that an appointed Governor had exercised high constitutional authority by dissolving an elected Assembly without much thought or care. Three other judges, writing their separate opinions, joined Justice A.S. Salam in his dissent and agreed with him that the majority judgment of the Peshawar High Court should be upheld.[44]

These four judges were joined by Justice Dr Nasim Hasan Shah to the extent that lack of notice to the Attorney-General did not render the judgment of the Peshawar High Court as nullity.[45] Justice Ajmal Mian, agreeing with the dissenting judges and upholding the judgment of the Peshawar High Court, denied the relief of restoring the dissolved Assembly and the dismissed Cabinet.

Dissolution of the Provincial Assembly of Sindh: Challenge before the Sindh High Court

On 6 August 1990, the Governor of Sindh dissolved, in his discretion, the Provincial Assembly of Sindh and the following order was passed:

> The Governor having considered the situation in the province of Sindh and the prevailing facts and circumstances, is of the opinion that the Government of the Province cannot be carried on in accordance with the provisions of the Constitution and an appeal to the electorate is necessary among others for the reasons mentioned below:-
>
> (a) The Government of the Province of Sindh has failed in its duty to maintain law and order, and to protect the life, honour, dignity, and property of the people who have been constantly subjected to indiscriminate killings, rape, terrorism, dacoities, kidnapping for ransom, politics of violence and vengeance amongst citizens throughout the Province and also failed to ensure the rights of citizens in a just, equitable, and non-discriminating manner leading to accentuation of political and ethnic polarisation affecting the welfare of the people and endangering the integrity of the Province.
>
> (b) The mandate, effectiveness, and purpose of the Provincial Assembly in Sindh as a representative institution under the Constitution is defeated by widespread corruption including misapplication of public funds in the Provincial Government, its functionaries, the statutory authorities/bodies operating under its control, the holders of representative offices for political gain and furtherance of personal interests, to such extent that the orderly functioning of the Government in accordance with the provisions of the Constitution including the requirements of oath prescribed therein and the law, is no longer possible and further the Assembly has failed to take remedial action in this behalf, and has lost the confidence of the people.
>
> (c) The Government of the Province has undermined the Civil Services in violation of Articles 240 and 242 of the Constitution and subjected the services to undue pressures and threats and further the authority of agencies and resources of the Government of the Province and statutory bodies/corporations under its control have been misused for political ends and purposes and for personal gains.
>
> Now, therefore, I, Mehmood A. Haroon, Governor of the Province of Sindh, in exercise of the powers conferred on me by Clause (2)(b) of Article 112 of the Constitution of the Islamic Republic of Pakistan, with the previous approval of the President of Pakistan, hereby dissolve the Provincial Assembly of Sindh with immediate effect, and the Chief Minister and the Cabinet have ceased to hold office forthwith.[46]

This order of dissolution of the Provincial Assembly of Sindh was challenged by the former Chief Minister of Sindh.[47] The Sindh High Court dismissed the constitution petition holding that the grounds mentioned in the order of the Governor for dissolving the Provincial Assembly were quite clear and specific and clearly showed the failure and breakdown of Constitutional machinery of provincial government inasmuch as it had totally failed to protect the life, liberty, honour, and property of the inhabitants of the province. The Court took notice of the correspondence between the President, the

Prime Minister, and the Governor of Sindh in connection with the 'Pucca Qila' incident in Hyderabad and the demand for extension of provisions of Article 245 of the Constitution to the territory of Sindh. The Court observed that the refusal of elected representatives of urban areas of Sindh to attend the Assembly session, including the budget session, on the ground of threat to their lives; the allegation against sitting ministers and MNAs regarding their involvement in heinous crimes like kidnapping for ransom and harbouring of dacoits; and the exchange of kidnapees between the PPP and MQM, the two major political forces in the province, under the aegis of army authorities, could only reflect failure of the working of constitutional government in the province. The Court also took notice of large-scale irregular appointments in the services of provincial government in violation of service laws and disposal of government land in violation of rules for political considerations. As such, the material brought before the Court was found adequate and reasonable for passing the order of dissolution by the Governor.

General Elections, October 1990

In the general elections held in October 1990, the Islami Jamhoori Ittehad won 105 seats in the National Assembly. The Pakistan Democratic Alliance, which also included Pakistan People's Party, captured only forty-five seats. MQM (Haq Prast) and Awami National Party headed by Wali Khan, who lost his one seat in the election, got fifteen and six seats, respectively. Of the remaining seats, three went to JUP (Noorani), two each to Jamhoori Watan Party and Pakistan National Party, and one to Pakhtoon-Khwah Milli Party.

Prominent party leaders including Wali Khan, former Speaker Meraj Khalid, veteran leader Nasrullah Khan, Maulana Fazlur Rahman, Minister for Information and Broadcasting Syeda Abida Husain, former NWFP Chief Minister, Aftab Ahmad Sherpao, Mumtaz Bhutto, and Hafiz Pirzada lost in the elections. The leaders who won included Muhammad Khan Junejo, Ghulam Mustafa Jatoi, Nawaz Sharif, Benazir, Nusrat Bhutto, Ghulam Mustafa Khar, and former Speakers Hamid Nasir Chattha and Syed Fakhar Imam.[48]

Final Party Position

	IJI	PDA	MQM	JUI	ANP	PNP	JUP (N)	PK MAP	JWP	Indepen-dents	Total
NWFP	8	5	-	4	6	-	-	-	-	3	26
FATA	-	-	-	-	-	-	-	-	-	8	8
FCT	1	-	-	-	-	-	-	-	-	-	1
Punjab	91	14	-	-	-	-	3	-	-	6	114
Sindh	3	24	15	-	-	-	-	-	-	4	46
Balochistan	2	2	-	2	-	2	-	1	2	-	11
	105	45	15	6	6	2	3	1	2	21	206

It was alleged by the PDA that the general elections had been rigged on a massive scale with the objective of defeating PDA and installing an IJI government. It was alleged that Ishaq Khan had played a major role in the rigging of elections. He made a speech on television on the eve of the elections in which he asked the people to vote against the PDA. Under instructions from Ishaq, an 'election cell' was set up in the President's secretariat in Aiwan-e-Sadar 'in order to apprise the President with the latest position about elections to the national assembly and provincial assemblies'. This cell was headed by General (Retd.) Rafaqat. Similar cells were set up at the provincial and local levels. It was alleged that Ishaq made appointments of such people to the Election Commission whose duty it was to ensure the defeat of PDA candidates.[49]

It was also alleged in the White Paper that caretaker governments at the federal and provincial levels played an active role in defeating the PDA by the misuse of state media, violation of election rules, disinformation campaign, misuse of public servants, misuse of public funds, and misuse of government facilities. The caretakers placed all kinds of administrative hurdles in the way of the PDA in the matter of issuance of identity cards, manipulation of boundaries of constituencies, and disruption of PDA rallies. The caretakers, it is alleged, used the power of transfer and posting of public servants to the advantage of the IJI and to the complete disadvantage of the PDA, particularly in certain critical constituencies. They applied pressure on subordinate officials in the administration and threatened them with dire consequences if they did not participate in rigging.[50]

The Election Commission was alleged to have acted in a partisan manner by appointing partisan staff and allowing irregularities. The Commission was alleged to have changed the procedure at the last moment on the instructions of the President and the caretaker government. It was alleged to have allowed bogus voting with fake identity cards. Other irregularities alleged included use of ballot papers without serial numbers, preventing PDA voters from entering polling stations, refusal to give PDA polling agents the official result sheets, changing election results in transit from presiding officer to returning officer, and the presence of unauthorized police at polling stations.[51]

No doubt, most of the allegations in the PDA White Paper are correct and the election was allowed to be held in a manner totally adverse to the PDA and favourable to the IJI. The President was a clear partisan who was hell-bent on ensuring the defeat of the PDA and did everything within his power and resources to achieve this end. The caretaker governments were manned by the IJI. Nevertheless, the PDA was also responsible for its defeat. Its performance during its 20-month rule did not inspire confidence and many voters switched their loyalties to the IJI. The PDA did not contest the election with any concerted planning. They appeared to be demoralized and emotionally defeated. Had they planned properly and contested the elections with spirit and vigour, they could have obtained much better results than they did despite all the difficulties posed by the President and the caretakers, who were actually meant to be its undertakers.

NOTES

1. In the general elections of 1988, 20 seats were reserved for women and 10 seats for minorities.
2. Article 91(2).
3. Article 91(2A).
4. Article 91(3).
5. Bhargava, G.S., *Benazir—Pakistan's New Hope*, 1989, Arnold Publishers, New Delhi, pp. 17 and 26.
6. Bhutto, Zulfiqar Ali, *My Dearest Daughter — A Letter from the Death Cell*, Published in 1989 by Benazir Bhutto, p. 56.
7. *The Nation*, 13 December 1988.
8. Article 130 (2) and (2A).
9. Muhammad Anwar Durrani v Province of Baluchistan, PLD 1989 Quetta 25.
10. PLD 1989 S.C. 166.
11. Muhammad Akram Sheikh v Federation of Pakistan, PLD 1989 S.C. 229.
12. It is interesting to note that judgment of eleven judges of the Supreme Court was reviewed by four judges only.
13. *The Muslim*, Islamabad, 24 October 1989.
14. Ibid.
15. Ibid.
16. Ibid., 26 October 1989.
17. Ibid., 26 October 1989.
18. Ibid., 28 October 1989 and 29 October 1989.
19. Ibid., 2 November 1989.
20. Article 101.
21. Article 48(1).
22. 1989 Civil Law Cases 1369.
23. A bench of 11 Judges was hearing the case and division appeared to be 7 to 4 in favour of the Prime Minister—reckoned from the remarks openly made by the judges in the Court during the proceedings. Undoubtedly, interest of the judges or at least some of them on the Bench, was involved in the outcome of the case. Even the appointment of the next Chief Justice, due in January 1990, was on the line. The two sides even resorted to canvassing the judges on the Bench. One of the judges on the Bench later told the author that he was visited by the then Chief Minister of the Punjab, Nawaz Sharif, with his brother Shahbaz, at his residence in Lahore who requested him to side with the President in the verdict. His refusal to oblige resulted in the severance of his long-time relationship with Nawaz Sharif.
24. Federal Government of Pakistan v M.D. Tahir, 1990 SCMR 189.
25. This agreement is reproduced in the judgment of Justice Ajmal Mian on pages 271 to 274 in Al-Jehad Trust v Federation of Pakistan, PLJ 1997 S.C. 209.
26. Reproduced on pages 66 to 68 of PLD 1991 Karachi 1.
27. Bhutto, Benazir, *Daughter of the East*. 1988, Hamish Hamilton, London. She took pains in writing about her sufferings and privation at the hands of the military regime which might be true. The people of Pakistan vindicated her by voting her into power in 1988.
28. Reference No. 4 of 1990 (President of Pakistan v Mohtarama Benazir Bhutto). It was alleged against her that she, in her note on 10 April 1989, ordered that certain applicants should be preferred in the grant of Liquified Petroleum Gas licence because they had suffered unduly during the past dictatorial regime.

    Reference No.11 of 1990 (President of Pakistan v Mohtarama Benazir Bhutto). It was alleged against her that about Rs 100 million were spent out of the secret funds on horse trading around the time when the resolution for vote of no confidence was moved against her in the National Assembly. All these references were dismissed when the PPP came back into power in 1993.
29. Mst. Sakina Bibi v Federation of Pakistan, PLD 1992 Lahore 99.

30. Hakim Khan v Government of Pakistan, PLD 1992 S.C. 595.
31. Benazir was obliged to retain Sahabzada Yaqub Khan as Foreign Minister, who did not belong to her political party.
32. Zardari was tried for terrorist activities before a Special Court constituted under Suppression of Terrorist Activities (Special Courts) Act, 1975.
33. Thousands of jobs were given under the Placement Bureau without proper scrutiny and without resorting to the method of selection provided under the law. Hundreds of plots were allotted to her partymen in the C.D.A. Schemes.
34. A political party claiming to represent refugees from India (not Indian Punjab) mostly settled in urban areas in Sindh. This party had massive support in Karachi, Hyderabad, and other urban centres of Sindh.
35. The President, in the broadcast to the nation a day before the polls, appealed to the voters to reject PPP. He used the expression that he had already put them (PPP) in the coffin and it was for the nation to bury them.
36. Ahmad Tariq Rahim v Federation of Pakistan, PLD 1990 Lahore 505 is the short Order in the case. Detailed judgment in this case is reported as PLD 1991 Lahore 78.
37. Khalid Malik v Federation of Pakistan, PLD 1991 Karachi 1.
38. PLD 1992 S.C. 646.
39. Reproduced on pages 197-8 of PLD 1990 Peshawar 192.
40. Aftab Ahmad Khan Sherpao v The Governor of NWFP, PLD 1990 Peshawar 192.
41. Within minutes of the announcement of this judgment, a petition was presented before a single judge of the Supreme Court of Pakistan, who happened to be available in Peshawar (in the building of the Peshawar High Court), and he suspended the operation of this judgment. Later on, this petition was presented before a full Bench of the Supreme Court at Karachi and the order of suspension of operation of the judgment was continued.
42. The Chief Justice, Sardar Fakhre Alam, who presided over the full Bench, and Justice Inayat Elahi Khan, were not elevated to the Supreme Court and instead a judge junior to them and who had not even completed five years as a judge of the High Court, was elevated to the Supreme Court. A third judge, Justice Nazir Ahmad Bhatti, was banished to the Federal Shariat Court. Justice Qazi Mohammad Jamil, who was an additional judge, was not made a permanent judge. The only dissenting judge, Justice S. Ibne Ali who was an additional judge, was rewarded and made a permanent judge.
43. Federation of Pakistan v Aftab Ahmad Khan Sherpao, PLD 1992 S.C. 723.
44. These three judges being Abdul Qadeer Chaudhry, Ajmal Mian, and Sajjad Ali Shah, JJ.
45. The full Bench was composed of twelve judges. On merits, there were four dissenting judge. On the question of notice to the Attorney-General, there were five dissenting judges.
46. Reproduced on p. 62 of PLD 1991 Karachi 1.
47. Khalid Malik v Federation of Pakistan, PLD 1991 Karachi 1. The Sindh High Court disposed of, by one order, all constitution petitions challenging the dissolution of the National Assembly passed by the President and the dissolution order of the Provincial Assembly of Sindh passed by the Governor of Sindh. The Constitutional Petitions thus disposed of included the petition filed by the former Chief Minister of Sindh, Syed Qaim Ali Shah.
48. *The Nation*, 26 October 1990.
49. *How A Election Was Stolen*, The PDA White Paper on the Pakistan Elections, 1990. Published by Pakistan Democratic Alliance, Islamabad, September 1991.
50. Ibid.
51. Ibid.

32

THE FIRST NAWAZ GOVERNMENT: CONSTITUTIONAL DUEL OVER THE PUNJAB

Commanding an overwhelming mandate, Nawaz Sharif, President of the IJI, was elected prime minister with 153 votes, which meant a two-thirds majority in the parliament. He promised to introduce fundamental changes in economic policy thus paving the way to greater prosperity. He specially emphasized the following points:

1. Pakistan would maintain friendly relations with all its neighbouring countries, especially with the People's Republic of China, Turkey, Iran, Saudi Arabia, other countries of the Gulf, and Bangladesh, and of course, the United States of America.
2. Government would endeavour to secure the right of self determination for subjugated Kashmiri Muslims according to the United Nations resolutions.
3. Good neighbourly relations with India would be worked on.
4. Pakistan would endorse and give full support to the rights of Muslims all over the world.
5. The power crisis which had been generated on account of the rise in oil prices had made it incumbent on Pakistan to further its peaceful nuclear programme. Government would discharge its obligations in this regard in accordance with national feelings and aspirations. Massive industrialization could not be accomplished without a peaceful nuclear energy programme.
6. A wide-ranging national reconstruction plan would be undertaken and ad hocism would be shunned.
7. Denationalization of sick industries would be undertaken for economic uplift.

Provincial Governments Formed

As a result of elections to the provincial assemblies, the following position emerged:[1]

Party Position

Party/Province	Punjab 240	Sindh 100	NWFP 80	Balochistan 40	Total Seats 460
IJI	211	6	32	7	256
PDA	13	48	6	3	70
PDP	2	-	-	-	2
ANP	-	-	21	-	21
JUI(F)	-	-	2	5	7
JWP	-	-	-	11	11
PNP	-	-	-	3	3
PKMP	-	-	-	3	3
BNM	-	-	-	2	2
IND	14	18	14	4	50
MQM	-	28	-	-	28
Results declared	240	100	75	38	453

The IJI completely swept the polls in the Punjab winning 211 out of the 240 general seats. After suffering a humiliating defeat at the hands of the IJI in the polls for the National Assembly, the PDA, appeared to have resigned to its fate when the polls to the provincial assemblies were held three days later. Thus PDA fared much worse in the polls for provincial assemblies than those of the National Assembly. It seemed like a loss of nerve. There was no effort on their part to hold their own and the decline was clearly discernable. In the three days intervening between the national and provincial assemblies polls, the PDA had directed its energy on crying itself hoarse about rigging and laid the blame for it on the establishment. No attempt was made to seriously face the challenge of the provincial assembly polls.

In the Punjab, the PDA won fourteen seats in the National Assembly out of 115 seats but in the Provincial Assembly, it could only win thirteen out of 240. If the law of averages in the National Assembly could be applied to the result in the provincial assemblies polls, the PDA should have won around thirty seats. Similarly, in the NWFP, the PDA won five seats in the National Assembly out of a total of twenty-six, but in the Provincial Assembly, it could only win six out of seventy-five seats for which polling was held.[2] Applying the law of averages in the NWFP, PDA should have won fifteen seats in the Provincial Assembly.

In Sindh, PDA paid heavily for its tardiness in handling the polls for the Provincial Assembly. Having won twenty-four out of forty-six seats reserved for the National Assembly in Sindh (52 per cent of the seats), thereby losing its majority in the Provincial Assembly of Sindh. It could win forty-eight out of the 100 Provincial Assembly general seats. The MQM won twenty-eight seats, IJI six seats, and eighteen seats went to the independents. With the aid, assistance, and abetment of Ishaq, coupled with the manoeuvering and manipulation of Jam Sadiq Ali, the PDA was rendered into a minority despite being the largest party in the Assembly.

Having swept the polls in the Punjab with 211 out of 240 seats in the Provincial Assembly, the IJI formed the government with an overwhelming majority, and elected Ghulam Haider Wyne as chief minister. In the NWFP, it won thirty-two seats followed by twenty-one by ANP, its ally, out of eighty seats. Thus, IJI formed government in the NWFP in coalition with ANP, with Mir Muhammad Afzal as the chief minister. In Sindh, Jam Sadiq Ali, in collusion with Ishaq and Mahmood A. Haroon, made a coalition with the MQM and won over all the independents. He even won over some members from the PDA in the Sindh Assembly. The result was that Jam Sadiq Ali was elected chief minister without contest and PDA members left the House when the election to the office was held.[3]

Legislations Concerning Economic Reforms

The Nawaz government introduced economic reforms which included privatization of nationalized industries, free movement of foreign exchange in and out of the country, and incentives to foreign and Pakistani entrepreneurs to invest in industry and other sectors of the economy.

The principal legislation concerning economic reforms introduced in August 1991 was Protection of Economic Reforms Ordinance, 1991 which was followed by two Ordinances in December 1991 and April 1992 in the same terms.[4] Finally, an Act of Parliament in the same terms was passed in July 1992 called Protection of Economic Reforms Act, 1992[5] which covered the following economic reforms introduced by Nawaz:

One, all citizens of Pakistan resident in or out of Pakistan and all other persons would be entitled to hold, sell, transfer, and take out foreign exchange within or out of Pakistan in any form. All foreign exchange transactions were protected

Two, all citizens and other persons resident in or outside Pakistan and holding foreign currency accounts in Pakistan, would be immune from any enquiry from the Income Tax Department or any other taxation authority as to the source of financing of the foreign currency accounts.

Three, banks would maintain complete secrecy regarding transactions in foreign currency accounts.

Four, no restriction would be imposed on deposits in and withdrawals from the foreign currency accounts and all existing restrictions stood withdrawn forthwith.

Five, balances in the foreign currency accounts and income therefrom would be exempted from levy of wealth tax and income tax.

Six, fiscal incentives provided by the government through statutory orders from time to time could not be altered to the disadvantage of investors.

Seven, the ownership, management, and control of any banking, commercial, manufacturing, or other company, establishment, or enterprise transferred by the government to any person under any law would not be compulsorily acquired or taken over by the government for any reason whatsoever. No foreign industrial or commercial enterprise established or owned in any form by a foreign or Pakistani investor for private gain in accordance with law, and no investment in share or equity of any company, firm or enterprise and no commercial bank or financial institution established, owned or acquired by any foreign or Pakistani investor should be compulsorily acquired or taken over by the government.

Eight, secrecy of bonafide banking transactions was required to be strictly observed by all banks and financial institutions by whomsoever owned, controlled, or managed them.

Denationalization and Privatization

In November 1990, Nawaz declared his policy on privatization based on the following methodology:

1. Sale of individual state-owned enterprises (SOEs) by inviting bids from the private sector.
2. Sale of shares of SOEs in suitable tranches through the Stock Exchange at a price per share to be determined through an evaluation process to ensure broad-based ownership and participation of foreign institutional investors.
3. Encouraging employees to constitute Employee Management Groups and negotiating with them a market price per share on the basis of an evaluation of assets, liabilities, and net worth, besides promoting the concept of ESOP (Employees' Stock Ownership Plan).
4. Encouraging prospective investment managers to form Modaraba Companies and raise funds for purchasing shares of SOEs on the basis of a negotiated market price.
5. Entering into a management contract with a Modaraba Company, leasing or contracting of management to private entrepreneurs for a specified period, and so forth.
6. Entering into a lease management contract with employees for a specified period to enable them to buy out units.[6]

The Nawaz government took bold decisions to privatize not only industrial units and banks which had been taken over from the private sector but also the public sector including DFIs and industrial units, whether taken over initially from the private sector or not. In order to enforce the government's policy, an amending ordinance for transfer of managed establishments was promulgated which authorized the government to invite bids for the sale of shares and proprietary interest in the SOEs through public advertisement.[7] On receipt of bids, the government was required to offer to sell shares and proprietary interest, equal to the highest bid in an auction, to previous owners. In case of a refusal to accept such an offer, the government could sell them to others on such terms and conditions as the government deemed fit. This ordinance was further amended by another ordinance whereby on receipt of bids, if the workers' bid was the highest, the unit would be sold to them.[8]

There were two broad categories of industrial units involved in denationalization and disinvestment from the public to the private sector under the privatization scheme. The first category comprised industrial units set up by the federal government with public funds called state established units. The second category comprised such industrial units as had been initially taken over from the private sector and subsequently acquired under the Economic Reforms Order, 1972. Both these categories of industrial units were treated as Managed Establishments under the relevant law. The government privatization scheme made no distinction between the two.

By the first notification of the Finance Division, Government of Pakistan, No. F.5(1)-Admn-1/91, dated 22 July 1991, the President of Pakistan established a Privatization Commission for Industries with the following terms of reference:

1. To invite applications for the total or partial privatization of public sector industries and enterprises and ensure widest possible participation.
2. To evaluate bids received according to criteria prescribed by the government and formulate recommendations for consideration by the government.
3. To recommend to the government such labour/ manpower rehabilitation programmes as might be necessary whilst privatizing units and to develop a roster of such employees who might need rehabilitation or develop self-employment on the basis of small financing.
4. To advise the government on implementing a development programme for improvement of public sector units till their privatization.
5. To assist in the implementation of government policies on deregulation and privatization and advise the government on deregulating the economy to the maximum possible extent; and
6. To review and recommend measures for the revival and rehabilitation of those industries which were closed and were under the control of the NCBs and DFIs.

The above task was assigned to civil servants whose official net emoluments after deduction of accommodation and other allowances ranged between 1500–12000 rupees, that is, 50–400 US dollars per month. Hence, professionals with relevant knowledge and experience would not be attracted to join the civil service. Consequently, apart from the sale of managed establishments and a number of irregularities inherent in such transactions, the terms of reference were not implemented.

By the second notification of the Finance Division, Government of Pakistan No. F.5(4)-Admn.1/92, dated 10 May 1992, the President established a Privatization Commission (Power Sector) with the following terms of reference:

1. To undertake privatization in the power sector in accordance with the privatization policy of the government.
2. To determine suitable modalities for carrying out privatization transactions keeping in view the government's objectives.
3. To appoint consultants for privatization.

4. To evaluate the offers received from the private sector and to make recommendations for the government's consideration and approval.
5. To hold negotiations with prospective buyers and to sign agreements after approval by the government.
6. To propose a regulatory framework for the government's approval. This framework was to ensure smooth and efficient operation of privatized units and protect the interests of the consumers.
7. To safeguard the genuine interests of the employees of the entities proposed to be privatized and devise suitable packages for their welfare including possible participation in ownership.
8) To suggest measures as might be considered necessary to ensure modernization and expansion of the privatized units to meet the growing demand from consumers.

While the bureaucratic set-up of the Privatization Commission was busy in formulating and following their set procedures, the cartels were busy devising ways and means to take over certain industries so as to retain a monopoly within a particular sector. For instance, a number of cement industries were acquired by the same group by bidding through Calicon Pvt. Ltd. and other companies incorporated under the Companies Ordinance, 1984, as a means of hiding their identities. In practice, it so happened that companies A, B, and C all owned by one group placed three different bids for a certain cement industrial unit which were considered to be the first, the second, and the third highest respectively. Under the bidders' plan, companies A and B did not comply with the letters of intent forwarded to them by the Privatization Commission in accordance with a pre-planned procedure and forfeited their deposits, company C was enabled to purchase the unit for a very low price. In some cases, the sale price was even lower than the commercial value of the land on which the unit was built. It is common knowledge that the cartels made windfall profits following divestiture of cement factories.[9]

Zahid Sarfraz, one of the ministers of the Nawaz government is reported to have said[10]

> almost all the industrial units which are sold to the private sector were making profits and did not fall in the category of financially insolvent enterprises. Privatization is used as a vehicle for providing economic benefits to those industrialists who have supported Mr Nawaz Sharif in securing him political supremacy in the country. Mr Nawaz Sharif is trying to create monopolies and cartels of high profit earning industrial products which will ultimately lead to the concentration of economic resources of the country in the hands of four or five families or groups.

The former Chairman of the Privatization Commission, Lieutenant-General Saeed Qadir, is on record as having said that concentration of economic power was inevitable and suggested that 'It is not always a bad thing'. He failed to realize that, in Britain, whose privatization programme had been accepted as a model for other countries, the primary objective was stated to be the improvement of living standards of the people.

The second front used by cartels as a vehicle to gain ownership and control was the trade union of employees working in the target industry since according to the Transfer of Managed Establishment (Amendment) Act, 1992, if the highest bid was made by the employees of a managed establishment, a letter of intent to sell the unit had to be forwarded to the employees' union by the Privatization Commission. Ironically, there were only 500 employees working in Pak-Saudi Fertilizer who were interested in purchasing the unit at as high a price as 400 million rupees. Similarly, Pakistan Switchgear Ltd. was supposed to have been purchased by Pakistan Switchgear Employees' Association. However, it subsequently transpired from a Lahore High Court writ petition No. 2263 of 1993 filed by the said Association against the former Secretary and his brother that the former Secretary's brother and his associates were behind the facade of workers' buy-out scheme in the deal.

It is interesting to note that Clause 2 of the Instructions to Bidders concerning the source of financing says:

> The Government shall not enquire about the source of financing from any of the bidders.

Clearly, such an exemption would extend even to illicit funds generated from the sale of drugs. Consequently, objections were raised by different circles regarding the cover provided for black money under Clause 2 of the Instructions to Bidders.

One of the major criticisms levied against the divestiture process was that bidders were not provided with all the relevant information. The bidders were expected to be ready within thirty days, which was unrealistic. The World Bank had written to the Government of Pakistan in September 1993 expressing doubts about the rationale of rapid privatization, adding that a successful sale effort required at least eighteen months to prepare a comprehensive programme that would cover all aspects of privatization. One wonders why the World Bank failed to point to the lack of a legislative framework as well as legal cover for the Privatization Commission which could have taken that long to go through parliamentary procedure. Considering the fact that it took Britain ten years to privatize approximately sixty units, France five years for sixty-five units, and Malaysia seven years for fifty-four units, accelerated privatization in Pakistan was made possible through bypassing parliamentary approvals unlike the process in Britain and other countries and the slipshod manner of privatizing SOEs. The fact that the bids were either too low or too high points to an incorrect method of evaluation.[11]

During September-October 1993, the World Bank mission comprising a Senior Private Sector Development Specialist and Project Adviser, visited the Privatization Commission. After perusing relevant material and holding discussions with staff members, it provided the Commission with a formal report, the salient points of which were:

- The first wave of the privatization programme should be deemed a success and the former Privatization Commission be commended for it.
- Privatization was carried out in a decisive manner.

- Privatization Commission was relatively free from bureaucratic hassles and red tape.
- The mandate of the Privatization Commission was clear and limited.
- The government and the Privatization Commission were able to overcome initial opposition to privatization from many vested interests, but it managed to win labour to its side.
- Strong political commitment of the Prime Minister and the Finance Minister guaranteed the success of the privatization process.
- On average, the process was probably more transparent than in most other developing countries.
- Shortcomings identified in the report included:
  - The speed imposed on the privatization process was unrealistic.
  - There was a lack of preparation of transactions.
  - There was inadequate availability of information to bidders.
  - Obligations were not disclosed after closing of bids were imposed on buyers.
  - The quality of contractual agreements was deficient.
  - In some cases, accounts and financial statements given to buyers did not reflect a true picture.
  - In some cases, information was provided to some bidders but not to all.[12]

In Pakistan, the term 'irregularity' equates with what is considered a white-collar crime in other countries. Irregularities can be classified in the following two different categories:

> Either, irregularities committed through omission due to indolence or lack of sufficient knowledge about legal consequences arising out of such omission;
> Or, irregularities committed in furtherance of a pre-planned scheme aimed at seeking some pecuniary or other advantage for the perpetrator or his relatives or associates, knowing well that doing so is unlawful and using intricate methods to conceal them.[13]

It is not possible to enumerate all the irregularities that crept into the process of denationalization and privatization. Some of the major ones noticed were:

1. Financial statements prepared by the Privatization Commission to arrive at a reference price were done in a disorganized manner and were not based on any objective criterion.
2. There was interference by bureaucrats, particularly by some federal secretaries, who wanted to benefit their own relatives and, of course, themselves in the process.
3. Privatized units were handed over to new owners without the settlement of workers' dues.
4. The management of some privatized units was handed over without receiving payment of the bid value. In one case, the requirement was payment of 40 per cent of the bid value before transfer of management but this was not done and the management was transferred on receipt of only 26 per cent of the bid value.

5. In some cases, the management was handed over to the new owners without obtaining acceptable bank guarantees for the balance 60 per cent of the bid value.
6. In some cases, bids were not opened at the scheduled date and time but later, in a clandestine manner, in the interest of favourites.
7. There were frequent defaults in the payment of the balance amount of the bid price and no serious effort was made to recover it or to repossess the unit.
8. Exorbitant fees were paid to legal consultants who were appointed on political considerations.[14]

Thus the process of denationalization and privatization was contaminated by those involved in it, obviously out of consideration for their own interest or the interest of their political bosses, without any regard for the common national interest.

Presidential References

As discussed earlier, the PDA did not accept the results of the elections which, according to the White Paper issued by it, were massively rigged at the instance of Ishaq, in association with the caretaker governments at the centre and in the provinces. However, the PDA decided to sit in the opposition in the national as well as in the provincial assemblies. It is rumoured that Benazir offered Nawaz co-operation in her attempt to repeal the Eighth Amendment, thus withdrawing the power of the President to dissolve one National Assembly at his discretion. This proposal was not accepted by Nawaz who was obviously obliged to Ishaq for dismissing Benazir and for paving the way to his rise to power.

The opposition initially attacked the President for rigging the general elections of 1990 and for instituting presidential references against Benazir for misconduct. Benazir's husband, Asif Ali Zardari, was also involved in several criminal cases, remained in jail for more than two years during the pendency of proceedings against him. All these references were filed under a special law introduced in the year 1977 for the disqualification of members of Parliament and provincial assemblies.[15] Some of the references filed are listed below:

Reference Number One pertained to a contract awarded for the expansion and augmentation of KESC (Karachi Electric Supply Corporation). This project was financed by an Asian Development Bank (ADB) loan of 100 million US dollars. It was alleged that Benazir, disregarding the opinion of the Minister for Water and Power, the decision of the Competent Board of Directors of KESC, and the concurrence of ADB, made every attempt to exclude the lowest and the most qualified bidder of the tender, namely M/s Lahmeyar, and tried to award the contract to M/s Fichtner at a higher rate, and thereby attempted to cause a loss to the government of Pakistan to the extent of 101.3 million ruppees.[16]

Reference Number Two pertained to the sale of raw cotton bales. It is alleged that Benazir, disregarding advice from the CEC (Cotton Export Corporation), the Secretaries

Committee and the Ministry of Commerce, and the clamour of KCA (Karachi Cotton Association) and APTMA (All Pakistan Textile Mill Owners Association) regarding the impropriety of the deal, violated the established rules and procedures for the sale of cotton, thereby abusing her power and position as Prime Minister and Chairman ECC (Economic Coordination Committee of the Cabinet). She manipulated the ECC to enter into a contract with Ralli Brothers, a predesignated firm, causing a loss of approximately 4.6 million US dollars, that is over 10 crore rupees.[17]

Reference Number Four pertained to the allotment of land for the Lake View Hotel Project. It was alleged that disregarding the CDA (Capital Development Authority) Ordinances/Regulations/Rules thereunder, in violation of the CDA Master Plan and by ignoring the available expert advice of CDA officials, Benazir had the letter of intent issued to M/s IGTC (International Guarantee Trust Company) for their proposal at extremely low rates and then made an attempt to issue a letter of allotment, which action was eventually frustrated by order of status quo by the Lahore High Court. It was also alleged that in order to achieve the purpose of showing undue favours to M/s IGTC at the cost of the CDA, Benazir removed the Chairman CDA and Mr Sehwani, Member Planning, and also changed the CDA Regulations to facilitate this transaction. She created a committee for the allotment and dispensed with the well-established system of auction. Had this deal gone through, it would have caused a loss of hundreds of crores of rupees to the CDA and the Exchequer and an equivalent, undue gain to IGTC. It was widely rumoured that Zardari had substantial interest in the deal and IGTC was only a front since the real profits would have been milked by Zardari and his collaborators.[18]

Reference Number Five pertained to the allocation of Liquified Petroleum Gas quota. It was alleged that allocation of Liquified Petroleum Gas quota by Benazir, besides being in breach of statutory rules, was arbitrary, discriminatory, and without reasonable basis. It was also a case of favouritism, nepotism, wilful maladministration and abuse of power and position.[19]

Reference Number Ten pertained to the misuse of Pakistan Air Force planes during the no-confidence motion against Benazir. It was alleged that various MNAs were transported from Chaklala to Saidu Sharif and from Peshawar to Saidu Sharif. This constituted misconduct through wilful misappropriation and diversion of public money and resources.[20]

Reference Number Eleven pertained to the disbursement of secret service funds. It was alleged that Benazir disbursed millions of rupees from the secret service funds for unauthorized purposes, including the effort to win as many members of the National Assembly as possible, for winning election of the prime minister of Azad Kashmir, and to win as many members of the Provincial Assembly of NWFP as possible. It was alleged that the misconduct of Benazir in this matter resulted in a considerable loss of 95.1 million rupees to the national exchequer in the financial years 1988/89 and 1989/90.[21]

Reference Number Thirteen pertained to appointments made through the Placement Bureau. It was alleged that Benazir committed acts of favouritism and wilful maladministration and/or otherwise acts of misconduct as Prime Minister and Minister in charge of Establishment Division in abuse of her power and position in appointing, or causing to be appointed members and sympathisers of her political party and others to public office in violation of the civil service laws, the rules framed thereunder, and other establishment and relevant procedures, and that in order to ensure implementation of her unlawful orders, threatened disciplinary action against senior officers to act contrary to the law/rules, thereby undermining the civil services.[22]

All these references lingered on for so long that, before they could be decided, Benazir returned to power in 1993. Consequently, the references were not prosecuted and were eventually dismissed. There are always serious difficulties in proving allegations of a factual nature, particularly when bureaucrats and other interested parties to shady deals do not cooperate and did everything within their power to frustrate and defeat such proceedings. This is perhaps the reason why no serious accountability of politicians, senior bureaucrats, and army Generals could take place in Pakistan. After all, the charges were not wholly concocted.

The Twelfth Amendment

It has been discussed earlier that one of the consequences of the Afghan war was the spread of violence throughout Pakistan. Street crimes and car snatching, hitherto a rare phenomena in Pakistan, became common occurrences. Robberies and dacoities on highways and break-ins in residential areas spread widely. One of the solutions to this thought out by the Nawaz government was to create special courts for the trial of heinous offences. Special courts for speedy trials had been established during Junejo's government but the laws creating them had expired. It was considered important by Nawaz that such courts be given a constitutional cover.

Consequently, the Twelfth Amendment to the Constitution was passed by Parliament in July 1991, the main purpose of which was the establishment of Special Courts for the trial of heinous offences. For this purpose, Article 212B was added to the Constitution.[23] It read:

212B Establishment of Special Courts
for trial of heinous offences:

1. In order to ensure speedy trial of cases of persons accused of such of the heinous offences specified by law as are referred to them by the Federal Government, or an authority or person authorized by it, in view of their being gruesome, brutal, and sensational in character or shocking to public morality, the Federal Government may by law constitute as many Special Courts as it may consider necessary.
2. Where the Federal Government constitutes more than one Special Court, it shall determine the territorial limits within which each one of them shall exercise jurisdiction.
3. A Special Court shall consist of a judge, being a person who is, or has been, or is qualified for appointment as a judge of a High Court and is appointed by the Federal Government after consultation with the Chief Justice of the High Court.
4. A person other than a judge of a High Court who is appointed as a judge of a Special Court shall hold office for the period this Article remains in force and shall not be removed from office except in the manner prescribed in Article 209 for the removal from office of a judge and, in the application of the said Article for the purpose of this clause, any reference in that Article to a judge shall be construed as a reference to a judge of a Special Court.

5. The law referred to in clause (1) shall make provision for the constitution of as many Supreme Appellate Courts as the Federal Government may consider necessary and for an appeal against the sentence or final order of a Special Court being preferred to a Supreme Appellate Court which shall consist of —
   (a) a Chairman, being a judge of the Supreme Court to be nominated by the Federal Government after consultation with the Chief Justice of Pakistan; and
   (b) two judges of the High Courts to be nominated by the Federal Government after consultation with the Chief Justice of the High Court concerned.
6. Where the Federal Government constitutes more than one Supreme Appellate Court, it shall determine the territorial limits within which each one of them shall exercise jurisdiction.
7. A Special Court and a Supreme Appellate Court shall decide a case or, as the case may be, an appeal within thirty days.
8. Notwithstanding anything contained in the Constitution, no court shall exercise any jurisdiction whatsoever in relation to any proceedings before, or order or sentence passed by a Special Court or a Supreme Appellate Court constituted under a law referred to in clause (1), except as provided in such law.

Other provisions of the Twelfth Amendment related to the enhancement of salaries of the judges of the Supreme Court and the High Courts under the Fifth Schedule to the Constitution. The Twelfth Amendment was a temporary amendment as far as Article 212B was concerned and was to last for a period of three years only. Article 212B thus became ineffective in July 1994.

The Twelfth Amendment created a hierarchy of courts parallel to the constitutional hierarchy consisting of the High Courts and the Supreme Court. A Special Court under this amendment was not subordinate to the High Court and the Supreme Court. The Supreme Appellate Court was an anomalous court ranking somewhere in between the High Courts and the Supreme Court. It had a Supreme Court judge as its chairman and two High Court judges as members.

Legislation Regarding the Separation of Judiciary from the Executive

Since Zia had suspended the operation of the Constitution, in particular the provisions regarding the separation of the judiciary from the executive, the matter remained in cold storage until 1985 when, under the RCO, the period was extended to fourteen years, which was to expire on 14 August 1987. The government at that time felt no urgency despite the fact that the period was reaching its expiry because it desired judicial powers to remain in the hands of executive magistrates.

Inaction on the part of the executive was challenged by members of the Bar immediately on the expiry of the fourteen years on 14 August 1987 before the High Courts in constitutional jurisdiction, and they prayed for mandamus against the federal and provincial governments to fulfil the constitutional dictate of separating the judiciary from the executive. A full Bench of the Sindh High Court consisting of seven judges accepted the writ petition filed by Sharaf Faridi[24] and other advocates by a majority of six to one. The Court held that the separation of the judiciary from the executive would mean:[25]

(a) that the executive should place adequate annual funds at the disposal of the judiciary for operating it without any interference by any agency of the executive;
(b) that the appointment of the Chief Justice and judges of the Supreme Court and Chief Justices and judges of High Courts by the President, in consultation with the Chief Justice of Pakistan and Chief Justice of the concerned High Court, as the case may be, should be meaningful;
(c) that transfer of a High Court judge to another High Court without his consent or his appointment to the Federal Shariat Court without his consent, militates against the concept of independence/separation of judiciary as envisaged by the Constitution;
(d) that denial and failure to establish independent courts and tribunals by separating them from the executive would negate the fundamental right of life and liberty guaranteed to citizens by the Constitution.

The Court held that since after the enforcement of the Constitution, the various federal and provincial governments had failed to do what they were required to under the Constitution, a direction under Article 199 could be issued to them. The Court emphasized that in order to bring the laws in conformity with Article 175 and similar provisions, not only administrative but also some legislative measures were needed. Since it was contestable whether direction could be issued to legislatures to discharge their constitutional obligation, a direction could be issued to the federal and provincial governments to initiate legislative measures for bringing existing laws in conformity with Article 175.

The Court issued the following directions to the government of Sindh:

1. to issue necessary notification for bifurcating the magistracy into judicial and executive magistrates and to place the judicial magistrates under the administrative control of the High Court within a period of six months;
2. to issue necessary notification for placing the judicial magistrates under the departmental control of the High Court including their disciplinary matters; and
3. to initiate legislative measures within a period of six months in order to make necessary amendments in the relevant statutes to bring them in conformity with Articles 175 and 203 of the Constitution.

The federal government was directed to initiate all legislative and administrative steps to bring existing laws relating to or affecting the judiciary in accordance with Articles 175 and 203 of the Constitution within a period of six months.

The dissenting judge, Justice Mamoon Kazi, held that the provisions of Article 175(3) could not be construed as self-executory and, therefore, Article 175(3) was not enforceable nor did it confer any power on the High Court to issue directions for its implementation.

The Supreme Court upheld the majority judgment of the Sindh High Court in nearly all its material details.[26] The Court held:

> The independence of the judiciary means
> (a) that every judge is free to decide matters before him in accordance with his assessment of the facts and his understanding of the law without improper influences, inducements or pressures, direct or indirect, from any quarter or for any reason; and
> (b) that the Judiciary is independent of the Executive and Legislature, and has jurisdiction, directly or by way of review, over all issues of a judicial nature.

On financial independence of the judiciary, the Supreme Court laid down the following guidelines:

> Financial independence of the judiciary can be secured if the funds allotted to the Supreme Court and High Courts (by the Parliament and the Provincial Assemblies in their respective annual budgets) are allowed to be disbursed within the limits of the sanctioned budget by the respective Chief Justices of these Courts without any interference by the Executive (in practical terms without reference to and seeking the approval of the Ministry of Finance/the Provincial Finance Department). Thus, the Chief Justice would be competent to make reappropriation of the amounts from one head to another, create new posts, abolish old posts or change their nomenclature, and to upgrade or downgrade etc. as per requirements of their respective Courts and this should be possible without being obliged to seek the approval of the Ministry of Finance or the Provincial Finance Departments as the case may be, provided of course the expenditure that is incurred by them falls within the limits of the budget allocation for their Courts. To ensure financial discipline, an Accounts Officer of the Accountant-General may sit in all Courts for pre-audit and issue of cheques. In this way, the control of the executive over the judiciary in this important sphere will be eliminated and the judiciary enabled to function independently.

The Supreme Court also held that:

> The following directions consistent with the mandate contained in Article 175 of the Constitution would suffice to secure the separation of the judiciary from the executive, namely:
> (i) The Governments of Sindh and Punjab shall issue the requisite notifications in terms of subsection (2) of section 1 of Law Reforms Ordinance (XII of 1972) for enforcing the provisions of the aforesaid Ordinance by 23 March, 1994, for bifurcating the magistracy into Judicial Magistrates and Executive Magistrates and place all the Judicial Magistrates under the administrative control of the Court; and
> (ii) The Federal Government as also the provincial governments of Sindh, Punjab, NWFP, and Balochistan shall not require the Supreme Court and the High Courts of the provinces to seek their approval to incur expenditure on any item from the funds allowed for them in the annual budgets, provided the expenditure incurred falls within the limit of the sanctioned budgets, as is more fully explained in the body of the judgment. Necessary instructions to enable compliance with this direction shall be issued by the federal government and the provincial governments to all concerned by 1-12-1993.

Differences between the President and the Prime Minister

To begin with, the relationship between the President and the Prime Minister had been cordial, but in 1993 it turned sour. It was rumoured that Prime Minister Nawaz Sharif wanted to amend the Constitution so as to undo the discretionary powers of the President to dissolve the National Assembly and also to appoint chiefs of armed forces. The President publicly defended such powers under the Eighth Amendment and vowed to fight for their retention in the Constitution. The relationship between the two further deteriorated till finally, the Prime Minister came out publicly on 17 April 1993, and attacked the President, alleging that he was actively encouraging intrigues and conspiracies to destabilize his government. Nawaz vowed not to resign, not to advise the dissolution of the National Assembly, and not to take any dictation from the President.

One of the immediate causes of the differences between the two men was disagreement over the appointment of the Chief of Army Staff. General Asif Nawaz, Chief of Army Staff, had died suddenly in January 1993 and his successor had to be chosen. Nawaz wanted a General of his choice but Ishaq did not want any encroachment on his discretion to appoint the army chief. Earlier, the relationship between Nawaz and General Asif Nawaz had soured and it was felt that Nawaz and his family wanted to have their way with the armed forces so that his stay in power was not threatened.[27] This conflict came to a head when Ishaq appointed General Abdul Waheed Kakar as army chief without consulting or even informing Nawaz Sharif. The Prime Minister saw this as a clear affront to him.

Dissolution of the National Assembly

It has been discussed earlier that in his address to the nation on television and radio on 17 April 1993, Nawaz openly criticized Ishaq and threatened to act in future without consultation with the President. Ishaq, an old warrior and already 78-years-old, was not going to take such a threat lying down. He immediately started collecting his advisers around him to make his own move at the earliest. For his assistance, Ishaq called Syed Sharifuddin Pirzada who, as Law Minister and Attorney-General during Zia's regime, had earned a reputation as someone adept at distorting the Constitution and framing laws in order to suit the convenience of his master.

On 18 April 1993, the day following Nawaz Sharif's speech, Ishaq retaliated by ordering the dissolution of the National Assembly and dismissed the Prime Minister and his Cabinet. A caretaker prime minister and cabinet were immediately installed. The President gave the following reasons for his action in his address to the nation on television and radio: [28]

1. The constitutional, political, and economic crisis facing the country was to be averted;
2. The situation around Pakistan, and internationally, was most unsatisfactory;
3. The former Prime Minister tried to hide the misdeeds of his government while he dared to jeopardize Pakistan's highest constitutional office, national integrity, prestige, dignity, and honour of the country;

4. Most of the federating units (provinces) were vociferously protesting against the attitude and predominance of the federal government;
5. The Council of Common Interests (CCI) had been relegated to a meaningless status despite all propagation to the contrary;
6. Complaints were being received from all the provinces about the functioning of the National Finance Commission;
7. The former Prime Minister interfered personally and gave orders in small matters thus paralysing the administrative machinery, and this had practically destroyed the chain of command;
8. Although the government had drummed up its economic reforms, in actual fact its measures were leading the country's economy towards a deep abyss and reaching a point of no return;
9. National wealth was being concentrated in a few hands and national resources were being monopolized by a few favourites. In a frenzy of making the rich richer, the poor were being rendered poorer; and
10. Sensitive departments like PTCL, PIA, WAPDA, and Railways, which constituted the backbone of the national economy, were being denationalized.

Order of Dissolution

The Order of Dissolution is reproduced below:

> The President, having considered the situation in the country, the events that have taken place and circumstances, the contents and consequences of the Prime Minister's speech on 17 April 1993 and among others for the reasons mentioned below, is of the opinion that the Government of the Federation cannot be carried on in accordance with the provisions of the Constitution and an appeal to the electorate is necessary:
>
> (a) The mass resignation of the members of the Opposition and of considerable numbers from the Treasury Benches, including several ministers, *inter alia*, showing their desire to seek fresh mandate from the people have resulted in the Government of the Federation and the National Assembly losing the confidence of the people, and that the dissension therein, has nullified its mandate.
>
> (b) The Prime Minister held meetings with the President in March and April and the last on 14 April 1993, when the President urged him to take positive steps to resolve the grave internal and international problems confronting the country, and the nation was anxiously looking forward to the announcement of concrete measures by the government to improve the situation. Instead, the Prime Minister in his speech on 17 April 1993, chose to divert the people's attention by making false and malicious allegations against the President of Pakistan who is Head of State and represents the unity of the Republic. The tenor of the speech was that the government could not be carried on in accordance with the provisions of the Constitution, and he advanced his own reasons and theory for the same, which reasons and theory, in fact, are unwarranted and misleading. The Prime Minister tried to cover up the failures and defaults of the government although he was repeatedly apprised of the real reasons in this behalf,

which he even accepted and agreed to rectify by specific measures on urgent basis. Further, the Prime Minister's speech is tantamount to a call for agitation and in any case the speech and his conduct amounts to subversion of the Constitution.

(c) Under the Constitution, the Federation and the Provinces are required to exercise their executive and legislative authority as demarcated and defined and there are specific provisions and institutions to ensure its working in the interests of the integrity, sovereignty, solidarity, and well-being of the Federation and to protect the autonomy granted to the Provinces by creating specific constitutional institutions consisting of Federal and Provincial representatives; but the Government of the Federation has failed to uphold and protect these, as required, in that, *inter alia*:
   i. The Council of Common Interests under Article 153 which is responsible only to Parliament has not discharged its constitutional functions to exercise its powers as required by Article 153 and 154, and in relation to Article 161, and particularly in the context of privatisation of industries in relation to item 3 of Part II of the Federal Legislative List and item 34 of the Concurrent Legislative List.
   ii. The National Economic Council under Article 156, and its Executive Committee, has been largely by-passed, *inter alia*, in the formulation of plans in respect of financial, commercial, social, and economic policies.
   iii. Constitutional powers, rights, and functions of the provinces have been usurped, frustrated, and interfered with in violation of *inter alia*, Article 97.

(d) Maladministration, corruption, and nepotism have reached such proportions in the Federal Government, its various bodies, authorities, and other corporations including banks supervised and controlled by the Federal Government, the lack of transparency in the process of privatization and in the disposal of public government properties, that they violated the requirements of the oath(s) of the public representative together with the Prime Minister, the Ministers, and Ministers of State prescribed in the Constitution and prevent the Government from functioning in accordance with the provisions of the Constitution.

(e) The functionaries, authorities and agencies of the Government under the direction, control, collaboration, and patronage of the Prime Minister and Ministers have unleashed a reign of terror against the opponents of the government including political and personal rivals/relatives, and mediamen, thus creating a situation wherein the government cannot be carried on in accordance with the provisions of the Constitution and the law.

(f) In violation of the provisions of the Constitution:
   i. The Cabinet has not been taken into confidence or decided upon numerous Ordinances and matters of policy.
   ii. Federal Ministers have for a period even been called upon not to see the President.
   iii. Resources and agencies of the Government of the Federation, including statutory corporations, authorities, and banks, have been misused for political ends and purposes and for personal gain.
   iv. There has been massive wastage and dissipation of public funds and assets at the cost of the national exchequer without legal or valid justification resulting in increased deficit financing and indebtedness, both domestic and international, and adversely affecting the national interest including defence.
   v. Articles 240 and 242 have been disregarded in respect of the Civil Services of Pakistan.

(g) The serious allegations made by Begum Nuzhat Asif Nawaz as to the high-handed treatment meted out to her husband, the late Army Chief of Staff, and the further allegations as to the circumstances culminating in his death indicate that the highest functionaries of the Federal Government have been subverting the authority of the Armed Forces and the machinery of the Government and the Constitution itself.

(h) The Government of the Federation for the above reasons, *inter alia*, is not in a position to meet properly and positively the threat to the security and integrity of Pakistan and the grave economic situation confronting the country, necessitating the requirement of a fresh mandate from the people of Pakistan.

Now, therefore, I, Ghulam Ishaq Khan, President of the Islamic Republic of Pakistan, in exercise of the powers conferred on me by Clause (2)(b) of Article 58 of the Constitution of the Islamic Republic of Pakistan, and all other powers enabling me, hereby dissolve the National Assembly with immediate effect; and dismiss the Prime Minister and the Cabinet who shall cease to hold office forthwith.[29]

Order of Dissolution Challenged

The Order of Dissolution was challenged by the Speaker of the National Assembly, Gohar Ayub, before the Lahore High Court. While his constitutional petition was pending, Nawaz Sharif, the deposed Prime Minister, filed a constitutional petition under Article 184(3) of the Constitution directly before the Supreme Court, challenging the order of dissolution of the National Assembly on the ground of violation of fundamental rights. This petition was heard by a Bench of eleven judges, headed by the Chief Justice Nasim Hasan Shah, on a day-to-day basis. The Supreme Court accepted the constitutional petition by a majority of ten to one on 26 May 1993, holding in its short order that the impugned order of dissolution did not fall within the ambit of the powers conferred on the President in this behalf and was, therefore, not sustainable under the Constitution. The National Assembly, the Prime Minister and his Cabinet were thus restored and were held entitled to function with immediate effect. The appointment of the caretaker government was held to be of no legal effect. However, all actions taken and orders passed by the caretaker government, which were in accordance with the Constitution and which were required to be done and taken for the ordinary orderly running of the State were held to be valid.

The Supreme Court, in its detailed judgment,[30] gave several reasons for setting aside the order of dissolution passed by the President. Some of the major reasons that prevailed with the Supreme Court in the judgment of the majority are enumerated below:

1. In the scheme of the Constitution, the Prime Minister, in administering the affairs of the government, is neither answerable to the President, nor is in any way subordinate to him. He is answerable only to the National Assembly. It is the President who is bound by the advice of the Prime Minister or the Cabinet in all matters concerning formulation of policies and administration of affairs of the government and not the other way about. The President and the Prime

Minister are expected to work in harmony and despite personal rancour, ill-will, and incompatibility of temperament, no deadlock, no stalemate, no breakdown can arise if both act in accordance with the terms of the respective oaths taken by them while occupying their high offices.

2. Regarding the speech of the Prime Minister made on 17 April 1993, it was held that the material placed before the Court satisfied it that the opinion formed by the Prime Minister that the President had ceased to be a neutral figure and had started to align himself with his opponents and was encouraging them in their efforts to destabilize his government, was indeed one that could be reasonably entertained.
3. No man, howsoever high, can destroy an organ consisting of chosen representatives of the people unless cogent, proper, and sufficient cause exists for taking such a grave action and that no such situation had arisen or could be said to have arisen on account of the Prime Minister.
4. The speech of the Prime Minister did not amount to subversion of the Constitution, nor could it create a complete deadlock or stalemate resulting in collapse of constitutional machinery. If a speech does not create lawlessness, disorder, or threat to security or disruption, it would hardly amount to subversion of the Constitution.
5. Resignations from the Cabinet could not be a sure indication of lack of confidence in the government, nor do they affect or impair the smooth functioning of parliamentary democracy. The resignations of the ministers would be wholly irrelevant while taking into consideration or forming grounds for taking action under Article 58(2)(b) of the Constitution.
6. The ground of lack of 'transparency' in administration or privatization was held as vague criteria, not referable to any statutory provision, thus making the satisfaction of the empowered authority subjective and not objective. Such a ground for taking action under Article 58(2)(b) was held to be far-fetched, a matter of degree and quite unjustified, particularly in an environment of secrecy of financial transactions and non-existence of freedom to obtain information.
7. The allegations of corruption, maladministration, incorrect policies being pursued in matters financial, administrative, and international, were held to be neither independently decisive nor within the domain of the President for action under Article 58(2)(b) and thus wholly extraneous.
8. The President had no authority to receive resignations of the members of the National Assembly which had to be handed over personally by the members concerned to the Speaker of the National Assembly. Thus, resignations handed over to the President had no constitutional validity or value and these documents could not form the basis for arriving at the conclusion that the National Assembly had lost its representative capacity.
9. The requirements of Article 58(2)(b) of the Constitution are all objective and relatable to the various constitutional provisions.
10. The grounds mentioned in the dissolution order of 18 April 1993, neither collectively nor individually, justified the inference that a situation had arisen

in which the government of the federation could not be carried on in accordance with the provisions of the Constitution and an appeal to the electorate was necessary.

Justice Saad Saood Jan, while agreeing with the majority view on the merits of the case, held that the petition was not maintainable under Article 184(3) of the Constitution. Justice Muhammad Rafiq Tarar went to the extent of observing that the President had no power to dismiss a prime minister, directly or indirectly, howsoever illegal, unconstitutional, or against public interest his actions might look to him. The President, according to him, by removing the Prime Minister under the cloak of the powers contained in Article 58(2)(b) and dissolving the National Assembly might be accused of subverting the Constitution within the meaning of Article 6 of the Constitution. Nine judges out of the majority held that the petition was maintainable having reference to enforcement of the fundamental rights or any of them. Justice Shafiur Rehman, rendering the leading judgment, ventured into the determination of the discretionary power of the President to appoint chiefs of the armed forces. Although this was not apparently a list before the Court, the learned judge proceeded to hold that the President's discretionary power was restricted to the appointment of the Chairman of the Joint Chiefs of Staff and the appointment of the three Chiefs of Army, Air, and Naval Staff could only be made by the President on the advice of the Prime Minister. This interpretation appears to be very attractive on the face of it, but with due respect to the learned judge who undoubtedly has been one of the competent judges in Pakistan, it does not appear to be correct applying the established principle of statutory interpretation to the plain reading of the language of Article 243(i)(c) as amended by the RCO (PO 14 of 1985) that amendment made in a statute becomes part and parcel of the parent statute and cannot be read separately therefrom.

Justice Sajjad Ali Shah, the lone dissentor, came up with a strong opinion differing with his colleagues, both on the question of merit as well as on the question of maintainability of the petition. He held that the petition could not be filed straightway in the Supreme Court because Article 184(3) could not be invoked for the reason that there was no fundamental right available to the petitioner to continue the government till the tenure came to an end. He made a comparison between the case of Ahmad Tariq Rahim in order to show that the material produced in the present case was both qualitatively and quantitatively superior to that of the case of Tariq Rahim. He observed that the same yardstick for evaluation of material and interpretation of Article 58(2)(b) should be followed and no departure should be made from the guidelines laid down in the cases of Haji Saifullah and Ahmad Tariq Rahim by the Supreme Court. He took notice of the fact that Islami Jamhoori Ittehad, an amalgam of several parties, jointly contested the elections and formed government but the several parties dissociated themselves from it and even the Muslim League was split into two groups, the Nawaz Sharif Group and the Junejo Group. Hence, he held that IJI was not, at the time of dissolution, the same group of political parties which had been voted into power. He held that the prime minister and the president, have to work together in an atmosphere of congeniality to run the daily affairs of the government. The fact that a situation creating stalemate in the working relationship of the two pillars of the government had become a *fait accompli* validly enabling the President to exercise his discretionary power under Article 58(2)(b). Regarding the grounds of maladministration, corruption, and nepotism, the learned judge took notice of the sale of Muslim Commercial Bank and eight cement factories to the Mansha Group, a favourite of Nawaz Sharif. The learned judge observed that there was no difference in the case of Ahmad Tariq Rahim and the one in hand in so far as allegations, grounds of dissolution, and material produced in support thereof were concerned, and that a departure was made and the same yardstick of evaluation of material was not applied. He lamented that 'seemingly it so appears that two prime ministers from Sindh were sacrificed at the altar of Article 58(2)(b) of the Constitution but when the turn of a prime minister from the Punjab came, the tables were turned'.

While rendering his incisive dissenting opinion, the learned judge appeared to have forgotten that he was also making a departure from his own earlier dissenting opinion in the case of Ahmad Tariq Rahim. Was he not expected or required to apply the same yardstick as he had done in his earlier judgment? After holding the two cases similar and liable to similar result, was he not bound by his opinion in Ahmad Tariq Rahim's case holding the order of the President invalid?

The Caretaker Government

When the President and the Prime Minister fell apart in 1993, and Nawaz Sharif's government was sacked, the power to appoint a caretaker cabinet was abused to the maximum. Balakh Sher Mazari, who had fallen out with Nawaz and had formed a group hostile to him within the Muslim League, was appointed caretaker prime minister. Benazir and her husband, against whom the Pesident had filed cases alleging corruption, abuse of power, and resorting to terrorist activities, were invited to participate in the caretaker cabinet, an offer that she and her husband readily accepted. Bhutto had her husband appointed federal minister, against whom several cases for corruption and terrorist activities were pending. Ishaq, in his moment of desperation, did not hesitate to administer oath as federal minister to a person whom he had accused of serious acts of terrorism and corruption. Benazir Bhutto also got several of her partymen appointed federal ministers and advisers. The number of ministers and advisers in the federal cabinet broke all previous records.[31] Preparations were afoot to repeat the performance of 1990, this time to keep Nawaz out of power, in the aborted elections of July 1993. The leader and members of the PPP who had been crying hoarse the previous three years against the injustices done to them by Ishaq, were suddenly his main supporters trying to do unto their opponents in 1993 exactly what had been done unto them in 1990. The caretaker cabinet became a spectre of unethical, ad hoc government without any care or consideration for principles or even basic dignified behaviour. The Supreme Court ended this political feast amongst strange bedfellows by restoring the dismissed federal government and by setting aside the order of dissolution of the National Assembly.

A lot can be said about this judgment, but the fact remains that it constitutes a judicial milestone in the history of Pakistan. It was a heartening departure from all the previous spineless judgments by the Courts. It is widely believed that the Courts in Pakistan, at various crucial times in history, have failed to stand up to men in power and their acts or orders, howsoever atrocious, have been upheld on one line of reasoning or another. In a couple of cases, where acts or orders of a person in power were actually disregarded by the Courts, the judgments came only after the death or departure from power of such a person.

It is unfortunate that the gains of this judgment were soon eroded by the vengeful President, in collusion with the provincial governments, and the restored federal government could not even last for two months. The positive effects of the judgment cannot be ignored or underestimated. In future, any president will have to think a hundred times before dissolving the National Assembly. The unfettered power of the president has been checked, clipped, and fettered. It went to the credit of judges who sat long hours every day to hear the case on priority basis, even at the cost of their personal concerns.[32] It would have been so much the better if some of the judges on the Bench had exercised restraint in making remarks and observations in the open court, thus disclosing their ideas rather prematurely.[33]

Constitutional Duel over the Punjab

After the dismissal of the Nawaz government, Wattoo managed to oust Wyne as Chief Minister of the Punjab and assume office.

The situation changed on 26 May 1993 when the Supreme Court restored the National Assembly and the federal cabinet headed by Nawaz Sharif who now felt that he could not run the federal government in the face of a hostile government in Punjab. Besides, he was indebted to the Chaudhris of Gujrat who had stood by him during his removal from office and perhaps he had made a deal with them to support their nominee, Parvez Elahi, for election to the office of chief minister of Punjab. Soon after the resumption of office on 26 May, he came to Lahore and launched a campaign to win over a majority of the members of the Provincial Assembly. With Nawaz in the saddle as Prime Minister and Shujaat Husain[34] as Federal Minister for Interior, an enterprise that was backed by big money, the position of Chief Minister Wattoo started sagging and large-scale defections began to take place from his camp to the opposite camp. Preparations were being made to table a vote of no-confidence against him. Pitted agains such heavy odds, Wattoo threw in the towel on 29 May 1993, and tendered advice to the Governor Altaf Husain[35] for dissolution of the Provincial Assembly, who immediately complied. Simultaneously, his opponents were gearing up to table a vote of no-confidence in order to incapacitate him from tendering advice to the Governor to dissolve the Assembly under explanation to Article 112(1) of the Constitution. The explanation under this Article disentitles the chief minister against whom a notice of resolution for vote of no-confidence had been moved in the Provincial Assembly, but has not been voted upon, from tendering advice to the governor to dissolve the Provincial Assembly. These events led to two conflicting claims and versions, one being that the advice to dissolve was tendered earlier and the other that the notice of motion for vote of no-confidence was delivered to the Secretary of the Provincial Assembly earlier. The first version was supported by the Chief Minister and the Governor, and the second by Parvez Elahi and his supporters who included former chief minister, Ghulam Haider Wyne.

Parvez Elahi challenged the order of dissolution of the Provincial Assembly of Punjab before the Lahore High Court in a constitutional petition which was heard by a full Bench of five judges. The Court made a detailed, factual enquiry into the conflicting versions of the parties and recorded evidence which included the statements of the Chief Minister, a former chief minister, and some senior bureaucrats. The petitioner contended that the order of dissolution was void because:

1. the notice of the resolution of a vote of no-confidence was delivered to the Secretary of the Provincial Assembly of the Punjab at his residence at 12:00 noon on 29 May 1993;
2. at the time the advice was tendered by the Chief Minister to the Governor, he was disentitled to do so as a notice of a resolution for vote of no-confidence against him had already been given;
3. the advice, as also the impugned order of dissolution based thereon, were fabricated subsequent to the delivery of the notice aforementioned; and
4. the advice and the order of dissolution are collusive and malafide.

On behalf of the respondents, it was controverted that the notice of resolution for vote of no-confidence was given at 12:00 noon or any time prior to the tender of advice for dissolution. It was asserted that the Chief Minister had tendered his advice to the Governor to dissolve the Assembly which was received by him at 11:35 a.m. on 29 May 1993 and on the basis thereof, the Assembly was dissolved at 4:00 p.m. on the same date, even if any notice had been served for a resolution for vote of no-confidence at 12:00 noon, the same day, it was of no legal effect.

The Lahore High Court accepted the constitutional petition and declared the order of the Governor dissolving the Provincial Assembly of Punjab without lawful authority, and of no legal effect, with the result that the Assembly stood restored.[36] After a lengthy examination and discussion of the evidence, the Court was led to the inference that neither the receipt of notice nor the tendering of advice and the passing of the order of dissolution had been established to have taken place at the said timings. However, it was concluded that the notice of resolution of no-confidence was delivered to the secretary at a time prior to the tendering of advice. The Court also held the advice tendered by the Chief Minister as malafide in law for the following reasons:

1. It was tendered solely to keep himself in power and to forestall any attempt to dislodge him.
2. The action was contrary to the assurances given by the Chief Minister even until 28 May 1993 that the Assembly would not be dissolved.
3. There was no issue on which an appeal to the electorate was necessary to curtail the normal constitutional life of the Assembly.

4. It did not lie with the Chief Minister to advise dissolution as a measure of punishment to those who had elected him, especially when it was with the help of those very members that he toppled the previous leader of the House and became the chief minister.
5. The advice was made apparently with a view to disturbing the functioning of a constitutional organ and the government machinery as an aftermath of the judgment delivered by the Supreme Court in the case of *Mian Mohammad Nawaz Sharif v the Federation of Pakistan,* etc. (PLD 1993 SC473) whereby the National Assembly and the federal government were restored on 26 May 1993.

Attempt to Impose Federal Government Rule in the Punjab

However, this judgment was immediately frustrated because, only an hour or two after its announcement, the Chief Minister again advised the dissolution of the Assembly and the Governor dissolved it forthwith. In the face of this situation, the federal government resorted to a proclamation under Article 234 of the Constitution to take over the administrative control of the Punjab. This proclamation was issued on the basis of a resolution passed at a joint sitting of the two Houses of the Parliament but was never sent to the President for his approval because the position taken by the federal government was that if such a proclamation was based on the resolution of Parliament in a joint sitting, then it could be issued without sending it to the President. On the contrary, the President's standpoint was that the matter had to be referred to him because only he could issue such a proclamation. This led to another serious constitutional crisis. The federal government appointed its representative to take over the provincial government in Punjab and ordered the federal force of Rangers to help him take over the government and to forcibly eject the Governor and/or the Chief Minister, if necessary. The Chief Minister, at the behest of the President, ordered the provincial police force to resist all such efforts. The Rangers force was forbidden by the Army High Command to get involved in any showdown with the police because the office of Judge Advocate General of the Army felt that the position taken by the President was legally correct.

After the frustration of this proclamation, another constitutional petition was filed by Parvez Elahi which was heard by a full Bench of eleven judges but before the hearing could proceed any further, a compromise between the President and the Prime Minister was brokered by the Army High Command on 18 July 1993 under which the President and the Prime Minister had to quit and neutral caretaker governments were installed at the federal and provincial levels to hold free and fair general elections.

Dissolution of the NWFP Provincial Assembly, 1993

Simultaneous to the dissolution of the Provincial Assembly of Punjab, the Provincial Assembly of the NWFP was dissolved by the Governor on the advice of the Chief

Minister. The situation in NWFP was somewhat similar to that of the Punjab and the opponents of the Chief Minister, Mir Muhammad Afzal, were trying to overthrow his government bringing a resolution for a vote of no-confidence against him. Obviously, the federal government headed by Nawaz was instrumental in doing so because the Chief Minister was believed to be sympathetic to the President. This dissolution was also challenged through a constitutional petition before the Peshawar High Court, which was heard by a full Bench of five judges.

The Peshawar High Court dismissed the constitutional petition holding that the advice for dissolution by the Chief Minister was tendered before a notice for a vote of no-confidence was given.[37] The Court also rejected the plea of the petitioners for liberal and progressive interpretation of Clause (1) of Article 112 read with the Explanation thereto. The Court was of the view that the sensitive nature of the dissolution and its political repercussions demand that nothing more than what was already there in Article 112(1) and the Explanation thereto should be read into them. The Court thus held

1. It is nowhere mentioned in this Clause and the Explanation that the Chief Minister should record reasons that prompted him to tender the advice for dissolution of the Assembly.
2. It is also nowhere mentioned that the Governor, instead of dissolving the Assembly forthwith on receipt of the advice, should hold an inquiry about the existence of a resolution for a vote of no-confidence against the advising Chief Minister or to require him to reconsider the advice or place it before the Cabinet or to ask him to obtain a vote of confidence from the Provincial Assembly.
3. It is also not provided that a Chief Minister, under the threat of a vote of no-confidence was disqualified to tender advice.
4. The notice of a resolution for a vote of no-confidence cannot be given outside the Assembly. Such notice, if oral, must be given on the floor of the House so that the Speaker is in a position to ascertain that it has been given by twenty per cent of the total membership of the Provincial Assembly. If the notice is in writing, it must be given either on the floor of the House to the Speaker or in the Assembly Secretariat to the Secretary of the Provincial Assembly. The meanings of the Assembly Secretariat cannot be extended so as to include the residence of the secretary and the additional secretary.

Exit of the President and the Prime Minister

The dramatic confrontation between Ishaq and Nawaz had its drop scene on 18 July 1993. The Prime Minister advised dissolution of the National Assembly and then resigned. The President passed the order of dissolution of the National Assembly and stepped down. The Chairman of the Senate, Wasim Sajjad, took over as Acting President. This compromise was evidently brokered by the army, with Chief of Army Staff General Abdul Waheed, playing a leading role. It also spoke volumes for the incompetence and timidity of Nawaz Sharif who mishandled the situation when everything was going in his favour. He had a two-thirds majority in the Parliament, the judiciary stood by him and had restored his government, and Ishaq was a lame duck president due to retire in six months time. But this mindless confrontation with the outgoing president and sordid efforts to oust the Punjab government through hasty horse trading, led to the fall of his government. When cornered by the President, the provincial government and, finally, the military leadership, Nawaz demonstrated no courage and meekly bowed out.[38] If he had shown the courage to refuse to resign, it was highly unlikely that the military leader would have forced him out. In fact, they might have been forced to help his government against the unruly pronvinces of the Punjab and the NWFP where the governments had lost all legal and moral authority to continue in office. But courage is not a quality to be found in those who are nurtured and planted into power by the establishment. In particular, those who have to save their financial empires can show little courage in the face of adversity, that is why conventional wisdom has always held that men who have widespread financial interests are not suitable for political office because, at the time of crisis, they run into the conflict of personal interest against national interest.

Performance of the Nawaz Government, 1990–93

Nawaz Sharif started his political career as a provincial minister under the Martial Law regime of Zia. It is said that his father had old ties with Lieutenant-General Ghulam Jilani Khan, Governor of Punjab, who patronized and introduced him to the inner circle of the generals around Zia. Nawaz Sharif soon won their confidence, which facilitated his appointment as Chief Minister of Punjab in 1985 while he was still in his thirties. He remained loyal to the military leadership and, in the differences that rose between Zia and Junejo resulting in the dismissal of Junejo's government, Nawaz took sides with Zia. He was thus retained as caretaker chief minister of Punjab and was encouraged by the military High Command to take on Junejo and challenge his leadership within the Muslim League.

It is generally believed that IJI, which included other political parties like Jamaat-e-Islami, was formed with the assistance of Inter Services Intelligence (ISI), and Nawaz Sharif was installed as its president to circumvent the stranglehold of the Muslim League headed by Junejo. It is also widely believed that it was due to the shrewd planning of the ISI that Nawaz Sharif emerged as the principal leader against the PPP which ultimately paved his way to the prime ministership of Pakistan in his early forties.

When Nawaz Sharif took over as the prime minister, he presented a package of liberal economic reforms which included privatization of nationalized industries, free movement of foreign exchange in and out of the country, and incentives to foreign and Pakistani capitalists for investment in Pakistan. He also did away with most of the restrictions of customs duty on goods being brought in by Pakistanis as accompanied baggage. It cannot be denied that these policies were, on the face of it, progressive and, if properly implemented, could have led to economic development.

The main reason whey they failed was the inherent conflict between the personal interests of Nawaz and his family on the one hand, and national interests on the other. His family was a medium-size industrial group successful around 1980 in steel works like iron re-rolling, when Nawaz Sharif entered politics. Since then, his family has built an industrial empire running into a large number of steel units, cotton textile mills, sugar mills, and so on. His official positions as a minister, chief minister, and then as prime minister, have come in handy in the process of building the family empire. The family has also benefited from lucrative land deals made from time to time with insider information about the policies of government regarding the setting up of industrial estates.

The second cause of the failure of the Nawaz government was political corruption. Nawaz is believed to have started his career as a businessman, where bribing officials belonging to government departments is a way of life. He apparently brought these skills into politics and refined it under mentors like Zia and Ghulam Jilani Khan. He is alleged to have used money, urban plots of lands, and other material favours to win over members of Parliament and the Provincial Assembly of NWFP to destabilize the federal government and the provincial government of NWFP when these were headed by the PPP. At the height of the confrontation between the federal government headed by Benazir and the Punjab government headed by Nawaz, there developed a war of urban plots of land between them. The federal government was using Capital Development Authority (CDA) plots, and the Punjab government was using Lahore Development Authority's (LDA) plots to grant political favours and to destabilize the governments of one another.

During his tenure as Chief Minister of the Punjab from 7 March 1985 to 6 August 1990, he allotted 1111 plots in various development schemes of LDA and 2027 plots in different schemes of the Housing and Physical Planning Department of the Punjab. He allotted or directed the allotment on lease of eight pieces of prime property with timberwood in Murree to different people, including some political figures. A few of them allegedly established their businesses after clearing the timber. As Chief Minister, he converted twenty to seventy plots, mostly commercial and some community property as well, into residential plots and allotted them to people of his choice at nominal prices. In the Johar Town Scheme of the LDA, he allotted sixty-six one-kanal plots against the chief minister's discretionary quota of twenty one-kanal plots.[39]

Nawaz is also known for his generosity in using public funds for obtaining political favours. As Prime Minister, he obtained 200 million rupees out of the Bait-ul-Mal Fund for the year 1992–93 and distributed 73 million rupees to the so-called needy, poor, widows, orphans, and others. The amount distributed per head varies from 500 rupees to lacs. Out of 862 beneficiaries, thirty-six got 50,000 rupees each, seven people got 200,000 rupees each, five people got 150,000 rupees each, a lucky widow got 300,000 rupees and a lucky man from Lahore got 500,000 rupees. These beneficiaries include some well-known motor dealers. This distribution was without any authorization under the law because, in the Pakistan Bait-ul-Mal Act, 1991, the prime minister does not figure in any capacity and it is only the Management Board of the Bait-ul-Mal which is competent to spend money in accordance with the purposes of the Act. In any case, the prime minister is allowed to spend 400,000 rupees as annual discretionary grant under the Prime Minister's Salary, Allowances, and Privileges Act, 1975. There seems to be no systematic and equitable method of selecting the poor and needy for the distribution of funds, nor was any criteria laid down for the allocation of funds per head. So this project meant nothing more than public posturing and self promotion.[40]

The privatization of nationalized industries, undoubtedly a good policy, was done in a not very commendable manner. There was no transparency to it and it clearly degenerated into favouritism and nepotism where favourites were given industrial units at a fraction of their real value. Mian Mansha, an unknown businessman but apparently a crony of Nawaz, could buy a nationalized bank and large cement plants at a subsidized price and become a tycoon overnight. Other friends and relatives were also having an open season, at the cost of national wealth. Nawaz introduced what is known as the 'Yellow Cab' scheme. It is said that valuable foreign exchange amounting to nearly 750 million US dollars was poured into it. For a political rather than economic cause it provided employment to a few at a price that was very high. The concessions given under the scheme were widely abused. Nawaz seemed to be running Pakistan as his personal fiefdom with a licence to do whatever he felt like with its national resources.

Nawaz and some members of his cabinet are believed to be deeply involved in the co-operative societies scandal where 17 billion rupees of the people's savings were siphoned off. The motorway from Lahore to Islamabad, costing nearly one billion US dollars, came under severe criticism as an example of misplaced priorities and extravagant policies. It is said that for this money, the long-awaited Indus Highway could have been constructed and the National Highway could have been doubled.

The foreign policy of Nawaz Sharif was another example of failure. There appeared to be no direction to it and Pakistan was increasingly isolated in the world. Relations with neighbouring countries hit a new low. Foreign aid was fast drying up. Nawaz had little understanding of and exposure to the management of foreign affairs. He could have made up for this deficiency by appointing a competent and experienced foreign minister. Instead, he allowed the bureaucrats with little initiative and limited perspective to conduct the foreign policy with obviously disappointing results.

Despite being the blue-eyed boy of the establishment and having been beholden to Ishaq, Nawaz Sharif finally fell out with him apparently on the appointment of the Chief of Army Staff. The gulf between the two widened until, on 18 April 1993, the National Assembly was dissolved under Article 58(2)(b) and Nawaz and his Cabinet were dismissed. His government was restored by the Supreme Court on 26 May 1993. Nawaz Sharif addressed the nation and promised to let bygones be bygones but old habits die hard. He was soon involved in horse-trading to topple the provincial government in Punjab which led to an open confrontation between the federal and the provincial governments, particularly in Punjab and the NWFP. These provincial governments were clearly aided by Ishaq. This tension and confrontation heightened to a point where opposition parties decided to march on the capital by giving a nationwide call for a 'long march' on 16 July 1993. This might have led to an ugly situation, possibly resulting in violent confrontation, had the army not intervened. Army leaders forced the opposition parties to call off the march, forced Nawaz to quit as prime minister and, at the same time, prevailed upon Ishaq to step down. The chairman of the Senate took over as acting President and caretaker governments were formed at the centre as well as in the provinces comprising mostly faceless bureaucrats who held out the promise to hold free, fair, and transparent general elections in October 1993.

The Caretaker Government

To everyone's surprise, Moeen Qureshi, a retired bureaucrat who had served for a long time outside the country in the World Bank, was appointed Caretaker Prime Minister. He was totally unknown in Pakistan and there were doubts about his Pakistani credentials. His only merit appeared to be that he was a political outsider and therefore expected to be neutral. Moeen Qureshi's experience, connections, and clout in the international community, particularly in international economic institutions, was to come in handy in resolving the economic mess Pakistan found itself in. For the caretaker government, governors and caretaker chief ministers were all taken from amongst retired civil and military bureaucrats.

Despite the fact that Qureshi was new to the political and social milieu in Pakistan, he made his presence felt. In the short period of ninety days, he tried to expose the misdeeds of the previous governments and published a list of defaulters of bank loans, exposing those who used their influence to abuse the banking system and used the depositors' money literally as their own by obtaining big loans without any intention of repayment. Moeen Qureshi also published a list of tax-payers that exposed many affluent people who were dodging the tax collectors while the burden was being borne by less fortunate tax-payers. The imposition of nominal tax on agricultural income was another significant step that earlier regimes kept shying away from to avoid the displeasure of the feudals. Moeen Qureshi made the State Bank of Pakistan an autonomous body with the objective of keeping political interference out of commercial banks. Ordinances were passed which made Pakistan Radio and Television autonomous, a step towards greater freedom of speech and expression. Other commendable steps of the caretakers included cutting down the size of the bloated administrative machinery, abolishing the discretion of the prime minister and the chief ministers in the allotment of residential plots, and concerted moves against drug traffickers. Qureshi initiated a campaign against the defaulters of bank loans but he had only limited success. His endeavour to collect unpaid utility bills also met with little success. It goes to his credit that at least he made a serious effort to recover government dues. The only blemish on Moeen Qureshi was that on his last day, he made a large number of promotions and other administrative decisions which included a favour to his brother and some other relations.

General Elections, October 1993

The general elections to the National Assembly were held on schedule on 6 October 1993. Results as were officially declared on 7 October 1993 of 201 constituencies, are as under:

Party	Punjab	NWFP	Sindh	Balochistan	Total
PPP	47	5	33	1	86
PML(N)	52	9	10	(Islamabad 1)	72
PML(J)	6	-	-	-	6
PIF (Pakistan Islamic Front)	-	2	1	-	3
ANP	-	3	-	-	3
JWP (Jamhoori Watan Party)	-	-	-	2	2
Islami Jamhoori Mahaz	-	2	-	2	4
Pakhtoon-Khwah Milli Awami Party	-	-	-	3	3
BNM (Hayee)	-	-	-	1	1
BNM (Mengal)	-	-	-	1	1
NPP	-	-	1	-	1
NDA	1	-	-	-	1
Pakhtoon-Khwah Qaumi Party	-	1	-	-	1
United Dini Mahaz	1	1	-	-	2
Independents	5	1	1	1	8

In addition, seven seats in the Federally Administered Tribal Areas went to the independents.

It is interesting to note that there was a very low turn out of voters in the general elections to the National Assembly. The overall percentage of voters was only 40.54 per cent. The province-wise breakdown is as under:[41]

Province	Votes cast	Registered voters	Turn out percentage
Punjab	14,197,173	29,539,003	48.75
Sindh	3,111,091	11,198,777	27.50
NWFP	1,981,941	5,849,409	34.10
Balochistan	668,025	2,753,029	23.00
Total	19,958,230	49,340,218	40.45%

The low turnout of voters compared to previous elections demonstrated a lack of interest and apathy on the part of the common citizen, who had discovered to his dismay that successive general elections did not bring any real change in his life and that all governments that came and went were inefficient, corrupt, and indifferent towards the problems of the people. When there is only a change of faces at the polls, there is hardly any motivation for the voter to go cast his vote.

As a result of elections to the National Assembly, no political party or political alliance emerged with a clear majority in the National Assembly. PPP and PML(N) stood as equal political forces in the country. Religious parties, including Pakistan Islamic Front (PIF), led by Jamaat-i-Islami, suffered a humiliating electoral defeat. PPP emerged as the largest party with eighty-six seats, followed by PML(N) with seventy-two seats. The number of votes taken by the PPP were 7,563,909 (38.1 per cent of the total votes cast) against 7,890,676 (39.7 per cent of the total votes cast) taken by PML(N). Nawaz thus claimed that his party had won a popular vote.

There are two factors worth mentioning have that tilted the balance in favour of the PPP. The first one was the PIF which secured only three seats in the National Assembly but was instrumental in the defeat of PML(N) in at least fourteen constituencies where there was a close race between the PPP and the PML(N). PIF, which was previously an ally of PML(N) in the IJI, took away enough votes from the PML(N) to ensure its defeat at the hands of PPP candidates with very narrow margins in fourteen closely contested seats. Had it not been so, the results would have been just the opposite. The second factor was MQM's boycott of the elections. The result was that in Karachi, thirteen seats were divided by PML(N) and PPP, each getting six seats and one going to PIF. Had MQM participated in the elections, all thirteen seats would have been taken by it. It has remained a political mystery why the MQM boycotted elections to the National Assembly, especially since they participated in the elections to the Provincial Assembly of Sindh three days later. The MQM has paid dearly for this political lapse. One explanation generally proffered in political circles is that they were forced by the armed forces not to participate in elections to the National Assembly. This explanation is at best speculation.

On 9 October 1993, elections were held to 459 seats of the provincial assemblies of four provinces. Once again, PPP and PML(N) emerged as the principal parties in the provincial polls. The voter turnout was slightly better, with twenty-two million voters casting their ballots and the percentage of turn out was 43.10 per cent. An important factor that might have made the difference of 2.5 per cent in voter turn out between the National and Provincial Assembly polls could be the MQM. The MQM participated in the local polls with the result that it swept Karachi and Hyderabad, once again winning twenty-seven seats in the Sindh Assembly.

The respective party positions in the four provinces were as under:[42]

Party	Punjab	NWFP	Sindh	Balochistan	Total
PPP	94	22	56	3	175
PML(N)	106	15	8	6	135
PML(J)	18	4	-	-	22
ANP	-	21	-	1	22
BNM (Haqiqi)	-	-	-	4	4
BNM (Mengal)	-	-	-	2	2
MQM (Haq Prast)	-	-	27	-	27
PIF	2	4	-	-	6
IJM	-	1	-	3	4
JWP (Jamhoori Watan Party)	-	-	-	4	4
NDA	2	-	-	-	2
JMP (Jamiat Mashaish Pakistan)	-	1	-	-	1
NPP	-	-	2	-	2
Independents	17	11	5	9	42
PNP	-	-	-	2	2
Dehati Ittehad	-	-	-	1	1
PKMAP	-	-	-	4	4
Bhutto Shaheed Committee	-	-	1	-	1
MDM	1	1	-	1	3
Total	240	80	99	40	459

Before the general elections, an understanding or alliance had been reached between the PPP and PML(J) on the one hand, and the PML(N) and ANP on the other. The position that emerged after the provincial polls was that PPP had an absolute majority in Sindh with fifty-six out of ninety-nine seats for which elections were held. The other party with a substantial following in Sindh was MQM (Altaf Group or Haq Prast) which won twenty-seven seats. In the Punjab, the PPP and PML(J) alliance had an edge over PML(N) with 112 against 106 seats respectively. In NWFP, the PML(N) and ANP alliance had a clear edge with thirty-six seats over the PPP and PML(J) who had together won twenty-six seats. PML(N) had emerged as the single largest party in the Punjab with 106 seats as against 94 taken by the PPP. In NWFP, the PPP was the largest single party with twenty-two seats, with a slight edge over the ANP which had twenty-one seats. Balochistan was a hotch-potch with nine out of forty seats going to independents and the remaining thirty-one seats divided amongst eleven parties. PML(N) won six seats which was more than any other single party. Pakistan Islamic Front (PIF) led by Jamaat-i-Islami, once again fared very poorly in the provincial polls. It only made its presence felt in the NWFP with two seats in the National Assembly and four seats in the NWFP Assembly. In the Punjab, PIF did not win any seat in the National Assembly and only had two seats in the Provincial Assembly. It did not win any seat in the provincial assemblies of Sindh and Balochistan.

NOTES

1. *The Nation*, 29 October 1990.
2. The actual number of seats in the Provincial Assembly of the NWFP are eighty-three, out of which eighty belong to regional constituencies and three to minorities.
3. *The Nation*, 6 November 1990.
4. Protection of Economic Reforms Ordinance, 1991 (Ordinance XXVI of 1991) PLD, 1991 Central Statutes 494. Protection of Economic Reforms Ordinance, 1991 (Ordinance XXXIX of 1991), PLD 1992 Central Statutes 55. Protection of Economic Reforms Ordinance, 1992 (Ordinance III of 1992), PLD 1992 Central Statutes 166.
5. Protection of Economic Reforms Act, 1992 (Act XII of 1992) PLD 1992 Central Statutes 250.
6. Mirza, S.A. *Privatization in Pakistan*, 1995, Ferozsons (Pvt) Ltd., Lahore, pp. 32-3.
7. Transfer of Managed Establishments (Amendment) Ordinance, 1991 (Ordinance XV of 1991), PLD 1991 Central Statutes 338. This Ordinance was later substituted by Transfer of Managed Establishments (Amendment) Act, 1991 (Act XXII of 1991), PLD 1992 Central Statutes 47.
8. Transfer of Managed Establishments (Second Amendment) Ordinance, 1991, (Ordinance XXXIII of 1991), PLD 1991 Central Statutes 551. The amendment contained in this Ordinance was subsequently incorporated in Transfer of Managed Establishments (Amendment) Act, 1992 (Act V of 1992). PLD 1992 Central Statutes 224.
9. Mirza, S.A. *Privatization in Pakistan, supra*, note 6, pp. 76-7.
10. Ibid., p. 77.
11. Ibid., pp. 78-9.
12. Ibid., pp. 90-91.
13. Ibid., p. 93.
14. Ibid., Chapter V, pp. 93-114.
15. Parliament and Provincial Assemblies (Disqualification of Membership) Order, 1977. President's (Post-Proclamation) Order 17 of 1977, PLD 1978 Central Statutes 17.
16. Jafri, Sadiq, *Benazir Bhutto on Trial*, 1993, Jang Publishers, Lahore 15-64.
17. Ibid., pp. 65-90.
18. Ibid., pp. 91-125.
19. Ibid., pp. 127-231.
20. Ibid., pp. 233-78.
21. Ibid., pp. 279-317.
22. Ibid., pp. 319-46.
23. Constitution (Twelfth Amendment) Act, 1991, Act XIV of 1991, PLD 1991 Central Statutes 461.
24. Mr Sharaf Faridi was a prominent lawyer from Karachi. He was elected to the Pakistan Bar Council for three consecutive terms and was elected President, Sindh High Court Bar Association for four consecutive years. He died in office in January 1994 after performing commendable services for the lawyer community in Pakistan.
25. Sharaf Faridi v The Federation of Islamic Republic of Pakistan etc., PLD 1989 Karachi 404.
26. Government of Sindh v Sharaf Faridi, PLD 1994 S.C. 105.

27. Asif Nawaz, under whom military action was initiated against terrorists in Sindh, felt that there was a lack of cooperation with the armed forces on the part of the government, particularly in the action against the MQM in Karachi.
28. *The News*, Lahore, 19 April 1993.
29. The text is reproduced on pages 572 to 575 of 'Mohammad Nawaz Sharif v President of Pakistan', PLD 1993 S.C. 473.
30. Muhammad Nawaz Sharif v Federation of Pakistan, PLD 1993 S.C. 473.
31. At one point in time, there were sixty-three members of the federal cabinet and more were coming if the Supreme Court did not restore Nawaz's government.
32. The devotion to duty on the part of Justice Shafiur Rehman must be noted. He did not waste a day of the Court and continued hearing the case despite the shocking death of his young son in Lahore by accidental electrocution.
33. 'Justice Sajjad Ali Shah, in his dissenting opinion, has taken note of indications given at the very beginning of the proceedings that decision of the Court would be such which would please the nation', The Chief Justice, Dr Nasim Hasan Shah reportedly observed in open court during the course of the proceedings that he would not like to be remembered as Munir, obviously referring to the former Chief Justice who earned discredit in the cases of Maulvi Tamizuddin and Dosso. The speech of the Chief Justice in June 1993 at the dinner hosted by the Lahore High Court Bar Association praising the judgment was not received well by the lawyers and the press. It is an established practice that judges do not publicly discuss their own judgments.
34. A cousin of Ch. Parvez Elahi, who was an aspirant for the chief ministership of the Punjab.
35. An obscure former MNA from Jhelum, a nominee of the PPP.
36. Parvez Elahi v Province of Punjab, PLD 1993 Lahore 518. The detailed judgment is cited as PLD 1993 Lahore 595.
37. Nawabzada Mohsin Ali Khan v Government of NWFP and others, PLD 1993 Peshawar 207.
38. It is rumoured that when he was pressed by the military generals to resign, Nawaz twice requested that he be allowed to consult his father. One of the generals reportedly said, 'Come on, who is the Prime Minister, you or your father?'
39. Habib-ul-Wahab-al Khairi v Mian Manzoor Ahmad Wattoo and others, Writ Petition No.7459 of 1993, decided by Justice A.M. Tiwana of the Lahore High Court. In this case, Wattoo submitted his written statement in which he alleged that Nawaz, on 6 August 1990, the day the Punjab Assembly was dissolved, allotted 600 plots valued about 600 million rupees to his favourites, mostly MNAs, MPAs, Senators, politicians, and other influential people in order to gain political dividends. It is alleged that in his effort to win over the political loyalties of some fair-weather politicians, he did not spare the open spaces meant for public sites, schools, hospitals, and so on, in different development schemes of the LDA. These plots were allotted at a throwaway price of 90,000 rupees per *kanal* as against their market value ranging from 20 lac rupees to 50 lac rupees per *kanal*. He also asserted that the Chaudhris of Gujrat and the Sharifs of Model Town had been operating as property dealers and grabbed valuable plots of the LDA in Garden Town, Allama Iqbal Town, Gulberg, Faisal Town, New Muslim Town, and Model Town Extension.
40. The judgment of Justice A. M. Tiwana of the Lahore High Court in Writ Petition No. 9781 of 1993. It is mentioned in the judgment that Mr Ghulam Haider Wyne and his successor Mian Manzoor Ahmad Wattoo were frittering away big chunks of the Punjab Bait-ul-Mal Fund and the Jahez Fund. However, the dissipation of Wattoo was more callous because he and his colleagues were investing the money meant for the poor to hatch a conspiracy against the federation along with top civil servants and senior police officers supported by hired armed bandits. Wyne, during the period when he was Chief Minister of the Punjab, paid 45 million rupees out of the Jahez Fund including amounts like 590 thousand rupees and 480 thousand rupees paid on the recommendations of two of his favourite MPAs. He paid 3 million rupees to Idara, Merkezi Anjuman Mian Channun, which was his constituency. Wattoo played this game more callously. On the recommendation of his close associates, he sanctioned payment of 3 million rupees for Misali School, 1.5 million rupees to Haleem Institute, 5 million rupees to Idara Markezi Darool Aloom Ghousia, Model Town, 5

million rupees to Cadet School Lahore. (Except for Haleem Institute, all these schools are unknown.) These cheques were generally handed over to close associates, some of whom got the major part of the money transferred to their own names. Two close relatives of Wattoo were given 6 million rupees for distribution, two of his favourites received 472,450 rupees and 376 thousand rupees for treatment abroad. Such was the callous use of funds that kitchen expenses for the chief minister house in two months came to 3,875,825 rupees and the annual provision in the budget was 1,138,000 rupees. He took 1 million rupees out of the Bait-ul-Mal Fund to his hometown for distribution as *Eidi.* IG Punjab, DIG Lahore and SSP Lahore were awarded 5 lac rupees, 5 lac rupees and 2 lac rupees respectively for their meritorious services on 30 June 1993 (for frustrating the Resolution of the Parliament under Article 234). These figures are taken from the statement of Mr G. M. Sikandar, Principal Secretary to the Chief Minister, recorded by Justice A.M. Tiwana in Writ Petitions Nos. 9781/1993, 7459/1993, 8622/1993 and 8623/1993 being heard together.

41. *Pakistan Year Book, 1993-94*, published by Book Talk in 1994, Mian Chambers, 3-Temple Road, Lahore. These figures are taken from pages 446-7.
42. Ibid., pp. 447-8.

33

BENAZIR'S SECOND TERM: THE JUDICIAL CRISIS

As a result of the general elections in 1993, the PPP secured eighty-six seats and the PML(N) seventy-three seats. In addition, the PML(J) secured six seats and formed an alliance with the PPP at the centre and in the Punjab. With the help of independent members and some small parties, Benazir was elected prime minister on 19 October 1993 (with 121 votes as against seventy-two polled by Nawaz).[1]

In the Punjab, Mian Manzoor Wattoo of the PML(J) was elected chief minister (with 131 votes against 105 polled by Shahbaz Sharif). In Sindh, the PPP had an absolute majority in the Provincial Assembly, where it formed the government. Syed Abdullah Shah was elected Chief Minister of Sindh. In the NWFP, the PML(N) had an electoral alliance with the Awami National Party (ANP) which did well and won thirty-six out of eighty seats in the Provincial Assembly. Pir Sabir Shah of the PML(N) was elected Chief Minister of NWFP (with forty-eight votes against twenty-nine polled by Aftab Sherpao). In Balochistan, Nawab Zulfiqar Magsi was elected chief minister with the support of the PML(N) and the ANP alliance. All his opponents withdrew their nominations papers.[2]

After the formation of the governments at the centre and in the provinces, the next step was the election of the president, which was held on 13 November 1993. Initially, a number of candidates, including some leading political figures like former President Ishaq, Nawabzada Nasrullah Khan, Nawab Akbar Bugti, Air Marshall (Retd) Asghar Khan, Yahya Bakhtiar, Balakh Sher Mazari, and others filed their nomination papers. Later on, however, they dropped out of the race one by one and only two candidates were left in the field, Acting President Wasim Sajjad, a nominee of the PML(N), and Farooq Ahmad Leghari, a nominee of the PPP. Leghari was elected with 274 votes cast in his favour against 168 votes polled by Sajjad. In a goodwill gesture unknown to Pakistani politicians, Sajjad conceded defeat and congratulated Leghari on his election.

In his first speech, Leghari stated that the sooner the Eighth Amendment was lifted, the better it would be.[3] Benazir said that with the election of Leghari as President, the Eighth Amendment had become ineffective for at least five years. She promised to present a Bill for the repeal of the Eighth Amendment which, according to her, would expose Nawaz who had bitterly criticized the Amendment after the dismissal of his government but was not now willing to co-operate with Benazir for its repeal.[4] Despite this statement, no Bill was ever presented by her government.

The Sabir Shah Case

It was difficult for the PPP government at the centre to countenance opposition parties forming the provincial government in the NWFP and the coalition government of the PML(N) and the ANP under Sabir Shah was a thorn in the side of the PPP. The PPP tried to destablize it by constitutional subterfuge. After all, it had its own nominee elected as President which would come in handy for the purpose. The PPP had to overcome the obstacle of the majority in the coalition and to somehow reduce it to a minority. This could not happen as long as Sabir Shah and his government was in office. Therefore, it was imperative to have the government suspended, providing an interregnum for the PPP in the NWFP headed by Aftab Sherpao to win over members of the Provincial Assembly, thus reducing Sabir Shah and his supporters into a minority.

Ultimately, a constitutional solution was found to accomplish this. The emergency powers of the President were pressed into service. A report was obtained from the Governor of NWFP that a situation had arisen in which the government of NWFP could not be carried on in accordance with the provisions of the Constitution. On 25 February 1994, the President issued a proclamation under Article 234 of the Constitution directing the Governor to assume the functions of the government of NWFP declaring that the powers of the Provincial Assembly should be exercised by Parliament. It was also ordered that the Chief Minister and the provincial ministers should forthwith cease to hold office. Governor rule was lifted to allow the PPP to form a government in NWFP through blatant horse trading. PPP operators armed with large sums of money enticed and ultimately won over enough borderline members of the ruling coalition to weaken and thus bring down Sabir Shah's government.[5]

Sabir Shah challenged the validity of the Proclamation before the Supreme Court of Pakistan under Article 184(3) of the Constitution on the grounds, firstly, that the dissolution of his government was malafide as he had a majority in the House; secondly, that there was peace in the province, the only political problem being the defection of two members of the Assembly belonging to his political party to the PPP; thirdly, that the report on the basis of which the President acted was made by the Acting Governor whose appointment was unconstitutional; fourthly, that the President under Article 234 could not terminate the offices of chief ministers and other ministers; fifthly, that the proclamation deprived the elected representatives of their fundamental right to govern themselves in violation of Article 17 of the Constitution of Pakistan; and sixthly, that the sole purpose of the proclamation was to topple the duly constituted government with the assistance of the two defected members.

The respondents pleaded firstly that the validity of the proclamation could not be challenged in view of Article 236(2) of the Constitution of Pakistan; secondly, that the petition was misconceived as no fundamental right was involved; thirdly, that the President and the Governor could not be impleaded in view of Article 248 of the Constitution of Pakistan; fourthly, that the petitioner's government was weak as seven ministers and advisers had resigned their posts; fifthly, that the appointment of the Governor was valid and the report submitted by him legal; and sixthly, that the defection of the two members was sub judice. The petition was accepted by the Supreme Court by a majority of seven to two holding that the proclamation—to the extent that it purported to declare that the Chief Minister and his Cabinet would cease to hold office beyond the period of currency of the proclamation—was in excess of the power conferred on the President under Article 234 of the Constitution of Pakistan and that on the revival of the Provincial Assembly on the lapse of the proclamation, the Chief Minister and the Cabinet would stand revived. The Court clarified that it would be open to the Governor to re-fix a date and time in accordance with Article 130(5) of the Constitution of Pakistan requiring the Chief Minister to obtain a vote of confidence from the Assembly.

The Supreme Court held that:[6]

1. The ouster clause of Article 236(2) would not save a proclamation issued under Article 234 which is without jurisdiction, *coram non judice* or malafide, and the superior court in exercise of its judicial power can examine the validity of the proclamation.
2. The validity of the appointment of an incumbent of a public officer cannot be impugned through collateral proceedings. Therefore, it is not necessary to hold whether the Acting Governor was validly appointed or not for the reason that the actions taken or orders passed by the Acting Governor were covered by the *de facto* doctrine.
3. Under Article 234, receipt of a report by the President from the Governor is not a condition precedent to the issuance of proclamations. The President may act on the basis of information received by him from any other source. The word 'otherwise' in Article 234(1) has a wide connotation.
4. There were clearly conflicting efforts on the part of the opposition to oust the Chief Minister and his Cabinet, and on the part of the Chief Minister and his party to continue in office. The Speaker in this situation had declined to re-fix the date pursuant to the notice issued by the Governor under Article 130(5) of the Constitution requiring the Chief Minister to obtain a vote of confidence. Such a situation necessitated the taking of a temporary measure under Article 234 of the Constitution in order to provide a cool-down period to both the parties. The President was justified in these circumstances in issuing the proclamation under Article 234 of the Constitution.
5. Refusal of the Speaker to allow the Assembly to meet in pursuance of the order of the Governor and declaration of the Chief Minister that he would not seek a vote of confidence created a situation where the exercise of the constitutional powers of the Governor were being obstructed and a person who had possibly lost the confidence of the Assembly was insisting on continuing in office as Chief Minister. The Governor was, therefore, justified in advising the President that the government of the province was not being carried on in accordance with the provisions of the Constitution.

6. The President under article 234 of the Constitution can only suspend the Chief Minister and his Cabinet for a period of two months. But he has no power to dismiss or remove them from office.
7. The Governor was competent under Article 130(5) of the Constitution to require the Chief Minister to obtain a vote of confidence.
8. 'Satisfaction' of the President under Article 234 with regard to the existence of a situation in which the government of the province cannot be carried on in accordance with the provisions of the Constitution cannot be treated subjectively; it must be based on the existence of objective conditions justifying the issue of the proclamation. If the Court finds that the material used by the President in arriving at his satisfaction bears nexus to the object of proclamation, it cannot interfere with the proclamation on the ground that there was not sufficient material before the President to express his satisfaction with regard to the existence of a condition which would justify issuance of the proclamation.

Public Hangings Banned

Election 10 of the Special Courts for Speedy Trials Act, 1992, allowed the government to fix the place of execution of the death sentence. The government could order a public hanging under the law in order to create a deterrent effect. The Supreme Court of Pakistan took *suo moto* notice of this law and held that public hanging is violative of the dignity of man as enshrined in Article 14 of the Constitution of Pakistan.[7] The Supreme Court of Pakistan also held that public hanging is violative of Article 7 of the 'Universal Declaration of Human Rights in Islam', a document prepared by a number of leading Muslim scholars and published in London on 12 April 1980. The relevant portion of Article 7 reads:

> The right of protection from torture:
>
> It is not permitted to torture the criminal, still less the suspect: 'God will inflict punishment to those who have inflicted torture in this world.'

Implementation of Decision to Separate the Judiciary from the Executive

The Supreme Court of Pakistan had ordered the immediate separation of the judiciary from the executive in Sharaf Faridi's case. However, Benazir's government was dragging its feet over it. The Supreme Court of Pakistan was approached for an extension of time which was denied to the government. Ultimately, steps were taken to implement the decision by the promulgation of Legal Reforms Ordinance, 1996 on 20 March 1996. This was followed by succeeding ordinances after every four months till it became an Act of Parliament on 3 July 1997.[8] The Ordinance provided for 'Executive Magistrates' and 'Judicial Magistrates' who would work under the District Magistrate and the Sessions Judge respectively. Judicial Magistrates were given the power to try offences under the Pakistan Penal Code and other criminal law statutes. Executive Magistrates could try cases of offences against public tranquility, contempts of the lawful authority of public servants, offences relating to weights and measures, and offences affecting public health, safety, convenience, decency, and morals. Executive Magistrates were conferred with the power to award punishment for a term of up to three years.

These provisions of the law have come under strong criticism by legal circles who believe that such powers to an Executive Magistrate are a negation of the dictates of the Constitution of Pakistan to separate the judiciary from the executive and the judgment of the Supreme Court of Pakistan given in Sharaf Faridi's case.

The Local Bodies Case

Local bodies are regarded as the backbone of a democratic order. Zia, who was averse to elections otherwise, relied heavily on local bodies elections to introduce a new cadre of leadership throughout Pakistan and succeeded largely in this attempt. The new leaders, particularly the PML(N), had emerged from local bodies elections which speaks volumes for their calibre and understanding of statecraft. People who should not have risen above the level of municipal corporations and district councils became federal ministers, chief ministers, and governors, particularly in the Punjab.

When Nawaz resigned as prime minister on 18 July 1993, the caretaker government decided to undo his main support in the masses which came from the local bodies. The local bodies elections had been held on 28 December 1991 in the Punjab for a term of four years which expired at the end of 1995. However, on 15 August 1993, the term of office of the local councilors was curtailed with immediate effect through a notification of the Governor of the Punjab. It was directed that fresh elections to the local bodies would be held in the month of January 1994. Elected officials were replaced by civil servants.

This notification was challenged through a number of constitutional petitions before the Lahore High Court by office bearers of local councils. The petitions were allowed by a single Bench on 30 January 1994, but the local councils were not restored and the provincial government was given two months to hold elections, failing which, the local councils elected on 28 December 1991 were to be restored.[9] The petitioners were not satisfied and filed Intra-Court Appeals, challenging non-restoration of the local councils. During the pendency of these Appeals, an Ordinance was promulgated on 5 April 1994 by the Governor of the Punjab declaring that the government had, and should be deemed always to have had, the power to control the term of local councils regardless of the duration of the residual term.[10] The Ordinance also validated the notification set aside by a single judge of the Lahore High Court.

The Intra-Court Appeals were dismissed on 9 April 1994 on the grounds that another notification had been issued fixing a fresh date, 27 July 1994, for elections to the local councils in supersession of the earlier impugned notification.[11]

However, this judgment was set aside by the Supreme Court of Pakistan with the direction to allow the appellants to amend their appeals. After the remand, these Intra-Court Appeals were disposed of through a judgment dated 19 February 1995. Provincial government was given a period of three months to hold fresh elections to the local councils subject to the consideration that, in case of failure on the part of the provincial government to do so, all local councils in the province would stand restored. The validating Ordinance was held as invalid law and notifications issued thereunder were also held to be invalid.[12]

This judgment was challenged in appeals before the Supreme Court of Pakistan which were allowed on 26 June 1996 and all the local bodies/councils in the province of Punjab were ordered to be restored to enable them to complete their term up to 9 February 1997.[13] On the following day, 27 June 1996, the Provincial Assembly of Punjab passed the Punjab Local Government (Repeal) Act, 1996 (Act VI of 1996), repealing the Punjab Local Government Ordinance, 1979 declaring that all members of the local councils would cease to hold office. It was soon followed by the Punjab Local Government Act, 1996,[14] providing for re-structuring and continuance of local government institutions.

The Punjab Local Government (Repeal) Act, 1996 was challenged before the Supreme Court of Pakistan on the plea that it was an exercise of legislative powers in as much as the intention was to keep the elected members of the local councils out of office and to defeat the earlier judgment of Supreme Court restoring the elected members to office. The Supreme Court upheld the validity of the Punjab Local Government (Repeal) Act, 1996 because it had been passed by the elected representatives of the people, that is, members of the Provincial Assembly under the power conferred upon them by the Constitution of Pakistan. The Court also held that it was not at liberty to inquire into the motives or malafide intent on the part of the legislature. Once a statute is made competently, the Court is not entitled to question the wisdom or fairness of the legislature. Nor can the Court refuse to enforce a law made on the ground that the result would be to nullify its own judgment.[15]

Thus came to an end the story of the struggle between the erstwhile elected members of the local bodies to regain their positions and Benazir's government in preventing it, even if it entailed frustrating the judgments of the Courts. It goes to the discredit of Benazir's government that during its three years in office, it did not hold elections to the local bodies nor did it allow the restoration of the elected members/ office bearers.

Wattoo Government Sacked: Lahore High Court Verdict

In a bid to keep the PML(N) out of power in the Punjab, though it held more seats than any other political party in the Assembly, the PPP entered into a coalition with the PML(J) to form a government in the Punjab. The PPP had to take the bitter pill of accepting Manzoor Ahmad Wattoo from the PML(J) as the chief minister even though his party only held eighteen seats in the House of 248. This uneasy coalition continued for nearly two years by which time PPP members of the Punjab Assembly had had enough of him. They could not come to terms with his arrogant and autocratic style of governance. Ultimately, Benazir gave in and plans were made to sack Wattoo. It was going to be a repeat performance of what was done in the NWFP for the removal of Sabir Shah.

A report was obtained from the Governor of Punjab against Wattoo on the basis of which on 5 September 1995 the President issued the following Proclamation under Article 234 of the Constitution of Pakistan:

> Whereas I, Farooq Ahmad Khan Leghari, President of the Islamic Republic of Pakistan, on receipt of report from the Governor of the Punjab and other information made available, am satisfied that a situation has arisen in which the Government of the Punjab cannot be carried on in accordance with the provisions of the Constitution.
>
> i. Now, therefore, in exercise of the powers conferred by Article 234 of the Constitution, I hereby:-
>   (a) direct the Governor of the Punjab to assume on my behalf the functions of the Government of that Province; and all or any of the powers vested in, or exercisable by, any body or authority in the Province, other than Provincial Assembly;
>   (b) make the following incidental and consequential provisions which appear to be necessary or desirable for giving effect to the subjects of this Proclamation:-
>
> ii. The Chief Minister and Provincial Ministers of that Province shall forthwith cease to perform functions of their respective offices; and
>
> iii. In the exercise of the functions which the Governor has been directed to assume as hereinbefore stated, the Governor shall act to such extent and subject to such conditions as I shall, from time to time, deem fit to give or impose.[16]

After the above Proclamation, the control of the affairs of the province were assumed by the Governor on behalf of the President.

The Governor then called upon Wattoo to obtain a vote of confidence from the Provincial Assembly in a session hurriedly summoned by him on 12 September 1995. Wattoo did not participate in the session and the Speaker informed the Governor that Wattoo failed to obtain a vote of confidence as a consequence of which he was removed from the office of the chief minister of Punjab.

Wattoo's removal did not solve Benazir's problems, who wanted someone from the PPP to be the chief minister of Punjab. But the PPP fell short of the requisite majority in the Provincial Assembly and had to depend upon the support of the PML(J) in order to form the government. the PML(J), which had tasted power for two years, was not ready for anything less than chief ministership. After making several offers, Benazir had to succumb to the demands of the PML(J) and conceded to her junior coalition partner. Agreement was reached on appointing a weak and pliable person, Sardar Muhammad Arif Nakai. Under the agreement, a PPP nominee was made the senior minister, sharing several of the powers of the chief minister, particularly those pertaining to administration. Nakai was only too happy to become the chief minister, even if only in name.

On 13 September 1995, Nakai was elected unopposed as Chief Minister of the Punjab with 152 votes. He took oath of office the same day and on 14 September 1995 obtained a vote of confidence with 148 votes to his credit. On 13 September 1995, the President revoked the Proclamation of Emergency issued on 5 September 1995. In this way, once again, emergency provisions were used to dislocate one chief minister and elect another.

The Proclamation of Emergency under Article 234 of the Constitution and the order of the Governor for obtaining a vote of confidence were challenged before the Lahore High Court as illegal and unconstitutional. The constitutional petition was finally heard and accepted by a full Bench of the Lahore High Court *vide* judgment dated 30 October 1996.

The Court held that the power to issue a Proclamation of Emergency in case of failure of constitutional machinery in a province is in the nature of an exception and should be used sparingly and strictly construed. Such a power constitutes an inroad into provincial autonomy and, if not properly used, can destroy the equilibrium between the federation and the federating units, causing a sense of deprivation in the provinces which would not be healthy for the federation. The power, the Court held, is not unbridled or uncontrolled. It is circumscribed by two conditions; firstly, that the President must be satisfied, and satisfaction must be objective and based on material relevant to Article 234; and secondly, that the satisfaction must be to the effect that the affairs of the province cannot be run in accordance with the Constitution. The satisfaction must be objective and based on some material within the nexus of Article 234. Although the Court could neither sit in appeal over the satisfaction of the President, nor could it substitute its own opinion for that of the President, yet it must be shown that the material on the basis of which he had acted was relevant to the conditions mentioned in Article 234. In order to show that the affairs of the province could not be carried on in accordance with the Constitution, it must be demonstrated that there was a deadlock or a constitutional breakdown or existence of a situation not contemplated by the Constitution, and it did not otherwise cater for or provide remedy. If a situation could be remedied under other provisions of the Constitution, action under Article 234 could not be taken.

The Court repelled the contention that since a number of ministers had resigned, a constitutional deadlock had occurred or functioning of the government had been impaired. It was held that the mere resignation of some or most provincial ministers did not constitute a situation which could legally mean that 'the affairs of the province cannot be carried on in accordance with the provisions of the Constitution'. Even if information was available with the governor that the chief minister had lost the confidence of the members of the Provincial Assembly, it would be irrelevant for the purpose of Article 234. In such a situation, the proper course of action for the governor would be to put the chief minister to a floor test by directing him to obtain a vote of confidence under Article 130(5).

The Court also held that only a functional chief minister could be directed to obtain a vote of confidence. Since Wattoo had ceased to function as chief minister after the proclamation of Article 234, he could not have been asked to obtain a vote of confidence in such circumstances. The Court also observed that although no time limit had been prescribed for obtaining a vote of confidence, reasonable time should have been allowed to him to do so. It was held that sixteen hours were not sufficient for the Chief Minister to obtain a vote of confidence, particularly when there were as many as 248 members of the Provincial Assembly.

The Court repelled the argument that the matter being a political question, fell outside the constitutional jurisdiction of the Court. The Court held that if the question before it is political in nature and involves interpretation of consitutional provisions, the Court would be entitled to resolve the controversy. Having taken oath to preserve and defend the Constitution, it becomes a duty of the superior courts to enforce the Constitution with its full might and majesty and in doing so, they should not hesitate in striking down unconstitutional actions/orders and to grant constitutional relief flowing therefrom. No expediency or other consideration should be allowed to stand in its way nor can a deviation or contravention of the Constitution be condoned or allowed to be perpetuated.

Applying the above tests, the Proclamation of the President dated 5 September 1995 under Article 234 was declared to be without lawful authority. The election of Nakai as chief minister was held to be without lawful authority. As a consequence, Wattoo stood restored as Chief Minister on 5 September 1995. The Governor could call upon Wattoo to obtain a vote of confidence by giving him not less than two clear days to do so. It was, however, undertaken by Wattoo not to advise the Governor to dissolve the Assembly before obtaining a vote of confidence.[17] Finally, it was ruled that if Wattoo failed to obtain a vote of confidence, Nakai would stand restored as Chief Minister without any fresh election or other formalities.

Rejoicing over the restoration proved to be very short lived. The judgment was announced on 3 November 1996. The same day, eighty-five members of the Provincial Assembly moved a resolution for a vote of no-confidence against him. On 5 November 1996, Benazir's government was dismissed. Wattoo appealed before the Supreme Court for an extension to obtain a vote of confidence. The Supreme Court extended the time from ten to thirteen days. Consequently, Wattoo was required to obtain a vote of confidence by 16 November at the latest. The motion for vote of no-confidence was also fixed for 16 November. On 16 November, the motion for vote of no-confidence was withdrawn by the movers, thus forcing Wattoo to obtain a vote of confidence from the Provincial Assembly. That very day, ninty-three members of the Provincial Assembly from the PML(N) tendered their resignations. Thus, Wattoo was left high and dry without any prospect of getting a vote of confidence. He therefore resigned from chief ministership of the Punjab that day on the pretext that he did not want to be a hurdle in the way of elections.[18]

Confrontation with the Judiciary

Justice Sajjad Appointed Chief Justice

Appointments to the Superior Courts in Pakistan have been made generally on considerations other than merit, being decided on the basis of political affiliations, nepotism, or favouritism. There has been a tacit understanding between the judiciary and successive governments on this issue. Governments could get their political favourites appointed to high judicial offices who, in return, obliged them and their colleagues by appointing their relatives and favourites. This dubious co-operation between the two organs of the State continued for quite some time until differences between the two developed into a major confrontation.

Before Benazir took over as prime minister in 1993, she promised reforms regarding the appointment of judges who would, in future, be made on merit. It did not take her long to renege on her promise. In order to understand the confrontation that subsequently took place between the judiciary and the executive, it is important to understand the experiences of Benazir with the judiciary that might have shaped her opinion, attitude, and policy towards the superior judiciary.

Benazir's first encounter with the superior judiciary was at the trial of her father in the Lahore High Court, followed by the rejection of his appeal by the Supreme Court of Pakistan which she later termed a 'judicial murder' in her book *Daughter of the East*. She thus perceived the judiciary to be a hostile institution.

Benazir also noticed that the judiciary was hand-in-glove with the Martial Law regime of General Zia and submitted meekly to humiliation at his hands. After all, the Supreme Court of Pakistan had conferred legitimacy on Zia's Martial Law in Nusrat Bhutto's Case and even allowed him to amend the Constitution of Pakistan unilaterally, a power he exercised recklessly, maliciously, and capriciously, at all times to the detriment of the PPP.

Although Benazir got relief from the Supreme Court of Pakistan in the Political Parties Case in 1988, she faced hostile courts when her government was dismissed by Ishaq in 1990. Except for the Peshawar High Court, the other High Courts comprehensively upheld the dismissal of her government and the government of the PPP in Sindh. The Supreme Court of Pakistan upheld these judgments and reversed the judgment of the Peshawar High Court favouring the PPP in the NWFP. Not only this, Benazir had also noticed that her arch rival and his party were always given favourable verdicts from the High Courts and the Supreme Court, once again with the sole exception of the Peshawar High Court.

She had thus taken over the reigns of power in 1993 with the determination that she would change the situation in favour of the PPP by inducting people into it who would be favourably predisposed to it and weed out those judges whom she perceived as hostile. To begin with, Benazir had to contend with Chief Justice Nasim Hasan Shah, whom she obviously did not like for being a member of the Bench of the Supreme Court that upheld the death sentence of Zulfiqar Ali Bhutto. In any case, his tenure was short as he was due to retire in April 1994. Benazir got her sweet revenge by having him sacked as the President of the Pakistan Cricket Board, a position that he had ardently sought from the Nawaz government.

Her major test came after the retirement of Shah. The obvious thing was to appoint Justice Saad Saood Jan as the chief justice, who was the senior-most judge of the Supreme Court, in keeping with the forty-year-old practice and precedent of appointing the senior-most judge of the Supreme Court as chief justice. This, unfortunately, was not to be. Jan was kept as Acting Chief Justice from 14 April till the end of May 1994 and, in the meantime, the Supreme Court was packed with ad hoc judges.

Justice Jan was put to an acid test when the government asked him to recommend two advocates for direct appointment as judges to the Supreme Court. The government also wanted him to recommend two retired judges of the Lahore High Court for appointment to the Supreme Court. Justice Jan faced a dilemma. He was convinced that the advocates recommended for direct appointment to the Supreme Court did not deserve it on merit. One of them was a senior member of the PPP and the other was a former colleague of Leghari in the civil service and, of course, a close friend. Jan finally made the bold but fateful decision of speaking his mind, regardless of consequences.

In a note written on 2 June 1994, Justice Jan stated that he did not regard the two advocates fit for direct appointment to the Supreme Court. In his opinion, such appointment should be open only to those advocates who are acclaimed internationally as outstanding jurists. Regarding the two retired judges of the Lahore High Court, he wrote that there was nothing outstanding about them or their record. He did not favour the appointment of retired judges of the High Courts to the Supreme Court and recommended the names of the Chief Justice and two senior judges of the Lahore High Court out of whom any two could be appointed to the Supreme Court.[19]

This note proved to be the proverbial last straw that broke the camel's back. On 5 June 1994, Justice Jan was shocked to learn that he had been ignored for appointment as the Chief Justice of Pakistan and instead Justice Sajjad Ali Shah, who was junior to him and to two other colleagues,[20] was appointed Chief Justice of Pakistan. Thus, a forty-year-old practice of appointing the senior-most judge as the Chief Justice was arbitrarily dispensed with. In any other country, senior judges would have resigned in protest, but in Pakistan there is no such tradition. Justice Jan went on long leave and came back to work after that.[21]

What were the factors behind the appointment of Justice Sajjad as Chief Justice? The main reason appears to be the short-sighted, narrow-minded, and parochial approach of Benazir and her government.[22] She was perhaps carried away by his two dissents apparently in favour of the PPP. First, in Ahmad Tariq Rahim's case, in which the dismissal of Benazir's government by Ishaq in 1990 was challenged, Justice Sajjad was one of the two dissenting judges and held that Ishaq's order to dissolve the National Assembly was invalid. He observed that the purpose of the dissolution was to get rid of the government of the PPP.[23] In Nawaz Sharif's case, where the dismissal of the Nawaz government by Ishaq was under challenge, Justice Sajjad was the lone dissenter out of eleven judges on the Bench who upheld the order as valid and expressed disapproval of the way in which Chief Justice Nasim Hasan

Shah had announced at the beginning of the proceedings that the nation was about to hear 'good news'. He also made a pungent remark at the end of his judgment saying that when two prime ministers from Sindh were removed under the discretionary powers of the president, the Supreme Court did not restore them but when it was the turn of a prime minister from the Punjab, the tables had been turned.[24] These remarks must have rankled in Benazir's mind while deciding on his appointment. She may have thought that, being a Sindhi and a sympathizer of the PPP (as it appeared apparently from the said judgments), he would go along and protect the interests of her government.

Subsequent events have repelled this impression and established Justice Sajjad as a man of his own mind. His remarks in those judgments reflected his own thinking and not a bias in favour of the PPP, as was perhaps assumed. The assumption was based on myopic thinking that if someone disagrees or opposes one major political party, even out of honest belief, he belongs to the opposite camp. It was under such a mistaken belief that the PPP government took the fateful decision of appointing Justice Sajjad as the Chief Justice of Pakistan.

PPP's Rough Handling of Superior Courts

After this, the PPP government went on a rampage against the judiciary. The Chief Justices of the Lahore and Sindh High Courts, whom the government believed to be opposed to the PPP or sympathetic to the political party in opposition, were removed and appointed as judges of the Federal Shariat Court. The Chief Justice of the Sindh High Court accepted the humiliating appointment, but the Chief Justice of the Lahore High Court refused to do so and retired. They were replaced by two Supreme Court judges who were appointed as Acting Chief Justices of the two High Courts. In Sindh, Justice Abdul Hafiz Memon was first appointed a judge of the Sindh High Court and subsequently as an Acting Chief Justice. On discovering that his appointment as a judge of the High Court had made him the junior-most judge and thus he could not be the Acting Chief Justice, the notification was immediately rescinded. He was then notified as a judge of the Supreme Court, followed by another notification appointing him as the Acting Chief Justice of the Sindh High Court.[25]

The Lahore High Court suffered a similar fate. After the removal of the Chief Justice, the PPP government brought back a retired judge of the Lahore High Court, Justice Muhammad Ilyas, who was then serving as a judge of the Federal Shariat Court and was deeply aggrieved from the previous government which, in his reckoning, had denied him appointment as Chief Justice of the Lahore High Court. He was appointed, as a judge of the Supreme Court and was then sent as Acting Chief Justice to the Lahore High Court. The Peshawar High Court was also headed by an Acting Chief Justice not drawn from the Supreme Court.

With three High Courts headed by Acting Chief Justices, the PPP government embarked upon the second phase of its plan which was to pack the High Courts with political appointees. Nine judges were appointed to the Sindh High Court, most of whom were either political appointees or favourites of the PPP bosses. A majority of them either did not qualify for appointment or were not fit for appointment because of a lack of requisite experience at the Bar of the High Court. In August 1994, the Lahore High Court was packed with twenty appointees. Out of these two were from amongst the sessions judges and the remaining were supposedly taken from the Bar. Only six or seven judges could justify their appointment on merit. Another three or four could be considered marginal cases. Eight or nine of these appointments were simply outrageous. Four or five of them had never or seldom appeared in the High Court as advocates.[26] One of them is said to have seen the building of the High Court for the first time when he came to take the oath of office. Four or five of them did not have the requisite experience of ten years at the Bar of the High Court. Even amongst these political appointees, there were clear cases of nepotism. The Governor of Punjab got his younger brother appointed to the post. The Chief Minister had one of his old friends appointed. A powerful MNA got his own son appointed, one who had never been known to practise law. There seemed to be some kind of quota for governor, chief minister, and president. Leghari appointed a friend from his native district.[27]

In the Supreme Court as well, the courts were packed with ad hoc judges. At one point in time, there were as many as seven ad hoc judges against ten permanent judges, including the Chief Justice, with two out of these permanent judges serving as Acting Chief Justices of the High Courts. Thus the permanent judges and ad hoc judges in the Supreme Court were nearly equal in number at the time.

Acting Chief Justices of the High Courts were made simple rubber stamps, recommending all that the government desired. They had virtually abdicated their role as judicial consultees under the Constitution. Chief Justice Sajjad went along with all this up to a point. Initially, he was even supportive of PPP appointees and issued contempt notices against those who spoke or wrote against such appointments.[28] Ultimately, he balked when things began to cross all levels of tolerance. He parted ways with the PPP government on a number of issues, including the appointment of a judge of the Sindh High Court from amongst sessions judges ahead of many others senior to him.[29] He decided to resist when he thought that the actions of the PPP were harmful to the judiciary as an institution.

The Judges' Judgment

The Supreme Court of Pakistan granted leave to appeal against the appointment of twenty judges to the Lahore High Court so as to consider the constitutionality of such appointments. After considerable arguments spread over several months, a Bench of the Supreme Court of Pakistan comprising five judges, gave a majority judgment of four to one,[30] accepting the appeal against such appointments. The Supreme Court held as under:[31]

1. Appointment of ad hoc judges against permanent vacancies of the Supreme Court violates the Constitution.

2. Appointment of Acting Chief Justices can only be a stop-gap arrangement for a short period and not, in any case, exceeding a period of 90 days.
3. An Acting Chief Justice cannot be a consultee for the purposes of appointment of judges, and the appointments made on the recommendation of an Acting Chief Justice were invalid and unconstitutional.
4. An additional judge of a High Court acquires a reasonable expectancy to be considered for appointment as permanent judge, and if he is recommended by the Chief Justice of Pakistan, he is to be appointed as such in the absence of strong reasons to the contrary to be recorded by the President/Executive which would any way be justiciable.
5. All permanent vacancies in the judiciary, particularly those of the Chief Justices, should be filled in advance if they are normal ones (like arising out of retirement) and in any case, not later than 30 days after their occurrence. If a vacancy occurs on account of death or for any unforeseen cause, it should be filled, at the most, within 90 days.
6. The senior most judge of a High Court has a legitimate expectancy to be considered for appointment as Chief Justice. He is entitled to be appointed as Chief Justice of that Court in the absence of very strong reasons to the contrary to be recorded by the President/Executive.
7. That sending of a Supreme Court judge to a High Court as an Acting Chief Justice would be undesirable, particularly in view of adverse observations in the judgment of the Supreme Court in Abrar Hassan v Government of Pakistan (PLD 1976 S.C. 315).
8. The words 'after consultation' occurring in Articles 177 and 193 of the Constitution involve a participatory consultative process between the consultees and the Executive. It should be effective, meaningful, purposive, and consensus oriented, leaving no room for complaint of arbitrariness or unfair play. The Chief Justice of a High Court and the Chief Justice of Pakistan are well-equipped to assess the knowledge and suitability of a candidate for judgeship of the superior Courts. The opinion of the Chief Justices as constitutional consultees was held to be binding on the Executive, and if the Executive disagreed with the view of the Chief Justice of Pakistan and the Chief Justice of a High Court, it should record strong reasons which would be justiciable. The Court found it to be a consistent practice that has acquired the status of convention during the pre-partition days of India as well as the post-partition period, that the recommendations of the Chief Justice of a High Court and the Chief Justice of the Supreme Court, in India as well as in Pakistan, have been consistently accepted and acted upon except in very rare cases.[32]
9. The requirement of ten years practice as an Advocate of the High Court for appointment as judge of the High Court does not mean mere enrolment for that period as an advocate, but actual practice/experience as an advocate of the High Court for such period.
10. If a person of unimpeachable integrity and sound knowledge of law is recommended by the Chief Justice of the High Court and the Chief Justice of

Pakistan, his past political affiliation would not be a disqualification because a person of integrity and sound knowledge normally severs his past connections with the political party with which he had affiliation and decides the matter purely on merits. However, it would be desirable not to appoint a person who is a strong activist in a political party and for him, it would not be possible to erase an unconscious tilt in favour of his party.

11. The power to transfer judges from one High Court to another cannot be invoked by the President/Executive for any purpose other than public interest, and that too only after consultation with the Chief Justice of Pakistan. The power of transfer cannot be pressed into service for the purpose of inflicting punishment on a judge or for any other extraneous consideration.

The Supreme Court directed the government to appoint permanent Chief Justices to High Courts where acting Chief Justices were working within thirty days of the judgment. The permanent Chief Justices were directed to process the cases of those judges whose appointment had been held invalid/unconstitutional under the judgment for regularization of the appointment of those judges who were qualified or fit to be so appointed. It meant that those amongst the appointees who had been confirmed on the recommendations of the acting Chief Justices and found to be not qualified or fit for appointment were to be dropped.

This judgment proved to be a red rag to the bull. Benazir took it as a personal affront to her. She could no longer make arbitrary appointments to the judiciary and those already made by her were re-opened for review. Once again, the judicial establishment had done her in. After all, these appointments were not the first of their kind. The previous government had also made similar and, at times, equally outrageous appointments. It was all the more painful that this was done to her by someone whom she had favoured by appointing him ahead of his senior colleagues. Her reaction to the judgment was confrontational. She criticized, even ridiculed, the judgment publicly before Parliament and the press. She made no secret of her feeling that she had been betrayed by a person who was her beneficiary. Even during the course of the hearing, there were strong rumours (and some of them were even reported in the press), that the government was trying to pressure the Chief Justice through various means.[33] All this did not make an impression on the Chief Justice whose resolve only hardened. What began as a difference of opinion developed into a bitter personal feud, which became one of the main reasons for the downfall of Benazir's government.

The Judges' Judgment is indeed an important milestone in the judicial history of Pakistan. It made consultation with chief justices on the matter of appointment of judges effective and meaningful. The undesirable practices of appointing ad hoc judges to the Supreme Court and Acting Chief Justices of the High Courts was done away with. Such appointments had degenerated into vehicles for rendering the judiciary subservient to the wishes of and pressures from the executive. Recognition of the convention/practice of appointment of the senior-most judge of a High Court as its Chief Justice was a step in the right direction. This would eliminate the possibility of in-fighting or bickering amongst judges and would render the superior judiciary self-operative, free from fear of and inducement from the executive. Continuation in office by the judges was no longer left to the vagaries of changing governments. Their appointment as permanent judges, after having served as Additional Judges was, to some extent, made self-operative.

The threat to independent judges, rather to the independence of the judiciary, by their transfer to the Federal Shariat Court or to other High Courts without their consent was removed. This could enhance public confidence in the judiciary by making its independence obvious and transparent. The continuous abuse of the practice of appointing a judge with the requisite qualification of ten years as a judge of a High Court was curbed. Subversion of this constitutional requirement by successive governments had become very painful, particularly to the Bar, which had been repeatedly shocked by having to face political appointments to the Bench who they had not known as practising advocates. Political participation was made subordinate to the merit and integrity of candidates for judicial office.

Nevertheless, the judgment was not without its shortcomings. It suffered from the inherent defect of being passed in a case where the judges were interested in its outcome. Certain interpretations of constitutional provisions were beyond the recognized principles of statutory or constitutional interpretation and bordered on re-writing the constitutional provisions concerned. It was laid down that the appointment/confirmation of judges on the consultation of an Acting Chief Justice would be invalid, but the same principle was not extended to those appointed/confirmed as judges on the consultation of the Acting Chief Justices during Zia's government. It is quite unusual in the annals of constitutional law for one provision of the Constitution to have superceded another. It is also unusual that a provision of the Constitution is held to be inoperative and ineffective.

Be that as it may, the overall impact of the judgment was healthy and it restored the eroding public confidence in judicial institutions. The judgment became instantly popular in the public at large and attracted a lot of attention from the press and other public fora. When Benazir's government offered resistance to its implementation, it became a rallying point for the political parties in opposition. The Bar Councils and the Bar Associations throughout Pakistan passed resolutions in its favour and became the vanguard of the movement for its implementation.

Benazir's government adopted a self-destructive attitude towards the judgment. While it agreed to implement the judgment and actually took certain steps towards it's implementation, it adopted a hostile attitude towards the judges responsible for it, particularly towards the Chief Justice.

Despite her resentment, the Judges' Judgment was implemented. Permanent chief justices were appointed in the three High Courts within thirty days. Ad hoc judges in the Supreme Court were relieved and repatriated to their respective High Courts. A number of High Court judges appointed during Benazir's government who did not meet the criteria were laid off. On 16 May, the government filed a Presidential Reference[34] in which the validity of the incumbency of Chief Justice Sajjad was also questioned. The following questions were raised:

i. What is the test for determining the existence of constitutional conventions in a country governed by a written constitution? Can the convention, if any, be read in the written constitution in alteration of the express provisions?

ii. Would all those provisions of the Constitution which were enacted by the framers of the Constitution prevail over those which were incorporated by the Chief Martial Law Administrator?

iii. While the case about the appointment of the Chief Justice of Pakistan remains sub-judice, what is the course appropriate in law for the Federal Government to adopt, for the appointment/confirmation of judges in the High Court/Supreme Court in the interim period, as the Chief Justice of Pakistan is one of the consultees in the process of appointment/confirmation of judges in the High Court/Supreme Court?

iv. What is the position of the judges who were appointed/ confirmed as judges in the superior courts by the Acting Chief Justices during the period of Martial Law (1977–85) and during 1986-88.

v. Keeping in view the overwhelming condemnation of the Doctrine of Necessity as a legal precept and its categorical rejection as an accepted principle of constitutional law by the Supreme Court of Pakistan, its subsequent revival by the Supreme Court (*vide* majority opinion para 55) may open the doors for extra-constitutional actions with dubious motives at the hands of interested elements and may tend to subvert the Constitution. What is the extent and reach of this doctrine in the sphere of the functioning of constitutional organs/functionaries and how is it possible to avoid the deleterious effects of this doctrine resulting in undesirable consequences on the survival of the democratic process?

vi. In the recent Judges case, the Chief Justice of Pakistan constituted a Bench which included himself, while the question of appointment of the Chief Justice of Pakistan was disputed and also raised during the course of arguments. What is the effect of Article IV of the Code of Conduct issued under Article 209(8) of the Constitution which prohibits a judge from acting in a case involving his own interest, in a judgment or decision rendered by such a judge?

The primary focus of the government in filing the reference was to embarrass Justice Sajjad, whose appointment as Chief Justice and even as a High Court judge was brought into question. When he was recommended for appointment in 1978 as judge of the Sindh High Court, the Court was headed by an Acting Chief Justice. Most of the other judges on the Bench were also recommendees of Acting Chief Justices when initially appointed. It was requested in the reference that the matter being urgent and important, it should be considered by a full court at an early date.[35]

The Presidential Reference was returned by the office of the Supreme Court of Pakistan because it did not bear the signature of President Leghari. Benazir's government took it as a slight because it considered the signature of the President irrelevant since he was supposed to act on the advice of the Prime Minister. The reference was re-filed after obtaining the signature of Leghari. It was followed by a review application by the government seeking a review of the Judges' Judgment of 20 March 1996 on the same grounds as raised in the President's Reference.[36] The review was sought on eleven points which were: the question and meaning of consultation; provisions of Islam regarding the appointment of judges; independence of the judiciary; conventions regarding appointment of Chief Justices on seniority basis; the question of advice of the acting Chief Justice; justiciability of the President's decisions regarding the appointment of judges; principle of federalism; the appointment of additional judges; transfer of judges to Shariat Court and other High Courts; and time frames fixed by the Court. Ultimately, both the reference and review petitions were withdrawn by the government's counsel when Justice Sajjad refused to accept two objections raised by the government which were: reconstitution of the Bench hearing these matters and withdrawing Justice Sajjad therefrom because he was alleged to be an interested party, and that the affected judges be made party to the proceedings. The Advocates General of Punjab and Sindh also withdrew their review petitions for the same reasons.[37]

After trying to retain the judges who, after scrutiny by the Chief Justice, were recommended to be dropped, this six month struggle came to an end on 30 September 1996. Benazir advised the President to notify the regularization of twenty-nine judges of the High Courts, which included fourteen judges of the Lahore High Court, ten of the Sindh High Court, and five of the Peshawar High Court. Those who were not regularized and thus laid off were eleven in all, including seven judges of the Lahore High Court, three of the Sindh High Court, and one of the Peshawar High Court. Another seven judges who were not recommended for regularization had already resigned. Their resignations were secured by the government. The President accepted those resignations which were received by him before 21 September, 1996. He returned five which he received after that date.[38]

Benazir and her government did not give in easily. There were certain other political events in September 1996 that led to the surrender of her government. On 20 September 1996, Benazir's brother Murtaza Bhutto was shot and killed in Karachi near his residence, apparently in a police encounter. The government, and Benazir's husband Zardari in particular, were blamed for the death. Another factor was the rift between Benazir and Leghari which had been brewing for some time, but came to the surface on 21 September 1996 when Leghari filed a reference on his own before the Supreme Court seeking its opinion on the question of whether he was bound by the advice of the prime minister in appointing judges to the superior courts.

Leghari-Benazir Rift: President's Reference No. 2

Differences had been brewing between Leghari and Benazir over several months, particularly on the implementation of the Judges' Judgment. It led to an open confrontation between the two which became public on the filing of the President's Reference No. 2 of 1996 on 21 September 1996,[39] in which events since the judgment of 20 March 1996 were recounted and it was stated that the prime constitutional objective of securing the independence of the judiciary required that the President should be the effective appointing authority of judges in accordance with the judgment given by the Supreme Court in that case. It was also stated that the impasse in the implementation of the Supreme Court judgment had assumed urgent public importance and that delay in the implementation was hurting public interest, a controversy that needed to be speedily resolved once and for all.

The President referred the following question of law for the consideration and opinion of the Supreme Court: whether the powers of the President to make appointments to the Supreme Court and the High Courts under Articles 177 and 193 of the Constitution are subject to the provisions of Article 48(1) of the Constitution.

This Reference was initially resisted by Benazir on the ground that it could not be filed without the advice of the prime minister. The President had engaged his own counsel to represent him in the fear that the Attorney-General may withdraw or oppose it. The situation created some bizarre scenes in court, when the Attorney-General appeared to object that being the chief law officer of the federation, only he could conduct the case and any other lawyer could only appear on his authorization. This problem was overcome by the dismissal of Benazir's government and the new Attorney-General withdrew this objection and supported the standpoint of the President.

The Supreme Court held that on the question of the appointments of judges, as contemplated under Articles 177 and 193 of the Constitution, the advice of the cabinet or prime minister under Article 48(1) of the Constitution of Pakistan is attracted but it is qualified by and subject to the ratio decided in the Judges' Judgment in which it was held that in the appointment of judges, the opinion of the Chief Justice of Pakistan and Chief Justice of the concerned High Court as to the fitness or suitability of a candidate for judgeship is entitled to be accepted in the absence of very sound reasons to be recorded by the President/Executive.[40]

In support of the conclusion that the president is bound by the advice of the prime minister or the cabinet, it was observed that amendments introduced by the Eighth Amendment did not change the form of government from parliamentary to presidential, although more powers were conferred on the president to carve out an effective role for him.

While agreeing with the conclusion that the president is bound by the advice of the prime minister in the matter of appointment of judges, Justice Ajmal Mian discussed various options that the president could exercise. He could agree with the reasons recorded by the prime minister for not accepting the recommendations of the Chief Justice or Chief Justices, he could refer the matter back to the prime minister for reconsideration, he could refer the matter for the consideration of the cabinet, he could convene a meeting of the prime minister and the Chief Justices concerned for resolving the issue by a participatory consensus-oriented consultative process, or make a reference to the Supreme Court under its advisory jurisdiction for soliciting its opinion.

The Court also took into consideration the eventuality of the judgment of the Supreme Court in the matter of appointment of judges not being implemented. The Chief Justice observed that it would be the constitutional duty of the President to see to it that the judgment is implemented and that there is no violation or non-compliance of Article 190 of the Constitution which makes it mandatory for all executive and judicial authorities throughout Pakistan to act in aid of the Supreme Court. If the judgment is not implemented, then such a situation could be construed as an impasse or deadlock and would amount to the failure of the constitutional machinery, and one would be justified to say that a situation had arisen in which a government of federation could not be carried on in accordance with the provisions of the Constitution. Justice Saiduzzaman Siddiqui, in his separate opinion, went a step further. He observed that if the prime minister fails to tender his advice within the time-frame fixed in the judgment in Al-Jehad Trust Case, he or she shall be deemed to have agreed to the recommendation of the Chief Justice of Pakistan and that of the Chief Justice of the Provincial High Court, as the case may be, and the President may proceed to make the final appointment on that basis.

Dismissal of Benazir's Government

Apart from the confrontation with Leghari that developed in September 1996, there were other developments that bedevilled Benazir's government and made it vulnerable. The disclosure of corruption at the highest level, particularly the purchase of 'Rockwood', a mansion in Surrey, for 2.7 million pound sterling by Benazir and Zardari shocked the people. Although several stories were afloat about corruption, graft, kickbacks, and commissions by Zardari, such blatant international proof and possibility of corruption seriously embarrassed her. There were other disclosures of purchase of property abroad by Zardari and his father.

Misgovernance by Benazir was no secret. The Pakistani rupee was being repeatedly devalued and the balance of payments was becoming increasingly adverse. The International Monetary Fund (IMF) had informed the government in September 1996 that its continued support would be made dependent on the administration imposing a tax on agricultural income, or a sizeable reduction in military expenditure, or the removal of regulator import duties, or the slashing of tariffs, and the management of flexible exchange rates.[41]

The murder of Murtaza Bhutto on 30 September further embarrassed Benazir and her government. Murtaza's widow, Ghinwa, openly blamed Zardari for his death. Even her mother, Nusrat, initially made some direct accusations but soon thereafter patched up with Benazir and stood by her side. Benazir tried to deflect the controversy and blamed Murtaza's murder on a planned conspiracy 'to sell out the country's interests'.[42] She insinuated that Leghari was behind such a conspiracy and referred to his acts following the killing. She particularly referred to the events of 21 September (the date when President's Reference Number 2 was filed) and 26 September (when Leghari met Nawaz).[43]

Another development was Leghari's overtures towards the opposition. He met the opposition leader, Nawaz, on 26 September when the latter requested that Leghari dismiss the government because it had forfeited its mandate, and to order fresh elections under a neutral caretaker government. Nawaz also asserted that the government was not being run in accordance with the Constitution and action should, therefore, be taken under Article 58(2)(b) of the Constitution. Leghari responded by saying that this was a matter that lay at his discretion, adding that he would act in accordance with the constitutional provisions if the supreme national interest so demanded. Nawaz assured Leghari that the PML(N) would counter any move against him.[44]

Leghari also encouraged other opposition forces to rally against Benazir. The Jamaat-i-Islami led a procession to the Parliament building in Islamabad on 27 October 1996. Declaring that the PPP government had created lawlessness in the country, the demonstrators questioned whether any of the country's institutions would be left intact if it were allowed to remain in power. The meeting and subsequent protests were quelled by the use of force. Nawaz convened a meeting in Islamabad of all the major opposition parties on 29 October 1996 in which a decision was taken to call upon all opposition members in the National Assembly to resign and to increase pressure on the government by holding street rallies throughout the country. All such activities had the obvious blessings of Leghari who was building a case for the dismissal of Benazir's government.

The restoration of Wattoo as Chief Minister of the Punjab by the Lahore High Court on 3 November 1996 was another serious blow to Benazir's government. She had to prepare a game plan to oust Wattoo by moving a resolution of vote of no-confidence by eighty-five MPAs from the PPP and its allies, minutes after his restoration. Zardari was immediately despatched to Lahore for executing the game plan. However, before any further showdown in Punjab, Leghari struck in the night between 4 and 5 November by dissolving the National Assembly under Article 58(2)(b) thereby dismissing the government. Meraj Khalid, a founder member of the PPP, a former Speaker of the National Assembly, and a former chief minister of Punjab, was appointed caretaker prime minister.

The following is the text of the dissolution order:

> Whereas during the last three years thousands of persons in Karachi and other parts of Pakistan have been deprived of their right to life in violation of Article 9 of the Constitution. They have been killed in police encounters and police custody. In the speech to Parliament on 29 October 1995, the President warned that the law enforcing agencies must ensure that there is no harassment of innocent citizens in the fight against terrorism and that human and legal rights of all persons are duly protected. This advice was not heeded. The killings continued unabated.
>
> The government's fundamental duty to maintain law and order has to be performed by proceeding in accordance with law. The coalition of political parties which comprise the government of the Federation are also in power in Sindh, Punjab, and NWFP but no meaningful steps have been taken either by the government of the Federation or, at the instance of the Governments of the Federation, by the Provincial Governments to put an end to the crime of extra-judicial killings which is an evil abhorrent to our Islamic faith and all canons of civilized government. Instead of ensuring proper investigation of these extra-judicial killings, and punishment for those guilty of such crimes, the government has taken pride that, in this manner, the law and order situation has been controlled. These killings coupled with the fact of wide-spread interference by the members of the government, including members of the ruling parties in the National Assembly, in the appointment, transfer, and posting of officers and staff of the law-enforcing agencies, both at the Federal and Provincial levels, has destroyed the faith of the public in the integrity

and impartiality of the law-enforcing agencies and in their ability to protect the lives, liberties and properties of the average citizen.

And whereas on 20 September 1996 Mir Murtaza Bhutto, the brother of the Prime Minister, was killed at Karachi along with seven of his companions including the brother-in-law of a former Prime Minister, ostensibly in an encounter with the Karachi Police. The Prime Minister and her government claim that Mir Murtaza Bhutto has been murdered as a part of a conspiracy. Within days of Mir Murtaza Bhutto's death the Prime Minister appeared on television insinuating that the Presidency and other agencies of State were involved in this conspiracy. These malicious insinuations, which were repeated on different occasions, were made without any factual basis whatsoever. Although the Prime Minister subsequently denied that the Presidency or the Armed Forces were involved, the institution of the Presidency, which represents the unity of the Republic, was undermined and damage caused to the reputation of the agencies entrusted with the sacred duty of defending Pakistan. In the events that have followed, the widow of Mir Murtaza Bhutto and the friends and supporters of the deceased have accused Ministers of the Government, including the spouse of the Prime Minister, the Chief Minister Sindh, the Director of the Intelligence Bureau and other high officials of involvement in the conspiracy which, the Prime Minister herself alleges led to Mir Murtaza Bhutto's murder. A situation has thus arisen in which justice, which is a fundamental requirement of our Islamic Society, cannot be ensured because powerful members of the Federal and Provincial Government who are themselves accused of the crime, influence and control the law-enforcing agencies entrusted with the duty of investigating the offences and bringing to book the conspirators.

And whereas on 20 March 1996 the Supreme Court of Pakistan delivered its judgment in the case popularly known as the Appointment of Judges case. The Prime Minister ridiculed this judgment in a speech before the National Assembly which was shown more than once on nation-wide television. the implementation of the judgment was resisted and deliberately delayed in violation of the Constitutional Mandate that all executive and judicial authorities throughout Pakistan shall act in aid of the Supreme Court. The directions of the Supreme Court with regard to regularization and removal of judges of the High Courts were finally implemented on 30 September 1996 with a deliberate delay of six months and ten days and only after the President informed the Prime Minister that if advice was not submitted in accordance with the judgment by the end of September 1996 then the President would himself proceed further in this matter to fulfil the constitutional requirement.

The Government has, in this manner, not only violated Article 190 of the Constitution but also sought to undermine the independence of the judiciary guaranteed by Article 2A of the Constitution read with the Objectives Resolution.

And whereas the sustained assault on the judicial organ of state has continued under the garb of a Bill moved in Parliament for prevention of corrupt practices. This Bill was approved by the Cabinet and introduced in the National Assembly without informing the President as required under Article 46(c) of the Constitution. The Bill proposes *inter alia* that on a motion moved by fifteen per cent of the total membership of the National Assembly, that is any thirty-two members, a judge of the Supreme Court or High Court can be sent on forced leave. Therefore, if on reference made by the proposed special committee, the Special Prosecutor appointed by such committee, forms the opinion that the judge is prima facie guilty of criminal misconduct, the special committee is to refer this opinion to the National Assembly which can, by passing a vote of no confidence, remove the judge from office.

The decision of the cabinet is evidently an attempt to destroy the independence of the judiciary guaranteed by Article 2A of the Constitution and the Objectives Resolution. Further, as the Government does not have a two-third majority in Parliament and as the opposition parties have openly and vehemently opposed the Bill approved by the cabinet, the government's persistence with the Bill is designed not only to embarrass and humiliate the superior judiciary but also to frustrate and set at naught all efforts made, including the initiative taken by the President, to combat corruption and to commence the accountability process.

And whereas the judiciary has still not been fully separated from the executive in violation of the provisions of Article 175(3) of the Constitution and the deadline for such separation fixed by the Supreme Court of Pakistan.

And whereas the Prime Minister and her government have deliberately violated, on a massive scale the fundamental right of privacy guaranteed by Article 14 of the Constitution. This has been done through illegal phone-tapping and eavesdropping techniques. The phones which have been tapped and the conversations that have been monitored in this unconstitutional manner include the phones and conversations of judges of the superior courts, leaders of political parties, and high-ranking military and civil officers.

And whereas corruption, nepotism, and violation of rules in the administration of the affairs of the government and its various bodies, authorities, and corporations has become so extensive and wide-spread that the orderly functioning of government in accordance with the provisions of the Constitution and the law has become impossible and in some cases, national security has been endangered. Public faith in the integrity and honesty of the government has disappeared. Members of the government and ruling parties are either directly or indirectly involved in such corruption, nepotism, and rule violations. Innumerable appointments have been made at the instance of members of the National Assembly in violation of the law declared by the Supreme Court that allocation of quotas to MNAs and MPAs for recruitment to various posts was offensive to the Constitution and the law and that all appointments were to be made on merit, honestly and objectively, and in the public interest. The transfers and postings of government servants have similarly been made, in equally large numbers, at the behest of members of the National Assembly and other members of the ruling parties. The members have violated their oaths of office and the government has not for three years taken any effective steps to ensure that the legislators do not interfere in the orderly executive functioning of government.

And whereas the Constitutional requirement that the Cabinet together with the Ministers of State shall be collectively responsible to the National Assembly has been violated by the induction of a Minister against whom criminal cases are pending which the Interior Minister has refused to withdraw. In fact, at an earlier stage, the Interior Minister had announced his intention to resign if the former was inducted into the cabinet. A cabinet in which one minister is responsible for the prosecution of a cabinet colleague cannot be collectively responsible in any manner whatsoever.

And whereas in the matter of the sale of Burmah Castrol shares in PPL, and BONE/PPL shares in Qadirpur Gas Field involving national assets valued in several billions of rupees, the President required the Prime Minister to place the matter before the cabinet for consideration/re-consideration of the decisions taken in the matter by the ECC. This has still not been done, despite lapse of over four months, in violation of the provisions of Articles 46 and 48 of the Constitution.

And whereas for the foregoing reasons, taken individually and collective, I am satisfied that a situation has arisen in which the government of the Federation cannot be carried on in accordance with the provisions of the Constitution and an appeal to the electorate is necessary.

Now therefore, in exercise of my powers under Article 58(2)(b) of the Constitution, I, Farooq Ahmad Khan Leghari, President of the Islamic Republic of Pakistan, do hereby dissolve the National Assembly with immediate effect and the Prime Minister and her cabinet shall cease to hold office forthwith. Further, in exercise of my powers under Article 48(5) of the Constitution, I hereby appoint 3 February 1997, as the date on which general elections shall be held to the National Assembly.'[45]

Benazir's Second Term Reviewed

When Benazir came into power for the second time, it was hoped that she had learnt her lesson. It was expected that she would keep Zardari at bay and would try to run a clean administration.[46] But the performance of her government was, once again, very disappointing. This time, she did not have any excuse whatsoever. The PPP had its own nominee as President and the military leadership, by and large, stood by it.

The law and order situation deteriorated daily, particularly in Karachi, and thousands of innocent citizens were murdered in deliberate acts of terrorism. Mosques and other places of congregation were bombed and innocent worshippers were shot in the manner of execution by sectarian terrorists. Despite all this, Benazir and her ministers kept chanting that everything was alright and under control.

The PPP had been horse trading once again. Sabir Shah's government in the NWFP was overthrown through questionable constitutional means and Aftab Sherpao formed the government there through political horse trading. Manzoor Wattoo was also removed as Chief Minister of the Punjab by using constitutional subterfuge.

The judiciary had a rough deal at the hands of the second PPP government. Although it was part of the manifesto of the PPP in the 1993 general elections to introduce judicial reforms and lay down objective standards for the appointment of judges,[47] the steps that were taken only led to a further deterioration of the judicial structure.

Benazir failed even in the conduct of foreign policy. Despite dozens of trips abroad as Prime Minister at a very heavy cost to the exchequer, Pakistan's relations with other countries suffered a serious setback. Even traditional friends and neighbours like Iran and China drifted away and moved closer to India. The situation in Afghanistan did not improve and anarchy continued to prevail. The government had been propagating its Kashmir policy but it yielded no results. The government lost face twice by withdrawing resolutions from the United Nations for condemning India on human rights abuses and crimes against humanity in occupied Kashmir. Even relations with the United States of America remained in a state of uncertainty. Benazir failed to retrieve 658 million US dollars paid to the USA for the purchase of F-16 fighter aircrafts.

Zardari was, once again, at the centre of the stories circulating about corruption in high places. Federal ministers, federal secretaries, and other high ranking officials were having an open season in bribery, kickbacks, and commissions. Some of the contracts awarded during the previous regime were cancelled without any justification. Benazir and Zardari signed several memorandums of understanding (MOUs) particularly regarding power generation projects. It was rumoured that Zardari received large sums in kickbacks on the MOUs. Some of the financial indiscretions of Benazir became embarrassingly public; disclosures included the purchase of the Surrey mansion for 2.7 million pound sterling, two luxury flats in London's prestigious and fashionable district of Belgracia, a mortgage account in the Channel Island of Guernsey, and an apartment in London for Hakim Ali, Zardari's father, valued at 200,000 pound sterling.[48]

Benazir's handling of the economy was highly inept. There was virtually no economic policy and she failed to attract any appreciable foreign investment. The only area in which some progress was made was the energy sector which was at a very heavy cost to the consumers of electricity in Pakistan. Power purchase agreements signed in this behalf were detrimental to the national interest. It was self-evident that the rates at which electricity was to be purchased would ruin the economy. WAPDA would go bankrupt paying the heavy bill of power purchase and consumers would be burdened by raising the tariff of electricity manifold. Industry would not afford electricity at that rate and industrial units would have to close. Despite such obvious problems, the PPP government proceeded to sign such power purchase agreements. Consequently, WAPDA, a national institution, is tottering on the brink of bankruptcy.

Textiles, the most important of the industries in Pakistan, suffered from deep recession and a large number of textile units were either closed down or were running at a heavy loss. Export earnings took a nosedive generally, textiles and carpets in particular. No new industrial units were set up and old ones were closing down. New taxes were being levied and the country was faced with the prospect of runaway inflation. There was political interference with the normal functioning of nationalized banks and bank credit fell into the wrong hands. No serious efforts were made to recover bank loans and bad debts were piling up every day.

The only accomplishment of Benazir's government was the restoration of peace in Karachi, but it was achieved through questionable means. The law enforcement agencies were given a free hand in dealing with the MQM and there were serious allegations of extra-judicial killings and excesses by police and other law enforcing agencies.

Benazir's government was also undermined by family feuds. Her brother Murtaza Bhutto became an open critic of her government and of her husband, whom he accused of embezzlement and looting. Her mother, Nusrat, sided with Murtaza Bhutto, the only surviving male heir of the Bhutto legacy. Benazir fell out with her mother and removed her as Chairperson of the PPP. The division in the family became absolute with Benazir and her husband Zardari on one side and Murtaza Bhutto and his mother Nusrat on the other. After Murtaza's murder, the differences became acute and the widow of Murtaza, Ghinwa, headed the party of her husband, PPP (Shaheed Bhutto group). She openly blamed Benazir and Zardari for the death and participated in general elections in February 1997 to undermine Benazir's party in Sindh. Her party was instrumental in the defeat of the PPP in Sindh in closely contested races.

In short, Benazir's second term in office became the symbol of corruption and incompetence. A growing number of Pakistanis questioned whether she had any coherent vision of the future of the country at all.[49] The legacy of her government has been corruption, high inflation, political and economic uncertainty, disillusionment, and widespread apathy amongst the common citizens.

NOTES

1. *The News*, 20 October 1993.
2. *The News*, 21 October 1993.
3. *The News*, 14 November 1993.
4. *The News*, 5 December 1993.
5. Ziring, Lawrence, *Pakistan in the Twentieth Century — A Political History*, 1997, Oxford University Press, Karachi, pp. 556-7.
6. Sabir Shah v Federation of Pakistan, PLD 1994 S.C. 738.
7. In re: Suo Moto Constitutional Petition, 1994 SCMR 1028.
8. Legal Reforms Ordinance, 1996 (Ordinance XL of 1996), gazetted on 2 March 1996, reported as PLD 1996 Central Statutes 300. It was followed by Legal Reforms Ordinance, 1996 (Ordinance XXII of 1996), gazetted on 4 July 1996, reported as PLD 1996 Central Statutes 1800. It was then followed by Legal Reforms Ordinance, 1996 (Ordinance XCIV of 1996) gazetted on 2 November 1996, reported as PLD 1997 Central Statutes 102. Another Ordinance, Legal Reforms Ordinance, 1997 (Ordinance XL of 1997) was gazetted on 4 March 1997 and reported as PLD 1997 Central Statutes (unreported Statutes Volume) 288. Finally, it was enacted as Legal Reforms Act, 1997 (Act XXIII of 1997), gazetted on 3 July 1997 and reported as PLD 1997 Central Statutes 402.
9. Mian Abdul Majeed v Province of Punjab, 1994 CLC 1244.
10. Punjab Local Government (Amendment and Validation) Ordinance 1994. Punjab Ordinance VI of 1994. PLD 1994 Punjab Statutes 51.
11. Mehr Zulfiqar Ali Babu v Government of Punjab, 1994 CLC 1794.
12. Muhammad Aslam v Punjab Government, NLR 1995 Civil 630.
13. Mehr Zulfiqar Ali Babu v Government of Punjab, 1997 SCMR 117.
14. Punjab Act VII of 1996, PLJ 1996 Punjab Statutes 43.
15. Mehr Zulfiqar Ali Babu v Government of the Punjab, PLJ 1997 S.C. 175.
16. The Proclamation as reproduced on page 51 of the report of the case titled 'Manzoor Ahmad Wattoo v Federation of Pakistan', PLD 1997 Lahore 38.
17. The counsel of Wattoo had requested the Court to allow him sixty days to obtain a vote of confidence, the period allowed to a newly elected Chief Minister. The request was declined by the Court because it was a matter of restoration of office.
18. *The News*, 17 November 1996.
19. Justice Saad Saood Jan showed a copy of this note to the author.
20. Justice Sajjad Ali Shah was also junior to Justice Ajmal Mian and Justice Abdul Qadeer Chaudhry.
21. In India, during Indira Gandhi's prime ministership, the senior-most judge of the Supreme Court was ignored in favour of someone fourth in seniority and the three senior judges resigned/retired in protest. Reportedly, Justice Ajmal Mian and Justice Abdul Qadeer Chaudhry offered Justice Jan their resignations in his support if the latter would do so. Justice Jan did not accept the offer.

22. The author learnt from a very influential member of the PPP who said that he was consulted in this matter. He claimed that he supported Justice Jan for appointment as the chief justice. Soon after the note of 2 June 1994, he was summoned by Benazir to Lahore and was shown the note in the Governor's House. He was then sent to the Supreme Court Rest House in Lahore where he found Justice Sajjad sitting with Asif Ali Zardari, Benazir's husband, and assuring the latter that he would do what the PPP government desired him to do.
23. PLD 1992 S.C. 646.
24. PLD 1993 S.C. 473.
25. Such was the state of confusion that the law ministry issued three successive notifications regarding the Chief Justice of the Sindh High Court, Justice Nasir Aslam Zahid, superceding one after the other on the same day. In one, he was appointed ad hoc judge of the Supreme Court, in the second, he was appointed permanent judge of the Supreme Court, and in the third and final, after rescinding the two notifications, he was appointed as a judge of the Federal Shariat Court.
26. Some of those appointed did not even go through the ordinary process of recommendation by the Chief Justice and the Governor. They were actually never recommended by a constitutional consultee. Some of the names are reported to have been added at the last minute. Their names were faxed from the Prime Minister House to the Law Ministry requiring the latter to include them in the notification to be issued in this behalf.
27. As the story goes, there were three brothers from Rajanpur who were practising lawyers. The oldest of them was close to Leghari and he was offered an appointment as a judge. Being nearly sixty-one years of age, the man could hardly serve for a year or so. Leghari then asked him to decide amongst the three of them as to who should be judge. The three brothers decided in favour of the youngest who incidently was the least known of them and had no appearance before the High Court. What favoured him was his age because he could serve as judge for five or six years.
28. He issued notices for contempt of court to a number of lawyers and journalists, including Mr Ardeshir Cowasjee who wrote for the daily *Dawn*, for criticizing such judicial appointments.
29. Agha Rafiq is said to have close relations with Asif Ali Zardari who tried to manage his appointment out of turn. When the Chief Justice objected to his appointment, the story goes, he was rudely reminded of his own appointment ahead of three senior judges.
30. The dissenting judge, Justice Mir Hazar Khan Khoso, was the only ad hoc judge in the Bench and his appointment as such was being adversely affected by the verdict of the majority.
31. Al-Jehad Trust v Federation of Pakistan, PLD 1996 S.C. 324.
32. The Supreme Court, on this point, has heavily relied upon judgment of the Indian Supreme Court in the Supreme Court Advocates-on-Record Association v the Union of India. AIR 1994 S.C. 268.
33. One of the instances commonly known is the police raid on the residence of his daughter with the motive to involve his son-in-law in a corruption case.
34. President Reference No. 1 of 1996.
35. *The News*, 17 May 1996.
36. *The News*, 20 May 1996.
37. *The News*, 8 July 1996.
38. *The News*, 1 October 1996.
39. There were also other factors that led to such confrontations. The arrogant attitude of Benazir and her husband towards Leghari was mainly responsible for the rift. It is also rumoured that the attempt on the part of Zardari to wire-tap the phone of Leghari's daughter made the rift deeply personal and bitter.
40. Al-Jehad Trust v Federation of Pakistan, PLD 1997 S.C. 84.
41. Ziring, Lawrence, *Pakistan in the Twentieth Century—A Political History, supra*, note 5, p. 572.
42. *The News*, 27 September 1996.
43. Ibid.
44. Ibid.
45. The text taken from the daily *The News*, 5 November 1996.

46. A source close to Benazir disclosed that on assuming power in October 1993, Benazir asked her husband to keep a low profile. Zardari argued that she should rather emulate her arch rival, Nawaz, who during the previous fifteen years in power had multiplied his industrial empire, made himself a multi-billionaire, employed all kinds of unethical and unscrupulous political methods, indulged in all-out bribery, profiteering, commissions, kickbacks and other corrupt practices, and got away with them. He did not serve a day in jail and was still a national leader and vote-getter. Benazir, it is said, bought the argument and decided to give him a free hand to meddle in politics and to indulge in shady financial deals.
47. While replying to the offer of cooperation being made to the then Prime Minister Nawaz on 29 May 1993 on the floor of the National Assembly, Benazir referred to the need for changing the method of appointment of judges of the superior courts. She repeated the proposal in her interview before national television prior to the general elections of October 1993.
48. Ziring, Lawrence, *Pakistan in the Twentieth Century—A Political History, supra*, note 5, p. 571.
49. Weekly *Time* of 17 April 1995, p. 16.

34

UNDER THE SHADOW OF THE EIGHTH AMENDMENT

A founder member of the PPP, Meraj Khalid, former Speaker of the National Assembly, and former Chief Minister of Punjab, was sworn in as Caretaker Prime Minister. The caretaker cabinet included Sahabzada Yaqub Khan, a former Foreign Minister, Abida Hussain, a former Federal Minister from PML(N), and Shahid Javed Burki as chief economic adviser, a role he had played earlier in the caretaker government of Moeen Qureshi. Burki was taken in order to restore the confidence of financial markets in Pakistan and abroad.[1] Fakharuddin G. Ibrahim, a highly respected lawyer, was taken as Federal Law Minister. The rest of the cabinet was the selection of Leghari who packed it with his old friends and cronies, particularly from the civil service batch of 1964 to which he belonged, his class-fellows from the days of Aitchison College, and his relatives.

All the provincial assemblies were dissolved within days and caretaker chief ministers were appointed everywhere. The Governor of Punjab was removed and replaced by another old friend and class-fellow of Leghari, Ahmad Tariq Rahim. The most startling appointment was that of Mumtaz Bhutto as caretaker Chief Minister of Sindh. Asif Ali Zardari, who was in the Governor's House Lahore during the night between 4 and 5 November 1996, plotting the overthrow of Wattoo, was taken into custody.[2]

Benazir, who was initially placed under 'protective custody', was soon allowed to move freely. She wasted no time in condemning the President's actions as undemocratic and unconstitutional. Claiming she had been illegally detained and her husband 'kidnapped', Benazir said she would fight Leghari's actions in the highest courts and questioned why Nawaz Sharif, a Punjabi, could be reinstated by the judiciary while Sindhi leaders, from Bhutto to Junejo to herself, were never the recipients of similar justice. Revealing an abiding persecution complex, Benazir also took the opportunity afforded by her freedom to indirectly implicate Leghari in the death of her brother Murtaza. If not the operator of a conspiracy, asked Benazir, why did the President make a point of Murtaza's murder in his dismissal order, and why was the judiciary so determined to operate against her? Though her statements were made in a highly emotional state, Benazir's questions were aimed at undermining the credibility of Leghari.[3] Forced to the conclusion that she had been betrayed, Benazir still refused to acknowledge her own wrong and how it might have led to the prevailing situation.

Law of Accountability

During the year 1996, with public disclosures every day of corruption in Benazir's government, there was a general outcry for the accountability of those who had served in public office and had personally enriched themselves by abuse of power and authority. Imran Khan, a national hero due to his achievements as a cricket superstar, launched a political movement in April 1996 called 'Pakistan Tehrik-e-Insaf' and called for the accountability of corrupt public officials and the retrieval of stolen public money. He was joined soon thereafter by Jamaat-i-Islami, led by Qazi Hussain Ahmad. Sensing a positive response from the general public, the PML(N) whose own record had been dismal, joined the chorus.

Leghari justified his dismissal of Benazir's government by rolling the process of accountability. The Ehtesab Ordinance, 1996 was promulgated on 18 November, purportedly for the eradication of corrupt practices from public offices and to provide effective measures for prosecution and speedy disposal of cases involving corruption.[4]

The provisions of the Ehtesab Ordinance would apply to a person who: '(i) has been the President or the Governor of a Province; (ii) is, or has been the Prime Minister, Chairman Senate, Speaker National Assembly, Deputy Chairman Senate, Deputy Speaker National Assembly, Federal Minister, Minister of State, Attorney-General and other Law Officers appointed under the Central Law Officers Ordinance, 1970 (VII of 1970), Adviser to the Prime Minister, Special Assistant to the Prime Minister, Federal Parliamentary Secretary, Member of the Parliament, Auditor-General, Political Secretary, Adviser or Consultant to the Prime Minister, Federal Minister or Minister of State or attached with any Ministry or Division, holder of a post of or office with the rank or status of a Federal Minister or Minister of State; (iii) is, or has been, the Chief Minister, Provincial Minister, Adviser to the Chief Minister, Special Assistant to Chief Minister, Provincial Parliamentary Secretary, Member of the Provincial Assembly, Advocate-General including Additional Advocate General and Assistant Advocates-General, Political Secretary, Adviser, or Consultant to the Chief Minister, Provincial Minister, or attached to any department of the Province, holder of a post or office with rank or status of a Provincial Minister; (iv) is, or has held an office or post in Basic Pay Scale 20 or above, in the service of Pakistan or any service in connection with the affairs of the Federation or of a Province or in equivalent pay scale of management in corporation, banks, financial institutions, firms, concerns, undertakings or any other institutions, or organization established, controlled or administered by or under the Federal Government or a Provincial Government'.

The Ordinance gave a wide definition of 'corruption' and 'corrupt practices' which included all kinds of activities such as bribery, graft, fraud, misappropriation, enrichment and possessing resources in one's own name or another's beyond known means. An office in the name of Chief Ehtesab Commissioner was created who would be appointed by the President for a period of four years after consultation with the Prime Minister, Leader of the Opposition in the National Assembly, and the Chief Justice of Pakistan. The Chief Ehtesab Commissioner (CEC) would be a serving or retired judge of the Supreme Court of Pakistan. The proceedings under the Ordinance had to be initiated by the CEC on his own, or upon receipt of a reference received from a government, federal or provincial, or a complaint. He could undertake inquiry or investigation into any complaint through any person or authority including a public officer. After due inquiry or investigation, the CEC could send a reference to the High Court which would be heard by a Bench of three judges.

The punishments included sentencing to a term of imprisonment of up to seven years, imposition of fine, forfeiture of property, disqualification to contest elections to Parliament or a Provincial Assembly or, if an incumbent member of Parliament or a Provincial Assembly was found guilty, he could lose his seat. A private complainant could be rewarded if a public office holder was convicted on his complaint. Such a complainant could be punished if his complaint was found to be false or malafide. The appeal against any sentence by the High Court would lie before the Supreme Court of Pakistan. The Court was vested with the power to freeze the property, movable or immovable, of the accused pending the proceedings against him.

The Ehtesab Ordinance was amended and cases under the Ordinance could be heard by a Bench of two judges as well.[5] It was provided that an accused could be arrested after reference against him by the CEC to the Court. The provisions regarding bail to the accused were made very stringent and the cases were required to be heard daily and disposed of within sixty days.

The law of accountability was indeed the need of the hour, keeping in view the misdeeds of succeeding governments. It was criticized because it made an exception in favour of the incumbent president and governors. The idea of making a judge, retired or serving, a CEC was however, ill conceived. A job like this should have gone to a lawyer well-versed in the art of prosecution like special prosecutors appointed in the USA with the power to investigate the President and to prosecute him if need be. Still, it was the first step in the right direction.

Election Laws Amended

The dismissal of Benazir's government was taken with indifference by the general public which felt that successive governments had grown insensitive to their needs and leaders of both the major parties had done nothing for them but enriched themselves. Everybody believed that corrupt leaders and bureaucrats should be brought to justice. They took a sigh of relief when Leghari indicated that he would make the forthcoming elections subject to the process of accountability and disqualify those found guilty, and that he would take steps to eliminate big spending by the candidates. With these objectives in view, election laws were amended introducing the following requirements:[6]

1. Every candidate had to declare in his nomination papers that no loan obtained by him from any bank or other financial institution in his own name or in the name of his spouse, dependent children, or dependent parent, remained unpaid for more than one year from the due date or had been written off. He had also to declare that

he and his relatives stated above were not in default for over six months in payment of taxes. Similarly, he had to declare that he and his such relatives were not in default of any government dues or utilities for over six months.

2. A candidate was also required to make a statement of assets and liabilities of his own, his spouse, and dependents. He was also required to make statement specifying income tax and wealth tax during the preceding three assessment years.
3. A candidate could however make payment of any loan, tax, government dues, or utilities before the rejection of his nomination papers.
4. The election expenses were restricted to one million rupees for election to a seat in the National Assembly and six hundred thousand rupees to that of a Provincial Assembly. The return of election expenses had to be filed before notification of the election result and such returns would remain subject to inspection by any member of the public.
5. The election expenses by a political party for a national election campaign were restricted to thirty million rupees. The political parties were required to submit the return of their expenses within thirty days of the poll.
6. Affixation of hoardings, posters or banners of any size or wall chalkings were completely prohibited. There was also a ban on the hoisting of party flags on any public property or public places.

These measures, although commendable, were inadequate. The machinery for implementation and monitoring was defective. Most of the returns filed were patently wrong and all of the ill-reputed politicians got away. One of the most important electoral reforms regarding the ban on transportation of voters by candidates on election day was omitted. This could only be achieved by a total ban on private transport on polling day, as is the case in India. The transportation of voters on election day is the single most important factor that gives a huge advantage to resourceful candidates, particularly feudals in rural constituencies.

Leghari-Nawaz Secret Pact: Justice Fakharuddin Resigns

The dismissal of Benazir's government was the first major step taken by Leghari on his own. Previously, Leghari was known to play second fiddle to Benazir. In the beginning, he had publicly promised to be neutral and to carry out the process of accountability even-handedly. But subsequent events proved that Leghari wilted under the pressure of incessant and persistent attacks from Benazir. He made a secret pact with Nawaz hoping that the latter would protect him from Benazir. He made significant concessions to Nawaz to enable him to contest the election and to succeed with the co-operation of the establishment.

The secret deal between the two became public because of two important events. One was the softening of the rigors of law for defaulters on public loans. Under the reforms brought in electoral laws, an unpaid loan from a bank or a financial institution taken in the name of any business concern mainly owned by a candidate, would make him a defaulter unable to participate in the elections. The expression 'mainly owned' was defined as the holding or controlling of a majority interest in a business concern. Another ordinance was promulgated on 19 December 1996 which re-defined the expression as referring to someone who was a director, a partner, or sole proprietor in a business concern at the time the loan was written off.[7] This amendment was made to help Nawaz and his brother Shahbaz participate in the elections. They had obtained a number of loans in the past for their business concerns which had been written off because of their power, authority, and influence. They had cleverly avoided becoming directors or partners in such concerns but owned major shares in their own names or in the names of immediate family members.

The other event was the resignation by Fakharuddin G. Ibrahim, the Federal Law Minister, who was the most respected member of the caretaker government. He made a public statement[8] to the effect that Leghari had reneged on his promise to the nation to hold fair and even-handed accountability and had joined hands with Nawaz in a deal to bring him to power. The changes in election laws proved the allegations levelled by Fakharuddin to the hilt.

Dissolution of National Assembly Challenged

The dissolution of the National Assembly was challenged before the Supreme Court of Pakistan under its original jurisdiction by Syed Yousaf Raza Gilani, Speaker of the National Assembly on 11 November 1996. Leghari and the Caretaker Prime Minister Meraj Khalid were made respondents in person. The grounds taken in the petition included the following:

1. That the powers conferred by Article 58(2)(b) of the Constitution were not to be subjectively applied but required the existence of such objective conditions that showed that the government of the Federation could not be carried out in accordance with the Constitution. Total collapse of the constitutional machinery was visualized and it was not enough to merely allege that the Government was not being run in accordance with the Constitution of Pakistan.
2. That the reading of the grounds of dissolution order tantamounts to personal indictment of the Prime Minister and that as if she is being punished for the alleged misdemeanour in the past.
3. That from none of the grounds alleged in the dissolution order could it be discerned that the government of the Federation could not be carried on in accordance with the provision of the Constitution neither was there any allegation of constitutional deadlock nor that the machinery of the Government had broken down completely and its authority eroded.
4. That the major criticism in the impugned order was levelled against the Government and not against the National Assembly. The National Assembly having requisitioned a session to discuss and finalize the proposal of the President in his message to the Assembly and the President could not but for the *malafide* reasons foreclose the proposed legislation by the Parliament.

5. That the issuing of the impugned order at midnight, between 4th and 5 November 1996 clearly showed that the order was passed hurriedly without a proper and judicious application of mind.
6. That the delayed speech delivered by the President the next day again by midnight clearly reflected the President's *malafide* motives. It was the speech of a person who was out to take revenge and punish the Prime Minister for the deeds and actions which were closed and past.

Two days after the filing of the petition of Speaker Gilani, Benazir also filed a petition challenging the order of dissolution of the National Assembly and the dismissal of her government. The allegations made by the President in the dissolution order were responded to as under:

1. Regarding the ground of extra judicial killings in Karachi, it was submitted that the observation of the President was entirely misconceived and contrary to the facts. This ground was not cogent or relevant to the question of the dissolution of the National Assembly. It related to the provinces, as law and order being not a subject in the Federal domain. The President had thus proceeded on an entirely ill-advised and irrelevant premise. Reference was also made to a number of speeches made by Leghari, from time to time, supporting the actions of the government in restoring law and order in Karachi. It was also observed that the Federal Government had entered into negotiations with the MQM so as to try to bring peace to the city of Karachi, a gesture appreciated by the President in his address to Parliament of 29 October 1995.
2. Regarding the ground that Benazir had insinuated implication of the President in a conspiracy of murder of Murtaza Bhutto, it was questioned that on what basis did the President assume that the death of Murtaza was 'ostensibly in an encounter with the Karachi Police'. It was asserted that an assumption of a conspiracy is far more credible than the assumption of a police encounter. It was lamented that the President was trying to take political edge on account of a tragic event. Attacking Leghari for falsely and maliciously accusing Benazir of complicity in the brutal death of her brother, it was highlighted that Leghari was guilty of uncharitable haste in filing a Reference in the Supreme Court of Pakistan on a day when she was burying her brother, and the offices of the Supreme Court were closed. Taking a strong exception to the harsh and defamatory nature of the language used by the President, it was urged that this ground was sufficient for setting aside of the Dissolution Order, as was held in the case of Nawaz Sharif (PLD 1993 SC 473).
3. Regarding the ground of ridiculing the judgment of the Supreme Court of 20 March 1996 and deliberate delay in its implementation, it was denied that the judgment was ridiculed. Whatever was said was fair comment on the judgment, and the authors of the judgment were themselves broad-minded not to take any umbrage upon any statement made by the petitioner. How could the President do so? Anyhow, the speech of Benazir could not form the basis of packing up of all the members of the National Assembly. Even otherwise, speeches in Parliament are constitutionally protected.

   As to the implementation of the judgment, it was pointed out that it has never been resisted or delayed. It must not be forgotten that besides the learned Chief Justices, the Governors of the respective Provinces were also Constitutional consultees. They also had to give their opinions, and although they were advised specifically by letter of the

Law Ministry of on or about 10 July 1996 to expedite their consideration, they were in a quandary. A dispute had been raised by some of the affected judges concerning the observations of the learned Chief Justices of the High Courts. This was particularly cogent, it seemed, with respect to the allegations/insinuation of corruption and/or the findings of the number of years that some had practised in the High Courts. The Governors felt themselves obliged to give definite opinions as these were indeed serious matters affecting the reputation and character of those concerned. These proceedings might have led to some delay, but it was not unjustified. There were other issues which were not specifically dealt with in the judgment, and required resolution. These included the mode of resignation/termination of the affected judges after scrutiny, the retrospective appointment of two judges, the appointments of the Provincial Chief Justices, particularly of Mr Nasir Aslam Zahid (to the Supreme Court or the High Court). One issue still remained unresolved, the validation of the appointment of the present Chief Justice whose appointment obviously came under the cloud of the judgment as it rejected supersession outright and upheld the principle of seniority.

In any case, the first few of the issues named above entailed several meetings between the President and the Prime Minister, and with the Chief Justice himself. Benazir's desire that the judgment be implemented in full and without any reservations, was thus reflected by her seeking guidance both from the President and the Chief Justice. And it was in furtherance of this objective alone that she had several meetings with the President and the Chief Justice, and also exchanged with them letters/communications in this regard.

4. In response to the allegation that there was sustained assault on the judicial organ of State in the garb of a Bill moved in Parliament for disciplining judges, it was submitted that the presumption that there has been any 'sustained assault on the judicial organ' was wholly misconceived and malafide. In any case, the mere moving of a motion or a Bill in Parliament could not form the basis of any punitive action. If anything, the mere allegation is a violation of the privilege of Parliament. If parliaments began to be dissolved on the mere fact that the presidents did not agree with a particular Bill tabled in the House by a party, or member, there would be no House that would remain. As the President himself has noted, the government did not in fact have a two-thirds majority in Parliament, no (alleged) harm could have been done. Then why dissolve the entire National Assembly on a ground that could not have fructified by the President's own showing?
5. In reply to the allegation that the judiciary had not been separated from the executive in violation of Article 175(3) of the Constitution of Pakistan and the deadline for such separation fixed by the Supreme Court of Pakistan, it was submitted that the ground was misconceived and could not form the basis for the dissolution order. A high-powered committee was formed for the purpose which held a number of meetings, including the final one presided over by the President himself, and took decisions. Accordingly, the Law Reforms Ordinance, 1996 was promulgated before the cut-off date prescribed by the Supreme Court itself. Subsequently, all provinces issued notifications required under the Ordinance for its promulgation. The Ordinance was laid in the National Assembly and passed in a record period of eight days. In fact, even the Chief Justice of Pakistan had expressed his satisfaction upon the process of separation of the judiciary. Reference may be made to the daily *Dawn* dated 4 October 1996.

6. The ground that the Prime Minister and her Government deliberately violated, on a massive scale, the fundamental right of privacy guaranteed by Article 14 of the Constitution through illegal phone-tapping and eaves-dropping techniques. This charge was denied saying that they never authorized any phone-tapping. Benazir claimed herself to be a victim of phone-tapping.
7. Regarding the allegation that corruption, nepotism, and violation of rules in the administration of the affairs of the Government and its various bodies, authorities and corporations, had become so extensive and widespread that the orderly functioning of Government in accordance of the provisions of the Constitution of Pakistan and the law had become impossible, it was submitted that this ground was in utter disregard of the previous judgments of the Court in which the Court has consistently ruled that allegations of corruption, nepotism, and violation of roles (even though reprehensible), did not constitute a ground that was sufficient in itself to justify an order under Article 58(2)(b). Mere unsubstantiated allegations cannot form the basis of any dissolution or punitive action. If this be the case, then the President ought to have resigned when the Opposition came out with the allegation of his alleged corruption in the Mehran Bank case, and also published a pamphlet purporting to give specific details and copies of cheques. That which applies to the National Assembly or the Government, must also apply to the President. By entrusting all the important offices in the caretaker set-up to his relatives (brother-in-law), room-mates and batch-fellows in the Academy (the batch of 1964), and to school-fellows (the Aitchisonians), did the President not violate his oath of office? And is any oath different in sanctity from any other?
8. In response to the allegation that the Constitutional requirement that all the Cabinet together with the Ministers of State should be collectively responsible to the National Assembly was violated by the induction of a Minister against whom criminal cases are pending which the Interior Minister had refused to withdraw, it was submitted that the charge was misconceived. The President had himself been a member of a Cabinet wherein two of his own colleagues were under trial on the false charges of murder. Not only that, in April 1993, the President as Caretaker Finance Minister, himself met and requested the then President Ishaq Khan to appoint Mr Asif Ali Zardari as Federal Minister even though there were cases pending against Mr Zardari in those days. And the President had selected and appointed/approved the appointment of Mr Mumtaz Ali Bhutto as the Caretaker Chief Minister, Sindh, who had himself been an accused and absconder in FIR No. 24 at PS Khanoth, District Dadu, under trial in the Court of the Judge Special Court II, S.T.A. Hyderabad. Another Chief Minister appointed/approved by the President was one of the main defaulters of the bank loans, a practice that the President wanted to be removed in his message to the National Assembly and the Senate. In any case, a person is innocent until proven guilty. This is the salutary principle of law and justice. The ground is not relatable to Article 58(2)(b).
9. In reply to the allegation that in the matter of the sale of Burmah Castrol shares in PPL and BONE/PPL shares in Qadirpur Gas Field involving national assets valued in several billions of rupees, the President required the Prime Minister to place the matter before the Cabinet for consideration/re-consideration of the decisions taken in this matter by the ECC, which was not done. It was submitted that the ground was not tenable at all nor was it germane to the impugned order.

With respect to the above transactions, to the best recollection of the petitioner, it may be further submitted that the government of Nawaz Sharif had given approval to

Burmah to sell its shares in PPL and BONE without any restrictions to another foreign investor in 1992, which was approved by the Benazir government and the President himself. The transactions were challenged in the Balochistan High Court and the Supreme Court of Pakistan by Senator Abdul Haye and the government of Balochistan respectively.

The President was and is fully aware of the pending cases before the Superior Courts of Pakistan and therefore, inclusion in the Dissolution Order of the PPL/BONE matter is in contempt of court.

By making the transaction part of the Dissolution Order, the President has not only exhibited that there was no application of the mind in the framing of the Order but has also exhibited his insensitivity to the issue of foreign investment in Pakistan.

10. Regarding final paragraph of the President's order that for the foregoing reasons, taken individually and collectively, he was satisfied that a situation had arisen in which the government of the Federation cannot be carried on in accordance with the provisions of the Constitution and an appeal to the electorate was necessary, it was stated that none of the reasons was either individually or collectively sufficient to provide the foundation of the dissolution order. The petitioner enjoyed the support of the majority and no appeal to the electorate was necessary. In fact repeated and premature elections weaken democratic institutions and the system. They also burden the exchequer and the people with a huge expense. They cause instability and uncertainty. It was held in the case of Nawaz Sharif (PLD 1993 SC 473 at p.568), that to apply this clause that the Government could not be carried on in accordance with the provisions of the Constitution, the action could not be based on mere likes and dislikes, or on surmises. For this clause to be applicable, there must be an actual breakdown, a stalemate, a deadlock. How could the Court depart from this view particularly when in this case a deadlock was not even alleged. In any case, the caretaker appointments made and the other measures taken against Benazir and her husband would indicate that the President did not propose to make a fair appeal to, or obtain a fair verdict from the electorate.

Dissolution Upheld

Confrontation over the implementation of the Judges' Judgment inevitably brought the Chief Justice to centre stage. He had become a symbol of resistance and opposition to Benazir's government and a hero for all opposition forces in the country. The popularity of Justice Sajjad was not without its toll. It transformed his personality and he assumed an air of arrogance. He enjoyed making press statements and could not stay away from a show of partisanship. When Benazir challenged the order of the dissolution of the National Assembly, his attitude was clearly hostile. He returned her petition twice on flimsy procedural grounds. It appeared that he wanted to delay and frustrate the petition. He also had the petition so fixed that it would be heard after other constitutional petitions pending at that time which were, of course, not as urgent. He pulled out old cases pending against the validity of the Eighth Amendment and fixed them ahead of the dissolution cases. He made another significant departure with this petition. On all previous occasions, the cases of dissolution of Assemblies were heard by all available judges of the Supreme Court of Pakistan but this time he constituted a Bench of only seven judges, keeping a number of senior judges out of the Bench. Such manoeuvres resulted in the dismissal of the petition only four days before the general elections, which proved to be the last nail in the coffin of the PPP, whose members were already disillusioned, demoralized, and dejected. It was thus routed in the general election held on 3 February 1997.

The Supreme Court, by a majority of six to one, upheld the order of the President dissolving the National Assembly and dismissing Benazir's government.[9] The reasons that prevailed with the majority are briefly quoted below:

1. For the President to objectively form the opinion that a situation had arisen in which the government could not be carried on in accordance with the provisions of the Constitution is the availability of material in support of the ground of dissolution. The discretionary power of the President in this behalf, though exercisable in an objective manner, cannot be equated with that of a court of law. He is rather required to act according to the rules of prudence. There is no requirement of a standard of proof of evidence as in a trial in a court of law.
2. The Court is only required to examine whether or not the President had exercised his power in accordance with provisions of Article 58(2)(b) and that action taken by him was bonafide. The Court has no concern with quantity or sufficiency of material nor can it sit in approval on the dissolution order.
3. Article 58(2)(b) requires 'opinion' and not 'satisfaction' of the President. 'Opinion' can be formed without the touch of finality. It lacks the dissent of absolutism and can always be differentiated from 'satisfaction', which has the touch of finality, containing absolutism. In other words, it can be said that opinion has lesser responsibility than satisfaction from the point of view of burden of proof.
4. There was deliberate non-compliance, rather defiance, on the part of the Prime Minister in acting on the joint recommendation of the Chief Justice of Pakistan and the Chief Justice of the concerned High Court. The instances mentioned here are those of Justice Rana Bhagwan Das and Justice Javed Nawaz Khan Gandapur of the Sindh and Peshawar High Courts respectively who were not confirmed despite recommendations of the Chief Justice, but were extended as Additional Judges for six months.
5. There is no protection available to an individual member of a legislative assembly to ridicule a judgment of the Supreme Court in the garb of fair comment. Constitution Fifteenth Amendment Bill was introduced in Parliament for initiating the process of accountability of judges by sending them on forced leave if fifteen percent of the members moved a motion against them, was designed to humiliate and embarrass the superior judiciary and ran counter to Article 209 meant for action against judges by the Supreme Judicial Council.
6. There was a general impression that all official acts were motivated by corruption, favouritism, and nepotism. The actions of a government, about which such an impression has been created and commonly perceived, lose authority, legality, and validity. Such action though purported to be done

under provisions of the law or the Constitution but motivated by private impulses, benefits, and corruption, cannot be termed as performed under the Constitution. There is overwhelming evidence made manifest from the enormous record produced in the case to establish that persons holding the highest posts in government were guilty of corrupt practices and gross abuse of power on the basis of which it could be concluded that the government could not be carried on in accordance with provisions of the Constitution.

7. Relying on press clippings, it was held that there was sufficient material (distinguished from evidence) that there were extra-judicial killings, custodial deaths, illegal arrests, torture, illegal searches and seizures on the orders of the government and its functionaries. It was held that such instances were so numerous that the President was justified in forming the opinion that government could not be carried on and was not being carried on in accordance with the provisions of the Constitution. Such extra-judicial killing, seizure and search, it was observed, not only violate the right to life but also infringe on the dignity of man and the privacy of the home and denying treatment according to law and equal protection of laws. Thus fundamental rights under Articles 4, 9, 14, and 25 were clearly violated.
8. Relying on Abdul Wali Khan's case (PLD 1976 S.C. 57), newspaper cuttings were relied upon as relevant material.
9. There was no law that could permit intelligence agencies to tap, tape or eavesdrop on the telephones of judges or other persons against whom there was no allegation of being suspect or anti-State. Since reports of such tapped conversations were regularly transmitted to Benazir, which were examined or read by her and no action was taken against these agencies, therefore, it proves her direction for and participation in such illegal acts.
10. Analysing the grounds, particularly the extra-judicial killings, ridiculing the judiciary, corruption, bribery, withdrawal of money from Bait-ul-Mal and the banks, it is established that the people had lost faith in the services, the administration and in the impartiality and legality of the Assembly as well. The members of the Assembly are not required to remain mere spectators of violations of the Constitution and infringement of fundamental rights at a massive scale. They have a duty to discharge as required by the Constitution to prevent such violations and infractions. In these circumstances, the President was justified in forming an opinion that an appeal to the electorate was necessary.

In brief, the majority held that there was sufficient material available on the record in support of the following grounds mentioned in the order of dissolution:

1. Extra-judicial killings.
2. Non-implementation of the judgment of the Supreme Court in the case of appointment of judges.
3. Harassment of judges by introduction of the Bill in the National Assembly proposing to send a judge on forced leave if 15 per cent of the total members of the National Assembly moved a complaint of misconduct against him.

4. Non-separation of the judiciary from the executive as required under Article 175(3) of the Constitution within the time stipulated which was so set by the Supreme Court in the judgment.
5. Violation of Article 14 by tapping the telephones of judges, leaders of political parties, and high-ranking military and civil officials.
6. Corruption in government departments and corporations, and making appointments in violation of rules and regulations.

The Court declined to consider the material regarding the murder of Murtaza Bhutto and the sale of Burma Castrol shares in PPL and BONE/PPL shares in Qadirpur Gas Field for the reason that the cases were pending in the courts of law and, therefore, such matters were sub-judice. The Court excluded from consideration the material in support of the allegation against Hakim Ali Zardari for having purchased property in a foreign country since he was not part of the government as the transactions took place earlier than that period. It was also held that so far as allegations against Nawaz Khokhar and his inclusion in the Cabinet in spite of resistance and opposition by the Interior Minister was concerned, the material not sufficient and this ground was not adequate for the dissolution of the National Assembly but it could be considered along with the material produced on the other grounds, as it did not promote and advance good government.

The Court repelled the objection of non-maintainability by relying on Nawaz Sharif's case (PLD 1993 S.C. 324), holding therein that the petition was directly maintainable before the Supreme Court under Article 184(3) of the Constitution.

Justice Zia Mahmood Mirza wrote a strong dissent and noted in particular that:

1. There was no material available with the President at the time of passing of the dissolution order in support of the allegation of phone-tapping and eaves-dropping.
2. Mere moving of a Bill in the Assembly cannot be made a ground for dissolving the National Assembly. It is for the Parliament to adopt it or reject it. If National Assembly which is the highest elected/representative body in the country is allowed to be dissolved on premises that a Bill was moved therein which the President disapproved, then there would be no end to it and no Assembly would survive.
3. The power under Article 58(2)(b) should only be exercised when the constitutional machinery of the government completely breaks down, making it impossible for representative government to function in accordance with provisions of the Constitution.
4. Since there were no proceedings for contempt or disqualification under Article 63 of the Constitution pending against Benazir, therefore, the ground of ridiculing the judgment in the Judges case and its non-implementation/deliberate delay in its implementation was not available to the President for taking drastic action of dissolving the National Assembly.
5. The ground of extra-judicial killings was neither legally nor factually available to the President. He having remained actively associated with government policies regarding the situation in Karachi for a period of three years and having all along applauded and appreciated policies of the government and steps taken by it to combat terrorism and violence in Karachi, was precluded from pressing this ground into service.

6. The involvement of Benazir or of the federal government in extra-judicial killings did not appear to have been substantiated on record.
7. That the provision empowering the President to dissolve the National Assembly at his discretion, being drastic in nature, is to be construed strictly and this power must be exercised sparingly and only in an extreme situation when no other option is available within the framework of the Constitution.
8. That the situation envisaged in sub-clause (b) of Article 58(2) viz. that the government of the Federation could not be carried on in accordance with the provisions of the Constitution contemplates a situation where the machinery of the Government is completely broken down and its authority eroded and the Government could not be carried on in accordance with the provisions of the Constitution (as held in the case of Haji Muhammad Saifullah PLD 1989 SC 166); breakdown of Constitutional mechanism, a stalemate, a deadlock in ensuring the observance of the provisions of the Constitution (as interpreted/explained by Shafiur Rehman J. in his separate note recorded in the case of Haji Muhammad Saifullah, or as observed in Ahmad Tariq Rahim's case, PLD 1992 SC 646); where there is an actual or imminent breakdown of the Constitutional machinery, where there takes place extensive, continued and pervasive failure to observe numerous provisions of the Constitution creating an impression that the country was being governed by extra-Constitutional methods.

Eighth Amendment Held Valid: Mahmood Achakzai's Case

The Eighth Amendment to the Constitution in 1985 had been at the centre of political controversy, particularly in relation to the discretionary powers of the President to dissolve the National Assembly and to dismiss the federal government. This power was exercised on four occasions and each time after being thoroughly judicially reviewed by the superior courts. On two occasions, the exercise of such presidential power was upheld and on the other two occasions, it was held that the power was exercised invalidly. However, on one occasion only the National Assembly and the federal government was restored.

A number of citizens, or their organizations, had challenged the Eighth Amendment. Some of these appeals were pending before the Supreme Court since 1990. As discussed earlier, Chief Justice Sajjad decided to hear all such cases ahead of the cases concerning the dissolution of the National Assembly. The reason apparently was that if the Eighth Amendment is held to be invalid, then the discretionary power to dissolve the National Assembly would not be available and dissolution orders would consequently become void and unconstitutional.

The main arguments raised by the petitioners were as under:

(a) The decision of the Supreme Court in Nusrat Bhutto's case (PLD 1977 S.C. 657) was violated by Zia in promulgating and enforcing amongst others Provisional Constitution Order, 1981 and Referendum Order, 1984. This being so, the National Assembly and the Provincial Assemblies elected in 1985 and their functioning thereafter could not be taken to be duly elected bodies under the Constitution. Consequently, the Eighth Amendment passed by such a National Assembly would be invalid.

(b) The basic structure of the Constitution of Pakistan has been given in the Objectives Resolution and any amendment that violates such a basic structure would itself be invalid. The Eighth Amendment being violative of such basic structure by having altered its parliamentary character was liable to be struck down as invalid.

(c) The National Assembly, elected on a non-party basis in 1985, was unconstitutional and illegal and could not thus amend the Constitution.

The Counsels for the federation raised the following objections in response:

i. That the judges hearing the cases had taken oath under the Constitution as amended by the Eighth Amendment. Therefore, they could not question it or allow it to be questioned.

ii. That all the petitions were hit by the doctrine of political question. Since the question of balance of power between the President and the Prime Minister, because of its political sensitivity, is political question, therefore, the Court could not determine the same.

iii. That doctrine of *de facto* would favour the validation of the Eighth Amendment as it has been in force for so long. Its invalidation after more than twelve years would affect large number of orders made or actions taken thereunder.

The Supreme Court after hearing all the parties at length, upheld the validity of the Eighth Amendment.[10] The main findings of the Court were as under:

1. Although Article 239 confers unlimited power to the Parliament to amend the Constitution, yet it cannot amend in complete violation of Islam, nor can it convert democratic form into undemocratic. Similarly, courts cannot be abolished through amendment in the Constitution. It is an emerging legal theory that even if the Constitution is suspended or abrogated, the judiciary continues to hold its position to impart justice and protect rights of the people.
2. The salient features of the Constitution as reflected in the Objectives Resolution are federation and parliamentary form of government blended with Islamic provisions. As long as such salient features are retained and not altered in substance, amendments can be made as per procedure prescribed in Article 239 of the Constitution. The Court held that the Eighth Amendment did not alter the basic features of the Constitution and was, therefore, valid.
3. The National Assembly elected on a non-party basis was held to be constitutional and legal. Parliament having been validly constituted, Constitution (Eighth Amendment) Act, 1985 introduced in and passed by such Parliament was a competently enacted piece of legislation.
4. Article 58(2)(b) of the Constitution only brought about balance between the powers of the President and the Prime Minister in parliamentary form of government as is contemplated under a parliamentary democracy. There was nothing unusual about it and such provisions enabling the President to exercise such power could be found in various parliamentary democratic constitutions

like those of Australia, Italy, India, France, and Portugal. This provision in fact has shut the door on Martial Law for ever.

5. By recognizing certain basic features and characteristics of the Constitution, it does not mean that the Supreme Court has impliedly accepted the theory of the basic structure of the Constitution. Only a limited application of the theory has been made to save prominent features found within the realm of the Constitution itself.
6. On the objection regarding the doctrine of political question, it was held that any question being a political question would not deter the Court from determining it on the touchstone of the Constitution. Courts should not adopt a 'political question doctrine' for refusing to determine difficult and knotty problems barring political overtures. It would amount to abdication of judicial power which neither the Constitution permits nor the law allows. The crucial factor is that the action impugned is shown to be violative of the Constitution.
7. The Eighth Amendment was incorporated into the Constitution in 1985 after which three elections were held on a party basis and the resultant Parliaments did not touch this Amendment. It amply demonstrated that this Amendment was ratified by implication and had come to stay in the Constitution unless amended in the manner prescribed in Article 239.

General Elections, February 1997

It was expected that there would be a low turnout of voters at these hurriedly called elections, but the turnout was even less. Leghari appeared on Pakistan Television (PTV) on the evening on 3 February 1997, the polling day, and said that turnout in urban areas had been 26 per cent and in rural areas 27 per cent. Subsequently, he resiled and stated that it was much more. Observers felt that his initial statement was correct and later figures of higher turnout were a result of padding and fabrication.

According to the election results, the PML(N) won a two-thirds majority in the National Assembly, about 90 per cent of the seats in the Punjab Assembly, and a near majority in the NWFP Assembly. In Sindh and Balochistan, no party had an absolute majority though in Sindh, the PPP had obtained more seats than any other party. Benazir denounced the election results as being 'engineered'.[11] Qazi Hussain Ahmad, leader of the Jamaat-i-Islami, declared that the low turnout was a rejection by the voters of the corrupt electoral process and said that Jamaat would not recognize the government formed as a result thereof.[12]

The results of the elections are tabulated as under:[13]

PARTY POSITION

	NA	PP	PS	PF	PB
PML(N)	134	212	15	31	5
PPP	19	2	36	4	1
HPG (Haq Prast Group)	12	0	28	0	0
ANP (Awami National Party)	9	0	0	28	0
BNP (Balochistan National Party)	3	0	0	0	9
JUI(F) (Jamiat-i-Ulema-i-Islam)	2	0	0	1	6
JWP (Jamhoori Watan Party)	2	0	0	0	6
NPP (National People's Party)	1	0	3	0	0
PPP(SB) (Shaheed Bhutto)	1	0	2	0	0
BNM	0	0	0	0	2
PDP (Pakistan Democratic Party)	0	1	0	0	0
PKMAP (Pakhtoon-Khwah Milli Awami Party)	0	2	0	0	2
PML(J)	0	2	0	2	1
UNA	0	0	1	0	0
Independents	19	21	15	11	8
Total	202	238	100	77	40

NOTES

1. Ziring, Lawrence, *Pakistan in the Twentieth Century—A Political History*, 1997, Oxford University Press, Karachi, p. 585.
2. It was widely rumoured that Zardari was caught with a lot of cash in foreign currency and gold bullion which he was keeping with him to win over MPAs in the Punjab to oust Wattoo. However, despite the outcry about this rumour, the government did not come up with anything.
3. She called Leghari 'Farooq-ul-Haq' to make him sound like Ziaul Haq, implying the similarities between the two for betraying their benefactors.
4. Ordinance CXI of 1996, PLD 1996 Central Statutes 1954,
5. Ehtesab (Amendment) Ordinance, 1997 (Ordinance VII of 1997), PLD 1997 Central Statutes 255.
6. Representation of the People (Fourth Amendment) Ordinance, 1996 (Ordinance CVII of 1996), PLD 1997, Central Statutes 6.
7. Representation of the People (Fifth Amendment) Ordinance, 1996. Ordinance CXIX of 1996, PLD 1997 Central Statutes 215.
8. *The News*, 19 December 1997.
9. Benazir Bhutto v Farooq Ahmad Leghari, PLJ 1998 S.C. 27.
10. Mahmood Khan Achakzai v Federation of Pakistan, PLD 1997 S.C. 426.
11. *The News*, 4 February 1997.
12. Ibid.
13. *The News*, 6 February 1997.

35

NAWAZ'S SECOND TERM: STORMING THE SUPREME COURT

The PML(N) had obtained more than two-thirds majority in the National Assembly and consequently, Nawaz Sharif, the leader of the PML(N) was elected prime minister by the National Assembly. In his acceptance speech, he made special mention of the need for accountability at all levels, like Benazir before him had done. He obtained a vote of confidence from the National Assembly on 18 February 1997 and the federal government was formed in coalition with the ANP and the MQM.

In the Punjab, the PML(N) had completely swept the polls and there was no opposition worth the name. It was expected that the chief ministership of Punjab would go to Parvez Elahi who had been so promised in 1993 after the reinstatement of the Nawaz government by the Supreme Court of Pakistan. Nawaz and his family had second thoughts about offering the Punjab government to the Chaudhris of Gujrat. They had a bitter experience with Wattoo in 1993 and decided not to risk Punjab at any cost. Besides, with such an overwhelming majority in the Punjab Assembly, Nawaz had little to fear from any group inside the party. So, it was decided to keep the chief ministership of the Punjab within the family and Shahbaz Sharif, the brother of Nawaz, was chosen for the post. Parvez Elahi was offered the office of Speaker of the Provincial Assembly of the Punjab as compensation. The Chaudhris of Gujrat had little choice but to accept what was offered them.

In the NWFP, a coalition government of the PML(N) and the ANP was formed, headed by Mahtab Abbasi of the PML(N). In Sindh, a coalition government of the PML(N) and the MQM was formed, headed by Liaquat Ali Jatoi of the PML(N). In Balochistan, no party had a majority and a coalition headed by Akhtar Mengal was formed.

End to the Eighth Amendment

After the general elections, Leghari emerged very powerful. He got away with the dismissal of Benazir's government and had a government of his own choice inducted. Leghari assumed an assertive air and got an old friend and civil service colleague appointed as Governor of Punjab, apparently against the wishes of Nawaz and his colleagues in the Parliament, without realizing that his position was quite vulnerable with Nawaz having a two-thirds majority in both Houses of Parliament.

Nawaz struck soon, using his overwhelming majority in the Parliament, and did away with the discretionary powers of the President. The Constitution (Thirteenth Amendment) Act, 1997[1] was moved and passed in a matter of minutes on 4 April 1997 by relaxing the usual rules regarding constitutional amendment, particularly those concerning advance consideration and repeated readings.

The most significant amendment was the omission of Article 58(2)(b) of the Constitution vesting discretionary power in the President to dissolve the National Assembly. The corresponding power of the Governors to dissolve the Provincial Assembly under Article 112(2)(b) was also done away with. The power of the president to appoint governors was watered down. Previously, such appointments were made by the president 'after consultation with' the prime minister. After the Thirteenth Amendment, such power was exercisable 'on the advice of' the prime minister. This change made all the difference because the advice of the prime minister is binding on the president. By the amendment of Article 243 of the Constitution, the discretionary powers of the president to appoint chiefs of armed forces was also taken away.

There has been a consensus amongst political parties and legal circles that power under Article 58(2)(b), introduced by the Eighth Amendment, did enormous harm. None of the governments elected in the general elections of 1985, 1988, 1990, and 1993 could complete their five year term primarily because of the exercise of discretionary powers of the President to dissolve the National Assembly. The manner in which the Thirteenth Amendment was hurriedly introduced and passed made it suspect. If it were not for the fact that the Amendment had been passed in the late hours of the night, the President, the armed forces, or the judiciary might have intervened and stopped it.[2] The Thirteenth Amendment was passed unanimously because both the major parties had suffered under at the hands of the President.

The Thirteenth Amendment proved to be the end of the Eighth Amendment. Once again, the President became the titular head with only ceremonial powers as envisaged by the original Constitution of 1973. The discretionary powers of the President to appoint the Chief Election Commissioner were not touched, intentionally or otherwise. It is an irony that the Eighth Amendment was undone within a few months of its being held valid by the Supreme Court.

End to Defections

The problem of defection and political horse trading had assumed alarming proportions in the past. It has been discussed how the government of Ghulam Haider Wyne in the Punjab was overthrown in 1993 by Wattoo's defection. Benazir had defeated the motion for vote of no confidence against her in 1989 by winning over certain MNAs from the opposition. The overthrow of Sabir Shah's government in NWFP in 1994 by Sherpao was another example of blatant bribery causing defections.

With two-thirds majority in both Houses of Parliament, Nawaz had the Constitution (Fourteenth Amendment) Act, 1977 passed on 3 July 1997.[3] This amendment was apparently introduced in order to put to an end to the problem of defections. Like the Thirteenth Amendment, this one too was also bulldozed through Parliament in a matter of minutes around midnight.[4] All rules were once again relaxed, and despite protests by the opposition of being taken unawares and of being confronted with the draft of the amendment when they came to attend the session, it was passed unanimously.

The Fourteenth Amendment added Article 63-A to the Constitution. It provides that if a member of Parliament or Provincial Assembly defects, then the head of the political party to which he belongs or on whose ticket he was elected himself or through another person authorized in this behalf may give notice to him to show cause within seven days why disciplinary action be not taken against him. After the show cause notice, the disciplinary committee of the party would decide the matter if it pertains to breach of party discipline such as violation of the party constitution, code of conduct, or declared policies. In case of a decision against such a member, he can appeal to the head of the party whose decision would be final. In case a member votes contrary to any direction issued by the parliamentary party to which he belongs, or abstains from voting against party policy in relation to any Bill, the head of the party concerned, after examining his explanations, would determine whether or not such member has defected. The presiding officer of the House[5] to which the member concerned belonged would be sent the decision who would transmit it within two days to the Chief Election Commissioner who, in turn, would give effect to the decision within seven days of its receipt.

The action of the party head cannot be challenged before any court, including the Supreme Court or a High Court. This constitutional bar has made heads of political parties in Parliament and the provincial assemblies virtual dictators. Such an Amendment was passed because all party heads wanted to keep dissenting members in line.

Although defections in the political parties had become a problem and needed to be addressed, yet the solution offered went beyond the problem. The Fourteenth Amendment silenced dissent within political parties rather than defections therefrom. Voting within the party on a Bill or abstention from voting on a bill, is not unusual in established democracies and has never been equated with defection. Nawaz and Benazir tried to kill all dissension, thus reducing the members of the Parliament voting for the amendment to mere rubber stamps.

New Accountability Law

The Ehtesab Ordinance, 1996 has been discussed earlier. It was replaced by another Ordinance on the subject in February 1997[6] which was repealed by the Ehtesab Act, 1997.[7] Certain important departures have been made in the Act from the previous Ordinance on the subject. They are:

(a) The scope and ambit of the law was extended to include the incumbent or former government servants holding posts in Basic Pay Scales 17 or above. The Ordinance included the holders of posts in Basic Pay Scales 20 or above.

(b) The Ehtesab Cell was provided for which was to be set up by the Federal Government for the purpose of investigation and enquiry of offences under this Act. This Cell took over the responsibility of enquiries and investigations to the exclusion of any other agency or authority of the government. It can, however, require the assistance of any agency, police officers, or other officials, if it so deems fit. After completion of the enquiry or investigation, the Ehtesab Cell is required to communicate to the Chief Ehtesab Commissioner its appraisal of the material and evidence in the form of reference to him. The effect of such reference is that the Chief Ehtesab Commissioner can direct that the accused be arrested and the case referred to the Court for trial.

The primary purpose of the government in creating the Ehtesab Cell was to take all investigations into its own hands and to undermine the powers and position of the Chief Ehtesab Commissioner. The developments that followed the Act prove that the Ehtesab Cell had become more powerful than the Ehtesab Commissioner and all resources had been placed at the disposal of the Cell. It was headed by Saif-ur-Rahman Khan, a close confidant of Nawaz. This precluded the accountability of Nawaz and his cronies, making it a selective weapon used to victimize any member of the opposition that the Cell chose to proceed against. It goes to the credit of the Cell that it did uncover certain foreign exchange accounts of Benazir, Zardari, and other members of the Bhutto family in Britain and in Switzerland. It also uncovered properties purchased by Benazir and Zardari in their own names or in the names of their frontmen. Benazir had the audacity to deny this in one breath and admit it, somehow, in another. She moved the courts in foreign countries to lift injunctions against the operation of these accounts.

Confrontation with the Judiciary

Although Justice Sajjad was a benefactor of the PML(N) and had paved the way for its coming back into power, it did not take long before serious differences arose between him and the new prime minister. Trouble started when he took *suo moto* notice of the hand-cuffing of certain officers of Water & Sanitation Agency in Faisalabad on the verbal orders of the Prime Minister. Justice Sajjad later set them free on bail.[8] Differences deepened with the enforcement of the Anti-Terrorist Law which he strongly opposed. His point of view was that the money being spent on the establishment of new anti-terrorist courts could be better spent on the existing court structure and that sessions judges could be spared from hearing cases against terrorist acts on a daily basis. Nawaz and his government were committed to the idea of a parallel court structure of anti-terrorist courts to obtain quick results and also to accommodate some PML(N) members as special judges. Consequently, the anti-terrorist law was introduced and special courts were established. Appeals against their sentences did not lie before High Courts but before special appellate courts, consisting of High Court judges. Since the appellate forum was not the High Court, therefore, no further appeal would lie to the Supreme Court and, in this way, the High Courts and the Supreme Court were excluded from the due process under the anti-terrorism law.

The situation came to a head on 28 August 1997 when Justice Sajjad recommended five judges from three High Courts for elevation to the Supreme Court.[9] Under the Judges' Judgment, the recommendation of the chief justice is binding on the executive, which may differ but would have to record reasons in writing which, in turn, would be justiciable. There was strong resistance to these recommendations from the executive, particularly from the Prime Minister. The reason apparently was that two of the judges recommended were not acceptable to Nawaz because one of them had decided a number of cases against his industrial empire while Nawaz was out of power, and the other had served as federal law secretary during Benazir's government. Both of them were perceived by him as being hostile to his government. Once again, personal and family interests stood in the way of his decision making. The recommendations were not acted upon, though only thirty days were available to the government to do so. The government could not give any reasons in writing because they would clearly be perceived as being personal in nature.

In order to defeat the recommendations, the government notified a reduction in the number of judges of the Supreme Court from seventeen to twelve, a number fixed as far back as in 1986. This was done to preclude the making of appointments altogether. However, Justice Sajjad struck back and suspended the notification.[10] The government had to eat humble pie and withdraw the notification on 16 September 1997, but it continued to resist making the appointments. Various proposals came from government quarters including one that said that the two recommendees under dispute be sent on long leave and the other three be appointed. The proposal, although absurd on the face of it, had its rationale. Nawaz was convinced by now that Justice Sajjad was on the war path and should not have judges sympathethic to him because that would only strengthen him. After intense confrontation, Nawaz backed down but not before Justice Sajjad, heading a Bench of three judges, suspended the Fourteenth Amendment to the Constitution in this constitutional war of attrition. On 30 October 1997, a three-member Bench headed by Justice Sajjad passed an order invoking Article 190 of the Constitution asking the President to appoint the five judges since the government had failed to do so. The President warned the government that he might be compelled to notify the elevation of the judges. At this, Nawaz capitulated and ordered notification of appointment of these judges.

The appointment of the five judges according to Justice Sajjad's recommendations proved to be a high point for him in this confrontation and a low point for Nawaz. The latter was perceived to have led the country to unnecessary confrontation over a period of two months for reasons clearly personal to him. It was a victory for Justice Sajjad because he appeared to be fully justified.

Although a lot was said about the enforcement of this judgment but, to be realistic, Justice Sajjad did not always play by the rule. The first three appointments to the Supreme Court after this judgment were in violation of the seniority rule laid down in the judgment. The three judges drawn from Lahore, Peshawar, and Sindh High Courts were not the senior-most judges in their respective High Courts. He also violated the ruling that a permanent vacancy should be filled within thirty days of its occurrence. He was following his own schedule for such appointments and not the thirty-day rule. These five vacancies did not occur overnight but were allowed to remain vacant over a long period of time. Only three appointments to the Supreme Court were recommended in a period of one year, one being that of the Chief Justice of the Balochistan High Court, and two of the Chief Justices of the Lahore High Court. One such appointment was out of punishment and the other was a reward, so, the question was: why were all five appointments made together and so suddenly? Certainly, the power to recommend appointments to the Superior Courts had become a weapon in the armoury of the Chief Justice in the war of dominance with the executive which was being used rather blatantly to further his own agenda.

Another important development that had taken place during one-and-a-half years of confrontation with succeeding governments was that the Chief Justice had antagonized many people within the judiciary. His growing arrogance and autocratic style were alienating the judges of his own Court since he was becoming increasingly intolerant of any difference of opinion or dissent within the Court. He was also promoting partisanship within the ranks of the judiciary and patronizing the judges of the superior courts who were drawn from the subordinate judiciary and are generally known as service judges. This caused differences with a Chief Justice of the Lahore High Court who tried to persuade him that a majority of judges should be drawn from amongst the lawyers, as has always been the practice, and also tried to demonstrate that the performance of service judges in the past left much to be desired. He forced the Chief Justice of the Lahore High Court to recommend more service judges and an unprecedented appointment of five service judges out of a batch of seven was made. Not only that, he appointed the Chief Justice to the Supreme Court of Pakistan which was obviously done as punishment. There was another point of difference between the two. The Chief Justice of the Lahore High Court did not recommend two sessions judges for such an appointment because, according to his information, they did not enjoy a good reputation. However, his successor, under pressure from Justice Sajjad, recommended them and they were appointed in the following batch. He was subsequently rewarded by being elevated to the Supreme Court a few days before his retirement. When the next Chief Justice of the Lahore High Court made contradictory statements about not being consulted about the appointment of special judges to the newly established anti-terrorist courts, Justice Sajjad took serious exception to this and decided to oust him as Chief Justice by having him appointed to the Supreme Court.

Another cause for resentment amongst the judges of the Supreme Court was the departure from the tradition of consulting senior judges in important matters who were being kept out of the Benches constituted for hearing important constitutional cases. The same judges were being unnecessarily humiliated by being despatched to registries against their consent and by withdrawing various facilities from them. When Justice Sajjad went to perform *Umra* in Saudi Arabia, seven Supreme Court judges requisitioned a meeting of a full court to consider various matters and requested the Acting Chief Justice Ajmal Mian, on 10 October 1997 to call a meeting on 13 October 1997, during the absence of Justice Sajjad. When Justice Sajjad learnt of this, he decided to cut short his visit and rushed home before the meeting could take place and had it cancelled.[11] He did not even bother to go to Islamabad and stayed back in Karachi and gave orders by telephone to the Registrar that the meeting was cancelled. The requisitionist judges had to cut a sorry figure by being embarrassed for moving a requisition while the Chief Justice was away. While the move was not right on their part, Justice Sajjad should have taken it as a warning and ought to have taken steps to build bridges with them. After all, it was his responsibility to carry his colleagues along with him and not to go it alone.

After a few days, on 17 October, another requisition was moved by seven judges for a full court meeting which was rejected by Justice Sajjad. Not only that, he retaliated against the requisitionists and sent them packing to registries at provincial headquarters. The judges who found favour with him were kept at the Principal Seat in Islamabad. This further intensified the divide within the Supreme Court and brought in differences to the boil which was reflected in the letter written by five dissident judges to the President, airing their differences with the Chief Justice.

When the Fourteenth Amendment to the Constitution was suspended by a three-member Bench headed by the Chief Justice, there was a strong reaction from the Prime Minister and members of his Cabinet, members of Parliament from the PML(N) and its allied parties. In his press conference, the Prime Minister called the order of suspension 'illegal' and 'unconstitutional'. There were speeches in Parliament in which strong remarks were made against the Chief Justice and the members lamented that the order was violative of the supremacy and sovereignty of Parliament. These speeches led to contempt proceedings against the Prime Minister and members of Parliament before the Supreme Court. Nawaz made an appearance in these proceedings before the Supreme Court on two occasions, 17 and 18 November, before a Bench of five judges headed by the Chief Justice himself. Though he did not tender an unqualified apology, he expressed his regrets in a written statement over the remarks made. The matter could have been dropped at that stage, but Justice Sajjad once again proved that he did not understand the practical limitations to his power. Little did he realize that a prolongation of the contempt proceedings would only go in favour of Nawaz who was rapidly gaining popularity due to the common public perception that the Chief Justice was being bull-headed. What was being said against the Prime Minister before the appointment of the five judges was now being said about the Chief Justice.

It was at this stage that the President became openly partisan. In order to protect the Prime Minister from punishment in the contempt proceedings, Parliament passed the Contempt of Court (Amendment) Bill making any order of punishment for contempt of court by a Bench of the Supreme Court appealable before another Bench comprised of the remaining judges of the Supreme Court. It was also provided that such a sentence would not be effective for thirty days, during which an appeal could be filed and further that the sentence would automatically be suspended till the final decision of the appeal. When asked to give assent to the Bill by the government, Leghari avoided it on the ground that he would do so provided the Supreme Court did not prevent him, which was a clear signal to Justice Sajjad who took the cue. On an application made on this issue, a Supreme Court Bench headed by Justice Sajjad issued an interim order restraining the President from signing the Bill and went further to direct that if the Bill were signed into law, it should be considered suspended. In this episode as well, all the parties concerned behaved unreasonably. Nawaz and his colleagues were unreasonable in pressuring Leghari to sign the Bill forthwith. The Constitution gave thirty days to the President to give his assent and he could use his discretion to wait until the thirtieth day or to send it back to the Parliament for reconsideration. Leghari was also unreasonable in giving a tacit signal to the Chief Justice that he should be legally restrained from signing the Bill. This was a clear indication that the President and the Chief Justice were acting on an agenda of their own. The order of the Supreme Court restraining the President from giving assent to the Bill was also a very unusual step. There is no precedent of a president being restrained from giving assent to a Bill passed by a parliament, although the courts can review it judicially after it becomes a law to test its constitutionality.

The confrontation had spread and battle lines were drawn between the executive and the Parliament on the one hand, and the President and the Chief Justice on the other. At this point, the military leadership was sucked into the situation. It was the army chief who became an arbitrator between the Prime Minister, the President and the Chief Justice. He earned a respite for the Prime Minister by getting the contempt case and other cases against him adjourned for about a week, from 20 November to 27 November.

Fall of Justice Sajjad Ali Shah

The government used the respite of one week (20–27 November) to its full advantage. It was fully aware of the differences and the rising resentment amongst the judges of the Supreme Court against the Chief Justice. Leaders of the PML(N), known to be past masters in the art of wheeling and dealing, got down to what they did best. On 18 November, a two-member Supreme Court Bench in Quetta had entertained a petition against the appointment of the Chief Justice on the ground that he was not the senior-most judge when appointed. However, no interim order had been passed on the petition and the case was referred to the Chief Justice for constituting a full court to decide the matter. It was indeed a warning to him of things to come. They stopped short of restraining the Chief Justice from performing his functions, but this did not prevail for long. On 26 November, a day before the hearing on the contempt case against the Prime Minister was to resume, a petition was presented before the Registry of the Supreme Court in Quetta, challenging the appointment of Justice

Sajjad as Chief Justice. Initially, the petition was not entertained by the office in Quetta because under the Supreme Court Rules, a petition under the original jurisdiction can only be filed and entertained at the Principal Seat in Islamabad. Subsequently that day, the Bench of two judges in Quetta entertained it and passed an interim order restraining the Chief Justice from performing his functions.[12]

> Appreciating the contention that recognition had been given to constitutional convention by the judgment in the Judges' case to the effect that the senior-most judge of the Supreme Court had always been appointed chief justice with the exception of Justice Sajjad, operation of the notification dated 5 June 1994 appointing him as the Chief Justice of Pakistan was ordered to be held in abeyance until further orders and that the Chief Justice should cease to perform judicial and administrative functions and powers of the Chief Justice till further orders.[13]

This restraining order touched off the most bizarre events. The Chief Justice and the judges opposed to him simply ran amok. Justice Sajjad, sitting alone in Chamber in Islamabad, suspended the judicial order of the Quetta Bench through an administrative order. This led to another proceeding at the Quetta Bench the same evening in which a third judge also joined in and suspended the suspension order of the Chief Justice on the evening of 26 November 1997 at the Judges' Rest House in Quetta. In this three-member-Bench judgment,[14] it is stated that the petition of Asad Ali was not originally entertained at the Quetta Registry on the ground that petitions under Article 184(3) of the Constitution, as per practice generally followed, are to be filed at the main Registry, Islamabad.[15] However, despite such practice, the Senior Judge in Quetta, Justice Irshad Hassan Khan, directed the Assistant Registrar on 26 November 1997 to entertain the petition of Asad Ali, diarize it in the relevant register, and place it before the Court for appropriate orders. The judgment takes notice of the administrative order of the Chief Justice, faxed to the Quetta Registry at 6:00 p.m. on 26 November 1997, which had held that the judges at the Quetta Registry had acted without lawful authority and the Assistant Registrar Quetta Registry was directed not to fix any cases before them for disposal until further orders.

On 28 November 1997, the petition of Asad Ali was fixed before the judges in Quetta, namely Justice Irshad Hassan Khan, Justice Nasir Aslam Zahid, and Justice Khalil-ur-Rehman Khan. Sharifuddin Pirzada, who until then was working behind the scenes, now surfaced as *amicus curiae*. Relying on the judgment of 27 November 1997 of the sister Bench consisting of two judges in Peshawar, it was held that the rule requiring presentation of the petition for enforcement of fundamental rights at the main Registry, Islamabad, was regulatory in nature and could be dispensed with. Even the judgment of the five-judges Bench in Islamabad setting aside the orders dated 26 November 1997 of the Quetta Bench (of two judges and three judges) was ignored on the basis of a dialogue between an advocate and the dissenting judge as reproduced in an English daily.

Simultaneous to the events in Quetta, a similar petition was presented before the Peshawar Registry of the Supreme Court. A two-judge Bench in Peshawar entertained a petition on 27 November 1997 under Article 184(3) of the Constitution and dispensed with the rule requiring the presentation of such a petition at the main Registry, Islamabad, and passed an interim order restraining Justice Sajjad from passing any judicial or administrative order in his capacity as the Chief Justice of Pakistan. The Bench consisting of Justice Saiduzzaman Siddiqui and Justice Fazal Ilahi Khan also directed the Registry of the Supreme Court to take immediate steps and place the matter forthwith before the senior puisne judge, Justice Ajmal Mian, in Karachi and obtain appropriate instructions of the Bench for hearing such cases[16] (entertained in Quetta and Peshawar).

Subsequently, on 28 November 1997, Justice Saiduzzaman Siddiqui, after being informed that the senior-most judge, Justice Ajmal Mian, had declined to assume the office of Acting Chief Justice, assumed unto himself the administrative powers of the Chief Justice and ordered the constitution of a full fifteen-member Bench (excluding the Chief Justice and Justice Ajmal Mian) in Islamabad to hear the petition against the Chief Justice.[17]

On 27 November, the Quetta decision of the three judges, passed on the evening of 26 November 1997, was suspended, this time by a five-member Bench in Islamabad, headed by Justice Sajjad himself, by a majority of four to one. Some of the PML lawyers who were also members of Parliament created a scene in the courtroom, becoming altogether hysterical. They kept shouting that the Chief Justice had been suspended and, therefore, could not preside over the Bench. Amongst those seen shouting in the courtroom, were non-lawyers or lawyers not enrolled as advocates of the Supreme Court of Pakistan. One of them was the political secretary to the Prime Minister. Though he was temporarily removed from the position thereafter, he was soon reinstated.

The five-judges Bench took notice of the fact that when it was learnt on 26 November 1997 that the order restraining the Chief Justice from performing his duties was passed by the Quetta Bench, the remaining five judges of the Bench were present with the Chief Justice in his chamber. The Bench also noticed that the Court, during the hearing on 27 November 1997, was jampacked with members of Parliament and supporters of the PML(N) and had raised objections to the sitting of the Chief Justice on the Bench and pointed out that there was no Supreme Court and the Bench was not properly constituted. It was also observed that several advocates who addressed the Court criticizing the constitution of the Bench, had behaved in a manner which was not only unruly but also uncalled for. It was thus directed that the orders passed by the Quetta Bench would not be given effect to, as the matter would be heard at the Principal Seat.[18] The dissenting judge, Justice Mamoon Kazi, held that since the orders of the Supreme Court cannot be appealed against and can only be reviewed, therefore, it would have been appropriate to constitute a Bench consisting of all Judges (including those whose orders were being reviewed). He lamented that if the order passed by one Bench was interfered with by another Bench, it would create further division amongst the judges seriously eroding the credibility of decisions given by the apex Court. He also observed that the Chief Justice should have refrained from hearing the case himself since the order in question directly concerned him.

Storming the Supreme Court

On 28 November, the Supreme Court Bench headed by the Chief Justice took up the contempt case against the Prime Minister. Under a pre-planned move, PML workers stormed the Supreme Court building, thus preventing the Bench from continuing the hearings. It was indeed one of the most despicable assaults on the courts in judicial history, obviously sponsored by the government and led by its ministers and members of Parliament and provincial assemblies. PML workers from various places in the Punjab were taken to Islamabad in buses under the leadership of their respective MNAs and MPAs. They attacked the building and the police contingent present there stood aside like spectators.

The Supreme Court (a Bench of five judges headed by Justice Sajjad) described the incident in the following words:[19]

> While the proceedings were in progress, one of the contemners came forward and whispered something in the ear of Mr S. M. Zafar who told him that since he was not his advocate, he could not make a request on his behalf. Meanwhile, Raja Muhammad Akram got up and came to the rostrum and stated that he was representing Khawaja Muhammad Asif and requested for leave of his client's absence on the ground that he had to attend some very important work. He was allowed to go. A little later a big commotion was heard as if there was a riot outside the court room and slogans were being raised. It appeared that a big mob wanted to rush into the court room. In fact, a few persons did succeed in doing so and one of them informed the judges that they should rise and go away, as a fully charged mob behind him was forcing entry into the court-room to take the Chief Justice into custody. This was supported by the persistent commotion and highpitched slogans of people who were in the process of raiding the courtroom. In such circumstances, there was no other alternative for the Court but to adjourn the proceedings and the judges retired. Even outside there was a flurry of activities as people were running here and there and some policemen escorted the judges to the chamber of the Chief Justice.
>
> Later on, the Registrar came and informed us in a state of shock, that he had been manhandled and a big mob got unruly and made a raid on the courtroom where the contempt case was being heard against the respondents, including the parliamentarians.

After the storming of the building, the Chief Justice wrote to the President requesting army protection. In his letter, he alleged that the attack was led by the government's ministers whose faces had been recorded by the closed circuit television cameras inside the Supreme Court building. It was also alleged that after the attack, the assailants were asked by the PML leaders to have lunch at the Punjab House where reportedly they were addressed and, of course, applauded by the chief minister of the Punjab as if they had just won a war. The Chief Justice also asked the President to send a reference against the five Supreme Court judges at the Quetta and Peshawar Registries to the Supreme Judicial Council for misconduct.[20]

In response to the letter of the Chief Justice, the President wrote a letter to the Prime Minister asking him to provide army protection to the Chief Justice. The Prime Minister ignored the advice and the Chief Justice wrote directly to the Chief of Army

Staff. Two separate cause lists were issued for Supreme Court hearings on 1 December, one by the Chief Justice of five judges Bench and the other by Justice Siddiqui of ten judges Bench. The Chief Justice annulled the administrative order of Justice Siddiqui calling for a full Bench hearing of the Chief Justice's case on 1 December. Ten judges issued a statement terming the Chief Justice's annulment order illegal.

Subsequently, a Bench of three judges of the Supreme Court held an inquiry into the matter of storming of the Court on 28 November 1997. It examined a large number of witnesses under oath and, by its order of 3 July 1998, the Bench held that twenty-six people, including two MNAs and three MPAs of the PML(N), the Prime Minister's private secretary, ten office bearers and activists of the PML(N), and ten members of administration in the police, were prima facie guilty of gross contempt of the Supreme Court, of violation of the applicable law, and of being involved in, or aiding and abetting, or facilitating the storming of the Supreme Court. In pursuance of this finding, the Supreme Court directed that show cause notices be issued calling upon them to explain why action should not be taken against them for contempt of the Supreme Court.

A Divided Judiciary

In the face of such a situation, a delegation of Bar representatives belonging to the Pakistan Bar Council, Supreme Court Bar Association, Lahore High Court Bar Association, and the Punjab Bar Council, went to the Supreme Court on 1 December 1997 to make a final effort to save the Court from complete dissipation and humiliation. Unfortunately, they found the Supreme Court totally divided. The Chief Justice and four other judges present in his chamber were ready to sit as a Bench on his order. Ten judges led by Justice Siddiqui had assembled in his chamber. Justice Ajmal Mian wisely stayed out of this conflict and was alone in his chamber. The air was filled with tension. The Chief Justice having realized by now that the battle was lost, had mellowed down and was receptive to the Bar delegation. He immediately accepted the suggestion that in order to show solidarity they would not be working that day. However, he kept insisting that if others assembled as a Bench, then he would along with the other four judges also sit as a Bench. He was prepared to confer with all the judges to address their grievances and iron out the differences. The other group of judges was in an aggressive mood. Initially, their response to the bar delegation was negative but after some persuasion, they accepted the suggestion to sit with the Chief Justice and other colleagues to discuss their differences.

In these circumstances, it was a major achievement to bring together all seventeen judges of the Supreme Court in the same room.[21] It seemed that they had not met one another for quite some time. The Bar representatives sat and had tea with them. Abid Hassan Minto, President of the Supreme Court Bar Association, and the leader of the delegation, requested all the judges to sort out their differences and save the image of the judiciary from being tarnished. He also stated that, in the view of the bar, Justice

Sajjad was the chief justice and should be accepted as such by his colleagues for the good of the institution. However, the Chief Justice was requested to address the genuine grievances of his colleagues. After that, the Bar representatives left the room, hoping that something good would come out of the meeting. The meeting went on for one-and-a-half hours. It lowered the tension for the time being and it was decided that, in deference to the wishes of the Bar delegation, no Bench would function that day.

Initially, a formula was evolved under which three Benches were to be formed for the following day, a five-member Bench headed by the Chief Justice to hear cases against the Prime Minister, a seven-member Bench headed by Justice Siddiqui to hear cases against the Chief Justice, and another five member Bench for other cases. The underlying understanding was that the Bench of the Chief Justice would adjourn the cases against the Prime Minister and the cases against the Chief Justice would be disposed of. The formula did not work because some of the judges in the opposition demanded that the Chief Justice should adjourn all cases against the Prime Minister for three months so that, in the meantime, he would retire. The Chief Justice refused to accept the suggestion because he took it as dictation and a deadlock ensued. It became an open secret that the origin of the differences between the two groups of judges was not within, but outside the Court, and that they were working on their respective agendas of protecting or advancing conflicting interests. The institution of the Supreme Court had obviously fallen prey to such interests.

On 2 December 1997, the Supreme Court committed collective suicide and rival Benches met in the Supreme Court building. The Chief Justice, instead of taking steps to diffuse the situation, became even more erratic. Heading a three-member Bench, he suspended the Thirteenth Amendment without adequate hearing, thus restoring the President's powers to dissolve the National Assembly.[22] The rival ten-member Bench immediately held the order in abeyance and restrained the President from acting on such a ruling.[23] In a separate order, it was held that Justice Ajmal Mian should immediately assume the administrative and judicial powers and functions of the Chief Justice.[24] With various rumours circulating throughout the country that day, Leghari resigned in protest against what he termed the 'unconstitutional' demands of the government. Finally, the curtain was drawn on the high drama of the judicial and constitutional crises.

The Asad Ali Case

Justice Ajmal Mian took the oath of Acting Chief Justice of Pakistan after the order passed by the ten-member Bench of the Supreme Court on 2 December 1997. Soon after, the ten-member Bench headed by Justice Siddiqui commenced the hearing of Asad Ali's case. Surprisingly, Justice Sajjad decided to participate in the hearings of the case by appointing counsels to defend himself. He could have easily stayed out of these proceedings by denouncing them as *coram non judice*, the Bench not being competently constituted under the authority of the Chief Justice, but he lent legitimacy to these proceedings by his participation. The judgment was announced on 23 December 1997.

The first and foremost objection raised by the counsel of Justice Sajjad was bias on the part of several judges sitting on the Bench. Five judges on the Bench—Justice Siddiqui, Justice Fazal Ilahi Khan, Justice Irshad Hassan Khan, Justice Nasir Aslam Zahid, and Justice Khalil-ur-Rehman—were objected to as biased because, while sitting in the Quetta and Peshawar Registries, they had entertained petitions against Justice Sajjad for violating express provisions contained in the Supreme Court Rules on this matter. Justice Sheikh Riaz Ahmad was objected to as he was associated with the preparation of the summary for appointment of Justice Sajjad as the Chief Justice of Pakistan in his capacity as the federal law secretary. Justice Siddiqui was also objected to on two other counts: first, that he was an interested party to the controversy as he was the direct beneficiary of upholding of the rule seniority for appointment to the office of the chief justice because he would automatically be appointed chief justice on the retirement of Justice Ajmal Mian in 1999, and, secondly, because Justice Sajjad as Chief Justice had already made reference against him to the President of Pakistan for proceedings for misconduct before the Supreme Judicial Council.

The objections regarding bias or disqualification were repelled as under:[25]

1. The fact that a certain judge had admitted two petitions challenging the validity of the appointment of Justice Sajjad as the Chief Justice at Branch Registries neither displayed any bias on his part nor amounted to the expression of a final opinion on the controversy in the case.
2. Disqualification from hearing the case would arise only when a judge is shown to have a personal interest or a pecuniary interest, however small it may be, in the subject matter of the case before him. However, if the judge so disqualified has the exclusive jurisdiction in the matter and there is no other competent court available to hear the case or the quorum for hearing of the case could not be formed without the presence of the judge so disqualified, then in such circumstances, in spite of disqualifications, he can sit and hear the case under the doctrine of necessity to prevent failure of justice. In all other cases, where general bias or disqualification is alleged against a judge of a superior court, it is left to him to decide whether he would like to hear a particular case before him or not.
3. The mere fact that one of the judges sitting on the Bench was at one stage associated with the case of appointment of Justice Sajjad as the Chief Justice in his capacity as federal law secretary, could not debar him from hearing the case because there was no element of personal bias or prejudice.

An objection was raised to the maintainability of the petition because the petitioner, Asad Ali, had no *locus standi* to challenge the validity of the appointment of Justice Sajjad as Chief Justice. This objection was rejected on the rationale that the selection of a person to the high office of the Chief Justice of Pakistan is a pivotal appointment to maintain the independence of the judiciary and to provide free and unobstructed access to impartial and independent courts/tribunals to ordinary citizens. Therefore, it was reasoned, any deviation from the method prescribed under the Constitution for appointment to the office of Chief Justice would give rise to the infringement of the right of a citizen to have free, fair, and equal access to independent and impartial courts thus violating the rights guaranteed under Articles 9 and 25 of the Constitution.

To the contention that the appointment of Justice Sajjad as Chief Justice was a closed chapter, it was held that in view of the observations of the Supreme Court in the Al-Jehad case (PLD 1996 S.C. 324), the question relating to the validity of the appointment of the Chief Justice of Pakistan was a live controversy requiring an authoritative pronouncement by the Supreme Court. It was also observed that the Bench of the Supreme Court that decided the Al-Jehad case could not come to an effective decision on the controversy because it was presided over by the Chief Justice in question.

Another objection was raised to the effect that since the judges of the Supreme Court who had been superseded by Justice Sajjad did had not challenged his appointment but had served under him, they had acquiesced to his appointment. This objection was rejected on the reasoning that such a failure on the part of the superceded judges was for reasons of maintaining comity among the judges of the Supreme Court.

The objection that the ten-member Bench did not constitute a full court was disposed of with the observation that when, out of seventeen judges of the Supreme Court of Pakistan, one judge could not sit as he was a respondent in the case, another refused to sit as his personal interest was involved, and five other judges declined, the remaining ten judges constituted a Full Court. No judge could be compelled to participate in the Full Court proceedings against his wishes.

It was held that the senior most judge of the Supreme Coult of Pakistan, in the absence of any concrete or valid reason, has to be appointed the Chief Justice on the basis of convention. The appointment of Justice Sajjad as Chief Justice, superceding three judges of the Court who were senior to him, was made without any concrete or valid reason. Such an appointment was, therefore, unconstitutional, illegal, and contrary to the decision of the Supreme Court of Pakistan in the case of Al-Jehad Trust (PLD 1996 S.C. 324).

The Court ruled that Justice Sajjad would cease to hold the office of Chief Justice of Pakistan and ordered his reversion to the position of a judge of the Supreme Court in accordance with his seniority among the judges of the Supreme Court. The federal government was directed to denotify the appointment of Justice Sajjad as Chief Justice and notify the appointment of the senior most judge as the Chief Justice of Pakistan forthwith. All actions taken and orders passed by Justice Sajjad in his capacity as Chief Justice up to 25 November 1997 were to be deemed valid and passed and were not open to challenge on the ground of defect in his appointment. This was held on the basis of the *de facto* doctrine. However, all actions taken or orders passed by him as Chief Justice on and after 26 November 1997 were declared of no legal effect.

On 23 December 1997, the federal government denotified Justice Sajjad as Chief Justice and notified Justice Ajmal Mian as the Chief Justice of Pakistan who took oath on the same day.

Role of Leghari as President

Leghari resigned on 2 December 1997, and blamed Nawaz for the constitutional crisis.[26] His resignation brought to an end the high drama of conflict between the judiciary, the executive and the legislature. His resignation cut short the normal term of office of the president of five years by nearly one year.

Leghari was nominated by the PPP in 1993 as President with the tacit understanding that he would safeguard its interests. He lent his name, power, and prestige to the imposition of an emergency in the NWFP and the Punjab with the dubious intent of ousting the governments of Sabir Shah and Wattoo.

Leghari began his term with the reputation of being Mr Clean, but this was soon tarnished by the Mehran Bank scandal. There are rumours that his sons were involved in smuggling vehicles from Afghanistan and making huge gains in the process with the protection available to them due to the high office of their father. He was responsible for making inapproprirate appointments to the judiciary. Leghari condoned the corrupt ways of the PPP government but ran into conflict with Benazir and Zardari over more personal matters. Once he had dismissed Benazir's government, he went overboard to make a deal with Nawaz, helping him into power by putting the entire administration behind him in the general elections of February 1997. Later, when he realized the impact of the huge mandate he had helped Nawaz gain, he tried to undermine it by attempting to align the judiciary and the armed forces against Nawaz. Justice Sajjad went along with him to the very end but not everyone did. When the leaders of the armed forces refused to stand with Leghari in his conflict with Nawaz and he faced the prospect of being impeached, Leghari lost courage and resigned in disgrace.

After him, Wasim Sajjad, Chairman of the Senate, took over as Acting President. Initially, it was expected that since the Prime Minister hailed from the Punjab, the President would be nominated from another province. The federal cabinet discussed the names of various candidates in the meeting on 12 December but failed to reach a consensus.[27] According to the qualifications spelled out in the cabinet, the President must be from a smaller province. Candidates from the NWFP were in the lead, particularly Sartaj Aziz and Fida Muhammad Khan.[28] In a surprise move, it was announced by the federal cabinet on 15 December that Justice (Retd.) Muhammad Rafiq Tarar would be the PML(N) candidate for president. This appeared to be the personal choice of Nawaz and his family[29] and it was Nawaz who disclosed it to his Cabinet in a specially convened meeting on 15 December.

Tarar Elected President

Tarar's election as president was not free from difficulties. His nomination papers were rejected by the Acting Chief Election Commissioner, Justice Mukhtar Junejo, on 18 December for propagating an opinion and acting in a manner prejudicial to the integrity or independence of the judiciary in Pakistan or defaming or bringing into ridicule the institution of the judiciary.[30] Reliance was placed on press statements made by Tarar in which he made strong remarks against Justice Sajjad and went to the extent of calling him a 'judicial terrorist'. Tarar challenged the decision of the Acting Chief Election Commissioner before the Lahore High Court and, in an unprecedented order, a single judge suspended the order of rejection of his nomination papers and referred the matter to a larger Bench. A full Bench of three judges was constituted which, apart from a senior judge, Justice Malik Qayyum, had two of the most junior judges on it. This was unprecedented because generally a Bench of senior judges is constituted in a case of public importance. The Bench, on hearings held on 24 and 29 December, adjourned the case but extended the interim order of suspension of nomination papers of Tarar.[31]

Nawaz did not want to take a risk with Justice (Retd.) Mukhtar Junejo as Acting Chief Election Commissioner and replaced him with Justice (Retd) Abdul Qadeer Chaudhry, a retired judge of the Supreme Court, on 27 December 1997. The election was held on 31 December 1997 and Tarar won with a huge margin. He secured 374 votes out of a total of 457 votes polled. His nearest rival, Aftab Shaaban Mirani, a PPP nominee, secured only fifty-eight votes.[32]

The Constitution petition filed by Tarar was accepted by the full Bench of the Lahore High Court on 12 January 1998.

Justice (Retd) Rafiq Tarar was a sure winner to be elected as President. Coming from Gujranwala in central Punjab, Tarar had a short stint at law practice there before being appointed district and sessions judge.[33] At that time, there was a quota amongst advocates for direct appointment as district and sessions judges. He was one of the last such appointees.

Later, Tarar was a judge in labour courts in various districts of Punjab before being appointed additional judge of the Lahore High Court in October 1974, at only 45 years of age. He was confirmed judge in 1977. In December 1989, he became Chief Justice of the Lahore High Court after fifteen years on the Bench. In January 1991, he was elevated to the Supreme Court, where he served until his retirement in October 1994. After retirement, Tarar entered politics and joined the PML(N) when he was later elected Senator in March 1997.

Although Tarar had a long career in the judiciary, he did not make a mark as a judge. He dealt mostly with criminal cases and rarely sat on a Bench that decided important issues of constitutional law. However, he was respected for being an honest judge, an amiable character with a pleasant demeanour, and is known for his peculiar rustic sense of humour.

A deeply religious man, Tarar, is also known to be a man of strong views and prejudices and makes no secret of them. He is a man of conviction and once he believes in something, right or wrong, he pursues it with an intensity and passion. His dislike of the PPP and its leaders has never been a secret.

Although his judgments on constitutional matters are few, they are clearly indicative of being favourable to martial law and, later, to the IJI. His first significant judgment came immediately after the Provisional Constitution Order of 1981 (PCO). In a division Bench judgment titled *Tajammal Hussain Malik v Federal Government of*

Pakistan (PLD 1981 Lahore 462), he held that the PCO did not impinge upon or undermine the powers and functions of the judiciary. This finding was clearly against the language and effect of the PCO, which had humiliated the judges by forcing upon them an unconscionable oath, sacked independent judges, and withheld all powers from the judiciary to question any judgment, order, or sentence of any martial law authority or military court.

In 1990, as Chief Justice of the Lahore High Court, Tarar presided over a full Bench hearing the writ petition against the President's order of 6 August 1990, dissolving the National Assembly and dismissing the first Benazir government. He upheld the order of dissolution in *Kh. Ahmad Tariq Rahim v Federation of Pakistan* (PLD 1991 Lahore 78).

The most significant constitutional judgment of his career was *Mohammad Nawaz Sharif v President of Pakistan* (PLD 1993 SC 473). He was a member of the Bench of eleven judges of the Supreme Court which, by a majority of ten to one, invalidated the order of the President dated 18 April 1993, dissolving the National Assembly and dismissing the Nawaz government. He agreed with the majority but wrote a separate judgment in which he went a step further. He held that the dissolution order was passed by the President in a fit of anger and vengeance. He also held that the President had no power to dismiss a prime minister, directly or indirectly, howsoever illegal, unconstitutional, or against public interest his actions might seem to him. The President, according to him, by removing the Prime Minister under Article 58(2)(b), might be accused of subverting the Constitution within the meaning of Article 6.

Tarar had been a vocal opponent of Justice Sajjad ever since the latter's appointment as Chief Justice in June 1994, ahead of his three senior colleagues. On his retirement in October 1994, he refused to accept a farewell reference from his colleague judges because he believed that the Supreme Court was presided over by someone who had been wrongly appointed as chief justice. He gave a press statement on his retirement that he would only accept the reference if the office of the chief justice was given to someone rightly entitled to it. After his retirement, he continued to be a critic of Justice Sajjad. It is widely rumoured that he was instrumental in influencing some judges of the Supreme Court that led to the judicial mutiny resulting in the ouster of the Chief Justice. He is said to have flown to Quetta on 26 November, resulting in the Quetta Bench verdict against Justice Sajjad.

Tarar was neither a politician of standing nor had he ever been a distinguished judge. The office of President being a symbol of the State should have gone to someone well acquainted with statecraft. Tarar did not qualify on any of these counts. The only reason for his nomination that appears to have prevailed with the Prime Minister could be his unflinching personal loyalty to Nawaz and his family which seems to have outweighed the political logic of a regional political balance among the offices of the president and the prime minister, requiring that they be from different provinces.[34]

Important Constitutional Cases

A large number of petitions for contempt of court had been filed against Benazir, Nawaz, parliamentarians, journalists, and some advocates. The contempt proceedings against Nawaz, S. Muhammad Asif, Asfandyar Wali, and others were in progress when PML(N) workers stormed the building of the Supreme Court on 28 November to stop them. After the ouster of Justice Sajjad, it was decided by the Supreme Court to take up pending cases.

A Bench headed by Chief Justice Ajmal Mian was formed which heard all these cases at length for a number of days, concluding on 2 March 1998, and delivered a comprehensive judgment. This judgment took into account all the leading judgments on the subject of contempt of court in Pakistan, India, England, and in other countries. The judgment authored by Justice Ajmal Mian is a monumental piece of work recording the history and development of contempt of court law and is virtually a book of reference on the subject. The judgment leads to the inescapable conclusion that the laws of contempt of court have undergone radical changes conceptually. Courts around the world are becoming less sensitive to the utterances that were once taken to be contemptuous. This liberalization has much to do with the march of history, particularly in the twentieth century, conferring high sanctity and respect for the freedom of speech, expression, and the press. The Court defined that the objective of clubbing all contempt cases together was to lay down the parameters of contempt law in the light of the fundamental rights of freedom of speech, expression, and the press.[35]

The Court proceeded to determine the cases of the two prime ministers and members of Parliament. The Court expressed displeasure with Nawaz and Benazir saying that when out power, they make reckless expressions about the judiciary merely because certain judgments, otherwise lawfully passed, did not suit their temperament. However, contempt proceedings against Nawaz were dropped because (1) his replies when minutely examined suggested feelings of dejection, despondency, and despair or semblance of desperation; (2) all the questions and answers viewed in their entirety did not appear to be crossing the boundaries of the Constitution and law; (3) he categorically repeated his respect for the judiciary and the Chief Justice; and (4) in his written reply had also affirmed his respect of the Court while he also expressed regrets if someone's feelings had been injured. The contempt proceedings against Benazir were dropped on the grounds of (1) lapse of many years without action since the filing of the petition; (2) she was no longer in power, and (3) she was already facing too many cases.

The Court, after examining the highly charged speeches on the floor of the Parliament by Khawaja Asif, Asfandyar Wali, and others, came to the conclusion that these speeches did constitute contempt of court but exonerated them on the ground that 'they were under the mistaken belief that their speeches on the floor of the House are protected by Article 66 of the Constitution' which gives members of Parliament the right to freedom of expression. As far as cases against Khalid Anwar, Minister of Law, Senator Ajmal Khattak, and others were concerned, it was observed that they had unequivocally expressed great regard and respect for the Court while repudiating the allegations against them. Therefore, it was held that in the absence of any reasonable cause, tangible and admissible versions and categoric affirmation of these respondents regarding respect of the Court, there did not appear any plausible cause for the accusation and that the proceedings against them were *ex facie* misconceived.

There is some valid criticism against the judgment of the Supreme Court on contempt, particularly the following:[36]

One, the statement of Nawaz (relied upon by the Court to drop proceedings against him) was neither unconditional nor did it signify complete submission to the authority of the Court, nor had it been accompanied by an expression of resolution that he would not repeat it again.

Two, as far as the dropping of proceedings against Benazir was concerned, the reasoning that there was a delay in the prosecution of proceedings does not inspire confidence. There are so many criminal and civil cases pending in the Supreme Court for years without action being taken and yet this long pendency does not furnish grounds for dropping the proceedings. Benazir had not even expressed her regret at offending the Court.

Three, if the mistaken belief about the law, even by the law minister, is accepted as valid grounds for exoneration, then every rustic illiterate charged with serious offences can plead mistaken belief regarding the penal provisions of law being applied against him.

Despite the criticism against the verdict, it cannot be denied that the judgment is liberal and progressive in nature and has duly considered modern trends towards greater tolerance by the Courts in matters of contempt law. It is indeed adherence to the change aptly expressed by Lord Denning in the following words:

> It is a jurisdiction which undoubtedly belongs to us but which we will most sparingly exercise, more particularly as we ourselves have an interest in the matter. Let me say at once that we will never use this jurisdiction as a means to uphold our own dignity. That must rest on surer foundations. Nor will we use it to suppress those who speak against us. We do not fear criticism, nor do we resent it for there is something far more important at stake. It is not less than freedom of speech itself. It is the right of every man, in Parliament or out of it, in the press or over the broadcast, to make fair comment, even outspoken comment, on matters of public interest. Those who comment can deal faithfully with all that is done in a Court of Justice. They can say that we are mistaken, and our decisions erroneous, whether they are subject to appeal or not. All we would ask is that those who criticise us will remember that, from the nature of our office, we cannot reply to their criticisms. We cannot enter into public controversy. We must rely on our conduct itself to be its own vindication.[37]

Supreme Court Upholds the Thirteenth Amendment

It has been mentioned above that a three-member Bench of the Supreme Court headed by Justice Sajjad had suspended the operation of the Thirteenth Amendment to the Constitution on 20 December 1997 which was in turn immediately suspended by a ten-member Bench of the Supreme Court. This petition was finally heard by a seven-member Bench of the Supreme Court headed by Chief Justice Ajmal Mian. Neither the petitioner, Syed Iqbal Haider, nor his counsel, was present when the case was taken up on 16 March 1998. Consequently, the petition was dismissed for non-prosecution.[38]

Supreme Court Verdict on the Fourteenth Amendment

The Fourteenth Amendment was suspended in October 1997 by a Bench headed by Chief Justice Sajjad restraining party heads from taking adverse actions against members who spoke their minds and expressed an independent opinion in the Parliament.

A seven-member Bench of the Supreme Court, headed by Chief Justice Ajmal Mian, declared the Fourteenth Constitutional Amendment as *intra-vires* and valid under the Constitution by a six to one majority judgment.[39]

The Chief Justice, writing for four members of the Bench, held that the freedom of speech in a parliamentary form of government, subject to reasonable restrictions, was *sine qua non* and Article 63-A could not be construed in a manner which would defeat the basic feature of the parliamentary form of government. He observed that different clauses of the Amendment should be interpreted in conjunction with Articles 66 (privilege of members) and Article 19 (freedom of speech) and efforts should be made to preserve the right of freedom of speech on the floor of the House, subject to reasonable restrictions without which a parliamentary form of government cannot be run effectively.

The Court held that there had been a consistent view from the very beginning in Pakistan that a provision of the Constitution cannot be struck down by holding that it was violative of any prominent feature, characteristic, or structure, and that it has no application to strike down a constitutional amendment.

Attending to the argument that the Fourteenth Amendment has abridged fundamental rights and violates Article 8 which prohibits the federal government, *Majlis-e-Shoora* (Parliament), a provisional government, and a provincial assembly, from making any law which takes away or abridges such fundamental rights and declares that law-making to the extent of such contravention shall be void, the Court held that such limitation is on the legislation. However, quoting Article 8(2) of the Constitution of Pakistan, the Chief Justice observed that by employing the words 'any law in the provision', the intention of the Constitution seems to be that Article 8 of the Constitution would apply to all laws made by the parliament be it general or any law to amend the Constitution. Likewise, no enactment can be made in respect of the provisions of the Constitution relating to the judiciary by which the independence of the judiciary or its separation from the executive was undermined or compromised. These are built-in limitations in the Constitution, completely independent from political morality and force of the public, the Chief Justice said.

The Chief Justice, speaking for a majority of four members of the Bench, assumed that he was unable to agree that the explanation of Article 63-A would also include the conduct of the legislators outside the House. The principle of interpretation that a penal provision should be construed strictly and its scope should not be extended unless it was so required by the clear language used therein or by necessary intent, therefore a legislator cannot be declared disqualified under Article 63-A for misconduct committed outside the precinct of the parliament. He said that Article 63-A(ii) of the Constitution also does not debar a High Court or the Supreme Court from examining any order passed or action taken against a member.

In Pakistan, instead of adopting the basic structure theory or declaring provisions of the Constitution as *ultra-vires* to any of the fundamental rights, the apex court has pressed into service the rule of interpretation that if there is a conflict between two provisions of the Constitution which are not reconcilable, the provision which contains a lesser right must yield in favour of a provision which provides higher rights. This rule was also applied in the Al-Jehad Trust case,[40] the Chief Justice recalled. Thus the Court would adopt an interpretation which was more in consonance or nearest to the provisions of the Constitution guaranteeing fundamental rights, independence of judiciary, and democratic principles blended with Islamic provisions. The Chief Justice also referred to Hakam Khan's case,[41] where the Court held that no provision of the Constitution could be declared *ultra-vires* on the ground that the same was in conflict with Article 2-A of the Constitution.

Concerning arguments that Article 63-A has the potential of abuse, it was held that at this juncture, it cannot be assumed that Article 63-A could be exploited or misused by the leader of a political party. There seems to be no conflict between paragraphs (a) to explanation to clause (i) of Article 63-A with Articles 19 and 66 of the Constitution as these do not expressly provide that a member cannot express his views in exercise of his right under Article 66 on any matter which is brought before the House.

Justice Saiduzzaman Siddiqui and Justice Irshad Hassan Khan, though concurring otherwise, differed with the Chief Justice about findings regarding clauses (A), (B), and (C) of explanations to Article 63 and A(1) and declared them independent of each other. They held that clause (a) of Article 61-A covers the acts of an elected member of a political party both inside and outside the House only, while clauses (b) and (c) relate to his actions outside the House. He noted that the act of defiance by an elected member of a political party of the Constitution code of conduct and declared policies of the party outside the Assembly is as much damaging to the image and working of that party as his conduct inside the Assembly. A division was looked upon with suspicion by the people and was likely to lose the confidence of its electorate. A member of the political party who, after his election to the Assembly on the ticket of that party, publicly denounces the Constitution, code of conduct, or declared policy of the party cannot claim the right to represent that party in the Assembly on any moral, ethical, or legal grounds. They, however, held that the right of honest dissent cannot be held to include defiance and denunciation of the discipline, code of conduct, and declared policies of the party. If an elected member of a political party feels so strongly that he cannot stand by the policies of the party on account of his convictions on these issues, he may shed his representative character as is required of him for having been elected on the ticket of that party.

Justice Mamoon Kazi dissented from the majority judgment and declared the amendment as violative of the fundamental rights and, therefore, void and unenforceable.

After this pronouncement, the head of a political party has been made stronger and a member can be disqualified if he commits a breach of the party discipline, violates the code of conduct and the party's declared policies, or votes contrary to any direction issued by the parliamentary party to which he belongs or absents from voting in the House against the party policy or in relation to any Bill. However, the breach of party discipline would be presumed only when a member commits such violation inside the parliament. The judgment has reserved the right of freedom of speech for a member in the House subject to the reasonable restrictions envisaged under Article 66 (privilege of members) read with Article 19.

Supreme Court Strikes Down Anti-Terrorist Law

It has been discussed above that the introduction of the anti-terrorist law in June 1997 became one of the major causes leading to the confrontation between the judiciary and the executive. The law, Anti-Terrorism Act, 1997 (ATA), was challenged before the Lahore High Court as unconstitutional. A full Bench of the Lahore High Court upheld the law as valid by a majority of four to one. This verdict was challenged before the Supreme Court which, in its judgment released on 15 May 1998, struck down twelve provisions of the Act as invalid and brought special courts at par with ordinary courts working within the existing judicial system. Among other things, the five-member Bench in a unanimous short order held that the power to law enforcement agencies to open fire on suspicion of terrorism, and accepting of a confession before a DSP as a valid piece of evidence, were untenable and needed to be suitably amended.

The Court also directed the government to make suitable amendment in the ATA to vest the appellate power in a High Court instead of an appellate tribunal. According to legal experts, after this decision of the apex court, those convicted under the ATA will also be able to approach the Supreme Court after a High Court.

The ATA provisions which were held to be invalid in their present form were sections 5(2)(i), 10, 14, 19(10(b), 24, 25, 26, 27, 28, 35, and 37. The short order of the Supreme Court is reproduced as under:[42]

For the reasons to be recorded later on, we dispose of the above cases as under:

i. Section 5(2)(i) is held to be invalid to the extent it authorizes the officer of police, armed forces, and civil armed forces charged with the duty of preventing terrorism, to open fire or order for opening of fire against person who in his opinion in all probability is likely to commit a terrorist act or any scheduled offence, without being fired upon;

ii. Section 10 of the Anti-Terrorism Act, 1997, hereinafter referred to as the Act, in its present form is not valid. The same requires to be suitably amended as to provide that before entering upon a premises which is suspected to have material or a recording in contravention of Section 8 of the Act, the concerned officer of police, armed forces, or civil armed forces shall record in writing his reasons for such belief and serve on the person or premises concerned a copy of such reasons before conducting such search;

iii. Section 19(10)(b) of the Act, which provides for trial of an accused in absentia on account of his misbehaviour in the court, is violative of Article 10 of the Constitution and, therefore, is declared as invalid.

iv. Sections 24, 25, 27, 28, 30, and 37 of the Act are also not valid in their present form as they militate against the concept of independence of judiciary and Articles 175 and 203 of the Constitution. They need to be amended as to vest the appellate power in a High Court instead of appellate tribunal and to use the words 'High Court' in place of 'Appellate Tribunal'.

v. Section 26 of the Act is not valid in its present form as it makes admissible the confession recorded by a police officer not below the rank of a Deputy Superintendent of Police as it is violative of Articles 13(b) and 21 of the Constitution and that the same requires to be suitably amended by substituting the words 'by a police officer not below the rank of a Deputy Superintendent of Police' by the words 'Judicial Magistrate'.

vi. That the offences mentioned in the Schedule should have nexus with the objects mentioned in Sections 6, 7, and 8 of the Act.

vii. Section 35 of the Act in its present form is not valid as it militates against the concept of the independence of judiciary and is also violative of Articles 175 and 203 of the Constitution and, therefore, it needs to be suitably amended inasmuch as the power to frame rules is to be vested in the High Court to be notified by the Government.

viii. Section 14 of the Act requires to be amended as to provide security of the tenure of the judges of the Special Courts in consonance with the concept of independence of judiciary.

Lahore High Court Upholds Ehtesab Act

A five-member full Bench of the Lahore High Court, headed by the Chief Justice, upheld all but one provision of the Ehtesab Act of 1997. The provision struck down sought to validate references involving offences committed before the cut off date of 6 November 1990, laid down by the Act itself.[43]

Two references against former ministers, chief ministers, and several bureaucrats were sent back to the Lahore High Court Benches set up under the Ehtesab Act for which hearings had been suspended in view of the full Bench proceedings. The Court held that 'No exception can be taken to the process of accountability and the legislative measure adopted to give effect to it'. The cut-off date of 6 November 1990, which marks the induction of the first Nawaz Sharif government at the centre, was also upheld. The Bench had observed in the course of proceedings that it had the merit of embracing one tenure each of Mian Nawaz Sharif and Ms Benazir Bhutto as prime ministers.

The full Bench upheld the establishment of the Ehtesab Bureau in the Prime Minister's Secretariat and the appointment of Senator Saif-ur-Rehman Khan as its chairman for the reason that it would work under the overall supervision of the Chief Ehtesab Commissioner; that the Chief Ehtesab Commissioner has the power to investigate a case by an agency independent of the Bureau under sections 15 and 22 of the Ehtesab Act; that he alone can order arrest of an accused; and that he is the ultimate authority to decide whether or not to file a reference.

The cut-off date was indeed arbitrary and discriminatory as it excluded the period of the first Benazir government and five years of Nawaz as Chief Minister of the Punjab, from the process of accountability. The first Ehtesab Ordinance promulgated by the caretaker government in November 1996 provided for across-the-board accountability from 31 December 1985, the day when constitutional rule was restored after a long spell of martial law. It was not acted upon though it was revived on 1 February 1997 through a succeeding ordinance. The Ehtesab Act was enacted on 31 May 1997 by the new parliament. It brought forward the cut-off date to 6 November 1990. However, while repealing the Ehtesab Ordinances of 1996 and 1997, it saved all the proceedings taken up or pending under the Ordinances even if they involved pre-1990 offences.

Nuclear Tests: Declaration of Emergency

On coming into power, Nawaz Sharif opened a dialogue with the Indian government headed by moderate politician, Inder Kumar Gujral. Talks were held at the levels of prime ministers and foreign secretaries, and although not much could be achieved because of deadlock over Kashmir, the tension level between the two countries was brought down considerably. Unfortunately this did not last very long. The general elections held in India in February/March 1998 brought the Bharatiya Janata Party (BJP) as the largest party in Parliament. The BJP, a Hindu nationalist party, along with its allies, held 250 seats out of a total of 545 in the Lok Sabha. It was able to form the government by making coalitions with regional parties. The government was shaky and unstable, but its programme was radical, which included the development of nuclear weapons, undoing of the special status of Jammu and Kashmir under article 370 of the Indian Constitution, and the construction of Ram Mandir at the site of Babri Masjid which was demolished by BJP supporters in 1992.

The BJP embarked upon its ambitious programme by detonating three nuclear devices in the Pokhran desert in Rajasthan on 11 May 1998 and another two nuclear devices on 13 May 1998 at the same site. Following these tests, the Indian government adopted a belligerent attitude towards Pakistan with its leaders making bellicose statements indicating their intention to invade Azad Jammu and Kashmir.

Although there was strong reaction from the USA, Canada, and Japan, other western powers had a lukewarm response to the nuclear tests. Russia openly supported India. In the G-8[44] meeting held immediately after the explosions, no consensus could be arrived at amongst these powers regarding sanctions against India. France and Germany openly opposed the sanctions. Only USA and Japan took some half-hearted measures and applied minor sanctions.

In this situation, all political parties in Pakistan came to a consensus that in order to provide an effective defence and to deter Indian adventurism, it was imperative that Pakistan respond with its own nuclear tests.

On 28 May 1988, Pakistan held five successful tests of nuclear devices in the Chagi region of Balochistan province. The entire nation rejoiced and supported the government in this step expressing their approval of the policy of nuclear deterrence. Another test was conducted on 30 May 1998.

On 28 May 1998, while the people were still rejoicing, the government took a hasty decision. For reasons best known to the government, an emergency was proclaimed throughout the country under Article 232 of the Constitution. This proclamation was followed the same day, 28 May 1998, by an Order by the President under Article 233(2) of the Constitution declaring:

> The right to move any court including a High Court or the Supreme Court, for the enforcement of all the Fundamental Rights conferred by Chapter I of Part II of the Constitution, and all proceedings pending in any court for the enforcement, or involving the determination of any question as to the enforcement of any of the said rights would remain suspended for the period during which the said Proclamation would be in force.

Another very unfortunate step taken by the government rather hurriedly was the freezing of all foreign currency accounts in local banks regardless of whether they belonged to residents or non-residents. This was clearly in violation of the guarantee given to foreign currency account holders under the Protection of Economic Reforms Act, 1992. This step has completely destroyed the credibility of the government and the economy of the country, which was already in considerable difficulty. The Pakistani rupee went into free fall against the US dollar and other leading currencies in the world. The value of the Pakistani rupee against the US dollar fell from 44 rupees to more than 55 rupees in a matter of one month. Remittances from overseas Pakistanis were drastically reduced. Overseas Pakistanis have reacted adversely to the appeal of the Prime Minister for foreign currency. Despite intense propaganda for people to make contributions to the Prime Minister's austerity fund, there has been little response. Even where protection was offered to non-resident Pakistanis the response has been cold. Repeated circulars from the State Bank of Pakistan offering new incentives and concessions for new foreign currency accounts or deposits in the foreign currency accounts, has not helped matters. The government has lost credibility in the eyes of the people of Pakistan.

The performance of the second Nawaz government has been very disappointing. Despite what has reportedly been called a huge mandate, the failures of the Nawaz government are pronounced and obvious.

One, the government was a failure in the political sense. It failed miserably in holding on to political alliances. It broke its long-time political partnership with the Awami National Party (ANP) which has now turned hostile. The issue that has estranged them was the renaming of the Frontier Province. ANP proposed 'Pakhtoonkhwa' as the name for the NWFP. It claimed that Nawaz had promised this name and was now backing out under pressure from the hawks in his party. This allegation is not without substance. Nawaz's government was also in trouble with its other political allies, the MQM, and the BNM led by Akhtar Mengal, Chief Minister of Balochistan.

Two, the Nawaz government failed to check terrorism and the deteriorating law and order situation. The situation in Karachi remained grave with warring factions of the MQM on a rampage. Hundreds of people have been killed while the federal and provincial governments have been helpless spectators. Nawaz reversed the policy of Benazir for Karachi which had achieved relative peace there, although with questionable means. With no policy of his own on Karachi, lawlessness reigns supreme as a result. The law and order situation in Punjab has deteriorated extremely. Sectarian killings, murders, dacoities, and other crimes are on the rise. The introduction of Anti-Terrorist Courts has done little to check rising crime.

Three, the Nawaz government caused great harm to the federation by alienating smaller provinces from the Punjab. The acts and policies of his government only strengthened the perception that Punjab dominates other provinces which were not given their due. Since top constitutional positions like those of the president, the prime minister and the chairman of the senate, have all gone to the Punjab, this view has only gained further strength and credence. By raising the issue of the construction of Kalabagh Dam without consensus amongst all the provinces, tension between the Punjab and other provinces has accentuated. Whether Nawaz has been parochial in his outlook or not, his approach in public life is reflective of a lack of political sensitivity.

Four, Nawaz has done incalculable harm to the judiciary. In his confrontation with Justice Sajjad, he went beyond all limits creating a schism within the Supreme Court and, in this way, divided and destroyed the Court. He did not stop short of engineering an assault by his party workers on the Supreme Court to pre-empt a decision on the contempt of court case against him. Nawaz is condemned to go down in history with this shameful act to his name.

Five, Nawaz's economic policies have been a complete failure. Despite the pretension of being an economic wizard and claiming the support of the business community, he failed to revive and regenerate economic activity after the disastrous years of Benazir's government. The economy is still in dire straits and, after the nuclear tests, the country has come to the brink of economic disaster. Nawaz reneged on his own policy of opening the economy by freezing foreign currency accounts in Pakistan. The country is likely to commit default on its foreign obligations. The spectre of economic sanctions in the wake of nuclear tests has further depressed future economic prospects.

Six, Nawaz concentrated on keeping all power his own hands. He has further personalized the system of governance by holding open courts instead of strengthening state institutions. Nawaz Sharif ruled the country like a private fiefdom. He could trust no one but his own brother, Shahbaz, for chief ministership of the Punjab. His father, Mian Sharif, interfered with his decision-making in a big way. The running of the State became a family concern for Nawaz.

Seven, the exercise of accountability undertaking by Nawaz's government failed miserably. The only creditable achievement being the uncovering of some foreign bank accounts of Benazir, Zardari, and other members of the family. Otherwise, the process of accountability has been conducted selectively by his close confidants in order to ensure that his family members and important leaders of the PML(N) are saved.

NOTES

1. Act I of 1997, PLD 1997 Central Statutes 323.
2. Nawaz visited Leghari in his home-town, Choti, in Dera Ghazi Khan, a few hours before the introduction of the Amendment Bill to inform him that the PML(N) Parliamentary Committee had decided to do away with his discretionary powers. Leghari, who was initially not willing to grant him an audience, was shocked to learn the news of the castigation of presidential powers. The Parliamentary Committee had met under great secrecy and the news had not leaked to him.
3. Act XXIV of 1997, PLD 1997 Central Statutes 324.
4. Two Senators from the PPP told the author that they received the draft of the Fourteenth Amendment when they went to the Parliament to attend the session. They did not know that the session was called to consider such an amendment.
5. The Presiding Officer of the House means Speaker of the National Assembly in case of an MNA, the Chairman of the Senate in case of a Senator, and Speaker of the concerned Provincial Assembly in case of an MPA.
6. Ordinance XX of 1997, PLD 1997 Central Statutes 140 (Unreported Statutes volume).
7. Act IX of 1997, PLD 1997 Central Statutes 369.
8. It is learnt on good authority that when the Attorney-General tried to argue that hand-cuffing was a result of the FIRs registered against these officers, an audio-tape was played on the order of Justice Sajjad in his chamber where the proceedings were being held. It was clearly audible that a police officer whispered in the ear of Nawaz, when the latter had ordered hand-cuffing, that the FIR had not been registered. Nawaz replied using crude vernacular that he did not care.
9. *Herald*, December 1997, p. 32.
10. A Bench of the Supreme Court headed by Justice Sajjad admitted a petition filed by Supreme Court Bar Association on 5 September 1997 challenging the notification for reduction in the number of judges of the Supreme Court. The notification was also suspended in this order.
11. Justice Sajjad had to catch a Saudi Air flight after being denied a confirmed seat on PIA. See *Herald* of December 1997, p. 32.
12. It is widely rumoured that the Quetta verdict was obtained after two retired judges of the Supreme Court and a chief minister were flown in to Quetta on a special plane and that Sharifuddin Pirzada, privy to the whole plan, was also present there.
13. Asad Ali v Federation of Pakistan, 1998 SCMR 122.
14. Asad Ali v Federation of Pakistan, 1998 SCMR 15.
15. It is not a matter of practice alone. It is a requirement of Rule 1 of Order XXV of the Supreme Court Rules, 1980 that a petition for enforcement of fundamental rights under Article 184(3) should be filed at the main Registry.
16. Akhunzada Behrawar Saeed v Sajjad Ali Shah, 1998 SCMR 115.
17. Ibid., pp. 118-19. Prior to this administrative order, the Peshawar Bench passed an order on 28 November 1997, taking notice of the refusal of Justice Ajmal Mian to be Acting Chief Justice,

calling upon the next senior judge to constitute the Full Court for hearing in terms of the earlier order. Akhunzada Behrawar Saeed v Mr Justice Sajjad Ali Shah, 1998 SCMR 173.

18. In re: Constitutional Petition No. 248-Q of 1997, 1998 SCMR 127.
19. Muhammad Ikram Chaudhry v Mian Muhammad Nawaz Sharif, 1998 SCMR 176.
20. The text of the letter dated 28 November 1998 of Justice Sajjad to Leghari has been printed in *Dawn*, 16 May 1998 at page 9.
21. The author, being a member of the Pakistan Bar Council, was a member of the bar delegation.
22. Syed Iqbal Haider v Federation of Pakistan, 1998 SCMR 181. In this order, the happenings like rowdyism in the Court on 27-11-1997 and storming of the Court on 28-11-1997 are recorded.
23. Syed Iqbal Haider v Federation of Pakistan, 1998 SCMR 179.
24. Asad Ali v Federation of Pakistan, 1998 SCMR 119.
25. Asad Ali v Federation of Pakistan, PLD 1998 S.C. 161.
26. *Dawn*, 3 December 1997.
27. *Dawn*, 13 December 1997.
28. *Dawn*, 14 December 1997.
29. It is believed that the father of Nawaz, Mian Muhammad Sharif, prevailed in this choice.
30. Article 63(g) of the Constitution.
31. *Dawn*, 25 December 1997 and *Dawn*, 30 December 1997.
32. *Dawn*, 1 January 1998.
33. Tarar owed his appointment as Sessions Judge in 1966 to his old friend Anwar Bhinder from his native Gujranwala. At that time Bhinder was Speaker of the Provincial Assembly of West Pakistan. In that capacity, he was able to help his otherwise briefless lawyer friend to be appointed as Sessions Judge.
34. Ever since the promulgation of the Constitution of 1973, a convention had developed that presidents and prime ministers came from different provinces. From 1973 to 1977, Prime Minister Bhutto was from Sindh and President Fazal Elahi from Punjab. From 1985 to 1988, Prime Minister Junejo came from Sindh and President Zia from Punjab. From 1988 to 1990, Prime Minister Benazir hailed from Sindh and President Ishaq from NWFP. From 1990 to 1993, Prime Minister Nawaz hailed from Punjab and President Ishaq from NWFP. From 1993 to 1996, Prime Minister Benazir came from Sindh and President Leghari from the Punjab.
35. Syed Masroor Ahsan v Ardeshir Cowasjee, PLD 1998 SC 823.
36. Haque, Ikramul, 'Implications of contempt verdict', Article appearing in *Dawn*, 18 April 1998.
37. This quotation of Lord Denning has been taken from the book of A.G. Chaudhry titled 'Lectures on Constitutional Law' published by Irfan Law Book House, Lahore, 1996, pp. 200-201.
38. *Dawn*, 17 March 1998.
39. Wukala Mahaz Barai Tahafaz Dastoor v Federation of Pakistan, PLD 1998 S.C. 1263.
40. PLD 1996 S.C. 324.
41. PLD 1992 S.C. 590.
42. Mehram Ali v Federation of Pakistan, PLJ 1998 S.C. 1415.
43. *Dawn*, 27 March 1998.
44. It stands for the Group of Eight most industrialized nations, namely USA, Canada, UK, Germany, France, Italy, Japan, and Russia.

PART VIII

CONSTITUTIONAL AND POLITICAL ISSUES IN PAKISTAN

36

CONSTITUTIONAL AND POLITICAL ISSUES

Unfortunately, the lesson offered by fifty years of a chequered constitutional and political history is that governments in Pakistan seem determined not to learn from history. Successive governments have adopted the same course, repeated identical mistakes, and pushed the country deeper and deeper into uncertainty and insecurity.

It should be recognized that Pakistan is a pluralist society with different ethnic, linguistic, cultural, religious, sectarian, and parochial segments of the population living together. All such groups have their own distinct demands and aspirations to which the constitutional and legal set-up must respond with clarity, sincerity, and transparency. Political demands and issues cannot be pulled under the rug by assuming that diversity is of no consequence in view of the fact that 98 per cent of the population is Muslim.

This commonality has advantages in the political sense in forging integration, provided the issues of diversity are adequately addressed. In order to accomplish this objective, the constitutional provisions regarding due process of law (Article 4), freedom of religion (Article 20), equality before law, and equal protection of law (Article 25), safeguard against discrimination in services (Article 27), preservation of language, script, and culture (Article 28), and other similar provisions have to be made a living reality and have to be enforced in letter and in spirit. Political problems and issues need to be resolved politically. An attempt to resolve them by force has only resulted in the most unfortunate consequence of the breakup of Pakistan and the secession of East Pakistan.

For instance, the violent suppression of the MRD movement in Sindh in 1983 left deep political scars in the province which are noticeable even today. The law and order situation in the interior has not returned to the normalcy prevailing there prior to 1983. Military action in Balochistan (1973–77), only alienated a large segment of the Baloch and their political leaders. Attempts made in 1990 to resolve the political problems of Karachi and other urban centres in Sindh through administrative and military means have not borne fruit either. Instead, they have led to anarchy and colossal economic loss to the country. The aspirations of the people of Karachi can only be satisfied by giving them their due share in the federal, provincial, and local governments and their due quota in the services. The repeated imposition of martial law has only added to constitutional and political problems and resolved nothing. Martial law is responsible for the weakening and undermining of constitutional and political institutions in the country.

Political parties have failed to develop along institutional lines. Parliamentary traditions have not taken root and members of the legislature have failed to perform their paramount duty of law-making, reducing themselves to pawns on the chessboard of power politics. The judicial organ of the State has been emaciated and subordinated to the executive as a result of repeated interference with its smooth working by making judicial appointments on considerations other than merit. Members of the bureaucracy have been reduced to self-seekers, yes-men, and sycophants. Any independent voice in the civil bureaucracy is quickly silenced. People have little respect for and confidence in the Constitution and the institutions functioning thereunder. People have in general been alienated by these regimes because of being denied participation in the political process. Economic activity has been hampered because of corruption, want of accountability, and reckless and disproportionately high expenditures on defence and administration.

Martial law regimes have thus been a major cause of political instability and constitutional floundering in Pakistan. The electoral process could not gain credibility because, in order to keep itself in power, every regime has used the administrative machinery to manipulate elections in its favour. After every general election (or even a by-election), the losing parties allege rigging at the polls. The military and its intelligence agencies have generally played a negative role during general elections by attempting to tamper with the results. Except for the general elections of 1970, which were followed by events leading to the breakup of Pakistan, the outcome of all other elections have been disputed by the party or parties that lost, or were declared to have lost, at the polls.

Minorities in Pakistan have always felt alienated and insecure because they have been made to feel that they are not equal participants in the political process and in public affairs. All members of the Assemblies belonging to the minorities voted against the Objectives Resolution which was apparently bulldozed against their will without making any attempt to allay their fears or reach any political accommodation with them on matters that they had reservations about. The Second Amendment to the Constitution of 1973 has only created greater fears among members of the minorities. Ordinance XX of 1984 restricting the religious practices of the Ahmadis, further added to the fears of the minorities. Separate electorates have been imposed upon them without their consent and clearly against their will. Their political voice has been stifled and they have been deprived of any effective role in national affairs. Christians have been deprived of their educational institutions in the name of nationalization and the promise of returning these institutions to the original owners has not been honoured in their case.

The judiciary, being the third organ of the State under the Constitution, has been relegated to a position inferior to the executive. Constitutional provisions regarding the appointment of judges have been blatantly and consistently abused. Political or personal considerations have taken precedence over merit. As a result, the judiciary has been infected by self-seekers and incompetent, pliable men. People are losing faith in the judiciary and its ability to dispense justice. This alone is most alarming.

Widespread corruption in subordinate courts and in the superior courts has further undermined the confidence of the people in the judicial process, which they perceive to be an instrument in the hands of the rich, the privileged, and the powerful. Failure to dispense justice has been a fundamental cause of disaffection not only towards governments but also in the political system. The appointment of acting chief justices and ad hoc judges of the superior courts has eroded the credibility of the judiciary in the public mind. The recent assertion of the Supreme Court in the matter of appointment of judges to superior courts and its confrontation with the executive over this has helped the judiciary to regain some respect and credibility in the eyes of the common citizen but subsequent events of 1997 destroyed it egain. It is difficult to predict if the judiciary will retain its primacy in the matter of appointment of judges.

Provincial autonomy has been a constant subject of debate and discussion for constituent assemblies while framing the Constitution. A number of provisions were made, particularly in 1956 and in 1973, with the avowed object of guaranteeing autonomy to the provinces, but they have never been put into effect and have remained dead letters. The federal government has endeavoured to maintain its dominance over the provinces. The political party in power at the centre has rarely tolerated or even countenanced a provincial government headed by a party in the opposition. Provincial governments have been forced to remain dependent on the central government and have not been allowed to function autonomously. In 1971, this was a major cause for the alienation and ultimate secession of East Pakistan from the federation. In 1973, the provisional governments in NWFP and Balochistan were unfairly dismissed and the fiat of the central government was imposed on them. This led to an armed revolt in Balochistan which had to be controlled by military action.

Democracy, the system ostensibly given by the various constitutions in Pakistan, has never been allowed to function effectively. Governments in power have been destabilized through intrigue and conspiracies. The opposition has never been allowed to play its democratic role. Members of the opposition have generally been harassed through the coercive machinery of the State. False criminal cases are registered against the opposition members and they have been made to languish in jail with the sole object of breaking their will and forcing them to forego loyalty to their political parties. The governments in power have tried to win over the members of the opposition through inducements at State expense. Horse-trading is rampant and loyalties of the members of Parliament and provincial assemblies are openly bought and sold. Successive governments have thus been mired in corruption and coercion and democratic values have counted for little.

The military stands established as the true repository of power in the State structure. Even after the lifting of martial law in 1985, it is the military that calls the shots. The concept of the *troika* (sharing of power between the president, the prime minister, and the military command), though clearly an extra-constitutional development, became a fact of life in Pakistan after the death of Zia. The role of the military in the affairs of governance is now beyond dispute and every successive government has accepted it. Hence, constitutional working has been largely subverted and the price being paid to appease the military by a disproportionately high allocation in the budget has caused stagnation in all social sectors like education, health, and housing. Corruption has virtually eaten into the State structure in Pakistan. It is endemic throughout government at all levels and its scale is outrageous. No country, least of all a poor and underdeveloped one like Pakistan, can afford to live with such a high degree of corruption. Funds allocated to development and aid received from international financial institutions like the World Bank and the Asian Bank have been unscrupulously devoured by corrupt politicians and bureaucrats. Loans obtained from abroad have greased the palms and fattened the pockets of politicians and bureaucrats. It is no longer taboo for the governments to be corrupt. Parties that are in power or have been in power, feel no pangs of conscience at their acts of corruption or their reputation as such. The entire bodypolitic is infested with corruption and this situation has brought the State structure to the verge of collapse.

Instability of Political Parties

For any healthy constitutional and political system to function smoothly, strong and well-entrenched political parties are essential. They ensure capable, honest, and motivated leadership and train the political cadre from amongst whom future political leaders are drawn. They guarantee the continuity of the political process at the national, provincial, and local levels. Political parties act as bridges between peoples of different provinces, regions, ethnic, and linguistic groups. They lend stability to the political system, thus ensuring the smooth functioning of the Constitution.

Unfortunately, political parties in Pakistan have failed to develop into strong vehicles of national political will. They have generally been weak and unstable and are easily manipulated. Most of the political parties have been top heavy with leaders but without any cadres at the grass roots or at the intermediate levels. At the time of the creation of Pakistan, there was only one national political party, the Muslim League, whose position was undisputed in view of its having led the movement for independence and the creation of Pakistan. It was the party of Muhammad Ali Jinnah who once remarked that he would be leaving behind two legacies for people: Pakistan and the Muslim League.

Unfortunately, he did not live long enough to organize the party. Even for the year he lived after Independence, Jinnah was too unwell to concentrate on building the party. His guidance was essential at that point in time because political parties which organize mass movements for liberation from foreign dominance are not necessarily qualified for the serious task of governance. The change-over from agitational politics to administration of national affairs is generally slow and painful and full of teething problems which have to be resolved by an honest and competent leadership. Jinnah, who alone could have provided such leadership, did not have the time and the health to do so. He realized, even during his grave illness, that the lower rung of leadership under him was not up to the task. He was disappointed with Liaquat, whom he had groomed over the years to take his place.

During the last few months of his life, Jinnah's relationship with Liaquat had been strained. He was exasperated at the infighting amongst political leaders of his party in the Punjab and in Sindh–particularly the Mamdot-Daultana feud in Punjab. He was forced to remark that he had false coins in his pocket. The language issue in East Bengal became a test of the popularity of the Muslim League and it started losing ground politically. At the time of Jinnah's death, the Muslim League had started showing signs of losing control over political affairs. After Jinnah, Liaquat became the pre-eminent leader of Pakistan. He had the stature and the clout to hold the Muslim League together but he was, however, not very successful in achieving this. Suhrawardy became its chief opponent in East Bengal who separated his party from the Muslim League and named it Awami Muslim League and, later, Awami League.[1]

Bhashani was another man who arose as a leader of stature in East Bengal, heading political forces hostile to the Muslim League which became the target of attacks by all other political parties in East Bengal. The Muslim League could not afford to test its popularity at the polls in East Bengal and provincial elections had to be postponed. When the elections were finally held in 1954, all other political parties formed an alliance known as the 'Jugtu Front' against the Muslim League and routed it at the polls. From this point onwards, the Muslim League ceased to be a political force of any consequence in East Pakistan. The situation for the Muslim League was not very happy in West Pakistan either. Political infighting between Mamdot and Daultana had weakened it in the Punjab and the party had fallen prey to intrigue and manipulation. Liaquat, instead of acting as a statesman to resolve the dispute, became partisan. He sided with Daultana and tacitly approved the rigging of the polls during elections in the Punjab in 1951.

Daultana was aware of the weakness of his party in the Punjab which led him to condone the rigging and laid the foundation of the destruction of confidence in and credibility of the electoral process. What Daultana did not forsee was that when you ask the administration to rig the polls for you, you cannot expect it to remain loyal and play second fiddle to you. The bureaucracy demanded its share in political power. When Liaquat died, they got their representative, Malik Ghulam Muhammad, appointed Governor-General. The rest is history. How he destroyed the political process in Pakistan by dismissing the government of Khawaja Nazimuddin without any justification, and replacing him by a bureaucrat from East Bengal, Muhammad Ali Bogra, has been discussed earlier. His dissolution of the Constituent Assembly in 1954 stymied the political process in the country. To make matters worse, he was replaced by another bureaucrat, Iskandar Mirza, who was a past master in intrigue.

More bureaucrats followed. Chaudhri Mohammad Ali was inducted as the prime minister. Though much can be said about the services of Mohammad Ali to the cause of Pakistan, the fact remains that he was a career bureaucrat and did not become prime minister through the political process. He was adopted by the Muslim League as its chief which speaks volumes for the political bankruptcy of the party. He was forced out through intrigue in 1956 with the active involvement of Iskandar Mirza, who had become the President on adoption of the Constitution on 23 March 1956.

Suhrawardy had a short stint as prime minister, leading a coalition government headed by the Awami League. He was soon ousted by Mirza through intrigue. His ouster was followed by short-lived, weak and unstable coalition governments of Chundrigar and Feroz Khan Noon. From 1951 to 1958, national affairs were in the hands of a large number of political parties. The Muslim League lost its pre-eminent position and became a hangout of intriguers and self-seekers, unscrupulous and ambitious people who wanted power at any price. Their Machiavellian methods brought about the downfall of the party and it lost its support amongst the people of Pakistan.

East Pakistan saw the rise of a number of political parties during this period. Awami League, headed by Suhrawardy, and National Awami Party, led by Bhashani, being the main ones. The political scene in West Pakistan was even worse. Bureaucrats were busy destroying whatever was left of political parties. They created a party of lackeys and sycophants called 'The Republican Party' which had no grass root support or even organization. It was a creation of the establishment which feudals and political opportunists had joined with their own axe to grind. They were active in the formation, destabilization, and the fall of governments to please Iskandar Mirza. When martial law was declared in October 1958, this party evaporated into thin air and nothing was heard of it any more. Nevertheless, it caused incalculable harm to the institution of political parties in Pakistan and paved the way for martial law.

Martial law further eroded whatever shabby political party structure had survied till October 1958. Political parties were banned and several leaders were disqualified from contesting the elections. Martial law was lifted in 1962 and political parties were revived under severe restrictions imposed under the Political Parties Act 1962. Ayub was totally averse to political parties and made no secret of his hostility towards them. Later, he discovered, much to his chagrin, that it was not possible to run a civilian government under a Constitution without political parties. He finally decided to make his own political party and applied for the name of Muslim League, which seemed most convenient since it had been associated with the creation of Pakistan. The earlier Muslim Leaguers were not ready to accept him as the head of the party. Consequently, the Muslim League split into two factions identified as Convention Muslim League, comprising those who accepted Ayub as their leader, and Council Muslim League, comprising those who did not.

In the presidential election of 1965, all parties other than the Convention Muslim League (including Council Muslim League), formed an alliance and nominated Fatima Jinnah as its candidate for presidency. This alliance did not have anything in common except opposition to Ayub. It included such diverse elements as the Khudai Khidmatgars of Ghaffar Khan in NWFP, the Jamaat-i-Islami of Maudoodi, the National Awami Party (NAP) of Bhashani, and the Awami League of Mujib. No effort was made to forge this alliance into a single political party or even into a long term political alliance. Consequently, the alliance fell apart after the presidential elections into several small, weak, unstable and at the same time warring and contending factions ready to go for each other's throat at the first opportunity.

Convention Muslim League was hardly a political party in the real sense. It had no programme or following. There was no organization at the grass-root level or even above. It was a gathering of self-serving, unscrupulous, and power hungry politicians who had joined Ayub for a ride in power. They had no real allegiance or loyalty even to him, but were there to enjoy the fruits, perks, and spoils of power. When Ayub was ousted in 1969, this party fell like a house of cards. Its remnants ran around to join other political parties or to secure the gains they had made during the Ayub regime. That was the end of the Convention Muslim League. No wonder that in this political environment, Bhutto, who had gained popularity amongst the masses during the Indo-Pak war of 1965, received a warm response from the people. The political party that he created, the Pakistan People's Party (PPP), became popular throughout West Pakistan and did well in the national polls in 1970, winning a majority of seats in the National Assembly in West Pakistan and in the Provincial Assembly of Punjab, and emerged as the largest party in the Provincial Assembly of Sindh. A real political party of the masses was born in West Pakistan. Other political parties received a drubbing at the polls in 1970, except for the National Awami Party (NAP) which made a strong showing at the polls in NWFP and in Balochistan.

In East Pakistan, the Awami League led by Mujib swept the polls in 1970 to both the National and the Provincial Assembly. The events that followed in East Pakistan led to the unfortunate breakup of Pakistan, and the Awami League is a consign of history as far as Pakistan is concerned. In the Pakistan that was left after 1971, the PPP emerged as a major party with a nationwide following. Its initial pretensions were socialist in nature since it had amongst its ranks socialists and left-leaning political workers. Its intellectual mentor was a former civil servant, J.A. Rahim, who was deeply influenced by the methods of communist parties in China and the Soviet Union. The slogans adopted by the party and the display of its banners and flags were on the same lines as the communist parties in China, the Soviet Union, and North Korea. But Bhutto, who came from the feudal class of Sindh, ultimately inducted the feudals of Sindh and Southern Punjab into his party. This inherent contradiction between the feudals and left-leaning politicians had to come to a head with the result that, by 1976, the socialist left had either been weeded out or had become ineffective and inconsequential.

Even J.A. Rahim was ousted. Feudals from other political parties joined the PPP and by 1977, when general elections were called, the party had changed completely. PPP lost its popular base due to the strong arm political tactics of Bhutto who victimized, jailed, and harassed political opponents. NAP, the leading opposition party, was banned and the leader of the opposition, Wali Khan, was detained and prosecuted for treason. The provincial governments headed by opposition parties in NWFP and Balochistan were dismissed in 1973 without any justification, which led to the armed insurgency in Balochistan.

Another factor that hurt the PPP was Bhutto's dependence on bureaucratic channels rather than on party cadre. He did not organize the party on democratic lines and no internal elections were held, all party offices being filled through nominations. The heads of security forces and bureaucrats around him became very powerful and party leaders and workers were sidelined. A time came when party workers could only reach

Bhutto through the bureaucrats around him. He relied on the reports of the intelligence agencies and civil servants at district and divisional levels in order to decide about the party candidates for national and provincial assemblies. The structure of the PPP was thus weakened. Other political parties during Bhutto's government were either harassed and kept on the run, or forced into some kind of accommodation with the PPP. When general elections were called in 1977, nine opposition parties formed an alliance called Pakistan National Alliance (PNA). Prominent among them were the Muslim League, Jamaat-i-Islami, Tehrik-i-Istiqlal, Jamiat-i-Ulema-i-Islam (JUI—led by Mufti Mahmood who was selected as head of the PNA), and National Democratic Party (a successor of the NAP which had been banned). This alliance had all shades of ideology and opinion in it, ranging from religious parties like Jamaat-i-Islami and JUI, to socialist/secular parties like NDP and Tehrik-i-Istiqlal. Their only common objective was opposition to Bhutto and the PPP. The PNA did hold together during the nationwide agitation against Bhutto from March to June 1977, but when martial law was imposed in July 1977, its internal schisms and contradictions spread and it started coming apart at the seams. Tehrik-i-Istiqlal was the first political party to quit the alliance, and by the middle of 1979, the PNA had all but disappeared as a political alliance.

The component parties of the PNA, small and divided, became victims of their diverse interests. Some, like Jamaat-i-Islami and Pagara Muslim League, became accomplices of Zia's martial law and enjoyed the perks and privileges granted by the government in power. Others like Tehrik-i-Istiqlal and Jamiatul Ulema-i-Pakistan, became bitter opponents of the martial law regime and ultimately joined the PPP in 1981 in a new alliance known as the Movement for the Restoration of Democracy (MRD). Others like the NDP, re-emerged as the Awami National Party (ANP) on the release of Wali Khan, and the JUI went their own way, staying clear of martial law and the MRD. Subsequently, JUI headed by Fazlur Rahman, the son of Mufti Mahmood, joined MRD. The MRD suffered from the same drawback as earlier political alliances, that is, with nothing in common except hostility towards a government or its head. Nevertheless, the MRD waged a commendable struggle for the lifting of martial law, the restoration of the Constitution and democracy, and for the holding of elections. Its movement in Sindh in 1983 made a nationwide impact and obliged Zia to proceed with his plan to hold general elections in February 1985, albeit partyless ones. The parties in the MRD did not participate in the polls of 1985 because they stood for party-based general elections. When Benazir returned to the country in April 1986, the MRD became increasingly irrelevant and the political scene was again dominated by the PPP. The partyless polls of 1985 led to the formation of governments at the federal and provincial levels headed by the nominees of the president and the governors respectively.

Just like Ayub, Junejo soon learnt that it is not possible to run a civilian government without a parliamentary structure. Thus, the new prime minister, Junejo, was forced to create a political party from amongst those members of the Parliament and the Provincial Assemblies who had been elected on a non-party basis. This was considered essential for proper governance at the national and provincial levels. Junejo, originally belonging to the Convention Muslim League of Ayub, gave the name of Muslim

League to the political outfit that he was creating from amongst the members of the Parliament and the Provincial Assemblies. This Muslim League, despite a lot of infighting, has survived thanks to the support of the establishment and the Inter Services Intelligence (ISI), from time to time. Its dominant group is headed by Nawaz Sharif and the party faction under him is known as the Pakistan Muslim League (Nawaz)–PML(N). Its smaller splinter group, formed after the death of Junejo, is known as the Pakistan Muslim League (Junejo)–PML(J). The latter faction split further, some time ago. However, during the period from 1988 onwards (after the death of Zia), the main contending parties, the PPP and PML, formed alliances with smaller parties either at the goading of the establishment or out of a need for protection. In the general elections of 1988, fearing the success of the PPP, the establishment, managed to forge an alliance of the PML, Jamaat-i-Islami, and some small parties, and named it Islami Jamhoori Ittehad (IJI), which was successful in containing the PPP at the polls to the National Assembly and produced better results at the provincial polls for the Punjab Assembly. When the PPP government was dismissed by Ishaq in 1990, the IJI contested general elections as an alliance and won a landslide to the National Assembly and Provincial Assemblies of Punjab and the NWFP. The governments formed at the federation and in these provinces were headed by Nawaz Sharif from the PML and his nominees at the provincial level. When the PPP was ousted from government in 1990 and lost in the elections, it formed an alliance with some small political parties like the PDP led by Nawabzada Nasrullah, and the PML(Q) led by Malik Qasim. This alliance, known as the Pakistan Democratic Alliance (PDA), was apparently made to protect PPP leaders from persecution at the hands of the party in power. The PDA contested the polls in the general elections of 1993 as an alliance after including the dissident elements of the PML known as PML(J). The IJI did not last long as a political alliance and broke up before the polls of 1993.

Jamaat-i-Islami, which was the second most important political party in the alliance, withdrew from the IJI and decided to go its own way, forging an electoral alliance of its own for the general elections of 1993 by the name of Pakistan Islamic Front (PIF). However, this alliance made a very poor showing and was routed at the polls.

Another political party of consequence and worthy of mention is the Muhajir Qaumi Movement (MQM). An ethnic organization, it came into existence in 1985-1986 with the ostensible objective of safeguarding the rights of *mohajirs* in Karachi and other urban areas of Sindh. Its creation is reputed to be the brainchild of Zia, particularly the ISI, designed to weaken the hold of the PPP in Sindh. It was beyond the wildest imagination of its creators that one day it would become a *djin* which could not be put back into the bottle from which it was released. The MQM quickly caught up with mohajirs who had migrated from parts of India other than the Punjab in 1947 and afterwards, and became their sole voice. In the general elections of 1988, the MQM swept the polls in the urban areas of Karachi and Hyderabad. Initially, a coalition was formed between the PPP and the MQM at the federal and the provincial levels (in Sindh), but soon after, the MQM fell out with the PPP and became its bitter opponent. It has continued to be so. The MQM fared well in the urban areas of Karachi and Hyderabad in the polls of 1990.

The MQM had good relations with the Nawaz government but did not sustain it. Military operations were ordered against the reportedly terrorist activities of its militant wing, an operation which continues in some form or the other. The MQM has broken into factions, the main one being led by Altaf Husain, a fugitive in England, known as MQM(A), the other consisting of the dissidents known as the MQM (Haqiqi). Without doubt, it is the MQM (A) which has the support of the mohajir community and the MQM (H) is only used by the government as a counterweight.

Looking closely at the political landscape in Pakistan and at its leadership, one is compelled to say that political parties have failed to lend stability to the country. The reasons can be summarized as under:

The Muslim League, as it stood at the time of independence, did not get the chance to organize itself properly. It was in bad shape in 1937 when it performed miserably at the polls held under the Government of India Act, 1935. Under the able guidance of Jinnah, it became an effective organization and passed the resolution for independence and for the partition of India in March 1940. It led a movement for the creation of a Muslim homeland from 1941 to 1947, particularly in the years 1944 to 1947. Leading a movement and organizing a political party are two different things. The demands of a liberation movement generally engage the attention of the party leaders and leave little time for concentration on matters of internal organization and raising and training of a political cadre. During the liberation movement, it is generally difficult to judge the credentials of those joining the party and, in any case, a liberation movement needs support from all quarters. In this situation, self-seekers get an opportunity to join the ranks of the party and play a negative role when the liberation movement comes to an end and the party faces the serious business of governance. This is what happened to the Muslim League, particularly at the hands of the feudals of the Punjab. They were, as a class, hostile to the Muslim League which was initially a party of the middle class. Later, they opposed the Muslim League and supported the Unionist party which believed in a united India, but when the popularity of the Pakistan movement led by the Muslim League became irresistible in 1945–46, many feudals in Punjab decided to jump on the bandwagon of the Muslim League. When Pakistan came into existence, their machinations destroyed the party and rendered it unpopular amongst the people. Hence, from the very beginning, the political party system was not allowed to take root in Pakistan.

The meddling of bureaucrats in politics in the early and mid-fifties destroyed whatever party structure existed. They created new political parties and alliances, encouraged floor crossing in the legislatures, manoeuvred temporary and unstable alliances and coalitions, and destabilized them when it suited their interests. Political parties and their internal structures became instruments in the hands of manipulators who used them for their own self-advancement and perpetuation.

Repeated imposition of martial law liquidated whatever party structure existed in 1958. The creation of political parties became the domain of martial law regimes. The political structure was turned upside down. Instead of political parties coming up from the grass roots, they became creatures of patronage by the military generals and their underlings. The party structure was imposed from above and political operatives and self-seekers joined them with the sole objective of self-aggrandizement and self-advancement. This situation suited the military dictators who desired a political proxy for their deeds, but the parties they created had neither a democratic internal structure nor popular support in the masses. They could hardly lend political stability to the country.

There has been a clear and significant trend over more than twenty years, for political leaders to personalize rather than institutionalize their parties. This is evident from the way Bhutto, Benazir, and Nawaz Sharif handled their affairs. They have tended to keep all power in their own hands or with family members, leaving party officials and party channels devoid of any power in decision-making. This style is reflected in the way they have run their governments. Instead of institutionalizing decision-making in the appointment of government servants and an extension of their contracts, they have personally taken such decisions. This is a serious flaw in their line of thinking. Little do they realize that individuals die and perish but institutions live on. It is inconvenient for them and the country suffers because their valuable time in office is lost in petty decision-making and important national issues and policies are often ignored.

Another reason for the weakness of party structures is the lack of democracy in the ranks themselves. Major political parties like the PPP and the PML(N) hold no internal elections to party offices which are filled through nominations and appointments. Hence, party officials are not representatives of the workers who feel frustrated about this imposition from the top. Party officials tend to come from the ruling classes and care little about the workers and the need for remaining in touch with the problems of the common citizen. They turn into sycophants for the leader at the top and end up isolating and insulating him from political realities, thus achieving their own ends of self-advancement. It is then observed that party structures are alienated from the common man whose voice does not reach the leadership.

Debate Over Form of Government

Debate over the merits of the parliamentary or the presidential forms of government is as old as democracy itself. The two models owe their origin to Great Britain and the United States of America (USA), and have spread to other countries of the world.

The parliamentary form of government in Great Britain had its beginnings in the victory of Parliament over the Royalists and the beheading of King Charles. It was further strengthened by the passing of the Bill of Rights in 1688 and the abdication of King James. With the passage of time, the King (or the Queen) of England lost nearly all powers (in practical terms) and became a figurehead only. The Cabinet, headed by the Prime Minister, became the true instrument of power. Development of the party system in Britain, particularly the predominance of two major political parties greatly strengthened the parliamentary system which became a model to follow in all those countries which had colonial ties with Great Britain at some point in time. That is why countries like Australia, Canada, India, and New Zealand adopted it. It also served as a model for countries in Europe when they became Republics after they had thrown away the yoke of monarchy or dictatorship. Germany, Italy, Spain, Austria, Greece, Sweden, Denmark, and Norway have all adopted the parliamentary form of government and have made phenomenal material progress under this system. Japan, in Asia, also adopted the parliamentary system after its defeat in the Second World War, in its Constitution of 1951.

The presidential form of government, as we understand it today, owes its origin to the Constitution of the USA. On gaining independence after the expulsion of British colonists, thirteen original States formed into a confederation and adopted Articles of Confederation. The arrangement of government under the confederation was loose and weak causing serious problems of governance and national solidarity. Finally, a Constitutional Convention was called in 1787 which adopted a Federal Constitution for the United States of America (USA) which has worked very successfully for more than two hundred years. This Constitution created a very powerful President in the dual role of head of State and chief executive. The presidential system has given stability to the government in the USA and the system has survived crucial times like the American Civil War of 1861–65 and the two World Wars in the present century. It has been adopted in countries with strong American influence like the Philippines and South Korea or by autocratic governments in countries of Central and South America like Mexico, Brazil, Argentina, Peru, Chile, and others.

France has had a different historical experience in this regard. After the French Revolution in 1789, a brief experiment was made in democracy during the period known as the First Republic. It was short-lived (1793–99), unstable, and uncertain in its features. After about fifty years of dictatorship and monarchy, France once again became a democracy known as the Second Republic (1848–52).

Its Constitution was prepared and adopted on the American model which again proved short-lived and met its end when Louis Napoleon, who had been elected as President under the Second Republic, was proclaimed Emperor. On the fall of Paris and the defeat of France in the Franco-Prussian War (1870–71) and abdication of Napoleon III, France became a democracy once again and has stayed as such ever since. A Republican Constitution was adopted in the year 1875 which lasted until 1940, when it ended due to the fall of Paris in the Second World War. This period is known as the Third Republic and the Constitution was based on the parliamentary form of government. This period is known for unstable governments due to the multi-party political system in France. Mostly, coalition governments were formed which fell frequently. The government in 1940 is discredited with the defeat of France in the Second World War due to its indecision and confusion. After the Second World War, the Constitution of the Fourth Republic was adopted in 1946 which was again based on a parliamentary system, and the governments formed under it once again proved to be unstable. Twenty-three governments were formed over a span of only twelve years.

To avoid an army coup against parliamentary institutions, leading parliamentarians called upon Charles de Gaulle to form a government. De Gaulle agreed to do so if he was allowed to draw up a new Constitution giving much greater powers to the executive.[2] De Gaulle was elected as the first president under the new Constitution.

This Constitution provided for a mixed form of parliamentary and persidential systems where the President is directly elected for a period of seven years on the basis of universal suffrage and is very powerful with full control over the departments of defence and foreign relations. The President can appoint the Prime Minister but the latter has to obtain a vote of confidence from the legislature.

Debate on this question has raged ever since the creation of Pakistan. It is, however, generally believed that the founding fathers of Pakistan favoured the parliamentary form of government. Jinnah desired to see Pakistan being governed under a parliamentary democratic system. That is why, when he became the Governor-General of Pakistan, he allowed a parliamentary system to work under him with Liaquat as the first prime minister. It was only after his death that things took a serious turn in Pakistan, particularly in constitution making. The Constituent Assembly, instead of framing a Constitution at the earliest, started dragging its feet over it with the obvious intention of perpetuating itself. It was involved in heated debates and deadlocks over issues like the choice of national language, bicameral or unicameral legislatures, joint or separate electorates, and so forth. The first prime minister was assassinated in October 1951 and was replaced by the Governor-General, Khawaja Nazimuddin. The office of Governor-General was somehow taken over by a senior bureaucrat, Malik Ghulam Muhammad. This office was provided under the Government of India Act, 1935, which was the constitutional document in vogue at that time, as adapted by the Governor-General under the Indian Independence Act of 1947.

The Governor-General was empowered to dissolve the Assembly and to dismiss the ministers at his discretion. Unfortunately, this power was exercised arbitrarily and capriciously by Governor-General Ghulam Muhammad. He dismissed the government of Khawaja Nazimuddin in 1953. Nazimuddin was then succeeded by Muhammad Ali Bogra and, while he was prime minister, in 1954 the Governor-General dissolved the Constituent Assembly (elected in 1947 for framing the first Constitution of Pakistan) only a few days after the Assembly had adopted a final draft. This led to a serious constitutional crisis and the matter was hotly contested in courts, culminating in the controversial decision of the Federal Court in Moulvi Tamizuddin Khan's case upholding the action of the Governor-General. After the retirement of Ghulam Muhammad, Major-General (Retired) Iskandar Mirza, again a senior bureaucrat, assumed the office of Governor-General. On the promulgation of the first Constitution of Pakistan in March 1956, he became the first President under the new Constitution. He, too, was fond of meddling in politics and destablizing successive governments. As a result, between March 1956 and October 1958 (when martial law was imposed), Pakistan had four prime ministers. He actively participated in intrigues which led to the fall of the government of Mohammad Ali who had to ultimately resign when he lost the confidence of a majority of the members of the National Assembly in August 1956.

He was succeeded by Suhrawardy, a consummate politician, but even his government did not last for more than a year and Iskandar Mirza, once again through intrigue and manipulation, destabilized his government and forced him to resign. He was then succeeded by Chundrigar, who was ousted after two months due to loss of confidence of the majority in the National Assembly occasioned once again by manipulations on the part of the President and his cronies. He was succeeded by Malik Feroz Khan Noon, whose government was ultimately dismissed on 7 October 1958 on the declaration of martial law and the abrogation of the Constitution by Iskandar Mirza. Iskandar Mirza himself became the first casualty of martial law and was removed as President within a few days. The office of prime minister was dispensed with and General Ayub installed himself as President in addition to being Chief Martial Law Administrator. He introduced indirect elections under what he called Basic Democracy. He got 80,000 Basic Democrats elected from as many small constituencies of 500 to 1000 voters each. These 80,000 Basic Democrats (40,000 each from the provinces of East and West Pakistan) formed an electoral college for the election of the president. He was elected in this manner in February 1960 through a referendum and also obtained a mandate for giving a new Constitution to Pakistan. He had little respect for parliamentary democracy and clearly favoured the presidential form of government which was suitable to his aspirations and character. He appointed a Constitution Commission, headed by Justice Shahabuddin, then Chief Justice of Pakistan, to examine the causes of failure of parliamentary government in Pakistan and to make recommendations for a new Constitution. After making thorough enquiries through questionnaires, tours and interviews, the Commission submitted its report on 29 April 1961.

The Commission held lack of leadership, well-organized and disciplined political parties, general lack of character in politicians and their undue interference in the administration, as the real causes of the failure of parliamentary democracy in Pakistan. The Commission recommended the presidential form of government as suitable to the conditions in Pakistan. Except for this recommendation, the report of the Shahabuddin Commission was not to the liking of Ayub. He kept the report in cold storage for a long time and appointed a committee of his own ministers (headed by Manzoor Qadir with Mohammad Shoaib and Bhutto as its members), which made recommendations entirely to his liking. He accepted the recommendations of the committee of his ministers in preference to that of the Shahabuddin Commission. The Constitution of 1962 approved the presidential form of government, but the president and members of national and provincial assemblies were elected indirectly by the electoral college consisting of the Basic Democrats. In the agitation against Ayub in 1968–69, all political parties rejected the presidential form of government and demanded the restoration of parliamentary democracy in the country.

In the general elections held in December 1970 to elect a Constituent Assembly (for framing a new constitution), all the major political parties, including the Pakistan People's Party (PPP), promised the introduction of parliamentary democracy under the Constitution to be framed. When Yahya resigned in December 1971, Bhutto took over as the President of Pakistan. It appears that the presidential system was to his liking as well. The Interim Constitution, introduced on 21 April 1972, also provided for the presidential form of government. When the time came to frame a permanent

Constitution, efforts were made and hints were dropped that Bhutto favoured the presidential system.

Mian Mahmood Ali Kasuri, who was the law minister at the time, resisted the idea and took the position that although he personally favoured the presidential system, he thought that the Pakistan People's Party (PPP) had committed itself to the nation to give a Constitution based on the parliamentary form of government. This led to an ugly confrontation between him and ministers of the PPP government who made personal attacks on him and attempts were made in the press to malign his name. This ultimately forced him to resign as law minister and to quit the PPP. This controversy forced the PPP to give a Constitution in 1973 based on the parliamentary form of government. On the promulgation of the Constitution in August 1973, Bhutto became prime minister and Chaudhry Fazal Elahi was elected president. The office of president under the 1973 Constitution in its original form was very weak. The prime minister was the chief executive and held all the executive powers of the federation under the Constitution. Bhutto was not happy with this situation and wanted to amend the Constitution to adopt the presidential system had he won a two-thirds majority in the National Assembly in 1977.

On the imposition of martial law in July 1977, the debate over the merits of the two systems of government was once again encouraged, obviously at the behest of Zia and his coterie. The blame for the political crises in 1977 was laid squarely on the parliamentary system and a weak presidency. It was widely publicized that had the president been strong, the political crises in 1977 could have been resolved without the imposition of martial law. Zia called for an amendment of the Constitution to create a balance in the powers between the president and the prime minister with the help of government controlled media and the press. Revival of the Constitution of 1973 Order (RCO) and the Eighth Amendment became the culminating point of this campaign and this Amendment strengthened the position of the president by conferring wide powers on him including the discretionary dissolution of the National and Provincial Assemblies and the appointment of Chiefs of Armed Forces.

Increase in the powers of the president under RCO and the Eighth Amendment was thus the price extorted from a helpless parliament for the lifting of martial law and the restoration of civilian government. The impact of the Eighth Amendment on the Constitution of Pakistan, particularly in relation to the discretionary power of the president to dissolve the National Assembly, has become the dominant constitutional issue in Pakistan of late. This discretionary power has been exercised rather too often.

In a span of eight years (from 29 May 1988 to 5 November 1996), the President dissolved the National Assembly four times in exercise of this discretionary power. For the first time, on 29 May 1988, Zia dissolved the National Assembly and dismissed Junejo's government. The second occasion was 6 August 1990, when Ishaq dissolved the National Assembly and dismissed Benazir's government. The third occasion was 18 April 1993, when Ishaq once again dissolved the National Assembly and dismissed the government of Nawaz Sharif. The fourth occasion was 5 November 1996 when Leghari dissolved the second Benazir government. As a result, of the frequent exercise of this power, the National Assembly elected in 1985 for a period of five years did not last for more than three years and two months, the National Assembly elected in November 1988, did not last for more than twenty months. The National Assembly elected in October 1990, was dissolved after twenty-nine months, and the National Assembly elected in October 1993 was dissolved after thirty-six months. These powers have finally been laid to rest under the Thirteenth Amendment to the Constitution passed in April 1997.

The debate over the system of government continues. Every strong man in politics, including Ayub, Bhutto, Zia, and Nawaz has had a predisposition towards the presidential from of government. Those who fear the autocracy and dictatorial inclinations of leaders with extraordinary powers have always opposed the idea and favoured the parliamentary system. Politicians, who have limited political influence or are associated with small or regional political parties like Nawabzada Nasrullah, Jatoi, Daultana, and Wali Khan, have opposed the presidential system. The parliamentary form of government is better attuned to smaller parties, splinter groups, or regional and ethnic parties which become suddenly important due to a struggle between the larger parties for dominance and formation of the government. At times, they hold the entire system hostage and wrest undue advantages for themselves and their cronies. Wattoo's government in the Punjab is a classic example of such political blackmail by a small party. He became chief minister with less than ten per cent of the seats in the Punjab Assembly, using the PPP's fears of a PML(N) government. In all fairness, Pakistan's experience with the presidential system has not been good. As a result, it is perceived by the people as something akin to dictatorship, mostly because it is identified with three periods of martial law.

Even the constitutional period of the presidential system, 1962–1969 is perceived as an extension of Ayub's martial law. In any case, Ayub's presidential Constitution was not given by a popularly elected Constituent Assembly or Convention and was imposed by a military dictator against the will of the people. Furthermore, the system given under the 1962 Constitution was stained by concepts like limited electorates, guided democracy, indirect elections to the presidency and the legislatures, and lack of participation by the people in the system. This, of course, is not the true picture of a democratic presidential system which has the following advantages:

One, it lends certainty and stability to the government. A president is elected for a fixed term of office and cannot be removed but for misbehaviour or misconduct through a difficult impeachment procedure. He thus has full opportunity to formulate long-term policies and to execute them. He can work single-mindedly for the country without any fear of losing a majority in the legislature. He can even pursue, or at least advance, unpopular policies for some time if they are in the long-term interest of the country. His continuance in office is not subject to intrigue and manipulation.

Two, in times of emergencies, the presidential system has the ability to respond quickly and effectively by resorting to firm measures. It is not hostage to changing and fluctuating majorities in the legislature. While based on democratic principles, it has the advantages of monarchy and dictatorship. It promotes strict separation of power amongst the three organs of the State and the legislature has the opportunity to concentrate on its primary function of law-making. This is not so in the parliamentary system, where the legislatures are involved in the assumption, exercise, and transfer of executive power. In a parliamentary system, legislative functions, are relegated to a secondary position. Despite such basic and important advantages of the presidential over the parliamentary system, it has been noticed that the presidential system can be more prone to corruption, favouritism, and misuse of power. The family members of the president and the coterie around him tend to misuse the position. Scandals abound in countries with presidential systems like Mexico, Indonesia, Philippines, and Brazil. Collor, the President of Brazil, had to resign on charges of corruption and misuse of power after a long and concerted national movement against him. Suharto, the President of Indonesia, ruled with an iron hand for thirty-two years and resigned recently. His family is reported to have accumulated one of the biggest fortunes ever, anywhere between forty to fifty billion dollars. Keeping in view Pakistan's constitutional and political experience and the heterogeneity of the population and its division into linguistic, parochial, and ethnic groups, the presidential system may not be appropriate for Pakistan. What it has going against it may be listed as follows:

One, the presidential system is likely to promote feelings of neglect and alienation amongst the people of smaller provinces. Punjab, being the largest province with a majority of the population may be perceived as having an advantage over all other provinces put together. There could be continuing bickering and confrontation between Punjab on the one hand, and the smaller provinces, on the other.

Two, the question of provincial autonomy is likely to be raised. In a federal presidential system, the provinces are supposed to be autonomous with their own elected heads. In case the Constitution allows elected governors for the provinces, it may lead to serious friction or maybe even confrontation between the federation and a province if the president and the governor of that province belong to different political parties. The election campaign for gubernatorial office could lead to the raising of provincial and parochial issues as opposed to national issues. This situation can exist anywhere in a presidential system but in Pakistan, where the provinces have their own separate linguistic and ethnic identities and groups, the situation could become serious and might run contrary to the interest of national integrity and solidarity.

Three, in case the Governors are appointed by the President as executive heads of the provinces, the Constitution would cease to be a federal one. It would virtually mean denial of the will of the people in the provinces and they would be denied the right to elect their own provincial administrations. The provincial administration would be perceived to be imposed by the centre, as was the case during Ayub. This situation would be diametrically opposed to the concept of provincial autonomy and the federal system.

Four, corruption and abuse of authority, already endemic in our political system, would accentuate in a presidential system where accountability is minimal. One can only shudder at the prospect of the near relatives and close friends of a president let loose on the economic resources of the country.

Five, persecution and victimization of political opponents, a common phenomenon in Pakistan's politics, are likely to increase in a presidential system. In a parliamentary system, the opposition can protest in the Parliament which the prime minister and the ministers have to listen to. In a presidential system, there would be no such opportunity.

For these reasons, one cannot avoid the conclusion that the parliamentary system, with all its drawbacks and disadvantages, may still be more suitable to Pakistan's condition. Efforts should, therefore, be made to curtail the vices and excesses of the parliamentary system, such as floor crossing, and destabilization of government by outside forces like the military and the bureaucracy, since dispensing with the parliamentary system altogether may not be in the best interest of Pakistan.

Role of Legislatures: Sovereign, Subordinate, or Advisory?

Under the parliamentary form of government, the legislatures are theoretically sovereign. They can pass any law within their constitutional competence and the president or the governor has no authority to veto them. In the United Kingdom, it is said that Parliament is so sovereign that it may declare a man a woman, and a woman a man. This concept owes its origin to the unwritten character of the British Constitution. Even where there are written constitutions in a parliamentary democracy, the legislatures are sovereign in their respective domains. Does this apply to Pakistan? An attempt to answer this question can be made by examining the following constitutional developments.

It has been discussed above that the Objectives Resolution of 1949 is the basic constitutional document of Pakistan. It was adopted with some modifications as the preamble to all the three Constitutions (of 1956, 1962, and 1973). It has now become an operative part of the Constitution with the incorporation of Article 2A which declared the Objectives Resolution, reproduced in the Annex, as a substantive part of the Constitution and took effect accordingly. The resolution declares at the very beginning:

> Whereas sovereignty over the entire universe belongs to Allah Almighty alone and the authority which He has delegated to the State of Pakistan, through its people for being exercised within the limits prescribed by Him is a sacred trust.

This declaration sets at rest the British concept of the absolute sovereignty of the Parliament as far as its application to Pakistan is concerned. The Parliament is not sovereign but subject to the authority of Allah Almighty which He has delegated to the State of Pakistan to be exercised within the limits prescribed by Him. This declaration in the Constitution is subject to two interpretations. Those who want Pakistan to be a theological state would like to interpret it to mean that the entire Constitution and the laws formed thereunder are subject to the general principles of Islam and have to be read as such. This would mean that the Constitution would lose its paramountcy and its provisions can be struck down or ignored in order to enforce the principles of Islam. This interpretation is likely to result in reducing the

Constitution and its provisions to secondary importance and making them subject to the concepts of Islam as propounded by various schools. The Supreme Court has for the time being curbed such interpretation and held, setting aside a judgment of the Lahore High Court to the contrary, that one provision of the Constitution (Article 2A) cannot override another provision (Article 45).[3]

The other and narrower interpretation would mean that the Constitution as the basic law of the country, cannot be ignored or marginalized through judicial review and those laws, or provisions thereof, framed by competent legislatures, can be struck down if they are found to be repugnant to clear injunctions of the Holy Quran and *Sunnah*. Such interpretation clearly narrows down the scope of judicial review and appears to be in consonance with the intent of the Objectives Resolution itself expressed as under:

> Wherein the Muslims shall be enabled to order their lives in the individual and collective spheres in accordance with the teachings and requirements of Islam as set out in the Holy Quran and the *Sunnah*.

This view of the Constitution and laws framed thereunder finds further support from the following portion of the Objectives Resolution as well.

> Wherein the State shall exercise its powers and authority through the chosen representatives of the people.

It is, therefore, self evident that the Objectives Resolution did not intend to make the legislatures subordinate or secondary institutions but sovereign ones within their respective spheres under the Constitution subject, of course, to the restriction that while framing laws, they should not transgress the limits set out in the Holy Quran and *Sunnah*.

One violence done by Zia to the language of the Constitution was the introduction of the expression '*Majlis-e-Shoora*' for Parliament in the Revival of the Constitution of 1973 Order, 1985 (P.O. 14 of 1985). The Parliament, while adopting the Eighth Amendment in 1985, should not have countenanced this but it appears to have taken this substitution rather lightly. Majlis-e-Shoora gives the impression that Parliament is an advisory and not a sovereign body. '*Shoora*' is an Arabic word arising out of the root which means advice. Actually, this expression has been frequently used in Muslim countries which have monarchies and the function of such a *Majlis* is not to make laws but to advise the king or emperor in matters of law-making. Zia had constituted a '*Majlis-e-Shoora*' in 1981 consisting of his nominees and appointees which was nothing but a rubber stamp body acting on the wishes and to the convenience of a dictator. This was obviously his view of Parliament and this expression should not have been allowed to be introduced in the Constitution. Nevertheless, Parliament is performing its functions as a legislature rather than an advisory body even after the Eighth Amendment.

Another such transgression of the Constitution was the Federal Shariat Court established through Constitutional Amendment in 1980 which created a parallel system of judiciary. Initially, in 1979, the provincial High Courts were vested with jurisdiction to declare any law, or any provision thereof, repugnant to the injunctions of the Holy Quran and *Sunnah*. After having done so, there was no necessity of creating a new and parallel court for the exercise of such jurisdiction. Appeals against the decisions of this court do not lie to the Supreme Court generally, as in other cases, but to its Special Bench, known as Shariat Appellate Bench, the composition of which includes two members who are not judges of the Supreme Court but style themselves as *Ulema*.

This Court system completely by-passes the Supreme Court and the High Courts. The Federal Shariat Court was further strengthened by vesting jurisdiction in it to hear appeals against the judgments and sentences passed by the trial Courts in *Hudood* cases. Thus, the jurisdiction of the provincial High Courts was curtailed in this behalf. The Federal Shariat Court has also infringed upon the independence and sovereignty of Parliament and the Provincial Assemblies. The Court has jurisdiction to examine and determine the question of whether or not any law or provision of law is repugnant to the injunctions of Islam as laid down in the Holy Quran and the *Sunnah* of the Holy Prophet (PBUH). Only those laws or provisions of law can be struck down as un-Islamic which are clearly repugnant to the injunctions of the Holy Quran and *Sunnah*. Hence, the role of this court was somewhat limited and restricted but, over the years, it has extended this role rather radically. It has ventured to give its opinion on anything and everything and even those laws which do not violate any injunctions of the Holy Quran and *Sunnah* have been interfered with. It has done great violence to the laws of pre-emption in the country with the resultant negation of the rights of the citizens acquired over the years under statutes and customary law.[4] Hence, the Federal Shariat Court and its Shariat Appellate Bench have assumed the role of a super-legislature unto themselves, correspondingly reducing the legislatures, federal as well as provincial, to a subordinate position.

Another factor undermining the Constitution has been the ordinance-making powers of the president and the governor over subjects assigned to Parliament and the provincial assemblies, respectively. The power was designed to be exercised in the eventuality of an emergency, particularly when the national or provincial assemblies were not in session. Ordinance-making was to be an exceptional mode of legislation and that also on temporary basis, four months in case of a President's Ordinance and three months in case of a Governor's Ordinance. Unfortunately, Ordinance-making has become the rule rather than an exception in law-making. The legislatures have virtually abdicated their primary function and duty of law-making in favour of the executive, and their members have busied themselves with the power game. The legislatures have been reduced to subordinate bodies which belatedly rubber stamp the ordinances framed by the executive. The inefficiency and indifference of the legislatures can be judged from the fact that the ordinances laid before them are allowed to lapse and are promulgated periodically and repeatedly till such time that the appropriate legislature may find time or condescend to rubber stamp them.

Role of the Judiciary: Independent or Docile?

The judiciary is one of the three organs of the State, executive and legislature being the other two. It is the final arbiter of the Constitution and protector of fundamental rights and civil liberties of the citizens. Its role is vital for a healthy nation and a democratic society. With such a basic role in a constitutional set-up, the judiciary's position as an independent institution cannot be over emphasized. On independence, Pakistan inherited a healthy judicial system with a reputation for integrity and competence. This was mainly attributable to a fair system of appointment of judges wherein appointments were generally made on merit.

The first Chief Justice of Pakistan, Mian Abdur Rashid, was a man of unimpeachable character and reputation and shunned appearance in public functions and gatherings. His successor, Muhammad Munir, became highly controversial due to certain judgments of his but his later successors, particularly Shahabuddin and A.R. Cornelius, maintained high standards of judicial conduct. Appointments to superior courts during the times of British India were made with extreme care. There were two channels of such appointments—the Indian Civil Service and the leading lawyers. With a few exceptions, the judges of High Courts in British India had a reputation for integrity and competence. If anyone faltered, it was due to his innate weaknesses and shortcomings and not because of lack of qualification at the time of appointment. The quality of the judgments was high. The judges generally led secluded lives, carefully avoiding any allegations of bias or favouritism. It is in this perspective that Pakistan, in its first Constitution in 1956, adopted the system of judicial appointments prevalent during the times of British India.

The Chief Justice of the Supreme Court was appointed by the President and other judges of the Supreme Court were appointed by the President after consultation with the Chief Justice. The Chief Justice of the High Court was appointed by the President in consultation with the Chief Justice of Pakistan and the Governor of the concerned province. Other judges of the High Court were appointed by the President in consultation with the Chief Justice of Pakistan, the Governor of the concerned province, and the Chief Justice of the concerned High Court. These provisions of the Constitution of 1956 were more or less repeated in the Constitutions of 1962 and 1973. The process of appointment of High Court judges has, in practice, worked in this manner. The Chief Justice of a High Court initiates the process by preparing a list of names consisting of leading advocates in the province and senior judicial officers amongst the subordinate judiciary whom he recommends for appointment as judges. This file is then forwarded to the Governor of the province (of course, through the Chief Minister) who adds his own comments and recommendations thereon. The file is then sent to the federal law ministry, from where it goes to the Chief Justice of Pakistan.

The Chief Justice makes his own comments and recommendations on the proposed names (or perhaps adds new names) before sending it back to the federal law ministry. The law ministry then sents the file to the Prime Minister and finally to the President. The rationale behind this system was that the Chief Justices of the concerned High

Courts and the Supreme Court were in a better position to assess the ability, reputation, and integrity of advocates appearing before them and of the members of the subordinate judiciary working under them. The participation of executives like the President (and the Prime Minister) and Governors of the provinces (and their Chief Ministers) was to ensure that there were no negative reports about the recommendees relating to their personal integrity and loyalty to the nation. The presumption behind this system is that all the constitutional functionaries involved in the process are fair and impartial, free from personal interest, bias or prejudice, capable of applying objective standards, and committed to the independence of the judiciary. Unfortunately, our historical experience in this regard establishes that such rationales and presumptions have eroded or ceased to exist over the years and the constitutional functionaries involved have repeatedly misused their powers. Unfortunately, the system has been corrupted over the years by State functionaries. The chief justices concerned have often used the system to get their relatives or favourites appointed to high office. Constitutional functionaries from the executive involved in the process have used it to have their own favourites and the members of their own political parties appointed.

The slide started, in particular, during the government of Ayub who made a number of judicial appointments on political or personal considerations. Ayub appointed a member of the National Assembly to the High Court in return for his vote on a matter which was highly sensitive to the government in power and a brother of a prominent politician who had helped him in the presidential election of 1965 as judge of a West Pakistan High Court. Another judge was appointed on the recommendation of a *pir* of Ayub. He used to hold interviews for the recommendees which led to arbitrary and highly subjective selections. Ayub also became susceptible to political pressure. At times, groups of politicians from his party prevailed upon him to make appointments of people they recommended.

Not many judicial appointments were made during the martial law regime of Yahya. There was hardly any improvement in the time of Bhutto. His government dealt with the judiciary with a heavy hand which was expected to commit itself to the goals of the government in power. The responsibility for the Fifth Amendment did not lie entirely with Bhutto, but some members of the judiciary also contributed to it. The Chief Justice of the Lahore High Court at that time, Sardar Muhammad Iqbal, wanted to continue as chief justice and repeatedly refused elevation to the Supreme Court. The judge next to him in seniority, Maulvi Mushtaq Husain, also refused elevation to the Supreme Court with his eyes on the office of Chief Justice of the Lahore High Court. Judges of the Lahore High Court junior to both of them were being elevated to the Supreme Court and a bad precedent was being established. The Court was rife with factionalism with each of them promoting their respective favourites among the judges and members of the Bar.

In 1975, there were protests from the representatives of the Bar against favouritism and unjust enrichment of the relatives of judges who were practising at the Bar. Instead of taking corrective steps and tolerating criticism which was not untrue and reflected the feelings of a majority of members of the Bar, the judges tried to crush the criticism by using the weapon of law of contempt of court, sentencing the representatives of the bar to terms in prison. The government took advantage of the situation in order to weaken and undermine the independence of the judiciary by introducing the Fifth Amendment in the Constitution, limiting the term of office for Chief Justices of the Supreme Court and the High Courts to a fixed period. The only redeeming feature of the struggle was a new law of contempt of court which softened the rigours of the previous law and allowed critical but fair comments on judgments and the judicial system made in temperate language.

The real trial of the judiciary began during Zia. In the beginning, there was a marriage of convenience between the Martial Law regime and the superior courts. The chief justices were appointed acting governors of their respective provinces. The Chief Justice of the Lahore High Court, who had presided over the Bench which sentenced Bhutto to death, was given a free hand in the appointment of judges. This power was grossly abused. He got two batches of nine additional judges each appointed in the years 1978 and 1979. Barring a few of them who deserved such appointment on merit, others were unknown lawyers. Most of them were his former associates or favourites whom he wanted to promote in order to strengthen his group within the Lahore High Court. These groups met a tragic end because, by the time these appointees were ripe for confirmation/appointment as permanent judges, Chief Justice Maulvi Mushtaq had fallen from favour with the Martial Law regime and had been unceremoniously removed and replaced by Justice Shamim Hussain Qadri, who was hostile to him and his appointees.[5] Out of eighteen appointees, only eight (including four who were drawn from the subordinate judiciary) were confirmed. Thus, only four out of the fourteen lawyers appointed in these two batches, were confirmed as permanent judges.

This was followed by the Provisional Constitution Order of 1981 which rendered the judiciary totally worthless. A number of self-respecting judges did not take the oath and went into retirement. Some of the others whom the Martial Law regime regarded as antagonistic or independent were sacked by not being invited to take oath. The terms of the oath were extremely humiliating, but Zia was confident that they would submit to any terms, howsoever humiliating they may be, to continue in office. This situation led to a race amongst ambitious lawyers to get into the good books of the generals who could help appoint them as judges.

One *mofussil* lawyer who had hardly appeared before the High Court but was a friend of the governor, was appointed judge. It became a practice with Zia not to appoint permanent chief justices of the Supreme Court and the High Courts. In this way, he thought he could control the judiciary better. At a given point in time, all the superior courts in the country were headed by Acting Chief Justices.

During Martial Law, politicians lost all influence in the matter of appointment of judges. In their place, judges, whether serving or retired, had close relations with Zia and his military *junta*. This power was exercised without any regard to the dignity and independence of the judiciary. Judges planned the careers of their sons or sons-in-law and got their relatives appointed as Assistant Advocates-General or Additional Advocates-General. They were then promoted to Advocates-General or Additional

Advocates-General, thus paving the way to their appointment as judges of the High Courts. For relatives who had become somewhat senior in the legal profession, appointment as Deputy Attorney-General was preferred as a stepping stone to appointment as a High Court judge. In this way, the offices of the Attorney General and Advocates-General became nurseries and launching pads for appointment to the superior courts that were restricted to the near relatives of the judges and other influential men. After the lifting of Martial Law and during the government of Junejo, the situation improved a little bit.[6]

The practice of appointing Acting Chief Justices was once again resorted to in the Lahore High Court. The retiring Chief Justice was appointed as a Supreme Court judge in the first place and was then sent back to the High Court as Acting Chief Justice. This obviously caused great resentment amongst other judges, particularly those who were next in line awaiting appointment as chief justice, but the government in power wanted to ensure that the Court remained in the hands of someone it considered reliable.

During the first government of Ms Benazir Bhutto, practically no appointments were made to the judiciary. There was a tug of war between the President and the Prime Minister at that time on this issue. The President was of the view that the power to appoint judges was his, but the Prime Minister insisted that the President was bound under the Constitution to accept her advice in this matter. The question was raised and remained pending for some time before the Supreme Court but no decision was made as the federal government withdrew the appeal pending before the Court, presumably under pressure from Ishaq. The first Nawaz Sharif government (1990–1993) also made no improvement on this. The chief justices had their own favourites appointed and the politicians their own. Generally, a deal was struck between the constitutional functionaries involved in this process accommodating their respective favourites.[7]

Efforts were made to win over the loyalty of the judges by allotting them residential plots from discretionary quotas and by offering them other material benefits. During this period, there were a number of constitutional cases decided by the Supreme Court and the High Courts and the decisions generally went against the People's Party. Ms Benazir Bhutto, then leader of the opposition, publicly denounced the method of appointment of judges and demanded that it be radically reformed so that people of independent opinion and disposition were appointed. She supported the idea of a parliamentary committee to verify the credentials of the nominees before appointment, giving the right of public hearing to members of the Bar and the public. It was indeed a progressive idea with the potential of making the entire process open and transparent. This idea formed part of the manifesto of the PPP in the general elections of 1993. Unfortunately, when the PPP came back into power, this promise to the nation was conveniently forgotten.

It appears that Benazir was advised against it on the grounds that it would require a constitutional amendment. Another factor was the ambition of members of the party who sought appointment as judges without going through a screening process. Their argument was that they had been waiting for sixteen long years while their political opponents had been getting appointed. If their political opponents had not been through any screening procedures, they reasoned, why should they? Eventually, the PPP government took to the path that had been adopted by its predecessors and even went overboard. Out of a large number of appointments made to the superior Courts in 1994 and 1995, a majority were made either for political considerations or were based on nepotism and favouritism.[8] Several appointees were not qualified for appointment as judges since they had not practised as advocates and only remained enrolled as such or, if they had practised, then they had not completed ten years of practice. There was also wholesale interference with the independence of the judiciary. The practice of appointing Acting Chief Justices to the High Courts and ad hoc judges to the Supreme Court, generally associated with Zia, was liberally resorted to. In the appointment of Chief Justice of the Supreme Court, a forty-year-long convention of appointing the senior-most judge as Chief Justice was dispensed with. The judges in disfavour were banished to the Federal Shariat Court. Most of the additional judges who were appointed during the first Nawaz government, were not confirmed. In retaliation, Nawaz Sharif threatened to throw out those judges who had been appointed during Benazir's government. Judges thus became pawns on the political chess-board.

The Supreme Court, in its judgment in the case of Al Jehad Trust,[9] tried to correct the situation which was going out of hand. From 1994 to 1996, three out of the four High Courts were headed by Additional Chief Justices, two of them drawn from the Supreme Court. During 1995–1996, there were seven ad hoc judges in the Supreme Court as against nine permanent judges. Thus, nearly half of the strength of the Supreme Court was manned by ad hoc judges. The Supreme Court condemned the practice of appointment of Acting Chief Justices of High Courts and ad hoc judges of the Supreme Court and upheld the expectation of the senior-most judge of a Court to be appointed as Chief Justice to be a legitimate one.

The Supreme Court thus terminated all ad hoc appointments to the Supreme Court and directed the government to appoint permanent Chief Justices of High Courts within thirty days. The judgment declared all the appointments to the High Courts made on the recommendations of Acting Chief Justices as invalid and unconstitutional and the Chief Justices of the High Courts were directed to initiate a process within thirty days of the judgment. It goes without saying that this judgment restored some prestige, respect, and credibility to the judiciary.

Although it brought the judiciary into conflict with the executive, it enjoyed widespread public support and was appreciated as a sign of the independence of the judiciary. Only time will tell if the judiciary continues on this course or relapses into its unhappy past of being a pliable tool of government. Some of the appointments made after the judgment do not conform to the standards laid down in the judgment.

This résumé of the history of the judiciary, particularly in reference to the appointment of judges, has been given to trace the gradual degeneration of this institution in Pakistan. The system of appointment of judges is of paramount importance for the independence of the judiciary because it is human resources that make or mar any institution. It is the integrity and competence of judges that ensures credibility and public confidence in the institution which has, unfortunately, eroded over the years. Every successive government has contributed to its degeneration and decline. Short-term considerations of having pliable judges has weighed more with every succeeding government than the long-term need of an independent judiciary. In this process, there are no heroes. Not only have the politicians failed the judiciary, but even the judges have undermined the institution.

The judges have generally offered no serious resistance to any government trying to undermine the judiciary as an institution. The judges who were superceded did not resign in protest. Those who were sent to the Federal Shariat Court have meekly submitted to the maltreatment. The perks and privileges of office matter more to them than the ultimate good of the institution to which they belong. Even giving a free hand to the chief justices in the matter of appointment of judges is not without difficulty. It has been noticed that, in the past, Chief Justices have not acquitted themselves well. They have used this authority to promote their own relatives, favourites, or colleagues. There is little to choose between political appointees on the one hand and relatives and favourites of the judges on the other. All such appointments have been for the wrong reason. Despite this, it cannot be denied that a number of people who have served as judges were of some merit. They have sustained the system, but merit was accidental rather than an objective in such cases. If some political appointees or relatives of the judges have developed into good judges, it was only due to their individual capabilities and merit. The system has not required them to do so.

The discussion on this issue would not be complete without mention of the Supreme Judicial Council. In several countries, including the United States of America, India, and Pakistan under the 1956 Constitution, the power of impeachment of judges is conferred in Parliament. The idea of a Supreme Judicial Council was the brain-child of the late Manzoor Qadir who believed that a council of senior judges would be most appropriate for the accountability of judges. He thought that such a Council would ensure the independence of the judiciary.

Therefore, the idea of a Supreme Judicial Council was adopted in the 1962 and 1973 Constitutions of Pakistan, consisting of five judges; with the Chief Justice of Pakistan as its chairman, two senior-most judges of the Supreme Court and two senior-most judges of the High Courts. In our experience of the last thirty-six years with this Council, it has been found that the idea did not succeed in practice. It has failed to regulate and discipline the judges for which it was primarily meant and has degenerated into a judges club meant primarily to protect rather than punish judges for their wrongdoings. It has only dealt with three cases in all these years, and these also during the times of Martial Law, which smacked of victimization. It is time that the Supreme Judicial Council is done away with and replaced by a Judicial Commission composed of judges, members of Parliament, including those from the opposition and representatives of the Bar.

This situation is all the more unfortunate in a country where the police is corrupt and brutal and the administration indifferent. In these circumstances, the judiciary necessarily becomes the last resort and hope for the common citizen and if the institution loses its credibility, then it is indeed tragic. At least, in the matter of appointment of judges, political parties would lay aside their differences and evolve an objective and credible method which should ensure that the process is open and transparent. Since the process has been secretive over the years, it has given rise to serious abuses and malpractices. A lid has been kept over the entire system in which rank opportunism, favouritism, nepotism, and political patronage have flourished. In order to restore credibility to the system, the judiciary should be exorcized of these demons. The entire system may have to be radically restructured for this purpose. However, it cannot be denied that the judiciary in Pakistan has been repeatedly called upon to perform an exceptionally difficult task.

Due to the lack of political stability in the country, irresponsible governments, frequent martial laws, and constitutional interruptions, the judiciary has been burdened with the task of determining questions which in a stable constitutional set-up would be left to the politicians and parliamentarians to resolve. The courts have been repeatedly obliged to decide difficult issues of validity of dissolution of Assemblies or the legitimacy of a martial law regime. The exercise of decision-making in such cases becomes all the more cumbersome when the courts are under threat and individual judges are faced with the prospect of being relieved from office by an authoritarian and unscrupulous government. Oftentimes there have been physical threats to them and to their families. Such conditions are hardly conducive to the impartial and just administration of justice. It is indeed the failure of the political system that unjustly burdens the judiciary with the resolution of issues that belong to the realm of the political process and not the judicial one. It is generally believed that the judiciary in Pakistan has always gone along with the establishment. The judgments in the Moulvi Tamizuddin and Dosso cases are generally cited in support of this allegation. Asma Jilani's case hardly helps because it was delivered long after the military dictator had been overthrown. In three out of four cases of dissolution of the National Assembly and dismissal of government, it is alleged that they were not restored because the establishment did not wish it. The only time when the National Assembly and the government were restored by the Supreme Court, it is believed, the establishment was divided over the President's action. This situation provided opportunity to the Supreme Court to act independently.[10]

> The Courts thus confront two worlds concurrently. Their role is to interpret the state's constitutive framework for the polity and to provide the citizens with the opportunity to voice their opinion and redress their grievances—a responsibility in the first instance to the polity. Were the source of state sovereignty firmly based in the people, this role would be primarily hermeneutic, deciphering meaning from contexts of intent and effect. But because the polity has so often been divorced from the state, the judicial role has been more conflictual than judges would like or occasionally are willing to recognize.
>
> The courts have developed over the last half century of Pakistan's existence as arenas for relatively open political debate. As institutions of judgment, however, they more often support than challenge state power. Those who approach the courts in political cases are keen to dissent, and their desire to be heard can override their faith in the results; the means are more important than the end, and in the same way, are the end. At the same

> time, the politically aggrieved have turned to the courts not only to provide relief against an unsympathetic state, but also to find a way to express alternative constitutions, polities and parties.[11]

In such an environment, the judiciary has become an intensely controversial institution. The courts bear the burden of constitutional and political developments beyond their share and role in the State. They have frequently been made into scapegoats by political parties for their own failures and mistakes. The courts have more often than not become part of the tug of war between the forces that control State power and those opposed to them. These forces also perceive the role of the courts according to their respective needs. Those in power would like the courts to exercise judicial restraint and those in opposition would want the courts to have an activist role. Those in power would like the courts to be committed to their goals and those in opposition would want to see them independent, as a check on the excessive or abusive exercise of authority. No wonder, every government in office tends to appoint chief justices or judges of the superior courts with the understanding that their judgments would not destabilize the government. This is why the independence of the judicial organ has always been in jeopardy. It is ironic that the judiciary, manned by people whose appointments have generally been made on considerations other than merit, are called upon to decide basic questions relating to the State structure or the future to the State itself. These are the constraints and vicissitudes that the judiciary in Pakistan has gone through in the last fifty years. The independence of the judiciary has been a myth rather than a reality. Successive governments and members of the judiciary have caused incalculable harm to the institution.

Its role has at times been relegated from that of an organ of the State to that of a department of government. It has been the object of manipulation by the executive and is perceived by the people as docile. Its assertion of independence in the judges' case was a ray of hope for the citizens. The hope proved to be short-lived and was dashed soon afterwards when the Supreme Court stood divided against itself and the chief justice was overthrown. This short-lived change was just an episode in the judicial history of Pakistan. The perception of docility continues to mar the image of the judiciary.

Role of the Military: Meddling in Politics?

The armed forces are raised and equipped to defend the country from external aggression. They are supposed to have no political role and are required to take orders from the civilian authorities that work under the Constitution. They are not generally allowed any special role in a democratic Constitution. Countries with a democratic tradition have endeavoured hard to establish the subordination of the armed forces to civilian authorities. President Truman of the USA is credited with the firm decision to sack a great general and a war hero, General McArthur, in 1951 for insubordination during the Korean war. It is said that 'war is too important to be left to generals alone'.

The basic reason is that the armed forces are not trained to take political decisions and military solutions are certainly not conducive to the settlement of internal or even international disputes. The final answers to internal problems are political, and to foreign aggression diplomacy. Unfortunately, third world countries generally have failed to establish the supremacy of civilian authority over the armed forces with the result that military coups became commonplace all over the third world. Pakistan is one of the rank examples of domination of the armed forces in the affairs of the State. It all began in 1954 when Governor-General Ghulam Muhammad offered Ayub, Commander-in-Chief of the Army, to impose martial law and take over the administration of the country. Ayub first refused but later accepted a place in the Cabinet of Muhammad Ali Bogra in 1954 as defence minister. This was the turning point in the history of Pakistan when the leadership of the armed forces started considering the option of taking over power through a *coup d 'etat* and Ayub made no secret of it in his political autobiography *Friends not Masters*.

In October 1958, the decisive step was taken, martial law was imposed, and the Constitution was abrogated. From then onwards, governments have functioned and affairs of the State have been run under the shadow of the military, either by directly taking over State power or by indirectly throwing its weight around to accomplish its desired objectives. It has already been discussed in detail how three martial laws were imposed, their impact on national affairs, and disruptions in the constitution. There is no doubt in the public mind that it is the power that matters most in national affairs. It calls all the shots and has the final say on principal matters of national concern. It is pathetic to note that civilian authority over the years has meekly submitted to the domination of military authority.

The post-Zia stand-off in the civilian military relationship deserves mention at some length. For many years, Zia insisted on a constitutional role for the armed forces in the affairs of the State. He perhaps had the Turkish model in mind, wherein the armed forces are assigned a role under Article 118 of the Turkish Constitution.[12] The argument frequently given in favour of such a role is that modern Turkey owes its existence and independence to the armed struggle waged by its armed forces led by Kamal Ataturk against invaders and alien intruders at the end of the First World War.

This rationale does not apply to Pakistan where independence came as a result of a popular struggle and mass movement of Muslims in India for their homeland, led by Jinnah and his political party, the Muslim League. In this perspective, assigning any constitutional role to the armed forces in Pakistan should have been anathema not only to democracy but also to the history of its freedom movement. Zia translated his idea into practice by providing for the establishment of a National Security Council which would include the Chairman Joint Chiefs of Staff Committee and the three chiefs of the armed forces. This was introduced under the RCO but later dropped under the Eighth Amendment. Nevertheless, the RCO had made other provisions regarding the armed forces which included, (a) supreme command of Armed Forces to vest in the President and (b) discretionary appointment by the President of the Chairman, Joint Chiefs of Staff Committee, and the three chiefs of the armed forces. These provisions were retained under the Eighth Amendment. The office of president was thus made preponderant *vis-à-vis* the prime minister because the appointment of leader of the armed forces was now in his hand. After Zia's death, who contained in himself the offices of the President and Chief of Army Staff, the position changed. The armed forces had tasted power and were not willing to give it up. Mirza Aslam Beg, who became Chief of Army Staff, supported the transition of power under the Constitution to Ishaq but also extracted the price of power sharing with a final say in matters of national importance. This power-sharing arrangement was never addressed in writing but it emerged as a reality. It has been given the name of a 'troika' between the President, the Prime Minister, and the Chief of Army Staff.

A decisive role was played by the armed forces in the events of 1993 by forbidding the Rangers to execute the proclamation of emergency in the Punjab by the Joint Houses of Parliament to help the federal government take over the provincial administration in Punjab. It was the leadership of the armed forces that brokered the arrangement between the President and the Prime Minister which led to the resignation of the Prime Minister, the dissolution of the National Assembly, and the resignation of the President. What Zia failed to achieve directly has been accomplished indirectly through the decisive role of the armed forces in the affairs of State.

It is unfortunate that even Benazir, who has the pretensions of having the support of the masses as her power base rather than the backing of the armed forces, easily capitulated to this arrangement. She visited the armed forces headquarters before and after becoming the prime minister and involved the Chief of Army Staff in decision-making in matters of national importance. She left no doubt in the minds of anyone that the military has the superior role in decision-making. The Thirteenth Amendment wresting the discretionary power of the President to dissolve the National Assembly under Article 58(2)(b) and to appoint Chairman Joint Chiefs of Staff Committee and Chiefs of Army, Naval, and Air Staff has certainly given a major jolt to the troika. The office of President was the medium through which leaders of the armed forces could force their will and control governments. After the weakening of the office of the President, the military establishment will have to find new channels for the exercise of its will.

Role of the Bureaucracy: Masters or Servants of the People?

Since its birth, Pakistan has been governed by its bureaucratic, military, and political elites. The bureaucratic elite gradually became more assertive, steadily increasing their power at the expense of the political elite. An important contributory factor in this development was the fact that, at an early stage in the history of Pakistan, some erstwhile bureaucrats helped themselves to the high state offices of Governor-General and Prime Minister. They brought with them the tradition, outlook, and attitudes typical of bureaucrats, and their sympathies were slanted towards the bureaucracy rather than towards political institutions. The military governments installed in 1958, 1969, and 1977 had to fall back on civil bureaucracy, further strengthening its power. At the same time, the civil bureaucracy has suffered noticeable decline over the years in its standards, traditions, and professionalism. It is now characterized by inefficiency, irresponsibility, and corruption.

The bureaucracy in Pakistan can trace its origin to the year 1792 when the East India Company, having acquired Diwani of Bengal, Bihar, and Orissa, started revenue collection and administration of justice through its own employees. The Company organized its administrative agency for this purpose. Under the East India Company Act, 1793, the Company formulated rules and procedures for appointment to service and other terms and conditions of service of its employees such as, seniority, promotion, and retirement benefits. The Act divided the service into two groups: covenanted and uncovenanted. The term 'civil service' was used for the first time by the East India Company for its civilian employees in contra-distinction to military forces which the Company maintained to defend its fortifications and carry out offensive operations in pursuit of its economic interests. Civil servants were put to extensive training in administration. For this purpose, Fort William College was established in Calcutta in 1800. Six years later, the Company shifted its training programme to England and opened its own training institution, called Hailebury College. Thenceforth, trainees were sent to England for a two year course in the arts and humanities. The Fort William College, continued to offer training in oriental languages. After the transfer of authority from the Company to the British Crown in 1858, Hailebury was closed down and a new system of recruitment to the service was put in place.

This new system was the selection of candidates in England through a competitive examination held by the Public Service Commission. Key posts, both in the executive and in the judicial departments were reserved for members of the Indian Civil Service who were almost entirely Englishmen. In 1870, with a view to giving the service an Indian flavour, the British Crown created a new 'statutory civil service' recruited from amongst the Indians. This class of civil servants was assigned middle grade positions in the executive and judicial branches of administration.

On the recommendation of the Aitchison Commission in 1887, the British government reorganized the Indian Civil Service into two classes, namely, the Imperial Civil Service (ICS) and Provincial Civil Service (PCS). The former consisted predominantly of Englishmen recruited in England and the latter consisted of Indians and European residents of India. The ICS was a *corps d'élite* enjoying higher prestige and occupying key positions with higher emoluments and better terms and conditions of service. The PCS were assigned subordinate posts and made to operate under the administrative control of the ICS. As the demand for Indianization of the service increased, the British government took steps to enhance the induction of Indians into the civil service. For this purpose, it reserved the lower posts for the natives.

On the recommendations of the Islington Commission (1915), the British government divided the service into two classes, Class I and II. Class I Officers were defined as those who held positions at executive or administrative levels and Class II officers as those who held posts at operational levels. Each class was to be recruited separately. This policy enabled the Indians to enter the civil service in greater numbers but their rise to higher posts was still difficult, and overall control of the administration lay in the hands of British ICS officers. Some natives did make it to higher posts but their number was very small and they were given these positions only after they had undergone a complete transformation in personality and character through intensive training at British institutions. The policy of reserving important posts for ICS officers and maintaining their firm hold over the civil service establishment was supported by the Report of the Simon Commission (1930).

Simon justified this policy in view of increased communal tension in India which, he observed, necessitated intelligent and impartial handling of the situation. This policy was obviously suited to the colonial government because its ICS officers controlled the entire civil administration in India and its loyalty was beyond question. It was through its civil service that the British government maintained a stronghold over Indian affairs—administrative, political, and social. The civil service of India was instrumental in sustaining colonial rule, the rule by so few over so many for so long. This service played its role effectively and efficiently. Its members were known for their honesty, integrity, and dedication to work.

After independence, the civil service of Pakistan continued the same system of colonial administration. It retained the same class structure, the same elite character and the same colonial pattern of administration. The All Pakistan Services consisted of various services, prominent among them being the Civil Service (called CSP) and Police Service (known as PSP). The CSP, regarding itself as the successor of the former ICS, retained its elite character and was the most pampered, patronized, and protected class of civil servants.

Following the tradition of its predecessors, CSP officers continued to hold top positions in the Service hierarchy. All important positions at the highest level—federal, provincial, and even autonomous bodies and corporations were reserved for members of this service. The number of Muslims in the superior services in British India was very limited. Due to better educational opportunities and encouragement by their colonial masters, Hindus took most of the positions in the superior services in British India, particularly the civil service, police service, audits and accounts, income tax, and customs and excise services. The departure of Hindu administrators from the areas that formed part of Pakistan left a void in the administrative structure in the newly formed state. Pakistan, therefore, encouraged all Muslims in the erstwhile superior services of British India, whether serving or already retired, to opt for or come to Pakistan and fill in the administrative void. This situation gave an opportunity to senior civil servants who had opted for Pakistan not only to fill in higher administrative posts, but also to keep an eye on high political offices, particularly since the Muslim League, which was more of a political movement, did not have a trained cadre to occupy high political positions in the area of finance and commerce.

The above situation led to the entry of higher civil servants into positions like that of finance minister to bureaucrats. Chaudhri Mohammad Ali, Malik Ghulam Muhammad, and Iskandar Mirza came into politics through that gateway. Once they got into cabinet positions, they had an opportunity through manoeuvre and intrigue to move into higher positions like those of Governors-General and Prime Minister. They could sense the weaknesses of the political party structure and political leaders which opened a gate for bureaucratic intrigue and manipulation, particularly when there was internal cohesion amongst senior bureaucrats.

It is common knowledge that Ghulam Muhammad and Iskandar Mirza played havoc with the constitutional and political infrastructure in the initial years of Pakistan. The country has paid a very heavy price in the form of repeated martial laws and other constitutional and political upheavals on account of their doings. The traumatic conditions at the time of independence coupled with the ongoing tension with India followed by political crisis in the country, left very little time and energy with the government to devise and execute any major overhaul of the administrative system in Pakistan. All that could be done was to commission a few studies and write a few reports on the subject.

First of all the Pay and Services Commission, headed by Justice Muhammad Munir, the Chief Justice of the Lahore High Court, submitted its report in 1948. This was followed by three reports, one by Rowland Edgar in 1953, another by Bernard Cladieus in 1955, and the third one by Paul Becket in 1957. This was again followed by the Report of Pay and Services Commission (1959–62), headed by Justice A.R. Cornelius, the then Chief Justice of Pakistan. All these reports emphasized the need for reforming the outmoded administrative system in Pakistan.

Successive governments have either ignored the recommendations contained in these studies or adopted them only marginally. Consequently, the civil service of Pakistan, both structurally as well as functionally, retained its colonial character. It continued to be imperialistic, elitist, and arrogant. The fact that the people had attained freedom and the country had become independent had little or no effect on the style, attitude, and attributes of the bureaucrat. During the Ayub government, the civil service was at the peak of its powers and privileges. They administered Pakistan in the manner of colonial rulers. Since a majority of the civil servants were drawn from West Pakistan, their manner and style of governance completely alienated the East Pakistanis. They became one of the major causes for the secession of East Pakistan. Even in West Pakistan, there was widespread resentment against them and the people demanded extensive reforms in the civil administrative structure. It was in this perspective that Bhutto introduced a new package of administrative reforms in 1973. These reforms were in two parts; first, change in the structure of the bureaucracy; and second, change in the law affecting the civil service. The salient features of the structural reforms were as follows:

1. The abolition of service labels such as CSP and PSP;
2. The abolition of classes, namely, Class I, II, III, and IV.
3. The merger of all services and cadres into a Single Unified Grade Structure;
4. The introduction of unified 23 grade National Pay Scales;
5. Provision for lateral entry into government service for talented individuals from the private sector;
6. Eligibility for horizontal movement from one post/cadre to another; and
7. A commitment to introduce scientific career planning on the basis of merit, job description, and evaluation.

These changes were of a comprehensive nature and broad implications transformed the hierarchy of the civil service. The service was given a new complexion and orientation. The philosophy behind the reforms was to create a public-oriented administration, efficient and professional in outlook and responsive and accountable to the people. The reforms were accompanied by constitutional and legislative measures aimed at creating a new legal structure for the civil service.

The new measures had two prominent features: one, the previous practice of providing constitutional guarantees and safeguards as to tenure and other terms and conditions of service of the civil servants was dispensed with and the Parliament or the provincial legislatures were empowered to deal with the terms and conditions of the service of the government servants; and, two, administrative tribunals were established to decide cases involving the terms and conditions of service of the civil servants including disciplinary matters. The implementation of Bhutto's service reforms altered the cadre system of the bureaucracy in several important ways. The CSP class was abolished and its membership was dispersed into the newly created District Management Group, Tribal Areas Group, and the Secretariat Group. The practice of designating non-CSP officers as 'listed post holders' in the All Pakistan Service was also abolished. As a consequence, the centuries-old practice of the reservation of posts for members of the CSP and other elite services was discontinued.

The former accounts services (PAAS, PMAS, and PRAS) were merged into a single Accounts Group. Finally, the composition of the Pakistan Foreign Service (PFS) was greatly modified and expanded to form the Foreign Affairs Group. In each of these instances, the cadre system as it was inherited from the British and as it developed since independence was significantly modified. Given the previous impervious nature of the cadre system, such modification was indeed 'revolutionary'.

The reform of the cadre system left the overall scheme of Pakistan's administrative system unaltered and the organization of the bureaucracy into semi-functional occupational groups has persisted. The promotional prospects and relative status of officers are still determined pre-ponderantly by group affiliation. The reforms did not modify the contractual importance of the cadre system to the bureaucracy of Pakistan nor did it challenge the nature of the cadre system *per se,* but only modified the prevailing relationship between the membership of different cadres. The net result is that the colonial structure of the services, although modified, did not change materially. Its relationship with the common citizen continues to be that of the rulers and the ruled. The reforms, though radical on paper, could not render the administrative structure a public oriented service. Some of the reasons for this failure are discussed below.

The idea of lateral entry into the services at every level was very good provided it was pursued properly and honestly. A few lateral entry examinations were held but their standards left much to be desired. At the end of the day, most of the selectees appeared to have been taken on the consideration of favouritism, nepotism, or *sifarish.* Most of the selectees had the backing of one politician or the other. Several other selections for lateral entry were made even without the formalities of holding any competitive examination. Loyalty to the People's Party became a criterion for selection into such sensitive services like the police service or the foreign service. Thus, the idea of getting talent on merit from the private sector through lateral entry degenerated into the formation of a *sifarish* group of government servants mostly composed of the incompetent and inefficient who knew well that they did not owe their selection to merit. The old CSP and other superior services cadre had not taken the service reforms with favour and were completely hostile to lateral entry into what they regarded as their exclusive domain. They still retained a good deal of internal cohesion and did everything to discredit and defame the bureaucratic reforms and those inducted through lateral entry. They had a stake in undoing these reforms. Thus, a fine idea was killed by its defective application.

Bhutto's government did not last long enough to implement its own reforms. Zia, who overthrew him in 1977, was hostile to everything that was associated with Bhutto. He, therefore, took steps to undo the bureaucratic reforms introduced by Bhutto and in this endeavour, he was fully helped and encouraged by the erstwhile CSP class, which had a personal grievance against these reforms. Members of this class held important positions under Zia and went ahead with his blessing to demolish the structure which Bhutto had tried to build through bureaucratic reforms.

It is the necessity of all military regimes to depend upon the civil bureaucracy. Such regimes have no public support and need the expertise of the civil services to run the affairs of the country. The civil bureaucracy thus becomes most powerful during military governments. These regimes give opportunity to the civil bureaucracy to add to its powers and privileges and assume the character of a ruling class. Zia's government offered an opportunity to the higher civil bureaucracy to reorganize itself to regain its former colonial character.

There was an influx of military officers into the civil bureaucracy during Zia's government. It was considered a matter of great fortune for a young military officer to be inducted into the civil bureaucracy, particularly into District Management and Police Service groups. Such inductions generally went to close relatives of the generals or those who happened to win their favours. The induction has continued even after Zia, but its percentage has gone down.

Even during pseudo-democratic governments, the powers of the bureaucracy have not in any way dwindled. Political parties that come to power do not have trained cadres for higher or even medium level administrative positions. The ministers are generally inexperienced and corrupt and regard their office as an opportunity to make money. To accomplish this they need the advice and help of bureaucrats serving under them. This provides an opening to the bureaucrats to help themselves to a lion's share in the money being made in this manner. This unfortunate development has led to further degeneration and corruption in the bureaucratic cadre. Honest and well-intentioned bureaucrats are relegated to unimportant and ineffective positions and are eventually weeded out of service. After fifty years of independence, the bureaucracy continues to have the character of a ruling class neither responsive nor accountable to the people. The change it has undergone is only for the worse for it has ceased to be a professional, efficient, or dedicated outfit and has degenerated into a highly corrupt and inefficient force lacking in dedication and purpose that is oppressive and callous in its approach. The bureaucracy in Pakistan believes and practises the belief that it is meant to rule and not to serve the people.

Issue of Provincial Autonomy

Since the creation of Pakistan, there has been a continuing debate on the grant of autonomy to the provinces. At the time of independence, there were three provinces in the western wing of the country and one in the eastern wing. Punjab, a very large province of British India, was divided into two, the western part coming to Pakistan. Sindh, which was part of the Bombay Presidency until 1937, became a separate province under the Government of India Act, 1935 on the basis of a long standing demand of Indian Muslims. The North-West Frontier Province (NWFP) had been a separate province in which there was an anti-Muslim League government at the time of independence and a referendum was held in the province to determine whether the people wanted to join either Pakistan or India. Subsequently, Balochistan, with a large territory and very small population was also recognized as a separate province of Pakistan which raised the number of provinces in the western wing to four. East Pakistan consisted of the eastern part of the large province of Bengal in British India which, like Punjab, was partitioned along communal lines.

The eastern part, named East Bengal, with a predominant Muslim population, became the fifth province of Pakistan. This situation gave rise to a strange anomaly. East Bengal, a single province, had 55 per cent of the total population but only 15 per cent of the total land area of Pakistan. The four provinces in West Pakistan had 85 per cent of the land area, but a minority of the population accounting for 45 per cent of the total population of Pakistan. This situation made the task of the constitution-makers very difficult. They had to grapple with various equations regarding the representation of the provinces in Parliament, balancing the lopsidedness of the population on the one hand, and safeguarding the interest and identity of the provinces on the other.

This situation was also faced by the constitution-makers of the United States in 1787. Out of the original thirteen states forming the federation, three or four were very large ones, like New York, Virginia, and Pennsylvania, and three or four very small states like Rhode Island, New Hampshire, and Vermont. Other states fell between the two. The larger states demanded representation in the federal legislature on the basis of population and the smaller ones asserted that each state should be given equal representation on the basis of separate individual identity. The argument was that each state was autonomous and was voluntarily joining the federation on the basis of equality. This difficulty was resolved through a constitutional compromise which satisfied everyone. The Congress (federal legislature of the USA) was made bicameral. In the Upper House, or the Senate, all the States were given equal representation, that is, two Senators were to be elected from each State.

In the Lower House, the House of Representatives, representation was given on the basis of population. Hence, the smaller states had equal weightage with the larger ones in the Upper House and larger states had greater weightage in the Lower House. This is very much like the situation that presented itself to the first Constituent Assembly of Pakistan.

The First Constituent Assembly, in its long deliberations spread over seven years, discussed various solutions and contemplated the idea of a bicameral legislature with greater representation to East Pakistan in the Lower House, that is, the National Assembly, according to the ratio of population and greater representation to West Pakistan in the Upper House giving equal representation to each of the provinces without any consideration of the size and population. Ultimately, the matter was resolved by the second Constituent Assembly after the merger of the four provinces of West Pakistan into one unit, thus forming a single province of West Pakistan. The Constituent Assembly agreed on parity between the two provinces, one larger in size and the other greater in population. Under the 1956 Constitution, a unicameral legislature was provided with an equal number of seats to East and West Pakistan.

The Constitution of 1962 also adopted the principle of parity between the two provinces of East and West Pakistan. When the Constituent Assembly met for framing the Constitution of 1973, the problem of striking a balance between the eastern and western wings had ceased to exist due to the unfortunate secession of East Pakistan. A formula, similar to that of the US Constitution, was evolved in the Constitution of 1973 creating a bicameral legislature with the Upper House called the Senate having equal representation from each of the four provinces, and the Lower House called the National Assembly with representation on the basis of population.

The second aspect of provincial autonomy is sharing of powers between the centre and the provinces. It is a primary test of provincial autonomy. Theoretically, a federation is a voluntary creation of federating units/provinces who agree, under contract, to relinquish some of their powers to the federation like defence, currency, foreign relations, inter-provincial communications, and so on. Under this concept, the provinces are the real and ultimate repository of all powers, out of which they cede some voluntarily to the federation. This conceptual situation did not exist in Pakistan at the time of independence. It was not that all the provinces of British India got freedom on their own and then got together to form two federations, one in Pakistan and the other in India. India won its freedom on the basis of two parallel freedom movements, one led by the Indian Congress and the other by the Muslim League. The latter won a Muslim homeland in India based on the formula that those provinces which had a majority population of Muslims would join together to form Pakistan. The remaining provinces formed the federation of India. Some provinces had already existed and others came into existence as a result of the partition of the provinces of Bengal and Punjab at the time of independence. Pakistan was a composite of provinces at the time of independence and the Constituent Assembly was under the obligation of framing a Constitution keeping in view this reality by dividing powers between the centre and the provinces. Conceptually speaking, in a federal Constitution, only subjects assigned to the federal government and the central legislature are expressly and specifically stated because such subjects and powers are specially ceded by the province to the federation. All other subjects belong to the provinces. As mentioned above, Pakistan was not a federation in that sense of the word, therefore, the Constitution of 1956 did not provide for a federal list alone. Three lists were provided under the Constitution of 1956 under its Fifth Schedule: the federal list, concurrent list, and the provincial list. The provincial legislature was conferred exclusive power to legislate on residuary subjects, that is, those subjects which were not enumerated in any of the three legislative lists. This distribution of powers had the attributes of a federal Constitution because the provincial legislature could exclusively legislate on ninety-four subjects mentioned in the provincial list, legislate concurrently on nineteen subjects with the federal legislature, and in addition could also legislate on residuary subjects. The federal legislature was very powerful and dominant because it could legislate exclusively on thirty subjects of wide and far reaching importance, legislate concurrently with the provincial legislatures on nineteen other very important subjects, and on the concurrent list, the federal legislature had overriding powers over the provincial legislatures in the sense that a law passed by the federal legislature on a subject would override a law made by the provincial legislature on the same subject if the latter was inconsistent or repugnant to the former. Correspondingly, the federal government was very powerful under the 1956 Constitution in relation to the provincial governments.

The Constitution of 1962 followed a similar division of powers between the centre and the provinces. The Third Schedule to the Constitution provided for forty-nine subjects (of comprehensive and far reaching importance) upon which the central legislature had exclusive power to make laws. Provincial legislatures had power to make laws for provinces or any part thereof on subjects not enumerated in the Third Schedule. Although the 1962 Constitution followed the classical pattern of distribution of powers in a federation, it was in reality an eye-wash. The central legislature possessed the power to legislate in the national interest on all subjects not even enumerated in the Third Schedule. Furthermore, a provincial law was to become invalid if it was inconsistent with a central law. There was complete domination and preponderance of federal legislature over the provincial ones. Correspondingly, the federal government was very powerful compared to the provincial governments. The Constitution of 1962 was federal in name only. The executive authority in a province was vested in the Governor who was an appointee of the president and served during his pleasure. Thus the provincial executive authority was totally dependent on the central executive authority. The Constitution of 1973 has provided for two legislative lists under its Fourth Schedule: the federal legislative list and the concurrent legislative list.

Provincial legislatures have exclusive power to legislate on subjects not enumerated in the two lists but the federal legislature is very powerful because it can legislate exclusively on sixty-seven subjects of far reaching importance. It is of interest to note that eight subjects mentioned in Part II of the federal legislative list are those in which the provinces have special interest or pertain to interaction between the centre and the provinces. As for the subjects in the concurrent legislative list, the laws passed by the federal legislature override the laws passed by the provincial legislatures on the same subject to the point of inconsistency. Correspondingly, the federal government is very powerful in relation to the provincial governments under this Constitution.

Under the Constitution of 1956, the executive authority of a province extended to all matters over which provincial legislatures had power to make laws. The Constitution did not make many provisions which would safeguard the provinces from the excesses of the centre. The National Finance Commission was to be constituted which would be composed of the federal and provincial finance ministers and other persons to be appointed by the president in consultation with the governors of the provinces. This Commission was to deal with the distribution of taxes between the federation and the provinces, grants-in-aid by the federal government to the governments of the provinces, and other matters relating to finance. The allocation of taxes to the provinces was to be made according to the recommendation of the Commission. A provincial government had to exercise its executive authority to ensure compliance with the federal laws and to facilitate the exercise of authority by the federal government. Any dispute that might arise between the federal government and one or more provincial governments or between the provincial government which did not fall under the jurisdiction of the Supreme Court could be referred to a tribunal to be appointed by the Chief Justice of Pakistan. The report of the tribunal, if found in order by the chief justice, was forwarded to the president who could pass orders to give effect to the report. An Inter-Provincial Council was to be constituted by the president to investigate and discuss subjects of common interest to the federation and the provinces and to make recommendations for better coordination of policy and action with respect to that subject. The Constitution of 1962 also provided that the executive authority of a province extended to all matters with respect to which the legislature of the province had power to make laws. Regarding the National Finance Commission, provisions similar to the Constitution of 1956 were made. A National Economic Council was to be constituted by the president to review the overall economic position of Pakistan and to formulate plans with respect to financial, commercial and economic policies, and the economic development of Pakistan. The primary object of the Council in formulating the plans was to ensure that disparities between the provinces and between different areas within a province in relation to income per capita were removed.

The Constitution of 1973 was framed in the aftermath of a movement for provincial autonomy that was waged by the Awami League led by Mujib, which unfortunately resulted in the breakup of Pakistan. The Six Point Programme of Mujib was an extreme statement for provincial autonomy bordering on confederational arrangement. Even political parties, like the NAP and the JUI, which made substantial gains in the general elections of 1970 in these provinces, wanted a guarantee for autonomy for these provinces. In these circumstances, some additional provisions were made in this Constitution providing greater voice and weightage to the provinces. A Council of Common Interests was introduced to be constituted by the president which would be comprised of the chief ministers of the provinces and an equal number of members from the federal government to be nominated by the prime minister from time to time. The Council would formulate and regulate policies in relation to the subjects like railways, water, electricity, oil and natural gas, and industrial development. It could also exercise supervision and control over institutions responsible for such subjects. The powers of the Council included hearing of complaints regarding use, distribution, or control of water supplies to the provinces. Such a complaint could be heard and decided by the Council itself or it could refer it to a Commission of experts for report and, on the receipt of such a report, could make its decisions. The National Economic Council was retained in this Constitution but with provincial representation. Under the 1962 Constitution, the National Economic Council was to be nominated by the president without any requirement of provincial representation.

In the 1973 Constitution, the president is required to nominate one member from each province on the recommendation of the government of that province. The Council reviews the overall economic conditions of the country and formulates financial, commercial, social, and economic policies. Provisions similar to those of previous Constitutions were made in this Constitution as well as in the National Finance Commission. Special provisions were made in this Constitution regarding provincial rights regarding the supply and distribution of electricity, requirements of natural gas, and broadcasting and telecasting. For the first time, the federal duty of excise on natural gas and royalty collected by the federal government had been made payable to the province where the well-head of natural gas was situated. Similarly, the net profits earned by the federal government from the bulk generation of power at a hydro-electric station became payable to the province in which the hydroelectric station was situated. These were indeed major material gains made by the provinces under the 1973 Constitution.

Having considered the constitutional provisions in relation to provincial autonomy, it is important to examine how these provisions have been enforced practically. In the first place, it can be said that the 1962 Constitution cannot be regarded as a federal Constitution with autonomy for the provinces. It was not given by a Constituent Assembly with representatives from the provinces. The provincial governments were in no way autonomous under this Constitution but are headed by Governors who were appointees of the President, serving at his pleasure and removed by him at any time. Hence, provincial governments were run by the central government through its nominees and appointees, the Governors. The 1962 Constitution, for all practical purposes, gave a unitary form of government. However, the Constitutions of 1956 and 1973 can be regarded as federal Constitutions, at least on paper. The provincial governments were designed to be autonomous within their own spheres of exercise of powers and legislation. The question is: could the provinces under these Constitutions have been autonomous in practice?

Regardless of the debate on provincial autonomy in the last fifty years, there has been a persistent tendency towards centralization rather than decentralization. Despite the fact that the country was divided into two nearly equal wings a thousand miles apart between 1947 and 1971, the central government, under the two Constitutions of 1956 and 1962, held and controlled all the important subjects, departments, and revenue heads. This situation certainly accentuated the feeling of alienation amongst the people in East Pakistan who saw West Pakistan dominating the centre and in this way, East Pakistan. The people of East Pakistan, who were the vanguard of the freedom movement, were made to feel that they had very little say in matters that concerned their lives and that they were dictated from Karachi and later from Rawalpindi. Mujib, who was essentially a man without much intellect but a shrewd demagogue, exploited these feelings to the utmost. He is reported to have said repeatedly at public meetings that he could smell jute (manufactured in East Pakistan) from the roads of Karachi. In his Six Points Programme he emphasized the need for control on the financial resources of the province, including the proceeds from exports. The ultimate frustration of the Six Points Programme led to the breakup of Pakistan. The importance of the issue of provincial autonomy cannot be over-emphasized in the constitutional and political affairs of Pakistan.

Although the Constitution of 1973 made elaborate provisions for safeguarding the interests of the provinces, in practice, most of these provisions have not been acted upon. The provinces did gain in royalties and net profits from natural gas and hydroelectric generation within their territories but the Council of Common Interests which was designed to monitor provincial autonomy and to safeguard the interests of the provinces in vital areas like distribution of water, electricity, and national resources, has remained ineffective. It is either not constituted at all or, if constituted, is not summoned to meet regularly and frequently. The provincial government in Punjab was forced to invoke the jurisdiction of the superior courts in 1989, seeking the direction of the federal government to call a meeting of the Council to deliberate on the issues concerning the provinces. The federal government fully resisted such a request on the part of the provincial government. The failure to call a meeting of the Council was one of the principal charges levelled by the President in his order to dismiss the federal government and to dissolve the National Assembly in 1990. Even later, there has been little progress regarding the resolution of problems of the provinces through the Council. Hence, whatever may be the state of provincial autonomy on paper under the constitutions, the governments at the centre have almost always frustrated the effort towards decentralization or exercise of greater powers by the provinces. They have always ensured a strong centre. This is the main reason why central governments have never tolerated provincial governments run by political parties in the opposition and efforts have always been made to destabilize and overthrow them. Hence, provincial autonomy in Pakistan, regardless of the sanctimonious statements of politicians on the subject from time to time, is a dream that has practically eluded Pakistan.

Religion and the State

The commonwealth, according to Locke, is a society of men who gather together to further their civil interests. These interests include 'life, liberty, health and indolence of body, and the possession of outward things, such as money, lands, houses, furniture and the like'.[13] Like the Commonwealth, the Church is a form of society, and as such it requires laws, but just as the commonwealth has no business making laws for the

Church or legislating on the subject of salvation, neither should ecclesiastical discipline extend outside its own proper sphere. Thus, Church law should not be concerned with civil and worldly goods, even if the Church thinks there is a direct connection between worldly goods and eternal salvation. Similarly, the Church should not use physical power to enforce its views on salvation, the use of physical power should be limited to the civil magistrate. This 'separation of Church and State', based on a radical narrowing of the functions of both religion and politics, makes co-existence of Church and State possible, but it is important to understand that this co-existence occurs largely on the State's terms: it is based on the view that the Church should never interfere with the business of politics by compelling its members to accept the Church's understanding of what is right and wrong with respect to the things of this world.[14] These were the views of the seventeenth-century British philosopher Sir John Locke on the separation of religion and state. Thomas Jefferson, the third President of the USA, expressed similar views about the separation of religion and state in his letter addressed to his Attorney-General:

> Believing with you that religion is a matter solely between man and his God, that he owes account to none other for his faith or his worship, that legislative powers of government reach actions only, and not opinions, I contemplate that sovereign reverence that act of the whole American people which declared that this legislature should "make no law respecting an establishment of religion, or prohibiting the free exercise thereof", thus building a wall of separation between Church and State.[15]

Implicit in the partial separation of religious and political identities is the possibility of a third pattern of relationship–religious systems that are set sharply apart from the state. Religious specialists may develop ideas that contradict secular claims and values. This seems to occur under conditions of persistent social changes, social contact, and widespread and prolonged suffering.[16]

Thus the possibility of conflict between the religion and State. Proponents of the separation of State from religion rely on the distinction between actions and opinions. Religions concur themselves with views, beliefs, or opinions and the States concern themselves with actions. Religious opinion rests upon the conscience of man for which he is answerable to God. The legitimate powers of government on the other hand, extend to such acts as are injurious to others. However, when opinions translate themselves into actions or reactions, they enter the sphere of the State. What determines whether the expression of religious belief should be provided by the State depends on the question of whether its mere expression constitutes an overt act against peace and good order. It has thus developed into an established doctrine of democratic societies that religious opinion should be protected by the State, but not seditious or blasphemous preaching, which has the potential to disturb peace and tranquility which the State has a duty to maintain. Hence, belief itself falls outside the domain of the State, but expression of belief can be considered to be an overt action to be judged by its effect on civil society. All this is subject to tolerance by the majority of the religious beliefs of the minorities, their expression, as well as propagation. What appears to be restricted is not the positive statement of a religion, but public criticism and condemnation of religious beliefs of others.

With the development of democracy and written democratic constitutions, constitution makers were forced to contend with the issue of the relationship between religion and the State. Historical experience, particularly in Europe, has proved that where religious clergy prevailed over state power, it led to religious wars between countries with different religions or different dogmas of the same religion. It is also a lesson of history that state power in the hands of the religious clergy leads to victimization and persecution of religious minorities within the state. No wonder one of the causes of the French Revolution was the excessive power and wealth in the hands of the Church which made the people feel that they were oppressed equally by the State and the Church. Constitution makers had, therefore, to tread carefully between the fear of promoting a religion at the cost of the minorities and to guarantee the people freedom of religion, its practice, and propagation and establishment of religious institutions. While persecution and oppression in the name of religion is highly regrettable, denial of the right to openly profess, practice, and propagate religions (like it used to be in some communist countries) is even more reprehensible.[17]

A democratic constitution thus has the objective of guaranteeing to the people freedom to freely and openly profess, practice, and propagate their religions. The right also includes the freedom to the people to order their lives in accordance with the teachings and tenets of their religions. The real test about close interaction of religion and state comes when the constitution of a state establishes a state religion. Prohibition against establishment of religion by the state is generally understood as under:[18]

> A government should not provide any financial aid to a religion or to the sect of a religion if such aid or assistance would tend to establish a religion. However, non-discriminatory forms of assistance would not fall within this prohibition.
>
> The State should not pass laws which would advance one religion or all religions or prefer one religion over another.
>
> A government should not force or influence a person to go to or to remain away from the places of worship against his will or force him to confess a belief or disbelief in any religion.
>
> No tax in any amount should be levied to support any religious activities or institutions, by whatever name they might be called, or whatever form they might adopt to teach or practice religion.

While examining a statute on the touchstone of the 'establishment of religion' and 'free exercise thereof' clauses of the First Amendment to the US Constitution, the Supreme Court held:[19]

> The test may be stated as follows: What are the purpose and the primary effect of the enactment? If either is the advancement or inhibition of religion, then the enactment exceeds the scope of legislative power as circumscribed by the Constitution. That is to say, that to withstand the strictures of the Establishment Clause, there must be a secular legislative purpose and a primary effect that neither advances nor inhibits religion.

In a nutshell, establishment of a religion means to promote a religion by the state, to prefer one religion over the other, to tax people in aid of a religion and to force people to practice or not to practice a religion. Separation of religion and state would essentially mean the denial of such an establishment.

It is commonly asserted that in Islam, unlike in Christianity and other religions, there is no separation of religion and politics. In strict textual and formal legal terms, this may be true, but this standard generalization is not helpful in comprehending Muslim political praxis either historically or contemporaneously. In its most fundamental sense, politics involves a set of active links, both positive and negative, between civil society and institutions of power. In this sense, there has been little separation, certainly none in our time, between religion and politics anywhere. For example, all those countries where Christians are in the majority observe Christmas as a public holiday. Similarly, in all countries where Muslims are in majority, Eids are observed as public holidays. Although the origins of these festivals are religious, they have become an integral part of the ethos and cultures of these societies. Their observance does not in any way indicate the inter-mixing of religion and politics. In a narrow perspective, the relationship of politics and religion may be discussed in terms of the links between religion and state power. In this sense, separation between state and religion has existed in the Muslim world for at least eleven of Islam's fourteen centuries. The organic links between religion and state power ended in AD 945 when a Buwayhid prince, Muiz al-Dawla Ahmad, marched into the capital city of Baghdad and terminated the Abbasid caliph's dual role as the temporal and spiritual leader of the Islamic nation. One is generous in dating the effective separation of religion and state power from the Buwayhid intervention of 945. The fundamentalist *ulema* take a somewhat more conservative view. They believe that no Muslim state has been Islamic since the accession to power of the Umayyad dynasty in 650. To them, the Islamic state effectively ended with the first four caliphs who had been companions of the Prophet Mohammad (PBUH). However, the minority Shi'ite *ulema*, who believe that legitimate succession belonged only to the blood relatives and descendants of the Prophet, definitely do not regard two of the four caliphs (Umar and Usman) as legitimate rulers. The orthodox *ulema's* rejection of the Islamic character of Muslim states after 650 is based primarily on three factors. The first concerns the presumed impiety of all but a few exceptional rulers (that is, 'Umar Ibn Al-'Aziz, 717-20). The second relates to the historic prevalence of secular laws and practices in Muslim statecraft. The third involves the actual fragmentation of the Islamic world into multiple political entities historically, sultanates, emirates, khanates, sheikhdoms, empires and now, republics. All theologians agree on the principle of a single '*umma*' (Muslim nation) and a single caliph (or *imam*) as essential to a truly Islamic polity governed according to divine laws and the example of the Prophet. Lacking all three conditions of the ideal Islamic polity, Muslim peoples have for more than a millennium accepted as legitimate the exercise of state power by temporal governments, as long as they observe the basic norms of justice and fair play and rule with some degree of consent from the governed. This generalization applies also to the overwhelming majority of *ulema* and local religious leaders. In fact, the most renowned theologians of Islam, Al-Mawardi (d. 1058), Al-Baghdadi (d. 1037), Al-Ghazzali (1058-1111), and Ibn Jama'a (1241-1333) have developed a large body of exegeses to justify, explain, and elaborate on this historic compromise between the Islamic ideal and Muslim political realities.

There is an inherent problem in the establishment of religion by the State. The question would necessarily arise as to which creed is going to be sanctioned by the State: Sunni or Shia? In case it is the Sunni sect, then which of various Sunni schools of thought would be preferred by the State? In any case, any attempt to impose the *shariat* of one sect over the other, one school of thought over the others within the sect, is bound to be met with stiff resistance from those who belong to the excluded sect or excluded school of thought or jurisprudence. In the past, the Muslim community has resisted state sponsorship of a creed or even a school of religious thought. Thus, two of the greatest Muslim rulers encountered popular resistance when they unsuccessfully attempted to sponsor an official creed. The Abbasid caliph, Al-Mamum (786-833), son of Harun-al-Rashid and founder of the House of Wisdom in Baghdad (where many of the translations and commentaries on Greek works were completed and later contributed to the European Renaissance) adopted the Mu'tazilite's doctrines as official creed. This rationalist school of religious thought in Islam was beginning to flourish when it received the sponsorship of the State. At the time the caliphate was in its prime, resistance to it mounted rapidly in the Islamic community. It was thus that the Mu'tazilites acquired the dubious distinction in Islamic history of engaging in the first significant practice of repression on theological grounds. Similarly, Akbar (1542–1605), the most illustrious of the Mughul emperors in India, met with widespread resistance from his Muslim subjects when he promulgated his own eclectic creed, *Din-i-Ilahi* (1582). The establishment or even sponsorship of religion or any particular school of religious thought has not met with favour in Muslim history because there always existed diversity of religious thought amongst the *umma*. Such diversity was seen with favour even by the Holy Prophet (PBUH) himself, who declared 'differences within the *umma* to be a blessing'.

A fusion of religion and political power was and remains an ideal in the Muslim tradition, but the absence of such a fusion is a historically experienced and recognized reality. The tradition of statecraft and the history of Muslim peoples have been shaped by this fact. The many manifestations of this reality are important in comprehending the Muslim polity. A few of these need to be mentioned here. As a religious and proselytizing medieval civilization, the Islamic *umma* evinced a spirit of tolerance towards other faiths and cultures that has been rare in history. It is important to acknowledge, for the sake of historical veracity as well as for a desperately needed reinforcement of non-sectarian and universalist values in Muslim civilization, that non-Muslims, especially Christians, Jews, and Hindus, have been an integral part of the Islamic enterprise. In the pre-colonial period, Muslim law and practice reflected a certain separation and autonomy of religious and social life along confessional lines. Admittedly, there were also instances of excesses against and oppression of the non-Muslim population under Muslim rule, yet the greatest achievements of Islamic civilization in science, philosophy, literature, music, art, and architecture, as well as statecraft, have been the collective achievements of Christians, Jews, Hindus, and others participating in the cultural and economic life of the 'Islamicate'. In fact, the most creative periods of Muslim history have been those that witnessed a flowering in the collaborative half of our ecumenical relations. This secular fact of Muslim political praxis, from Indonesia and India through the Fertile Crescent and Egypt to Spain, is generally neglected in the writings both of the *ulema* and the Orientalists. Yet it is more relevant to understanding Islam's relationship to politics than the antics of any current 'Islamic' political leader.[20]

The pragmatists in Islam denote an attitude of viewing religious requirements as being largely unrelated to the direct concerns of states and governments and of dealing with affairs of state in terms of the political and economic imperatives of contemporary life. The regulation of religious life is left to civil society and to private initiatives. This approach has not been opposed by the reconstructionist school of intellectuals. As discussed earlier, it parallels the historical Muslim experience. As such, it is accepted both by the masses and the majority of the *ulema*. Thus, wherever popular attitudes have been tested in open and free elections, pragmatist political parties and secular programmes have gained overwhelming victories over their fundamentalist adversaries. Thus, through the twentieth century, the political heroes of the Muslim world and the liberators and founding fathers of contemporary Muslim nations, have been secular and generally westernized individuals. For example, Kemal Ataturk (1881–1938), founder of modern Turkey, Muhammad Ali Jinnah (1876–1948), founding father of Pakistan, Ahmed Sukarno (1901–70), first president of Indonesia, Gamal Abdul Nasser (1918–70), second president of the republic of Egypt, Habib Bourguiba (b.1903), of Tunisia, and the Seven Historic Chiefs of the Algerian Revolution, are regarded as the most popular and decidedly historic Muslim leaders of the twentieth century. The movements and political organizations they led were secular and were heavily influenced by modern, largely western, ideas.

In Pakistan, the historical development of the inter-relation and interaction of religion and state may be studied through its constitutional embodiment.

The first expression of an opinion on the subject of separation of religion and state was made by the founder of the nation himself in his speech to the Constituent Assembly on 11 August 1947. Jinnah made it clear that, with partition, Muslims ceased to be Muslims and Hindus ceased to be Hindus, not in the religious sense but in the political sense. It was indeed a very strong statement on the separation of religion and state, but since the very rationale of Pakistan was to avoid Hindu hegemony in united India, it could not be argued that Pakistan would be dominated by a Muslim majority. That is why such an assurance was extended to the minorities by Jinnah to assure them that religion would not be politically exploited in the new nation. Then came the Objectives Resolution in 1949 after the death of Jinnah. This created a lot of controversy and misgivings on the part of the minorities. It was passed with a divisive vote on religious lines, all Muslim members voting for it and all non-Muslims voting against it. The anti-Ahmediya movement of 1953 brought to the forefront the issue of state interference in the matter of religion because those responsible for the movement wanted the Ahmedis to be declared non-Muslims. The *Munir Report* clearly disparaged such a demand, holding that there could be no consensus on the definition of who is a Muslim. It was observed in the report that no two sects of Islam, rather no two *ulema*, agreed on one definition of 'Muslim'. Things came to a head in 1974 on account of another anti-Ahmediya movement. This time, Bhutto, with all his secular pretensions, succumbed to the pressure of the clergy and made a constitutional amendment setting out the definition of a 'non-Muslim' that included all 'Ahmedis' belonging to Qadiani or Lahori groups. The provision was further amended in 1985, now giving the definitions of both the terms 'Muslim' and 'non-Muslim'. This development can certainly be called a step towards the establishment of religion by the state. but it may not be sufficient for the establishment of religion by the state. India, which has always made lofty claims about its secular constitution, has ventured to define who is and who is not part of the majority community of Hindu. The term has not been specifically defined but is stated indirectly in Article 25 which proclaims that Hindus include the Sikh, Jain, or Buddhist religions and their institutions would be deemed to be Hindu religious institutions. It may be argued that mere definition of membership of a religion, whether of inclusion therein or exclusion thereof, does not *per se* evidence the establishment of religion by State.

Another aspect of establishment of the religion by the State is its formal aspect: that is, the declaration. All three constitutions in Pakistan have declared the republic to be the Islamic Republic of Pakistan. This declaration alone does not make the State of Pakistan a theocratic one. It only declares the obvious: that the state of Pakistan is predominantly populated by Muslims. The other aspect relates to the declaration of a religion as the state religion. The Constitutions of 1956 and 1962 did not make any formal declaration to the effect that 'Islam is the state religion of Pakistan'. Certain general statements were made with regard to the promotion of Muslim unity and Islamic principles in the Chapter on 'Directive Principles of State Policy'. Article 2 of the Constitution of 1973 has, however, declared Islam to be the State religion of Pakistan in categorical terms, which is a clear departure from the previous Constitutions.

Historically, it was in 1949 when the Objectives Resolution was passed that religious minorities felt the encroachment of religion over the secular institution of the state. Members of the first and second Constituent Assemblies were cognizant of the fact that the Objectives Resolution was a declaratory instrument meant to give broad constitutional guidelines and that these would not be entirely free from controversy. This is the reason why the Objectives Resolution was incorporated in the first Constitution as its preamble. This was followed in the Constitutions of 1962 and 1973. Zia, in order to further substantiate his Islamic credentials, went a step further and added Article 2A to the Constitution under the RCO, making the principles and provisions set out in the Objectives Resolution, as reproduced in the annex, as a substantive and effective part of the Constitution.[21] This development has brought to the forefront the possibility of Article 2A taking precedence over other provisions of the Constitution.

Benazir, on assumption of office as prime minister in 1988, granted clemency under Article 45 of the Constitution, including commutation of all death sentences awarded by the military courts or other courts up to 6 December 1988, to life imprisonment, as a mark of celebration on being elected. This order of clemency was challenged before the Lahore High Court. The Court held that such an order was repugnant to Article 2A and in cases in which death sentences had been awarded, the president had no power to commute, remit, or pardon such sentences because, under Islam, the power of pardon in such cases only vests with the heirs of the deceased.[22] On appeal, the Supreme Court set aside the judgment of the High Court.[23] It was observed that if the Court finds that Article 45 of the Constitution contravenes the injunctions of Islam in some respect, it has to bring the transgression to the notice of Parliament which alone was competent to amend the Constitution, and could initiate remedial legislation to bring the impugned provision in conformity with the injunctions of Islam.

The Objectives Resolution envisaged an Islamic democratic state where powers and authority of the State would be exercisable through 'chosen representatives' of the people. This declaration is the principal guarantee for the democratic characters of the State. It pre-empts the argument advanced by some that only those who are qualified as *mujtahids* should exercise the State powers and authority in an Islamic State. Apart from two 'Islamic' clauses (pertaining to observance of principles of democracy, freedom, equality, tolerance, and social justice as enunciated by Islam, and the Muslims ordering their lives in the individual and collective spheres in accordance with the teaching and requirements of Islam as set out in the Holy Quran and *Sunnah*, the constitutional programme set forth in the resolution follows the pattern of a constitutional democracy on modern occidental lines. Federalism (autonomy of the federating units), fundamental rights and minority protection, rule of law (through independence of judiciary) are emphasized. Judged by itself, the Resolution could as well figure as a constitutional plan for a secular state.[24]

The Constitutions of 1956 and 1962 (and the 1973 Constitution in its original form), introduced institutions for research and promotion of Islam like the Islamic Ideology Council and Islamic Research Institute. These Constitutions prohibited the enactment of any law repugnant to the injunctions of Islam as laid down in the Holy Quran and *Sunnah*. As a result of amendments, made by Zia in the Constitution of 1973 which were later incorporated in the Eighth Amendment, a machinery has been provided through the Federal Shariat Court and its appellate forum for declaring laws repugnant to the injunctions of Islam as laid down in the Holy Quran and *Sunnah* as void. This of course, was a major step towards the establishment of religion as part of the polity in Pakistan. In the Constitution of 1956, the president was required to be a Muslim. However, there was no such requirement for the prime minister. The Constitution of 1962 also required the president to be a Muslim. The Constitution of 1973 provides for the president to be a Muslim. In the Constitution of 1973, as it was originally, it was provided that the National Assembly would elect one of its Muslim members as the prime minister. However, this requirement has been dispensed with under the RCO as modified by the Eighth Amendment. Although subsequent amendments like the Second Amendment declaring Ahmedis to be non-Muslim, provisions for a Federal Shariat Court and making the Objectives Resolution an operative part of the Constitution, have all added to the Islamic character of the Constitution, as far as the requirement of the prime minister to be a Muslim is concerned, subsequent amendments have backtracked.

The Constitution of 1973, as amended from time to time, has the necessary ingredients for the establishment of religion by the state. The rationale is that Pakistan was created in the name of Islam and, therefore, the establishment of Islam as the state religion under the Constitution is only a logical end and objective of its creation. This rationale is not without question. Jinnah, in his various speeches, clearly declared that members of various religions would cease to be so in the political sense and that Pakistan should not be a theocratic state. It may be inferred that he did not desire the establishment of religion by the state and believed that there should be no prohibition or obstruction in the free exercise of any religion. Pakistan was conceived as a safe haven for Muslims to freely practise their faith without any fear of the majority belonging to another and, at times, hostile religion. Pakistan was also conceived as a country where the civil rights of Muslims would be respected without the possibility of a brute majority violating them with impunity. Some of the fears that were expressed during the freedom movement have been confirmed and have come true in India where Muslims, who form the largest minority, have suffered rough treatment at the hands of a Hindu majority despite the secular character of the Constitution. Muslims in India live in an environment of fear and oppression. They face victimization in the exercise of their civil rights, particularly in government employments. Sikhs have lost their religious identity and have been classified as Hindus under the Constitution. This was one of the major reasons for the Khalsa movement in India. But this does not mean that the Muslim majority in Pakistan should do unto the minorities what they feared would have been done unto them had they been a minority in India or the way Indian Muslims have been treated over the years. Zia, who at best had a raw and rudimentary understanding of Islam, played into the hands of reactionary religious forces and mutilated the text and spirit of the Constitution, thus accentuating the divisions in the population based on religion. Once the state establishes a religion, it leads to confrontation between various sects, schisms, and schools within the faith about whose concepts and dogmas would prevail over the others. No wonder we are watching the divisions between Shias and Sunnis becoming sharpened and being increasingly expressed in violent terms through their political parties and militant wings. Even within the Sunnis, there are sharp, and at times violent, divisions amongst their various schools, particularly the Deobandis, the Barelvis, and the Wahabis. This confirms the wisdom that mankind had learnt over the centuries that to ensure peaceful conditions in a polity, religion and state should be kept separate. It is also conducive to the peaceful development of various schools of religious thought without their being brought into violent confrontation.

Issue of Joint or Separate Electorates

The question of whether electorates should be separate or joint has been an important constitutional issue in the history of the country. It was debated at great length in the deliberations of the first Constituent Assembly. The proponents of separate electorates argued that they formed the very basis of the creation of Pakistan since during British rule, it was a consistent demand of the Muslims that they be allowed elections on the basis of separate electorates because their representation proportionate to their ratio in the total population of India could only be ensured through this method. Muslims rejoiced when they were allowed separate electorates because they formed nearly one-fourth of the total population in India, and had very little representation in the legislatures since in more than eighty per cent of the general constituencies, they were outnumbered by the Hindus. The Muslim League made a very strong showing in the constituencies for Muslim seats in the general elections of 1946 which ultimately paved the way for the creation of Pakistan. After Independence, the position was reversed and Muslims in Pakistan were in a predominant majority (about eighty-five per cent to ninety per cent). They had no reason or justification to demand separate electorates. It was only the minorities in Pakistan who could demand separate electorates for self-protection but no such demand was made and, therefore, the Constitution of 1956 did not provide for a separate electorate. The Constitution Commission headed by Chief Justice Shahabuddin, in its report, however, recommended separate electorates, but there appeared to be little justification for such a recommendation and Ayub rejected it.

In the 1973 Constitution, as it was originally, a joint electorate was provided for. Subsequently, through an amendment, provisions were made for special seats for minorities in the national as well as in the provincial assemblies. The politics of electorate came to a head in 1977 when the opposition PNA composed of some religious parties felt that it was at a disadvantage in the system of joint electorate. It was widely felt that voters belonging to the minorities generally sided with the PPP, primarily because of its liberal and leftist views. This proved crucial in closely contested races. It was felt particularly by the religious parties like Jamaat-i-Islami, Jamiatul Ulema-i-Pakistan, and Jamiat-i-Ulema-i-Islam, that disenfranchising the members of the minorities in elections to the general seats would be to their advantage and correspondingly to the detriment of the PPP.

Zia, who feared the resurgence of the PPP and would not hesitate in taking any step that would go to its disadvantage, bought the idea. He introduced separate electorates through an Amendment (in 1979) in the Representation of the Peoples Act 1976. Ultimately, separate electorates also found their way into the Constitution through the RCO in 1985. Clause (4A) of Article 51 and Clause (5) of Article 106 were substituted providing for election of members of the national and provincial assemblies respectively, belonging to minorities on the basis of a separate electorate. This was indeed unfortunate, particularly in view of the fact that there was no demand on the part of the minorities in Pakistan for separate electorates. The system was thus imposed by the majority on the unwilling minorities who had never rejected a joint electorate with the Muslim majority. They only demanded the reservation of special seats under the Constitution, which was a justified demand. Separate electorates have considerably reduced the voice and weightage of the minorities. The example of India is worth studying. Indian Muslims, who are about 15 per cent of the total population in India, have a voice and weightage of much more than 15 per cent due to a joint electorate. The Muslim vote can affect the result of the election by 30 to 40 per cent of the constituencies, particularly in close races. If separate electorates are imposed on them, then their voice and role would be reduced to 15 per cent or maybe even less. They will no longer be courted by the political parties at the national level and Muslims elected against special seats would be running after political parties to accommodate them. This is what separate electorates can do to the minorities. It goes to the discredit of the PPP that its leadership has done nothing to reverse separate electorates under the law and the Constitution.

The system of separate electorates as enforced and administered in Pakistan is highly unfair and inconvenient since there are no separate constituencies for the minorities and they have to contest against multiple seats constituencies. For example, Christians have four seats in the National Assembly for which an electoral roll of Christians throughout Pakistan is prepared and the candidates for these seats have to run around all over Pakistan to canvas voters. The candidates who secure the first four positions throughout Pakistan are declared elected. This process exposes the candidates to a lot of hassle, expense, and inconvenience. Similar is the case for election to such seats in the Provincial Assemblies. For good reason, separate electorates should yield to a joint electorate in Pakistan unless the minorities themselves demand separate electorates.

Partisan Conduct of Elections

Elections in Pakistan during the last fifty years have been lacking in credibility. Results of most of the general elections have been disputed with allegations of rigging and manipulation by the opposition parties. It started with provincial elections held in Punjab in 1951 during the lifetime of Liaquat, when there were serious allegations that the Chief Minister of the Punjab, Mumtaz Daultana, had used the official machinery to influence the result of elections in certain constituencies to obtain desired results. Provincial elections in East Bengal held in 1954 were, by and large, considered fair because the ruling party was badly defeated. National elections scheduled for January 1959 under the Constitution of 1956 were never held because martial law was imposed in October 1958.

During Ayub's regime, two elections were held to the national and provincial assemblies in 1962 and 1965 based on indirect electorate consisting of basic democrats only, with 500 to 600 electors voting for a seat in the National Assembly and 250 to 300 electors voting for a seat in the Provincial Assembly. Even the results of these elections were disputed, though it was not difficult for the government to influence a small number of electors by threat or inducement which was done particularly in

West Pakistan under the iron hand of the then Governor, Amir Muhammad Khan of Kalabagh.

The only presidential election held in Pakistan was between Ayub and Fatima Jinnah in 1965 which has been widely denounced as rigged, even though the electorate was limited to 80,000 basic democrats. The extent of rigging and the means and methods applied to influence the vote and to achieve the desired results have been discussed earlier in the book. General elections held in December 1970 by Yahya's government are universally accepted as fair and impartial. The reason was perhaps that none of the members of the government contested the elections and so the government was not interested in any particular results. The results of the general elections held in March 1977 were vehemently challenged and disputed and became the cause for the PNA to launch a nationwide movement that resulted in the imposition of martial law and the overthrow of Bhutto. General elections held in February 1985 were not held on a party basis and most political parties barring one or two, did not participate in them. The results of the elections had little bearing on the outcome, and although there were allegations of rigging here and there, these were all instances of individual candidates indulging in malpractices.

The general elections of November 1988 were party-based and can be considered fair and impartial. There is evidence that the intelligence agencies, particularly the ISI, played a role in influencing the outcome of the elections. The general elections of 1990 were definitely not fair and impartial. The President was clearly hostile to the PPP, whose government he had just dismissed. The interim government was also hostile to the PPP and was virtually a nominee of the IJI, the other major participant in the elections. The entire government machinery was geared to ensure a crushing defeat for the PPP and the success of IJI. The President himself made an appeal to the nation in a broadcast on the eve of the general elections to reject the PPP. The general elections of 1993 can be described as relatively fair and impartial. These were held by a caretaker government composed of technocrats and bureaucrats who did not themselves participate in the election. All the parties were given adequate opportunity to campaign and the results were also more or less correctly tabulated. There were cases of malpractice but mainly at individual and local levels. The general elections of 1997 were heavily loaded in favour of the PML(N) since President Leghari, after dismissing Benazir's government in November 1996, was clearly hostile to her party. The establishment under him, including the caretaker government, was favourably inclined towards the PML(N). Much before that, voters had become estranged from the PPP because of the corruption and mis-government during its three years in government from 1993 to 1996. There was a very low turn-out at the polls comprising people who were transported to the polling stations by a political party. The turn-out was barely between 20 to 25 per cent and Leghari appeared on television after the closure of the poll, stating that the turn out was between 26 and 27 per cent. Later, however, the turn-out was shown to be more than 36 per cent. It is suspected that 10 per cent was added on later and the results were manipulated. There are serious questions about the credibility of elections that were clearly one-sided and in which the PML(N) swept the polls throughout Pakistan.

In Pakistan, the legitimacy of every successive government has become suspect due to the disputed results of the elections. Unless adequate measures are taken to ensure the credibility of the electoral process, constitutional functioning will always remain a problem. As soon as a government is inducted into office, the opposition starts crying hoarse against its legitimacy and usually raises a demand for fresh elections. The opposition indulges in agitation which results in a situation of political confrontation between the government and the opposition, thus paralyzing democratic functioning.

Some of the reasons for this may be enumerated below:

One, official machinery has often been used to influence the result in favour of the party in power. This means the involvement of the administrative machinery at all levels, particularly at the district level where it matters the most. Candidates with the government's blessings are given all kinds of facilities to obtain votes, including the assistance of the police, which deals leniently with those supporting the government candidate and severely with those opposing him. This goes to the extent of conjuring up false cases against the opponents and letting off supporters who have actually indulged in criminal activity. Deputy commissioners and assistant commissioners provide similar facilities to government candidates at the district and sub-divisional levels. On and before the polling day, the district administrations extend help to government candidates by providing transport and other facilities to them. Other government departments are also deployed to facilitate party candidates. Electricity, water, and gas connections are provided in constituencies during the election campaign to win over votes for government-backed candidates. Opposition candidates are left to face considerable odds and inconvenience in these circumstances.

Two, Although, for some time now, judicial officers have been appointed as returning officers, the presiding officers and other staff at the polling stations are mostly drawn from the official cadre working under the district administration, who take orders from the deputy commissioner and assistant commissioners rather than from the district judge and civil judges. There have been instances when presiding officers and polling officers have taken the result sheets of their respective polling stations to the deputy commissioners or assistant commissioners, where they may be changed or interpolated before being submitted to the returning officers. Manipulation is allegedly done in the result sheets and there are instances when a candidate had won unofficially but was later declared unsuccessful after the result sheets were changed at certain polling stations. Even judicial officers who are appointed as returning officers are not all free from fault. Many of them are very ambitious and want to curry favour with the government in power. They are thus willing to cooperate with the government to achieve its desired ends.

The composition of the Election Commission leaves much to be desired. Although the Chief Election Commissioner is generally appointed for a fixed term, the Election Commission itself is not a permanent body. It is constituted only when general elections to the national and provincial assemblies are to be held. This gives the government a lot of leverage in influencing the composition of the Election Commission. In addition to the Chief Election Commissioner, two judges of High

Courts are appointed to the Commission and the government in power generally ensures that they are favourably predisposed. In any case, the Election Commission is too small a body to control the conduct of elections throughout the country and has to fall back upon the administration which is already party to the manipulation of results. The Election Commission is helpless in trying to prevent malpractices or to punish the transgressions. In the general elections held in February 1997, the law completely prohibited the affixation of hoardings, posters, or banners of any size or wall chalking as a part of the election campaign of a candidate. This provision of law was openly and blatantly flouted by candidates of the PPP and the PML(N) and with impunity. Similarly, the law also restricted election expenses to 1,600,000 rupees for national and provincial assembly candidates, but this was also openly contravened. It is an open secret that candidates of the two parties spent many times the amounts legally prescribed on the expenses of the election day alone. False returns of the expenses were filed before the returning officers but no action has been taken against anyone. Transportation of voters to the polling stations by the candidate is a corrupt practice under election laws, but this was openly indulged in.

The media, particularly television and radio, are controlled by the government, and blatantly used to the advantage of the candidates of the party in power and to the detriment of the candidates of the parties in opposition. Very little coverage, and that also with a slant, is given to the opposition parties.

It is beyond doubt that fair and impartial general elections cannot be held by a government whose future is at stake. Only an impartial government with no stakes in the elections can hold fair polls. A caretaker government consisting of people with a good reputation and appointed with the consensus of the major parties contesting the elections need to be appointed before the holding of any general election. The Election Commission needs to be made a permanent body with sufficient staff to cover the general elections independently and effectively. Laws need to be enacted to give adequate and equitable time over the media to the parties participating in the elections to put forward their respective manifestos. The transportation of voters to the polling stations should be effectively checked. There should be a complete ban on the private vehicles being used on polling day so that wealthy candidates do not have an unfair advantage over others.

Issue of Insecure Minorities

At the time of independence, there were a substantial number of non-Muslims living in Pakistan, particularly in the provinces of East Bengal and Sindh. In Punjab, due to widespread disturbances, a near complete ouster of minorities had taken place. Nearly all non-Muslims living in areas forming West Punjab migrated to India and nearly the entire Muslim population living in areas now forming East Punjab were violently forced out and pushed into Pakistan, with the result that the presence of minorities in West Punjab was negligible. In all fairness, it must be said that minorities were not maltreated till the breakup of Pakistan in 1971. They had special seats in the National and Provincial Assemblies and participated in the national life and politics due to a joint electorate. Their rights were guaranteed under the Constitution. Even in the anti-Ahmediya movement of 1953 the government imposed martial law and the demands of the agitators were not accepted. Things changed radically after 1971.

The minorities form about 4 per cent of the total population, constituting about five million people. They got a rough deal during the martial law imposed by Zia. Minorities in Pakistan have been guaranteed freedom to profess, practise, and propagate their religions under the Constitution and all the religious denominations and their sects have been guaranteed the right to establish, maintain, and manage their religious institutions.[25] The Objectives Resolution of 1949 envisaged adequate provisions to be made for the minorities to freely profess their religions, to develop their cultures, and to safeguard their legitimate interests. Christians are perhaps largest in number amongst the minorities in Pakistan. They were seriously hit by the nationalization of private schools and colleges in 1972. A large number of educational institutions had been established throughout Pakistan by various Christian missions. Under Martial Law Regulation (MLR) No.118 these institutions were nationalised although properties under such institutions were not touched for about six or seven years and Christians continued to occupy them. From 1979 onwards, the government decided to expropriate the properties in the garb of the provisions contained in MLR 118. The properties under such institutions were ordered to be transferred in the name of the provincial governments in the revenue records and Christian occupants in these properties were given notices to vacate them. The Supreme Court finally came to the rescue of the Christians by holding that MLR 118 neither intended nor had the effect of making the government owner of the properties under such institutions.[26] Despite this ruling and the promise made by Junejo as prime minister in this behalf in a function held by Christians, these nationalized educational institutions in the Punjab were not returned to the Christians for quite some time because certain religious parties forced the government to renege on the commitment publicly made by the prime minister.

Ahmedis became a constitutional minority under the Constitution (Second Amendment) Act, 1974. They came under real difficulty after the enforcement of Ordinance XX of 1984 Anti-Islamic Activities of Qadiani Group, Lahori Group and Ahmedis (Prohibition and Punishment) Ordinance, 1984.[27] which prohibited them from using epithets, descriptions, and titles reserved for holy personages or places of the Muslims and it was made a punishable offence. In a case of grant of bail, the Supreme Court held that *ex facie* use of certain expressions (commonly used by the Muslims) does not create any feeling of hurt, offence, or provocation in Muslims and bail was granted to those accused of using such expressions.[28] However, in another case, the Supreme Court, upheld the *vires* of Ordinance XX of 1984 by a majority opinion as a valid piece of legislation not violative of the fundamental rights of the citizens to profess, practise, and propagate their religion.[29] In this background, the minorities are justified in feeling insecure and vulnerable. The introduction of Article 2A by the RCO and the Eighth Amendment only added to their anxiety and apprehension. Article 2A makes the principles and provisions set out in the Objectives

Resolution (reproduced in the annex) as a substantive part of the Constitution. The Objectives Resolution of 1949 has been reproduced in the annex but with one little change. The sixth paragraph of the Objectives Resolution reads as follows:

> Wherein adequate provision shall be made for the minorities freely to profess and practise their religions and develop their cultures.

While reproducing the above paragraph in the annex, the word 'freely' has been omitted. This is the only omission in the annex from the Objectives Resolution and is, therefore, conspicuous and significant. The minorities can understandably feel apprehensive about this omission, particularly in view of the continuously deteriorating standard of judicial appointments and the expanding role of religious parties in national politics. The above mentioned constitutional and statutory developments coupled with the forcible introduction of separate electorates has made the minorities feel with some justification that they have been relegated to the status of second class citizens. It is imperative that fears and apprehensions of the minorities should be assuaged to allow them full participation in national life.

Women in the Assemblies

The Constitution of 1956 provided for special seats for women—five each from East and West Pakistan to the National Assembly for a period of ten years.[30] This Constitution also provided for ten special seats each in the Provincial Assemblies of East and West Pakistan.[31] The Constitution of 1962 provided for six special seats for women (three each from East and West Pakistan) in the National Assembly.[32] It also provided for five special seats for women in each Provincial Assembly.[33] The Constitution of 1973, in its original form, provided for ten reserved seats for women in the National Assembly. Similar provision was made in the provincial assemblies and seats reserved for women in each provincial assembly equal to five per cent of the number of members elected from the province from general/Muslim seats. The seats specified for minorities in a province were not to be included for the purpose of computing the number of seats to be reserved for women. This provision was a temporary one, limited to a period of ten years from the commencing day (that is, 14 August 1973) or the holding of the second general election to the assemblies, whichever occurred later. These provisions were also amended by the Eighth Amendment though not to the detriment of women. The number of reserved seats for women in the National Assembly was raised from ten to twenty but no change was made in the number of seats reserved for women in the provincial assemblies. Although the period for the enforceability of these provisions remained ten years from the commencing date, it was indirectly extended by making this provision enforceable till the holding of the third general election to the assemblies. The electoral college for election to these reserved seats in each assembly was the concerned assembly itself. The members of each assembly would elect women against the reserved seats by proportional representation on the basis of a single transferable vote.

The provisions regarding reserved seats expired on the holding of general elections in November 1988, which was reckoned as the third general election under the Constitution of 1973 (general elections of March 1977 and February 1985 having been reckoned as the first and the second general elections respectively). Consequently, there were no reserved seats for women in the National and Provincial Assemblies in the general elections held in October 1990, October 1993 and February 1997. There is a nationwide demand for the restoration of reserved seats for women. Nearly all leading organizations representing women have voiced this demand and most political parties have supported it. Nawaz Sharif came up with a proposal in 1994 that seats for women should be reserved but elections against such seats should be held directly, with women forming electorates in the constituencies delimited for the purpose, and that separate electoral rolls should be prepared for the purpose. This proposal was widely criticized as unworkable and impracticable. If there are twenty special seats for women in the National Assembly to be elected in this manner it would mean that each constituency would be spread over an area and population of ten general constituencies which means a population of about five million. It would also mean voters equal to about five general constituencies, that is, about two to two and a half million. Such a system would be highly inconvenient, unfair, complex, and expensive for candidates seeking election. The proposal also introduces something conceptually new and unusual–separate electorate on the basis of sex. Nothing has been heard of this proposal and even the PML(N) is considering the revival of women seats in the Assembly, particularly with its present strength in Parliament enabling it to amend the Constitution at will. The proposal of reviving reserved seats for women with the assemblies forming the electorate for their election is not free from drawbacks. The women elected in this manner cannot be true representatives of women in the country since they would represent their own colleagues in the assemblies and bear their political stamp. They cannot be expected to truly advance the cause of women in society and would only play second fiddle to their male colleagues.

It cannot be denied that there should be reserved seats for women in the Assemblies because women have not yet reached the stage when they could play an effective role in the elections to the general seats. In the general elections of 1993 and 1997, only four women out of 207 general seats were elected on both occasions, which included Benazir and her mother Nusrat. It is indeed true that one of the main indicators of a country's potential to develop and prosper is the state of its women. In particular, the crucial test is: How much do women participate or contribute to national affairs as equals of men? Pakistan clearly fails in this test. Its women are far too backward and oppressed as compared to their fellow male citizens in education, health, human rights and liberties, and other social, economic, and political power-wielding.

It goes without saying that women need uplift so as to become equal partners with men in national affairs. One of the ways of achieving this end is by ensuring their adequate representation in the assemblies, provided such representation is meaningful and not cosmetic. Only those condidates who are elected by women themselves can espouse and advance their cause effectively for equality of opportunity. Till such time as a better method is evolved or women are brought up to the level of their male counterparts educationally, socially, and economically, the previous system of reserving seats in the assemblies for women elected on the basis of proportional representation by single transferable vote should be revived. Some restrictions should be imposed so that candidates in the elections to such seats should not be related to any member of the assembly electing such women representatives.[34]

Separation of the Judiciary from the Executive

Separation of powers is one of the cardinal doctrines of democratic constitutions in the world today. In the presidential form of government, such separation is more clearly defined where all parts of the state; the executive, the legislature, and the judiciary, function in their respective fields autonomous from one another. In the parliamentary form of government, such separation is not that well-defined, particularly between the executive and the legislature. The cabinet, headed by the prime minister, constitutes the executive which is elected from amongst the members of the legislature and can only function if it has the confidence of a majority.

The Government of India Act, 1935, which was used as the interim constitution in the first nine years of Pakistan, did not provide for a judiciary separate from the executive. This situation was inherently unfair and undemocratic and it should have been dispensed with immediately on independence. Unfortunately, no such step was taken and the country continued to be governed in the manner desired by the erstwhile colonial masters when there was no separation of the executive from the judiciary, at least at the magisterial level. This was deliberately so. The British had reason to ensure that the magistracy was under their control. The deputy commissioner was the kingpin of their system and he had two other capacities as the district executive: those of the district magistrate and the collector. As collector, he was in charge of land revenue in his district. As district magistrate, he controlled the entire magisterial establishment within his district. All magistrates in the district worked under him. In that capacity, he had to ensure that magistrates under him performed dual functions: the maintenance of law and order and the prevention of its breach, which is an executive function along with hearing and determinating cases arising out of such breach of law and order which is a judicial function. It was with the exercise of these two functions concurrently by the same authority that the colonial rulers ensured peace and stability as demanded by imperial interest. Anyone arrested by a magistrate for breach of peace was tried and punished by the same magistrate. A person so arrested could be kept behind bars as long as the administration desired because the magistrate would grant bail only if the administration permitted him to do so. In the exercise of his judicial functions a magistrate had little option but to follow the instructions of the colonial masters passed to him through the district magistrate.

When the first Constitution of Pakistan was enacted in 1956, due attention was not paid to this important matter. The separation of the judiciary from the executive was only mentioned as a desired objective in the Chapter of Directive Principles of State Policy in these words:

> The State shall separate the Judiciary from the Executive as soon as possible.[35]

A matter of such basic importance was not included in the operative part of the Constitution and was put into cold storage without any indication of the time frame within which the object was to be achieved. Perhaps the ruling classes in Pakistan did not want to lose the handle which had kept the colonialists in the saddle for so long.

The 1962 Constitution did not mention the separation of the judiciary from the executive. The Constitution of 1973 took the major step of fixing a time frame for the separation of judiciary from the executive in the following words:

> The Judiciary shall be separated progressively from the Executive within three years from the commencing day.[36] Article 175(3).

Although a period of three years should have been enough if the government wanted to accomplish this objective in earnest, the Bhutto government was in no urgency to do so. Under the Fourth Amendment to the Constitution, the period of three years was extended to five, thus taking it upto August 1978. The objective was not accomplished by the time the Bhutto government was overthrown in July 1977.

Since Zia's government had suspended the operation of the Constitution, in particular this provision, the matter remained in cold storage until 1985 when under the RCO, the period of such separation was extended to fourteen years, which was to expire on 14 August 1987. The government at that time felt no urgency despite the fact that the constitutional deadline was nearing expiry. The government appeared to be least concerned with this constitutional imperative because the delay was in its interest. The inaction on the part of the executive was challenged by the members of the Bar immediately on the expiry of fourteen years on 14 August 1987 before the High Court in writ jurisdiction and with a prayer for mandamus against the federal and provincial governments to fulfil the constitutional dictate of separation of the judiciary from the executive. A full Bench of the Sindh High Court consisting of seven judges accepted the writ petition filed by Sharaf Faridi by a majority of six to one.[37] The Court held that separation of the judiciary from the executive would mean:[38]

(a) that executive should place adequate annual funds at the disposal of the judiciary for operating them without any interference by any agency of the executive;
(b) that appointment of the Chief Justice and judges of the Supreme Court and Chief Justices and judges of High Courts by the President, in consultation with the Chief Justice of Pakistan and Chief Justice of the concerned High Court, as the case may be, should be meaningful;

(c) that transfer of a High Court judge to another High Court without his consent or his appointment to the Federal Shariat Court without his consent, militates against the concept of independence/separation of the judiciary as envisaged by the Constitution;

(d) that denial and failure to establish independent courts and tribunals by separating them from the executive would negate the fundamental right to life and liberty guaranteed to citizens by the Constitution.

The Court held that since the various federal and provincial governments after the enforcement of the Constitution failed to do what they were required to do under the Constitution, a direction under Article 199 could be issued to them to do the same. The Court emphasized that in order to bring laws in conformity with Article 175 and similar provisions, not only some administrative actions were required to be taken but also some legislative measures were needed. Since it would be debatable whether direction could be issued to legislatures to legislate in order to discharge its constitutional obligation, a direction could be issued to the federal and provincial governments to initiate legislative measures for bringing existing laws in conformity with Article 175.

The Court issued the following directions to the government of Sindh:

1. to issue necessary notification for bifurcating magistrates into judicial and executive magistrates and to place the judicial magistrates under the administrative control of the High Court within a period of six months;
2. to issue necessary notification for placing the judicial magistrates under the departmental control of the High Court including their disciplinary matters;
3. to initiate legislative measures within a period of six months in order to make the necessary amendments in the relevant statutes to bring them in conformity with Articles 175 and 203 of the Constitution.

The federal government was directed to initiate all legislative/administrative steps/measures to bring the existing laws relating or affecting the judiciary in accordance with Articles 175 and 203 of the Constitution within a period of six months. The dissenting judge, Justice Mamoon Kazi, held that the provisions of Article 175(3) could not be construed as self-executing and, therefore, neither was Article 175(3) enforceable nor did it confer any power on the High Court to issue directions for its implementation.

The Supreme Court upheld the majority judgment of the Sindh High Court in nearly all its material details.[39] The Court held:

> The independence of the judiciary means
>
> (a) that every judge is free to decide matters before him in accordance with his assessment of the facts and his understanding of the law without improper influences, inducements or pressures, direct or indirect, from any quarter or for any reason; and
>
> (b) that the Judiciary is independent of the Executive and Legislature, and has jurisdiction, directly or by way of review, over all issues of a judicial nature.

On financial independence of the judiciary, the Supreme Court laid down the following guidelines:

> Financial independence of the judiciary can be secured if the funds allotted to the Supreme Court and High Courts (by the Parliament and the Provincial Assemblies in their respective annual budgets) are allowed to be disbursed within the limits of the sanctioned budget by the respective Chief Justices of these Courts without any interference by the Executive (in practical terms without reference and seeking the approval of the Ministry of Finance/the Provincial Finance Department). Thus, the Chief Justice would be competent to make reappropriation of the amounts from one head to another, create new posts, abolish old posts or change their nomenclature and to upgrade or downgrade etc. as per requirements of their respective Courts and this should be possible without being obliged to seek the approval of the Ministry of Finance or the Provincial Finance Departments as the case may be, provided of course the expenditure that is incurred by them falls within the limits of the budget allocation for their Courts. To ensure financial discipline, an Accounts Officer of the Accountant-General may sit in all Courts for pre-audit and issue of cheques. In this way, the control of the executive over the judiciary in this important sphere will be eliminated and the judiciary enabled to function independently.

The Supreme Court also held that:

> The following directions consistent with the mandate contained in Article 175 of the Constitution would suffice to secure the separation of the Judiciary from the Executive, namely:
>
> i. The Governments of Sindh and Punjab shall issue the requisite notifications in terms of subsection (2) of section 1 of Law Reforms Ordinance (XII of 1972) for enforcing the provisions of the aforesaid Ordinance by 23rd March, 1994, for bifurcating the magistracy into Judicial Magistrates and Executive Magistrates and place all the Judicial Magistrates under the administrative control of the High Court; and
>
> ii. The Federal Government as also the Provincial Governments of Sindh, Punjab, NWFP, and Balochistan shall not require the Supreme Court and the High Courts of the Provinces to seek the approval to incur expenditure on any item from the funds allowed for them in the annual budgets provided the expenditure incurred falls within the limit of the sanctioned budgets, as more fully explained in the body of the judgment. Necessary instructions to enable compliance with this direction shall be issued by the Federal Government and the Provincial Governments to all concerned by 1-12-1993.

The Supreme Court gave its judgment on 31 March 1993, but the federal and provincial governments continue to drag their feet in its implementation. The provincial governments applied to the Supreme Court for an extension in time to implement this judgment which was categorically denied to them. All the provincial governments are moving at a snail's pace on this matter which is based on a constitutional dictate. Bureaucrats are trying their best to frustrate this judgment by telling the government that it would be left powerless and ineffective if the judiciary is separated from the executive as dictated by the Supreme Court. The inaction and delay on the part of the government is indeed a negation of their constitutional duty and a blatant violation of a clear verdict by the highest court in the country.

Fundamental Rights and Civil Liberties

'Fundamental rights are those which have their origin in the express terms of the Constitution or which are necessarily to be implied from those terms'.[40] In the opinion of Justice A.R. Cornelius, in *State v Dosso*, fundamental rights are more important than the Constitution itself, because a Constitution does not create these rights but only recognizes them as these are rights of all human beings accepted over centuries of civilized human existence. 'Civil liberties' is defined by Blackstone to be nothing other than natural liberty: 'So far restrained by human laws, and no further, as is necessary and expedient for the general advantage of the public'.[41]

The expression 'civil liberties' implies the existence of an organized society maintaining public order without which it would be prey to the excesses of unrestrained abuses. The two expressions 'fundamental rights' and 'civil liberties' have at times been taken as synonymous although 'fundamental rights' are more comprehensive than 'civil liberties' which is the concern with the rights of life, liberty, and property. More elaborately, these include the rights of due process of law; freedom of speech and writing; freedom of religion; freedom of movement, association, and assembly; the inviolability of human dignity and protection against double jeopardy; and freedom to acquire, hold, and dispose of property. Fundamental rights include all these and many others like freedom of trade, occupation, and profession; equality before law and equal protection of laws; protection of languages and culture, and so on.

The first Constituent Assembly of Pakistan attached special importance to the inclusion of fundamental rights in the Constitution for Pakistan and appointed a Committee on Fundamental Rights and on matters relating to minorities. This Committee, at its first meeting on 26 May 1948, decided to appoint two separate sub-Committees to deal with matters relating to (1) Fundamental Rights and (2) Minorities. The sub-Committee on Fundamental Rights submitted a report on 26 June 1948 and a further report on 17 June 1949 to the Committee which, in turn, presented its interim report to the Constituent Assembly on 28 September 1948.[42] The report, with some modifications, was adopted by the Constituent Assembly in October 1950. It was on the basis of this Report that a wide variety of rights of citizens were included in the Constitution of 1956 as 'fundamental rights'. Part II of the Constitution was devoted to the fundamental rights which were elaborately defined and described. These include equality before law and equal protection of laws; due process of law; protection against retrospective offences or punishment; safeguards as to arrest and detention; freedom of speech, assembly, association, and movement; freedom of trade, business or profession; freedom to profess, practise, and propagate any religion and the right to maintain religious institutions and educational institutions for receiving religious instruction; right to acquire, hold and dispose of property; non-discrimination in respect of access to public places; prohibition of slavery and forced labour; safeguard against discrimination in services; preservation of culture, script and language; and abolition of untouchability. These fundamental rights were quite comprehensive and covered civil liberties known to civilized societies. These include the rights recognized and adopted in the English Bill of Rights 1688 and various basic rights guaranteed by the US Constitution in the first ten Amendments and thirteenth and fourteenth Amendments. The Constitution declared that all laws inconsistent with or in derogation of the fundamental rights would be void. These rights were made enforceable by the Supreme Court by issuance of directives, orders, or writs including writs in the nature of habeas corpus, mandamus, prohibition, *quo warranto* and *certiorari*.[43] The High Courts were also empowered to issue such writs for enforcement of fundamental rights conferred under the Constitution.[44]

The Constitution of 1962 originally omitted the fundamental rights. There was an outcry against this and rightly so because it was repugnant to the principles of constitution-making for a civilized society in the modern world. Undoubtedly, the omission occurred because the Constitution had been given by a military dictator. Ultimately, the Constitution was amended and a chapter on fundamental rights was added by the Constitution (First Amendment) Act, 1963. The fundamental rights included in the 1962 Constitution were the same and similarly worded as those in the 1956 Constitution. It was provided that all laws inconsistent with or in derogation of the fundamental rights would be void. These were made enforceable through directives, orders, and writs to be issued by the High Courts.[45] However, no writ jurisdiction was conferred on the Supreme Court for enforcement of such fundamental rights.

The Constitution of 1973 included a chapter on fundamental rights which were similar to and similarly worded as those in the previous Constitutions. All laws inconsistent with, repugnant to or in derogation of the fundamental rights could be declared void. These were made enforceable through orders, directives, and writs of the High Courts.[46] The Supreme Court was conferred with the original jurisdiction to issue such orders, directives, and writs.[47] The Constitution of 1956 provided for suspension of fundamental rights and the enforcement mechanism on the proclamation of emergency by the president on account of war or internal disturbance.[48] The Constitution of 1962 also made a similar provision.[49] The Constitution of 1973 made only a slight departure in this behalf. The president, in his proclamation of emergency, has to specify which of the fundamental rights and their enforcement would stand suspended during the period of emergency.[50] The Constitution also permits legislation repugnant to certain fundamental rights like freedom of speech, movement, assembly, association, trade, business, or profession; and protection of property rights during the currency of the period of emergency. Such laws would, however, be deemed to have been repealed on the revocation of the emergency.

Although fundamental rights and civil liberties are given recognition, protection, and enforcement under the Constitution, the citizens of Pakistan remained deprived of fundamental rights and their enforceability through courts for a very long period of time. The Constitution of 1956 came into force on 23 March 1956 and was abrogated on 7 October 1958 by the proclamation of martial law, so the fundamental rights were only in force for two and a half years. The Constitution of 1962, which came into force on 7 June 1962, did not include fundamental rights which were added through an amendment which came into force on 10 January 1964. The fundamental rights were suspended on the proclamation of emergency on 6 September 1965 due to the Indo-Pakistan war and remained suspended till the Constitution itself was abrogated on 25 March 1969. Fundamental rights were also extended under the Interim Constitution of 1972 but they never came into force because of the continuation of the emergency proclaimed on 23 November 1971 due to the Indo-Pakistan war of 1971.

This proclamation of emergency of 1971 was continued under the Constitution of 1973. A joint sitting of the two Houses of Parliament passed a resolution on 5 September 1973, approving the continuation of emergency proclaimed in 1971 for a period of six months. On 6 September 1973, another resolution was passed in a joint sitting approving the President's Order of 14 August 1973 (the day the Constitution went into force), suspending the enforcement of the fundamental rights and continued such suspension for six months. The emergency and suspension of fundamental rights was continued by Parliament for another six months. However, the order suspending fundamental rights was finally rescinded on 14 August 1974.[51] The emergency, however, continued indefinitely because the requirement of periodic extensions for six months of the emergency in the joint meeting of the two Houses of Parliament was dispensed with on 13 February 1975 by the Third Amendment to the Constitution. In a nutshell, the emergency proclaimed in 1971 remained in force during the period from 14 August 1973 to 5 July 1977 when Bhutto was ousted by Zia. Even fundamental rights remained suspended for a full year after the enforcement of the Constitution. The fundamental rights remained suspended during the martial law of Zia (from 5 July 1977 to 30 December 1985). On 30 of December, 1985, Junejo, in a heroic announcement, declared the revocation of emergency and thus allowed enforcement of fundamental rights through the courts. Therefore, before 31 December 1985, the fundamental rights under the three Constitutions were justiciable for the following periods only:

23 March 1956 to 7 October 1958	two years,	six months,	fourteen days.
10th January 1964 to 6 September 1965	one year,	seven months,	twenty-six days.
14 August 1974 to 5 July 1977	two years,	ten months,	twenty-one days.
	seven years,	one month,	one day.

Once again emergency was proclaimed and all fundamental rights have been suspended by the President on 28 May 1998, the day five nuclear tests were held and the citizens are again on a course of uncertainty as to their fundamental rights and civil liberties.

Hence, from 23 March 1956 to 30 December 1985, a period of about thirty years, fundamental rights were enforceable through courts for only seven years, and the citizens of Pakistan remained deprived of their fundamental rights and civil liberties for more than half the period of its existence.

Corruption and Coercion in the Corridors of Power

Corruption and coercion in the body politic are nothing new. They have existed throughout history in nearly every country and in every system but in different degrees, intensity, and extent. Dictatorial regimes are more prone to these aberrations because there is little accountability in such regimes. Democratic regimes are expected to be less prone to corruption and coercion because of the transparency of the system of governance. The stipulations of the Constitution and a free press are meant to expose all elements of misgovernment and keep them in check. The health of a Constitution and the system of government that it provides are determined from the system of checks and balances it contains between the various organs of state and various state functionaries. This has been the eternal dilemma of constitution makers everywhere because the Constitution creates and regulates state power and we all know that power corrupts and absolute power corrupts absolutely. It is, therefore, imperative that the power conferred on any functionary should not be absolute but circumscribed. The rationale of the concept of 'separation of powers' is to ensure a balance between various institutions of the state thus checking, limiting, and containing one another. In the monarchical system, the king had absolute power. He was the chief executive, the law giver and the supreme judge. Historical evidence suggests that concentration of all power in one hand tends to create tyranny and corruption of the worst kind, witnessed during the corruption of the Roman and Byzantium empires. It was thus considered by political philosophers like Montesqueie, Locke, and Rousseau, to be imperative for a healthy state that these three basic state functions be divided and given into different hands so that they may keep an eye on one another and create a balance of state power.

'Corruption', as applied to public office holders, is a difficult word, not always accurately understood, covering a multitude of delinquencies great and small. The term broadly covers 'incompetency, corruption, gross immorality, criminal conduct amounting to felony, malfeasance, misfeasance or non-feasance in office'.[52] However, for the purpose of the present study, certain forms of corruption will be discussed in particular. Pakistan started with a clean slate headed by Jinnah, a man of unimpeachable character and conduct. Even other politicians of the early days of Pakistan like Liaquat, Nazimuddin, Chaudhri Mohammad Ali, Suhrawardy, and Chundrigar, despite their other shortcomings, were not tainted by monetary corruption or financial impropriety. All these leaders lived modestly and did not leave behind big fortunes or fat bank balances in Pakistan or abroad. Even the most detested political/bureaucratic characters of that time, Ghulam Muhammad and Iskandar Mirza, were not known for accepting bribes, commissions, or kickbacks.

It started with Ayub. He can be regarded as the pioneer of political corruption and coercion in Pakistan. With the declaration of martial law, he started picking at the politicians and was not above personal rancour. One of his first acts was to arrest and detain Ayub Khuhro on a false charge, primarily to avenge his (Khuhro's) attitude as defence minister towards him (Ayub) as Commander-in-Chief. It is said that Khuhro, as defence minister, used to make Ayub wait outside his office for hours. He then gave a Draconian law, Elective Bodies Disqualification Order (EBDO), for excluding those politicians from political life whom he did not eye with favour. Under this law, several national politicians like Suhrawardy and Qayyum Khan, were disqualified for seven years (till 31 December 1965). The matter did not stop there. His sons and relatives like General Habibullah, whose daughter was married to Ayub's son, became a big time industrialist during the Ayub regime and took full advantage of the name and influence of Ayub to become an industrial tycoon. His sons resigned from the army to become industrialists by obtaining big loans from government banks. One of them, Gohar Ayub, became a leading industrialist and even tried his hand at politics. After the controversial victory of Ayub at the presidential polls in 1965, he went on a rampage in Karachi along with his political cronies to avenge his father's defeat at the polls. Gohar and his lackeys indulged in excesses which were deeply resented by the people of Karachi. Ayub, a man with a humble background, grew very rich while in power. His government is also known for repression of student unions through the University Ordinance of 1963 and its strangulation of the press through the Press and Publications Ordinance, 1963. His self-righteous airs and holier-than-thou attitude did not make him realize that he was indulging in coercion and corruption. He justified enrichment of his family by saying that his sons had every right to go into business and industry and to obtain loans.

Yahya, another military man in politics, is discredited for taking steps that led to the breakup of Pakistan. He was notorious for being a drunkard and a womanizer who behaved irresponsibly in his public statements and at international gatherings and summits. Despite his other faults, he and his associates are not known to have indulged in financial improprieties. He is not known to have left any sizeable fortune behind.

Then came Bhutto. His regime has a very poor human rights record. Repression of political opponents was something common in his days in power. All his political opponents suffered detention, false involvement in criminal cases, and personal humiliation. He allowed his political underlings like Mustafa Khar and Mumtaz Bhutto to victimize their political opponents and encouraged the use of terrorist tactics to subdue any dissent within party ranks. Even in the matter of financial conduct, his regime is not known to have been clean. He is rumoured to have whisked away large sums to his foreign exchange accounts abroad. Some of the members of his cabinet were known to be thoroughly unprincipled. Corruption in public life became widespread in his regime and industrial and commercial licences, public offices like ambassadorships, and even depots for rationing of essential commodities were used as tools of political bribery. His government also dealt heavy-handedly with dissenting lawyers and journalists.

Then came Zia, whose government took coercion and corruption to new heights. He was an ardent believer in the carrot and stick policy and oppressed political rivals, particularly those who belonged to the PPP. The jails were full of political prisoners. But Zia would also offer public offices, lucrative business licences, and expensive plots of land to lure others to his side. He allowed his generals to grow rich overnight by making shady land deals and by accepting big commissions and kickbacks. Some of his generals were so corrupt that they could put Byzantine regimes to shame. Some international magazines called them the richest generals in the world, and with justification. Despite his Islamic pretentions, Zia had no reservations about using unfair means to perpetuate his power. He bribed generals, bureaucrats, and politicians alike to keep them in line. He 'gifted' expensive commercial plots in Islamabad, Lahore, and Karachi as part of political bribery. Cantonment lands became easy prey for his generals and other high-ranking military officials. Intelligence funds were swindled. Funds for the Afghan war were diverted to personal accounts. Even military hardware like missiles were secretly sold to Iran (during the Iran-Iraq war) to enrich Zia and some of his closest colleagues. The generals in the *junta* around him became rich beyond recognition. The politicians who cooperated with him had a great time too. As long as no one questioned his claim to power, he could get away with misappropriation of public funds, graft, bribery, commissions, and kickbacks.

Even the civilian government of Junejo was not free from corruption. Junejo, himself a decent and relatively honest man, had to indulge in political corruption to keep himself in power. He introduced political bribery to the members of Parliament and the Provincial Assemblies by allocating development funds to them on a yearly basis. Junejo knew all too well that these so-called development funds would be misappropriated and swindled anyway, but he sanctioned them as political bribery to keep members of Parliament loyal to him. During his government, commercial and residential plots were used as political bribes.

Even after the death of Zia, his shadow looms large over the political culture of Pakistan. The governments of Benazir and Nawaz that followed are models of political corruption. Both these governments have pulled out all the stops on corruption. The Sharif family became industrial tycoons and billionaires while in power. The Bhuttos and Zardaris are not far behind. Regardless of the bitter political rivalry between Benazir and Nawaz, their methods are identical and their objectives similar. They do not oppose one another in terms of different visions of the future of the country but for personal gain. Those out of power lament the loss of handsome amounts every day that they could have made by way of bribes, commissions, or kickbacks. The scale of corruption by these two governments alone is mind boggling. Huge amounts have been deposited abroad and national wealth has been looted. Expensive properties in England and Europe are being purchased with the funds from the public treasury in Pakistan. In addition, they have adopted a royal style of government. These regimes have imported fleets of Mercedes and other expensive cars for their use and bought aeroplanes for the prime minister and chief ministers. Nawaz Sharif illegally occupied seventy-two kanals of public land around his private residence in Lahore. Similarly, land around Bilawal House in Karachi has been occupied through questionable means.

These leaders, their families and relatives, and close associates regard themselves above the law and this poor country as their personal fiefdom.

Corruption has taken many forms in Pakistan. so much so, that it can be studied under different heads. Electoral corruption is one of its various forms, which refers to corrupting of the electoral process ever since the general elections in 1985, and the elections of 1988 in particular. In the partyless elections of 1985, it was imperative for a candidate to spend millions of rupees to get elected to a seat in the National or the Provincial Assembly. There were cases where tens of millions were spent for a seat in the National Assembly. The heads of expenditure in this regard included a huge bribe to the major *pirs* in the constituencies who could influence voters with the payment depending upon the extent of influence wielded by the *pir*; payment to principal supporters or those who wielded influence in various areas like village heads or heads of *biradaris* (brotherhoods); publicity through expensive colour hoardings, banners, and posters; and feasting throughout the election month for supporters and for the public at large. Such expensive campaigning drove away political workers belonging to the middle class who aspired to a seat in the Assemblies. Only the very rich could think of venturing into the electoral process.

The general elections of 1988 brought some hope for the middle-rung political workers and people from the middle class because these elections were being held on a party basis. However, the principal contending political parties, namely the PPP and IJI, disappointed the people because, barring a few cases, party tickets were virtually put on sale where the highest bidder could buy himself a party ticket. There were stories circulating about briefcases full of cash being left at the offices or residences of influentials in the allotment of party tickets. What happened in the general elections of 1988 was repeated with greater intensity in the general elections of 1990 and 1993. Compaign expenses simply sky-rocketed. In some constituencies, the candidates were rumoured to have spent as much as fifty million rupees, some of them having spent from their own pockets to build roads, give electrical connections, and indulge in other ad hoc developmental work. This situation was at its worst during the Benazir government from 1988 to 1990, with a hostile provincial government headed by Nawaz. The PPP was making all efforts to win over the loyalty of IJI members in the Punjab Assembly so as to tip the balance in its favour and destabilize the Nawaz government. The IJI, with the help of then President Ishaq, was trying to win over members supporting the PPP government at the centre and in the province of NWFP. The methods employed were no secret. Loyal members were kept captive in places like Murree, Changa Manga, and other resorts to avoid their being bought over by the other party. The PPP promised expensive plots of land in Islamabad and Karachi to keep their own members in line while the IJI government promised expensive plots in Lahore to buy the loyalties of members supporting the PPP at the centre and in the NWFP. It was rumoured that a Senator from IJI was sent to Peshawar with a lot of cash in briefcases to bribe members of the NWFP Assembly and destabilize Sherpao's government. The Senator was carrying on with his negotiations when his room was forcibly entered by thugs sent by the Sherpao government who made away with the briefcases in his room. In one day in Murree, twenty plots of land in the LDA scheme were said to have been allotted to members of the NWFP Assembly to win over their loyalties. During the no-confidence motion against Benazir in 1989, some MNAs from the IJI crossed the floor and opposed the motion of their own party. They were later rewarded with ministerships or parliamentary secretaryship. There are allegations that money was diverted to pay off the members of the National Assembly either to buy their loyalty or keep them in line.

After the dismissal of the Nawaz government at the federal level in April 1993, Pakistan witnessed its worst example of horse trading in the Punjab. Ghulam Haider Wyne, a loyalist of Nawaz, was not popular with a number of members of the Punjab Assembly and Manzoor Wattoo, Speaker of the Punjab Assembly at that time, pounced upon this opportunity and managed to get a motion of no-confidence passed against Wyne in a rather unusual and hurried manner. This was followed by Wattoo getting himself elected as Chief Minister of the Punjab. The situation changed on the restoration of the Nawaz government by the Supreme Court on 26 May 1993. Nawaz was obliged to the Chaudhris of Gujrat and wanted their nominee, Parvez Elahi, to be elected as Chief Minister. In any case, he did not trust Wattoo who had taken undue advantage of his ouster from power. He came into action and launched a campaign to win over a majority of the members of the Punjab Assembly for Parvez Elahi. With Nawaz in the saddle as Prime Minister and Shujaat Husain as Interior Minister, and above all backed by big money, the position of Wattoo started sagging and large scale defections took place from his camp. The majority shifted against him and a vote of no-confidence was imminent. He, therefore, advised the Governor to dissolve the Assembly to avoid facing a motion for vote of no-confidence. While the dispute over the validity of dissolution of the Assembly remained pending before the High Court, a majority of the members of the Punjab Assembly were virtually kept as guests, or captives of Parvez Elahi in a five star hotel in Islamabad in the hope that the Assembly would be revived by the Court and that these members would go to Lahore to pass a motion of no-confidence against Wattoo and for Parvez Elahi as chief minister. This never happened because of the dissolution of all the assemblies on 18 July 1993, although a majority of the members of the Punjab Assembly enjoyed the hospitality of Parvez Elahi in five star hotels of Islamabad and Bhurban for weeks together.

Another incidence of horse trading was the overthrow of the provincial government of the NWFP headed by Sabir Shah. Some of the members of the assembly were won over and later made ministers by Sherpao, who became the chief minister as a result. Even the Supreme Court failed to prevent such blatant horse trading. The practice of horse trading and floor crossing became a challenge for the Constitution and polity in Pakistan which the Fourteenth Amendment to the Constitution has tried to rectify but only time will tell if such a reprehensible practice can be cured by constitutional amendment.

Pakistan at the Crossroads

Political activity in Pakistan has been confused and clouded by non-issues that have been blown out of all proportions. So much time and energy has been spent debating problems that do not actually exist. Rhetoric and hyperbole have taken the place of serious discussion on real problems confronting the people. Cliches rather than accurate statements have been the stuff of political life. Serious thinking is not going into identifying the real issues and problems and the so-called think tanks within political parties are busy coining empty but high sounding slogans. The objective of the major political parties is to somehow achieve power and then consider what to do with it. There is nothing behind any party except for the bloated egos and thirst for power of the leaders. As a result, political parties do not have any serious manifestos–only hollow slogans. But even slogans, in order to be attractive, have the tendency not to focus on problems but on attractive catchwords during election campaigns and political rallies. Apart from the constitutional and political issues discussed above, there are other very important issues that are outside the scope of the present work. They are economic and social issues like poverty, illiteracy, over-population, lack of medical care, housing shortage, unplanned urbanization, pollution of air and water resources, deforestation, and others, which require immediate attention and focussing. Apart from making some general statements about these problems, successive governments have failed to address them. These issues have been treated as low priority and the budget allocation for them has been embarrassingly little. Whatever is allocated is not actually spent and budget allocations usually fall prey to top-heavy bureaucracy and greedy politicians. The funds never reach the place or the people for whom they were meant. No wonder the problems are only becoming more and more acute with the passage of time.

One of the favourite slogans of political parties is that if they are allowed to make society truly Islamic, everything would resolve itself. This is the slogan which had been used by Zia for over eleven years. Islam is neither the problem nor the controversy in Pakistan. More than ninety-five per cent of the population is Muslim and the minorities hardly matter. There is absolutely no threat to Islam. Nobody can dare do anything un-Islamic in Pakistan. The people will not allow that. Over-emphasizing this non-issue has created serious problems in the country. The Sunnis and Shias, who have lived peacefully together for centuries, are now at each other's throat. The schools within the Shia and Sunni sects are also at war with one another. The militant wings of these sectarian political parties are responsible for so many deaths and so much destruction. They have destroyed the peaceful life of the citizens and particularly the environment of educational institutions. At one point, Parliament busied itself over the debate of whether under Islam, the head of government could be a woman or not. In a democratic system, this debate is pointless because the verdict has to be given by the electorate. There are other political parties and groupings which have raised slogans against obscenity and pornography. These do not exist as issues or problems in Pakistan. The citizens are generally devout Muslims and do not accept these cultural values. It is, therefore, necessary that time and energy should not be wasted on non-issues and attention be focussed on the real issues bedeviling the polity. It is imperative that the problems are clearly identified, and only after such identification can their true solutions be found.

Democracy is that form of government in which sovereign power resides in and is exercised by the whole body of free citizens, directly or indirectly through a system of representation.[53] But democracy does not come overnight. It has to evolve in a society over a long period of time. It has to take root slowly amongst the people and become part of their culture. It cannot be imposed from above. Otherwise, it would remain alien in the body politic and would be prone to gross abuse. Pakistan is a classic example of the democratic form being imposed from above without any content. Those who run the system do not believe in it. They see it as an object of exploitation for their own narrow ends. They think that election to a democratic office is a licence to abuse power and to repress civil rights. They deny rule of law to the people and deprive them of individual liberty. A democracy without constitutional liberation is not only inadequate but dangerous, bringing with it erosion of liberty, the abuse of power, ethnic divisions, and even war. This is where Pakistan stands after fifty years of its creation. Since independence, Pakistan has experimented with the constitution, government, and the structure of the state. To date, the military has seized power three times and has ruled directly or indirectly for more than half the life of the country. Ostensibly, the withdrawal of military rule was followed by representative democracy with assemblies, cabinets, political parties, a free press, and other symbols of democracy, but the reality of Pakistan's political life remained unchanged. Every political government, since the death of Liaquat, has bowed to the authority of *la pouvoir*, the permanent reality of military dictate, and refrained from challenging it because they know it is their will which is ultimately obeyed by the citizens. Bhutto made the fatal mistake of ignoring this reality. He tried to assert the supremacy of the civilian government, paid dearly for it, and went to the gallows.

How does one categorize the polity of Pakistan which is democratic in the strictly formal sense of the term? On paper, at least, it meets all the criteria of liberal democracy that guarantees basic rights. In actual fact, people have lost faith in the electoral machinery, in the judicial system where judges try to match their constitutional ideas to the exigencies of corrupt politics, sometimes going against the interest of citizens; where no incumbent elected government allows the people to express political preferences from time to time in an atmosphere free from fear, coercion, or intimidation; where known corrupt people, tax evaders, smugglers, and robber barons are foisted upon a poor, illiterate electorate unable to make an informed political choice, and then are sworn in as ministers; where elections throw up not the best, not the noblest, not the fittest, not the most deserving, but the scum of the community only because they are the richest, the most corrupt, the most unprincipled and the most unscrupulous; where government loyalists and goons storm the country's Supreme Court, the guardian of the Constitution and protector of citizens' rights, and force the judges to flee for safety with no one to protect them; where no incumbent elected government ever loses an election for reasons that are too well known to dilate upon; where no elected central government, whatever its majority, has ever lost power on the floor of the House after a vote of no-confidence was brought against it; where parliamentary strength does not guarantee the stability or the survival of government, and loss of power is brought about by extraneous forces; where ultimate power, that is the highest power, resides neither in the people, nor the electorate, nor the parliament, nor the executive, nor the judiciary, nor even in the Constitution, which theoretically has superiority over all the institutions it creates; where a shadow military state lurks behind a corrupt civilian facade; where all major decisions are made by the military and civil governments merely follow; where neither the government, nor the opposition, nor the judiciary is interested in accountability; where political opponents are hounded, harassed and persecuted in the name of accountability; where acts of gross misconduct, abuse of power, betrayal of people's trust, rampant corruption, and violation of the oath of office by holders of public office go unpunished; where Parliament is gagged, does not represent the general will and aspirations and hopes of the people and nobody sheds any tears when it is dissolved and an elected government sacked; and where the only way to get rid of a corrupt, unpopular, and thoroughly discredited elected government is to follow Lenin's maxim that voting with the citizens' feet is more effective than voting through elections. It is axiomatic that elections alone even if they are free, fair, and impartial, do not make a political democracy. Isn't it, therefore, a misnomer to describe such a government as democratic? Talking about ballot box democracy, the saying of Stalin seems to be so true in the context of democracy in Pakistan: 'It doesn't matter who votes or how many vote. What matters is who does the counting.'[54]

Having ventured into a narrative of the constitutional and political history of Pakistan over the past fifty years and having discussed the various constitutional and political issues, there is ample reason to feel grim. Our lesson from history is that we do not learn from history. We are prone to make the same mistakes repeatedly with ever more disastrous consequences each time. It is noticeable that despite the lapse of fifty years, in which period three permanent constitutions were adopted and as many interim or provisional constitutions framed, basic constitutional and political issues remain unresolved. By now, these issues should have been history and the public office should be focussing on more vital issues of poverty alleviation, agricultural uplift, industrial expansion, environmental damage control, full literacy and higher education, foreign investment, medical care and cover for citizens, improved infrastructure and means of communications, and better standards of living for the people. Instead, we are still going round and round in circles.

Mind boggling corruption and endemic inefficiency has wiped out any confidence in the state structure that ever existed. Citizens do not seek the protection of the police, they rather seek protection from the police. The basic relationship and function between the state and the citizens of protector and protected has ceased to exist. The judiciary has lost its credibility and people do not expect justice from the court system because it has degenerated over the years. The administration is seen by the citizen as an oppressor and an instrument in the hands of a corrupt bureaucracy and unscrupulous politicians, which is used to enrich the corrupt and impoverish and oppress the populace. The state structure has all but crumbled.

People have lost all confidence in the political leadership. There is a consistent pattern of decline in the percentage of voter turn-out in every succeeding general elections. People do not expect any improvement in their conditions as a result of general elections. Major political parties and groupings do not offer any healthy alternatives. People are then forced to make a choice between two groups of political gangsters and rogues. The electoral system and structure on which democracy is supposed to rest has lost its moral standing.

The political system has degenerated into a contest between feudal and industrial powers. The PPP, originally a populist party, represents feudal interest in the country and the PML(N) is the stronghold of industrialists, traders, and businessmen. The interests of these classes are intrinsically in conflict with the national interest. The feudals have a stake in keeping the country backward, illiterate, dependent, and retrogressive so that they can reign supreme. Industrialists and businessmen are trained to maximize their profits and for them, politics is business. They advance their personal interests at the expense of the national interest, but for a few statements here and there and a few cosmetic steps as window dressing, they have little concern for the problems of the common man.

Overall, progressive political forces are losing ground to retrogressive ones. This is a great betrayal of the people of Pakistan who have repeatedly rejected those who advocate an obscurantist, theocratic state. It is also a betrayal of the vision of the founder of the nation who wanted Pakistan to take an honoured place in the comity of nations as a developed and enlightened State. It is a fact of history that Muslims progressed, prospered, invested, discovered, and enjoyed peace during times when religion was not imposed from above by the State. It is universally acknowledged that Muslims in the eras of the Abbasids in Baghdad, the Mughals in India, and the Ottomans in Turkey, were at the peak of their civilization while contemporary Europe was steeped in ignorance and prejudice. It is noticeable, particularly after the Second World War, that those countries which adopted democratic constitutions and modern systems of governance have prospered economically while those which had military or civilian dictatorial regimes have stagnated and suffered from corruption at the hands of their own rulers. Whatever the shortcomings of democracy, it has produced better results than any other system of governance devised in the course of human history. Seen in the light of historical experience and contemporary realities, it can be concluded that Pakistan can progress and prosper only as a modern progressive democratic state.

NOTES

1. The word 'Muslim' was later shed from the name, making it Awami League.
2. Finer, S.E.; Bogdanor, Vernon; Rudden, Bernard, *Comparing Constitutions*, 1993, Oxford University Press, Oxford, pp. 8–10.
3. Hakim Khan v Government of Pakistan, PLD 1992 S.C. 595.
4. See Government of NWFP v Said Kamal, PLD 1986 S.C.360. The statutes of pre-emption in Punjab and NWFP were struck down by the Shariat Bench of the Supreme Court on the notions of the members of the Bench themselves. This judgment was followed by a number of other judgments on the subject which foreclosed the right of the citizens acquired under the statutes that were struck down.

5. He is reported to have said in open court that 'Chicks will go with the hen', meaning thereby the appointees of Maulvi Mushtaq would meet the same fate that he himself had met.
6. One appointment was made solely on the consideration that the father of the appointee was a close friend of the father of a chief minister. A federal law minister, though with better credentials, got his uncle and an old friend, who had practically given up law practice, appointed as judges of the High Court.
7. A governor succeeded in having one of his relatives appointed. The law minister interfered by giving his opinion on the files of the nominees largely based on political considerations.
8. A governor got his brother appointed as a High Court judge. Even an MNA got his son, totally unknown in legal circles, appointed as such.
9. PLD 1996 S.C. 324.
10. Newberg, Paula, *Judging the State*. 1995, Cambridge University Press Cambridge, p. 235.
11. Ibid., p. 248.
12. Article 118 of the Turkish Constitution provides for a National Security Council composed of the Prime Minister, the Chief of the General Staff, the Ministers of National Defence, Internal Affairs and Foreign Affairs, the Commanders of the Army, Navy, and the Air Force, and the General Commander of Gendarmerie, under the chairmanship of the President of the Republic. The Council submits reports to the Council of Ministers on National Security of the State and the Council of Ministers is obliged to give priority in consideration to the decisions of the National Security Council.
13. Malbin, Michael J., *Religion and Politics*, American Enterprise Institute for Policy Research, Washington D.C. Edition 1978, pp. 29–30 quoting Locke.
14. Ibid., p. 30.
15. Ibid., p. 33.
16. *Encyclopedia Britannica*, 1974, Volume 15, p. 248.
17. US Constitution in the First Amendment resolved this dilemma by providing as under:
'Congress shall make no law respecting an establishment of religion, or prohibiting the free exercise thereof.'
18. The statements made are based on the interpretation of the establishment clause by the US Supreme Court in a number of cases including Everson v Board of Education, 330 US 1 (1947), Zorach v Clauson 343 US 306 (1952).
19. Abington School District v Schempp, 374 US 203 (1963).
20. Ahmad, Eqbal, 'Islam and Politics'. An article in the book titled Islam, Politics and State edited by Air Marshall (R) Asghar Khan, Zed Book Pubslishers, London. This book was reprinted in 1985 by Vanguard Book Ltd. Lahore with the title 'The Pakistan Experience—State of Religion', pp. 1-28.
21. This was not done without doing violence to the language of the Objectives Resolution. In the sentence 'wherein adequate provision shall be made for the minorities to freely profess and practise their religions and develop their cultures, the word 'freely' was dropped in the annex.
22. Mst. Sakina Bibi v Federation of Pakistan, PLD 1992 Lahore 99.
23. Hakim Khan v Government of Pakistan, PLD 1992 S.C. 595.
24. Conrad, Dieter, 'Conflicting legitimacies in Pakistan. The changing role of the Objectives Resolution (1949) in the Constitution'. This Article has appeared in the compilation 'Legitimacies and Conflicts in South Asia', from pages 122 to 157, edited by Subrata K. Mitra and Dietmar Rothermund, published by South Asia Institute, New Delhi Branch, Heidelberg University as South Asian Studies No. XXXI, printed by Manohar Press, New Delhi, 1997.
25. Article 20 of the Constitution.
26. Board of Foreign Missions v Government of the Punjab, PLJ 1987 S.C. 464 and Christian Educational Endowment Trust v Deputy Commissioner, PLJ 1987 S.C. 473.
27. Anti–Islamic Activities of Qadiani Group, Lahori Group and Ahmadis (Prohibition and Punishment) Ordinance, 1984.
28. Nasir Ahmed v The State, PLJ 1993 S.C. 1.

29. Zaheer-ud-din v The State, 1993 SCMR 1718.
30. Article 44.
31. Article 77.
32. Article 20.
33. Article 71.
34. In 1977, Bhutto, got his wife Nusrat elected against one of the reserved seats for women in the National Assembly.
35. Article 30.
36. Article 175(3).
37. Mr Sharaf Faridi was a prominent lawyer from Karachi. He was elected to the Pakistan Bar Council for three consecutive terms. He was elected as President, Sindh High Court Bar Association for four consecutive years and he died in office in January 1994. He performed commendable services for the lawyer community in Pakistan.
38. Sharaf Faridi v The Federation of Islamic Republic of Pakistan etc., PLD 1989 Karachi 404.
39. Government of Sindh v Sharaf Faridi, PLD 1994 S.C.105.
40. Black's Law Dictionary, Fifth Edition, p. 248.
41. *Words and Phrases*, Permanent Edition West Publishing Co., St. Paul, Minnesota, Volume 7, pp. 413–14.
42. Pirzada, S. Sharifuddin, *Fundamental Rights and Constitutional Remedies in Pakistan*, Edition 1966, published by All Pakistan Legal Decisions, Lahore, p. 30.
43. Article 22.
44. Article 170.
45. Article 98(2) (c).
46. Article 199(1) (c).
47. Article 184(3).
48. Article 192.
49. Article 30(9).
50. Article 233.
51. S.R.O. 1093(I)/74 dated 14 August 1974, Gazette of Pakistan, 1974, Extraordinary, Part II, p. 1548.
52. *Words and Phrases*, Volume 9A, Permanent Edition, 1960, West Publishing Co., St. Paul, Minnesota.
53. Black's Law Dictionary, Fifth Edition, 1979, West Publishing Co., St. Paul, Minna. pp. 388–9.
54. Khan, Roedad, 'Bonapartists and fake democracies', *Dawn*, 13 May 1998.

EPILOGUE

The manuscript of the book was sent to the publisher in July 1998. The process of publication has taken more than two years during which period certain important constitutional and political developments have taken place in the country. The military takeover of the government on 12 October 1999 is the most important event in recent history with far reaching consequences. Although the event is too recent for any historical analysis or profound judgment at this stage, the military takeover itself and the judgment of the Supreme Court upholding it have necessitated this epilogue.

Supreme Court Judgment on Proclamation of Emergency

Before discussing the military takeover and its aftermath, certain important constitutional and political developments during the Nawaz regime between June 1998 and October 1999 deserve mention. It has been mentioned before that a nation-wide emergency was proclaimed throughout the country on 28 May 1998, the day when nuclear tests were conducted in Pakistan. All the fundamental rights of the citizens were suspended under the proclamation. All the foreign currency accounts with banks in Pakistan were frozen. The imposition of emergency and suspension of the fundamental rights were challenged amongst others, by a number of political leaders including Farooq Leghari, Imran Khan and Manzoor Wattoo. All these petitions were filed directly before the Supreme Court on the original side under Article 184(3) of the Constitution.

The Supreme Court accepted the petitions partly and a seven judge bench headed by the Chief Justice Ajmal Mian held unanimously that:

1. That the petitions were maintainable.
2. That the materials placed before the Court and shown to the judges in Chambers *prima facie* indicated that the President was justified in issuing the Proclamation under clause (1) of Article 232 of the Constitution.
3. That keeping in view the effect of the Proclamation provided for in clause (1) of Article 233 of the Constitution, which authorizes the State to make any law or to take any executive action in deviation of Articles 15, 16, 17, 18, 19 and 24 of the Constitution and also keeping in view the language of Articles 10, 23 and 25 (which are hedged with qualifications), an order under clause (2) of Article 233 of the Constitution for suspending the enforcement of the Fundamental Rights was without justification.
4. That the Supreme Court would have jurisdiction to review/re-examine the continuation of Emergency at any subsequent stage, if the circumstances so warrant.

(Sardar Farooq Ahmad Khan Leghari and others v Federation of Pakistan and others, PLD 1999 S.C. 57)

Courts Decide Matter of Freezing of Foreign Currency Accounts

The matter of freezing of foreign currency accounts was also challenged before the Courts. A single judge of the Lahore High Court upheld the action of the government (Zahoor Ahmad v. The Federation of Pakistan, PLD 1999 Lahore 139). In appeal a full bench of Lahore High Court held that the action of freezing of the foreign currency accounts under Foreign Exchange (Temporary Restrictions) Act, 1998 was *ultra vires* of the Constitution being repugnant to equal protection clause as well as on account of excessive, unguided and arbitrary powers conferred on the functionaries of the State Bank of Pakistan (Shaukat Ali Mian v. Federation of Pakistan, 1999 CLC 607). It was argued on behalf of the federal government that the foreign currency accounts maintained with banks in Pakistan (amounting to approximately 11 billion U.S. Dollars on 28 May 1998) had actually been stripped of foreign currency and all the foreign currency deposited by the account holders had been acquired by the State Bank of Pakistan and that more than 80% of the foreign exchange had already been spent by the successive governments since 1991 and that there was very little foreign exchange actually available to be returned to the account holders. Another step taken by the federal government required that where any foreign currency account had been put under lien as security for the payment of any bank loan, the same should be converted into Pak rupees by 31 July 1998 so that the amount thus obtained be used to liquidate the loan for which it was held as collateral. This was regardless of the fact that such a loan was due for payment or not.

The Supreme Court, in appeal, upheld the findings of the full bench of the Lahore High Court with certain modifications as under:

1. It was violation of the assurance given by the Legislature in the Protection of Economic Reforms Act, 1992 to the effect that "The State Bank of Pakistan or other banks shall not impose any restrictions on deposits in and withdrawals from the foreign currency accounts and restrictions, if any, shall stand withdrawn forthwith". The improper utilization of the foreign exchange deposits of the foreign currency account holders by successive governments constitutes breach of the above solemn commitment. The State Bank of Pakistan also failed to perform its statutory duty of protecting the interest of the foreign currency account holders, thereby creating a situation where it became practically impossible to honour the above solemn statutory undertaking.
2. No power was conferred on the federation or on the State Bank of Pakistan under the Foreign Exchange (Temporary Restrictions) Act 1998 to compel foreign currency account-holders to liquidate their accounts into Pak Rupees where foreign exchange holdings had been accepted by the respective banks as security against any loans or other facilities extended to them.

3. That the foreign currency account-holders were entitled to receive interest/profits in foreign exchange on their deposits at rates already agreed as per original arrangements between them and the respective banks.
4. That the non-resident Pakistanis and foreigners maintaining foreign currency accounts as on 28.5.1998 would be entitled to utilize the interest/profits, payable to them under the above arrangements between them and the banks concerned, in any manner, including the right to remit the same abroad.
5. That in order to restore the confidence of the existing/prospective foreign currency account-holders, the federation/State Bank of Pakistan should evolve a scheme within a reasonable period keeping in view the foreign exchange position of the country for gradual removal of restrictions on operation of foreign currency accounts.

(Federation of Pakistan v Shaukat Ali Mian, PLD 1999 S.C. 1026)

Supreme Court Declares Military Courts as Unconstitutional

During the Nawaz government, the law and order situation was gradually deteriorating and sectarian killings were taking place all over the country. The situation in Karachi was getting out of control particularly when Hakim Saeed, a highly respected public figure, was murdered in broad daylight. The blame for his murder was put on MQM and Nawaz decided to crack down on the MQM. In this behalf, Pakistan Armed Forces (Acting in Aid of the Civil Power) Ordinance, 1998 (Ordinance XII of 1998) was promulgated on 20th November 1998. This Ordinance allowed establishment of military courts for trial of civilians charged with offences mentioned in the schedule to the Ordinance. The MQM leadership challenged the Ordinance under Article 184(3) of the Constitution as violative of the Constitution. The Supreme Court accepted the petition in the following terms:

1. The Ordinance No. XII of 1998 as amended up to date in so far as it allowed the establishment of military courts for trial of civilians charged with the offences mentioned in the said Ordinance was unconstitutional and that the cases in which sentences had already been awarded but not yet executed would stand set aside and the cases should stand transferred to the Anti-Terrorist Courts in terms of the guidelines provided hereunder for disposal in accordance with the law. However, the evidence already recorded in the pending cases should be read as evidence in the cases so transferred provided that it would not affect any of the powers of the Presiding Officer in this regard available under the law. However, the sentences and punishments already awarded and executed would be treated as past and closed transactions.
2. However, solution to menace of terrorism in Karachi, that had already taken toll of thousands of innocent lives and had adversely affected the economy of the entire country, should be found within the framework of the Constitution.

3. The following guidelines were laid down for achievement of the above objective:
   i. Cases relating to terrorism be entrusted to the Special Courts already established or which might be established under the Anti-Terrorism Act, 1997 or under any law in terms of the judgment of this Court in the case of Mehram Ali v. Federation of Pakistan (PLD 1998 SC 1445)
   ii. One case be assigned at a time to a Special Court and till judgment is announced in such a case, no other case be entrusted to it;
   iii. The concerned Special Court should proceed with the case entrusted to it on day to day basis and pronounce judgment within a period of 7 days;
   iv. Challan of a case should be submitted to a Special Court after full preparation and after ensuring that all witnesses would be produced as and when required by the concerned Special Court;
   v. An appeal arising out of an order/judgment of the Special Court should be decided by the appellate forum within a period of 7 days from the filing of such appeal;
   vi. Any lapse on the part of the investigating and prosecuting agencies should entail immediate disciplinary action according to the law applicable;
   vii. The Chief Justice of the High Court concerned should nominate one or more judges of the High Court for monitoring and ensuring that the cases/ appeals are disposed of in terms of these guidelines;
   viii. That the Chief Justice of Pakistan could also nominate one or more judges of the Supreme Court to monitor the implementation of these guidelines.

(Sh. Liaquat Hassan v Federation of Pakistan (PLD 1999 S.C. 504)

The Supreme Court by striking down the law for establishment of military courts for civilian offences did a great service to the nation. Undoubtedly the step taken by the government in this behalf was inherently unconstitutional. However, Nawaz publicly expressed his dissatisfaction with the judgment. His reaction exposed his claims to democratic credentials.

Constitution (Fifteenth Amendment) Bill

In August 1998, the impulsive Nawaz regime suddenly came up with a plan to virtually undo the Constitution through introduction of Fifteenth Constitutional Amendment Bill on 28 August 1998 which read as under:

> WHEREAS sovereignty over the entire universe belongs to Almighty Allah alone and the authority which He has delegated to the State of Pakistan through its people for being exercised through their chosen representatives within the limits prescribed by Him is a sacred trust;
>
> AND WHEREAS the Objectives Resolution has been made a substantive part of the Constitution;

AND WHEREAS Islam is the State religion of Pakistan and it is the obligation of the State to enable the Muslims of Pakistan, individually and collectively, to order their lives in accordance with the fundamental principles and basic concepts of as set out in the Holy Quran and Sunnah;

AND WHEREAS Islam enjoins the establishment of a social order based on Islamic values, of prescribing what is right and forbidding what is wrong (amr bil ma'roof wa nahi anil munkar);

AND WHEREAS in order to achieve the aforesaid objective and goal, it is expedient further to amend the Constitution of the Islamic Republic of Pakistan;

NOW, THEREFORE, it is hereby enacted as follows:

1. Short title and commencement:—(1) This Act may be called the Constitution (Fifteenth Amendment) Act, 1998.
2. Addition of new Article 2B in the Constitution:- In the Constitution of the Islamic Republic of Pakistan, hereinafter referred to as the said Constitution, after Article 2A, the following new Article shall be inserted, namely:

   '2B. Supremacy of the Quran and Sunnah:-

   (1) The Holy Quran and Sunnah of the Holy Prophet (peace be upon Him) shall be the supreme law of Pakistan.

   Explanation:- In the application of this clause to the personal law of any Muslim sect, the expression 'Quran and Sunnah' shall mean the Quran and Sunnah as interpreted by that sect.

   (2) The Federal Government shall be under an obligation to take steps to enforce the Shariah, to establish salat, to administer zakat, to promote amr bil ma'roof and nahi anil munkar (to prescribe what is right and to forbid what is wrong), to eradicate corruption at all levels and to provide substantial socio-economic justice, in accordance with the principles of Islam, as laid down in the Holy Quran and Sunnah.

   (3) The Federal Government may issue directives for the implementation of the provisions set out in clauses (1) and (2) and may take the necessary action against any state functionary for non-compliance of the said directives.

   (4) Nothing contained in this Article shall affect the personal law, religious freedom, traditions or customs of non-Muslims and their status as citizens.

   (5) The provisions of this Article shall have effect notwithstanding anything contained in the Constitution, any law or judgment of any Court'.
3. Amendment of Article 239 of the Constitution:- In the Constitution, in Article 239, after clause (3) the following new clauses shall be inserted, namely:-

   (3A) Notwithstanding anything contained in clause (1) to (3), a Bill to amend the Constitution providing for the removal of any impediment in the enforcement of any matter relating to Shariah and the implementation of the Injunctions of Islam may originate in either House and shall, if it is passed by a majority of the members voting in the House in which it originated, be transmitted to the other House; and if the Bill is passed without amendment by the majority of the members voting in the other House also, it shall be presented to the President for assent.

   (3B) If a Bill transmitted to a House under clause (3A) is rejected or is not passed within ninety days of its receipt or is passed with amendment it shall be considered in a joint sitting.

(3C) If the Bill is passed by a majority of the members voting in the joint sitting, with or without amendment, it shall be presented to the President for assent.

(3D) The President shall assent to the Bill presented to him under clause (3A) or clause (3C) within seven days of the presentation of the Bill".

The Bill generated heated debate throughout the country. The opposition in the Parliament was almost united against the Bill and there was even some resistance from within the PML(N). Nawaz called upon the members of the Parliament from his party, who were opposed to the Bill, to resign. Consequently the opposition within the party caved in under such threat. Though the Bill was somewhat modified to appease such party, the main provisions were retained. The clauses relating to executive directives and the constitutional amendment by simple majority were withdrawn. The Bill was tabled before the National Assembly on 9 October 1998 and it passed by 151 in favour and 16 against it. The members of the National Assembly voting in favour of the Bill included 143 from PML(N), seven FATA members and Hasil Bizenjo from Balochistan. Members belonging to the MQM remained absent from the House. The members belonging to minorities were present in the House but they did not participate in the vote. ANP and PPP members present in the House voted against the Bill.

The Bill was not presented before the Senate because Nawaz government did not have the required two-third majority there. The Bill was initially kept back to be tabled after March 2000, when elections to halve the membership of the Senate were due to be held and it was expected PML(N) would then acquire two-third majority in the Senate.

The Fifteenth Amendment Bill was apparently a blatant attempt by Nawaz to introduce dictatorship in the country in the name of Islam. This Amendment was unnecessary because the Islamic provisions included in the Constitution were adequate for the purpose of bringing the existing laws or any future legislation in conformity with the Injunctions of Islam. The Amendment would have empowered the centre more and weakened the provinces thus jeopardizing the provincial autonomy further. It would have created more divisions, accentuated the existing ones, and might have led to more sectarian and other violence. The Constitution would have lost its efficacy and would have been rendered into a meaningless document. The directives issued by the executive would have prevailed over the constitutional provisions. The law of the land would have slided into uncertainty jeopardizing the fundamental rights and civil liberties of the citizens. The Parliament and the Provincial Assemblies would have lost their character as law making bodies and the legislation would have ceased to be the business of the chosen representatives of the people. The Judiciary would have been undermined as an independent organ of the State and its decisions would have been openly flouted and overridden by the executive through directives issued in the name of Islam. Such directives would have been beyond correction through the process of judicial review. The freedom of press and speech would have been drastically curtailed and draconian censorship might have been clamped. The already difficult position of women in society would have been rendered untenable. The rights and legitimate interests of the minorities would have been further jeopardized and they would have suffered from greater insecurity. In a nutshell it was a naked attempt to impose dictatorial rule based on predesired fatwas obtained from favourite faqih or ulema. It would have set the clock back, pushing the country back into the dark ages.

The act of the Nawaz government in withholding Fifteenth Amendment Bill after its passage in the National Assembly was unusual and apparently malafide and unconstitutional. Article 239(1) reads:–

> A Bill to amend the Constitution may originate in either House and when the Bill has been passed by the votes of not less than two-thirds of the total membership of the House, it shall be transmitted to the other House.

Thus the Constitution requires (immediate) transmission of a Constitution Amendment Bill, after its passage from one House to the other. The period for such transmission has to be reasonable and not beyond ninety days in any case. Withholding the Bill after its passage from the National Assembly in October 1998 till after March 2000 (about one and a half years) would have been clearly contrary to the letter and spirit of the Constitution. Reference to Article 70 of the Constitution in this regard would be relevant which requires that a Bill (of an ordinary law) after its passage from one House, should be transmitted to the other House and the latter House has ninety days either to reject it, pass it without amendment or pass it with amendments. If the period of ninety days is allowed for consideration of a Bill by the House to which such Bill is transmitted, then how can the period of transmission itself be more than ninety days.

Supreme Court Storming Case Decided

It has been discussed above that a number of Parliament and Punjab Assembly members from the PML(N) and certain others from the PML(N) stormed the Supreme Court building in Islamabad on 28.11.1997 in order to disrupt the contempt proceedings against Nawaz. The Chief Justice Ajmal Mian appointed one of the judges of the Supreme Court, Abdur Rahman Khan to hold an inquiry into the incident. In this report dated 18.2.1998 he held that those individuals who had forced their entry into the court premises and raised slogans against the judiciary were prima facie guilty of gross contempt of court. He recommended that since most of such individuals had to be identified, it would be appropriate that a Bench of the Supreme Court be constituted for initiating contempt proceedings for the outrageous incident.

Accordingly a Bench of three judges of the Supreme Court consisting of Nasir Aslam Zahid, Munawar Ahmad Mirza and Abdur Rahman Khan was constituted by the Chief Justice to hold contempt proceedings against persons responsible for the incident. This Bench examined 53 witnesses, perused a large number of documents and watched the video cassettes containing coverage of the incident. By order dated 3

July 1998, Show Cause notices for contempt of court were issued to 26 persons including two members of the National Assembly (MNAs) and three members of the Punjab Assembly (MPAs).

Ultimately, the charges for contempt of court were framed against seven persons including the said two MNAs and three MPAs. The remaining persons were either discharged after issuance of warning or cases against them were postponed indefinitely. The Court held that the action of the day was not spontaneous but planned and the purpose was to disturb the Court which was conducting contempt proceedings at that time. However, all the accused were acquitted despite reaching the conclusion that the action of the mob/crowd amounted to a flagrant type of contempt of court. The reason given for the acquittal was that the evidence did not specifically point out any of the respondents to the extent that it could be said that the case against any one of them had been established beyond reasonable doubt.

(State v Tariq Aziz MNA and 6 others, 2000 SCMR 751)

The judgment in the storming case came as a deep disappointment to the people of Pakistan. The judgment was contradictory and confused in its reasoning and findings. It sermonized the government to jealously guard the independence of the judiciary while at the same time letting off the leading members of the government party holding representative positions responsible for committing gross contempt of court. On the one hand the court lamented that the court storming had undermined independence of judiciary but on the other hand it itself weakened and undermined the institution of judiciary by acquitting those responsible for the incident. However, in appeal, a five-member bench of the Supreme Court convicted seven persons belonging to PML(N), including two MNAs and four MPAs, for contempt of court for storming the Supreme Court building in November 1997 and sentenced each of them to do one month simple imprisonment.

(Shahid Orakzai v Pakistan Muslim League etc., Criminal Appeal No. 162 of 1999, decided on 28 September 2000)

Confrontation with the Military and Kargil Crisis

Nawaz in his endeavour to acquire more power for himself, soon ran into serious difficulty with the leadership of the Armed Forces. The Chief of Army Staff, General Jehangir Karamat, in his address to the Naval War College on 5 October 1998, proposed the establishment of a National Security Council for addressing important national issues. On 7 October 1998, General Karamat was forced to resign as Army Chief of Staff for making the proposal. He was replaced by General Pervez Musharraf, who was selected ahead of his senior colleagues. However, the sudden resignation of Gen. Jehangir Karamat caused resentment in the rank and file of the Army because the same was seen by many as a humiliation of the Armed Forces. On the other hand, his resignation was drummed up as a personal triumph for Nawaz who was now portrayed by the media as the most powerful Prime Minister that Pakistan ever had.

He was seen as someone who had stripped the President of his powers through the Thirteenth Amendment, neutralized the Parliament through the Fourteenth Amendment, forced a President to resign his office and driven out a Chief Justice from office. Now he had prevailed over the leadership of the Army by sacking its Chief of Staff. This state of affairs certainly went to his head leading to the future events that proved to his undoing.

In February 1999, Nawaz took a major initiative towards normalization of the relationship with India. Prime Minister Atal Behari Vajpayee of India visited Lahore on a bus in February 1999 thus launching a regular bus service between the cities of Lahore and Delhi. He was met at Wagah border by Nawaz and a joint communique known as 'Lahore Declaration' was signed between the two leaders spelling out various steps to be taken by the two countries towards normalization of relations. Except for Jamaat-i-Islami, whose workers demonstrated against the move, the visit of Vajpayee was not opposed by any other political or social elements in Pakistan. The move of Nawaz to normalize relations with India was generally seen with favour by opinion makers in Pakistan.

Unfortunately good relations between the two countries did not last for long. Within a few months of the Lahore Declaration, the two countries ran into a bitter confrontation within the disputed territory of Kashmir. Certain mountain peaks in the region of Kargil, from where Pakistani forces were ejected by the Indians some years ago, were occupied by the Mujahedeen (the freedom fighters) backed by Pakistan's Armed Forces. The Indian Army was badly trapped but India successfully opened a propaganda front at international level accusing Pakistan of aggression. Indian propaganda was so successful that Pakistan was left virtually without friends on the international scene. Even old friends like China refused to come to the aid of Pakistan. Faced with such a dire situation and acute isolation, Nawaz hurriedly appealed to President Clinton of the USA to bail him out. Consequently on 4 July 1999, Nawaz rushed to Washington DC and unilaterally (without participation of India) signed an accord with the USA for withdrawal of forces from Kargil and to respect the line of control in Kashmir in future. Consequently, Army personnel and Mujahedeen were withdrawn from Kargil under very humiliating circumstances. India came out with flying colours because most of the accusations it made stood admitted by Nawaz government in the Washington Accord. Bharatia Janata Party (BJP), Vajpayee's party, became the beneficiary of Pakistan's misadventure in Kargil and was returned to power with greater strength in the Lok Sabha this time in the general elections that were held in September 1999. The question as to who was responsible for the Kargil debacle, Nawaz government or the leadership of the Armed Forces, boggles the mind. It is, however, clear that Pakistan suffered a terrible setback and international humiliation. Nawaz in a recent statement blamed the Army leadership for the Kargil misadventure (*The News* of 13 June 2000). Nevertheless, Nawaz, being at the helm of affairs, cannot escape responsibility for the Kargil fiasco.

The Military Takes Over

In the aftermath of the Kargil crisis, the relationship between the Nawaz government and the leadership of the Armed Forces grew extremely tense. It was rumoured that Nawaz was preparing to sack another Army Chief and to appoint in his place someone of his own personal choice. In the middle of such rumours arrived the fateful day of 12 October 1999. General Pervez Musharaf was in Sri Lanka on an official visit on that day, when Nawaz tried to promote Lt. Gen. Zia ud Din (who was junior to several of his colleagues) to General and appoint him as Chief of Army Staff. The formalities of the appointment were somewhat carried out but the Army Corps Commander did not allow him to take over the charge of his new position. An announcement was made on national television about the appointment but it was soon interrupted and the television went off the air for a few hours. People were anxious to know what was actually happening. After a few hours, the TV screens displayed the announcement that the Nawaz government had been dismissed and that General Pervez would soon be addressing the nation. It later transpired that while the Army Commanders were taking over the TV stations, Prime Minister House, Governor Houses and other sensitive places and installations, an attempt was being made by Nawaz and his officials not to allow the PIA plane, with General Pervez aboard, to land at the Karachi Airport. It was ordered to be taken away to a destination either in the Gulf States or India. When the pilot informed that the plane was running out of fuel and could not make the journey, it was diverted to Nawabshah. However, before it could land there, the control of the airport at Karachi was taken over by the Army and the plane returned to land at Karachi

In a delayed broadcast to the nation (in the early hours of 13 October 1999) General Pervez announced that the Nawaz government had been removed and the Armed Forces had moved in and taken control of the affairs of the country. Later on it was decided by the military leadership that martial law would not be imposed and a new set-up would soon be announced. On 14 October 1999, General Pervez proclaimed emergency throughout Pakistan and assumed the office of the Chief Executive. He proclaimed that the Constitution would be held in abeyance but the President would, however, continue in office. It was also announced that the National Assembly, the Senate, and the four Provincial Assemblies would stand suspended and their speakers and chairmen were also suspended. Provisional Constitution Order (PCO) was promulgated which provided that notwithstanding the abeyance of the provisions of the Constitution, Pakistan (subject to PCO and other orders made by the Chief Executive) would be governed, as nearly as may be, in accordance with the Constitution. All courts in existence would continue to function and to exercise their respective powers and jurisdiction provided that the Supreme Court, High Courts or any other court would not have the power to make any order against the Chief Executive or any person exercising power or jurisdiction under his authority. The fundamental rights under the Constitution, not in conflict with the Proclamation of emergency or any order made thereunder from time to time, would continue to be in force. The President was to act on the advice of the Chief Executive. No court could pass any judgment, decree, writ, order or process whatsoever against the Chief Executive or any authority designated by him. All laws other than the Constitution would continue in force until altered, amended or repealed by the Chief Executive or any authority designated by him. All the persons who were members of the services would continue in office.

General Pervez in his speech of 13 October 1999 appealed to the people of Pakistan to remain calm and support the armed forces which had moved in as a last resort to prevent any further destabilization of the country. He stated that the Armed Forces would preserve the integrity and sovereignty of the country at any cost. In his address to the nation on 17 October 1999, he announced that he would head a six-member National Security Council, whose members would be the Chief of Naval Staff, the Chief of Air Staff, a specialist each in law, finance, foreign policy and national affairs. He also announced the following seven-point agenda:

1. Re-building of national confidence and morale;
2. Strengthening of the federation by removal of inter provincial disharmony and restoration of national cohesion;
3. Revival of economy and restoration of investors' confidence;
4. Ensuring law and order and dispensing speedy justice;
5. Depoliticization of state institutions;
6. Devolution of power to grass-root level, and
7. Ensuring swift and across-the-board accountability.

Military Government Confronts the Judiciary

The judiciary was not initially touched by the change. The military government promised the judiciary its independence and full powers and jurisdiction under the Constitution, subject to certain restraints on jurisdiction in regard to acts or orders of the Chief Executive or authorities acting under him. The judges of the superior courts were not required to take oath under the PCO and were allowed to continue to perform their functions and exercise their jurisdiction under the Constitution. The question as to what oath should be given to judges of superior courts came up at the time when retirement of the Chief Justice of the Peshawar High Court became due in the first week of January 2000. It was agreed that the new Chief Justice of that Court would take an oath under the Constitution. This was reaffirmed through Oath of Office (Judges) Order 1999 (promulgated on 31 December 1999) wherein it was provided that the judges of the superior courts would take the oath specified in the Constitution and in the appropriate form set out in the Third Schedule to the Constitution.

This situation was not to stay for long. A number of petitions had been filed by Nawaz and other PML(N) leaders in the Supreme Court under Article 184(3) of the Constitution challenging the military takeover on 12 October 1999 and seeking restoration of the Assemblies. All these petitions had been entertained and were fixed for hearing on 31 January 2000. As the date of hearing approached, the government started panicking. It was strongly rumoured that these petitions might be accepted and that the Assemblies might be restored and the Nawaz government reinstated. On 25 January 2000, Oath of Office (Judges) Order, 2000 was promulgated in which all the judges of the superior courts were required to make oath to the effect that they would discharge their duties and perform their functions in accordance with the Proclamation of Emergency of 14 October 1999 and the PCO as amended from time to time. However, it was provided that if a judge would not be given oath or would not take oath within the time fixed by the Chief Executive for the purpose, he would cease to hold office. In pursuance of this Order, the Chief Justice of Pakistan, Justice Saiduzzaman Siddiqui refused to take oath. His standpoint was that the military regime had given solemn undertaking to the judiciary that it would not interfere with its independence and it would be allowed to function under the Constitution. On his refusal to take oath, he was virtually put under house arrest until 11.00 A.M. on 26 January 2000 so that he might not influence those judges who were willing to take the oath. Four judges of the Supreme Court who originally hailed from Sindh, namely Nasir Aslam Zahid, Mamoon Kazi, Wajeehuddin Ahmad and Kamal Mansoor Alam, following the example of the Chief Justice, did not take oath. Khalil-ur-Rehman Khan, a Supreme Court Judge from Punjab, also refused to take oath in support of the standpoint of the Chief Justice. Only seven judges of the Supreme Court took oath and the senior most amongst them, Irshad Hassan Khan was appointed the Chief Justice. Two judges of the Lahore High Court, three judges of the Sindh High Court and two judges of the Peshawar High Court were not given oath and thus they ceased to hold office. None of the judges of the High Courts refused to take oath voluntarily.

Accountability Under the Military Government

The military government on taking over the affairs of the government made tall claims about holding accountability of corrupt politicians and bureacrates across the board. National Accountability Bureau (NAB) Ordinance, 1999 was promulgated for the purpose which contained quite a few draconian provisions particularly those relating to bail and detention. A National Accountability Bureau (NAB) was set up under this Ordinance headed by a serving General. So far, its performance has left much to be desired and the process of accountability appears to be selective and not across the board as claimed. Even the campaign for recovery of bank dues did not produce the desired results. This campaign had been drummed up in such a manner that it raised the expectations of the people in a big way. The government gave 16 November 1999 as the deadline for payment of bank dues and it was given to understand that the government would take very strong measures against those who did not pay by that date. However, the campaign for recovery of dues fizzled out after the said deadline and less than ten percent of the dues have been recovered.

Trial of Nawaz for Hijacking

Another important event was the trial of Nawaz along with six others for the hijacking of the PIA plane on 12 October 1999 with General Pervez on board. This high profile trial held in Karachi by Special Judge Mr Rehmat Hussain Jaffri ended with a verdict of guilty against Nawaz on 6 April 2000. He was awarded the sentence of life imprisonment. All his co-accused were acquitted. The appeals against his conviction and acquittal of others are pending in the Sindh High Court.

Supreme Court Upholds Military Takeover

The petitions against the military takeover and for restoration of the Assemblies were heard by a Bench of 12 judges of the Supreme Court headed by Chief Justice Irshad Hassan Khan. After months of hearing, judgment was announced as 12 May 2000 disposing of all the petitions with the following findings:

1. On 12 October, 1999 a situation had arisen for which the Constitution provided no solution and the intervention by the Armed Forces through an extra-constitutional measure became inevitable. Sufficient corroborative and confirmatory material had been produced by the Federal Government in support of the intervention by the Armed Forces through extra-constitutional measures. Thus, the intervention was validated on the basis of the doctrine of State necessity and the principle of *salus populi suprema lex* as embodied in Begum Nusrat Bhutto's case.
2. All past and closed transactions, as well as such executive actions as were required for the orderly running of the State and all acts, which tended to advance or promote the good of the people, were also validated.
3. That the 1973 Constitution remained the supreme law of the land subject to the condition that certain parts thereof were held in abeyance on account of State necessity
4. That the Superior Courts would continue to function under the Constitution. The mere fact that the Judges of the Superior Courts had taken a new oath did not in any manner derogate from this position because the Courts had originally been established under the 1973 Constitution.
5. i) That General Pervez, through Proclamation of Emergency dated the 14 October 1999 followed by PCO 1 of 1999, had validly assumed power by means of an extra-constitutional step. He was held entitled to perform all such acts and promulgate all legislative measures as enumerated hereinafter as under:
   (a) All acts or legislative measures which would be in accordance with, or could have been made under the 1973 Constitution, including the power to amend it;
   (b) All acts which tend to advance or promote the good of the people;

(c) All acts required to be done for the ordinary orderly running of the State; and

(d) All such measures as would establish or lead to the establishment of the declared objectives of the Chief Executive stated in his speeches of 13 and 17 October 1999

ii) That constitutional amendments by the Chief Executive could only be resorted to if the Constitution does not provide a solution for attainment of his declared objectives.

iii) That no amendment should be made in the salient features of the Constitution i.e. independence of judiciary, federalism, parliamentary form of government blended with Islamic provisions.

iv) That fundamental rights provided in the Constitution should continue to hold the field but the State would be authorized to make any law or take any executive action in deviation of Articles 15, 16, 17, 18, 19 and 24 of the Constitution.

v) That these acts, or any of them, could be performed or carried out by means of orders issued by the Chief Executive or through Ordinances on his advice.

vi) That the Superior Courts would continue to have the power of judicial review to determine the validity of any act or action of the Armed Forces, if challenged, in the light of the principles underlying the law of State necessity. These powers under Article 199 of the Constitution would remain available to their full extent, notwithstanding anything to the contrary contained in any legislative instrument enacted by the Chief Executive and/or any order issued by the Chief Executive.

vii) All orders made, proceedings taken and acts done by the Chief Executive or any authority on his behalf including the legislative measures, would be subject to judicial review by the superior courts on the touchstone of the State necessity.

6. That the cases of former Chief Justice and judges of the Supreme Court, who had not taken oath under the Order 1 of 2000, and those judges of the High Courts, who were not given oath, could not be re-opened having been hit by the doctrine of past and closed transaction.

7. That the Government should accelerate the process of accountability in a coherent and transparent manner justly, fairly, equitably and in accordance with law.

8. That the judges of the superior Courts would also be subject to accountability in accordance with the methodology laid down in Article 209 of the Constitution.

9. General Pervez, Chief of the Army Staff and Chairman Joint Chiefs of Staff Committee was held to be holder of Constitutional post. His purported arbitrary removal in violation of the principle of *audi altram partem* was held as *ab initio void* and of no legal effect.

10. Old legal order had not been completely suppressed or destroyed, but it was merely a case of constitutional deviation for a transitional period so as to enable the Chief Executive to achieve his declared objectives.
11. That the current electoral rolls were out-dated and fresh elections could not be held without updating them which as per report of the Chief Election Commissioner would take two years. Obviously, after preparation of the electoral rolls some time would be required for delimitation of constituencies and disposal of objections, etc. Hence three years period was allowed to the Chief Executive with effect from the date of the Army take-over i.e. 12 October, 1999 for holding general elections and achieving his declared objectives.
12. That the Chief Executive would appoint a date, not later than 90 days before the expiry of the aforesaid period of three years, for holding of a general election to the National Assembly and the Provincial Assemblies and the Senate of Pakistan.
13. That the Supreme Court would have jurisdiction to review/re-examine the continuation of the Proclamation of Emergency dated 12 October 1999 at any stage if the circumstances so warrant.

The military government could not have asked for more. The Supreme Court went all the way to justify the military takeover of 12 October 1999. The government was allowed a period of three years to accomplish its seven-point programme spelled out in the speech of General Pervez on 17 October 1999. The court did not appreciate that the programme was so comprehensive that it may not even be accomplished in many more years. The court also ignored the bitter experience of the past when Zia as head of a military regime was allowed to amend the Constitution. He made frequent use of this power and mostly in a wanton and irresponsible manner. He virtually changed the face of the Constitution particularly when he introduced amendments/alterations/additions/substitutions in 65 Articles of the Constitution under the Revival of the Constitution of 1973 Order 1985 (RCO). Conferrment of the same power on the Chief of Army Staff under the judgment of 12 May 2000 raises a spectre of similar abuse once again. The Supreme Court, in its eagerness to validate the military regime, ventured into matters which were not an issue before the court. The validity of the removal of General Pervez as Chief of Army Staff on 12 October 1999 was not directly an issue in the case but the court went out of its way to invalidate his removal on the principles of natural justice. Most unusual was the finding regarding the judges of the Supreme Court who did not take oath voluntarily or judges of the High Courts who were not given oath. The matter of not taking or being given oath was declared as a closed and past transaction. The matter was not an issue before the court. Besides, the finding was clearly against the principles of natural justice. None of these judges were heard or even represented before the court and they have all been virtually condemned unheard.

Conclusion

The events of 12 October 1999 and the judgment of 12 May 2000 have brought Pakistan back to square one. It stands today where it was in 1977 when martial law was upheld by the Supreme Court on the basis of the doctrine of necessity in Nusrat Bhutto's case. The head of military government has once again been given the power to amend the Constitution. So once again the country is at a cross-roads seething with discontent and faced with an uncertain future. The military government has also proposed a system of devolution of power through district governments which looks attractive on paper but is weak keeping in view practical political realities. It may turn out to be another useless and time wasting experiment which Pakistan can ill-afford. The military government has already spread itself thin by opening too many fronts which is fast eroding its support amongst people who are getting disillusioned with the regime after the initial euphoria of high expectations that military government might bring in real change in the lives of the people.

The military government appears to be lacking in direction and is getting into the pitfall of trying to do every thing at the same time with the potential to fail comprehensively. It can achieve results if its focus is limited. It might make progress in the area of accountability provided that, in the limited period available to it, it focuses on the major cases of corruption and accountability. Electoral reforms is another area in which it can achieve results. The government has already taken a few steps in the right direction by announcing certain electoral reforms which include preparation of new electoral lists; issuance of new identity cards based on physical verification; reduction of the age of the voter from 21 to 18; and empowering of the Election Commission and making it independent in its working. The future of democracy in Pakistan largely depends upon the efficacy and implementation of these reforms. Under no circumstances should the time frame given by the Supreme Court for return to democracy be violated or any attempt be made to seek any extension in time through breach of the judgment or by applying for the purpose to the Supreme Court. It is of paramount importance that the country returns at the earliest to the democratic process and civilian rule.

BIBLIOGRAPHY

Afzal, M. Rafique, *Political Parties in Pakistan 1958-69*, Volume II, 1987, National Institute of Historical and Cultural Research, Islamabad.

Ahmad, Professor Ghafoor, *'Phir Marshall Law Aa Gaya'*, 1988, Jang Publishers, Lahore.

Ahmad, Syed Sami, *The Judgement that Brought Disaster,* 1991, Justice Kayani Memorial Law Society, Karachi.

Ahmad, Qadeeruddin, *Pakistan—Facts and Fallacies,* 1979, Royal Book Company, Karachi.

Ahmad, Mushtaq, *Government and Politics in Pakistan,* 1959, Pakistan Publishing House, Karachi.

Arif, Gen. Khalid Mahmood, *Working with Zia: Pakistan's Power Politics, 1977-1988,* 1995, Oxford University Press, Karachi.

Azad, Maulana Abul Kalam, *India Wins Freedom,* 1959, Orient Longman, Calcutta.

Aziz, K.K., *Party Politics in Pakistan—1947-1958,* 1976, National Commission on Historical and Cultural Research, Islamabad.

Baxter, Craig & Wasti, Syed Razi, *Pakistan—Authoritarianism in 1980s,* 1991, Vanguards Books, Lahore.

Bhargava, G.S., *Benazir: Pakistan's New Hope,* 1989, Arnold Publishers, New Delhi.

Bhutto, Benazir, *Daughter of the East,* 1988, Hamish Hamilton, London.

Bhutto, Zulfiqar Ali, *If I am Assassinated,* 1979, Vikas Publishing House, New Delhi.

———, *My Dearest Daughter—A letter from the death cell,* published in 1989 by Benazir Bhutto.

———, *The Great Tragedy,* 1971, Pakistan People's Party Publication, Vision Publications Ltd., Karachi.

Birdwood, Sir George, *Report of the Old Records of India Office,* Calcutta.

Bokhari, Abrar Hussain, *Constitutional History of Indo-Pakistan,* 1964, M. Muhammad Suleman Qureshi & Sons, Lahore.

Bolitho, Hector, *Jinnah: Creator of Pakistan,* 1954, John Murray, London.

Brohi, A.K., *Fundamental Law in Pakistan,* 1958, Din Muhammad Press, Karachi.

Burki, Shahid Javaid, *Pakistan under Bhutto 1971-1977,* 1988, McMillan Press, Hong Kong.

———, Baxter, Craig, *Pakistan under the Military—Eleven years of Zia ul Haq,* 1991, Westview Press, Boulder, Colorado.

Burney, I.H, 'The March 1977 Elections: An Analysis', *Pakistan Economist*, 23 July 1977.

Chaudhri, Nazir Hussain, *Chief Justice Muhammad Munir—his life, writings and judgements,* 1973, Research Society on Pakistan, University of the Punjab, Lahore.

Chaudhri, Mohammad Ali, *The Emergence of Pakistan,* 1988, Services Book Club, Lahore.

Chaudhry, Barrister A.G., *The Leading Cases in Constitutional Law,* 1995, Sehar Publishers, Lahore.

Choudhry, G.W., *Constitutional Development in Pakistan,* 1969, Lowe and Brydone (Printers) Ltd. London.

———, *Documents and Speeches on the Constitution of Pakistan,* 1967, Green Book House, Dhaka.

______, *The First Constituent Assembly of Pakistan (1947-1954)*, 1956, Columbia University, New York.

______, *Democracy in Pakistan,* 1963, Green Book House, Dacca.

______, *The Last Days of United Pakistan.* A Personal Account, published in 49 International Affairs (1973).

Clark E.H. & Ghafoor, M., *An Analysis of Private Tubewell Costs* (Research Report No. 79), 1969, Pakistan Institute of Development Economics, Islamabad.

Collins, Larry and Lapierre, Dominque, *Freedom at Midnight,* 1975, Harper Collins Publishers Great Britain.

Conrad, Dieter, 'Conflicting Legitimacies in Pakistan' in the compilation *Legitimacy and Conflicts in South Asia,* 1997, South Asia Institute, New Delhi Branch, Heidelberg University, Heidelberg, Germany.

Constitutional Documents (Pakistan), Volumes I, II, III, IV, IV-A & V, 1964, Published by the Manager of Publications, Government of Pakistan, Karachi.

Dunbar, Sir George, *The History of India,* 1936 & 1990, Low Price Publications, Delhi.

Durant, Will, *Our Oriental Heritage—The Story of Civilization: Part I,* 1954, Simon & Schuster, New York.

Feldman, Herbert, *A Constitution for Pakistan,* 1955, Oxford University Press, London.

______, *From Crisis to Crisis: Pakistan 1962-1969*, 1972, Oxford University Press, London.

______, *The End and the Beginning: Pakistan 1969-1971*, 1975, Oxford University Press, London.

Gauhar, Altaf, *Ayub Khan—Pakistan's First Military Ruler,* 1994, Sang-e-Meel Publications, Lahore.

Gopal, Ram, *Indian Muslims: A Political History,* 1959, Asia Publishing House, Bombay.

Harrison, Selig, 'Nightmare in Baluchistan', *Foreign Policy,* Fall 1978.

Hayes, Louis D., *Politics in Pakistan—The Structure for Legitimacy,* 1984, Westview Press, Boulder and London.

Hodson, H.U., *The Great Divide,* 1969, London.

Hussain, Mushahid, *Pakistan's Politics—The Zia years,* 1990, Progressive Publishers, Lahore.

Hymen, Anthony, *Pakistan: Zia and After,* 1989, Abbinab Publications, New Delhi.

Jafri, Sadiq, *Benazir Bhutto on Trial,* 1993, Jang Publishers, Lahore.

Jalal, Ayesha, *The State of Martial Rule,* 1990, Cambridge University Press, Cambridge.

______, *The Sole Spokesman—Jinnah, The Muslim League and the Demand for Pakistan,* 1985, Cambridge University Press Cambridge.

Jennings, Sir Ivor, *Constitutional Problems in Pakistan,* 1957, Cambridge University Press, Cambridge.

______, *Approach to Self-Government,* 1956, Cambridge University Press, Cambridge.

Joshi, V.T., *Pakistan: Zia to Benazir,* 1995, Konark Publishers, New Delhi.

Kapur, Anup Chand, *Constitutional History of India (1765-1970)*, 1970, Nirhj Prakashan, New Delhi.

Keesing's Research Report, *Pakistan: From 1947 to the Creation of Bangladesh,* 1973, Keesing's Publications, New York.

Keith, A.B., *A Constitutional History of India, 1600-1935*, 1937, Central Book Depot, Allahbad.

Kennedy, Charles H., *Bureaucracy in Pakistan,* 1987, Oxford University Press, Karachi.

Khan, Muhammad Zafarullah, *The Forgotten Years,* 1991, Vanguard Books Ltd. Lahore.

Khan, Salahuddin, *Had there been no Jinnah,* 1989, Pan Graphics, Islamabad.

Khan, Air Marshall (R) Muhammad Asghar, *Generals in Politics: Pakistan 1958-1982*, 1983, Vikas Publishing House, New Delhi.

______, *Islam, Politics and State,* 1985, Zed Book Publishers, London.

Khan, Hamid, *Eighth Amendment—Constitutional and Political Crisis in Pakistan,* 1994, Wajidalis Ltd. Lahore.

______, *Administrative Tribunals for Civil Servants in Pakistan,* 1990, Progressive Publishers, Lahore.

Khan, Muhammad Ayub, *Friends, Not Masters: A Political Autobiography,* 1967, Oxford University Press, London.

Khan, Wali, *Facts are Facts—The Untold Story of India's Partition,* 1987, Vikas Publishing House, New Delhi.

Khan, Lt.-Gen. Gul Hassan, *Memoirs,* 1993, Oxford University Press, Karachi.

Khan, Sirdar Shaukat Hayat, *The Nation that Lost its Soul,* 1995, Jang Publishers, Lahore.

Khan, Roedad, *Pakistan: A Dream Gone Sour,* 1998, Oxford University Press, Karachi.

Lifschultz, Lawrence, *Bangladesh: The Unfinished Revolution,* 1979, Zed Press London.

Mahajan, V.D., *History of Indo-Pakistan,* 1985

______, *The Constitution of Pakistan,* 1965, Munawar Book Depot Lahore.

Mahmood, Safdar, *Pakistan Divided,* 1984, Ferozsons Ltd. Lahore.

______, *Constitutional Foundations of Pakistan,* 1990, Jang Publications, Lahore.

Mahmood, M. Dilawar, *The Judiciary and Politics in Pakistan,* 1992, Idara-e-Mutala-e-Tareekh, Lahore.

Malbin, Michael J., *Religion and Politics,* 1978, American Enterprise Institute for Policy Research, Washington D.C.

Maluka, Zulfiqar Khalid, *The Myth of Constitution in Pakistan,* 1995, Oxford University Press, Karachi.

Mascarenhas, Anthony, *The Rape of Bangladesh,* 1971, Vikas Publications, New Delhi.

Mirza, S.A., *Privatization in Pakistan,* 1995, Ferozsons Ltd., Lahore.

Misra, K.P., *Pakistan's Search for Constitutional Consensus,* 1967, Impex, New Delhi.

Munir, Muhammad, *From Jinnah to Zia,* 1980, Vanguard Books Ltd., Lahore.

______, *Constitution of Islamic Republic of Pakistan,* 1965, All Pakistan Legal Decisions, Lahore.

Nayyar, Kuldip, *Distant Neighbours,* 1972, Vikas Publishing House, Delhi.

Newberg, Paula R., *Judging the State—Courts and Constitutional Politics in Pakistan,* 1995, Cambridge University, Cambridge.

Niazi, Kausar, *'Aur line kat gai'*, 1987, Jang Publications Lahore.

Papanek, Gustov F., *Pakistan, Development, Social Goals and Private Incentive,* 1967, Harvard University Press, Cambridge.

Pirzada, S. Sharifuddin, *Fundamental Rights and Constitutional Remedies in Pakistan,* 1966, PLD Publishers, Lahore.

Rashid, Rao Abdul, *'Jo mein nay dekha'*, 1985, Atishfishan Publications, Lahore.

Rashid, Akhtar, *Election'77 - Aftermath: A Political Appraisal,* 1981, P.R.A.A.A.S. Publications, Islamabad.

Report of the Commission on International Development, Partners in Development, 1969, Praeger, New York.

Report on the General Elections 1985, Volume II, published by Election Commission of Pakistan, Islamabad.

Report of the Constitution Commission, published in 1961, Government of Pakistan.

Saharay, H.K., *A Legal State of Constitutional Development in India,* 1970, Nababharat Publishers, Calcutta.

Salik, Siddique, *Witness to Surrender,* 1977, Oxford University Press, Karachi.

Salim, Ahmad, *Pakistan of Jinnah—The Hidden Face,* 1993, Brothers Publishers, Lahore.

Sayeed, Khalid Bin, *Pakistan: The Formative Face,* 1968, Oxford University Press, Karachi.

______, *Politics in Pakistan: The Nature and Direction of Change,* 1980, Praeger Publishers, U.S.A.

Shah, Askar Ali, 'The Coalition without the anxiety', *Outlook*, 19 August 1972.

Shahab, Qudratullah, *Shahabnama,* 1992, Sang-e-Meel Publications, Lahore.

Shahab, Rafiullah, *History of Pakistan,* 1992, Sang-e-Meel Publications, Lahore.

Shahabuddin, Late Mr Justice Muhammad, *Recollections and Reflections,* 1975, PLD Publishers, Lahore.

Smith, Vincent A., *Oxford History of India,* 1981, Oxford University Press, Karachi.

Stephens, Ian, *Pakistan: Old Country, New Nation,* 1963, Ernest Benn Limited, London.

Syed, Anwar H., *The Discourse and Politics of Zulfiqar Ali Bhutto,* 1992, McMillan Press Ltd. Hong Kong.

Symonds, Richard, *Making of Pakistan*, 1966, Faber & Faber Limited, London.

Taseer, Salman, *Bhutto—A Political Biography,* 1980, Vikas Publishing House Ltd., New Delhi.

The New Encyclopaedia Britannica, 1974.

Vorys, Karl Von, *Political Development in Pakistan,* 1965, Princeton University Press, Princeton.

Waseem, Muhammad, *Politics and the State in Pakistan,* 1989, Progressive Publishers, Lahore.

Wilcox, Wayne Ayres, *Pakistan—The Consolidation of a Nation,* 1963, Columbia University Press, New York.

______, *The Emergence of Bangladesh,* 1973, American Enterprise Institute for Policy Research, Washington.

Williams, L.F. Rushbrook, *The State of Pakistan,* 1966, Faber & Faber, London.

______, *The East Pakistan Tragedy,* 1972, Tom Stacey Limited, London.

Wolpert, Stanley, *Jinnah of Pakistan,* 1984, Oxford University Press, Karachi.

______, *Zulfi Bhutto of Pakistan—His Life and Times,* 1993, Oxford University Press, New York.

Zaheer, Hassan, *The Separation of East Pakistan,* 1994, Oxford University Press, Karachi.

Ziring, Lawrence, *The Ayub Khan Era,* 1971, Syracuse University Press, U.S.A.

______, *Pakistan in the Twentieth Century—A Political History*, 1997, Oxford University Press, Karachi.

INDEX